iGA

Financial Instruments – IAS 39 and related Standards

iGAAP 2016

Financial Instruments – IAS 39 and related Standards

VOLUME C

Deloitte.

Wolters Kluwer

Published by Wolters Kluwer (UK) Ltd
145 London Road
Kingston upon Thames KT2 6SR
United Kingdom
Telephone +44 (0)844 561 8166
Facsimile +44 (0)208 247 2638
Email: cch@wolterskluwer.co.uk
Website: www.cch.co.uk

ISBN 978-1-78540-233-3

British Library Cataloguing-in-Publication Data

A catalogue record for this book is available from the British Library

Typeset by Innodata Inc., India.

Printed and bound by CPI Group (UK) Ltd, Croydon, CR0 4YY

Foreword

It is a pleasure once again to introduce *iGAAP*, Deloitte's guide to International Financial Reporting Standards. A significant enhancement in the content this year is the introduction of Volume D, an online volume containing disclosure examples drawn from a wide sample of IFRS reporters globally.

Although no major IFRSs have been issued since the release of our last edition, the past year has seen significant activity in many areas of financial reporting. In particular, many companies have started to prepare for the transition to two recently-completed Standards, IFRS 9 *Financial Instruments* and IFRS 15 *Revenue from Contracts with Customers*. Following an amendment to IFRS 15, both Standards are now effective from 1 January 2018 – which sounds a long way off but will be upon us before we know it. Both Standards are important and both will present significant implementation challenges.

Revenue is one of the most significant measures used by investors and the implementation of IFRS 15 will be a major exercise for many. IFRS 15 should result in a consistent measure of revenue irrespective of industry or jurisdiction. It provides more guidance than previous Standards and requires an appropriate use of professional judgement. A joint IASB/FASB Transition Resource Group (TRG), bringing together preparers, auditors, standard-setters and others, has been working to identify, evaluate and resolve implementation issues so as to ease transition and ensure consistent application.

Financial services entities are keenly focused on the implementation of IFRS 9, but this Standard should not be overlooked by others. The rules on impairment apply to all financial assets, including trade accounts and investments. IFRS 9 allows for the consideration of a broader range of information in determining credit loss estimates, and requires recognition of lifetime expected credit losses for those loans that have experienced a significant increase in credit risk. Here, too, the IASB has established the Impairment Transition Resource Group (ITG), whose remit is similar to the TRG established for IFRS 15.

Both IFRS 9 and IFRS 15 will require management and audit committees to consider the transition to the new Standards holistically, because both will require changes to information systems, business processes, compensation and other contractual arrangements. IFRS 15 provides for either a fully retrospective or a modified retrospective transition, and that choice will require careful evaluation. The transition to IFRS 9 will also need careful planning, particularly in deciding whether to continue to apply IAS 39 to hedging relationships. Presentation and disclosure in the financial statements will also be critical for both IFRSs.

Looking forward, two significant projects are nearing completion: *Leases* and *Insurance Contracts*. For the leases Standard, much hinges on the definition of a lease, which is still being refined as we go to press. All leases, as defined and subject to the short-term lease exception, will be on-balance sheet, with the accounting being similar to IAS 17's finance lease requirements. Lessor accounting will not change significantly from that in IAS 17.

Having made significant progress, the IASB expects to issue the insurance Standard late in 2016. The interaction between this IFRS and IFRS 9, in particular how to manage the gap between the effective dates of the two Standards, is a current concern. The IASB has recently issued proposals to mitigate this issue (including a possible deferral of the effective date of IFRS 9 for particular entities), with any amendment to IFRS 9 expected in mid-2016.

In financial reporting more generally, the IASB's Disclosure Initiative continues to bear fruit, with a draft Practice Statement on Materiality released in October 2015 and a major discussion paper on the Principles of Disclosure expected in early 2016.

Our aim in writing iGAAP is to provide you with a clear, practical guide to applying IFRSs, helping you get to grips with the issues and complexities that arise. The interpretative guidance provided draws on the wealth of experience of IFRS specialists and clients from around the globe. Our thanks to them for their generous and valuable input.

Veronica Poole

Global IFRS Leader
Deloitte

Principal authors

Veronica Poole

Veronica is a Senior Accounting Technical Partner at Deloitte. She is the UK National Head of Accounting and Corporate Reporting and the firm's Global IFRS Leader. Veronica is a member of the UK Accounting Council, the Financial Reporting Advisory Board to HM Treasury, CBI Companies Committee and the Hundred Group Financial Reporting Committee. She also chairs the Financial Reporting Faculty Advisory Board at the ICAEW.

Andrew Spooner

Andrew is the lead partner on IFRS financial instruments globally across Deloitte. He is a partner of the UK firm advising UK and multinational clients, with particular focus on financial services. Andrew is also a member of the European Securities and Markets Authority's Consultative Working Group for the Corporate Reporting Standing Committee, the Technical Expert Group of the European Financial Reporting Advisory Group and the Financial Reporting Faculty Board of the ICAEW.

Phil Barden

Phil is a partner in Deloitte's UK IFRS Centre of Excellence, assisting UK and multinational clients on a wide range of financial reporting issues. He is a member of the IASB/FASB Joint Transition Resource Group for Revenue Recognition and leads Deloitte's global Expert Advisory Panel on revenue recognition. Phil chairs the Financial Reporting Editorial Board of the ICAEW, and is a member of the Institute's Financial Reporting Committee.

Kush Patel

Kush is a partner in Deloitte's UK IFRS Centre of Excellence and specialises in the accounting for financial instruments. He advises financial and non-financial corporates on complex transactions and emerging accounting issues. He is a member of the ICAEW Financial Instruments Working Group and Deloitte's global Expert Advisory Panel on financial instruments.

Ken Rigelsford

Ken is the Director responsible for UK statutory reporting in Deloitte's UK technical department. He has been closely involved in the development of the new UK GAAP and is a member of the FRC's UK GAAP Technical Advisory Group. Ken is a member of the Financial Reporting, Business Law and Company Law Committees of the ICAEW. He chairs the Distributable Profits Working Party (a joint working party of the ICAEW and the ICAS) and is regarded as one of the leading experts in this field.

Norma Hall

Norma Hall is the team leader of the author team. She is a Director in Deloitte's IFRS Global Office and Editor of the firm's International Accounting Manual. She was formerly a partner in Deloitte's Hong Kong office, with extensive experience of the application of IFRSs to commercial transactions.

Amy Haworth

Amy Haworth is the team leader for UK GAAP volumes. She is a member of the UK IFRS Centre of Excellence and of Deloitte's global Expert Advisory Panel on revenue recognition.

Contributors

The authors would like to express their thanks to Deloitte's Global IFRS Leadership Team and the members of the UK technical department, with particular appreciation to the following for their contributions.

Kristin Bauer (USA)
Hanna Ben Fekih (France)
Jens Berger (Germany)
Mark Bolton (USA)
Robert Carroll (UK)
Evangelina Chatzitsakou (UK)
Chris Chiriatti (USA)
Elizabeth Chrispin (UK)
Brandon Coleman (USA)
Svetlana Cox (UK)
Anna Crawford (Australia)
Mark Crowley (USA)
Chris Cryderman (USA)
Kerry Danyluk (Canada)
Eric Dard (France)
Trevor Derwin (South Africa)
Shivanthi Edwards (USA)
Trevor Farber (USA)
Colin Fleming (UK)
Candy Fong (China)
Adrian Geisel (Germany)
Claudio Giaimo (Argentina)
Richard Gillin (UK)
Tracey Gordon (UK)
Clair Grindley (Canada)
Markus Hahn (UK)
Karen Higgins (Canada)
Tom Hopkins (UK)
Shinya Iwasaki (Japan)
Ryszarda Kingston (UK)
Tim Kolber (USA)
Frank Kroesch (USA)
Nadine Kusche (UK)
Christine Lallouette (France)
An Lam (Canada)
Elise Lambert (USA)
Sarah McWhirter (UK)
Miguel Millan (Mexico)
Jane Miller (Chile)
Jo Mithen (UK)
Robert Morris (USA)
Anthony Mosco (USA)
Rogerio Mota (Brazil)
Shan Nemeth (USA)
Magnus Orrell (USA)
Martine Pelletier (France)
Disna Perera (UK)
Sean Prince (USA)
Linda Riedel (UK)
Laurence Rivat (France)
Estela Rodenstein (UK)
James Rogers (UK)
Helen Shaw (UK)
Melissa Sim (Australia)
Amanda Swaffield (UK)
Nura Taef (Canada)
Stephen Taylor (China)
Alan Texeira (UK)
Jeffrey Thomas (USA)
Vicki Tibbitts (UK)
Robert Uhl (USA)
Maryse Vendette (Canada)
Henri Venter (Australia)
Debra Wan (Australia)
Peter Westaway (UK)
Kenichi Yoshimura (Japan)

Standards covered

This book covers the following Standards that are effective for reporting periods beginning on or after 1 January 2015:

- International Accounting Standard 32 – *Financial Instruments: Presentation* (IAS 32)
- International Accounting Standard 39 – *Financial Instruments: Recognition and Measurement* (IAS 39)
- International Financial Reporting Standard 1 – *First-time Adoption of International Financial Reporting Standards* (IFRS 1)
- International Financial Reporting Standard 7 – *Financial Instruments: Disclosures* (IFRS 7)
- International Financial Reporting Standard 13 – *Fair Value Measurement* (IFRS 13)

This book does not reflect the requirements of International Financial Reporting Standard 9 *Financial Instruments* (IFRS 9), nor the consequential amendments to IAS 39 and other Standards arising from IFRS 9.

This book incorporates relevant discussions from meetings of the International Accounting Standards Board and IFRS Interpretations Committee that took place up to 1 September 2015.

Table of Contents

C1 Scope

Contents

1 Introduction

In IFRS accounting literature, three Standards deal with the accounting for financial instruments.

- IAS 32 *Financial Instruments: Presentation* deals with the presentation and classification of financial instruments as financial liabilities or equity, and sets out requirements regarding the offset of financial assets and financial liabilities in the statement of financial position.
- IAS 39 *Financial Instruments: Recognition and Measurement* contains the key guidance regarding the recognition and measurement of financial instruments other than equity.
- IFRS 7 *Financial Instruments: Disclosures* sets out the disclosures required in respect of financial instruments.

In July 2014 the IASB finalised IFRS 9 *Financial Instruments*. This new IFRS replaces IAS 39. IFRS 9 is effective for annual reporting periods beginning on or after 1 January 2018 with early adoption permitted. This volume does not include the requirements of IFRS 9.

iGAAP 2016 Financial Instruments: IFRS 9 and related Standards – Volume B, Deloitte's companion volume for this manual, provides equivalent guidance regarding the application of the requirements of IFRS 9.

The definition of a financial instrument is broad; a financial instrument is defined as any contract that gives rise to a financial asset of one entity and a financial liability or equity instrument of another entity. Trade receivables and payables, bank loans and overdrafts, issued debt, ordinary and preference shares, investments in securities (e.g. shares and bonds), and various derivatives are just some examples of financial instruments. In addition, some contracts to buy and sell non-financial items that would not meet the definition of financial instruments are specifically brought within the scope of the financial instruments Standards on the basis that they behave and are used in a similar way to financial instruments (see **section 2.5**).

This chapter explains which items that meet the definition of a financial instrument are scoped out of IAS 32 and/or IAS 39 and IFRS 7. The detailed scope exclusions of IFRS 7 are discussed in more detail in **section 2** of **chapter C12**.

The scoping paragraphs of the three Standards (IAS 32, IAS 39 and IFRS 7) differ slightly so that:

- all financial instruments that are scoped out of IAS 32 are also scoped out of IAS 39;

- financial instruments that an entity issues with a discretionary participation feature are accounted for under IFRS 4 *Insurance Contracts* and are scoped out of IAS 39. Such instruments are within the scope of IFRS 7 and IAS 32 except that, for such contracts, the requirements of IAS 32 regarding the distinction between financial liabilities and equity instruments are not applicable;
- IAS 39 has some additional scope exclusions that go beyond the scope exclusions in IAS 32 (see **section 3**); and
- IAS 39 excludes all instruments classified as equity from its scope, whereas IFRS 7 appears to exclude only those derivatives over own equity, puttable instruments and instruments that impose on the entity an obligation to deliver a pro rata share of the net assets upon liquidation that are classified as equity, making no reference to other non-derivative instruments such as ordinary shares. It appears that this difference does not have any practical effect (see **3.1**).

2 Financial instruments scoped out of IAS 32, IAS 39 and IFRS 7

The following table summarises the scope of IAS 32, IAS 39 and IFRS 7 with respect to financial instruments only.

Financial instrument	**Within scope of IAS 32?**	**Within scope of IFRS 7?**	**Within scope of IAS 39?**
Interests in subsidiaries, associates and joint ventures accounted for in accordance with IAS 27, IAS 28 or IFRS 10	No	No	No
Interests in subsidiaries, associates and joint ventures accounted for in accordance with IAS 39 as permitted by IAS 27:10(b), IAS 28:44 or IFRS 10:31	Yes	Yes	Yes
Investments in equity securities (either as available-for-sale investments or at fair value through profit or loss)	Yes	Yes	Yes
Investments in debt securities (as available-for-sale investments, at fair value through profit or loss, loans and receivables or held-to-maturity investments)	Yes	Yes	Yes
Trade receivables and payables	Yes	Yes	Yes
Finance lease receivables of a lessor	Yes	Yes	No(1)

Financial instrument	**Within scope of IAS 32?**	**Within scope of IFRS 7?**	**Within scope of IAS 39?**
Construction contract receivables that do not qualify as financial instruments and are accounted for under IAS 11 *Construction Contracts* (see **2.7**)	No	No	No
Cash and cash equivalents	Yes	Yes	Yes
Borrowings and other financial liabilities (e.g. preference shares classified as financial liabilities)	Yes	Yes	Yes
Derivatives (and non-closely related embedded derivatives)	Yes	Yes	Yes
Derivatives over interests in subsidiaries, associates and joint ventures in individual financial statements	Yes	Yes	Yes
Derivatives over interests in associates and joint ventures in consolidated financial statements	Yes	Yes	Yes
Contracts over non-financial items that do not meet the purchase, sale or usage exemption in IAS 39:5	Yes	Yes	Yes
Contingent consideration in a business combination (acquirer or vendor) (2)	Yes	Yes	Yes
Deferred consideration in a business combination (acquirer or vendor)	Yes	Yes	Yes
Financial guarantee contracts for the writer that are not accounted for as insurance contracts	Yes	Yes	Yes
Finance lease obligations of a lessee	Yes	Yes	No(3)
Own equity shares	Yes	No(4)	No
Derivatives over own equity shares that are classified as equity (including derivatives over shares in non-controlling interest in the consolidated financial statements)	Yes	No	No
Forward contracts between an acquirer and a vendor in a business combination to buy or sell an acquiree at a future date	Yes	Yes	No
Loan commitments that cannot be settled net in cash or another financial instrument, are not designated as financial liabilities at fair value through profit or loss, or are not a loan commitment at a below market rate of interest	Yes	Yes	No
Employer's rights and obligations under employee benefit plans covered by IAS 19	No	No	No

Financial instrument	Within scope of IAS 32?	Within scope of IFRS 7?	Within scope of IAS 39?
Share-based payment arrangements covered by IFRS 2	No	No	No
Insurance contracts for the writer or holder of insurance (settled in cash or other financial assets)	No	No	No

(1) Except for the requirements on derecognition, impairment and embedded derivatives.

(2) Assumes that IFRS 3 *Business Combinations* (as revised in 2008) is being applied. Contingent consideration in a business combination is not in the scope of any of the three Standards for the acquirer if it arose in a business combination accounted for under the previous version of IFRS 3. Contingent consideration is always in the scope of all three Standards for the vendor.

(3) Except for the requirements on derecognition and embedded derivatives.

(4) Scope exclusion refers only to derivatives over own equity, certain puttable instruments and instruments that impose on the entity an obligation to deliver a pro rata share of the net assets upon liquidation but can be applied broadly to all equity instruments of the issuer – see **3.1**.

IAS 32 applies to all financial instruments except for the following:

- interests in subsidiaries, associates and joint ventures (see **section 2.1**);
- employers' rights and obligations under employee benefit plans (see **2.2**);
- rights and obligations arising under insurance contracts as well as financial instruments that are within the scope of IFRS 4 because they contain a discretionary participation feature (see **2.3**); and
- financial instruments, contracts and obligations under share-based payment arrangements (see **2.6** for further guidance and exceptions).

IAS 39 also scopes out these instruments, but has some additional scope exemptions (see **section 3**).

In addition, all three standards include within their scopes some contracts to buy or sell non-financial assets (see **section 2.5**) even though they do not meet the definition of a financial instrument.

Each of the above is considered in turn.

2.1 Interests in subsidiaries, associates and joint ventures

Interests in subsidiaries, associates and joint ventures that are accounted for under IAS 27 *Separate Financial Statements*, IAS 28 *Investments in Associates and Joint Ventures* or IFRS 10 *Consolidated Financial Statements* are not within the scope of IAS 32. However when, in the circumstances specified by those standards an entity accounts for its interests in subsidiaries, associates and/or joint ventures in accordance with

IAS 39, then those interests in subsidiaries, associates and/or joint ventures are also brought within the scope of IAS 32 and IFRS 7 (see **2.1.1** below). In such circumstances, the relevant disclosure requirements of IAS 27 and IFRS 12 *Disclosure of Interests in Other Entities* apply in addition to those of IFRS 7. For example, in the parent's separate financial statements, if the parent chooses to recognise its investment in its subsidiary in accordance with IAS 39 as an available-for-sale financial asset (see **chapter C2**), then that investment, having been clearly scoped into IAS 39, also falls into the scope of IFRS 7.

Derivatives that are linked to interests in subsidiaries, associates and joint ventures are always within the scope of IAS 32. If a derivative on an interest in a subsidiary meets the definition of equity in the consolidated financial statements in accordance with IAS 32 (see **chapter C3**), that derivative is scoped out of IAS 39 and IFRS 7 and is accounted for as equity under IAS 32. This treatment applies for a derivative over shares in a subsidiary when the derivative will be settled by delivery of a fixed amount of shares for a fixed amount of cash or other financial asset. The derivative meets the definition of equity in the consolidated financial statements because shares in a subsidiary in the consolidated financial statements are presented as non-controlling interests which are part of consolidated equity. In contrast, shares in an associate or joint venture are never considered part of equity in the consolidated financial statements and, therefore, in consolidated financial statements a derivative over an interest in an associate or joint venture will never meet the definition of equity and, consequently, will always be within the scope of IAS 39 and IFRS 7.

When derivatives over interests in subsidiaries, associates and joint ventures are within the scope of IAS 39, they are covered by the normal measurement requirements for derivatives as detailed in **chapter C4**.

Example 2.1A

Written call over equity of subsidiary (1)

Parent X and Subsidiary Y are part of Group Z.

Subsidiary Y writes a call option to an entity outside the group over a fixed number of its own equity shares that is exclusively physically settled in all cases and the strike price of the option is a fixed amount of cash. For Subsidiary Y, the written call option meets the definition of equity in accordance with IAS 32 and, therefore, in the financial statements of Subsidiary Y it is treated as an equity item.

In the consolidated financial statements of Group Z, the instrument is within the scope of IAS 32 because it is a derivative over an interest in a subsidiary. It is outside the scope of IAS 39 and IFRS 7 because the instrument meets the definition of equity in the financial statements of Subsidiary Y in accordance with IAS 32 and, therefore, it is presented within non-controlling interests in the consolidated financial statements of Group Z.

Example 2.1B

Written call over equity of subsidiary (2)

The facts are as in **example 2.1A** except that Parent X writes the call option over a fixed number of shares in Subsidiary Y for a fixed amount of cash.

In the separate financial statements of Parent X, the written call option is a derivative that is in the scope of IAS 39 and IFRS 7 because it does not meet the definition of equity in Parent X's financial statements (because the derivative does not relate to Parent X's equity).

In the consolidated financial statements of Group Z, the written call option is within the scope of IAS 32 because it is a derivative over an interest in a subsidiary which is presented within non-controlling interests. The instrument is outside the scope of IAS 39 and IFRS 7 because the instrument meets the definition of equity.

2.1.1 Investments in subsidiaries, associates and joint ventures in separate financial statements

When an entity prepares separate financial statements (as defined in IAS 27), an investment in a subsidiary, associate or joint venture should be accounted for either:

[IAS 27:10]

(a) at cost;

(b) in accordance with IAS 39; or

(c) using the equity method as described in IAS 28.

In August 2014, the IASB amended IAS 27 to allow an entity preparing separate financial statements to account for investments in subsidiaries, joint ventures and associates using the equity method as described in IAS 28. Prior to this an entity could only account for these investments at cost or in accordance with IAS 39. The amendments apply retrospectively for annual periods beginning on or after 1 January 2016. Earlier application is permitted in which case disclosure that the entity has applied the requirements for an earlier period is required.

The entity is required to apply the same accounting for each category of investments.

If the investment is accounted for in accordance with IAS 39, then it will be classified as either at fair value through profit or loss or available-for-sale (see **sections 3.1** and **3.5** of **chapter C2**).

Investments that cease to be subsidiaries, but that do not become associates or joint ventures, are accounted for in accordance with IAS 39 from the date they cease to be subsidiaries.

Similarly, investments that cease to be associates, but that do not become subsidiaries or joint ventures, are accounted for in accordance with IAS 39 from the date the entity ceases to have significant influence. Investments that cease to be joint ventures, but that do not become subsidiaries or associates, are accounted for in accordance with IAS 39 from the date the entity ceases to have joint control.

Venture capital organisations, mutual funds, unit trusts, investment-linked insurance funds and similar entities may, upon initial recognition, choose to designate their interests in associates and joint ventures as at fair value through profit or loss or classify them as held for trading in accordance with IAS 39 in the entity's individual or consolidated financial statements. [IAS 28:18] A venture capital organisation or similar entity is not permitted to apply IAS 39 to its investments in subsidiaries in the consolidated financial statements.

In October 2012 the IASB issued *Investment Entities – Amendments to IFRS 10, IFRS 12 and IAS 27*. The amendments require that Investment Entities shall not consolidate entities that they control subject to meeting specified criteria. Instead, Investment Entities shall measure those entities, along with their interests in associates and joint ventures, at fair value through profit or loss in accordance with IAS 39.

2.1.2 Interests in associates and joint ventures partially held by a venture capital organisation or similar entity

A group may consist of a venture capital entity (or similar) and other operations. This is common in large financial institutions when the organisation consists of a venture capital business as well as other banking operations, such as retail and investment banking.

IAS 28:19 states when an entity has an investment in an associate, a portion of which is held indirectly through a venture capital organisation, or a mutual fund, unit trust and similar entities including investment-linked insurance funds, the entity may elect to measure that portion of the investment in the associate at fair value through profit or loss in accordance with IAS 39 regardless of whether the venture capital organisation, or the mutual fund, unit trust and similar entities including investment-linked insurance funds, has significant influence over that portion of the investment. If the entity makes that election, the entity shall apply the equity method to any remaining portion of its investment in an associate that is not held through a venture capital organisation, or a mutual fund, unit trust and similar entities including investment-linked insurance funds.

In October 2012 the IASB issued *Investment Entities – Amendments to IFRS 10, IFRS 12 and IAS 27*. The amendments require that Investment Entities shall not consolidate entities that they control subject to meeting specified criteria. Instead, Investment Entities shall measure those entities, along with their interests in associates and joint ventures, at fair value through profit or loss in accordance with IAS 39. The amendments do not permit a parent to not consolidate an entity it controls if the parent is not itself an investment entity. Therefore a parent that is not an investment entity, but has investment entities in its group, must consolidate all entities it controls and cannot apply the investment entity exemption.

2.2 Employers' rights and obligations under employee benefit plans

Employers' rights and obligations under employee benefit plans are outside the scope of IAS 32, IAS 39 and IFRS 7. They are within the scope of IAS 19 *Employee Benefits*. IAS 19:153(a) specifically notes that 'other long-term employee benefits' include long-service benefits. Consequently, these liabilities should follow the accounting and disclosure requirements set out in IAS 19, and not IAS 32.

2.3 Rights and obligations arising under insurance contracts

Contracts that meet the definition of an insurance contract in IFRS 4 *Insurance Contracts* are outside the scope of IAS 32, IAS 39 and IFRS 7 (see **2.3.1**).

In addition, financial instruments that are within the scope of IFRS 4 because they contain a discretionary participation feature are outside the scope of IAS 32 and IAS 39. A discretionary participation feature is the right to receive, in addition to guaranteed benefits, significant further benefits that are at the discretion of the issuer and are based on the performance of a specified pool of contracts, investment returns or profit or loss of a company, fund or other entity that issues the contract. [IFRS 4:2 & Appendix A] The issuer of such instruments is exempt from applying the paragraphs in IAS 32 with respect to the distinction between financial liabilities and equity instruments. However, these instruments are subject to all of the other requirements of IAS 32. Furthermore, IAS 32 applies to derivatives embedded in these instruments that are required to be separately accounted for in accordance with IAS 39 (see **2.3.2**).

2.3.1 Definition of an insurance contract

An insurance contract is defined in IFRS 4 as a contract under which one party (the insurer) accepts significant insurance risk from another party (the policyholder) by agreeing to compensate the policyholder if a specified uncertain future event (the insured event) adversely affects the policyholder. [IFRS 4:Appendix A] An insurance risk is a pre-existing risk that the policyholder transfers to the insurer and is a risk other than financial risk, i.e. other than a risk of a possible future change in either a financial variable (e.g. interest rate, commodity price, credit rating) or a non-financial variable that is not specific to a party to the contract. The insurance risk has to be significant; it has to have a discernible effect on the economics of the transaction, i.e. significant additional benefits including claims handling and assessment costs could become payable. An adverse effect on a policyholder as a result of an insured event is a precondition for payment; however, the payment itself does not have to be limited to the financial loss suffered by the policyholder.

IFRS 4 contains numerous examples of insurance contracts, and also examples of contracts that do not meet the definition of an insurance contract and may fall within the scope of IAS 32, IAS 39 and IFRS 7.

Example 2.3.1

Insurance risk

A life insurance contract in which the insurer bears no significant mortality risk and that creates financial assets or financial liabilities will be in the scope of IAS 39. [IFRS 4:B19]

2.3.2 Derivatives embedded in insurance contracts

Derivatives embedded within insurance contracts are within the scope of IAS 32, IAS 39 and IFRS 7 if they are required to be separated in accordance with IAS 39. The only exception is if a derivative embedded in an insurance contract is itself an insurance contract. [IFRS 4:7]

Example 2.3.2

Embedded derivatives in insurance contracts

[IFRS 4:IG4, Example 2.16]

A contractual feature within an insurance contract provides a return that is contractually linked (with no discretion) to the return on specified assets. The embedded derivative is not an insurance contract and is not closely related to the contract (IAS 39:AG30(h)). Fair value measurement is required [*i.e. the embedded derivative will be separated from the insurance contract and fair valued*].

2.3.3 Financial guarantee contracts (issuer accounting)

If an entity has issued a financial guarantee to a third party, the entity will need to consider whether that instrument meets the definition of a financial guarantee contract as set out in IAS 39. The Standard defines such contracts as those that require the issuer to make specified payments to reimburse the holder for a loss it incurs because a specified debtor fails to make payment when due in accordance with the original or modified terms of a debt instrument. The issuer of such a contract should, in accordance with the requirements of IAS 39, initially recognise the financial guarantee contract at fair value and subsequently measure it at the higher of:

[IAS 39:47(c)]

- the amount determined in accordance with IAS 37 *Provisions, Contingent Liabilities and Contingent Assets*; and
- the amount initially recognised less, when appropriate, the cumulative amount of income recognised in accordance with the principles of IFRS 15 *Revenue from Contracts with Customers*.

This treatment in respect of initial recognition and subsequent measurement applies with the following three exceptions:

- if the financial guarantee contract was entered into or retained on a transfer of a financial asset and prevented derecognition of the financial asset or resulted in continuing involvement (see **3.3** and **3.4** in **chapter C8** for further details); [IAS 39:47(b)]
- if the financial guarantee contract was designated as at fair value through profit or loss at inception (see **7.1.2** in **chapter C3** for further details); [IAS 39:47(a)] and
- if the issuer has previously asserted explicitly that it regards such contracts as insurance contracts and has used accounting applicable to insurance contracts; in such circumstances, the issuer may elect to apply either IAS 39 or IFRS 4 *Insurance Contracts*. This election may be made on a contract-by-contract basis, but once made it is irrevocable. [IAS 39:2(e)]

An entity may have written financial guarantee contracts but not as a core business activity. It may have historically considered these contracts as insurance and asserted that they were insurance contracts or, alternatively, it may have made such an assertion at the time of transition to IFRSs.

The following decision tree summarises the treatment of issued financial guarantees.

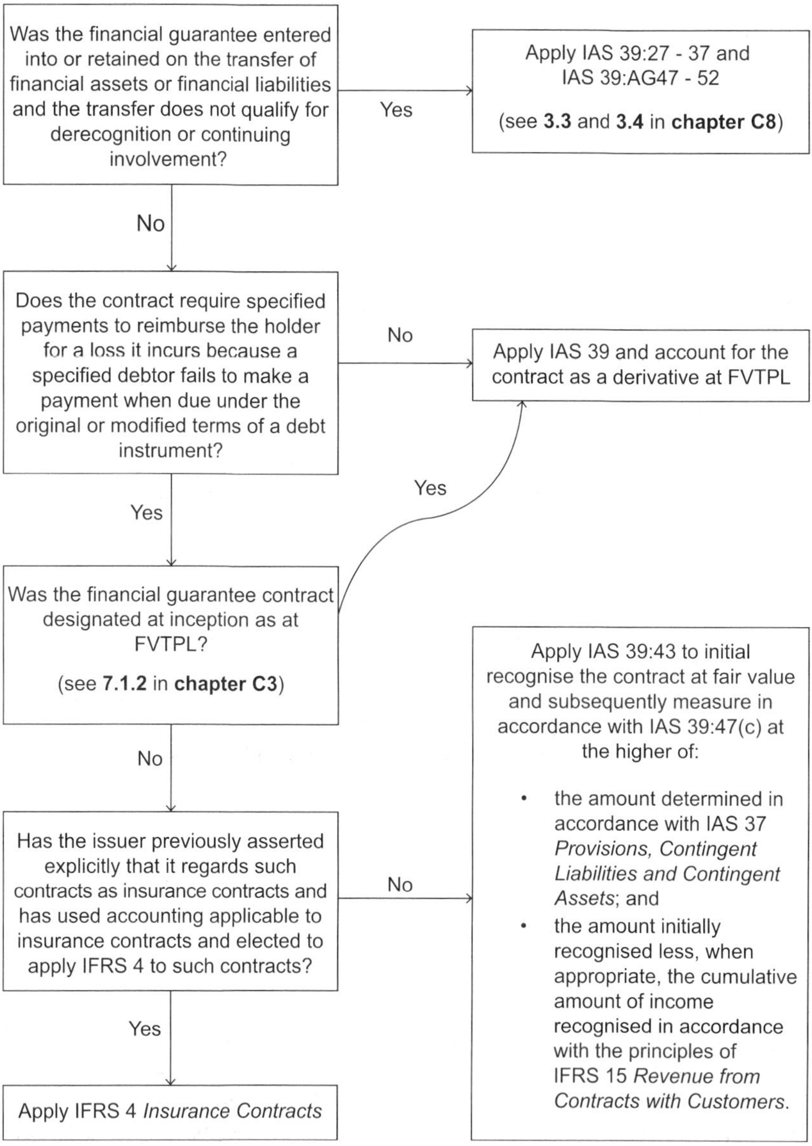

Example 2.3.3A

Financial guarantee contracts (1)

Entity A owns CU100 million of Entity X bonds that mature in 20 years. Entity X is rated BBB by the rating agencies. Entity A is concerned that Entity X may be downgraded, resulting a decline in value for the bonds. To protect against such a decline, Entity A enters into a contract with Entity B that will pay Entity A for any decline in the fair value of the Entity X bonds related to a credit downgrade to BB or below. The contract is for a five-year period, and Entity A pays CU2 million to enter into the contract. Because the contract pays Entity A in the event of a downgrade, and not in the event of a failure by Entity X to meet its payment obligations under the issued bonds, it is a derivative instrument within the scope of IAS 39 for Entity B and a derivative instrument within the scope of IAS 39 for Entity A.

Example 2.3.3B

Financial guarantee contracts (2)

Entity X owns CU100 million of single family residential mortgage loans. Entity X is concerned that defaults may increase as a result of a recession and, consequently, purchases a guarantee contract from Entity B, a mortgage insurance entity. The contract requires Entity B to pay Entity X for losses suffered as a result of mortgage defaults when Entity X forecloses on the mortgage. The contract has a CU5 million cap. Entity X pays Entity B a CU2 million fee for the contract. Because the contract provides for specified payments to be made to reimburse Entity X for a loss it incurs in the event of a failure of a specified debtor to pay when due, the contract meets the definition of a financial guarantee contract.

For the writer of the financial guarantee contract (Entity B), the instrument is within the scope of IAS 39. Unless the contract is designated as at fair value through profit or loss at inception, the contract will be recognised initially at fair value and then measured at the higher of the amount determined in accordance with IAS 37 and the amount initially recognised less, when appropriate, the cumulative amount of income recognised in accordance with the principles of IFRS 15 *Revenue from Contracts with Customers*. However, if Entity B has previously asserted explicitly that it regards such contracts as insurance contracts and used accounting applicable to insurance contracts, it could elect to apply either IAS 39 or IFRS 4 to the specific contract. If such an election is made, it is irrevocable in respect of the contract with Entity X but it does not affect Entity B's options for the treatment of other similar contracts.

Example 2.3.3C

Financial guarantee contracts (3)

Entity A has a wholly-owned subsidiary, Entity B. Entity B enters into a third-party bank loan. Entity A writes a financial guarantee contract to the bank over the loan. In the separate financial statements of Entity A, the financial guarantee contract is accounted for as set out in **example 2.3.3B**. In the consolidated financial statements of Group A, the financial guarantee contract is not separately recognised because the group as a single entity has simply borrowed money from a third party.

If Entity A instead provides a guarantee directly to Entity B in respect of its bank loan, in the separate financial statements of Entity A the guarantee is not recognised separately. The arrangement is such that Entity A has agreed to contribute more money to its subsidiary which will generally be accounted for as a capital contribution as and when it is contributed. The promise by the parent to inject money at a future date is not recognised up-front.

2.3.4 Financial guarantee contracts (holder accounting)

Financial guarantee contracts held, as opposed to those issued, are specifically outside the scope of IAS 39. [IAS 39:IN6]

IAS 39 does not specifically address the accounting by a holder of a financial guarantee contract (such as Entity X in **example 2.3.3B**). Although IAS 39:IN6 states that "financial guarantee contracts held are not within the scope of the Standard", there is no reference in the body of the Standard to the scoping-out of financial guarantee contracts held. In January 2008, as part of editorial changes to Standards, the IASB amended the wording of IAS 39:IN16 to clarify that financial guarantee contracts held are outside the scope of IAS 39 because they are insurance contracts. Given that IAS 39 scopes outs 'rights' under a financial instrument that meets the definition of an insurance contract in IFRS 4, it is reasonable to conclude that purchased financial guarantee contracts are outside the scope of IAS 39. The scope exclusion does not state which Standard should be applied for purchased financial guarantee contracts.

Given that financial guarantee contracts held are not in the scope of IAS 39, they are generally recognised as an asset equal to the premium paid and the asset is amortised to profit or loss over the period in which the benefit of the guarantee is obtained. Only if the entity considers it virtually certain that its claim under the financial guarantee contract will be successful will the asset be remeasured upwards to reflect the claim in accordance with IAS 37. Such contracts are not accounted for in accordance with IFRS 4 because that Standard only applies to the accounting by the issuer of insurance contracts, not the holder.

2.3.5 General guarantees of subsidiary obligations

In some jurisdictions, regulatory or statutory requirements state that an ultimate parent company or subsidiary (the guarantor) must, or can elect to, make representations that it will make payments to unspecified parties outside the group if a subsidiary (the obligor) fails to make payments under its obligations to those parties. The guarantor agrees to make a payment to the creditor equal to the amount that the obligor has failed to pay. The representation is open-ended (i.e. it relates to all currently recognised obligations as well as to all obligations that the subsidiary may enter into in the future) and does not have a specified counterparty. Care needs to be taken in determining whether such representations by the guarantor are financial guarantee contracts in the guarantor's financial statements.

Before considering whether the representation meets the definition of a financial guarantee contract in accordance with IAS 39:9, the entity must consider whether the instrument meets the definition of a financial instrument. If it does not, the instrument is not within the scope of IAS 39 and cannot be a financial guarantee contract.

Representations to unspecified parties do not meet the definition of a financial instrument because they are not a contractual arrangement between the guarantor and a specified third party or parties. IAS 32:13 states that a contract is "an agreement between two or more parties that has clear economic consequences that the parties have little, if any, discretion to avoid, usually because the agreement is enforceable by law". A representation to meet the subsidiary's obligations if the subsidiary fails to do so is a representation of unspecified amounts held by unspecified parties. As such, the representation is not a contractual arrangement and is outside the scope of IAS 32 and IAS 39. In addition, IAS 32:AG12 clarifies that "liabilities or assets that are not contractual (such as income taxes that are created as a result of statutory requirements imposed by governments) are not financial liabilities or financial assets". Therefore, the guarantor would apply IAS 37 and recognise a provision in accordance with the requirements of that Standard if the criteria in IAS 37:14 are met.

If the representation is a contractual arrangement between the guarantor and a specified third party over a specified amount and, therefore, it does meet the definition of a financial instrument and is within the scope of IAS 39, the entity must consider whether the instrument meets the definition of a financial guarantee contract in IAS 39:9. A financial guarantee contract only exists when the guarantor agrees to make specified payments to reimburse the holder for a loss it incurs because a specified debtor fails to make payment when due in accordance with the original or modified terms of a debt instrument. If the guarantor has not explicitly stated that it regards financial guarantee contracts as insurance contracts under IFRS 4, it must measure the contract as described earlier in this section.

A contractual arrangement that does meet the definition of a financial instrument but does not meet the definition of a financial guarantee contract is measured at fair value through profit or loss because the contractual arrangement meets the definition of a derivative in IAS 39:9. Such a contractual arrangement meets the definition of a derivative because: (1) the initial investment received by the guarantor is small compared with the amount that could be required to be paid if a claim is made under the contractual arrangement, (2) the fair value of the arrangement is driven by the credit risk of the obligor, and (3) the arrangement will be settled either at a future date (if the holder make a claim against the guarantor) or at its maturity (because expiration at maturity is a form of settlement). [IAS 39:IG.B.7]

2.3.6 Parent committed to future contributions to subsidiary (separate financial statements)

An arrangement whereby a parent agrees to make future contributions or to lend to a subsidiary is not a financial guarantee contract for the parent in its separate financial statements because the parent is not agreeing to make payments in the event that the subsidiary suffers loss on a specified debt instrument. Even if the subsidiary only makes a claim from the parent when it is in financial difficulty, the exercise of the claim is more in the nature of a claim under a loan commitment (and written and purchased loan commitments are outside the scope of IAS 39 – see **3.5**) or a commitment for a capital contribution which by analogy to loan commitment accounting would also be considered outside the scope of IAS 39.

2.3.7 Obligation to make payments when the counterparty to a derivative contract fails to make payment

A contract that requires an entity to make payments when the counterparty to a derivative contract (e.g. a foreign currency forward contract or an interest rate swap) fails to make payment is not a financial guarantee contract. A financial guarantee contract is a contract "that requires the issuer to make specified payments to reimburse the holder for a loss it incurs because a specified debtor fails to make payment when due in accordance with the original or modified terms of a debt instrument". [IAS 39:9] Because a derivative is not a debt instrument, the contract does not meet the definition of a financial guarantee contract.

2.3.8 Weather derivatives

Contracts requiring payments based on climatic, geological or other physical variables are inside the scope of IFRS 4 if they meet the definition of an insurance contract. Those based on climatic variables are sometimes referred to as 'weather derivatives'. Examples of climatic, geological and other physical variables include:

- the number of inches of rainfall or snow in a particular area;
- temperature in a particular area or for a specified period of time; and
- the severity of earthquakes.

If these contracts are not within the scope of IFRS 4, and they meet the definition of a derivative in **chapter C4**, they are within the scope of IAS 32, IAS 39 and IFRS 7.

2.3.9 Instruments issued by Real Estate Investment Trusts (REITs)

In January 2010, the IFRIC (now the IFRS Interpretations Committee) issued an agenda decision on IFRS 4 and IAS 32, *Scope Issue for Investments in REITs*. In some jurisdictions, a Real Estate Investment Trust (REIT) is a tax or regulatory designation used for an entity investing in real estate that meets certain criteria, for example to attain preferential income tax status. The contractual terms of the ownership units of some such REITs require them to distribute 90 per cent of their total distributable income; distribution of the remaining 10 per cent of distributable income is at the discretion of management. The IFRIC received a request to provide guidance on whether the discretion to distribute the remaining 10 per cent of total distributable income met the definition of a discretionary participation feature as defined in IFRS 4. If the discretionary participation feature definition is met, IFRS 4 permits the ownership units to be classified as liabilities, rather than assessing the instrument for financial liability and equity components in accordance with IAS 32.

The IFRIC noted that the objective of IFRS 4 is to specify the financial reporting for insurance contracts and that the definition of discretionary participation feature in Appendix A of IFRS 4 requires, among other things, that the instrument provides the holder with guaranteed benefits and that the discretionary participation feature benefits are additional to those guaranteed benefits. Further, the IFRIC noted that there must be guaranteed benefits to the holder for the definition to be met and that such guaranteed benefits are typically those present in insurance activities. The IFRIC noted that providing guidance on this issue would be in the nature of application guidance, rather than interpretative guidance. Consequently, the IFRIC decided not to add the issue to its agenda.

2.4 Contracts for contingent consideration in a business combination

Under IFRS 3(2008), contracts for contingent consideration which meet the definition of a financial instrument are within the scope of IAS 32, IAS 39 and IFRS 7 for both the acquirer and the seller. Paragraph BC349 in the Basis for Conclusions accompanying IFRS 3(2008) states that "the boards noted that most contingent consideration obligations are financial instruments, and many are derivative instruments".

Contracts for contingent consideration in a business combination that relate to business combinations accounted for in accordance with IFRS 3(2004) are excluded from IAS 32, IAS 39 and IFRS 7. They are subject to the requirements of IFRS 3(2004). This exemption applies only to the acquirer, not to the seller.

Improvements to IFRSs, issued by the IASB in May 2010, amended IFRS 3(2008) to make clear that contingent consideration balances arising from business combinations for which the acquisition date preceded the adoption of IFRS 3(2008) remain subject to the requirements of IFRS 3(2004) and, therefore, are not within the scope of IAS 32, IAS 39 or IFRS 7.

Irrespective of whether IFRS 3(2008) has been adopted, a seller's contract for contingent consideration is within the scope of IAS 32, IAS 39 and IFRS 7. The seller will recognise a financial asset arising from the contract for contingent consideration. The measurement of this financial asset will depend on the facts and circumstances of the contractual arrangement. Because the cash flows under the contract for contingent consideration are often derived from an underlying such as the future performance of the entity that has been sold, the asset will often meet the definition of a derivative in its entirety (see **chapter C4**) and will therefore be measured at fair value through profit or loss. Alternatively, the contingent consideration asset may be partly a loan and receivable measured at amortised cost to the extent that part of the consideration is not contingent with a non-closely related embedded derivative measured at fair value through profit or loss (see **chapter C5**) if the whole contingent consideration is not designated as at fair value through profit or loss at initial recognition.

2.5 Contracts to buy or sell non-financial items

IAS 32, IAS 39 and IFRS 7 deal primarily with contracts that are financial items; however, they also capture some contracts to buy or sell non-financial items. Contracts to buy or sell non-financial items that can be settled net (either in cash or by exchanging financial instruments) are within the scope of IAS 32, IAS 39 and IFRS 7 unless they were entered into, and continue to be held, for the purpose of the receipt of the non-financial item in accordance with the entity's expected purchase, sale or usage requirements. [IAS 39:5]

2.5.1 Net settlement

Net settlement can be in cash, another financial instrument, or by exchanging financial instruments. It can be achieved in many ways:

[IAS 39:6]

(a) the contractual terms may permit either party to settle net in cash or by exchanging financial instruments;

(b) settlement may not be explicit under the terms of the contract, but the entity may have a past practice of net settling similar contracts (see **2.5.3**);

(c) for similar contracts, the entity may have a past practice of taking delivery of the underlying and selling it within a short period after delivery for the purpose of generating a profit from short-term price fluctuations or from dealer's margin; or

(d) the non-financial item that is the subject of the contract may be readily convertible to cash.

2.5.2 Non-performance penalties

The terms of a contract need to be evaluated in detail because net settlement provisions may be implicit rather than explicit.

A non-performance penalty in a purchase order, when the amount of the penalty is calculated by reference to changes in the price of the item that is the subject of the contract, is an example of an implicit net settlement provision.

Example 2.5.2A

Non-performance penalty equivalent to net settlement

Entity A enters into a forward purchase agreement with Entity B to buy 100 units of a commodity at CU1.00 per unit. Entity A defaults on the forward contract when the prevailing market price of the commodity is CU0.75 per unit. Under the terms of the contract, Entity A is required to pay Entity B a non-performance penalty of CU25, i.e. 100 x (CU1.00 – CU0.75). The non-performance penalty represents an implicit net settlement provision.

Conversely, fixed penalties or normal handling fees do not amount to net settlement.

Example 2.5.2B

Non-performance penalty not equivalent to net settlement

Entity A enters into a contract to purchase wheat which will be used in its manufacturing operations. The delivery contract stipulates a non-performance penalty of CU1 million if Entity A fails to take delivery of the wheat. This is a fixed penalty and does not provide for net settlement because the amount of CU1 million is not based on changes in the price of wheat (the reference asset).

2.5.3 Past practice

Contracts where there is a past practice of either net settling or purchasing and selling the underlying within a short period after delivery with a view to making a short-term profit (i.e. (b) or (c) in the list in **2.5.1**) are always within the scope of the financial instruments Standards. It cannot be argued that such contracts have been entered into and continue to be held for the purpose of the receipt or delivery of the non-financial item in accordance with the entity's expected purchase, sale or usage requirements, because the entity's activities clearly indicate that this is not the case.

Example 2.5.3A

Rolling contracts until physical delivery

Entity C is in the business of milling maize and using it in its production process. Entity C's procurement strategy for maize includes purchasing futures on a futures exchange. Due to the significant quantity of maize needed, Entity C enters into forward purchases of maize to secure the level required for the running of its business. The intention at the outset is to take physical delivery of the maize under these contracts.

In January 20X6, Entity C secures maize for its 20X6 requirements. The longest available maturity of maize futures contracts is to July 20X6. Entity C's purchasing policy requires it to secure maize at least for 9 months, i.e. as far out as September 20X6. Accordingly, Entity C enters into a larger number of July 20X6 contracts with a view to rolling some of them to September 20X6.

In April 20X6, Entity C will close out some of its July 20X6 futures at market value at the time, and take out September 20X6 futures. As a result, Entity C will take physical delivery of the maize under the September contracts only.

Entity C's practice of net settling some of its July futures contracts (i.e. its practice of net settling similar contracts) prevents it from arguing that it enters into futures contracts for the receipt of maize in accordance with its expected purchase, sale or usage requirements. Accordingly, both the July and September contracts are within the scope of IAS 39.

Example 2.5.3B

Choice of cash or physical settlement (1)

[Extract from IAS 39:IG.A.1]

Entity XYZ enters into a fixed price forward contract to purchase one million kilograms of copper in accordance with its expected usage requirements. The contract permits XYZ to take physical delivery of the copper at the end of twelve months or to pay or receive a net settlement in cash, based on the change in fair value of copper.

If XYZ intends to settle the contract by taking delivery and has no history for similar contracts of settling net in cash or of taking delivery of the copper and selling it within a short period after delivery for the purpose of generating a profit from short-term fluctuations in price or dealer's margin, the contract is not accounted for as a derivative under IAS 39. Instead, it is accounted for as an executory contract [*i.e. outside the scope of IAS 39*].

Example 2.5.3C

Choice of cash or physical settlement (2)

Entity A is a copper manufacturer. Entity A enters into forward contracts to sell its copper cathode to its customers. The forward contracts are homogenous and permit Entity A to either:

- provide physical delivery of copper at the end of the contract; or
- pay or receive a net settlement in cash based on the change in fair value of copper.

Based on its inventory levels and its production capacity, Entity A is able to meet the obligation to deliver copper if it decides to provide physical delivery of copper for all of its outstanding forward sales contracts.

The stated intention in entering into the forward sales contracts is for the purpose of delivery of copper in accordance with its sales requirements. Historically, Entity A has a practice of net settling a portion of similar forward contracts, provided that the contracts are in the money. For contracts that are out of the money, historically Entity A has opted for physical delivery.

These contracts are all homogenous and the fact that Entity A has a past practice of net settling a portion of similar forward contracts means that it cannot assert that the contracts are held for the purpose of the delivery of copper in accordance with its expected sale requirements. Accordingly, the forward contracts are in the scope of IAS 39 and will be accounted for as derivatives.

In some circumstances, an entity will net settle as part of its normal operating cycle, as opposed to net settling in order to generate profits from short-term movements in prices. This is particularly common for utility entities that need to balance the demand from their customers with their supply contracts. For example, a retail gas supplier purchases gas under long-term take-or-pay contracts where if it does not take physical delivery of gas it has to pay a fixed monetary amount per unit. The buyer's intent is to use the contracted volumes it takes delivery of to serve its customers. However, the demand in certain periods (usually in the summer months) may fall below the minimum required contractual take. In this case, the buyer is forced to settle net, i.e. pay amounts without receiving gas, because the relative scarcity of natural gas storage capacity makes it difficult to store it for later use (storage of electricity is effectively impossible, so a similar situation is likely under a power contract). This 'balancing' activity is common for gas and power entities serving retail customers because customer demand forecasts cannot be precise. The practice of net settling similar contracts needs to be considered in determining whether the long-term contracts meet the definition of own-use requirements contracts for the purpose of applying the IAS 39 scope exemption.

It is a matter of judgement what is past practice of net settlement. An entity will need to consider its historical behaviour, reasons for past net settlement, and relative frequency. In some cases, it may be argued that an occurrence of a net settlement in the past was the result of an isolated non-recurring event that could not have been reasonably anticipated.

2.5.4 Written options

In addition to the restriction on contracts when there is a past practice of settling net or a practice of taking delivery of the underlying and selling it within a short period after delivery, a written option to buy or sell a non-financial item that can be settled net contractually or when the non-financial item is readily convertible to cash is always within the scope of IAS 39.

Example 2.5.4A

Written call option with no net settlement

Entity XYZ owns an office building. It writes Entity ABC an option, allowing Entity ABC to purchase the office building for a fixed price on a future date. The terms of the contract do not allow for it to be net settled, and the office building is not readily convertible to cash. Therefore, although Entity XYZ has written an option, the option does not fall within the scope of IAS 39.

Example 2.5.4B

Written put with possible net settlement

[Extract from IAS 39:IG.A.2]

Entity XYZ owns an office building. Entity XYZ enters into a put option with an investor that permits XYZ to put the building to the investor for CU150 million. The current value of the building is CU175 million. The option expires in five years. The option, if exercised, may be settled through physical delivery or net cash, at XYZ's option.

XYZ's accounting depends on XYZ's intention and past practice for settlement. Although the contract meets the definition of a derivative, XYZ does not account for it as a derivative [*i.e. the contract would not be in the scope of IAS 39*] if XYZ intends to settle the contract by delivering the building if Entity XYZ exercises its option and there is no past practice of settling net (IAS 39:5 and IAS 39:AG10).

The investor, however, cannot conclude that the option was entered into to meet the investor's expected purchase, sale or usage requirements because the investor does not have the ability to require delivery (IAS 39:7). In addition, the option may be settled net in cash. Therefore, the investor has to account for the contract as a derivative [*i.e. within the scope of IAS 39*]. Regardless of past practices, the investor's intention does not affect whether settlement is by delivery or in cash. The investor has written an option, and a written option in which the holder has a choice of physical settlement or net cash settlement can never satisfy the normal delivery requirement for the exemption from IAS 39 because the option writer does not have the ability to require delivery.

IAS 39 does not define a written option, with only limited discussion of written options provided in the context of hedge accounting. IAS 39:AG94 states that the potential loss on an option an entity writes could be significantly greater than the potential gain in value of a related hedged item.

There are different schools of thought as to what is considered to be a written option in the context of contracts over non-financial items. Some focus on the existence of a premium received. This treatment is analogous to the approach described in the hedge accounting guidance, under which the receipt of a premium (whether up-front or over the life of the option), indicates that the party to the option is taking on a greater risk of loss and, therefore, is being compensated by a premium. However, in the context of contracts over a non-financial item, this approach has its difficulties, largely because it can be extremely difficult to ascertain whether a premium is received over the life when this 'premium' may be included in the pricing of the non-financial item that will be delivered under the contract.

An alternative approach is to consider whether the holder of the option has the ability to exercise the option in order to make a profit. This approach assesses the pay-off characteristics of the contract. In circumstances where the behaviour of the holder in exercising the option is independent of price (i.e. the holder exercises the option for reasons other than the value of the underlying being greater than the strike price under the option), it could be argued that the holder exercises the option not in order to profit, but to take delivery of the non-financial item so as to meet the expected purchase, sale or usage requirements. Examples of this are electricity supply contracts to retail customers because generally electricity is considered to be readily convertible to cash in the hands of the writer of the option. As the holder of the option, the retail customer has no ability to take delivery of the electricity, store it, and sell the electricity on at a profit (i.e. the holder is unable to realise a profit from the contract). The holder's behaviour is driven simply by the need for electricity to meet its usage requirements. From the perspective of the writer of the option (i.e. the electricity seller), it can then be argued that it has not written an option.

In March 2007, the IFRIC (now the IFRS Interpretations Committee) issued an agenda decision on IAS 39, *Written Options in Retail Energy Contracts*. The IFRIC discussed what is meant by a 'written option' within the context of IAS 39:7. The discussion was primarily concerned with the accounting for energy supply contracts to retail customers. The agenda decision states that, following an analysis of such contracts, the IFRIC believes that in many situations these contracts do not meet the net settlement criteria laid out in IAS 39:5 & 6 and, if this is the case, such contracts would not be considered to be within the scope of IAS 39. It is not entirely clear from the IFRIC's agenda decision whether they considered these contracts as written options over an underlying that is not readily convertible into cash (and, therefore, not net settled per IAS 39:6(d)), or whether they did not consider them written options at all (and, therefore, viewed an analysis of ready convertibility of the underlying into cash as irrelevant).

In March 2010, the IFRIC (now the IFRS Interpretations Committee) issued an agenda decision on IAS 39, *Unit of Account for Forward Contracts with Volumetric Optionality*. The IFRIC had received a request to provide guidance on whether a contract that:

(a) obliges an entity to deliver (sell) at a fixed price a fixed number of units of a non-financial item that is readily convertible to cash and

(b) provides the counterparty with the option to purchase, also at a fixed price, a fixed number of additional units of the same item

can be assessed as two separate contracts for the purpose of applying IAS 39:5 - 7.

For example, an entity enters into an agreement to buy 100 units of a non-financial item that is readily convertible into cash, which includes a right to purchase a further 15 units at the same contracted price. These contracts are often referred to as having 'volumetric flexibility'.

The IFRIC recognised that diversity exists in practice and noted that the Board has accelerated its project to develop a replacement for IAS 39. At the time of its decision the IFRIC expected the IASB to issue a comprehensive replacement Standard by the end of 2010. The agenda decision stated the Board will consider the scope of IAS 39, including the guidance about contracts to buy or sell non-financial items in IAS 39:5 - 7, as part of the replacement Standard. Consequently, the IFRIC decided not to add this issue to its agenda.

At the date of writing, the IASB had not reconsidered the guidance on contracts to buy or sell non-financial items as part of its project to replace IAS 39.

Because IAS 39 assesses financial instruments on a contract-by-contract basis, when assessing whether the terms of the arrangement meet the own use and net settlement requirements in IAS 39:5 - 7, it is appropriate to view the unit of account as the whole contract. Using the example described above, if the seller concludes that the option on the 15 units is a written option, then the whole contract for 115 units is a written option. The contract is a single contract over 115 units and, therefore, it is not appropriate to split it into (1) a forward over 100 units classified as a normal usage requirements contract outside the scope of IAS 39, and (2) a written option over 15 units within the scope of IAS 39.

2.5.5 Expected purchase, sale and usage requirements

Non-optional contracts or purchased options over non-financial items where either the terms of the contract permit net settlement, or where the non-financial item that is subject to the contract is readily convertible to cash (e.g. many commodity contracts) must be assessed to see if they were entered into for the receipt or purchase of the item in accordance with the entity's expected purchase, sale or usage requirements.

Example 2.5.5

Purchase contract with possible net settlement

Entity X enters into a fixed price forward contract to purchase one million tonnes of copper. Copper is traded on the London Metals Exchange and is readily convertible to cash. The contract permits Entity X to take physical delivery of the copper at the end of 12 months or to pay or receive a net settlement in cash, based on the change in fair value of copper. Entity X does not have a practice of settling similar contracts net or taking physical delivery of copper and selling it within a short period after delivery for the purposes of generating a profit from short-term fluctuations in price.

In order for the contract to be scoped out of IAS 39, Entity X needs to demonstrate that the contract was entered into and continues to be held for the purpose of the receipt of copper in accordance with its expected purchase or usage requirements. In addition to past practice, factors like the quantities involved, quality and grades of the commodity, and delivery locations would need to be considered.

If the reporting entity, rather than the counterparty, has the choice of net cash settlement, the reporting entity may be able to demonstrate that it does not intend to exercise its right to net cash settlement and, therefore, the existence of the net cash settlement feature does not result in the arrangement being scoped into IAS 39. If the choice of net cash settlement is with the counterparty, it will generally not be possible for the reporting entity to demonstrate that the non-financial item will be delivered under the contract because the reporting entity does not control the cash settlement decision. If the reporting entity cannot insist that the counterparty delivers the non-financial item, the reporting entity cannot demonstrate that it intends to receive the non-financial item in accordance with its expected purchase, sale or usage requirements.

Each contract must be evaluated in its entirety. For example, an entity may have a contract for 100 units, but its expected usage requirement is only 80 units. The entity intends to net settle the part of the contract it does not need in its normal course of business. Such partial net settlement can be achieved in different ways (e.g. by entering into an offsetting contract for 20 units, or by taking delivery of all 100 units and selling 20 immediately). The entire contract falls within the scope of IAS 39 because the entire contract cannot be argued to be in accordance with the entity's expected usage requirements.

The following decision tree illustrates how to evaluate whether contracts to buy or sell non-financial items are within the scope of IAS 32, IAS 39 and IFRS 7.

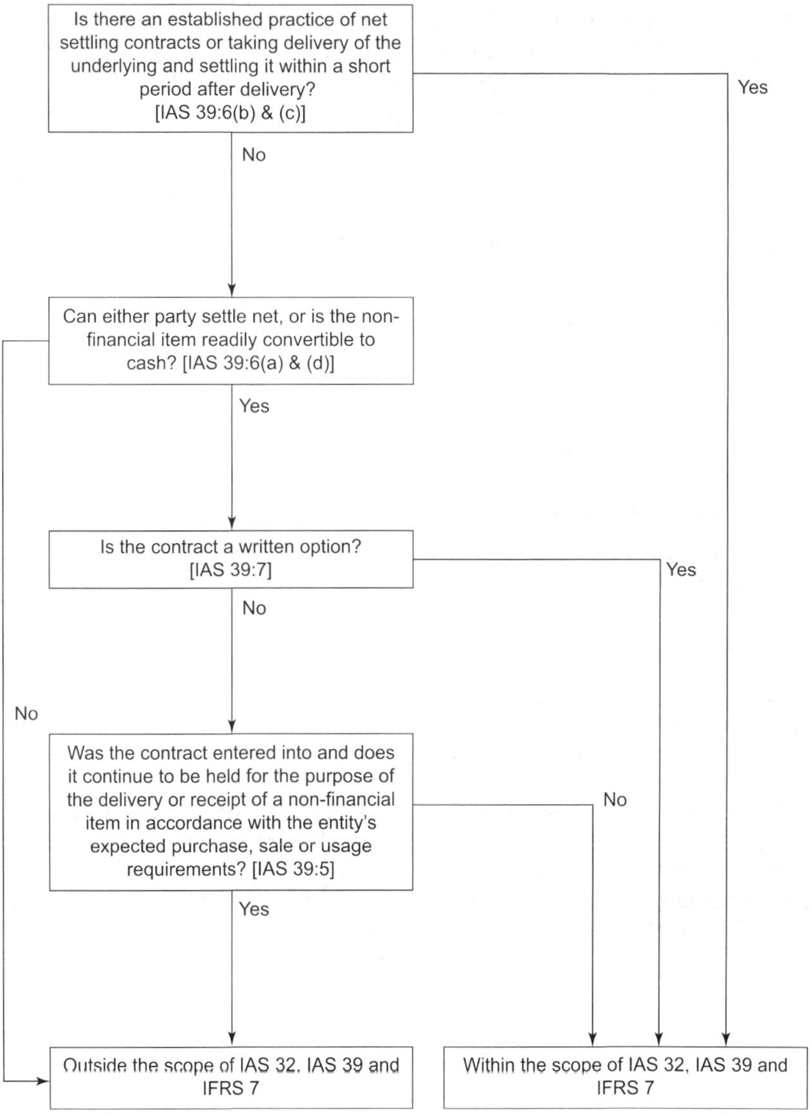

Entities may enter into multiple contracts with the same contractual terms for different reasons. Care needs to be taken in determining whether the contracts themselves should have the same accounting treatment or not. One subsidiary in a group may enter into contracts to buy non-financial items that are used in the group's production processes for the provision of finished goods and that are always physically delivered. A separate part of the group may enter into contractual arrangements with the same contractual terms but that are not always physically delivered (e.g. this separate business may cash settle the contracts or enter into offsetting contracts as part of a trading strategy). From a group perspective, it may be possible to differentiate the two portfolios of contracts in the two separate businesses and, therefore, account for them differently; such differentiation will only be appropriate if (1) the contracts are entered into separately and not in contemplation of each other, (2) there are no transfers between the businesses within the group, (3) the businesses are managed independently of each other, and (4) the strategies of the businesses are sufficiently different that the different settlement behaviour of each business is reasonable. In practice, it is unlikely that such a distinction is possible because different parts of a group often choose to transact with each other rather than entering separately into offsetting transactions outside the group, which would result in additional transaction costs.

2.5.6 Change of settlement terms

The terms of a contract, or the intentions of an entity, may change over time. A contract outside the scope of IAS 39 will continue to be treated as such only if it continues to be held for the purpose of the receipt or delivery of a non-financial item in accordance with the entity's expected purchase, sale or usage requirements.

Example 2.5.6

Change of terms to include net settlement

Two parties enter into a contract for the delivery of a non-financial asset. There is no net settlement provision in the contract, no established market mechanism or side agreement, and no history of net settlement.

Subsequently, the parties agree to settle the contract net. From the time the decision to settle net is taken, the contract will be recognised and measured under IAS 39 because, from that time, the contract no longer continues to be for the purpose of the receipt of the non-financial asset in accordance with the expected purchase, sale or usage requirements.

2.6 Share-based payments

IAS 32, IAS 39 and IFRS 7 exclude from their scope financial instruments, contracts and obligations under share-based payment arrangements to which IFRS 2 *Share-based Payment* applies, except for contracts over non-financial items that are within the scope of IAS 39 (see **section 2.5**). However, the scope of IAS 32 makes it clear that treasury shares that are purchased, sold, issued or cancelled in connection with employee share option plans, employee share purchase plans, and all other share-based payment arrangements are in the scope of IAS 32 (see **section 5** of **chapter C3**).

2.7 Construction contract receivables

Construction contract receivables are measured and presented in accordance with IFRS 15 *Revenue from Contracts with Customers*. The financial instruments Standards do not specifically scope out these contracts and, therefore, consideration must be given as to whether such receivables are financial instruments. A right to cash or another financial asset is a critical component of the definition of a financial asset. In construction contract arrangements, the amount of work carried out by the contractor may be in excess of the amount that is billed. Where only the passage of time is required before consideration is due, IFRS 15:108 requires that a receivable is recognised in the statement of financial position. Where there is a further conditional requirement before payment is due, for example certification of work done, IFRS 15:107 requires that a contract asset is recognised in the statement of financial position. In either case the amount recognised is subject to the impairment requirements of IAS 39. An entity must consider whether the amount recognised in accordance with IFRS 15 can be contractually billed or recovered.

Example 2.7

Gross amount due from customer for contract work

Entity A has entered into a contract with Entity B for the construction of a building. The contract is within the scope of IFRS 15, and is specifically not within the scope of IFRIC 12 *Service Concession Arrangements*. Entity A has assessed that the revenue from the contract will be recognised over time in accordance with IFRS 15. At the end of the reporting period, costs incurred plus recognised profits (less recognised losses) exceed progress billings and Entity A presents a contract asset in its statement of financial position.

Under the terms of the contract, Entity A is only able to invoice Entity B when specific work performed by Entity A has been certified as completed. These invoiced amounts are recognised in the statement of financial position as a separate financial asset because they represent a contractual right to receive cash and, therefore, meet the definition of a financial asset in IAS 32:11. Until that point the contract asset is not a financial asset because it is not

> "a contractual right... to receive cash or another financial asset from another entity". [IAS 32:11]

IAS 39 and IFRS 7 do not apply to an asset that is not a financial instrument as defined in IAS 32.

3 Additional scope exclusions of IAS 39

In addition to the scope exclusions discussed above, IAS 39 sets out a number of further exclusions, as follows:

- financial instruments issued by the entity that meet the definition of equity instruments in accordance with IAS 32 (see **3.1**);
- forward contracts to buy or sell an acquiree in a business combination (see **3.2**);
- certain reimbursement rights (see **3.3**);
- rights and obligations under leases, although in certain circumstances the derecognition, impairment and embedded derivative requirements of IAS 39 apply (see **3.4**); and
- certain loan commitments (see **3.5**).

Each of these items is considered in turn in the following sections.

3.1 Equity instruments of the entity

Financial instruments issued by an entity that meet the definition of equity instruments in IAS 32 (see **section 2** of **chapter C3**) are outside the scope of IAS 39. This exemption includes stand-alone equity instruments (e.g. ordinary shares), as well as derivatives over own equity that exchange a fixed amount of cash or other financial asset for a fixed number of equity instruments. The exemption applies only to the issuer of the equity instrument. The holder of the instrument should apply the recognition and measurement criteria of IAS 39.

> **Example 3.1**
>
> **Classification of equity instruments held as an economic hedge**
>
> Entity F is a large financial institution whose shares are included in the FTSE 100 Index. Entity F issues a bond whose principal amount varies with the movement in the FTSE 100 share index (an 'index tracker bond'). In order to hedge economically the equity derivative that is embedded in the bond, Entity F purchases a portfolio of the shares contained in the FTSE 100 index and wishes to classify them as held for trading. However, because IAS 39.2(d) excludes instruments that meet the definition of equity in IAS 32 from the scope of the Standard, Entity F cannot recognise its own purchased shares

as financial assets. IAS 32 requires that treasury shares be presented in the statement of financial position as a deduction from equity and not as financial assets, and that no gain or loss should be recognised in profit or loss on such equity instruments.

Following the amendment to IAS 32 *Puttable Financial Instruments and Obligations Arising on Liquidation*, issued in February 2008, some instruments previously classified as financial liabilities are classified as equity (see **2.1.2.1** and **2.1.3** in **chapter C3**). The IAS 32 amendment also amended IFRS 7 to exclude these instruments classified as equity from the scope of IFRS 7. [IFRS 7:3(f)]

IFRS 7 scopes out derivatives over own equity that meet the definition of equity. IFRS 7 does not appear to have a scope exception for non-derivative instruments classified as equity, such as ordinary shares. This appears to be an oversight in the drafting of the Standard because IFRS 7:BC8 states that the scope of IFRS 7 is intended to be the same as IAS 32 (which included disclosure requirements for financial instruments prior to IFRS 7 being issued) with one exception, namely "derivatives based on interests in subsidiaries, associates or joint ventures if the derivatives meet the definition of an equity instrument in IAS 32". The Basis for Conclusions justifies the exclusion of such derivatives by stating that these instruments are not remeasured and hence "do not expose the issuer to balance sheet and income statement risk" and that the disclosures about the significance of financial instruments for financial position and performance are not relevant to equity instruments. In addition, IFRS 7:BC8 states that these instruments are excluded from the scope of IFRS 7, but they are within the scope of IAS 32 for the purpose of determining whether they meet the definition of equity instruments. It appears reasonable to conclude that the scope exclusions for derivatives over own equity that meet the definition of equity also applies to non-derivatives that meet the definition of equity because the justification in the Basis for Conclusions of IFRS 7 would be equally relevant.

3.2 Forward contracts to buy or sell an acquiree in a business combination

Forward contracts between an acquirer and a selling shareholder in a business combination to buy or sell an acquiree that will result in a business combination within the scope of IFRS 3 *Business Combinations* are outside the scope of IAS 39. The term of the forward contract should not exceed a reasonable period normally necessary to obtain any required approvals and to complete the transaction. The application of IAS 39:2(g) is assessed at the time the holder enters into the derivative contract. If the contract is a forward contract, whether partly prepaid or not, which will lead to a certain business combination, the exemption applies and the forward contract is outside the scope of IAS 39. Contracts that have settlement alternatives that may not result in all cases in the delivery of shares to the acquirer will be within the scope of IAS 39 because the exemption within IAS 39:2(g) will not apply.

The above scenarios should be distinguished from contracts between an acquirer and vendor that are options to buy or sell a business in the future. IAS 27(2008) provides guidance as to whether an option represents a 'potential voting right that is currently exercisable or convertible'. If the option is currently exercisable but is not an in-substance present ownership interest, the appropriate accounting will depend on whether control currently exists. IFRS 10 requires an assessment of whether substantive potential voting rights alone, or in combination with other rights, can give an investor the current ability to direct the relevant activities of the entity and potentially control the entity. For both IAS 27(2008) and IFRS 10, if control does exist, the parent's proportion of the acquiree in the consolidated financial statements is determined taking into account the present ownership interests which do not reflect the possible exercise or conversion of potential voting rights. In such circumstances, the ownership interest that excludes the exercise of the currently exercisable option is a subsidiary because there is control and, therefore, it will be necessary to consider whether the currently exercisable option (to acquire a non-controlling interest) meets the definition of equity in the consolidated financial statements (see **section 6** in **chapter C3**). If the option meets the definition of equity, it is outside the scope of IAS 39. Otherwise, it will be within the scope of IAS 39 and the exemption in IAS 39:2(g) does not apply.

If the option is currently exercisable and it gives the holder the ability to control the target entity, and it is an in-substance present ownership interest, then in accordance with IAS 27(2008) and IFRS 10:B90 control exists and the parent's proportion of the acquiree in the consolidated financial statements is determined reflecting the in substance present ownership interest. The option is not subject to the requirements of IAS 39 in such circumstances because it is treated as a present ownership interest rather than being a derivative to acquire such an interest in the future.

If the option is not currently exercisable and would give the holder the ability to control the target entity only when it becomes exercisable, the scope exemption within IAS 39:2(g) also does not apply. The option will not always result in a business combination to buy or sell an acquiree at a future date and therefore is in the scope of IAS 39.

The IAS 39:2(g) exemption applies equally to the acquirer and the vendor. Therefore, if the acquirer applies the exemption on the basis that the contract will result in a future business combination, the vendor equally applies the exemption and scopes out its contract to sell its subsidiary to the acquirer in its consolidated financial statements. Irrespective of IAS 39:2(g), the contract may be outside the scope of IAS 39 for the vendor because the contract may meet the definition of equity when the contract is a forward sale of shares in a subsidiary for a fixed amount of functional currency.

In 2007, the IFRIC (now the IFRS Interpretations Committee) was asked to interpret whether the IAS 39:2(g) scope exemption applies only to binding contracts to acquire shares that constitute a controlling interest in another entity within the period necessary to complete a business combination, or if it applies more widely, and also whether it applies to similar transactions, such as those to acquire an interest in an associate. In January 2008, the IFRIC acknowledged that the wording in IAS 39:2(g) was ambiguous and could lead to diversity in practice. For this reason, the IFRIC referred the issue to the IASB. In April 2009, the IASB issued *Improvements to IFRSs*, which amended IAS 39:2(g). As amended, IAS 39:2(g) states that the scope exception applies only to forward contracts between an acquirer and a selling shareholder to buy or sell an acquiree that will result in a business combination at a future acquisition date. The term of the forward contract should not exceed a reasonable period normally necessary to obtain any required approvals and to complete the transaction.

Following the amendment made by *Improvements to IFRSs*, IAS 39:BC24D makes clear that the exception in IAS 39:2(g) should not be applied by analogy to investments in associates and similar transactions because an investment in an associate does not represent an acquisition of the constituent assets of the investee. The purpose of IAS 39:2(g) is to exempt from the provisions of IAS 39 contracts for business combinations that are firmly committed to be completed. Once the business combination is consummated, the entity follows the requirements of IFRS 3. IAS 39:2(g) applies only when completion of the business combination is not dependent on further actions of either party (and only the passage of a normal period of time is required). This contrasts with option contracts, which allow one party to control the occurrence or non-occurrence of future events depending on whether the option is exercised.

3.3 Certain reimbursement rights

Rights to payments to reimburse the entity for expenditure it is required to make to settle a liability that it recognises as a provision in accordance with IAS 37 *Provisions, Contingent Liabilities and Contingent Assets*, or for which, in an earlier period, it recognised a provision in accordance with IAS 37, are outside the scope of IAS 39. [IAS 39:2(j)] Such rights are within the scope of IAS 37 and are recognised as a separate asset when, and only when, it is virtually certain that the reimbursement will be received if and when the entity settles the liability. [IAS 37:53]

3.4 Rights and obligations under lease contracts

Rights and obligations under lease contracts may meet the definition of a financial instrument. In a finance lease, a lease receivable recognised by the lessor represents the lessor's right to receive a stream of cash flows. This receivable is substantially the same as blended payments of principal and interest under a loan agreement. Accordingly, a finance lease is a contract that gives rise to a financial asset from the lessor's perspective and also gives rise to a financial liability from the lessee's perspective. Operating leases, on the other hand, are generally regarded as uncompleted contracts whereby lessors provide the use of assets in exchange for a fee for their service. Accordingly, an operating lease is not regarded as a financial instrument (except as regards individual payments currently due and payable). This continues to be the case even if the operating lease is regarded as an onerous contract and a provision has been recognised in accordance with IAS 37. IAS 17 *Leases* sets out the accounting framework for leases and, consequently, leases are, for the most part, outside of the scope of all four financial instruments Standards. However:

- lease receivables recognised by a lessor are subject to the derecognition and impairment requirements of IAS 39 (see **section 3** of **chapter C8** and **section 5** of **chapter C6** respectively);
- finance lease payables recognised by a lessee are subject to the derecognition requirements of IAS 39 (see **section 4** of **chapter C8**);
- derivatives embedded in lease contracts are subject to the embedded derivative requirements of IAS 39 (see **section 9** of **chapter C5**); and
- finance leases are subject to the disclosure and presentation requirements of IFRS 7 and IAS 32.

3.5 Loan commitments

Loan commitments that cannot be settled net in cash or another financial instrument are outside the scope of IAS 39, unless the entity designates them as financial liabilities at fair value through profit or loss. If an entity has a past practice of selling the asset resulting from a loan commitment shortly after its origination, it should apply IAS 39 to all loan commitments in the same class.

Loan commitments that can be settled net in cash or another financial instrument are derivatives within the scope of IAS 39. Instalment payments do not constitute net settlement. Thus, for example, a mortgage construction loan that is paid out in instalments in line with the progress of the construction is not within the scope of IAS 39. [IAS 39:2(h)]

A financial institution may write a loan commitment to a large corporate borrower as a lead lender with the expressed intention of selling part of the loan to other financial institutions immediately when lent. The intention to sell part of the loan is part of the financial institution's predetermined credit risk management. At the inception of the loan commitment, the financial institution cannot assert that it does not have a past practice of selling the asset resulting from a loan commitment shortly after its origination and, therefore, it cannot consider the loan commitment wholly outside the scope of IAS 39. The financial institution may be able to demonstrate that, consistent with its predetermined credit risk management, only part of the loan that may be originated from the loan commitment is intended to be sold and, if so, that only that proportion of the loan commitment is in the scope of IAS 39 and is measured at fair value through profit or loss. If the loan is originated, the part of the loan commitment that is measured at fair value through profit or loss will be derecognised and will be incorporated into the initial carrying amount of the resulting loan.

If an entity commits to providing a loan at a below-market interest rate, it should initially recognise the commitment at fair value. Subsequently, the commitment is measured at the higher of:

[IAS 39:47(d)]

(i) the amount determined under IAS 37 *Provisions, Contingent Liabilities and Contingent Assets*; and

(ii) the amount initially recognised less, when appropriate, the cumulative amount of income recognised in accordance with the principles of IFRS 15 *Revenue from Contracts with Customers*.

Loan commitments can either be optional (i.e. provide a borrower with the right to borrow in the future from a specified lender) or non-optional (i.e. the borrower must borrow from the specified lender). In all cases, the lender will lend funds to the borrower either when the borrower exercises its right to borrow or, in the case of non-optional loan commitments, in accordance with the specified conditions in the contract. If a contract requires or gives an option for an entity to *acquire* a debt instrument, as opposed to lending funds to the borrower under the commitment, this arrangement is not a loan commitment because a lending will not take place. The arrangement is a derivative financial instrument which will be measured at fair value through profit or loss except if it meets the regular way exemption as described in **2.2** in **chapter C8**.

The scoping out of loan commitments as described above applies equally to the holder (the borrower) as it does to the writer (the lender). If a loan commitment is not within the scope of IAS 39, the writer accounts for it in accordance with IAS 37 and IFRS 15; however, all loan commitments are subject to the derecognition provisions of IAS 39.

3.5.1 Measurement of loan commitment outside the scope of IAS 39 (holder)

IFRSs do not provide specific guidance on the measurement of a loan commitment that is outside the scope of IAS 39 from the perspective of the holder. When the holder of the loan commitment pays the writer of the loan commitment compensation for entering into the loan commitment, the fair value of the compensation should be recognised as an asset. From the holder's perspective, the asset represents the right for the entity to borrow in the future on pre-specified terms which may be favourable. For the holder, the asset should be released to profit or loss on a systematic basis reflecting the periods over which the holder has the right to exercise the loan commitment.

If the loan commitment is fully drawn down by the holder and no further amounts can be drawn down, it would be appropriate to recognise the remaining unamortised loan commitment asset as part of the carrying amount of the borrowing on initial recognition as a transaction cost (see **2.1** in **chapter C6**). If the loan is not measured at fair value through profit or loss, this will form part of the instrument's effective interest rate (see **4.1** in **chapter C6**).

When the fee paid by the holder is more in the nature of a facility fee such that the amounts and timing of the draw-down and the repayment of the borrowing can vary at the discretion of the borrower (e.g. an overdraft fee), it would not be appropriate to capitalise the fee as a transaction cost when amounts are drawn down. The fee is not specific to an amount borrowed and, therefore, a systematic release of the fee over the period of the facility is more appropriate.

3.5.2 Loan commitment where the loan includes a non-closely related embedded derivative

When the loan to be originated under a loan commitment will be in the scope of IAS 39 and will include a non-closely related embedded derivative (see **section 3** in **chapter C5**), the question arises as to whether it is still permissible for the loan commitment to be scoped out of IAS 39 for the writer or the holder of the loan commitment. Once the loan is originated under the commitment, if it is under IAS 39 the non-closely related embedded derivative will be separated from the host loan contract and separately accounted for at fair value through profit or loss (unless the whole loan is designated at fair value through profit or loss at initial recognition – see **3.1** in **chapter C2** and **7.1.2** in **chapter C3**). It could be argued that applying the scope exemption in such circumstances creates a measurement inconsistency between the measurement of the loan commitment (outside the scope of IAS 39 and not measured at fair value) and the subsequent measurement of the loan (within the scope of IAS 39 and either wholly at fair value through profit or loss if so designated or in part measured at fair value in the case of a separately recognised embedded derivative). However, it should be noted that IAS 39 already allows such a measurement inconsistency when a loan commitment that will result in a loan not containing any embedded derivatives is outside the scope of IAS 39 (and not measured at fair value) and the loan subsequently originated under the commitment is designated at fair value through profit or loss under certain conditions. Therefore, it seems appropriate that the scope exemption for loan commitments that will result in loans with separately accounted embedded derivatives under IAS 39 should still apply if the relevant conditions are met (i.e. the loan commitment cannot be settled net in cash, the entity has not designated it as at fair value through profit or loss, and the entity does not have a past practice of selling the assets resulting from loan commitments shortly after origination).

To illustrate, Entity X may enter into a firm commitment to lend to Entity Y. The loan to be originated under the commitment will be a loan that the lender can convert into a fixed number of equity shares of the borrower. Once originated, the lender will have a loan asset with a separate non-closely related embedded derivative if the analysis in the paragraph above would apply. For Entity X the loan commitment would be outside the scope of IAS 39.

From Entity Y's perspective, the loan commitment is a right jointly to borrow cash and issue a derivative over its own equity. The loan commitment is partly a derivative over debt and partly a derivative over a derivative over own equity. The definition of a financial liability (see **section 2** in **chapter C3**) makes it clear that a derivative over a derivative over own equity would itself not meet the definition of equity and, therefore, it could be argued that the loan commitment can be considered to be within the scope of IAS 39. However, IAS 39:BC15 recognises that all loan commitments are in fact derivatives that are excluded from the scope of IAS 39. Consequently, it is reasonable to consider such a loan commitment for Entity Y as also being outside the scope of IAS 39.

4 Future developments

In July 2014 the IASB finalised IFRS 9. When IFRS 9 is effective it will replace IAS 39. The effective date of IFRS 9 is for annual reporting periods beginning on or after 1 January 2018, with early application permitted.

The scope of IFRS 9 and IAS 39 are substantially aligned. A major difference is IFRS 9 extends the scope of financial instruments accounting to include more non-financial contracts than are permitted in IAS 39. IFRS 9 permits, at initial recognition, to irrevocably designate as measured at fair value through profit or loss a contract to buy or sell a non-financial item that can be settled net in cash or another financial asset, or by exchanging financial instruments, as if the contract was a financial instrument, that was entered into for the purpose of the receipt or delivery of a non-financial item in accordance with the entity's expected purchase, sale or usage requirements. An entity may make this designation only if doing so eliminates or significantly reduces a recognition inconsistency (sometimes referred to as an 'accounting mismatch') that would otherwise arise from not recognising that contract because it is excluded from the scope of IFRS 9.

A further difference between the scope of IFRS 9 and IAS 39 is that the impairment requirements of IFRS 9 apply to all issued loan commitments that are not measured at fair value through profit or loss as compared to the scope of IAS 39 which requires issued loan commitments to be measured in accordance with IAS 37 if they are not in the scope of IAS 39.

C2 Financial assets

Contents

1 Introduction

IAS 39 prescribes how financial assets should be classified, which then drives how they should be measured subsequent to recognition.

All financial assets are required to be classified into one of the four primary classification categories; two of these categories ('held-to-maturity' and 'loans and receivables') are measured at amortised cost, and the other two categories ('fair value through profit or loss' and 'available-for-sale') are measured at fair value.

2 Definition of a financial asset

IAS 32:11 defines a financial asset as "any asset that is:

(a) cash;

(b) an equity instrument of another entity;

(c) a contractual right:

  (i) to receive cash or another financial asset from another entity; or

  (ii) to exchange financial assets or financial liabilities with another entity under conditions that are potentially favourable to the entity; or

(d) a contract that will or may be settled in the entity's own equity instruments and is:

  (i) a non-derivative for which the entity is or may be obliged to receive a variable number of the entity's own equity instruments; or

  (ii) a derivative that will or may be settled other than by the exchange of a fixed amount of cash or another financial asset for a fixed number of the entity's own equity instruments. For this purpose the entity's own equity instruments do not include puttable financial instruments classified as equity instruments in accordance with paragraph IAS 32:16A and 16B, instruments that impose on the entity an obligation to deliver to another party a pro rate share of the net assets of the entity only on liquidation and are classified as equity instruments in accordance with IAS 32:16C and 16D or instruments that are contracts for the future receipt or delivery of the entity's own equity instruments."

A deposit of cash with a bank or similar institution is a financial asset because it represents the contractual right of the depositor to obtain cash from the institution or to draw a cheque or similar instrument against the balance in favour of a creditor in payment of a financial liability.

Common examples of financial assets that represent a contractual right to receive cash in the future are trade accounts receivable, notes and loans receivable, and debt securities. An example of a financial asset that represents a contractual right to receive a financial asset other than cash is a note payable in treasury bonds which gives the holder the contractual right to receive treasury bonds.

Gold bullion is not a financial instrument, it is a commodity. Although bullion is highly liquid, there is no contractual right to receive cash or another financial asset inherent in the bullion. [IAS 39:IG.B.1] When the anticipated future economic benefit is the receipt of goods or services (e.g. prepaid expenses), the asset is not a financial asset. Also, assets that represent rights to receive cash that are not contractual (e.g. tax receivables) are not financial assets because they arise from statutory requirements. [IAS 32:AG12]

The definition of a financial asset also includes some derivative and non-derivative contracts indexed to, or settled in, an issuer's equity instruments, as illustrated in **example 2**.

Example 2

Derivative financial asset

On 1 February 20X0, Entity E enters into a contract with Entity F under which Entity E will receive the fair value of 1,000 of its own ordinary shares in exchange for a payment of CU104,000 in cash (i.e. CU104 per share) on 31 January 20X1. Under the terms of the contract, settlement will be net in cash. The market price per share of Entity E's ordinary shares on 1 February 20X0 is CU100.

The fair value at initial recognition of the forward contract on 1 February 20X0 is zero. On 31 December 20X0, Entity E's share price has increased and, as a result, the fair value of the forward contract has increased to CU6,300. Entity E should revalue the derivative asset to CU6,300 at 31 December 20X0.

For further detail on the classification of contracts indexed to or settled in an entity's own equity instruments as derivative assets or liabilities, gross liabilities or equity, by the issuer, see **section 6** in **chapter C3**.

3 Classification of financial assets

Every financial asset that falls within the scope of IAS 39 should be classified into one of the following four primary categories:

- at fair value through profit or loss (FVTPL);
- held to maturity (HTM);
- loans and receivables (L&R); or
- available-for-sale (AFS);

This classification is important because it drives the subsequent measurement of the asset (i.e. either at fair value or amortised cost).

Assets classified at FVTPL and AFS are measured at fair value, while those classified as HTM or L&R are measured at amortised cost. The only exception to this rule arises in respect of equity instruments that do not have a quoted market price in an active market and whose fair value cannot be reliably measured (and derivatives that are linked to and must be settled by delivery of such unquoted equity instruments), which are instead held at cost (see **3.1.6** in **chapter C6**).

Different classification categories that may apply for various financial asset types are illustrated in the following table.

	Type of financial asset		
Classification	**Investment in a debt security**	**Investment in an equity security for which fair value can be reliably measured**	**Derivatives and embedded derivatives**
FVTPL			
• held for trading	■	■	■
• designated as at FVTPL	■	■	
Loans and receivables	■		
Held-to-maturity	■		
Available-for-sale	■	■	

3.1 Financial assets at fair value through profit or loss (FVTPL)

FVTPL has two sub-categories.

- The first category comprises any financial asset that is designated on initial recognition as one to be measured at fair value with fair value changes recognised in profit or loss (see **3.1.1**).
- The second category comprises financial assets classified as held for trading (see **3.1.2**). All derivative assets are held for trading financial assets measured at FVTPL, except for derivatives that are designated and effective hedging instruments (see **chapter C9**).

3.1.1 Designation as at FVTPL

There are many reasons why an entity may wish to designate a financial instrument as at FVTPL:

- it eliminates an accounting mismatch;
- it allows an entity to avoid the burden of hedge accounting requirements (e.g. the requirements to designate, asses, and measure effectiveness – see **chapter C9**), because designation of both items as at FVTPL

achieves a similar result as if fair value hedge accounting had been applied;

- it de-emphasises interpretative issues regarding when an item is appropriately considered to be 'held for trading'; or
- when applied to hybrid instruments (see **chapter C5**), it eliminates the burden of separating embedded derivatives that are not considered to be closely related to the host contract because the fair value of the whole contractual arrangement is then recognised in profit or loss.

A financial asset or a financial liability may upon initial recognition be designated as at FVTPL only if it meets one of the following conditions:

(a) it eliminates or significantly reduces a measurement or recognition inconsistency that would otherwise arise from measuring assets or liabilities or recognising the gains and losses on them on different bases (commonly referred to as an 'accounting mismatch');

(b) a group of financial assets, financial liabilities or both is managed and its performance is evaluated on a fair value basis, in accordance with a documented risk management or investment strategy, and information about the group is provided internally on that basis to the entity's key management personnel (as defined in IAS 24 *Related Party Disclosures*); or

(c) in the case of a hybrid contract containing one or more embedded derivatives, an entity may designate the entire hybrid (combined) contract as a financial asset or financial liability as at FVTPL unless:

   - the embedded derivative does not significantly modify the cash flows that otherwise would be required by the contract; or
   - it is clear with little or no analysis when a similar hybrid instrument is first considered that separation of the embedded derivative is prohibited (e.g. a prepayment option embedded in a loan that permits the holder to prepay the loan for approximately its amortised cost – see **7.1** in **chapter C5**).

The election to designate a financial instrument as at FVTPL must be made at initial recognition of the financial instrument and cannot subsequently be revoked. This is the case even if the instrument giving rise to an accounting mismatch is derecognised. This is different from the approach taken when employing hedge accounting (see **chapter C9**) when an entity is free to revoke such a designation at any time.

The fair value option is not available for investments in equity instruments and derivatives that are linked to and must be settled by delivery of equity instruments, where the equity instrument does not have a quoted market price in an active market for which fair value is reliably determinable (see **3.1.6** in **chapter C6**).

It should be noted that the requirements for determining a reliable measure of the fair value of a financial asset or a financial liability apply equally to items that are measured at fair value and to those that are only disclosed at fair value.

The decision by an entity to designate a financial asset or a financial liability as at FVTPL is similar to an accounting policy choice in that the result of applying the fair value option should provide reliable and more relevant information about the effects of transactions, other events and conditions on the entity's financial position, financial performance or cash flows. [IAS 39:AG4C] However, an important difference between an accounting policy choice and the fair value option is that the latter is applied on an instrument-by-instrument basis.

The fair value option must be applied to a financial instrument in its entirety – it cannot be applied to only part of a financial instrument.

3.1.1.1 Eliminates or significantly reduces an accounting mismatch

The following are examples of the application of the fair value option so as to significantly reduce a measurement or recognition inconsistency.

- In the absence of designation as at FVTPL, a financial asset would often be classified as available-for-sale (with most changes in fair value recognised in other comprehensive income) while a related liability would often be measured at amortised cost (with changes in fair value not recognised). In such circumstances, an entity may conclude that its financial statements would provide more relevant information if both instruments were classified as at FVTPL. [IAS 39:AG4D]
- An entity's liabilities may have cash flows that are contractually linked to the performance of assets that would often be classified as available-for-sale. For example, an insurer may have liabilities that pay benefits based on realised / unrealised investment returns on a specified pool of the insurer's assets. If the measurement of those liabilities reflects current market prices, designating the assets as at FVTPL means that changes in the fair value of the financial assets are recognised in profit or loss in the same period as related changes in the value of the liabilities. [IAS 39:AG4E(a)]
- An entity may have liabilities under insurance contracts whose measurement incorporates current information (as permitted by IFRS 4 *Insurance Contracts*), and related financial assets would often be classified as available-for-sale or measured at amortised cost. Designating the assets as at FVTPL means that changes in the fair value of the financial assets are recognised in profit or loss in the same period as related changes in the value of the liabilities. [IAS 39:AG4E(b)]
- An entity may have financial assets, financial liabilities, or both, that share a risk (e.g. interest rate risk) that gives rise to opposite changes in fair value that tend to offset each other. However, only some of the instruments (e.g. derivatives) are measured at FVTPL. The requirements

for hedge accounting may not be met (e.g. because the requirements for effectiveness are not met). Designating the assets and liabilities as at FVTPL will achieve an accounting offset that reflects the existing natural economic offset. [IAS 39:AG4E(c)]

- An entity may have financial assets, financial liabilities, or both, that share a risk (e.g. interest rate risk) that gives rise to opposite changes in fair value of those assets and liabilities that tend to offset each other. The assets and liabilities may be measured on a different basis and hedge accounting cannot be applied because none of the instruments is a derivative. Designating the assets and liabilities as at FVTPL will achieve an accounting offset that reflects the existing natural economic offset. [IAS 39:AG4E(d)]

Example 3.1.1.1A

Fair value option: acquired fixed rate debt

Entity A acquires a fixed rate debt instrument. In order to economically hedge the fair value risk associated with interest payments on the fixed rate debt, Entity A concurrently enters into an interest rate swap with a bank (receive-floating pay-fixed) which has the same terms and payment dates as the debt. The interest rate swap is a derivative that must be measured at FVTPL. Entity A does not wish to apply fair value hedge accounting because it does not wish to prepare any hedge documentation and it does not have the processes in place to monitor hedge effectiveness. By designating the fixed rate debt as at FVTPL on initial recognition, the entity will achieve a natural substantial offset in profit or loss against the fair value movements on the held for trading derivative. Because the instruments share a common risk (interest rate risk), Entity A will seek to demonstrate that applying the fair value option results in more relevant information because it significantly reduces a measurement inconsistency that would otherwise arise from measuring the derivative at FVTPL and the debt at amortised cost. [IAS 39:9]

Example 3.1.1.1B

Fair value option: intragroup derivative

A subsidiary acquires a 5-year fixed rate bond. To hedge against interest rate risk, the subsidiary enters into a receive-floating pay-fixed interest rate swap with its parent. In the subsidiary's financial statements, the bond is designated as at FVTPL. The designation cannot be applied in the consolidated financial statements because the interest rate swap is eliminated on consolidation. If the parent or another group entity has a derivative instrument with a third party that shares a common risk with the bond, the group may be able to designate the bond in the consolidated financial statements provided that the designation is made at initial recognition.

In the examples above, the entity need not have entered into all of the assets and liabilities giving rise to the measurement or recognition inconsistency at exactly the same time. The fair value option is available provided that

(1) each asset or liability is designated as at FVTPL at its initial recognition, (2) the delay between entering into the separate transactions is reasonably short and (3) when each transaction is initially recognised, any remaining transactions are expected to occur. [IAS 39:AG4F]

It would not be acceptable to designate only some of the financial assets and financial liabilities giving rise to an inconsistency as at FVTPL if to do so would not eliminate or significantly reduce the inconsistency and would therefore not result in more relevant information. However, it would be acceptable to designate only some of a number of similar financial assets or financial liabilities if to do so would achieve a significant reduction (and possibly a greater reduction than other allowable designations) in the inconsistency. [IAS 39:AG4G]

Example 3.1.1.1C

Fair value option: lack of accounting mismatch

Entity B buys an equity share for CU100 which does not meet the definition of held for trading. At the same time, Entity B buys a put option for CU20 over the same share with a strike price of CU100. Entity B is contemplating whether it could designate the equity share as a financial asset at FVTPL at initial recognition by claiming that such designation would eliminate or significantly reduce an accounting mismatch that arises as a result of entering into the put option.

If the fair value option is not applied, the share will be measured at fair value with gains and losses recognised in other comprehensive income (unless an impairment is recognised, in which case the cumulative losses are reclassified from equity to profit or loss prior to derecognition of the share). The put option will be accounted for at FVTPL (assuming no hedge accounting).

In considering whether an accounting mismatch is eliminated or significantly reduced, Entity B considers various share price scenarios.

- If the share price increases above CU100, the increase in the fair value of the share will be recognised in other comprehensive income, while the decrease in the fair value of the option will be recognised in profit or loss. However, it should be noted that while the share price could rise well above CU120 (i.e. the fair value gain could be in excess of CU20), the corresponding potential fall in the value of the option is limited to CU20 (because the value of the purchased put option cannot decline below zero). Gains from the share that arise from increases in the share price above CU120 will not be reflected in corresponding losses from the put option. Therefore, the degree of offset between the share and the option if the fair value option is applied is limited to certain share price scenarios only. In addition, when the share price increases to between CU100 and CU120, the decline in fair value of the option will not be linear compared with the increase in the fair value of the share price because the option's fair value reflects time value whereas the share's does not.
- If the share price falls, and the fall is not considered significant or prolonged, then the fair value loss will be recognised in other comprehensive income

> while the increase in the fair value of the option will be recognised in profit or loss. As noted above, the increase in fair value of the option will not be fully offset by the decrease in the fair value of the share because the option's fair value will also reflect changes in time value.
>
> If an impairment loss arises, the cumulative loss recognised in other comprehensive income will be reclassified from equity to profit or loss as a reclassification adjustment (see **section 5** in **chapter C6**). Once the impairment loss has been recognised, future falls in the fair value of the shares and further increases in the intrinsic value of the option will be recognised in profit or loss and will achieve the same accounting result as if the fair value option had not been applied. In the period when the impairment loss is recognised, not applying the fair value option would result in a greater one-off loss in profit or loss as a result of reclassification from equity compared to the net loss when applying the fair value option.
>
> Considering all the various scenarios, it is not appropriate for Entity B to claim that applying the fair value option would eliminate or significantly reduce an accounting mismatch.

3.1.1.2 Managed and performance evaluated on a fair value basis

The following are examples of the application of the fair value option on the basis that financial assets, financial liabilities, or both, are managed and their performance is evaluated on a fair value basis, in accordance with a documented risk management or investment strategy.

- An entity that is a venture capital organisation, mutual fund, unit trust or similar entity whose business is investing in financial assets with a view to profiting from the total return in the form of interest or dividends and changes in fair value may designate such investments as at FVTPL, provided that it does not hold a controlling interest in them. [IAS 39:AG4I(a)]
- An entity may have financial assets and financial liabilities that share one or more risks and those risks are managed and evaluated on a fair value basis in accordance with a documented policy of asset and liability management. An example could be an entity that has issued 'structured products' containing multiple embedded derivatives and that manages the resulting risks on a fair value basis using a mix of derivative and non-derivative financial instruments. [IAS 39:AG4I(b)] This is particularly evident for investment banks that issue structured medium-term note programmes linked to a basket of equities or corporate bonds, when the bank economically hedges its liability by purchasing equity and corporate bonds in the cash market, and/or enters into derivative contracts where the underlying is the referenced equities or corporate bonds. It is common for investment banks to manage their portfolios of assets and liabilities on a fair value basis.
- An insurer holds a portfolio of financial assets, manages it so as to maximise its total return (i.e. interest/dividends and changes in fair

value), and evaluates its performance on that basis. For example, a portfolio may be held to back specific liabilities, in which case the investment policy and evaluation on a fair value basis may apply to both the assets and liabilities, or to the assets alone. [IAS 39:AG4I(c)]

- An entity that designates financial instruments as at FVTPL on the basis that it manages and evaluates their performance on that basis must designate all eligible financial instruments that are managed and evaluated together, i.e. it cannot cherry-pick. [IAS 39:AG4J]

The risk management or investment strategy must be documented, although documentation need not be extensive. For example, if the performance management system as approved by the entity's key management personnel clearly demonstrates that the performance is evaluated on a total return basis, no additional documentation is required. The documentation does not need to be on an item-by-item basis (it may be on a portfolio basis), or at the level of detail required for hedge accounting.

3.1.1.3 Contracts containing one or more embedded derivative

IAS 39:11A allows a hybrid contract containing one or more embedded derivatives to be designated in its entirety at FVTPL unless:

- the embedded derivative does not significantly modify the cash flows that otherwise would be required by the contract; or
- it is clear with little or no analysis when a similar hybrid instrument is first considered that separation of the embedded derivative is prohibited (e.g. a prepayment option embedded in a loan that permits the holder to prepay the loan for approximately its amortised cost - see **7.1** in **chapter C5**).

Example 3.1.1.3

Fair value option: commodity-linked debt

Entity Q acquires a debt instrument that has interest payments linked to a basket of commodity prices. The link to commodity prices is considered to be a non-closely related embedded derivative that would require separation and measurement at FVTPL. Entity Q may choose at initial recognition to designate the whole debt instrument as at FVTPL to avoid separating out the embedded derivative.

IAS 39 applies to financial instruments within its scope. However, some of the Standard's requirements (e.g. those in respect of embedded derivatives) apply to a wider range of contracts.

The question arises as to whether the fair value option is available in respect of hybrid contracts where the host contract is a non-financial item or a financial item outside the scope of IAS 39 (e.g. an operating lease that is not a financial instrument may have an embedded derivative that is separately recognised in the statement of financial position). The IFRIC (now the IFRS Interpretations Committee) has considered this question and, in November 2007, recommended that the IASB should clarify IAS 39:11A by specifying whether it applies only to contracts with embedded derivatives that have financial hosts, or whether the fair value option can be applied to all contracts with embedded derivatives. In August 2008, the IASB issued an exposure draft, *Improvements to IFRSs*, which proposed amending IAS 39:11A to clarify that the fair value option could only apply to financial instruments within the scope of IAS 39. In the basis of conclusions to the exposure draft, the Board acknowledged that the wording in paragraph 11A was not clear. The Board noted that prior to the restricted fair value option issued in June 2005 that continues to apply in IAS 39, the Standard had an unrestricted fair value option which could only be applied to financial instruments within the scope of IAS 39. The objective of the fair value option introduced in 2005 was to restrict, not broaden, an entity's ability to designate financial instruments as at FVTPL. At its January 2009 meeting, the IASB decided to defer its redeliberations on the fair value option for a future period.

At its January 2010 meeting, the IFRIC decided to remove the item, without finalisation, from the Annual Improvements project. The IFRIC believes that the issue will be incorporated as part of the Board's broader decisions on replacing IAS 39 and, therefore, should not be considered on a piecemeal basis. It is of note that the fair value option included within IFRS 9 only relates to those contractual arrangements that are wholly within the scope of that Standard.

It would be surprising to reach a different conclusion from that proposed by the IASB in the 2008 exposure draft, because the alternative interpretation would allow host contracts outside the scope of IAS 39 (which, in many cases, have been deliberately excluded by IAS 39:2) to be measured at FVTPL and this would override the recognition and measurement guidance of more specific Standards (e.g. IAS 17 *Leases* and IFRS 4 *Insurance Contracts*). It would also mean that executory host contracts (e.g. sale and purchase contracts) would be 'grossed up' in the statement of financial position.

The rules on embedded derivatives contained in non-financial host contracts were introduced as an anti-abuse measure to stop entities from stapling financial instruments on to non-financial contracts. Once an embedded derivative has been separated, that part of the hybrid instrument falls within the scope of IAS 39 but the host contract always remains outside the scope of IAS 39. The fair value option is made available under IAS 39 (a Standard that deals with financial instruments and contracts that behave like financial instruments) and therefore, for embedded derivatives, it seems logical to conclude that the fair value option is available only when the host contract is in the scope of IAS 39.

IFRIC 9 *Reassessment of Embedded Derivatives* allows an entity to reconsider whether an embedded derivative is closely related only if there is a change in the terms of the contract that significantly modifies the cash flows that otherwise would be required under the contract (or if the instrument is a hybrid (combined) financial asset that is reclassified out of FVTPL and an assessment of embedded derivatives is performed for the first time). Because the fair value option can only be applied at initial recognition, only if the cash flows are modified sufficiently for the original instrument to be derecognised would an entity be able to designate the modified instrument as at FVTPL (see **section 3** in **chapter C5**).

The revised version of IFRS 3 *Business Combinations* issued in January 2008 (effective for business combinations for which the acquisition date is on or after the beginning of the first annual reporting period beginning on or after 1 July 2009) clarified that if a contractual arrangement is acquired as part of a business combination, the acquirer must determine what is the classification of the contractual arrangement at the date of acquisition because this is the date of initial recognition (see **section 5** below). At the date of acquisition, the acquirer will need to consider whether the contractual arrangement has any embedded derivatives that require separation. The acquirer is not *reassessing* an embedded derivative at this point because the acquirer is recognising the contractual arrangement for the first time and will be able to apply the fair value option election when appropriate.

3.1.1.4 Fair valuing through alternative designations

In some circumstances, an entity can achieve fair value accounting through profit or loss by using alternative designation strategies. The choice of that designation strategy must be made at initial recognition of the instruments concerned.

Example 3.1.1.4A

Fair value option: alternative designations (1)

Bank A issues structured notes that contain non-closely related embedded derivatives linked to specific securities. Bank A manages the risk of these embedded derivatives by immediately investing in the underlying securities (which do not meet the definition of held for trading). Bank A also manages the performance of the portfolio of underlying securities and issued structured notes on a fair value basis.

Bank A has a number of choices:

(a) designate the portfolio of financial assets (underlying securities) and financial liabilities (structured notes) as at FVTPL because it is managed on a fair value basis; or

(b) designate the hybrid financial liabilities (structured notes) as at FVTPL because they contain non-closely related embedded derivatives; or
(c) designate the financial assets (underlying securities) as at FVTPL because there is an accounting mismatch with the embedded derivative that is separately accounted for at FVTPL; or
(d) designate the financial assets (underlying securities) as at FVTPL because there is an accounting mismatch with the financial liabilities if they are designated as at FVTPL under (b) above.

In some scenarios, a particular choice of designation will produce more meaningful information about the effects of transactions, other events and conditions on the entity's financial position, financial performance or cash flows. Because the decision to designate an instrument is similar to an accounting policy choice, the entity should choose the designation strategy that results in reliable and the *most* relevant information.

Example 3.1.1.4B

Fair value option: alternative designations (2)

Entity B issues a mandatorily convertible instrument that at maturity converts into shares of Entity D. The instrument consists of a debt host contract and a non-closely related embedded derivative (i.e. a forward contract to deliver Entity D's shares). Entity B economically hedges its exposure to Entity D by acquiring shares in Entity D. The shares in Entity D are not held for trading because Entity B does not intend to sell them in the short-term, but rather intends to deliver the shares to the holder of the mandatorily convertible instrument. If the fair value option were not applied, the investment in Entity D's shares would be classified as available-for-sale.

Entity B has a non-closely related embedded derivative in its issued mandatorily convertible instrument that relates to Entity D's share price. This embedded derivative will be measured at FVTPL. Entity B may choose to designate Entity D's shares as at FVTPL because this will significantly reduce the recognition inconsistency that would have existed from gains or losses in Entity D's shares being recognised in other comprehensive income.

Arguably, Entity B could choose to designate the mandatorily convertible instrument as at FVTPL on initial recognition because it has an embedded derivative that is not closely related. If Entity B measured the entire hybrid instrument at FVTPL, there would still be a recognition inconsistency because the investment in the shares is an available-for-sale investment with fair value gains or losses recognised in other comprehensive income. A further election to designate Entity D's shares as at FVTPL would significantly reduce this inconsistency, but the reduction in the inconsistency is less than would be achieved if Entity B applies the fair value option designation as described in the previous paragraph. Designating the entire hybrid instrument would result in the fair value of the entity's credit risk being recognised in profit or loss which would not be the case if Entity B does not apply the fair value option.

3.1.2 Held for trading financial assets

A financial asset is classified as held for trading if:

[IAS 39:9]

- it is acquired principally for the purpose of sale in the near term;
- on initial recognition it is part of a portfolio of identified financial instruments that are managed together and for which there is evidence of a recent actual pattern of short-term profit-taking; or
- it is a derivative (except for a derivative that is a designated and effective hedging instrument).

Held for trading financial assets are measured at FVTPL.

Examples of held for trading financial assets are:

- equity securities bought and sold by defined benefit pension plans and investment companies that are actively traded by the entity;
- a portfolio of debt and/or equity securities managed by a trading desk;
- reverse repurchase agreements that form part of a trading book; or
- derivative financial instruments that are not effective hedging instruments.

In May 2009, the IFRIC (now the IFRS Interpretations Committee) issued an agenda decision on IAS 39 titled *Classification of Failed Loan Syndications*. The IFRIC was asked to consider whether a loan amount resulting from a loan syndication that the originator intends to sell in the near term must always be classified as held for trading. The question arises when loans are originated with an intention of syndication but the arranger fails to find sufficient commitments from other participants (failed syndications). The arranger then tries to sell the surplus loan amount to other parties in the near term rather than holding it for the foreseeable future.

The IFRIC noted that the definitions of 'loans and receivables' and financial asset or financial liability at FVTPL in IAS 39:9 determine the classification of a loan in such circumstances. The definition of loans and receivables explicitly requires a loan (or portion of a loan) that is intended to be sold immediately or in the near term to be classified as held for trading on initial recognition. IAS 39:AG14 describes characteristics that generally apply to financial instruments classified as held for trading. The IFRIC noted, however, that these general characteristics are not a prerequisite for all instruments the Standard requires to be classified as held for trading.

The IFRIC also noted that, in accordance with IAS 39:50D, an entity would be permitted to consider reclassifying the surplus loan amount that it no longer intends to sell. Given the specific requirements in IAS 39, the IFRIC did not expect significant diversity in practice. Therefore, the IFRIC decided not to add this issue to its agenda.

3.1.2.1 A portfolio with a recent actual pattern of short-term profit taking

Although the term 'portfolio' is not explicitly defined in IAS 39, the context in which it is used suggests that a portfolio is a group of financial assets that are managed together as part of a group. [IAS 39:IG.B.11 & 12] If there is evidence of a recent actual pattern of short-term profit taking on financial instruments included in such a portfolio, those financial instruments qualify as held for trading even though an individual financial instrument in the portfolio may in fact be held for a longer period of time. [IAS 39:IG.B.11]

Note that classification as held for trading on this basis is only permitted if the non-derivative financial instrument is included in such a portfolio *on initial recognition*.

3.1.2.2 Indicators of trading activities

The term 'trading' generally suggests active and frequent buying and selling. Determining whether or when an entity is involved in trading activities is a matter of judgement that depends on the relevant facts and circumstances, which should be assessed based on an evaluation of various activities of the entity rather than solely on the terms of the individual transactions. Inherent in that assessment is an evaluation of the entity's intent in entering into financial instrument contracts and using particular types of financial instruments. Indications that financial instruments are entered into for trading purposes are set out below. The absence of any or all of the indicators in any category, by itself, would not necessarily avoid the classification of financial assets or liabilities as held for trading. All available evidence should be considered to determine whether, based on the weight of that evidence, an operation is involved in trading activities.

Organisational characteristics (nature of operations):

- the primary assets/liabilities of the operation are financial instrument contracts;
- the operation does not use its own capital as the primary source of funding for its activities but instead makes extensive use of other techniques such as leveraging and credit enhancement as sources of risk capital;
- the operation develops and utilises its own proprietary models to price the financial instrument contracts that it offers or trades; and
- the operation offers financial instruments as a dealer, not as a 'user'.

Customers, counterparties and competitors:

- the majority of the counterparties to the financial instrument contracts and competitors are banks, brokers/traders or fund managers;
- the volume and prevalent direction (buying/selling) of transactions are indicative of trading;
- the change in the value of financial instrument contracts is expected to move in a direction that does not mitigate or offset the risk of other exposures;
- the volume of transactions differs significantly from the operation's historical requirements for such contracts;
- there has been a change in the volume of transactions that is significant relative to the change in demand arising from the entity's primary operating environment and financial structure;
- contracted quantities far exceed normal needs and exposure levels or result in opposite exposures;
- the operation does not consume the financial instruments to meet its normal needs (or make use of physical delivery to settle the contracts); and
- there is a high turnover rate in the portfolio of financial instrument contracts.

Management and controls:

- compensation and/or performance measures are tied to the short-term results generated from financial instrument transactions (i.e. the operation is measured based on trading profits or changes in the market values of its positions);
- the operation communicates internally in terms of 'trading strategy' (i.e. management reports identify contractual positions, fair values, hedging activities, risk exposure etc.);
- the operation sets limits on market positions and related strategies, sets policies governing what types of contracts it will transact in, and sets the controls it will follow; in addition, management is involved in reviewing compliance with those limits, strategies, policies, and controls on a daily or frequent basis;
- the word 'trading' appears in the name of or documentation of the operation for internal or external purposes;
- employees of the operation are referred to as 'traders' or 'dealers' or have prior experience in banking, broking, derivatives trading or risk management activities;
- the net market positions of the operation are assessed on a regular and frequent basis (e.g. hourly or overnight);

- the infrastructure of the operation is similar to that of the trading operation of a bank or an investment bank's front office, middle office and back office (i.e. there is segregation between back-office processing and front-office trading functions);
- an infrastructure exists that enables the operation to capture price and other risks on a real-time basis;
- the activities are managed on a portfolio or 'book' basis; and
- management searches for opportunities to take advantage of favourable price spreads, arbitrage opportunities, or outright positions in the marketplace.

Transactions/contracts:

- the operation has a history of pairing off (entering into offsetting contracts) or otherwise settling the transactions without physically receiving or delivering the underlying item. In other words, past practices of the operation have resulted in net cash settlement, offsetting, as well as netting out, and the type of settlement has changed quickly from one type to another to maximise profits/ mitigate losses;
- the contracts do not permit physical delivery and must be settled net in the market or in cash; and
- the financial instrument contracts are not customarily used for general commercial (operational) business purposes or by the industry in general.

3.1.3 Reclassification into the FVTPL category

Reclassification into the FVTPL category after initial recognition is prohibited by IAS 39:50. Reclassifications out of the FVTPL category are permitted for non-derivative financial assets subject to meeting specified criteria (see **section 4.2**).

The following changes in circumstances are not reclassifications:

[IAS 39:50A]

- a derivative that was previously a designated and effective hedging instrument in a cash flow hedge or net investment hedge no longer qualifies as such;
- a derivative becomes a designated and effective hedging instrument in a cash flow hedge or net investment hedge; and
- financial assets are reclassified when an insurance company changes its accounting policies in accordance with IFRS 4:45.

It should be noted that a change in the basis for measuring fair value (e.g. a change from using quoted market prices to using an alternative valuation technique when quoted market prices are no longer available) is not a reclassification. This applies when an item is classified as at FVTPL or as an available-for-sale financial asset.

3.2 Held-to-maturity investments (HTM)

HTM investments are financial instruments with fixed or determinable payments and fixed maturity that an entity has the positive intention and ability to hold to maturity, other than:

[IAS 39:9]

- those that the entity upon initial recognition elects to designate as at FVTPL;
- those that the entity designates as available-for-sale; and
- those that meet the definition of loans and receivables.

HTM investments are measured at amortised cost using the effective interest method.

An asset cannot be classified as HTM if it can be contractually prepaid or otherwise extinguished by the issuer in such a way that the holder would not recover substantially all of its recorded investment (i.e. those contracts where the issuer has a right to settle at an amount significantly below amortised cost). In addition, a debt security where the issuer has a right to redeem early should be evaluated to determine whether it contains an embedded derivative that must be accounted for separately (see **chapter C5** on embedded derivatives).

Some host debt instruments from which an embedded derivative has been separated can be classified as HTM.

3.2.1 Fixed or determinable payments and fixed maturity

HTM investments are financial instruments with fixed or determinable payments and fixed maturity, which means that the contractual arrangement defines the amounts and dates of payments to the holder, such as interest and principal payments.

Equity instruments cannot be HTM investments either because they have an indefinite life (e.g. ordinary shares) or because the amounts the holder may receive can vary in a manner that is not predetermined (e.g. share options, warrants and similar rights). [IAS 39:AG17]

Preference shares with fixed or determinable payments and a fixed maturity (e.g. mandatorily redeemable preference shares) determined to be financial liabilities in accordance with IAS 32 for the issuer can be classified as HTM by the holder.

A debt instrument with a variable interest rate can satisfy the criteria for a HTM investment. [IAS 39:AG17] The terms of the contract determine the amounts and dates of payments to the holder. An example is a five-year debt instrument which pays a variable rate of interest specified as LIBOR plus 150 basis points, with interest payments receivable semi-annually in arrears.

Example 3.2.1A

HTM: debt host contract (1)

Entity G has a bond asset with interest payments indexed to the price of gold. The bond has a fixed payment at maturity and a fixed maturity date.

Interest payments contain an embedded derivative (indexation to gold) that is separated and accounted for as a derivative at fair value (unless Entity G elects on initial recognition to designate the bond as a financial asset at FVTPL or it cannot separate and measure the embedded derivative, in which case the whole instrument is designated as at FVTPL). Once the embedded derivative is separated, the host debt instrument can be classified as HTM provided that Entity G has the positive intention and ability to hold the bond to maturity.

Example 3.2.1B

HTM: debt host contract (2)

Entity A purchases a 5-year equity indexed-linked note that is quoted in an active market with an original issue price of CU10 at a market price of CU12 at the time of purchase. At maturity, the note requires payment of the original issue price of CU10 plus a supplemental redemption amount that depends on whether a specified share price index exceeds a predetermined level at the maturity date. The supplemental amount paid at redemption is a formula that incorporates the change in the share index. If the share price index does not exceed or is equal to the predetermined level, no supplemental redemption amount is paid. Entity A has the positive intention and ability to hold the note to its maturity.

Entity A can classify the note as HTM because it has a fixed payment of CU10 and fixed maturity and Entity A has the positive intention and ability to hold it to maturity. However, the equity index feature is an embedded derivative that is not closely related to the debt host, and must be separated. The purchase price of CU12 is allocated between the host debt instrument and the embedded derivative. For example, if the fair value of the embedded option at acquisition is CU4, the host debt instrument is measured at CU8 on initial recognition. In this case, the discount of CU2 that is implicit in the host bond (principal of CU10 minus the original carrying amount of CU8) is amortised to profit or loss over the term to maturity of the note using the effective interest method. [IAS 39:IG.B.13]

It is important to note in this example that the instrument has a floor on the redemption equal to CU10. If that floor were not in place, Entity A would not be able to assert an intention to hold to maturity, because an issuer's right to settle a financial asset at an amount significantly below its amortised cost precludes an entity from asserting a positive intention to hold to maturity. [IAS 39:AG16]

If the terms of a 'perpetual' debt instrument (such as perpetual bonds, debentures and capital notes) provide the holder with the contractual right to receive payments of interest at fixed dates into perpetuity, the instrument cannot be classified as HTM because the instrument does not have a fixed maturity date.

It can be argued that a perpetual debt instrument with fixed or determinable payments for which the only cash payments under the terms of the instrument are interest payments during a limited period (e.g. 10 years) can be classified as HTM provided that the amount invested is recovered through fixed or determinable payments, and the rights to zero interest after Year 10 have no present value at inception. In such circumstances, one would need to argue that the final date on which interest is paid is in effect the maturity date of the financial instrument. Despite the legal form being a perpetual instrument, the substance is that of a finite life instrument.

3.2.2 Positive intention and ability to hold to maturity

An entity cannot classify a financial asset as HTM if the entity intends to hold the financial asset for only an undefined period. A debt security, for example, should not be classified as HTM if the entity anticipates that the security would be available to be sold in response to:

[IAS 39:AG16(b)]

- changes in market interest rates and related changes in the investment's prepayment risk;
- liquidity needs (e.g. due to the withdrawal of deposits, increased demand for loans, surrender of insurance policies, or payment of insurance claims);
- changes in the availability of and the yield on alternative investments;
- changes in funding sources and terms; or
- changes in foreign currency risk.

In summary, classification of an investment as HTM means that the entity is indifferent to future opportunities to profit from changes in the asset's fair value.

For this reason, IAS 39 prohibits the hedging of a HTM investment for interest rate risk or prepayment risk because, in classifying the investment as HTM, the entity has effectively expressed its commitment to retaining the financial asset and collecting all of its contractual cash flows, irrespective of the impact of changes in market interest rates on the asset's fair value and any option the issuer may have to redeem the asset prior to its contractual maturity.

IAS 39 states that an asset is not classified as HTM if it can contractually be repaid or otherwise extinguished by the issuer in such a way that the holder of the asset would not recover substantially all of its recognised investment. Any premium paid and capitalised transaction costs are considered in determining whether the carrying amount would be substantially recovered. In the circumstances where the holder will recover substantially all of its investment (e.g. in the case of a debt instrument where the issuer exercises its call option on the asset and the option's exercise price is approximately equal to the instrument's amortised cost), the debt instrument's maturity date is viewed as being accelerated. The issuer's exercise of a call feature in such circumstances does not invalidate the holder's treatment of the investment as HTM, provided that the holder intends to hold the investment until it is called.

Convertible debt instruments generally bear a lower interest rate than debt instruments without a conversion feature because the investor pays for the right to benefit from the appreciation in value of the option embedded in the debt instrument. The conversion feature would normally be separated out from the debt host contract and accounted for as an embedded derivative. If the conversion feature can be exercised only at maturity of the instrument, then it may be reasonable for the holder to argue that it has the positive intention and ability to hold the debt host contract to maturity. However, generally, it would be contradictory to assert a positive intention to hold the debt host contract to its maturity if the conversion right that has been purchased by the holder allows the holder to convert the instrument into equity at any time. In the latter case, the holder does not have the positive ability to hold the debt host contract to maturity because exercising the option prior to maturity of the instrument would extinguish the debt host contract early.

For a debt instrument held that is subject to a purchased put option, the existence of the option will prima facie undermine any statement of intention to hold the instrument to maturity. Paying for a put feature is inconsistent with expressing an intention to hold the financial asset until maturity. An entity should not classify a financial asset as HTM if it has the intention to hold the instrument for only an undetermined period or if it stands ready to sell the asset in response to general market conditions. Therefore, unless the terms of the put option are such that it can be exercised only in one of the permitted, isolated, non-recurring circumstances (see **3.3.2**), it will not be acceptable to classify a puttable security as HTM. [IAS 39:AG19]

Example 3.2.2A

HTM: sale due to credit rating triggers

An investment fund holds high-yield debt securities (bonds etc.). The portfolio's guidelines specify that the fund will only sell an asset if the credit rating of the asset deteriorates below a certain specified level. The fund's assets cannot be classified as HTM because the fund cannot claim at initial recognition that there is a positive intention to hold the assets to maturity - the intention is to hold the assets only while their credit rating is within the prescribed parameters.

Note that a general policy of this nature to dispose of assets when specified credit rating triggers occur will not fall within the scope of the exception in IAS 39:AG22 (see **3.3.2**) allowing disposals in response to a significant deterioration in credit worthiness considered to be an isolated non-recurring event.

Example 3.2.2B

HTM: managing debt duration

Entity X has a portfolio of debt securities and wishes to classify the investments as HTM. The investment policy allows management to transfer every HTM security to a more liquid portfolio at a specific predetermined date (e.g. 24 months prior to each security's stated maturity). The policy is designed to permit Entity X the flexibility to sell debt securities and thereby manage the duration of the portfolio.

Entity X's policy would preclude classification of its debt securities as HTM because Entity X does not have the positive intention to hold the securities to maturity; its intention is to hold the securities until the date 24 months prior to stated maturity and that date is not sufficiently close to maturity to qualify under the exceptions from the general tainting rules (see **3.3.2**).

Example 3.2.2C

HTM: regulatory constraint (1)

Entity P would like to designate as HTM its portfolio of high quality assets held for the purpose of complying with regulatory requirements on liquidity.

It is not acceptable for Entity P to designate the portfolio as HTM because Entity P cannot claim that there is a positive intention to hold the assets to maturity; the intention is to hold the assets as long as they continue to be of an appropriate quality and Entity P is not required to realise them for regulatory purposes.

A significant risk of default by the issuer does not preclude classification of a financial asset as HTM provided that its contractual payments are fixed or determinable and the other criteria for classification as HTM are met. [IAS 39:AG17]

There may be a significant risk of default on interest and principal on a bond (e.g. due to significant business, financial or economic uncertainties) and this risk may be evidenced, for instance, by a low-grade rating of the bond issue. However, the likelihood of default is not a consideration in qualifying for the HTM category as long as there is an intention and ability to hold the instrument to maturity, notwithstanding the concerns at the acquisition date regarding the potential for default.

When an entity classifies a high-credit risk debt security as HTM knowing that the security may be sold if there is a further downgrade in credit rating, it may be difficult to substantiate that a significant sale in response to a subsequent credit deterioration does not 'taint' the HTM portfolio (other than, for example, if a bankruptcy occurs).

Securities that have been pledged as collateral for borrowings or are subject to a repurchase agreement or securities lending agreement (i.e. they have been transferred to another party under a repo or securities lending transaction but continue to be recognised by the reporting entity) can be classified as HTM provided that the entity intends and expects to be able to repay the borrowings without being required to dispose of the asset. [IAS 39:IG.B.18]

For financial assets classified as HTM, management should consider whether the entity has both the financial ability and the regulatory ability to avoid disposing of HTM investments prior to maturity. The assessment of an entity's financial ability should consider such factors as its funding position and its ability to maintain any over-collateralisation requirements. The assessment of an entity's financial ability should also take into account such factors as its regulatory capital requirements, its liquidity position (including specified holdings of liquid assets), its loans-to-one-borrower ratio, growth prospects and related financing requirements and its investment authority (including permitted asset-mix).

Example 3.2.2D

HTM: regulatory constraint (2)

Entity Q, a regulated entity, would like to classify certain of its securities as HTM. However, the securities in question are regarded by Entity Q's regulators as high-risk securities and the regulator may require Entity Q to sell the securities as a result of changes in credit risk.

Entity Q cannot classify the securities as HTM. Even though Entity Q may have the positive intention to hold the securities to maturity, it does not have the ability to do so because the regulator can require it to dispose of the securities.

It is not uncommon for regulators of financial institutions to designate specific financial instruments such as certain collateralised mortgage obligations

(CMOs) and other, similar stripped securities (e.g. interest-only and principal-only securities) as high-risk securities that are required to be disposed of in specified circumstances. If a financial instrument is subject to such regulatory requirements, classification as HTM is generally inappropriate.

3.2.3 Frequency of assessment of positive intention and ability to hold to maturity

Both the positive intention and ability to hold investments to maturity are required to be reassessed at the end of each reporting period. [IAS 39:AG25]

Example 3.2.3

HTM: sale after the reporting period

Entity X, with a 31 December year end, has a portfolio of financial assets classified as HTM. Early in January 20X2, prior to the issuance of the 20X1 financial statements, Entity X sells a portion of the financial assets held, and the factors motivating the sale do not qualify under the exceptions set out in **3.3.2**.

The entire HTM securities portfolio is required to be reclassified as available-for-sale in the statement of financial position as at 31 December 20X1 because the actions in January undermine the entity's assertion of intent at the end of the reporting period.

3.3 Tainting of the HTM portfolio

'Tainting' is the term used to describe the effect of disposing of or reclassifying a HTM investment before its maturity date in situations where such disposal or reclassification disqualifies the entity from continuing to use the HTM classification for the remaining portfolio of securities held. Except for specified limited circumstances described in **3.3.2**, a sale or reclassification of a HTM investment casts doubt on the entity's stated intention or ability to hold the rest of its HTM portfolio to maturity. As a consequence, when an entity has, during the current year, sold or reclassified more than an insignificant amount of HTM investments before maturity (i.e. tainting of the HTM portfolio has occurred), all of the entity's HTM investments generally must be reclassified into the available-for-sale category. Furthermore, the entity is prohibited from classifying any investments as HTM for the next two financial years. [IAS 39:9]

Example 3.3

HTM: sale of single asset

Entity X has a portfolio of HTM financial assets comprising both municipal and corporate bonds. A sale or transfer of a single corporate bond which comprises more than an insignificant amount of the portfolio other than in one of the exceptional circumstances described in **3.3.2** would result in tainting of all remaining bonds, both municipal and corporate.

3.3.1 Sub-categorisation for the purposes of applying the 'tainting' rule

An entity cannot create two different categories of HTM financial assets (e.g. debt securities denominated in US dollars and debt securities denominated in Euros). The 'tainting rule' applies to the portfolio of HTM investments in its entirety. If an entity has sold or reclassified more than an insignificant amount of HTM investments, it cannot classify any financial assets as HTM financial assets. [IAS 39:IG.B.20]

3.3.2 Sales or reclassifications of HTM financial assets which do not taint the HTM portfolio

Sales or reclassifications in strictly defined and limited circumstances specified in IAS 39 do not taint the remaining HTM portfolio. These are sales or transfers that:

[IAS 39:9]

- are so close to maturity or the financial asset's call date (e.g. less than three months before maturity) that changes in the market rate of interest would not have a significant effect on the financial asset's fair value;
- occur after the entity has collected substantially all of the financial asset's original principal through scheduled payments or prepayments;
- are attributable to an isolated event that is beyond the entity's control, is non-recurring and could not have been reasonably anticipated by the entity; or
- do not involve 'more than insignificant' amount of the entity's HTM portfolio (more than insignificant in relation to the total amount of HTM investments).

Selling an asset close enough to its maturity does not taint the remaining HTM portfolio if the effect of movements in interest rates between the repurchase date and the maturity is expected to have an insignificant impact on the fair value of the asset. For instance, if an entity sells a financial asset less than three months prior to maturity, the present value of the amount received from the sale usually will not be significantly different from the amount received at maturity. This is unlikely to be the case if the instrument's maturity is several months away.

IAS 39 does not provide guidance as to what is considered to be 'substantially all' of the financial asset's original principal. Prior to the 2004 revisions to IAS 39, Implementation Guidance included an example illustrating that the collection of 90 per cent or more of the original principal was considered to be 'substantially all'. In the amended Implementation Guidance, this interpretation has been removed and, therefore, judgement must be applied on a case-by-case basis in determining what is considered to be 'substantially all'.

For an event to be considered as isolated, non-recurring, beyond the entity's control and could not have been reasonably anticipated, the event would need to be extremely remote and unlikely to occur in practice. Not many events are likely to meet these conditions.

A sale, or a transfer of a HTM investment due to one of the following isolated, non-recurring events is not considered to be inconsistent with its original classification as HTM and does not raise a question about the entity's intention to hold other investments to maturity:

[IAS 39:AG22]

(a) a significant deterioration in the issuer's credit-worthiness;

(b) a change in tax law that eliminates or significantly reduces the tax-exempt status of interest on the HTM investment (but not a change in tax law that revises the marginal tax rates applicable to interest income);

(c) a major business combination or major disposal (such as sale of a segment) that necessitates the sale or transfer of HTM investments to maintain the entity's existing interest rate risk position or credit risk policy (although the business combination is an event within the entity's control, the changes to its investment portfolio to maintain an interest rate risk position or credit risk policy may be consequential rather than anticipated);

(d) a change in statutory or regulatory requirements significantly modifying either what constitutes a permissible investment or the maximum level of particular types of investments, thereby causing an entity to dispose of a HTM investment;

(e) a significant increase in the industry's regulatory capital requirements that causes the entity to downsize by selling HTM investments; and

(f) a significant increase in the risk weights of HTM investments used for regulatory risk-based capital purposes.

Note that a disaster scenario that is only remotely possible (e.g. a run on a bank or a similar situation affecting an insurance company) is not something that is assessed by an entity in deciding whether it has the positive intention and ability to hold an investment to maturity. [IAS 39:AG21]

Catastrophic losses or high levels of policy surrenders are 'reasonably probable' of occurring in the insurance industry. They cannot be considered to be non-recurring or isolated and would not meet the exception under IAS 39:9. As a result, the sale of investments classified as HTM in order to meet excessive levels of claim obligations or because of policyholder withdrawals would taint the entity's HTM category.

The following factors, amongst others, would be relevant in determining whether there has been a significant deterioration in the issuer's creditworthiness. [IAS 39:AG22(a)]

The deterioration in the issuer's creditworthiness should have occurred after the security was acquired. Low credit ratings or concerns regarding creditworthiness existing at acquisition would generally lead to a conclusion that a subsequent not insignificant sale from the HTM category taints the rest of the HTM portfolio.

There should be evidence of actual deterioration of the issuer's creditworthiness. A downgrading by a rating agency may provide objective evidence of a significant credit deterioration. An expectation of deterioration should be supported by objective evidence. Some of the financial measures that may provide objective evidence are:

- cash flows from operations (i.e. decline in cash flows, available cash flows, liquidity);
- broker/analyst reports on the issuer;
- adverse performance compared to projections;
- sustained decline in earnings or other key measures; and
- violation of covenants or other evidence that the issuer is in peril of violating covenants.

An increase in yield relative to a risk-free rate may be indicative of a change in the market's evaluation of the risk associated with holding the issuer's debt. In many situations, an effective measure of a significant deterioration is a significant increase in the yield on the debt of an entity when compared to the change in the yield of a risk-free security of a similar maturity.

Guidance used in determining impairment may also be useful in assessing a significant decline in the issuer's creditworthiness (see **5.1** of **chapter C6**). Information affecting the issuer (e.g. the current and near-term projected financial condition and performance of the issuer, the issuer's dividend payment and earnings performance, the general market conditions and prospects of the region and industry in which the issuer operates, and specific adverse news or events) may provide objective evidence of impairment that may be indicative of a significant decline in the issuer's creditworthiness.

To provide evidence of a significant deterioration in the issuer's creditworthiness, general market or industry factors should have a direct or demonstrable effect on a specific issuer. For example, widespread difficulties experienced by others in the industry (e.g. due to over-leveraging or weak assets) that are not expected to affect the issuer are not relevant.

In contrast, the development of severe competition, adverse tax or regulatory developments, or declining markets may have a direct bearing on the creditworthiness of specific issuers.

A sale of a HTM investment following a downgrade of the issuer's credit rating by a rating agency would not necessarily raise a question about the entity's intention to hold other investments to maturity. A downgrade indicates a decline in the issuer's creditworthiness. IAS 39 specifies that a sale due to a significant deterioration in the issuer's creditworthiness could satisfy the condition in IAS 39 and, therefore, not raise a question about the entity's intention to hold other investments to maturity. However, the deterioration in creditworthiness must be significant judged by reference to the credit rating at initial recognition. A credit downgrade of a notch within a class or from a rating class to the immediately lower rating class could often be regarded as reasonably anticipated. If the rating downgrade in combination with other information provides evidence of impairment, the deterioration in creditworthiness often would be regarded as significant. [IAS 39:IG.B.15]

A permitted (i.e. non-tainting) sale in accordance with IAS 39:AG22(a) should be in response to an actual deterioration rather than in advance of a deterioration in creditworthiness and should not be based on mere speculation or in response to industry statistics.

The deterioration should be supported by evidence about the issuer's creditworthiness though the entity need not await the formal notification of an actual downgrading in the issuer's published credit rating or inclusion on a 'credit-watch' list.

When an entity uses internal ratings for assessing exposures, changes in those internal ratings may help to identify issuers for which there has been a significant deterioration in creditworthiness, provided that the entity's approach to assigning internal ratings and changes in those ratings give a consistent, reliable and objective measure of the credit quality of the issuers.

If an entity does not sell a debt instrument immediately in response to a significant credit deterioration, but continues to classify the instrument in the HTM portfolio, a sale of that instrument at a future date would not satisfy the conditions for permitted sales. Because an entity is required to make an ongoing assessment of its ability and intent to hold an instrument to its maturity, by not reclassifying the instrument out of HTM when the credit deterioration occurred, the entity effectively reconfirmed its intent to hold the instrument to its maturity.

An exchange of debt securities classified as HTM pursuant to a bankruptcy generally qualifies as a permitted sale out of HTM because bankruptcy is the ultimate form of credit deterioration. However, if the investor had anticipated the bankruptcy at the acquisition date and was able to control the outcome, then such a sale would not satisfy the conditions for permitted sales due to a significant deterioration in the issuer's creditworthiness.

Example 3.3.2A

HTM: sale due to cash need

Entity P, an insurance entity, sells financial assets that have been classified as HTM due to cash needs arising from the failure of one of its principal reinsurers.

A sale from the HTM portfolio for this reason would be inconsistent with the positive intent and ability to hold the security to maturity. This situation is not analogous to significant deterioration in an issuer's creditworthiness, because the deterioration does not relate specifically to the issuer of the security sold but to the entity's reinsurer.

Example 3.3.2B

HTM: counterparty restructuring

Entity N, a life insurance entity, purchased a debt security in a private placement offering. At acquisition, Entity N classified the debt as HTM. The issuer, a private entity, is currently in bankruptcy proceedings and is restructuring its debt. The issuer is contemplating swapping its debt security to Entity N for new debt and shares. Entity N has no control over the outcome of the issuer's restructuring arrangements.

Prior to the issuer's determination of the final restructuring arrangements, Entity N can continue to classify the debt security as HTM. The HTM classification is acceptable because the issuer's termination of the original debt is not under Entity N's control. The restructuring is analogous to an issuer's call option. In some circumstances, it may not be possible to hold a security to its original stated maturity, such as when the security is called by the issuer prior to maturity. The issuer's exercise of the call option effectively accelerates the security's maturity and is not viewed as being inconsistent with the HTM classification. Under these circumstances, the maturity date is accelerated to the date of early redemption or when the debt security is exchanged. Accordingly, Entity N's classification as HTM is appropriate. Entity N should determine whether an impairment loss has arisen and, if so, recognise that impairment loss (see **section 5** of **chapter C6**).

Prior to the issuer's determination of the final restructuring arrangements, Entity N could have transferred the debt security from the HTM to the AFS category if the intention and ability to hold to maturity is no longer appropriate, without tainting its HTM portfolio, because a transfer resulting from evidence of a significant deterioration in the issuer's creditworthiness will not call into question Entity N's intent to hold other financial assets to maturity.

Sales out of HTM in anticipation of future tax law changes that have not become law will taint the HTM portfolio if sales are significant in comparison to the HTM portfolio. To reduce the risk of tainting, the tax change must already have become law prior to the disposal of the assets.

Example 3.3.2C

HTM: change in tax treaty

Entity X, an entity operating in Canada, has a portfolio of financial assets classified as HTM, which contains a Malaysian bond issue. At the date that Entity X purchased the security, a tax treaty existed between the Canadian tax jurisdiction and Malaysia which Entity X anticipated would continue for the foreseeable future and at least for as long as the bonds were outstanding. This treaty allowed the use of Canadian foreign tax credits to reduce the onerous tax consequences that would otherwise result from inclusion of interest on the Malaysian security in taxable income in both tax jurisdictions (assuming Entity X is also taxed on the income in Malaysia).

Entity X cannot reclassify the security from its HTM category in anticipation of the treaty's expiration without calling into question the intent to hold other HTM financial assets to maturity. If the treaty does expire, however, reclassification may be permitted which will not taint any remaining HTM securities.

A disposal out of HTM is permitted if it is consequential to a major business combination or disposal of a business and affects existing interest rate risk or credit risk positions which must be maintained in accordance with risk management policies. Therefore, an entity may reassess the classification of HTM securities concurrently with or shortly after a major business combination and not necessarily call into question its intent to hold other securities to maturity in the future. As time passes, it becomes increasingly difficult to demonstrate that the business combination, and not other events or circumstances, necessitated the transfer or sale of HTM securities.

Sales in anticipation of a business combination (e.g. for the purpose of financing it) will taint the HTM category.

Sales out of the HTM category as a result of a change in senior management in connection with a restructuring of the entity will result in tainting. A change in management is not identified as an instance of sales or transfers from HTM that does not compromise the classification as HTM because a change in management or a restructuring cannot be argued to be an isolated, non-recurring event that could not have been reasonably anticipated. [IAS 39:IG.B.16]

In some countries, regulators of banks or other industries may set capital requirements on an *entity-specific* basis based on an assessment of the risk in that particular entity.

Sales of HTM investments in response to an unanticipated significant increase by the regulator in the *industry's* capital requirements do not taint the entity's intent to hold remaining investments to maturity. However, sales of HTM investments imposed by regulators due to a significant increase in *entity-specific* capital requirements applicable to a particular entity, but not to the industry, will generally 'taint' the entity's intent to hold other financial assets as HTM. Entity-specific capital requirements could only be disregarded in exceptional cases if it can be demonstrated that the sales result from an increase in capital requirements which is an isolated event that is beyond the entity's control and that is non-recurring and could not have been reasonably anticipated by the entity. [IAS 39:IG.B.17]

In consolidated financial statements, intragroup sales of HTM investments between group entities generally would not taint the HTM portfolio from a group perspective, as long as the business purpose of the transfer and the investment policies of the 'buyer' are consistent with a continued positive intention and ability to hold to maturity. The impact on each entity's stand-alone financial statements should be assessed separately; in the financial statements of the selling entity, the stated intention of holding securities to maturity will have been undermined, even though the sale was made to another entity within the consolidated group.

Note that an entity cannot apply the conditions separately to HTM financial assets held by different entities in a consolidated group, even if those group entities are in different countries with different legal or economic environments. If the consolidated entity in total across the group has sold or reclassified more than an insignificant amount of investments classified as HTM, it cannot classify any financial assets as HTM investments in its consolidated financial statements unless such sales and transfers do not taint the HTM portfolio.

As a remedy to protect the investor from the issuer's violation of a debt covenant, a contractual right of foreclosure that was negotiated at arm's length at the issuance date would not preclude an investor classifying an investment as HTM. Similarly, the exercise of such a right or foreclosure on the violation of a substantial covenant would not taint an investor's remaining HTM portfolio.

Example 3.3.2D

HTM: sale following acceptance of tender offers

Entity A, an insurance company, initially classified 100 per cent of its property liability fixed income portfolio as AFS, 50 per cent of its life fixed income securities portfolio as HTM, and 50 per cent as AFS. Entity A considered various factors in making these classifications, including its investment policy, security characteristics, liquidity needs, and asset-liability management strategy.

In a subsequent year, Entity A began receiving unsolicited tender offers from issuers with respect to its fixed income portfolio (including its HTM portfolio) prompted by a very volatile interest rate environment. Entity A accepted certain tender offers involving the exchange of debt securities classified as HTM because these exchanges were on economically favourable terms.

As a consequence, Entity A is required to transfer 100 per cent of previously classified HTM securities to AFS because it can no longer assert it has the positive intent to hold all of these securities to maturity. The sale of a security in response to a tender offer typically is motivated not by a need for cash, but instead by the investor's desire for additional possible profit – a motive inconsistent with the HTM classification. Further, none of the exceptions for sales that do not taint HTM portfolio applies in these circumstances.

In the context of open-ended funds (e.g. a mutual fund) where investors do not have an investment in equity shares in the fund, but own 'units' in the fund, and can require redemption of their share of the net assets of the fund in cash, it is difficult to argue that the possibility of unit-holders asking for redemption of their units is a non-recurring situation that could not have been reasonably anticipated.

In fact, it could reasonably be argued that the entity (e.g. the mutual fund) is "subject to an existing legal or other constraint that could frustrate its intention to hold the financial asset to maturity" and, therefore, that HTM classification of the fund's portfolio of investments would be inappropriate.

When a large number of unit-holders require redemption of their share in the net assets of the fund, the fund could be obliged to sell assets in order to fulfil its obligation to deliver cash to the unit-holders exiting the fund. Although IAS 39:AG21 states that a "disaster scenario that is only remotely possible, such as a run on a bank or a similar situation affecting an insurer, is not something that is assessed by an entity in deciding whether it has the positive intention and ability to hold an investment to maturity", the possibility of unit-holders asking for their redemption in cash (and in large numbers), thereby forcing the sale of fund assets, does not constitute a disaster scenario but is readily possible in the course of the operation of a mutual fund and, consequential, liquidity needs have to be considered by the fund manager at any time.

A sale or transfer of a security classified as HTM for reasons other than those that are specifically permitted does not indicate that the previous financial statements were issued in error. Because the accounting for financial assets as HTM is based primarily on a representation of intent by management, the sale or transfer of a security classified as HTM does not represent an error of previously issued financial statements, provided that no evidence existed at the time the financial statements were issued demonstrating that the entity did not have the positive intent and ability to hold the security to maturity. However, such a sale or transfer may call into question the entity's intent to hold other debt securities to maturity in the future.

If 'tainting' of the HTM portfolio occurs in a period, resulting in reclassification of the portfolio as AFS (see **4.6**), comparative amounts for the previous period are not restated for the reclassification because this would disguise the consequences of 'tainting.'

If an entity plans to sell a security from the HTM category in response to one of the permitted conditions that do not taint the HTM portfolio, the entity may continue to classify the security as HTM. There is no requirement in IAS 39 for the security to be reclassified as AFS if an entity intends to sell in response to one of the permitted conditions.

3.4 Loans and receivables

Loans and receivables are non-derivative financial assets with fixed or determinable payments that are not quoted in an active market, other than those the entity intends to sell immediately or in the short-term (which must be classified as held for trading), and those that the entity on initial recognition designates as either at FVTPL or AFS. [IAS 39:9]

Note that financial assets that do not meet the definition of loans and receivables may still satisfy the criteria for classification in the HTM category because the HTM definition is different from the loans and receivables definition (see **section 3.2** on HTM assets).

Loans and receivables are measured at amortised cost using the effective interest method (see **4.1** of **chapter C6**).

A financial asset cannot be classified as a loan and receivable if it can be contractually prepaid or otherwise extinguished by the issuer in such a way that the holder would not recover substantially all of its recorded investment, other than because of credit deterioration. [IAS 39:9] Such assets are accounted for as available-for-sale or at FVTPL.

For example, a fixed rate interest-only strip created in a securitisation and subject to prepayment risk cannot be classified as a loan and receivable because there is a risk that the purchaser may not recover substantially all of its investment due to prepayment.

Loans and receivables are created by providing money, goods or services to a debtor. Examples are deposits held in banks, trade receivables and loan assets (including loans originated by the entity, loans acquired in a syndication, and other loans purchased in a secondary market provided that the market is not active and the loans are not quoted). Investments in debt securities that are not quoted in an active market can also be classified as loans and receivables.

When banks make term deposits with a central bank or other banks and the proof of deposit is negotiable, the deposit meets the definition of loans and receivables unless the depositor bank intends to sell the deposit immediately or in the near term, in which case the deposit must be classified as held for trading.

Financial assets purchased after origination qualify for classification as loans and receivables provided that they meet all of the criteria for loans and receivables. However, an interest in a pool of assets that are not themselves loans and receivables (e.g. an interest in a mutual fund or a similar fund) should not be classified as loans and receivables.

The principal difference between loans and receivables and HTM investments is that loans and receivables are not subject to the tainting provisions that apply to HTM investments. Loans and receivables not held for trading can be classified as such even if an entity does not have the positive intention and ability to hold them until maturity. As a consequence, the ability to measure a financial asset at amortised cost without consideration of the entity's intention and ability to hold the asset until maturity is only appropriate when there is no active market for that asset. [IAS 39:BC27]

Example 3.4

Loan in security form

An entity acquires a debt security issued by a government at original issuance. The debt security will be quoted in an active market.

The debt security does not qualify for classification as loans and receivables because the debt security is quoted in an active market. The definition of loans and receivables in IAS 39 does not distinguish between loans that take the form of securities and those that do not. However, only debt securities that are not quoted in an active market can be classified in the 'loans and receivables' financial asset category.

As with any financial asset, the characteristics of an item classified as loans and receivables should be evaluated to determine whether the contractual arrangement contains an embedded derivative that must be accounted for separately (see **chapter C5**).

Following the separation of an embedded derivative from a debt host contract, the debt host contract may be accounted for as loans and receivables provided that the classification criteria for loans and receivables are met.

3.4.1 Definition of loans and receivables: equity security

Equity instruments (such as ordinary shares, share options, warrants and similar rights) should not be classified as loans and receivables because the amounts the holder may receive can vary in a manner that is not predetermined. A preference share that is a non-derivative equity instrument of the issuer with fixed or determinable payments can be classified in the loans and receivables category for the holder provided that it is not quoted in an active market. [IAS 39:IG.B.22] An example of such a preference share is a mandatorily redeemable preference share.

3.4.2 Securitised loans

A purchased interest in a pool of assets that are themselves loans and receivables can be classified as loans and receivables if it meets the criteria for such classification. If an entity acquires a beneficial interest in a securitised pool of loans and receivables, this would not meet the definition of loans and receivables if the beneficial interest is quoted in an active market.

3.5 Available-for-sale financial assets (AFS)

AFS financial assets are those non-derivative financial assets that are designated as AFS, or that are not classified as loans and receivables or HTM investments, are not held for trading and are not designated as at FVTPL on initial recognition.

AFS financial assets are measured at fair value with fair value gains or losses recognised in other comprehensive income. On sale or impairment of the asset, the cumulative gain or loss previously recognised in other comprehensive income is reclassified to profit or loss as a reclassification adjustment.

However, interest calculated using the effective interest method on interest-bearing AFS financial assets, impairment losses and foreign exchange gains and losses on monetary AFS financial assets are recognised in profit or loss (see **chapter C6** on measurement).

Dividends are recognised in profit or loss only when:

(a) the entity's right to receive payment of the dividend is established;

(b) it is probable that the economic benefits associated with the dividend will flow to the entity; and

(c) the amount of the dividend can be measured reliably.

Examples of AFS financial assets are equity investments that are not designated on initial recognition as at FVTPL, debt securities that are quoted in an active market (which may or may not have put features that would also prohibit them from being classified as HTM) and other financial assets held for liquidity purposes.

Example 3.5

Held for trading versus available-for-sale

[IAS 39:IG.B.12]

Entity A has an investment portfolio of debt and equity instruments. The documented portfolio management guidelines specify that the equity exposure of the portfolio should be limited to between 30 and 50 per cent of total portfolio value. The investment manager of the portfolio is authorised to balance the portfolio within the designated guidelines by buying and selling equity and debt instruments. Is Entity A permitted to classify the instruments as available for sale?

It depends on Entity A's intentions and past practice. If the portfolio manager is authorised to buy and sell instruments to balance the risks in a portfolio, but there is no intention to trade and there is no past practice of trading for short-term profit, the instruments can be classified as available for sale. If the portfolio manager actively buys and sells instruments to generate short-term profits, the financial instruments in the portfolio are classified as held for trading.

In July 2014, the IFRS Interpretations Committee issued an agenda decision on IAS 39 titled *Classification of a hybrid financial instrument by the holder*. The Committee was asked to clarify the classification by the holder of a hybrid financial instrument with a revolving maturity option, an early settlement option and a suspension of interest payments option (all at the option of the issuer). Specifically, the submitter raised the question of whether the host of such a financial instrument should be classified by the holder as equity, or as a debt instrument under IAS 39.

On the basis of the responses to the outreach request, the Interpretations Committee observed that the issue is not widespread. The Interpretations Committee also noted that the financial instrument described in the submission is specific and it would not be appropriate to provide guidance on this particular issue.

The Interpretations Committee considered that its agenda criteria are not met. Consequently, the Interpretations Committee decided not to add this issue to its agenda.

4 Reclassifications

IAS 39 permits limited reclassifications of certain financial assets subject to meeting specified criteria. Reclassifications are not permitted for financial liabilities, derivatives or financial assets for which the fair value option has been selected.

4.1 Into FVTPL

IAS 39:50 prohibits any reclassification of a financial instrument into the FVTPL category after initial recognition.

Although IAS 39:50 is categorical that reclassifications into FVTPL are prohibited, there does appear to be one exception to this prohibition, which is described in IAS 39:12. If an entity is not able to measure an embedded derivative separately at a financial reporting date subsequent to acquisition, the entity is required to designate the entire hybrid (combined) contract as at FVTPL. Because embedded derivatives are only required to be separated from contracts that are not measured at FVTPL, the situation described in IAS 39:12 would appear to be a reclassification from a measurement category other than FVTPL to FVTPL.

4.2 Out of FVTPL

As described in **section 3.1**, financial assets may be classified at initial recognition as at FVTPL if specified conditions are met. In some cases, this classification is mandatory (e.g. in the case of derivatives that are not designated as effective hedging instruments or non-derivative financial assets that are deemed held for trading). In other cases, the classification is by election (e.g. when an entity applies the fair value option). IAS 39 only permits reclassification out of FVTPL, subject to specified criteria, for non-derivative financial assets that were originally classified as at FVTPL because they met the definition of held for trading. Financial assets that are classified as at FVTPL because they are derivatives or because they are designated as at FVTPL under the fair value option cannot be reclassified under any circumstances.

Loan commitments that are within the scope of IAS 39 and recognised and measured as at FVTPL cannot be reclassified because they meet the definition of derivatives and derivatives cannot be reclassified. In addition, a financial asset cannot be reclassified if it is designated as at FVTPL under the fair value option which would also prohibit reclassification of loan commitments designated as at FVTPL in accordance with IAS 39:4(a). Also, in the case of written loan commitments, they are financial liabilities and financial liabilities cannot be reclassified.

The first condition to be met in order to reclassify a financial asset from FVTPL is that the financial asset is no longer held for the purpose of selling or repurchasing it in the near term. [IAS 39:50(c)] This criterion applies irrespective of whether the asset was initially classified as held for trading because (i) it was acquired principally for the purpose of selling in the near term or (ii) because it is part of a portfolio of identified financial instruments that are managed together and for which there is evidence of a recent actual pattern of short-term profit-taking.

If an entity wishes to reclassify a financial asset that was classified as held for trading because it was part of a portfolio of identified financial instruments that are managed together and for which there was evidence of a recent actual pattern of short-term profit-taking, the entity must demonstrate that the specific asset subject to reclassification is not intended to be sold in the near term. For an asset that forms part of a portfolio of assets, this may be difficult to demonstrate unless the asset has been isolated from the portfolio or the mandate of the portfolio has changed such that there is no longer evidence of short-term profit-taking.

IAS 39:50(c) refers to "selling or repurchasing it in the near term" which is the same terminology that is used in the held for trading definition. Both selling *and* repurchasing is relevant in the held for trading definition as the held for trading definition applies to both financial assets and financial liabilities. The reference to "repurchasing" in IAS 39:50(c) appears to be superfluous because this relates to financial liabilities and financial liabilities cannot be reclassified.

The second condition to be considered in order to reclassify a financial asset from FVTPL is whether the financial asset meets the definition of loans and receivables. If it does, the financial asset may be reclassified out of FVTPL if the entity has the intention and ability to hold the financial asset for the foreseeable future or until maturity. [IAS 39:50D] If it does not meet the definition of loans and receivables, it may be reclassified out of FVTPL only in rare circumstances. [IAS 39:50B]

The following summarises the criteria for reclassifying out of FVTPL.

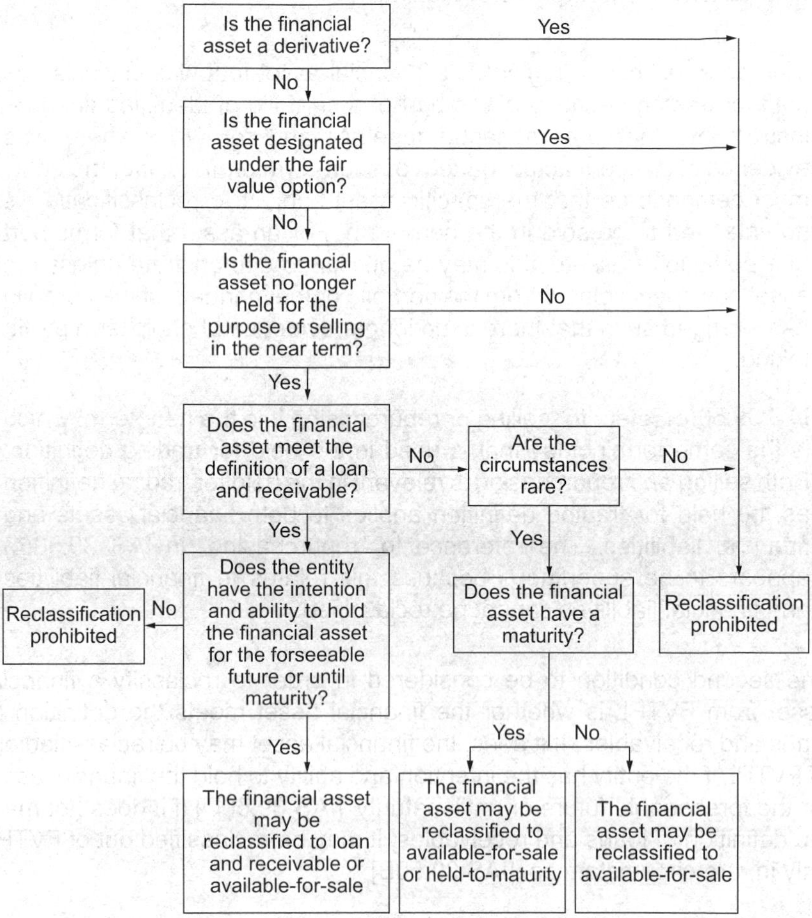

IAS 39 does not state explicitly at what date an entity should determine whether the financial asset meets the definition of loans and receivables when assessing whether the financial asset can be reclassified. Two interpretations are acceptable:

(i) assess the definition of loans and receivables at the date of initial recognition of the financial asset; or

(ii) assess the definition of loans and receivables at the date of reclassification of the financial asset. This is particularly relevant for financial assets that would not have met the definition of loans and receivables at initial recognition (e.g. because the instrument was traded in an active market), but that meet the definition at the date of reclassification.

An entity should decide on the appropriate interpretation and apply it consistently as an accounting policy choice to all reclassification assessments that require the entity to apply the definition of loans and receivables. If the accounting policy is considered relevant for the understanding of the financial statements, it should be disclosed in accordance with IAS 1:117.

The financial asset reclassified from FVTPL should be reclassified at its fair value on the date of reclassification. Any gain or loss recognised in profit or loss up until the date of reclassification should not be reversed. The fair value of the financial asset on the date of reclassification becomes its new cost (in the case of equity instruments) or amortised cost (in the case of debt instruments). [IAS 39:50C]

For financial assets reclassified out of FVTPL, the entity will start to apply the impairment guidance described in IAS 39:58 - 70 for that asset. Prior to the date of reclassification, an assessment of impairment was not required because the asset was measured at FVTPL. Because the instrument's fair value at the date of reclassification becomes its new deemed cost or deemed amortised cost, impairment losses recognised after the reclassification date may differ from the impairment losses that would have been recognised had the instrument never been previously measured at FVTPL (see **5.4.3** in **chapter C6** for more detail).

A financial asset reclassified out of FVTPL is subject to extensive disclosure requirements (see **4.1.4** in **chapter C12**).

4.2.1 Rare circumstances

IAS 39 does not provide any specific guidance as to how an entity should determine whether the circumstances under which reclassification is being contemplated are 'rare'. However, the Board expressed in IAS 39:BC104D that rare circumstances arise from a single event that is unusual and highly unlikely to recur in the near term. In a press release that accompanied the issuance of the amendment to IAS 39, *Reclassification of Financial Assets*, in October 2008 the IASB stated that "the deterioration of the world's financial markets that has occurred during the third quarter of this year is a possible example of rare circumstances cited in these IFRS amendments".

In order for circumstances to be considered rare, there should be cause and effect between those circumstances and the financial assets held that are subject to reclassification. In the second half of 2008, some markets for asset-backed securities became in effect closed because of the stark reduction in new instruments being issued and very low trading volumes for existing instruments, partly due to a lack of price transparency and lack of investor appetite. An entity with investments in asset-backed securities in those markets, which had originally been classified as held for trading, may have ceased to intend to hold the investments for trading purposes and, due to the rare circumstances in those markets, been unable to sell the assets. Depending on the specific facts and circumstances reclassification may be acceptable.

The mere reduction in the price of assets is generally not evidence of rare circumstances because falling prices, even in a stock market crash, are not in themselves rare. In addition, the reduction in the value of an asset (e.g. an investment in an equity security) does not necessarily have an effect on the intentions or investment strategy of the holder of the instrument. Often the only effect is the fair value loss that would be realised if the entity disposed of the asset, and the realisation of a fair value loss is not in itself rare.

4.2.2 Foreseeable future

IAS 39 does not provide guidance on how an entity should assess whether it intends to hold the financial asset for the foreseeable future.

'Foreseeable future' is not a new term introduced in the IAS 39 amendment because it is a term used in other IFRSs. IAS 21:15 permits the foreign exchange gains/losses on a monetary item that is a receivable from or a payable to a foreign operation to be recognised in other comprehensive income if settlement is neither planned nor likely to occur in the foreseeable future. Paragraph 39 of IAS 12 *Income Taxes* allows an exemption from recognising certain 'controllable' deferred tax liabilities in circumstances where it is probable that temporary differences will not reverse in the foreseeable future.

What is regarded as the 'foreseeable future' will depend on the facts and circumstances and intentions of the entity and the specific asset that is being assessed for reclassification. If an entity is actively marketing the asset in an attempt to sell it, this activity would be inconsistent with the assertion that the entity does not intend to sell the asset in the foreseeable future. An entity may at the date of reclassification have the intention to retain the asset for the foreseeable future, but later it may receive an unsolicited offer and choose to sell the asset. An entity determines the foreseeable future at the date of reclassification and it does not need to revisit this assessment. However, to the extent that an entity sells reclassified assets shortly after the reclassification date, this would call into question the entity's assertion that it has the intention to hold other assets that it wishes to reclassify until the foreseeable future.

4.2.3 Assessing embedded derivatives

Hybrid contracts that are financial instruments may contain embedded derivatives which were not separately accounted for because these hybrid contracts are measured at FVTPL (see **section 3** in **chapter C5**) may be reclassified out of FVTPL subject to meeting specific criteria. As the embedded derivative was not separated out at initial recognition a question arises whether IFRSs require or prohibit an entity from assessing the separation of the embedded derivative at the date the financial asset is reclassified.

In March 2009, the IASB issued amendments to IAS 39 and IFRIC 9 titled *Embedded Derivatives*. The amendments state that, upon reclassification of a financial asset out of FVTPL, an entity is required to assess whether embedded derivatives should be separated from the host financial contract. In addition, if an entity is unable to measure separately the embedded derivative that would have to be separated on reclassification of a hybrid (combined) contract out of the FVTPL category, that reclassification is prohibited. In such circumstances, the hybrid (combined) contract remains classified as at FVTPL in its entirety. The Board noted that when IFRIC 9 was issued, reclassifications out of the FVTPL category were prohibited and, therefore, IFRIC 9 did not consider the possibility of such reclassifications. The Board believed it was appropriate that embedded derivatives should be assessed at the date of reclassification. Not to require this would allow an entity to circumvent the requirement to assess embedded derivatives by classifying a financial asset initially as at FVTPL and subsequently reclassifying the asset.

The amendments also state that when assessing for embedded derivatives at the date of reclassification, the assessment should be made on the basis of the circumstances that existed at the later of when the entity first became a party to the contract and the date of change in the terms of the contract that significantly modifies the cash flows that otherwise would have been required under the contract. The Board considered that looking to circumstances when the entity became party to the contract was consistent with one of the stated purposes of embedded derivative accounting which is to prevent circumvention of the recognition and measurement requirements for derivatives and provide some degree of comparability. Furthermore, because the terms of the embedded features in the hybrid (combined) financial instrument have not changed, the Board did not see a reason for arriving at an answer on separation different from what would have been the case at initial recognition of the hybrid (combined) contract.

The Board's decision to look to circumstances when an entity became party to the contract when determining whether an embedded derivative is closely related to the host financial contract will be most relevant when determining whether put options, call options, or other prepayment options in debt instruments are closely related. IAS 39:AG30(g) requires such options to be separated from the host contract if the option's exercise price is not approximately equal to the amortised cost of the host debt instrument. At the date of reclassification, an entity will be required to make the embedded derivative assessment it would have made had the debt instrument not been initially classified as at FVTPL, i.e. the entity will need to determine the instrument's amortised cost for all dates when the instrument may be put, called, or prepaid and compare the amortised cost with the exercise price of the option on those dates.

4.3 Into AFS investments

A debt or equity instrument may be reclassified out of held for trading (part of the FVTPL category) into AFS in accordance with IAS 39:50 (see **section 4.2**). Because the instrument is measured at fair value both before and after reclassification, there is no gain/loss on reclassification and all amounts previously recognised in profit or loss prior to the date of reclassification are retained in profit or loss.

An entity must reclassify a debt instrument from HTM to AFS if there is no longer the intention and ability to hold the debt instrument to maturity. Also, all debt instruments must be reclassified out of HTM into AFS when there are sales or reclassifications of more than an insignificant amount of HTM investments that do not meet any of the conditions in IAS 39:9 (see **4.6**). At the date of reclassification, the difference between the carrying amount of such investments and their fair value should be recognised in other comprehensive income. [IAS 39:52]

If the fair value of an investment in an unquoted equity instrument becomes sufficiently reliable following a period during which the investment was measured at cost in accordance with IAS 39:53, resulting in the measurement of that investment at fair value, this is not a reclassification between financial asset categories. Investments in equity instruments can only ever be classified in either FVTPL or AFS (both of which are required to be measured at fair value) and IAS 39 does not have a fifth classification category. Therefore, although IAS 39:53 refers to financial assets that became reliably measurable when the measure was not previously available and this paragraph is included in the section titled 'Reclassifications', it is not apparent what category such assets could be reclassified to. It is reasonable to consider such assets as continuing to belong to the same classification category to which they were originally classified, but that their basis of measurement has been changed to fair value. The difference between cost and fair value at the date the fair value becomes reliably measureable should be recognised in other comprehensive income if the asset is classified as an AFS asset (see **4.10** and **4.11**).

4.4 Out of AFS investments

Investments in debt instruments may be reclassified out of AFS. Investments in equity instruments classified as AFS cannot be reclassified.

If the fair value of an investment in an unquoted equity instrument classified as an AFS asset becomes unreliable and, therefore, an entity ceases to measure this investment at fair value and begins to measure it at cost in accordance with IAS 39:54, this is not a reclassification between financial asset categories. Investments in equity instruments can only ever be classified in either FVTPL or AFS (both of which require measurement at fair value) and IAS 39 does not have a fifth classification category. Therefore, although IAS 39:54 refers to examples where the fair value of an investment in an unquoted equity instrument becomes unreliable, and this paragraph is included in the section of the Standard titled 'Reclassifications', it is not apparent what category such assets could be reclassified to. It is reasonable to consider such assets as continuing to belong to the same classification category to which they were originally classified, but that their basis of measurement has been changed to cost (see **4.10** and **4.11**).

A financial asset classified as AFS may be reclassified to HTM if the entity has the intent and ability to hold the asset to maturity. The asset may be reclassified during the instrument's life except during the two-year tainting period (see **section 3.3**) if the entity has disposed of more than an insignificant amount of held-to-maturity assets.

A financial asset classified as AFS may be reclassified out of the AFS category to the loans and receivables category if it meets the definition of loans and receivables and the entity has the intention and ability to hold the financial asset for the foreseeable future or until maturity.

As described in **4.2**, an entity should determine an accounting policy with respect to the date it determines whether a reclassified AFS debt instrument meets the definition of loans and receivables. Two interpretations are acceptable:

(i) assess the definition of loans and receivables at the date of initial recognition of the financial asset; or

(ii) assess the definition of loans and receivables at the date of reclassification of the financial asset.

An entity should decide on an appropriate interpretation and apply it consistently as an accounting policy choice to all reclassification assessments that require the entity to apply the definition for loans and receivables. If the accounting policy is considered relevant for the understanding of the financial statements, it should be disclosed in accordance with IAS 1:117.

If an entity's accounting policy is to assess the definition of loans and receivables at the date of initial recognition, then the entity will not be able to reclassify an AFS debt instrument where that AFS debt instrument was classified as such because it did not meet the definition of loans and receivables at initial recognition due to the fact that it was traded in an active market.

If an entity's accounting policy is to assess the definition of loans and receivables at the date of reclassification, then the debt instrument may no longer be traded in an active market and so the entity may be able to reclassify the AFS debt instrument even though it did not meet the definition of loans and receivables at initial recognition.

The following summarises the criteria for reclassifying out of AFS.

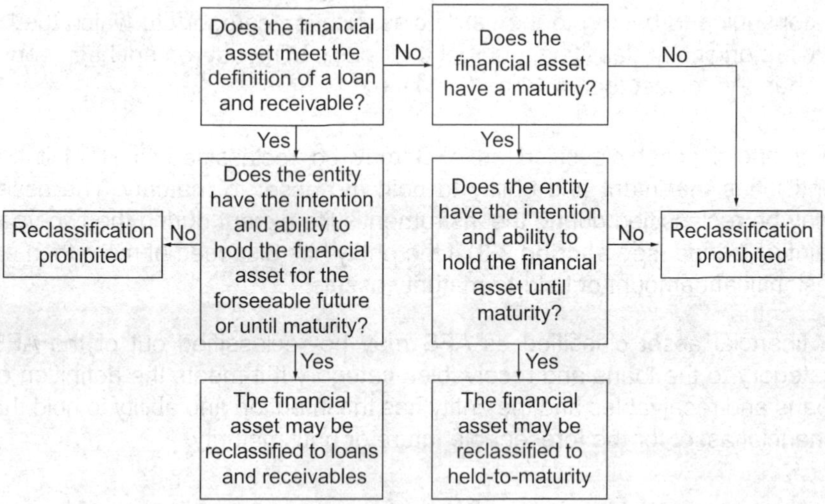

A financial asset reclassified from AFS should be reclassified at its fair value on the date of reclassification. Any gain or loss already recognised in profit or loss should not be reversed. The fair value of the financial asset on the date of reclassification becomes its new amortised cost.

Any previous gain or loss on an AFS asset that has been recognised in other comprehensive income should be amortised to profit or loss over the remaining life of the investment using the effective interest method in the case of an instrument with a fixed maturity. Any difference between the new amortised cost (being the asset's fair value at the date of reclassification) and its maturity amount should also be amortised over the remaining life of the financial asset using the effective interest method, similar to the amortisation of a premium or a discount. In the case of a financial asset that does not have a fixed maturity (e.g. a perpetual debt instrument reclassified from AFS to loans and receivables), the gain or loss should be recognised in profit or loss when the financial asset is sold or otherwise disposed of or impaired. If the reclassified financial asset is subsequently impaired, any previous gain or loss that has been recognised in other comprehensive income is reclassified from equity to profit or loss irrespective of whether or not the asset has a fixed maturity. [IAS 39:54]

A financial asset reclassified out of AFS to loans and receivables is subject to extensive disclosure requirements (see **4.1.4** in **chapter C12**).

4.5 Into HTM investments

A financial asset classified as at FVTPL may be reclassified to HTM if the financial asset is no longer held for the purpose of selling or repurchasing it in the near term [IAS 39:50(c)] and it meets the definition of a HTM investment. The criteria for reclassification are described in **section 4.2**.

A financial asset classified as AFS may be reclassified to HTM if the entity has the intent and ability to hold the asset to maturity. The asset may be reclassified during the instrument's life except during the two-year tainting period if the entity has disposed of more than an insignificant amount of HTM assets. When the two-year period subsequent to the period in which tainting occurred has passed, the entity is allowed to reclassify the assets back into HTM provided that it intends and is able to hold these assets to maturity. On the date of reclassification, an asset's carrying amount (i.e. its fair value at the date of reclassification) becomes the asset's new amortised cost. [IAS 39:54] Any previous fair value gain or loss on the asset that has been accumulated in equity is amortised to profit or loss over the remaining life of the financial asset using the effective interest method.

4.6 Out of HTM investments

When, as a result of a change in intention or ability, it is no longer appropriate to classify an investment as HTM, it is reclassified to AFS and remeasured at fair value. [IAS 39:51] The 'tainting' provisions of IAS 39 (see **section 3.3**) apply not only to sales but also to reclassifications of HTM investments. Therefore, reclassifications of more than an insignificant amount of HTM investments, which do not meet any of the conditions for permitted sales, taint the HTM portfolio and all remaining HTM investments must be reclassified into AFS.

On reclassification out of HTM into the AFS category, as a consequence of tainting, any difference between an asset's carrying amount and its fair value is recognised in other comprehensive income. [IAS 39:51 and IAS 39:55(b)] This difference must be disclosed in addition to the reason for reclassification. [IFRS 7:12]

When an entity taints its HTM portfolio in the current reporting period, and is required to reclassify all of its HTM investments into the AFS category, it does not restate its comparatives for the reporting period to reflect this change of classification, because this would conceal the impact of 'tainting' the portfolio.

4.7 Into loans and receivables

Reclassifications of financial assets classified either as at FVTPL or as AFS to the loans and receivables category are permitted in certain circumstances. The criteria for reclassifying out of these categories are described in **sections 4.2** and **4.4**.

4.8 Out of loans and receivables

Although IAS 39 provides explicit guidance on reclassifications into loans and receivables, it is silent as to whether and when reclassifications out of loans and receivables are permitted or required. As the loan and receivable definition requires that the instrument is not quoted in an active market the Standard is not clear whether reclassification is permitted or required if the instrument becomes quoted in an active market after it is classified as a loan and receivable. Reclassification would only be permitted to an available-for-sale financial asset as reclassifications into the fair value through profit or loss category are expressly forbidden by IAS 39:50.

Due to the lack of specific guidance in IAS 39 an entity should determine an accounting policy whether financial assets should be reclassified from loans and receivables to available-for-sale financial assets in the case where the loans and receivables definition is no longer met. This policy should be applied consistently for similar events and circumstances for all loans and receivables. If an entity chooses reclassification as its accounting policy, it will need to reclassify as available-for-sale all items classified as loans and receivables that become quoted in an active market; it would not be appropriate for an entity to reclassify only some of its loans and receivables that become quoted in an active market. The date of reclassification should be the date when the market for the financial asset becomes active.

4.9 Summary of reclassifications

The summary of reclassifications below excludes investments in equity instruments (or derivatives linked to them and settled by delivery of an unquoted equity instrument) for which fair value is unreliable (see **4.10** and **4.11**).

Out of	Into	Criteria	Example
FVTPL	L&R	*Debt instrument meets the definition of L&R* The asset is no longer held for the purpose of selling in the near term and the entity has the intention and ability to hold the financial asset for the foreseeable future.	A trade receivable that at initial recognition was intended to be sold when that intent no longer applies.

Out of	Into	Criteria	Example
FVTPL	HTM	*Debt instrument does not meet the definition of loans and receivables (if the instrument met the definition of L&R it could not be reclassified to HTM because the HTM definition specifically excludes L&R)* The asset is no longer held for the purpose of selling in the near term and the entity has the intention and ability to hold the financial asset until maturity (this requirement applies for all HTM assets) and the circumstances are rare.	A debt security that at initial recognition was intended to be sold in the near term and is a security that is traded in an active market (e.g. corporate debt, government bond) and where the entity now considers it has the intent and ability to hold to maturity. The circumstances for the reclassification are deemed rare.
FVTPL	AFS	*Debt instrument meets the definition of L&R* The asset is no longer held for the purpose of selling in the near term and the entity has the intention and ability to hold the financial asset for the foreseeable future.	A trade receivable that at initial recognition was intended to be sold where the intent no longer applies.
FVTPL	AFS	*Equity instrument or debt instrument does not meet the definition of L&R* The asset is no longer held for the purpose of selling in the near term and the circumstances are rare.	A debt security that at initial recognition was intended to be sold and is a security that is traded in an active market (e.g. corporate debt, government bond). The circumstances for the reclassification are deemed rare.
AFS	L&R	*Debt instrument meets the definition of L&R* The entity has the intention and ability to hold the financial asset for the foreseeable future.	A trade receivable that at initial recognition was designated as AFS.

Out of	Into	Criteria	Example
AFS	HTM	*Debt instrument does not meet the definition of L&R* The asset is held with the intention and ability to hold to maturity.	A debt security that at initial recognition was intended to be sold prior to maturity and is a security that is traded in an active market (e.g. corporate debt, government bond) and where the entity now considers it has the intent and ability to hold to maturity.
AFS	FVTPL	Not permitted	Not permitted
HTM	AFS	Debt instrument is no longer held with the intent and ability to hold to maturity. If there are more than an insignificant amount of sales or reclassifications of HTM assets the HTM portfolio is 'tainted' and the whole portfolio must be reclassified to AFS.	A debt security that at initial recognition was considered traded in an active market (e.g. corporate debt, government bond) and the entity had the intent and ability to hold to maturity but the intent or ability no longer applies.
HTM	L&R	Not permitted	Not permitted
HTM	FVTPL	Not permitted	Not permitted
L&R	HTM	Not permitted	Not permitted
L&R	AFS	Accounting policy choice whether to reclassify if the L&R is no longer met. This policy should be applied to all L&Rs.	A debt security that was not quoted in an active market becomes quoted in an active market subsequent to initial recognition, or subsequent to being reclassified to L&R.
L&R	FVTPL	Not permitted	Not permitted

4.10 Investments in equity instruments for which a reliable measure of fair value is no longer available

In the rare circumstances that a reliable measure of fair value is no longer available, so that it is no longer appropriate for an unquoted equity instrument (or derivative linked to it and settled by delivery of an unquoted equity instrument) to be measured at fair value, then the instrument must be measured at cost. The carrying amount of the asset on this date becomes its cost. [IAS 39:54] Any fair value gains and losses recognised in profit or loss to that date will not be reversed; equally any fair value gains and losses that were included in equity will remain in equity until the financial asset is sold, at which point these movements will be reclassified to profit or loss. However, even when the asset is carried at cost, it is still subject to an impairment assessment (see **section 5** in **chapter C6**).

4.11 Investments in equity instruments for which fair value becomes reliably determinable

When, subsequently, a reliable measure becomes available for an equity instrument (or derivative that is linked to and must be settled by delivery of an unquoted equity instrument) that was previously held at cost, the asset is measured at fair value. [IAS 39:53]

The difference between the financial asset's carrying amount and its fair value is recognised in profit or loss for assets classified as at FVTPL and in other comprehensive income for assets classified as AFS.

5 Classification of financial assets acquired in a business combination

When financial assets are acquired in a business combination, those assets must be classified in the consolidated financial statements of the acquirer into one of the permitted categories described in **section 3** above. It is entirely possible that the classification of a financial asset for these purposes may differ from its classification in the financial statements of the acquiree. For example, the acquirer in its consolidated financial statements may choose to designate a financial asset as at FVTPL or as an AFS asset on initial recognition even though the acquiree may have classified it otherwise when it first recognised the asset. Also, the acquirer may choose to classify an asset as HTM that the acquiree did not. There are many other variations where the acquirer's classification can differ from the acquiree's classification for the same financial asset. These differences can arise because 'initial recognition' from the acquirer's perspective is the date of acquisition of the subsidiary and its classification decisions are made at that date.

The revised version of IFRS 3 *Business Combinations* issued in January 2008 provides clear guidance stating that, at the acquisition date, the acquirer should make any classifications or designations concerning financial assets acquired or financial liabilities assumed in a business combination in accordance with pertinent conditions (e.g. contractual terms, economic conditions, acquirer's operating or accounting policies) at that date. IFRS 3(2008) applies prospectively to business combinations for which the acquisition date is on or after the beginning of the first annual reporting period beginning on or after 1 July 2009.

6 Future developments

In July 2014 the IASB issued IFRS 9 *Financial Instruments*. The Standard replaces the classification and measurement requirements in IAS 39 *Financial Instruments: Recognition and Measurement* for financial assets which are discussed in this chapter. IFRS 9 is effective for annual periods beginning on or after 1 January 2018 with early adoption permitted.

IFRS 9 requires entities to classify financial assets as being measured at either amortised cost or fair value. Gains and losses on assets measured at fair value are recognised either in (i) profit or loss ("fair value through profit or loss") or (ii) for certain designated investments in equity instruments and certain debt instruments if held in a business model in which assets are managed both in order to collect contractual cash flows and for sale, in other comprehensive income ("fair value through other comprehensive income"). The criteria for amortised cost and fair value through other comprehensive income measurement differs to IAS 39 in that there is greater focus on the entity's business model in determining how financial assets are classified.

The requirements of IFRS 9 are described at length in *iGAAP 2016 Financial Instruments – IFRS 9 and related Standards – Volume B*.

C3 Financial liabilities and equity

Contents

1 Introduction

IAS 32 *Financial Instruments: Presentation* requires an issuer of a financial instrument to classify the financial instrument, or its component parts, as a financial liability or as equity in accordance with the substance of the contractual arrangement and the definitions of a financial liability and an equity instrument. The overriding principles are that when the issuer does not have an unconditional right to avoid the obligation to deliver cash or another financial asset, and when the contract does not, in substance, evidence a residual interest in the net assets of the issuer after deducting all of its liabilities, the instrument is not an equity instrument (see **section 2**).

A more complex area, in respect of which the Standard provides additional guidance, is the treatment of derivative and non-derivative contracts indexed to, or settled in, an entity's own equity instruments. The definitions of a financial asset and a financial liability also include certain contracts on own equity and are applied to evaluate whether such contracts are, in substance, equity, financial liabilities or derivatives (derivatives can be either financial assets or financial liabilities). For example, a written put option on own shares that will be settled, if the option is exercised by the holder, by delivering cash in exchange for the entity's own shares, is a financial liability because the entity will have an obligation to deliver cash (see **section 6**).

This chapter addresses the application of the financial liability and equity definitions to various types of financial instruments issued in practice and contracts indexed to and settled in an entity's own equity. It also indicates the implications of classification as either debt, equity or a derivative for the measurement of that contract or its component parts.

2 Principles of liability/equity classification

A financial instrument or its component parts should be classified upon initial recognition as a financial liability or an equity instrument according to the substance of the contractual arrangement, rather than its legal form, and the definitions of a financial liability and an equity instrument. [IAS 32:15 & 18] For some financial instruments, although their legal form may be equity, the substance of the arrangements is that they are liabilities. A preference share, for example, may display either equity or liability characteristics depending on the substance of the rights attaching to it.

The appropriate classification as a financial liability, equity or a combination of both, is determined by the entity when the financial instrument is initially recognised and that classification is not generally changed subsequently unless the terms of the instrument change. As exceptions to this general principle, **section 8** discusses a number of circumstances in which reclassification may be appropriate even though the terms of the instrument have not changed. In addition, when the specific requirements for puttable instruments and instruments that contain an obligation to deliver a pro rata share of net assets at liquidation described in **2.1.2.1** and **2.1.3** respectively no longer apply or start to apply, reclassification may be appropriate.

When classifying a financial instrument in consolidated financial statements, an entity should consider all of the terms and conditions agreed upon between members of the group and the holders of the instrument. For example, a financial instrument issued by a subsidiary could be classified as equity in the subsidiary's individual financial statements and as a liability in the consolidated financial statements if another group entity has provided a guarantee to make payments to the holder of the instrument.

IAS 32 defines a financial liability as any liability that is:

[IAS 32:11]

(a) a contractual obligation:
   (i) to deliver cash or another financial asset to another entity (e.g. a payable); or
   (ii) to exchange financial assets or financial liabilities with another entity under conditions that are potentially unfavourable to the entity (e.g. a financial option written by the entity); or

(b) a contract that will or may be settled in the entity's own equity instruments and is:
   (i) a non-derivative contract for which the entity is or may be obliged to deliver a variable number of its own equity instruments (e.g. an instrument that is redeemable in own shares to the value of the carrying amount of the instrument); or
   (ii) a derivative contract over own equity that will or may be settled other than by the exchange of a fixed amount of cash (or another financial asset) for a fixed number of the entity's own equity instruments (e.g. a net-share settled written call over own shares). For this purpose, rights, options or warrants to acquire a fixed number of the entity's own equity instruments for a fixed amount of any currency are equity instruments if the entity offers the rights, options or warrants pro rata to all of its existing owners of the same class of its own non-derivative equity instruments. Also for these purposes, the entity's own equity instruments do not include puttable financial instruments that are classified as equity instruments in accordance with IAS 32:16A and 16B, instruments that impose on the entity an obligation to deliver to another party a pro rata share of the net assets of the entity only on liquidation and are classified as equity instruments in accordance with IAS 32:16C and 16D, or instruments that are contracts for the future receipt or delivery of the entity's own equity instruments.

As an exception, an instrument that meets the definition of a financial liability is classified as an equity instrument if it has all the features and meets the conditions in IAS 32:16A and 16B or IAS 32:16C and 16D.

The Standard defines an equity instrument as any contract that represents a residual interest in the assets of an entity after deducting all of its liabilities.

In May 2008, the IFRIC (now the IFRS Interpretations Committee) issued an agenda decision on IAS 32, *Deposits on Returnable Containers.* The IFRIC was asked to provide guidance on the accounting for the obligation to refund deposits on returnable containers. In some industries, entities that distribute their products in returnable containers collect a deposit for each container delivered and have an obligation to refund this deposit when containers are returned by the customer. The issue is whether the obligation should be accounted for in accordance with IAS 39.

The IFRIC noted that IAS 32:11 defines a financial instrument as "any contract that gives rise to a financial asset of one entity and a financial liability or equity instrument of another entity". Following delivery of the containers to its customers, the seller has an obligation only to refund the deposit for any returned containers. In circumstances in which the containers are derecognised as part of the sale transaction, the obligation is an exchange of cash (the deposit) for the containers (non-financial assets). Whether that exchange transaction occurs is at the option of the customer. Because the transaction involves the exchange of a non-financial item, it does not meet the definition of a financial instrument in accordance with IAS 32. In contrast, when the containers are not derecognised as part of the sale transaction, the customer's only asset is its right to the refund. In such circumstances, the obligation meets the definition of a financial instrument in accordance with IAS 32 and is therefore within the scope of IAS 39. In particular, IFRS 13:47 states that "the fair value of a financial liability with a demand feature (e.g. a demand deposit) is not less than the amount payable on demand, discounted from the first date that the amount could be required to be paid."

2.1 Contractual obligation to deliver cash or another financial asset

The key feature in determining whether a financial instrument is a liability is the existence of a contractual obligation of one party (the issuer) to deliver cash or another financial asset to another party (the holder), or to exchange financial assets or liabilities under conditions that are potentially unfavourable. In contrast, in the case of an equity instrument (e.g. ordinary shares) the right to receive cash in the form of dividends or other distributions is at the issuer's discretion and, therefore, there is no obligation to deliver cash or another financial asset to the holder of the instrument. There is an exception to this rule for certain puttable instruments and instruments with an obligation to deliver a pro rata share of net assets only at liquidation (see **2.1.2.1** and **2.1.3**).

Items such as deferred revenue and warranty obligations require delivery of goods or services rather than an obligation to deliver cash or another financial asset and, therefore, are not financial liabilities. [IAS 32:AG11] Obligations to pay tax, company registration fees and other similar charges are obligations to pay cash. However, these are statutory rather than contractual requirements and, therefore, they are not financial liabilities. Similarly, constructive obligations (as defined in IAS 37 *Provisions, Contingent Liabilities and Contingent Assets*) do not arise from contracts and are not financial liabilities. [IAS 32:AG12]

Liability characteristics are established in practice in a number of ways, as discussed in the following sections.

In November 2012 the IFRS Interpretations Committee received a request to clarify the classification of the liability for prepaid cards issued by a bank in the bank's financial statements and accounting for the unspent balance of the prepaid cards with the following contractual features:

(a) no expiry date;

(b) cannot be refunded, redeemed or exchanged for cash;

(c) redeemable for goods or services only;

(d) redeemable only at selected merchants, which, depending upon the card programme, range from a single merchant to all merchants that accept a specific card network; and

(e) no back-end fees, which means that the balance on the prepaid card does not reduce unless spent by the holder.

The Interpretations Committee was asked to consider whether the liability for those prepaid cards is a non-financial liability because the issuing bank does not have an obligation to deliver cash to the cardholder.

At its November 2014 meeting, the Interpretations Committee discussed the submission and observed that the liability for prepaid cards with features as explained above would meet the definition of a financial liability, because the issuing bank has a contractual obligation to deliver cash to the merchant that is conditional upon the cardholder using the prepaid card to purchase goods or services. In such a circumstance, an issuing bank would apply the guidance in IAS 39 to determine when to derecognise the liability for prepaid cards. However, the Interpretations Committee was concerned about other similar arrangements, such as customer loyalty programmes or prepaid cards issued by a non-banking entity that can be redeemed for goods or services of the issuing entity or of other entities, and requested the staff to analyse those other similar arrangements.

In January 2015, the Interpretations Committee discussed the staff's analysis and requested further analysis on more complex arrangements which, at the time of writing, had yet to be presented to the Interpretations Committee.

2.1.1 Mandatory redemption and/or mandatory interest payments

When an instrument requires mandatory redemption by the issuer for a fixed or determinable amount, a contractual obligation to deliver cash at redemption exists and, therefore, the instrument includes, and is presented as, a liability. An exception to this principle applies for certain puttable instruments and certain instruments that contain an obligation to deliver a pro rata share of net assets at liquidation as described in **2.1.2.1** and **2.1.3**.

Example 2.1.1A

Mandatorily redeemable preference shares

Entity A issues preference shares that are mandatorily redeemable at par in ten years. A contractual obligation to deliver cash exists for the repayment of principal – the issuer cannot avoid the outflow of cash in Year 10. Therefore, the preference shares should be classified as a financial liability.

Perpetual instruments provide the holder with no right to require redemption. However, the terms of such instruments often require the issuer to make coupon payments into perpetuity. A perpetual instrument with a mandatory coupon is a liability in its entirety because the whole of its value is derived from the stream of future coupon payments.

Example 2.1.1B

Perpetual coupon-bearing preference shares

A perpetual instrument is issued at a par amount of CU100 million requiring coupon payments of 6 per cent to be made annually. Provided that 6 per cent is the market rate of interest for this type of instrument when issued, the issuer has assumed a contractual obligation to make a future stream of 6 per cent interest payments. The net present value of the interest payments is CU100 million and represents the fair value of the instrument. The preference shares should be classified as a financial liability.

Many traditional debt instruments such as bonds and bank loans involve both mandatory redemption and mandatory interest payments.

Other instruments may require a mandatory distribution of a percentage of the profits of an entity (to the extent that such profits are generated) rather than a traditional interest payment. Such an instrument meets the definition of a liability because it is a contractual obligation of the issuer to deliver cash or another financial asset to the holder. The issuer has no discretion over paying out a percentage of its profits.

A distinction must be drawn between those circumstances in which the issuer genuinely contractually has no discretion over payment of interest (or dividends) and those in which payment may be avoided but this decision will have consequences (even if significant). For example, an entity may issue instruments under which it contractually retains the discretion regarding the distribution of a percentage of profits but, if the distribution is not paid, the entity ceases to benefit from a favourable tax treatment. Such arrangements are common for Real Estate Investment Trusts (REITs) in some jurisdictions. In such circumstances, although the entity may intend to pay dividends in order to retain the significant tax benefits, it has no contractual obligation to deliver cash (or another financial asset) to the holder of the instrument and, therefore, the instrument is not a financial liability.

The terms of shares issued by REITs may differ and each situation should be assessed on its own merits. The scope of REITs from the perspective of the issuer is also discussed in **2.3.9** in **chapter C1**.

2.1.2 Puttable instruments

A puttable instrument is defined as a financial instrument that gives the holder the right to put the instrument back to the issuer for cash or another financial asset or that is automatically put back to the issuer on the occurrence of an uncertain future event or the death or retirement of the instrument holder. [IAS 32:11]

2.1.2.1 Puttable instruments presented as equity

Because puttable instruments contain a contractual obligation for the issuer to deliver cash or another financial asset to the holder, such instruments are generally classified as financial liabilities. However, certain puttable instruments that meet specified criteria must be presented as equity. The criteria for equity classification are extensive and restrictive.

The requirements regarding equity classification for some puttable instruments originated from an amendment to IAS 32 issued in February 2008, *Puttable Financial Instruments and Obligations Arising on Liquidation*. The purpose of the amendment was to provide a limited scope exception to the definition of a financial liability that would apply to certain financial instruments that contain obligations but that, in the IASB's view, also represent a residual interest in the net assets of the issuing entity. The exception applies to puttable instruments (described in this section) as well as to instruments containing an obligation to deliver a pro rata share of the net assets of the entity only on liquidation (see **2.1.3**). Because the requirements of the amendment are designed as an exception, they should be applied narrowly and should not be used by analogy (IAS 32:96B). Failure to meet one of the requirements results in failure to qualify for the exception, in which case the instrument will not meet the criteria for classification as equity.

A puttable instrument is classified as equity if it meets all of the following criteria:

[IAS 32:16A]

(a) the holder is entitled to a pro rata share of the entity's net assets in the event of the entity's liquidation;

The entity's net assets are those assets that remain after deducting all other claims on its assets. A pro rata share is determined by: (i) dividing the entity's net assets on liquidation into units of equal amount; and (ii) multiplying that amount by the number of the units held by the financial instrument holder. The IASB decided that the instrument must entitle the holder to a pro rata share of the net assets on liquidation because the net assets on liquidation represent the ultimate residual interest in the entity. [IAS 32:BC57]

An instrument that has a preferential right on liquidation of the entity is not an instrument with an entitlement to a pro rata share of the net assets of the entity. An instrument has a preferential right on liquidation, for example, if it entitles the holder to a fixed dividend on liquidation in addition to a share of the entity's net assets, when other instruments in the subordinate class with a right to a pro rata share of the net assets of the entity do not have the same right on liquidation. [IAS 32:AG14C]

(b) the instrument is in the class of instruments that is subordinate to all other classes of instruments;

For an instrument to be in the most subordinate class, the financial instrument must have no priority over other claims to the assets of the entity on liquidation and must not need to be converted into another instrument before it is in the class of instruments that is subordinate to all other classes of instruments. [IAS 32:BC58] The instrument must be in the class of instruments that is subordinate to all other classes of instruments on liquidation in order to represent the residual interest in the entity.

When determining whether an instrument is in the subordinate class, an entity evaluates the instrument's claims on liquidation as if liquidation were to occur on the date when the instrument is classified. The initial classification should be reassessed if there is a change in relevant circumstances. For example, if the entity issues or redeems another financial instrument, this may affect whether the instrument under consideration is in the class of instruments that is subordinate to all other classes. [IAS 32:AG14B]

If an entity has only one class of financial instruments, that class is treated as if it were subordinate to all other classes. [IAS 32:AG14D]

In some circumstances, the most subordinate class of instruments is immaterial compared to the overall capital structure of the entity. This is particularly so when the most subordinate instruments are 'founder shares' (i.e. shares issued when the entity was formed) but the entity is capitalised by other issued instruments (e.g. puttable instruments issued after the founder shares were issued). The founder shares in this case, although immaterial, cannot be ignored in determining whether the puttable instruments should be classified as equity. Because the puttable instruments are not the most subordinate instruments issued by the entity, they are not classified as equity.

Example 2.1.2.1A

Immaterial founder shares

Entity A is capitalised principally by issue of puttable instruments whose contractual terms meet the requirements of IAS 32:16A for classification as equity except for the criterion of IAS 32:16A(b) that such an instrument be subordinate to all other classes of instruments. This is due to the existence of 'founder shares' (i.e. shares issued when Entity A was formed), the value of which is immaterial compared to the puttable instruments and the overall capital structure of the entity. The puttable instruments rank ahead of the ordinary shares on liquidation of Entity A.

Entity A should classify the puttable instruments as liabilities. IAS 32:16A(b) requires that for a puttable instrument to be classified as equity it must be in the class of instruments that is subordinate to all other classes of instruments.

In the circumstances described, although immaterial, the founder shares cannot be ignored in determining whether the puttable instruments should be classified as equity. Because the puttable instruments are not the most subordinate instruments issued by Entity A, they should not be classified as equity.

(c) all financial instruments in the class of instruments that is subordinate to all other classes of instruments have identical features. For example, they must all be puttable, and the formula or other method used to calculate the repurchase or redemption price is the same for all instruments in that class;

In January 2009, the IFRIC (now the IFRS Interpretations Committee) issued an agenda decision on IAS 32, *Classification of Puttable and*

Perpetual Instruments. The IFRIC considered whether a puttable instrument is subordinate to all other classes of instruments when an entity also has perpetual instruments that meet the definition of equity instruments.

The IFRIC noted that a financial instrument is first classified as a liability or equity instrument in accordance with the general requirements of IAS 32. That classification is not affected by the existence of puttable instruments. As a second step, if a financial instrument would meet the general definition of a liability because it is puttable to the issuer, the entity considers the conditions in IAS 32:16A & 16B to determine whether it should be classified as equity. Consequently, the IFRIC noted that IAS 32 does not preclude the existence of several classes of equity.

The IFRIC also noted that IAS 32:16A(c) applies only to "instruments in the class of instruments that is subordinate to all other classes of instruments". IAS 32:16A(b) specifies that the level of an instrument's subordination is determined by its priority in liquidation. Accordingly, the existence of the put option does not of itself imply that the puttable instruments are less subordinate than the perpetual instruments.

(d) apart from the contractual obligation for the issuer to repurchase or redeem the instrument for cash or another financial asset, the instrument does not include any contractual obligation to deliver cash or another financial asset to another entity, or to exchange financial assets or financial liabilities with another entity under conditions that are potentially unfavourable to the entity, and it is not a contract that will or may be settled in the entity's own equity instruments as set out in subparagraph (b) of the definition of a financial liability; and

The requirements of IAS 32:16A(d) restrict equity classification to instruments where the only obligation in the instrument is the put right held by the holder; the limited scope exception cannot be applied to puttable instruments containing contractual obligations in addition to the put right because the holder may have a claim to some of the net assets in preference to other instrument holders and, consequently, such instruments may not represent a residual interest in the entity. [IAS 32:BC60]

(e) the total expected cash flows attributable to the instrument over the life of the instrument are based substantially on the profit or loss, the change in the recognised net assets or the change in the fair value of the recognised and unrecognised net assets of the entity over the life of the instrument (excluding any effects of the instrument).

Profit or loss and the change in the recognised net assets should be measured in accordance with relevant IFRSs. [IAS 32:AG14E]

For a puttable instrument to be classified as equity, in addition to meeting the above criteria in IAS 32:16A, the issuer must have no other financial instrument or contract that has:

[IAS 32:16B]

(a) total cash flows based substantially on the profit or loss, the change in the recognised net assets or the change in the fair value of the recognised and unrecognised net assets of the entity (excluding any effects of such instrument or contract); and

(b) the effect of substantially restricting or fixing the residual return to the puttable instrument holders.

When applying IAS 32:16B(a) & (b), the issuer is not required to consider non-financial contracts with a holder of an instrument described in IAS 32:16A that have contractual terms and conditions that are similar to the contractual terms and conditions of an equivalent contract that might occur between a non-instrument holder and the issuing entity.

The application guidance issued with IAS 32 (which is an integral part of the Standard) provides guidance on how to determine whether transactions and arrangements were entered into by the instrument holder other than as an owner of the entity. The general principle is that a transaction or arrangement between the instrument holder and the issuing entity will only be considered to have been entered into by the instrument holder in a capacity other than as an owner if the cash flows and contractual terms and conditions of the transaction or arrangement are similar to an equivalent transaction that might occur between a non-instrument holder and the issuing entity; in other words, the arrangement must be similar to an arrangement that could have been entered into with a non-owner.

If an instrument holder is also an employee of the issuing entity, the cash flows payable to the instrument holder in his or her capacity as an employee are ignored because those cash flows do not arise in their capacity as an owner. Similarly, a profit- or loss-sharing arrangement that allocates profit or loss to the instrument holders on the basis of services rendered or business generated during the current or prior years are arrangements with instrument holders in a non-owner role and should not be considered when assessing the features listed in IAS 32:16A. However, if the profit- or loss-sharing arrangement allocates profit or loss based on the nominal amount of the instrument holder's interest relative to others in the class, this would represent an arrangement with the holders in their capacity as owners and should be considered when applying IAS 32:16A. [IAS 32:AG14H]

IAS 32:AG14G provides a further example of a partnership structure where some partners provide a guarantee to the entity and are remunerated for that guarantee. In determining whether the partners' interests in the partnership are identical, the guarantee is ignored because the guarantee is not provided by the partners in their capacity as owners.

IAS 32:AG14J provides examples of some instruments and arrangements that, when entered into on normal commercial terms with unrelated parties, are unlikely to prevent instruments that otherwise meet the criteria in IAS 32:16A from being classified as equity:

(a) instruments with total cash flows substantially based on specific assets of the entity;

(b) instruments with total cash flows based on a percentage of revenue;

(c) contracts designed to reward individual employees for services rendered to the entity; and

(d) contracts requiring the payment of an insignificant percentage of profit for services rendered or goods provided.

In May 2010, the IFRS Interpretations Committee considered a request for clarification of guidance relating to the classification of puttable financial instruments that include contractual obligations to provide pro rata distributions. The request proposed an amendment to the guidance in IAS 32 as part of *Improvements to IFRSs* to clarify that a puttable instrument can be classified as equity if it has a contractual obligation to deliver cash, or another financial asset, to all existing holders of the instrument on a pro rata basis.

The Interpretations Committee decided not to propose an amendment to IAS 32 because they considered that the identified unique circumstances that justified amending IAS 32, titled *Classification of Rights Issues* (see **6.1.1**), did not apply in this case. Further, an amendment to IAS 32 in this regard would introduce an additional exception to the general definition of a financial liability, which would be beyond the scope of the annual improvements process. At the date the decision was made, the Committee considered that an amendment would only be effective for annual periods beginning on or after 1 January 2012 and this was expected to be after the IASB had issued a final *Financial Instruments with Characteristics of Equity* (FICE) Standard.

Since the IFRIC reached the agenda decision the FICE project has been deferred and has been included in the IASB's research programme. See future developments in **9.2**.

If a puttable instrument is presented as equity, IAS 1 *Presentation of Financial Statements* requires the following disclosures:

[IAS 1:136A]

- summary quantitative data about the amount classified as equity;
- the entity's objectives, policies and processes for managing its obligation to repurchase or redeem the instruments when required to do so by the instrument holders, including any changes from the previous period;

- the expected cash outflow on redemption or repurchase of that class of financial instruments; and
- information about how the expected cash outflow on redemption or repurchase was determined.

When a puttable instrument is presented as equity, but subsequently fails to meet any of the criteria detailed in IAS 32:16A & 16B, the entity should reclassify it from the date when the instrument ceases to have all of the features or meet all of the conditions set out in those paragraphs. The financial liability should be measured at the instrument's fair value at the date of reclassification with any difference between the carrying amount of the equity instrument and the fair value of the financial liability at the date of reclassification recognised in equity. Similarly, if an entity redeems all of its issued non-puttable instruments and any puttable instruments that remain outstanding have all of the features and meet all of the conditions in IAS 32:16A & 16B, the entity should reclassify the puttable instruments as equity instruments from the date when it redeems the non-puttable instruments. The reclassification to equity should be at the carrying amount of the financial liability at the date of reclassification. [IAS 32:16E & 16F]

IAS 1 requires that when an entity reclassifies a puttable financial instrument between financial liabilities and equity, it should disclose the amount reclassified into and out of each category, and the timing and reason for that reclassification. [IAS 1:80A(a)]

Because the presentation of some puttable instruments as equity, rather than as financial liabilities, is an exception to the principles in IAS 32, the Standard does not permit the extension of this amendment to the classification of non-controlling interests in the consolidated financial statements. Therefore, puttable instruments presented as equity in the separate or individual financial statements that represent non-controlling interests in the consolidated financial statements are classified as financial liabilities in the consolidated financial statements.

Example 2.1.2.1B

Puttable instruments held by non-controlling interests

Entity P controls Entity Q, which therefore is included in Entity P's consolidated financial statements. Entity Q's capital structure consists of puttable instruments (partly held by Entity P and partly by other external investors) which meet the requirements for equity classification in its individual financial statements. Entity P's interest in the puttable instruments is eliminated on consolidation. Even though the puttable instruments held by the non-controlling interests meet the definition of equity in Entity Q's individual financial statements, they are presented as a financial liability in the consolidated financial statements of Entity P.

The prohibition on equity classification in the consolidated financial statements for certain puttable instruments presented as equity in the subsidiary financial statements appears at odds with the general principles in IFRS 10 *Consolidated Financial Statements* under which equity instruments issued by subsidiaries not held by the parent are presented as non-controlling interests. This is further evidence that the requirement to present certain puttable instruments as equity is a limited scope exception that not only overrides the general definition of a financial liability, but also overrides other principles within IFRSs.

2.1.2.2 Puttable instruments presented as financial liabilities

A puttable instrument that does not meet the definition of equity as described in **2.1.2.1** will be classified either wholly as a financial liability, or partly as a financial liability in the case of an instrument that is a compound instrument (i.e. the instrument consists partly of a financial liability and partly an equity component). In considering whether an instrument is a financial liability or equity, an entity must first apply the criteria in **2.1.2.1** to determine whether the instrument is equity. If it is not, this section is relevant.

The fact that the contractual put right in a puttable instrument is conditional upon the holder exercising its right to require redemption does not negate the existence of a financial liability, because the issuer does not have the unconditional right to avoid delivering cash or another financial asset. [IAS 32:19(b)] An obligation is not negated if the instrument gives the holder the right to a residual interest in the assets of the issuer as is the case, for example, for a unit in a mutual fund. [IAS 32:18(b)]

Example 2.1.2.2A

Preference shares puttable at par

An entity issues preference shares that are puttable at par for cash at the option of the holder at a particular date.

The preference shares contain a financial liability element which should be measured at the present value of the obligation to redeem the preference shares for par in cash.

The fact that the contractual put right in a puttable instrument is conditional upon the holder exercising its right to require redemption does not negate the existence of a financial liability element, because the issuer does not have the unconditional right to avoid delivering cash or another financial asset. Further, the instrument does not meet the exception to the definition of a financial liability in IAS 32:16A & 16B to be presented as equity.

Example 2.1.2.2B

Instrument puttable at net asset value

Entity A issues Class B shares which allow the holder to put the shares back to Entity A at any time at a price equal to the holder's proportional share of the net assets of Entity A. This price is calculated as the number of Class B shares owned, divided by the total number of Class B shares outstanding, multiplied by the net assets of Entity A (excluding the Class B shares from the net asset calculation).

The Class B shares do not entitle the holder to a pro rata share of Entity A's net assets in the event of liquidation and are not the most subordinate class of shares. As such, the criteria of IAS 32:16A are not met.

Although Class B shareholders might receive returns that would typically be associated with equity holders in that they participate in the performance of the net assets of Entity A, the fact that Entity A has a contractual obligation to pay the holder of the Class B shares cash if the holder chooses to put the instrument back to Entity A, and the fact that the terms of the Class B shares do not meet the criteria to be classified as equity in IAS 32:16A, mean that Entity A should classify the Class B shares as financial liabilities.

Example 2.1.2.2C

Discretion to refuse redemption

Entity A has instruments in issue that allow the holders to request redemption of their instrument at specified dates and amounts. Entity A's governing charter states that the entity has a choice whether or not to accept the holder's request. There are no other conditions on the level of redemptions or any limitations on the entity's discretion to redeem or make payments to holders. In its history, Entity A has never refused to redeem the instruments when requested to do so by a holder. All other characteristics of the instrument are equity.

Because Entity A has no obligation to transfer cash or another financial asset, the instrument should be classified as equity. A history of, or intention to make, discretionary payments does not trigger liability classification. [IAS 32:AG26]

Under IAS 32, interests in many open-ended mutual funds, unit trusts, partnerships and some co-operative entities, which embody the right of the holder to require the issuer to redeem the interests for a cash amount equivalent to their share of net assets, but which do not meet the narrow criteria for equity classification described in **2.1.2.1**, should be classified as financial liabilities. This may lead to a situation where some entities have no equity capital in their financial statements. IAS 32 permits the use of an appropriate description of the line item relating to puttable instruments and provides an illustrative example of such presentation, which is reproduced below.

Example 2.1.2.2D

Presentation of an entity without equity

[Extracts from IAS 32 Illustrative Examples: Example 7]

Statement of financial position as at 31 December 20X1

		20X1		**20X0**
	CU	**CU**	**CU**	**CU**
ASSETS				
Non-current assets (classified in accordance with IAS 1)	91,374		78,484	
Total non-current assets		91,374		78,484
Current assets (classified in accordance with IAS 1)	1,422		1,769	
Total current assets		1,422		1,769
Total assets		92,796		80,253
LIABILITIES				
Current liabilities (classified in accordance with IAS 1)	647		66	
Total current liabilities		(647)		(66)
Non-current liabilities excluding net assets attributable to unitholders (classified in accordance with IAS 1)	280		136	
		(280)		(136)
Net assets attributable to unitholders		91,869		80,051
Statement of comprehensive income for the year ended 31 December 20X1				
Revenue		2,956		1,718
Expenses (classified by nature or function)		(644)		(614)
Profit from operating activities		2,312		1,104
Finance costs:				
– other finance costs		(47)		(47)
– distributions to unitholders		(50)		(50)
Change in net assets attributable to unitholders		2,215		1,007

When an entity has no instruments classified as equity, the usual requirements for presenting specified gains and losses in other comprehensive income continue to apply. For example, the effective portion of hedging gains and losses on cash flow hedges (see **2.2** in **chapter C9**) and net investment hedges (see **2.3** in **chapter C9**), and gains and losses on AFS investments (see **3.5** in **chapter C2**) are recognised in other comprehensive income following the general recognition and measurement rules.

IFRIC Interpretation 2 *Members' Shares in Co-operative Entities and Similar Instruments* provides guidance on the application of IAS 32's principles to the classification of members' shares in a co-operative entity as liabilities. The Interpretation clarifies the following.

- The contractual right of a member to request redemption of contracts identified as members' shares does not, in itself, give rise to a liability. Rather, the entity must consider all of the terms of the contract in determining classification as a liability or equity (including relevant local laws, regulations and the entity's governing charter in effect at the date of the classification). However, expected future amendments to those laws, regulations or the entity's charter should not be considered. [IFRIC 2:5]
- Members' shares that give the member a right to request redemption are equity of the entity if the entity has an unconditional right to refuse redemption. [IFRIC 2:7]
- Local laws, regulations or the entity's governing charter can impose prohibitions on the redemption of members' shares that are unconditional or dependent on certain conditions being met (or not met) (e.g. prohibitions based on liquidity criteria). If redemption is unconditionally prohibited, members' shares are equity. However, provisions in local laws, regulations or the entity's governing charter that prohibit redemption only if conditions (e.g. liquidity constraints) are met (or not met) do not result in members' shares being equity. [IFRIC 2:8]
- An unconditional prohibition may be absolute (i.e. all redemptions are prohibited) or partial (i.e. redemption of members' shares prohibited if redemption would cause the number of shares or paid-in capital from members' shares to fall below a specified level). In the case of a partial prohibition, members' shares in excess of the prohibition against redemption are liabilities, unless the entity has an unconditional right to refuse redemption, or the members' shares meet the criteria allowing certain puttable instruments (see **2.1.2.1**) and obligations arising on liquidation (see **2.1.3**) to be classified as equity. [IFRIC 2:9]

Example 2.1.2.2E

Limited discretion to refuse redemption

Local laws governing the operation of co-operatives prohibit co-operative entities from redeeming members' shares if, by such redemption, an entity would reduce paid-in capital from members' shares below 90 per cent of the highest amount of paid-in capital from members' shares. The highest amount for a particular co-operative is CU1,000,000. With the exception of the 90 per cent restriction, the paid-in capital for this co-operative is redeemable at the option of the member.

At 31 December 20X0 the balance of paid-in capital represented by the issued shares is CU900,000; at 31 December 20X1, the balance has increased to CU950,000.

At 31 December 20X0, the entire balance of CU900,000 is classified as equity.

At 31 December 20X1, CU900,000 is classified as equity and CU50,000 as a financial liability.

In some cases, the number of shares or the amount of paid-in capital subject to a redemption prohibition may change over time. If this is the case, such a change may lead to a transfer between financial liabilities and equity. [IFRIC 2:9]

Example 2.1.2.2F

Reclassification due to change in local law

Continuing with **example 2.1.2.2E**, at 31 December 20X2, the local laws governing the operation of co-operatives are amended so that redemption of members' shares is permitted up to 20 per cent of the highest amount of members' shares, rather than 10 per cent. If, at that date, the entire balance of paid-in capital remained unchanged from 31 December 20X1 at CU950,000, the entity would reclassify an additional CU100,000 from equity to financial liabilities so that CU800,000 is classified as equity and CU150,000 is classified as a financial liability, with no gain or loss resulting at the date the transfer is made. The entity should disclose separately the amount, timing and reason for the transfer.

Consistent with the requirements of IAS 39, demand deposits, including current accounts, deposit accounts and similar contracts that arise when members act as customers, are financial liabilities of the entity. [IFRIC 2:6]

2.1.3 Instruments containing an obligation to deliver a pro rata share of the net assets of the entity only on liquidation

When liquidation of an entity is certain to occur and is outside the control of the entity (e.g. an entity with a limited life) or is not certain to occur but is at the option of the holder of an instrument issued by the entity (e.g. in some partnership interests), the entity has a contractual obligation to pay cash or another financial asset that the entity cannot avoid. Therefore, such entities will generally recognise a financial liability with respect to the amounts payable by the entity on liquidation. However, IAS 32 has an exception for certain instruments, or components of instruments, when the issuer has an obligation to deliver to another party a pro rata share of the net assets of the entity only on liquidation. This limited scope exception was introduced at the same time as the equivalent limited scope exception for puttable instruments described in **2.1.2.1**.

The criteria for equity classification are similar to, but not the same as, the criteria described in IAS 32:16A & 16B for puttable instruments. The instrument must meet all of the following criteria to be presented as equity:

[IAS 32:16C]

(a) it entitles the holder to a pro rata share of the entity's net assets in the event of the entity's liquidation;

(b) it is in the class of instruments that is subordinate to all other classes of instruments; and

(c) all financial instruments in the class of instruments that is subordinate to all other classes of instruments must have an identical contractual obligation for the issuing entity to deliver a pro rata share of its net assets on liquidation.

The three criteria above are equivalent to the criteria in IAS 32:16A(a) - (c) for puttable instruments. The shaded boxes that accompany the criteria described in **2.1.2.1** apply equally to the criteria in IAS 32:16C reproduced immediately above.

For an instrument, or component of a financial instrument, containing an obligation to deliver a pro rata share of the net assets of the entity only on liquidation, to be classified as equity, in addition to meeting the above criteria in IAS 32:16C, the issuer must have no other financial instrument or contract that has:

[IAS 32:16D]

(a) total cash flows based substantially on the profit or loss, the change in the recognised net assets or the change in the fair value of the recognised and unrecognised net assets of the entity (excluding any effects of such instrument or contract); and

(b) the effect of substantially restricting or fixing the residual return to the instrument holders.

When applying (a) and (b) above, the issuer should not consider non-financial contracts with a holder of an instrument described in IAS 32:16C that have contractual terms and conditions that are similar to the contractual terms and conditions of an equivalent contract that might occur between a non-instrument holder and the issuing entity. If the entity cannot determine that this condition is met, it should not classify the instrument as an equity instrument.

IAS 32:16D reproduced immediately above is equivalent to IAS 32:16B for puttable instruments. The guidance and shaded boxes that accompany IAS 32:16B for puttable instruments, and the inability to classify puttable instruments held by non-controlling interests as equity in the consolidated financial statements (as described in **2.1.2.1**), apply equally to instruments containing an obligation to deliver a pro rata share of the net assets of the entity only on liquidation.

The Board acknowledged in its Basis for Conclusions that many of those requirements, and the reasons for them, are similar for puttable financial instruments and instruments that contain an obligation to deliver a pro rata share of the net assets only at liquidation. As highlighted in IAS 32:BC67, the criteria for the latter instruments differ from the former because:

(a) there is no requirement that there be no other contractual obligations;

(b) there is no requirement to consider the expected total cash flows throughout the life of the instrument; and

(c) the only feature that must be identical among the instruments in the class is the obligation for the issuing entity to deliver to the holder a pro rata share of its net assets on liquidation.

The Standard explains that the reason for the differences is the timing of settlement of the obligation. In the case of obligations settled only on liquidation, the life of the financial instrument is the same as the life of the issuing entity because the extinguishment of the obligation can occur only on liquidation. Therefore, the IASB concluded that it was appropriate to focus only on the obligations that are triggered on liquidation. The instrument must be subordinate to all other classes of instruments and represent the residual interests only at that point in time. However, if the instrument contains other contractual obligations, those obligations may need to be accounted for separately in accordance with the requirements of IAS 32 (i.e. the instrument may be a compound instrument containing a financial liability and equity component).

IAS 1 requires that when an entity reclassifies between financial liabilities and equity an instrument that imposes on the entity an obligation to deliver to another party a pro rata share of the net assets of the entity only on liquidation, it should disclose the amount reclassified into and out of each category (financial liabilities or equity), and the timing and reason for that reclassification. [IAS 1:80A(b)]

In the case of a limited life entity, disclosure is required of information regarding the length of the entity's life. [IAS 1:138(d)]

2.1.4 Restrictions on ability to satisfy contractual obligation

A restriction on the contractual obligation of the entity to deliver cash or another financial instrument, such as the need to obtain regulatory approval for payment, does not in itself negate that obligation. In such cases, the entity does not have an unconditional right to avoid delivering cash or another financial asset. [IAS 32:19(a)]

Example 2.1.4

Inability to satisfy put feature

Entity A issued preference shares that are puttable for CU1 million by the holders to Entity A at any time after a specified date. Under the terms of the shares, Entity A is required to satisfy its obligation under the put option from its distributable reserves.

The preference shares include a liability that reflects the put option feature that creates an obligation for Entity A. The possibility that Entity A might not be in a position to satisfy the obligation under the put option if it were to find that it has insufficient distributable reserves does not negate the obligation (however likely this is to occur).

2.1.5 Contractual obligation that is not explicit

An obligation may be established indirectly through the instrument's terms and conditions. IAS 32 gives two examples of how such an obligation could be created.

- A financial instrument may contain a non-financial obligation that must be settled if, and only if, the entity fails to make distributions or to redeem the instrument. If the entity can avoid a transfer of cash or another financial asset only by settling the non-financial obligation, the financial instrument is a financial liability. [IAS 32:20(a)]
- A financial instrument is a financial liability if it provides that, on settlement, the entity will deliver either cash or another financial asset, or its own shares whose value is determined to exceed substantially the value of the cash or other financial asset. Although the entity does not have an explicit obligation to deliver cash or another financial asset, the holder of the asset has in substance been guaranteed a minimum amount equal to at least the cash/other financial asset settlement option amount. [IAS 32:20(b)]

In March 2006, the IFRIC (now the IFRS Interpretations Committee) discussed the role of contractual and economic obligations in the classification of two different financial instruments under IAS 32. The first instrument was an irredeemable, callable financial instrument with dividends payable only if dividends are paid on the ordinary shares of the issuer which included a 'step-up' dividend clause that would increase the dividend at a pre-determined date in the future unless the instrument had previously been called by the issuer. The second instrument was an irredeemable, callable financial instrument with dividends that must be paid if interest is paid on another, linked, instrument.

The IFRIC agreed that IAS 32 is clear that a contractual financial obligation was necessary in order that a financial instrument be classified as a liability (ignoring the classification of financial instruments that may or will be settled in the issuer's own equity instruments). Such a contractual obligation could be established explicitly or indirectly. However, the obligation must be established through the *terms and conditions* of the financial instrument. IFRIC also noted that IAS 32 is clear that an economic obligation (commonly known as *economic compulsion*), by itself, would not result in a financial instrument being classified as a liability. The IFRIC also discussed the role of 'substance' in the classification of financial instruments. It noted that IAS 32 restricted the role of 'substance' to consideration of the contractual terms of an instrument, and that anything outside the contractual terms was not considered for the purpose of assessing whether an instrument should be classified as a liability under IAS 32. These points were subsequently confirmed by the IASB through their discussions in June 2006.

In September 2013 the IFRS Interpretations Committee dealt with a request to clarify how an issuer would classify three financial instruments in accordance with IAS 32. None of the financial instruments had a maturity date but each gave the holder the contractual right to redeem at any time. The holder's redemption right was described differently for each of the three financial instruments; however in each case the issuer had the contractual right to choose to settle the instrument in cash or a fixed number of its own equity instruments if the holder exercised its redemption right. The issuer was not required to pay dividends on the three instruments but could choose to do so at its discretion.

The Interpretations Committee noted that IAS 32:15 requires the issuer of a financial instrument to classify the instrument in accordance with the substance of the contractual arrangement. Consequently, the issuer cannot achieve different classification results for financial instruments with the same contractual substance simply by describing the contractual arrangements differently.

IAS 32:11 sets out the definitions of both a financial liability and an equity instrument. IAS 32:16 describes in more detail the circumstances in which a financial instrument meets the definition of an equity instrument.

The Interpretations Committee noted that a non-derivative financial instrument that gives the issuer the contractual right to choose to settle in cash or a fixed number of its own equity instruments meets the definition of an equity instrument in IAS 32 as long as the instrument does not establish an obligation to deliver cash (or another financial asset) indirectly through its terms and conditions. IAS 32:20(b) provides the example that an indirect contractual obligation would be established if a financial instrument provides that on settlement the entity will deliver either cash or its own equity instruments whose value is determined to exceed substantially the value of the cash.

The Interpretations Committee also acknowledged that financial instruments, in particular those that are more structured or complex, require careful analysis to determine whether they contain equity and non-equity components that must be accounted for separately in accordance with IAS 32.

The Interpretations Committee noted that if the issuer has a contractual obligation to deliver cash, that obligation meets the definition of a financial liability.

The Interpretations Committee considered that in the light of its analysis of the existing IFRS requirements, an interpretation was not necessary and consequently decided not to add the issue to its agenda.

In January 2014 the IFRS Interpretations Committee dealt with a request to clarify how an issuer would classify in accordance with IAS 32 a financial instrument that is mandatorily convertible into a variable number of shares (subject to a cap and a floor) but gives the issuer the option to settle by delivering the maximum (fixed) number of shares.

The Interpretations Committee discussed how an issuer would assess the substance of a particular early settlement option included in a financial instrument in accordance with IAS 32. The instrument has a stated maturity date and at maturity the issuer must deliver a variable number of its own equity instruments to equal a fixed cash amount, subject to a cap and a floor. The cap and the floor limit and guarantee, respectively, the number of equity instruments to be delivered. The issuer is required to pay interest at a fixed rate. The issuer has the contractual right to settle the instrument at any time before maturity. If the issuer chooses to exercise that early settlement option, it must:

(i) deliver the maximum number of equity instruments specified in the contract; and

(ii) pay in cash all of the interest that would have been payable if the instrument had remained outstanding until its maturity date.

The Interpretations Committee noted that the definitions of financial asset, financial liability and equity instrument in IAS 32 are based on the financial instrument's contractual rights and contractual obligations. However, IAS 32:15 requires the issuer of a financial instrument to classify the instrument in accordance with the substance of the contractual arrangement. Consequently, the Interpretations Committee noted that if a contractual term of a financial instrument lacks substance, that contractual term would be excluded from the classification assessment of the instrument.

The Interpretations Committee noted that the issuer cannot assume that a financial instrument (or its components) meets the definition of an equity instrument simply because the issuer has the contractual right to settle the financial instrument by delivering a fixed number of its own equity instruments. The Interpretations Committee noted that judgement will be required to determine whether the issuer's early settlement option is substantive and thus should be considered in determining how to classify the instrument. If the early settlement option is not substantive, that term would not be considered in determining the classification of the financial instrument.

The Interpretations Committee noted that the guidance in IAS 32:20(b) is relevant because it provides an example of a situation in which one of an instrument's settlement alternatives is excluded from the classification assessment. Specifically, the example in that paragraph describes an instrument that the issuer will settle by delivering either cash or its own shares and states that one of the settlement alternatives should be excluded from the classification assessment in some circumstances.

The Interpretations Committee noted that to determine whether the early settlement option is substantive, the issuer will need to understand whether there are actual economic or other business reasons that the issuer would exercise the option. In making that assessment, the issuer could consider, along with other factors, whether the instrument would have been priced differently if the issuer's early settlement option had not been included in the contractual terms. The Interpretations Committee also noted that factors such as the term of the instrument, the width of the range between the cap and the floor, the issuer's share price and the volatility of the share price could be relevant to the assessment of whether the issuer's early settlement option is substantive. For example, the early settlement option may be less likely to have substance – especially if the instrument is short-lived – if the range between the cap and the floor is wide and the current share price would equate to the delivery of a number of shares that is close to the floor (i.e. the minimum). That is because the issuer may have to deliver significantly more shares to settle early than it may otherwise be obliged to deliver at maturity.

The Interpretations Committee considered that in the light of its analysis of the existing IFRS requirements, neither an interpretation nor an amendment to a Standard was necessary and consequently decided not to add the issue to its agenda.

Example 2.1.5

Perpetual instrument with coupon step-up and dividend pusher

Bank A issues a perpetual instrument with the following terms.

- €100 million notional with annual 8 per cent interest payments for 8 years. Bank A has a call option embedded in the instrument that allows the instruments to be repurchased at the end of Year 8, and each year thereafter, for €100 million.
- If the instrument is not called by Bank A at the end of Year 8, the interest on the instrument increases to 14 per cent per annum (commonly referred to as a 'step-up' feature).
- The interest payments (both before and after the call date) are only payable if Bank A pays a dividend on its ordinary shares (commonly referred to as a 'dividend pusher'); the ordinary shares are classified wholly as equity.
- Bank A has consistently chosen to pay dividends on its ordinary shares. When the perpetual instrument is issued, Bank A's cost of borrowing for a similar debt instrument is approximately 8 per cent.

Bank A does not have an indirect or a direct obligation to deliver cash or other financial asset in respect of the perpetual instrument. The instrument is therefore classified wholly as equity.

Bank A has no obligation to pay interest because it can always avoid paying interest by exercising its discretion and not paying dividends on its ordinary shares. Bank A has no obligation to exercise its right to call the instrument at the end of Year 8 because the call right is an option and Bank A can always choose not to exercise that right. Because the instrument is perpetual, there is no redemption date and, therefore, the instrument does not contain any contractual obligation to deliver cash or another financial asset.

In determining the substance of the contractual arrangement, an entity must assess whether the terms of the instrument provide the issuer with discretion as to whether to deliver cash or another financial asset. In the circumstances described, Bank A has discretion as to whether or not it wishes to pay an ordinary dividend. Even though it may be highly likely that Bank A will choose to pay ordinary dividends and, as a result, will be required to pay interest under the perpetual instrument, the high likelihood is of itself not sufficient for the instrument to be classified as a financial liability. Similarly, although it may be very likely that Bank A will pay interest on the perpetual instrument and will exercise its call option at the end of Year 8 (thus making the instrument economically equivalent to an 8-year loan), this likelihood of itself is not sufficient for the instrument to be classified as a financial liability.

2.1.6 Shares to the value of, or issuer settlement option

Some instruments may contain an obligation for the issuer to deliver a variable number of its own equity instruments such that the fair value of the entity's own equity delivered under the arrangement equals the amount of the contractual obligation. The amount of the contractual obligation may be fixed or may fluctuate in part or in full in response to a variable other than the market price of the issuer's own equity.

Such instruments do not meet the definition of equity because the issuer is merely using its own shares as currency to extinguish its obligation. The contract therefore does not evidence a residual interest in the entity's assets after deducting all of its liabilities. [IAS 32:21]

Example 2.1.6A

Variable number of shares to the value of a fixed obligation

Entity A issues CU0.01 nominal preference shares that will pay out CU1 over three years. Entity A will pay the CU1 in its own ordinary shares so that the number of shares issued will vary to equate to CU1 in value.

The instrument is a financial liability because Entity A issues shares such that the fair value of the shares delivered is always equal to the amount of the contractual obligation (i.e. a variable number of shares).

Example 2.1.6B

Variable number of shares to the value of a variable obligation

Entity B issues an instrument for CU100 that pays no interest before maturity. At maturity, Entity B is required to deliver as many of its own equity instruments as are equivalent in value to the original issue price of CU100 plus a supplemental redemption amount depending on whether a designated share price index has increased between issuance of the instrument and the maturity date. The supplemental amount is determined as a multiple of the percentage increase in the share price index from the date of issue of the instrument to maturity and the original issue price. If the share price index has fallen over the life of the instrument, equity instruments equivalent in value to CU100 are delivered.

The instrument is a financial liability in accordance with IAS 32:11 because the instrument will be settled by delivery of a variable number of Entity B's equity instruments.

As stated in IAS 39:AG30(d) equity-indexed payments are not closely related to a debt instrument in which they are embedded. Accordingly, this feature needs to be separated out from the host contract and accounted for separately in accordance with IAS 39:11 - 13.

2.1.7 Contingent settlement provisions

Financial instruments may be structured such that the obligation to deliver cash or another financial instrument arises only on the occurrence or non-occurrence of uncertain future events (or on the outcome of uncertain circumstances) that are beyond the control of both the issuer and the holder of the instrument. The issuer does not have an unconditional right to avoid the obligation to deliver cash or another financial instrument and, therefore, such instruments are financial liabilities of the issuer unless:

[IAS 32:25]

- the contingent settlement provision that could require payment in cash or another financial asset is not genuine; or
- settlement in cash or another financial asset can only be required in the event of liquidation of the issuer; or
- the instrument meets the specified criteria for a puttable instrument or an obligation arising on liquidation to be classified as equity (see **2.1.2.1** and **2.1.3** respectively).

'Genuine' is generally understood to be not spurious or counterfeit, i.e. a genuine provision is one that is authentic and has commercial substance. A provision that is extremely rare, highly abnormal and very unlikely to occur is not considered genuine. [IAS 32:AG28]

Future events that are beyond the control of both the issuer and the holder of the instrument include:

(a) a change in macroeconomic, industry and other indices such as a stock market index, consumer price index, growth in Gross Domestic Product or total sector production;

(b) changes in law, government regulations, and other regulatory requirements (such as changes in taxation, pricing controls or accounting requirements); and

(c) changes in the key performance indicators of the issuer that are beyond the control of both the issuer and the holder such as revenues, net income or debt to equity ratio.

Example 2.1.7A

Contingent settlement provisions: change in accounting or tax law

Entity A issues preference shares bearing 5 per cent non-cumulative dividends payable at the discretion of the issuer. The shares will be redeemed if the applicable taxation or accounting requirements were to change.

The contingent event of a change in taxation or accounting requirements is deemed to be genuine.

The requirement for redemption on change of taxation or accounting requirements represents a contingent settlement provision (i.e. it is an uncertain future event beyond the control of both the issuer and the holder of the instrument).

Because the contingent event is genuine and can result in the issuer having to deliver cash or another financial asset at a time other than Entity A's liquidation, the instrument is classified as a financial liability. [IAS 32:25].

However, the 5 per cent dividend is payable at the discretion of Entity A and, consequently, is equity of Entity A. Therefore, the preference share contains both debt and equity features, i.e. it is a compound instrument (see **section 3**).

Example 2.1.7B

Contingent settlement provisions: shares redeemable on initial public offering

Entity B issues shares for CU1 million. Dividends are discretionary. Entity B is obliged to redeem the shares for par in the event of a flotation/initial public offering (IPO) of the entity. Entity B cannot guarantee a successful flotation/IPO, but it does have discretion as to whether to instigate proceedings to float or to seek an IPO. Given that Entity B can avoid redeeming the shares by avoiding a flotation/IPO, the instrument is classified as equity.

Example 2.1.7C

Contingent settlement provisions: shares redeemable in the absence of an initial public offering

Entity C issues shares for CU1 million. Entity C is obliged to redeem the shares at par in the event that Entity C is not subject to a successful flotation/Initial Public Offering (IPO) within five years from the date of issue of the shares. Entity C cannot guarantee a successful flotation/IPO, but it does have discretion as to whether to instigate proceedings to float or to seek an IPO.

Given that the contingent event (a successful flotation/IPO) is not in the control of Entity C, it is a contingent settlement provision. The contingent settlement provision is considered genuine, it is potentially payable other than at liquidation, and the shares do not meet the puttable exception in IAS 32 and therefore IAS 32:25 applies. Because Entity C cannot avoid redeeming the shares for cash, the instrument contains an obligation to pay cash that creates a financial liability.

Example 2.1.7D

Contingent settlement provisions: change of control

Entity D issues preference shares for CU1 million. Entity D is obliged to redeem the preference shares at par in the event that control of Entity D changes. A change in control is defined in the terms of the preference shares as a change in ownership of at least 51 per cent of the ordinary shares of Entity D.

Given that the contingent event (the sale of ordinary shares in Entity D by one set of shareholders to another) is not in the control of the Entity D, it is a contingent settlement provision. Because Entity D cannot avoid redeeming the preference shares for cash, the instrument contains an obligation to pay cash that creates a financial liability.

2.2 Equity instruments

In classifying a financial instrument as a liability or equity, equity classification is appropriate only if the instrument fails the definition of a financial liability as detailed in **section 2**.

The key requirement in determining whether an instrument is equity is the issuer's unconditional ability to avoid delivery of cash or another financial asset. That ability is not affected by:

- the history of making distributions;
- an intention to make distributions in the future;
- a possible negative impact on the price of ordinary shares of the issuer if the distributions are not made on the instrument concerned;
- the amount of the issuer's reserves;
- an issuer's expectations of a profit or loss for the period; or
- an ability or inability of the issuer to influence the amount of its profit or loss for the period.

Provided that dividends are at the discretion of the issuer, it is irrelevant whether dividends are cumulative or non-cumulative. [IAS 32:AG26]

Once a dividend is properly declared and the issuer is legally required to pay it, a contractual obligation to deliver cash comes into existence and a financial liability for the amount of the declared dividend should be recognised. Similarly, a liability arises upon liquidation to distribute to the shareholders the residual assets in the issuer, i.e. any remaining assets after satisfying all of its liabilities.

The existence of an option whereby the issuer can redeem equity shares for cash does not trigger liability classification because the issuer retains an unconditional right to avoid delivering cash or another financial asset. A contractual obligation would only arise at the point when the issuer exercised its right to redeem. This principle applies to all instruments that are not derivatives over own equity.

Specific rules apply to derivatives over own equity. For example, a purchased call option over a fixed number of shares will allow the issuer to buy back shares at a fixed price in the future. The issuer always has a choice as to whether it wishes to pay cash, because it always has a choice as to whether it wishes to exercise its option. However, this instrument is only treated as equity if it is gross physically settled in all cases when the issuer chooses to exercise, i.e. the option can never be net settled.

Instruments are frequently issued with a link to dividend payments on other types of instruments, most commonly ordinary shares. A 'dividend stopper' is a contractual term that requires no dividend to be paid on the ordinary shares if the payment is not made on another specified instrument. A 'dividend pusher' is a term that requires a dividend to be paid on a specified instrument if a dividend payment is made on ordinary shares.

Provided that the link is to the dividends on an instrument like an ordinary share where the issuer has discretion as to whether or not to pay a dividend, neither a 'dividend pusher' nor a 'dividend stopper' of itself results in the instrument concerned being classified as a liability. This is because the issuer retains discretion as to whether or not to pay on the instrument, albeit that the decision will need to be made in conjunction with the decision on whether to pay dividends on ordinary shares. The issuer continues to have an unconditional right to avoid the outflow of cash (or other financial assets).

Example 2.2A

Dividend stopper

Entity Y issues 6 per cent cumulative, non-redeemable preference shares with discretionary dividends that are subject to the availability of distributable reserves. The directors of Entity Y decide at each period end whether and the extent to which a dividend will be paid on the preference shares. The terms of the instrument include a dividend stopper, i.e. if no dividend is paid on the preference shares, then no dividend is paid on Entity Y's ordinary shares.

The payment of dividends on the preference shares is entirely at Entity Y's discretion (albeit the decision will need to be made in conjunction with the decision regarding whether to pay dividends on ordinary shares). For this reason, Entity Y continues to have an unconditional right to avoid an outflow of cash (or another financial asset) and, therefore, the preference shares should be classified as equity.

Example 2.2B

Dividend pusher

Entity M issues non-redeemable preference shares bearing 6 per cent discretionary non-cumulative dividends that are subject to the availability of distributable reserves. The directors of Entity M decide at each period end whether and the extent to which a dividend will be paid on the preference shares. The payment of dividends on Entity M's ordinary shares is also discretionary. However, the terms of the instrument include a dividend pusher, i.e. if a dividend is paid on Entity M's ordinary shares, then a dividend must be paid on the preference shares.

Because the payment of dividends on its ordinary shares is discretionary, Entity M continues to have an unconditional right to avoid an outflow of cash (or another financial asset) and, therefore, the preference shares should be classified as equity.

In March 2010, the IFRIC (now the IFRS Interpretations Committee) issued an agenda decision *IAS 32 Financial Instruments: Presentation – Shareholder Discretion*, in response to a request for guidance on whether a financial instrument in the form of a preference share that includes a contractual obligation to deliver cash is a financial liability or equity, if the payment is at the ultimate discretion of the issuer's shareholders.

The IFRIC noted that:

- IAS 32:AG26 identifies that when distributions to holders of preference shares are at the discretion of the issuer, the shares are equity instruments;
- diversity may exist in practice in assessing whether an entity has an unconditional right to avoid delivering cash if the contractual obligation is at the ultimate discretion of the issuer's shareholders and, consequently, whether a financial instrument should be classified as a financial liability or equity; and
- the IASB is currently undertaking a project to improve and simplify the financial reporting requirements for financial instruments with characteristics of equity. The main objectives of this project are to develop a better distinction between equity and non-equity instruments and converge IFRSs and US GAAP.

Consequently, the IFRIC recommended that the IASB address this issue as part of its project on *Financial Instruments with Characteristics of Equity* (FICE). At the time, the IASB's project was expected to address the distinction between equity and non-equity instruments in a shorter period than the IFRIC would require to complete its due process.

Since the IFRIC reached the agenda decision the FICE project has been deferred and has been included in the IASB's research programme. See future developments in **9.2**.

3 Compound instruments

The terms of a financial instrument may be structured such that it contains both equity and liability components (i.e. the instrument is neither entirely a liability nor entirely an equity instrument). Such instruments are defined in IAS 32 as compound instruments. An example of a compound instrument is a bond that is convertible, either mandatorily or at the option of the holder, into a fixed number of equity shares of the issuer. Compound instruments come in many forms and are not restricted solely to convertible instruments. The liability and equity components of a compound instrument are required to be accounted for separately. [IAS 32:28]

The requirement to separate out the equity and financial liability components of a compound instrument is consistent with the principle that a financial instrument must be classified in accordance with its substance, rather than its legal form. A compound instrument takes the legal form of a single instrument, while the substance is that both a liability and an equity instrument exist.

For example, a convertible bond that pays fixed coupons and is convertible by the holder into a fixed number of ordinary shares of the issuer has the legal form of a debt contract; however, its substance is that of two instruments:

- a financial liability to deliver cash (by making scheduled payments of coupon and principal) which exists as long as the bond is not converted; and
- a written call option granting the holder the right to convert the bond into a fixed number of ordinary shares of the entity.

The economic effect of the instrument is substantially the same as issuing simultaneously (i) a debt instrument with an early settlement provision and (ii) warrants to issue ordinary shares.

Example 3

Instrument exchangeable into equity of a subsidiary

Entity P issues to independent investors, zero coupon guaranteed exchangeable bonds for cash of CU2 billion. The bonds are exchangeable into the existing ordinary shares of a subsidiary of Entity P, Entity S, at a fixed conversion price of CU25 per share (80 million shares). The functional currency of both Entity P and Entity S is Currency Units (CU).

At maturity, the bondholders will choose to either (1) redeem the bonds in cash at 109.10 per cent of their issued amount, or (2) convert the bonds into equity shares of Entity S at the fixed exercise price. If the bond holders choose to convert the bonds into equity, Entity P will deliver existing ordinary shares of Entity S, reducing Entity P's interest in Entity S from 100 per cent to a minimum of 90 per cent.

The conversion option is classified as equity in Entity P's consolidated financial statements because it provides for the exchange of a fixed amount of cash for a fixed number of Entity S's shares. IAS 32:22 states that "a contract that will be settled by the entity (receiving or) delivering a fixed number of its own equity instruments in exchange for a fixed amount of cash or another financial asset is an equity instrument." In consolidated financial statements, this applies to equity instruments of a subsidiary as well as of the parent entity.

Assuming that Entity P does not lose control of Entity S, any transfer of Entity S's shares on conversion of bonds will be accounted for as an equity transaction in accordance with IFRS 10:23.

The treatment of a convertible bond denominated in a currency that is not the functional currency of the entity that issued the instrument and/or the entity whose shares will be delivered on conversion is discussed in **3.8.1**.

3.1 Separating the liability and equity components

Separation of the instrument into its liability and equity components is made upon initial recognition of the instrument and is not subsequently revised. The method used is as follows:

- firstly, the fair value of the liability component is calculated, and this fair value establishes the initial carrying amount of the liability component; and
- secondly, the fair value of the liability component is deducted from the fair value of the instrument as a whole, with the resulting residual amount being recognised as the equity component.

This method of allocating the liability and equity components is consistent with the definition of equity as a residual interest in the assets of an entity after deducting all of its liabilities. It ensures that no gain or loss arises on the initial recognition of the two components.

The fair value of the liability component on initial recognition is the present value of the contractual stream of future cash flows (including both coupon payments and redemption amount) discounted at the market rate of interest that would have been applied to an instrument of comparable credit quality with substantially the same cash flows, on the same terms, but without the conversion option.

Example 3.1A

Convertible debt

Entity A issues 2,000 convertible bonds on 1 January 20X5. The bonds have a 3-year term, and are issued at par with a face value of CU1,000 per bond, resulting in total proceeds of CU2 million. Interest is payable annually in arrears at an annual interest rate of 6 per cent. Each bond is convertible, at the holder's discretion, at any time up to maturity into 250 ordinary shares. When the bonds are issued, the market interest rate for similar debt without the conversion option is 9 per cent.

On initial recognition, the contractual cash flows of the liability component are valued first, and the difference between the proceeds of the bond issue (being the fair value of the instrument in its entirety) and the fair value of the liability is assigned to the equity component. The present value (i.e. fair value) of the liability component is calculated using a discount rate of 9 per cent (i.e. the market interest rate for similar bonds with the same credit standing having no conversion rights). The calculation, which excludes the income tax entries, is illustrated below.

	CU
Present value of principal at the end of 3 years*	1,544,367
Present value of interest (CU120,000 payable annually in arrears for 3 years**)	303,755
Total liability component (B)	1,848,122
Residual equity component (A-B)	151,878
Proceeds of bond issue (A)	2,000,000

* present value of principal amount at 9 per cent:

2,000,000/(1.09)^3 =	1,544,367

** present value of interest (CU120,000) payable at the end of each of 3 years:

interest at end of year 1: 120,000/1.09 =	110,092
interest at end of year 2: 120,000/$(1.09)^2$ =	101,002
interest at end of year 3: 120,000/$(1.09)^3$ =	92,661
Total net present value of interest payments	303,755

Upon initial recognition of the convertible instrument in the financial statements of the issuer, the following entries are recorded.

		CU	CU
Dr	Cash	2,000,000	
Cr	Financial liability		1,848,122
Cr	Equity		151,878

To recognise the convertible instrument.

Any transaction costs are allocated between the debt component and the equity component using their relative fair values.

The financial liability component will be subsequently measured in accordance with the measurement requirements in IAS 39 depending on its classification (either as a financial liability at FVTPL, or as an 'other' liability, measured at amortised cost using the effective interest method).

The equity component will not be remeasured.

Example 3.1B

Perpetual interest-bearing preference shares

Entity A, a CU functional currency entity, issues non-redeemable preference shares. The preference shares have a cumulative, mandatory dividend fixed at CU424 per share per year. If earnings are not sufficient to cover the dividend in any given year, such dividends will be paid in future years. Additional dividends may be declared but only if dividends of the same amount are declared on the other classes of shares.

The preference share is a compound financial instrument that contains both liability and equity components. The liability is the contractual obligation by the issuer to deliver cash (CU424 per year), while the equity component is represented by the holder's right to receive an equity return in the form of additional dividends, if declared.

The fair value of the liability will be calculated as the present value of the mandatory dividend of CU424 per share per year in perpetuity discounted at the market interest rate for a similar instrument that does not entitle the holder to additional discretionary dividends. The equity component is calculated as the residual amount after deducting from the fair value of the instrument as a whole the amount separately determined for the liability component.

3.2 Separating the liability and equity components when the instrument has embedded derivatives

In addition to the financial liability and equity components, a compound instrument may also have embedded derivatives (see **chapter C5**). For example, the instrument may contain a call option exercisable by the issuer. The value of any such embedded derivative features must be allocated to the liability component. [IAS 32:31] Thus, the carrying amount of the liability component is established by measuring the fair value of a similar liability (with similar terms, credit status and embedded non-equity derivative features) but without an associated equity component. The carrying amount of the equity component is then determined by deducting the fair value of the liability component from the fair value of the compound instrument as a whole.

A further assessment is required to establish whether the embedded derivative is closely related to the liability component (see **chapter C5**). This assessment is made before separating the equity component. No gain or loss arises from initially recognising the components of the instrument separately.

Example 3.2A

Convertible debt with issuer call

A CU functional currency entity issues a bond with a principal amount of CU60 million carrying a coupon of 5 per cent payable annually in arrears. The instrument is issued for proceeds of CU60 million. The instrument is convertible into a fixed number of equity shares of the issuer after a specified date. The instrument has no fixed maturity. However, it contains an issuer call option that allows the issuer to redeem the bond at par at any point in time.

It is established that the value of a similar bond (of similar credit status with similar features except that it does not contain a call or equity conversion option) at current market rates would be CU57 million. Based on an option pricing model, it is further determined that the value of the issuer purchased call option on a similar bond without a conversion option is an asset of CU2 million.

The value allocated to the liability and equity components should be as follows.

Liability component: CU55 million (CU57 million less CU2 million)

This reflects the inclusion of the value of the additional embedded derivative feature (asset) in the liability component.

Equity component: CU5 million (CU60 million – CU55 million)

This represents the equity residual arrived at by subtracting from the fair value of the whole instrument the fair value of the liability component (which includes the value of the embedded derivative feature in the form of the purchased call feature).

The guidance in IAS 39:AG27 - AG33 will need to be considered in assessing whether the embedded derivative is closely related to the host contract or whether, subsequent to issuance of the bond, it will be accounted for separately at fair value through profit or loss.

In **example 3.2A**, the initial amortised cost of the financial liability is established as the fair value of issued callable debt. Assuming the call feature over the debt instrument is not separated, the effective interest rate applied at inception and throughout the life of the instrument is the same rate of interest that would apply to plain callable debt. To the extent that interest rates change subsequent to issue, this will impact the likelihood that the callable debt will be called by the issuer and, therefore, the carrying amount will be updated (see **4.1** in **chapter C6**).

Example 3.2B

Convertible debt with issuer call and holder put

Entity X issued a convertible debt instrument in May 20X1 with a contractual maturity of 8 years. One bond allows the holder to obtain, at any time, one share of the issuer (the conversion option). The coupon is 2 per cent payable annually. The issue price is 100 per cent and the redemption price is 140 per cent.

The instrument is puttable by the holders on three different dates during the life of the instrument (May 20X3, May 20X5 and May 20X7).

The instrument is also callable by the issuer, starting 20X3, if the price of the issuer's shares increases beyond 125 per cent of the redemption price.

In the case of exercise of the put/call option, the redemption price is equivalent to the amortised cost of the issued instrument (prior to the equity conversion option being separated). The embedded call/put options, therefore, are closely related to the instrument and are not accounted for as derivatives with changes in fair value recognised in profit or loss. On initial recognition, Entity X considers

> that there is a very high probability that the instrument will be redeemed by the holders on the first exercise date of the put (i.e. 20X3), given the low price of its shares.
>
> Entity X will account for the issued bond as a compound instrument. On initial recognition, Entity X needs to consider the contractual cash flows in order to measure the value of the debt component of the compound instrument.
>
> The fair value of the plain debt instrument without a call/put or equity conversion option is equivalent to the present value of the contractually determined stream of future cash flows until maturity (in this case 20X9) discounted at the rate of interest that applies to instruments of comparable credit quality and providing substantially the same cash flows on the same terms but without the call, put or conversion option (i.e. debt instruments with a 20X9 maturity date).
>
> Entity X then determines the value of the call and put options embedded in the debt instrument using an option pricing model. The call and put options are valued as if they were a call and a put embedded in a debt instrument that did not have any equity conversion feature. Both the purchased call and the written put are deducted and added to the debt in order to obtain the fair value of the total liability component.
>
> Finally, Entity X determines the value of the embedded conversion option (equity component) by subtracting the total liability component from the total net proceeds received on issuance.

If the financial liability is not designated as at FVTPL, the effective interest rate must be applied in determining amortised cost. If an entity designates financial instruments as at FVTPL, it should have a policy as to whether it recognises the effective interest rate in profit or loss separately for such items (see **4.3.1** in **chapter C12**). An issuer must apply the effective interest rate to the financial liability ignoring the likelihood that the financial liability may be forgiven if the equity conversion is exercised. This treatment is consistent with the principle that the likelihood of conversion is reflected in the value of the conversion option and is recognised as a separate financial instrument in equity.

3.3 Conversion of a compound instrument

Upon conversion of a compound instrument, equity is issued and the liability component is derecognised. The original equity component recognised at inception remains in equity (although it may be reclassified from one line item of equity to another). No gain or loss is recognised on conversion. [IAS 32:AG32]

Example 3.3A

Convertible debt: issue of new shares

Assume the facts are as in **example 3.1A**, but the date now is 31 December 20X6 (i.e. the end of Year 2 of the instrument's life). Assume that, due to a rapid rise in Entity A's share price, all holders of the bonds exercise their right to convert their holdings into a fixed number of equity instruments of Entity A at 31 December 20X6.

The liability has been accounted for at amortised cost using the effective interest method (see **4.1** in **chapter C6**).

At 31 December 20X6, the following applies:

- the amortised cost carrying amount of the liability (determined using the effective interest method) immediately prior to conversion is CU1,944,954;
- the original equity component immediately prior to conversion still stands at the original CU151,878; and
- upon conversion, 500,000 equity shares will be issued (250 equity shares per bond x 2,000 bonds issued) with each equity share having a nominal value of CU1.

The accounting entries on conversion are as follows.

		CU	CU
Dr	Bond liability	1,944,954	
Cr	Equity		1,944,954

To remove the liability from the statement of financial position and recognise the issue of shares as a result of conversion.

The original component of equity, CU151,878, may be reclassified to another line item within equity.

Example 3.3B

Convertible debt: issue of treasury shares

Assume the facts are as in **example 3.1A** except that, instead of issuing new shares upon conversion, Entity A satisfies the requirement for equity shares to be delivered to the bondholders through the use of treasury shares. Rather than issuing 500,000 new equity shares, Entity A delivers to the bondholders upon conversion 500,000 of its own shares that it had previously repurchased and held as treasury shares.

The accounting entries in these circumstances would be as follows.

		CU	CU
Dr	Bond liability	1,944,954	
Cr	Equity		1,944,954

To remove the liability from the statement of financial position as a result of conversion and remove the treasury shares from equity.

The original component of equity (CU151,878) and the amount deducted from equity (as required by IAS 32:33) on acquisition of the treasury shares may be reclassified to another line item within equity upon conversion.

3.4 Early redemption of a compound instrument

When an entity redeems or repurchases a convertible instrument before its maturity through a tender offer (without altering the conversion feature), the consideration paid (including any transaction costs) is allocated to the liability and equity components at the date of the early redemption/early repurchase. The method used to make this allocation is the same as that used to make the original allocation of the proceeds of the issue of the instrument between the liability and equity components upon initial recognition. [IAS 32:AG33]

To the extent that the amount of the consideration allocated to the liability component exceeds the carrying amount of the liability component at that time, a loss is recognised in profit or loss. Conversely, to the extent that the consideration allocated to the liability component is smaller than its carrying amount, a gain is recognised in profit or loss.

The amount of consideration allocated to equity is recognised in equity with no gain or loss being recognised (the equity component that is not eliminated may be reclassified to another line item within equity).

Example 3.4

Convertible debt: repurchase

Assume the facts are as in **example 3.1A** and that one year has elapsed since the convertible bonds were issued and it is now 31 December 20X5.

In respect of the first year (year ended 31 December 20X5), the following accounting entries will have been recorded.

		CU	CU
Dr	Interest expense	166,331	
Cr	Bond liability		166,331

To recognise the interest expense and amortised cost of the bond using an effective interest rate of 9 per cent.

		CU	CU
Dr	Bond liability	120,000	
Cr	Cash		120,000

To recognise the payment of interest in cash.

This gives a carrying amount for the liability at the end of the first year of CU1,894,453.

	CU
Initial carrying amount at inception	1,848,122
Accretion in Year 1 using the effective interest method	166,331
Cash coupon payment at end of Year 1	(120,000)
Carrying amount at end of Year 1	1,894,453

At the end of the first year, Entity A repurchases the convertible bonds for a cash amount of CU2,100,000. It is established that, at the date of repurchase, Entity A could have issued a non-convertible instrument with a term of 2 years bearing a coupon rate of 7 per cent.

The consideration paid is allocated to the liability and equity components using the same method as was used on initial recognition of the convertible bonds; the fair value of consideration paid is first allocated to the liability component with the residual being assigned to the repurchase of the equity component:

	Fair value of repurchase consideration	**Carrying amount prior to repurchase**	**Difference**
	CU	**CU**	**CU**
Liability component:			
Present value of two remaining interest payments of CU120,000 discounted at 7 per cent and 9 per cent respectively	216,963	211,093	
Present value of principal amount due in two years' time of CU2 million discounted at 7 per cent and 9 per cent respectively	1,746,877	1,683,360	
	1,963,840	1,894,453	69,387
Equity component	136,160*	151,878	(15,718)
Total	2,100,000	2,046,331	53,669

* The amount of CU136,160 represents the difference between the repurchase price of CU2,100,000 and the amount of the consideration paid allocated to the liability component.

Having completed the allocation of the repurchase price, the following entries are recorded by Entity A in respect of the repurchase of the bonds.

		CU	CU
Dr	Bond liability	1,894,453	
Dr	Debt extinguishment loss (profit or loss)	69,387	
Cr	Cash		1,963,840

To recognise the repurchase of the bond liability and the resulting loss.

		CU	CU
Dr	Equity	136,160	
Cr	Cash		136,160

To recognise the portion of the cash paid in respect of the repurchase of the equity component.

The remaining balance of CU15,718 for the equity component may be reclassified to another line item within equity upon redemption.

3.4.1 Early redemption of convertible bond by the issuer exercising an embedded call option

Repurchase of convertible debt through a tender offer is explicitly addressed in the application guidance to IAS 32 as described above, but early redemption via the issuer exercising an embedded call option is not. This is considered in the following example.

Example 3.4.1

Early redemption of convertible bond by the issuer exercising an embedded call option

Entity B (whose functional currency is CU) issues a convertible bond for CU10 million on 1 January 20X0. The bond is redeemable at the par amount of CU10 million at 31 December 20X9. The bond pays interest of 4 per cent on the par amount on 31 December throughout its life. The holder can convert the bond into a fixed number of equity shares at any point from 1 January 20X5 to 31 December 20X9. In addition, under the terms of the call option embedded in the convertible bond, Entity B may redeem the instrument early by paying the par amount of CU10 million at any point between 1 January 20X5 and 31 December 20X9. Once notice is given that the call option is to be exercised the call option is settled immediately thereafter.

The convertible bond is classified as a compound instrument with a financial liability and equity components. The call option is deemed to be closely related to the debt instrument (see **7.1** in **chapter C5**) and is therefore not separately accounted for on the basis of a comparison of the exercise price of the option (amount repayable if called) to the amortised cost of the instrument before separating the equity component under IAS 32.

Entity B exercises its call option on 1 January 20X5 and redeems the instrument under the terms of the option at this date.

One way of accounting for the exercise of the call option would be to account for it as part of the debt instrument to which it is closely related. This would necessitate remeasuring the amortised cost of the financial liability component of the convertible debt under IAS 39:AG8 (see **4.1.2** in **chapter C6**). This would involve discounting the revised estimate of cash flows payable under the instrument (to include the CU10 million that will be payable immediately under the terms of the option) at the original effective interest rate established at initial recognition of the financial liability component of the convertible debt. The difference between the previous amortised cost carrying amount and the newly remeasured amount would be recognised in profit or loss. This would have the effect of recognising a loss equal to par less the carrying amount from the prior reporting period.

Alternatively, it may be argued that the guidance under IAS 32:AG33 should be applied because this refers to redemption. Under this approach, the consideration paid to redeem the convertible debt would be allocated to the financial liability and equity components upon early redemption using the same method as that used to make the allocation between the financial liability and equity component on initial recognition of the compound instrument. However, because the fair value of the financial liability component once the option has been exercised is likely to be equal to the redemption price, this method would allocate all of the consideration (i.e. the redemption price) to the financial liability component. Therefore, the effect would be likely to be substantially the same as the remeasurement under IAS 39:AG8 as discussed in the previous paragraph.

3.5 Amendment of the terms of a compound instrument to induce early conversion

An entity may amend the terms of a convertible instrument during its life so as to make conversion more attractive through either offering a more favourable conversion ratio, paying additional consideration in the event of conversion before a specified date, or a combination of both. In such circumstances, the difference between the fair value of the consideration that the holder receives upon conversion under the revised terms and the fair value of the consideration that the holder would have received upon conversion under the original terms, measured at the date when the terms are amended, should be recognised in profit or loss as a loss. [IAS 32:AG35]

Example 3.5

Convertible debt: inducement to convert

Assume the facts are as in **example 3.1A**, but at 31 December 20X5 (i.e. the end of Year 1 of the instrument's life), to induce holders to convert promptly,

Entity A amends the terms in one of two ways in respect of conversions that take place prior to 1 March 20X6.

Scenario 1: Entity A alters the terms such that each of the 2,000 bonds converts into 300 equity shares of Entity A, instead of 250 equity shares as under the original conversion terms (assume the market value of the equity shares at the date of the amendment is CU5).

Scenario 2: Entity A states that it will pay an additional CU1 in cash in relation to each share converted.

The liability and equity components have the following carrying amounts in the statement of financial position at 31 December 20X5.

	CU
Liability component:	
– present value of two remaining interest payments of CU120,000 discounted at 9 per cent	211,093
– present value of principal amount of CU2 million due in two years' time discounted at 9 per cent	1,683,360
	1,894,453
Equity component	151,878*
Total	2,046,331

* The equity component remains unchanged since the allocation on initial recognition.

The following entries will be needed to recognise the amendment of the terms of the convertible bonds.

Scenario 1

Number of equity shares to be issued to bondholders under the *amended* conversion terms:	
– number of bonds issued	2,000
– number of shares to be issued per bond on conversion	300
Total number of equity shares to be issued on conversion	600,000
Number of equity shares to be issued to bondholders under *original* conversion terms:	
– number of bonds issued	2,000
– number of shares to be issued per bond on conversion	250
Total number of equity shares to be issued on conversion	500,000

Number of incremental equity shares to be issued to bondholders upon conversion: 100,000.

Value of incremental equity shares to be issued to bondholders upon conversion: 100,000 × CU5 = CU500,000

Therefore, the entry needed to record the amendment of the terms is as follows.

		CU	CU
Dr	Expense on amendment of terms of convertible bonds (profit or loss)	500,000	
Cr	Equity		500,000

To recognise the amendment of the terms of the convertible bonds.

Upon conversion, the accounting would follow the approach laid out in **example 3.3A**. If the instrument were not converted no further gain or loss would be recognised.

Scenario 2

The additional consideration to be paid in the event of conversion would amount to: 500,000 × CU1 = CU500,000

This would be recognised through the following entry upon amendment of the terms of the convertible bonds.

		CU	CU
Dr	Expense on amendment of terms of convertible bonds (profit or loss)	500,000	
Cr	Financial liability		500,000

To recognise the amendment of the terms of the convertible bonds.

On conversion, the accounting would follow the approach laid out in **example 3.3A** except that an additional entry would be required to recognise the payment of the additional cash inducement as follows.

		CU	CU
Dr	Financial liability	500,000	
Cr	Cash		500,000

To record the payment of the additional cash inducement.

If the instrument were not converted, an entry would be required to derecognise the inducement that the holder has not exercised.

		CU	CU
Dr	Financial liability	500,000	
Cr	Gain upon non-exercise of inducement (profit or loss)		500,000

To derecognise the liability for the inducement that has not been exercised.

As described in **3.3**, upon conversion of a compound instrument, equity is issued and the liability component is derecognised. The original equity component recognised at inception remains in equity (although it may be reclassified from one line item of equity to another) and no gain or loss is recognised on conversion. This treatment equally applies for conversion of a compound instrument where previously there was an inducement and an expense in profit or loss and increase in equity was recognised. Upon conversion of the compound instrument, the financial liability is derecognised and reclassified to equity. Equity will therefore consist of the original equity component recognised on issue of the compound instrument, the amount recognised in equity as a result of the inducement, plus the reclassification of the liability upon conversion. Amounts may be transferred within equity from one line item to another upon conversion of the compound instrument.

3.6 Treatment of mandatorily convertible instruments

An entity may issue an instrument that at the end of its life is mandatorily convertible into a fixed number of its equity shares (rather than conversion being at the option of the holder). This instrument is, in substance, a prepaid forward purchase of the entity's equity shares. Because the instrument carries an obligation for the issuer to make fixed interest payments during the life of the mandatorily convertible instrument, the instrument includes a financial liability component. The following example illustrates the entries for a mandatorily convertible debt instrument.

Example 3.6

Mandatorily convertible instrument

A CU functional currency entity issues a mandatorily convertible instrument for CU100,000 on 1 January 20X5. The instrument obliges the entity to make cash coupon payments of CU5,000 on both 31 December 20X5 and 31 December 20X6. On 31 December 20X6, the instrument will mandatorily convert into 5,000 ordinary shares of the entity.

At the inception of the instrument, the following two elements will be separated.

- A liability component arising from the coupon payments of CU5,000 to be made on both 31 December 20X5 and 31 December 20X6. This will be determined as the present value of the payments discounted at the rate that would have been applicable if the entity had issued a debt instrument with similar features and of similar credit standing, but without the mandatory conversion feature.
- An equity component representing the delivery of equity in the future. This amount will be determined as the residual amount after the liability component is deducted from the fair value of the whole compound instrument at inception (CU100,000).

If, using this methodology, it is determined that the liability component at inception is, for example, CU9,000 (based on a discount rate of 7.32 per cent), the following entries will be required on initial recognition of the instrument:

		CU	CU
Dr	Cash	100,000	
Cr	Financial liability		9,000
Cr	Equity		91,000

To recognise the mandatorily convertible instrument.

Over the life of the instrument, the following entries will be made with respect to the liability so that, by the end of the instrument's life, the liability component will have been extinguished.

Year end 31 December 20X5

		CU	CU
Dr	Interest expense	659	
Cr	Financial liability		659

To recognise the interest expense to account for the liability at amortised cost using the effective interest rate of 7.32 per cent.

		CU	CU
Dr	Financial liability	5,000	
Cr	Cash		5,000

To record the cash coupon payment of CU5,000.

Year end 31 December 20X6

		CU	CU
Dr	Interest expense	341	
Cr	Financial liability		341

To recognise the interest expense to account for the liability at amortised cost using the effective interest rate of 7.32 per cent.

		CU	CU
Dr	Financial liability	5,000	
Cr	Cash		5,000

To reflect the cash coupon payment of CU5,000.

Upon mandatory conversion of the instrument into 5,000 ordinary shares of the entity via the issue of new shares, local company law may require some reclassification of the balance within equity. However, no gain or loss is recognised on conversion in accordance with IAS 32:AG32.

In May 2014, the IFRS Interpretations Committee issued a final agenda decision on IAS 32, *Classification of a financial instrument that is mandatorily convertible into a variable number of shares upon a contingent 'non-viability' event.*

The Interpretations Committee discussed how an issuer would classify a particular mandatorily convertible financial instrument in accordance with IAS 32. The financial instrument did not have a stated maturity date but was mandatorily convertible into a variable number of the issuer's own equity instruments if the issuer breached the Tier 1 Capital ratio (i.e. described as a 'contingent non-viability event'). The financial instrument is issued at par and the value of the equity instruments that will be delivered at conversion is equal to that fixed par amount. Interest payments on the instrument are payable at the discretion of the issuer.

Specifically the Interpretations Committee discussed the following issues:

(i) whether the financial instrument meets the definition of a financial liability in its entirety or must be classified as a compound instrument comprised of a liability component and an equity component (and, in the latter case, what those components reflect); and

(ii) how the financial liability (or liability component) identified above in bullet (i) would be measured.

The Interpretations Committee decided not to add this issue to its agenda. The Interpretations Committee noted that the scope of the issues raised in the submission is too broad for it to address in an efficient manner.

3.7 Convertible debt with multiple settlement options

Throughout **section 3** so far, it has been assumed that the equity conversion option can only be gross physically settled, i.e. a fixed number of shares is delivered on conversion of the bond. However, this may not always be the case. As explained in **section 6**, if the settlement of the call option can be achieved in ways other than by delivery of a fixed number of shares for a fixed amount of cash, the call option is treated as a derivative and is carried at fair value with gains and losses recognised in profit or loss.

Some convertible debt instruments include cash settlement options. The contractual terms of such instruments allow that if the holder of the instrument invokes the conversion option, the issuer has a choice over the manner in which the call option is settled: the issuer may deliver either a fixed number of shares to the holder, or an amount of cash equal to the market value of the fixed number of shares on the date of conversion or an average price in a period before conversion. Because the issuer will not always deliver a fixed amount of equity for receipt of a fixed amount of cash upon conversion, the conversion feature does not meet the definition of equity. The written call option is accounted for as a derivative liability. The convertible debt is a hybrid instrument containing a host debt contract and an embedded derivative liability (written call option over own shares).

The embedded derivative is measured at fair value with changes in fair value recognised in profit or loss. The treatment of hybrid instruments is explained in **chapter C5**.

Example 3.7

Convertible debt: cash settlement choice at conversion

On 1 January 20X1, Entity X issues a convertible bond with a face value of CU10 million at par. The instrument has a maturity of 10 years and pays an annual coupon of 5 per cent on 31 December. The bond is convertible at maturity at the discretion of the holder. However, if the holder does exercise the right to convert, Entity X can either:

- deliver a fixed number of Entity X's ordinary shares; or
- pay an amount of cash equal to the fixed number of shares under the conversion option multiplied by the average share price of Entity X's ordinary shares in the 10 days immediately preceding maturity.

IAS 32:26 states that when a derivative financial instrument gives one party a choice regarding how it is settled, it is a financial asset or a financial liability unless all of the settlement alternatives would result in it being an equity instrument.

In the circumstances described, Entity X has an obligation to pay cash for interest payments and to redeem the instrument at maturity and, because the written call option within the convertible instrument may be settled in cash rather than through the delivery of a fixed number of shares, the equity conversion feature does not meet the definition of equity. The convertible debt is therefore a financial liability in its entirety.

Entity X does not designate the instrument at initial recognition as at fair value through profit or loss, and therefore the hybrid instrument must be separated between a debt host contract measured at amortised cost and the equity conversion feature measured at fair value through profit or loss.

The difference between the fair value of the total hybrid instrument and the fair value of the embedded derivative is assigned to the host contract, with the host accounted for at amortised cost.

Assuming that the fair value of the written call option is CU1.5 million at 1 January 20X1, the entries on that date would be as follows.

		CU	CU
Dr	Cash	10,000,000	
Cr	Financial liability (host contract)		8,500,000
Cr	Derivative financial liability		1,500,000

To recognise the convertible debt and written call option.

Entity X will account for the host contract at amortised cost by applying the effective interest rate of 7.15 per cent, and the derivative will be remeasured to its fair value. On 31 December 20X1, the amortised cost of the host debt contract is CU9,107,750 and the fair value of the embedded derivative is CU2,450,000. Therefore, the entries required are as follows.

		CU	CU
Dr	Interest expense	607,750	
Cr	Financial liability (host contract)		607,750
Dr	Financial liability (host contract)	500,000	
Cr	Cash		500,000

To recognise the interest expense on the host debt contract measured at amortised cost using the effective interest rate of 7.15 per cent and payment of contractual coupon.

		CU	CU
Dr	Derivative loss	950,000	
Cr	Derivative financial liability		950,000

To recognise the fair value movement on the embedded derivative in profit or loss.

3.8 Foreign currency denominated convertible debt

An entity may issue an instrument denominated in a foreign currency (a currency other than the functional currency of the entity) that is convertible into a fixed number of ordinary shares of the entity. Such an instrument contains a written option to exchange a fixed number of equity instruments for a fixed amount of cash that is denominated in a foreign currency.

As explained in **section 6** of this chapter, a derivative contract over an entity's own equity is accounted for as equity only when it will be settled exclusively by the entity delivering (or receiving) a fixed number of its own equity instruments in exchange for a fixed amount of cash or another financial asset.

For foreign currency denominated convertible debt, the question arises as to whether the equity conversion option meets the definition of equity when the consideration the issuer receives for issuing a fixed number of shares is forgiveness of a debt instrument that is variable in functional currency terms. The same question also applies to free-standing instruments (e.g. a stand-alone physically settled written call over own shares that will be settled at exercise through an exchange of a fixed number of own shares for a fixed amount of foreign currency cash).

A gross physically settled derivative over a fixed number of own equity shares meets the definition of equity only if the amount of cash or financial assets paid or received is fixed in the *functional currency* of the issuer (the one exception relates to certain rights issues as described in **6.1.1**). The following guidance is relevant.

- A derivative over a fixed number of equity shares that is exchanged for a variable amount of cash is a derivative, and not equity. For example, an instrument that requires an exchange of a fixed number of equity shares for a variable amount of cash calculated to equal the value of 100 ounces of gold is a derivative because the fair value of the derivative is driven from movements in the gold price as well as the equity price. [IAS 32:24]
- IAS 39 considers that, although foreign denominated monetary items and foreign currency forecast transactions are fixed in foreign currency terms, they are variable in functional currency terms and, therefore, they are eligible to be designated in a cash flow hedge. [IAS 39:IG.F.3.3 & F.3.4]

Applying this guidance to foreign currency denominated convertible debt, it is clear that (1) the foreign currency convertible, while fixed in foreign currency terms, is variable in functional currency terms and, therefore, a fixed number of shares will be delivered in exchange for a variable amount of cash; and (2) conversion will occur based on the interaction of not only the equity price, but also the foreign currency value of the bond that is forgiven.

The IFRIC (now the IFRS Interpretations Committee) referred the classification of foreign currency denominated convertible debt to the IASB and, in September 2005, the Board explored whether to amend IAS 32 to permit contracts to be classified as equity if they are to be settled by an entity delivering a fixed number of its own equity instruments for a fixed amount of cash or another financial asset denominated in a foreign currency. The Board noted that the amendment would result in equity and foreign exchange features whose values are interdependent being recognised in equity, and that excluding from equity the value attributable to the foreign exchange features would require arbitrary rules. The Board also noted that allowing dual indexed contracts (to share price and foreign exchange rates) to be classified as equity would require additional and detailed guidance to avoid structuring opportunities aimed at obtaining a desired accounting result. The Board therefore decided not to proceed with an amendment to IAS 32.

Example 3.8

Foreign currency denominated convertible debt

Entity A has a functional currency of Sterling. Entity A issues a convertible bond denominated in US dollars that, if converted, will result in the gross physical delivery of a fixed number of Entity A's shares.

The convertible bond will be classified in its entirety as a financial liability because, upon conversion, a fixed amount of shares will be delivered in exchange for a variable amount of functional currency cash, being the forgiveness of the bond obligation.

3.8.1 Different entities in a group issue convertible debt and the shares delivered on conversion when debt is in a foreign currency

A convertible debt instrument might be issued under which the shares to be delivered on conversion will not be those of the legal entity that issued the instrument, but those of another entity in the same group (e.g. the parent or subsidiary of the issuer). Further, the debt may be denominated in a currency that is different from the functional currency of either the entity that issued the instrument, the entity whose shares will be delivered on conversion, or both.

If a parent and subsidiary have the same functional currency and either the parent issues a foreign currency denominated convertible bond that is convertible into a fixed number of the subsidiary's shares, or the subsidiary issues a foreign currency convertible bond that is convertible into a fixed number of the parent's shares, the instrument in both cases would be classified wholly as a liability in the consolidated financial statements because a fixed number of shares is exchanged for a variable amount of functional currency cash.

The accounting for convertible debt issued by an entity in the group that is convertible into a fixed number of equity instruments of another entity in the group is more complex when the two entities have different functional currencies and the bond is denominated in one of those currencies. The IFRIC (now the IFRS Interpretations Committee) discussed this scenario but did not take the issue onto its agenda because the issue was considered to be too narrow. In the absence of specific guidance, it is not clear whether a group should look to the functional currency of the issuer of the fixed number of shares or the functional currency of the issuer of the convertible bond. For the purposes of assessing such convertible instruments, a group should establish a policy as to how it determines what is a fixed amount of functional currency cash when different entities in the group issue the convertible instrument and the shares. This policy should be applied consistently to all similar instruments.

3.8.2 Functional currency of the issuer 'pegged' to the currency of the debt

When the functional currency of the issuer is 'pegged' to the currency in which the convertible debt instrument is denominated, the currency in which the convertible debt is denominated is not regarded as a 'foreign' currency.

Example 3.8.2

Functional currency of the issuer 'pegged' to the currency of the debt

A Hong Kong dollar functional entity issues a convertible debt instrument denominated in US dollars. At the date of issue, the Hong Kong dollar and US dollar are subject to a fixed peg (i.e. the exchange rate between the US dollar and the Hong Kong dollar is fixed).

Because there is no variability in the carrying amount of the US dollar financial liability in the functional currency of the issuer, the US dollar is not regarded as a foreign currency. Accordingly, the convertible debt is treated as a compound instrument containing a financial liability and an equity component.

As discussed in **section 8**, there is no clear guidance on when it is appropriate to reconsider the liability/equity classification in circumstances when there has been no change in the terms of the instrument. Thus, if following the issue of the convertible debt, the Hong Kong dollar and the US dollar cease to be subject to a fixed peg, resulting in the US dollar being regarded as a foreign currency, the issuer should determine an appropriate accounting policy and apply it consistently.

3.9 Anti-dilutive provisions in convertible debt

Convertible bonds will often include anti-dilutive provisions within the contractual terms of the instrument to ensure that the bondholder's potential interest in the equity of the issuer is not diluted in specified circumstances. If these provisions are triggered, the number of shares that would be delivered to the bondholder is adjusted.

For an equity conversion feature to be considered equity, it must result in the exchange of a fixed amount of cash or other financial asset for a fixed number of equity instruments (the 'fixed-for-fixed criterion').

IAS 32 does not provide any guidance on which types of anti-dilutive provision in convertible debt result in the equity conversion feature failing equity treatment.

Many anti-dilutive provisions are structured so as to 'make-whole' the holder of the convertible bond if specified events occur such that the holder of the convertible debt instrument remains in the same position relative to existing ordinary shareholder before and after the event. If this is the case, such provisions are not deemed to breach the fixed-for-fixed criterion. A different conclusion would be reached if the adjustment to the conversion ratio benefited the convertible bondholder at the expense of the existing ordinary shareholders.

To the extent that shares are issued at a discount or repurchased at a premium (i.e. the shares are not issued or repurchased at their fair value), the convertible bondholders that are potential shareholders of the entity will be disadvantaged relative to the existing shareholders. An anti-dilutive provision that makes-whole for the discount on issue or premium on repurchase will not breach the fixed-for-fixed criterion. Consider the following examples:

Conversion option adjusted for bonus issue of shares to existing ordinary shareholders

If the issuer decides to issue additional ordinary shares to existing ordinary shareholders while the convertible debt is outstanding (e.g. through a bonus issue for nil consideration), the conversion feature will be adjusted to reflect the increased number of shares in issue. This adjustment attempts to put the convertible debt holder in the same economic position relative to existing ordinary shareholders as was the case immediately prior to the issue of the new shares and, as such, does not breach the fixed-for-fixed criterion.

Conversion option adjusted for share buyback

The same principle can be applied when the number of shares under the conversion option is reduced due to the issuer entering into a buyback of its own shares at a premium to their market price when the convertible debt is outstanding. If the adjustment to the conversion ratio only reflects the degree to which the shares are purchased a premium to their market price and so the convertible bondholder does not gain any advantage, the existence of the anti-dilution feature would not breach the fixed-for-fixed criterion.

Conversion option is adjusted for special dividends

Anti-dilutive provisions linked to dividend payments are also common. If the issuer pays dividends on its existing ordinary shares, there may be an adjustment to the conversion ratio which attempts to compensate the holder of the convertible debt when dividends paid are in excess of a specified level. Such provisions attempt to compensate the holder of the convertible bond when a 'special dividend' is paid which is in the nature of a return of capital to the existing ordinary shareholders. In such circumstances, the conversion ratio that was determined when the convertible bond was issued assumes a certain level of dividend payments between the date when the instrument was issued and the date when conversion can occur. The adjustment to the conversion feature makes whole the difference between the amount of the special dividend and the amount of the dividends expected to be paid.

Alternatively, the number of shares under the conversion feature may be adjusted for the actual dividend paid in a period while the convertible bond is outstanding. In this instance, the conversion ratio that was determined when the convertible bond was issued assumed no dividend payments between the date when the instrument was issued and the date when conversion can occur. The number of shares to be delivered under the conversion feature is adjusted so that the conversion price is equal to that which would have been determined had the issuer known at inception exactly what dividends would be paid in the future. Neither of these anti-dilutive provisions is considered to breach the fixed-for-fixed criterion because they both exist to retain parity between the existing ordinary shareholders (who have received dividends) and holders of the convertible debt (who have not).

Down-round protection

An example of a provision that would breach the fixed-for-fixed criterion is 'down-round protection'. Under these arrangements, the number of shares receivable under the conversion option increases if the strike price of the conversion option is adjusted downwards or if shares are subsequently issued at a lower price. Such arrangements are designed to protect the holders of convertible debt from adverse movements in share price at the expense of the existing ordinary shareholders and, as such, result in a transfer of value (in relative terms) from the existing ordinary shareholders to convertible debt holders. For this reason, they are not purely 'anti-dilutive' in nature and result in the equity conversion feature not meeting the definition of equity.

3.10 Other variations in convertible debt

It is not practicable to provide an exhaustive list of different variations in conversion features in convertible debt. However, some further examples and discussion of the accounting analysis are set out below.

3.10.1 Discounted convertible debt

Convertible debt may be issued such that the investor receives some of the interest on the instrument in the form of fixed cash coupons and some in the form of accretion up to the par amount. The accretion up to the par amount is not regarded as variable, i.e. not fixed, consideration and therefore will not breach the 'fixed-for-fixed' criterion. This is because, firstly, the par amount remains constant and, therefore, the nominal value of the bond remains unchanged (as referred to in IAS 32.22, the bond has a 'fixed stated principal amount'). Secondly, the unwinding of the discount to par is part of the interest on the bond component. When compared to conventional fixed rate convertible debt issued at par (i.e. without a discount), the conversion option always results in the holder giving up a variable amount of future interest receipts. As the instrument's life shortens, the amount of interest forgiven by the holder reduces. Such variability in the amount forgiven by the holder is not considered variability in cash in determining whether the conversion option meets the definition of equity.

Example 3.10.1

Discounted convertible debt

Entity A issues convertible debt for CU90 that is convertible into a fixed number of equity shares at any time and pays an annual cash coupon of 1 per cent based on the par amount of CU100. If the holder does not choose to convert the instrument into the fixed number of equity shares, the bond will be redeemed at maturity for the par amount of CU100. Consequently, the holder of the instrument receives some of the interest on the instrument in the form of fixed cash coupons and some in the form of the additional CU10 received following accretion up to the par amount.

The conversion option meets the fixed-for-fixed criterion and should be classified because equity as the nominal amount of the bond given up on conversion is fixed.

3.10.2 Convertible debt: interest linked to benchmark interest rate

Convertible debt usually carries a fixed rate of interest or, as described above, it may be partly issued at a discount and, therefore, economically pays a fixed amount of interest at maturity. If the interest on convertible debt is linked to a benchmark interest rate (e.g. LIBOR) and the instrument is not issued at a discount, then all interest flows are variable. It could be argued that the conversion feature breaches the 'fixed cash' criterion because the interest forgiveness is always changing. Similar to the analysis above for a discounted convertible bond, it would be inappropriate to consider variable interest as a breach of the 'fixed cash' criterion. Firstly, the par amount remains constant (as referred to in IAS 32:22, the bond has a 'fixed stated principal amount'). Secondly, IAS 32:22 specifically states that "changes in the fair value of a contract arising from variations in market interest rates that do not affect the amount of cash or other financial assets to be paid or received … on settlement of the contract" do not preclude equity classification. If the fixed cash is considered the par amount and the variable interest is considered to be merely servicing, the 'fixed cash' criterion is not breached. Such an instrument would therefore be treated as a compound instrument that contains a financial liability and an equity component.

If the interest payments were driven not by a benchmark interest rate but, instead, by another variable that was not a market rate of interest (e.g. changes in the profitability of the entity), the same conclusion would not be appropriate and, therefore, the instrument would be treated as a financial liability in its entirety. The issuer would need to consider whether the variable basis of interest payments was a closely related embedded derivative if the instrument was not classified as at FVTPL. Guidance on embedded derivatives is set out in **chapter C5**.

3.10.3 *Convertible debt: conversion to a variable number of shares dependent on the share price at the date of conversion*

Convertible debt that permits the holder to convert the instrument into a variable number of shares dependent on the share price at the date of conversion is not a compound instrument. For example, the conversion feature may be forgiveness of a fixed amount of functional currency debt (i.e. principal and any future interest) for a fixed number of shares (say 10.0 shares if the share price is above CU100 but below CU110, but 9.5 shares if the share price is above CU110 but below CU120, and 9.0 shares if the share price is above CU120). The number of shares to be delivered is based on a sliding scale that reduces as the share price increases. In such circumstances, the conversion feature does not meet the definition of equity because the conversion does not result in the delivery of a fixed number of shares.

In the example set out in the previous paragraph, it is not appropriate to consider the conversion feature as three separate conversion features that each have a right to convert the same fixed amount of cash (being principal and interest) for a fixed amount of shares because the conversion features are mutually exclusive. Only one conversion feature can ever be exercised (equally, there can only ever be one fixed amount of cash that is forgiven as consideration for the issue of shares) because, once conversion has occurred, the instrument is extinguished.

3.10.4 *Convertible debt: conversion to a fixed number of shares or variable number of shares to the value of the debt component*

Consider an example where convertible debt permits the holder to convert into a fixed number of shares before the debt's contractual maturity date when the share price is above a specified level, but also allows the holder to forgive the debt component (being principal and interest) by electing for a variable number of shares equal to the par value of the debt component when the share price is below that specified level. On the face of it, and consistent with the example described in **3.10.3**, because the instrument does not always result in the delivery of a fixed number of shares, it could be argued that the instrument does not have any equity element (i.e. the entire instrument is a financial liability).

However, the right for the holder to require repayment of debt in a variable number of shares equal in value to the debt component is not itself a conversion feature; rather, it is a settlement alternative inherent in the debt component. The payment of interest and principal, regardless of whether it is settled in cash or in shares of an equal value, is a financial liability. The inclusion of a feature that permits the holder to early redeem the instrument by requiring the issuer to deliver a variable number of shares equal in value to the par amount of the debt when the share price is below a specified level is merely an early redemption option. Put another way, when the share price is below a specified level, the holder can require the convertible debt to be early redeemed and the issuer is required to use its own shares as currency for this early redemption.

The right to convert into a fixed number of shares when the share price is above the specified level is an equity instrument because it permits the holder to require the issuer to deliver a fixed amount of shares in exchange for a fixed amount of cash (being the principal and interest, and the 'shares to the value of' settlement alternative on that principal and interest).

3.10.5 Convertible debt: convertible only on the occurrence of a contingent event

The issuer of convertible debt that is convertible only upon the occurrence of a contingent event that is outside the control of the holder and the issuer must first determine whether, if the event occurs, the conversion would result in the delivery of a fixed number of equity instruments for a fixed amount of functional currency cash. Put another way, ignoring the contingent element, would the instrument be a compound instrument with an equity and a debt component? If the answer to this question is yes, then the fact that the holder can only convert if a contingent event occurs does not prevent the conversion feature being presented as equity.

The inclusion of the contingency merely reduces the likelihood of the conversion occurring and, therefore, for a stated amount of proceeds would result in the residual amount of net proceeds allocated to the equity component being lower when compared to an equity component of convertible debt without the contingency. This is because the fair value of the debt component would be higher due to a corresponding higher contractual interest rate on the debt component when the conversion option is contingent compared to when it is not.

3.10.6 Convertible debt: conversion into a variable number of shares but subject to a specified minimum and/or maximum number of equity shares

In May 2014, the IFRS Interpretations Committee issued a final agenda decision on IAS 32, *Accounting for a financial instrument that is mandatorily convertible into a variable number of shares subject to a cap and a floor.*

The Interpretations Committee discussed how an issuer would account for a particular mandatorily convertible financial instrument in accordance with IAS 32 and IAS 39. The financial instrument has a stated maturity date and, at maturity, the issuer must deliver a variable number of its own equity instruments to equal a fixed cash amount – subject to a cap and a floor, which limit and guarantee, respectively, the number of equity instruments to be delivered.

The Interpretations Committee noted that the issuer's obligation to deliver a variable number of the entity's own equity instruments is a non-derivative that meets the definition of a financial liability in IAS 32:11(b)(i) in its entirety. IAS 32:11(b)(i) of the definition of a liability does not have any limits or thresholds regarding the degree of variability that is required. Therefore, the contractual substance of the instrument is a single obligation to deliver a variable number of equity instruments at maturity, with the variation based on the value of those equity instruments. Such a single obligation to deliver a variable number of own equity instruments cannot be subdivided into components for the purposes of evaluating whether the instrument contains a component that meets the definition of equity. Even though the number of equity instruments to be delivered is limited and guaranteed by the cap and the floor, the overall number of equity instruments that the issuer is obliged to deliver is not fixed and therefore the entire obligation meets the definition of a financial liability.

Furthermore, the Interpretations Committee noted that the cap and the floor are embedded derivative features whose values change in response to the price of the issuer's equity share. Therefore, assuming that the issuer has not elected to designate the entire instrument under the fair value option, the issuer must separate those features and account for the embedded derivative features separately from the host liability contract at fair value through profit or loss in accordance with IAS 39. The Interpretations Committee considered that in the light of its analysis of the existing IFRS requirements, an Interpretation was not necessary and consequently decided not to add the issue to its agenda.

Example 3.10.6

Convertible bond convertible into a variable number of shares but subject to a specified minimum and/or maximum number of equity shares

Entity A (CU functional currency) issues a convertible debt instrument with a maturity of five years that pays interest at 5 per cent on a nominal value of CU10,000. At the option of the holder, the instrument may be converted at maturity into ordinary shares of Entity A as follows:

- if the ordinary share price is under CU100 at the convertible instrument's maturity date, into 100 ordinary shares; or
- if the ordinary share price is above CU150 at the convertible instrument's maturity date, into 67 ordinary shares; or
- if the ordinary share price is between CU100 and CU150 at the convertible instrument's maturity date, into the number of ordinary shares that are equivalent in value to CU10,000.

The ordinary shares meet the definition of equity instruments in IAS 32.

The convertible debt instrument is entirely a financial liability as the number of equity instruments to be delivered on conversion is not fixed. The variability in the number of shares to be issued is limited; Entity A may actually deliver a fixed number of shares such as a minimum (floor) or maximum (cap) number of shares depending on its future ordinary share price. However, the conversion feature of the instrument still fails the definition of equity because the number of shares to be delivered on conversion varies.

It is not appropriate to consider the instrument as containing three separate conversion features, two of which convert into a fixed number of shares (being the cap and the floor), because the conversion features are mutually exclusive. Only one of the three possible conversion features can ever arise on exercise because, following conversion, the debt instrument (including the other two conversion features) is extinguished.

Consequently, the convertible instrument is a hybrid financial liability in its entirety consisting of two separate obligations: (1) an obligation to pay interest at 5 per cent on a principal of CU10,000 throughout the life of the instrument and to repay the principal of CU10,000 at maturity and (2) a derivative conversion option that fails the definition of equity because the issuer is obliged to deliver a variable number of equity instruments if the holder exercises the conversion option.

If the instrument is not measured at fair value through profit or loss in its entirety, the appropriate accounting for Entity A in accordance with IAS 39 is as follows:

- the derivative conversion feature should be separated out as a non-closely related embedded derivative and measured at fair value through profit or loss; and
- the debt host contract (i.e. the obligation to pay interest and principal) should be measured at amortised cost.

3.10.7 Convertible debt: change of control clauses

Many convertible debt instruments contain change of control protection clauses. One common example of a protection clause attempts to provide the convertible bondholder with an enhanced conversion ratio following a change of control of the issuer in order to compensate the convertible bondholder for the loss of time value in the option in the event that the bondholder chooses to exercise the conversion option early. Such instruments will often grant to the issuer a right to redeem the convertible bond early, at par, for a period immediately following a change of control. It is this issuer call option that may incentivise the convertible bondholder to convert early and, in doing so, receive an additional number of shares to reflect the fact that, absent conversion, the issuer will buy back the convertible bond at par and the convertible bondholder will lose the remaining value of the conversion option.

The terms and conditions of the instrument will generally either stipulate a predetermined adjusted conversion ratio which varies depending on when the change of control occurs during the life of the instrument (with the adjustment to the conversion ratio being reduced the closer the date of the change of control is to the maturity date of the instrument) or include a formula which attempts to determine the value of the remaining time value in the conversion option at the date of change of control and adjusts the conversion ratio to reflect this value.

Change of control clauses vary considerably and it is not possible to generalise as to their effect on the classification of convertible debt. The terms and objective of the clause must be carefully considered to determine whether the objective of the change in the conversion ratio is to preserve the rights and value of the bondholders following a change of control by providing additional shares on conversion equal to the remaining time value of the conversion option on the date of change of control. If this is the case, this feature would not breach the fixed-for-fixed criterion.

3.11 Reverse convertible instruments

A conventional convertible bond entitles the holder to convert the bond into shares of the issuer. If the conversion option meets the definition of equity, the conversion option is recognised in equity and the bond component is recognised as a financial liability. The accounting treatment for this is clear in IAS 32 and reflects the fact that, until conversion, the issuer always has an obligation to pay the bond component, which will either be settled by paying cash or another financial asset or be forgiven by the holder if the holder chooses to exercise its conversion option.

The accounting treatment under IAS 32 is less clear for 'reverse' convertible instruments where the issuer (rather than the holder) has the choice as to whether to settle a bond with cash or another financial asset or to deliver a fixed number of shares. In this case, the holder does not have a choice as to whether to convert. This raises the question as to whether the issuer ever has an obligation to pay cash because the issuer can always choose to deliver shares.

Example 3.11

Reverse convertible bond

Entity X is a CU functional currency entity and issues a reverse convertible instrument for CU100 million. The instrument has a maturity of five years. The instrument has non-discretionary annual interest payments over its life of CU10 million. At maturity, the issuer has a choice of either:

(i) paying cash equal to the principal amount (CU100 million); or

(ii) issuing a fixed number of 15 of its own equity shares. The value of 15 shares at issue of the instrument does not substantially exceed the value of the cash settlement alternative under (i).

Given the lack of clear guidance in IAS 32, two approaches are considered to be acceptable. Whichever approach is adopted, Entity X should apply it consistently as an accounting policy choice.

Approach 1

From Entity X's perspective, the instrument is a compound instrument analysed as (a) an obligation to pay cash as interest during the life and principal at maturity, which is a financial liability, and (b) a purchased put option over its own shares (i.e. an option to exchange the obligation to pay CU100 million for a fixed number of shares), which is equity. Economically, the high interest payments represent the interest rate on a plain vanilla bond (without the conversion feature) plus the option premium in respect of the purchased put spread over the life. This approach is consistent with the approach taken for conventional convertible debt where the holder has the choice of conversion. The equity component of the reverse convertible bond will be determined as the difference between the fair value of the instrument as a whole and the fair value of the financial liability (comprising the obligation to pay cash in relation to interest and principal).

Approach 2

From Entity X's perspective, the instrument is a compound instrument analysed as (a) an obligation to pay cash in respect of interest over the life and (b) an option to either pay CU100 million or issue 15 shares at maturity in settlement of the principal. Because Entity X can avoid paying cash in relation to the principal amount through delivery of a fixed number of own equity shares, this feature does not give rise to a financial liability.

This approach views the reverse convertible bond as different from a conventional convertible bond under which the holder has the choice regarding conversion and the issuer always has an obligation to pay the principal in cash because it cannot control whether the conversion option is exercised. In the case of the reverse convertible bond, the issuer can avoid the outflow of cash by exercising its right to convert and delivering the fixed number of equity shares.

Supporters of this approach view it as being consistent with IAS 32:20(b), which states that an entity has a financial liability if the terms of the instrument provide that, on settlement, the entity will deliver either:

(i) cash or another financial asset; or

(ii) its own shares whose value is determined to exceed substantially the value of the cash or other financial asset.

Because IAS 32:20(b) only requires financial liability treatment if the value of the shares is determined to exceed substantially the value of the cash alternative, the settlement choice at maturity for this reverse convertible bond is not a financial liability.

The equity component of the reverse convertible bond will be determined as the difference between the fair value of the instrument as a whole and the fair value of the financial liability (comprising only the obligation to pay cash in relation to interest).

In some cases, careful judgement is needed in order to determine whether a contractual arrangement is a derivative over own equity, and therefore is equity if it meets the 'fixed-for-fixed' requirements (see **section 6**) or whether it is a non-derivative, and therefore is equity if it is contains no obligation to pay cash or another financial asset.

Consider the following example. Entity A enters into an arrangement with an investor whereby it receives CU100 on Day 1. Under the terms of the arrangement, Entity A has a choice of either delivering a fixed number of equity shares of Entity A to the potential investor or returning the CU100 to the investor.

This arrangement is most akin to a reverse convertible bond and, as such, two different approaches are considered to be acceptable.

The first approach is to view the arrangement as an instrument that will be settled by Entity A either delivering cash or issuing a fixed number of own shares and not to apply the rules regarding derivatives over own equity. Viewed in this way, the arrangement should, on initial receipt of CU100, be accounted for as equity because Entity A has the unconditional right to avoid delivering cash by choosing to deliver own shares. This is the case only if the value of the alternative to deliver shares instead of cash is not determined to exceed substantially the value of the cash alternative. [IAS 32:21] A financial liability would only be recognised at the point when Entity A has chosen not to deliver own shares and has therefore incurred an obligation to deliver cash. If the value of the share settlement was determined to exceed substantially the value of the cash, the instrument would be considered a financial liability because, in substance, the holder has been guaranteed receipt of an amount that is at least equal to the cash alternative.

The second approach is to view the instrument as a debt host contract (being the obligation to deliver CU100) and an embedded purchased put option which permits the issuer to deliver its own equity shares as extinguishment for the debt host contract. Because the number of shares delivered by the issuer and the debt host contract forgiven is fixed, the purchased put option would meet the definition of equity.

4 Treatment of interest, dividends, gains and losses and other items

The classification of a financial instrument or a component of a financial instrument as either a financial liability or an equity instrument determines the treatment of interest, dividends, and other gains and losses relating to that instrument or component of that instrument. Interest, dividends, losses and gains relating to a financial liability, or to a component of a compound instrument that is a financial liability, are recognised as income or expense in profit or loss. Distributions to holders of equity instruments shall be recognised directly in equity. Similarly, transaction costs of an equity transaction are accounted for as a deduction from equity. [IAS 32:35] Income tax relating to distributions to holders of an equity instrument and to transaction costs of an equity transaction shall be accounted for in accordance with IAS 12 *Income Taxes*. [IAS 32:35A]

The following items are treated as income or expense in profit or loss:

[IAS 32:35 - 37]

- interest payments on a bond issued by an entity;
- dividend payments on preference shares that are classified as financial liabilities;
- gains and losses associated with redemption or refinancing an instrument classified as a financial liability (notwithstanding the fact that the instrument may take the legal form of a share);
- gains and losses related to the carrying amount of an instrument that is a financial liability notwithstanding the fact that the instrument gives the holder a right to participate in the residual interest of an entity (e.g. certain puttable instruments such as units in a mutual fund that fail equity classification); and
- costs of an equity transaction that is abandoned.

Dividends classified as an expense in profit or loss may be presented either with interest on other liabilities or as a separate item.

Dividends that are non-discretionary represent a financial liability (or, depending on the other terms of the shares, a component of a larger financial liability) to provide cash (or another financial asset) to shareholders. In accordance with IAS 32:35, such dividends are recognised as income or expense in profit or loss.

The obligation to pay non-discretionary dividends will be measured either at amortised cost (using the effective interest method) or at fair value depending on the classification of the financial liability to which the dividends relate. Unlike discretionary distributions to holders of equity instruments, recognition does not depend on declaration of the dividend.

The following items are accounted for within equity:

[IAS 32:35 & 37]

- dividend payments on shares classified wholly as equity; and
- incremental directly attributable costs incurred in successfully issuing or acquiring an entity's own equity instruments (including transaction costs, regulatory fees, amounts paid to regulatory, legal, accounting and other professional advisers, printing costs, stamp duties).

The amount of transaction costs accounted for as a deduction from equity in the period is disclosed in line with the requirements of IAS 1 *Presentation of Financial Statements*. [IAS 32:39] IAS 32 does not specify where in equity the transaction costs should be recognised and this may depend on local legal requirements.

In May 2012, the IASB issued *Annual Improvements to IFRSs 2010–2012 Cycle* which clarified the intention of IAS 32 was to follow the requirements in IAS 12 for accounting for income tax relating to distributions to holders of an equity instrument and to transaction costs of an equity transaction. Paragraph 35A was added and paragraph 39 amended in order to do this.

Example 4A

Effective interest rate and dividends for a compound instrument

Entity A issues a non-cumulative preference share that is mandatorily redeemable for cash of CU10 million in 10 years' time. During the life of the instrument, dividends are payable at the discretion of Entity A. The non-cumulative preference share is issued for CU8 million.

The non-cumulative redeemable preference share is a compound instrument. The liability component is determined as the present value of the eventual redemption amount of CU10 million discounted at the rate at which the entity could issue a similar instrument with a similar credit standing but without the feature of discretionary dividends during its life.

Assuming the liability component is equal to CU7.8 million, the residual amount of CU0.2 million will be treated as the equity component. The unwinding of the discount (between the redemption of CU10 million and its present value of CU7.8 million) on the liability component is accounted for using the effective interest method as an interest expense and reported in profit or loss. Any discretionary dividends declared and paid are treated as relating to the equity component and, therefore, are classified as an equity distribution.

Transaction costs that are incremental and directly attributable to the issue of a compound financial instrument (i.e. they would have been avoided if the compound instrument had not been issued) are allocated to the liability and equity components in proportion to the allocation of the proceeds (see **3.1**). Costs that relate jointly to more than one transaction (for instance a joint and concurrent offering of some equity instruments and an issue of instruments classified as liabilities) are allocated using a basis that is rational and consistent with similar transactions. [IAS 32:38]

Example 4B

Transaction costs: placing and new issue of shares

Entity B places its privately held ordinary shares that are classified as equity with a stock exchange and simultaneously raises new capital by issuing new ordinary shares on the stock exchange. Transaction costs are incurred in respect of both transactions. Because the issue of new shares is the issue of an equity instrument, but the placing of the existing equity instruments with the exchange is not, the transaction costs will need to be allocated between the two transactions. Transaction costs in respect of the new shares issued will be recognised in equity whereas the transaction costs incurred in placing the existing shares with the stock exchange will be recognised in profit or loss.

In July 2008, the IFRIC (now the IFRS Interpretations Committee) issued an agenda decision on IAS 32, *Transaction Costs to be Deducted from Equity*. The IFRIC received a request for guidance on the extent of transaction costs to be accounted for as a deduction from equity in accordance with IAS 32:37 and on how the requirements of IAS 32:38 to allocate transaction costs that relate jointly to more than one transaction should be applied. The issue related specifically to the meaning of the terms 'incremental' and 'directly attributable'.

The IFRIC noted that only incremental costs directly attributable to issuing new equity instruments or acquiring previously outstanding equity instruments are considered to be related to an equity transaction under IAS 32. The IFRIC also noted that judgement will be required to determine which costs are related solely to other activities undertaken at the same time as issuing equity, such as becoming a public company or acquiring an exchange listing, and which costs are related jointly to both activities and, therefore, are required to be allocated in accordance with IAS 32:38. In view of the existing guidance, the IFRIC decided not to add this issue to its agenda.

5 Treasury shares

When an entity reacquires its own shares, those shares (known as treasury shares) are deducted from equity. No gain or loss is recognised in profit or loss on the purchase, sale, issue or cancellation of an entity's own equity instruments. The acquisition and subsequent resale by an entity of its own equity instruments represents a transfer between owners (specifically between those who have given up their equity interest and those who continue to hold an equity instrument) rather than a gain or loss to the entity. Accordingly, any consideration paid or received is recognised in equity. [IAS 32:33]

Example 5A

Acquisition of equity

Entity A buys back 100,000 of its own equity shares in the market for CU5 a share. The shares will be held as treasury shares to enable Entity A to satisfy its obligations under its employee share option scheme. The following entry will be made to recognise the purchase of the treasury shares as a deduction from equity.

		CU	CU
Dr	Equity	500,000	
Cr	Cash		500,000

To recognise treasury shares as a deduction from equity.

Example 5B

Treasury shares held as an economic hedge

Entity F is a large financial institution whose shares are included in the FTSE 100 index. Entity F issues a bond whose principal amount varies with the movement in the FTSE 100 share index (an 'index tracker bond'). In order to hedge economically the equity derivative that is embedded in the bond, Entity F purchases a portfolio of the shares contained in the FTSE 100 index and wishes to classify them as held for trading. Within that portfolio are a number of Entity F's own shares.

Entity F cannot classify its own purchased shares as held for trading in order to hedge economically the index tracker bond. IAS 39 excludes from its scope instruments issued by an entity that meet the definition of equity in IAS 32.

Furthermore, IAS 32 requires that treasury shares be presented in the statement of financial position as a deduction from equity and not as assets, and that no gain or loss should be recognised in profit or loss on such shares.

The amount of treasury shares held is disclosed separately either in the statement of financial position or in the notes in accordance with IAS 1. An entity provides disclosure in accordance with the requirements of IAS 24 *Related Party Disclosures* when an entity reacquires its own equity instruments from related parties. [IAS 32:34]

When an entity holds its own shares on behalf of others (as is the case when a financial institution holds its own shares on behalf of a client as a custodian), this represents an agency relationship and, consequently, the shares are not included in the statement of financial position of the entity. [IAS 32:AG36]

6 Derivatives over own equity

A derivative contract over an entity's own equity is accounted for as equity *only* when it will be settled by the entity delivering (or receiving) a fixed number of its own equity instruments and receiving (or delivering) a fixed amount of cash or another financial asset. Any consideration received (such as the premium received in relation to written options over own shares or warrants on the entity's own shares that satisfy the above condition) is added directly to equity. Similarly, any consideration paid for such an instrument (such as premium paid for a purchased option that satisfies the above condition) is deducted from equity. Changes in fair value of the equity instrument are not recognised in the financial statements. [IAS 32:22] At a group level, derivatives over own equity include derivatives over shares of subsidiaries.

In January 2010, the IFRIC (now the IFRS Interpretations Committee) issued an agenda decision titled *IAS 32 Financial Instruments: Presentation – Application of the 'Fixed-for-Fixed' Condition*. The IFRIC received requests for guidance on the application of IAS 32:22 which states that "except as stated in paragraph 22A, a contract that will be settled by the entity (receiving or) delivering a fixed number of its own equity instruments in exchange for a fixed amount of cash or another financial asset is an equity instrument" (often referred to as the 'fixed-for-fixed' condition).

As part of the IFRIC's discussions grouped the questions on the fixed-for-fixed condition into two broad groups: those related to the denomination of the fixed amount of cash being in a foreign currency and those where the fixed amount of cash or shares is not fixed, but predetermined. The IFRIC identified that diversity may exist in practice in the application of the fixed-for-fixed condition to these situations and also other situations. However, the IFRIC decided not to add this item to its agenda in anticipation of finalisation of the Board's *Financial Instruments with Characteristics of Equity* (FICE) project. Since the IFRIC reached the agenda decision the FICE project has been deferred and has been included in the IASB's research programme. See future development in **9.2**.

Example 6A

Purchased call option

On 1 February 20X5, Entity A, a CU functional currency entity, purchases for CU5,000 a call option over 1,000 of its own ordinary shares. The option is exercisable at a strike price of CU102 per share only on 31 January 20X6 (i.e. it is a 'European type' option).

The option is gross physically settled, i.e. Entity A takes delivery of 1,000 of its own shares in exchange for an amount of cash paid to the counterparty equal to the option exercise price of CU102,000 (CU102 per share × 1,000 shares).

1 February 20X5

On inception of the contract, the following entry will be recorded in order to recognise the cash paid in exchange for the right to receive a fixed number of own shares in exchange for a fixed amount of cash.

		CU	CU
Dr	Equity	5,000	
Cr	Cash		5,000

To recognise the call option.

The premium is recognised in equity because the call option gives a right to receive a fixed number of the entity's own shares in exchange for a fixed amount of cash and, therefore, meets the definition of an equity instrument.

31 December 20X5

No entry is recorded on 31 December 20X5 because no cash is paid or received. The fair value of the option is irrelevant because the equity instrument is not remeasured.

31 January 20X6

The entity exercises the call option and the contract is gross physically settled through the entity taking delivery of 1,000 of its own shares in exchange for a payment of CU102,000 to the counterparty. This is recognised with the following entry.

		CU	CU
Dr	Equity	102,000	
Cr	Cash		102,000
To record the exercise of the call option.			

With the exception of instruments that meet the exception from financial liability presentation in IAS 32:16A & 16B, or IAS 32:16C & 16D, a contract that contains an obligation for an entity to purchase its own equity instruments for cash or another financial asset gives rise to a financial liability for the present value of the redemption amount (for example, for the present value of the forward repurchase price, option exercise price or other redemption amount). This is the case even if the contract itself is an equity instrument. [IAS 32:23] This is commonly referred to as 'gross obligation accounting'.

Examples of instruments that give rise to a liability include forward contracts to buy own equity and written put options that allow the holder to put the shares back to the entity at a fixed or variable amount (e.g. a fixed amount plus inflation). At inception, such contracts are recognised at an amount equal to the present value of the obligation inherent in the contract. This treatment is required notwithstanding the fact that the contract itself may be an equity instrument (as it can be settled only through the entity delivering a fixed amount of cash in exchange for a fixed number of its own shares). [IAS 32:23] This is similar to taking delivery of own shares today but with an obligation to still pay the cash under the share buy-back to the counterparty.

IAS 32:23 requires the financial liability arising from the obligation to buy back own equity to be measured at the *present value* of the redemption amount but does not specify the discount rate that should be used in deriving the present value. In the absence of specific guidance a reasonable approach would be to reflect in the discount rate:

- interest rate risk – being the benchmark interest rate for the term to the earliest redemption date for the relevant currency of the obligation; and
- the credit risk associated with the issuer because the issuer is the obligor under the arrangement.

The discount rate should not reflect:

- the risk associated with potential changes in cash flows, to the extent that this risk is already taken into consideration in developing the cash flows used to establish the redemption price and by adjusting the liability each period for the change in variability of cash flows; or
- the likelihood that the option will be exercised, because the basis for the measurement of liability assumes the amount is payable.

The financial liability is subsequently remeasured through profit or loss (i.e. interest is accrued in accordance with the effective interest method up to the share redemption amount). In the case of a gross liability based on a variable amount of cash, the remeasurement of the amount of the eventual liability (e.g. for changes in inflation) would also be recognised through profit or loss.

If the contract expires without delivery, the carrying amount of the financial liability is reclassified to equity; amounts recognised in profit or loss up to the date of extinguishment are not reversed in profit or loss.

Recognition of a gross obligation for the present value of the redemption amount is required where the contract is exclusively gross physically settled by the entity delivering cash or another financial asset in exchange for the entity's equity instruments or if the counterparty to the arrangement has the right to require the entity to pay the counterparty cash or another financial asset in exchange for the entity's equity instruments.

Where the entity has a choice how the contract is settled and one of the settlement choices is for the entity (not the holder) to choose gross physical settlement, IAS 32 is less clear how the contract should be presented. There are two acceptable approaches and an entity should choose an approach as an accounting policy applied consistently to all similar transactions.

Presentation as a derivative at FVTPL

This presentation may be applied on the basis that:

- the entity can choose not to gross settle and therefore is not obligated to settle the contract by delivering cash or another financial instrument in acquiring its own equity instruments; and
- the settlement alternatives other than gross physical settlement will not result in the exchange of a fixed number of equity instruments for a fixed amount of cash or another financial asset and therefore meet the definition of a financial asset and financial liability in IAS 32:11.

Presentation as a gross obligation

Presentation as a gross obligation equal to the present value of the amount potentially payable under the contract may be applied on the basis that:

- if the contract may be gross settled, irrespective of which party may choose that settlement choice, the entity has a potential obligation to pay cash or another financial asset in acquiring its equity instruments; and
- the illustrative examples in the implementation guidance of IAS 32, specifically IAS 32:IE6 and IAS 32:IE31, include a forward purchase

and written put over equity instruments with settlement alternatives where one of the settlement choices is gross settlement. Both examples state: "[i]f one of the settlement alternatives is to exchange cash for shares, Entity A recognises a liability for the obligation to deliver cash. Otherwise, Entity A accounts for the forward contract as a derivative." The examples do not distinguish between gross settlement at the choice of the entity or choice of the holder.

Example 6B

Forward purchase contract

Assume the facts are as in **example 6A** except that, instead of purchasing a call option over own shares that will be gross physically settled, on 1 February 20X5 Entity A enters into a forward contract to buy 1,000 of its own ordinary shares on 31 January 20X6 for CU104 per share.

This contract will be gross physically settled, i.e. Entity A will take delivery of 1,000 of its own shares in exchange for paying to the counterparty a share redemption amount of CU104,000 (CU104 per share × 1,000 shares).

1 February 20X5

The entity has an unconditional obligation to deliver CU104,000 in cash in one year's time to the counterparty in exchange for a fixed number of its own equity shares. The following entry is made to recognise this obligation to deliver CU104,000 in one year at its present value of CU100,000 discounted using an appropriate interest rate which is determined to be 4 per cent.

		CU	CU
Dr	Equity	100,000	
Cr	Liability		100,000

To recognise the forward contract.

31 December 20X5

The following journal entry is made to accrue interest in accordance with the effective interest method.

		CU	CU
Dr	Interest expense	3,660	
Cr	Liability		3,660

To accrue interest at the effective interest rate of 4 per cent.

31 January 20X6

The following journal entry is made to accrue interest for the month of January 20X6 in accordance with the effective interest method.

		CU	CU
Dr	Interest expense	340	
Cr	Liability		340

To accrue interest at the effective interest rate of 4 per cent.

On the same date, the following entry is made to recognise the settlement of the liability for the share redemption amount.

		CU	CU
Dr	Liability	104,000	
Cr	Cash		104,000

To recognise payment of the share redemption amount.

Local company law may also require some reclassification of the balance within equity on receipt by Entity A of its own shares.

Example 6C

Written put option

On 1 February 20X5, Entity A writes a put option over 1,000 of its own ordinary shares and receives in exchange a premium of CU5,000. The option is exercisable at a strike price of CU98 per share only on 31 January 20X6 (i.e. it is a European type option). The option will be gross physically settled, i.e. if the option is exercised, the entity will receive 1,000 of its own shares in exchange for paying to the counterparty an amount equal to the option exercise price of CU98,000 (CU98 per share × 1,000 shares).

1 February 20X5

At the inception of the contract, the following entry is recorded to recognise the cash received in exchange for writing the put option and the present value of the CU98,000 obligation to be settled on 31 January 20X6 (discounted using an appropriate interest rate determined to be 3.2 per cent) giving the counterparty the right to receive a fixed amount of cash in exchange for a fixed number of Entity A's shares.

		CU	CU
Dr	Cash	5,000	
Dr	Equity	90,000	
Cr	Liability		95,000

To recognise the premium received and the present value of the liability under thc put option.

31 December 20X5

The following entry is recorded to accrue interest on the liability in accordance with the effective interest method.

		CU	CU
Dr	Interest expense	2,745	
Cr	Liability		2,745

To accrue interest at the effective interest rate of 3.2 per cent.

31 January 20X6

The following journal entry is recorded to accrue interest on the liability for the remaining month of January 20X6 in accordance with the effective interest method.

		CU	CU
Dr	Interest expense	255	
Cr	Liability		255

To accrue interest at the effective interest rate of 3.2 per cent.

On the same date, if the written put option is exercised by the counterparty, the following entry is recorded to recognise the settlement of the liability for the strike price of the written put option.

		CU	CU
Dr	Liability	98,000	
Cr	Cash		98,000

To recognise payment of the strike price.

If the written put option is not exercised by the counterparty, the following entry is recorded instead.

		CU	CU
Dr	Liability	98,000	
Cr	Equity		98,000

To record the expiry of the put option.

When an acquirer acquires less than 100 per cent of the shares of a subsidiary in a business combination, it is common also to enter into a written put option with the seller that permits the seller to put its remaining interest in the subsidiary to the acquirer at a specified price. These put options are written by the acquirer to allow the seller an exit mechanism for the remaining shares. The acquisition of shares that results in the interest being recognised as a subsidiary will be accounted for in accordance with IFRS 3 *Business Combinations*. If the written put option can be physically settled (i.e. the subsidiary's shares are physically delivered and paid for by cash or other financial asset), irrespective of whether the strike price of the put option is a fixed or variable price, a gross obligation must be recognised at an amount equal to the present value of the amount that could be required to be paid to the counterparty in accordance with IAS 32. Changes in the measurement of the gross obligation due to the unwinding of the discount or changes in the amount that the acquirer could be required to pay are always recognised in profit or loss. It is not acceptable to adjust these gains or losses against the goodwill that arose on the acquisition because changes in the value of the gross obligation relate to the potential *future* purchase of the remaining shares in the subsidiary.

In November 2006, the IFRIC (now the IFRS Interpretations Committee) considered the classification and presentation of written put options and forward purchase arrangements entered into by a parent over shares of a subsidiary, otherwise known as puts and forwards over non-controlling interests (previously known as 'minority interests'). The IFRIC confirmed that in the consolidated financial statements, a financial liability must be recognised in accordance with IAS 32:23 for the obligation to pay cash in the future to purchase the shares held by non-controlling interests (NCI), even if the payment of that cash is conditional on the option being exercised by the holder. After initial recognition, any liability to which IFRS 3 is not being applied will be accounted for in accordance with IAS 39. The parent will reclassify the liability to equity if the put option expires unexercised.

The IFRIC recognised that there is likely to be divergence in practice in how the related debit to equity is presented. However, the IFRIC did not believe that it could reach a consensus on this matter on a timely basis and, therefore, it decided not to add this item to its agenda.

The debit recognised in equity on initial recognition of the written put or forward purchase over an NCI may be presented as either a deduction from NCI or from other reserves (within Entity Q's equity) alongside NCI. The subsequent attribution of profit or loss and other comprehensive income between the equity of the ultimate parent and NCI may be affected by this decision.

In May 2010, the IFRS Interpretations Committee started to discuss how an entity should account for changes in the carrying amount of a financial liability for a put option written over NCI. The request to the Interpretations Committee focused on the accounting for an NCI put option after the amendments to IFRS 3 *Business Combinations* and IAS 27 *Consolidated and Separate Financial Statements* in 2008 and IAS 39. The request considered whether there was a potential conflict between these amendments and the financial instruments guidance.

In September 2010, the IFRS Interpretations Committee issued a tentative decision not to take the issue on to its agenda. That tentative decision stated that the Committee observed that IAS 32:23 requires the financial liability recognised for an NCI put option to be subsequently measured in accordance with IAS 39. The Committee observed that IAS 39:55 & 56 require changes in the carrying amount of financial liabilities to be recognised in profit or loss. However, the Committee noted that additional accounting concerns exist relating to the accounting for NCI put options and that these would be best addressed as part of the IASB's *Financial Instruments with Characteristics of Equity* (FICE) project.

Many respondents to the tentative agenda decision did not agree with the Interpretations Committee's approach. Further, as the Board did not have the capacity to devote time necessary to deliberate issues relating to the FICE project the Committee decided to add the issue to its agenda with the objective of addressing on a timely basis the current significant diversity that exists in practice.

In January and March 2011 the Interpretations Committee discussed possible ways to resolve the issue through a potential scope exception from IAS 32 for written put options over NCI. The scope exclusion would change the measurement basis of NCI puts to that used for other derivative contracts, i.e. FVTPL, thereby not recognising a financial liability at the present value of the option exercise price as currently required by IAS 32:23. The scope exclusion would apply only to the consolidated financial statements of the controlling shareholder. In addition, the scope exclusion would apply only to NCI puts with the following features:

- the NCI put is not embedded in another contract, and
- the NCI put contains an obligation for an entity in the consolidated group to settle the contract by delivering cash or another financial asset in exchange for the interest in the subsidiary.

The Interpretations Committee recommended that the Board should consider making an amendment to the scope of IAS 32. The proposal was rejected by the IASB. The Board noted that, ideally, the accounting for derivatives written on an entity's own equity instruments should be addressed comprehensively within the context of its project on *Financial Instruments with Characteristics of Equity*. Although the Board decided not to amend IAS 32 to change the accounting for NCI puts at this time, it asked the Interpretations Committee to address the issue that was submitted by clarifying the existing accounting requirements for the subsequent measurement of the financial liability that is recognised for an NCI put.

The Interpretations Committee responded to the Board's request by issuing Draft IFRIC Interpretation DI/2012/2 *Put Options Written on*

Non-controlling Interests in May 2012. The draft IFRIC Interpretation states for written puts on NCI a financial liability is initially measured at the present value of the redemption amount in the parent's consolidated financial statements. Subsequently, the financial liability is measured in accordance with IAS 39. IAS 39:55 & 56 require that changes in the measurement of that financial liability are recognised in profit or loss. The changes in the measurement of that financial liability do not change the relative interests in the subsidiary that are held by the parent and the non-controlling-interest shareholder and therefore are not equity transactions (i.e. they are not transactions with owners in their capacity as owners) as described in IFRS 10:23.

Feedback received on the Draft IFRIC was reported by the Interpretations Committee to the IASB, which in June 2014 decided that this project should be incorporated into the broader project looking at the distinction between liabilities and equity (see **9.2**).

Example 6D

Written put option over equity of subsidiary

On 1 January 20X8, Entity Q, the ultimate parent of Group Q, acquires a 60 per cent interest in Entity P from Entity O. As part of the acquisition agreement, Entity Q also writes a put option over the remaining 40 per cent of shares in Entity P to Entity O. Entity Q pays CU1,000 million under the purchase agreement. The written put option allows Entity O to put the 40 per cent interest in Entity P to Entity Q at CU275 million plus 20 per cent of Entity P's post-acquisition cumulative profits. The put option can be exercised by Entity O at 1 July 20Y0 and at every anniversary thereafter until 1 July 20Y2. Cumulative profits are determined based on audited financial statements of Entity P up to the year ended immediately prior to exercise of the put option. Group Q's reporting period end is 31 December.

At 1 January 20X8, the fair value of 60 per cent of the shares in Entity P is CU1,100 million and the fair value of the written put option is CU100 million. At that date, Group Q measures non-controlling interests at CU200 million, which is their proportionate share of the acquiree's identifiable net assets. Entity Q's estimation of profits of Entity P for the two-year period ending 31 December 20X9 is CU50 million. Entity Q determines that an appropriate discount rate for use in measuring the financial liability relating to the put option is 10 per cent.

At 31 December 20X8, the fair value of the written put option is CU90 million. Entity Q revises its estimate of Entity P's profits for the two-year period ending 31 December 20X9 to CU80 million.

Entity Q separate financial statements

The written put option is over a third party's equity and, therefore, it does not meet the definition of equity for Entity Q. The put option will therefore be classified as at fair value through profit or loss (FVTPL).

1 January 20X8

		CU million	CU million
Dr	Cost of investment	1,100	
Cr	Cash		1,000
Cr	Written put option – FVTPL		100

To recognise the cost of investment in the subsidiary and the written put option at fair value at initial recognition.

31 December 20X8

		CU million	CU million
Dr	Written put option – FVTPL	10	
Cr	Gain (profit or loss)		10

To recognise the remeasurement of the put option.

Group Q consolidated financial statements

The written put option permits a third party, Entity O, to put up to 40 per cent of the shares in a subsidiary of Group Q to Group Q. Because Group Q could be required to pay cash or other financial assets as settlement for the acquisition of shares in a subsidiary (in this case, non-controlling interests in the group), Group Q is required to recognise a gross obligation for the potential future acquisition of these equity shares.

1 January 20X8

At the date of acquisition, Group Q consolidates Entity P and recognises a 40 per cent non-controlling interest (NCI). The fair value of consideration used to acquire 60 per cent of the shares in Entity P for the purposes of determining any goodwill arising on acquisition is CU1,100 million. The difference between this amount and the total consideration paid to Entity O is the premium that Entity Q received for writing the put option.

The estimated present value of the amount Group Q could be required to pay Entity O should Entity O exercise its put option on 1 July 20Y0 is CU225 million. This is determined as follows: [CU275 million + (CU50 million x 20 per cent)] x $1/(1.1^{2.5})$.

		CU million	CU million
Dr	Net assets acquired and goodwill	1,300	
Cr	NCI		200
Dr	Equity	125	
Cr	Cash		1,000
Cr	Gross obligation under put option		225

To recognise the acquisition of the subsidiary and the recognition of the present value of the gross obligation under the written put option over the non-controlling interest.

The debit recognised in equity on initial recognition of the written put option over Entity P's shares may be presented as either a deduction from NCI or from other reserves (within Entity Q's equity) alongside NCI. The subsequent attribution of profit or loss and other comprehensive income between the equity of Entity Q and NCI may be affected by this decision.

31 December 20X8

The estimated present value of the amount Group Q could be required to pay Entity O, should Entity O exercise its put option at the earliest opportunity, being 1 July 20Y0, is CU252 million. This is determined as follows: [CU275 million + (CU80 million x 20 per cent)] x $1/(1.1^{1.5})$.

		CU million	CU million
Dr	Profit or loss	27	
Cr	Gross obligation under put option		27

To recognise the remeasurement of the present value of the gross obligation under the written put option over the non-controlling interest.

All derivatives over own equity (other than forward purchases and written puts) where settlement is not exclusively by the exchange of a fixed number of equity shares for a fixed amount of cash (or another financial asset) are treated as derivatives (derivative financial assets or liabilities) and are accounted for in accordance with the requirements of IAS 39; the fair value of the instrument is recognised in the statement of financial position with changes in fair value recognised in profit or loss unless it is designated as an effective hedging instrument in a cash flow hedge or a hedge of a net investment in a foreign operation. A forward purchase or a written put option that may result in the entity receiving its own equity shares and being obligated to deliver cash (or another financial asset) is recognised as a financial liability that represents the entity's gross obligation to deliver cash or another financial asset to the counterparty. All other forward purchase and written put option contracts over own shares are measured at fair value through profit or loss.

Therefore, the following derivatives over own equity are accounted as derivatives that are fair valued through profit or loss:

- those that are exclusively net settled in cash (or other financial assets);
- those that are exclusively net settled in own equity shares; and
- any derivative over own equity which gives either party a choice over how it is settled unless all the settlement alternatives result in the exchange of a fixed number of own shares for a fixed amount of cash or another financial asset (or in the case of a forward purchase or written put over own shares where one of the settlement alternatives can require the issuer to gross physically settle).

Example 6E

Forward sale contract: net share settlement

On 1 February 20X5, Entity A, a CU functional currency entity, enters into a forward sale contract over 1,000 of its own ordinary (equity) shares on 31 January 20X6 at a fixed price of CU18 per share. The terms of the contract are that it will be net settled in shares, i.e. on 31 January 20X6, Entity A will receive (if the share price is below CU18) or deliver (if the share price is above CU18) shares with an aggregate market value equal to 1,000 times the difference between the market price per share at that date and the fixed price in the contract of CU18.

1 February 20X5

The price per share when the contract is entered into on 1 February 20X5 is CU18. The initial fair value of the forward contract on 1 February 20X5 is zero. Therefore, no entry is recorded because the fair value of the derivative is zero and no cash is paid or received.

31 December 20X5

On 31 December 20X5, the market price per share has increased to CU24 and, as a result, the fair value of the forward contract has decreased to a liability of CU6,000 [(CU24 – CU18) x 1,000)].

The following entry is recorded to recognise the decrease in the fair value of the forward contract.

		CU	CU
Dr	Loss (profit or loss)	6,000	
Cr	Forward liability		6,000

To recognise the decrease in the fair value of the forward contract.

31 January 20X6

On 31 January 20X6, the market price per share has decreased to CU20. The fair value of the forward contract is a liability of CU2,000 ([(CU20 – CU18) x 1,000]. Therefore, the following entry is recorded to recognise the decrease in the fair value of the forward liability.

		CU	CU
Dr	Forward liability	4,000	
Cr	Gain (profit or loss)		4,000

To recognise the decrease in the fair value of the forward liability.

On the same day, the contract is settled net in shares (with Entity A delivering 100 of its own shares to the counterparty to settle its obligation to deliver shares with an aggregate value of CU2,000). The following entry is therefore recorded to recognise the settlement of the contract net in own equity shares.

		CU	CU
Dr	Forward liability (100 shares x CU20)	2,000	
Cr	Equity		2,000

To recognise the settlement of the contract net in own equity shares.

For illustrative purposes only, the effect of time value is excluded from the calculation of the fair value of the forward contract.

Example 6F

Total return swap

An entity enters into a total return swap ('TRS') over 1,000 of its own equity shares on 1 February 20X5. The contract matures on 31 January 20X6. Due to the nature of the total return swap (whose fair value is driven by changes in the entity's share price), gross settlement is not possible and it will be settled net (either in cash or in a variable number of shares). Therefore, the instrument does not qualify as an equity instrument and it will be accounted for as a derivative.

1 February 20X5

The initial fair value of the swap on 1 February 20X5 is zero. No entry is recorded because the fair value of the derivative is zero and no cash is paid or received.

31 December 20X5

The fair value of the swap at 31 December 20X5 is CU4,500; therefore, the following entry is recorded to recognise the increase in fair value.

		CU	CU
Dr	Swap asset	4,500	
Cr	Profit or loss		4,500

To recognise the increase in fair value of the swap asset.

31 January 20X6

The fair value of the swap at 31 January 20X6 is CU3,750; therefore, the following entry is recorded to recognise the decrease in fair value.

		CU	CU
Dr	Profit or loss	750	
Cr	Swap asset		750

To recognise the decrease in fair value of the swap asset.

The entries to be recorded upon settlement will depend on which of the two methods of net settlement is chosen. If net share settlement is chosen, the following entry will be made.

		CU	CU
Dr	Equity	3,750	
Cr	Swap asset		3,750

To recognise the net share settlement.

In this scenario, settlement will take place through the entity taking receipt of 150 of its own shares (CU3,750/CU25) (the market value of the entity's share on this date is CU25).

If net cash settlement is chosen, the following entry will be made at settlement of the contract.

		CU	CU
Dr	Cash	3,750	
Cr	Swap asset		3,750

To recognise the net cash settlement.

The following decision tree summarises the classification of derivatives over own equity instruments. In making this determination, it should also be noted that:

- in consolidated financial statements, derivatives over the equity of subsidiaries are treated in the same way as derivatives over the equity of the parent entity;
- recognition of a financial liability for an obligation to purchase own equity for cash (or another financial asset) is required even if the obligation is conditional on the holder exercising its right to sell the shares to the entity and notwithstanding the fact that the contract itself may be an equity instrument (because it can be settled only through the entity delivering a fixed amount of cash in exchange for a fixed number of its own shares); [IAS 32:23] and
- a derivative over own equity when the underlying equity instrument meets the requirements for equity classification in accordance with either IAS 32:16A & 16B (puttable instruments) or IAS 32:16C & 16D (instruments that impose on the entity an obligation to deliver to another party a pro rata share of the net assets of the entity only on liquidation) of IAS 32 cannot be classified as equity. [IAS 32:22A]

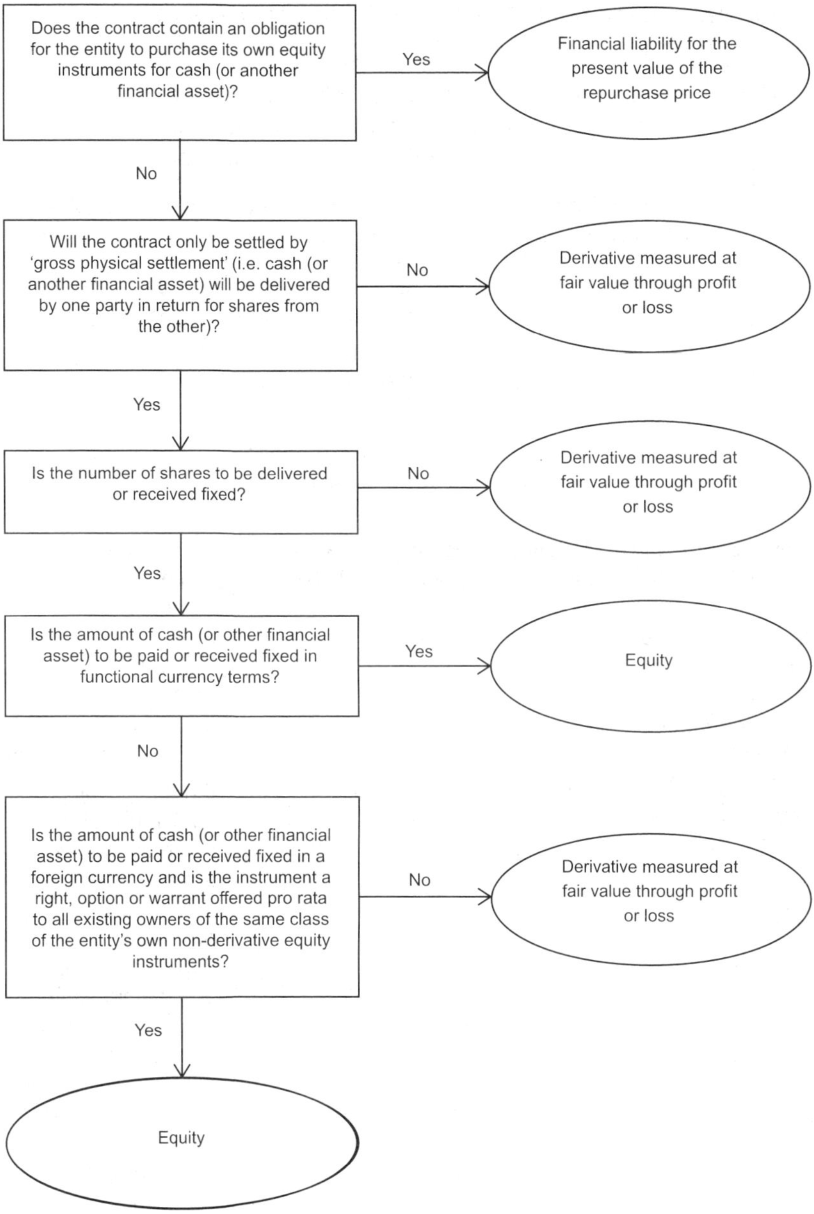

The following table illustrates the application of IAS 32 to different derivatives over own equity, with different settlement mechanisms. The settlement mechanisms are described as follows.

(1) **Net cash settlement**. When one party's net gain/loss is settled in cash and no shares are exchanged.

(2) **Net share settlement (shares for shares)**. A variable number of shares is delivered/received having an aggregate current fair value equal to the amount of the gain/loss to the relevant party.

(3) **Gross physical settlement**. The buyer/seller delivers/receives cash in return for shares from the seller/buyer.

(4) **Settlement options**. When either the issuer or the holder has a right to choose among two or more of the above ways of settlement.

	Settlement options available			
	Net cash settlement only	**Net share settlement only**	**Gross physical settlement only**	**Settlement options**
Forward contract to buy equity shares (the forward contract may be over a fixed or variable number of equity shares for a fixed or variable amount of functional or foreign currency cash)	Derivative financial asset/ liability	Derivative financial asset/ liability	Gross liability	If gross physical settlement exists as an alternative at the election of the counterparty, financial liability for the present value of the repurchase price. If gross physical settlement exists as an alternative at the election of the reporting entity (issuer), two approaches are acceptable as an accounting policy choice. Either (i) financial liability for the present value of the repurchase price, or (ii) derivative financial asset/ liability. If gross physical settlement does not exist as an alternative for either party, treat as a derivative financial asset/liability.

	Settlement options available			
	Net cash settlement only	**Net share settlement only**	**Gross physical settlement only**	**Settlement options**
Forward contract to sell a fixed number of equity shares for a fixed amount of functional currency cash	Derivative financial asset/ liability	Derivative financial asset/ liability	Equity	Derivative financial asset/liability
Forward contract to sell a fixed number of equity shares for a fixed or variable amount of foreign currency cash or a variable amount of functional currency cash	Derivative financial asset/ liability	Derivative financial asset/ liability	Derivative financial asset/ liability	Derivative financial asset/liability
Forward contract to sell a variable number of equity shares for a fixed or variable amount of functional or foreign currency cash	Derivative financial asset/ liability	Derivative financial asset/ liability	Derivative financial asset/ liability	Derivative financial asset/liability
Purchased call option on a fixed number of equity shares for a fixed amount of functional currency cash	Derivative financial asset	Derivative financial asset	Equity	Derivative financial asset
Purchased call option on a fixed number of equity shares for a fixed or variable amount of foreign currency cash or variable amount of functional currency cash	Derivative financial asset	Derivative financial asset	Derivative financial asset	Derivative financial asset

	Settlement options available			
	Net cash settlement only	**Net share settlement only**	**Gross physical settlement only**	**Settlement options**
Purchased call option on a variable number of equity shares for a fixed or variable amount of functional or foreign currency cash	Derivative financial asset	Derivative financial asset	Derivative financial asset	Derivative financial asset
Written call option on a fixed number of equity shares for a fixed amount of functional currency cash	Derivative financial liability	Derivative financial liability	Equity	Derivative financial liability
Written call option on a fixed number of equity shares for a fixed or variable amount of foreign currency cash or a variable amount of functional currency cash	Derivative financial liability	Derivative financial liability	Derivative financial liability	Derivative financial liability
Written call option on a fixed number of equity shares for a fixed amount of foreign currency cash that is offered pro rata to all of the issuer's existing owners of the same class of its own non-derivative equity instruments. See **6.1.1**.	Derivative financial liability	Derivative financial liability	Equity	Derivative financial liability

	Settlement options available			
	Net cash settlement only	**Net share settlement only**	**Gross physical settlement only**	**Settlement options**
Written call option on a fixed number of equity shares for a fixed amount of foreign currency cash that is *not* offered pro rata to all of the issuer's existing owners of the same class of its own non-derivative equity instruments. See **6.1.1**.	Derivative financial liability	Derivative financial liability	Derivative financial liability	Derivative financial liability
Written call option on a variable number of equity shares for a fixed or variable amount of functional or foreign currency cash	Derivative financial liability	Derivative financial liability	Derivative financial liability	Derivative financial liability
Purchased put option on a fixed number of equity shares for a fixed amount of functional currency cash	Derivative financial asset	Derivative financial asset	Equity	Derivative financial asset
Purchased put option on a fixed number of equity shares for a fixed or variable amount of foreign currency cash or variable amount of functional currency cash	Derivative financial asset	Derivative financial asset	Derivative financial asset	Derivative financial asset
Purchased put option on a variable number of equity shares for a fixed or variable amount of functional or foreign currency cash	Derivative financial asset	Derivative financial asset	Derivative financial asset	Derivative financial asset

	Settlement options available			
	Net cash settlement only	Net share settlement only	Gross physical settlement only	Settlement options
Written put option on equity shares (the option may be over a fixed or variable number of equity shares for a fixed or variable amount of functional or foreign currency cash)	Derivative financial liability	Derivative financial liability	Gross liability	If gross physical settlement exists as an alternative at the election of the counterparty, financial liability for the present value of the repurchase price. If gross physical settlement exists as an alternative at the election of the reporting entity (issuer), two approaches are acceptable as an accounting policy choice. Either (i) financial liability for the present value of the repurchase price, or (ii) derivative financial liability. If gross physical settlement does not exist as an alternative for either party, treat as a derivative financial liability.

6.1 Other variations of terms of derivatives over own equity

As described immediately above, the guidance on multiple settlement alternatives for stand-alone derivatives over own equity is consistent with the multiple settlement alternatives guidance for convertible debt described in **3.7**. The guidance is consistent because, in order to determine whether an equity conversion option in convertible debt is considered to be equity for the issuer, the guidance regarding derivatives over own equity is applied. As a result, the guidance on foreign currency convertible debt described in **3.8** equally applies to stand-alone derivatives over own equity, i.e. for a derivative over own equity to meet the definition of equity it must be an exchange of a fixed number of shares for a fixed amount of functional currency cash. The one exception to this is the accounting for certain rights denominated in a foreign currency (see **6.1.1**). The guidance on anti-dilutive provisions in **3.9** also applies to stand-alone derivatives over own equity.

It is not possible to provide an exhaustive list of different variations in the terms of derivatives over own equity. However, some examples and the accounting analysis are included below.

6.1.1 Foreign currency denominated rights issues

In October 2009, the IASB issued an amendment to IAS 32 titled *Classification of Rights Issues*. The amendment changes the presentation for certain rights issues denominated in a foreign currency that, prior to the amendment, would have failed the definition of equity and would have been presented as a financial liability. Following the amendment, rights, options and warrants that will be settled only by the issue of a fixed number of shares for a fixed amount of cash or other financial asset *in any currency* are presented in equity if the entity offers the rights, options or warrants pro rata to all of its existing owners of the same class of its own non-derivative equity instruments. [IAS 32:11(b)(ii)] Prior to the amendment, rights, options and warrants that result in the receipt of currency other than the functional currency of the issuing entity would not meet the definition of equity and would therefore be presented as a derivative financial liability as at FVTPL.

It is common for rights issues to have an exercise price in a currency other than the functional currency of the issuer if the issuer is listed in more than one jurisdiction or might be required to do so by law or regulation. As part of its deliberations, the IASB agreed that a contract with an exercise price denominated in a foreign currency would not result in the entity receiving a fixed amount of cash and, therefore, would fail the definition of equity. However, the IASB considered that with respect to foreign currency denominated rights issues, the accounting treatment was inconsistent with the substance of the transaction because the Board considered such transactions to partially resemble dividends paid in shares as the rights issue is offered only to existing shareholders on the basis of the number of shares they already own. In addition, the Board considered that such arrangements are a transaction with an entity's owners in their capacity as owners and, therefore, the transaction should be recognised in equity with no impact in comprehensive income. It is for these reasons that the IASB decided to make an 'extremely narrow amendment' (IAS 32:BC4J) by amending the definition of a financial liability to exclude such arrangements.

Example 6.1.1

Foreign currency denominated rights issue

Entity D's ordinary shares are listed on multiple stock exchanges. Entity D offers all its existing shareholders the right to buy one ordinary share in Entity D for every two shares held (a '1 for 2' rights issue). The price payable to Entity D for the issue of ordinary shares under the rights issue (the strike price) is at a 30 per cent discount to the share price at the rights offer date (a fixed price in the currency of the strike price). Because Entity D's ordinary shares are listed on multiple stock exchanges, Entity D structures the rights issue so that the strike price for the rights in a particular jurisdiction matches the currency of that jurisdiction.

The rights issue should be classified as equity because the discounted shares are offered pro rata to all ordinary shareholders and therefore the condition in IAS 32:11(b)(ii) is met.

The limited amendment to IAS 32 only relates to 'rights, options and warrants'. [IAS 32:11(b)(ii)] Therefore, contractual arrangements that are non-optional (e.g. forward contracts or other arrangements where the counterparty is not given the choice as to whether to acquire equity instruments of the issuer) are not subject to the exemption included in the amendment. Because the amendment to IAS 32 only applies to certain rights issues that meet the specific criteria for equity classification, it is not possible to analogise to other arrangements that do not meet these criteria and classify those arrangements as equity.

6.1.2 Contracts under which the number of own equity shares or amount of cash is predetermined but still subject to variability

Derivatives over own equity may be structured so that they can be exercised at various points in time and the number of shares or the amount of cash is predetermined up-front but varies with time. One must consider whether such derivatives involve an exchange of a fixed amount of cash or other financial asset for a fixed amount of equity. The following example illustrates this point.

Entity A, which has a currency unit (CU) functional currency, enters into two stand-alone contracts to deliver its own equity to a third party.

- Contract 1 is a written call option that gives the counterparty the right to buy equity of Entity A for CU100 on any of three fixed dates over a 3-year period. The number of shares that will be delivered to the counterparty on exercise will depend on when the counterparty exercises the option. If the counterparty exercises the option one year after issuance, 10 shares will be delivered; if two years after issuance, 11 shares; and if three years after issuance, 12 shares. If the option is not exercised on any of these dates, the call option will expire and there is no further right to buy shares under the arrangement.
- Contract 2 is also a written call option that gives the counterparty the right to buy equity of Entity A for CU100 on any of three fixed dates over a 3-year period. The number of shares that will be delivered to the counterparty on exercise will depend on when the counterparty exercises the option and the rate of LIBOR on that date. If the counterparty exercises the option one year after issuance, the

number of shares to be delivered is 10 × (1 + LIBOR); if two years after issuance 10 × $(1 + \text{LIBOR})^2$ and, if three years after issuance 10 × $(1 + \text{LIBOR})^3$. If the option is not exercised on any of these dates, the call option will expire and there is no further right to buy shares under the arrangement.

Contract 1 meets the definition of an equity instrument because, if exercised, the issuer will receive a fixed amount of cash for delivering a fixed amount of its own equity. Even though the number of shares that the instrument may be converted into varies, it only varies with the passage of time and not with other variables (i.e. the number of shares is fixed at inception of the contract). The arrangement is considered to be an exchange of a fixed number of shares for a fixed amount of cash. Therefore, the premium received for writing the call option is credited to equity and subsequent changes in the fair value of the instrument are not recognised in the financial statements.

Contract 2, on the other hand, does not meet the definition of equity because, if exercised, the issuer will deliver a variable number of shares for a fixed amount of cash. Even though the number of shares is determinable (i.e. it is determined by a specified index, in this case LIBOR), the number of shares is not fixed in advance and varies due to factors other than the passage of time (in this case, interest rates). The contract is not, therefore, an exchange of a fixed number of shares for a fixed amount of cash. The written option meets the definition of a derivative in IAS 39:9 and should be measured at fair value through profit or loss.

6.1.3 *Contract to exchange a fixed number of shares of a parent for a fixed number of shares in a subsidiary*

In the consolidated financial statements, a contract to exchange a fixed number of shares of a parent for a fixed number of shares in a subsidiary is an exchange of a fixed number of shares of the issuer (the parent), which are equity instruments, for a fixed number of shares of a subsidiary (held by a non-controlling interest), which are also equity of the group. IAS 32 does not address this fact pattern because the Standard assumes that, for a derivative over equity to be classified as equity, the exchange will always involve receipt or delivery of a fixed amount of cash (or other financial asset) for a fixed amount of equity. Because the arrangement is an exchange of a fixed number of two equity instruments, at the consolidated level it is reasonable that the instrument be presented as equity because the holder is exchanging one fixed amount of residual interest in one group entity for another.

6.2 Share buy-back arrangements

An entity may enter into arrangements with a third party, usually with a financial institution, for that third party to buy back the entity's equity shares in the market for delivery to the entity. It is important to determine for such arrangements whether the third party is acting as principal or as an agent for the entity. If the third party is acting as agent, then the contractual arrangement between the entity and the third party is not a financial instrument. In such cases, only when shares are acquired by the third party will the entity recognise a financial liability to pay the third party and a debit in equity for the shares to be delivered; and when the shares are delivered to the entity will the entity settle the financial liability with cash or other financial asset and re-present within equity that treasury shares have been acquired or shares cancelled.

Example 6.2

Share buyback arrangement

Entity A enters into an arrangement immediately prior to its period end which allows a financial institution to acquire equity shares in Entity A in the market and then deliver these shares to Entity A at the price the financial institution paid subject to a fee.

The financial institution must acquire a number of shares between a minimum (the 'floor') and maximum (the 'cap') amount, and there is a maximum number of shares which may be acquired in a trading day. Within these boundaries, the financial institution has full discretion to buy shares and Entity A cannot refuse to purchase those shares once they are acquired by the financial institution.

Entity A enters into this arrangement to ensure that its share buyback programme continues during the 'quiet period', (the period, also referred to as a 'close period' between the entity's period end and the release of its financial results) without breaching regulatory rules.

At the period end, Entity A will need to recognise a financial liability for the obligation to acquire its own equity (i.e. a 'gross obligation'). This financial liability will be initially recognised at the present value of the maximum amount that Entity A could be required to pay to the financial institution, with a corresponding debit in equity.

Changes in the present value of this liability (e.g. due to the unwinding of any discount applied or to changes in the market price of the Entity A's shares), will be recognised in profit or loss.

If the arrangement limits the maximum amount the entity can pay to the financial institution, the financial liability will be initially measured at the present value of this amount. In this case, Entity A may not have variability in the amount it will pay due to changes in its share price because Entity A could always be required to pay the maximum amount to the financial institution.

When the financial institution buys the shares in the market and delivers them to Entity A and Entity A settles the obligation with cash or another financial asset, Entity A will derecognise the part of the financial liability equal to the amount that has been paid.

If, at the end of the buyback period, the financial institution has not acquired the maximum amount of shares or utilised the maximum amount that Entity A can spend on buying back shares, the financial liability remaining at that point should be reversed with a corresponding credit in equity to show that it has been extinguished.

7 Classification of financial liabilities

All financial liabilities are required to be classified and subsequently measured at amortised cost using the effective interest rate (see **section 4** of **chapter C6**), except for:

[IAS 39:47]

- financial liabilities at fair value through profit or loss (FVTPL) (see **section 7.1**);
- financial liabilities that arise when a transfer of a financial asset does not qualify for derecognition or when the continuing involvement approach applies (see **7.2** and **3.4** of **chapter C8**);
- financial guarantee contracts not designated as at FVTPL that are not accounted for under IFRS 4 *Insurance Contracts* (see **2.3.3** of **chapter C1**); and
- commitments to provide a loan at a below-market interest rate (see **3.5** of **chapter C1**).

Financial liabilities that are designated as hedged items are subject to the hedge accounting requirements (see **chapter C9**).

7.1 Financial liabilities at FVTPL

This class of financial liabilities can further be divided into two sub-categories:

- financial liabilities classified as held for trading; and
- financial liabilities designated by the entity as at FVTPL.

7.1.1 Financial liabilities classified as held for trading

A financial liability is held for trading if it falls into one of the following categories:

[IAS 39:9]

- financial liabilities incurred principally for the purpose of repurchasing them in the near term;
- financial liabilities that on initial recognition form part of a portfolio of identified financial instruments that are managed together and for which there is evidence of a recent actual pattern of short-term profit-taking; and
- derivative liabilities, unless the derivative is a financial guarantee contract or it forms part of a designated and effective hedging relationship (see **chapter C9**).

The fact that a liability is used to provide funding for trading activities does not of itself mean that liability is to be classified as held for trading. [IAS 39:AG15] Thus, a borrowing that a bank uses to fund its trading portfolio of debt and equity securities is not automatically classified as held for trading.

The following are examples of liabilities that would be classified as held for trading and thus included in the FVTPL category:

- an interest rate swap that has negative fair value and is not accounted for as a hedging instrument;
- a derivative liability incurred upon writing a foreign exchange option that is not accounted for as a hedging instrument;
- an obligation to deliver financial assets borrowed by a short seller (i.e. an entity that sells financial assets it has borrowed and does not yet own); and
- a quoted debt instrument that the issuer plans to buy back in the near term depending on movements in the debt instrument's fair value, i.e. a financial liability that is incurred with an intention to repurchase it in the near term.

IAS 39:47 states that derivatives (including derivatives embedded in other non-derivative arrangements) are not measured at fair value if they are linked to and must be settled by the delivery of an unquoted equity instrument whose fair value cannot be reliably measured. Such instruments are measured at cost. In the case of non-optional derivatives (e.g. forward contracts), the cost may be nil. In the case of written options, there will normally be a cost which reflects the option's time value.

Because IAS 39 states that subsequent measurement must be at cost, it does not appear to allow an entity to amortise the carrying amount of the liability measured at cost to profit or loss over the period of the derivative. Therefore, to the extent that the derivative liability has a cost, it will be recognised in profit or loss only on derecognition of the derivative liability (i.e. when the instrument is extinguished). This will typically be when the obligation is discharged by transferring the obligation to a third party, settlement by delivering or receiving the unquoted equity instrument, or expiration in the case of an option that matures unexercised.

7.1.2 Financial liabilities designated as at FVTPL

The option to designate a financial liability as at FVTPL is available in limited circumstances notwithstanding the fact that, in the absence of such a choice, the liability would have been classified and measured other than at FVTPL. A financial liability can only be designated as at FVTPL when it meets one of three specified criteria (see **3.1.1** in **chapter C2**). The designation is irrevocable so that, once it has been made, the liability cannot subsequently be reclassified into another category during its life.

The ability to designate a financial liability as at FVTPL is restricted to those financial liabilities that are in the scope of IAS 39 (see **3.1.1.3** in **chapter C2**).

If an entity has designated a financial liability as at FVTPL, it must disclose the amount of change in its fair value that is due to credit risk which can be determined as the amount of change that is not attributable to changes in market conditions that give rise to market risk (i.e. benchmark interest rate). [IFRS 7:10] (See **4.1.3** in **chapter C12**.)

7.2 Financial liabilities arising from continuing involvement accounting and failed derecognition

When an entity transfers an asset but neither retains nor transfers substantially all of the risks and rewards of ownership of a financial asset, and retains control of that asset, the entity continues to recognise the asset to the extent of its continuing involvement (see **3.4** in **chapter C8**). A corresponding liability is also recognised in accordance with IAS 39:31 and measured in such a way that the net carrying amount of the asset and the liability is:

- the amortised cost of the rights and obligations retained, if the asset is measured at amortised cost; or
- the fair value of the rights and obligations retained, if the asset is measured at fair value.

The specific measurement guidance as described above means that a continuing involvement liability cannot be classified as at FVTPL. This is reinforced in IAS 39:35 which states that, if the transferred asset is measured at amortised cost, an entity is prohibited from designating the associated financial liability as at FVTPL.

When an entity transfers an asset but retains substantially all the risks and rewards of ownership of the asset, a financial liability is recognised equal to the consideration received. IAS 39 is not clear whether this 'failed sale' financial liability can be designated as at FVTPL. The recognition of such financial liabilities is common in the case of repurchase obligations ('repos') or in structured transactions where an asset is legally transferred but the risks and rewards related to the transferred asset are passed back to the transferor via guarantees and/or derivatives. IAS 39:47 requires all financial liabilities to be measured at amortised cost with some exceptions that include liabilities measured at fair value through profit or loss (whether held for trading or designated as at FVTPL) and financial liabilities that arise when a transfer of a financial asset does not qualify for derecognition. In the case of a financial liability initially recognised at the fair value of the consideration received on a failed derecognition transaction, the terms of the liability are imputed from the transfer arrangement and the liability is regarded as an in-substance collateralised borrowing. IAS 39:29 states that the transferor should recognise any income on the transferred asset that continues to be recognised in the transferor's statement of financial position "and any expense incurred on the financial liability". Because the Standard is not clear whether 'expense' is limited to interest expense only on the deemed collateralised borrowing or whether it could include fair value gains/losses, it is reasonable that an entity can designate the financial liability as at FVTPL if all the criteria for designation are met.

7.3 Reclassification

Reclassifications of financial liabilities in and out of the FVTPL category are prohibited. The following changes in circumstances are not reclassifications:

[IAS 39:50A]

- a derivative that was previously a designated and effective hedging instrument in a cash flow hedge or net investment hedge no longer qualifies as such; and
- a derivative becomes a designated and effective hedging instrument in a cash flow hedge or net investment hedge.

7.4 Classification of financial liabilities acquired in a business combination

When financial liabilities are assumed in a business combination, those liabilities must be classified in the consolidated financial statements of the acquirer into one of the permitted categories described in **section 7**. It is entirely possible that the classification of a financial liability for these purposes may differ from its classification in the financial statements of the acquiree. For example, the acquirer in its consolidated financial statements may choose to designate a financial liability as at FVTPL at initial recognition even though the acquiree may have classified it otherwise when it first recognised the liability. These differences can arise because 'initial recognition' from the acquirer's perspective is the date of acquisition of the subsidiary and its classification decisions are made at that date.

IFRS 3 *Business Combinations* provides clear guidance stating that, at the acquisition date, the acquirer should make any classifications, designations concerning financial assets acquired or financial liabilities assumed in a business combination in accordance with pertinent conditions (e.g. contractual terms, economic conditions, acquirer's operating or accounting policies) at that date.

8 Reassessing classification

The liability-equity classification made at initial recognition is reconsidered if there are changes to the contractual terms of the instrument. In November 2006, the IFRIC (now the IFRS Interpretations Committee) issued an agenda decision that included a reassessment of liability-equity classification in the case of a change in terms of the instrument that resulted in a financial liability being reclassified to equity. IFRIC 2:5 also states that in determining liability-equity classification, the entity should consider all terms and conditions at the date of classification "but not expected future amendments to those laws, regulations or charter". The IFRIC noted that Example 3 in IFRIC 2 provides an example of reclassification from equity to financial liability following a change in the entity's governing charter.

IAS 32 is less clear in what circumstances it is appropriate to reconsider the liability-equity classification in circumstances where the terms of the instrument do not change. Generally, an entity would not reconsider the classification of the arrangement. However, there are instances where it is acceptable to reconsider classification, and other cases where it is required.

Reconsideration as an accounting policy choice

Where there is a change in the functional currency of the issuer of convertible debt following the initial recognition of the instrument by the issuer IAS 32 is not clear whether the financial liability and equity classification should be reconsidered. This could be the case where the fixed amount of cash nominally received under the conversion option in the convertible debt is in the functional currency of the issuer when the instrument is issued, but following initial recognition the cash is deemed to be in a foreign currency because the functional currency of the issuer changes. Another example is where the fixed amount of cash nominally received under the conversion option in the convertible debt is in a foreign currency when the instrument is issued, but following initial recognition is in the functional currency of the issuer because the functional currency of the issuer changes.

We consider there are two acceptable approaches in these circumstances and an entity should determine an appropriate accounting policy and apply it consistently in accordance with IAS 8 *Accounting Polices, Changes in Accounting Estimates and Errors*.

One approach is that the classification of the convertible debt should not be reconsidered after initial recognition if the terms of the instrument do not change. This view is supported by the fact that IAS 32 only prescribes that an entity should classify the instrument, or its component parts, on initial recognition, and that the Standard is silent regarding any requirement to re-assess the original classification after initial recognition when there is no change in the contractual terms of the instrument.

The second approach is that the classification of the convertible debt should be reconsidered after initial recognition if the terms of the instrument do not change. This view focuses on the requirement under IAS 39:39 that an entity should derecognise a financial liability (or part of a financial liability) when, and only when, it is extinguished (i.e. when the obligation specified in the contract is discharged or cancelled or expires). When a change in functional currency above occurs and, as a consequence, the conversion feature no longer meets the definition of financial liability, reclassification is considered to be appropriate because the obligation has been discharged or cancelled. Further, if the equity component recognised at initial recognition no longer meets the definition of equity following the change in functional currency this supports the view that it should be reclassified as a financial liability.

The accounting policy would equally apply in the case of a standalone derivative over equity shares (rather than a conversion feature within a debt instrument as described above).

Examples of the application of the two approaches are included in **example 8A**.

Example 8A

Convertible debt with change in functional currency

Entity B, a US dollar functional currency entity, issues a Euro denominated convertible bond that is convertible at the holder's choice into a fixed number of equity shares of Entity B. Because the conversion feature is not in the functional currency of Entity B, it will not be settled by the exchange of a fixed amount of functional currency cash for a fixed number of shares and the conversion feature is classified as a derivative financial liability in accordance with IAS 32:11.

One year after the date of issue, Entity B's functional currency changes to the Euro. The terms of the convertible bond do not change. Following the change in functional currency, the conversion feature will be settled by the exchange of a fixed amount of functional currency cash (Euros) for a fixed number of shares.

If Entity B's functional currency had been the Euro at the date of issue of the bond, the instrument would have been classified as a compound instrument under IAS 32:28 because the conversion feature would have met the definition of equity.

Entity B needs to determine an accounting policy in accordance with IAS 8 whether to reclassify its financial liability and equity classification in response to a change in functional currency and apply it consistently.

- Policy one would not reclassify the convertible bond after initial recognition.
- Policy two would be to require reclassification of the convertible bond after initial recognition.

If the fact pattern is reversed so that Entity B's functional currency at the date of issue of the bond is the Euro, the convertible bond is classified as a compound instrument at the date of issue. If Entity B's functional currency subsequently changes to US dollar, the same accounting policy choice is available.

Where the number of equity instruments to be delivered under a standalone derivative (or a derivative embedded in another instrument) is variable for a specified period, but with certainty will be fixed in a following period and that period runs until the end of the instrument's life, IAS 32 is not clear whether the entity is permitted, or is required, to reassess the financial liability and equity classification in the second period when the number of equity shares is known to be fixed. Similar to the change of functional currency described above there is no change in terms of the contract and consequently we consider it is acceptable to determine a consistently applied accounting policy in accordance with IAS 8 as to whether the financial liability and equity classification should be reassessed after initial recognition of the instrument.

Example 8B

Convertible debt with conversion price becoming fixed with passage of time

On 1 January 20X1, Entity Y, a CU functional currency entity, issued CU denominated convertible bonds with a par of CU30 million. The convertible bonds will mature on the third anniversary of the date of issue at par value unless they are converted into ordinary shares prior to maturity. The conversion price is the lower of CU4 and 133 per cent of the issue price of ordinary shares issued for less than CU3 by Entity Y between 1 January 20X1 and 1 January 20X3. In effect, therefore, the conversion price is subject to variability until 1 January 20X3 and becomes fixed from that date onwards.

On initial recognition of the instrument on 1 January 20X1, the equity conversion option will not result in the delivery of a fixed amount of cash for a fixed number of equity shares and, therefore, does not meet the definition of equity. Because the number of shares that may be delivered under the instrument is variable, the instrument is not a compound instrument; it is a hybrid financial instrument wholly in the scope of IAS 39. The equity conversion option is an embedded derivative that is not closely related to the debt host contract. Accordingly, unless the convertible bond is designated as at FVTPL, it will be recognised separately from the debt host contract and measured at FVTPL with the debt host contract measured at amortised cost.

On 1 January 20X3 the number of shares that will be delivered under the conversion option ceases to be variable. Therefore, there is a question as to whether at this point in time Entity Y should reconsider its liability-equity classification of the conversion option. In the absence of specific guidance in IAS 32 and IAS 39 two approaches (as discussed below) are considered acceptable. Whichever approach is selected by Entity Y, it should be applied consistently as an accounting policy choice.

Approach 1 no reconsideration of classification

Entity Y could choose a policy of not reconsidering the classification when the contractual terms of the instrument do not change and there has been no change in the circumstances of the entity. If this accounting policy is adopted, Entity Y should continue to account for the equity conversion option as a non-closely related embedded derivative measured at FVTPL.

Approach 2 reconsideration of classification

Entity Y could choose a policy of reconsidering the classification when the contractual terms of the instrument do not change and there has been no change in the circumstances of the entity. This approach would be justified on the basis that the liability classification of the conversion option at initial recognition was based on the presence of the contractual feature that gave rise to variability in the number of shares. Because this feature expires at 1 January 20X3 purely with the passage of time, although there has been no change to the contractual terms of the instrument, the contractual terms that are effective for the remainder of the life of the conversion option have changed. Under this approach, the change in the effective terms makes it appropriate to reconsider the classification. At 1 January 20X3 the conversion option meets the definition of equity because it will always result, if converted, in the exchange of a fixed number of shares for a fixed amount of functional currency cash. If this accounting policy is adopted, Entity Y will reclassify the embedded derivative financial liability (representing the conversion option) to equity at its fair value with no gain or loss in profit or loss at the date of reclassification.

Reconsideration required

An alternative fact pattern that we consider would require reconsideration of the financial liability and equity classification where the terms have not changed is where the underlying shares to be delivered under a derivative (or derivative embedded in another instrument) cease, or start, to be a non-controlling interest in the consolidated financial statements after the instrument is initially issued. An example would be a convertible bond where the shares to be delivered upon conversion are a fixed number of shares of a subsidiary. In the consolidated financial statements the conversion feature meets the definition of equity, however, if after initial classification of the convertible debt the consolidated entity disposes of its subsidiary, the shares to be delivered under the convertible debt no longer meet the definition of equity as they are no longer shares of a non-controlling interest. It would not be appropriate to regard the conversion feature as meeting the definition of equity when the shares to be delivered under the conversion feature are no longer an equity instrument.

Example 8C

Derivative over interest in a subsidiary with subsequent disposal of the subsidiary

Entity C is a CU functional currency entity. It has a 60 per cent owned subsidiary, Entity D, that currently has 1 million equity shares in issue. Entity C acquires a call option enabling it to purchase a further 100,000 equity shares of Entity D; the option is not exercisable until the end of Year 2. The option can only be exercised through gross physical settlement (i.e. through receipt of a fixed number of shares for a fixed amount of CU cash).

Upon entering into the call option, Entity C determines that the call option meets the definition of equity in the consolidated financial statements because it will be settled exclusively through the exchange of a fixed amount of functional currency cash for a fixed number of equity shares.

Subsequent to entering into the call option but before the option is exercisable at the end of Year 2, Entity C disposes of half of its 60 per cent interest in Entity D such that, following the disposal it has a 30 per cent shareholding and the pre-existing purchased call option over 100,000 shares (equivalent to an additional 10 per cent). Control is lost at the date of disposal, but Entity C retains significant influence over Entity D.

Following the disposal, the purchased call option is no longer considered to be an option over the group's own equity instruments because Entity D is no longer a member of Entity C's group (its status has changed from a subsidiary to an associate). Consequently, the purchased call option no longer meets the definition of equity in Entity C's consolidated financial statements.

At the date of disposal, the purchased call option must be reclassified from equity to a derivative measured at fair value through profit or loss. Any difference between the fair value at the date of reclassification and the original amount recognised in equity is retained in equity because it is analogous to a cancellation of the equity instrument.

Although, in the circumstances described, there has been no change in the terms of the purchased call option, this fact cannot be used as a basis for not reclassifying the option (unlike in circumstances such as those discussed in **example 8A** (change of functional currency) and **example 8B** (conversion price becoming fixed with the passage of time) when the transaction/event only affects whether the 'fixed for fixed' criterion is met). This is because the disposal has affected the 'nature' of the option such that it is no longer an option over the entity's own shares.

If Entity C's interest in Entity D were originally an investment in an associate, the purchased call option would have not met the definition of equity at initial recognition and would have been measured at fair value through profit or loss.

If Entity C subsequently acquired a further 30 per cent interest in Entity D (independent of the call option), and thus acquired control of Entity D, the purchased call option would at that point meet the definition of equity and would be reclassified to equity at its fair value at the date of acquisition.

9 Future developments

9.1 Own credit risk

In October 2010, the IASB issued amendments to IFRS 9, *Financial instruments*, which changed the presentation requirements of financial liabilities designated as at FVTPL. These amendments are also included in the finalised completed version of IFRS 9 issued in July 2014. The amendments require that gains or losses on a financial liability, other than a loan commitment or financial guarantee contract, designated as at FVTPL shall be presented as follows:

[IFRS 9:5.7.7 & 8]

(a) the amount of change in the fair value of the financial liability that is attributable to changes in the credit risk of that liability shall be presented in other comprehensive income, and

(b) the remaining amount of change in the fair value of the liability shall be presented in profit or loss unless the treatment of the effects of changes in the liability's credit risk described in (a) would create or enlarge an accounting mismatch in profit or loss (in which case all gains or losses are recognised in profit or loss).

All gains and losses on loan commitments and financial guarantee contracts that are designated as at FVTPL are recognised in profit or loss. [IFRS 9:5.7.9]

The amendments also provide guidance on distinguishing credit risk from asset-performance risk. This is particularly relevant in determining the component of the fair value change attributable to changes in credit risk for certain special purpose entities.

The amendment to IFRS 9 does not change the accounting for financial liabilities for entities that have not adopted IFRS 9 and therefore continue to apply IAS 39 in classifying and measuring financial liabilities.

IFRS 9 is effective for accounting periods beginning on or after 1 January 2018 with early application permitted. Instead of early adopting the whole Standard, IFRS 9:7.1.2 permits early adoption of the requirements for the presentation of gains and losses on financial liabilities designated as at FVTPL only.

The detailed requirements of IFRS 9 are contained in *iGAAP 2016 Financial Instruments: IFRS 9 and related Standards – Volume B.*

9.2 Financial instruments with the characteristics of equity

In response to the views received on the 2011 Agenda Consultation the IASB agreed in May 2012 to initiate a research programme that would include financial instruments with the characteristics of equity. At the date of writing the research project was in the development stage which means that the IASB has completed its assessment work, has begun its discussions, and the next step is likely to be the issuance of a discussion paper.

C4 Derivatives

Contents

1 Introduction

IAS 39 *Financial Instruments: Recognition and Measurement* requires that all derivatives are accounted for in the statement of financial position at fair value, irrespective of whether they are used as part of a hedging relationship. Changes in fair value are recognised in profit or loss unless the contract is designated in an effective hedging relationship under which some or all of the derivative gains and losses are required to be presented in other comprehensive income (e.g. in a cash flow hedge or a hedge of a net investment in a foreign operation) (see **chapters C9** and **C10** on hedge accounting).

Because the definition of a derivative is broad (see **section 2**), many contracts are likely to be caught and, therefore, will have to be accounted for at fair value. For example, certain contracts to buy or sell non-financial items fall within the scope of IAS 39 and meet the definition of a derivative (see **2.5** in **chapter C1**).

A fixed price commitment to buy or sell a financial instrument at a future date meets the definition of a derivative financial instrument. However, as a practical expedient, these are not accounted for as derivatives as at FVTPL if the commitment has a short duration accepted by market convention. Such commitments are referred to as 'regular way' purchases or sales. Regular way contracts are subject to special accounting rules which are discussed in **2.2** in **chapter C8**.

2 Definition of a derivative

IAS 39 defines a derivative as a financial instrument or other contract within the scope of the Standard with all three of the following characteristics:

[IAS 39:9]

- its value changes in response to the change in a specified interest rate, financial instrument price, commodity price, foreign exchange rate, index of prices or rates, credit rating or credit index, or other variable, provided in the case of a non-financial variable that the variable is not specific to a party to the contract (sometimes called the 'underlying');
- it requires no initial net investment or an initial net investment that is smaller than would be required for other types of contracts that would be expected to have a similar response to changes in market factors; and
- it is settled at a future date.

The definition of a derivative is important because it is used in determining the classification and measurement of financial instruments. Those instruments that meet the definition of a derivative are required to be classified as at FVTPL unless the instrument is designated and is highly effective as a hedging instrument. The definition of a derivative is also relevant in accounting for embedded derivatives in contractual arrangements and hedge accounting, because financial assets and liabilities are only permitted to be designated as hedging instruments in hedging risks other than foreign currency risk if they meet the definition of a derivative.

2.1 Underlying

An underlying is a variable that, along with either a notional amount or a payment provision, determines the settlement amount of a derivative.

Examples of underlyings include:

- a security price or security price index;
- a commodity price or commodity price index;
- an interest rate or interest rate index;
- a credit rating or credit index;
- a foreign exchange rate or foreign exchange rate index;
- an insurance index or catastrophe loss index;
- a climatic or geological condition (e.g. temperature, earthquake severity or rainfall), another physical variable, or a related index; or
- another variable (e.g. volume of sales).

The value or cash flows of all assets, liabilities, and purchase and sale commitments change in response to changes in the market factors in which they are founded. There is nothing unique in this regard about derivatives, except that the market factor is referred to as an index, a variable or an underlying and, in many instances, the referenced underlying is not delivered at settlement but is used as a basis for computing a settlement amount, usually in cash.

Prior to the issue of IFRS 4 *Insurance Contracts*, IAS 39 scoped out derivatives when the variable is based on climatic, geological and other physical variables. However, when IFRS 4 was issued, IAS 39 was amended so that these contracts are now within its scope unless they meet the definition of an insurance contract (see **2.3** in **chapter C1**). If an insurance contract contains an embedded derivative that needs to be separately accounted for, then it is only the embedded derivative part of the insurance contract that will be accounted for as a derivative in accordance with IAS 39. Embedded derivatives are considered in **chapter C5**.

Additionally, a derivative where the underlying is a specific commodity (e.g. oil) may be scoped out of IAS 39 if the contract is considered a normal purchase, sale or usage requirement contract (see **2.5** in **chapter C1**). Whether the instrument is scoped in or out of IAS 39 is dependent on the entity's normal business requirements as well as the settlement terms of the instrument, the entity's past practice, and whether the instrument is a written option and the underlying is readily convertible to cash.

The definition of a derivative was amended by the IASB when it issued IFRS 4 *Insurance Contracts* to scope out contracts over non-financial variables that are specific to a party to the contract. This amendment was required to ensure that insurance risk was scoped out of IAS 39 and instead accounted for in accordance with IFRS 4.

Yet since then there have been differing views as to whether the term 'non-financial variable specific to a party to the contract' is limited to scoping just insurance contracts or is broader than that.

In October 2007, the IASB issued an exposure draft, *Improvements to International Financial Reporting Standards*, which proposed to amend IAS 39's definition of a derivative by deleting the term 'non-financial variable specific to a party to the contract', so that contracts linked to non-financial variables specific to a party to a contract would be within the scope of the definition. In its Basis for Conclusions on those proposed amendments, the IASB observed that the phrase highlighted above was introduced when IFRS 4 was issued "to exclude from the scope of IAS 39 contracts within the scope of IFRS 4".

Following feedback on the exposure draft, in October 2008, the IASB tentatively decided not to proceed with the amendment, noting that the Board will consider the issue in a future project. Yet, in issuing IFRS 9 in 2009 and 2010, the IASB did not specifically consider the issue and carried forward the existing definition in IAS 39.

In September 2012, the IFRS Interpretations Committee considered various accounting questions in respect of the restructuring of Greek Government Bonds. As part of the restructuring the holders of these bonds received a security issued by the Hellenic Republic for which the return was indexed to the country's GDP. The Committee noted that the fact pattern submitted was based on the assumption that indexation to the issuer's GDP is a non-financial variable specific to a party to the contract. IFRIC Update September 2012 states:

> "The Interpretations Committee noted that the question of what constitutes an underlying that is a non-financial variable specific to a party to the contract had been considered on several previous occasions by itself and by the IASB. Consequently, the Interpretations Committee was concerned that it would not be able to resolve the issue efficiently within the confines of existing IFRSs and the Conceptual Framework and the demands of the Interpretation process and that it was not likely that it would be able to reach a consensus on the issue on a timely basis. The Interpretations Committee

therefore considered that the question of whether the assumption in the submission is appropriate would remain open."

IAS 39 nor any other IFRS provides a clear answer as to whether the term 'non-financial variable specific to a party to the contract' in the definition of a derivative is limited to the scoping out of insurance contracts or is broader. Both the IASB and the IFRS Interpretations Committee have considered this question in the past, but to date no clarifying guidance has been issued.

Given the lack of specific guidance on this topic and the IFRS Interpretations Committee's decision to leave open the assumption made in the submission received on Greek Government Bonds, it is acceptable to adopt either of the approaches set out below as an accounting policy choice. In developing the accounting policy, entities may need to take into consideration specific requirements by local regulators, if any.

Accounting policy one

The inclusion of the term 'non-financial variable specific to a party to the contract' is limited to excluding insurance contracts from the definition of a derivative. Therefore, unless a contract meets the definition of an insurance contract in IFRS 4, the contract is not scoped out of the definition of a derivative if the contract is either fully (or partly, in the case of an embedded derivative) in the scope of IAS 39.

This approach is consistent with the IASB's tentative view included in the 2007 exposure draft (see above). It is also supported by:

- IAS 39:IG.A.2 *Option to put a non-financial asset where an option to put an office building* that can be either physically settled or net cash settled is a derivative,
- IAS 39:IG.B8 *Definition of a derivative: foreign currency contract based on sales volume* where a contract based on foreign currency and sales volume is a derivative.

Accounting policy two

The inclusion of the term 'non-financial variable specific to a party to the contract' is broader than simply excluding insurance contracts from the definition of a derivative. Therefore, a contract (other than an insurance contract) that is either fully or partly in the scope of IAS 39 may have a non-financial variable that is specific to a party to the contract and, consequently, it may be excluded from the definition of a derivative.

This approach, in line with the agenda decision noted in the September 2012 IFRIC Update, recognises that because the IASB has not fully resolved this question different views could validly be held.

If such an approach is applied, it is then necessary to assess what is 'specific to a party' and which variables are considered 'non-financial' (as these terms are not defined by IFRSs).

For an underlying to be specific to a party to the contract the underlying must be unique to the party. For example, an entity's real estate is non-financial that is specific to the party to the contract. However, commodities may not be specific to the party when they are readily tradable and are homogenous. An entity's inventory of gold may not be specific to the party to the contract as it is not distinguishable from a different party holding the same commodity.

For some variables the determination of non-financial may be relatively straightforward when the variable has no financial element to it (for example, the tonnage of ore extracted from a mine or the number of units sold by a motor vehicle manufacturer). It is less straightforward whether a variable based on an amount derived from the financial statements of a party to the contract (for example, revenue, EBITDA or net assets) is 'non-financial'. Again, the views of local regulators may need to be considered in developing a policy.

2.2 Notional amounts and payment provisions

While neither a notional amount nor a payment provision is an essential characteristic of a derivative instrument, derivative instruments usually contain a notional amount or a payment provision each of which may interact with the underlying to determine the settlement amount of the derivative instrument. A notional is often an amount of currency, a number of shares, a number of units of weight or volume or other units specified in the contract. A payment provision is a provision which requires a fixed payment or payment of an amount that can change (but not proportionally to a change in the underlying) as a result of some future event that is unrelated to a notional amount.

Example 2.2A

Payment provision based on interest rates

Entity ABC receives CU200 to enter into a contract that requires it to pay CU500 if 6-month LIBOR increases by 75 basis points over the next six months. Even though this contract does not have a notional amount, it contains a payment provision that does not move proportionally with the underlying.

Example 2.2B

Payment provision based on share price

Entity XYZ enters into a contract that requires it to pay CU10 million if Entity ABC's share price increases by CU5 per share during a 6-month period; conversely Entity XYZ will receive CU10 million if Entity ABC's share price decreases by CU5 per share during the same six-month period.

In this example, the underlying is the price of Entity ABC's shares. There is no notional amount to determine the settlement amount. Instead, there is a payment provision that does not move proportionally with the underlying. The absence of a notional amount does not preclude the instrument from meeting the definition of a derivative because there is a payment provision.

It is sometimes the case that a contract has neither a notional amount nor a fixed payment provision. In addition, a contract may have multiple underlyings.

Example 2.2C

Foreign currency forward contract linked to sales

Entity X, a Euro functional currency entity, sells products in Switzerland. The sales are denominated in Swiss francs. Entity X enters into a contract with an investment bank to convert Swiss francs to Euros at a fixed exchange rate. The contract requires Entity X to remit Swiss francs based on its sales volume in Switzerland in exchange for Euros at a fixed exchange rate of 1.60.

The contract with the bank has two underlyings (sales volume and the Euro/ Swiss franc exchange rate). The contract does not have a specified notional amount or a fixed payment provision, but still meets the definition of a derivative.

2.3 Interaction of notional amounts with the underlying

The settlement amount of a derivative instrument with a notional amount is determined by the interaction of that notional amount with the underlying. The interaction may be simple multiplication, or it may involve a formula with leverage factors or other constants.

Example 2.3

Interest rate swap

XYZ enters into an interest rate swap that requires XYZ to pay a fixed rate of interest and receive a variable rate of interest. The fixed interest rate amount is 7.5 per cent, while the variable interest rate amount is 3-month LIBOR, reset on a quarterly basis. The notional amount of the swap is CU100 million.

The underlying is an interest rate index, 3-month LIBOR. Net regular settlements are calculated by applying the difference between 7.5 per cent and 3-month LIBOR to the notional amount of CU100 million.

2.4 Initial net investment

The second part of the definition of a derivative is that there is either no initial net investment, or that any initial investment is smaller than would be required for other contracts that are expected to have a similar response to changes in market factors. This is a comparative measure, and excludes any margin accounts (which are instead treated as collateral). Various examples are set out in the following sections.

2.4.1 Interest rate swaps

Example 2.4.1

Interest rate swap

Entity B enters into a contract with a counterparty that requires it to pay a LIBOR-based variable rate of interest, and receive a fixed rate of 8 per cent. The contract is an interest rate swap with a notional amount of ¥10 billion. Entity B did not pay or receive cash at inception (i.e. the contract is at market at inception) and, therefore, does not require an initial net investment by either party.

In some instances, the terms of the interest rate swap may be favourable or unfavourable and may require one of the parties to make an up-front initial investment in the contract. If the initial investment represents a premium or discount for market conditions, the initial net investment would normally still be smaller than the notional amount on the debt instrument from which the interest rate cash flows are derived, and so would satisfy the initial net investment criterion of a derivative.

2.4.1.1 Interest rate swap with fixed leg prepaid

Example 2.4.1.1

Prepaid fixed leg

Entity X enters into an 8-year pay fixed at 7 per cent, receive LIBOR interest rate swap on CU100 million. It prepays the fixed leg at inception. The amount it pays is calculated as CU7 million (CU100 million x 7 per cent) for eight years, discounted at market rates.

This initial payment is significantly less than the amount Entity X would have to pay to acquire an instrument that would have a similar response to changes in market factors. Entity X would need to acquire CU100 million debt with a LIBOR return in order to replicate the return on the floating rate leg of the swap.

Therefore, the swap with a prepaid fixed leg will still meet the definition of a derivative.

If the fixed rate payment obligation on the interest rate swap is prepaid after initial recognition, the payment would be considered termination of the old swap and an origination of a new instrument that would need to be classified for the first time. [IAS 39:IG.B.4]

2.4.1.2 Interest rate swap with floating leg prepaid

Example 2.4.1.2

Prepaid floating leg

Entity A enters into a 6-year pay LIBOR, receive fixed 5 per cent interest rate swap on CU100 million. It prepays the variable leg at inception. The cash inflows that the entity continues to receive are akin to those of a financial instrument with a fixed annuity of 5 per cent per year for the next six years.

Because the amount prepaid will be about the same as what would have been paid to purchase a fixed annuity instrument paying 5 per cent over the next six years, the initial net investment test is failed. The contract will not be accounted for as a derivative, but instead as a loan made by Entity A. [IAS 39:IG.B.5]

2.4.2 Options

For an option, the premium paid could be significant. However, it is likely to be smaller than the amount that would be required to buy an instrument with a similar response to changes in market factors, i.e. the underlying instrument to which the option relates.

Example 2.4.2A

Deep in the money option (1)

Entity A purchases, for CU1.1 million, an option to buy 80,000 shares in Entity B at CU75 per share in three months' time. When Entity A purchases the option, Entity B's shares are trading at CU70 per share. The cost of the option, CU1.1 million, is less than what it would cost to buy 80,000 shares in Entity B, so it meets this part of the definition. This will even be the case for many deep in the money options, as demonstrated below.

Example 2.4.2B

Deep in the money option (2)

Entity XYZ purchases a deep in the money call option on Entity ABC shares. Entity ABC's share price is €100 per share. The option is an American option with a 180-day maturity. The option has a strike price of €10 per share and Entity XYZ pays a premium of €91. The initial investment in the option of €91 is less than the notional amount applied to the underlying, i.e. €100 (the notional amount is one share and the underlying is €100 per share).

Although the option has a significant initial net investment, it is smaller than the investment that would be required for other types of contracts that would be expected to have a similar response to changes in market factors. The invested amount of €91 does not approximate the notional amount applied to the underlying (€100) and, therefore, the option meets the initial net investment criterion for a derivative instrument.

2.4.3 Currency swap

Currency swaps typically require an initial exchange of currencies. These swaps will still satisfy the initial net investment criterion because the exchange is of amounts with an equal fair value, so that on a net basis the fair value at inception is zero.

Example 2.4.3

Currency swap

Entity X enters into a 3-year currency swap with Bank Z. At inception, when the Sterling/Euro exchange rate is 1.5, the swap results in Entity X paying Bank Z £100 million and Bank Z paying Entity X €150 million. Although there has been an exchange of cash, the amounts exchanged are of equal fair value.

2.4.4 Prepaid forward contract

Example 2.4.4

Prepaid forward contract

Entity X enters into a forward contract to purchase one million ordinary shares in Entity T in one year. The current market price of Entity T's shares is €50 per share, and the 1-year forward price is €55 per share. Entity X prepays the forward contract at inception with a €50 million payment.

The initial net investment approximates the investment that would be required for other types of contracts that would be expected to have a similar response to changes in market factors because one million of Entity T's shares could be purchased at inception for the same price of €50 million. Accordingly, the prepaid forward contract does not meet the initial net investment criterion for a derivative instrument. [IAS 39:IG.B.9]

2.4.5 Offsetting loans

Two or more non-derivative contracts should be considered together when the substance of the aggregate position is that of a derivative. IAS 39:IG.B.6 states that indicators of such a situation are when the contracts are:

- entered into at the same time and in contemplation of each other;
- have the same counterparty;
- relate to the same risk; and
- there is no apparent economic need or substantive business purpose for structuring the transactions separately that could not also have been accomplished in a single transaction.

Example 2.4.5

Offsetting loans

Entity A makes a 5-year fixed rate loan to Entity B on market terms. Simultaneously, Entity B makes a 5-year variable rate loan to Entity A on market terms over the same notional amount. The combination of these two loans is similar in effect to an interest rate swap. Even if amounts are exchanged at inception of the two loans, the net fair value of the amounts exchanged is zero. Therefore, the loans should be considered together and the entire arrangement accounted for as a derivative.

2.5 Future settlement

The third part of the definition of a derivative is that it is settled at a future date. Settlement can occur in different ways, either gross or net [IAS 39:IG.B.3], and does not just mean exchange of cash. For example, it may be expected that an out of the money option will not be exercised. However, expiry of the contract is a form of settlement, even if at maturity of the instrument no cash or underlying changes hands. [IAS 39:IG.B.7]

3 Scoped-in contracts

Certain contracts to buy or sell non-financial items are within the scope of IAS 39 (see **2.5** in **chapter C1**). If a contract to buy or sell a non-financial item is within the scope of IAS 39 and meets the definition of a derivative, it will be recognised at fair value.

Example 3

Contract over a non-financial item

Entity A enters into a futures contract to purchase 1,000 bushels of corn for CU1 per bushel in three months. No cash is paid at inception. Assuming the contract is within the scope of IAS 39 (i.e. because it is not entered into for the purpose of the receipt of the corn bushels), the contract meets the definition of a derivative.

It has an underlying (the price of corn bushels), there is no initial investment, and the contract will be settled in the future. The contract must be recognised in

Entity A's statement of financial position at fair value, with changes in fair value recognised in profit or loss unless the contract qualifies as a hedging instrument in an effective hedge relationship.

4 Examples of contracts that meet the definition of a derivative

Some common examples of derivatives are set out in the following table.

Contract	Notional amount/ payment provision	Underlying	Initial investment	Future settlement
A futures contract to buy 1,000 barrels of crude oil at $60 a barrel in one month and the contract is not entered into for the physical delivery of oil for the entity's normal business usage requirements	1,000 barrels of crude oil	Price of oil barrels	$0	Yes – one month
A forward to buy $500 for £300 in one year	$500 (or £300)	£/$ exchange rate	£0	Yes – one year
An option to buy 80,000 shares in Entity B at CU75 per share in one month. The option costs CU1.1 million	80,000 shares	Entity B's share price	CU1.1 million	Yes – one month
A pay LIBOR + 25 basis points, receive fixed 5 per cent interest rate swap over CU100 million, settled quarterly	CU100 million	LIBOR	CU0	Yes – quarterly
A pay floating £ on £100 million, receive floating US$ on $170 million currency swap, settled annually	£100 million or $170 million	£/$ exchange rate	£0	Yes – annually
A contract to receive CU10 million if Entity A's share price increases by CU5 per share at the end of six months. The initial investment is CU1 million.	Payment provision	Entity A's share price	CU1 million	Yes – six months

Contract	**Notional amount/ payment provision**	**Underlying**	**Initial investment**	**Future settlement**
A pay variable Euro amount based on the entity's sales, receive £ at a fixed exchange rate of €1.5:£1 based on the entity's sales, settled monthly	Variable notional	€/£ exchange rate and sales volume	£0	Yes – monthly
A 5-year interest rate cap over CU100 million. The cap will pay if LIBOR increases beyond 8 per cent. The premium paid to enter into the cap is CU1 million.	CU100 million	LIBOR	CU1 million	Yes – if, during the 5-year period, LIBOR exceeds 8 per cent.

The definition of a derivative is very broad and, therefore, can capture many contractual arrangements that traditionally would not be considered derivatives. One example is bets in the gaming industry. A bookmaker will take a bet from a customer on the outcome of a specified event (e.g. a horse race, general election or football match) in cash for stated or variable odds. When the event occurs, depending on the outcome, the bookmaker will pay any winnings to the customer. The contract for the bet is no different from a derivative contract without a notional amount and with a payment provision. The bookmaker has written an option to the customer, where the bookmaker will receive an up-front premium in return for bearing potential downside risk should the uncertain event occur.

When the customer does not 'fix' the odds (i.e. has variable odds), the derivative will be far less sensitive to changes in the probability of the uncertain event occurring and, therefore, the derivative will be far less sensitive to changes in market prices. However, when the holder of the bet 'fixes' the odds, the fair value of the bet will change with changes in the probability of the uncertain event occurring.

The bookmaker will take bets on many different outcomes for one event and expects to make a profit irrespective of that event's outcome. If a bookmaker has taken too many bets from customers on one outcome, it may 'lay off' bets with another bookmaker (i.e. it enters into an offsetting bet to lay off the risk). This is a form of economic hedging. The bookmaker cannot apply hedge accounting because a derivative is not a qualifying hedged item (see **3.6** in **chapter C9**). As such, in accordance with IAS 39, bookmakers should recognise all bets, whether written or purchased, as derivative assets and liabilities measured at fair value through profit or loss.

In May 2007, the IFRIC (now the IFRS Interpretations Committee) issued a rejection notice on gaming transactions stating that an unsettled wager is likely to meet the definition of a derivative and will therefore be accounted for under IAS 39. The IFRIC recognised that, in other situations, a gaming institution does not take a position against a customer but instead provides services to manage the organisation of games between two or more gaming parties. In these circumstances, the gaming institution earns a commission regardless of the outcome of the wager and, therefore, it is likely that the commission would meet the definition of revenue and would be recognised when the conditions in IAS 18 *Revenue* (now IFRS 15 *Revenue from Contracts with Customers*) were met.

5 Presentation of derivatives

5.1 Current versus non-current

Where assets and liabilities are not presented in the statement of financial position in order of liquidity, derivatives will need to be presented as current and non-current assets, and current and non-current liabilities in accordance with IAS 1 *Presentation of Financial Statements*.

A derivative that has a maturity of less than 12 months from the end of the reporting period or has a maturity greater than 12 months but is expected to be settled within 12 months should be presented as a current asset or liability in the statement of financial position. A derivative that has a maturity of more than 12 months from the end of the reporting period and is not intended to be settled within 12 months will be presented as a non-current asset or liability.

Prior to the issue of *Improvements to IFRSs* in May 2008, there was ambiguity as to whether derivatives with a maturity greater than 12 months that are not intended to be settled within 12 months and were not part of a designated and effective hedge accounting relationship could be presented as non-current because these instruments also met the definition of held for trading in IAS 39:9. An amendment to IAS 1 included as part of *Improvements to IFRSs* clarified that, in such instances, the derivatives should be presented as non-current because the derivative is not held primarily for trading purposes.

For guidance on the presentation of embedded derivatives see **section 13** of **chapter C5**.

5.2 Presentation in profit or loss

5.2.1 Fair value gains and losses on derivatives in hedge accounting relationships

IAS 39 provides limited guidance on the appropriate presentation in profit or loss of gains and losses on derivatives in highly effective hedge accounting relationships. However, an analogy can be drawn with the principle in IAS 39:IG.G.2 that describes how cash flows arising from hedging instruments should be classified in statements of cash flows. The implementation guidance states that cash flows arising from hedging instruments are classified as operating, investing or financing activities on the basis of the classification of the cash flows arising from the hedged item. Therefore, it appears appropriate that gains and losses in highly effective hedge accounting relationships are presented in the same line in the statement of comprehensive income as the hedged item affects profit or loss. If gains and losses are material, separate presentation of those gains and losses in profit or loss would be required. An item that is not sufficiently material to warrant separate presentation on the face of the statement of comprehensive income may nevertheless be sufficiently material for it to be presented separately in the notes. [IAS 1:30]

5.2.2 Fair value gains and losses on derivatives that are economic hedges

IAS 39 requires gains and losses on derivatives to be reported in profit or loss when hedge accounting is not applied. However, the Standard does not specify where such gains and losses would be presented within profit or loss.

Example 5.2.2

Presentation of non-hedge accounting derivative

Entity A enters into a derivative contract (forward contract) to hedge a foreign currency cash flow under a highly probable forecast revenue stream. The entity does not apply hedge accounting.

Presentation of the gains and losses on the derivative within revenue or elsewhere in operating profit is not precluded, provided that the chosen presentation is applied consistently from period to period to all similar items and follows the nature of the transaction to which it is linked. The policy adopted should be disclosed in the financial statements.

C5 Embedded derivatives

Contents

1 Introduction

The definition of an embedded derivative and the principle of separation of embedded derivatives are relatively simple, but the application is complicated because most of the guidance in IAS 39 is provided by means of examples. Furthermore, the scope is wide because an entity will need to consider whether embedded derivatives may reside in contracts other than financial instruments. Embedded derivatives can be found in any contract, such as a lease, an insurance contract, or a sale or a purchase contract.

The challenge extends beyond searching for all embedded derivatives. Once an embedded derivative has been found, it must then be determined whether the embedded derivative needs to be separately accounted for under IAS 39. Not all embedded derivatives are required to be separated out from the host contract in which they reside.

Embedded derivatives that are required to be separated are accounted for in the same way as stand-alone derivatives, i.e. at fair value with gains and losses recognised in profit or loss at each measurement date, unless the embedded derivative qualifies as an effective hedging instrument in a cash flow or a net investment hedge of a foreign operation.

Entities are required to assess *all* contractual arrangements for embedded derivatives, whether or not those contractual arrangements are in the scope of IAS 39.

2 Definitions

IAS 39 defines an embedded derivative as a component of a hybrid (combined) instrument that also includes a non-derivative host contract – with the effect that some of the cash flows of the combined instrument vary in a way similar to a stand-alone derivative. An embedded derivative causes some or all of the cash flows that otherwise would be required by the contract to be modified according to a specified interest rate, financial instrument price, commodity price, foreign exchange rate, index of prices or rates or other variable (provided in the case of a non-financial variable that the variable is not specific to a party to the contract, see **2.1** in **chapter C4**). [IAS 39:10]

The hybrid contract is the entire contract, within which there is an embedded derivative. The host contract is the main body of the contract, excluding the embedded derivative. The diagram and examples below illustrate the application of these terms.

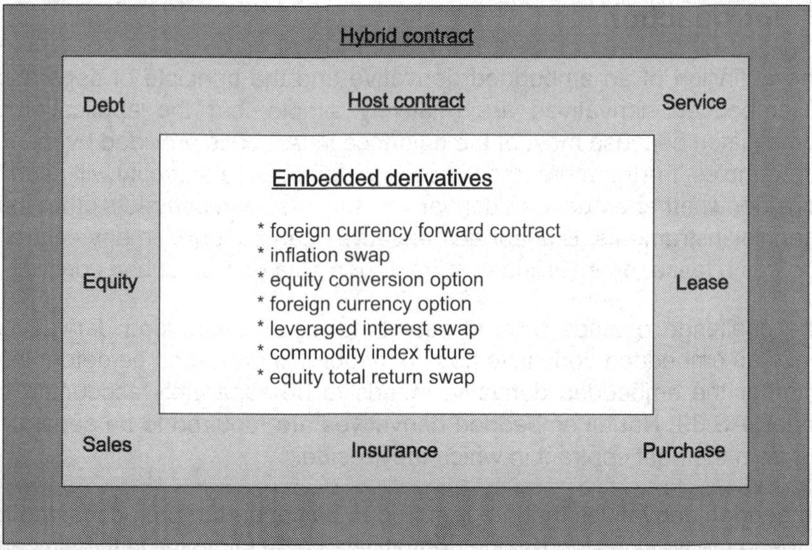

Example 2A

Debt host contract

Entity X issues a bond that is convertible into ordinary shares of Entity Y. The hybrid contract is the convertible bond; the host contract is the bond liability, and the embedded derivative is the conversion option.

Example 2B

Lease host contract

Entity A enters into a lease with an inflation factor, such that each year rentals are adjusted for changes in a retail price index. The hybrid contract is the entire lease; the host is the lease contract, and the embedded derivative is the adjustment to the retail price index.

Example 2C

Executory host contract

Entity T, a UK entity whose functional currency is Sterling, enters into a contract to sell a non-financial item in US dollars. The hybrid contract is the entire sales contract which will be settled in US dollars; the host contract is the Sterling sales contract; the embedded derivative is the foreign exchange Sterling/US dollar forward contract.

A derivative that is attached to a financial instrument but is contractually transferable independently of that instrument, or has a different counterparty from that instrument, is not an embedded derivative but a separate financial instrument. [IAS 39:10]

Example 2D

Contractually separate derivative

Entity A issues floating rate debt. To protect itself against rising interest rates, it purchases an interest rate cap, capping interest payable at 8 per cent. The cap is contractually separate from the debt, so that it is not an embedded derivative but a free-standing derivative.

Entity A could have instead issued floating rate debt, where the debt instrument itself is capped such that, once interest rates rise above 8 per cent, interest payable is restricted to 8 per cent until rates fall below that level. In this case, there is an embedded derivative within the debt (i.e. the interest rate cap), and this cap would need to be assessed to see if it should be separately accounted for.

3 Separation conditions

Not all embedded derivatives should be separated from their host contracts. An embedded derivative is separated from its host contract and accounted for separately as a stand-alone derivative when all of the following criteria are met:

[IAS 39:11]

(a) the economic characteristics and risks of the embedded derivative are not closely related to the economic risks and characteristics of the host contract;

(b) a separate instrument with the same terms as the embedded derivative would meet the definition of a derivative; and

(c) the hybrid instrument is not measured at fair value with changes in fair value recognised in profit or loss (i.e. a derivative that is embedded in a financial liability at fair value through profit or loss is not separated).

Condition (b) above means that an embedded feature should only be separated from its host contract if it meets the definition of a derivative, i.e.:

- it has an underlying;
- it involves no initial net investment (or an initial net investment that is smaller than would be required for other types of contracts that would be expected to have a similar response to changes in market factors); and
- it is settled at a future date.

See **chapter C4** for a detailed discussion on the definition of a derivative.

Example 3A

No underlying

A lease contract contains a provision that rentals increase by CU100 each year. The price adjustment feature does not meet the definition of a derivative on a stand-alone basis because its value does not change in response to changes of some 'underlying'; there is no underlying.

The condition in IAS 39:11(c) (see above) means that any financial asset or financial liability that is held at fair value with changes in fair value recognised through profit or loss should not be assessed to see if it contains any embedded derivatives. Any embedded derivative that is not closely related to its host and meets definition of a derivative will be accounted for as if it were a stand-alone derivative – i.e. measured at fair value, with changes in fair value recognised in profit or loss. If the entire contract is currently accounted for at fair value, the embedded derivative is automatically accounted for at fair value and, therefore, it is not required to be separated.

An entity can elect to designate a hybrid instrument in the scope of IAS 39 as at FVTPL at initial recognition even though the instrument would not meet the definition of held for trading (see **3.1** in **chapter C2**). This option is available when the financial instrument is a hybrid contract containing one or more embedded derivatives, unless;

[IAS 39:11A]

(a) the embedded derivative does not significantly modify the cash flows that otherwise would be required by the contract; or

(b) it is clear with little or no analysis when a similar hybrid instrument is first considered that separation of the embedded derivative is prohibited, as in the case of a prepayment option embedded in a loan that permits the holder to prepay the loan for approximately its amortised cost (see **7.1**).

Designating a hybrid instrument as at FVTPL may provide benefit to entities with more complex instruments where the search for and analysis of embedded derivatives significantly increases the cost of compliance with IAS 39. This approach will also benefit entities that issue structured products or acquire structured products (e.g. equity-linked notes or callable range-accrual notes) which may contain more than one embedded derivative that is not closely related to the host contract. For issuers of these instruments, who normally invest in derivatives as an economic hedge of the issued notes, fair valuing the hybrid instrument reduces the accounting mismatch that would have resulted had the host contract been measured at amortised cost. Furthermore, for these more complex instruments, the fair value of the combined contract may be significantly easier to measure and, therefore, provide more reliable information than the fair value of only those embedded derivatives that are required to be separated. [IAS 39:BC77A - 78]

Example 3B

FVTPL measurement of a contract over a non-financial item

An entity enters into a forward contract to purchase wheat. The contract meets the definition of a derivative, but does not meet the 'expected purchase, sale or usage requirements' scope exemption because the entity has a history of net cash settling similar contracts (see **2.5** in **chapter C1**). Embedded in the forward contract is a price adjustment feature that if the retail price index increases by 3 per cent during the term of the contract, the contracted price will be doubled.

Because the contract is within the scope of IAS 39 and meets the definition of a derivative, it will be accounted for at FVTPL. The embedded derivative will automatically be accounted for at FVTPL and, therefore, no further consideration of embedded derivatives is necessary.

The condition in IAS 39:11(a) (see above) is the most difficult of the three bifurcation criteria to assess because there is no definition of 'closely related'. Rather than define 'closely related', the appendix to IAS 39 provides two illustrative lists: one of examples of embedded derivatives that are closely related to their hosts and the other of examples of embedded derivatives that are not closely related to their hosts.

When an embedded derivative is not included in one of these two lists, a significant degree of judgement will be required and conclusions may need to be drawn by analogy to the specific examples given. Ultimately, the conclusion reached should be consistent with the underlying principle that an embedded derivative should be separated from its host contract when its economic characteristics and risks differ from those of the host contract.

In summary, the following decision tree can be used to determine whether an embedded derivative needs to be separated from its host contract.

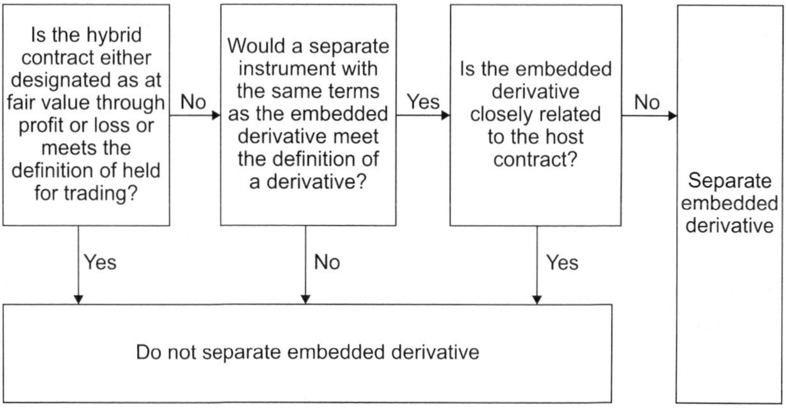

If it is determined that an embedded derivative is closely related to the host contract, it should not be separated from the host contract because the entire hybrid contract is accounted for in accordance with the relevant Standard that deals with the host contract. For example, if an embedded derivative in a lease contract is deemed to be closely related to the lease host, then the entire contract is accounted for in accordance with IAS 17 *Leases*.

If an identified embedded derivative is not closely related to the host contract, then it must be separately accounted for as if it were a free-standing derivative. This is considered further in **section 12**.

IFRIC Interpretation 9 *Reassessment of Embedded Derivatives* provides guidance on whether an entity should assess whether embedded derivatives are closely related at the time the entity first becomes a party to the contract or on an ongoing basis. The Interpretation clarifies the following.

- An entity is generally prohibited from reassessing its conclusion as to whether an embedded derivative needs to be separated from the hybrid contract after it is initially recognised.
- An entity is required to revisit its assessment if there is a change in the terms of the contract that significantly modifies the cash flows that would otherwise be required under the (original) contract. The significance of the change in cash flows is evaluated by considering the extent of the change in the cash flows of the embedded derivative, the host contract or both, and whether these changes are significant relative to the previously expected cash flows of the contract.
- An entity is required to revisit is assessment when a financial asset is reclassified out of the FVTPL category.

The Interpretation does not apply to embedded derivatives acquired in:

[IFRIC 9:5 & 12]

- a business combination (as defined in IFRS 3 *Business Combinations*);
- a combination of entities or businesses under common control as described in IFRS 3:B1-B4; or
- the formation of a joint venture as defined in IAS 31 *Interests in Joint Ventures* and joint arrangement as defined in IFRS 11 *Joint Arrangements*

or their possible reassessment at the date of acquisition.

IFRIC 9:5 includes a footnote stating that IFRS 3 addresses the acquisition of contracts with embedded derivatives in a business combination.

The guidance in IFRIC 9:5 and the footnote are curious from the perspective of the acquirer because, at the date of acquisition of a subsidiary, the acquirer is not *reassessing* embedded derivatives, but rather it is *assessing* them for the first time; for the purposes of the consolidated financial statements, the date of acquisition is the date the acquirer first becomes party to the acquiree's contractual arrangement. IFRS 3 states that if a contractual arrangement is acquired as part of a business combination, the acquirer must determine what is the appropriate classification of the contractual arrangement at the date of acquisition because this is the date of initial recognition. At the date of acquisition, for contracts that are not measured at fair value through profit or loss, the acquirer will need to consider whether the contractual arrangement includes any embedded derivatives that require separation.

For the acquiree, the accounting for a hybrid contract is not affected by the acquisition as in the acquired entity the contractual arrangements in the acquiree continue to be recognised, i.e. the acquisition date is not the initial recognition date for the acquiree. Unless the terms of the hybrid contract are changed as a result of the acquisition, with the effect that the cash flows are significantly modified, any embedded derivative will not be reassessed.

The acquirer's determination as to whether or not an embedded derivative is closely related to a host contract at the date of acquisition may differ to the determination arrived at by the acquiree when it first recognised the same contract. Differences are not uncommon because the determinations are based on the economic conditions and particular circumstances at different dates.

A first-time adopter of IFRSs is required to make its assessment on the basis of conditions existing at the later of the date it first became a party to the contract and the date a reassessment is required. In all cases, IFRIC 9 should be applied retrospectively.

Example 3C

Reassessment of embedded derivatives: common currency

Entity G operates in Country Y and had entered into long-dated supply contracts denominated in US dollars. When Entity G entered into the contracts, an assessment was made as to whether the US dollar was considered to be a 'common currency' per IAS 39:AG33(d)(iii) with a view to establishing whether an embedded derivative would need to be separated out. At the time Entity G entered into the contracts, the US dollar was considered a common currency for Country Y. The functional currency of Entity G and the counterparty to the contracts is not US dollars.

At the end of the current reporting period, the US dollar is no longer considered a common currency in Country Y. Entities within that country now use the domestic currency instead because the domestic currency is now traded cross-border and is considered a 'hard' currency by other countries.

Entity G should not revisit the embedded derivative assessment it made when it originally entered into the contracts because the terms of the arrangement have not changed. The accounting treatment is unchanged even though, if Entity G entered into the same contract at the end of the current reporting period, the US dollar would not be considered a common currency and an embedded derivative would need to be recognised.

It should be noted that, as part of the IASB's annual improvements project, the Board proposed amending the requirements of IAS 39:AG33(d)(iii). However, after issuing the exposure draft of annual improvements, the IFRIC (now the IFRS Interpretations Committee) agreed to remove the issue from its agenda (see **10.5**).

Example 3D

Reassessment of embedded derivatives: change in correlation of energy prices

Entity T, a coal-fired power station, entered into contracts to supply electricity prior to the deregulation of the energy market. The price paid for the supply of electricity was partly linked to the gas price. Entity T always intended to physically deliver electricity to the counterparty and, therefore, the supply contract was always considered to be an executory contract outside the scope of IAS 39. At the date the contract was entered into, the prices for gas and electricity were highly correlated and, therefore, Entity T considered the linkage to gas prices was a closely related embedded derivative.

Following deregulation of the market, the two prices are no longer highly correlated and, if Entity T entered into the contract today, it would conclude that the linkage to gas prices is an embedded derivative that is not closely related to the electricity supply contract. Entity T does not revisit its assessment regarding embedded derivatives made when it entered into the electricity supply contract because the terms of the arrangement are unchanged. This is the case even though, if Entity T entered into the same contract today, it would conclude that the embedded derivative should be separated.

Example 3E

Reassessment of embedded derivatives: novation within group

Group A has a US dollar functional currency subsidiary, Subsidiary B, which enters into contracts to sell non-financial items at a fixed future date with a Euro functional third-party counterparty, Entity D. The contract is denominated in US dollars.

The foreign currency embedded derivative is not separately recognised because Subsidiary B has a US dollar functional currency and is a substantial party to the contract. In Group A's consolidated financial statements, the same treatment is applied.

> Sometime later, Subsidiary B novates the contract to a fellow subsidiary, Subsidiary C, which has a Sterling functional currency. At the date of novation, there are no changes to the terms of the contract other than that Subsidiary C has stepped into Subsidiary B's place as the seller. Subsidiary C is a principal to the transaction following the novation.
>
> In the individual financial statements of Subsidiary C, at the novation date it becomes a party to the contract for the first time and, therefore, must consider whether the contract has any embedded derivatives. The contract is not denominated in either Subsidiary C's or Entity D's functional currency and, therefore, a non-closely related embedded derivative must be recognised by Subsidiary C, being a currency forward contract between Sterling and US dollar.
>
> In Group A's consolidated financial statements, because the group is presented as a single economic entity, there has been no change in the contractual terms of the contract and, therefore, the group would not reassess the embedded derivative assessment it made when Subsidiary B entered into the arrangement.

In March 2009, the IASB issued amendments to IFRIC 9 and IAS 39 titled *Embedded Derivatives*. The amendments clarify that, upon reclassification of a financial asset out of FVTPL to loans and receivables, AFS financial assets or HTM investments (see **section 4** in **chapter C2**), an entity is required to assess whether embedded derivatives should be separated from the host financial contract. In addition, if an entity is unable to measure separately the embedded derivative that would have to be separated on reclassification of a hybrid (combined) contract out of the FVTPL category, that reclassification is prohibited. In such circumstances, the hybrid (combined) contract remains classified as at FVTPL in its entirety.

The Board noted that when IFRIC 9 was issued, reclassifications out of the FVTPL category were prohibited and, therefore, IFRIC 9 did not consider the possibility of such reclassifications. The Board believed it was appropriate that embedded derivatives should be assessed at the date of reclassification. Not to require this would allow an entity to circumvent the need to assess embedded derivatives by classifying a hybrid contract initially as at FVTPL and subsequently reclassifying it. The Board noted that the inability to reclassify if the embedded derivative that would have to be separated cannot be measured separately would prevent reclassification of a hybrid (combined) financial asset out of that category between financial reporting dates and, therefore, avoid a requirement to reclassify the hybrid (combined) financial asset back into the FVTPL category at the end of the financial reporting period.

The amendments also state that, when assessing for embedded derivatives at the date of reclassification, the assessment should be made on the basis of the circumstances that existed at the later of when the entity first became a party to the contract and a change in the terms of the contract that significantly modifies the cash flows that otherwise would have been required under the contract. The Board considered that looking to circumstances when the entity became party to the contract was consistent with one of the stated purposes of embedded derivative accounting which is to prevent circumvention of the recognition and measurement requirements for derivatives and provide some degree of comparability. Furthermore, because the terms of the embedded features in the hybrid (combined) financial instrument have not changed, the Board did not see a reason for arriving at an answer on separation different from what would have been the case at initial recognition of the hybrid (combined) contract.

IFRIC 9 does not address remeasurement issues arising from a reassessment of embedded derivatives. [IFRIC 9:4] This will require careful consideration depending on particular facts and circumstances.

Example 3F

Reassessment of embedded derivatives: modification to terms

Entity B, a Euro functional currency entity, is party to a contract to purchase a fixed quantity of electricity at a future date for £10 million (€12 million at the spot rate at inception of the contract of €1.2:£1). The electricity will always be physically delivered under the contract and will be used for Entity B's production processes. The contract is a hybrid contractual arrangement containing a host contract that is an executory contract to purchase electricity in Euros and a non-closely related embedded foreign currency derivative based on the guidance in **10.5**. The two elements are:

(i) non-closely related embedded €/£ forward with an initial fair value of zero to buy €12m, sell £10m; and

(ii) host purchase contract to buy a set quantity of electricity with a purchase price of €12m (that matches the Euro leg of the foreign currency forward in (i) above).

Upon entering into the contract, Entity B separates out the non-closely related foreign currency embedded derivative and measures it at FVTPL.

At a later date, there is a contractual modification to the terms such that the currency in which the contract is denominated changes to the functional currency of Entity B, i.e. Euro. The embedded derivative had a negative fair value at the date of modification of €1 million. Due to the redenomination of the currency of the contract, Entity B pays the counterparty €1 million which is equal to the value of the change in contractual terms of the arrangement. Entity B derecognises the embedded derivative.

The change in denomination of the contract in this case is a significant modification of the contract's cash flows that triggers reassessment under IFRIC 9. Because the denomination of the contract after modification is in the functional currency of Entity B, the contract no longer has a non-closely related embedded derivative and the entire arrangement will be accounted for prospectively as an executory contract outside the scope of IAS 39.

Care is needed in determining how the carrying amount of an embedded derivative is treated when the embedded derivative is no longer closely related. This is particularly relevant when the modification occurs without cash consideration or when the cash consideration differs from the value of the embedded derivative derecognised. The carrying amount of the embedded derivative, being its fair value, at the date of modification of the contract, will be recognised in profit or loss, remain in the statement of financial position or be recognised in other comprehensive income in the period or future periods depending on the substance of the modified terms of the contract. Consideration will need to be given as to whether the pricing of the remaining contract is modified to reflect the value of the change in terms of the arrangement; whether any other goods or services are provided or received as part of the modification; or an equity transaction occurs between the entity and the counterparty.

Consideration will also need to be given to the substance of the modification when a non-closely related embedded derivative is recognised for the first time following the modification of a contract where previously the embedded derivative was closely related. The substance of the arrangement will determine whether, having recognised the derivative at fair value, the counter-entry affects profit or loss, the statement of financial position or other comprehensive income.

4 Terms of the embedded derivative and the debt host contract

The term 'debt host contract' that is applied below includes debt instruments that are issued by an entity (and, therefore, are financial liabilities) as well as debt instruments that an entity may invest in that are recognised as financial assets.

The terms of the host contract must reflect the stated or implied terms of the hybrid contract (i.e. the embedded feature must be clearly present in the hybrid contract). In the absence of implied or stated terms a judgement may have to be made, but an entity cannot create cash flows that do not contractually exist.

Example 4A

Fixed versus floating debt host contract (1)

Entity A issues floating rate debt. The contract cannot be seen as fixed rate debt with an embedded interest rate swap that swaps fixed rate cash flows into floating rate cash flows. The terms of the contract do not contain any fixed cash flows, so there can be no embedded feature with fixed rate cash flows.

Example 4B

Fixed versus floating debt host contract (2)

A 5-year debt instrument has fixed annual payments, and a principal repayment at the end of the contract which is conditional on changes in the FTSE 100 index. This instrument must be treated as a host fixed rate debt contract with an embedded equity feature. It cannot be classified as floating rate debt with an embedded equity swap that has an offsetting floating rate leg. The host is a fixed rate contract because there are no variable interest rate payments in it.

Embedded non-optional derivatives must be determined so that they have a fair value of zero at inception of the contract. If this was not stipulated, it would be possible to split one instrument into an infinite number and variety of hosts with embedded derivatives. This could be done by separating embedded derivatives with terms that create leverage, asymmetry or another risk exposure that does not exist in the hybrid contract. [IAS 39:AG28 & IG.C.1]

Embedded optional derivatives will not necessarily have a fair value (or intrinsic value) of zero at inception. The fair value of such an embedded derivative will depend on its strike price or rate. Therefore, the separation of an option from a hybrid contract should be based on the stated terms of the option feature. [IAS 39:AG28 & IG.C.2)]

5 Determination of host contract: debt vs. equity

If a hybrid contract has both debt and equity features, a determination must be made as to whether the host contract is debt or equity. Often, this will be a relatively straightforward task because the 'majority' of the contract will behave either more like debt or more like equity.

From the perspective of the holder of a contract, if the host contract has no stated or predetermined maturity and represents a residual interest in the net assets of the issuer, then its economic characteristics and risks are those of an equity instrument. Any embedded derivative would need to possess equity characteristics of the issuer to be regarded as closely related. If the host contract is not an equity instrument and meets the definition of a financial asset or liability, then its economic characteristics and risks are those of a debt instrument. [IAS 39:AG27]

More commonly, the host contract will not represent a residual interest in an entity and, thus, the economic characteristics and risks of a financial host contract will be considered that of a debt instrument. For example, even though an overall hybrid instrument may provide for repayment of the principal linked to the market price of the issuer's ordinary shares, the host contract may not involve any existing or potential residual rights in the net assets of the issuer (i.e. rights of ownership) so would not be an equity instrument. The host contract is a debt instrument, and the embedded derivative (the indexation to the market price of the issuer) is not closely related to the host contract.

Example 5A

Debt host contract (1)

Entity A purchases a five-year 'debt' instrument issued by Entity B with a principal amount of CU1 million that is indexed to the share price of Entity C. At maturity, Entity A will receive from Entity B the principal amount plus or minus the change in the fair value of 10,000 shares of Entity C. No separate interest payments are made by Entity B. Entity A classifies the debt instrument as available for sale. Entity A concludes that the instrument is a hybrid instrument with an embedded derivative because of the equity-indexed principal.

The host contract is a debt instrument because the hybrid instrument has a stated maturity, i.e. it does not meet the definition of an equity instrument (IAS 32:11 and IAS 32:16). The embedded non-optional derivative is separated so as to have an initial fair value of zero (see IAS 39:IG.C.1). Because the embedded derivative has a fair value of zero, an amount equal to the purchase price, being the fair value of the entire instrument at initial recognition, is recognised as a debt instrument. The debt instrument is accounted for as a zero coupon debt instrument. Thus, in accounting for the host instrument, Entity A imputes interest over five years being the difference between the amount allocated to the debt instrument at initial recognition and the redemption amount of the debt host contract.

Example 5B

Debt host contract (2)

Entity A invests in instruments that are classified as AFS that are issued by Entity B. The instruments have the legal form of shares, and embedded within them is a put option allowing Entity A to put the 'shares' back to Entity B for the higher of:

(i) the fair market value of the shares; and

(ii) an amount based on the initial investment with compounded interest based on LIBOR.

The option is exercisable five years after the initial investment is made.

While the instruments have the legal form of shares, they do not evidence a residual interest in Entity B. Entity A will receive a rate of return that is at least equal to the return on a debt instrument. Entity A should account for the instruments as a debt host contract with an embedded derivative not closely related to the host contract.

In January 2007, the IFRIC (now the IFRS Interpretations Committee) issued a rejection notice on the classification by the holder of financial instruments that are puttable by the holder at an amount other than fair value. The issuer accounts for the instrument as a financial liability in accordance with IAS 32. The IFRIC was asked whether the holder's accounting in IAS 39 should be symmetrical with that of the financial statements of the issuer. The IFRIC noted that IAS 32 and IAS 39 do not directly address whether the accounting for financial instruments in the financial statements of the holder should be symmetrical with that of the issuer. However, the IFRIC noted that the issuer of a financial instrument is required to classify it in accordance with IAS 32, whereas the holder of the financial instrument is required to classify and account for it in accordance with IAS 39. The IFRIC also noted that IAS 39 requires the holder to identify embedded derivatives in hybrid financial instruments and requires separate accounting for the embedded derivatives if all the conditions in IAS 39:11 are met. These requirements apply to the holder regardless of whether any embedded derivatives are accounted for separately in the financial statements of the issuer. In the light of the existing guidance in IAS 39, the IFRIC decided that the issue should not be taken onto its agenda.

6 Multiple embedded derivatives

It is possible for a contract to contain more than one embedded derivative. In such circumstances, each embedded derivative should be individually assessed to see if it is closely related to the host contract.

Example 6A

Conversion feature and put option

Entity A holds convertible bonds. In addition to the conversion feature, Entity A can choose to put the bonds back to the issuer. When assessing for embedded derivatives, it will be necessary to consider both the conversion option and the put option.

When contracts contain multiple embedded derivatives, they are generally treated as a single compound embedded derivative. Only if the embedded derivatives relate to different risk exposures and are readily separable and independent of each other are they accounted for separately from each other. [IAS 39:AG29]

IAS 39:AG29 clearly states that the embedded derivatives should only be accounted for separately from each other when (1) they relate to different risk exposures and (2) they are readily separable and independent of each other. However, it is not clear whether the requirement to treat multiple embedded derivatives as a single compound derivative applies both to the assessment of whether the embedded derivatives are closely related to the host contract and the accounting for bifurcated derivatives, or whether it applies solely to the accounting for bifurcated derivatives. Accordingly, two accounting treatments are acceptable.

The first approach is to regard IAS 39:AG29 as applying to the assessment of the embedded derivatives and the accounting for bifurcated derivatives. The second approach is to regard IAS 39:AG29 as applying only in accounting for bifurcated derivatives. Because both approaches can be supported under IFRSs, an entity should determine as an accounting policy choice whether multiple embedded derivatives should be assessed as a single compound instrument or assessed individually. The accounting policy selected should be applied consistently to all hybrid instruments.

Example 6B

Multiple embedded derivative with the same risk

Entity Y issues debt for CU100 with a par value of CU100 and a maturity of 10 years. Key terms of the debt instrument are as follows.

- Interest rate – the interest rate is a floating rate of 3-month LIBOR plus a fixed margin.
- Interest rate floor (embedded derivative 1) – the interest rate will not be lower than X per cent for any period. The rate is set such that the interest rate floor is in the money at issuance of the debt (i.e. the floor is above the market rate of 3-month LIBOR plus the fixed margin at issuance of the contract).
- Prepayment options (embedded derivative 2) – Entity Y may at any time, voluntarily prepay the principal and related accrued interest outstanding in whole or in part plus a penalty amount of 1 per cent of the amount prepaid.

The entire instrument is not accounted for at fair value through profit or loss (FVTPL) because it is neither held for trading nor designated as at FVTPL. Other than the two embedded derivatives described, there are no other embedded derivatives and no transaction costs associated with the instrument.

A question arises whether both embedded derivatives should be assessed as a single compound instrument in determining if they are closely related to the host contract, or should they be assessed individually?

Approach 1 – IAS 39:AG29 applies to the assessment of the embedded derivatives and the accounting for bifurcated derivatives.

If this approach is applied in the circumstances described, the two embedded derivatives should be assessed as a single compound embedded derivative because they both relate to the same risk (interest rate risk), and they are not independent of each other because the likelihood of the prepayment option being exercised depends on whether the interest rate floor is in the money. Because a component of the compound embedded derivative (the interest rate floor) is not closely related (based on the floor being in the money at inception and the guidance in IAS 39:AG33(b)) (see **7.7.3**), the compound embedded derivative as a whole is assessed as not closely related and bifurcated from the host contract (assuming the other criteria in IAS 39:11 are met). Applying this approach, the prepayment option is not individually assessed to determine if it is closely related.

Approach two – IAS 39:AG29 applies only in accounting for bifurcated derivatives.

Under this approach, only embedded derivatives that individually meet all of the criteria for separation under IAS 39:11 should be treated as embedded derivatives subject to separation. IAS 39:AG29 only applies to the resulting embedded derivatives that meet all of the IAS 39:11 criteria for separation (i.e. it applies after assessment of what needs to be separated and not before).

When assessed individually, the interest floor is determined not to be closely related (based on the floor being in the money at inception and the guidance in IAS 39:AG33(b)). Therefore, assuming that the other IAS 39:11 criteria are met, the interest rate floor should be accounted for separately from the host debt contract. The prepayment option also needs to be assessed individually to determine if it is closely related on the basis of the guidance in IAS 39:AG30(g) (see **7.1**). Only if that individual assessment results in the prepayment option being considered not closely related will the floor and the prepayment option be viewed as a compound embedded derivative.

Assuming Entity Y chooses as its accounting policy to assess the two embedded derivatives individually (i.e. approach two above) the interest rate floor that has been identified as a non-closely related embedded derivative will be separated. However, when assessing whether the prepayment option is individually closely related, IAS 39:AG30(g)(i) requires a comparison of the exercise price of the option to the "amortised cost of the host debt instrument". For the purpose of this assessment, should the host debt contract include the non-closely related interest rate floor?

IAS 39:AG30(g) states that the assessment of whether a call or put option is closely related to the host contract is made before separating the equity element of a convertible debt instrument in accordance with IAS 32 *Financial Instruments: Presentation*. However, it is not clear whether this paragraph establishes a specific exception that applies only in the case of an issuer of a compound instrument when an equity element is separated or whether this paragraph can be applied by analogy to other situations. Accordingly, two accounting treatments are acceptable.

Approach (a) – IAS 39:AG30(g) applies only in the case of an issuer of a compound instrument when an equity element is separated. Under this approach, the exception in IAS 39.AG30(g) is not relevant in this scenario and the prepayment option is assessed against the host contract excluding the interest rate floor. This is consistent with the general principle that the interest rate floor will be accounted for separately and therefore should not form part of the assessment of the remaining terms (i.e. the debt host including the prepayment option but without the floor).

The effect of excluding the floor from the host debt contract is that the amortised cost of the host instrument for the purpose of applying IAS 39:AG30(g)(i) would be determined as the difference between the fair value of the entire hybrid contract and the fair value of the embedded interest rate floor (liability) written by Entity Y. In the circumstances described, this results in an increased risk of the prepayment option being assessed as not closely related because the amortised cost of the host contract (excluding the floor) will be smaller.

Approach (b) – IAS 39:AG30(g) can be applied by analogy to other circumstances. Under this approach, the amortised cost of the instrument should include the interest rate floor. In the circumstances described, this would mean the amortised cost of the host contract for the purposes of the assessment under IAS 39:AG30(g) would start at the amortised cost of the entire hybrid contract (CU100) even though the interest rate floor will be recognised separately on the statement of financial position at initial recognition.

Because both approaches can be supported under IFRSs, an entity should determine an accounting policy choice to be applied consistently to all hybrid instruments.

If an embedded derivative must be separated from its host contract, but it cannot be valued, the entity must first determine both the fair value of the whole contract and the fair value of the host contract. The difference represents the fair value of the derivative instrument to be separated. [IAS 39:13] If an entity is unable to compute the fair value of the derivative on this basis, the entity must designate the entire instrument as at FVTPL. [IAS 39:12]

7 Embedded derivatives in debt host contracts

Financial liabilities are discussed at some length in **chapter C3**. These include traditional debt contracts like bonds and bank borrowings, and also certain other securities that are in substance liabilities (e.g. mandatorily redeemable preference shares). IAS 39 also requires entities to assess for embedded derivatives in debt host contracts that are financial assets.

7.1 Put, call and prepayment options

Contractual terms that allow either party to terminate the contract early and accelerate the repayment of the outstanding principal, either in whole or in part, are often embedded derivatives. Examples of such terms include call options of the issuer, put options of the holder, and prepayment features.

These embedded derivatives are not closely related to the host debt contract unless the exercise price is approximately equal to the debt host contract's amortised cost on each exercise date. [IAS 39:AG30(g)]

From the perspective of the issuer of a convertible debt instrument with an embedded call or put option feature, the assessment of whether the call or put option is closely related to the host debt contract is made before separating the equity element under IAS 32 as discussed in **section 3** of **chapter C3**. [IAS 39:AG30(g)(i)]

Example 7.1A

Issuer call option

Entity A issues a five-year zero-coupon bond for CU75 million, with a face value of CU100 million. Embedded in the debt is a call option allowing Entity A to repay the debt after three years for CU90 million, when its amortised cost will be CU89 million. Because the repayment amount is approximately equal to its amortised cost on that date, the call option is closely related to the host contract and so is not separated from it. This is the case for both the issuer and holder of the bond.

If the terms were instead such that Entity A could call the debt at any time, but would have to redeem it at a fixed amount (e.g. at par of CU100 million), the call option would not be closely related because the repayment amount would not approximately equal the amortised cost on each date that the call can be exercised. For example, the week after issuing the bond (when the bond's amortised cost is approximately CU75 million), Entity A could call it back but would have to pay CU100 million to do so. This situation arises because the bond was issued at a substantial discount and, therefore, its amortised cost will not approximate to its par value except in the years close to its maturity.

Example 7.1B

Investor put option

Entity X issues 10-year bonds with a par value of CU1 million for proceeds of CU1 million. The bonds have a coupon of 10 per cent. Embedded in the bonds is a clause that allows the investors to put the bonds back to Entity X for CU1 million in the event the FTSE declines by 5 per cent. It is reasonably possible that the FTSE will decline by 5 per cent in the near future. The issue costs are insignificant.

The embedded put option would not be accounted for separately, even though the put option is contingent on an event that is not related to the host instrument (i.e. a trigger other than interest rates or credit). The tests in IAS 39 relate to the exercise price (settlement amount), not the trigger. The likelihood of the put option being exercised is also irrelevant in determining whether the embedded derivative is closely related, although this will affect valuation. In this case, the bonds will be put back at an amount that approximates amortised cost. It is not relevant that the put option only becomes exercisable if an equity index performs in a particular manner.

Example 7.1C

Investor contingent put option

Entity A issues CU100 million 7 per cent cumulative preference shares. Dividends are payable quarterly subject to the availability of distributable profits. Issue costs are insignificant. The preference shares are puttable at par to Entity A for cash if interest rates move by 150 basis points. Any dividend that remains accumulated and not paid becomes payable when the shares are put to Entity A.

The embedded put option would not be separated from the host contract under the embedded derivative requirements. The preference shares are classified as a liability under IAS 32 (see **chapter C3**). The put feature is an option that is considered to be closely related to the host because the exercise price of the put option is the amortised cost of the preference shares.

Sometimes derivatives may be 'embedded' subsequent to the issuance of the instrument.

Example 7.1D

Remarketable put bonds

Entity X issues 10-year bonds with a 6 per cent coupon to a bank and receives proceeds of €103 million. The debt is puttable by the holder at the end of three years. The 3-year debt rate for vanilla debt instruments (i.e. those without put or call features) is 6 per cent. The bank staples a call option and sells the two instruments to an investor. This call option enables the bank to reacquire the bonds in the event that it wishes to exercise its put option inherent in the bond issued by Entity X.

A party other than the issuer (i.e. the bank) has stapled the call option into the debt instrument. Thus, an investor would not be able to consider the call option to be closely related to the host debt instrument. The holder of the call option would have a free-standing derivative that would be recognised at fair value.

Note that Entity X does not have to consider the accounting for the call option because Entity X is not a party to the call option.

A debt instrument that may be called by the issuer, or put or prepaid by the holder, must be assessed in order to determine whether these features are considered to be closely related. The outcome of this assessment is dependent on comparing the strike price under the option (i.e. the amount the issuer would pay the holder on exercise of the option) with the amortised cost of the instrument. What is less clear is whether call, put and prepayment options that are likely to be exercised should be taken into account in determining amortised cost.

Consider the following example. A fixed rate debt instrument is issued at par with a 10-year term. The debt can be put by the holder any time after Year 5 for an amount equal to 110 per cent of par. If the issuer at initial recognition considers it likely that the holder will put at Year 5, the host contract could be considered a 10-year host redeeming at 100 per cent or a 5-year host that early redeems at 110 per cent. If the former approach is taken, the put option is not closely related because 110 per cent is not approximately equal to 100 per cent whereas, if the latter approach is taken, the put option would be closely related because 110 per cent would be equal to 110 per cent.

The above example illustrates that when a significant penalty is payable on early redemption, the accounting can differ depending on which approach is taken. Ironically, if an entity did take into account a put option that is likely to be exercised in determining the host contract, it would result in that put option not being recognised. If the put option were less likely to be exercised, it would result in the put option being recognised.

Extending the example above, assume the holder can put at any time in the 10 years for an amount equal to 110 per cent of par. The issuer still believes it is most likely the holder will put at Year 5. If the issuer were to consider the 5-year put option as part of the amortised cost of the host contract, and thereby not recognise an embedded derivative for that put option, it would still need to consider whether the put options from Years 2 to 4 are closely related. If the host contract is considered a discounted instrument, issued for 100 per cent and redeemable at 110 per cent at Year 5, some of the put options between Years 2 and 4 would be non-closely related embedded derivatives because their exercise price of 110 per cent would not be approximately equal to amortised cost.

If an early redemption feature in a debt instrument is reflected in the host contract's amortised cost when determining whether that feature is closely related, it is not clear how an entity should account for the instrument if there is a subsequent change in the likelihood that the early redemption feature will be exercised. Applying the example above, if the issuer subsequently estimated the put option was now likely to be exercised after Year 5, two views exist. The first view is that the change in timing of cash flows is simply a remeasurement of estimated cash flows and the revised changes in cash flows should be discounted by the original effective interest rate in accordance with IAS 39:AG8. An alternative view is that the host contract is deemed a five year instrument; therefore, the right for the holder to put the instrument after Year 5 is equivalent to a term extension option which, if the extension is not at market interest rates, would be considered a non-closely related embedded derivative.

Certain specific prepayment options embedded in a debt host contract that are designed to ensure the lender is compensated for loss of interest when the borrower prepays are closely related to the debt host contract. Such prepayment options are not equal to the amortised cost of the debt host contract because the amount prepaid will include an adjustment to reflect the then market interest rate. IAS 39:AG30(g)(ii) states that a prepayment option is closely related to the host debt contract if the exercise price of the prepayment option reimburses the lender for an amount up to the approximate present value of lost interest for the remaining term of the host contract. Lost interest is the product of the principal amount prepaid multiplied by the interest rate differential. The interest rate differential is the excess of the effective interest rate of the host contract over the effective interest rate the entity would receive at the prepayment date if it reinvested the principal amount prepaid in a similar contract for the remaining term of the host contract.

A further consideration is whether the option is a prepayment option over an interest-only or principal-only strip. The embedded derivative will be closely related provided that the host contract:

[IAS 39:AG33(e)]

(i) initially resulted from separating the right to receive contractual cash flows of a financial instrument that itself did not contain an embedded derivative; and
(ii) does not contain any terms not present in the original host debt.

Example 7.1E

Interest-only strip: no additional terms

A pool of floating rate mortgages is split into an interest-only and principal-only strip, with different entities acquiring each part. The terms of the mortgages allow the borrower to prepay the mortgage at amortised cost prior to the contractual maturity of the mortgage. Because this prepayment option is at amortised cost, it does not require separation.

Entity K purchases an interest-only strip from the pool of floating rate mortgages. The floating rate interest-only strip has the same terms as the floating rate on the original instrument. Entity K must consider whether the interest-only strip has embedded derivatives that require separation.

Because the interest-only strip does not contain any terms not present in the original host debt contract and the prepayment option was not separated in the accounting for the original mortgage, the prepayment option is considered closely related to the interest-only strip and, therefore, is not separated. [IAS 39:AG33(e)]

Example 7.1F

Interest-only and principal-only strip: additional terms

Transferor X securitises CU100 million of mortgage loans with an 8 per cent coupon in a securitisation structure that meets the requirements for derecognition (derecognition is discussed further in **chapter C8**). The issued beneficial interests consist of a principal-only strip of CU100 million and an interest-only strip that pays 8 per cent based on the principal amount.

Transferor X received proceeds of CU60 million for the principal-only strip. If market 30-year mortgage rates exceed 10 per cent, the coupon on the interest-only strip increases to 10 per cent. The additional 2 per cent will be paid from the principal-only cash receipts. The conditional 2 per cent payment is an option, sometimes referred to as a caplet.

The embedded caplet is required to be separated because it was not present in the original financial instrument.

7.2 Term-extending features

When the term of the debt is extendable, and there is no concurrent adjustment to the approximate current market rate of interest at the time of the extension, the embedded term-extension option is not closely related to the host debt contract. To be closely related, the reset to market rates must result in a reset of both current interest rates and current credit spread for the issuer.

If an entity issues a debt instrument and the holder of that debt instrument writes a call option on the debt instrument to a third party, the issuer regards the call option as extending the term to maturity of the debt instrument provided that the issuer can be required to participate in or facilitate the remarketing of the debt instrument as a result of the call option being exercised. [IAS 39:AG30(c)]

Example 7.2A

Term-extension feature (1)

Entity X issues CU10 million fixed rate debt with an 8 per cent coupon and maturity of five years. At the end of five years, Entity X has an option to extend the term for an additional three years. If extended, the coupon will remain at 8 per cent. If the option is exercised, it will significantly extend the term of the debt and the coupon will not reset to current market rates. Therefore, this term-extending option is an embedded derivative that is not closely related to the host contract.

Example 7.2B

Term-extension feature (2)

Entity X issues debt of CU10 million with an 8 per cent coupon and a maturity of five years. If LIBOR increases by 200 basis points within any one year, the maturity of the bonds will be extended for another three years at the same 8 per cent coupon rate. The embedded derivative would be accounted for separately from the host contract because the coupon following extension does not reset to the current market rate.

The likelihood of LIBOR increasing by 200 basis points in a year is not a consideration when determining whether the embedded derivative is closely related. It will, however, affect the valuation of the embedded derivative. If the possibility of LIBOR increasing by 200 basis points is considered low, the value of the embedded derivative will be relatively small.

5-year fixed rate debt with an option to extend for three years (as described in **example 7.2A**) is economically no different from 8-year fixed rate debt that is puttable at the end of five years. However, the criteria for determining whether there is an embedded derivative in these instruments are different. As IAS 39 has specific guidance on the accounting for prepayment options and term extension options, and that guidance differs, two instruments that are economically the same may be treated differently. An entity cannot separate a prepayment option if the debt is prepayable at its amortised cost, but would be required to separate out a term-extending option if that option did not result in the interest being reset to market rates.

An alternative accounting treatment for term-extension options is to treat them as loan commitments that may be outside the scope of IAS 39. A term-extension option is a right to extend existing financing for a new period and therefore it can be argued is akin to a commitment to lend. Although a loan commitment meets the definition of a derivative, if it were to also meet the definition of a loan commitment and be outside the scope of IAS 39 as described in IAS 39:4 then it would not be subject to the embedded derivative requirements in IAS 39 as an embedded derivative only requires separation if it is a derivative in the scope of IAS 39. Such an approach would result in not applying the guidance on term-extension options as described above and detailed in IAS 39:AG30(c).

If an entity elects to apply the loan commitment exemption to term-extending features, this election should be a consistently applied accounting policy to all similar term-extending features that in the absence of applying that policy would be subject to IAS 39:AG30(c).

7.3 Indexed interest and principal payments

When interest or principal payments in a debt contract are indexed to changes in a specified security price, commodity price, foreign exchange rate, or index of prices or rates, the host debt contract contains an embedded derivative.

Such an embedded derivative will not be closely related to the host debt contract if the amounts of interest or principal are indexed to the price of a commodity or to the change in value of an equity instrument. [IAS 39:AG30(d) & (e)]

Example 7.3A

Commodity price adjustment

Entity X issues 10-year notes with no stated coupon. Embedded in the notes is a clause that adjusts the interest paid by reference to changes in the price of corn.

The embedded derivative would be accounted for separately because the adjustment to interest payments based on changes in corn prices is not closely related to the host debt instrument.

Example 7.3B

Equity price adjustment

Entity X issues 10-year notes to a bank. The terms of the notes require interest paid to be adjusted based on changes in the share price of Entity Y.

The embedded derivative will be separated because the interest payments are indexed to changes in the share price of Entity Y and, therefore, the adjustment is not closely related to the host debt instrument.

Generally, an embedded derivative that adjusts interest and/or principal amounts paid on the debt contract will not be closely related to the host debt when the underlying that drives the value of the derivative is different from the economic factors that drive the value of the host debt contract. The guidance would equally apply to indexation to a basket of commodities or share indices like the FTSE 100.

Example 7.3C

Equity index adjustment

A bank issues 10-year notes with a coupon of 5 per cent to an entity. At maturity, the entity receives cash equal to the higher of the initial proceeds and an amount based on the Standard and Poor's 500 (S&P 500).

The embedded cash-settled S&P 500 call option is an embedded derivative that is not closely related to the host debt contract.

Even if the interest or principal payments are determined by changes in underlyings that are typically associated with debt (e.g. interest rates, inflation or creditworthiness of the issuer), there may still be an embedded derivative that is not closely related to the host debt contract (e.g. when interest or principal repayments are determined based on leveraged, complex or formulaic features).

With respect to interest rate and interest rate index features these features must be such that *either* the holder would not recover substantially all of its recognised investment *or* the issuer would pay more than twice the market rate of the host contract at inception (of issuing the instrument) *and* could result in a rate of return that is at least twice what the market return would be for a similar host contract (sometimes referred to as the 'double-double test'). [IAS 39:AG33(a)]

The test is based on the contractual terms, so the determination is made for both parties to the contract based on the return or loss to the investor. Thus, if the holder separately accounts for an embedded derivative because it could lose substantially all of its initial investment, the issuer should generally do the same.

Example 7.3D

Recovery of recognised investment (1)

Entity X issues CU10 million in debt with an 8 per cent coupon. However, if LIBOR increases by 500 basis points within any one year, the bonds mature and the holder receives CU8 million in total.

An embedded derivative exists and should be separately accounted for because there is a payment provision that may cause the holder not to recover substantially all of its recognised investment if LIBOR increases by 500 basis points.

In **example 7.3D**, the likelihood of LIBOR increasing by 500 basis points is not relevant when making this determination. The test in IAS 39 is based around the possibility of the holder not recovering its recognised investment or obtaining double its initial rate of return. Even if it is unlikely that LIBOR will increase by 500 basis points, the contingent embedded derivative must be separated from the host contract. However, if the probability of this event occurring is low then the fair value of the embedded derivative at inception will be relatively small compared to the fair value of the host contract.

The condition that the holder will not recover substantially all of its recognised investment is only met if the holder can be forced to accept a settlement amount that is substantially below its recognised investment. If the terms of the contract permit, but do not require, the holder to settle the instrument in such a manner, then the feature is closely related to the host contract.

The 'double-double test' is performed at the date that the hybrid instrument is initially recognised. The first step is to determine whether there is a possible future interest rate scenario, no matter how remote, in which the embedded derivative would at least double the investor's initial return on the host contract. In making this assessment, it is important to differentiate the return on the host contract from the return on the hybrid contract. The host contract has terms identical to the hybrid contract being tested, except that it does not contain the embedded derivative. IAS 39:AG33(a) describes this step as requiring that the embedded derivative could at least double the holder's initial rate of return on the host contract. An embedded derivative that does not breach this threshold would be considered closely related to its host. If the embedded derivative does breach the threshold, a second step must be performed to determine whether it is closely related to the host contract. The second step is to review each interest rate scenario identified in the first step for which the investor's initial rate of return on the host contract would be doubled, and determine whether, for any of the scenarios, the embedded derivative would at the same time result in a rate of return that is at least twice what otherwise would be the then-current market return for a contract that has the same terms as the host contract and that involves a debtor with a credit quality similar to the issuer's credit quality at inception. If the embedded derivative does not breach the threshold, it would be considered closely related to its host contract. If the threshold is breached in any one of the scenarios then the embedded derivative would be considered not closely related to the host contract and it must be separated.

A vanilla variable rate debt instrument does not contain an embedded derivative even though the investor could pay a rate more than twice the rate at inception. A rate that is always equal to the current market rate is not an embedded derivative.

Example 7.3E

Double-double interest rate test (1)

On 1 January 20X1, an entity issues a bond where interest payments are linked to LIBOR. The bond also incorporates an interest rate cap whereby if LIBOR equals or exceeds 8 per cent at any interest rate reset date, the investor will receive a return of 10 per cent. On the date the entity issues the bond, it also could issue at par a variable rate bond not containing a cap that pays LIBOR minus 1 per cent. At 1 January 20X1, LIBOR is 5 per cent. The bond cannot be contractually settled such that the investor would not recover substantially all of its initial recorded investment in the bond.

To perform the first test in paragraph IAS 39:AG33(a), the issuer must determine whether there is any interest rate scenario, no matter how remote, under which the embedded derivative (the cap) would at least double the investor's initial rate of return on the host contract. This analysis is summarised in the following table.

A	B	C	D	
Interest rate change	**Return reflecting the effect of the cap**	**Initial rate of return on the host (LIBOR – 1%)**	**Initial rate of return on the host doubled**	**Is the first test met, i.e. is B > D?**
0 – 7.99%	0 – 7.99%	4%	8%	No
8% and up	10%	4%	8%	Yes

Because the first test is met, the issuer must perform the second test described in paragraph IAS 39:AG33(a) to determine whether the embedded cap is closely related to its bond host. For this test, the issuer must determine, for each interest rate scenario identified above for which the investor's initial rate of return on the host contract would be doubled, whether the embedded cap would simultaneously result in a rate of return that is at least twice what otherwise would be the then-current market return for a contract that has the same terms as the host contract (i.e. has the same credit quality as the issuer at inception). The analysis for this test can be summarised as follows.

A	B	C	
Interest rate scenario identified in the first test above for which the cap would at least double the investor's initial rate of return on the host contract	**Return reflecting the effect of the cap under the interest rate scenario in A**	**Current market rate of return for the host contract under the interest rate scenario in A (LIBOR – 1%)**	**Is the second test met (i.e. is B at least twice C for any scenario)?**
8% and up	10%	7%	No

Because the first test in IAS 39:AG33(a) is met, but the second test is not, the embedded cap is considered closely related to the bond host.

Example 7.3F

Double-double interest rate test (2)

Entity A invests in 30-year variable rate debt issued by Entity B. The debt is indexed to the 3-month LIBOR rate plus 4 per cent. As of the date of issuance, the 3-month LIBOR rate was 2 per cent. The debt's terms also specify that if the 3-month LIBOR rate increases to 5 per cent, the debt issuer is required to pay 23 per cent for the remaining term of the bonds. The bond cannot be contractually settled such that the investor would not recover substantially all of its initial recorded investment in the bond.

If Entity B were to issue 30-year variable rate debt without any embedded derivatives (i.e. the interest rate reset feature), it would pay a coupon of 3-month LIBOR plus 6 per cent. Consequently, the initial rate of return on the host contract is 8 per cent (3-month LIBOR of 2 per cent plus 6 per cent). It is necessary to determine whether the embedded derivative could at least double the investor's initial rate of return on the host contract, which was 8 per cent at the date of issuance, in any of the possible interest rate environments. Therefore, when 3-month LIBOR increases to 5 per cent, the 23 per cent interest rate feature more than doubles the initial rate of return of 8 per cent on the host contract.

It is then necessary to perform an analysis to determine whether the embedded derivative results in a rate of return that is at least twice what otherwise would be the then-current market rate of return for a host contract when 3-month LIBOR is at 5 per cent. When 3-month LIBOR increases to 5 per cent, the rate of return on the host contract would be 11 per cent (3-month LIBOR of 5 per cent plus 6 per cent) for a bond of similar credit quality that does not contain any embedded derivatives. Therefore, when 3-month LIBOR increases to 5 per cent, the 23 per cent interest rate feature is more than twice the then-current market rate of return of the host contract of 11 per cent (3-month LIBOR of 5 per cent plus 6 per cent.)

Entity A and Entity B each would be required to treat the feature as a non-closely related embedded derivative.

Example 7.3G

Double-double interest rate test (3)

Entity A issues CU10 million debt with a coupon of 8 per cent and a term of 10 years. Entity A's market rate for 10-year debt is 8.25 per cent. Embedded in the debt is an interest rate adjustment that resets the interest rate to 16.40 per cent if 3-month LIBOR increases to 7 per cent or greater during the first three years of the debt.

The adjustment feature is an embedded derivative, but it would not be accounted for separately. The derivative could not cause the rate of return on the host contract to double.

Example 7.3H

Recovery of recognised investment (2)

Entity X issues CU10 million in debt with a coupon of 8.25 per cent and a term of 10 years. Entity X's market rate for 10-year debt is 8 per cent. Embedded in the debt is a clause stating that, if interest rates increase beyond a specified level, the holder of the debt must give the issuer an additional CU1 million in borrowings maturing in 10 years on which the holder will receive no interest.

The adjustment feature is a written option issued by the holder. The issuer pays for this option through a higher interest cost when compared to debt without the option. The embedded derivative would not be accounted for separately by the issuer (or by the holder) because the holder will recover all of its recognised investment, being CU10 million advanced at inception and CU1 million if it is advanced at a later date. In all cases, the investor will recover all its recognised investment. There is no circumstance that can result in the issuer paying a rate that is more than double the market rate of the host contract at inception.

Note the 'recognised investment' is based on the amount advanced by the holder. The likelihood of the option being exercised and the present value of the loan are not considered when determining whether the holder will recover its recognised investment.

7.4 Inflation features

IAS 39 does not specifically address whether an inflation feature within a debt contract that is in the scope of IAS 39 is closely related to the host contract. When an embedded derivative is not specifically addressed by the Standard, significant judgement will need to be used. In these situations, drawing analogies to specific examples given will often prove helpful.

IAS 39 does address inflation features within lease contracts. Finance lease contracts are similar to debt contracts and, therefore, the guidance below is based on the examples given for contracts with lease hosts.

Example 7.4

Inflation-linked bond

Entity X issues an inflation-linked bond. The bond pays a coupon of 4 per cent annually, with a repayment of principal on maturity of the bond. The principal payment is indexed to the domestic retail price index but cannot decrease below par.

Because the bond is denominated in the local currency, the indexation of the principal payment to domestic inflation rates is closely related to the host contract.

An inflation feature in a host debt contract in the scope of IAS 39 is closely related to the host provided that the inflation index is not leveraged, cannot cause the investor not to recover substantially all of its initial investment, and is the inflation rate of the economic environment for the currency in which the debt is denominated.

Inflation features that are leveraged will not be closely related to a host debt contract. This is discussed further in the context of a lease host contract in **9.1**.

7.5 Credit derivatives and liquidity features

IAS 39 does not explicitly address adjustments to the terms of a debt instrument in the scope of IAS 39 as a result of issuer default, changes in the issuer's credit rating or creditworthiness. It does, however, provide guidance on embedded credit derivatives that relate to other reference entities. Further, certain credit sensitive contracts embedded in other instruments may meet the definition of a financial guarantee contract (see **2.3.3** in **chapter C1**).

7.5.1 Adjustment for issuer's credit risk

IAS 39 does not provide specific guidance regarding when the cash flows on debt instruments in the scope of IAS 39 are adjusted for changes in the issuer's creditworthiness.

It is reasonable to conclude that credit features that relate to the credit quality of the issuer (e.g. the issuer's credit rating, default or ratios indicative of its credit status) should be viewed as closely related to the host debt contract if the credit feature is not leveraged and is designed to reflect the approximate credit risk borne by the lender. In economic terms, such features directly affect the value of the host debt contract.

Example 7.5.1A

Interest adjustment: debt covenants

Entity X issues bonds with a BBB rating. The terms of the bond are such that if Entity X violates a specified debt-to-equity ratio covenant, or Entity X's credit rating is downgraded, the interest rate will reset to the then-current market rate for Entity X.

The interest rate reset is considered to be closely related to the host contract because it relates to default in a credit risk-related covenant and Entity X's own credit rating and, therefore, the embedded derivative would not be accounted for separately.

Example 7.5.1B

Interest adjustment: credit risk and share price

Entity Y issues bonds with a BBB rating. The terms of the bond are such that if both of the following conditions are met, the coupon on the bond will be reduced by 50 basis points:

(a) the rating of the bonds by a specific rating agency is upgraded to at least BBB+; and

(b) the average share price of the ordinary shares of Entity Y exceeds a specified level over a specified 20-day period.

Because the adjustment to the interest payments only occurs if both conditions are met, it is appropriate to consider the provision as a single embedded derivative in line with IAS 39:AG29 as discussed in **section 6** above, rather than two embedded derivatives. Although one of the underlyings of the derivative is related to credit quality of the issuer (i.e. Entity Y's credit rating) and the other underlying relates to Entity Y's equity price, the whole derivative would be considered not to be closely related to the host debt contract. This is because one of the underlyings (i.e. equity price) is considered not to be closely related to the economic characteristics and risks of debt (see **7.3** above).

By contrast, if the feature operated such that there were two independent adjustments to the interest paid on the bond (of 25 basis points each), one of which is triggered by changes to Entity Y's credit rating and the other by movements in Entity Y's equity price, it would be appropriate to treat the two features as separate embedded derivatives. The credit-rating triggered feature would be closely related but the equity-triggered feature would not be closely related to the debt host contract and, as a consequence, would be accounted for separately at FVTPL.

7.5.2 Adjustment for liquidity of issuer's debt

IAS 39 does not provide specific guidance when the cash flows of a debt instrument in the scope of IAS 39 are adjusted for changes in the relative liquidity of that debt instrument. Provided that the adjustments are not leveraged, the adjustment is likely to be closely related to the debt host contract because the liquidity of the instrument is inherent in the debt host contract.

Example 7.5.2

Interest adjustment: liquidity

Entity X issues a debt instrument that is repayable at par at maturity that pays a fixed rate of interest. On issue of the debt, the instrument is not listed. The debt instrument contains a contractual provision specifying that if the debt instrument ever becomes listed the rate of interest payable on the instrument will decrease by 0.5 per cent. The interest rate will be reset to its initial level in the event that the debt instrument is subsequently delisted.

The listing of the debt instrument is likely to increase the liquidity of the debt instrument. The lower liquidity of an unlisted instrument is a cost borne by the holders because it limits their ability to sell their holding of the debt instrument when the borrower's ability to meet its obligations as they fall due is in question. The listing of the debt instrument is likely to improve its liquidity and to provide the holders with an exit mechanism before maturity. The holder's willingness to accept a reduction in the interest rate in exchange for increased liquidity would be considered closely related to the host debt contract.

7.5.3 Adjustment for third party credit

IAS 39 views a credit derivative that transfers credit risk of a particular reference asset (which the entity, the 'beneficiary', may not own) to another party (the 'guarantor') as not closely related to the host debt contract when the host is in the scope of IAS 39. [IAS 39:AG30(h)]

Example 7.5.3A

Credit-linked note

Entity X issues credit-linked bonds. The bonds are linked to the performance of a portfolio of third-party corporate bonds held by a third-party bank. The bonds pay a rate of interest in excess of Entity X's normal cost of funds because, in the event that one of the referenced corporate bonds defaults, Entity X will pay a reduced principal to the holders.

The embedded credit-related provision would be accounted for separately because the credit of a third party entity is not considered to be closely related to the debt host contract issued by Entity X.

Example 7.5.3B

Cash versus synthetic credit default obligations

Collateralised debt obligation (CDO) special purpose entities (SPEs) are set up to issue notes to investors which pay based on the performance of specified named corporate debt. The interest and principal on the assets is used to service and repay the CDO liability. If there is default under the named corporate debt, then the investors of the CDO notes will suffer loss. The losses are shared by investors in a pre-agreed manner, often with the most junior notes suffering most of the expected loss.

There are two types of structures:

- the assets in the SPE are actual corporate debt (e.g. GM & Ford corporate bonds), referred to as 'cash CDOs' because the SPE has to own the actual cash instruments; or
- the assets in the SPE are derivatives over the corporate debt (e.g. credit default swaps (CDS) over GM & Ford), referred to as 'synthetic CDOs' because the SPE will or may hold synthetic instruments rather than holding cash instruments.

A CDO is illustrated below.

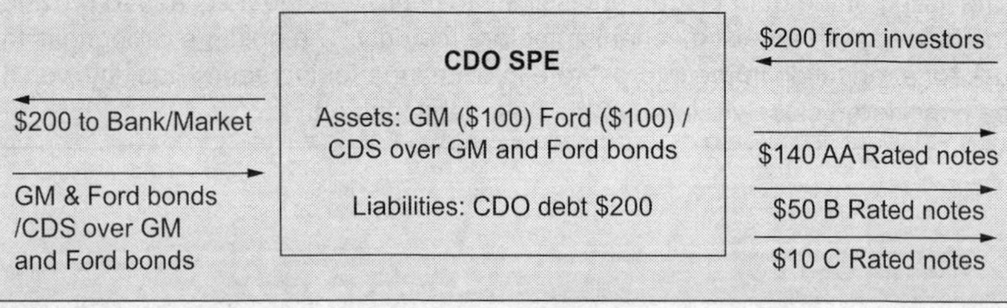

Whether the CDO structure is cash or synthetic will affect the accounting for the notes.

Cash CDO

If an issued CDO liability is not measured at FVTPL, the SPE will need to assess whether the CDO liability has embedded credit derivatives that require separation. Because the entity must own the underlying cash instruments, the issued CDO liability does not have a credit derivative that requires separation. The beneficiary (the SPE) is transferring the credit risk of its referenced assets to a guarantor (the investor in the CDO notes).

Synthetic CDO

Because the SPE is required to pay returns on the CDO liability that is linked to the performance of corporate bonds, but without actually needing to own these cash instruments (e.g. it can purchase credit derivatives over the reference corporate bonds), the notes issued by the SPE have credit embedded derivatives that require separation. The beneficiary (the SPE) is transferring the credit risk of referenced assets to a guarantor (the investor of the CDO notes) but does not own the underlying referenced assets.

The guidance on whether to separate an embedded derivative in CDOs applies to the issuer and holder of the CDO notes.

7.6 Foreign currency features

Debt contracts in the scope of IAS 39 may require the issuer to make payments of interest or principal in a foreign currency. An example of such a contract is a dual currency bond where the principal is paid in a foreign currency but interest is paid in the entity's functional currency. The foreign currency feature in a dual currency bond is an embedded derivative (foreign currency swap or foreign currency forward) but it is not separated from the host debt instrument because foreign currency gains and losses on a dual currency bond are already recognised in profit or loss following the requirements of IAS 21 *The Effects of Changes in Foreign Exchange Rates*.

Certain currency features may need to be separated. A debt contract may, for example, include a provision that would allow the holder to choose to receive interest payments in an alternative currency. This provision is a foreign currency option, written by the issuer.

Foreign currency option features are generally viewed by IAS 39 as taking on an additional foreign currency risk that is not normally present in transactions and will not be fully reflected by the requirements of IAS 21. Such an option in a debt host contract is not closely related and needs to be accounted for separately.

7.7 Caps, floors and collars on interest rates

Floating rate debt contracts often include features that 'cap', 'floor' or 'collar' the amount of interest payable on the debt.

7.7.1 *Definitions*

A 'cap' is an option contract that puts an upper limit on a floating interest rate. The purchaser of the cap is paid the difference between the current floating interest rate and the strike rate of the cap whenever the current floating rate exceeds the strike rate.

Example 7.7.1

Interest rate cap

Entity A purchases an interest rate cap, paying a premium of CU1 million. The cap has a notional amount of CU100 million and a strike rate of 6 per cent. Currently, LIBOR is 4.5 per cent.

The cap will pay Entity A the difference between LIBOR and 6 per cent whenever LIBOR exceeds 6 per cent. Thus, if LIBOR moves to 6.5 per cent, the cap will pay Entity A CU500,000, i.e. 0.5 per cent (the difference between LIBOR and 6 per cent) applied to the notional amount of the cap (CU100 million).

A 'floor' is an option contract that puts a lower limit on a floating interest rate. The writer of the floor will pay the difference between the current floating interest rate and the strike rate of the floor whenever the current floating rate drops below the strike rate. A floor is effectively the opposite of a cap. The writer of a floor will receive a premium which compensates it for the risk it has taken on (i.e. the risk that rates drop below a certain level).

Entities often want to protect themselves against rises in interest rates, so they purchase caps. However, these can be expensive. To reduce or limit the cost, entities will often simultaneously write a floor. Thus, they have achieved an interest rate collar. A 'collar' is an instrument that combines a cap and a floor. The holder of an interest rate collar will be exposed to interest rate movements only within a specified range. It protects the holder against a significant rise in interest rates, but limits the benefits of a drop in interest rates.

7.7.2 *'In the money' and 'out of the money' caps, floors and collars*

A cap is 'in the money' if its strike rate is lower than the market rate of interest. It is 'out of the money' if its strike rate is higher than the market rate of interest. If a cap has a strike rate of 6 per cent, it will be in the money whenever interest rates are above 6 per cent and out of the money whenever interest rates are below 6 per cent.

A floor is in the money if its strike rate is higher than the market rate of interest. It is out of the money if its strike rate is lower than the market rate of interest. If a floor has a strike rate of 4 per cent, it will be in the money whenever interest rates are below 4 per cent and out of the money whenever interest rates are above 4 per cent.

A collar has two strike prices, the upper and lower limits. A collar is out of the money if interest rates are between these two strike rates; it is in the money otherwise.

7.7.3 Embedded caps, floors and collars

An embedded cap or floor on the interest rate of a debt instrument, where the cap or floor is not leveraged, is closely related to the host debt contract provided that the cap is at or above the market interest rate and the floor is at or below the market interest rate when the instrument is issued. The assessment as to whether an embedded cap or floor is closely related to a host debt contract is made at issuance and is not subsequently revised. [IAS 39:AG33(b)]

Example 7.7.3

Embedded interest rate cap

Entity X issues CU100 million debt with a 5-year maturity. The interest is payable at LIBOR plus a credit spread of 150 basis points. LIBOR at issuance is 4.5 per cent and, therefore, the rate at inception of the debt is 6 per cent. There is a provision in the debt contract that if LIBOR were to rise, the rate payable on the debt would not rise above 7 per cent.

The cap is an embedded derivative that is closely related to the host debt contract because, at the time of the issuance of the debt, the cap is out of the money.

While the Standard does not specifically address a collar embedded in a debt contract, a simple analogy to caps and floors can be made. If a debt contract has an embedded collar which caps interest rates at 7 per cent and has a floor of 4 per cent, the collar will be closely related to the host debt contract provided that both the cap and the floor are out of the money when the debt is issued and the collar is not leveraged.

7.8 Conversion and equity features

A conversion feature that allows the holder of the debt contract to convert the outstanding amount into equity of the issuer is an embedded derivative that is not closely related to the host debt contract for the holder. The conversion option is also not closely related for the issuer if the conversion feature fails the definition of equity. Assessing whether the conversion feature meets the definition of equity for the issuer is complex and is addressed in **chapter C3**.

Example 7.8

Equity conversion feature

Entity X issues debt that is convertible into a fixed number of its ordinary shares in five years. The conversion feature represents an embedded written call option on the shares of Entity X, settled in a fixed number of shares.

For Entity X, because the conversion feature meets the definition of equity, the convertible debt is a compound instrument that should be split into its liability and equity components. Entity X will not account for the written call option as an embedded derivative because the option is an equity instrument of Entity X (see **chapter C3**).

The investor will account for the embedded purchased option separately because the equity conversion feature is not closely related to the host debt contract.

Another form of equity embedded derivative is an 'equity kicker'. These are debt instruments which provide for the lender to receive shares of the borrower for nothing, or a very low amount, if the borrower lists its shares on a stock exchange. The debt remains outstanding following the delivery of the shares. Typically, the lender is a venture capitalist. Similar to convertible debt, debt with an equity kicker carries a coupon that is lower than the rate on a comparable debt without the equity kicker.

The equity kicker meets the definition of a derivative because its value will change in response to changes in the borrower's share price, it has little initial net investment, and it is settled at a future date. This is true even though the right to receive the shares is contingent on an unrelated event. [IAS 39:IG.C.4]

For the holder, the embedded derivative is not closely related to the host debt contract and therefore will require separation at FVTPL. For the issuer, if the equity kicker fails the definition of equity for the issuer, it will also be recognised as an embedded derivative that is not closely related to the host debt contract and therefore will require separation at FVTPL.

7.9 Non-cash settlement of interest or principal

Debt contracts that allow for the payment of interest or principal in non-cash consideration may contain embedded derivatives that are not closely related to the host debt contract. In some cases the embedded derivative feature may be outside the scope of IAS 39 because it results in the delivery of a non-financial item in accordance with the entity's purchase, sale or usage requirements (see **2.5** in **chapter C1**).

Example 7.9

Non-cash settlement of interest

Entity A lends Entity B, a newspaper publisher, CU10 million for 10 years. Each year instead of paying interest, Entity B agrees to give Entity A a predetermined amount of free advertising space in a newspaper. For Entity B, selling newspaper advertising space falls within its normal sale requirements and, therefore, that part of the contractual arrangement is outside the scope of IAS 39. The debt instrument, excluding the fair value of the free advertising space, is in the scope of IAS 39 and will be measured at fair value at initial recognition. The fair value of the debt instrument will be less than the proceeds borrowed reflecting the fair value of the non-cash consideration included in the loan agreement.

If the sale of advertising space did not meet the normal purchase, sale or usage requirements exemption for Entity B (e.g. because Entity B was not a newspaper publisher), then that feature would be in the scope of IAS 39. The delivery of non-cash consideration embedded in the loan meets the definition of a derivative because it has an underlying (the price of the advertising space), no initial net investment, and it will be settled at future dates. The economic characteristics and risks of the embedded derivative and debt are not closely related and, therefore, the non-cash consideration feature would be separated and measured at FVTPL.

7.10 Unit-linking features embedded in host debt instrument

A unit-linking feature embedded in a host debt instrument in the scope of IAS 39 is closely related to the host debt instrument if the unit-denominated payments are measured at current unit values that reflect the fair values of the assets of the fund. A unit-linking feature is a contractual term that requires payments denominated in a unit of an internal or external investment fund. [IAS 39:AG33(g)]

IFRS 4:IG Example 2:2.15 provides the example of a policyholder option to surrender a contract for account value equal to the fair value of a pool of equity investments, possibly after deducting a surrender charge. The example makes reference to IAS 39:AG33(g) and states that if such a feature is embedded in a host investment contract then, if the insurer regards the account value as the amortised cost or the fair value of that portion of its obligation, no further adjustment is needed for the option (unless the surrender value differs significantly from the account value). Otherwise the embedded derivative feature would be required to be classified separately as at FVTPL. A host investment contract is described in IFRS 4:IG4 as a financial instrument that does not meet the definition of an insurance contract.

The above guidance suggests that unit-linking features would only be considered closely related where the unit denominated payments are measured in such a way that they reflect the fair value of the assets of the fund to which they are linked. In any case, even if the unit-linking feature is determined to be closely related to a debt host contract IAS 39:AG8 would be applicable for subsequent measurement of the hybrid instrument if it was measured at amortised cost (see **4.1.2** in **chapter C6**). Applying IAS 39:AG8 would result in the carrying amount of the hybrid instrument reflecting the amount expected to be paid or received which would incorporate the unit linking feature.

7.11 Further examples of embedded derivatives in host debt contracts

The table below provides further examples of derivative instruments embedded in debt host contracts.

Type of instrument	Economic characteristics	Embedded derivative	Closely related?
Inverse floater	Bond accrues interest at 5.25 per cent for three months to July 20X4; thereafter, at 10.75 per cent less 6-month LIBOR to January 20X5.	Forward starting fixed-to-floating rate interest rate swap	No. IAS 39:AG33(a)
Leveraged inverse floater	Bond accrues interest at 6 per cent to June 20X5; thereafter, at 14.55 per cent – (2.5 × 3-month LIBOR).	Forward starting leveraged interest rate swap	No. IAS 39:AG33(a)
Ratchet floater	Bond accrues interest at 3-month LIBOR + 50 basis points. In addition to having a lifetime cap of 7.25 per cent, the coupon will be collared each period between the previous coupon and the previous coupon plus 25 basis points. 3-month LIBOR at inception is 4 per cent.	Combinations of purchased and written options that create changing caps and floors	Yes. IAS 39:AG33(b)
Fixed-to-floating note	A bond that pays a varying coupon (first-year coupon is fixed; second- and third-year coupons are based on LIBOR).	Forward-starting interest-rate swap	Yes. IAS 39:AG33(a)

Type of instrument	Economic characteristics	Embedded derivative	Closely related?
Equity-indexed note	A bond for which the return of interest, principal, or both is tied to a specified equity security or index (e.g. the Standard and Poor's 500 (S&P 500) index). This instrument may contain a fixed or varying coupon rate and may place all, or a portion, of principal at risk.	Forward exchange contracts or option contracts	No. IAS 39:AG30(d)
Variable principal redemption bond	A supplemental principal payment will be paid to the investor, at maturity, if the final S&P 500 closing value (determined at a specified date) is less than its initial value at date of issuance and the 10-year constant maturity treasuries (CMT) is greater than 2 per cent as of a specified date. In all cases, the minimum principal redemption will be 100 per cent of face amount.	Option contract	No. IAS 39:AG30(d)
Crude-oil knock-in note	A bond that has a 1 per cent coupon and guarantees repayment of principal with upside potential based on the strength of the oil market.	Option contract	No. IAS 39:AG30(e)
Gold-linked bull note	A bond that has a fixed 3 per cent coupon and guarantees repayment of principal with upside potential if the price of gold increases.	Option contract	No. IAS 39:AG30(e)
Step-up bond	A bond that provides an introductory above-market yield that is less than twice the market rate at inception and steps up to a new coupon, which will be below then-current market rates or, alternatively, the bond may be called, at an amount that approximates the amortised cost of the debt instrument, in lieu of the step-up in the coupon rate.	Interest rate swap and call option	Yes. IAS 39:AG30(g) and AG33(a)

Type of instrument	Economic characteristics	Embedded derivative	Closely related?
Credit-sensitive bond	A bond that has a coupon rate of interest that resets based on changes in the issuer's credit rating.	Conditional exchange contract or option	Yes. IAS 39:AG33(a)
Inflation bond	A bond with a contractual principal amount that is indexed to the non-leveraged inflation rate of the economic environment of the issuer, but cannot decrease below par; the coupon rate is below that of traditional bonds of a similar maturity.	Inflation-linked swap with embedded floor	Yes. IAS 39:AG33(a) and (f)(i)
Specific equity-linked bond	A bond that pays a coupon slightly below that of traditional bonds of similar maturity; however, the principal amount is linked to the stock market performance of an equity investee of the issuer.	Series of forward contracts or option contracts	No. IAS 39:AG30(d)
Dual currency bond	A bond providing for repayment of principal in one currency (e.g. Euro) and periodic interest payments denominated in a different currency (e.g. Yen).	Foreign currency forward	Yes. IAS 39:AG33(c)
Short-term loan with foreign currency option	A US lender issues a loan at an above-market interest rate. The loan is made in US dollars, the borrower's functional currency, and the borrower has the option to repay the loan early in US dollars or in a fixed amount of a specified foreign currency.	Foreign currency option	No. IAS 39:AG30(g)

8 Embedded derivatives in equity host contracts

Embedded derivatives are not limited to debt hosts; they can also be embedded in equity host contracts. **Chapter C3** provides guidance on identifying the host contract as either debt or equity because sometimes it may be difficult to determine whether the host contract is debt or equity.

The identification of an equity or debt host contract is particularly relevant for entities classifying and measuring financial assets, rather than those classifying and measuring financial liabilities. The identification of whether the host contract is equity or debt is relevant in determining whether the economic characteristics and risks of the host contract are similar to that of the embedded derivative.

From the perspective of an issuer, it is very uncommon to issue a host contract that meets the definition of equity and contains an embedded derivative that needs to be separated out as a financial asset or liability as at fair value through profit or loss (see **example 8B**). In some cases both the embedded derivative and the host contract meet the definition of equity as neither conveys any obligation to pay cash or other financial assets.

Example 8A

Contingent share conversion based on interest rates (1)

Entity A issues €100 million of perpetual, irredeemable preference shares that pay a fixed dividend rate of 10 per cent which is payable at the discretion of the entity. The shares meet the definition of equity under IAS 32.

The shares include a provision stating that if interest rates increase by 200 basis points, the holders will additionally receive 100,000 ordinary shares in Entity A.

The embedded option is not separated by the issuer because it and the host instrument are both equity instruments of the issuer. Although the option is triggered by a change in interest rates, the value of the option is indexed to the change in fair value of, and is settled in, the issuer's shares. Equally, from the perspective of a holder the embedded option is closely related to the host.

Example 8B

Contingent cash payment based on interest rates (2)

Entity A issues US$100 million of perpetual, irredeemable preference shares that pay a discretionary, fixed dividend rate of 8 per cent. Because the entity has discretion as to whether or not, and the extent to which, dividends are paid, the host contract meets the definition of equity in IAS 32. Embedded in the shares is a provision that states if LIBOR increases to 12 per cent or more, the holders will become entitled to receive a one-off payment of cash calculated by a predetermined formula.

The issuer cannot avoid an outflow of cash in respect of the amount prescribed by the formula if LIBOR reaches 12 per cent, i.e. the embedded feature is an embedded derivative liability. Both the holder and the issuer account for this derivative separately from the host instrument. Accounting for the host instrument by the issuer is different from that by the holder because, for the issuer, equity is outside the scope of IAS 39.

Example 8C

Convertible preference shares

Entity X issues perpetual preference shares where any dividends issued are entirely at the discretion of the issuer. The preference shares are convertible into a fixed number of ordinary shares at any time after a specified date. The preference shares meet the definition of equity under IAS 32.

The preference shares are equity of Entity X. The conversion feature represents an embedded call option on Entity X's ordinary shares that also meets the definition of equity. Entity X does not account for the embedded option separately because both the option and the host are equity instruments of Entity X.

The same considerations apply to the investor; however, the accounting in the investor's books will be different from that of the issuer because, for the issuer, equity is outside the scope of IAS 39. For the holder, the perpetual preference share is a financial asset which consists of an equity host contract with a closely related equity embedded derivative.

From the perspective of the holder, if a hybrid instrument has an equity host and is puttable at a fixed amount or an amount determined on the basis of an index that is unrelated to the fair value of the equity host (e.g. the price of gold) then the put option would not have equity characteristics and, therefore, would not be closely related. In the case of a put option with a fixed strike price, the investor has downside protection and, therefore, does not share in a residual interest in the net assets of the issuer, and, in the case of a strike price linked to a variable other than the net assets of the issuer, the investor is not exposed to the residual net assets of the entity. The put option would not be considered closely related to the equity host contract and, therefore, would be separated and classified as at FVTPL.

From the perspective of the holder of a hybrid instrument, judgement is required in determining whether the put feature in puttable shares is closely related to the equity host contract when the host contract is classified as an AFS asset in the scope of IAS 39. (If the hybrid instrument is classified as at FVTPL, the embedded derivative guidance is not applicable because the whole instrument is fair valued through earnings.)

If the shares are puttable at fair value, it may be argued that the amount received by the holder upon exercise of the put option (being the fair value of the shares) represents the fair value of the equity host, because the amount payable to the holder is the fair value of the residual interest in the assets of the entity after deducting all of its liabilities and therefore, by definition, it has equity characteristics. The put option would be closely related because its risk characteristics are similar to those of the equity host. The whole hybrid instrument would be classified as AFS with gains and losses recognised in other comprehensive income and no embedded derivative would be recognised. This treatment could also apply where the issuer is an unquoted entity and the strike price for the put option is derived from a formula designed as a surrogate for the fair value of the shares of the issuing entity. Greater care would need to be taken in determining whether the strike price for the put option is equivalent to the fair value of the underlying shares and, therefore, whether the put option could be considered closely related.

If the shares are puttable at a fixed amount or an amount determined on the basis of an index that is unrelated to the fair value of the equity host (e.g. the price of gold), the put option would not have equity characteristics and, therefore, would not be closely related. Because the investor can force the issuer to pay an amount not equal to the proportionate share of the net assets of the entity, the holder has downside protection and, therefore, is not exposed to the residual net assets of the entity. The put option would be accounted for separately at FVTPL and the host contract would be classified as an AFS asset.

In March 2014 the IASB's Interpretations Committee received a request to clarify the classification by the holder of a hybrid financial instrument with a revolving maturity option, an early settlement option and a suspension of interest payments option (all at the option of the issuer). Specifically, the submitter raised the question of whether the host of such a financial instrument should be classified by the holder as an equity or as a debt instrument under IAS 39 *Financial Instruments: Recognition and Measurement*.

On the basis of the responses to the outreach request, the Interpretations Committee observed that the issue is not widespread. The Interpretations Committee also noted that the financial instrument described in the submission is specific and it would not be appropriate to provide guidance on this particular issue.

The Interpretations Committee noted that IFRS 9 *Financial Instruments* would resolve the question of whether the instrument should be classified before or after identifying the embedded derivatives, because it would not require bifurcation for hybrid contracts with financial asset hosts and a holder would be required to classify the instrument as a whole. As a result, the Interpretations Committee considered that developing accounting guidance on this issue would not be effective for a reasonable time period.

The Interpretations Committee considered that its agenda criteria are not met. Consequently, the Interpretations Committee tentatively decided not to add this issue to its agenda.

9 Embedded derivatives in lease contracts

Embedded derivatives can exist in lease contracts, whether an entity is acting as a lessee or a lessor in either a finance or an operating lease.

9.1 Inflation factors

An embedded derivative in a host lease contract is closely related to the host contract if the embedded derivative is an inflation-related index (e.g. if lease payments are indexed to a retail price index), provided that the index is not leveraged, and the index relates to inflation in the entity's own economic environment. [IAS 39:AG33(f)(i)]

9.1.1 Entity's economic environment

IAS 39 does not give any guidance as to what constitutes 'the entity's own economic environment'. It is reasonable to assume that when an entity operates in a certain country and enters into a lease agreement on, say, a property located in that country, the inflation of the country concerned will be the relevant inflation index because that index is related to the value of the lease and is present in the environment in which the entity operates.

Example 9.1.1

Inflation-adjusting lease payments

Entity X, a UK entity, has extensive operations in Europe and the US. Entity Y, Entity X's subsidiary, leases property in Paris with a lease term of 10 years. The functional currency of Entity Y is the Euro. Lease payments are to be made in Euros. Embedded in the lease is a provision that requires the lease payments to be adjusted every two years for the change in the UK consumer price index, which is not the index of the economic environment of Entity Y.

The embedded inflation indexed payment would be accounted for separately because, although the rate of inflation is not leveraged, the inflation index is in a different economic environment from the entity entering into the lease.

9.1.2 Leverage factors

The second consideration when assessing whether an inflation adjustment in a lease contract is an embedded derivative that should be separately accounted for is leverage. IAS 39 does not define leverage in the context of inflation. However, the concept of leverage is used in the assessment of the features present in debt contracts. For debt contracts, a leverage feature that can double the holder's initial rate of return and could result in a rate of return that is at least twice what the market return would be for a contract with the same terms as the host contract is not closely related to the host debt contract.

By analogy, it can be argued that an inflation adjustment for two times or more of the inflation index will be seen as leveraged. Careful consideration of the terms of the lease is required for a decision on whether any inflation adjustment included in it is indeed leveraged.

Example 9.1.2

Leveraged inflation-adjusting lease payments

Entity X, a UK entity, leases property in London with a lease term of 10 years. Lease payments are to be made in Sterling. Embedded in the lease is a provision that requires the lease payment to be adjusted annually for three times the changes in UK's retail price index.

The embedded inflation adjustment is not closely related to the host contract and will be accounted for separately because it is leveraged.

In **example 9.1.2**, it is quite clear that there is a leveraged inflation feature that needs to be separated. However, what is less clear is whether the derivative that needs separation is the total inflation adjustment (i.e. three times the retail price index) or just the leveraged portion (i.e. two times the retail price index).

The argument for the latter is that adjustment by the retail price index is seen as closely related. However, there are two counter-arguments to that: firstly, separation of only a portion of the embedded derivative amounts to splitting the derivative into two parts which is not generally permitted under IAS 39; secondly, separation could be argued to create cash flows that are not evident in the contract, which also is not the general practice under IAS 39. Accordingly, the total inflation adjustment (i.e. three times the retail price index) should be split out.

9.2 Foreign currency features

There are no specific rules addressing currency features in lease contracts. There are two pieces of guidance included in IAS 39 which analyse foreign currency features embedded in contracts: foreign currency derivatives embedded in host debt instruments; and foreign currency derivatives embedded in a host contract that is not a financial instrument.

For the former, the foreign currency feature is not separately accounted for because the instrument is a monetary item and, under IAS 21, foreign currency gains and losses are already recognised in profit or loss. For the latter, the assessment is more complicated. A foreign currency derivative embedded in a host contract that is not a financial instrument is closely related to the host provided it is not leveraged, does not contain an option, and requires payments denominated in:

- the functional currency of any substantial party to the contract;
- the currency in which the price of the related good or service that is acquired or delivered is routinely denominated in commercial transactions around the world; or
- a currency that is commonly used in contracts to purchase or sell non-financial items in the economic environment in which the transaction takes place.

It can be argued that trade receivables and payables recognised under finance leases are in the nature of a debt host and, therefore, are covered by the same requirements in IAS 21 to recognise foreign currency gains and losses in profit or loss on monetary items. Therefore, it would be reasonable to analogise from the foreign currency guidance on debt contracts when considering foreign currency features in finance lease payables and receivables.

Operating leases are non-financial instruments. Therefore, the considerations that apply to non-financial items detailed in **10.5** will equally apply to operating leases. These considerations include foreign currency options, leverage factors, the functional currency of substantial parties to the contract, and the currency that is commonly used in contracts in the economic environment in which the transaction takes place.

9.2.1 Examples of embedded foreign currency features

The following examples apply the analysis in **9.2** above.

Example 9.2.1A

Operating lease denominated in functional currency of a party

Entity X, a Dutch entity, leases property from Entity Y, a UK entity, under an operating lease. The lease payments are denominated in Sterling. The functional currency of Entity X is the Euro and the functional currency of Entity Y is Sterling.

The denomination of the lease payments in Sterling would not require separate accounting because Sterling is the functional currency of a substantial party to the contract, Entity Y.

Example 9.2.1B

Operating lease not denominated in functional currency of a party

Entity X, a New Zealand entity, leases property under an operating lease from Entity Y, an Australian entity. The lease payments are denominated in US dollars. The functional currency of Entity X is the New Zealand dollar and the functional currency of Entity Y is the Australian dollar.

The denomination of the lease payments in US dollars would require separate accounting because it is not the currency of the primary economic environment of either counterparty to the contract, and the price of this asset is not denominated routinely in that currency in international commerce.

If the property were leased under a finance lease (which is a financial instrument), the lease payments would represent monetary items and, therefore, be within the scope of IAS 21. The embedded derivative would not be separated.

Example 9.2.1C

Choice of settlement in foreign currencies

A lease contract between Entity A (Sterling functional currency) and Entity B (US dollar functional currency), whereby the lessee can choose to make payments in either Sterling or US dollars, contains an embedded option that is not closely related to the host lease contract. This is true even though both of the settlement currencies are functional currencies of one of the counterparties to the lease. This answer would apply regardless of whether the lease was an operating or finance lease.

9.2.2 Substantial party

A 'substantial party' to the contract in the examples above is a party acting as a principal under the contract. The criterion for a 'substantial party' would not be satisfied if the party is an agent that is being engaged by one of the transacting entities solely to comply with the requirement that payments be denominated in the functional currency of any substantial party to the contract.

Example 9.2.2

Substantial party

Entity X would like to lease property from Entity Y under an operating lease and have the payments denominated in US dollars. The functional currency of both entities is Sterling. To accomplish a US dollar-denominated lease, Entity Y leases the property to an investment bank whose functional currency is US dollars. The investment bank then subleases the property to Entity X. The sublease agreement requires Entity X to pay US dollars. The investment bank is indemnified by Entity Y for any losses incurred due to a default by Entity X. The investment bank is acting solely as an agent for Entity X and, accordingly, is not at risk. The bank cannot be viewed as a substantial party to the lease. Therefore, the embedded foreign currency derivative requires separate accounting.

9.3 Referenced underlyings

A lease with contingent rentals that are based on related sales or on variable interest rates contain an embedded derivative (linkage to sales or interest) which is deemed to be closely related to the host lease contract.

9.3.1 Contingent rentals based on variable interest rates

Example 9.3.1

Lease linked to interest rates

Entity A, a UK entity, enters into a lease under which the payments are indexed to 6-month LIBOR. The embedded derivative does not need to be separated because the indexation is to interest rates inherent in Entity A's local economy.

IAS 39 does not provide guidance on what constitutes a variable interest rate. It is reasonable to assume that when an entity operates in a particular jurisdiction and enters into a lease agreement in that jurisdiction, a variable interest rate would be similar to the benchmark interest rate that would be payable on a debt instrument where the proceeds received from the debt instrument are invested in the leased asset and the debt is secured on the leased asset.

9.3.2 Contingent rentals based on related sales

Example 9.3.2A

Lease linked to sales

Entity X leases a property, which it uses as a retail outlet, selling custom-made umbrellas. Embedded in the lease is a clause requiring lease payments to increase for each additional 1,000 umbrellas sold after the first 100,000.

Contingent rentals based on related sales are considered to be closely related to the host lease contract; accordingly, the sales-related derivative should not be separated from the lease.

Example 9.3.2B

Lease linked to throughput

Entity Y leases shop premises in an airport terminal on an operating lease. The lease payments are contingent on the number of passengers who pass through the terminal.

While the contingent rentals are not based directly on related sales, it is clear that sales are directly affected by the number of passengers passing through the terminal. Therefore, the embedded derivative is closely related to the host lease contract and separate accounting is not required.

9.3.3 Contingent rentals based on other measures

IAS 39 states that contingent rentals based on related sales are closely related to the host lease contract. However, no guidance is given on contingent rentals based on other measures, such as profit or net assets or based on ratios. Entities will need to consider their accounting policy with respect to the definition of derivative, see **2.1** in **chapter C4**, in determining whether contingent rentals linked to such measures are a "non-financial variable that is specific to a party to the contract". The application of the accounting policy may in some cases lead to a conclusion that the contingent feature does not meet the definition of a derivative and therefore cannot be considered an embedded derivative.

Example 9.3.3

Lease linked to profits

Entity Z, a UK entity, leases a retail unit in a large shopping mall located in the UK. Under the lease, lease payments will increase for each £1,000 profit after tax made over £1,000,000.

Under Entity Z's accounting policy, it does not regard its own profits as a "non-financial variable specific to a party to the contract" and therefore a separate contract with contingent payments linked to profits would meet the definition of a derivative (see **2.1** in **chapter C4**).

While contingent rentals based on related sales are closely related to a host lease contract, the same is not true of contingent rentals based on profit after tax. Several of the balances that are added together to reach profit after tax (such as cost of sales and tax) do not have economic characteristics and risks similar to those of the lease contract. Therefore, the embedded derivative is not closely related to the host lease contract and separate accounting is required.

9.3.4 Other referenced underlyings

A lease contract under which payments are determined by changes in a referenced underlying that is not generally connected with the normal pricing of a traditional lease contains an embedded derivative that is required to be separated. Examples of referenced underlyings include security prices, commodity prices, an unrelated index of prices or rates, credit ratings or a credit index.

Example 9.3.4

Lease linked to share price index

Entity A has several investments in FTSE 100 shares. It enters into a lease contract and negotiates a clause whereby lease payments are indexed to changes in the FTSE 100.

Contingent rentals based on changes in the FTSE 100 are not closely related to the host lease contract; consequently, the embedded derivative would need to be separated from the host lease.

10 Embedded derivatives in purchase, sale and service contracts

There is very little guidance on assessing embedded derivatives in executory contracts that either are not net settleable or meet the own use scope exception, particularly service contracts. The appropriate accounting will need to be determined by analogising from the guidance and principles applicable to other host contracts.

10.1 Adjustments for ingredients

Pricing of sales, purchase and service contracts is often structured so as to pass on to customers the cost of an ingredient used in the production or delivery of an asset or service.

There is no guidance from which to draw an analogy. Hence, the assessment of a particular contract should be based on an analysis of the economic characteristics and risks of that contract. This should include a combination of qualitative and quantitative factors.

For example, a physically delivered contract to purchase electricity is assessed and found to be a purchase, sale and usage requirement contract that is outside the scope of IAS 39. However, there is a pricing adjustment with respect to a different commodity, gas. Gas is used as an ingredient in the production of the electricity that will be physically delivered. The pricing adjustment is achieved through a formula that incorporates many other pricing inputs and variables. The prices of gas and electricity in this case are not highly correlated.

Commodity-based contracts that are entered into and continue to meet the entity's expected purchase, sale, or usage requirements are outside the scope of IAS 39 and are therefore not financial instruments. (This is discussed further in **2.5** of **chapter C1**.) However, even if a contract is not a financial instrument in its entirety, it may include an embedded derivative that is potentially required to be accounted for separately.

The guidance in IAS 39 focuses on economic characteristics and risks in determining whether the embedded derivative is closely related. The guidance does not specifically refer to a purely quantitative assessment, nor does it refer to a purely qualitative assessment of the relationship. Therefore an entity would need to determine whether both quantitative and qualitative factors are relevant in determining whether the pricing adjustment is closely related to the host contract or not.

In the circumstances described, a quantitative assessment would establish that the economic characteristics are different, due to a lack of correlation between the pricing adjustment and the price of the commodity that is delivered under the contract. However, this quantitative assessment is not necessarily the only factor in the determination as to whether the embedded derivative is closely related, because qualitative factors may also be relevant to the decision. If the supplier of the electricity (who is the counterparty to the arrangement) is a gas-powered power station, then this qualitative characteristic is relevant in determining whether the pricing adjustment should be separately accounted for. Because the pricing adjustment is specifically relevant to the production of the commodity to be delivered under the contract, then the pricing adjustment is considered to be closely related to the host contract. However, if it cannot be demonstrated that the pricing adjustment is directly relevant to the counterparty (e.g. the counterparty is an electricity exchange/broker and did not use the indexed commodity (gas) in the production of the commodity (electricity) that was to be physically delivered, or the counterparty is a nuclear-powered electricity supplier and does not use gas in the production of the electricity), then this pricing adjustment does not have qualitative merit and, therefore, a quantitative assessment should take precedence.

10.2 Inflation factors

There is no specific guidance on inflation factors within purchase, sale or service contracts, but an analogy can be established with lease contracts. An embedded inflation-related index in a host lease contract is closely related to the host contract provided that the index is not leveraged and the index relates to inflation in the entity's own economic environment.

Example 10.2

Executory contract linked to inflation

Entity A, a UK entity, enters into a long-term service contract under which it agrees to clean and maintain specified buildings owned by Entity B for the next 10 years. All the buildings are located within the UK. Entity A receives a fixed annual fee. Embedded in the contract is a clause providing for a one-off adjustment half-way through the contract such that the fee receivable is adjusted for changes in the UK's retail price index from the beginning of the contract. Thereafter, the fee remains fixed at the new amount.

The embedded inflation-indexed payment is closely related to the host service contract because the rate of inflation is not leveraged, and the inflation index is that of the local economic environment.

In determining whether the inflation feature within a sale, purchase or service contract is leveraged or is that of the entity's local environment, similar considerations to those used when assessing host lease contracts should be applied (see **9.1**).

10.3 Adjustments for unrelated factors

Purchase and sales contracts in which payments are determined by changes in a referenced underlying that is not generally connected with the normal pricing of such contracts contain embedded derivatives that need to be separated. Examples of pricing adjustments of this type include adjustments by reference to interest rates, security prices, unrelated commodity prices, and various indices of prices or rates.

Example 10.3

Executory contract linked to share price index

Entity A contracts to buy goods from Entity B for a fixed amount plus or minus an indexation feature linked to movements in the FTSE 250. The embedded derivative based on the FTSE 250 is not closely related to the host contract and would need to be separated from the host purchase contract.

10.4 Caps, floors and collars

In some purchase, sales and service contracts, the price is set as a market price at the time of the payment, but is 'capped', 'floored', or 'collared' within a range. The concepts of caps, floors and collars are explained in the context of interest rates in **7.7**.

Similar consideration can be applied here, i.e. terms included in a contract to purchase or sell an asset that establish a cap and a floor on the price to be paid or received for the asset are closely related to the host contract if both the cap and the floor are out of the money at inception and are not leveraged. [IAS 39:AG33(b)] This can be extended to collars included in purchase and sales contracts, i.e. collars are closely related to the host contract if they are out of the money at inception.

The assessment is made at inception of the contract, and is not subsequently revised.

Whilst IAS 39 does not specifically mention caps, floors and collars embedded in service contracts, it is reasonable to analogise to the guidance given on purchase and sales contracts.

Example 10.4

Executory contract with embedded cap

Entity A enters into a contract to purchase tin in 12 months at the market price of tin at the date of purchase. Embedded in the contract is a cap that puts an upper limit on the price Entity A will be required to pay. The cap is out of the money at inception of the contract (i.e. the cap is set above the current price for tin).

The cap is closely related to the host purchase contract and, accordingly, it will not be separated. The cap is closely related to the host contract for the life of the contract, irrespective of whether tin prices rise so that the cap becomes in the money.

10.5 Foreign currency features

An embedded foreign currency derivative in a host contract that is not a financial instrument is closely related to the host contract provided that it is not leveraged, does not contain an option feature and requires payments denominated in one of the following currencies:

[IAS 39:AG33(d)]

(i) the functional currency of any substantial party to the contract;

(ii) the currency in which the price of the related good or service that is acquired or delivered is routinely denominated in commercial transactions around the world (such as the US dollar for crude oil transactions); or

(iii) a currency that is commonly used in contracts to purchase or sell non-financial items in the economic environment in which the transaction takes place (e.g. a relatively stable and liquid currency that is commonly used in local business transactions or external trade)

The three criteria in IAS 39:AG33(d) are not mutually exclusive. For example, an entity in Country Y may export oil in US dollars. One, two or all three of the following may apply: the exporting entity may have the US dollar as its functional currency; oil is considered a non-financial item that is routinely denominated in US dollars throughout the world; and the US dollar may be a common currency for either internal or external transactions for Country Y.

The term 'substantial party' is discussed further in **9.2.2**.

The assessment of the functional currency of a substantial party to the contract in (i) above requires careful consideration. For example, a substantial party to a contract may be a subsidiary of a larger group. The presentation currency of the group (see IAS 21 *The Effects of Changes in Foreign Exchange Rates*) is not relevant to this assessment, because it is the functional currency of the subsidiary that is relevant. In many cases, judgement will be required when the subsidiary is in a jurisdiction that does not produce individual entity financial statements under IFRSs or an equivalent GAAP and, therefore, its functional currency is not evident. Too much reliance should not be placed on the country of incorporation or geographical location of a substantial party to the contract because the evaluation of the functional currency under IAS 21 includes many other factors.

A currency in which the price of the related goods or services is routinely denominated in commercial transactions around the world can only be a currency that is used for similar transactions all around the world, not just in one local area. For example, if cross-border transactions in natural gas in North America are routinely denominated in US dollars and such transactions are routinely denominated in Euros in Europe, neither the US dollar nor the Euro is the currency in which the goods or services are routinely denominated in commercial transactions around the world. [IAS 39:IG.C.9]

By definition, a currency in which the price of goods or services is routinely denominated around the world has to be one currency. However, the existence of a relatively small proportion of transactions in one or two markets, or in a particular jurisdiction, that are denominated in a local currency does not preclude a non-financial item from being considered to be routinely denominated in a particular currency in commercial transactions around the world.

The number of non-financial items that would qualify under IAS 39:AG33(d)(ii) is likely to be limited. In practice, such items will primarily be commodities that are traded in US dollars in commercial transactions throughout the world.

For certain types of commodity transactions, contracts may be based on a dominant currency (such as the US dollar) but may be denominated in local currencies in certain markets for regulatory or other reasons, i.e. the price is translated at the spot rate into local currencies (a 'convenience translation' mechanism). For example, although the dominant currency for crude oil transactions as noted in IAS 39:AG33(d)(ii) is the US dollar, some contracts for crude oil may be denominated in Canadian dollars in Canada, when the Canadian dollar price is a convenience translation of the US dollar crude oil price. A simple convenience translation into a local currency of the price of a commodity that is routinely denominated in a dominant currency would not negate the view that the price of the commodity is routinely denominated in a single currency in commercial transactions around the world. On the other hand, if a commodity transaction is regularly denominated in various currencies in commercial transactions around the world where such foreign currency prices are not convenience translations of a dominant currency price, that price of that commodity would not be considered to be routinely denominated in a particular currency.

The existence of an organised commodity exchange where a commodity is traded in a single currency provides a useful starting point in determining the dominant currency in which transactions in that commodity are denominated and, accordingly, whether the price of the commodity can be considered to be 'routinely denominated' in that particular currency. The organised commodity exchanges may establish liquid markets for commodities quoted in a particular currency, and transactions between counterparties that are not conducted through the exchange are also denominated in that particular currency, because to do otherwise would present arbitrage opportunities. For example, copper and gold are traded in US dollars on organised commodity exchanges and transactions between various counterparties that are not conducted through the exchange are also denominated in US dollars given the liquid markets established by the exchanges.

Certain commodities are not traded on organised exchanges, but global pricing forums exist that publish 'spot' prices denominated in a dominant currency for that particular commodity. Transactions between market participants are based on those published spot prices. For example, certain organisations independently may monitor market activities and publish US dollar prices that have become generally accepted as spot prices for the given commodity. Contracts between market participants are denominated in US dollars based on these published spot prices. In Japan and Europe, transactions may be conducted in Japanese Yen or Euros, respectively, but such Yen and Euro price equivalents are convenience translations of the US dollar spot price. Accordingly, in such circumstances, the price of the given commodity would be considered to be routinely denominated in US dollars in commercial transactions around the world.

The concept of a 'currency that is commonly used in contracts to purchase or sell non-financial items in the economic environment in which the transaction takes place' as described in IAS 39:AG33(d)(iii) was introduced to address situations where entities operate in economies in which it is common for business contracts to be denominated in a foreign currency. [IAS 39:BC39]

'Economic environment' should be considered for the country concerned as a whole. It may be the case that more than one currency is commonly used. The Standard provides an example of a common currency as a "relatively stable and liquid currency that is commonly used in local business transactions *or* external trade" (emphasis added). Therefore, a currency that is common for *either* external or internal transactions will be considered common for that country.

Looking at external trade, it may be possible that a country has multiple currencies that are commonly used to purchase or sell non-financial items. For instance, import and export transactions in and out of a small country (with counterparties in other small countries) may be commonly denominated in a range of internationally liquid, stable currencies (such as the Euro and the US dollar) rather than just one internationally liquid, stable currency. In such circumstances, if there is a significant level of transactions in each of the currencies, it may be possible that more than one currency is commonly used in the economic environment of external trade for that country.

Similarly, it may be possible that in certain hyperinflationary economies more than one foreign currency is used in local business transactions (because large sections of the general population view amounts in terms of one foreign currency and significant other sections of the population view amounts in another foreign currency). Also, this may be the case where a particular industry dominates the economy and commonly uses a foreign currency in local business transactions while the entirety of the remaining part of the economy uses the local currency. The judgement as to whether there is more than one common currency will depend on how significant the use of a particular currency is with respect to the local or external trade transactions of the country as a whole.

In determining whether a currency is common in a particular jurisdiction, the analysis should focus on *all* transactions in that jurisdiction. For example, in determining whether external trade is commonly denominated in Euros, transactions with the Euro zone should not be excluded from the analysis. Equally, if an entity is determining whether a country with large oil exports is considered to have US dollars as a common currency, the analysis of that country should not exclude exports of oil which would be expected to be denominated in US dollars because oil is routinely denominated in US dollars throughout the world.

In May 2007, the IFRIC (now the IFRS Interpretations Committee) published a tentative rejection notice in response to a submission on the application of IAS 39:AG33(d)(iii) regarding, in particular, what is the economic environment when determining whether a currency is commonly used in contracts to buy or sell non-financial items. In the draft rejection notice, the IFRIC noted that the paragraph requires an entity to identify where the transaction takes place and to identify currencies that are commonly used in the economic environment in which the transaction takes place. The IFRIC was proposing not to take the issue on to its agenda because any guidance developed would be more in the nature of application guidance than an interpretation.

Following responses by constituents and further debate at IFRIC, the IFRIC agreed to refer the matter to the Board for amendment to clarify the Standard and eliminate any diversity in practice. At its December 2007 meeting, the IASB noted that IAS 39:AG33(d) is intended to prohibit the separation of embedded foreign currency derivatives if the embedded derivatives are integral to the contractual arrangement. The IASB noted that embedded foreign currency derivatives are likely to be integral to the contractual arrangement if the foreign currency has one or more of the characteristics of a functional currency as set out in IAS 21:9. Accordingly, the Board decided to amend IAS 39:AG33(d)(iii) to refer to a currency that has one or more of the characteristics of a functional currency as set out in IAS 21:9.

At its January 2009 meeting, the Board decided to defer its redeliberations of the proposal relating to the bifurcation of an embedded foreign currency derivative to a future period.

At its January 2010 meeting, the IFRIC decided to remove the item, without finalisation, from the annual improvements project. The IFRIC believe that the issue will be incorporated as part of the Board's broader decisions on replacing IAS 39 and, therefore, should not be considered on a piecemeal basis. However, this issue was not brought back to the Board's attention as part of its deliberations in replacing IAS 39. The IASB transferred all the guidance on embedded derivatives from IAS 39 to IFRS 9 in October 2010 as part of its project to replace IAS 39 but this guidance was left unchanged.

The following examples demonstrate the application of the guidance in IAS 39:AG33(d).

Example 10.5A

Routinely denominated currency (1)

Two entities, both of whose functional currency is the Japanese Yen, enter into a 3-year supply contract. If payments were either denominated in or linked to the US dollar, and the US dollar is not the currency in which the service is routinely denominated in commercial transactions around the world, the embedded foreign currency forward would need to be separated from the host supply contract.

When a transaction is denominated in a currency that is a common currency in the economic environment of one or both of the substantial parties to the contract, it is reasonable to consider the currency denomination of the contract is closely related for both parties.

Contracts where a party has the option over which currency the contract may be settled in contain foreign currency features that are not closely related to the host purchase or sale contract.

Example 10.5B

Choice of settlement in foreign currencies

Entity A, a car dealership, contracts to purchase cars from Entity B, a car manufacturer. The functional currencies of Entities A and B are Sterling and Euro respectively. The purchase agreement allows Entity A to choose whether to settle the contract in a fixed amount of either Sterling or Euros.

The embedded foreign currency option must be separated from the host purchase contract. This treatment applies even though both settlement currencies are functional currencies of counterparties to the sales agreement.

Example 10.5C

Leveraged foreign currency adjustment

Entity X, a UK entity, enters into a sales contract with Entity Z, a US entity. Payments are in US dollars, but embedded in the contract is a clause such that payments are adjusted for twice the change in the US dollar exchange rate for the period that the payment is outstanding.

The sales contract contains an embedded derivative that is not closely related to the host sales contract because leveraged foreign currency features are not closely related to host sales contracts.

Example 10.5D

Routinely denominated currency (2)

Entity A, a UK entity, contracts to buy oil from Entity B, also a UK entity. The functional currency of both entities is Sterling; however, the contract is to be settled in a fixed number of US dollars.

The embedded foreign currency feature is closely related to the host purchase contract, even though it is not in the functional currency of either counterparty to the contract. This is because the price of oil is routinely denominated in US dollars in commercial transactions around the world. Therefore, two Sterling functional currency entities can transact in oil in US dollars and the foreign currency embedded derivative is deemed to be closely related to the host purchase or sale contract.

Example 10.5E

Common currency in local economic environment

Entity A operates in a South American country that is assessed as having a high inflation economy. Like all other local businesses, it chooses to conduct its business in US dollars, a relatively stable currency. Thus, all purchase and sales contracts are denominated in US dollars.

The embedded foreign currency derivative does not need to be separated from the host purchase or sales contract because these contracts are denominated in a currency that is commonly used in the local economic environment.

If Entity A chose to use the Euro when all other local businesses use the US dollar, this exemption would not be available. To avoid separation of the embedded derivative, Entity A would have to demonstrate that it met one of the other exemptions noted above.

Example 10.5F

Common currency: sales contract indexed to a foreign currency

Two entities based in Country A both have a functional currency of US Dollars. The entities enter into a construction contract whose price is fixed at the inception in Euros. Progress billings under the contract will be invoiced and paid in US Dollars. The amount of US Dollars payable/receivable will vary and be equal to the fixed Euro amounts converted to US Dollars based on the Euro/US Dollar exchange rate at each payment date. The Euro is the currency commonly used in contracts in the economic environment in which the transaction takes place.

As the amount of US Dollars varies to equal the fixed amount of Euros at the payment date, the contract is considered a Euro denominated contract.

The contract contains an embedded derivative because the payment terms are equivalent to entering into the contract in US Dollars and then entering into a Euro/US Dollars foreign currency derivative. However, the embedded derivative is considered to be closely related and, therefore, does not need to be accounted for separately as a derivative in accordance with IAS 39:AG33(d)(iii) because the Euro is a currency that is commonly used in the economic environment in which the transaction takes place.

Determination of contractual terms of the separated embedded derivative should be done by reference to the contractual terms of the non-financial host contract. For example, if a foreign currency derivative that is required to be separated is embedded in a purchase contract of a non-financial item which specifies delivery in two months' time, the maturity of the foreign currency derivative is two months.

The purchase contract stops being an executory (non-financial) contract once the delivery of the non-financial item takes place and a financial instrument (a foreign currency payable) comes into existence. The foreign currency translation of the payable is recognised in profit or loss in accordance with IAS 21 because it is a foreign currency denominated monetary item. When the non-financial item is recognised, the embedded derivative is derecognised and its carrying amount is included in the cost of the non-financial item (see **section 12**).

11 Embedded derivatives in insurance contracts

As discussed at **2.3** in **chapter C1**, derivatives embedded in insurance contracts are within the scope of IAS 39 if they require separation in accordance with IAS 39, except if a derivative embedded in an insurance contract is itself an insurance contract. [IFRS 4:7] An insurance contract is a contract under which one party (the policyholder) accepts significant insurance risk from another party by agreeing to compensate the policyholder if a specified uncertain future event adversely affects the policyholder.

As an exception to IAS 39, an insurer is not required to separate and measure at fair value a policyholder's option to surrender an insurance contract for a fixed amount (or for an amount based on a fixed amount and an interest rate), even if the exercise price differs from the carrying amount of the host insurance liability. However, the requirement in IAS 39 does apply to a put option or cash surrender option embedded in an insurance contract if the surrender value varies in response to the change in a financial variable (such as an equity or commodity price or index), or a non-financial variable that is not specific to a party to the contract. Furthermore, this requirement also applies if the holder's ability to exercise a put option or cash surrender option is triggered by a change in such a variable (e.g. a put option that can be exercised if a stock market index reaches a specified level). This applies equally to options to surrender a financial instrument containing a discretionary participation feature. [IFRS 4:8 & 9]

IFRS 4:IG Example 2: 2.15 provides the example of a policyholder option to surrender a contract for account value equal to the fair value of a pool of equity investments, possibly after deducting a surrender charge. The example makes reference to IAS 39:AG33(g) and states that if such a feature is embedded in a host insurance contract and if the insurer measures that portion of its obligation at account value, no further adjustment is needed for the option (unless the surrender value differs significantly from account value). Otherwise the embedded derivative is to be measured separately as at FVTPL.

A unit-linking feature embedded in a host insurance contract is closely related to the host contract if the unit-denominated payments are measured at current unit values that reflect the fair values of the assets of the fund. A unit-linking feature is a contractual term that requires payments denominated in a units of an internal or external investment fund. [IAS 39:AG33(g)] For equivalent guidance on debt host contracts, see **7.10**.

This is a complex area, and must be considered in conjunction with IFRS 4 *Insurance Contracts*. The following examples are applications of embedded derivative features in insurance contracts.

Example 11A

Surrender value indexed to share price index

A policyholder has an option to surrender an insurance contract for a surrender value based on the FTSE 100. The option is not closely related to the host contract (unless the option is life-contingent to a significant extent) and should be separated from the host contract and accounted for as a derivative.

Example 11B

Death benefit linked to share price index

A host insurance contract contains a death benefit linked to equity prices or equity index, payable only on death or annuitisation and not on surrender or maturity. The equity-index feature is an insurance contract (unless the life-contingent payments are insignificant), because the policyholder benefits from it only when the insured event occurs. Thus, the contract is outside the scope of IAS 39.

Example 11C

Surrender value linked to interest rates

A host insurance contract contains an embedded guarantee of minimum interest rates to be used in determining its surrender or maturity values.

If the guarantee is in the money on issue, or is leveraged, then the embedded guarantee is not an insurance contract (unless the embedded guarantee is life-contingent to a significant extent) and should be separated from the host contract.

Example 11D

Dual-indexed payout feature

Entity A purchases an insurance contract that contains a dual trigger such that payment is contingent on a breakdown in power supply that adversely affects the holder (first trigger) and a specified level of electricity prices (second trigger). The contingent payment is made only if both triggering events occur.

The embedded derivative is an insurance contract (unless the first trigger lacks commercial substance). A contract that qualifies as an insurance contract, whether at inception or later, remains an insurance contract until all rights and obligations are extinguished or expire. Therefore, although the remaining exposure is similar to a financial derivative after the insured event has occurred, the embedded derivative is still an insurance contract.

A derivative embedded in an insurance contract is closely related to the host insurance contract if the embedded derivative and host insurance contract are so interdependent that an entity cannot measure the embedded derivative separately (i.e. without considering the host contract). [IAS 39:AG33(h)]

12 Measurement of embedded derivatives at initial recognition

If an embedded derivative is separated from its host contract (because it is not closely related to the host), then it must be accounted for as if it were a free-standing derivative. The embedded derivative should be recognised in the statement of financial position at fair value, with changes in fair value recognised in profit or loss as they arise, unless it is designated as an effective hedging instrument in a cash flow or a net investment hedge (see **chapter C9**).

The host contract is accounted for under IAS 39 if it is a financial instrument within the scope of the Standard; otherwise it is accounted for under the appropriate Standard (e.g. under IAS 17 if it is a lease contract).

Example 12

Accounting for foreign currency derivative embedded in executory contract

Entity A, a UK-based entity with Sterling as its functional currency, enters into a contract to purchase cocoa from a local supplier, Entity B, in six months for a fixed amount of US dollars. The US dollar is not the functional currency of either party to the transaction. The cocoa will be delivered and used over a reasonable period in the normal course of business.

Because the cocoa will be physically delivered and is for use in the normal course of business, the contract qualifies for the purchase requirements scope exception and therefore is not wholly in the scope of IAS 39. This means that the entire contract is not a derivative recognised in the statement of financial position at fair value with changes in fair value recognised in profit or loss.

The contract still needs to be assessed for embedded derivatives. The contract contains an embedded foreign currency forward that is not closely related because the contract will be settled in US dollars and US dollars is neither the functional currency of either counterparty to the contract nor the currency in which the price of cocoa is routinely denominated in commercial transactions throughout the world. It is also not the currency commonly used in contracts to purchase or sell non-financial items in the UK. This embedded derivative must be separated from the host purchase contract and accounted for in the statement of financial position at fair value. Changes in fair value (arising from changes in the Sterling/US dollar exchange rate) will be recognised in profit or loss.

Assume the contract is entered into on 1 January 20X5. The contract is over a specified amount of cocoa for US$150,000. The 6-month forward exchange rate is US$1.5:£1. The 3-month forward exchange rate on 31 March 20X5 (Entity A's year end) is US$1.2:£1, and the spot exchange rate on 30 June 20X5 (when the cocoa is delivered) is US$1.25:£1. From the point of view of Entity A, the contract will be accounted for as a foreign currency forward contract to sell US dollars and buy Sterling, and an unrecognised executory contract to sell Sterling and buy inventories.

There are no entries on 1 January because the embedded derivative is a non-optional derivative with a fair value of zero at inception. At 31 March, the forward exchange rate has moved and so Entity A now expects US$150,000 to be equivalent to £125,000, rather than £100,000. There is a fair value loss on the forward contract, so the entry is as follows.

	£	£
Dr Profit or loss	25,000	
Cr Forward liability		25,000

To record the remeasurement of the forward liability.

On 30 June, the forward liability has decreased in value, because US$150,000 will cost £120,000. The entry is as follows.

	£	£
Dr Forward liability	5,000	
Cr Profit or loss		5,000

To record the remeasurement of the forward liability.

Entity A now pays US$150,000 to buy the cocoa under the purchase contract.

	£	£
Dr Inventories	120,000	
Cr Cash		120,000

To record the purchase of cocoa.

Entity A must also remove the embedded derivative from its statement of financial position.

		£	£
Dr	Forward liability	20,000	
Cr	Inventories		20,000

To eliminate the embedded derivative.

The inventories are recognised in the statement of financial position at £100,000. This is US$150,000 translated at the forward rate contracted on 1 January. When the inventories are sold, the cost of sales will be £20,000 lower than expected (based on cash paid on 30 June). This is because a £20,000 loss has already been recognised in profit or loss as a result of fair valuing the embedded derivative.

Note: for illustrative purposes only, this example ignores the time value of money for the purpose of valuing the forward contract.

12.1 Allocating proceeds to the embedded derivative at inception

At inception, an entity must determine the fair value of the embedded derivative first. The difference between the consideration paid or received to acquire the entire contract and the fair value of the embedded derivative is assigned to the host contract.

Example 12.1

Allocating the proceeds to the embedded derivative

Entity A invests CU1 million in a convertible bond. The bond has a coupon of 6 per cent, a maturity of five years, and is convertible into a fixed number of equity shares at maturity of the bond. Using a Black-Scholes model, it is determined that the fair value of the conversion option is CU100,000. Assuming that the entire bond is not carried at FVTPL, separation of the embedded derivative is necessary. The amount assigned to the bond is determined by subtracting the fair value of the option from the consideration paid to purchase the bond. The entry on purchasing the asset is as follows.

		CU	CU
Dr	Bond	900,000	
Dr	Equity conversion option	100,000	
Cr	Cash		1,000,000

To record the purchase of the convertible bond.

It will not always be easy to establish the fair value of embedded derivatives, but there is little room for manoeuvre. If an embedded derivative needs to be separately accounted for, but the entity is unable to determine reliably the fair value of the embedded derivative on the basis of its terms and conditions (e.g. because the embedded derivative results in the delivery of an unquoted equity investment), the entity must determine the fair value of the whole contract and the fair value of the host contract, and the balance represents the derivative instrument. [IAS 39:13] If an entity is unable to do this, the entity must designate the whole contract as at FVTPL. [IAS 39:12] The entity might conclude, however, in the above example of an equity embedded derivative that results in the delivery of unquoted equity investment, that the equity component of the combined instrument may be sufficiently significant to preclude it from obtaining a reliable estimate of the fair value of the entire instrument. In such circumstances, the combined instrument is measured at cost less impairment. [IAS 39:IG.C.11]

13 Presentation of embedded derivatives

IFRSs do not provide specific guidance on the presentation of embedded derivatives in the statement of financial position or in profit or loss. IAS 39:11 has an explicit statement articulating that IFRSs do not address whether an embedded derivative should be presented separately in the statement of financial position.

It seems appropriate for an entity to choose as an accounting policy whether it presents a hybrid contract in its statement of financial position as a single contractual arrangement or non-closely related embedded derivatives as separate financial assets or liabilities. The policy should be applied consistently to all hybrid contracts.

If an entity chooses to present the embedded derivative(s) and the host contract as a single contractual arrangement, it must still comply with IFRS 7:8 & 20(a), which require an analysis of the carrying amounts of financial instruments, and of gains or losses in the period, by IAS 39 classification category. Irrespective of the policy adopted for presentation (as discussed in the previous paragraph), the embedded derivative component will always be classified as at FVTPL for measurement purposes (except if it is designated in a qualifying and effective hedge relationship); the host contract, if it is a financial instrument in the scope of IAS 39, will be in a different category, such as loans and receivables, AFS or HTM.

In addition, an entity must determine if the embedded derivative is current or non-current under IAS 1 *Presentation of Financial Statements* when an entity does not present assets and liabilities in order of liquidity. Two accounting policies are considered acceptable, as set out below.

Policy 1

Separate presentation of the host and the embedded derivative, but assessment regarding classification as current or non-current based on the cash flows of the whole hybrid arrangement because embedded derivatives cannot be settled separately from the host contract.

Policy 2

No separate presentation of the host and the embedded derivative, and assessment regarding classification as current or non-current based on the cash flows of the whole hybrid arrangement because embedded derivatives cannot be settled separately from the host contract.

Example 13

Presentation of embedded derivative in the statement of financial position

Consider the application of the two policies described immediately above in the following five examples in which the embedded derivative would be separately accounted for under IAS 39:

Scenario 1

Issued debt with maturity in five years with a separated embedded put option that allows the holder to put the debt instrument back to the issuer every six months' time at an amount not approximately equal to the debt host contract's amortised cost.

Scenario 2

Same as Scenario 1 except that the issuer has a call option (rather than the holder having a put option). The issuer does not expect the call to be exercised in the next 12 months.

Scenario 3

Issued debt with maturity in five years with no put or call options but principal payment depends on the performance of a specified equity index.

Scenario 4

An executory contract to buy a non-financial item in five years when the price paid is based on a non-closely related foreign currency. The non-financial host contract is treated as an executory contract outside the scope of IAS 39. The embedded non-closely related foreign currency derivative is separately recognised at fair value through profit or loss.

Scenario 5

An operating lease with five years to maturity with a non-closely related embedded inflation derivative (e.g. the lease rentals are linked to leveraged inflation).

Depending on the entity's accounting policy, the presentation options are as follows.

	Policy 1	**Policy 2**
Scenario	Separate presentation of host contract and derivative, but assessment of current/non-current based on the whole hybrid arrangement because the embedded cannot be settled separately from the host contract.	No separate presentation of host contract and embedded, and assessment of current/non-current based on the whole hybrid arrangement because the embedded cannot be settled separately from the host contract.
1 Debt with written put	Derivative (D): current liability; Host (H): current liability	Whole instrument: current liability
2 Debt with purchased call	D: non-current asset*; H: non-current liability	Whole instrument: non-current liability*
3 Debt linked to equity index	D: non-current asset/liability; H: non-current liability	Whole instrument: non-current liability
4 Executory contract with foreign currency derivative	D: non-current asset/liability; H: not recognised	D: non-current asset/ liability; H: not recognised
5 Operating lease with inflation derivative	D: non-current asset/liability; H: not recognised	D: non-current asset/ liability; H: not recognised

* Because the issuer does not expect to call the debt in the 12 months after the reporting date, the derivative and host contract are both non-current. If the issuer expected to call the debt in the 12 months following the reporting date the derivative and host contract would be both presented as current in the statement of financial position.

The list of scenarios above is not intended to be exhaustive.

C6 Measurement

Contents

1 Introduction

IAS 39 has a different measurement approach at initial recognition and for subsequent measurement for certain financial instruments. The Standard requires all financial instruments to be measured at initial recognition at fair value, but for subsequent measurement it requires a mixed measurement model with some assets and liabilities measured at fair value and others at amortised cost or cost. The model is based on the classification of financial assets and liabilities as discussed in **chapters C2** and **C3**.

The requirements on fair value measurement at initial recognition and for financial instruments subsequently measured at fair value are contained in **chapter C7**. That chapter covers the requirements of IFRS 13 *Fair Value Measurement*.

This chapter focuses on financial instruments measured at amortised cost, cost and also deals with the accounting for AFS assets. It sets out the detailed impairment requirements that apply to all financial assets that are not measured at FVTPL.

This chapter begins with the guidance on how to account for transaction costs at initial recognition before moving onto the subsequent measurement requirements.

2 Initial recognition

2.1 Transaction costs

IAS 39:43 requires that, except for trade receivables that do not have a significant financing component (determined in accordance with IFRS 15 *Revenue from Contracts with Customers*), all financial instruments are initially recognised at fair value (see **section 3** in **chapter C7**) plus or minus, in the case of a financial asset or liability that is not classified as at FVTPL, transaction costs that are directly attributable to the acquisition or issue of the asset or liability. Trade receivables that do not have a significant financing component at initially recognised at their transaction price.

The consequences of this requirement are summarised below.

(a) For financial instruments that are measured subsequent to initial recognition at amortised cost (see **section 4**), transaction costs are included in the calculation of the effective interest rate – in effect, they are amortised through profit or loss over the term of the instrument.

(b) For financial assets classified as AFS, when the effective interest method is applied (see **section 4.1**), transaction costs will initially be recognised as part of the carrying amount of the financial asset. The transaction costs will be amortised through profit or loss over the term of the instrument under the effective interest method as with assets and liabilities measured at amortised cost. If the AFS asset does not have fixed or determinable payments or has an indefinite life and, therefore, the effective interest rate is not applied (e.g. the asset is an investment in an equity security), transaction costs are recognised in profit or loss only when an impairment loss is recognised or on derecognition of the asset.

(c) For financial instruments classified as at FVTPL, transaction costs are recognised in profit or loss immediately on initial recognition.

Transaction costs are defined as incremental costs that are directly attributable to the acquisition, issue or disposal of a financial asset or a financial liability. An incremental cost is one that would not have been incurred if the entity had not acquired, issued or disposed of the financial instrument. [IAS 39:9]

Transaction costs include fees and commissions paid to agents (including employees acting as selling agents), advisers, brokers and dealers, levies by regulatory agencies and security exchanges, and transfer taxes and duties. However, debt premiums or discounts, financing costs, internal administrative costs and holding costs are not transaction costs. [IAS 39:AG13] In practice, the interpretation of this definition may require significant judgement. A particular issue arises in relation to the treatment of origination fees (see **4.1.3**).

2.2 Settlement date accounting

The accounting for regular way trades is considered at **2.2** in **chapter C8**. When an entity uses settlement date accounting for an asset that is subsequently measured at either cost or amortised cost, the asset is recognised initially at the settlement date, but at the fair value that existed at the trade date (discussed further in **3.5**). Movements in fair value between trade and settlement date are not recognised (other than impairment losses). For assets measured at fair value subsequent to initial recognition, the change in fair value between trade and settlement date is recognised in profit or loss if the asset is measured at FVTPL, and in other comprehensive income if the asset is classified as AFS. [IAS 39:57]

3 Subsequent measurement

3.1 Financial assets

The classification of financial instruments determines how they are subsequently measured. As discussed in **section 3** of **chapter C2**, IAS 39 requires financial assets to be classified into one of four categories: fair value through profit or loss (**3.1.1**), held-to-maturity (**3.1.2**), loans and receivables (**3.1.3**) and AFS financial assets (**3.1.4**).

3.1.1 Financial assets at fair value through profit or loss (FVTPL)

Assets classified as at FVTPL are measured at fair value. Gains and losses that arise as a result of changes in fair value are recognised in profit or loss, except for those arising on derivatives that are designated in effective cash flow hedges or hedges of a net investment in a foreign operation. Fair value measurement is described in detail in **chapter C7**.

Gains and losses that arise between the end of the last reporting period and the date an instrument is derecognised do not constitute a separate 'profit/loss on disposal'. Such gains and losses will have arisen prior to disposal, while the item is still being measured at FVTPL, and should be recognised in profit or loss when they occur.

Transaction costs that might be incurred when the asset is disposed of in the future are *not* deducted from fair value in determining the carrying amount. Some argue that this is inconsistent with the use of exit prices (i.e. fair value) for measurement purposes, but the Standard is clear that such costs are viewed as being related to the act of disposal and, therefore, are recognised only in the period of disposal itself.

3.1.2 Held-to-maturity investments

Held-to-maturity investments are measured at amortised cost using the 'effective interest method'. This method is discussed in detail in **section 4**.

3.1.3 Loans and receivables

Loans and receivables are also measured at amortised cost using the effective interest method, as discussed in **section 4**.

3.1.4 Available-for-sale financial assets (AFS)

Financial assets classified as AFS are measured at fair value. Fair value measurement is described in detail in **chapter C7**. As with financial assets measured at FVTPL, no deduction is made for transaction costs that might be incurred when the asset is disposed of in the future.

Gains and losses that arise as a result of changes in fair value in AFS financial assets are recognised in other comprehensive income, with three exceptions:

(i) interest, calculated using the effective interest method, is recognised in profit or loss (see **section 4**);

(ii) impairment losses are recognised in profit or loss (see **section 5**); and

(iii) foreign exchange gains and losses on monetary financial assets (the approach adopted in relation to foreign currency gains and losses is discussed in **3.3**).

When an AFS asset is derecognised, the cumulative gain or loss previously recognised in other comprehensive income is reclassified from equity to profit or loss. This reclassification of previous fair value gains and losses is frequently referred to as 'recycling'.

Example 3.1.4

Available-for-sale debt instrument

A zero coupon bond is acquired for its fair value of CU95 on 1 January 20X0 and classified as AFS. Transaction costs arising on acquisition are CU5. The bond is due to be redeemed for CU130 on 31 December 20X4. On 31 December 20X0, the bond's fair value is CU103. On 31 December 20X1, the entity sells the bond for its fair value of CU108.

In 20X0, the entity records the following entries.

(1) Initial recognition (at fair value, including transaction costs)

		CU	CU
Dr	Asset	100	
Cr	Cash		100

To recognise the zero coupon bond.

(2) Interest income (calculated under the effective interest method – the rate of 5.39 per cent is calculated so as to include transaction costs as explained in **section 4.1**)

		CU	CU
Dr	Asset	5.39	
Cr	Interest income		5.39

To recognise interest income.

(3) Fair value adjustment (such that the asset is stated at its fair value of CU103)

		CU	CU
Dr	Other comprehensive income	2.39	
Cr	Asset		2.39

To record the remeasurement of the asset to fair value.

In 20X1, the entity records the following entries.

(1) Interest income (calculated under the effective interest method)

		CU	CU
Dr	Asset	5.68	
Cr	Interest income		5.68

To recognise interest income.

(2) Fair value adjustment (such that the asset is stated at its fair value of CU108)

		CU	CU
Dr	Other comprehensive income	0.68	
Cr	Asset		0.68

To record the remeasurement of the asset to fair value.

(3) Sale of asset

		CU	CU
Dr	Cash	108	
Cr	Asset		108

To record the disposal of the asset.

(4) Reclassification to profit or loss of fair value losses previously recognised in other comprehensive income and accumulated in equity

		CU	CU
Dr	Profit or loss	3.07	
Cr	Other comprehensive income		3.07

To reclassify losses previously recognised in other comprehensive income and accumulated in equity.

3.1.4.1 Available-for-sale financial asset exchanged for another available-for-sale financial asset

If an AFS asset is derecognised, with the consideration received being another AFS asset, the fair value gain or loss previously recognised in other comprehensive income should nonetheless be reclassified to profit or loss. Because the original asset has been derecognised, the deferred gain or loss is not attributable to the new asset and does not remain in equity. [IAS 39:IG.E.3.1]

Example 3.1.4.1A

Available-for-sale equity instrument – group restructuring (1)

Entity A has a directly-held wholly-owned subsidiary, Entity B. Entity A accounts for its investments in subsidiaries in accordance with IAS 39 in its separate financial statements as permitted by IAS 27(2008):38(b) and IAS 27(2011):10(b). Entity A designates its investment in Entity B as an AFS investment in its separate financial statements and, therefore, measures its investment at fair value with fair value gains/losses recognised in other comprehensive income.

As part of a group reorganisation, a new holding entity, Entity C, is created whose shares are issued to Entity A in return for Entity A's investment in Entity B. Entity C has no other assets or liabilities or transactions other than the issue of shares to Entity A and the acquisition of shares in Entity B. At the date of the group reorganisation, Entity A has accumulated gains in equity attributable to the increase in value of Entity B. The group structure is illustrated below.

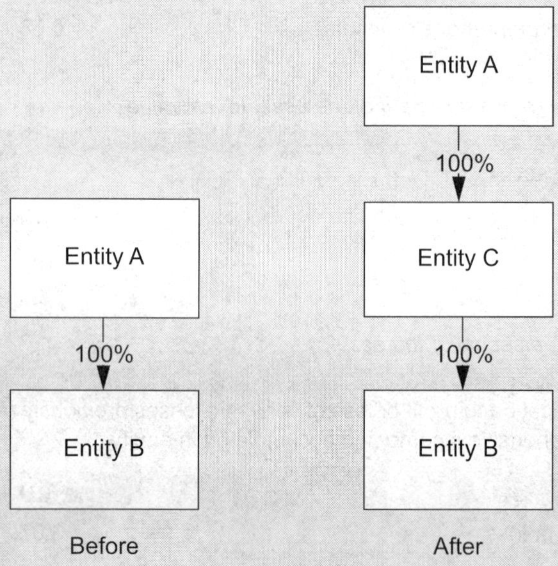

In its separate financial statements, Entity A will not derecognise its investment in Entity B. Although Entity A has transferred its contractual rights to receive cash flows under the Entity B shares in accordance with IAS 39:18(a), Entity A has not transferred substantially all the risks and rewards of ownership of the Entity B shares in accordance with IAS 39:20(b) because the consideration received for transferring the shares in Entity B are shares in Entity C, whose only asset is the investment in Entity B. Entity A's exposure to the risks and rewards of Entity B are unchanged. Because Entity A has not derecognised the shares in Entity B, the fair value gain previously recognised in other comprehensive income and accumulated in the AFS reserve in equity will not be reclassified to profit or loss at the date of the group reorganisation.

Example 3.1.4.1B

Available-for-sale equity instrument – group restructuring (2)

Entity X purchases 100 equity shares of Entity Y, a listed entity, for CU1,000 (i.e. at a price of CU10 per each share). The investment is classified as AFS. At Entity X's period end, 31 December 20X1, Entity Y's share price has increased to CU20 per share. As a result, the fair value of Entity X's holding has increased to CU2,000 with Entity X recognising a fair value gain on its AFS financial asset of CU1,000 in other comprehensive income.

On 1 January 20X2, Entity Y undergoes a corporate restructuring such that certain assets, liabilities and activities of Entity Y are transferred into a newly-created Entity Z whose shares will be distributed to the shareholders of Entity Y. The restructuring means that Entity Y will continue with certain core activities while Entity Z will undertake certain other activities that were previously undertaken by Entity Y. As part of the demerger, shareholders in Entity Y will receive 1 new share in Entity Z (in addition to retaining their existing shares in Entity Y) for each share owned in Entity Y. After the reorganisation, Entity X will hold 100 shares in Entity Z in addition to the 100 shares it originally owned in Entity Y. Following the demerger, the assets and liabilities within Entity Y and Entity Z are those originally within Entity Y with no new assets or liabilities introduced. The shares in Entity Z are not listed. At the time of the demerger, the share price of Entity Y decreases to CU5 per share.

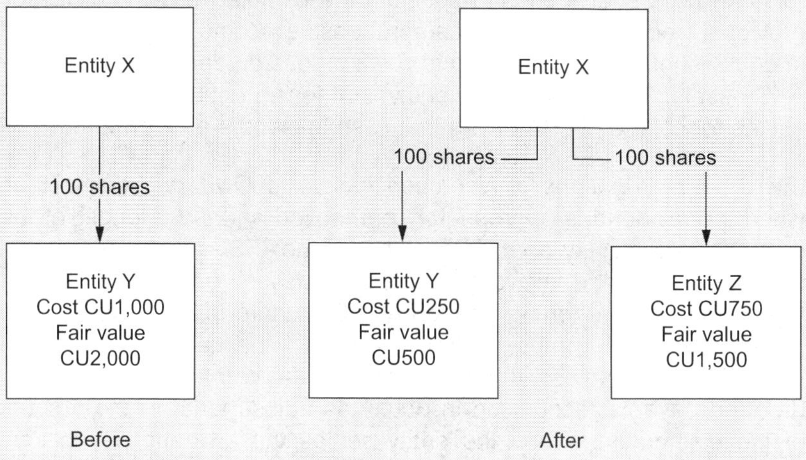

On receipt of the additional shares in Entity Z, the balance in the AFS reserve should not be reclassified to profit or loss because the original financial asset (shares of Entity Y) does not meet the requirements for derecognition. Entity X has not transferred the contractual rights to receive cash flows from the Entity Y shares nor has it retained the contractual rights to receive the cash flows of the financial asset, but assumed a contractual obligation to pay the cash flows to one or more recipients in an arrangement that meets the pass through conditions (IAS 39:18). At the point of the demerger, from the point of view of Entity X, some of the value of the Entity Y shares has been distributed to the newly-established Entity Z. In addition, Entity X's investment in Entity Y is not considered to be impaired because the reduction in fair value of Entity Y shares is only the result of a redistribution of assets to existing shareholders for nil consideration.

Although the gain of CU1,000 previously recognised in other comprehensive income should not be reclassified to profit or loss at the point of the demerger, Entity X will need to take the following actions.

(i) Recognise the shares in Entities Y and Z at their fair values upon the demerger. The fair value of the Entity Y shares upon demerger will be equal to CU500 (fair value of CU5 multiplied by 100 shares). In the absence of a quoted market price, the fair value of the shares in Entity Z should be estimated using a valuation technique. In the event that the fair value of Entity Z shares cannot be estimated reliably, the shares will be held at cost less impairment; the cost will be deemed to equal CU1,500 (i.e. the value of Entity Y shares prior to the demerger (CU2,000) less the value of those shares upon demerger (CU500)).

(ii) Allocate the gain of CU1,000 previously recognised in other comprehensive income in relation to the investment in Entity Y shares across the shares in

Entity Y and Z. This allocation should be made in proportion to the values established in (i) above.

3.1.4.2 Distribution of available-for-sale financial assets as dividends

If an entity distributes AFS assets to owners as dividends-in-kind (also known as 'dividends in specie'), the cumulative gains or losses previously recognised in other comprehensive income and accumulated in equity should be reclassified to profit or loss on derecognition of the AFS assets. This treatment is equivalent to the entity selling the AFS assets for cash and distributing that cash to owners as a dividend.

IFRIC 17 *Distributions of Non-cash Assets to Owners* requires that, when the dividend is appropriately authorised and is no longer at the discretion of the entity, a liability to distribute the AFS assets as a dividend is recognised at the fair value of the AFS assets to be distributed. At the end of each reporting period and at the date of settlement of the dividend, the entity must review and adjust the carrying amount of the dividend payable, with any changes in the carrying amount of the dividend payable recognised in equity as adjustments to the amount of the distribution. When the entity settles the dividend payable by delivering the AFS assets, any amount previously recognised in other comprehensive income is reclassified to profit or loss.

3.1.4.3 Dividends receivable from available-for-sale financial assets

Dividends are recognised in profit or loss only when:

(a) the entity's right to receive payment of the dividend is established;

(b) it is probable that the economic benefits associated with the dividend will flow to the entity; and

(c) the amount of the dividend can be measured reliably.

Dividends are defined in IAS 39:9 as '[d]istributions of profits to holders of equity instruments in proportion to their holdings of a particular class of capital.'

Example 3.1.4.3

Dividends on available-for-sale equity instruments

On 1 January 20X0, Entity X acquires an equity instrument of Entity Y for its fair value of CU100; the instrument is classified as an AFS financial asset. Entity Y immediately declares a dividend of CU10 and, consequently, the fair value of the equity instrument in Entity Y decreases to CU90. Entity X records the following entries.

(1) Initial recognition

		CU	CU
Dr	Asset	100	
Cr	Cash		100

To recognise the equity instrument.

(2) Dividend income

		CU	CU
Dr	Cash	10	
Cr	Dividend income (profit or loss)		10

To recognise the dividend income.

(3) Fair value adjustment (such that the asset is stated at its fair value of CU90)

		CU	CU
Dr	Other comprehensive income	10	
Cr	Asset		10

To record the remeasurement of the equity instrument.

The accounting treatment in the example above appears unfortunate, because the realisation of part of the value of an asset will lead to the recognition of two offsetting amounts – one in profit or loss and the other in other comprehensive income. Nevertheless, IAS 39 explicitly requires that dividends received are recognised in profit or loss. In addition, an entity would need to consider in all cases whether the reduction in fair value recognised in other comprehensive income needs to be reclassified to profit or loss because the asset is impaired (see **5.1.2**).

Instead of being paid in cash, a dividend may be structured so that it is payable in shares of the issuer. This is often termed a 'stock dividend', a 'share dividend' or a 'scrip dividend'. When the dividend is payable exclusively in shares of the issuer (i.e. there is no cash or other settlement alternative), the investor does not regard the dividend as revenue in profit or loss. Rather, the pro-rata receipt of additional shares in the issuer, from the investor's perspective, is in the nature of a bonus issue of shares whereby the investor's economic interest remains unchanged. The number of shares held by the investor increases, but the value of its total interest is unchanged because its economic interest is distributed over a greater number of shares (i.e. the increase in the number of shares results in a concurrent reduction in the value of each share).

When the investor is given a choice of settlement between shares of the issuer or cash (or another settlement alternative that is not shares of the issuer) the dividend is recognised as revenue at the date the dividend is authorised and is measured at the higher of the value of the shares offered and the value of the cash alternative. This reflects the fact that the investor would be expected to opt for the most economically advantageous alternative. From the date of authorisation of the dividend until the date on which the investor elects to receive cash or shares, the estimated revenue should be adjusted to reflect changes in the fair value of the shares but it should never fall below the value of the cash alternative. On the date that the investor makes its final election, the revenue amount becomes fixed.

When the dividend is structured so that it is certain that all shareholders will decide to take the shares rather than cash (i.e. the cash alternative does not have substance), the dividend is in effect a pure stock dividend and should be accounted for accordingly. When the market value of the share alternative is above the cash alternative, the dividend is often referred to as an 'enhanced stock dividend'. Careful judgement will be necessary, based on the specific facts and circumstances, to determine whether a dividend involving an enhanced stock dividend is in substance a distribution to owners recognised in profit or loss or a pure stock dividend.

3.1.5 Hedged items

IAS 39 includes specific requirements to be applied when accounting for a financial asset that is a hedged item. These requirements are discussed in detail in **chapters C9** and **C10**.

3.1.6 Unquoted equity instruments

IAS 39 requires investments in equity instruments and derivatives (whether assets or liabilities) that are linked to and must be settled by delivery of unquoted equity instruments [IAS 39:46(c)] that do not have a quoted market price in an active market, and whose fair value cannot be reliably measured, to be measured at cost. Examples of such derivatives would include purchased call options over a third party's equity shares requiring physical settlement, or a forward purchase of such shares.

The application guidance issued with the Standard (IAS 39:AG80 & AG81) makes it clear that it will normally be possible to estimate the fair value of an asset that has been acquired from an outside party. Cost should be used *only if* there is a significant range of possible fair value estimates and the probabilities of the various estimates cannot be reasonably assessed.

3.1.7 Instruments whose fair value is 'unreliable'

If IAS 39 requires a financial instrument to be measured at fair value, no exception from measurement on that basis is permitted except in relation to certain unquoted equity instruments as described in **3.1.6**. In all other cases, fair value is deemed to be reliably measurable.

In November 2006, the IFRIC (now the IFRS Interpretations Committee) issued an agenda decision on IAS 39, *Valuation of Electricity Derivatives*. The decision related to electricity derivatives that fail to meet the normal purchase, sale or usage exemption in IAS 39:5 and, therefore, are wholly within the scope of IAS 39. The question asked was whether such contracts fell under the exception from fair valuation that applies to derivatives linked to unquoted equity instruments. Valuation issues arise because the derivatives under consideration have a variable notional amount and the term of a derivative might extend well beyond the period for which there is any observable market data. The IFRIC noted that the only exception in IAS 39 from the requirement to measure derivatives at fair value after initial recognition is given in IAS 39:46(c) (amplified by IAS 39:AG80 & AG81) which addresses unquoted equity investments, and that it was not appropriate to extend this exemption to other derivatives. The IFRIC noted further that IAS 39 contains general principles on how to measure fair value. The IFRIC decided that it should not seek to develop more detailed guidance on this topic because the subject was too specific.

3.1.8 Negative fair value

If the fair value of a financial instrument previously recognised as a financial asset falls below zero, it becomes a financial liability and is measured as discussed in **section 3.2**.

3.2 Financial liabilities

Financial liabilities are measured at amortised cost using the effective interest method (see **section 4**), with the following exceptions:

- financial liabilities at FVTPL (see **3.2.1**);
- financial liabilities that arise when a transfer of a financial asset does not qualify for derecognition or when the continuing involvement approach applies (see **3.2.2**)
- written financial guarantee contracts not designated as at FVTPL that are not accounted for under IFRS 4 *Insurance Contracts* (see **2.3.3** of **chapter C1**);
- commitments to provide a loan at a below-market interest rate (see **3.5** of **chapter C1**); and
- hedged items (see **3.2.3**).

3.2.1 *Financial liabilities at fair value through profit or loss (FVTPL)*

Financial liabilities at FVTPL, which include those classified as held for trading and derivative liabilities that are not designated as effective hedging instruments, and those designated as at FVTPL, are measured at their fair value with gains and losses recognised in profit or loss. Fair value measurement is described in detail in **chapter C7**. However, a derivative liability that is linked to, and must be settled by delivery of, an unquoted equity instrument whose fair value cannot be reliably measured is measured at cost (discussed further in **3.1.6**).

A consequence of including a financial liability in this category is that the effect of an entity's own credit risk will be reflected in profit or loss. For example, if an entity that has elected to measure its issued debt at fair value experiences financial difficulties, it is likely to recognise a gain in profit or loss reflecting the instrument's worsening creditworthiness.

3.2.2 *Financial liabilities arising on the transfer of a financial asset*

A liability may arise when a transfer of a financial asset does not qualify for derecognition or is accounted for using the 'continuing involvement' approach. The approach required for measuring such liabilities is discussed in **chapter C8**.

3.2.3 *Hedged items*

IAS 39 includes specific requirements to be applied when accounting for a financial liability that is a hedged item. These requirements are discussed in detail in **chapters C9** and **C10**.

3.3 Foreign currency

When a financial asset or liability is a monetary item, foreign exchange gains and losses should be recognised in profit or loss in accordance with IAS 21 *The Effects of Changes in Foreign Exchange Rates*. Monetary items are defined as units of currency held and assets and liabilities to be received or paid in a fixed or determinable number of units of currency. [IAS 21:8]

3.3.1 *Financial assets and liabilities measured at fair value through profit or loss*

For financial assets and liabilities that are measured at FVTPL, the requirement to recognise foreign currency gains or losses is straightforward because all gains and losses are recognised in profit or loss as part of the fair value gain or loss. The fair value is determined firstly in the foreign currency in which the item is denominated and that foreign currency amount is subsequently translated into the entity's functional currency using the closing rate. The accounting treatment is the same irrespective of whether the item is monetary or non-monetary.

3.3.2 Amortised cost

For financial assets and financial liabilities measured at amortised cost (which will only include monetary items), foreign currency gains or loss are calculated by determining the amortised cost in the foreign currency in which the item is denominated and the foreign currency amount is subsequently translated into the entity's functional currency using the closing rate. This approach applies to both financial assets and financial liabilities that are measured at amortised cost.

3.3.3 Cost

In the limited circumstances in which IAS 39 requires financial instruments to be measured at cost (some investments in unquoted equity instruments and derivatives that are linked to and will result in the delivery of an unquoted equity instrument – see **3.1.6**), any such investment that is denominated in a foreign currency should be translated at the historical rate. [IAS 21:23(b) & IAS 39:46(c)] Therefore, no foreign currency gains or losses arise.

3.3.4 Exceptions

IAS 21 specifically excludes from its scope the measurement of foreign currency items that are subject to hedge accounting, because IAS 39 is more specific. If a financial asset or financial liability is designated as a hedged item in a fair value hedge of the exposure to changes in foreign currency rates under IAS 39, the hedged item is remeasured for changes in foreign currency rates even if it would otherwise have been recognised using a historical rate under IAS 21. [IAS 39:89] This exception applies to non-monetary items that are carried in terms of historical cost in the foreign currency and are hedged against exposure to foreign currency rates. [IAS 21:23(b)]

Foreign currency gains or losses on monetary items are recognised in profit or loss except if the monetary item is designated as a hedging instrument in either a cash flow hedge (see **2.2** in **chapter C9**) or a hedge of a net investment (see **2.3** in **chapter C9**). [IAS 39:AG83]

The foreign currency translation of AFS financial assets in IAS 39 is particularly complex. If the item is monetary (e.g. an investment in a debt security), the foreign currency translation recognised in profit or loss is based on an amortised cost amount (even though the instrument is measured at fair value rather than amortised cost). [IAS 39:AG83] Other changes in the carrying amount are recognised in other comprehensive income under IAS 39:55(b). The effect of this is that the cumulative gain or loss recognised in other comprehensive income is the difference between the amortised cost (adjusted for impairment, if any) and the fair value of the instrument in the functional currency of the reporting entity. IAS 39:IG.E.3.2 illustrates the approach and is reproduced below.

Example 3.3.4

IAS 39 and IAS 21 – Available-for-sale financial assets: separation of currency component

[IAS 39:IG.E.3.2]

For an available-for-sale monetary financial asset, the entity recognises changes in the carrying amount relating to changes in foreign exchange rates in profit or loss in accordance with IAS 21:23(a) and IAS 21:28 and other changes in the carrying amount in other comprehensive income in accordance with IAS 39. How is the cumulative gain or loss that is recognised in other comprehensive income determined?

It is the difference between the amortised cost (adjusted for impairment, if any) and fair value of the available-for-sale monetary financial asset in the functional currency of the reporting entity. For the purpose of applying IAS 21:28 the asset is treated as an asset measured at amortised cost in the foreign currency.

To illustrate: on 31 December 20X1 Entity A acquires a bond denominated in a foreign currency (FC) for its fair value of FC1,000. The bond has five years remaining to maturity and a principal amount of FC1,250, carries fixed interest of 4.7 per cent that is paid annually (FC1,250 × 4.7 per cent = FC59 per year), and has an effective interest rate of 10 per cent. Entity A classifies the bond as available for sale, and thus recognises gains and losses in other comprehensive income. The entity's functional currency is its local currency (LC). The exchange rate is FC1 to LC1.5 and the carrying amount of the bond is LC1,500 (= FC1,000 × 1.5).

Dr	Bond	LC1,500
Cr	Cash	LC1,500

On 31 December 20X2, the foreign currency has appreciated and the exchange rate is FC1 to LC2. The fair value of the bond is FC1,060 and thus the carrying amount is LC2,120 (= FC1,060 × 2). The amortised cost is FC1,041 (= LC2,082). In this case, the cumulative gain or loss to be recognised in other comprehensive income and accumulated in equity is the difference between the fair value and the amortised cost on 31 December 20X2, i.e. LC38 (= LC2,120 – LC2,082).

Interest received on the bond on 31 December 20X2 is FC59 (= LC118). Interest income determined in accordance with the effective interest method is FC100 (=1,000 × 10 per cent). The average exchange rate during the year is FC1 to LC1.75. For the purpose of this question, it is assumed that the use of the average exchange rate provides a reliable approximation of the spot rates applicable to the accrual of interest income during the year (IAS 21:22). Thus, reported interest income is LC175 (= FC100 × 1.75) including accretion of the initial discount of LC72 (= [FC100 – FC59] × 1.75). Accordingly, the exchange difference on the bond that is recognised in profit or loss is LC510 (= LC2,082 – LC1,500 – LC72). Also, there is an exchange gain on the interest receivable for the year of LC15 (= FC59 × [2.00 – 1.75]).

Dr	Bond	LC620
Dr	Cash	LC118
Cr	Interest income	LC175
Cr	Exchange gain	LC525
Cr	Fair value change in other comprehensive income	LC38

On 31 December 20X3, the foreign currency has appreciated further and the exchange rate is FC1 to LC2.50. The fair value of the bond is FC1,070 and thus the carrying amount is LC2,675 (= FC1,070 × 2.50). The amortised cost is FC1,086 (= LC2,715). The cumulative gain or loss to be accumulated in equity is the difference between the fair value and the amortised cost on 31 December 20X3, i.e. negative LC40 (= LC2,675 – LC2,715). Thus, the amount recognised in other comprehensive income equals the change in the difference during 20X3 of LC78 (= LC40 + LC38).

Interest received on the bond on 31 December 20X3 is FC59 (= LC148). Interest income determined in accordance with the effective interest method is FC104 (= FC1,041 × 10 per cent). The average exchange rate during the year is FC1 to LC2.25. For the purpose of this question, it is assumed that the use of the average exchange rate provides a reliable approximation of the spot rates applicable to the accrual of interest income during the year (IAS 21:22). Thus, recognised interest income is LC234 (= FC104 × 2.25) including accretion of the initial discount of LC101 (= [FC104 – FC59] × 2.25). Accordingly, the exchange difference on the bond that is recognised in profit or loss is LC532 (= LC2,715 – LC2,082 – LC101). Also, there is an exchange gain on the interest receivable for the year of LC15 (= FC59 × [2.50 – 2.25]).

Dr	Bond	LC555
Dr	Cash	LC148
Dr	Fair value change in other comprehensive income	LC78
Cr	Interest income	LC234
Cr	Exchange gain	LC547

When some portion of the change in carrying amount is recognised in other comprehensive income and some portion is recognised in profit or loss (e.g. if the amortised cost of a foreign currency bond classified as AFS has increased in value foreign currency terms (resulting in a gain in profit or loss) but its fair value has decreased in the functional currency (resulting in a loss in other comprehensive income)), an entity cannot offset those two components for the purposes of determining gains or losses that should be recognised in profit or loss or in other comprehensive income. [IAS 39:IG.E.3.4]

For AFS financial assets that are not monetary items under IAS 21 (e.g. an investment in an equity investment), the gain or loss that is recognised in other comprehensive income includes any related foreign currency component. The foreign currency translation will be reclassified from equity to profit or loss when the asset is impaired or derecognised.

3.3.5 Summary of foreign currency accounting

A summary of how foreign currency is treated for the various financial instrument classifications in IAS 39 is set out in the following table.

Classification	Monetary or non-monetary item	Foreign currency gains and losses from remeasurement (prior to its disposal)*
Available-for-sale	Monetary item (e.g. debt security)	Profit or loss
Available-for-sale	Non-monetary item (e.g. equity security)	Other comprehensive income
Loan and receivable	Always a monetary item	Profit or loss
Held-to-maturity	Always a monetary item	Profit or loss
Fair value through profit or loss	Not applicable	Profit or loss
Liability carried at amortised cost	Always a monetary item	Profit or loss
* Assumes that the item is not being hedged for foreign currency, or is not a hedging instrument in a foreign currency hedge.		

3.3.6 Dual currency bonds

IAS 39:AG33(c) states that a foreign currency derivative that provides a stream of principal or interest payments denominated in a foreign currency and that is embedded in a host debt instrument (e.g. a dual currency bond) is closely related to the host debt instrument. Such a derivative is not separated from the host instrument because IAS 21 requires foreign currency gains and losses on monetary items to be recognised in profit or loss. This is relevant for dual currency bonds held and issued that are not classified at FVTPL.

Neither IAS 39 nor IAS 21 provides specific guidance regarding how to measure dual currency bonds. Because IAS 39 states that the foreign currency gains and losses are accounted for under IAS 21, it is reasonable to assume that the accounting treatment is equivalent to isolating the foreign currency cash flows and measuring them as if they were a separate instrument. For example, if interest is denominated in a foreign currency, but the principal is not, an entity could measure the interest flows as if it was a foreign currency denominated interest rate strip and apply the effective interest method and treat the principal cash flow as a functional currency denominated zero coupon bond. Conversely, if the principal is denominated in a foreign currency, but the interest is not, an entity could measure the principal as if it was a foreign currency denominated zero coupon bond and apply the effective interest method and treat the interest flows as a functional currency denominated interest rate strip (see **example 3.3.6**).

Example 3.3.6

Accounting for a dual currency bond

Entity A, a Sterling functional currency entity, issues a dual currency bond on 1 January 20X4 under which the interest is denominated in Sterling but the principal is denominated in US dollars. The bond has a notional amount of US$200m, has a maturity of three years and is issued at par.

Entity A determines the carrying amount of a US$-denominated 3-year zero coupon bond at inception by discounting US$200m by the 3-year US$ zero coupon rate reflecting Entity A's credit quality which is 10 per cent (US$200m / 1.1^3 = US$150.26m). Entity A then converts this amount into its functional currency at the US$:£ spot rate at inception (US$150.26m / US$2:£1 = £75.13m). The difference between this amount and the functional currency equivalent net proceeds received from issuing the dual currency bond is allocated to the functional currency interest only strip [(US$200m / US$2:£1) – £75.13m = £24.87m]. Each period, the US$ effective interest rate of 10 per cent is applied to the US$-denominated zero coupon bond in US$ and this US$ carrying amount is converted into Sterling in accordance with IAS 21.

Entity A determines the Sterling effective interest rate for the interest only strip which is the 3-year interest rate for an equivalent 3-year amortising loan. For illustration purposes, this interest rate is also assumed to be 10 per cent (although, in practice, the interest rates for the respective currencies will differ).

The foreign exchange rates for the three periods are as set out below.

	Period end rate (US$:£)	**Average rate (US$:£)**
20X3	2.00	–
20X4	1.80	1.90
20X5	2.10	1.95
20X6	1.90	2.00

The carrying amount of the foreign currency zero coupon bond in US$ is determined by applying the US$ effective interest rate in US$.

	20X4	**20X5**	**20X6**
Opening carrying amount (US$)	150.26	165.29	181.82
Interest at 10 per cent (US$)	15.03	16.53	18.18
Closing carrying amount(US$)	165.29	181.82	200.00

The carrying amount of the foreign currency zero coupon bond in Sterling is determined by converting the opening carrying amount in US$ at the opening rate, adding interest at the average rate, adding/subtracting foreign exchange gains or losses so that the closing value in Sterling is equal to the US$ closing value at the period end rate.

	20X4	20X5	20X6
Opening carrying amount (£)	75.13	91.83	86.58
Interest at average rates (£)	7.91	8.48	9.09
Foreign currency (gains) losses (£)	8.79	(13.71)	9.59
Closing carrying amount (£)	91.83	86.58	105.26

The carrying amount of the interest only strip in Sterling is determined by adding the effective interest rate and deducting the cash payments for each period.

	20X4	20X5	20X6
Opening carrying amount (£)	24.87	17.36	9.10
Interest at 10 per cent (£)	2.49	1.74	0.90
Less cash paid (£)	(10.00)	(10.00)	(10.00)
Closing carrying amount (£)	17.36	9.10	–

The entries are summarised below.

	Description	Cash	Debt	Interest expense	Foreign currency gain/(loss)
		£	£	£	£
1/1/X4	Issue debt	100.00	(100.00)		
20X4	Interest on US$ zero coupon bond		(7.91)	7.91	
	Foreign currency movement		(8.79)		(8.79)
	Interest on interest only strip	(10.00)	7.51	2.49	
20X5	Interest on US$ zero coupon bond		(8.48)	8.48	
	Foreign currency movement		13.71		13.71
	Interest on interest only strip	(10.00)	8.26	1.74	
20X6	Interest on US$ zero coupon bond		(9.09)	9.09	
	Foreign currency movement		(9.59)		(9.59)
	Interest on interest only strip	(10.00)	9.10	0.90	
31/12/X6	Repayment of dual currency bond	(105.26)	105.26		

3.4 Reclassifications

The measurement consequences at the date of reclassification of reclassifying financial assets under IAS 39 are discussed in **section 4** of **chapter C2**. After reclassification, the financial asset will generally be accounted as it had always been included within the new classification. The exceptions are:

- measurement of the effective interest rate for debt instruments reclassified out of FVTPL when a new effective interest rate is determined at the date of reclassification;
- measurement of the effective interest rate for debt instruments reclassified out of AFS when, if the instrument has a fixed maturity, a new effective interest rate is determined at the date of reclassification to ensure any gain or loss that has been recognised in other comprehensive income is amortised to profit or loss. If the asset is subsequently impaired, the entire gain or loss recognised in other comprehensive income that has not yet been reclassified to profit or loss is reclassified from equity to profit or loss;
- assets reclassified out of AFS to loans and receivables, in circumstances when there is an increase in the recoverability of cash flows following the date of reclassification (see **4.1.2.4**); and
- determining impairment for equity and debt instruments reclassified out of FVTPL (see **sections 5.4.1** and **5.4.3** respectively).

3.5 Settlement date accounting

When an entity uses settlement date accounting for an asset that is subsequently measured at cost (in the case of some investments in unquoted equity instruments in IAS 39) or amortised cost, no accounting entries are required between the trade date and the settlement date (other than impairment losses). In the case of financial assets measured at amortised cost, the effective interest rate is applied from the settlement date.

When an entity uses settlement date accounting for an asset that is subsequently measured at fair value, changes in value between the trade date and the settlement date for assets that are subsequently measured at fair value are recognised:

(i) in profit or loss for financial assets classified as at FVTPL; and

(ii) in other comprehensive income for AFS financial assets.

This subject is discussed in greater detail at **2.2** in **chapter C8**.

4 Amortised cost

On acquisition, the carrying amount of a financial instrument, being its fair value (normally the transaction price), represents the discounted amount of the expected future cash flows that will arise under that instrument. For financial assets and liabilities measured at amortised cost, the unwinding of that discount is included in profit or loss as interest income or interest expense.

Amortised cost is defined as the amount at which the financial asset or financial liability is measured at initial recognition minus principal repayments, plus or minus the cumulative amortisation using the effective interest method of any difference between that initial amount and the maturity amount, and minus any reduction (directly or through the use of an allowance account) for impairment or uncollectibility. [IAS 39:9]

The effective interest method is discussed in **section 4.1**.

Amortised cost measurement is required for financial assets that are classified as either 'loans and receivables' or 'HTM investments'. Amortised cost measurement is required for all recognised financial liabilities except those at FVTPL and other limited exceptions listed in **section 3.2**. In addition, while interest-bearing AFS financial assets are measured at fair value, with changes in fair value recognised in other comprehensive income, IAS 39 nonetheless requires interest income or expense (calculated on an amortised cost basis) to be included in profit or loss. This approach is illustrated in **example 3.1.4**. For financial assets or liabilities at FVTPL, interest is effectively wrapped up in the fair value adjustment that is included in profit or loss in each accounting period and is not required to be separately disclosed, although an entity may choose to do so as an accounting policy choice.

When IFRS 13 was issued it consequentially amended IAS 39 by deleting IAS 39:AG79 which previously stated that short-term receivables and payables with no stated interest rate may be measured at the original invoice amount if the effect of discounting is immaterial.

In December 2013 the IASB issued *Annual Improvements to IFRSs 2010-2012 Cycle*. This introduced IFRS 13:BC138A which states the IASB did not intend to change the measurement requirements for those short-term receivables and payables, noting that IAS 8:8 already permits entities not to apply accounting policies set out in accordance with IFRSs when the effect of applying them is immaterial.

4.1 The effective interest method

IAS 39 requires that the amortised cost of a financial asset or liability be calculated using the 'effective interest method'. This method allocates interest income/expense over the relevant period by applying the 'effective interest rate' to the carrying amount of the asset or liability. The effective interest method is also applied in determining the interest recognised on an interest-bearing AFS asset.

The effective interest rate is defined as the rate that exactly discounts estimated future cash payments or receipts through the expected life of the financial instrument (or, when appropriate, a shorter period) to the net carrying amount of the financial asset or financial liability. When calculating the effective interest rate, an entity should estimate cash flows considering all contractual terms of the financial instrument (e.g. prepayment, call and similar options) but should not consider future credit losses. The calculation includes all fees and points paid or received between parties to the contract that are an integral part of the effective interest rate, transaction costs, and all other premiums or discounts. There is a presumption that the cash flows and the expected life of a group of similar financial instruments can be estimated reliably. However, in those rare cases when it is not possible to estimate reliably the cash flows or the expected life of a financial instrument (or group of financial instruments), the entity should use the contractual cash flows over the full contractual term of the financial instrument (or group of financial instruments). [IAS 39:9]

Because transaction costs are taken into account when determining the initial net carrying amount, their recognition in profit or loss is effectively spread over the life of the instrument.

Example 4.1

Effective interest rate

On 1 January 20X0, an entity acquires a bond for CU90, incurring additional transaction costs of CU5. Interest of CU4 is receivable annually over the following five years (31 December 20X0 to 31 December 20X4). The bond has a mandatory redemption of CU110 on 31 December 20X4. The bond is measured at amortised cost.

Year	Carrying amount b/f	Interest income at 6.96%	Cash flow	Carrying amount c/f
	CU	CU	CU	CU
20X0	95.00	6.61	(4.00)	97.61
20X1	97.61	6.79	(4.00)	100.40
20X2	100.40	6.99	(4.00)	103.39
20X3	103.39	7.19	(4.00)	106.58
20X4	106.58	7.42	(114.00)	0.00

The effective interest rate of 6.96 per cent is the rate that discounts the expected cash flows on the bond to the initial carrying amount, i.e.:

$4/1.0696 + 4/1.0696^2 + 4/1.0696^3 + 4/1.0696^4 + 114/1.0696^5 = 95$

The effective interest rate is determined based on the initial carrying amount of the financial asset or liability. Therefore, the effective interest rate applied to any financial instrument (including interest bearing AFS assets) is not recalculated to reflect fair value changes in the carrying amount of the asset.

Under some economic conditions, the overall effective interest rate on some financial assets may be negative. For example, during an economic downturn, strong demand for 'safe harbour' assets can increase their prices sufficiently to result in negative yields. Another example of this phenomenon arises in jurisdictions where, as a matter of monetary policy, negative central bank interest rates are set, resulting in the origination of financial assets with negative interest rates.

In January 2015, the IFRS Interpretations Committee issued a final agenda decision on IAS 39 and IAS 1 *Presentation of Financial Statements*, regarding the presentation, in the statement of comprehensive income, of income and expenses arising on financial instruments with a negative yield.

The Interpretations Committee noted that interest resulting from a negative effective interest rate on a financial asset does not meet the definition of interest revenue in IAS 18 *Revenue*, because it reflects a gross outflow, instead of a gross inflow, of economic benefits (the same conclusion would apply under IFRS 15 *Revenue from Contracts with Customers*). Consequently, the expense arising on a financial asset because of a negative effective interest rate should not be presented as interest revenue, but in an appropriate expense classification. The Interpretations Committee noted that in accordance with IAS 1:85 & 112(c), the entity is required to present additional information about such an amount if that is relevant to an understanding of the entity's financial performance or to an understanding of this item.

The Interpretations Committee considered that in the light of the existing IFRS requirements an interpretation was not necessary and consequently decided not to add the issue to its agenda.

4.1.1 Cash flows

When calculating the effective interest rate, the *estimated* cash flows arising from the asset or liability (or, where relevant, the group of assets or liabilities) should be used. IAS 39 explicitly states that all contractual terms of the instrument (e.g. prepayment, call and similar options) should be considered, but that future credit losses should *not* be taken into account. This last point is consistent with the fact that the impairment model adopted in IAS 39 requires impairment losses to be recognised as they are incurred, rather than when they are expected (see **section 5**).

In contrast, credit losses that have already been incurred on an instrument by the time it is acquired by the reporting entity should be taken into account when calculating the effective interest rate. This might be the case where a financial asset is acquired at a deep discount because credit losses that have occurred are reflected in the transaction price. As mentioned above, IAS 39 requires impairment losses to be recognised as incurred. If previously incurred losses are not factored into the calculation, an overstated interest income amount would be offset by the recognition of impairment losses that have already been incurred.

If an asset or liability in the form of debt instrument has a prepayment, put, or call feature embedded in the terms of the instrument, the entity must firstly determine whether that feature is an embedded derivative that needs to be separately accounted for. See **7.1** in **chapter C5** for further guidance on embedded derivatives. Briefly, such embedded derivatives will be separately accounted for unless the option's exercise price is approximately equal to the instrument's amortised cost on each exercise date, or the exercise price reimburses the lender for an amount up to the approximate present value of lost interest for the remaining term. [IAS 39:AG30(g)]

If the embedded derivative is accounted for separately, the impact of this feature must not be used in determining the estimated cash flows of the debt host contract when determining the effective interest rate. If the feature was taken into account, it would result in double counting of the prepayment, put or call feature in profit or loss because it would be included in the effective interest rate on the debt host contract as well as in the fair value movements of the embedded derivative.

4.1.2 Changes in cash flows

For floating rate instruments, when cash flows are re-estimated to reflect movements in market rates of interest, the effective interest rate is updated. If the instrument is initially recognised at an amount equal to the amount receivable or payable on maturity, re-estimating future cash flows for this reason will not normally have a significant effect on the carrying amount of the instrument. [IAS 39:AG7]

The re-estimation of future cash flows for any other reason or in the case of an instrument that is not a floating rate instrument will normally result in a change in carrying amount because the revised estimated cash flows are discounted at the instrument's original effective interest rate. The required adjustment is recognised in profit or loss. [IAS 39:AG8] The one exception to recognising an immediate gain or loss in profit or loss for changes in cash flows when applying IAS 39:AG8 is for certain financial assets that are reclassified out of the FVTPL category or reclassified from AFS to loans and receivables (see **4.1.2.4**). With the exception of such reclassified debt instruments, the changes in estimated cash flows will immediately affect profit or loss. For example, this will be the case for an instrument where the timing or amount of interest or principal payments varies due to the presence of an embedded derivative but the embedded derivative feature is not accounted for separately as an embedded derivative and the instrument is also not considered a floating rate instrument.

The difference in approach in IAS 39:AG7 & AG8 reflects the fact that varying interest receipts/payments are a contractual term of a floating rate instrument. In this situation, it would be inappropriate to determine at inception a single rate to discount estimated future cash flows. Instead, the Standard requires an entity to reflect changes in the interest rate in profit or loss as such changes occur.

Judgement is required in determining what constitutes a floating rate debt instrument. A debt instrument may have variable cash flows linked to market interest rates which differ from standard floating rate debt instruments. If the instrument is considered a floating rate debt instrument then IAS 39:AG7 is applied; if it is not, then IAS 39:AG8 applies.

4.1.2.1 Changes in cash flows linked to changes in an inflation index

In 2008, the IFRIC (now the IFRS Interpretations Committee) received a request for guidance on the application of the effective interest method to a financial instrument with future cash flows linked to changes in an inflation index. The IFRIC did not add the issue to its agenda but recommended that the Board should consider clarifying or expanding the relevant guidance in IAS 39. As part of its annual improvements project, in October 2008 the IASB decided tentatively that a floating rate financial instrument is an instrument with contractual variable cash flows arising from changes in market variables, however, it decided not to define the term market variable. The proposed amendment to IAS 39 was expected to be included in the exposure draft of proposed annual improvements issued in the second half of 2009; however, the IASB agreed to instead incorporate it into IFRS 9 *Financial Instruments* as part of reforming the amortised cost and impairment requirements. However, when IFRS 9 was published as finalised it largely copied the guidance on the effective interest rate from IAS 39 to IFRS 9 and therefore no new guidance was issued.

In the absence of specific guidance, the choice between applying IAS 39:AG7 and AG8 continues to be available for inflation-linked debt. It is an accounting policy choice and must be applied consistently to similar instruments.

Consider an example of a Sterling functional currency entity that has issued a Sterling denominated bond where principal and interest payments are indexed to unleveraged UK inflation. The inflation-linking feature is considered a closely related embedded derivative (see **7.4** in **chapter C5**). If the entity chooses to apply IAS 39:AG8, the effective interest rate will be calculated at initial recognition of the bond as the rate that exactly discounts the expectations of inflation at initial recognition to the initial carrying amount (being fair value less transaction costs). This effective interest rate is never updated. At the end of each subsequent reporting period, the cash flows are re-estimated, reflecting the then current expectations of future inflation, and are discounted using the original effective interest rate. Any difference between the carrying amount of the instrument before and after such re-estimation is recognised in profit or loss.

If the entity chooses to apply IAS 39:AG7, it may follow one of two possible approaches. One approach is to update the expected cash flows at each period end in line with changes in expectations of inflation in the same way as applying IAS 39:AG8 but, unlike under IAS 39:AG8, the changes in expectations do not result in an immediate gain/loss in profit or loss. Instead, the effective interest rate is revised each period (i.e. the gain/loss is spread forward). At initial recognition, the effective interest rate is calculated at a rate that discounts the estimated cash flows of principal and interest (which include the estimation of future inflation) to the initial carrying amount. That initial effective interest rate is used to account for the instrument at amortised cost until the end of the next reporting period. The carrying amount at the end of the first reporting period will be equal to the initial carrying amount,, plus the effective interest on the carrying amount, less any cash payments/receipts in the period. The entity then determines a new effective interest rate as the rate that discounts the new estimated cash flows of the instrument (taking into account the revised estimation of future inflation) back to the period end carrying amount. This new effective interest rate is applied for the new reporting period. This approach is repeated at each subsequent reporting period until the instrument is derecognised.

An alternative approach in applying IAS 39:AG7 is for profit or loss to reflect only the accrued inflation for the period up to the reporting date (i.e. the effective interest rate is not determined by looking forward to expectations of future inflation). This approach is consistent with the tentative conclusion of the IASB at its Board meeting in October 2008 when the Board tentatively agreed that expectations (and changes in expectations) of future cash flows are not considered when calculating the effective interest rate for floating rate instruments.

Applying one of the IAS 39:AG7 approaches described above will result in a less volatile profit or loss when compared to applying IAS 39:AG8. The application of the latter approach results in changes in expectations of future inflation impacting profit or loss immediately at each re-estimation date.

4.1.2.2 'Interest' determined as a proportion of the profits of the issuer

In May 2009, the IFRIC (now the IFRS Interpretations Committee) issued an agenda decision on IAS 39, *Participation Rights and Calculation of the Effective Interest Rate*. The IFRIC was asked for guidance regarding how an issuer should account for a financial liability that contains participation rights under which the instrument holder's return is determined as a proportion of the results of the issuer. In the specific circumstances considered (1) the holder received a percentage of the issuer's net income and was allocated a proportionate share of the issuer's losses, (2) losses were applied to the nominal value of the instrument to be repaid on maturity, and (3) losses allocated to the holder in one period could be offset by profits in subsequent periods.

The IFRIC considered the issue without reconsidering the assumptions described in the request, namely that the financial liability:

- does not contain any embedded derivatives;
- is measured at amortised cost using the effective interest method; and
- does not meet the definition of a floating rate instrument.

The IFRIC noted that IAS 39:AG6 & AG8 provide the relevant application guidance for measuring financial liabilities at amortised cost using the effective interest method. The IFRIC also noted that it is inappropriate to analogise to the derecognition guidance in IAS 39 because the liability has not been extinguished. Because specific application guidance already exists, the IFRIC decided not to add this issue to its agenda.

Guidance on the accounting treatment of financial instruments where interest is determined as a proportion of profit of the issuer is referred to at **2.1** in **chapter C4** with respect to the definition of a derivative. This guidance is relevant for financial assets and financial liabilities.

4.1.2.3 Changes in expected cash flows due to embedded prepayment, put or call options

Changes in any expected cash flows that relate to an embedded prepayment, put or call option may not have an effect on the carrying amount for a hybrid financial liability or hybrid financial asset because one of the following two circumstances may apply.

(i) The embedded derivative is separately accounted for. As discussed in **4.1.1**, this means that the derivative is ignored when determining the effective interest rate of the host contract.

(ii) The embedded derivative is not separately accounted for because the option's exercise price is approximately equal to the instrument's amortised cost on each exercise date. In this situation, because prepayment/put/call can only occur at an amount (approximately) equal to amortised cost, the discounted amount of future cash flows will be (approximately) unaffected by any change in expectations with respect to the exercise of said options.

This statement is not applicable for embedded prepayment, put or call options embedded in compound instruments with a separated equity component because of the unique way in which the embedded prepayment, put or call options are assessed as being closely related and the way the liability component is separated from the instrument as a whole.

When a prepayment, put or call option is embedded in an issued compound instrument, the assessment of whether the prepayment, put or call option is considered closely related to the debt host contract is made *prior* to the instrument being split into liability and equity components (see **3.2** in **chapter C3**). If the exercise price of the prepayment, put or call option is approximately equal to the amortised cost (prior to splitting the instrument into its liability and equity parts) it is closely related and, therefore, it is not separately recognised. If the embedded derivative is not separately recognised, the embedded prepayment, put or call option is taken into account in determining the timing and amount of the expected cash flows for the liability component when determining its amortised cost in future periods. Because the liability is initially recognised at a discount to the proceeds of the instrument as a whole, yet in most cases it can be early redeemed at an amount equal to the proceeds of the instrument as a whole, changes in the likelihood that the prepayment, put or call option will be exercised will affect the liability's carrying amount.

Example 4.1.2.3A

Issuer call option and holder put option in convertible debt

Entity X issued a convertible debt instrument in May 20X2 with a contractual maturity of 16 years. Each bond allows the holder to convert, at any time, into one share of Entity X. The issue price is 100 per cent and redemption price at maturity is 140 per cent.

The instrument is puttable by the holders on three different dates during the life of the instrument (May 20X6, May 20Y0 and May 20Y4) at the amortised cost of the instrument prior to the equity conversion option being separated plus a penalty of 3 per cent of the redemption amount. At initial recognition, Entity X considers that there is a very high probability that the instrument will be redeemed by the holders at the first put date (i.e. May 20X6) given the low price of its shares. The instrument is also callable by Entity X, starting May 20X6, if the price of the issuer's shares increases beyond 125 per cent of the redemption price. Entity X does not expect to call the instrument.

All the embedded call and put options over the instrument (excluding the conversion option that is treated as equity) are considered closely related to the debt component because the exercise prices are approximately equal to the amortised cost of the instrument prior to the equity conversion option being separated. The embedded call and put options are therefore not separated and form part of the debt component recognised as a financial liability. The financial liability is not designated as at FVTPL; rather, it is subsequently measured at amortised cost.

The fair value of the debt component at initial recognition is the contractual cash flows of the instrument (i.e. interest and principal at maturity) discounted by the entity's normal borrowing rate, plus the fair value of the written put option less the fair value of the purchased call option. The effective interest rate is the rate that exactly discounts this carrying amount with the estimated early redemption payment, in this case at May 20X6. This is the instrument's *original* effective interest rate. The difference between the total liability that includes the written put option and the purchased call option and the net proceeds at issue is assigned to the equity component.

Assuming that the expectation of repayment in May 20X6 does not change, the carrying amount of the debt component will change only for the application of the effective interest rate, i.e. it will increase by the difference between the effective interest rate and interest paid in the period. At May 20X6, the carrying amount of the liability will therefore equal the redemption amount. If the put option is exercised as expected, the early redemption will result in nil gain or loss.

If, however, expectations of repayment were to change (e.g. a change in market conditions were to cause the issuer to consider that the bond will be put back to the issuer on May 20Y0 instead of May 20X6), a recalculation of the carrying amount of the liability component would be required. The new carrying amount of the liability would be the re-estimated cash flows, being interest up to, and principal payable in, May 20Y0, discounted by the *original* effective interest rate. Any difference between the new carrying amount and the old carrying amount will be recognised in profit or loss.

Example 4.1.2.3B

Example of calculating amortised cost using IAS 39:AG8 for a financial asset

Entity A lends CU1,000 for five years. The instrument has a principal amount of CU1,250 and carries fixed interest of 4.7 per cent that is paid annually (CU1,250 × 4.7 per cent = CU59 per year). The contract also specifies that the borrower has an option to prepay the instrument at the end of every year at an amount equal to the amount advanced plus accrued interest at 10 per cent less interest paid to date, plus a penalty of CU30. There are no transaction costs. At inception, the entity expects the borrower not to prepay and the prepayment feature is considered a closely related embedded derivative as the amount prepayable is approximately equal to the financial asset's amortised cost.

The table below provides information about the amortised cost, interest income and cash flows of the debt instrument in each reporting period.

Year	(a) Amortised cost at the beginning of the year	(b = a x 10%) Interest income	(c) Cash flows	(d = a + b+ c) Amortised cost at the end of the year
20X0	1,000	100	(59)	1,041
20X1	1,041	104	(59)	1,086
20X2	1,086	109	(59)	1,136
20X3	1,136	113	(59)	1,190
20X4	1,190	119	(1,250 + 59)	–

On the first day of 20X2 the entity revises its estimate of cash flows. It now expects that 50 per cent of the instrument will be prepaid at the end of 20X2 and the remaining 50 per cent at the end of 20X4. In accordance with IAS 39:AG8, the opening balance of the debt instrument in 20X2 is adjusted. The adjusted amount is calculated by discounting the amount the entity expects to receive in 20X2 being the prepayable amount ((CU1,136 * 50 per cent) + CU30 = CU598) plus interest of CU59 for the year, with the due interest in years 20X3 and 20X4 (CU59 * 50 per cent = CU30) and the remaining principal due in 20X4 (CU1,250 * 50 per cent), using the original effective interest rate (10 per cent). This results in the new opening balance in 20X2 of CU1,114. The adjustment is a gain of CU28 (CU1,114 – CU1,086) and is recorded in profit or loss in 20X2. The table below provides information about the amortised cost, interest income and cash flows as they would be adjusted taking into account the change in estimate.

Year	(a) Amortised cost at the beginning of the year	(b = a x 10%) Interest income	(c) Cash flows	(d = a + b + c) Amortised cost at the end of the year
20X0	1,000	100	(59)	1,041
20X1	1,041	104	(59)	1,086
20X2	1,086+28	111	(568+30+59)	568
20X3	568	57	(30)	595
20X4	595	60	(625 + 30)	–

4.1.2.4 Changes in cash flows following reclassification

The amendment to IAS 39 *Reclassification of Financial Assets* issued in October 2008 amended IAS 39:AG8 for debt instrument assets reclassified out of FVTPL, or AFS, to loans and receivables (see **sections 4.2** and **4.4** respectively in **chapter C2**). The amendment requires that any increases in estimates of future cash receipts as a result of increased recoverability of those cash receipts after the date of reclassification should be recognised as an adjustment to the effective interest rate from the date of the change in estimate rather than as an adjustment to the carrying amount of the asset at the date of the change in estimate. The impact of this amendment is to 'spread' the effect of increased recoverability of cash flows forward through a higher effective interest rate rather than recognising a gain in profit or loss at the time when the cash flows are re-estimated. The aim of the IASB in amending IAS 39:AG8 was to attempt to align the post-reclassification gains/losses on reclassified debt instruments with US GAAP as best it could, but acknowledging that there remain broader GAAP differences in this area that could not be eliminated as part of the amendment.

If there are changes in estimates of contractual cash flows other than as a result of increased recoverability (e.g. changes in prepayment estimates) but the recoverability of the contractual cash flows is unchanged, and the financial asset is not a floating rate instrument but has been reclassified, then the holder does not revise the effective interest rate as described immediately above. Instead, the holder estimates the future contractual cash flows and discounts them at the original effective interest rate (being the effective rate at the date of reclassification or a revised effective interest rate if the rate has been revised since the date of reclassification) and recognises any difference in profit or loss (see **4.1.2**). For reclassified floating rate assets, the guidance is less clear. In circumstances when there are changes in market interest rates and/or changes in prepayment speeds when there is no change in recoverable cash flows, it may be reasonable to update the effective interest rate for the changes in estimate contractual cash flows instead of recognising an immediate gain or loss as the instrument is regarded as a floating rate instrument in the scope of IAS 39:AG7.

In circumstances where there is an increased recoverability of contractual cash flows concurrently with other changes in estimates of contractual cash flows, the entity should revise the effective interest rate. IAS 39:AG8 requires revision of the effective interest rate for reclassified assets in cases of increased recoverability since the reclassification date. Therefore, an entity is not permitted to separate the changes in cash flows due to increased recoverability (and apply a revised effective interest rate for that component) from other changes in contractual cash flows (and apply the original effective interest rate to that component).

Example 4.1.2.4

Reclassification from FVTPL to L&R with subsequent increase in recoverability of cash flows

In June 20X0, Bank A purchases asset-backed securities that are linked to an underlying portfolio of corporate bonds held by the issuer of the asset-backed securities. The investment is known as a 'cash CDO'. The investment matures in 20Y0 at its par value of CU100 million although, depending on the performance of the underlying corporate bond portfolio, the asset-backed securities may be redeemed earlier. The investment is classified by Bank A as at FVTPL at initial recognition because it has the intent to trade the instrument.

At 30 June 20X3, the investment has declined in value to CU70 million and the asset-backed securities and the underlying portfolio of corporate bonds are no longer traded in an active market.

On 1 July 20X3, Bank A reclassifies the investment to the loans and receivables category because the entity has the intention and ability to hold the investment for the foreseeable future. Bank A has an accounting policy of applying the loans and receivables definition at the date of reclassification, as opposed to the date of initial recognition (see **4.2** in **chapter C2**). At the date of reclassification, its opening amortised cost equals its fair value, being CU70 million. Bank A estimates that it will recover the following contractual cash flows on the investment with an expected redemption in June 20X8.

Date	**Coupon**	**Principal**
	CU million	**CU million**
30 June 20X4	6	
30 June 20X5	6	
30 June 20X6	6	
30 June 20X7	6	
30 June 20X8	6	80

The effective interest rate that exactly discounts the estimated future cash flows to the fair value of the investment at the date of reclassification is 10.9 per cent. This new effective interest rate is used to amortise the difference between the amortised cost of the cash CDO at the date of reclassification and the redemption value until the expected maturity date. Accordingly, the amortised cost will accrete as follows.

	Amortised cost b/f	**Interest income at 10.9%**	**Coupon**	**Amortised cost c/f**
Date	**CU million**	**CU million**	**CU million**	**CU million**
30 June 20X4	70.0	7.6	(6.0)	71.6
30 June 20X5	71.6	7.8	(6.0)	73.4
30 June 20X6	73.4	8.0	(6.0)	75.4
30 June 20X7	75.4	8.2	(6.0)	77.6
30 June 20X8	77.6	8.4	(6.0)	80.0

On 30 June 20X6, Bank A estimates there is an increase in the recoverability of cash flows. Bank A expects that it will receive 90 per cent of principal, instead of 80 per cent as previously expected.

Date	**Coupon**	**Principal**
	CU million	**CU million**
30 June 20X7	6	
30 June 20X8	6	90

Because the increase in recoverability of cash flows occurred after a reclassification of a debt instrument, Bank A must determine a new effective interest rate in accordance with IAS 39:AG8. The effective interest rate that exactly discounts these future cash flows to the amortised cost carrying amount of the investment at 30 June 20X6 is 16.9 per cent. Accordingly, the amortised cost will accrete as follows.

	Amortised cost b/f	**Interest income at 16.9%**	**Coupon**	**Amortised cost c/f**
Coupon date	**CU million**	**CU million**	**CU million**	**CU million**
30 June 20X7	75.4	12.7	(6.0)	82.1
30 June 20X8	82.1	13.9	(6.0)	90.0

If the asset was subject to an impairment event in a future period, the effective interest rate that would be used to discount the expected recoverable cash flows to determine the impairment loss would be the revised effective interest rate, i.e. 16.9 per cent.

If the asset was instead subject to further increases in the recoverability of cash flows in a future period, the effective interest rate would once again be revised in accordance with IAS 39:AG8.

4.1.3 Fees

The definition of the effective interest rate states that "[t]he calculation includes all fees and points paid or received between parties to the contract that are an integral part of the effective interest rate". [IAS 39:9] IAS 39:AG8A includes a note of caution that the description of fees for financial services may not be indicative of the nature and substance of the services provided. Fees that are an integral part of the effective interest rate of a financial instrument include:

[IAS 39:AG8B]

Origination fees. Such fees arise on the creation or acquisition of a financial asset or are received on issuing financial liabilities measured at amortised cost. For assets this may include compensation for activities such as evaluating the borrower's financial condition, evaluating and recording guarantees, collateral and other security arrangements, negotiating the terms of the instrument, preparing and processing documents and closing the transaction. These fees are an integral part of generating an involvement with the resulting financial instrument. Origination fees received on issuing financial liabilities measured at amortised cost are included in the effective interest rate if they are an integral part of generating an involvement with a financial liability. Fees and costs should be distinguished between those that are an integral part of the effective interest rate for the financial liability from origination fees and transaction costs relating to the right to provide services, such as investment management services.

Commitment fees. Such fees are received on origination of a loan when the loan commitment is outside the scope of IAS 39 and it is probable that the entity will enter into a specific lending arrangement. These fees are regarded as compensation for an ongoing involvement with the acquisition of a financial instrument. If the commitment expires without the entity making the loan, the fee is recognised as revenue on expiry.

Fees that are not an integral part of the effective interest rate of a financial instrument and are accounted for in accordance with IFRS 15 *Revenue from Contracts with Customers* include:

[IAS 39:AG8C]

(a) fees charged for servicing a loan;

(b) commitment fees to originate a loan when the loan commitment is outside the scope of IAS 39 and it is unlikely that a specific lending arrangement will be entered into; and

(c) loan syndication fees received by an entity that arranges a loan and retains no part of the loan package for itself (or retains a part at the same effective interest rate for comparable risk as other participants).

The choice of the terms 'probable' and 'unlikely' for assessing whether commitment fees are an integral part of the effective interest rate in describing the two possible alternatives is slightly unusual. It is suggested that 'unlikely' should be interpreted as meaning anything less than probable.

4.1.4 Amortisation period

The definition of the effective interest rate (see **4.1**) requires the amortisation of premiums/discounts, fees, points paid or received and transaction costs (those that are taken into account in calculating the effective rate) over "the expected life of the financial instrument or, when appropriate, a shorter period". A shorter period will be appropriate if it is the period to which the relevant premiums/discounts, fees, points paid or received or transaction costs relate. [IAS 39:AG6] For example, if a fee is received as compensation for a discounted interest rate over an initial period (which ends with a repricing to market interest rates), then that fee should be amortised over that initial period rather than the expected life of the instrument. In general, when the variable to which the fee, transaction costs, discount or premium relates is repriced to market rates before the expected maturity of the instrument, a shorter period will be used. However, if it is another variable that is repriced, the expected life of the instrument will be used. This would be the case when the premium/discount on an instrument results from changes in the credit spread over the specified floating rate, but it is the interest rate that is repriced.

4.1.5 Measurement

There is a presumption that it will be possible to estimate reliably the cash flows and expected life of an instrument or group of similar instruments, such that the effective interest rate can be determined. However, in those 'rare cases' when this is not possible, the rate should be calculated based on the contractual cash flows over the full contractual term of the instrument. [IAS 39:9]

The application of the effective interest method is illustrated in the examples below.

Example 4.1.5A

Example of calculating amortised cost: debt instruments with stepped interest payments

[Extract from IAS 39:IG.B.27]

On 1 January 20X0, Entity A issues a debt instrument for a price of CU1,250. The principal amount is CU1,250 and the debt instrument is repayable on 31 December 20X4. The rate of interest is specified in the debt agreement as a percentage of the principal amount as follows: 6.0 per cent in 20X0 (CU75), 8.0 per cent in 20X1 (CU100), 10.0 per cent in 20X2 (CU125), 12.0 per cent in 20X3 (CU150), and 16.4 per cent in 20X4 (CU205). In this case, the interest rate that exactly discounts the stream of future cash payments through maturity is 10 per cent. Therefore, cash interest payments are reallocated over the term of the debt instrument for the purposes of determining amortised cost in each period. In each period, the amortised cost at the beginning of the period is multiplied by the effective interest rate of 10 per cent and added to the amortised cost. Any cash payments in the period are deducted from the resulting number. Accordingly, the amortised cost in each period is as follows:

Year	(a) Amortised cost at the beginning of the year	(b = a x 10%) Interest income	(c) Cash flows	(d = a + b – c) Amortised cost at the end of the year
20X0	1,250	125	75	1,300
20X1	1,300	130	100	1,330
20X2	1,330	133	125	1,338
20X3	1,338	134	150	1,322
20X4	1,322	133	1,250 + 205	–

Example 4.1.5B

Accounting for a loan with a separated embedded derivative

On 1 January 20X0, Entity B originates a loan of CU100. Interest of CU4 is receivable annually over the next five years (on 31 December 20X0 to

31 December 20X4). The loan is repayable at an amount of CU110 on 31 December 20X4. However, the borrower can prepay (at CU111 plus accrued interest for the year) at any time. Because the prepayment option will result in the loan potentially being prepaid by the borrower at an amount that is not approximately equal to the amortised cost, and the exercise price could compensate the lender for more than the approximate present value of lost interest for the remaining term of the host contract, the prepayment option is separately accounted for as an embedded derivative. The prepayment option is effectively an option written by the originator allowing the borrower to repay the borrowing at any time. Economically, the borrower can be expected to prepay the liability if the fair value of the instrument rises above CU111 (plus accrued interest).

On 1 January 20X0, the fair value of the prepayment option for the originator is a CU3 liability. Therefore, the remaining balance of CU103 is the host contract asset.

(1) Initial recognition at 1 January 20X0

		CU	CU
Dr	Asset	103.00	
Cr	Cash		100.00
Cr	Prepayment option		3.00

To recognise the loan.

The effective interest rate on the host contract is 5.11 per cent (calculated as the rate that exactly discounts interest of CU4 and principal of CU110 to the carrying amount of CU103).

At the end of 20X0, interest rates have fallen slightly, and the fair value of the option has risen from CU3 to CU5. The following entries are recorded in 20X0.

(2) Interest income

		CU	CU
Dr	Asset	5.26	
Cr	Interest income		5.26

To recognise interest income.

Interest income is determined at the effective interest rate of 5.11 per cent (5.11% x CU103.00).

(3) Interest receipt

		CU	CU
Dr	Cash	4.00	
Cr	Asset		4.00

To record receipt of interest.

The carrying amount of the loan as at 31 December 20X0 is therefore CU104.26.

(4) Embedded derivative

		CU	CU
Dr	Profit or loss	2.00	
Cr	Embedded derivative liability		2.00

To record the remeasurement of the embedded derivative.

By the end of 20X1, interest rates have fallen further so that, on 31 December 20X1, the borrower repays the borrowing early. At the year end, the fair value of the prepayment option is CU6.

(5) Interest income

		CU	CU
Dr	Asset	5.33	
Cr	Interest income		5.33

To recognise interest income.

Interest income is determined at the effective interest rate of 5.11 per cent (5.11% x CU104.26).

(6) Interest receipt

		CU	CU
Dr	Cash	4.00	
Cr	Asset		4.00

To record receipt of interest.

The carrying amount of the loan prior to early repayment is therefore CU105.59.

(7) Embedded derivative

		CU	CU
Dr	Profit or loss	1.00	
Cr	Embedded derivative liability		1.00

To record the remeasurement of the embedded derivative.

(8) Early repayment of loan

		CU	CU
Dr	Cash	111.00	
Dr	Embedded derivative liability	6.00	
Cr	Asset		105.59
Cr	Profit or loss		11.41

To record the repayment of the loan.

The credit in profit or loss on early repayment of the loan represents the cumulative catch-up of the fair value of the host contract. Because the host contract is not measured at fair value during its life, this results in a gain in profit or loss when the instrument is terminated, due to the impact of movements in interest rates that have not previously been recognised in the financial statements. Because interest rates have fallen considerably, the fair value of the host contract has risen.

The above example assumes that, at inception, the holder of the loan considers that the put option is not likely to be exercised. If the put option was considered likely to be exercised, there is an argument that the likely exercise of the put option would form part of the instrument's amortised cost and, therefore, would result in a different host contract being identified (see **7.1** in **chapter C5**).

Example 4.1.5C

Effective interest rate for fixed rate perpetual debt

An entity issues a perpetual debt instrument for consideration of CU100. Interest of CU6 is payable annually in perpetuity. The instrument is not redeemable. The effective rate (i.e. the rate that discounts CU6 annually in perpetuity to CU100) is 6 per cent. Interest of CU6 is recognised in profit or loss and there is no amortisation of the principal amount. This would also be the case for a floating rate instrument because, as discussed in **4.1.2**, the effective rate is adjusted for changes in market rates for floating rate instruments.

Example 4.1.5D

Effective interest rate for stepped fixed rate perpetual debt

An entity issues a perpetual debt instrument; the interest rate is fixed at 10 per cent for the first 10 years and 8 per cent for each year thereafter.

The 10 per cent interest payments in the first ten years represent a part payment of redemption. Consequently, when these payments are made, the difference between 10 per cent and 8 per cent is treated as a reduction in the carrying amount of the liability. In the period from Year 10, the effective interest will be recognised at 8 per cent because all payments relate to interest and not repayment of principal.

An alternative way of considering the higher payments in the first 10 years is the sum of the differential between the 10 per cent and 8 per cent represents repayments on an amortising loan. The value of the amortising loan at inception less the proceeds from the instrument as a whole represents the carrying amount of the perpetual debt instrument.

IAS 39:IG.B.25 has a similar fact pattern as **example 4.1.5D** except that after Year 10 the interest rate reduces to zero. The implementation guidance states that the amortised cost is zero after Year 10 because the present value of the stream of future cash payments in subsequent periods is zero.

An alternative argument to that used in the implementation guidance is that, after the final payment is made at Year 10, the financial liability is derecognised because the entity has fully discharged any obligation to pay cash or other financial asset.

4.1.6 Interaction of effective interest rate and fair value hedge accounting

When an entity applies fair value hedge accounting to a hedge of a debt instrument, the carrying amount of the debt is adjusted for movements in the hedged risk to the extent the hedge is highly effective. Fair value hedge accounting is explained in detail at **2.1** in **chapter C9**. IAS 39:92 requires the fair value adjustment to be amortised to profit or loss at the earliest when the adjustment is made and no later than when the hedged item ceases to be fair value adjusted. This amortisation is included as part of the revised effective interest rate. Therefore, if an entity chooses to amortise the fair value adjustment as soon as the adjustment is made then, assuming the fair value adjustment changes for each subsequent reporting period because there is a change in the fair value of the hedged risk and the hedge is highly effective, a revised effective interest rate will need to be determined at the start of each reporting period. Alternatively, if an entity chooses to start to amortise the adjustment when hedge accounting ceases, the entity will only need to recalculate the effective interest rate at that point.

In May 2008, the IASB issued *Improvements to IFRSs*. The improvements amended IAS 39 to make it clear that the effective interest rate that is used when applying IAS 39:AG8 when revisions in estimates of cash flows occur is the original effective interest rate, except when IAS 39:92 as described above applies, in which case the revised effective interest rate that includes the effects of the fair value hedge adjustment is used.

5 Impairment

IAS 39 requires all financial assets, with the exception of those measured at FVTPL, to be assessed for impairment. IAS 39 adopts different approaches to assessing and calculating impairment for different classification categories. The requirements to assess for impairment are summarised in the following table.

Financial asset	Impairment assessment required?	Section in this chapter
Investment in debt instruments		
Loans & receivables	Yes	**5.2**
Held-to-maturity investments	Yes	**5.2**
Available-for-sale financial assets	Yes	**5.4**

Financial asset	**Impairment assessment required?**	**Section in this chapter**
Fair value through profit or loss	No	–
Investment in equity instruments		
Fair value through profit or loss	No	–
Available-for-sale financial assets	Yes	**5.4**
Unquoted equity instruments measured at cost	Yes	**5.3**
Derivative instruments (including separated embedded derivatives)		
Fair value through profit or loss	No	–
Derivatives that result in physical delivery of unquoted equity investments measured at cost	Yes	**5.3**

The two most notable characteristics of the IAS 39 impairment model are that:

(i) impairment losses should be recognised when they are incurred, rather than as expected; and

(ii) an impairment loss should be regarded as incurred if, and only if, there is objective evidence of impairment as a result of one or more events that occurred after initial recognition (a 'loss event').

5.1 Evidence of impairment

IAS 39 requires an assessment, at the end of each reporting period, as to whether there is any objective evidence that a financial asset or group of financial assets is impaired. An asset is impaired, and an impairment loss recognised, if and only if, such evidence exists. [IAS 39:58]

5.1.1 Loss events

Impairment losses are incurred on a financial asset or a group of financial assets if, and only if, there is objective evidence of an impairment that results from one or more events that occurred after the initial recognition of the asset (a 'loss event'). [IAS 39:59]

The following points are important to note.

- Such loss events must have an impact on the estimated future cash flows of the asset, or group of assets, that can be reliably measured.
- An impairment may occur as the result of the combined effect of several events – it is not always possible to identify a single, discrete event that caused the impairment.
- Losses expected as a result of future events are not recognised (no matter how likely those events might be).

The Standard gives a number of examples of possible loss events:

[IAS 39:59]

(a) significant financial difficulty of the issuer or obligor;

(b) a breach of contract, such as a default or delinquency in interest or principal payments;

(c) the lender, for economic or legal reasons relating to the borrower's financial difficulty, granting to the borrower a concession that the lender would not otherwise consider;

(d) it becoming probable that the borrower will enter bankruptcy or other financial reorganisation;

(e) the disappearance of an active market for that financial asset because of financial difficulties; or

(f) observable data indicating that there is a measurable decrease in the estimated future cash flows from a group of financial assets since the initial recognition of those assets, although the decrease cannot yet be identified with the individual financial assets in the group, including:

  (i) adverse changes in the payment status of borrowers in the group (e.g. an increased number of delayed payments or an increased number of credit card borrowers who have reached their credit limit and are paying the minimum monthly amount); or

  (ii) national or local economic conditions that correlate with defaults on the assets in the group (e.g. an increase in the unemployment rate in the geographical area of the borrowers, a decrease in property prices for mortgages in the relevant area, a decrease in oil prices for loan assets to oil producers, or adverse changes in industry conditions that affect the borrowers in the group).

The following are not, in themselves, evidence of an impairment.

- In contrast to (e) above, the disappearance of an active market because an entity's financial instruments are no longer publicly traded.
- A downgrading of an entity's credit rating, in the absence of other information suggesting the occurrence of a loss event.
- A decline in the fair value of a financial asset below its cost or amortised cost (IAS 39 gives the example of a decline in the fair value of a debt instrument resulting from an increase in the risk-free interest rate).

A change in the fair value of a fixed rate debt investment due to movements in the *risk-free interest rate* would never by itself be objective evidence of impairment. Also, changes in the fair value of a fixed rate debt investment due to movements in market interest rates will generally not be indicative of impairment because movements in market interest rates are never specific to the credit quality of the investment that is held. [IAS 39:IG.E.4.10]

However, it is possible that a fall in fair value due to an increase in the borrower's specific interest rate (i.e. due to an increase in the credit spread of the borrower) could be indicative of impairment when considered with other evidence supporting that a loss event has been incurred. [IAS 39:AG22(a)]

In the case of an AFS debt instrument that has already been subject to recognition of impairment losses and where there continues to be evidence of impairment, a further decline in the fair value of the investment due to a change in the risk-free interest rate is evidence of impairment (see **5.4.3.2**).

Losses that are expected to arise as a result of future events are not recognised. This holds true no matter how likely such events might be. The most obvious example of an expected future event in this context is the future default of a counterparty if a default was expected already at origination. Often an entity will have reliable empirical evidence of the rate of default for a particular class of borrower. However, the existence of such evidence does not imply that an impairment loss should be recognised. Otherwise, a 'day-one' loss would be recognised upon the origination or acquisition of many financial assets (future cash flows used to calculate the effective interest rate do not reflect future credit losses – see **4.1.1**). At origination, the effective interest rate assumes the borrower will meet all its contractual obligations and will not default even though the probability of default is factored into the interest rate the lender will charge the borrower. This 'incurred loss' (as opposed to 'expected loss') approach is a key characteristic of the impairment model of IAS 39.

For example, if a financial asset is purchased at a discount to its initial issue price because there has been a worsening of the credit quality of the counterparty between the issue date and the acquisition date, but there is no loss event, the effective interest rate will reflect the rate that exactly discounts the cash flows until maturity without taking into account expected credit losses. The effective interest rate therefore will be higher than the rate that would have been achieved had the asset been purchased originally at the issue date. Even though the credit spread inherent in the effective interest rate is higher than it is at inception, this is not evidence of impairment itself. When a loss event occurs, only then will an impairment loss be recognised.

In some cases, financial assets are acquired at a deep discount that reflects incurred credit losses. Entities include such incurred credit losses in the estimated cash flows when computing the effective interest rate. [IAS 39:AG5]

It is not necessary to be able to identify a single, discrete event in order to conclude that an impairment loss has occurred. In addition to point (e) of the list above, the following factors should be considered in determining whether there is objective evidence that an impairment loss has been incurred:

[IAS 39:IG.E.4.1]

- information about the counterparty's liquidity, solvency and business and financial risk exposures;
- levels of and trends in delinquencies for similar financial assets;
- national and local economic trends and conditions; and
- the fair value of collateral and guarantees.

In assessing financial assets or groups of financial assets for impairment, an entity considers financial guarantees and any existing collateral. IAS 39:AG84 states that, when considering impairment, an entity should take into account the cash flows from the foreclosure of collateral. IAS 39:IG.E.4.1 states that, in determining whether there is objective evidence that an impairment loss has been incurred, the entity must consider the existence of guarantees over the financial asset. The appropriate accounting for financial guarantee contracts held is described at **2.3.4** in **chapter C1**.

5.1.2 Equity investments

In addition to the potential loss events discussed above, further factors will apply when considering the impairment of equity investments. Information about significant changes with an adverse effect that have taken place in the technological, market, economic or legal environment in which the issuer operates may constitute objective evidence of an impairment. A significant or prolonged decline in fair value (below cost) is objective evidence of impairment and, therefore, will result in the fair value loss being reclassified from other comprehensive income to profit or loss (see also **5.4.1**). [IAS 39:61] The determination of what constitutes a 'significant or prolonged' decline in fair value requires application of judgement.

In accordance with the requirements of IAS 1 *Presentation of Financial Statements* (paragraphs 122 - 123) and IFRS 7:20, an entity should provide disclosures regarding the judgements it has made in determining the existence of objective evidence of impairment and the amounts of impairment losses.

When considering what is a 'significant or prolonged decline in fair value' of an equity security below cost, the investor must compare the original cost in the investor's functional currency at the date of acquisition and the fair value of the equity security (also in the investor's functional currency) on the remeasurement date. If an entity purchased a listed foreign currency denominated equity security whose fair value in local currency terms has remained relatively stable since acquisition, but the currency depreciated significantly or has been depreciating for a prolonged period, this would constitute impairment, because losses that are attributable to foreign currency losses are a portion of the overall net fair value loss of an equity security.

In July 2009, the IFRIC (now the IFRS Interpretations Committee) issued an agenda decision on IAS 39, *Meaning of 'Significant or Prolonged'*. The IFRIC considered a number of practices and concluded as follows.

- The Standard cannot be read to require the decline in value to be both significant *and* prolonged. Thus, either a significant *or* a prolonged decline is sufficient to require the recognition of an impairment loss. The IFRIC noted that in finalising the 2003 amendments to IAS 39, the IASB deliberately changed the word from 'and' to 'or'.
- IAS 39:67 requires the recognition of an impairment loss on AFS equity instruments if there is objective evidence of impairment. IAS 39:61 states conclusively that a significant or prolonged decline in fair value of an investment in an equity instrument below its cost is objective evidence of impairment. Consequently, when such a decline exists, recognition of an impairment loss is required.
- The fact that the decline in the value of an investment is in line with the overall level of decline in the relevant market does not mean that an entity can conclude the investment is not impaired.
- The existence of a significant or prolonged decline cannot be overcome by forecasts of an expected recovery of market values, regardless of their expected timing. Consequently, an anticipated market recovery is not relevant to the assessment of 'significant or prolonged'.
- IAS 39:AG83 and IAS 39:IG.E.4.9 *Impairment of Non-monetary Available-for-Sale Financial Asset* both discuss the recognition of financial instruments denominated in foreign currencies. It is inappropriate to assess 'significant or prolonged' in the foreign currency in which the equity investment is denominated. That assessment must be made in the functional currency of the entity holding the instrument because that is how any impairment loss is determined.

The Standard contains separate rules for the measurement of impairment losses to be applied to financial assets that are carried at amortised cost, carried at cost, and classified as AFS.

5.2 Assets carried at amortised cost

The requirements outlined in this section are relevant for financial assets classified as either loans and receivables or HTM.

Once an impairment loss has been identified, its amount is measured as the difference between the asset's carrying amount and the present value of estimated future cash flows, discounted at the original effective interest rate. This amount is then recognised in profit or loss. The carrying amount of the asset is reduced, either directly or through use of an allowance account. [IAS 39:63] However, as a practical expedient, the impairment loss can be measured on the basis of an asset's fair value using an observable market price. [IAS 39:AG84]

In circumstances in which there is a range of possible amounts, a loss equal to the best estimate within that range should be recognised. When there is a continuous range of possible amounts, and each point in that range is as likely as any other, the mid-point of the range is used.

For collateralised assets, the estimated cash flows that should be used to calculate any impairment reflect the cash flows that might result from foreclosure, less the costs of obtaining and selling the collateral. [IAS 39:AG84] Collateral should not be recognised as a separate asset before foreclosure. [IAS 39:IG.E.4.8]

5.2.1 Discount rate

In calculating an impairment loss, expected future cash flows are discounted at the original effective interest rate. As a result, *only* the effect of the reduction in cash flows is recognised as a loss – that amount is not affected by other factors (e.g. changes in the market interest rate, or the credit rating of the borrower) that might affect the fair value of the asset.

When the terms of a loan are renegotiated due to the financial difficulties of the borrower/issuer, any impairment is still measured by reference to the original effective interest rate before the modification of terms. [IAS 39:AG84]

Two particular instances in which a different rate should be used are as follows.

(i) For a variable rate asset, impairment should be measured using the current effective interest rate determined under the contract (see **section 4.1.2**).

(ii) The carrying amount of an asset designated as a hedged item in a fair value hedge of interest rate risk will be adjusted for fair value changes attributable to interest rate movements. The original effective interest rate then becomes irrelevant and the rate is recalculated using the adjusted carrying amount of the loan. [IAS 39:IG.E.4.4]

The IAS 39 impairment model is illustrated in the simple example below.

Example 5.2.1A

Determining the amount of impairment for a loan

On 1 January 20X0, an entity originates a loan of CU100 that is measured at amortised cost. The loan attracts five annual repayments of CU25 on 31 December 20X0 to 31 December 20X4. Ignoring future credit losses, it is expected that all contractual cash flows will be received; therefore, the effective interest rate is 7.93 per cent and the following entries are recorded in 20X0.

(1) Initial recognition

		CU	CU
Dr	Asset	100.00	
Cr	Cash		100.00

To recognise the loan.

(2) Interest income

		CU	CU
Dr	Asset	7.93	
Cr	Interest income		7.93

To recognise interest income.

(3) Repayment

		CU	CU
Dr	Cash	25.00	
Cr	Asset		25.00

To record the repayment of the loan.

The carrying amount of the loan as at 31 December 20X0 is therefore CU82.93. On 1 January 20X1, the entity receives information regarding the future prospects of the sector in which the borrower operates. This information coincides with a downgrading of the borrower's credit rating. Together, these two occurrences are deemed to constitute a loss event and it is now expected that the 20X3 and 20X4 repayments will not be received.

The revised carrying amount of the loan is calculated by discounting the expected future cash flows (i.e. the 20X1 and 20X2 repayments) at the original effective interest rate:

$CU25/1.0793 + CU25/1.0793^2 = CU44.62$

Therefore, an impairment loss of CU38.31 (i.e. CU82.93 – CU44.62) is recognised, as follows.

		CU	CU
Dr	Profit or loss	38.31	
Cr	Asset		38.31

To recognise an impairment loss.

If an investment in a debt instrument is reclassified out of FVTPL or AFS, the entity must determine an effective interest rate at the date of reclassification because the fair value at the date of reclassification becomes its new deemed amortised cost. In the case of a debt instrument reclassified out of AFS, any amounts recognised in other comprehensive income must be amortised to profit or loss as part of the revised effective interest rate if the debt instrument has a maturity. If the reclassified debt instrument is subsequently impaired, any unamortised amounts in other comprehensive income must be reclassified from other comprehensive income to profit or loss along with the impairment loss. [IAS 39:54(a) & 50F]

In July 2010, the IFRS Interpretations Committee issued an agenda decision on IAS 39, *Impairment of Financial Assets Reclassified from Available-For-Sale to Loans and Receivables*. The Committee received a request for guidance on how an entity should account for the impairment of financial assets with a fixed maturity after they have been reclassified from the AFS category to loans and receivables.

The Committee noted that IAS 39:50F & 54 require that the fair value of a financial asset on the date of reclassification becomes its new cost or amortised cost. A new effective rate of interest is then calculated and applied to the financial asset. This is the rate that discounts the estimated future cash flows to the new carrying amount of the financial asset. The Committee also noted that, when an impairment loss is recognised, applying the requirements of IAS 39:54 would result in all gains or losses that have been recognised in other comprehensive income being reclassified from equity to profit or loss.

The Committee noted that IAS 39 provides sufficient guidance on financial assets that are reclassified from AFS to loans and receivables and that it does not expect diversity in practice. Consequently, the Committee decided not to add this issue to its agenda.

Example 5.2.1B

Reclassification from available-for-sale to loans and receivables, and subsequent impairment

In June 20X0, Bank A purchases asset-backed securities that are linked to an underlying portfolio of corporate bonds held by the issuer of the asset-backed securities. The investment is known as a 'cash CDO'. The investment matures in 20Y0 at its par value of CU100 million although, depending on prepayments and restructuring of the underlying corporate bond portfolio, the asset-backed securities may be redeemed earlier. The investment is classified by Bank A as AFS.

At 30 June 20X3, the investment has declined in fair value to CU70 million and the asset-backed securities and the underlying portfolio of corporate bonds are no longer traded in an active market. The AFS reserve in equity is CU30 million because the investment has not been subject to impairment.

On 1 July 20X3, Bank A reclassifies the investment to the loans and receivables category because the entity has the intention and ability to hold the investment for the foreseeable future. Bank A has an accounting policy of applying the loans and receivables definition at the date of reclassification, as opposed to the date of initial recognition (see **4.2** in **chapter C2**). At the date of reclassification, its opening amortised cost equals its fair value (i.e. CU70 million). Bank A estimates that it will recover all the contractual cash flows on the investment with an expected redemption in June 20X8. The contractual cash flows are as follows.

Date	**Coupon**	**Principal**
	CU million	**CU million**
30 June 20X4	6	
30 June 20X5	6	
30 June 20X6	6	
30 June 20X7	6	
30 June 20X8	6	100

The effective interest rate that exactly discounts these future cash flows to the fair value of the investment at the date of reclassification is 14.9 per cent. This new effective interest rate is then used to amortise the difference between the amortised cost of the CDO at the date of reclassification and the redemption value until the expected maturity date. Accordingly, the amortised cost will accrete as follows.

Date	**Amortised cost b/f**	**Interest income at 14.9%**	**Coupon**	**Amortised cost c/f**
	CU million	**CU million**	**CU million**	**CU million**
30 June 20X4	70.0	10.5	(6.0)	74.5
30 June 20X5	74.5	11.1	(6.0)	79.6
30 June 20X6	79.6	11.9	(6.0)	85.5
30 June 20X7	85.5	12.7	(6.0)	92.2
30 June 20X8	92.2	13.8	(6.0)	100.0

The debit in the AFS reserve in other comprehensive income of CU30 million is frozen at the date of reclassification and will be amortised to profit or loss over the remaining life of the CDO by applying an effective interest rate. As a result, the effect on profit or loss will be as follows.

Date	**AFS reserve b/f**	**Amortisation of AFS reserve in profit or loss**	**AFS reserve c/f**	**Interest income at 14.9%**	**Net interest income**
	CU million	**CU million**	**CU million**	**CU million**	**CU million**
30 June 20X4	(30.0)	(4.5)	(25.5)	10.5	6.0
30 June 20X5	(25.5)	(5.1)	(20.4)	11.1	6.0

Date	AFS reserve b/f	Amortisation of AFS reserve in profit or loss	AFS reserve c/f	Interest income at 14.9%	Net interest income
	CU million	CU million	CU million	CU million	CU million
30 June 20X6	(20.4)	(5.9)	(14.5)	11.9	6.0
30 June 20X7	(14.5)	(6.7)	(7.8)	12.7	6.0
30 June 20X8	(7.8)	(7.8)	0	13.8	6.0

On 30 June 20X6, Bank A estimates that there is a reduction in the recoverability of cash flows due to objective evidence of impairment. Bank A expects that it will no longer receive any coupon and that only 70 per cent of the principal amount will be recovered (i.e. CU70 million).

Applying IAS 39:54(a) & 67, Bank A reclassifies all of the residual AFS reserve (CU14.5 million) to profit or loss. Additionally, it recognises an impairment loss measured as the difference between the investment's carrying amount (CU85.5 million) and the present value of estimated future cash flows discounted at the investment's revised effective interest rate (i.e. the effective interest rate determined at the date of reclassification).

The present value of the expected future cash flows discounted using the effective interest rate determined at the date of reclassification (14.9 per cent) is CU53.0 million. The total impact on profit or loss is as follows.

Coupon date	Net interest income	Reclassification of AFS reserve to profit or loss	Impairment loss on the investment	Total impact on profit or loss
	CU million	CU million	CU million	CU million
30 June 20X6	6.0	(14.5)	(32.5)	(41.0)

The amortised cost of the investment will then accrete as follows.

Coupon date	Amortised cost b/f	Interest income at 14.9%	Coupon	Amortised cost c/f
	CU million	CU million	CU million	CU million
30 June 20X7	53.0	7.9	0	60.9
30 June 20X8	60.9	9.1	0	70.0

Following the impairment, the net amount recognised in profit or loss is only the interest income measured using the effective interest rate of 14.9 per cent because the entire AFS revaluation has already been reclassified to profit or loss.

5.2.2 Reversals

If the amount of a past impairment loss decreases and the decrease can be related objectively to an event occurring after the impairment was recognised, then the impairment is reversed through profit or loss. However, the carrying amount should not be increased to an amount that exceeds what the amortised cost would have been (at the date of the reversal) had the impairment not been recognised. [IAS 39:65] It should be noted that, to qualify for recognition, a reversal does *not* need to have resulted from the same factor that caused the original impairment.

5.2.3 Subsequent interest

Once an impairment loss has been recognised, subsequent interest income is recognised using the rate of interest used to discount the future cash flows in measuring that impairment. [IAS 39:AG93] In the case of fixed rate debt instruments measured at amortised cost, the discount rate will be the original effective interest rate. For floating rate debt instruments measured at amortised cost, the discount rate will be the effective interest rate at the date of impairment. IAS 39 does not allow for non-accrual of interest following impairment.

In the case of a floating rate financial asset, the rate used to discount future cash flows in measuring impairment will be the current effective interest rate because the effective interest rate is updated through the asset's life as the market rates change (see **5.2.1**). This is consistent with the requirements of IAS 39:AG93 which states that once a financial asset has been written down as a result of an impairment loss, interest income is thereafter recognised using the rate of interest used to discount the future cash flows for the purpose of measuring the impairment loss. In this case, the 'rate' of interest is a 'floating rate'. Entities may have a preference for 'freezing' the effective interest rate at the date of impairment, as opposed to updating the effective interest rate after the impairment date, but this is contrary to the principle in the Standard that interest income on floating rate loans is recognised at the current floating rate.

5.2.4 Groups of assets

IAS 39 contains specific requirements regarding the determination of impairment for a group of financial assets. It is first necessary to consider whether there is objective evidence of an impairment for financial assets that are 'individually significant'. Assets that are not individually significant may be assessed either individually or collectively. [IAS 39:64] There is no guidance on the appropriate interpretation of the term 'individually significant' and it is, undoubtedly, an area of considerable judgement for management.

Measurement of impairment on a portfolio basis may be applied to groups of small balance items and to financial assets that are individually assessed and found not to be impaired when there is indication of impairment in a group of similar assets and impairment cannot be identified with an individual asset in that group. [IAS 39:IG.E.4.7]

If a collective assessment is to be undertaken, it should include financial assets that have been considered individually, whether or not they are individually significant, for which no impairment has been recognised. Assets that have been considered individually, and for which an impairment is (or continues to be) recognised, are not included in the collective assessment.

When an asset is assessed for impairment individually and an impairment loss would have been recognised but for the existence of collateral, the asset is not impaired and is not included in the collective assessment of impairment. Had the same asset not been collateralised, an impairment loss would have been recognised on an individual basis, and the asset would also not be included in the collective assessment.

The asset groups used for collective assessment of impairment should be defined to include financial assets with similar credit risk characteristics. IAS 39:AG87 gives the example of using 'a credit risk evaluation or grading process that considers asset type, industry, geographical location, collateral type, past-due status and other relevant factors'. If groups sharing similar risk characteristics cannot be identified, the collective assessment cannot be performed.

In determining the impact of external factors on whether an impairment loss should be recognised on an individual or collective basis, each external factor needs to be considered carefully to determine whether that factor relates only to the specific counterparty to the asset under consideration, or more widely to the industry in which that counterparty operates in.

For example, the fact that an external factor affects the counterparty to a much greater degree than its competitors within the same industry may suggest that this factor is more relevant in an individual impairment analysis. The factor may need to be reapplied, along with other factors, on a collective impairment assessment if it also affects the rest of the industry.

It should be noted that the characteristics of assets that have been assessed individually and found not to be impaired will differ from those assets assessed only on a collective basis. This should be taken into account in performing the collective assessment and, as a result, a different amount of impairment may be required.

As soon as information is available that specifically identifies losses on individual assets, those assets are removed from the collective assessment. [IAS 39:AG88]

The application guidance to IAS 39 provides further guidance on how to perform a collective impairment assessment. [IAS 39:AG89 - AG92] The main elements of this guidance are as follows.

- Future cash flows for an asset group are estimated on the basis of historical loss experience for assets with similar credit risk characteristics to the group.
- Information about historical loss rates should be applied to groups that are defined in a manner consistent with the groups for which that information was observed.
- Peer-group experience is used if there is no, or insufficient, entity-specific loss experience.
- Historical loss experience is adjusted on the basis of current observable data so that it is consistent with current conditions.
- The methodology and assumptions used to estimate future cash flows are reviewed regularly.

Most importantly, collective assessments of impairment will still reflect the incurred loss model and will not result in the recognition of expected future losses. The aim is to reflect, on a portfolio basis, the effect of loss events that have occurred with respect to individual assets in the group (but have not yet been identified on an individual asset basis). IAS 39 provides an example of an entity that determines on the basis of historical experience that one of the main causes of default on credit card loans is the death of the borrower. The entity may observe that the death rate is unchanged from one year to the next. Nevertheless, some of the borrowers in the entity's group of credit card loans may have died in that year, indicating that an impairment loss has occurred on those loans, even if, at the year end, the entity is not yet aware which specific borrowers have died. It is appropriate for an impairment loss to be recognised for these 'incurred but not reported' losses. However, it would not be appropriate to recognise an impairment loss for deaths that are expected to occur in a future period, because the necessary loss event (the death of the borrower) has not yet occurred. [IAS 39:AG90]

Consistent with the principle of only recognising incurred but not reported losses, if a formulae-based approach or statistical method is employed, the method must not give rise to an impairment loss on initial recognition. Such methods may be used only if they are consistent with the guidance above and:

- incorporate the effects of the time value of money;
- consider the cash flows for the whole of the remaining life of an asset; and
- consider the age of loans within the portfolio.

It is not acceptable to set aside additional provisions or reserves in excess of the amount of impairment or bad debt losses that are recognised under IAS 39. [IAS 39:IG.E.4.6]

5.3 Assets carried at cost

Unquoted equity instruments (and derivatives that result in physical delivery of unquoted equity investments) whose fair value cannot be reliably measured are measured at cost (see **3.1.6**). For such instruments, if there is objective evidence of an impairment (as discussed in **section 5.1**), the amount of the impairment loss is measured as the difference between carrying amount and the present value of estimated future cash flows discounted at the current rate of return for a similar financial asset. [IAS 39:66]

Once an impairment loss has been recognised on a financial asset recognised at cost, a reversal of that impairment is not permitted.

5.4 Available-for-sale financial assets

If a decline in the fair value of an AFS financial asset has been recognised in other comprehensive income under the requirements discussed in **3.1.4**, and there is objective evidence of an impairment (as discussed in **5.1.1** for debt instruments and **5.1.1** and **5.1.2** for equity instruments), the cumulative loss that had been recognised in other comprehensive income is reclassified from equity to profit or loss. The amount of cumulative loss is the difference between the acquisition cost (net of principal repayments and amortisation for debt instruments) and the current fair value, less any impairment loss previously recognised in profit or loss. [IAS 39:67 & 68] Any portion of the cumulative net loss that is attributable to foreign currency movements that had been recognised in other comprehensive income in the case of a non-monetary item, e.g. for equity instruments, is also reclassified from equity to profit or loss. [IAS 39:IG.E.4.9]

5.4.1 Impairment measurement – equity instruments

An impairment of an AFS equity investment does not establish a new deemed cost for that investment. The test of whether there has been a "significant or prolonged decline in the fair value of an investment in an equity instrument below its cost" is with reference to the original cost on initial recognition (not the carrying amount after the previous impairment) and 'prolonged' should be evaluated against that period in which the fair value of the investment has been below original cost at initial recognition. IAS 39 does not allow entities to consider only the period since the last impairment loss was recognised in profit or loss nor does it allow entities to segregate different loss events in order to evaluate the significance and duration of each event separately. Therefore, once an impairment loss is recognised in profit or loss, any further decline in value must be recognised immediately in profit or loss. [IAS 39:IG.E.4.9] This was confirmed by the IFRIC (now the IFRS Interpretations Committee) in April 2005.

If an investment in an equity instrument is reclassified from FVTPL to AFS, consideration should be given as to whether "cost" is the original acquisition cost at initial recognition or the fair value at the date of reclassification. Prior to the IAS 39 amendment on reclassifications of financial assets, cost always meant 'acquisition cost' because it was not possible to reclassify an equity investment from one fair value measurement category to another and, therefore, the amount recognised in equity always represented the difference between the acquisition cost of the equity investment and its fair value. For an investment in an equity instrument reclassified from FVTPL to AFS, the amounts in equity will be the difference between the fair value at the date of the reclassification and the fair value at the end of the reporting period. The IAS 39 amendment on reclassifications introduced IAS 39:50C which states that the fair value at the date of reclassification "becomes its new cost". The requirements to assess impairment were not applicable prior to reclassification because any impairment is automatically included in profit or loss for assets carried at FVTPL. Therefore, subsequent to reclassification, in assessing whether the fair value of an equity investment is significantly below its cost it is appropriate to compare the fair value at the end of the reporting period with the fair value at the date of reclassification. Similarly, in assessing whether there has been a prolonged decline in fair value below cost, it is appropriate to look at how long the equity investment's fair value has been below the 'new cost' established at the date of reclassification.

It is unlikely that an entity could apply a portfolio approach for assessing impairment of AFS equity securities. Equity securities are issued by different entities and they are unlikely to have similar risk characteristics because their exposure to equity price risk will differ.

If an entity holds an investment in a fund that invests in equity securities, and the investment is classified as an AFS investment, the investor should assess impairment based on a comparison of cost and fair value of the investment in the fund, not by looking through the fund to the individual equity securities held by the fund.

5.4.2 Impairment reversals – equity instruments

Once an entity has recognised an impairment loss on an AFS equity investment, it is not permitted to recognise a reversal through profit or loss. [IAS 39:69] This approach differs from the approach for debt instruments where reversal is permitted (see **5.4.4**).

IAS 39:BC127 - BC130 explain the rationale for this difference in approach. Primarily, the IASB took the view that reversals of impairments in debt instruments are more objectively determinable than those in equity instruments. In particular, for equity instruments, the IASB "could not find an acceptable way to distinguish reversals of impairment losses from other increases in fair value". This is consistent with the approach taken for unquoted equity instruments measured at cost (see **5.3**).

A puttable instrument issued by an entity (e.g. a fund), under which the holder can put the instrument back to the issuer at any time for cash equal to a proportionate share of the net asset value of the entity, should be considered an equity instrument when establishing whether a reversal of impairment is appropriate. Because the instrument does not have specified payments and a fixed maturity it is an equity investment and, therefore, any reversal of a previously recognised impairment through profit or loss is not permitted if it is classified as an AFS financial asset.

5.4.2.1 Interim financial reporting and impairment

IFRIC Interpretation 10 *Interim Financial Reporting and Impairment*, published in July 2006, provides guidance on the interaction between the requirements of IAS 34 *Interim Financial Reporting* and the recognition of impairment losses for certain financial assets. In respect of investments in equity instruments or financial assets carried at cost, the Interpretation clarifies that an entity should not reverse an impairment loss recognised in a previous interim period.

Example 5.4.2.1

Interaction of impairment and interim financial reporting

On 1 January 20X1, Entity A and Entity B each buy small shareholdings of equity instruments of Entity X for CU100. Both entities classify their investments in the quoted equity instruments as AFS. Accordingly, IAS 39:55(b) requires gains and losses to be recognised initially in other comprehensive income except for impairment losses, which are recognised in profit or loss.

Entity A is listed on its national stock exchange which requires interim reports in accordance with IFRSs on a semi-annual basis. Entity B is required to prepare IFRS financial statements on an annual basis for statutory purposes. On 30 June 20X1, Entity X shows signs of severe financial difficulties with the share price declined to CU80. While preparing its interim report, Entity A concludes that its investment in Entity X is impaired and recognises an impairment loss of CU20 in profit or loss. Because Entity B is not required to prepare a semi-annual report, it does not review its equity instruments for evidence of impairment at that point in time.

On 31 December 20X1, the financial condition of Entity X has fully recovered due to a successful debt restructuring with the share price having risen to CU120.

Both Entity A and Entity B conclude that the original cost of the investment is recoverable. However, while Entity B does not recognise an impairment loss in its annual IFRS financial statements, Entity A is prohibited from reversing the impairment loss recognised in its interim report. The result is that Entity A and Entity B have different results for exactly the same equity instrument.

5.4.3 Impairment measurement – debt instruments

The amount of the impairment loss to be recognised on an AFS debt instrument is the cumulative fair value loss that has been recognised in other comprehensive income. The whole of this amount is reclassified from equity to profit or loss. Because the impairment loss is recognised on a fair value basis, this differs from a loss on a debt instrument measured at amortised cost where the loss is determined as the difference between the asset's carrying value and its recoverable amount calculated as the sum of the estimated future recoverable cash flows discounted at the asset's original effective interest rate. The reason for this difference is that the impairment loss on an AFS debt instrument includes a market participant's view of recoverable cash flows discounted at a rate that reflects current market interest rates, adjusted for liquidity and other factors a market participant would include in determining fair value.

If a debt instrument is reclassified from FVTPL to AFS, the impairment requirements in IAS 39:58 - 70 apply for the first time. Because the asset was previously measured at FVTPL an assessment of impairment was not required. If there is objective evidence of impairment following reclassification, an impairment loss is recognised and this is treated as the first impairment event irrespective of the history of the asset prior to the reclassification. Only gains/losses since the date of reclassification are reclassified to profit or loss.

5.4.3.1 Subsequent interest

IAS 39:AG93 requires that, following impairment for all debt instruments, interest is recognised using the rate of interest used to discount the future cash flows for the purpose of measuring the impairment loss. In the case of fixed rate debt instruments measured at amortised cost, the discount rate will be the original effective interest rate. For floating rate debt instruments measured at amortised cost, the discount rate will be the effective interest rate at the date of impairment. Because the impairment loss on an AFS debt instrument is equal to the fair value loss recognised in equity that is reclassified to profit or loss, the interest rate subsequent to the impairment loss is based on a market interest rate at the date of impairment. The market interest rate reflects the rate that was used in determining the asset's fair value. A further reason for applying a market interest rate for interest recognition subsequent to the date of impairment, as opposed to the original effective interest rate, is that, assuming there are no further impairment losses, or reversals of impairment losses, the amount in equity at maturity will be zero.

Examples 5.4.3.1 and **5.4.3.2** deal with investments in zero coupon bonds as opposed to interest-bearing debt instruments. This is for illustrative purposes only. An entity is required to revise the effective interest rate at the date of impairment for all AFS debt instruments.

Example 5.4.3.1

Interest recognition subsequent to impairment losses on AFS debt instruments

Entity B acquires a zero coupon bond debt security and classifies it as AFS at initial recognition at 1/1/X6. The instrument is acquired for CU82.6 and has a maturity in two years with a redemption of CU100. The effective interest rate is 10 per cent. Entity B has a calendar year reporting period end.

At 31/12/X6, Entity B determines that there is objective evidence of impairment. Entity B estimates the expected recoverable cash flows to be CU80 at maturity, instead of CU100. The fair value of the debt security is CU70. The difference between CU82.6 plus interest at the instrument's original effective interest rate of 10 per cent less its fair value of CU70 is a fair value loss of CU20.86 and is recognised in the AFS reserve in equity. In accordance with IAS 39:67 the fair value loss in equity is reclassified to profit or loss.

		CU	CU
Dr	AFS asset	8.26	
Cr	Interest income – profit or loss		8.26

To recognise interest income at the original effective interest rate of 10 per cent.

		CU	CU
Dr	Other comprehensive income	20.86	
Cr	AFS asset		20.86

To recognise the fair value loss in other comprehensive income.

		CU	CU
Dr	Impairment loss – profit or loss	20.86	
Cr	Other comprehensive income		20.86

To reclassify the impairment loss previously recognised in other comprehensive income and accumulated in equity to profit or loss.

Entity B must revise the instrument's effective interest rate at 1/1/X7. The effective interest rate is the rate that discounts the estimated recoverable cash flows, being CU80 in one year, to the instrument's carrying amount, being CU70. The revised effective interest rate is 14.3 per cent.

At the instrument's maturity at 31/12/X7, the cash flows received equalled Entity B's estimated recoverable cash flows at 31/12/X6, i.e. there were no further impairment losses or reversals of impairment losses.

		CU	CU
Dr	AFS asset	10.00	
Cr	Interest income – profit or loss		10.00

To recognise interest income at the revised effective interest rate of 14.3 per cent.

The amount in equity is zero because the instrument's carrying amount following recognition of the revised effective interest rate equals CU80, being its fair value at maturity.

For illustrative purposes only, had Entity B not revised the effective interest rate to 14.3 per cent from 10 per cent at the date of impairment loss, the interest income of CU7 (being CU70 x 10%) would be understated and the amount in equity would have been overstated being a credit of CU3 (CU77 – CU80).

If, following an impairment loss of an AFS debt instrument, there are further impairment losses and fair value losses are reclassified from equity to profit or loss, the effective interest rate for interest recognition subsequent to the further impairment will need to be revised. The basis for revising the effective interest rate is the same as with the first revision, being the rate that exactly discounts the estimated recoverable cash flows to the instrument's carrying value.

If, following an impairment loss, there is a reversal of an impairment loss that requires fair value gains previously recognised in other comprehensive income to be reclassified from equity to profit or loss, the effective interest rate will also need to be revised at that date. The revised effective interest rate will be used for subsequent interest recognition after the impairment reversal. The basis for revising the effective interest rate immediately following a reversal of an impairment loss is the same as for the first revision, being the rate that exactly discounts the estimated recoverable cash flows to the instrument's carrying amount (for reversals, see **5.4.4**).

5.4.3.2 Fair value losses subsequent to impairment

If an AFS debt instrument has been impaired and amounts have been reclassified from equity to profit or loss, and the asset continues to have an impaired status (i.e. the expected recoverable contractual cash flows to be received are lower than at initial recognition), further fair value losses recognised in other comprehensive income should also be reclassified from equity to profit or loss. Effectively, if an asset is impaired, IAS 39 does not distinguish between fair value losses that arise due to further declines in recoverability of cash flows, and those fair value losses that arise due to other factors (changes in risk-free interest rates, liquidity risk etc.).

Example 5.4.3.2

Fair value losses subsequent to impairment – debt instruments

Entity Q acquires an investment in an AFS debt instrument at 1/1/X1. Entity D has a calendar year end.

At 31/12/X3, Entity Q determines that there is objective evidence of impairment and the fair value loss previously recognised in other comprehensive income is reclassified from equity to profit or loss in accordance with IAS 39:67.

At 31/12/X4, a further fair value loss is recognised in other comprehensive income and Entity Q estimates the recoverable cash flows remaining due are lower than at 1/1/X1, i.e. the asset continues to be impaired. The fair value loss recognised initially in other comprehensive income in the period must be reclassified from equity to profit or loss.

5.4.4 Impairment reversals – debt instruments

If the fair value of an AFS debt instrument increases and the increase can be related objectively to an event occurring after the impairment was recognised, then the impairment is reversed through profit or loss. [IAS 39:70] It should be noted that, to qualify for recognition, a reversal does *not* need to have resulted from the same factor that caused the original impairment. The amount of the gain recognised in profit or loss on reversal of an impairment loss is unlikely to be equal to the amount of the original impairment loss recognised in profit or loss. This is because the amount of the original impairment loss and the reversal are based on the *fair value* loss and gain respectively that are recognised in other comprehensive income at the reporting date.

IAS 39:70 allows reversal of impairment losses on an AFS debt instrument if there is objective evidence of "an event occurring after the impairment was recognised". IAS 39:70 does not state what event is sufficient to warrant an impairment reversal. It is assumed the event must be a credit event as opposed to a non-credit event such as a change in the risk-free interest rate. This is consistent with the approach described in IAS 39:65 for amortised cost financial assets which looks specifically to an event like an improvement in the debtor's credit rating.

Example 5.4.4A

Impairment reversals – debt instruments (1)

Entity D acquires an investment in an AFS debt instrument at 1/1/X1. Entity D has a calendar year end.

At 31/12/X3, Entity D determines that there is objective evidence of impairment and the fair value loss recognised in other comprehensive income is reclassified from equity to profit or loss in accordance with IAS 39:67.

At 31/12/X4, there is objective evidence that the impairment loss has reversed and, therefore, the gain recognised in other comprehensive income is reclassified from equity to profit or loss. The amount of the gain recognised in profit or loss will not necessarily equal the amount of loss recognised in profit or loss at 31/12/X3.

Example 5.4.4B

Impairment reversals – debt instruments (2)

Entity E acquires a zero coupon bond debt security and classifies it as an AFS investment at initial recognition at 1/1/X1. The instrument is acquired for CU68 and has a maturity of five years with a redemption amount of CU100. The effective interest rate is 8.0 per cent. Entity E has a calendar year end.

At 31/12/X1, Entity E determines there is objective evidence of impairment. Entity B estimates the expected recoverable cash flows to be CU90 at maturity, instead of CU100. The fair value of the debt security is CU65. The difference between CU68 plus interest at the instrument's original effective interest rate of 8.0 per cent less its fair value CU65 is a fair value loss of CU8.5 recognised in other comprehensive income and accumulated in the AFS reserve in equity. In accordance with IAS 39:67, the fair value loss initially recognised in other comprehensive income is reclassified from equity to profit or loss as an impairment loss.

		CU	CU
Dr	AFS asset	5.5	
Cr	Interest income – profit or loss		5.5

To recognise interest income at the original effective interest rate of 8.0 per cent. The effective interest rate is applied to the instrument's opening fair value which also equals its opening amortised cost for the purposes of calculating the instrument's interest income.

		CU	CU
Dr	Other comprehensive income	8.5	
Cr	AFS asset		8.5

To recognise the fair value loss directly in other comprehensive income.

		CU	CU
Dr	Impairment loss – profit or loss	8.5	
Cr	Other comprehensive income		8.5

To reclassify the fair value loss initially recognised in other comprehensive income to profit or loss as an impairment loss.

Entity E must revise the instrument's effective interest rate at 1/1/X2. The effective interest rate is the rate that discounts the estimated recoverable cash flows, CU90 in four years, to the instrument's carrying amount, CU65. The revised effective interest rate is 8.5 per cent.

At 31/12/X2, Entity E determines there is further impairment due to a further decline in recoverable cash flows. Entity E estimates the expected recoverable cash flows to be CU85 at maturity, instead of CU90 as was previously estimated. The fair value of the debt security is CU66. The difference between CU65 plus interest at the instrument's revised effective interest rate of 8.5 per cent less its fair value of CU66 is a fair value loss of CU4.5 and is recognised initially in other comprehensive income and accumulated in the AFS reserve. In accordance with IAS 39:67, the amount initially recognised in other comprehensive income is reclassified from equity to profit or loss.

		CU	**CU**
Dr	AFS asset	5.5	
Cr	Interest income – profit or loss		5.5

To recognise interest income at the revised effective interest rate of 8.5 per cent. The effective interest rate is applied to the instrument's opening fair value, not the prior period's amortised cost, because the effective interest rate was reset following the reclassification of the impairment loss from equity to profit or loss.

		CU	**CU**
Dr	Other comprehensive income	4.5	
Cr	AFS asset		4.5

To recognise the fair value loss directly in other comprehensive income.

		CU	**CU**
Dr	Impairment loss – profit or loss	4.5	
Cr	Other comprehensive income		4.5

To record the reclassification of the fair value loss initially recognised in other comprehensive income from equity to profit or loss as an impairment loss.

Entity E must revise the instrument's effective interest rate at 1/1/X3. The effective interest rate is the rate that discounts the estimated recoverable cash flows, CU85 in three years, to the instrument's carrying amount, CU66. The revised effective interest rate is 8.8 per cent.

At 31/12/X3, there is objective evidence of a reversal of a credit event that has led to an increase in recoverability in cash flows. Entity E estimates the expected recoverable cash flows to be CU98 at maturity, instead of CU85 as was previously estimated. The fair value of the debt security is CU84. The difference between CU66 plus interest at the instrument's revised effective interest rate of 8.8 per cent less its fair value of CU84 is a fair value gain of CU12.2 and is recognised in other comprehensive income and accumulated in the AFS reserve. In accordance with IAS 39:70, the fair value gain initially recognised in other comprehensive income is reclassified from equity to profit or loss as a reversal of an impairment loss.

		CU	CU
Dr	AFS asset	5.8	
Cr	Interest income – profit or loss		5.8

To recognise interest income at the revised effective interest rate of 8.8 per cent. The effective interest rate is applied to the instrument's opening fair value, not the prior period's amortised cost, because the effective interest rate was reset following the reclassification of the impairment loss from equity to profit or loss.

		CU	CU
Dr	AFS asset	12.2	
Cr	Other comprehensive income		12.2

To recognise the fair value gain directly in other comprehensive income.

		CU	CU
Dr	Other comprehensive income	12.2	
Cr	Impairment reversal – profit or loss		12.2

To recognise the fair value gain initially recognised in other comprehensive income from equity to profit or loss as a reversal of an impairment loss.

Entity E must revise the instrument's effective interest rate at 1/1/X4. The effective interest rate is the rate that discounts the estimated recoverable cash flows, being CU98 in two years, to the instrument's carrying amount, being CU84. The revised effective interest rate is 8 per cent.

At 31/12/X4, the estimated recoverable cash flows remain unchanged since the last reporting period end. The fair value of the debt security is CU95. The difference between CU84 plus interest at the instrument's revised effective interest rate of 8.0% less its fair value CU95 is a fair value gain of CU4.3 and is recognised in other comprehensive income in the AFS reserve.

		CU	CU
Dr	AFS asset	6.7	
Cr	Interest income – profit or loss		6.7

To recognise interest income at the revised effective interest rate of 8 per cent. The effective interest rate is applied to the instrument's opening fair value, not the prior period's amortised cost, because the effective interest rate was reset following the reclassification of the fair value gain from equity to profit or loss upon reversal of the impairment loss.

		CU	CU
Dr	AFS asset	4.3	
Cr	Other comprehensive income		4.3

To recognise the fair value gain directly in other comprehensive income.

At 31/12/X5, the cash flows at maturity are equal to the estimated recoverable cash flows at the end of the prior reporting period. The fair value of the debt security is equal to its settlement amount of CU98. The difference between CU95 (being the prior period's closing fair value) plus interest at the instrument's revised effective interest rate of 8 per cent on the instrument's opening amortised cost less its fair value of CU98 is a CU4.3 loss that is recognised in the AFS reserve in other comprehensive income.

		CU	CU
Dr	AFS asset	7.3	
Cr	Interest income – profit or loss		7.3

To recognise interest income at the revised effective interest rate of 8 per cent. The effective interest rate is applied to the instrument's opening amortised cost (CU90.7, being CU84.0 + CU6.7), not the opening fair value, as the effective interest rate was not reset because there were no impairment losses or reversals of impairment losses in the previous period.

		CU	CU
Dr	Other comprehensive income	4.3	
Cr	AFS asset		4.3

To recognise the fair value loss directly in other comprehensive income.

At maturity, the AFS reserve in equity equals zero. A summary of the entries is illustrated below.

Date	Available-for-sale asset	Cash	Profit or loss Dr/(Cr)	Other comprehensive income Dr/(Cr)
Opening – 1/1/X1	68.0	(68.0)		
Interest	5.5		(5.5)	
Fair value loss	(8.5)			8.5
Impairment loss			8.5	(8.5)
Closing – 31/12/X1	65.0			
Interest	5.5		(5.5)	
Fair value loss	(4.5)			4.5
Impairment loss			4.5	(4.5)
Closing – 31/12/X2	66.0			
Interest	5.8		(5.8)	
Fair value gain	12.2			(12.2)
Reversal of impairment loss			(12.2)	12.2
Closing – 31/12/X3	84.0			
Interest	6.7		(6.7)	
Fair value gain	4.3			(4.3)
Closing – 31/12/X4	95.0			

Date	Available-for-sale asset	Cash	Profit or loss Dr/(Cr)	Other comprehensive income Dr/(Cr)
Interest	7.3		(7.3)	
Fair value loss	(4.3)			4.3
Closing – 31/12/X5	98.0	98.0		
	0	30.0	(30.0)	0

IAS 39:70 states that if, following an impairment of an AFS debt instrument, the fair value increases and the increase can be objectively related to an event occurring after the impairment loss was recognised in profit or loss, the impairment loss should be reversed and the amount of the reversal recognised in profit or loss. Although IAS 39:70 refers to increases in fair value, this paragraph should be applied to circumstances where there are fair value gains recognised in other comprehensive income following impairment. For example, a debt instrument may increase in fair value over the reporting period but will not necessarily result in a gain being recognised in other comprehensive income. If the increase in fair value over the reporting period is lower than the interest recognised by applying the effective interest rate less cash received in the period, the amount in other comprehensive income will be a fair value loss.

If there has been a decline in the recoverability of cash flows on an AFS debt instrument that has previously been impaired, the amount recognised directly in other comprehensive income may not necessarily be a fair value loss. Similar to above, if the decrease in fair value over the reporting period is smaller than the interest recognised calculated by applying the effective interest rate less cash received in the period, the amount in other comprehensive income will be a fair value gain. It would be inappropriate to reclassify this fair value gain from equity to profit or loss because there has not been a reversal of a credit event as described in IAS 39:70. Equally, even though there has been a decline in the recoverability in cash flows, there has not been an impairment loss that should be recognised in profit or loss because the amount in other comprehensive income is a fair value gain, not a fair value loss.

5.5 Measurement difficulties

The IASB acknowledges that, in some cases, the observable data required to estimate the amount of an impairment loss on a financial asset may not be available or relevant to current circumstances. [IAS 39:62] In such cases, the use of 'experienced judgement' is required. In a collective impairment assessment, **5.2.4** gives guidance on the approach to be adopted if measurement is less than straightforward.

5.6 Distressed debt

An entity must determine the effective interest rate of acquired distressed debt on the date the debt is acquired on the basis of the expected future cash flows considering incurred credit losses.

Example 5.6

Effective interest rate on distressed debt

Entity B acquires distressed debt. The fair value of the consideration paid to acquire the debt is CU60. The debt is contracted to redeem at par (CU100) at its maturity. The low consideration paid reflects the fact that prior to Entity B's acquisition of the debt, the debt was subject to impairment.

In order to determine the interest to be received on the debt Entity B must determine the effective interest rate at acquisition. The effective interest rate will incorporate the cash flows expected to be received on the debt (i.e. it will incorporate the impact of the impairment event) because incurred credit losses are considered in computing the effective interest rate for financial assets acquired at a deep discount. [IAS 39:AG5] This treatment is consistent with the prohibition on recognising expected future losses in the effective interest rate [IAS 39:59] as upon acquisition of the distressed debt, the impairment event had already occurred. [IAS 39:BC32]

To the extent the recoverability of the asset improves as a result of a reversal of factors that led to the original impairment, this should not be recognised as a reversal of impairment because the original impairment loss was not included in Entity B's financial statements. Instead, Entity B would revise its estimate of expected cash flows and recognise a cumulative catch-up in profit or loss to adjust the carrying amount of the asset by discounting the revised expected cash flows at the original effective interest rate (the effective interest rate computed at initial recognition when Entity B acquired the asset). [IAS 39:AG8]

In July 2012 the IFRS Interpretations Committee received a request for guidance on several accounting issues that resulted from the restructuring of Greek government bonds (GGBs). At its September 2012 meeting, the Interpretations Committee concluded that the GGBs surrendered in March 2012 should be derecognised, which means the new GGBs received as part of the debt restructuring are recognised as new assets. At the July 2012 and November 2012 meetings, the Interpretations Committee addressed the particular request to consider whether IAS 39:AG5 could apply when determining the effective interest rate on initial recognition of those new GGBs. Applying IAS 39:AG5 means that the effective interest rate would be determined at initial recognition using estimated cash flows that take into account incurred credit losses.

The Interpretations Committee noted that IAS 39:AG5 applies to acquired assets, which includes both purchased and originated assets.

The Interpretations Committee also noted that even though an origination of a debt instrument with an incurred loss is rather unusual, there are situations in which such transactions occur. For example, within the context of significant financial difficulty of an obligor, transactions can arise that involve originations of debt instruments that are outside the normal underwriting process but are instead forced upon already existing lenders by a restructuring process. This could include situations in which modifications of debt instruments result in derecognition of the original financial asset and the recognition of a new financial asset under IFRSs. In circumstances such as these, new financial assets could be recognised that have incurred losses on initial recognition. The Interpretations Committee noted that whether an incurred loss exists on initial recognition of an asset is a factual matter and that the assessment requires judgement. The Interpretations Committee also noted that the circumstances leading to the recognition of an asset with an incurred loss on initial recognition need not be limited to those in which debt instruments are effectively forced upon existing lenders, but could also arise in other transactions.

The Interpretations Committee considered that in the light of its analysis of the existing requirements of IAS 39 an interpretation was not necessary and consequently decided not to add the issue to its agenda.

6 Implications for business combinations

IFRS 3 *Business Combinations* requires the acquirer to recognise all identifiable assets and liabilities at fair value at the date of the business combination and to reassess classifications and designations of all contractual arrangements, with the exception of classification of leases as finance or operating leases and the classification of insurance contracts. In the consolidated financial statements, the acquirer will make all the classification decisions it would have made had the entity acquired the acquiree's financial instruments separately, i.e. not as part of a business combination.

It is worth noting that subsequent measurement of financial instruments by the acquirer in the consolidated financial statements may differ from the acquiree's financial statements. The acquirer may make different classification decisions than those that were originally made by the acquiree. For example, the acquirer may designate a financial instrument carried by the acquiree at amortised cost as at FVTPL, or as AFS. Even if classification and the measurement basis are the same (e.g. an asset is measured at amortised cost in both the acquiree's financial statements and the acquirer's consolidated financial statements), the amounts recognised in the consolidated statement of financial position and statement of comprehensive income in respect of that asset may be different from the amounts recognised by the acquiree. The acquirer recognises the asset at fair value at the time of acquisition and that amount may be different from the carrying amount of the asset in the financial statements of the acquiree both at initial recognition and at the date of acquisition. Thus, going forward, the acquirer will apply a different effective interest rate to that applied by the acquiree. This effective interest rate will affect interest recognition and the amount of any future impairment. Also, the acquiree may reverse an impairment loss in its own financial statements but the acquirer will not if the reversal is an impairment that occurred in the acquiree prior to the acquisition date.

The above illustrations are not exhaustive and there are many other differences that can arise when comparing the subsequent measurement of financial instruments by the acquiree and acquirer.

7 Future developments

In July 2014 the IASB issued IFRS 9 *Financial Instruments*. The Standard replaces IAS 39 *Financial Instruments: Recognition and Measurement*. IFRS 9 is effective for annual periods beginning on or after 1 January 2018 with early adoption permitted.

IFRS 9 requires entities to classify financial assets as being measured at either amortised cost or fair value. Gains and losses on assets measured at fair value are recognised either in (i) profit or loss ("fair value through profit or loss") or (ii) for certain designated investments in equity instruments and certain debt instruments if held in a business model in which assets are managed both in order to collect contractual cash flows and for sale, in other comprehensive income ('fair value through other comprehensive income'). The criteria for amortised cost and fair value through other comprehensive income measurement differs to IAS 39 in that there is greater focus on the entity's business model in determining how financial assets are classified. Also, for equity instruments designated at fair value through other comprehensive income reclassification of those gains or losses to profit or loss is prohibited.

The presentation of fair value gains and losses associated with movements in own credit for those financial liabilities designated as at FVTPL has also changed. IAS 39 requires all fair value gains and losses to be recognised in profit or loss. However, IFRS 9 requires that gains or losses on a financial liability, other than a loan commitment or financial guarantee contract, designated as at FVTPL should be presented as follows:

[IFRS 9:5.7.7 & 8]

(a) the amount of change in the fair value of the financial liability that is attributable to changes in the credit risk of that liability should be presented in other comprehensive income; and

(b) the remaining amount of change in the fair value of the liability should be presented in profit or loss unless the treatment of the effects of changes in the liability's credit risk described in (a) would create or enlarge an accounting mismatch in profit or loss (in which case all gains or losses are recognised in profit or loss).

All gains and losses on loan commitments and financial guarantee contracts that are designated as at FVTPL are recognised in profit or loss. [IFRS 9:5.7.9]

With respect to impairment of financial assets a new 'expected loss' approach has been introduced into IFRS 9 that is designed to result in earlier loss recognition compared to the 'incurred loss' approach in IAS 39.

IFRS 9 has a single model applying to all financial assets subject to measurement of expected credit losses as well as some loan commitments and financial guarantee contracts. For financial instruments on which the credit risk has increased significantly since initial recognition, the loss allowance is measured at an amount equal to lifetime expected credit losses. For purchased or originated credit impaired financial assets lifetime expected credit losses are included in determining the credit adjusted effective interest rate used to recognise interest income and a loss allowance is recognised for any change in lifetime expected losses. For all other financial instruments, the loss allowance is measured at an amount equal to the 12-month expected credit losses unless the simplified approach is elected to always measure the loss allowance at lifetime expected losses (available for trade receivables, contracts assets under IFRS 15 *Revenue from Contracts with Customers* and lease receivables). The estimate of expected credit losses reflects an unbiased and probability weighted amount (determined by evaluating the range of possible outcomes) as well as the time value of money. Depending on the status of a financial asset with regard to credit impairment (reflecting criteria similar to IAS 39 guidance), interest revenue is calculated in different ways.

The requirements of IFRS 9 are described at length in *iGAAP 2016 Financial Instruments – IFRS 9 and related Standards – Volume B.*

C7 Fair value measurement of financial instruments

Contents

1 Introduction

IAS 32, IFRS 7 and IAS 39 all permit or require the use of fair value measurement for initial recognition, subsequent measurement or disclosure of financial instruments. Fair values are central to the measurement of financial instruments because IAS 39 requires that all financial assets and financial liabilities are measured initially on the basis of 'fair value'. Fair value is also stipulated as the on-going measurement basis for all instruments that are held for trading, for derivatives and investments in equity investments, and for many debt instruments held as financial assets.

Detailed information about *when* a fair value measurement is required for financial instruments can be found in **chapters C2** and **C3**. This chapter primarily addresses *how* fair value is measured. This is relevant for fair value measurements of financial instruments recognised in the statement of financial position as well as fair value measurements for disclosure purposes. Guidance on fair value measurement of non-financial items is included in **chapter A6** of **Volume A** of this manual.

Prior to the issue of IFRS 13 *Fair Value Measurement* in May 2011, guidance on how to measure fair value for financial instruments was primarily included in the application guidance of IAS 39; guidance on the measurement of fair value for non-financial items was available in a number of other IFRSs. Most guidance on fair value measurement has been replaced by the requirements of IFRS 13, which is a comprehensive Standard applicable to the measurement of fair value for assets, liabilities and an entity's own equity instruments except as noted in IFRS 13:6 (see **section 2**). IFRS 13 also includes disclosure requirements applicable to all assets and liabilities measured at fair value after initial recognition except those listed in IFRS 13:7 (see **section 2**). These disclosure requirements replace many of the fair value measurement disclosures previously required under IFRS 7 as well as introducing additional disclosures. The disclosure requirements for financial instruments are discussed in **chapter C12**.

IFRS 13 incorporates into IFRSs, for the first time, authoritative guidance and requirements regarding fair value measurement "when the volume or level of activity for an asset or a liability has significantly decreased" [IFRS 13:B37] Previously similar guidance was set out in the October 2008 report by the IASB's Expert Advisory Panel titled *Measuring and Disclosing the Fair Value of Financial Instruments in Markets that are no Longer Active*, which had only educational status.

1.1 Summary of IFRS 13 framework

The table and flow chart below set out a step-by-step approach to applying the basic measurement principles of IFRS 13 to financial instruments. The table also provides a high level summary of some of the key concepts underlying IFRS 13 and illustrates the framework for measuring fair value. The summary does not address all of the requirements of the Standard – users should refer to the more detailed discussions later in this chapter and to the text of the Standard for a fuller understanding.

Note that Steps 2 to 4 do not necessarily occur in the order set out in the table and flow chart (i.e. they are inter-related).

#	Step	Explanation
1.	Identify the 'asset' or 'liability' being measured (i.e. the unit of account) (see **section 3.2**).	IFRS 13 notes that the asset or liability measured at fair value may be (1) a stand-alone financial asset or liability, (2) a group of financial assets or a group of financial liabilities, or (3) a group of assets and liabilities. The level at which fair value is measured will depend on the 'unit of account' specified in other IFRSs (typically, the level at which the asset or liability is aggregated or disaggregated for recognition or disclosure purposes). Under IAS 39, the unit of account is generally an individual financial instrument.
2a.	For financial assets and financial liabilities with offsetting market risks or counterparty credit risk, evaluate the criteria for the fair value exception and establish a policy (see **section 6**)	IFRS 13 permits an exception to the general fair value measurement requirements for financial assets and financial liabilities if an entity: • manages the group of assets and liabilities on the basis of its net exposure to market risks or counterparty credit risk; provides information on that basis to key management personnel; and • measures those assets and liabilities at fair value in the statement of financial position. In summary, the exception permits an entity to measure the fair value of the group of assets and liabilities (i.e. the portfolio) rather than the individual assets and liabilities within the portfolio. Details of the exception, including the detailed criteria for qualification, are set out in IFRS 13:48 - 56. The application of this exception is an accounting policy choice in accordance with IAS 8 *Accounting Policies, Changes in Accounting Estimates and Errors* and must be applied consistently from period to period for a particular portfolio. This exception does not change the unit of account (which continues to be the individual instrument determined under IAS 39), but changes the unit of measurement from the individual financial instrument to the group (portfolio) of financial instruments.

#	Step	Explanation
2b.	For financial liabilities and an entity's own equity instruments, assume the financial liabilities or equity instruments are transferred to market participants at the measurement date (see **section 5**)	IFRS 13 requires that the fair value of a financial liability or an entity's own equity instrument be based on an assumed transfer to a market participant even if the entity does not intend to transfer the liability or equity instrument to a third party or it is unable to do so. Under this assumption, the fair value of a financial liability should be measured on the basis that the liability would remain outstanding and the transferee would be required to fulfil the obligation; it should not be assumed that the financial liability would be settled or otherwise extinguished. Similarly, the fair value of an entity's own equity instrument should be measured on the basis that the equity instrument would remain outstanding and the transferee would take on the rights and responsibilities associated with the instrument; it should not be assumed that the instrument would be cancelled or otherwise extinguished. In addition, the measurement of financial liabilities and own equity instruments depends on whether identical liabilities or equity instruments are held by other parties as assets. However, an entity must measure the liability or equity instrument from the perspective of a market participant that holds the identical item as an asset if (a) a quoted price for an identical or similar instrument is not available and (b) the identical item is, in fact, held by another party (or by other parties) as an asset.
3.	Identify the market in which to price the financial asset or financial liability – i.e. either (1) the principal market or (2) if no principal market exists, the most advantageous market (see **section 3.3**).	The principal market is "[t]he market with the greatest volume and level of activity for the asset or liability". The most advantageous market is "[t]he market that maximises the amount that would be received to sell the asset or minimises the amount that would be paid to transfer the liability…". If there is a principal market for the financial asset or financial liability, the fair value measurement should reflect the price in that market, even if the price in a different market is potentially more advantageous at the measurement date. In the absence of evidence to the contrary, the market in which an entity would normally enter into a transaction to sell the asset or to transfer the liability is presumed to be the principal (or most advantageous) market. Therefore, an entity is permitted to use the price in the market in which it normally enters into transactions unless there is evidence that the principal (or most advantageous) market and that market are not the same. A market cannot be identified as the principal (or most advantageous) market unless the entity has access to that market at the measurement date.

#	Step	Explanation
4.	Develop assumptions that market participants in the principal (or most advantageous) market would use when pricing the financial asset or financial liability (see **section 3.3**).	'Market participants' are buyers and sellers in the principal (or most advantageous) market for the asset or liability that are (1) independent of each other, (2) knowledgeable, (3) able to enter into a transaction for the asset or liability, and (4) willing to enter into such a transaction. An entity need not identify specific market participants, but should identify characteristics that distinguish market participants generally.
5.	Estimate fair value using appropriate valuation techniques and related inputs (see **sections 8** & **9**).	When the price for a financial asset or a financial liability cannot be observed directly, it must be estimated using a valuation technique. Entities should use valuation techniques that are appropriate in the circumstances and for which sufficient data are available to measure fair value, maximising the use of relevant observable inputs and minimising the use of unobservable inputs. Highest priority should be given to unadjusted quoted prices in active markets for identical assets or liabilities. IFRS 13 refers to three widely used valuation techniques: • the market approach (see IFRS 13:B5 - B7); • the cost approach (see IFRS 13:B8 - B9); and • the income approach (see IFRS 13:B10 - B30). Any valuation technique used to measure fair value should be consistent with one or more of these approaches. IFRS 13 does not set out a hierarchy of valuation techniques because particular valuation techniques may be more appropriate in some circumstances than in others. The two most common valuation techniques used for financial instruments are the market approach and the income approach. The use of multiple valuation techniques may be appropriate in certain circumstances. In those cases, the results should be evaluated considering the reasonableness of the range of values indicated by those results. A fair value measurement is the point within that range that is most representative of the fair value in the circumstances. Once a valuation technique has been selected, it should be applied consistently. A change in a valuation technique or its application (e.g. a change in its weighting when multiple valuation techniques are used or a change in an adjustment applied to a valuation technique) is only appropriate if the change results in a measurement that is equally or more representative of fair value in the circumstances.

#	Step	Explanation
		An entity should evaluate the factors listed in IFRS 13:B37 (see **section 9.5**) to determine whether there has been a significant decrease in the volume or level of activity for the asset or liability relative to normal market activity. When such a decrease has occurred, this will affect the entity's selection of techniques and/or inputs and the weight placed on quoted prices.
6.	If the exception in Step 2a applies, allocate the fair value calculated in Step 5 (which might include several units of account) to the individual units of account that are the subject of the fair value measurement (as determined in Step 1 above) (see **section 6**).	If the fair value calculated in Step 5 is for multiple units of account, the fair value should be allocated to the individual units of account that are the subject of the fair value measurement on a reasonable and consistent basis.
7.	Classify the fair value measurement within the fair value hierarchy (see **section 10**) and prepare the disclosures required by IFRS 13 (see **chapter C12**).	IFRS 13 establishes a fair value hierarchy that categorises into three levels the inputs to valuation techniques used to measure fair value (see IFRS 13:72 - 90 for details). When several inputs are used to measure the fair value of an asset or a liability, those inputs may be categorised within different levels of the fair value hierarchy (e.g. the valuation may be based on some Level 2 and some Level 3 inputs). In such circumstances, the categorisation of the fair value measurement in its entirety is based on the lowest level input that is significant to the entire measurement. IFRS 13 sets out disclosure requirements in respect of fair value measurements. The disclosures vary depending on whether the assets or liabilities are measured at fair value on a recurring or non-recurring basis.

Fair value measurement framework

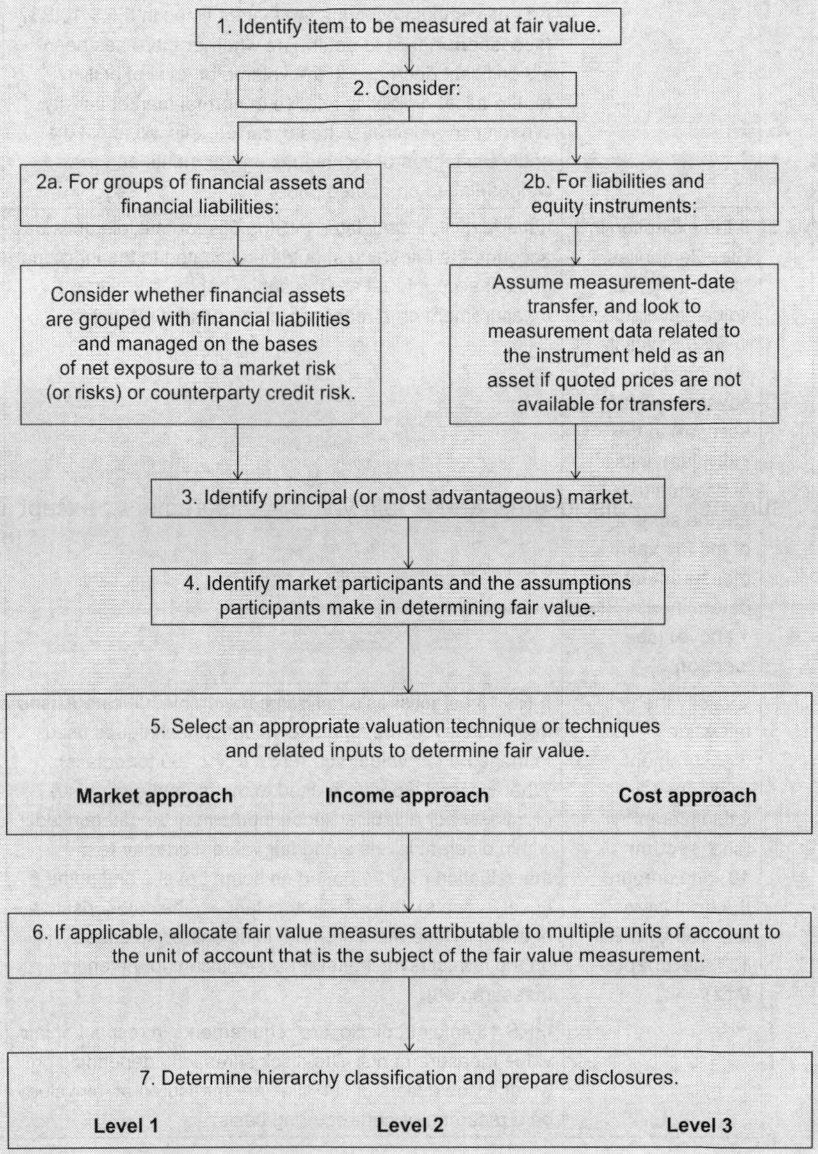

2 Objective and scope

2.1 Objective

The objective of IFRS 13 is to:

[IFRS 13:1]

- define fair value;
- set out in a single IFRS a framework for measuring fair value; and
- require disclosures about fair value measurements.

2.2 Scope

2.2.1 Scope – general

IFRS 13 applies when another IFRS either requires or permits fair value measurement or disclosures about fair value measurements except in limited circumstances specified in IFRS 13:6 & 7. [IFRS 13:5] None of the exceptions in IFRS 13:6 & 7 (which are listed in **chapter A6** of **Volume A** of this manual) applies to financial instruments in the scope of IAS 32, IAS 39, IAS 39 and IFRS 7. Consequently, all financial instruments in the scope of IAS 32, IAS 39 and IFRS 7 that are measured at fair value are subject to the fair value measurement and disclosure guidance contained in IFRS 13.

The measurement requirements in IFRS 13 apply in respect of:

- financial instruments that are measured at fair value in the statement of financial position; and
- financial instruments for which the fair value is disclosed, even if the item is not measured at fair value in the statement of financial position (e.g. financial instruments not measured at fair value but for which fair value is required to be disclosed under IFRS 7:25). [IFRS 13:BC25]

Some financial instruments are measured at fair value on an ongoing basis (IFRS 13 refers to this as 'fair value on a recurring basis') and some (e.g. financial assets meeting the criteria for amortised cost measurement in IAS 39:46 – see **section 3** in **chapter C2**) are measured at fair value only on initial recognition or for disclosure purposes. IFRS 13 applies in all of these circumstances (subject to the exceptions in IFRS 13:6 & 7).

2.2.2 Application of IFRS 13 to receivables and payables measured at initial recognition using present value techniques

All recognised financial instruments that are within the scope of IAS 39, excluding certain trade receivables, are required to be measured at fair value on initial recognition. This requirement applies irrespective of how the instrument is subsequently measured. The exception is for trade receivables that do not have a significant financing component (determined in accordance with IFRS 15 *Revenue from Contracts with Customers*) that are not initially measured at fair value, rather they are initially measured at their transaction price. In the case where receivables and payables are initially measured at fair value but subsequently measured at amortised cost, because fair value generally cannot be observed directly, present value techniques are used to estimate fair value at initial recognition. Accordingly, IFRS 13 (including the guidance in IFRS 13:B12 - B30 regarding the use of present value techniques to measure fair value) applies to such initial measurements.

Note, however, that IFRS 13's disclosure requirements do not apply to fair value measurements at initial recognition (see IFRS 13:91 & BC184).

2.2.3 Application of IFRS 13 to financial assets measured at amortised cost that are determined to be impaired

When a financial asset measured at amortised cost is determined to be impaired, the impairment loss is measured as the difference between the asset's carrying amount and the present value of the estimated future cash flows (see IAS 39:63).

For measurement in the statement of financial position IFRS 13 does not generally apply when an impaired financial asset is measured using this approach. The recognition of an impairment loss using the approach described results in the financial asset being remeasured at the present value of expected future cash flows discounted at the original effective interest rate. This amount may not be equivalent to fair value because a fair value measurement would incorporate a current market discount rate. Accordingly, the measurement and disclosure requirements of IFRS 13 do not generally apply to an impaired financial asset measured at amortised cost.

However, as a practical expedient, IAS 39:AG84 allows the impairment of a financial asset measured at amortised cost to be measured on the basis of the instrument's fair value using an observable market price. When this approach is adopted, it results in the financial asset being measured at fair value and, consequently, the requirements of IFRS 13 do apply.

In addition, IFRS 7:25 requires an entity to disclose the fair value of each class of financial assets and financial liabilities. Consequently, the fair value of financial assets measured at amortised cost is required to be disclosed. The amount disclosed should be measured in accordance with IFRS 13 and the disclosures required under IFRS 13:97 should be provided.

2.2.4 Application of IFRS 13 to a hedged item in a fair value hedge

Hedged items in a fair value hedge are not measured at fair value in the statement of financial position. The hedged item may be accounted for under an IFRS that specifies a measurement basis other than fair value (e.g. a debt instrument measured at amortised cost under IAS 39). In such circumstances, under the fair value hedge accounting rules, the underlying carrying amount of the hedged item is adjusted for relevant changes in the fair value of the hedged risk. The hedged risk could be (i) changes in the fair value of the hedged item (see **example 2.2.4A**) or (ii) changes in a portion of the fair value of the hedged item specific to a hedged risk (see **example 2.2.4B**). In both cases, the fair value hedge adjustment applied to the hedged item results in a 'hybrid' carrying amount for the hedged item.

In such circumstances, the fair value measurement principles in IFRS 13 should be used in determining the amount of the fair value hedge adjustment (i.e. the amount of the relevant changes in the fair value of the hedged risk).

When the relevant IFRS requires disclosure of the fair value of a hedged item that is not measured at fair value in its entirety in the statement of financial position:

- the measurement requirements of IFRS 13 apply to the amount disclosed as fair value; and
- the disclosure requirements of IFRS 13:97 apply.

Example 2.2.4A

Application of IFRS 13 to a hedged item in a fair value hedge (1)

On 1 January 20X1, Company A (which is not a broker-dealer) measures oil inventories of 100,000 barrels under IAS 2 *Inventories* at its cost of US$60 per barrel (US$6 million). The spot price for oil is US$65 per barrel. At that date, Company A enters into and designates oil futures contracts to sell 100,000 barrels of oil at US$65 per barrel as a fair value hedge of its oil inventories. The fair value of the oil futures contracts on 1 January 20X1 is zero. The oil futures contracts are measured at fair value at subsequent reporting dates in accordance with IAS 39.

At 31 December 20X1, the spot price for oil is US$63 per barrel. Assume, for simplicity, that Company A did not purchase or sell any oil in the period. The IAS 2 measurement of the oil inventories is unchanged, because the current spot price of US$63 per barrel is higher than the carrying amount of $60 per barrel (i.e. cost). However, as a result of the fall in the spot price from US$65 to US$63 per barrel, the fair value of the oil futures contract on 31 December 20X1 is an asset of US$200,000. For illustrative purposes, assuming Company A has a perfectly effective fair value hedge, the carrying amount of the inventories is therefore adjusted by US$200,000, resulting in an adjusted carrying amount of US$5.8 million (i.e. US$6 million less the fair value hedge adjustment of US$200,000).

This adjusted carrying amount of US$5.8 million is not the fair value of the inventories, and IAS 2 does not require that the fair value of the inventories be disclosed. Consequently, neither the measurement nor the disclosure requirements of IFRS 13 apply in respect of the inventories.

However, the fair value measurement principles in IFRS 13 should be used in determining the amount of the fair value hedge adjustment because the fair value hedge adjustment represents an adjustment for fair value movements in the hedged risk. In addition, both the measurement and the disclosure requirements of IFRS 13 apply in respect of the oil futures contracts because they are derivatives measured at fair value.

Example 2.2.4B

Application of IFRS 13 to a hedged item in a fair value hedge (2)

Entity Z issues fixed-rate debt at 6 per cent, which includes a credit spread of 100 basis points (i.e. the rate comprises a LIBOR rate of 5 per cent and a credit spread of 1 per cent). To hedge its exposure to interest rate movements, Entity Z enters into a receive-fixed rate at 5 per cent, pay-floating rate at LIBOR swap. The LIBOR portion of the 6 per cent fixed-rate debt is designated as the hedged item. At subsequent reporting dates, the interest rate swap is remeasured to fair value in accordance with IAS 39, with the fair value movement recognised in profit or loss. The carrying amount of the debt is adjusted for changes in the fair value of the debt arising from changes in the benchmark interest rate, LIBOR.

This adjusted carrying amount is not the fair value of the debt. Consequently, the measurement requirements of IFRS 13 do not apply to that carrying amount. However, the fair value measurement principles in IFRS 13 should be used in determining the amount of the fair value hedge adjustment because the fair value hedge adjustment represents an adjustment for fair value movements in the hedged risk.

Because the entity is required to disclose the fair value of the debt under IFRS 7:

- the measurement requirements of IFRS 13 apply to the amount disclosed as fair value; and
- the disclosure requirements of IFRS 13:97 also apply.

Both the measurement and the disclosure requirements of IFRS 13 apply in respect of the interest rate swap because it is a derivative measured at fair value.

2.2.5 Application of the disclosure requirements of IFRS 13 to assets and liabilities measured at fair value and included within a disposal group classified as held for sale

Under IFRS 5 *Non-current Assets Held for Sale and Discontinued Operations*, assets and liabilities that are excluded from the scope of the measurement requirements of that Standard may nevertheless be included within a disposal group classified as held for sale and the disposal group as a whole is subject to the measurement requirements and the classification and presentation requirements of IFRS 5 (see **section 2** of **chapter A20** of **Volume A** of this manual).

Items included within a disposal group that are not subject to the measurement requirements of IFRS 5 are measured in accordance with applicable IFRSs; some items (e.g. financial instruments) may be measured at fair value. If assets and liabilities that are measured at fair value on a recurring or non-recurring basis are part of a disposal group classified as held for sale, the question arises as to whether the disclosure requirements of IFRS 13 apply to those assets and liabilities.

The extent to which the disclosure requirements of other IFRSs apply to assets or liabilities included within disposal groups classified as held for sale is addressed in IFRS 5:5B which states that "[d]isclosures in other IFRSs do not apply to [non-current assets held for sale] (or disposal groups) unless those IFRSs require . . . disclosures about measurement of assets and liabilities within a disposal group that are not within the scope of the measurement requirement of IFRS 5".

For assets and liabilities excluded from the scope of the measurement requirement of IFRS 5 that are included within a disposal group classified as held for sale and that are measured at fair value, the effect of IFRS 5:5B is that the disclosure requirements of IFRS 13 apply *to the extent that those disclosure requirements relate to measurement*.

Given that IFRS 13 as a whole is concerned with the measurement of fair value, and with disclosures regarding the measurement of fair value, all of the disclosure requirements of IFRS 13 relate to 'measurement' and, consequently, should be applied.

When determining the classes of assets and liabilities as required by IFRS 13:94 (see **section 3** in **chapter C12**), and preparing the fair value measurement disclosures, an entity should distinguish assets and liabilities that are part of a disposal group classified as held for sale from its other assets and liabilities. The classes determined in accordance with IFRS 13:94 should be consistent with the major classes of assets and liabilities disclosed separately in accordance with IFRS 5:38 (see **7.3.1** in **chapter A20** of **Volume A** of this manual).

3 Definition of fair value

3.1 Definition of fair value – general

Fair value is defined as "[t]he price that would be received to sell an asset or paid to transfer a liability in an orderly transaction between market participants at the measurement date". [IFRS 13:Appendix A]

This basis for measuring fair value is commonly referred to as an *exit price* approach because it reflects the price at which a market participant that holds the asset or owes the liability could *exit* that asset or liability by selling the asset or transferring the liability to a third party.

Note that the definition assumes a hypothetical and orderly exchange transaction (i.e. it is not an actual sale or a forced transaction or distress sale). [IFRS 13:BC30]

Fair value as defined above is a market-based measurement (not an entity-specific value). [IFRS 13:2] It is therefore measured using the assumptions that market participants would use when pricing the asset or liability, including assumptions about risk. Consequently, an entity's intention to hold an asset or to settle or otherwise fulfil a liability is not relevant when measuring fair value. [IFRS 13:3]

IFRS 13's definition clarifies that fair value should reflect current market conditions (which reflect the current expectations of market participants about future market conditions, rather than those of the reporting entity). [IFRS 13:BC31]

The extent to which market information is available can vary between different types of assets and liabilities. For some assets and liabilities, observable market transactions or market information may be available. For other assets and liabilities, observable market transactions and market information may not be available. However, the objective under IFRS 13 in both circumstances is the same – to estimate the price at which an orderly transaction to sell the asset or to transfer the liability would take place between market participants at the measurement date under current market conditions. [IFRS 13:2] When a price for an identical asset or liability is not observable, an entity measures fair value using another valuation technique that maximises the use of relevant observable inputs and minimises the use of unobservable inputs. [IFRS 13:3]

A fair value measurement requires an entity to determine all of the following:

[IFRS 13:B2]

- the particular asset or liability that is the subject of the measurement (consistently with its unit of account);
- the principal (or most advantageous) market for the asset or liability; and
- the valuation technique(s) appropriate for the measurement, considering the availability of data with which inputs that represent the assumptions market participants would use when pricing the asset or liability and the level of the fair value hierarchy within which the inputs are categorised.

Key elements of the definition of fair value are discussed in the following sections, namely:

- the asset or liability that is being measured (see **section 3.2**);
- the market in which the transaction is assumed to occur (see **section 3.3**);
- the market participants that are assumed to enter into the transaction (see **section 3.4**); and
- the 'price' at which the transaction is assumed to occur (see **section 3.5**).

3.2 Identifying the asset or liability

3.2.1 Determining the appropriate unit of account

The asset or liability being measured at fair value may be (1) a stand-alone asset or liability (e.g. a financial instrument), (2) a group of assets or a group of liabilities, or (3) a group of assets and liabilities. The level at which fair value is measured will depend on the 'unit of account' (typically, the level at which the asset or liability is aggregated or disaggregated for recognition or disclosure purposes). [IFRS 13:13 and Appendix A]

The unit of account is determined in accordance with the IFRS that requires or permits the fair value measurement, except as provided in IFRS 13. [IFRS 13:14] For financial instruments, the unit of account is determined in accordance with IAS 32, IAS 39 or IFRS 7.

IFRS 13 does not generally prescribe the unit of account. The IASB concluded that IFRS 13 should describe *how* to measure fair value, not *what* is being measured at fair value. Other IFRSs specify whether a fair value measurement considers an individual asset or liability or a group of assets or liabilities (i.e. the unit of account). For example, under IAS 39 the unit of account is generally an individual financial instrument. [IFRS 13:BC47]

As IAS 39 requires that assets and liabilities be recognised and measured in accordance with their contractual terms the unit of account guidance in IAS 39 is therefore based on a stand-alone asset or liability rather than based on a group of assets and/or liabilities. Therefore, in applying IFRS 13 to financial instruments fair value is generally determined on a stand-alone basis. However, as described in **section 6**, IFRS 13 permits financial instruments that are managed together and that have offsetting risks to be valued based on the group of financial instruments rather than the fair value of individual financial instruments.

In September 2014, the IASB issued Exposure Draft ED/2014/4 *Measuring Quoted Investments in Subsidiaries, Joint Ventures and Associates at Fair Value*. The ED considers the unit of account for the purposes of measuring the fair value of investments in subsidiaries, joint ventures and associates when the investment is quoted in an active market. This issue is relevant in the following circumstances:

- an entity chooses to measure such investments at fair value in accordance IAS 39 in its separate financial statements;
- an acquirer acquires the controlling interest in an investee where the previously-held interest is required to be measured at fair value;
- an investment entity parent measures its investments in subsidiaries (other than subsidiaries that provide investment-related services or activities) at fair value in accordance with IFRS 10 *Consolidated Financial Statements*; and
- an entity is required to measure the fair value of its investment in a subsidiary, joint venture or associate as part of an impairment assessment in accordance with IAS 36 *Impairment of Assets*.

In the ED, the IASB proposes that the unit of account for investments in subsidiaries, joint ventures and associates is the investment as a whole, and that the fair value measurement of an investment composed of financial instruments quoted in an active market should be the product of the quoted price of the financial instrument (P) multiplied by the quantity (Q) of instruments held (i.e. P × Q) without adjustments. This is on the basis that the quoted prices in an active market provide the most reliable evidence of fair value. The comment period for the ED ended in January 2015 and at the time of writing the IASB was in the redeliberation phase of the project.

Given the ongoing debate there are two acceptable approaches to fair valuing interests in subsidiaries, joint ventures and associates when the individual investment is quoted in an active market. The unit of account can be considered the individual investment and therefore the interest is fair valued as the quantity multiplied by the price of an individual instrument (i.e. P x Q), or alternatively the unit of account can be considered as a whole and thus potentially the P x Q valuation can be adjusted to reflect the premium that would be paid for control, joint control or significant influence over an investee. It should be noted that any such adjustment would be unobservable (i.e., a 'Level 3' input). If significant, this would result in the entire fair value measurement being categorised as 'Level 3' and, therefore, additional disclosures stipulated by IFRS 13 with regard to Level 3 fair value measurement (for example, a description of the valuation process and inputs used and of sensitivity to changes in the unobservable input used) would be required. An entity should select its approach as an accounting policy and apply it consistently in fair valuing interests in subsidiaries, joint ventures and associates where the individual investment is quoted in an active market.

The following examples set out considerations for determining the appropriate unit of account for equity interests held by an entity in various scenarios and how the fair value of those interests should be measured.

Scenario	**Unit of account prescribed in the applicable IFRS**
Scenario 1	
Entity A owns a 16 per cent equity interest in Entity B (160 million ordinary shares). Entity B's ordinary shares are traded in an active market. The share price of each ordinary share at the measurement date is CU0.5. Entity A accounts for the 16 per cent equity interest at fair value at initial recognition and at the end of each reporting period in accordance with IAS 39.	IAS 39 is the applicable Standard that requires the fair value measurement. IFRS 13:80 specifically discusses a scenario where an entity holds a position in a single asset or liability (including a position comprising a large number of identical assets or liabilities) and the asset or liability is traded in an active market; in such circumstances, the unit of account is the individual financial instrument (see **section 10.3**). The fair value of such a holding of financial instruments is required to be measured within Level 1 as the product of the quoted price (P) for the individual financial instrument and the quantity (Q) held by the entity (i.e. P x Q). Therefore, in this scenario, the fair value of the 16 per cent equity interest in Entity B is measured as 160 million x CU0.5 = CU80 million.

Scenario	Unit of account prescribed in the applicable IFRS
Scenario 2	
Entity C owns a 54 per cent equity interest in Entity D (300 million ordinary shares). Entity D is a subsidiary of Entity C. Entity D's ordinary shares are traded in an active market. The share price of each ordinary share at the measurement date is CU0.5.	Based on Entity C's accounting policy, IAS 39 is the applicable Standard that requires the fair value measurement in Entity C's separate financial statements.
In its separate financial statements, Entity C has chosen to account for its investments in subsidiaries in accordance with IAS 39 at fair value at initial recognition and at the end of each reporting period.	Entity's C's accounting policy for fair valuing interests in subsidiaries, joint ventures and associates is to consider the unit of account as the individual investment. Therefore, the unit of account for Entity C's investment in Entity D is the individual share in Entity D, and the fair value of the 54 per cent equity interest in Entity D is determined as the product of the quoted price (P) for the individual shares and the quantity (Q) held by Entity C (i.e. P x Q = 300 million x CU0.5 = CU150 million). Note that this question concerns measurement in the separate financial statements of Entity C only. The accounting in the consolidated financial statements is specified in IFRS 10 *Consolidated Financial Statements*.

3.2.2 Determining the characteristics of an asset or a liability to be taken into account

3.2.2.1 Characteristics of an asset or a liability to be taken into account – general

When measuring fair value, the characteristics of an asset or a liability that should be taken into account are those that market participants would consider when pricing that asset or liability at the measurement date. Such characteristics could include, for example:

[IFRS 13:11]

- the condition and location of an asset; and
- restrictions, if any, on the sale or use of an asset.

The effect on the measurement arising from a particular characteristic will differ depending on how that characteristic would be taken into account by market participants. [IFRS 13:12]

3.2.2.2 Restrictions on the sale or use of an asset

Following the principle set out in IFRS 13:11 (see **3.2.2.1**), a legal or contractual restriction on the sale or use of an asset should be incorporated in the asset's fair value measurement if (1) the restriction is a characteristic of the asset, and (2) market participants would take the effect of the restriction into account when pricing the asset.

Example 8 accompanying IFRS 13, reproduced as **example 3.2.2.2**, illustrates the effect of restrictions on the fair value measurement of an asset. Example 8 considers a restriction that is a characteristic of the asset being measured and that would transfer to market participants with the asset; such restrictions should be taken into account when measuring the fair value of the asset. In contrast, a restriction that is specific to the entity holding the asset and that would not transfer to market participants should not be taken into account when measuring the fair value of the asset.

Example 3.2.2.2

Restriction on the sale of an equity instrument

[IFRS 13:IE28 – Example 8]

An entity holds an equity instrument (a financial asset) for which sale is legally or contractually restricted for a specified period. (For example, such a restriction could limit sale to qualifying investors.) The restriction is a characteristic of the instrument and, therefore, would be transferred to market participants. In that case, the fair value of the instrument would be measured on the basis of the quoted price for an otherwise identical unrestricted equity instrument of the same issuer that trades in a public market, adjusted to reflect the effect of the restriction. The adjustment would reflect the amount market participants would demand because of the risk relating to the inability to access a public market for the instrument for the specified period. The adjustment will vary depending on all the following:

(a) the nature and duration of the restriction;

(b) the extent to which buyers are limited by the restriction (e.g. there might be a large number of qualifying investors); and

(c) qualitative and quantitative factors specific to both the instrument and the issuer.

Sometimes it is immediately clear whether a restriction is a characteristic of an asset and would transfer to market participants. In other circumstances, significant judgement may be required to make the assessment and it may be necessary to obtain expert advice.

Consistent with **example 3.2.2.2**, when a restriction needs to be taken into account when measuring the fair value of the asset, this is achieved by adjusting the fair value of an identical unrestricted asset to reflect the 'compensation' that a market participant would require because of the restriction. The adjustment will vary depending on (1) the nature and duration of the restriction, (2) the extent to which buyers are limited by the restriction, and (3) qualitative and quantitative factors specific to the asset (including factors specific to the issuer of the asset, as appropriate).

When categorising the fair value measurement for the purposes of the fair value hierarchy under IFRS 13:72, an entity will need to evaluate the significance of any adjustment made to reflect a restriction on the sale or use of the asset (see **10.3.3.2** for additional guidance regarding such evaluations).

The following are additional common examples of restrictions on the sale of assets.

Restriction on the sale of securities specified in contractual terms When a restriction on the sale of securities (e.g. prohibiting sale of the securities to specified groups of investors or only permitting the securities to be sold to specified groups of investors) is embedded in the contractual terms of the securities, the restriction is a characteristic of the securities and would transfer to market participants. Consequently, the fair value measurement of the securities should reflect the asset-specific restriction.

Founders' shares Founder shareholders may be contractually prevented from selling their shares immediately following an initial public offering (IPO). Such a restriction may be outlined in the IPO prospectus. Assuming that the restriction is not embedded in the contractual terms of the shares (and, accordingly, would not transfer to a market participant in a hypothetical sale of the shares), the restriction is specific to the founder shareholders and is not a characteristic of the shares. In such circumstances, the restriction on the sale of the shares would not be taken into account when measuring the fair value of the shares.

Directors' shareholdings Assume that Company A owns ordinary shares issued by Company B and Company A is entitled to appoint a member of its management team to Company B's board of directors. Because Company A appoints a director of Company B, Company A is restricted from selling any of its shares in Company B during the period surrounding Company B's periodic release of earnings. Other market participants that are not directors of Company B or that do not have a right to appoint directors of Company B would not be subject to this restriction. Because the restriction is entity-specific (i.e. it is not a characteristic of the shares) and would not transfer with the shares, Company A should not reflect the effect of the restriction in the fair value measurement of its investment in Company B.

Assets pledged as collateral An entity may enter into a borrowing arrangement that requires assets to be pledged as collateral. The borrowing arrangement may restrict the entity from selling or transferring the assets during the term of the arrangement. Other market participants, however, would not be subject to this restriction. Because the restriction is entity-specific (i.e. it is not a characteristic of the assets) and would not transfer with the assets, it should not be reflected in the fair value measurement of the pledged assets.

3.3 Identifying the market in which to price the asset or liability

3.3.1 Principal market versus most advantageous market

IFRS 13 requires an entity to consider the market in which the sale of an asset or the transfer of a liability will take place. The Standard introduces the concepts of a 'principal market' and a 'most advantageous' market. Both terms are important in establishing the market in which the particular asset will be sold or the liability transferred and, consequently, in determining what price will be achieved if the sale or transfer occurs in that market at the measurement date.

A fair value measurement assumes that the transaction to sell the asset or transfer the liability takes place either:

[IFRS 13:16]

- in the principal market for the asset or liability; or
- in the absence of a principal market, in the most advantageous market for the asset or liability.

The *principal market* is the market with the greatest volume and level of activity for the asset or liability. The *most advantageous market* is the market that maximises the amount that would be received to sell the asset or minimises the amount that would be paid to transfer the liability, after taking into account transaction and transport costs. [IFRS 13:Appendix A]

Note that, although transaction costs are not deducted (for an asset) or added (for a liability) when measuring fair value, they are considered when identifying the most advantageous market for an asset or a liability (see **3.5.3**).

The principal market should be identified on the basis of the volume or level of activity for the asset or liability rather than the volume or level of activity of the reporting entity's transactions in a particular market. [IFRS 13:BC52] Therefore, the assessment as to which of two or more accessible markets is the principal market is made from the perspective of market participants rather than the entity.

Equally, in the absence of a principal market, the most advantageous market is identified using the assumptions that market participants would use.

A principal market may not exist, for example, when the volume or level of activity for the asset or liability is the same in two different markets to which the entity has access, or when there is no observable market for the asset or liability. In such circumstances, an entity needs to identify the most advantageous market or develop assumptions from the perspective of a market participant in a hypothetical most advantageous market.

IFRS 13 does not require an entity to conduct an exhaustive search of all possible markets to identify the principal market or (in the absence of a principal market, the most advantageous market) but an entity is required to take into account all information that is reasonably available. In the absence of evidence to the contrary, the market in which the entity would normally enter into a transaction to sell the asset or to transfer the liability is presumed to be the principal market (or most advantageous) market. [IFRS 13:17]

Therefore, an entity is permitted to use the price in the market in which it normally enters into transactions unless there is evidence that the principal market and that market are not the same. [IFRS 13:BC53]

If there is evidence that the market in which an entity would normally transact is not the principal (or most advantageous) market, the principal (or most advantageous) market should be identified by:

- firstly, identifying other markets to which the entity has access; and
- secondly, when relevant, assessing which of two or more accessible markets is the principal (or most advantageous) market.

If there is a principal market for the asset or liability, the fair value measurement should reflect the price in that market even if the price in a different market is potentially more advantageous at the measurement date. [IFRS 13:18]

3.3.2 Access to the market

To use the price in the principal (or most advantageous) market as the basis for measuring fair value, an entity must have access to that market at the measurement date. Because different entities (and businesses within those entities) with different activities may have access to different markets, the principal (or most advantageous) market for the same asset or liability might be different for different entities (and businesses within those entities). Therefore, the principal (or most advantageous) market should be considered from the perspective of the entity, thereby allowing for differences between and among entities with different activities. [IFRS 13:19]

Example 7 accompanying IFRS 13 (summarised at **section 7**) illustrates a scenario in which two entities measure the same instrument differently because each identifies its principal market on the basis of the market to which it has access.

Although an entity must be able to access the market, the entity does not need to be able to sell the particular asset or transfer the particular liability on the measurement date to be able to measure fair value on the basis of the price in that market. [IFRS 13:20]

For example, as discussed in **example 3.2.2.2**, an entity may be restricted from selling a particular asset at the measurement date. Nevertheless, if the entity has access to the principal market at that date, the entity could measure the asset's fair value using observed prices for sales of similar (but unrestricted) assets in that market. If the restriction is a characteristic of the asset (i.e. it would transfer with the asset in a hypothetical sale), an entity should make an adjustment to observed market prices for similar (but unrestricted) assets to reflect the restriction (see **3.2.2.2** for further discussion).

3.3.3 Measuring fair value when no apparent exit market exists

Even when there is no observable market to provide pricing information about the sale of an asset or the transfer of a liability at the measurement date, a fair value measurement should assume that a transaction takes place at that date, considered from the perspective of a market participant that holds the asset or owes the liability. That assumed transaction establishes a basis for estimating the price to sell the asset or to transfer the liability. [IFRS 13:21]

When an observable market for an asset or a liability does not exist, an entity must assume a hypothetical transaction at the measurement date. This is consistent with the fair value objective in IFRS 13 to measure fair value as "the price that would be received to sell an asset or paid to transfer a liability in an orderly transaction between market participants at the measurement date". [IFRS 13:Appendix A] See **3.4.3** for guidance on how an entity might identify market participants when no apparent exit market exists.

3.3.4 Factors indicating a change in the principal (or most advantageous) market

While it is presumed that the market in which an entity normally transacts is the principal (or most advantageous) market (see **3.3.1**), an entity should reassess the principal (or most advantageous) market for an asset or a liability at each measurement date based on reasonably available information. Factors indicating that there may have been a change in the principal (or most advantageous) market include the following (the list is not exhaustive):

- a significant change in market conditions;
- a decrease in the volume or level of activity relative to other markets;
- the development of a new market (see below);
- a change in the entity's ability to access particular markets (e.g. an entity loses access to a market or gains access to a market to which it did not previously have access); and
- when there is no principal market, a change in value such that the price for the asset or liability in a market previously considered most advantageous is no longer the most advantageous.

Events such as those listed above may indicate that there has been a change in the principal (or most advantageous) market for the asset or liability, or that circumstances have changed such that there is no longer a principal market for the asset or liability (in which case the entity should refer instead to the most advantageous market).

When a market first develops (e.g. for a new form of securities), it may operate primarily as a principal-to-principal or over-the-counter market. However, the volume and level of activity in the exchange market may increase over time. As the volume and level of activity change, and the balance of market activity shifts, an entity should take this into account when reassessing the principal (or most advantageous) market for an asset or a liability.

3.4 Market participants

3.4.1 Definition of market participants

Market participants are defined as "[b]uyers and sellers in the principal (or most advantageous) market for the asset or liability that have all of the following characteristics:

(a) They are independent of each other, i.e. they are not related parties as defined in IAS 24, although the price in a related party transaction may be used as an input to a fair value measurement if the entity has evidence that the transaction was entered into at market terms.

(b) They are knowledgeable, having a reasonable understanding about the asset or liability and the transaction using all available information, including information that might be obtained through due diligence efforts that are usual and customary.

(c) They are able to enter into a transaction for the asset or liability.

(d) They are willing to enter into a transaction for the asset or liability, i.e. they are motivated but not forced or otherwise compelled to do so". [IFRS 13:Appendix A]

3.4.2 Use of assumptions that market participants would use

IFRS 13 requires an entity to use the assumptions that market participants would use when pricing the asset or liability, assuming that market participants act in their economic best interest. [IFRS 13:22]

In developing those assumptions, an entity is not expected to identify specific market participants, but is expected to identify characteristics that distinguish market participants generally, considering factors specific to:

[IFRS 13:23]

- the asset or liability;
- the principal (or most advantageous) market for the asset or liability; and
- market participants with whom the entity would enter into a transaction in that market.

Example 3.4.2A

Use of assumptions that market participants would use

Entity F uses a discounted cash flow model to measure the fair value of a financial asset. Entity F has obtained information about the assumptions that market participants would use to measure the fair value of the asset. However, Entity F believes that some of those assumptions are not appropriate.

Entity F is not permitted to rely on its own internal data rather than use the assumptions that market participants would use. A fair value measurement is a market-based measurement and not entity-specific. IFRS 13:22 requires that the fair value of an asset or a liability should be measured using the assumptions that market participants would use when pricing the asset or liability, assuming that market participants act in their economic best interest.

When using a discounted cash flow model to measure the fair value of a financial asset, Entity F should incorporate relevant observable inputs whenever available. Any unobservable inputs used in the fair value measure (e.g. estimated future cash flows or risk adjustments incorporated into the discount rate) should be based on management's estimate of assumptions that market participants would use in pricing the asset in a current transaction at the measurement date. If market data from transactions involving comparable assets indicate, for example, that a significant liquidity discount applies at the measurement date to compensate for the difficulty in selling assets under current market conditions, Entity F should incorporate that information in its cash flow model (e.g. through an adjustment to the discount rate) even if management's internal data would not result in such a liquidity adjustment.

Example 3.4.2B

Use of assumptions that market participants would use

Entity A uses a discounted cash flow model as a valuation technique to measure the fair value of its investment in the debt securities of Entity X. No quoted price for identical securities is available. Entity A's valuation technique requires assumptions about default rates as inputs. Default rate assumptions can be readily derived from current relevant observable market data: for example, actively traded credit default swaps (CDSs) on publicly traded bonds of Entity X, or asset swap spreads (the differential between the bond yield and the LIBOR curve expressed in basis points) or issuer spreads on the basis of recent notes issuances.

In applying its valuation technique to measure fair value, Entity A should maximise the use of relevant observable inputs. Therefore, it cannot rely solely on its own historical default data for issuers with a credit quality similar to that of Entity X or on its own default assumptions, even if the default assumptions are 'stressed' (e.g. by changing the inputs to other reasonably possible alternative assumptions). Instead, Entity A should use the relevant default rate assumptions that are observable in the market.

Example 3.4.2C

Fair value measurement of loans and receivables – requirement to consider the credit standing of the borrower

Entity A (a lender) has a loan receivable from Entity B (a borrower). When measuring the fair value of the loan receivable, Entity A should take into account the credit standing of Entity B.

A lender is required to take into account a borrower's credit standing when measuring the fair value of a loan receivable in accordance with IFRS 13.

IFRS 13:22 states that "[a]n entity shall measure the fair value of an asset or a liability using the assumptions that market participants would use when pricing the asset or liability, assuming that market participants act in their economic best interest".

Market participants would incorporate the effect of a borrower's credit standing into the valuation of a loan receivable because the borrower's credit standing can be indicative of the amount that will be collected on the loan. Therefore, Entity A should make appropriate adjustments to the fair value measurement of its loan and receivable to reflect Entity B's credit standing.

These requirements are relevant when Entity A measures the loan receivable at fair value on initial recognition and/or at subsequent reporting dates. They are also relevant when Entity A measures the receivable at amortised cost at subsequent reporting dates because, subject to limited exceptions, IFRS 7 requires that the fair value of financial instruments be disclosed at each reporting date. The amount disclosed should be measured in accordance with IFRS 13 and the disclosures required under IFRS 13:97 should be provided.

3.4.3 Identifying market participants when no apparent exit market exists

IFRS 13:21 requires that, even when there is no observable market to provide pricing information about the sale of an asset or the transfer of a liability at the measurement date, a fair value measurement should assume that a transaction takes place at that date, considered from the perspective of a market participant that holds the asset or owes the liability. That assumed transaction establishes a basis for estimating the price to sell the asset or to transfer the liability (see **3.3.3**).

In such circumstances, the entity is not required to identify specific market participants. Instead, the entity should consider the characteristics of potential market participants who would purchase the asset or accept a transfer of the liability being measured. In addition, the entity should identify the assumptions that such market participants would make in a transaction that maximises the amount received to sell an asset or minimises the amount paid to transfer a liability.

Potential market participants for financial instruments include counterparties to a derivative instrument, investors maximising return, investors trying to establish a strategic relationship with an investee, or a range of other participants with a specific objective.

When identifying a potential market participant, care should be taken to ensure that the unit of account from the perspective of the market participant is consistent with the unit of account of the item being measured.

When developing assumptions that market participants would use in such a hypothetical transaction, an entity may start with its own assumptions and make adjustments for factors specific to the asset or liability being measured, including (the list is not exhaustive):

- growth rates and risk adjustments to reflect market participant assumptions; and
- performance and risk indicators (e.g. delinquencies, defaults, prepayment speeds and interest rates).

Market participant assumptions that are developed when no apparent market exists may be based on unobservable inputs or adjustments. An entity needs to evaluate the significance of these inputs or adjustments when determining the appropriate level in the fair value hierarchy within which the measurement should be categorised (see **10.3.3.2** for additional guidance regarding such evaluations).

3.5 The price at which a transaction is assumed to occur

3.5.1 Characteristics of the price at which a transaction is assumed to occur

The price at which a transaction is assumed to occur in the principal or most advantageous market is the price:

[IFRS 13:24]

- in an 'orderly' transaction (see **3.5.2**); and
- under current market conditions at the measurement date.

The price may be directly observable or estimated using another valuation technique (see **section 8**). [IFRS 13:24]

The price should not be adjusted for 'transaction costs', but it should be adjusted for 'transport costs' in specified circumstances (see **3.5.3**). [IFRS 13:25 & 26]

3.5.2 An 'orderly' transaction

A fair value measurement assumes that the asset or liability is exchanged in an 'orderly' transaction in the principal (or most advantageous) market. An orderly transaction is defined as "[a] transaction that assumes exposure to the market for a period before the measurement date to allow for marketing activities that are usual and customary for transactions involving such assets or liabilities; it is not a forced transaction (e.g. a forced liquidation or distress sale)". [IFRS 13:Appendix A]

Appendix B to the Standard provides additional guidance regarding the identification of orderly transactions (see **section 9.6**).

3.5.3 Transaction costs and transport costs

Transaction costs are defined as "[t]he costs to sell an asset or transfer a liability in the principal (or most advantageous) market for the asset or liability that are directly attributable to the disposal of the asset or the transfer of the liability and that meet both of the following criteria:

- They result directly from and are essential to that transaction.
- They would not have been incurred by the entity had the decision to sell the asset or transfer the liability not been made (similar to costs to sell, as defined in IFRS 5)". [IFRS 13:Appendix A]

Transaction costs do not include transport costs. [IFRS 13:26] Transport costs are defined as "[t]he costs that would be incurred to transport an asset from its current location to its principal (or most advantageous) market". [IFRS 13:Appendix A]

IFRS 13 specifies that, when measuring fair value, the relevant market price should *not* be adjusted for transaction costs. Because such costs are specific to a transaction and will differ depending on how an entity enters into a transaction for an asset or a liability, they are not considered to be a characteristic of the asset or liability. [IFRS 13:25]

Note, however, that transaction costs are considered when identifying the most advantageous market for an asset or a liability (see **3.3.1** and **example 3.5.3**).

The appropriate treatment for transaction costs should be determined in accordance with other relevant IFRSs. [IFRS 13:25] For financial instruments, transaction costs are accounted for in accordance with the requirements in IAS 32, IAS 39 and IAS 39 (see **section 2.1** in **chapter C6**). [IFRS 13:24 & 25]

In contrast, the price in the principal (or most advantageous) market used to measure the fair value of the asset or liability *is* adjusted for costs that would be incurred to transport the asset from its current location to that market *if* location is a characteristic of the asset. [IFRS 13:26]

Transport costs are relevant in determining the fair value of non-financial items. Because certain contracts that include the delivery or receipt of non-financial items are scoped into IAS 32, IAS 39, IAS 39 and IFRS 7 (see **2.5** in **chapter C1**), transport costs may be relevant in determining the fair value of a contract that is in the scope of the financial instruments Standards. This may be the case in determining the fair value of a commodity for delivery to a particular location where location is an attribute of the contract.

The appropriate treatments for transaction and transport costs are illustrated in the following example.

Example 3.5.3

Level 1 principal (or most advantageous) market

[IFRS 13:IE19 - IE22, Example 6]

An asset is sold in two different active markets at different prices. An entity enters into transactions in both markets and can access the price in those markets for the asset at the measurement date. In Market A, the price that would be received is CU26, transaction costs in that market are CU3 and the costs to transport the asset to that market are CU2 (i.e. the net amount that would be received is CU21). In Market B, the price that would be received is CU25, transaction costs in that market are CU1 and the costs to transport the asset to that market are CU2 (i.e. the net amount that would be received in Market B is CU22).

If Market A is the principal market for the asset (i.e. the market with the greatest volume and level of activity for the asset), the fair value of the asset would be measured using the price that would be received in that market, after taking into account transport costs (CU24).

If neither market is the principal market for the asset, the fair value of the asset would be measured using the price in the most advantageous market. The most advantageous market is the market that maximises the amount that would be received to sell the asset, after taking into account transaction costs and transport costs (i.e. the net amount that would be received in the respective markets).

Because the entity would maximise the net amount that would be received for the asset in Market B (CU22), the fair value of the asset would be measured using the price in that market (CU25), less transport costs (CU2), resulting in a fair value measurement of CU23. Although transaction costs are taken into account when determining which market is the most advantageous market, the price used to measure the fair value of the asset is not adjusted for those costs (although it is adjusted for transport costs).

IFRS 13 requires entities to ensure fair value measurements reflect characteristics specific to the asset or liability. Consequently, *if* location is a characteristic of an asset, an entity should consider transport costs when measuring the fair value of the asset.

4 Measuring the fair value of non-financial assets – highest and best use

The application of IFRS 13's requirements under this heading is limited to non-financial assets. This concept is not relevant for financial assets, liabilities or an entity's own equity instruments because those items do not have alternative uses as contemplated in IFRS 13. [IFRS 13:BC63] Consequently, this topic is not dealt with in this chapter but is discussed in **section 4** of **chapter A6 of Volume A** of this manual.

5 Measuring the fair value of financial liabilities and an entity's own equity instruments

5.1 Measuring the fair value of liabilities and an entity's own equity instruments – general

5.1.1 General principles

The fair value of a financial liability or an entity's own equity instruments (e.g. an equity share issued as part of the consideration in a business combination) is measured based on the assumption that the liability or equity instrument is transferred to a market participant at the measurement date. [IFRS 13:34]

For a financial liability, it is assumed that the liability would remain outstanding and the market participant transferee would be required to fulfil the obligation. It would not be settled with the counterparty or otherwise extinguished on the measurement date. [IFRS 13:34(a)]

IFRS 13 is clear that the fair value of a liability is based on a transfer amount, i.e. the amount the reporting entity would need to pay a third party to take on the obligation, and that obligation remains outstanding and contractually unaltered before and after transfer. Fair value is therefore *not* based on the premise of settling the liability with the counterparty at the measurement date.

For an entity's own equity instrument, it is assumed that the equity instrument would remain outstanding and the market participant transferee would take on the rights and responsibilities associated with the instrument. The instrument would not be cancelled or otherwise extinguished on the measurement date. [IFRS 13:34(b)]

IFRS 13 requires that the fair value measurement be based on an assumed transfer to a market participant even if an entity does not intend to transfer its liability or own equity instrument to a third party (e.g. because the entity has advantages relative to the market that make it more beneficial for the entity to fulfil the liability using its own internal resources) or it is unable to do so (e.g. because the counterparty would not permit the liability to be transferred to another party). [IFRS 13:BC81 & 82]

Even when there is no observable market to provide pricing information about the transfer of a liability or an entity's own equity instruments (e.g. because contractual or other legal restrictions prevent the transfer of such items), there might be an observable market for such items if they are held by other parties as assets (see **5.1.2**). [IFRS 13:35]

Consistent with the objective of fair value measurement and the prioritisation in the fair value hierarchy (see **section 10**), when measuring the fair value of a liability or an entity's own equity instrument at fair value, the entity should maximise the use of relevant observable inputs and minimise the use of unobservable inputs. [IFRS 13:36]

5.1.2 Liabilities and equity instruments held by other parties as assets

When a quoted price for the transfer of an identical or a similar financial liability or an entity's own equity instruments is not available, and the identical item is held by another party as an asset, an entity is required to measure the fair value of the financial liability or equity instrument from the perspective of a market participant that holds the identical item as an asset at the measurement date. [IFRS 13:37] This requirement could be relevant, for example, when measuring the fair value of corporate bonds or a call option on an entity's shares. [IFRS 13:35]

Determining the fair value of a financial liability or an entity's own equity instrument from the perspective of the counterparty holding the same instrument as an asset reinforces the notion that the fair value ascribed to the contract is the same irrespective of whether the entity is the issuer or the holder. This is based on the theory that fair value is based on a transaction in which the contract is transferred, as opposed, to being settled or extinguished with the holder. In all cases the fair value is based on the premise that the instrument remains outstanding and therefore is a theoretical transfer value.

In the circumstances described above, the appropriate bases for measuring the fair value of the liability or the entity's own equity instrument are listed below, in descending order of preference:

[IFRS 13:38]

(a) using the quoted price in an active market (see below) for the identical item held by another party as an asset, if that price is available;

(b) if that price is not available, using other observable inputs, such as the quoted price in a market that is not active for the identical item held by another party as an asset; and

(c) if the observable prices in (a) and (b) above are not available, using another valuation technique, such as:

    (i) an income approach (e.g. a present value technique that takes into account the future cash flows that a market participant would expect to receive from holding the liability or equity instrument as an asset; see **5.1.2**); or

    (ii) a market approach (e.g. using quoted prices for similar liabilities or equity instruments held as assets; see **section 8.4**).

An active market is defined as "[a] market in which transactions for the asset or liability take place with sufficient frequency and volume to provide pricing information on an ongoing basis". [IFRS 13:Appendix A]

A quoted price of a liability or an entity's equity instrument held by another party as an asset should be adjusted only if there are factors specific to the asset that are not applicable to the fair value measurement of the liability or equity instrument. An entity should ensure that the price of the asset does not reflect the effect of a restriction preventing the sale of an asset. [IFRS 13:39]

The Standard provides the following examples of factors that might indicate that the quoted price of the asset should be adjusted.

[IFRS 13:39]

- The quoted price for the asset relates to a similar (but not identical) liability or equity instrument held by another party as an asset. For example, the liability or equity instrument may have a particular characteristic (e.g. the credit quality of the issuer) that is different from that reflected in the fair value of the similar liability or equity instrument held as an asset.

- The unit of account for the asset is not the same as for the liability or equity instrument. For example, for liabilities, in some cases the price for an asset reflects a combined price for a package comprising both the amounts due from the issuer and a third-party credit enhancement. If the unit of account for the liability is not for the combined package, the objective is to measure the fair value of the issuer's liability, not the fair value of the combined package. In such circumstances, the entity would adjust the observed price for the asset to exclude the effect of the third-party credit enhancement.

5.1.3 Liabilities and equity instruments not held by other parties as assets

5.1.3.1 Liabilities and equity instruments not held by other parties as assets – general

When a quoted price for the transfer of an identical or a similar liability or entity's own equity instrument is not available, and the identical item is not held by another party as an asset, the fair value of the liability or equity instrument is required to be measured using a valuation technique from the perspective of a market participant that owes the liability or has issued the claim on equity. [IFRS 13:40]

For example, when applying a present value technique, an entity might take into account either of the following:

[IFRS 13:41]

- the future cash outflows that a market participant would expect to incur in fulfilling the obligation, including the compensation that a market participant would require for taking on the obligation (see **5.1.3.2**); or
- the amount that a market participant would receive to enter into or issue an identical liability or equity instrument, using the assumptions that market participants would use when pricing the identical item (e.g. having the same credit characteristics) in the principal (or most advantageous) market for issuing a liability or an equity instrument with the same contractual terms.

5.1.3.2 Estimating future cash outflows

IFRS 13's general guidance regarding the use of present value techniques is discussed in detail in **8.6.1** to **8.6.3**. This section covers the Standard's specific guidance for applying present value techniques to liabilities and an entity's own equity instruments not held by other parties as assets.

When using a present value technique to measure the fair value of a liability that is not held by another party as an asset, an entity should, among other things, estimate the future cash outflows that market participants would expect to incur in fulfilling the obligation. [IFRS 13:B31]

Those future cash outflows should include:

[IFRS 13:B31]

- market participants' expectations about the costs of fulfilling the obligation; and
- the compensation that a market participant would require for taking on the obligation.

The compensation that a market participant would require for taking on the obligation should include the return that a market participant would require for the following:

[IFRS 13:B31]

- undertaking the activity (i.e. the value of fulfilling the obligation – for example by using resources that could be used for other activities); and
- assuming the risk associated with the obligation (i.e. a risk premium that reflects the risk that the actual cash outflows might differ from the expected cash outflows).

IFRS 13 defines a risk premium (also referred to as a 'risk adjustment') as "[c]ompensation sought by risk-averse market participants for bearing the uncertainty inherent in the cash flows of an asset or a liability". [IFRS 13:Appendix A] A risk premium can be included in the fair value measurement of a liability or an entity's own equity instrument that is not held by another party as an asset in one of the following ways:

[IFRS 13:B33]

- by adjusting the cash flows (i.e. as an increase in the amount of cash outflows); or
- by adjusting the rate used to discount the future cash flows to their present values (i.e. as a reduction in the discount rate).

An entity should ensure that it does not double-count or omit adjustments for risk. For example, if the estimated cash flows are increased to take into account the compensation for assuming the risk associated with the obligation, the discount rate should not be adjusted to reflect that risk. [IFRS 13:B33]

5.2 Non-performance risk

5.2.1 Requirement to reflect the effect of non-performance risk

The fair value of a liability reflects the effect of non-performance risk. [IFRS 13:42]

Non-performance risk is defined as "[t]he risk that an entity will not fulfil its obligation. Non-performance risk includes, but may not be limited to, the entity's own credit risk". [IFRS 13:Appendix A] IFRS 7:Appendix A defines credit risk as "[t]he risk that one party to a financial instrument will cause a financial loss for the other party by failing to discharge an obligation".

Non-performance risk is assumed to be the same before and after the transfer of the liability. [IFRS 13:42]

The IASB acknowledges in the Basis for Conclusions of IFRS 13 that it is unlikely that non-performance risk is the same before and after the transfer of the financial liability. However, the IASB concluded that such an assumption was necessary when measuring the fair value of a financial liability in order for the transfer concept to apply. If the transferee, acting as a market participant, had a different credit standing to the transferor it would not take on the obligation of the transferor because either (1) in the case of the transferee's credit standing being worse than the transferor's, the counterparty to the obligation would not permit the transfer to take place, or (2) in the case of the transferee's credit standing being better than the transferor's, the transferee would not choose to take on the obligation without renegotiating the terms to reflect the difference in credit standing.

Furthermore, if it is assumed that market participants have different credit standings, this would result in fundamentally different valuations depending on the identity of the transferee. It was also noted that those that hold the entity's obligations as assets do consider the effect of an entity's credit risk and other risk factors when pricing those assets and, therefore, this effect should be equally reflected in the fair value of the entity's obligations to those holders of assets. [IFRS 13:BC94]

When evaluating the non-performance risk (including credit risk) of a financial liability for the purpose of measuring its fair value, it is useful to refer to the October 2008 report issued by the IASB's Expert Advisory Panel titled *Measuring and Disclosing the Fair Value of Financial Instruments in Markets That Are No Longer Active*. The report describes practices entities use when measuring financial instruments at fair value. In paragraph 35 of the report, the Panel noted that "[u] nderstanding the credit risk of a debt instrument involves evaluating the credit quality and financial strength of both the issuer and the credit support providers".

Paragraph 35 of the report also lists the following as some of the more common factors that an entity should consider.

"(a) **Collateral asset quality:** the assets to which the holder of an instrument has recourse in the event of non-payment or default could be either all of the assets of the issuing entity or specified assets that are legally separated from the issuer (ring-fenced). The greater the value and quality of the assets to which an entity has recourse in the event of default, the lower the credit risk of the instrument. Measuring the fair value of a debt instrument therefore involves assessing the quality of the assets that support the instrument (the collateral) and the level of the collateralisation, and evaluating the likelihood that the assigned collateral will generate adequate cash flows to make the contractual payments on the instrument.

(b) **Subordination:** the level of subordination of an instrument is critical to assessing the risk of non-payment of an instrument. If other more senior instruments have higher claims over the cash flows and assets that support the instrument, this increases the risk of the instrument. The lower the claim on the cash flows and assets, the more risky an instrument is and the higher the return the market will demand on the instrument.

(c) **Non-payment protection:** many instruments contain some form of protection to reduce the risk of non-payment to the holder. In measuring fair value, both the issuer and the holder of the instrument consider the effect of the protection on the fair value of the instrument, unless the entity accounts for the protection as a separate instrument. Protection might take the form of a guarantee or a similar undertaking (e.g. when a parent guarantees the debt of a subsidiary), an insurance contract, a credit default swap or simply the fact that more assets support the instrument than are needed to make the payments (this is commonly referred to as over-collateralisation). The risk of non-payment is also reduced by the existence of more subordinated tranches of instruments that take the first losses on the underlying assets and therefore reduce the risk of more senior tranches absorbing losses. When protection is in the form of a guarantee, an insurance contract or a credit default swap, it is necessary to identify the party providing the protection and assess that party's creditworthiness (to the extent that the protection is not accounted for separately). The protection will be more valuable if the credit risk of the protection provider is low. This analysis involves considering not only the current position of the protection provider but also the effect of other guarantees or insurance contracts that it might have written. For example, if the provider has guaranteed many correlated debt securities, the risk of its non-performance might increase significantly with increases in defaults on those securities. In addition, the credit risk of some protection providers moves as market conditions change. Thus, an entity evaluates the credit risk of each protection provider at each measurement date."

Although paragraph 35 of the Expert Advisory Panel report refers to the valuation of a 'debt instrument', the factors listed above would also be relevant in determining the non-performance risk for a derivative.

Example 5.2.1A

Impact of a guarantee by an acquirer on the fair value of an acquiree's loan

Entity A acquires 100 per cent of Entity B from Entity C in a business combination. One of the identifiable liabilities of Entity B is a loan owed to a third party. The loan was originally guaranteed by Entity C as part of the loan terms. However, as a result of the business combination, the terms of the loan are revised so that Entity A becomes the guarantor of the loan (i.e. the guarantee by Entity A becomes part of the revised loan terms).

IFRS 3 *Business Combinations* requires that the third party loan is measured at fair value at the date of acquisition. The measurement requirements of IFRS 13 apply.

There are no quoted prices available for the transfer of an identical or a similar liability.

When measuring the fair value of the loan at the date of acquisition for the purpose of preparing consolidated financial statements, Entity A should take into account the effect of its own guarantee of the loan because the guarantee is part of the loan terms.

As discussed at **5.1.1**, IFRS 13:37 requires that when a quoted price for the transfer of an identical or a similar liability is not available, and the identical item is held by another party as an asset, an entity should measure the fair value of the liability from the perspective of a market participant that holds the identical item as an asset at the measurement date.

In the circumstances described, the loan is guaranteed by Entity A from the date of acquisition. From the perspective of a market participant holding the loan as an asset, the fact that the loan is guaranteed by Entity A would be taken into account when measuring the fair value of the loan receivable because the market participant would expect to recover the loan from Entity A if Entity B defaulted on the loan. Consequently, when measuring the fair value of the loan, a market participant would take into account (1) the credit standing of Entity B, and (2) the guarantee provided by Entity A.

This is also consistent with the requirement in IFRS 13:43 (see below) that an entity should take into account the effect of its own credit risk (credit standing) and any other factors that might influence the likelihood that the obligation will or will not be fulfilled.

The effect of an entity's credit standing and any other factors that might influence the likelihood that the obligation will or will not be fulfilled may differ depending on the nature of the liability (e.g. whether it is a financial or a non-financial liability, or whether any credit enhancements are attached). [IFRS 13:43]

To understand non-performance risk, consideration has to be given to the specific terms of the instrument rather than simply looking at the overall credit rating or quality of the entity in its entirety. Looking at the latter will generally obscure the particular credit characteristics of the instrument itself, like credit enhancements, or fail to reflect the relative seniority or subordination of the liability relative to the liabilities of the entity.

Example 5.2.1B

Fair value of a financial liability – impact of credit rating

[IFRS 13:IE32]

Entity X and Entity Y each enter into a contractual obligation to pay cash (CU500) to Entity Z in five years. Entity X has a AA credit rating and can borrow at 6 per cent, and Entity Y has a BBB credit rating and can borrow at 12 per cent. Entity X will receive about CU374 in exchange for its promise (the present value of CU500 in five years at 6 per cent). Entity Y will receive about CU284 in exchange for its promise (the present value of CU500 in five years at 12 per cent). The fair value of the liability to each entity (i.e. the proceeds) incorporates that entity's credit standing.

Example 5.2.1C

Fair value of a financial liability – structured note

[IFRS 13:IE34 - Example 10]

On 1 January 20X7 Entity A, an investment bank with a AA credit rating, issues a five-year fixed rate note to Entity B. The contractual principal amount to be paid by Entity A at maturity is linked to an equity index. No credit enhancements are issued in conjunction with or otherwise related to the contract (i.e. no collateral is posted and there is no third-party guarantee). Entity A has designated this note as at fair value through profit or loss. The fair value of the note (i.e. the obligation of Entity A) during 20X7 is measured using an expected present value technique. Changes in fair value are as follows:

(a) Fair value at 1 January 20X7. The expected cash flows used in the expected present value technique are discounted at the risk-free rate using the government bond curve at 1 January 20X7, plus the current market observable AA corporate bond spread to government bonds, if non-performance risk is not already reflected in the cash flows, adjusted (either up or down) for Entity A's specific credit risk (i.e. resulting in a credit-adjusted risk-free rate). Therefore, the fair value of Entity A's obligation at initial recognition takes into account non-performance risk, including that entity's credit risk, which presumably is reflected in the proceeds (and is the same as the transaction price).

(b) Fair value at 31 March 20X7. During March 20X7 the credit spread for AA corporate bonds widens, with no changes to the specific credit risk of Entity A. The expected cash flows used in the expected present value technique are discounted at the risk-free rate using the government bond curve at 31 March 20X7, plus the current market observable AA corporate bond spread to government bonds, if non-performance risk is not already reflected in the cash flows, adjusted for Entity A's specific credit risk (i.e. resulting in a credit-adjusted risk-free rate). Entity A's specific credit risk is unchanged from initial recognition. Therefore, the fair value of Entity A's obligation changes as a result of changes in credit spreads generally. Changes in credit spreads reflect current market participant assumptions about changes in non-performance risk generally, changes in liquidity risk, and the compensation required for assuming those risks.

(c) Fair value at 30 June 20X7. As of 30 June 20X7 there have been no changes to the AA corporate bond spreads. However, on the basis of structured note issues corroborated with other qualitative information, Entity A determines that its own specific creditworthiness has strengthened within the AA credit spread. The expected cash flows used in the expected present value technique are discounted at the risk-free rate using the government bond yield curve at 30 June 20X7, plus the current market observable AA corporate bond spread to government bonds (unchanged from 31 March 20X7), if non-performance risk is not already reflected in the cash flows, adjusted for Entity A's specific credit risk (i.e. resulting in a credit-adjusted risk-free rate). Therefore, the fair value of the obligation of Entity A changes as a result of the change in its own specific credit risk within the AA corporate bond spread.

Example 5.2.1D

Fair value of a financial liability - debt obligation: quoted price

[IFRS 13:IE40 - 42 – Example 12]

On 1 January 20X1 Entity B issues at par a CU2 million BBB-rated exchange-traded five-year fixed rate debt instrument with an annual 10 per cent coupon. Entity B designated this financial liability as at fair value through profit or loss.

On 31 December 20X1 the instrument is trading as an asset in an active market at CU929 per CU1,000 of par value after payment of accrued interest. Entity B uses the quoted price of the asset in an active market as its initial input into the fair value measurement of its liability (CU929 × [CU2 million ÷ CU1,000] = CU1,858,000).

In determining whether the quoted price of the asset in an active market represents the fair value of the liability, Entity B evaluates whether the quoted price of the asset includes the effect of factors not applicable to the fair value measurement of a liability, for example, whether the quoted price of the asset includes the effect of a third-party credit enhancement if that credit enhancement would be separately accounted for from the perspective of the issuer. Entity B determines that no adjustments are required to the quoted price of the asset. Accordingly, Entity B concludes that the fair value of its debt instrument at 31 December 20X1 is CU1,858,000. Entity B categorises and discloses the fair value measurement of its debt instrument within Level 1 of the fair value hierarchy.

Example 5.2.1E

Fair value of a financial liability – debt obligation: present value technique

[IFRS 13:IE43 - 47 – Example 13]

On 1 January 20X1 Entity C issues at par in a private placement a CU2 million BBB-rated five-year fixed-rate debt instrument with an annual 10 per cent coupon. Entity C designated this financial liability as at fair value through profit or loss.

At 31 December 20X1 Entity C still carries a BBB credit rating. Market conditions, including available interest rates, credit spreads for a BBB-quality credit rating and liquidity, remain unchanged from the date the debt instrument was issued. However, Entity C's credit spread has deteriorated by 50 basis points because of a change in its risk of non-performance. After taking into account all market conditions, Entity C concludes that if it was to issue the instrument at the measurement date, the instrument would bear a rate of interest of 10.5 per cent or Entity C would receive less than par in proceeds from the issue of the instrument.

For the purpose of this example, the fair value of Entity C's liability is calculated using a present value technique. Entity C concludes that a market participant would use all of the following inputs (consistently with paragraphs B12-B30 of the IFRS) when estimating the price the market participant would expect to receive to assume Entity C's obligation:

(a) the terms of the debt instrument, including all of the following:
   (i) coupon of 10 per cent;
   (ii) principal amount of CU2 million; and
   (iii) term of four years.
(b) the market rate of interest of 10.5 per cent (which includes a change of 50 basis points in the risk of non-performance from the date of issue).

On the basis of its present value technique, Entity C concludes that the fair value of its liability at 31 December 20X1 is CU1,968,641.

Entity C does not include any additional input into its present value technique for risk or profit that a market participant might require for compensation for assuming the liability. Entity C's obligation is a financial liability, hence, Entity C concludes that the interest rate already captures the risk or profit that a market participant would require as compensation for assuming the liability. Furthermore, Entity C does not adjust its present value technique for the existence of a restriction preventing it from transferring the liability.

The fair value measurement for a liability should reflect the effect of non-performance risk based on the unit of account for financial reporting purposes specified in relevant IFRSs (see also **section 3.1**). The issuer of a liability issued with an inseparable third-party credit enhancement (e.g. a third-party guarantee of debt) that is accounted for separately from the liability should not include the effect of the credit enhancement in the fair value measurement of the liability; in such circumstances, the fair value measurement should reflect the credit standing of the issuer and not that of the third-party guarantor. [IFRS 13:44]

As required under IFRS 13:44, when an entity has a liability with a third-party guarantee, and the liability and the guarantee are accounted for separately under relevant IFRSs, the fair value of the liability should not reflect the effect of the guarantee. In such circumstances, the fair value of the liability from the issuer's perspective will not equal its fair value as a guaranteed liability held by another party as an asset. [IFRS 13:BC98]

5.2.2 Effect of collateral on fair value measurement of liabilities

When an entity has provided collateral in respect of a liability, this will affect the fair value measurement of the liability under IFRS 13. As discussed in **section 5.2**, IFRS 13:42 requires that the fair value of a liability should reflect the effect of non-performance risk, and that non-performance risk is assumed to be the same before and after the transfer of the liability. The definition of non-performance risk in IFRS 13:Appendix A (see **section 5.2**) clarifies that it encompasses an entity's own credit risk (credit standing) and any other factors that might influence the likelihood that the obligation will be fulfilled. One factor specifically mentioned in IFRS 13:43(b) is "the terms of credit enhancements related to the liability, if any".

Collateral is a form of credit enhancement that is contractually linked to a liability (i.e. the terms of the obligation require a lien on the collateral until settlement of the obligation). The fact that an entity has provided collateral typically means that the stated terms of the liability (e.g. the interest rate charged) differ from the terms of an identical liability that is not supported by collateral. The collateral is a characteristic of the liability and, consequently, it should be reflected in the fair value measurement of the collateralised liability.

Example 5.2.2 illustrates how collateral might affect the fair value of a liability on initial recognition.

Example 5.2.2

Effect of collateral on fair value measurement of liabilities

On 1 January 20X1, Company A borrows CU10 million repayable in five years. The fixed interest rate is one-year LIBOR plus 125 basis points. Company A is required to pledge specified property interests as collateral. Management estimates that Company A could have arranged a similar loan with no collateral at a 200 basis point spread to LIBOR. On 1 January 20X1, the one-year LIBOR rate is 1.5 per cent. For simplicity, transaction costs are ignored.

At 1 January 20X1, the fair value of the loan (including any impact from the collateral) is CU10 million. The present value of the loan's contractual cash flows, discounted at Company A's unsecured borrowing rate of 3.5 per cent (i.e. 1.5 per cent LIBOR plus 200 basis points), is CU9.7 million.

This example illustrates that the effect of an issuer's credit standing as well as the effect of credit enhancements should be taken into account in measuring the fair value of the liability. If Company A ignored the reduction in the interest rate attributable to the collateral, it would mistakenly conclude that the fair value of its debt was CU9.7 million rather than CU10 million.

5.2.3 Effect of changes in non-performance risk

Changes in the fair value of collateral or an entity's credit standing should be taken into account in measuring the fair value of a liability on an ongoing basis. This is to ensure that the fair value measurement reflects market participant assumptions at the measurement date.

Examples 5.2.3A and **5.2.3B** illustrate the effect of some of these factors on the fair value of collateralised obligations.

Example 5.2.3A

Effect of a decline in the fair value of collateral

On 1 January 20X1, Company B issues CU100 million of bonds collateralised by a portion of its aircraft fleet. On 30 September 20X3, there has been a substantial decline in the fair value of the aircraft that serve as collateral for the bonds. Assume that Company B's credit standing remains unchanged and all other stated terms of the bonds represent current market conditions for the remaining term of the obligation.

When measuring the fair value of the bonds at 30 September 20X3, Company B must do so from the perspective of a market participant that holds the bonds as an asset (i.e. a bondholder) – see **5.1.1**. [IFRS 13:37] A market participant would reflect the reduced level of collateral in the price at which a transfer of the bond would take place.

Company B determines that the hypothetical market participant would be willing to transfer the liability for only CU80 million. In other words, the fair value of the bonds has decreased by CU20 million due to the decline in value of the collateral even though Company B's credit standing remains unchanged.

Example 5.2.3B

Effect of a decline in the borrower's credit standing

Assume the same facts as in **example 5.2.3A** except that, at 30 September 20X3, the fair value of the aircraft pledged as collateral remains unchanged. Instead, the credit standing of Company B has declined from AAA to AA-.

When measuring the fair value of the bonds at 30 September 20X3, Company B is required to consider the effect of the decline in its credit standing but also the fact that the fair value of the collateral has not changed.

Company B observes that the wider credit spread for uncollateralised AA-corporate bonds suggests that the fair value of the bonds has declined by 10 per cent (i.e. to CU90 million). However, because the fair value of the collateral has not changed, the note remains well collateralised. Consequently, the fair value of the note may not have declined by as much as 10 per cent. Company B determines that the increase in non-performance risk arising from the decline in its own credit standing is partially offset by the collateral. Based on credit spreads observed for similar, collateralised bonds, Company B concludes that the fair value of the notes has decreased by CU7 million to CU93 million.

5.3 Restriction preventing the transfer of a liability or an entity's own equity instrument

When measuring the fair value of a liability or an entity's own equity instrument, no separate input or adjustment to other inputs should be included to reflect the existence of a restriction that prevents the transfer of the item. The effect of a restriction that prevents the transfer of a liability is either implicitly or explicitly included in the other inputs to the fair value measurement. [IFRS 13:45]

For example, at the transaction date for a liability, both the creditor and the obligor accepted the transaction price for the liability with full knowledge that the obligation includes a restriction that prevents its transfer. As a result of the restriction being included in the transaction price, a separate input or an adjustment to an existing input is not required at the transaction date to reflect the effect of the restriction on transfer. Similarly, a separate input or an adjustment to an existing input is not required at subsequent measurement dates to reflect the effect of the restriction on transfer. [IFRS 13:46]

5.4 Financial liability with a demand feature

The fair value of a financial liability with a demand feature (e.g. a demand deposit) is not less than the amount payable on demand, discounted from the first date that the amount could be required to be paid. [IFRS 13:47]

6 Measuring the fair value of financial assets and financial liabilities with offsetting positions in market risks or counterparty credit risk

An entity that holds a group of financial assets and financial liabilities is exposed to market risks (as defined in IFRS 7) and to the credit risk (as defined in IFRS 7) of each of the counterparties. If the entity manages that group of financial assets and financial liabilities on the basis of its net exposure to either market risks or credit risk, the entity is permitted to apply an exception to the general requirements of IFRS 13 for measuring fair value.

The exception permits an entity to measure the fair value of a group of financial assets and financial liabilities on the basis of the price that would be received to sell a net long position (i.e. an asset) for a particular risk exposure or to transfer a net short position (i.e. a liability) for a particular risk exposure in an orderly transaction between market participants at the measurement date under current market conditions. This fair value measure for the group of financial assets and financial liabilities should be consistent with how market participants would price the net risk exposure at the measurement date. [IFRS 13:48] This exception only applies to financial assets, financial liabilities and other contracts within the scope of IAS 39. [IFRS 13:52]

In December 2013 the IASB issued *Annual Improvements to IFRSs 2011–2013* Cycle that amended IFRS 13:52 to clarify that the portfolio exception applies to all contracts within the scope of IAS 39 regardless of whether they meet the definitions of financial assets or financial liabilities as defined in IAS 32. The clarification was in response to questions raised about whether the scope included contracts that are accounted for as if they were financial instruments, but that do not meet the definitions of financial assets or financial liabilities in IAS 32, such as contracts to buy or sell a non-financial item that can be settled net in cash or another financial instrument, or by exchanging financial instruments, as if the contracts were financial instruments.

An entity shall apply that amendment for annual periods beginning on or after 1 July 2014. An entity shall apply that amendment prospectively from the beginning of the annual period in which IFRS 13 was initially applied. Earlier application is permitted. If an entity applies that amendment for an earlier period it shall disclose that fact. [IFRS 13:C4]

An entity is permitted to apply the measurement exception in IFRS 13:48 to a portfolio that contains *only* financial assets (as opposed to a group of financial assets and financial liabilities) provided that the financial instruments have offsetting positions in market risks or counterparty credit risk and that the detailed conditions in IFRS 13:49 (see below) are met.

An example of a portfolio containing only financial assets is a portfolio of bonds measured at fair value and purchased credit default swaps also measured at fair value. The credit default swaps may provide an offset to the credit risk associated with the specific bonds.

An entity is permitted to use this exception only if the entity does all of the following:

[IFRS 13:49]

- it manages the group of financial assets and financial liabilities on the basis of the entity's net exposure to a particular market risk (or risks) or to the credit risk of a particular counterparty in accordance with the entity's documented risk management or investment strategy;
- it provides information on that basis about the group of financial assets and financial liabilities to the entity's key management personnel, as defined in IAS 24 *Related Party Disclosures*; and
- it is required or has elected to measure those financial assets and financial liabilities at fair value in the statement of financial position at the end of each reporting period.

This exception does not apply for financial statement presentation. When the basis for the presentation of financial instruments in the statement of financial position differs from the group basis for the measurement of financial instruments (e.g. if IAS 32 does not require the group of financial instruments to be presented on a net basis) an entity may need to allocate the portfolio-level adjustments to the individual instruments that make up the group. That allocation should be performed on a reasonable and consistent basis using a methodology appropriate in the circumstances. [IFRS 13:50]

A common example of an adjustment made at the portfolio level as contemplated in IFRS 13:48 is a credit valuation adjustment (CVA). An entity might incorporate the effect of exposure to a particular counterparty's credit risk by netting its derivative asset and liability contracts with a given counterparty in accordance with a master netting arrangement and then calculate a CVA on the basis of the net position with the counterparty.

Another example of a portfolio-level adjustment is a 'mid-to-bid' or 'mid-to-ask' adjustment. A derivatives dealer might initially compute the value of a portfolio of both its long (buy) and short (sell) derivative positions with the same underlying risk using the mid-point in the bid-ask spread. The derivatives dealer would then make a 'mid-to-bid' or 'mid-to-ask' adjustment at the portfolio level effectively to move the net open position of the portfolio to the bid or ask price depending on whether the portfolio is net long or net short by period.

The question arises as to how should an entity allocate a portfolio-level adjustment to the individual financial assets and financial liabilities in the portfolio.

IFRS 13:50 requires that an entity should allocate a portfolio-level adjustment to the individual financial assets and financial liabilities in the portfolio on a reasonable and consistent basis using a methodology appropriate in the circumstances.

The following table illustrates one approach to allocating a CVA to a group of derivative contracts under a master netting arrangement with a single counterparty.

	Asset/(Liability) in CU	**Hierarchy level (prior to allocation of CVA)**
Contract A	100	2
Contract B	200	3
Contract C	(175)	3
Net position before CVA	125	Not applicable
Credit valuation adjustment	(10)	See discussion below
Fair value of portfolio	115	Not applicable

The unit of account, in this example, is each individual derivative contract in its entirety. Accordingly, the CU10 CVA must be allocated to the units of account within the portfolio. For example, the entity might allocate the CU10 CVA on the basis of the relative fair value of the asset positions (Contracts A and B in the example above). The resulting fair value of Contract A would be CU97 (i.e. CU100 less 100/300 x CU10). The resulting fair value of Contract B would be CU193 (i.e. CU200 less 200/300 x CU10). Other approaches may also be appropriate depending on the circumstances.

When a portfolio-level adjustment is allocated to individual assets and/or liabilities in the circumstances described, this will affect the classification of the assets and/or liabilities within IFRS 13's fair value hierarchy (see **section 10**). An allocated portfolio adjustment is an input to the measurement of the fair value of the asset or liability. If such an input is not based on observable data and has a significant effect on the measurement of the fair value of an individual asset or liability, the fair value measurement is categorised in Level 3 of the fair value hierarchy.

Assume in the example above that, before the allocation of the CVA, the inputs used in determining the fair value of Contract A were based on observable market data. However, if the effect of the counterparty's credit risk is not considered observable market data, the allocated amount of CVA is a Level 3 input. In determining the classification of Contract A within the hierarchy, the entity must determine whether the amount of CVA allocated to Contract A is significant to the measurement of Contract A in its entirety (see **10.3.3.2** for discussion). Because the CVA is unobservable, if the allocated portion of the CVA for Contract A is considered significant, then Contract A would be classified in Level 3 in its entirety.

During the IASB and FASB's deliberations it was noted that some respondents requested additional guidance for allocating the bid-ask and credit adjustments to the individual assets and liabilities that make up the group of financial assets and financial liabilities. The Boards noted that although any allocation method is inherently subjective, it was concluded that a quantitative allocation would be appropriate if it was reasonable and consistently applied. Therefore, the Boards decided not to require a particular method of allocation. [IFRS 13:BC131]

The application of this exception is an accounting policy choice in accordance with IAS 8 and, when selected, should be applied consistently from period to period (including the entity's policy for allocating any portfolio adjustments). [IFRS 13:51]

In May 2013 the Interpretations Committee received a request to clarify the interaction between the use of Level 1 inputs and the portfolio exception set out in IFRS 13. The portfolio exception in IFRS 13 permits an entity to measure its net exposure to either market risks or credit risk arising from a group of financial assets and financial liabilities in specified circumstances. The portfolio exception was intended to align the valuation of financial instruments for financial reporting with an entity's internal risk management practices. In particular, the issue that was discussed by the Interpretations Committee was whether an entity is:

(a) permitted to apply the portfolio exception in IFRS 13 to measure the resulting net risk exposure of a portfolio made up solely with identical Level 1 instruments; or

(b) required to measure the financial assets and the financial liabilities of such a portfolio on an individual basis, using the corresponding Level 1 prices for each financial instrument.

In its discussions, the Interpretations Committee observed that, in relation to (a) above, the main question that needs to be addressed is whether an entity:

(a) would be required to measure such a net risk exposure on the basis of the Level 1 prices for the individual instruments that comprise that net risk exposure; or

(b) would be allowed to consider the net risk exposure as a whole and, consequently, consider adjusting it with any appropriate premiums or discounts.

The Interpretations Committee noted that there was insufficient guidance in the Standard for it to be able to answer this question and so it decided that this issue needs to be considered by the IASB. Accordingly it asked the staff to present the Interpretations Committee's concerns to the IASB.

The IASB also noted that this issue has similarities with the issue of the interaction between the use of Level 1 inputs and the unit of account that arises when measuring the fair value of investments in subsidiaries, joint ventures and associates (discussed above). Consequently, the IASB included this issue in Exposure Draft ED/2014/4 *Measuring Quoted Investments in Subsidiaries, Joint Ventures and Associates at Fair Value* issued in September 2014. In the ED the IASB included an illustrative example to illustrate the application of IFRS 13:48 to a group of financial assets and financial liabilities whose market risks are substantially the same and whose fair value measurement is categorised within Level 1 of the fair value hierarchy.

As part of the IASB's redeliberations following the publication of the ED, the illustrative example was discussed by the IASB in April 2015 when it decided that the example appropriately illustrates the application of IFRS 13:48. That is, if an entity elects to use the exception in IFRS 13:48, the appropriate fair value measurement of the net risk exposure arising from a group of financial assets and financial liabilities whose market risks are substantially the same, and whose fair value measurement is categorised within Level 1 of the fair value hierarchy, would be determined by multiplying the financial instruments included in the resulting net position by the corresponding unadjusted Level 1 price.

The IASB noted that the proposed illustrative example to IFRS 13 is non-authoritative, and the comments received did not reveal significant diversity in practice. Accordingly, the IASB concluded that it was unnecessary to publish the proposed illustrative example in IFRS 13 as a separate document. Therefore the illustrative example is not due to be published by the IASB.

The example below is taken from the IASB staff paper that was discussed by the IASB in April 2015 (agenda reference 6). It is based on the illustrative example from the ED but also includes changes proposed by the IASB staff following feedback received on the ED.

Example 6

Measuring the fair value of a portfolio of Level 1 financial assets and financial liabilities with offsetting risk positions

Entity A holds a group of financial assets and financial liabilities consisting of a long position of 10,000 financial assets and a short position of 9,500 financial liabilities whose market risks are substantially the same. Entity A manages that group of financial assets and financial liabilities on the basis of its net exposure to market risks. The fair value measurement of all financial instruments in the group is categorised within Level 1 of the fair value hierarchy.

The bid-ask spread is CU98-CU102, with the mid-price being CU100. The most representative bid price is CU99 and the most representative ask price is CU101.

Entity A applies the exception in IFRS 13:48 that permits Entity A to measure the fair value of the group of financial assets and financial liabilities on the basis of the price that would be received to sell, in this particular case, a net long position (i.e. an asset) for the exposure to market risks in an orderly transaction between market participants at the measurement date under current market conditions.

Since the market risks arising from the financial instruments are substantially the same, the measurement of the net exposure to market risks arising from the group of financial assets and financial liabilities coincides with the measurement of the net long position (500 financial assets). Consequently, Entity A measures the group of financial assets and financial liabilities on the basis of the price that it would receive if it would exit its outstanding net exposure to market risks as follows:

	Quantity held (Q)	Level 1 price (CU) (P)	(CU) P × Q
Net exposure to market risks, which in this case coincides with the measurement of the net long position	500	99	49,500

Entity A would also have achieved the same measurement of CU49,500 by measuring the net exposure to market risks at the mid-price (i.e. CU100 × 500 = CU50,000) adjusted by a bid-offer reserve (CU1 × 500 = CU500).

Since the basis for the presentation of the financial instruments in the statement of financial position differs from the basis for their measurement, Entity A subsequently allocates the portfolio-level adjustments (i.e. CU49,500) to the individual (10,000) financial assets and (9,500) financial liabilities. In accordance with IFRS 13:50 & 51, Entity A performs this allocation on a reasonable basis that is consistent with previous allocations of that nature using a methodology appropriate to the circumstances.

6.1 Exposure to market risks

Consistent with the normal fair value measurement requirements, when measuring the fair value of a group of assets and liabilities based on the net exposure to one or more market risks, IFRS 13 requires an entity to apply the price within the bid-ask spread that is most representative of fair value in the circumstances to the entity's net exposure to those market risks. [IFRS 13:53]

In order to measure a group of financial assets and financial liabilities on a net basis for a particular market risk, it is necessary for that market risk within that group of financial assets and financial liabilities to be substantially the same. For example, an entity would not combine the interest rate risk associated with a financial asset with the commodity price risk associated with a financial liability because doing so would not mitigate the entity's exposure to interest rate risk or commodity price risk. [IFRS 13:54]

In some cases, the market risk parameters will not be identical due to basis differences. In those cases the basis risk should be taken into account in the fair value measurement of the financial assets and financial liabilities within the group. [IFRS 13:54]

Similarly, the term of the entity's exposure to market risk arising from the financial assets and financial liabilities should be substantially the same. For example, an entity that uses a 12-month futures contract against the cash flows associated with 12 months' worth of interest rate risk exposure on a five-year financial instrument within a group made up of only those financial assets and financial liabilities measures the fair value of the exposure to 12-month interest rate risk on a net basis and the remaining interest rate risk exposure (i.e. Years 2-5) on a gross basis. [IFRS 13:55]

6.2 Exposure to the credit risk of a particular counterparty

When applying the fair value measurement exception described in **section 6** for financial instruments with the same counterparty, the entity should include the effect of the entity's net exposure to the credit risk of that counterparty or the counterparty's net exposure to the credit risk of the entity in the fair value measurement when market participants would take into account any existing arrangements that mitigate credit risk exposure (e.g. a master netting agreement with the counterparty or an agreement that requires the exchange of collateral on the basis of each party's net exposure to the credit risk of the other party) in the event of default. The fair value measurement should reflect market participant expectations about the likelihood that such an arrangement would be legally enforceable in the event of default. [IFRS 13:56]

Reflecting in the fair value measurement of the portfolio of items the net credit risk exposure with the same counterparty is appropriate where the two parties have an agreement that requires that in the case of default the reporting entity is only required to pay or receive the net amount of the various contracts that are owed to and due from the counterparty. Applying the fair value measurement exception in this case reduces the extent of credit risk included in the measurement of the portfolio of items relative to including credit risk in the measurement of each of the individual items and summing the assets and liabilities together.

Netting the credit risk exposure with the counterparty and reflecting only the credit risk associated with the net open credit risk position is often referred to as a CVA (credit valuation adjustment, or a 'positive CVA') in the case where the reporting entity has a net credit exposure to the counterparty, i.e. where the reporting entity is net owed amounts by the counterparty; or as a DVA (debit valuation adjustment, or a 'negative CVA') in the case where the counterparty has a net credit exposure to the reporting entity, i.e. where the reporting entity owes amounts to the counterparty.

7 Fair value measurement at initial recognition

7.1 Potential for difference between the transaction price and fair value at initial recognition

IAS 39:43 requires that all financial assets and financial liabilities, except certain trade receivables, should be recognised initially on the basis of 'fair value'. The exception applies to trade receivables that do not have a significant financing component (determined in accordance with IFRS 15 *Revenue from Contracts with Customers*) that are not initially measured at fair value, rather they are initially measured at their transaction price.

If the asset has been acquired, or the liability assumed, in a market transaction, it might be assumed that the transaction price (i.e. the price paid to acquire an asset or received to assume a liability) can be taken to be the fair value of the asset or the liability. However, the price paid to acquire an asset, or received to assume a liability, is an *entry* price and, consequently, it is not necessarily the same as the fair value of the asset or liability for IFRS 13 purposes (which is an *exit* price – see **section 3**). The Standard notes that entities do not necessarily sell assets at the prices paid to acquire them; nor do they necessarily transfer liabilities at the prices received to assume them. [IFRS 13:57]

7.2 Indicators that the transaction price differs from fair value at initial recognition

When determining whether the fair value at initial recognition equals the transaction price, an entity should take into account factors specific to the transaction and to the asset and liability. [IFRS 13:59]

In many cases the transaction price and the fair value will be equal (e.g. when the transaction date is the same as the measurement date and the asset is acquired in the market in which the asset would be sold). [IFRS 13:58] However, when the amounts are not equal, the asset or liability should be measured at fair value and the difference between the transaction price and fair value (generally referred to as a 'day 1 gain or loss', 'day 1 profit or loss' or as 'day 1 p&l') is required to be recognised as a gain or loss in profit or loss unless the relevant IFRS specifies otherwise. [IFRS 13:60] See **section 7.3** for the appropriate treatment of 'day 1 p&l' under IAS 39.

When determining whether the fair value at initial recognition equals the transaction price, an entity should take into account factors specific to the transaction and to the asset and liability. [IFRS 13:59]

IFRS 13:B4 lists a number of factors which may suggest that the transaction price is not the fair value of the asset or liability at initial recognition.

The following table repeats the factors listed in IFRS 13:B4 and provides examples for each. Note that this list of indicators is not exhaustive, and other factors may exist that should be considered in evaluating whether a transaction price represents fair value (see IFRS 13:BC133).

Factor (IFRS 13:B4)	**Example**
The transaction is between related parties, although the price in a related party transaction may be used as an input into a fair value measurement if the reporting entity has evidence that the transaction was entered into at market terms.	An entity purchases a portfolio of troubled loans from an unconsolidated investee. The parties meet the definition of related parties under IAS 24 *Related Party Disclosures*. The fact that the parties are related may indicate that the transaction price does not reflect fair value. However, this alone would not be determinative. Evidence that the transaction was entered into at market terms may include: • the appointment of third parties to negotiate or measure fair value; or • the terms of the transaction are consistent with available market data for similar transactions between unrelated parties; or • there is no evidence that one of the parties to the transaction is under duress (see the next factor).
The transaction takes place under duress or the seller is forced to accept the price in the transaction (e.g. if the seller is experiencing financial difficulty).	A hedge fund must sell all of its non-marketable assets in response to a spike in redemptions that may lead to a liquidity crisis. A liquidity crisis may be an indicator of financial difficulty. The factors in IFRS 13:B43 indicating that a transaction is not orderly (see **section 9.6**) may also indicate that the transaction price does not represent fair value.

Factor (IFRS 13:B4)	Example
The unit of account represented by the transaction price is different from the unit of account for the asset or liability measured at fair value. For example, this might be the case if the asset or liability measured at fair value is only one of the elements in the transaction (e.g. in a business combination), if the transaction includes unstated rights and privileges that are measured separately in accordance with another IFRS, or if the transaction price includes transaction costs.	IFRS 13:14 requires that the unit of account for an asset or a liability should be determined in accordance with the IFRS that requires or permits the fair value measurement, except as provided in IFRS 13 (see **3.2.1**). The following example illustrates a scenario in which the unit of account for the asset is different from the unit of account represented by the transaction price. On 30 June 20X1, Company A acquires a 3 per cent equity interest (3 million shares) in Company B from an independent third party. Quoted prices in an active market are available for Company B's shares. Company A pays CU100 million for the entire 3 per cent equity interest (the transaction price is determined based on a negotiated arm's length price for the entire 3 per cent equity interest). The quoted price for Company B's shares on 30 June 20X1 is CU36 per share. Company A needs to identify the unit of account in order to measure the fair value of the 3 per cent equity interest on initial recognition. In identifying the unit of account for fair value measurement purposes, IAS 39 is the applicable Standard. IFRS 13:BC47 states, in part, that "[i]n IAS 39 and IAS 39 the unit of account is generally an individual financial instrument". This guidance is also consistent with the guidance set out in IFRS 13:80 which states that "[i]f an entity holds a position in a single asset… and the asset… is traded in an active market, the fair value of the asset… shall be measured within Level 1 as the product of the quoted price for the individual asset… and the quantity held by the entity" Therefore, notwithstanding the fact that Company A paid a transaction price of CU100 million for the entire 3 million shares, the unit of account in this example is each individual share, not the entire 3 per cent equity interest acquired. Specifically, the fair value of the 3 per cent equity interest in Company B is measured as the product of the quoted price for each individual share and the quantity held ('P x Q') (i.e. CU108 million = 3 million shares x CU36 per share).

Factor (IFRS 13:B4)	Example
The market in which the transaction takes place is different from the principal market (or most advantageous market). For example, those markets might be different if the entity is a dealer that enters into transactions with customers in the retail market, but the principal (or most advantageous) market for the exit transaction is with other dealers in the dealer market.	*Entity A (a retail counterparty) enters into an interest rate swap in a retail market with Entity B (a dealer) for no initial consideration (i.e. the transaction price is zero). Entity A can access only the retail market. Entity B can access both the retail market (i.e. with retail counterparties) and the dealer market (i.e. with dealer counterparties). From the perspective of Entity A, the fair value at initial recognition is zero because Entity A does not have access to the dealer market. From Entity B's perspective, the transaction price of the interest rate swap (i.e. zero) does not represent fair value at initial recognition if prices observed or market participant assumptions in the dealer market (i.e. Entity B's principal market) indicate that fair value is something other than zero. Note: This final scenario is a summary of Example 7 from the illustrative examples accompanying IFRS 13 (see IFRS 13:IE24 - IE26).

7.3 Day 1 profit or loss

When there is a difference between the fair value at initial recognition and the transaction price, IFRS 13:60 states that any resulting gain or loss should be recognised in profit or loss unless another IFRS specifies otherwise.

With respect to financial instruments, an entity should understand the reason for any difference between the fair value at initial recognition and the transaction price. This difference may represent consideration for goods or services between the two entities or a capital contribution or deemed distribution in circumstances when one party is acting in its capacity as an owner. Other IFRSs will determine how such amounts are accounted for.

Example 7.3A

Interest-free loan (1)

On 1 January 20X0, Parent A grants a non-callable interest-free loan of CU100 to a wholly-owned subsidiary, Subsidiary B. The loan is repayable on 31 December 20X0 and is not callable prior to that date by Parent A. The market rate of interest for a loan to the subsidiary would be 8 per cent. Consideration paid is made up as follows:

(i) CU92.59 is the fair value of the financial asset (i.e. CU100/1.08).

(ii) CU7.41 is a capital contribution. This amount represents the fair value of Parent A's providing Subsidiary B with interest-free finance. The amount should be recognised by Subsidiary B directly in equity as a capital contribution because it does not meet the definition of income under paragraph 4.25 of the *Conceptual Framework for Financial Reporting*.

Example 7.3B

Interest-free loan (2)

On 1 January 20X0, Subsidiary C grants a non-callable interest-free loan of CU100 to its parent, Parent A. The loan is repayable on 31 December 20X0 and is not callable prior to that date by Subsidiary C. The market rate of interest for a loan to Parent A would be 8 per cent. Consideration paid is made up as follows:

(i) CU92.59 is the fair value of the financial asset (i.e. CU100/1.08).

(ii) CU7.41 is in substance a distribution from Subsidiary C to Parent A. This amount represents the fair value of the Subsidiary C's providing its parent with interest-free finance. The amount should be recognised by Subsidiary C directly in equity as a deemed distribution because it does not meet the definition of an expense under paragraph 4.25 of the *Conceptual Framework for Financial Reporting*.

When the difference is not consideration for goods or services, or a capital contribution or deemed distribution, IAS 39 sets out specific guidance as to whether that difference (often referred to as 'day 1 p&l') may be recognised in profit or loss at initial recognition.

If, in an arm's length transaction, the transaction price differs from fair value at initial recognition, the appropriate accounting for the difference depends on how fair value is determined in those circumstances. If the fair value is evidenced by a quoted price in an active market for an identical asset or liability (i.e. a Level 1 input) (see **10.2.1**) or based on a valuation technique that uses only data from observable markets, then the difference is recognised as a gain or loss on initial recognition (i.e. day 1 profit or loss). In all other cases, the fair value at initial recognition is adjusted to bring it in line with the transaction price. Consequently, the 'day 1 p&l' is deferred by including it in the initial carrying amount of the asset or liability. After initial recognition, the entity shall recognise that deferred difference as a gain or loss only to the extent that it arises from a change in a factor (including time) that market participants would take into account when pricing the asset or liability. [IAS 39:AG76(b)]

Example 7.3C

Day 1 p&l (1)

Bank A sells a 30-year cash-settled forward-sale contract over a commodity to Entity B.

Forward prices for the specific commodity are freely quoted in the market for 10, 15, and 20 year periods. Bank A uses an extrapolation technique and its proprietary pricing system to estimate the 30-year forward rate and incorporates an additional premium on top of this internal price. Some of the premium may be received in cash at inception and some may be included in the contracted price of the forward contract.

The valuation technique uses both the available forward prices and Bank A's estimates of the commodity prices between years 20 and 30. Because some of the inputs are entity-specific and not observable, a day 1 profit cannot be recognised.

Example 7.3D

Day 1 p&l (2)

Bank X issues credit-linked notes to institutional investors.

The credit-linked notes are debt instruments with an interest rate higher than normal bonds issued by Bank X because the performance of the notes is linked to the performance of a basket of underlying corporate bonds. The terms require that if a corporate bond in the basket defaults, then the notional principal will be reset on the next payment date to reflect the outstanding value of the remaining bonds in the basket. This term is commonly referred to as 'first-to-default', because it is the first bond in the basket that defaults that results in the early repayment of the notes at an amount less than was originally invested by the holder.

Bank X does not actually hold the corporate bonds that the credit-linked notes are linked to. Instead Bank X purchases a large number of credit default options over the individual corporate bonds. These purchased options serve as an economic hedge in case any of the referenced credits default. The remaining proceeds from issuing the credit-linked notes are invested in high quality government debt.

If the credit-linked notes are not traded in an active market, then Bank X must use a valuation technique to measure the financial liability. At inception the proceeds received from the issuance of the notes are equal to their fair value.

It would not be possible to recognise an up-front profit on initial recognition of the credit-linked notes, even if the sum paid to purchase the government bonds and the credit options is less than the proceeds from the notes if:

- there are no other observable current market transactions in the same credit-linked notes with the same terms over the same portfolio of corporate credits; or
- if the valuation of the credit-linked notes includes non-observable market data, e.g. default correlation data between the different corporate credits where this data is not sourced from observable markets.

The deferred gain or loss should be released to profit or loss such that it reaches a value of zero at the time when the entire contract can be valued using active market quotes or verifiable objective market information. IAS 39:BC222(v)(ii) notes that straight-line amortisation may be an appropriate method in some cases, but it will not be appropriate in others. In circumstances when the item acts in a non-linear fashion (e.g. option-based contracts), non-linear amortisation may be appropriate. An entity should determine a policy for amortisation. The following policies may be appropriate:

(i) calibrate unobservable inputs to the transaction price and recognise the deferred gain or loss as the best estimates of those unobservable inputs change based on observable information; or

(ii) release the day 1 gain or loss in a reasonable fashion based on the facts and circumstances.

Example 7.3E

Day 1 p&l (3)

Entity A writes a call option over a specified financial asset to Entity B and receives a premium from Entity B. The option can be exercised by Entity B at any time during the instrument's life. The written call option meets the definition of a derivative and is classified by Entity A as at FVTPL. Entity A uses its proprietary valuation model to fair value the written option because the instrument is not traded in an active market. The model uses observable inputs to the extent possible but also includes significant unobservable inputs. Entity A is not permitted to recognise an up-front gain or loss at initial recognition and measures the derivative at the transaction price. Entity A should recognise in profit or loss changes in the fair value of the derivative that have occurred subsequent to initial recognition.

To illustrate, Entity A received CU500 for the written call option and the entity's proprietary model valued the instrument at CU300. Entity A initially recognises a derivative liability at CU500 equivalent to the consideration received. At the next measurement date, using the same proprietary model, the fair value of the instrument has fallen by CU100 and this fair value gain is recognised in profit or loss.

Entity A must determine an accounting policy that is consistent with IAS 39:AG76A(b) for subsequent recognition of the initial difference of CU200 (CU500 - CU300) in profit or loss. Any amounts not recognised in profit or loss before the date of exercise or maturity will be recognised in profit or loss on that date.

8 Valuation techniques

8.1 Valuation techniques required to maximise the use of observable inputs

When the price for an asset or a liability cannot be observed directly, it must be estimated using a valuation technique. When used in the context of fair value measurement, 'valuation technique' is a generic term and its application is not limited to complex fair valuation models. For example, valuing an asset or a liability using quoted prices in an active market for identical assets and liabilities is a valuation technique. In other cases, when prices cannot be observed directly and more judgement is required, it will be appropriate to use more complex valuation techniques.

An entity is required to use valuation techniques that are appropriate in the circumstances and for which sufficient data are available to measure fair value, maximising the use of relevant observable inputs and minimising the use of unobservable inputs. [IFRS 13:61]

Observable inputs are defined as "[i]nputs that are developed using market data, such as publicly available information about actual events or transactions, and that reflect the assumptions that market participants would use when pricing the asset or liability". [IFRS 13:Appendix A]

Unobservable inputs are defined as "[i]nputs for which market data are not available and that are developed using the best information available about the assumptions that market participants would use when pricing the asset or liability". [IFRS 13:Appendix A]

8.2 Widely used valuation techniques

IFRS 13 refers to three widely used valuation techniques:

[IFRS 13:62]

- the market approach (see **section 8.4**);
- the cost approach (sometimes referred to as 'replacement cost') (see **section 8.5**); and
- the income approach (see **section 8.6**).

Any valuation technique used to estimate fair value should be consistent with one or more of the above approaches. [IFRS 13:62]

The two common valuation techniques used for financial instruments are the market approach and the income approach.

8.3 Selecting an appropriate valuation technique

IFRS 13 does not set out a hierarchy of valuation techniques; this is because particular valuation techniques might be more appropriate in some circumstances than in others. [IFRS 13:BC142]

Each valuation technique has its own merits and may or may not be suitable for measuring the fair value of a specified item or items in the given circumstances. In practice, different valuation techniques can give rise to different estimates of fair value and, therefore, it is important to select the most appropriate methodology for the particular circumstances.

Choosing a valuation technique requires judgement and involves the selection of a method, formulae and assumptions. The reliability of a fair value measurement derived from a valuation technique is dependent on both the reliability of the valuation technique and the reliability of the inputs used. Consequently, when selecting a valuation technique, it will be important to consider the availability of reliable inputs for that valuation (see **section 9**). In addition to selecting a technique that maximises the use of relevant observable inputs and minimises the use of unobservable inputs, an entity must also ensure that the best possible evidence is used to support unobservable inputs.

In assessing the appropriateness of each valuation technique, an entity should also evaluate all available inputs significant to the valuation technique and compare the technique with other valuation techniques. For example, in a given situation, an entity may conclude that it is appropriate to use a market approach rather than an income approach because the market approach uses superior market information as inputs.

An entity should consider using a valuation specialist.

See **section 8.7** for a discussion of when it is appropriate to use multiple valuation techniques.

Example 8.3 illustrates how an entity might approach the selection of a valuation technique (or techniques) for unquoted equity securities in specified circumstances.

Example 8.3

Selecting an appropriate valuation technique or techniques for unquoted equity securities

Company A holds equity investments in the following two entities – Company B and Company C. Company A measures these investments at fair value on a recurring basis.

- Company B is a clothing retailer that operates in the niche market of the baby clothing industry. Quoted prices are not available for Company B's shares. Most of Company B's competitors are either privately held or are subsidiaries of larger publicly traded clothing retailers. Company B is similar to two other organisations, whose shares are thinly traded in an observable market.
- Company C is a retailer that operates in the competitive consumer electronics industry. Although quoted prices are not available for Company C's shares, Company C is comparable to many entities whose shares are actively traded.

Because the prices of Company B's and Company C's shares cannot be observed directly, Company A must measure the fair value of these investments using a valuation technique (or techniques).

Company A is considering a market approach, an income approach or a combination of these two approaches. The market approach and the income approach are common valuation techniques for equity investments that are not publicly traded. Under the market approach, entities use prices and other relevant information generated by market transactions involving identical or comparable securities. Under the income approach, future amounts are converted into a single present amount (e.g. discounted cash flows model). Company A is not considering the cost approach to value its equity securities because it is not considered relevant. (See **sections 8.4 - 8.6** for detailed descriptions of these valuation techniques. See also **section 8.7** for a discussion of when it is appropriate to use multiple valuation techniques.)

Company A should select the valuation technique (or techniques) that is (are) appropriate in the circumstances and for which sufficient data are available to measure fair value, maximising the use of relevant observable inputs and minimising the use of unobservable inputs.

Investment in Company B

Using a market approach, the fair value measurement of Company A's investment in Company B would involve an analysis of market prices and other relevant information for the two similar organisations that are traded (albeit thinly) in an observable market. It is likely that the observable market data would need to be adjusted to reflect differences between Company B and the two similar organisations that are traded. For example, Company A might consider that market participants would incorporate significant entity-specific adjustments into the valuation of Company B's shares (e.g. adjustments to reflect the relative illiquidity of Company B's shares, profitability, net assets, unrecognised assets such as internally generated intangible assets, and differences in business model between Company B and the two traded organisations). These adjustments would be made using Company A's own assumptions. Consequently, in such circumstances, a market approach would rely on unobservable inputs that are significant to the fair value measurement.

Using an income approach based on discounted cash flows, the fair value measurement of Company A's investment in Company B would also be based on significant entity-specific assumptions in forecasting Company B's future cash flows. As a result, the income approach would also rely on unobservable inputs that are significant to the fair value measurement.

Based on the above information, it is likely that Company A would conclude that both the market approach and the income approach are appropriate techniques for measuring the fair value of its investment in Company B. In making its selection, Company A would consider the reliability of the evidence supporting the inputs used in each of the valuation techniques. Provided that relevant and reliable inputs are available, and there are no other factors indicating that one of the approaches is superior, it would seem appropriate to use a combination of both approaches, even if one approach is used only to corroborate the results of the other.

Investment in Company C

When selecting an appropriate approach to measure the fair value of its investment in Company C, Company A should perform an analysis similar to that outlined above.

Using a market approach, it is more likely that market participants would incorporate fewer unobservable adjustments into the valuation of Company C's shares because of the large number of comparable traded entities and the high trading volume of the shares of those comparable entities. However, Company A should consider whether to make an adjustment for illiquidity to reflect the fact that Company C's shares are unquoted whereas those of comparable entities in the same sector are listed and actively traded.

Using an income approach based on discounted cash flows, the fair value measurement of Company A's investment in Company C would be based on forecasted future cash flows. This forecast would include projections of future profitability and, therefore, would be likely to include entity-specific assumptions that are not observable.

As a result, it is likely that Company A would conclude that it is appropriate to measure the fair value of its investment in Company C using the market approach because it uses more observable inputs (i.e. in terms of the hierarchy described in **section 10**, 'Level 2' inputs vs. 'Level 3' inputs) with a significant effect.

8.4 Market approach

The 'market approach' is defined as "[a] valuation technique that uses prices and other relevant information generated by market transactions involving identical or comparable (i.e. similar) assets, liabilities or a group of assets and liabilities, such as a business". [IFRS 13:Appendix A]

A quoted price for an identical asset or liability in an active market that the entity can access at the measurement date provides the most reliable evidence of fair value. [IFRS 13:77] Quoted prices for the identical asset or liability are regarded as Level 1 inputs within the fair value hierarchy (see **10.2.1**). When a quoted price exists for an identical asset or liability, it should be used without adjustment, except in the circumstances described at **10.2.1**. [IFRS 13:77] When a quoted price for an asset or a liability exists in multiple active markets, it will be necessary to identify the market and price which represents fair value for the specific facts and circumstances.

Valuation techniques consistent with the market approach often use market multiples derived from a set of comparable assets or liabilities. A range of multiples may be derived, with a different multiple for each comparable asset or liability. The selection of the appropriate multiple within the range requires the exercise of judgement – with appropriate consideration of the qualitative and quantitative factors specific to the measurement. [IFRS 13:B6]

Valuation techniques consistent with the market approach include matrix pricing. Matrix pricing is a mathematical technique used principally to value some types of financial instruments, such as debt securities, without relying exclusively on quoted prices for the specific securities, but rather relying on the securities' relationship to other benchmark quoted securities. [IFRS 13:B7]

8.5 Cost approach

The 'cost approach' is defined as "[a] valuation technique that reflects the amount that would be required currently to replace the service capacity of an asset (often referred to as current replacement cost)". [IFRS 13:Appendix A] This method is often used to measure the fair value of tangible assets that are used in combination with other assets or with other assets and liabilities. [IFRS 13:B9]

The cost approach is not generally used when measuring the fair value of financial instruments. The cost approach considers the cost to replace the service capacity of an asset, a concept that is not relevant in the context of financial instruments.

8.6 Income approach

8.6.1 Income approach – general

The 'income approach' is defined as "[v]aluation techniques that convert future amounts (e.g. cash flows or income and expenses) to a single current (i.e. discounted) amount. The fair value measurement is determined on the basis of the value indicated by current market expectations about those future amounts". [IFRS 13:Appendix A]

Income approaches that are used for measuring the fair value of financial instruments include, for example:

[IFRS 13:B11]

- present value techniques (see below); and
- option pricing models, such as Black-Scholes-Merton formula or a binomial model (i.e. a lattice model), that incorporate present value techniques and reflect both the time value and the intrinsic value of an option.

IFRS 13 describes two types of present value techniques:

- the discount rate adjustment technique (see **8.6.4.2**) and
- the expected cash flow (expected present value) technique (see **8.6.4.3**).

IFRS 13 does not specifically require that one of these present value techniques be used. The most appropriate present value technique for the measurement of fair value in a particular scenario will depend on the facts and circumstances specific to the asset or liability being measured (e.g. whether prices for comparable assets or liabilities can be observed in the market) and the availability of sufficient data. [IFRS 13:B12]

8.6.2 Components of a present value measurement

Present value is a tool used to link future amounts (e.g. cash flows or values) to a present amount using a discount rate. A fair value measurement of an asset or a liability using a present value technique captures all of the following elements from the perspective of market participants at the measurement date:

[IFRS 13:B13]

- an estimate of future cash flows for the asset or liability being measured;
- expectations about possible variations in the amount and timing of the cash flows representing the uncertainty inherent in the cash flows;
- the time value of money, represented by the rate on risk-free monetary assets that have maturity dates or durations that coincide with the period covered by the cash flows and pose neither uncertainty in timing nor risk of default to the holder (i.e. a risk-free interest rate);
- the price for bearing the uncertainty inherent in the cash flows (i.e. a risk premium);

- other factors that market participants would take into account in the circumstances; and
- for a liability, the non-performance risk relating to that liability, including the obligor's own credit risk.

8.6.3 General principles underlying present value measurement

Present value techniques differ in how they capture the elements listed in **8.6.2**. However, all of the following general principles govern the application of any present value technique used to measure fair value.

[IFRS 13:B14]

- Cash flows and discount rates should reflect assumptions that market participants would use when pricing the asset or liability.
- Cash flows and discount rates should take into account only the factors attributable to the asset or liability being measured.
- To avoid double-counting or omitting the effects of risk factors, discount rates should reflect assumptions that are consistent with those inherent in the cash flows. For example, a discount rate that reflects the uncertainty in expectations about future defaults is appropriate if using contractual cash flows of a loan (i.e. a discount rate adjustment technique). That same rate should not be used if using expected (i.e. probability-weighted) cash flows (i.e. an expected present value technique) because the expected cash flows already reflect assumptions about the uncertainty in future defaults; instead, a discount rate that is commensurate with the risk inherent in the expected cash flows should be used.
- Assumptions about cash flows and discount rates should be internally consistent. For example, nominal cash flows, which include the effect of inflation, should be discounted at a rate that includes the effect of inflation. The nominal risk-free interest rate includes the effect of inflation. Real cash flows, which exclude the effect of inflation, should be discounted at a rate that excludes the effect of inflation. Similarly, after-tax cash flows should be discounted using an after-tax discount rate. Pre-tax cash flows should be discounted at a rate consistent with those cash flows.
- Care should be taken in determining a pre-tax discount rate by adjusting a post-tax rate. Because the tax consequences of cash flows may occur in different periods, the pre-tax rate of return is not always the post-tax rate of return grossed up by the standard rate of tax. See **8.4.2** in **chapter A10** of **Volume A** of this manual for further guidance on how to adjust a post-tax discount rate to arrive at a pre-tax discount rate. Discount rates should be consistent with the underlying economic factors of the currency in which the cash flows are denominated.

8.6.4 Risk and uncertainty

8.6.4.1 Risk and uncertainty – general

A fair value measurement using present value techniques is made under conditions of uncertainty because the cash flows used are estimates rather than known amounts. In many cases, both the amount and timing of the cash flows are uncertain. Even contractually fixed amounts, such as the payments on a loan, are uncertain if there is risk of default. [IFRS 13:B15]

Market participants generally seek compensation (i.e. a risk premium) for bearing the uncertainty inherent in the cash flows of an asset or a liability. A fair value measurement should include a risk premium reflecting the amount that market participants would demand as compensation for the uncertainty inherent in the cash flows. Otherwise, the measurement would not faithfully represent fair value. In some cases, determining the appropriate risk premium might be difficult. However, the degree of difficulty alone is not a sufficient reason to exclude a risk premium. [IFRS 13:B16]

Present value techniques differ in how they adjust for risk and in the type of cash flows they use. For example the discount rate adjustment technique described in **8.6.4.2** uses contractual, promised or most likely cash flows and a risk-adjusted discount rate. [IFRS 13:B17(a)]

Expected present value techniques incorporate the effects of risk and uncertainty in one of two ways. The calculation either uses risk-adjusted expected cash flows and a risk-free rate to discount them or uses expected cash flows that are not risk-adjusted and a discount rate adjusted to include the risk premium that market participants require (see **8.6.4.3**). That rate is different from the rate used in the discount rate adjustment technique described in **8.6.4.2**. [IFRS 13:B17(b) & (c)]

8.6.4.2 Discount rate adjustment technique

The discount rate adjustment technique uses a single set of cash flows from the range of possible estimated amounts, whether contractual or promised (as is the case for a bond) or most likely cash flows. In all cases, those cash flows are conditional upon the occurrence of specified events (e.g. contractual or promised cash flows for a bond are conditional on the event of no default by the debtor). The discount rate used in the discount rate adjustment technique is derived from observed rates of return for comparable assets or liabilities that are traded in the market. Accordingly, the contractual, promised or most likely cash flows are discounted at an observed or estimated market rate for such conditional cash flows (i.e. a market rate of return). [IFRS 13:B18]

The discount rate adjustment technique requires an analysis of market data for comparable assets or liabilities. Comparability is established by considering the nature of the cash flows (e.g. whether the cash flows are contractual or non-contractual and are likely to respond similarly to changes in economic conditions), as well as other factors (e.g. credit standing, collateral, duration, restrictive covenants and liquidity). Alternatively, if a single comparable asset or liability does not fairly reflect the risk inherent in the cash flows of the asset or liability being measured, it may be possible to derive a discount rate using data for several comparable assets or liabilities in conjunction with the risk-free yield curve (i.e. using a 'build-up' approach). [IFRS 13:B19]

Example 8.6.4.2

Deriving a discount rate using a build up approach

[Based on IFRS 13:B20 - B21]

Assume that Asset A is a contractual right to receive CU800 in one year (i.e. there is no timing uncertainty). There is an established market for comparable assets, and information about those assets, including price information, is available. Of those comparable assets:

(a) Asset B is a contractual right to receive CU1,200 in one year and has a market price of CU1,083. Thus, the implied annual rate of return (i.e. a one-year market rate of return) is 10.8 per cent [(CU1,200/CU1,083) – 1].

(b) Asset C is a contractual right to receive CU700 in two years and has a market price of CU566. Thus, the implied annual rate of return (i.e. a two-year market rate of return) is 11.2 per cent [(CU700/CU566)^0.5 – 1].

(c) All three assets are comparable with respect to risk (i.e. dispersion of possible pay-offs and credit).

On the basis of the timing of the contractual payments to be received for Asset A relative to the timing for Asset B and Asset C (i.e. one year for Asset B versus two years for Asset C), Asset B is deemed more comparable to Asset A. Using the contractual payment to be received for Asset A (CU800) and the one-year market rate derived from Asset B (10.8 per cent), the fair value of Asset A is CU722 (CU800/1.108). Alternatively, in the absence of available market information for Asset B, the one-year market rate could be derived from Asset C using the build-up approach. In that case, the two-year market rate indicated by Asset C (11.2 per cent) would be adjusted to a one-year market rate using the term structure of the risk-free yield curve. Additional information and analysis might be required to determine whether the risk premiums for one-year and two-year assets are the same. If it is determined that the risk premiums for one-year and two-year assets are not the same, the two-year market rate of return would be further adjusted for that effect.

When the discount rate adjustment technique is applied to fixed receipts or payments, the adjustment for risk inherent in the cash flows of the asset or liability being measured is included in the discount rate. In some applications of the discount rate adjustment technique to cash flows that are not fixed receipts or payments, an adjustment to the cash flows may be necessary to achieve comparability with the observed asset or liability from which the discount rate is derived. [IFRS 13:B22]

8.6.4.3 Expected present value technique

The expected present value technique uses as a starting point a set of cash flows that represents the probability-weighted average of all possible future cash flows (i.e. the expected cash flows). The resulting estimate is identical to expected value, which, in statistical terms, is the weighted average of a discrete random variable's possible values with the respective probabilities as the weights. All possible cash flows are probability-weighted, hence, the resulting expected cash flow is not conditional upon the occurrence of any specified event (unlike the cash flows used in the discount rate adjustment technique described in **8.6.4.2**). [IFRS 13:B23]

In making an investment decision, risk-averse market participants would take into account the risk that the actual cash flows may differ from the expected cash flows. Portfolio theory distinguishes between unsystematic (diversifiable) risk, which is the risk specific to a particular asset or liability, and systematic (non-diversifiable) risk, which is the common risk shared by an asset or a liability with the other items in a diversified portfolio. Portfolio theory holds that in a market in equilibrium, market participants will be compensated only for bearing the systematic risk inherent in the cash flows. In markets that are inefficient or out of equilibrium, other forms of return or compensation might be available. [IFRS 13:B24]

IFRS 13 describes two methods for applying the expected present value technique. Both methods are illustrated in **example 8.6.4.3**.

[IFRS 13:B25 & B26]

- Method 1 adjusts the expected cash flows of an asset for systematic (i.e. market) risk by subtracting a cash risk premium (i.e. risk-adjusted expected cash flows). Those risk-adjusted expected cash flows represent a certainty-equivalent cash flow, which is discounted at a risk-free interest rate. A certainty-equivalent cash flow refers to an expected cash flow (as defined), adjusted for risk so that a market participant is indifferent to trading a certain cash flow for an expected cash flow. For example, if a market participant was willing to trade an expected cash flow of CU1,200 for a certain cash flow of CU1,000, the CU1,000 is the certainty equivalent of the CU1,200 (i.e. the CU200 would represent the cash risk premium). In that case, the market participant would be indifferent as to the asset held.

- Method 2 adjusts for systematic (i.e. market) risk by adding a risk premium to the risk-free interest rate. Accordingly, the expected cash flows are discounted at a rate that corresponds to an expected rate associated with probability-weighted cash flows (i.e. an expected rate of return). Models used for pricing risky assets, such as the capital asset pricing model, can be used to estimate the expected rate of return. Because the discount rate used in the discount rate adjustment technique (see **8.6.4.2**) is a rate of return relating to conditional cash flows it is likely to be higher than the expected rate of return relating to expected or probability-weighted cash flows. [IFRS 13:B26]

Example 8.6.4.3

Present value techniques: Discounting risk adjusted expected cash flows by the risk-free rate vs. discounting unadjusted expected cash flows by a risk-adjusted discount rate

[Based on IFRS 13:B27 - B30]

Assume that an asset has expected cash flows of CU780 in one year determined on the basis of the possible cash flows and probabilities shown below. The applicable risk-free interest rate for cash flows with a one-year horizon is 5 per cent, and the systematic risk premium for an asset with the same risk profile is 3 per cent.

Possible cash flows	**Probability**	**Probability-weighted cash flows**
CU500	15%	CU75
CU800	60%	CU480
CU900	25%	CU225
Expected cash flows:		CU780

In this simple illustration, the expected cash flows (CU780) represent the probability-weighted average of the three possible outcomes. In more realistic situations, there could be many possible outcomes. However, to apply the expected present value technique, it is not always necessary to take into account distributions of all possible cash flows using complex models and techniques. Rather, it might be possible to develop a limited number of discrete scenarios and probabilities that capture the array of possible cash flows. For example, an entity might use realised cash flows for some relevant past period, adjusted for changes in circumstances occurring subsequently (e.g. changes in external factors, including economic or market conditions, industry trends and competition as well as changes in internal factors affecting the entity more specifically), taking into account the assumptions of market participants.

In theory, the present value (i.e. the fair value) of the asset's cash flows is the same whether determined by discounting the risk adjusted expected cash flows by the risk-free rate (Method 1) or by discounting the unadjusted expected cash flows by the risk-adjusted discount rate (Method 2).

Using Method 1, the expected cash flows are adjusted for systematic (i.e. market) risk. In the absence of market data directly indicating the amount of the risk adjustment, such adjustment could be derived from an asset pricing model using the concept of certainty equivalents. For example, the risk adjustment (i.e. the cash risk premium of CU22) could be determined using the systematic risk premium of 3 per cent (CU780 – [CU780 × (1.05/1.08)]), which results in risk-adjusted expected cash flows of CU758 (CU780 – CU22). The CU758 is the certainty equivalent of CU780 and is discounted at the risk-free interest rate (5 per cent). The present value (i.e. the fair value) of the asset is CU722 (CU758/1.05).

Using Method 2, the expected cash flows are not adjusted for systematic (i.e. market) risk. Rather, the adjustment for that risk is included in the discount rate. Thus, the expected cash flows are discounted at an expected rate of return of 8 per cent (i.e. the 5 per cent risk-free interest rate plus the 3 per cent systematic risk premium). The present value (i.e. the fair value) of the asset is CU722 (CU780/1.08).

When using an expected present value technique to measure fair value, either Method 1 or Method 2 could be used. The selection of Method 1 or Method 2 will depend on facts and circumstances specific to the asset or liability being measured, the extent to which sufficient data are available and the judgements applied.

8.7 Use of multiple valuation techniques

In some cases, it is appropriate to use a single valuation technique (e.g. when valuing an asset or a liability using quoted market prices in an active market for identical assets or liabilities). However, in other circumstances, it is appropriate to use multiple valuation techniques. [IFRS 13:63]

When multiple valuation techniques are used to measure fair value, the results (i.e. the fair value measurements) should be evaluated taking into account the reasonableness of the range of values indicated by those results. A fair value measurement is the point within that range that is most representative of the fair value in the circumstances. [IFRS 13:63]

In determining whether it is more appropriate to use a single approach or multiple approaches, an entity should consider the appropriateness (i.e. relevance and applicability) of each valuation technique and the observability of the available inputs that are significant to the valuation technique. If one valuation technique is clearly superior to the other techniques (e.g. because it uses more observable inputs), it may be appropriate to use a single valuation technique. Conversely, if no valuation technique is superior (e.g. because all techniques use unobservable inputs that are significant to the measurement), it may be appropriate to use a combination of valuation techniques provided that reliable and relevant inputs are available.

8.8 Calibration of valuation techniques

If the transaction price is fair value at initial recognition and a valuation technique that uses unobservable inputs will be used to measure fair value in subsequent periods, the valuation technique should be calibrated so that at initial recognition the result of the valuation technique equals the transaction price. Calibration ensures that the valuation technique reflects current market conditions, and it helps an entity to determine whether an adjustment to the valuation technique is necessary (e.g. there might be a characteristic of the asset or liability that is not captured by the valuation technique). After initial recognition, when measuring fair value using a valuation technique or techniques that use unobservable inputs, an entity should ensure that those valuation techniques reflect observable market data (e.g. the price for a similar asset or liability) at the measurement date. [IFRS 13:64]

Some IFRSs require or permit assets or liabilities to be recognised initially at fair value. When an asset is acquired or a liability assumed in a market transaction, it cannot be assumed that the price paid to acquire the asset or received to assume the liability (i.e. transaction or entry price) is the same as the fair value of the asset or liability in accordance with IFRS 13 (an exit price) (see **section 7** for further discussion).

IFRS 13:64, as discussed above, deals specifically with circumstances in which:

- a valuation technique that uses unobservable inputs is used to measure the fair value of an asset or a liability in subsequent periods; and
- the transaction price for the asset or liability *is* an appropriate measure of fair value at initial recognition in accordance with IFRS 13.

In such circumstances, IFRS 13:64 requires that the valuation technique should be calibrated (i.e. adjusted) so that, at initial recognition, the result of the valuation technique equals the transaction price.

If the transaction price is fair value at initial recognition, calibration of an entity's pricing model eliminates differences between the transaction price and the model's output (the 'inception difference'). IFRS 13 does not prescribe any specific method for the calibration of pricing models. Therefore, an entity should select the most appropriate method for the particular circumstances.

Factors to consider when selecting the calibration method include:

- the valuation technique used;
- the availability of information about market participant assumptions (e.g. relevant observable inputs, estimated timing of when unobservable inputs may become observable);
- the complexity involved (i.e. complexity in different calibration methods, or in the identification of the causes underlying differences between transaction price and fair value estimates based on the entity's pricing model);
- the terms of the instrument; and
- the nature of the entity's portfolio.

In outline, calibration might be approached in the following manner.

- **Step 1 –** Identify the source of the inception difference.
- **Step 2 –** Adjust the unobservable inputs or establish valuation adjustments such that the adjusted model result equals the transaction price at inception (i.e. the inception difference is eliminated).
- **Step 3 –** Changes in fair value measured using the entity's pricing model will be recognised subsequent to initial recognition. The adjustments identified at Step 2 may be reversed or modified when (1) unobservable inputs become observable or (2) unobservable inputs or valuation adjustments are adjusted to reflect new information (e.g. through subsequent calibration of the model or model inputs to reflect new transaction data).

Step 2 may result in either direct adjustment to model inputs or an adjustment to the model's output (a valuation adjustment).

When calibration is achieved through direct adjustment to model inputs, an entity should consider the impact of such adjustments on the valuation of other instruments in its portfolio (e.g. instruments valued using the same or similar pricing inputs). The calibration may affect the valuation of other instruments because the calibrated inputs may replace or supersede the assumptions previously used for unobservable inputs.

When calibration is achieved through a valuation adjustment, the entity should review the valuation adjustment periodically to ensure that the adjustment reflects any new information and that it is consistent with the exit price notion in IFRS 13.

See **example 8.8** for an illustration of a model calibration approach that may be acceptable when the inception difference can be isolated to a particular unobservable model input.

Example 8.8

Calibration of models or model inputs

Entity X enters into an electricity forward contract to purchase 100 megawatts of electricity (daily) for a 10-year term. The electricity forward contract is within the scope of IAS 39 and is measured at fair value.

No cash is exchanged between the parties at the inception of the forward contract. Using the guidance in IFRS 13:B4 (see **section 7**), Entity X determines that the transaction price equals the exit price (i.e. the fair value of the forward contract equals zero at inception).

Entity X develops its own valuation technique to measure the fair value of the forward contract at subsequent reporting dates. At inception, there are three years of observable forward prices available in the relevant market. Entity X's model uses estimated forward electricity prices beyond three years. At inception, and prior to calibration, the pricing model values the forward contract as an asset of CU1 million. Consequently, Entity X needs to calibrate its model so that the model result at inception equals the transaction price of zero.

In this simple scenario, Entity X might calibrate its model as follows.

- **Step 1** – Entity X establishes that the only unobservable input that significantly affects the model value is forward electricity prices. Consequently, Entity X attributes the inception difference of CU1 million (i.e. the difference between the model's result and the fair value of zero) to its estimate of unobservable forward electricity prices for Years 4 to 10 of the contract.
- **Step 2** – Entity X adjusts the unobservable forward price points at Years 4 to 10 on the forward price curve such that the model produces a fair value of zero.

  Because Entity X attributed the inception difference solely to the unobservable electricity prices in the relevant market, any calibration adjustment represents a calibration of these unobservable electricity prices to the most recent available information (the forward contract's transaction price). As a result, if Entity X owns a portfolio of contracts whose fair values are estimated using long-dated electricity prices in the same market, the calibration adjustment to the electricity forward prices would most likely also affect the fair value of those other long-dated contracts.

  Similar considerations are also relevant when a calibration results in valuation adjustments to the pricing model's output. In general, calibration adjustments provide updated information about assumptions used by market participants in assessing unobservable inputs or valuation adjustments. Therefore, calibration adjustments may have an effect beyond the recently executed transaction.
- **Step 3** – Assuming no other calibration adjustments are made and that observable forward prices remain available for the next three years, the calibration adjustments would be removed as the inputs for Years 4 to 10 become observable. (For example, at the end of Year 1 of the contract, observable forward prices would be available for Years 2 to 4, and unobservable inputs for Years 5 to 10 would be used. As a result, the calibration adjustments for Year 4 should be removed from the valuation as this input has become observable.) All calibration adjustments should be removed once all the unobservable inputs become observable (e.g. in the last 3 years of the contract). In addition, no calibration adjustments should remain in the model in a period in which settlement has occurred.

8.9 Changes in valuation techniques

Once a valuation technique has been selected, it should be applied consistently. A change in a valuation technique or its application (e.g. a change in its weighting when multiple valuation techniques are used or a change in an adjustment applied to a valuation technique) is only appropriate if the change results in a measurement that is equally or more representative of fair value in the circumstances. [IFRS 13:65]

The Standard provides the following examples of events that might appropriately lead to a change in valuation technique:

[IFRS 13:65]

- new markets develop;
- new information becomes available;
- information previously used is no longer available;
- valuation techniques improve; or
- market conditions change.

If a valuation technique does not use unadjusted quoted prices, and in a subsequent period a quoted price in an active market becomes available, the quoted price should be used because IFRS 13:77 states that "a quoted price in an active market provides the most reliable evidence of fair value and shall be used without adjustment to measure fair value whenever available", with limited exceptions.

Depending on the particular circumstances, a change from a valuation technique that uses unadjusted quoted prices to a different valuation technique (such as a discounted cash flow technique) may be appropriate when:

- quoted prices for an identical asset or liability are no longer available; or
- quoted prices are available, but the market is no longer active. Note, however, that prices from relevant observable transactions must be considered in determining fair value even if the market is not active (see **section 9.5**); or
- the entity no longer has access to the market in which the prices are quoted. The entity must be able to access the market in order to use a quote from that market without adjustment to reflect the lack of access, but the entity does not need to be able to sell the particular asset or transfer the particular liability on the measurement date (see **section 3.3** for further details); or
- quoted prices are no longer based on relevant observable market data and do not reflect assumptions that market participants would make in pricing the asset at the measurement date. As discussed at **section 9.7**, an entity cannot necessarily assume that a price provided by an external source is representative of fair value at the measurement date.

A decrease in the volume or level of activity in a market does not necessarily mean that the market is no longer active (see **10.2.1** for a discussion of active vs. inactive markets) and, consequently, that a change in the valuation technique is warranted.

In selecting another valuation technique, when appropriate, an entity should maximise the use of relevant observable inputs (e.g. quoted prices for a similar asset or liability with adjustments as appropriate) and minimise the use of unobservable inputs.

If there is a change in the valuation technique used or its application, any resulting difference should be accounted for as a change in accounting estimate in accordance with IAS 8 *Accounting Policies, Changes in Accounting Estimates and Errors*; however, the disclosures generally required under IAS 8 regarding a change in accounting estimate are not required for revisions resulting from a change in a valuation technique or its application. [IFRS 13:66]

9 Inputs to valuation techniques

9.1 Definition of inputs

Inputs are defined as "[t]he assumptions that market participants would use when pricing the asset or liability, including assumptions about risk, such as the following:

(a) the risk inherent in a particular valuation technique used to measure fair value (such as a pricing model); and

(b) the risk inherent in the inputs to the valuation technique". [IFRS 13:Appendix A]

Inputs may be observable or unobservable. [IFRS 13:Appendix A] Valuation techniques used to measure fair value are required to maximise the use of relevant observable inputs and minimise the use of unobservable inputs (see **section 8**). [IFRS 13:67]

Valuation inputs that are observable are more reliable than those that are unobservable (sometimes referred to as 'entity-specific' because these inputs are derived by an entity rather than by the 'market').

The inputs used should be consistent with the characteristics of the asset or liability that market participants would take into account in a transaction for the asset or liability (see **section 3.1**). [IFRS 13:69] Various factors may influence the fair value of a financial instrument. Below is a non-exhaustive list of factors that may be relevant in valuing non-derivative and derivative financial instruments:

- time value of money (i.e. interest at the risk-free rate);
- credit risk (both counterparty credit risk for a financial asset and own credit risk for a financial liability);
- liquidity risk;

- foreign currency exchange rates;
- commodity prices;
- equity prices;
- volatility;
- prepayment or surrender risk; and
- servicing costs.

9.2 Observable inputs

Examples of markets in which inputs might be observable for some assets and liabilities include the following.

[IFRS 13:B34]

- **Exchange markets** In an exchange market, closing prices are both readily available and generally representative of fair value (e.g. the London Stock Exchange).
- **Dealer markets** In a dealer market, dealers stand ready to trade (either buy or sell for their own account), thereby providing liquidity by using their capital to hold an inventory of the items for which they make a market. Typically, bid and ask prices (representing the price at which the dealer is willing to buy and the price at which the dealer is willing to sell, respectively) are more readily available than closing prices. Over-the-counter markets (for which prices are publicly reported) are dealer markets. Dealer markets also exist for some other assets and liabilities, including some financial instruments, commodities and physical assets (e.g. used equipment).
- **Brokered markets** In a brokered market, brokers attempt to match buyers with sellers but do not stand ready to trade for their own account. Brokers do not use their own capital to hold an inventory of the items for which they make a market. The broker knows the prices bid and asked by the respective parties, but each party is typically unaware of another party's price requirements. Prices of completed transactions are sometimes available. Brokered markets include electronic communication networks, in which buy and sell orders are matched, and commercial and residential real estate markets.
- **Principal-to-principal markets** In a principal-to-principal market, transactions (both originations and re-sales) are negotiated independently with no intermediary. Little information about those transactions may be made available publicly.

9.3 Applying a premium or discount

In some cases, the characteristics of an asset or a liability that market participants would take into account in a transaction for the asset or liability result in the application of an adjustment, such as a premium or discount (e.g. a control premium or non-controlling interest discount). However, a fair value measurement should not incorporate a premium or discount that is inconsistent with the unit of account in the IFRS that requires or permits the fair value measurement (see **section 3.2**). [IFRS 13:69]

Premiums or discounts that reflect size as a characteristic of the entity's holding (specifically, a blockage factor that adjusts the quoted price of an asset or a liability because the market's normal daily trading volume is not sufficient to absorb the quantity held by the entity) are not permitted in a fair value measurement. [IFRS 13:69]

For example, an investor holding one share that is quoted in an active market may receive a different amount of consideration per share compared to an investor that sells 15 per cent of the total equity shares. The difference between the two holdings is simply the size of the investor's holding, which is typically not a characteristic of the financial asset and thus is not considered in the fair value measurement in this circumstance. For both investors, the fair value measurement of the shares is the price for disposing of a single share multiplied by the quantity held.

In contrast, when measuring the fair value of a controlling interest, it is appropriate to incorporate a control premium because IFRS 13 regards the control premium as a characteristic of the asset or liability. [IFRS 13:69]

In all cases, if there is a quoted market price in an active market for an asset or a liability, the entity should use that price without adjustment when measuring fair value, except as specified in IFRS 13:79 (see **10.2.1**). [IFRS 13:69]

9.4 Bid price versus ask price inputs

9.4.1 Bid price and ask price inputs – general

If an asset or a liability measured at fair value has a bid price and an ask price (e.g. an input from a dealer market), IFRS 13 requires the price within the bid-ask spread that is most representative of fair value in the circumstances to be used to measure fair value regardless of where the input is categorised within the fair value hierarchy (i.e. Level 1, 2 or 3; see **section 10**).

IFRS 13 permits, but does not require, that asset positions may be measured at bid prices and that liability positions may be measured at ask prices. [IFRS 13:70]

IFRS 13 allows an entity to use mid-market pricing or other pricing conventions that are used by market participants as a practical expedient for fair value measurements within a bid-ask spread. [IFRS 13:71]

An entity does not need to meet any specific qualifying criteria to use mid-market pricing or other pricing conventions as a practical expedient for measuring fair value, provided that the selected pricing convention:

- is used by market participants (e.g. an industry-accepted pricing convention); and
- is consistent with the fair value measurement objective of IFRS 13. For example, it would not be appropriate to use ask prices for recognised assets or bid prices for recognised liabilities because such a pricing approach would be inconsistent with the IFRS 13 objective that fair value is an exit price.

The decision to use a particular pricing convention is an accounting policy choice that should be consistently applied from period to period and for assets or liabilities with similar characteristics and risk. The policy should also be disclosed, if appropriate.

Example 9.4

Mid-market prices

Entity X and Entity Y hold the same debt security as an asset. Entity Y, a broker-dealer, is a market-maker in the debt security. Entity X is not. The debt security is traded in an active market by Entity Y (and other broker-dealers) using bid and ask prices.

Even though Entity X would most likely sell the debt security at or close to the bid price, Entity X may select a policy to use the mid-market price as the fair value of the debt security as a practical expedient. However, it would not be appropriate to use the ask price for the debt security because this would be inconsistent with the objective of fair value being an exit price.

Even though Entity Y may be able to exit at a price greater than the bid price, Entity Y may choose as its policy to measure the debt security by using the bid price as a practical expedient.

IFRS 13 also contains detailed guidance for circumstances when an entity may fair value a portfolio of similar items together that have offsetting market risks and in doing so use mid-market prices for the offsetting market risks (see **section 6**).

9.4.2 Changes in the use of bid, ask or mid-market pricing or other pricing conventions

When an entity has in the past complied with the requirements of IFRS 13:70 (see above) and measured fair value at the price within the bid-ask spread that is most representative of fair value in the circumstances, it is not generally appropriate for the entity to change its accounting policy to using the practical expedient of mid-market pricing or another pricing convention as permitted by IFRS 13:71.

Once a valuation technique has been selected, it should generally be applied consistently. A change in a valuation technique is only appropriate if the change results in a measurement that is equally or more representative of fair value in the circumstances. [IFRS 13:65]

Having established a policy of measuring fair value at the price within the bid-ask spread that is most representative of fair value in the circumstances, a change to using a practical expedient such as mid-market pricing or another pricing convention would generally be inappropriate because it would not typically result in a measurement that is equally or more representative of fair value.

9.5 Measuring fair value when the volume or level of activity for an asset or a liability has significantly decreased

IFRS 13 notes that the fair value of an asset or a liability might be affected when there has been a significant decrease in the volume or level of activity for that asset or liability in relation to normal market activity for the asset or liability (or similar assets or liabilities). [IFRS 13:B37]

The consequence of a significant decrease in the volume or level of activity could be that a transaction price or a quoted price for that item is not representative of fair value. However, a decrease in the volume or level of activity on its own may not indicate that a transaction price or quoted price does not represent fair value or that a transaction in that market is not orderly. [IFRS 13:B38]

The following are examples of factors that can help determine whether, on the basis of evidence available, there has been a significant decrease in the volume or level of activity for the asset or liability:

[IFRS 13:B37]

- there are few recent transactions;
- price quotations are not developed using current information;
- price quotations vary substantially either over time or among market-makers (e.g. some brokered markets);

- indices that previously were highly correlated with the fair values of the asset or liability are demonstrably uncorrelated with recent indications of fair value for that asset or liability;
- there is a significant increase in implied liquidity risk premiums, yields or performance indicators (such as delinquency rates or loss severities) for observed transactions or quoted prices when compared with the entity's estimate of expected cash flows, taking into account all available market data about credit and other non-performance risk for the asset or liability;
- there is a wide bid-ask spread or significant increase in the bid-ask spread;
- there is a significant decline in the activity of, or there is an absence of, a market for new issues (i.e. a primary market) for the asset or liability or similar assets or liabilities; and
- little information is publicly available (e.g. for transactions that take place in a principal-to-principal market).

In assessing whether there has been a significant decrease in the volume or level of activity, an entity should evaluate the significance and relevance of factors such as those listed above. [IFRS 13:B37]

Note that the presence of one or more of the factors listed in IFRS 13:B37 alone is not sufficient to conclude that a market is not 'active' see **10.2.1** for further discussion).

If it is concluded that there has been a significant decrease in the volume or level of activity for the asset or liability in relation to normal market activity for the asset or liability (or similar assets or liabilities), further analysis of the transactions or quoted prices is needed. If it is determined that a transaction or quoted price does not represent fair value (e.g. there may be transactions that are not orderly), an adjustment to the transactions or quoted prices will be necessary if those prices are to be used as a basis for measuring fair value. The adjustment can be significant to the fair value measurement in its entirety. [IFRS 13:B38]

Adjustments also may be necessary in other circumstances (e.g. when a price for a similar asset requires significant adjustment to make it comparable to the asset being measured, or when the price is 'stale'). [IFRS 13:B38]

IFRS 13 does not prescribe a methodology for making significant adjustments to transactions or quoted prices. Consistent with valuation techniques discussed in **section 8**, appropriate risk adjustments should be applied, including a risk premium reflecting the amount that market participants would demand as compensation for the uncertainty inherent in the cash flows of an asset or a liability. Otherwise, the measurement does not faithfully represent fair value. In some cases, determining the appropriate risk adjustment may be difficult. However, the degree of difficulty alone is not a sufficient basis on which to exclude a risk adjustment. The risk adjustment should be reflective of an orderly transaction between market participants at the measurement date under current market conditions. [IFRS 13:B39]

If there has been a significant decrease in the volume or level of activity for the asset or liability, a change in valuation technique or the use of multiple valuation techniques may be appropriate (e.g. the use of a market approach and an income approach – see **sections 8.4** and **8.6**, respectively). When weighting indications of fair value resulting from the use of multiple valuation techniques, an entity should consider the reasonableness of the range of fair value measurements. The objective is to determine the point within the range that is most representative of fair value under current market conditions. A wide range of fair value measurements may be an indication that further analysis is needed. [IFRS 13:B40]

Even when there has been a significant decrease in the volume or level of activity for the asset or liability, the objective of a fair value measurement remains the same. Fair value is the price that would be received to sell an asset or paid to transfer a liability in an orderly transaction (i.e. not a forced liquidation or distress sale) between market participants at the measurement date under current market conditions. [IFRS 13:B41]

Estimating the price at which market participants would be willing to enter into a transaction at the measurement date under current market conditions if there has been a significant decrease in the volume or level of activity for the asset or liability depends on the facts and circumstances at the measurement date and requires judgement. An entity's intention to hold the asset or to settle or otherwise fulfil the liability is not relevant when measuring fair value because fair value is a market-based measurement, not an entity-specific measurement. [IFRS 13:B42]

If an entity is unwilling to transact at a price from an external source (such as a quoted market price or a price provided by a broker, pricing service or potential buyer), the entity's unwillingness to transact at that price is not sufficient evidence for the entity to disregard that price in measuring fair value. If the best information available in the circumstances indicates that market participants would transact at a price from an external source, an entity is not permitted to disregard that price simply because it is not willing to transact at that price.

Examples 9.5A and **9.5B** explore this issue further.

Example 9.5A

Assumptions can be readily derived from current observable market data

Entity A is using a valuation model to measure the fair value of its investment in privately placed corporate debt securities issued by Entity X. No quoted price for identical securities is available. Entity A's valuation model uses assumptions about default rates and discount rates. Default rate assumptions can be readily derived from current observable market data for actively traded credit default swaps on publicly traded bonds of Entity X. When measuring the fair value of its investment, Entity A cannot disregard this market data even if Entity A would not be willing to transact at a price consistent with this market data.

Example 9.5B

Active markets for similar securities

Entity A holds distressed debt securities. Transactions in the securities occur infrequently and there is no active market for the securities, but there are active markets for similar securities. Entity A's own valuation model, which is based on observable Level 2 inputs current at the measurement date, indicates that market participants would be willing to buy and sell the debt for CU30 at the measurement date. Entity A has calibrated the model to the best information available at the measurement date (including transaction prices in similar securities and risk premiums).

At the measurement date, a potential buyer provides an unsolicited bid to buy the securities for CU20. When measuring the fair value of the debt securities, Entity A can neither disregard this bid price simply because it is not willing to transact at that price, nor can it assume that the bid price provides better evidence of fair value than its own model. Although the bid price is the price one potential buyer would be willing to pay for Entity A's asset, it may not necessarily be the price at which market participants (buyers and sellers) would be willing to transact on the measurement date.

Valuation techniques to measure fair value should maximise the use of relevant observable inputs (i.e. Level 1 and Level 2 inputs that do not require significant adjustment) and minimise the use of unobservable inputs (Level 3 inputs). If the bid price is classified as a Level 3 input, it may be appropriate for Entity A to place less weight on the bid price in measuring the fair value of its debt securities given that Entity A's own model is based on Level 2 inputs. However, if Entity A obtains several bid prices and the fair value indicated by the valuation model is not in the range of the bid prices obtained, Entity A may need to consider whether its model is valid and identify the reasons for the discrepancy between the model amount and the bid prices.

IFRS 13 provides an illustrative example of estimating a market rate of return when the volume or level of activity for a financial asset has significantly decreased (see **example 9.5C**).

Example 9.5C

Estimating a market rate of return when the volume or level of activity for an asset has significantly decreased

[IFRS 13:IE48 - IE58 – Example 14]

This example illustrates the use of judgement when measuring the fair value of a financial asset when there has been a significant decrease in the volume or level of activity for the asset when compared with normal market activity for the asset (or similar assets).

Entity A invests in a junior AAA-rated tranche of a residential mortgage-backed security on 1 January 20X8 (the issue date of the security). The junior tranche is the third most senior of a total of seven tranches. The underlying collateral for the residential mortgage-backed security is unguaranteed non-conforming residential mortgage loans that were issued in the second half of 20X6.

At 31 March 20X9 (the measurement date) the junior tranche is now A-rated. This tranche of the residential mortgage-backed security was previously traded through a brokered market. However, trading volume in that market was infrequent, with only a few transactions taking place per month from 1 January 20X8 to 30 June 20X8 and little, if any, trading activity during the nine months before 31 March 20X9.

Entity A takes into account the factors in IFRS 13:B37 (see above) to determine whether there has been a significant decrease in the volume or level of activity for the junior tranche of the residential mortgage-backed security in which it has invested. After evaluating the significance and relevance of the factors, Entity A concludes that the volume and level of activity of the junior tranche of the residential mortgage-backed security have significantly decreased. Entity A supported its judgement primarily on the basis that there was little, if any, trading activity for an extended period before the measurement date.

Because there is little, if any, trading activity to support a valuation technique using a market approach, Entity A decides to use an income approach using the discount rate adjustment technique described in paragraphs IFRS 13:B18 - B22 to measure the fair value of the residential mortgage-backed security at the measurement date. Entity A uses the contractual cash flows from the residential mortgage-backed security.

Entity A then estimates a discount rate (i.e. a market rate of return) to discount those contractual cash flows. The market rate of return is estimated using both of the following:

- the risk-free rate of interest.
- estimated adjustments for differences between the available market data and the junior tranche of the residential mortgage-backed security in which Entity A has invested. Those adjustments reflect available market data about expected non-performance and other risks (e.g. default risk, collateral value risk and liquidity risk) that market participants would take into account when pricing the asset in an orderly transaction at the measurement date under current market conditions.

Entity A took into account the following information when estimating these adjustments:

(a) the credit spread for the junior tranche of the residential mortgage-backed security at the issue date as implied by the original transaction price.

(b) the change in the credit spread implied by any observed transactions from the issue date to the measurement date for comparable residential mortgage-backed securities or on the basis of relevant indices.

(c) the characteristics of the junior tranche of the residential mortgage-backed security compared with comparable residential mortgage-backed securities or indices, including all of the following:

  (i) the quality of the underlying assets (i.e. information about the performance of the underlying mortgage loans such as delinquency and foreclosure rates, loss experience and prepayment rates);

  (ii) the seniority or subordination of the residential mortgage-backed security tranche held; and

  (iii) other relevant factors.

(d) relevant reports issued by analysts and rating agencies.

(e) quoted prices from third parties such as brokers or pricing services.

Entity A estimates that one indication of the market rate of return that market participants would use when pricing the junior tranche of the residential mortgage-backed security is 12 per cent (1,200 basis points). This market rate of return was estimated as follows:

(a) Begin with 300 basis points for the relevant risk-free rate of interest at 31 March 20X9.

(b) Add 250 basis points for the credit spread over the risk-free rate when the junior tranche was issued in January 20X8.

(c) Add 700 basis points for the estimated change in the credit spread over the risk-free rate of the junior tranche between 1 January 20X8 and 31 March 20X9. This estimate was developed on the basis of the change in the most comparable index available for that time period.

(d) Subtract 50 basis points (net) to adjust for differences between the index used to estimate the change in credit spreads and the junior tranche. The reference index consists of subprime mortgage loans, whereas Entity A's residential mortgage-backed security consists of similar mortgage loans with a more favourable credit profile (making it more attractive to market participants). However, the index does not reflect an appropriate liquidity risk premium for the junior tranche under current market conditions. Thus, the 50 basis point adjustment is the net of two adjustments:

  (i) the first adjustment is a 350 basis point subtraction, which was estimated by comparing the implied yield from the most recent transactions for the residential mortgage-backed security in June 20X8 with the implied yield in the index price on those same dates. There was no information available that indicated that the relationship between Entity A's security and the index has changed.

  (ii) the second adjustment is a 300 basis point addition, which is Entity A's best estimate of the additional liquidity risk inherent in its security (a cash position) when compared with the index (a synthetic position). This estimate was derived after taking into account liquidity risk premiums implied in recent cash transactions for a range of similar securities.

As an additional indication of the market rate of return, Entity A takes into account two recent indicative quotes (i.e. non-binding quotes) provided by reputable brokers for the junior tranche of the residential mortgage-backed security that imply yields of 15–17 per cent. Entity A is unable to evaluate the valuation techniques or inputs used to develop the quotes. However, Entity A is able to confirm that the quotes do not reflect the results of transactions.

Entity A has multiple indications of the market rate of return that market participants would take into account when measuring fair value, hence, it evaluates and weights the respective indications of the rate of return, considering the reasonableness of the range indicated by the results.

Entity A concludes that 13 per cent is the point within the range of indications that is most representative of fair value under current market conditions. Entity A places more weight on the 12 per cent indication (i.e. its own estimate of the market rate of return) for the following reasons:

(a) Entity A concluded that its own estimate appropriately incorporated the risks (e.g. default risk, collateral value risk and liquidity risk) that market participants would use when pricing the asset in an orderly transaction under current market conditions; and

(b) the broker quotes were non-binding and did not reflect the results of transactions, and Entity A was unable to evaluate the valuation technique(s) or inputs used to develop the quotes.

9.6 Identifying transactions that are not orderly

The determination as to whether a transaction is orderly is more difficult if there has been a significant decrease in the volume or level of activity for the asset or liability in relation to normal market activity. In such circumstances, it is not appropriate to conclude that all transactions in that market are not orderly (i.e. forced liquidations or distress sales). [IFRS 13:B43]

IFRS 13 does not require an entity to undertake exhaustive efforts to determine whether a transaction is orderly, although, the entity should not ignore information that is reasonably available. However, the Standard does establish a presumption that, when an entity is a party to a transaction, it has sufficient information to conclude whether the transaction is orderly. [IFRS 13:B44]

An entity is expected to evaluate the circumstances to determine whether, on the weight of the evidence available, the transaction is orderly. [IFRS 13:B43]

The Standard identifies the following circumstances that may indicate that a transaction is not orderly:

[IFRS 13:B43]

- there was not adequate exposure to the market for a period before the measurement date to allow for marketing activities that are usual and customary for transactions involving such assets or liabilities under current market conditions;
- there was a usual and customary marketing period, but the seller marketed the asset or liability to a single market participant;
- the seller is in or near bankruptcy or receivership (i.e. the seller is distressed);
- the seller was required to sell to meet regulatory or legal requirements (i.e. the seller was forced); or
- the transaction price is an outlier when compared with other recent transactions for the same or a similar asset or liability.

If a transaction price is determined not be orderly, little if any weight (compared to other indications of fair value) is placed on that transaction price. [IFRS 13:B44(a)]

If a transaction price is determined to be orderly, that transaction price is taken into accounting in estimating fair value. However, the amount of weight placed on that transaction price when compared with other indications of fair value will depend on facts and circumstances such as:

[IFRS 13:B44(b)]

- the volume of the transaction.
- the comparability of the transaction to the asset or liability being measured.
- the proximity of the transaction to the measurement date.

If there is not sufficient information available to conclude whether a transaction is orderly, the transaction price should be taken into account in estimating fair value. However, the transaction price may not represent fair value and, consequently, would not necessarily be the sole or primary basis for measuring fair value or estimating market risk premiums and less weight should be placed on it when compared with other transactions that are known to be orderly. [IFRS 13:B44(c)]

Example 9.6

Determining whether a transaction is orderly

Entity A is acting as an administrator on behalf of the creditors of Entity B, which is subject to bankruptcy proceedings. The administrator's role is to seek to maximise the return to Entity B's creditors. As part of Entity A's responsibilities, it auctions a portfolio of Entity B's financial assets. Entity A promotes the auction to interested parties with the expectation of receiving bids for the financial assets over a specified period.

Even though the financial assets are being sold as part of bankruptcy proceedings, the auction process may be considered to be an orderly transaction provided that all of the necessary conditions are met.

IFRS 13:Appendix A defines an orderly transaction as "[a] transaction that assumes exposure to the market for a period before the measurement date to allow for marketing activities that are usual and customary for transactions involving such assets or liabilities; it is not a forced transaction (e.g. a forced liquidation or distress sale)".

In the circumstances described, it seems possible that the auction process may be considered to be an orderly transaction because the sale is not immediate and there is sufficient (i.e. usual and customary) time to market the assets to other market participants.

If transactions in assets or liabilities occur between willing buyers and sellers in a manner that is usual and customary for transactions involving such assets or liabilities, these should be considered to be orderly transactions. Persuasive evidence is required to establish that an observable transaction is not an orderly transaction.

9.7 Quoted prices provided by third parties

IFRS 13 does not preclude the use of quoted prices provided by third parties, such as pricing services or brokers, if it is determined that the quoted prices provided by those parties are developed in accordance with IFRS 13. [IFRS 13:B45]

However, if there has been a significant decrease in the volume or level of activity for the asset or liability, an entity is required to evaluate whether the quoted prices provided by third parties are developed using current information that reflects orderly transactions or a valuation technique that reflects market participant assumptions (including assumptions about risk). In weighting a quoted price as an input to a fair value measurement, an entity should place less weight (when compared with other indications of fair value that reflect the results of transactions) on quotes that do not reflect the result of transactions. [IFRS 13:B46]

Furthermore, the nature of a quote (e.g. whether the quote is an indicative price or a binding offer) should be taken into account when weighting the available evidence, with more weight given to quotes provided by third parties that represent binding offers. [IFRS 13:B47]

Broker or pricing service quotes are not necessarily determinative of fair value if an active market (as defined in IFRS 13:Appendix A –

see **10.2.1**) does not exist for the item being measured. In assessing whether a broker or pricing service quote appropriately represents fair value, an entity needs to understand how the broker or pricing service has arrived at the quoted price, and the inputs and other information used.

Quote based on information from an active market

Consistent with IFRS 13:77 (see **10.2.1**), when a broker or pricing service quote represents the unadjusted price quoted for an identical asset, liability or equity instrument in an active market to which the entity has access at the measurement date, the entity is required to use the quoted price without adjustment when measuring fair value, subject to limited exceptions as discussed in IFRS 13:79. Such a quote represents a Level 1 input.

If any adjustment is made to the broker or pricing service quote in the circumstances specified in IFRS 13:79, or in the absence of an active market, a broker or pricing service quote does not represent a Level 1 input. However, it may nevertheless be determinative of fair value.

Quote based on valuation technique(s)

If a quote is based on a valuation technique that is used by market participants and uses market-observable or market-corroborated inputs that reflect the assumptions of market participants, it is determinative of fair value if no significant adjustment to the quote is needed. If a significant adjustment is needed, the quote is not determinative of fair value but it could represent a relevant observable input into the entity's fair value measurement.

General considerations

In assessing whether a quote is determinative of fair value, the entity should consider all relevant circumstances, including the following questions (the list is not exhaustive).

- Are there differences between the asset or liability being measured and the item for which a quote is available (e.g. differences in the terms or risk attributes)? Such differences may necessitate adjustments to the price quoted by the broker or pricing service.
- Does the quote reflect currently occurring orderly transactions for the asset or liability being measured? That is, are market participants currently transacting in the asset or liability at the price quoted by the broker or pricing service or does the quote reflect 'stale' information or transactions that are not orderly? IFRS 13.B46 (see above) provides specific guidance for circumstances in which there has been a significant decrease in the volume or level of activity for the asset or liability.

- Is the broker or pricing service using a valuation technique that complies with the fair value measurement principles in IFRS 13? For example, does the valuation technique used by the broker or pricing service (1) reflect market participant assumptions, including assumptions about risk, (2) maximise the use of relevant observable inputs, and (3) minimise the use of unobservable inputs? If the valuation technique does not reflect the assumptions market participants would use in pricing the asset or liability, the price quoted by the broker or pricing service may need adjustment or may not be relevant to the entity's fair value measurement.
- Is the quote provided by the broker or pricing service an indicative price or a binding offer? That is, does the broker or another market participant stand ready to transact at the price quoted by the broker or pricing service? As noted above, IFRS 13:B47 indicates that more weight should be given to quotes based on binding offers. Typically, a quote obtained from a broker or pricing service is an indicative price and not a binding offer (unless the broker is a market-maker).
- Does the quote come from a reputable broker or pricing service that has a substantial presence in the market and the experience and expertise to provide a representationally faithful quote for the asset or liability being measured? An entity may place more weight on a quote from a broker or pricing service that has more experience and expertise related to the asset or liability being measured.

As the number of market transactions decreases, brokers or pricing services may rely more on proprietary models based on their own assumptions to arrive at a quote. The entity should evaluate how the quote has been arrived at and whether it reflects market participant assumptions, including assumptions about risk. This information may be difficult to obtain if quotes are based on proprietary models that brokers or pricing services may not be willing to share. However, even when brokers or pricing services do not wish to share detailed information about their models, it may still be possible to obtain information about the nature of the assumptions and the inputs used in the model. If the quote does not reflect assumptions that market participants would use in pricing the asset or liability, the quote will most likely not be determinative of fair value because adjustments may be required. In such cases, the quote may be an input to the entity's fair value measurement, but other indications of fair value may be equally or more useful when estimating fair value (e.g. a valuation based on the entity's own estimates of the inputs that market participants would use in pricing the asset or liability).

Multiple quotes

An entity may need to perform additional analysis when quotes for an individual asset or liability are obtained from different brokers or pricing services. Multiple quotes within a narrow range constitute stronger evidence of fair value than multiple quotes that are widely dispersed.

IFRS 13:B40 states that a wide range of measurements may be an indication that further analysis is needed. The entity should consider the reasonableness of the range of fair value measurements, with the objective of determining the point within the range that is most representative of fair value under current market conditions.

In addition, if an entity's own estimate of fair value is outside the range of broker or pricing service quotes, the entity should understand the reason(s) for such a difference. If the range of quotes provides strong evidence of fair value, the entity may need to make adjustments to its valuation technique to reflect current market information.

10 Fair value hierarchy

10.1 Fair value hierarchy – general

To increase consistency and comparability in fair value measurements and related disclosures, IFRS 13 establishes a fair value hierarchy that categorises into three levels the inputs to valuation techniques used to measure fair value, as follows:

[IFRS 13:72]

- Level 1 inputs comprise unadjusted quoted prices in active markets for identical assets and liabilities that the entity can access at the measurement date (see **10.2.1**);
- Level 2 inputs comprise other observable inputs not included within Level 1 of the fair value hierarchy (see **10.2.2**); and
- Level 3 inputs comprise unobservable inputs (including the entity's own data, which are adjusted, if necessary, to reflect the assumptions market participants would use in the circumstances) (see **10.2.3**)

Observable inputs are defined as "[i]nputs that are developed using market data, such as publicly available information about actual events or transactions, and that reflect the assumptions that market participants would use when pricing the asset or liability". [IFRS 13:Appendix A]

Unobservable inputs are defined as "[i]nputs for which market data are not available and that are developed using the best information available about the assumptions that market participants would use when pricing the asset or liability". [IFRS 13:Appendix A]

The fair value hierarchy gives the highest priority to Level 1 inputs and the lowest priority to Level 3 inputs. [IFRS 13:72]

For example, if a fair value measurement for an asset is based on an unadjusted quoted price in an active market for an identical asset that the entity can access at the measurement date, this is categorised within 'Level 1' of the fair value hierarchy. In contrast, a valuation based on unobservable inputs would be categorised within 'Level 3'. [IFRS 13:72]

When an entity approaches the measurement of an asset, or a liability, or an entity's own equity instrument, at fair value, it looks at the available valuation techniques and at the inputs available for those techniques. When selecting the techniques and inputs to be used, the entity is required to maximise the use of observable inputs and minimise the use of unobservable inputs (see **section 8**). Once the selection has been made, each of the inputs is categorised within the fair value hierarchy outlined above; **section 10.2** summarises IFRS 13's requirements regarding the categorisation of inputs.

When an entity has determined the appropriate categorisation of the inputs into a fair value measurement, and has arrived at a measure of fair value using those inputs, it is then necessary to determine the appropriate categorisation of the fair value measurement in its entirety; this topic is discussed in **section 10.3**.

10.2 Categorisation of inputs to valuation techniques within the fair value hierarchy

10.2.1 Level 1 inputs

10.2.1.1 Level 1 inputs – general

Level 1 inputs are quoted prices (unadjusted) in active markets for identical assets or liabilities that the entity can access at the measurement date. [IFRS 13:76 & Appendix A]

A quoted price for an identical asset or liability in an active market provides the most reliable evidence of fair value and should be used without adjustment to measure fair value whenever available, except in any of the circumstances described in IFRS 13:79 (see below). [IFRS 13:77]

An active market is defined as "[a] market in which transactions for the asset or liability take place with sufficient frequency and volume to provide pricing information on an ongoing basis". [IFRS 13:Appendix A]

Determining whether a market is active focuses on the trading activity for the individual asset or liability being measured and not on the general levels of activity in the market in which the asset or liability is traded. For example, a security listed on the FTSE in London or HKFx in Hong Kong could be considered to be traded in an inactive market if the security itself is traded infrequently.

IFRS 13:B37 sets out a list of factors that may indicate that there has been a significant decrease in the volume or level of activity for an asset or a liability relative to normal market activity for that asset or liability (or similar assets or liabilities) (see **section 9.5**).The presence of one or more of the factors listed in IFRS 13:B37 alone is not sufficient to conclude that a market is not active. An entity should evaluate the relevance and significance of these factors to the individual asset or liability measured at fair value in order to determine whether the market for that asset or liability is inactive. A market is not deemed inactive simply because of insufficient trading volume relative to the size of an entity's position.

The characterisation of a market as 'active' or 'inactive' may change as market conditions change. However, a decline in the volume of transactions for a particular asset or liability does not automatically mean that the market has become inactive. A market would still be considered active as long as the frequency and volume of relevant transactions are sufficient to provide ongoing pricing information.

Further, quoted prices from a market affected by a decline in the volume or level of activity should not be ignored unless the price is associated with a transaction that is not orderly. It is not appropriate to conclude automatically that all transactions occurring in a market exhibiting a significant decline in volume or level of activity are not orderly. IFRS 13:B43 sets out a list of factors that may indicate that a transaction is not orderly (see **section 9.6**). Very little weight should be given to prices observed for a transaction that is not orderly; more weight may be given to a price observed for an orderly transaction. However, the entity should evaluate carefully whether an adjustment may be needed to that price to ensure the fair value measurement is consistent with the objectives in IFRS 13.

When a financial asset or financial liability is exchanged in multiple active markets (e.g. on different exchanges), the entity will need to consider which market is the most relevant for measuring fair value. IFRS 13 states explicitly that the emphasis within Level 1 is on determining both of the following:

[IFRS 13:78]

- the principal market for the asset or liability or, in the absence of a principal market, the most advantageous market for the asset or liability (see **section 3.3**); and
- whether the entity can enter into a transaction for the asset or liability at the price in that market at the measurement date.

When a quoted price in an active market is available, it should not be adjusted except in the circumstances listed below.

[IFRS 13:79]

- When an entity holds a large number of similar (but not identical) assets or liabilities (e.g. debt securities) that are measured at fair value and a quoted price in an active market is available but not readily accessible for each of those assets or liabilities individually (i.e. given the large number of similar assets or liabilities held by the entity, it would be difficult to obtain pricing information for each individual asset or liability at the measurement date). In such circumstances, as a practical expedient, an entity may measure fair value using an alternative pricing method that does not rely exclusively on quoted prices (e.g. matrix pricing – see **section 8.4**). However, the use of an alternative pricing method results in a fair value measurement categorised within a lower level of the fair value hierarchy.

- When a quoted price in an active market does not represent fair value at the measurement date. That might be the case if, for example, significant events (such as transactions in a principal-to-principal market, trades in a brokered market or announcements) take place after the close of a market but before the measurement date. An entity shall establish and consistently apply a policy for identifying those events that might affect fair value measurements. However, if the quoted price is adjusted for new information, the adjustment results in a fair value measurement categorised within a lower level of the fair value hierarchy.

- When measuring the fair value of a liability or an entity's own equity instrument using the quoted price for the identical item traded as an asset in an active market and that price needs to be adjusted for factors specific to the item or the asset (see **5.1.1**). If no adjustment to the quoted price of the asset is required, the result is a fair value measurement categorised within Level 1 of the fair value hierarchy. However, any adjustment to the quoted price of the asset results in a fair value measurement categorised within a lower level of the fair value hierarchy.

If an entity holds a position in a single asset or liability (including a position comprising a large number of identical assets or liabilities, such as a holding of financial instruments) and the asset or liability is traded in an active market, the fair value of the asset or liability should be measured within Level 1 as the product of the quoted price for the individual asset or liability and the quantity held by the entity. That is the case even if a market's normal daily trading volume is not sufficient to absorb the quantity held and placing orders to sell the position in a single transaction might affect the quoted price. [IFRS 13:80]

10.2.1.2 Published net asset values for open-ended investment funds as Level 1 inputs

Some open-ended investments funds not listed on a stock exchange may publish daily quotations of their net asset values (NAVs) at which redemptions or purchases of units occur without any adjustments to the published NAV. The redemptions and unit purchases may take place regularly at the quoted NAVs and there is no secondary market for the units because they are not transferrable (i.e. the sole transactions are issuances and redemptions of the units by the fund). These quoted NAVs may meet the definition of a Level 1 input provided that all of the elements of the definition in IFRS 13:76 (see **10.2.1.1**) are met.

Consequently, the following criteria must be satisfied:

- the price must be quoted in an active market (see **10.2.1.1**);
- the price must be unadjusted;
- the price must be for an asset or a liability that is identical to the asset or liability being measured; and
- the entity must have access to the price at the measurement date.

For the price to be classified as a Level 1 input, it is not required that there be an active market between the holders of the financial instrument and other potential holders that are not the issuer of the financial instrument; it is possible that the financial instrument does not have an active market other than between the holders of the financial instrument and the issuer of the financial instrument.

Careful analysis is required when assessing whether such prices meet the definition of a Level 1 input. In particular, the assessment should include: (1) whether quoted prices are readily and regularly available; (2) whether transactions occur regularly; and (3) whether the regularly occurring transactions take place at the quoted (unadjusted price) on an arm's length basis.

10.2.2 Level 2 inputs

Level 2 inputs are inputs other than quoted prices included within Level 1 that are observable for the asset or liability, either directly or indirectly. [IFRS 13:81 & Appendix A]

Level 2 inputs include the following:

[IFRS 13:82]

- quoted prices for similar assets or liabilities in active markets.
- quoted prices for identical or similar assets or liabilities in markets that are not active.
- inputs other than quoted prices that are observable for the asset or liability, for example:
  - interest rates and yield curves observable at commonly quoted intervals;

  - implied volatilities; and
  - credit spreads.
- inputs that are derived principally from or corroborated by observable market data by correlation or other means (market-corroborated inputs).

Under IFRS 13:82 (see above), when an entity measures the fair value of an asset or a liability and no Level 1 inputs are available, it may use quoted prices for 'similar' assets or liabilities in active markets as a Level 2 input. Equally, under IFRS 13:79(a) (see **10.2.1**), entities holding a large number of 'similar' assets or liabilities for which a quoted price is not accessible for all of the assets and liabilities being measured, may measure fair value using alternative pricing (e.g. matrix pricing) as a practical expedient.

IFRS 13 does not provide any specific guidance as to what is meant by 'similar' in this context. The identification of a similar asset or liability involves the exercise of judgement and requires both:

- an understanding of the terms and other factors that affect the fair values of the asset or liability being measured and the asset or liability for which the quoted price exists; and
- an identification and assessment of any differences in the terms and other factors that affect the fair values of these assets or liabilities.

In October 2008, the IASB's Expert Advisory Panel issued a report *Measuring and Disclosing the Fair Value of Financial Instruments in Markets That Are No Longer Active* which describes practices entities use when measuring financial instruments at fair value. Paragraph 32 of the report (quoted below) provides examples of the basic terms of a financial instrument with contractual cash flows. Entities may consider these terms, and any associated differences, when assessing whether the instrument for which a quoted price exists is 'similar' to the instrument being measured.

"The basic terms of a financial instrument include, for example:

(a) **the timing of the cash flows:** when the entity expects to realise the cash flows related to the instrument.

(b) **the calculation of the cash flows:** for example, for a debt instrument the interest rate that applies (i.e. the coupon), or for a derivative instrument how the cash flows are calculated in relation to the underlying instrument or index (or indices).

(c) **the timing and conditions for any options in the contract:** for example:

(i) prepayment options (one or both parties can demand or make an early payment).

(ii) extension options (one or both parties can extend the period of the instrument).

(iii) conversion options (one or both parties can convert the instrument into another instrument).

(iv) put or call options (one or both parties can exchange the instrument for a defined amount of cash or other assets or liabilities).

(d) **protection of the rights of the parties to the instrument:** for example:

(i) terms relating to credit risk in debt instruments, such as collateral, event of default and margin call triggers.

(ii) subordination of the instrument, for example the priority of the instruments in the event of a winding up.

(iii) the legal enforceability of the cash flows."

Further, paragraph 33 of the report notes that "to measure the fair value of an instrument it is necessary to assess the return that market participants would require on the instrument to compensate for" certain risks. This principle is largely consistent with the fair value measurement principles in IFRS 13. Accordingly, any differences between the compensation that market participants would require for the risk associated with the instrument being measured and the compensation required for the instrument for which a quoted price exists should be considered in determining whether the instruments are similar and whether an adjustment to the quoted price is necessary.

If the asset or liability has a specified (contractual) term, a Level 2 input must be observable for substantially the full term of the asset or liability. [IFRS 13:82]

Example 10.2.2

Determining how an input is classified when the item being measured has a specified contractual term

Company X enters into a fixed-price six-year agreement to sell 50 megawatts (MW) of on-peak electricity for delivery at location ABC beginning on 1 January 20X1 and continuing through to 31 December 20X6. On 31 March 20X1, Company X is measuring the fair value of the fixed-price agreement. Active market quotes are available for forward contracts to sell electricity at location ABC for two years (31 March 20X1 to 31 March 20X3). Accordingly, Company X will use the two years of observable forward pricing data and develop an expectation for the remaining 3 years and nine months (i.e.1 April 20X3 to 31 December 20X6) using a model that relies on pricing data and weather patterns from the previous four years. The model also incorporates all relevant physical constraints (capacity of existing power plants and power plants expected to be completed near location ABC, projected supply and demand etc.).

In the circumstances described, the five-year and nine-month forward price curve represents a Level 3, rather than a Level 2, input.

An input for an item with a specified contractual term falls within Level 2 of the hierarchy only if it meets both of the following criteria:

- as required by IFRS 13:82 (see above), the input must be observable for substantially the full term of the asset or liability (see above); and
- the impact of the unobservable period must not be significant to the fair value of the asset or liability. The guidance set out in **10.3.3.2** should be applied when evaluating whether the effect of the unobservable period is significant.

IFRS 13:B35(b) cites as an example an interest rate swap with a term of10 years and for which the fair value is determined using a swap rate based on a yield curve that is observable at commonly quoted intervals for 9 years. The swap rate input is a Level 2 input provided that any reasonable extrapolation of the yield curve for Year 10 would not be significant to the fair value measurement of the swap in its entirety.

In contrast, in the circumstances described, Company X can observe forward prices for only 24 months of the remaining 69-month term of the agreement (i.e. 35 per cent of the term). Because this does not represent substantially the full term, the first criterion above is not met. An analysis of the second criterion is unnecessary; the forward price curve is considered a Level 3 input. However, if the forward price curve had been observable for substantially the full term, Company X would need to consider the second criterion (i.e. whether the effect of the unobservable term is significant to the fair value of the agreement) to determine whether the forward price curve is a Level 2 or Level 3 input.

Adjustments to Level 2 inputs will vary depending on factors specific to the asset or liability. Those factors include the following:

[IFRS 13:83]

- the condition or location of the asset;
- the extent to which inputs relate to items that are comparable to the asset or liability (including those factors described in IFRS 13:39 – see **5.1.1**); and
- the volume or level of activity in the markets within which the inputs are observed.

An entity should consider whether adjustments to the quoted price for a similar asset or liability are necessary to reflect differences between the terms of the items being compared and other factors that may affect the fair values of those items. For example, the entity may need to make adjustments to reflect differences in the condition, location or risks (including non-performance risk and liquidity risk) of the items being compared.

Under IFRS 13:37, when a quoted price for the transfer of an identical or similar liability is not available and the identical item is held by another party as an asset, the fair value of the liability is measured from the perspective of a market participant that holds the identical item as an asset at the measurement date. The value should only be adjusted for factors specific to the asset that are not applicable to the fair value measurement of the liability. IFRS 13:39 provides a number of examples of such factors (see **5.1.1**).

In addition, if an entity uses a quoted price for a similar item in its valuation technique, the entity may need to make adjustments to reflect differences in risk, including liquidity differences. For example, the item being measured may be in shorter supply (relative to demand) than the similar item for which a quoted price exists. In this situation, a liquidity risk premium exists for the item being measured that should be factored into the fair value measurement as an adjustment to the quoted price of the similar item.

An adjustment to a Level 2 input that is significant to the entire measurement might result in a fair value measurement categorised within Level 3 of the fair value hierarchy, if the adjustment uses significant unobservable inputs. [IFRS 13:84] See **10.3.3.2** for further discussion.

IFRS 13 provides the following examples of Level 2 inputs for particular assets and liabilities.

[IFRS 13:B35]

- **Receive-fixed, pay-variable interest rate swap based on the London Interbank Offered Rate (LIBOR) swap rate** A Level 2 input would be the LIBOR swap rate if that rate is observable at commonly quoted intervals for substantially the full term of the swap.
- **Receive-fixed, pay-variable interest rate swap based on a yield curve denominated in a foreign currency** A Level 2 input would be the swap rate based on a yield curve denominated in a foreign currency that is observable at commonly quoted intervals for substantially the full term of the swap. That would be the case if the term of the swap is 10 years and that rate is observable at commonly quoted intervals for 9 years, provided that any reasonable extrapolation of the yield curve for Year 10 would not be significant to the fair value measurement of the swap in its entirety (but see **example 10.2.2** for circumstances when observable data is not available for substantially the full term of the agreement).
- **Receive-fixed, pay-variable interest rate swap based on a specific bank's prime rate** A Level 2 input would be the bank's prime rate derived through extrapolation if the extrapolated values are corroborated by observable market data, for example, by correlation with an interest rate that is observable over substantially the full term of the swap.

- **Three-year option on exchange-traded shares** A Level 2 input would be the implied volatility for the shares derived through extrapolation to Year 3 if both of the following conditions exist:
  (i) prices for one-year and two-year options on the shares are observable
  (ii) the extrapolated implied volatility of a three-year option is corroborated by observable market data for substantially the full term of the option.

In that case, the implied volatility could be derived by extrapolating from the implied volatility of the one-year and two-year options on the shares and corroborated by the implied volatility for three-year options on comparable entities' shares, provided that correlation with the one-year and two-year implied volatilities is established. [IFRS 13:B35]

10.2.3 Level 3 inputs

Level 3 inputs are unobservable inputs for the asset or liability. [IFRS 13:86 & Appendix A]

Unobservable inputs should be used to measure fair value to the extent that relevant observable inputs are not available (e.g. when there is little, if any, market activity for the asset or liability at the measurement date). However unobservable inputs should reflect the assumptions that market participants would use when pricing the asset or liability, so as to achieve the general fair value measurement objective (i.e. an exit price at the measurement date from the perspective of a market participant that holds the asset or owes the liability). [IFRS 13:87]

Unobservable inputs should reflect, among others, assumptions that market participants would make about risk. Assumptions about risk include the risk inherent in a particular valuation technique used to measure fair value (such as a pricing model) and the risk inherent in the inputs to the valuation technique. A measurement that does not include an adjustment for risk would not represent a fair value measurement if market participants would include one when pricing the asset or liability. For example, it might be necessary to include a risk adjustment when there is significant measurement uncertainty (e.g. when there has been a significant decrease in the volume or level of activity when compared with normal market activity for the asset or liability (or similar assets or liabilities) and the entity has determined that the transaction price or quoted price does not represent fair value – see **sections 9.5** to **9.7**). [IFRS 13:88]

Unobservable inputs should be developed using the best information available in the circumstances, which might include an entity's own data. In developing unobservable inputs, an entity's own data, should be adjusted if reasonably available information indicates that other market participants would use different data or there is something particular to the entity that is not available to other market participants (e.g. an entity-specific synergy).

IFRS 13 does not require an entity to undertake exhaustive efforts to obtain information about market participant assumptions. However, the entity is required to take into account all information about market participant assumptions that is reasonably available. Unobservable inputs developed in the manner described above are considered market participant assumptions and meet the objective of a fair value measurement. [IFRS 13:89]

IFRS 13 provides the following examples of Level 3 inputs for particular assets and liabilities.

[IFRS 13:B36]

- **Long-dated currency swap** A Level 3 input would be an interest rate in a specified currency that is not observable and cannot be corroborated by observable market data at commonly quoted intervals or otherwise for substantially the full term of the currency swap. The interest rates in a currency swap are the swap rates calculated from the respective countries' yield curves.
- **Three-year option on exchange-traded shares** A Level 3 input would be historical volatility, i.e. the volatility for the shares derived from the shares' historical prices. Historical volatility typically does not represent current market participant expectations about future volatility, even if it is the only information available to price an option.
- **Interest rate swap** A Level 3 input would be an adjustment to a mid-market consensus (non-binding) price for the swap developed using data that are not directly observable and cannot otherwise be corroborated by observable market data.

10.2.4 Determining the level within the fair value hierarchy when broker or pricing service quotes are used

IFRS 13 allows the use of quoted prices provided by brokers or pricing services if the entity has determined that the quoted prices provided by a broker or pricing service are developed in accordance with IFRS 13. See **section 9.7** for more detailed guidance regarding when a quoted price provided by a broker or pricing service can be considered to be determinative of fair value.

When quoted prices are provided by a broker or pricing service, and are used by an entity in measuring the fair value of an asset or a liability, the following considerations are relevant for the entity's assessment of the level within the fair value hierarchy in which the quoted prices fall.

Level 1 inputs

Level 1 inputs are unadjusted quoted prices in active markets for identical assets or liabilities. If the quote provided by a broker or pricing service is a Level 1 input, the quoted price should be used to measure the fair value of the asset or liability without adjustment, subject to limited exceptions as discussed in IFRS 13:79 (see **10.2.1.1**).

If an adjustment is necessary in accordance with IFRS 13:79, or if the quoted price originates from a market that is not active, the broker or pricing service quote does not represent a Level 1 input.

In January 2015, the Interpretations Committee received a request to clarify under what circumstances prices that are provided by third parties would qualify as Level 1 in the fair value hierarchy in accordance with IFRS 13. The submitter noted that there are divergent views on the level within the hierarchy in which fair value measurements based on prices received from third parties should be classified.

The Interpretations Committee noted that when assets or liabilities are measured on the basis of prices provided by third parties, the classification of those measurements within the fair value hierarchy will depend on the evaluation of the inputs used by the third party to derive those prices, instead of on the pricing methodology used. In other words, the fair value hierarchy prioritises the inputs to valuation techniques, not the valuation techniques used to measure fair value. In accordance with IFRS 13, only unadjusted quoted prices in active markets for identical assets or liabilities that the entity can access at the measurement date qualify as Level 1 inputs. Consequently, the Interpretations Committee noted that a fair value measurement that is based on prices provided by third parties may only be categorised within Level 1 of the fair value hierarchy if the measurement relies solely on unadjusted quoted prices in an active market for an identical instrument that the entity can access at the measurement date.

The Interpretations Committee also observed that the guidance in IFRS 13 relating to the classification of measurements within the fair value hierarchy is sufficient to draw an appropriate conclusion on the issue submitted. Consequently, the Interpretations Committee decided not to add this issue to its agenda.

Level 2 inputs

Level 2 inputs are inputs other than quoted prices included within Level 1 that are observable for the asset or liability, either directly or indirectly. Observable inputs are defined in IFRS 13:Appendix A as "[i]nputs that are developed using market data, such as publicly available information about actual events or transactions, and that reflect the assumptions that market participants would use when pricing the asset or liability [or own equity instrument]".

If a quote from a broker or pricing service meets any of the following criteria, it represents a Level 2 input.

- The entity can determine that the broker or pricing service quote itself represents a quoted price for similar assets or liabilities in active markets.
- The entity can determine that the quote is based on quoted prices for identical or similar assets or liabilities in markets that are not active, from transactions that are orderly and for which adjustments are based only on information that is (1) observable, or (2) market-corroborated, or (3) unobservable, but insignificant to the measurement.
- The entity can determine that the quote was established using a valuation technique and that the inputs the broker or pricing service used to arrive at the quoted price are observable or market-corroborated and any unobservable inputs do not have a significant effect on the measurement.
- The entity can corroborate the broker or pricing service quote or inputs using prices (1) from orderly transactions in an active market or (2) from orderly transactions in an inactive market for which any adjustment needed to ensure the price is representative of fair value is insignificant to the measurement.

In some circumstances, adjustments to the Level 2 inputs may be necessary, for example if the quoted price is based on a similar (but not identical) asset or liability. If an adjustment is required, an entity should determine whether the adjustment is significant to the entire measurement and whether it is based on unobservable inputs (see **10.3.2.1**). If this is the case, the entire measurement will be categorised within Level 3.

Level 3 inputs

Level 3 inputs are unobservable inputs for the asset or liability. Broker or pricing service quotes meeting any of the following criteria are categorised in Level 3 of the fair value hierarchy.

- The entity can determine that the quote is based on a Level 1 or Level 2 input but an adjustment is required that is significant to the measurement and based on unobservable inputs.
- The entity can determine that the quote is based on unobservable inputs with a significant effect.

Regardless of whether the entity determines that the broker or pricing service quote is based on observable or unobservable inputs, it is not appropriate for an entity to accept, without further analysis, that the inputs used are appropriate in the circumstances. The entity must gain sufficient understanding of the inputs to be able to conclude that they reflect assumptions market participants would use, including assumptions about risks inherent in a particular valuation technique and the inputs used. Further, an entity must be able to conclude that the inputs used are based on the best information available. Adjustments should be made if reasonably available information, including the entity's own data, indicates that other market participants would use different inputs.

Other considerations

Depending on the asset or liability being measured at fair value, a quote from a broker or pricing service may be the only input, or one of many inputs, into an entity's fair value measurement of that asset or liability. All inputs must be considered before determining the level within the fair value hierarchy for measurement of the asset or liability (see **section 10.3**).

Other factors indicating that a broker or pricing service quote may be given more weight in the fair value measurement include that:

- the quote is binding on the entity making the quote; or
- the quote is available from more than one broker or pricing service.

Disclosure

IFRS 13:IE64(b) in the illustrative examples accompanying IFRS 13 suggests that, in order to comply with the disclosure requirements in IFRS 13:92(d), an entity may disclose "how third-party information such as broker quotes, pricing services, net asset values and relevant market data was taken into account when measuring fair value" as part of the entity's additional information about significant unobservable inputs. Further, IFRS 13:IE65(d) suggests that, in order to comply with the disclosure requirements in IFRS 13:93(g), an entity may disclose how the entity determined that third-party information, such as broker quotes or pricing services, used in the fair value measurement was developed in accordance with IFRS 13 as part of the entity's description of its valuation process for Level 3 fair value measurements.

10.3 Categorisation of fair value measurements within the fair value hierarchy

10.3.1 Categorisation of fair value measurements – general

The categorisation of a fair value measurement within the fair value hierarchy is a two-step process. Initially, the entity determines the appropriate categorisation of the inputs to the valuation techniques used in the fair value measurement (see **section 10.2**). Once the valuation techniques have been applied, and the fair value measured, it is then necessary to determine the appropriate categorisation of the fair value measurement in its entirety. This is required in order to arrive at the appropriate analysis of the fair value measurements for disclosure purposes (see **4.3.3.3** in **chapter C12**).

As can be seen from the discussion in **10.3.1** to **10.3.2**, the appropriate categorisation of a fair value measurement is determined by the 'mix' of inputs used. For example, if only Level 1 inputs are used, the fair value measurement will be categorised as a Level 1 measurement (see **10.3.1**). The same principle applies if only Level 2 or only Level 3 inputs are used. Alternatively, the fair value measurement may be derived from several inputs from different categories, in which case it will be necessary to consider the significance of each of those inputs (see **10.3.2**).

10.3.2 Categorisation of measurements made using Level 1 inputs

A fair value measurement can only be categorised as a Level 1 measurement when only Level 1 inputs are used, and no adjustments are made.

In any of the circumstances described in IFRS 13:79 (see **10.2.1**), a Level 1 input cannot be used without adjustment. IFRS 13:79 outlines the appropriate adjustments for each circumstance. Note that any adjustment to a Level 1 input, regardless of its significance, means that the resulting fair value measurement cannot be categorised as a Level 1 measurement.

Based on the definition in IFRS 13:76 and Appendix 1 (see **10.2.1**), for a fair value measurement to be categorised in Level 1 of the fair value hierarchy, the following criteria must be satisfied:

- the only input used must be a price (or prices) quoted in an active market;
- the price must be unadjusted. IFRS 13:79 (see above) requires that any adjustment to a fair value measurement (regardless of its significance) that would otherwise meet the Level 1 criteria results in the fair value measurement being categorised as a lower-level measurement;
- the price must be for an asset or liability that is identical to the asset or liability being measured (see **examples 10.3.2A** to **10.3.2D**); and
- the entity must have access to the price at the measurement date. For example, an entity has access to the price if it has the ability to transact at that price in an exchange market. In addition, an entity has access to the price if there are dealers who stand ready to transact with the entity at that price. However, broker quotes by themselves are not sufficient evidence that the entity has access to the price if the brokers do not stand ready to transact at that price. Any adjustment made to a quoted price in an active market

because the entity has limited or no access to that market results in a Level 2 or a Level 3 measurement, depending on the nature of the adjustment. Further, although a quoted price in an active market may be available, such pricing may not be readily accessible for all of the assets and liabilities being measured, if an entity holds a large volume of similar (but not identical) instruments. As a result, the entity may measure fair value using alternative pricing (e.g. matrix pricing) as a practical expedient, which would result in a lower level measurement in the fair value hierarchy.

Example 10.3.2A

Application of Level 1 classification criteria – debt security

Entity P holds a debt security that is traded in a dealer market in which bid and ask prices are available. The market is an active market and it is the principal market for the security. The market is accessible by Entity P. No adjustments have been made to the quoted price.

If the quoted price used to measure the fair value of the debt security is for a debt security identical to that held by Entity P, the measurement of the debt security should be classified within Level 1 of the fair value hierarchy. The fact that a price is derived from a dealer market (rather than an 'exchange' market) does not in itself preclude classification as a Level 1 measurement because such dealer markets may be active and accessible to the entity (see also **10.2.4**).

Example 10.3.2B

Application of Level 1 classification criteria – issued debt security with identical instrument traded as an asset

Entity Q has issued an exchange-traded debt security. Entity Q has elected to account for this instrument using the fair value option under IAS 39. A quoted price for the transfer of an identical or similar liability is not available; however, an identical instrument is currently trading as an asset in an active market. Entity Q uses the quoted price for the asset as its initial input for the fair value measurement of the issued debt security. Entity Q also evaluates whether the quoted price for the asset requires adjustment for factors, such as third-party credit enhancements, that would not be applicable to the issued debt security. Entity Q determines that no adjustments are required to the quoted price of the asset.

Because the quoted price used to measure the fair value of the issued debt security is for an identical debt security (e.g. the identical ISIN*) traded as an asset, and no adjustments to the quoted price of the instrument are required, the resulting measurement of the issued debt security should be classified as a Level 1 measurement in the fair value hierarchy.

* ISIN refers to the International Securities Identification Number, a 12-character alphanumerical code that does not contain information characterising financial instruments but serves for uniform identification of a security at trading and settlement.

Example 10.3.2C

Application of Level 1 classification criteria – 'look-alike' forward contract

Entity R holds an over-the-counter (OTC) 'look-alike' forward contract (i.e. it mirrors another contract). The counterparty to this contract is contractually obligated to settle it on the basis of the quoted price for a similar futures contract traded on an active futures exchange. The forward contract meets the definition of a derivative and is therefore measured at fair value.

While the look-alike forward contract mirrors the exchange-traded futures contract, and the value of the look-alike forward contract is intended to approximate the quoted price for the exchange-traded futures contract, the forward and futures contracts are not identical. Even if the parties to the forward contract both have the highest credit quality (resulting in the same level of credit risk as the exchange-traded futures contract), the forward contract is not considered identical because (1) the counterparties are different, and (2) Entity R cannot sell the forward contract on the futures exchange (i.e. the forward contract has different levels of counterparty and liquidity risk when compared to the futures contract). While the quoted price for the futures contract may be a Level 1 input (when the market for it is active), the fair value measurement of the look-alike forward contract can only be classified as Level 2 or 3.

Example 10.3.2D

Application of Level 1 classification criteria – interest rate swap

Entity S is a party to an interest rate swap that is transacted on an over-the-counter (OTC) market. The OTC market does not quote prices for interest rate swaps. Entity S would determine the fair value of the swap by using either (1) a discounted cash flow approach based on market-based yield curves, or (2) the price at which a similar swap was exchanged on the OTC market. While similar swaps may have been exchanged on the OTC market, the similar swaps would have different counterparties and would, therefore, not be identical to the swap held by Entity S.

The price at which Entity S would be able to sell the swap would result from a negotiated transaction contemplating the credit standings of the two parties to the swap as well as the terms of the specific swap. Because the swap held by Entity S is not identical to any similar swap for which there may be transactions on the OTC market, the measurement of the swap by Entity S would be classified as a Level 2 or 3 measurement, depending on the inputs that are significant to the measurement.

10.3.3 Determining the level within the fair value hierarchy when several inputs are used

10.3.3.1 Determining the level within the fair value hierarchy – general

When several inputs are used to measure the fair value of an asset or a liability, those inputs may be categorised within different levels of the fair value hierarchy (e.g. the valuation may be based on some Level 2 and some Level 3 inputs). In such circumstances, the categorisation of the fair value measurement in its entirety is based on the lowest level input that is significant to the entire measurement. [IFRS 13:73] See **10.3.3.2** for a discussion of the meaning of the term 'significant'.

Example 10.3.3.1

Classification of fair value measurements within the fair value hierarchy

Entity I holds an investment in equity instruments that are not traded in an active market (e.g. equity instruments issued by a private entity). In accordance with IAS 39, the investment is measured at fair value subsequent to initial recognition.

How should Entity I classify the fair value measurement of its investment within the fair value hierarchy (i.e. as Level 1, Level 2 or Level 3)?

The examples below illustrate the application of the guidance in IFRS 13 on the classification of measurements within the fair value hierarchy.

Note that, because the equity instruments are not traded in an active market, Level 1 inputs are not available.

Scenario 1 – Fair value is estimated based on recent transactions

If Entity I estimates the fair value of its investment based on recent transactions between independent third parties (e.g. quoted prices in an inactive market, privately negotiated acquisitions or disposals of the equity instruments etc.), these transaction prices would be considered Level 2 inputs if they meet the definition of fair value. This would be the case if the price represents an exit price for the equity instruments at the date of the transaction, the transaction is executed at terms that are consistent with how other market participants would transact, and the transaction is not executed under duress.

Similarly, prices based on recent transactions between Entity I and third parties may be considered Level 2 inputs if they meet the criteria above. For example, Entity I owns a 5 per cent equity investment in Entity X and measures that investment at fair value. Entity I acquires an additional 10 per cent of Entity X. If the transaction price for the additional 10 per cent meets the definition of fair value, Entity I may use that price as a basis for valuing its entire 15 per cent investment at the next reporting date.

In either case, it may be necessary to adjust the recent transaction price to measure the investment appropriately at fair value at the reporting date. For example, the recent transaction price should be adjusted for events or changes in the entity's financial position that have occurred since the date of the transaction that would affect the value of the equity investment in the entity. Unobservable adjustments to a Level 2 input that are significant to the entire measurement would change the categorisation to Level 3.

Scenario 2 – Fair value is determined based on a discounted cash flow technique

IFRS 13:B36(e) (see **10.2.3**) cites as an example of a Level 3 input "a financial forecast (e.g. of cash flows or earnings) developed using the entity's own data if there is no reasonably available information that indicates that market participants would use different assumptions". While certain information used in the model may be observable (e.g. interest rate curves), the entity's projected cash flows (which are not observable) would probably be significant to the entire fair value measurement. Therefore, the measurement of the investment would probably be classified as Level 3.

Scenario 3 – Fair value is determined based on a market-based multiple applied to a financial measure

IFRS 13:B35(h) (see **10.2.2**) cites as an example of a Level 2 input "a valuation multiple (e.g. a multiple of earnings or revenue or a similar performance measure) derived from observable market data, e.g. multiples derived from prices in observed transactions involving comparable (that is, similar) businesses, taking into account operational, market, financial, and non-financial factors". The market-derived multiple may thus be considered a Level 2 input. However, the historical financial measure (i.e. earnings or EBITDA) and any adjustments needed to reflect differences between the entity and comparable entities would probably be Level 3 inputs because they are entity-specific and are not considered market-observable data. Therefore, the measurement of the investment would probably be classified within Level 3 of the fair value hierarchy.

The availability of relevant inputs and their relative subjectivity might affect the selection of appropriate valuation techniques. However, the fair value hierarchy prioritises the inputs to valuation techniques, not the valuation techniques used to measure fair value. For example, a fair value measurement developed using a present value technique might be categorised within Level 2 or Level 3, depending on the inputs that are significant to the entire measurement and the level of the fair value hierarchy within which those inputs are categorised. [IFRS 13:74]

In other words, the categorisation of the fair value measurement in the fair value hierarchy is based on inputs, not on the valuation technique in which they are used.

If an observable input requires an adjustment using an unobservable input and that adjustment results in a significantly higher or lower fair value measurement, the resulting measurement is a Level 3 measurement. For example, if a market participant would take into account the effect of a restriction on the sale of an asset when estimating the price for the asset, an entity would adjust the quoted price to reflect the effect of that restriction. If that quoted price is a Level 2 input and the adjustment is an unobservable input that is significant to the entire measurement, the measurement would be categorised within Level 3 of the fair value hierarchy. [IFRS 13:75]

10.3.3.2 Determining the 'significance' of an input or an adjustment

The Standard does not expand on what is meant by 'significant' in the context of IFRS 13:73, other than to state that the assessment of the significance of a particular input to the entire measurement requires judgement, taking into account factors specific to the asset or liability. [IFRS 13:73]

To determine the level in which the fair value measurement should be categorised, an entity should aggregate the inputs to the measurement by level and determine the lowest level of inputs that are significant to the fair value measurement in its entirety. For example, a measurement that includes inputs with significant effect from Levels 2 and 3 would be classified in its entirety in Level 3, because Level 3 is the lowest level input with a significant effect.

Entities should establish a methodology for determining whether an input or aggregated inputs are significant to the measurement in its entirety. The methodology should be applied consistently.

In some cases, a qualitative assessment of the inputs used may be sufficient. For example, changes in discount rates generally have a significant effect on fair value measurements determined using a discounted cash flow model.

In other cases, a quantitative analysis of the inputs may be required. One quantitative approach might involve the following steps.

- **Step 1** – Select a threshold or percentage of the overall fair value measurement as a benchmark for significance.
- **Step 2** – Perform a sensitivity analysis, calculating the percentage change in the fair value measurement arising from reasonably possible changes to each input.
- **Step 3** – Compare the percentage change in the fair value measurement for each input calculated under Step 2 to the benchmark selected under Step 1. If the percentage change in the fair value measurement for a particular input exceeds the selected benchmark, that input would be considered significant. If none of the individual Level 3 inputs are considered significant, the combined effect of all the Level 3 inputs should be considered to determine whether they have a significant effect in aggregate on the fair value measurement.

When this approach is used, the benchmark should represent a percentage of the overall measurement and not a percentage of a particular component of the fair value measurement. In addition, the threshold should not represent a percentage of total assets, total liabilities, gains or losses, or other line items in the statement of financial position or the statement of comprehensive income because this would not be specific to the fair value measurement.

Example 10.3.3.2 illustrates this approach.

Example 10.3.3.2

Determining the significance of an input

Entity A holds a hybrid instrument which includes an embedded option. Entity A is measuring the instrument at fair value in its entirety. One of the inputs to its valuation model is the volatility of the embedded option for which market data are not available (i.e. it is unobservable and, consequently, a Level 3 input).

Entity A is evaluating whether the unobservable volatility input is significant to the overall fair value measurement for the hybrid instrument. In making its assessment, Entity A considers the significance of the volatility in relation to the hybrid instrument in its entirety and not solely in relation to the embedded option.

Entity A uses a quantitative methodology and selects a threshold or percentage of the overall fair value measurement of the hybrid instrument as a benchmark for significance. Entity A then performs a sensitivity analysis to determine how the volatility input affects the overall fair value of the hybrid instrument within a reasonably possible range of values for the volatility input.

If reasonable changes in the volatility input cause the percentage change in the fair value measurement of the hybrid instrument to exceed the selected threshold, Entity A would conclude that the unobservable volatility input is significant to the measurement in its entirety. In that case, the fair value measurement of the hybrid instrument would represent a Level 3 measurement within the fair value hierarchy.

10.3.4 Observable transactions in inactive markets

The level of market activity does not affect the IFRS 13 measurement objective, i.e. fair value is the price in an orderly transaction between market participants at the measurement date under current market conditions.

Observable transactions are relevant inputs to a fair value measurement when they reflect market participants' assumptions in orderly transactions and, thus, are representative of fair value. Relevant observable inputs should be given priority when measuring fair value in accordance with IFRS 13. IFRS 13:67 (see **section 9**) states that "[v]aluation techniques used to measure fair value shall maximise the use of relevant observable inputs and minimise the use of unobservable inputs". Further, IFRS 13:87 (see **10.2.3**) states, in part, that "[u]nobservable inputs [Level 3] shall be used to measure fair value to the extent that relevant observable inputs [Level 1 and 2] are not available...".

However, when the volume and level of activity in a market have significantly decreased and the market is not active, observable transactions may not be representative of fair value because of increased instances of transactions that are not orderly (e.g. forced liquidations or distress sales). Consequently, an entity should perform further analysis of the transactions or quoted prices available to determine whether they represent fair value. In some circumstances, a change in valuation technique or the use of multiple valuation techniques may be appropriate, as discussed below.

Transaction is not orderly

If the observable transactions are not orderly, IFRS 13:B44(a) states that "the entity shall place little, if any, weight (compared with other indications of fair value) on that transaction price" (see **section 9.6**). If an entity previously used quoted prices to measure fair value, and quoted prices from orderly transactions are no longer available, the entity may need to change its valuation technique or use multiple valuation techniques. If the entity measures fair value by using the price from a transaction that is not orderly, the price should be adjusted to reflect the assumptions that market participants would use in pricing the asset or liability in an orderly transaction. The resulting measurement would generally be classified as a Level 3 measurement.

Transactions are orderly

If the observable transactions are orderly, the entity should consider the transaction price when estimating fair value. However, the entity may also need to adjust the transaction price when measuring fair value to meet the measurement objective. IFRS 13:B44(b) states that the "amount of weight placed on that [orderly] transaction price when compared with other indications of fair value will depend on the facts and circumstances" (see **section 9.6**).

If an entity determines that it does not need to make any significant adjustment to the transaction price using unobservable inputs to arrive at the fair value of the asset or liability, the transaction price represents a relevant observable input and the measurement would be classified as a Level 2 measurement. However, if the entity determines that it needs to make a significant adjustment to the transaction price using unobservable inputs, the measurement would be classified as a Level 3 measurement.

Insufficient information to determine whether transactions are orderly

If an entity is unable to obtain, without undue cost and effort, sufficient information to determine whether the transaction is orderly, the entity must consider the transaction price in determining fair value; however, the transaction price may not be the 'sole or primary' basis for estimating fair value. In such circumstances, because the transaction price may not reflect the assumptions that market participants would use, a fair value measurement that has this price as its principal input would most likely represent a Level 3 measurement. As above, the use of multiple valuation techniques may be appropriate in this case.

C8 Recognition and derecognition

Contents

1 Introduction

The recognition requirements of IAS 39 address the question of whether or not a financial instrument is included in the statement of financial position. Derecognition, not surprisingly, is the reverse of recognition and is the removal of a previously recognised financial instrument from the statement of financial position.

In summary, IAS 39 stipulates that:

- a financial instrument (financial asset or financial liability) is recognised when, and only when, the entity becomes a party to the contractual provisions of the instrument;
- a previously recognised financial asset is derecognised when, and only when, either the contractual rights to the cash flows from that asset expire, or the entity transfers the asset such that the transfer qualifies for derecognition; and
- a financial liability is derecognised when, and only when, it is extinguished.

The criteria that are applied to transfers of financial assets are a mix of risks and rewards and control tests. IAS 39 establishes a hierarchy for the tests and provides many examples to clarify the meaning of the concepts used and application of the tests to various transfer transactions.

Although the broad principles of derecognition may appear simple, a significant degree of judgement is required when applying these principles in practice.

2 Initial recognition

2.1 General principle

An entity should only recognise a financial asset or a financial liability in its statement of financial position when it becomes a party to the contractual provisions of the instrument. [IAS 39:14]

Arrangements that are recognised as financial assets and liabilities are as follows:

- Unconditional receivables are recognised as an asset when the entity becomes a party to the contract and, as a consequence, has a legal right to receive cash. [IAS 39:AG35(a)]
- Issued debt is recognised as a liability when the entity that issues it becomes a party to the contractual terms of the debt and, consequently, has a legal obligation to pay cash to the debt holder.

- A derivative is recognised as an asset or a liability on the commitment date, rather than on the date on which settlement takes place. At inception, the fair values of the right and obligation created by the derivative may be equal, in which case the fair value of the derivative will be zero. [IAS 39:AG35(c)]

Arrangements that are not recognised as financial assets and liabilities are as follows.

- Planned future transactions, no matter how likely, are not assets and liabilities because the entity has not become a party to a contract. [IAS 39:AG35(e)]
- Derivative contracts to buy or sell non-financial items that are scoped out of IAS 39 are not recognised as financial assets and liabilities because they are executory contracts.
- Assets to be acquired and liabilities to be incurred as a result of a firm commitment are generally not recognised until at least one of the parties has performed under the agreement. [IAS 39:AG35(b)]

A firm commitment to acquire a non-financial item is not recognised until the asset is acquired if the commitment itself is deemed to be outside the scope of IAS 39 (see **2.5** in **chapter C1**). A firm commitment to buy a financial asset, or a commitment to buy a non-financial item where the commitment is in the scope of IAS 39, is generally recognised as a derivative on the date the commitment is entered into (see **chapter C4**) unless the 'regular way' exemption is applied (see **2.2**). If a previously unrecognised firm commitment is subject to a highly effective fair value hedge, changes in the fair value of the hedged risk of the firm commitment are recognised in the statement of financial position. This appears to run counter to the general principle of not recognising firm commitments. The argument for permitting such an approach is that all firm commitments are recognised, but generally at a historical cost of nil, and the fair value hedge requirements merely remeasure part of that commitment to fair value. [IAS 39:BC152]

If an entity transfers or receives cash as collateral for an arrangement, careful consideration is needed to determine whether the cash should be recognised as a financial asset in the hands of the recipient. If the cash received by the recipient is not legally segregated from the recipient's other assets and the recipient has an unfettered right to use the cash, then the cash meets the definition of an asset. This is because the ultimate realisation of a financial asset is its conversion into cash and, therefore, no further transformation is required before the economic benefits of the cash transferred by the provider of the collateral are realised by the recipient. In this case, the recipient would recognise the cash as a financial asset and recognise an equivalent financial liability to return the cash to the provider of the collateral. The provider of the collateral would derecognise the cash and recognise a receivable from the collateral holder. [IAS 39:IG.D.1]

Derivatives that prevent a transfer of financial assets from achieving derecognition are not recognised if recognising both the derivative and the asset that failed derecognition would amount to accounting for the same rights and obligations twice. [IAS 39:AG49] For example, if an entity transfers a financial asset but at the date of transfer agrees to repurchase the asset at a fixed price in the future, the forward contract to repurchase the asset is not recognised as a derivative at FVTPL as it is this repurchase arrangement that results in the entity retaining the risks and rewards of ownership and thereby continuing to recognise the transferred asset.

2.1.1 Linked transactions

IAS 39 does not contain any general guidance regarding when two separate financial instruments entered into concurrently should be recognised as a single combined instrument. IAS 39 does, however, provide specific implementation guidance in IAS 39:IG.B.6 regarding when a loan receivable and a payable should be as accounted for as a single transaction equivalent to an interest rate swap. It seems reasonable to apply the guidance in IAS 39:IG.B.6 to other transactions. Two financial instruments should therefore be recognised and measured as a single combined instrument if all of the following conditions are met:

- they are entered into at the same time and in contemplation of each other;
- they have the same counterparty;
- they relate to the same risk; and
- there is no economic need or substantive business purpose for structuring the transactions separately that could not also have been accomplished in a single transaction.

Transactions are commonly structured as two or more financial instruments, notwithstanding that their substance is that of a single arrangement, in order to generate specific tax benefits. It is difficult to see how it can be argued that structuring for the purposes of obtaining tax benefits is a substantive business purpose, particularly when those tax benefits derive from the accounting treatment adopted.

In March 2014, the IFRS Interpretations Committee issued a final agenda decision on IAS 39, *Accounting for a term-structured repo transactions.*

The Interpretations Committee received a request to clarify: (Issue 1) whether an entity (Entity A) should account for three transactions separately or aggregate and treat them as a single derivative; and

(Issue 2) how to apply IAS 39:IG.B.6 in addressing Issue 1. Some key features of the three transactions are as follows:

(a) Transaction 1 (bond purchase): Entity A purchases a bond (the bond) from another entity (Entity B).

(b) Transaction 2 (interest rate swap): Entity A enters into interest rate swap contract(s) with Entity B. Entity A pays a fixed rate of interest equal to the fixed coupon rate of the purchased bond in Transaction 1 and receives a variable rate of interest.

(c) Transaction 3 (repurchase agreement): Entity A enters into a repurchase agreement with Entity B, in which Entity A sells the same bond in Transaction 1 on the same day it purchases the bond and agrees to buy back the bond at the maturity date of the bond.

The Interpretations Committee noted that in order to determine whether Entity A should aggregate and account for the three transactions above as a single derivative, reference should be made to IAS 39:IG.B.6 and C.6 and IAS 32:AG39.

The Interpretations Committee also discussed Issue 2, i.e., how to apply IAS 39:IG.B.6 in addressing Issue 1. The Interpretations Committee noted that application of the guidance in IAS 39:IG.B.6 requires judgement. It also noted that the indicators in IAS 39:IG.B.6 may help an entity to determine the substance of the transaction, but that the presence or absence of any single specific indicator alone may not be conclusive.

The Interpretations Committee noted that providing additional guidance would result in the Interpretations Committee attempting to specify the accounting for a specific transaction, and that this would not be appropriate.

On the basis of the analysis above, the Interpretations Committee determined that, in the light of the existing IFRS requirements, neither an Interpretation nor an amendment to a Standard was necessary and consequently decided not to add this issue to its agenda.

2.1.2 *Modification that leads to initial recognition of a new instrument*

An entity may become a party to the contractual provisions of a financial instrument as a result of a substantial modification of the terms of an instrument that it already recognises in its statement of financial position. The entity will need to consider whether the modification results in derecognition of the existing instrument and recognition of a new instrument. Derecognition of financial assets is detailed in **section 3** and derecognition of financial liabilities is detailed in **section 4**.

Example 2.1.2

Initial recognition following modification

An entity had previously issued a perpetual instrument with an issuer option to redeem after 15 years. Under the terms of the instrument, the entity was entitled to defer interest payments indefinitely, except upon liquidation of the entity. The instrument met the definition of an equity instrument and was presented as equity at its net proceeds.

During the current reporting period, the entity and the holder of the instrument agree to modify the terms of the instrument so that, if a prescribed contingent event occurs any time after the date of modification, the entity will be required to pay all deferred interest and lose the right to defer future interest. This newly created contingent settlement provision is considered to be 'genuine' in accordance with IAS 32:25; consequently, after this modification, in accordance with IAS 32:25 the instrument is classified as a financial liability. The modification involves no compensation payment to the holders of the instrument and no change in the expected cash flows, and no fees in respect of the modification are paid.

All financial instruments are measured at fair value at initial recognition. In this example, the initial recognition date for the financial liability is the date of the modification because, at that date, the original equity instrument is derecognised and a new financial liability is recognised. Therefore, the entity must recognise the financial liability at its fair value, which will incorporate expectations of cash flows and market interest rates at the date of the modification. Any difference between the previous carrying amount recognised in equity and the fair value of the financial liability is recognised as an adjustment within equity.

If the entity does not designate the financial liability as at FVTPL, after initial recognition the liability is measured at amortised cost which will include any directly attributable transaction costs.

In November 2006, the IFRIC (now the IFRS Interpretations Committee) issued a rejection notice regarding changes in the contractual terms of an existing equity instrument that results in the instrument being reclassified as a financial liability for the issuer. Two issues were discussed:

(i) on what basis the financial liability should be measured at the date when the terms are changed; and

(ii) how any difference between the carrying amount of the previously recognised equity instrument and the amount of the financial liability recognised at the date when the terms are changed should be accounted for.

The IFRIC noted that the financial liability is initially recognised when the contractual terms are changed and that, on initial recognition, a financial liability is measured at its fair value in accordance with

IAS 39:43. The IFRIC observed that Example 3 of IFRIC 2 *Members' Shares in Co-operative Entities and Similar Instruments* deals with a similar situation. In that example, at the time when the financial liabilities are recognised as a result of a change in terms, they are recognised at their fair value.

The IFRIC observed that the change in the terms of the instrument results in the derecognition of the original equity instrument. The IFRIC noted that IAS 32:33 states that no gain or loss should be recognised in profit or loss on the purchase, sale, issue or cancellation of an entity's own equity instruments. The IFRIC therefore concluded that, at the time when the terms are changed, the difference between the carrying amount of the equity instrument and the fair value of the newly recognised financial liability should be recognised in equity.

2.2 Trade date and settlement date accounting

Under IAS 39:38, a 'regular way' (see below) purchase or and sale of financial assets can be recognised (and derecognised) using either trade date or settlement date accounting. The method used is required to be applied consistently for all purchases and sales of financial assets that belong to the same category of financial assets (AFS, HTM etc.). For this purposes, assets that are held for trading form a separate category from assets designated as at FVTPL. [IAS 39:AG53]

A 'regular way' purchase or sale is defined as a transaction whose contractual terms "require delivery of the asset within a timeframe established generally by regulation or convention in the marketplace concerned". [IAS 39:9] A marketplace is not limited to a formal stock exchange or organised over-the-counter market. Rather, it means the environment in which the financial asset is customarily exchanged. An acceptable timeframe would be the period reasonably and customarily required for the parties to complete the transaction and prepare and execute closing documents. [IAS 39:IG.B.28] The trade date is the date of the commitment to buy or sell the financial asset. The settlement date is the date of the delivery of the asset. If a transaction is considered 'regular way', a derivative is not recognised for the time period between the trade date and the settlement date.

When trade date accounting is applied, the entity recognises the financial asset to be received and the corresponding liability to pay for it at the trade date; on disposal, the financial asset is removed from the statement of financial position on the trade date. [IAS 39:AG55]

Under the settlement date accounting approach, the asset is recognised on the date on which it is received by the entity; on disposal, the asset is not derecognised until the asset is delivered to the buyer. When the purchase of an asset is accounted for using settlement date accounting, between the trade date and settlement date, although the asset itself is not yet recognised, the entity is required to account for changes in its fair value, applying the same measurement basis that will be used to account for the acquired asset once it is recognised; therefore, changes in fair value are recognised in profit or loss for assets to be classified or designated as at FVTPL, and in other comprehensive income (OCI) for assets to be classified as AFS, and not recognised for assets to be carried at cost or amortised cost. [IAS 39:AG56]

Example 2.2A

Trade and settlement date accounting for a purchase of an asset

The following example illustrates the amounts to be recognised for a purchase of a financial asset.

The dates and fair values that are relevant to the example are:

- trade date: 29 December 20X1 (fair value of asset 1,000);
- period end date: 31 December 20X1 (fair value of asset 1,002); and
- settlement date: 4 January 20X2 (fair value of asset 1,003).

The contracted price of the asset is set as the trade date fair value of 1,000.

TRADE DATE ACCOUNTING

Journal entries	Debt instrument measured at amortised cost (e.g. HTM investment or L&R)	AFS asset	FVTPL
29/12/20X1			
	Dr Asset 1,000	Dr Asset 1,000	Dr Asset 1,000
	Cr Liability 1,000	Cr Liability 1,000	Cr Liability 1,000
Description	*To recognise the asset and payable.*	*To recognise the asset and payable.*	*To recognise the asset and payable.*
31/12/20X1			
	–	Dr Asset 2	Dr Asset 2
	–	Cr OCI 2	Cr Profit or loss 2
Description		*To recognise the increase in fair value to date.*	*To recognise the increase in fair value to date.*
04/01/20X2			
	–	Dr Asset 1	Dr Asset 1
	–	Cr OCI 1	Cr Profit or loss 1
Description		*To recognise the increase in fair value to date.*	*To recognise the increase in fair value to date.*

TRADE DATE ACCOUNTING			
Journal entries	**Debt instrument measured at amortised cost (e.g. HTM investment or L&R)**	**AFS asset**	**FVTPL**
	Dr Liability 1,000	Dr Liability 1,000	Dr Liability 1,000
	Cr Cash 1,000	Cr Cash 1,000	Cr Cash 1,000
Description	*To record the payment for the asset at the contracted amount.*	*To record the payment for the asset at the contracted amount.*	*To record the payment for the asset at the contracted amount.*

SETTLEMENT DATE ACCOUNTING			
Journal entries	**Debt instrument measured at amortised cost (e.g. HTM investment or L&R)**	**AFS asset**	**FVTPL**
29/12/20X1			
	–	–	–
	–	–	–
31/12/20X1			
	–	Dr Receivable 2	Dr Receivable 2
	–	Cr OCI 2	Cr Profit or loss 2
Description		*To recognise the increase in fair value to date.*	*To recognise the increase in fair value to date.*
04/01/20X2			
	–	Dr Receivable 1	Dr Receivable 1
	–	Cr OCI 1	Cr Profit or loss 1
Description		*To recognise the increase in fair value to date.*	*To recognise the increase in fair value to date.*
	Dr Asset 1,000	Dr Asset 1,003	Dr Asset 1,003
	Cr Cash 1,000	Cr Cash 1,000	Cr Cash 1,000
	–	Cr Receivable 3	Cr Receivable 3
Description	*To recognise the asset and payment for the asset at the contracted amount.*	*To recognise the asset and payment for the asset at the contracted amount and its change in fair value since trade date.*	*To recognise the asset and payment for the asset at the contracted amount and its change in fair value since trade date.*

When the settlement provisions of a financial instrument differ between various active markets, the entity must apply the provisions that apply in the market in which the purchase or sale of the financial instrument actually takes place.

Example 2.2B

Regular way contracts: which customary settlement provisions apply?

[Extract from IAS 39:IG.B.30]

Entity XYZ purchases one million shares of Entity ABC on a US stock exchange, for example, through a broker. The settlement date of the contract is six business days later. Trades for equity shares on US exchanges customarily settle in three business days. Because the trade settles in six business days, it does not meet the exemption as a regular way trade.

However, if XYZ did the same transaction on a foreign exchange that has a customary settlement period of six business days, the contract would meet the exemption for a regular way trade.

When the regulation or convention for settlement differs between a derivative over the underlying (e.g. a call option over a share) and the underlying itself (e.g. the share), the regulation or convention that is used to determine whether the financial instrument is regular way would be the regulation or convention specific to that instrument. For example, if the call option over the share is regularly settled within 14 days of exercise of the option in the option markets, but a direct acquisition of a share requires three day settlement, the entity will look to the options market in determining whether an option is regular way or not. [IAS 39:IG.B.31]

Example 2.2C

Application of trade and settlement date accounting for different categories of financial asset

Entity P has an accounting policy of settlement date accounting for loans and receivables and trade date accounting for AFS financial assets. Entity P enters into a regular way transaction whereby it will sell a loan in exchange for an AFS equity instrument. At the date of entering into the arrangement, 30 March 20X8, both assets have the same fair value. The settlement date is 2 April 20X8. Entity P's reporting date is 31 March 20X8.

	Amortised cost	Fair value
	CU	CU
30 March 20X8		
Loans and receivables	10,000	
AFS asset		10,400
31 March 20X8		
Loans and receivables	10,005	
AFS asset		10,350
2 April 20X8		
Loans and receivables	10,015	
AFS asset		10,325

30 March 20X8

		CU	CU
Dr	AFS asset	10,400	
Cr	Financial liability		10,400

To recognise the AFS asset at trade date.

31 March 20X8

		CU	CU
Dr	Other comprehensive income (equity)	50	
Cr	AFS asset		50

To recognise the change in fair value of the AFS equity instrument.

		CU	CU
Dr	Loans and receivables	5	
Cr	Interest income		5

To recognise the interest earned on an effective interest rate basis.

2 April 20X8

		CU	CU
Dr	Loans and receivables	10	
Cr	Interest income		10

To recognise the interest earned on an effective interest rate basis.

		CU	CU
Dr	Other comprehensive income (equity)	25	
Cr	AFS asset		25

To recognise the change in fair value of the AFS equity instrument.

		CU	CU
Dr	Financial liability	10,400	
Cr	Loans and receivables		10,015
Cr	Profit or loss		385

To recognise the gain on disposal of the loan at the date of derecognition. The gain represents the difference between the proceeds received (i.e. the fair value of the AFS equity instrument at the date the contract is entered into) and the amortised cost of the loan at the settlement date.

Trade or settlement date accounting for regular way transactions is not limited to exchanges of securities for cash because exchanges of large amounts of foreign currency are also subject to market convention. For example, an entity may agree to exchange an amount of foreign currency cash recognised in its statement of financial position for an amount of functional currency cash at a predetermined foreign currency exchange rate but with deferred delivery, say, two days after the agreement date subject to normal market settlement convention.

If the market settlement convention is not deemed normal (i.e. this is not a regular way transaction), the entity would continue to recognise the foreign currency cash balance and recognise a foreign currency forward contract to sell foreign currency and buy functional currency in two days' time at FVTPL. At maturity of the foreign currency forward contract, the foreign currency cash and the foreign currency forward contract would both be derecognised and the functional currency recognised.

If the market settlement convention is deemed normal (i.e. the transaction is a regular way one), the accounting would depend on whether the entity's accounting policy is to apply trade or settlement date accounting.

Example 2.2D

Trade and settlement date accounting for an exchange of foreign currency cash

Entity A agrees to sell US$200 million that is recognised in its statement of financial position for £100 million with settlement two days after trade date ('t+2'). Entity A has a Sterling functional currency. t+2 is considered to be the normal market settlement convention for the size and type of asset being exchanged in the market in which the exchange takes place. Entity A concludes, therefore, that this is a regular way transaction.

The dates and currency rates that are relevant are as follows:

- trade date: 30 December 20X1; US$2:£1 spot rate;
- period end date: 31 December 20X1; and
- settlement date: 1 January 20X2.

If Entity A's policy is trade date accounting, the following entries would be recorded.

30 December 20X1

		£ million	£ million
Dr	Receivable – £	100*	
Cr	Cash – US$		100

To derecognise the US$ cash at the trade date and recognise a receivable for the Sterling amount to be received at 1 January 20X2.

* the balance should be discounted unless the effect is immaterial

31 December 20X1

Because the US$ asset has been derecognised, there is no foreign currency monetary item that requires translation (had the receipt been in a foreign currency, the receivable would be retranslated to Entity A's functional currency at the period end).

1 January 20X2

		£ million	£ million
Dr	Cash – £	100*	
Cr	Receivable – £		100

To derecognise the Sterling receivable and recognise the Sterling cash at the settlement date.

* the balance should be discounted unless the effect is immaterial

If Entity A's policy is settlement date accounting the following entries would be recorded.

30 December 20X1

No entries are required because the US$ cash remains recognised until settlement date.

31 December 20X1

Because Entity A has agreed to sell the US$ at 1 January 20X1 at a fixed amount of Sterling, it does not have exposure to foreign currency risk. Entity A does not retranslate the US$ to Sterling after the trade date. This is consistent with IAS 39:IG.D.2.2, which states "[a] change in the fair value of a financial asset that is sold on a regular way basis is not recorded in the financial statements between trade date and settlement date even if the entity applies settlement date accounting because the seller's right to changes in the fair value ceases on the trade date". Therefore, no entries are required.

1 January 20X2

		£ million	£ million
Dr	Cash – £	100	
Cr	Cash – US$		100

To derecognise the US$ cash and recognise the Sterling cash at the settlement date.

If an entity derecognises a financial asset using settlement date accounting but it receives a non-cash financial asset in exchange which, under the entity's generally policy for the category of non-cash financial asset received, will be recognised using trade date accounting, the entity must apply trade date accounting to the non-cash financial asset to be received.

Example 2.2E

Settlement date accounting: exchange of non-cash financial assets

[Extract from IAS 39:IG.D.2.3]

On 29 December 20X2 (trade date) Entity A enters into a contract to sell Note Receivable A, which is carried at amortised cost, in exchange for Bond B, which will be classified as held for trading and measured at fair value. Both assets have a fair value of CU1,010 on 29 December, while the amortised cost of Note Receivable A is CU1,000. Entity A uses settlement date accounting for loans and receivables and trade date accounting for assets held for trading. On 31 December 20X2 (financial year-end), the fair value of Note Receivable A is CU1,012 and the fair value of Bond B is CU1,009. On 4 January 20X3, the fair value of Note Receivable A is CU1,013 and the fair value of Bond B is CU1,007. The following entries are made:

29 December 20X2

Dr	Bond B	CU1,010
Cr	Payable	CU1,010

31 December 20X2

Dr	Trading loss	CU1
Cr	Bond B	CU1

4 January 20X3	
Dr Payable	CU1,010
Dr Trading loss	CU2
Cr Note Receivable A	CU1,000
Cr Bond B	CU2
Cr Realisation gain	CU10

In January 2007, the IFRIC (now the IFRS Interpretations Committee) issued a rejection notice on accounting for short sales of securities when the terms of the short sales require delivery of the securities within the timeframe established generally by regulation or convention in the marketplace concerned. A fixed price commitment between trade date and settlement date of a short sale contract meets the definition of a derivative. Because IAS 39:AG55 & AG56 only permit a choice of trade or settlement date accounting for recognition and derecognition of financial assets traded under regular way purchases and regular way sales of long positions, the Standard would require a short sale to be recognised as a derivative until delivery of the security. The IFRIC acknowledged that an interpretation that is applied in practice is that entities choose trade date or settlement date accounting for short sales rather than treat a short sale as a derivative. Specifically, practice recognises the short sales as financial liabilities at fair value with changes in fair value recognised in profit or loss. Under the industry practice, the same profit or loss amount is recognised as would have been recognised if short sales of securities were accounted for as derivatives but the securities are presented differently in the statement of financial position. The IFRIC acknowledged that requiring entities to account for the short positions as derivatives may create considerable practical problems for entities' accounting systems and controls with little, if any, improvement to the quality of the financial information presented. For these reasons and because there is little diversity in practice, the IFRIC decided not to take the issue onto its agenda.

IAS 39 does not provide guidance on whether the trade date exemption can be applied if an entity delivers a financial instrument under a regular way contract but the delivery date is delayed, and the asset is delivered outside the normal convention for that type of contract. For example, a contract has a delivery date of t+3 days, but there is a delay in delivery and the instrument is delivered at t+5. A delay should not preclude use of the regular way exemption if the delay is outside the control of the entity.

3 Derecognition of financial assets

A financial asset is derecognised (i.e. removed from the statement of financial position), when, and only when, either the contractual rights to the asset's cash flows expire, or the asset is transferred and the transfer qualifies for derecognition.

The decision as to whether a transfer qualifies for derecognition is made by applying a combination of risks and rewards and control tests. The risks and rewards tests seek to establish whether, having transferred a financial asset, the entity continues to be exposed to the risks of ownership of that asset and/or continues to enjoy the benefits that it generates. The control tests are designed with a view to understanding which entity controls the asset (i.e. which entity can direct how the benefits of that asset are realised).

The use of both types of tests is often criticised for being a mix of two accounting models that can create confusion in application. IAS 39 addresses this criticism by providing a clear hierarchy for application of the two sets of tests: risks and rewards tests are applied first, with the control tests used only when the entity has neither transferred substantially all the risks and rewards of the asset nor retained them.

Inherent in the IAS 39 derecognition model is the notion of 'stickiness', i.e. it is more difficult to remove an asset from an entity's statement of financial position than it is to recognise that asset in the first place. Derecognition cannot be achieved by merely transferring the legal title to a financial asset to another party. The substance of the arrangement must be assessed in order to determine whether an entity has transferred the economic exposure associated with the rights inherent in the asset (i.e. its risks and rewards) and, in some cases, control of those rights.

3.1 The IAS 39 derecognition decision tree

IAS 39 provides a decision tree, reproduced below, that clarifies the hierarchy for application of the derecognition tests.

[IAS 39:AG36]

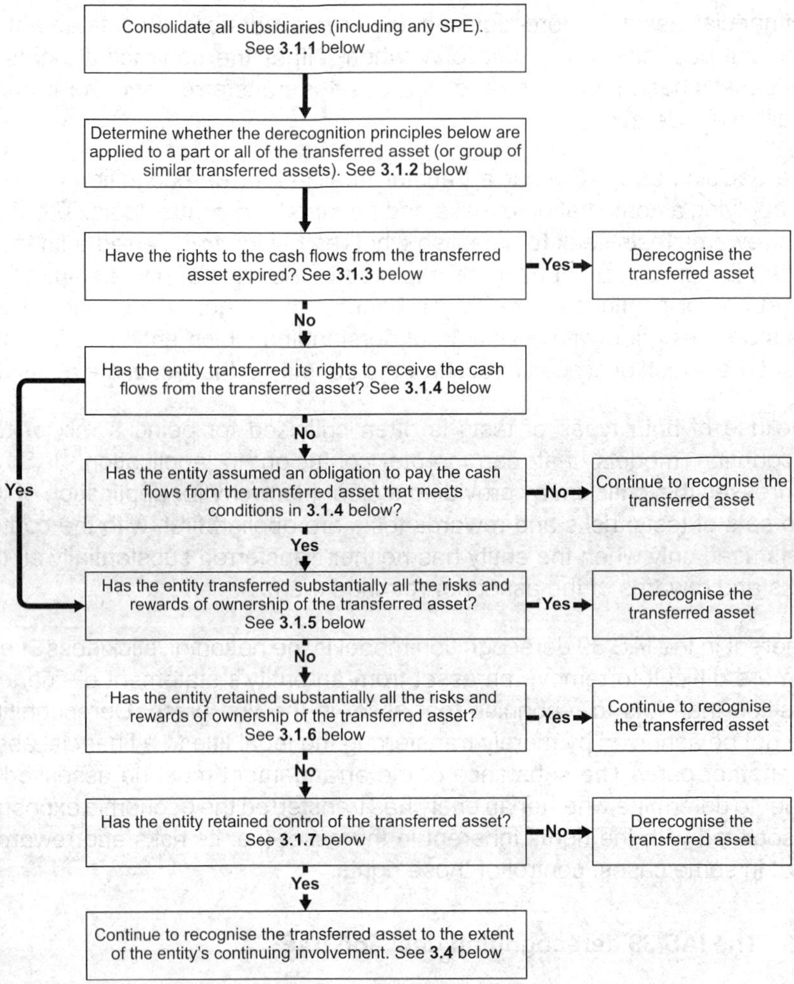

The steps of this decision tree are explained below.

3.1.1 Consolidate all subsidiaries

The first step is to define at which level the derecognition decision is to be applied – in the parent's separate financial statements or in the consolidated financial statements. When derecognition of financial assets is to be applied in the consolidated financial statements, the reporting group must first consolidate all subsidiaries in accordance with IFRS 10 *Consolidated Financial Statements*. [IAS 39:15]

This first step ensures that the derecognition decision is consistent regardless of whether the transfer of assets is direct to investors or through a consolidated structured entity that obtains the financial assets and, in turn, transfers those financial assets (or a portion of them) to third-party investors. [IAS 39:BC64]

IFRS 10 requires consolidation of all entities that are controlled by the reporting entity. An investor controls an investee when it is exposed, or has rights, to variable returns from its involvement with the investee and has the ability to affect those returns through its power over the investee.

Structured entities may take the form of a corporation, trust, partnership or unincorporated entity and are often created with legal arrangements that impose strict and sometimes permanent limits on the decision-making powers of their governing board, trustees or management over the operations of the structured entity. Frequently, these provisions specify that the policy guiding the ongoing activities of the structured entity cannot be modified, other than perhaps by its creator or sponsor (i.e. they operate on so-called 'autopilot').

Structured transactions, such as securitisations and certain other asset-based financing arrangements, typically seek, as their primary economic objective, to isolate legally the assets from the party providing them (and from that party's creditors) to avoid the investor having a credit exposure to the transferor. This isolation is often achieved through a structured entity. For many sellers of financial assets, structured arrangements that isolate the assets permit access to capital markets at more favourable prices than might otherwise be available because credit agencies and investors require a lower return from structures that avoid the consequences arising from bankruptcies. This ability is particularly important for those entities whose credit ratings may reflect the adverse effects of financial, operational or environmental risks not directly attributable to the assets being transferred. However, bankruptcy isolation does not automatically lead to the conclusion that the sponsor is not required to consolidate the structured entity.

A structured entity may issue different types of beneficial interests, multiple classes of interests and classes of interests with different maturities. Several forms of structured entities are common, depending on the asset being securitised, the securities issued by the entity and the legal framework governing the entity's operations. These include grantor trusts, owner trusts, revolving trusts, master trusts, structured corporations and REMICS (Real Estate Mortgage Investment Conduits).

Typically, the structured entity is prevented from selling, assigning or pledging its direct interest in any financial asset it holds; however, the owners of the beneficial interests generally have the right to pledge or exchange their beneficial interests.

3.1.2 Determine whether the derecognition principles are applied to part or all of an asset (or group of similar assets)

An entity needs to determine what is being evaluated for derecognition; this could be a whole financial asset, a group of financial assets, part of a financial asset, or part of a group of similar financial assets.

The derecognition principles are applied to part of a financial asset (or a group of similar financial assets) if the part comprises one of the following:

[IAS 39:16(a)]

- specifically identified cash flows (e.g. an interest or principal strip from a debt instrument);
- a fully proportionate share of the cash flows (e.g. the rights to the cash flows on 90 per cent of all cash flows arising from a debt instrument); or
- a fully proportionate share of specifically identified cash flows (e.g. 90 per cent of the cash flows that arise on the interest strip from a debt instrument).

In all other cases, the financial asset (or the group of financial assets) is considered in its entirety. [IAS 39:16(b)]

Example 3.1.2

Determining the part of a financial asset subject to transfer

Entity X, the transferor, transfers the right to the first CU90 of cash flows that are derived from a debt instrument; the fair value of the asset is CU100 on the date of transfer.

The transferor cannot apply the derecognition model to part of the asset because the transferor has neither transferred specifically identifiable cash flows nor a fully proportionate share of all or part of the cash flows. The transferor would apply the derecognition model to the asset in its entirety. The transferor effectively agrees to absorb the first CU10 of losses from the transferred asset.

It should be noted, however, that if the transferor had transferred a 90 per cent pro rata share of all cash flows from the asset, then the derecognition model could be applied to the part of the asset that has been transferred, i.e. 90 per cent. In that case, the transferor and the transferee would have agreed to participate in a fully proportionate share of losses.

IAS 39 does not provide any guidance regarding what makes assets 'similar'. 'Similar' generally means that the two instruments have contractually specified cash flows that are similar in amounts and timings, and have similar risk attributes. An entity should consider the similarity of terms (e.g. prepayment features, interest rates, currency denomination). By definition, there will always be some differences between similar instruments – otherwise they would be identical. A portfolio of mortgages transferred by a bank is often deemed to contain similar financial assets. Similarly, a portfolio of corporate bonds transferred by a bank is often deemed to contain similar financial assets. However, no two portfolios are ever precisely alike. A transfer of a portfolio of mortgages would need to be assessed separately from a transfer of a portfolio of corporate bonds even if the two transfers are made at the same time. With individual equity investments, the differences are so significant that no two equity investments are ever likely to be similar; the value is affected by intangibles and other 'soft' assets (e.g. reputation) that are not recognised in the statement of financial position or measured in any consistent way, but that do affect perceptions and, therefore, market price.

In September 2006, the IASB was asked by the IFRIC (now the IFRS Interpretations Committee) for input and advice on the meaning of 'similar' for group of financial assets (in IAS 39:16). The Board's view (subsequently used by the IFRIC as a basis for a tentative rejection wording in November 2006) was that they believed that derivative assets (which are often transferred together with non-derivative financial assets) are not 'similar' to non-derivative financial assets. Therefore, entities should apply the derecognition tests in IAS 39 to non-derivative financial assets (or groups of similar non-derivative financial assets) and derivative financial assets (or groups of similar derivative financial assets) separately, even if they are transferred at the same time. The Board also indicated that transferred derivatives that could be either assets or liabilities (such as interest rate swaps) would have to meet both the financial asset and the financial liability derecognition tests. This view was reaffirmed in the amendments to IAS 39, *Novation of Derivatives and Continuation of Hedge Accounting*, issued in June 2013 where paragraph BC220B was introduced which states that "a derivative should be derecognised only when it meets both the derecognition criteria for a financial asset and the derecognition criteria for a financial liability in circumstances in which the derivative involves two-way payments between parties (i.e. the payments are or could be from and to each of the parties)".

Following comments from constituents, at the IFRIC meeting in January 2007 the IFRIC decided to withdraw its tentative agenda decision and to add a project on derecognition to its agenda. However, in March 2009, the IFRIC decided to remove this topic from its agenda because the IASB accelerated its project to develop a replacement for the sections of IAS 39 dealing with derecognition. An exposure draft was published in March 2009 with the intention of issuing a final IFRS in the second half of 2010. However, in June 2010, the IASB announced its intention to proceed with a more limited project to issue new disclosure requirements regarding derecognition. These amendments to IFRS 7, *Transfers of Financial Assets*, were issued in October 2010 (see **4.1.5** in **chapter C12**).

3.1.3 Have the rights to the cash flows from the asset expired?

An entity derecognises a financial asset when the rights to the cash flows from that financial asset expire. [IAS 39:17]

The rights to the cash flows expire when, for example, a financial asset reaches its maturity and there are no further cash flows arising from that asset, or a purchased option reaches its maturity unexercised. An entity may have a right to receive certain or all cash flows from a financial asset over a specified period of time which may be shorter than the contractual maturity of that financial asset. In that case, the entity's right to the cash flows expires once the specified period expires.

In November 2014 the IASB's Interpretations Committee issued a final agenda decision on IAS 39, titled, *Holder's accounting for exchange of equity instruments*.

The Interpretations Committee received a request about the accounting by the holder of equity instruments in the circumstance in which the issuer exchanges its original equity instruments for new equity instruments in the same entity but with different terms. Specifically, this transaction involved equity instruments issued by a central bank and the exchange of instruments was imposed on the holders as a consequence of a change in legislation.

The submitter asked whether the holders of the equity instruments should account for this exchange under IAS 39 as a derecognition of the original equity instruments and the recognition of new instruments.

The Interpretations Committee observed that: (i) because of the unique nature of the transaction, the issue is not widespread; and (ii) the submitter had not identified significant diversity in accounting for this transaction among the holders of the equity instruments in question.

For these reasons, the Interpretations Committee decided not to add this issue to its agenda.

The Interpretations Committee additionally noted requests for more guidance in IAS 39 and IFRS 9 on the derecognition of financial assets that have been modified or exchanged. The staff observed that this more general matter had been raised previously with the IASB but that it had decided not to add such a project to its agenda. The Interpretations Committee asked the staff to perform further analysis to identify whether an issue of sufficiently narrow scope could be identified to be raised with the IASB. The staff's analysis is due to be considered at a future Interpretations Committee meeting.

3.1.4 Has the entity transferred its rights to receive the cash flows from the asset?

An entity may transfer the contractual rights to the cash flows that comprise a financial asset, or it may retain the contractual rights to the cash flows but assume a contractual obligation to pass on those cash flows to one or more recipients (often referred to as a 'pass-through' arrangement).

When an entity enters into a pass-through arrangement (i.e. the entity agrees to receive cash flows and has a concurrent obligation to pay those cash flows to the eventual recipient), the entity should treat the transaction as a transfer of a financial asset if, and only if, all of the following conditions are met:

[IAS 39:19]

- the entity has no obligation to pay amounts to the eventual recipients unless it collects equivalent amounts from the original asset (i.e. the entity does not benefit or suffer from performance or non-performance of the asset);
- the entity is prohibited by the terms of the transfer arrangement from selling or pledging the original asset other than as security to the eventual recipients for the obligation to pay them cash flows (i.e. the entity does not have control of the future economic benefits associated with the transferred asset); and
- the entity has an obligation to pass on or remit the cash flows that it has collected on behalf of the eventual recipients *without material delay*, is prohibited from reinvesting the cash flows received in the short settlement period between receiving them and remitting them to the eventual recipient in anything other than cash or cash equivalents (as defined in IAS 7 *Statement of Cash Flows*) and any interest earned on such investments must be passed on to the eventual recipients (i.e. the entity has no access to the benefits of the asset).

Transfers most commonly arise in respect of financial assets that represent a contractual right to receive cash. However, it is possible to transfer a financial asset that is a contractual right to receive a non-financial asset. For example, an entity may have a contractual right to receive oil to the value of CU100 million that fails the 'own use' exemption in IAS 39:5 and is accounted for under IAS 39 as a financial asset. The transfer criteria in IAS 39:18 state that a transfer can arise if the contractual right to receive 'cash flows' of the asset are transferred, or if the contractual right to the 'cash flows' of the financial asset are retained but a contractual obligation to pay the 'cash flows' to one or more recipients meets the pass-through conditions above. When a non-financial asset is receivable under a financial asset, that non-financial asset represents the "cash flows" for the purpose of applying IAS 39:18. As a result, an arrangement can fail to represent a pass-through if the obligation assumed does not require remittance of the non-financial asset. This is illustrated in the following example.

Example 3.1.4

Application of the pass-through test to an asset in the scope of IAS 39 that is settled by the receipt of a non-financial item

Entity A has an existing offtake agreement to purchase crude oil from an oil producer, Entity B, in the future. Under this arrangement, Entity A advances to Entity B cash of CU100 million and in return Entity B is obliged to deliver to Entity A on specified dates a variable amount of oil until Entity B has delivered oil equal in value to the amount of the advance (CU100 million) plus interest accrued at a rate of 10 per cent per annum. The value of the oil is determined based on the spot price at the date of delivery.

Entity A does not intend to use the oil as part of its usage requirements; it will either sell the oil spot on receipt, or forward in the future, or retain the physical oil for speculative purposes. Consequently, the advance does not qualify for the 'own use' exemption in IAS 39:5; even though it is settled with the receipt of a non-financial item, it is an asset in the scope of IAS 39.

Entity A enters into a separate agreement with Bank C under which it 'sells' its economic interest in the asset for CU100 million. This is achieved by Entity A assuming a contractual obligation to deliver to Bank C cash equivalent to the value of oil that it receives from Entity B. Entity A retains the contractual right to receive oil. When title to oil passes from Entity B to Entity A, this immediately triggers a cash payment from Entity A to Bank C (e.g. if Entity A receives CU12 million worth of oil on a specific date, Entity A is required to pay CU12 million in cash to Bank C on the same date).

The exposure to variability in timing of delivery of oil by Entity B is passed to Bank C because Entity A's obligation to pay Bank C is not triggered until Entity A receives oil from Entity B.

The arrangement with Bank C does result in a transfer by Entity A of its asset from Entity B under the 'pass-through' requirement of IAS 39:18(b).

Under IAS 39:18(b), a transfer arises if an entity both retains the contractual rights to receive the cash flows of the asset and assumes a contractual obligation to pay the cash flows to one or more eventual recipients.

Because Entity A's asset due from Entity B is exclusively physically settled in oil, the 'cash flows' for the purposes of applying IAS 39:18(b) are the contractual rights to receive oil. Therefore, in order to meet the second condition in IAS 39:18(b), it is necessary for Entity A to assume an obligation to pay to Bank C the same 'cash flows' (i.e. an equivalent physical amount of oil). However, the arrangements are such that Entity A receives physical oil from Entity B but pays cash to Bank C. The difference in the physical nature between receiving oil and paying cash means that the criteria for 'pass-through' in IAS 39:18(b) are not satisfied.

Entity A should instead recognise the cash proceeds from Bank C of CU100 million as a financial liability.

In September 2012 the IFRS Interpretations Committee considered the accounting treatment for various aspects of the restructuring of Greek Government Bonds (GGBs). One of the aspects the Committee received a request for guidance on was whether the restructuring of GGBs should result in derecognition of the whole asset, or only part of it, in accordance with IAS 39. Specifically, the Committee was asked whether the portion of the old GGBs that are exchanged for twenty new bonds with different maturities and interest rates should be derecognised, or conversely accounted for as a modification or transfer that would not require derecognition.

The Committee noted that the request has been made within the context of a narrow fact pattern. The narrow fact pattern highlighted the diversity in views that had arisen in relation to the accounting for the portion of the old GGBs that is exchanged for twenty new bonds with different maturities and interest rates. The submitter asked the Committee to consider whether these should be derecognised, or conversely accounted for as a modification or transfer that would not require derecognition.

In addition, the Committee has been asked to consider whether IAS 8 *Accounting Policies, Changes in Accounting Estimates and Errors* would be applicable in analysing the submitted fact pattern, and whether the exchange can be considered a transfer within the scope of IAS 39:17(b).

The Committee observed that the term 'transfer' is not defined in IAS 39. However, the potentially relevant portion of IAS 39:18 states that an entity transfers a financial asset if it transfers the contractual rights to receive the cash flows of the financial asset. The Committee noted that, in the fact pattern submitted, the bonds are transferred back to the issuer rather than a third party. Accordingly, the Committee believed that the transaction should be assessed against IAS 39:17(a).

In applying IAS 39:17(a), the Committee noted that in order to determine whether the financial asset is extinguished, it is necessary to assess the changes made as part of the bond exchange against the notion of 'expiry' of the rights to the cash flows. The Committee also noted that, if an entity applies IAS 8 because of the absence in IAS 39 of an explicit discussion of when a modification of a financial asset results in derecognition, applying IAS 8 requires judgement to develop and apply a n accounting policy. IAS 8:11 requires that, in determining an appropriate accounting policy, consideration must first be given to the requirements in IFRSs dealing with similar and related issues. The Committee noted that, in the fact pattern submitted, that requirement would lead to the development of an analogy to the notion of a substantial change of the terms of a financial liability in IAS 39:40.

IAS 39:40 sets out that such a change can be effected by the exchange of debt instruments or by way of modification of the terms of an existing instrument. Hence, if this analogy to financial liabilities is applied to financial assets, a substantial change of terms (whether effected by exchange or by modification) would result in derecognition of the financial asset.

The Committee noted that if the guidance for financial liabilities is applied by analogy to assess whether the exchange of a portion of the old GGBs for twenty new bonds is a substantial change of the terms of the financial asset, the assessment needs to be made taking into consideration all of the changes made as part of the bond exchange.

In the fact pattern submitted, the relevant facts led the Committee to conclude that, in determining whether the transaction results in derecognition of the financial asset, both approaches (i.e. extinguishment under IAS 39:17(a) or substantial change of the terms of the asset) would result in derecognition.

The Committee considered the following aspects of the fact pattern in assessing the extent of change that results from the transaction:

- A holder of a single bond has received in exchange for one portion of the old bond, twenty bonds with different maturities and cash flow profiles as well as other instruments in accordance with the terms and conditions of the exchange transaction.
- All of the bondholders received the same restructuring deal irrespective of the terms and conditions of their individual holdings. This indicates that the individual instruments, terms and conditions were not taken into account. The different bonds (series) were not each modified in contemplation of their respective terms and conditions but instead replaced by a new uniform debt structure.
- The terms and conditions of the new bonds are substantially different from those of the old bonds; this includes many different aspects such as the change in governing law, the introduction of contractual collective action clauses and the introduction of a co-financing agreement that affects the rights of the new bond holders, and modifications to the amount, term and coupons.

The Committee noted that the starting point that was used for its analysis was the assumption in the submission that the part of the principal amount of the old GGBs that was exchanged for new GGBs could be separately assessed for derecognition. The Committee emphasised that this assumption was more favourable for achieving partial derecognition than looking at the whole of the old bond. Hence, its conclusion that the old GGBs should be derecognised would apply even more so when taking into account that the exchange of the old GGBs was as a matter of fact the result of a single agreement that covered all aspects and types of consideration for surrendering the old GGBs. As a consequence, the Committee noted that partial derecognition did not apply.

Consequently, the Committee decided not to add the issue to its agenda.

3.1.4.1 Meaning of 'without material delay'

Without material delay does not mean instantaneously, nor does it imply an extended length of time. The contractual arrangement will need to be considered in full in order to make an assessment as to whether the timeframe between the collection of cash flows on the underlying assets and the point at which they are passed on to the eventual recipients is material in the context of the contractual arrangements of the transfer.

In some arrangements, the cash collected on the underlying assets occurs sporadically throughout a period of time. For example, if an entity retains the rights to the cash flows arising on a group of credit card receivables, the payments arising on those credit cards are likely to occur on any given day throughout the month. The contractual arrangement of the transfer may require that those cash flows are remitted to the eventual recipients on a weekly, monthly, quarterly or even annual basis. There is a trade-off between passing on the cash flows almost as soon as they arise and the administrative burden that goes along with passing on those cash flows. It is likely that half-yearly payments to the eventual recipients (and certainly annual payments) would be considered to be subject to a material delay because the conditions specified above fail and, therefore, derecognition would be inappropriate in these circumstances. It appears reasonable that the entity can invest the cash flows from the assets for up to three months without breaching the condition that all cash flows must be passed to the eventual recipient without material delay.

Any significant delay in passing on the cash flows of a transferred asset alters the credit risk characteristics for the eventual recipient when compared to the original transferred asset. The holder is exposed not only to the original transferred asset but to additional credit risk from the reinvestment of the cash flows from the original asset.

3.1.4.2 Pass-through arrangements structured with shares

When the contractual arrangement that passes the cash flows on the transferred asset to the eventual recipient is legally structured as a share, as opposed to a conventional obligation to a creditor, the form of the share may prevent the pass-through tests being met. For example, if a dividend under the share (i.e. the cash received under the transferred asset) is only required to be paid if there are sufficient distributable profits in the entity, then a lack of distributable profits will limit the transferor's ability to make payments to the eventual recipients without material delay. The potential for a dividend block in this case will prohibit the transferor meeting the pass-through criteria. Consideration should be given to other restrictions, either inherent in the terms of the instrument or in the articles of the entity, that would limit the entity's ability to pay amounts to the eventual recipients when due without material delay.

3.1.4.3 Consideration of the likelihood that the transferor will default

The likelihood that the transferor will default under the pass-through arrangements as a result of a default on other creditor obligations is not considered an impediment to meeting the pass-through criteria because the transferor is assumed to be a going concern. In many cases, the transferee may limit this risk by ensuring that the transferred assets reside in a bankruptcy remote structured entity so that the wider credit risk of the transferor is not borne by the transferee.

3.1.4.4 Pass-through arrangements with credit enhancement

A transferor may provide credit enhancement in a transfer arrangement so that it suffers the first loss on the asset up to a specified amount. In such circumstances, if the debtor fails to pay, the transferor absorbs the first loss fully, with the eventual recipient only suffering a loss after the first loss has been fully absorbed. A credit enhancement may be in the form of over-collateralisation or may be in the form of purchasing a subordinated interest in a consolidated structured entity (in the latter case, the entity is applying the pass-through tests at a consolidated level). Providing credit enhancement will not in itself result in failure of the pass-through tests if all cash received by the transferor on transferred assets is paid on to the eventual recipient, although the credit enhancement may result in failure of derecognition due to the transferor retaining substantially all the risks and rewards of ownership of the assets. The pass-through tests must be considered prior to considering the entity's exposure to risk and rewards.

If a greater amount of cash is realised on the assets than is needed to pay the eventual recipient (i.e. the eventual recipient's initial investment is fully paid), then the entity will retain the remainder of the cash and will not pass it on. In all cases the entity passes "any cash it collects on behalf of the eventual recipients".

Example 3.1.4.4

Pass-through arrangements with credit enhancement

Entity B enters into an arrangement with Entity C under which Entity C pays Entity B CU0.9 million in return for receiving cash flows on CU1.0 million of assets when expected losses on the assets are 10 per cent of all cash flows (interest and principal). Entity B retains the contractual rights to receive the cash flows from the assets but assumes an obligation to pay cash flows from the asset to Entity C. The maximum cash flows that Entity C can receive under the arrangement are interest and principal on a notional of CU0.9 million. If actual credit losses are lower than expected (say, only 5 per cent), Entity B will pay Entity C interest and principal on CU0.9 million and retain interest and principal on CU0.05 million.

Entity B will apply the derecognition model to the full CU1.0 million of assets (see **3.1.2**). Entity B will pass the pass-through tests, assuming all other conditions are met, because Entity B will pass interest and principal on a notional up to CU0.9 million of the cash flows to Entity C.

However, if the form of the transaction were different, in that Entity C pays Entity B CU1.0 million for the assets and purchases a financial guarantee contract from Entity B for CU0.1 million, then the pass-through tests would not be met because Entity B will pay the eventual recipient, Entity C, even when it does not collect the equivalent amount from the original assets.

3.1.4.5 Revolving structures

In a revolving structure, cash received on the assets is reinvested in buying new receivables assets. In other words, cash 'revolves' into new assets instead of being returned immediately to the investors. Upon maturity, the reinvested assets are used to repay the beneficial interest holders. Such 'revolving' structures do not meet the pass-through tests because they involve a material delay before the original cash is passed onto the eventual recipients and the reinvestment would typically be not in cash or cash equivalents. The treatment of revolving structures described above was confirmed by the IFRIC (now the IFRS Interpretations Committee) in September 2005.

3.1.4.6 Retention of servicing rights

An entity may enter into an arrangement with a third party to transfer the contractual rights to receive the cash flows of a financial asset, but also agree to continue to act as an agent to administer collection and distribution of cash flows to the recipient (i.e. it retains servicing rights on the cash flows).

IAS 39:18(a) focuses on whether an entity transfers the contractual rights to receive the cash flows from a financial asset. The determination as to whether the contractual rights to cash flows have been transferred is not affected by the transferor retaining the role of an agent to administer collection and distribution of cash flows. Retention of servicing rights by the entity transferring the financial asset does not, in itself, cause the transfer to fail the requirements in IAS 39:18(a). However, careful judgement must be applied to determine whether the entity providing servicing is acting solely as an agent for the owner of the financial asset (i.e. whether it has transferred all risks and rewards).

The IFRIC (now the IFRS Interpretations Committee) confirmed in September 2005 that the existence of servicing does not prevent an entity from transferring the contractual rights to the cash flows of the asset.

3.1.4.7 *Transfer of legal title*

When the Board considered a number of derecognition issues in September 2006 at the request of the IFRIC, it discussed whether any transfer in which legal ownership of the asset is not transferred can be considered an outright transfer of contractual rights under IAS 39:18(a). In other words, it considered whether the pass-through test is applicable to all transfers in which legal ownership of the financial asset is not transferred. The Board indicated that a transaction in which an entity transfers *all* the contractual rights *to receive the cash flows* [emphasis added in the IASB Update] (without necessarily transferring legal ownership of the financial asset), would not be treated as a pass-through and would be considered a transfer of contractual rights under IAS 39:18(a). An example might be a situation in which an entity transfers all the legal rights to specifically identified cash flows of a financial asset (e.g. a transfer of the interest or principal of a debt instrument). Conversely, application of the pass-through test would be required in situations in which the entity does not transfer all the contractual rights to cash flows of the financial asset, such as disproportionate transfers (see IAS 39:16(b)).

The Board's view in this case would mean that if an arrangement transferred all the legal rights to cash flows for a full proportionate interest in an asset (say 50 per cent of all cash flows), even though legal title of the asset was not transferred to the transferee, the transferor would apply paragraph 18(a) to the transfer and, therefore, would avoid the pass-through tests in paragraph 18(b).

3.1.4.8 *Conditional transfers*

The Board also discussed whether conditional transfers should be treated as pass-through transactions. Conditions attached to a transfer could include provisions ensuring the existence and value of transferred cash flows at the date of transfer or conditions relating to the future performance of the asset. The Board indicated that such conditions would not affect whether the entity has transferred the contractual rights to receive cash flows (under IAS 39:18(a)). However, the existence of conditions relating to the future performance of the asset might affect the conclusion related to the transfer of risks and rewards as well as the extent of any continuing involvement by the transferor in the transferred asset.

The Board's view on conditional transfers would allow the pass-through criteria to be met for a transfer of trade receivables even when there is a promise, say, to compensate the transferee should the transferor issue a credit note to the customer because the goods are returned. In this case, the transferor is obligated to pay cash to the transferee when the transferee did not collect cash from the asset.

The Board's views were included in a draft rejection notice issued by the IFRIC (now the IFRS Interpretations Committee) in November 2006. Following comments from constituents, at the IFRIC meeting in January 2007, the IFRIC decided to withdraw the rejection notice and add a project on derecognition to its agenda. However, in March 2009, the IFRIC decided to remove all of the outstanding derecognition issues from its agenda because the IASB accelerated its project to develop a replacement for the sections of IAS 39 on derecognition; the IASB published an exposure draft on this subject in March 2009 with the intention of issuing a final IFRS in the second half of 2010. However, in June 2010, the IASB announced its intention to proceed with a more limited project regarding new disclosure requirements in connection with derecognition. The resulting amendments to IFRS 7, *Transfers of Financial Assets*, were issued in October 2010 (see **4.1.5** in **chapter C12**).

3.1.5 Has the entity transferred substantially all of the risks and rewards of ownership of the asset?

Determining the extent to which the risks and rewards of the transferred asset have been transferred and retained is critical in determining the accounting outcome for a transfer. The greater the risks and rewards retained, the greater is the likelihood of continued recognition. The degree to which risks and rewards have been transferred and its effect on the accounting outcome can be illustrated as follows.

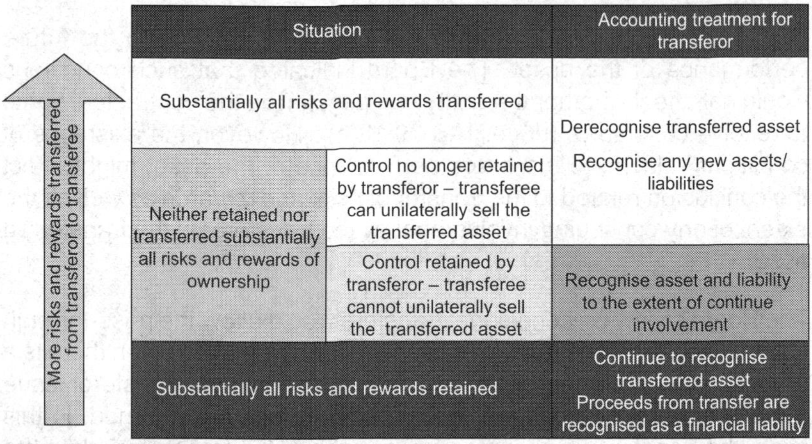

When the entity transfers substantially all of the risks and rewards of ownership of the financial asset, the asset should be derecognised. The entity may have to recognise separately any rights and obligations created or retained in the transfer. [IAS 39:20(a)]

There is no 'bright line' provided in IAS 39 as to what is meant by a transfer of 'substantially all' of the risks and rewards of ownership, and a significant degree of judgement is required when applying the risks and rewards test.

There are other references in the Standard to various yardsticks that need to be met when applying certain paragraphs. For example, when comparing the old and new terms of a financial liability, the terms are considered to be 'substantially different' if the present value of the cash flows under the new terms is at least 10 per cent different from the discounted present value of the remaining cash flows of the original financial liability (see **4.1**).

While IAS 39 does not apply the 90 per cent test to derecognition of financial assets, it would seem imprudent to conclude that substantially all the risks and rewards of ownership have been transferred when the computations show that the entity still retains more than 10 per cent of the exposure to the variability in present value of the expected future cash flows post transfer.

IAS 39 provides three examples of when an entity has transferred substantially all of the risks and rewards of ownership:

[IAS 39:AG39]

- an unconditional sale of a financial asset;
- a sale of a financial asset together with an option to repurchase the financial asset at its fair value at the time of repurchase; and

- a sale of a financial asset together with a put or call option that is deeply out of the money (i.e. an option that is so far out of the money that it is highly unlikely to be in the money before expiry).

In the first example, it is clear that there has been a transfer of all the risks and rewards of ownership of the asset. In the second example, the entity has sold the asset and, although it can call the asset back, this can only be done at the fair market value of the asset at the time of re-acquisition. The entity is in the same economic position as having sold the asset outright, with the ability to go into the market to reacquire the asset (i.e. it has transferred the full price risk of the asset). In the third example, the option is highly unlikely ever to be exercised and has very little value, which is substantially the same economic position as an unconditional sale.

Pass-through arrangements that meet the criteria in **section 3.1.4** may not satisfy the test regarding the transfer of substantially all of the risks and rewards of ownership.

Example 3.1.5A

Interaction of pass-through tests and risk and reward tests

Entity A originates a portfolio of five-year interest-bearing loans of CU10,000. Entity A enters into an agreement with Entity C whereby, in exchange for a cash payment of CU9,000, Entity A agrees to pay to Entity C the first CU9,000 (plus interest) of cash collected from the loan portfolio. Entity A retains rights to the last CU1,000 (plus interest), i.e. it retains a subordinated residual interest. If Entity A collects, say, only CU8,000 of its loans of CU10,000 because some debtors default, Entity A would pass on to Entity C all of the CU8,000 collected and Entity A keeps nothing. If Entity A collects CU9,500, it passes CU9,000 to Entity C and retains CU500. Expected losses are CU500.

Even though all cash flows that derive from the portfolio of assets are passed onto Entity C up to a maximum of CU9,000, Entity A has not transferred substantially all the risks and rewards of ownership because of the subordinated retained interest. The residual interest absorbs the likely variability in net cash flows, i.e. the expected losses.

IAS 39 acknowledges that in many cases it will be clear whether or not the entity has transferred substantially all of the risks and rewards of ownership following a transfer of an asset. When it is unclear whether or not there has been a transfer of substantially all of the risks and rewards of ownership of the financial asset, then the entity will have to evaluate its exposure before and after the transfer by comparing the variability in the amounts and timing of the net cash flows of the transferred asset. [IAS 39:21] If the exposure to the present value of the future net cash flows from the financial asset does not change significantly as a result of the transfer, then the entity has not transferred substantially all of the risks and rewards of ownership.

The computational comparison is made using an appropriate current market interest rate as the discount rate. All reasonably possible outcomes should be considered and a greater weight given to those outcomes that are more likely to occur. This is an expected cash flow model and should include all risks inherent in the cash flows.

There is no example in the Standard of the methodology to be used in performing the risks and rewards assessment. Whichever methodology is used, it should be consistently applied to all transfers that are similar in nature. It would be inappropriate to use multiple methodologies for similar transactions and to 'cherry pick' the methodology that indicated the desired degree of transfer of risks and rewards.

A common approach is to use a standard deviation statistic as the basis for determining how much variability has been transferred and retained by the transferor. To apply this approach, the transferor will need to consider various future scenarios that will impact the amount and timing of cash flows of the transferred assets and calculate the present value of these amounts both before and after the transfer. In the case of a transfer of debt instruments, scenarios will incorporate, among other factors:

- changes in the amount of cash flows due to changes in the rate of default by the borrower and recovery of any collateral in the case of default; and
- changes in the timing of when cash flows are received due to changes in prepayments rates.

The expected cash flows on the transferred assets will be allocated to the transferor and the transferee based on the rights and obligations following the transfer. For example, if the transferor guarantees part of the transferred assets or invests in a subordinated loan, a subordinated interest only strip or excess spread issued by the transferee, this will result in some of the exposure to the assets coming back to the transferor.

The transferor will need to assess the probability of the various scenarios occurring so that it can take the various present values described above and multiply them by those probabilities in order to determine probability weighted present values. These values are used for calculating the standard deviation, which can be thought of as the exposure, or volatility, that the transferor has to the transferred asset both before and after the transfer. This will form the basis for judging whether the transferor has retained or transferred substantially all the risks and rewards of ownership of the transferred assets.

The example below is aligned with the fact pattern included in the illustration in IAS 39:AG52, reproduced in **example 3.4.2**, where prepayable loans are transferred to a transferee in return for cash proceeds and an investment in a subordinated interest only strip, subordinated principal only strip, and an excess spread. The illustration in the Standard concludes that the transferor has neither retained nor transferred substantially all the risks and rewards of ownership.

Example 3.1.5B

Determining the extent of risk and reward transferred

Entity A has a portfolio of similar prepayable fixed rate loans with a remaining maturity of two years, a coupon and effective interest rate of 10 per cent. The principal and amortised cost is CU10,000. On 1/1/X0, Entity A transfers the loans for cash consideration of CU9,115 to Entity B, an entity not consolidated in Entity A's consolidated financial statements. In order to acquire the loans, Entity B issues a senior note, linked to the performance of the transferred assets, to third parties where the holders of the notes obtain the right to CU9,000 of any collections of principal plus interest thereon at 9.5 per cent. Entity A agrees to retain rights to CU1,000 of any collections of principal plus interest thereon at 10 per cent, plus the excess spread of 0.5 per cent on the remaining CU9,000 of principal. Collections from prepayments are allocated between the transferor and the transferee proportionately in the ratio of 1:9, but any defaults are deducted from Entity A's retained interest of CU1,000 until that interest is exhausted. Entity A's retained interest is therefore subordinate to the senior notes because it suffers the loss of any defaults on the transferred assets prior to the holders of the senior notes.

Interest is due on the transferred assets annually on the anniversary of the date of transfer.

In order to determine the extent to which Entity A has retained the risks and rewards of the transferred assets, Entity A considers a number of scenarios where amounts and timings of cash flows on the transferred assets vary and assigns a probability for each scenario occurring in the future. For illustration purposes, only four scenarios are included below although, in practice, a larger number of scenarios is likely to be required. A risk-free rate of 8.5 per cent is used to determine net present values. All amounts are denominated in CU.

Scenario		**Total**	**Senior note holders**	**Retained by Entity A**
1. All loans prepay immediately with no defaults. Probability is 20 per cent	1/1/X0 - undiscounted	10,000	9,000	1,000
	Total net present value	*10,000*	*9,000*	*1,000*
2. All loans prepay in one year with no defaults. Probability is 30 per cent	1/1/X0 - undiscounted	–	–	–
	1/1/X1 - undiscounted	11,000	9,855 (9.5% x 9,000) + 9,000	1,145 (0.5% x 9,000) + (10% x 1,000) + 1,000
	Total net present value	*10,138*	*9,083*	*1,055*

Scenario		Total	Senior note holders	Retained by Entity A
3. All loans run to their contractual maturity of 1/1/X2 with no defaults. Probability is 30 per cent	1/1/X0 - undiscounted	–	–	–
	1/1/X1 - undiscounted	1,000	855 (9.5% x 9,000)	145 (0.5% x 9,000) + (10% x 1,000)
	1/1/X2 - undiscounted	11,000	9,855	1,145
	Total net present value	*10,265*	*9,159*	*1,106*
4. All loans default at 1/1/X1 and due to immediate foreclosure and sale of the collateral, a total of CU10,741 is recovered. Probability is 20 per cent	1/1/X0 - undiscounted	–	–	–
	1/1/X1 - undiscounted	10,741	9,855	886 Proceeds from sale of collateral less amount paid to senior note holders
	Total net present value	*9,900*	*9,083*	*817*

The net present values for each scenario are multiplied by the probability of each scenario to determine a probability weighted present value. The variance before and after the transfer is determined using the profitability weighted present values as illustrated below.

Entity A's variability before the transfer

Scenario	**PV of cash flows**	**Probability**	**Probability weighted PV**	**Variability in PV**	**Probability weighted variability**
	a	b	c = a x b	e = a - d	f = e^2 x b
1	10,000	20%	2,000	(101)	2,040
2	10,138	30%	3,041	37	411
3	10,265	30%	3,080	164	8,069
4	9,900	20%	1,980	(201)	8,080
Total			10,101 [d]		18,600
Square root of f					136

Entity A's variability after the transfer

Scenario	**PV of cash flows**	**Probability**	**Probability weighted PV**	**Variability in PV**	**Probability weighted variability**
	a	b	c = a x b	e = a - d	f = e^2 x b
1	1,000	20%	200	(12)	29
2	1,055	30%	317	43	555
3	1,106	30%	332	94	2,651
4	817	20%	163	(195)	7,605
Total			1,012 [d]		10,840
Square root of f					**104**

Senior note holders' variability after the transfer

Scenario	**PV of cash flows**	**Probability**	**Probability weighted PV**	**Variability in PV**	**Probability weighted variability**
	a	b	c = a x b	e = a - d	f = e^2 x b
1	9,000	20%	1,800	(90)	1,620
2	9,083	30%	2,725	(7)	15
3	9,159	30%	2,748	69	1,428
4	9,083	20%	1,817	(7)	10
Total			9,090 [d]		3,073
Square root of f					**55**

Entity A determines whether substantially all of the risks and rewards of ownership of the transferred assets are retained by dividing the variability retained after the transfer by the variability of the portfolio as a whole [104/136 = 76%]. Consequently, Entity A concludes that substantially all the risks and rewards of ownership are neither transferred nor retained. Entity A would then need to address whether it has control of the transferred asset as described in detail in **3.1.7** to determine whether Entity A can derecognise the asset in full or continue to recognise its continuing involvement in the transferred assets.

It is worth noting that the sum of variability of Entity A after the transfer (CU104) plus variability of the senior note holders (CU55) is greater than the variability of the portfolio as a whole (CU136). This arises because the portfolio of loans as a whole has less risk due to the diversification of the loans within the portfolio. Some of this diversification is reversed when the portfolio is split into pieces. More complex mathematical techniques can be applied to show Entity B's variability to the loans after transfer that include the diversification effect that exists in the portfolio prior to the transfer. Such techniques are beyond the scope of this manual.

3.1.6 Has the entity retained substantially all of the risks and rewards of ownership of the asset?

If the entity has retained substantially all of the risks and rewards of ownership of a financial asset, the entity should continue to recognise that financial asset. [IAS 39:20(b)]

Once again, when it is unclear whether the entity has retained substantially all of the risks and rewards of ownership of the asset, it should look at its exposure before and after the transfer by comparing the variability in the amounts and timing of the net cash flows of the transferred asset. [IAS 39:21]

IAS 39 provides examples of transfers where substantially all of the risks and rewards of ownership have been retained and, therefore, derecognition is not permitted:

[IAS 39:AG40]

- a sale and repurchase transaction where the repurchase price is a fixed price or the sale price plus a lender's return;
- a securities lending transaction;
- a sale of a financial asset together with a total return swap that transfers the market risk back to the entity;
- a sale of a financial asset together with a deep in-the-money written put option or purchased call option (i.e. an option that is so far in the money that it is highly unlikely to go out of the money before expiry); and
- a sale of short-term receivables in which the entity guarantees to compensate the transferee for credit losses that are likely to occur.

In a typical repurchase agreement, the entity might, for example, own government securities that it sells to a third party with an agreement to repurchase the securities at a specified price, generally within a short period of time. At inception, the lender transfers the securities to the borrower and receives cash or other consideration as collateral; if the consideration is cash, it is then invested in other assets that earn a return. At a defined date, the transferor repurchases the securities. Dollar repurchase agreements (dollar rolls) are similar transactions in which the transferor repurchases similar but not identical assets to those originally sold. Economically, the lender is motivated in these transactions by the liquidity afforded by the agreement and/or the excess returns it expects to earn on the collateral.

Repurchase agreements are commonly referred to as 'repos'. In many countries, these are actively traded on listed exchanges or in the over-the-counter market and often are used as a source of funding or yield enhancement mechanism. The terminology, however, varies from country to country and the form taken, also, can be different. In some countries, a distinction is made between a repurchase agreement where legal title passes (also known as 'sell/buy-backs') and a 'carry' (typically, a short-term repo that is sometimes known as a classic repo) where title does not pass. Terminology also differs depending on which party is 'buying' or 'selling' the security (hence the use of terms such as 'reverse repos', 'inward carries' and 'outward carries').

In a securities lending transaction, the transferor (lender of the security) transfers a security to the transferee (borrower of the security) for a period of time. The transferee generally is required to provide collateral, which may be cash, other securities, or a standby letter of credit with a value that can be slightly higher than the value of the security borrowed (sometimes referred to as a 'haircut'). These transactions are typical when an entity needs a specific security to cover a short sale or a customer's failure to deliver securities sold. The transferor is compensated for lending the security by earning a fee or a return on the collateral invested if the collateral is cash.

A sale and repurchase transaction with a fixed price establishes a lending arrangement whereby the transferor is always going to reacquire the asset in the future. The fixed price is usually set to reflect the cost of borrowing over the period of the transaction. Because the transferor is required to reacquire the asset for a fixed price, the transferor is exposed to the market risk of the asset. The same analysis applies to a securities lending transaction. [IAS 39:AG51(a)]

A sale of a financial asset together with a total return swap that transfers the market risk back to the entity also establishes the economic equivalent of a lending arrangement. Under the terms of the total return swap, the transferor will usually pay an amount equivalent to a borrowing rate to the transferee over time and the transferee will reimburse the transferor for the performance of the asset. For example, the transferred asset may be an equity security; if the equity price goes up, the transferor receives the benefits of the rise in value of the transferred equity security from the transferee and pays an amount equivalent to a borrowing rate to the transferee; if the equity security price falls, the transferor pays an amount equivalent to a borrowing rate and, in addition, pays an amount equivalent to the fall in value of the equity security. The transferor continues to be exposed to the rise and fall in the equity security price after the transfer and hence, has retained substantially all of the risks and rewards of ownership of the asset. [IAS 39:AG51(o)]

When an entity sells an asset, but retains the right to buy the asset back at a price that is sufficiently low (option is deep in the money) that the option is highly likely to be exercised, the entity retains substantially all the risks and rewards of ownership. Similarly, when an entity sells an asset and gives the transferee the right to put the asset back at a sufficiently advantageous price (option is deep in the money) so that the option is likely to be exercised, the entity retains substantially all the risks and rewards of ownership. [IAS 39:AG51(f)]

Example 3.1.6A

Transfer of receivables with a deep in-the-money written put option (1)

Transferor X transfers receivables that are carried at amortised cost with a carrying amount of $90 and a put option which expires in 10 days to Transferee Y. Transferee Y pays $150 for the receivables, which have a fair value of $100. Under the terms of the put option, Transferee Y may put the receivables to Transferor X for $151. The possibility of the fair value of the receivables increasing to $151 in 10 days is considered remote and, therefore, exercise of the option appears virtually assured at inception.

Because, at inception, it is virtually certain that the put option will be exercised, Transferor X has retained substantially all of the risks and rewards of ownership over the receivables, and this transaction should be accounted for as a secured borrowing of $150 with the difference between the consideration received and the put strike price (i.e. $1), amortised to profit or loss using the effective interest method.

However, the same analysis is not appropriate when the option is not deep in the money and further derecognition tests should be applied.

In a sale of short-term receivables where the main risk of ownership is credit risk (i.e. the risk that the debtor will fail to pay), and the entity guarantees to compensate the transferee for credit losses that are likely to occur, the transferor has retained substantially all of the risks of ownership. [IAS 39:AG40(e)]

All the terms of a transfer need to be carefully evaluated. For example, penalty provisions attached to the agreement may affect the analysis of whether the risks and rewards have been transferred.

Example 3.1.6B

Transfer of receivables with a deep in-the-money written put option (2)

Transferor X transfers receivables with a carrying amount of $90 and a put option that expires in 10 days' time to Transferee Y. In the exchange, Transferee Y pays Transferor X $100, the fair value of the receivables. Under the terms of the put option, Transferee Y may put the receivables back to Transferor X for $101. However, if Transferee Y does not put the receivables back to Transferor X, Transferee Y must pay Transferor X an additional $50. The possibility of the fair value of the receivables increasing to $151 in 10 days is remote and, therefore, exercise of the option appears virtually assured at inception.

Because, at inception, it is virtually certain that the put option will be exercised, Transferor X has effectively retained substantially all the risks and rewards of ownership and, therefore, the transaction should be accounted for as a secured borrowing of $100 with the difference between the consideration received of

$100 and the put strike price of $101 amortised to profit or loss using the effective interest method.

Typical risks included in a risk and reward analysis are interest rate risk, credit risk (i.e. risk of default) and late payment risk. In many securitisation transactions, an entity (typically a structured entity) acquires assets and issues notes that are backed by those assets. The overall securitisation has liquidity risk associated with the fact that there is a mismatch in the timing of cash inflows and outflows. It is important to recognise that liquidity risk arising in the structured entity from differences in the contractual timing of cash flows of the assets and the notes issued to acquire the assets is not part of the transferred assets. This compares to late payment risk and credit default risk which is inherent in the assets. However, if an asset pays late, the transferee may not be able to meet its obligations under the notes. This liquidity risk is not part of the transferred assets because it only arises when the assets are placed inside the securitisation structure. The liquidity risk associated with late payment risk is therefore not included in the transferor's risk and rewards assessment in determining derecognition for the transferor. However, the impact of liquidity risk will be included in determining whether an entity should consolidate that structured entity, in particular in the assessment of whether the entity is exposed, or has rights, to variable returns from its involvement with the structured entity.

Derivatives are often included in contractual arrangements that transfer financial assets and may affect the analysis of whether the risks and rewards of those assets have been transferred. Their presence and contractual terms may not be obvious and careful review of all the terms of the transfer agreement is required.

In some instances, derivatives are included in a transfer or a securitisation structure and are not explicitly defined as derivatives. For example, the terms of a securitisation may call for the allocation of all principal cash flows to outside investors, with any remainder going to the retained interest of the seller. This provision may be in the form of a call option, put option, or forward contract. Identifying the implicit derivative in this example requires a thorough understanding of the transfer structure, terms, and conditions. A further assessment is required in these circumstances to determine the applicability of the embedded derivative provisions (see **chapter C5**).

Derivatives commonly found in transfers of financial assets include put options, call options, forward or repurchase contracts, forward sales contracts and swap agreements. Put options provide the transferee with the right to require the transferor to repurchase some or all of the financial assets that were sold (e.g. to repurchase delinquent receivables). Call options provide the transferor with the right to repurchase some or all of the financial assets sold to the transferee. Forward or repurchase agreements require the transferee to sell and the transferor to buy some or all of the financial assets that were sold before their scheduled maturity. Forward sales contracts require the transferor to sell and the transferee to buy additional financial assets in the future. Swap agreements effectively change one or more cash flows of the underlying transferred assets (or debt issued by a structured entity). For example, an interest rate swap may convert a variable rate asset to a fixed rate.

Derivatives can operate automatically or require exercise by one of the parties; they can be exercised freely or only after the occurrence of a future event. Such a future event may be certain of occurring (e.g. the passage of time), or may be conditional upon another event (e.g. a loan becoming delinquent). For conditional events, the certainty of occurrence varies – their occurrence may be considered to be probable, possible or remote. The exercise price of a derivative can be fixed above, below or equal to the market value of the financial assets at inception or it can be variable, equal to the market value at exercise date, or the result of a formula that is a function of market conditions or other future events. Derivatives can be combined to form different types of derivatives. Each of these factors impacts the extent to which risks and rewards have been retained by the transferor.

When a transferor transfers a fixed rate debt instrument for cash or other consideration, and at the same time enters into an interest rate swap with the transferee so that the transferor receives a fixed rate and pays floating rate based on a notional equal to the par amount of the transferred debt instrument, the interest rate swap does not preclude derecognition of the debt instrument as long as payments under the swap are not conditional on payments being made on the transferred debt. [IAS 39:AG51(p)] Even though the interest rate swap results in the transferor receiving cash flows similar to the underlying cash flows it would have received under the debt instrument, this does not prevent derecognition because the transferor's exposure before and after the transfer is different. Prior to the transfer, the transferor is exposed to fixed interest only and the credit risk of the issuer of the debt instrument. After the transfer, the transferor is exposed to the net of fixed and floating interest rates and the credit risk of the transferee to the extent that the transferee owes the transferor any amounts under the interest rate swap. If the cash flows under the swap were contingent on the cash flows received under the debt instrument, then the credit risk of the interest flows under the debt instrument would be retained by the transferor and a different derecognition conclusion would be likely to result.

When a transferor transfers a prepayable fixed rate debt instrument for cash or other consideration, and at the same time enters into an amortising interest rate swap with the transferee so that the transferor receives fixed rate and pays floating rate, the transferor will have retained prepayment risk if the repayment profile on the debt instrument matches the amortising profile of the interest rate risk. In this case, the transferor will either continue to recognise fully the fixed rate debt instrument or will recognise the transferred asset to the extent of its continuing involvement. If the amortisation of the notional amount of the swap is not linked to the principal amount outstanding of the transferred asset, the swap will not result in the transferor retaining prepayment risk on the asset. [IAS 39:AG51(q)] For the same reasons as described above for non-amortising swaps, as long as the interest flows on the swap are not conditional on the cash flows under the debt instrument, and the swap does not result in the transferor retaining any other significant risks and rewards of ownership, derecognition of the asset would be appropriate.

3.1.7 Has the entity retained control of the asset?

When an entity determines that it has neither transferred nor retained substantially all of the risks and rewards of ownership of the transferred assets, it needs to make an assessment as to whether or not it has retained control of the asset.

- If the entity has not retained control of the financial asset, the entity should derecognise the financial asset and recognise separately as assets or liabilities any rights and obligations created or retained in the transfer.
- If the entity has retained control of the financial asset, the entity should continue to recognise the financial asset to the extent of its continuing involvement in the financial asset. [IAS 39:20(c)]

An entity controls a financial asset when it is able to sell that asset. When the transferee has the *practical ability* to sell the asset in its entirety to an *unrelated* third party and is able to exercise that ability *unilaterally* and *without* the imposition of additional *restrictions* on the transfer, the transferee controls the asset and, therefore, the transferor must have relinquished control [emphasis added]. [IAS 39:23]

When the transferred asset is traded in an active market, the transferee generally has the practical ability to sell the asset. This is because there is a ready market and the transferee can repurchase the asset if and when it is required to return the asset back to the transferor. [IAS 39:AG42]

However, the fact that the transferred asset is traded in an active market is not in itself sufficient to conclude that the transferee has the 'practical ability' to sell the asset. For example, the settlement terms of repurchase, which are driven by the market conventions, may differ significantly from the settlement terms in the transfer agreement such that the transferee will not be able to gain access to the asset quickly enough to deliver the asset to the transferor so as to comply with the contractual provisions of the transfer agreement. In this case, the transferee is forced to hold the asset in order to ensure that it can deliver the asset back to the transferor when required.

Other factors may affect the entity's practical ability to sell the asset:

- a financial asset that would satisfy the call option or forward contract may have to be purchased from a third party at a price significantly above its estimated fair value, thus indicating that the assets are not liquid;
- financial assets available to satisfy the call option or forward contract may be held by one or a small number of investors, thus indicating that the assets are not liquid; or
- the quantity of financial assets necessary to satisfy the call option or forward contract may be too large compared to that traded in the market and the terms of the transfer do not allow delivery of the assets over a period of time.

Intuitively, the wider the range of assets that may be used to satisfy the call option, the more likely it is that the entity has practical ability to sell the asset. For instance, assets identical to those originally transferred may not be readily obtainable but, if the call option permits delivery of assets that are similar to the transferred assets, they may be readily obtainable. When a call option permits settlement in cash as an alternative to delivering the financial asset, and the cash settlement alternative does not contain an economic penalty rendering it unfeasible, the transferee has the practical ability to sell the asset as cash is a readily obtainable asset.

Unilateral and unrestricted ability to sell means that there can be no 'strings' attached to the sale. If the transferee has to attach a call option over the asset when it sells it, or introduce conditions over how the asset is serviced, in order to satisfy the terms of the original transfer, then 'strings' exist and the test of 'practical ability' is failed.

The 'strings' can be created by other instruments that form a contractual part of the transfer arrangement and are sufficiently valuable to the transferee, so that if the transferee were to sell the asset it would rationally include similar features within that sale. For example, a guarantee may be included in the initial transfer and may have such potential value to the transferee that the transferee would be reluctant to sell the asset and forgo any payments that may fall due under the guarantee.

The transfer agreement may have an explicit restriction that prohibits the transferee from selling the asset. When that restriction is removed or lapses, and as a result the transferee has the practical ability to sell the asset, derecognition would be appropriate.

The fact that the transferee may or may not choose to sell the asset should not form part of the decision making process; it is the transferee's practical ability to do so that is important.

Example 3.1.7A

Transfer of readily obtainable bonds with written put option

Transferor X sells South African government bonds that are readily obtainable in the market with a carrying amount of Rand 100 to Transferee Y for Rand 103. The transfer includes an option for Transferee Y to put the assets back to Transferor X up to one year after the transfer date at Rand 103.50. Transferee Y exercises its option 30 days after the initial sale. The option had a fair value of Rand 2 at the exchange date consisting of time value of Rand 1.50 and intrinsic value of Rand 0.50.

In this example, the transferor has neither transferred nor retained substantially all the risks and rewards of ownership because the option is neither deeply in nor deeply out of the money. The transferor has not retained control because the assets are readily obtainable. This put option does not therefore preclude derecognition.

Example 3.1.7B

Transfer of mortgage loans with right to call

Transferor X transfers a portfolio of mortgage loans to a third party, Transferee Y. The transferred loans can be repurchased by Transferor X at any time prior to their maturity. The agreement contains no explicit conditions restraining Transferee Y from selling, exchanging or pledging the assets to a third party.

Transferee Y does not have the practical ability to sell the portfolio of mortgage loans because it must have access to the original mortgage loans that were transferred in the event Transferor X exercises its right under the call option and the mortgage loans cannot be readily obtained from another source.

IAS 39 envisages circumstances when the transferee does not have the unilateral and unrestricted ability to sell the asset due to arrangements such as a call option held by the transferor. The Standard is less clear on the accounting treatment that should apply when a call option is held by a party other than the transferor. **Example 3.1.7C** illustrates this point.

Example 3.1.7C

Transfer of asset with purchased call option held by a third party

Bank A transfers loans to a non-consolidated structured entity. The funds that the structured entity used to purchase the loans were generated through a securitisation involving notes being issued by the structured entity to third parties. Bank A invests in a note that comprises an interest only strip on the transferred loans and also provides a subordinated loan to the structured entity.

Bank B (an independent third party relative to Bank A) holds substantive rights to direct the relevant activities of the structured entity, has provided a larger subordinated loan and invested in the most junior notes of the structured entity. Because it has the ability to use its power to affect its returns from its involvement with the structured entity, Bank B consolidates the structured entity. Bank B has a call on the assets of the structured entity that is exercisable at a fixed price.

Because Bank A has invested in the interest only strip and provided the subordinated loan, it is considered to neither have transferred nor retained substantially all of the risks and rewards of the transferred loans. Bank A must assess whether it has retained control of the asset, i.e. whether the *transferee* has the practical ability to sell the asset in its entirety to an unrelated third party and is able to exercise that ability unilaterally and without imposition of additional restrictions.

In this example, if the structured entity is considered to be the transferee, it does not have the practical ability to sell the loans without restrictions. If it were to sell the loans, it would need to attach restrictions such that it could honour its obligations under the call option which allows Bank B to call the remaining loans. The call option written by the structured entity limits the structured entity's ability to sell the asset. However, if the transferee in this case is viewed as the consolidated group of Bank B (which, therefore, includes the structured entity) then the transferee does have the unrestricted ability to sell the assets because the call option is eliminated on consolidation. Also, it can be argued that Bank A has not retained control of the asset, given that it has no mechanism within the arrangements for buying back the loans or being forced to acquire the loans. It is appropriate, therefore, for Bank A to derecognise the loans and not to apply continuing involvement accounting (see **section 3.4**), and instead initially recognise the interest only strip and subordinated loan at fair value.

3.2 Transfers that qualify for derecognition

When an entity concludes that derecognition of a financial asset is appropriate (the rights to the cash flows from the asset expired, or the entity has transferred substantially all of its risks and rewards, or the entity no longer retains control of the asset), the asset is removed from the statement of financial position and any new financial assets obtained, financial liabilities assumed and any servicing obligation are recognised at fair value. [IAS 39:25]

Often the transferor continues to service the transferred assets for a fee, which may take the form of part of the interest receipts on the transferred assets that an entity retains as compensation for servicing those assets.

Servicing refers to activities associated with the collection of cash flows from receivables or other financial assets after origination and the distribution of that cash to investors if the receivables are owned by other entities. Servicing may include the temporary investment and distribution to the financial asset owners of all or a portion of the cash collected. Servicing activities, also, may include monitoring delinquencies, advancing delinquent payments, restructuring receivables, and foreclosing on the collateral underlying the receivables when necessary. If the receivables are mortgage loans, servicing activities often include collecting and disbursing escrow payments for taxes and insurance. Servicing activities are inherent in all receivables; however, they do not need to be performed by the owner of the receivables. If the receivables are being serviced for another entity, the servicer generally receives a fee for performing these activities. This fee is usually a contractual amount received based on a fixed percentage of the outstanding receivables for the period. Servicers may also receive additional compensation by retaining late charges, other ancillary fees, and the float, which is the net interest earned on funds held by the servicer before disbursement. The compensation received by the servicer is referred to as the benefits of servicing.

If the benefits of servicing are not expected to cover the costs of servicing the assets, the entity should recognise a liability for the fair value of the service obligation entered into as a result of the transfer. [IAS 39:24] The servicing in this instance represents an obligation, because the servicer will either have to use its assets in the future to perform under the servicing contract or pay another entity to assume the servicing contract.

If the benefits of servicing exactly compensate the servicer for performing the servicing, but provide no additional benefits, the servicer has neither an asset nor a liability and the fair value of this servicing contract is zero.

A servicing contract with a positive fair value is considered to be one that would be favourable for a substitute servicer should one be required, and includes the profit that would be demanded in the marketplace. The amount allocated to a servicing right is treated as a retained interest and the amount allocated to it is determined by allocating the carrying amount of the larger financial asset. [IAS 39:24]

Example 3.2

Allocating consideration received between sold and retained interests

Entity A owns loans with a face amount of CU1 million that contractually yield 10 per cent interest over their life. The carrying amount of these loans after recognising impairment of CU20,000 is CU980,000. Entity A sells 90 per cent of the principal, plus the right to receive interest income of 8 per cent, without recourse to an investor for CU900,000 in cash. The part of the asset that has been transferred meets all the criteria for derecognition.

Entity A retains the right to service these loans, and the servicing contract stipulates a 1 per cent fee as compensation for performing the servicing. Entity A also retains an interest only strip for the portion of the interest coupon not sold (1 per cent). At the date of transfer, the fair value of the retained 10 per cent of the loan is CU100,000, the fair value of the servicing asset is CU15,000, and the fair value of the interest only strip is CU35,000.

The following table demonstrates the allocation of the carrying amount of the loans between the sold and retained interests assuming the entity has already determined that it has transferred substantially all the risks and rewards of ownership of the transferred assets (e.g. substantially all the credit losses and the majority of interest rate risk on the loans transferred).

Interest	Fair value	Percentage of total fair value	Allocated carrying amount[1]	Sold interests	Retained interests
	CU	%	CU	CU	CU
Loans sold	900,000	85.71	840,000	840,000	–
Loans retained	100,000	9.53	93,333	–	93,333
IO strip	35,000	3.33	32,667	–	32,667
Servicing asset	15,000	1.43	14,000	–	14,000
Total	1,050,000	100.00	980,000	840,000	140,000

[1] The allocated carrying amount is calculated as the percentage of total fair value multiplied by the aggregate carrying amount prior to the transfer (CU980,000).

The difference between:

- the carrying amount allocated to the part derecognised; and
- the sum of (i) the consideration received for the part derecognised (including any new asset obtained less any new liability assumed) and (ii), for AFS assets, any cumulative gain or loss allocated to it that had been recognised in other comprehensive income

is recognised in profit or loss. For AFS assets, a cumulative gain or loss that had been recognised in other comprehensive income is allocated between the part that is derecognised and the part that continues to be recognised on the basis of their relative fair values. [IAS 39:27]

In **example 3.2**, the assets were carried at amortised cost and the amount recognised in the profit or loss is calculated as the difference between the consideration of CU900,000 and the allocated carrying amount of the derecognised asset of CU840,000.

There are likely to be instances in which allocation based on the 'relative fair value method' is difficult because it is difficult to obtain the fair value of the parts of the asset that are subject to derecognition and continued recognition. The Standard acknowledges that when an entity has a historical practice of selling parts similar to the part that is continued to be recognised, or other market transactions for such parts exist, recent prices for actual transactions would best reflect the fair value of the parts. When there are no price quotes available, the best estimate of the fair value is the difference between the fair value of the larger financial asset as a whole and the consideration received from the transferee for the part of the asset that is derecognised. [IAS 39:28]

3.3 Transfers that do not qualify for derecognition

When a financial asset is precluded from being derecognised in its entirety (i.e. the transferor retains substantially all of the risks and rewards of ownership), the entity continues to recognise the asset in its entirety and recognises a financial liability for the consideration received. [IAS 39:29] The asset and liability cannot be offset and, similarly, any income arising from the asset cannot be offset against any expense incurred on the liability. [IAS 39:36] The asset's classification, measurement basis and income recognition does not change as a result of the transfer. This accounting treatment is often referred to as 'gross presentation' or 'secured borrowing' presentation.

Example 3.3

Transfer of receivables with credit guarantee

Entity X transfers short-term receivables to Entity Y and provides a credit guarantee to Entity Y over the expected losses of those receivables.

Entity X continues to recognise the receivables in its statement of financial position because it has retained substantially all the risks and rewards of ownership of the receivables. Entity X will recognise a financial liability for the proceeds received. The substance of the arrangement is that of a secured borrowing (i.e. short-term receivables provide security for the cash advanced by Entity Y).

When a derivative financial instrument forms part of the transfer arrangement and precludes the asset from being derecognised, the derivative is not accounted for separately because this would result in the rights to the cash flows being effectively counted twice. [IAS 39:AG49]

IAS 39 does provide some guidance on the transferee's accounting in circumstances where the transferor continues to recognise the asset in its entirety. To the extent that a transfer of a financial asset does not qualify for derecognition, the transferee does not recognise the transferred asset as its asset. The transferee derecognises the cash or other consideration paid and recognises a receivable from the transferor [IAS 39:AG50]. If the transferor continues to recognise the asset and, therefore, recognises a collateralised borrowing for the consideration received, then the transferee will not recognise the asset but will instead recognise a collateralised lending to the transferor. If a derivative is entered into between the transferor and the transferee as part of the arrangement, but it is not recognised by the transferor because it is an impediment to derecognition, then similarly the derivative will not be recognised by the transferee. The terms of the collateralised lending will include the cash consideration paid at the date of transfer, the contractual cash flows of the derivative, as well as the imputed repayment of principal.

3.4 Continuing involvement in the transferred assets

When an entity neither transfers, nor retains substantially all of the risks and rewards of ownership of a financial asset, and retains control of that asset, the entity continues to recognise the asset to the extent of its continuing involvement. Continuing involvement represents the extent to which the transferor continues to be exposed to the changes in the value of the transferred asset. A corresponding liability is also recognised and measured in such a way that the *net* carrying amount of the asset and the liability is:

[IAS 39:31]

- the amortised cost of the rights and obligations retained, if the asset is measured at amortised cost; or
- the fair value of the rights and obligations retained, if the asset is measured at fair value.

The liability that is recognised at the date of transfer will not necessarily equate to the proceeds received in transferring the asset which would ordinarily be the case if the asset continued to be fully recognised and the proceeds received were recognised as a collateralised borrowing. In some cases, the liability appears to be the 'balancing figure' that results from applying the specific guidance for continuing involvement accounting. IAS 39 acknowledges that measuring the liability by reference to the interest in the transferred asset is not in compliance with the other measurement requirements of the Standard. [IAS 39:31]

This requirement for consistent measurement of the asset and the associated liability means that the entity is not permitted to designate the liability as at FVTPL if the transferred asset is measured at amortised cost (see **7.2** in **chapter C3**).

The entity cannot offset the asset and the associated liability. Any subsequent changes in the fair value of the asset and the liability are measured consistently and are not offset. [IAS 39:33] Any income on the asset to the extent of the entity's continuing involvement and any expense incurred on the associated liability are not offset. [IAS 39:32]

When an entity transfers assets, but retains a guarantee over the transferred assets that absorb future credit losses, and that guarantee (as well as other continuing involvement) results in the transferor neither transferring nor retaining substantially all the risks and rewards of ownership, the transferor must recognise the guarantee as part of its continuing involvement.

Assuming, for illustrative purposes only, that the guarantee represents the transferor's only continuing involvement in the transferred asset, then:

- the transferred asset at the date of transfer will be measured at the lower of (i) the carrying amount of the asset and (ii) the maximum amount of the consideration received in the transfer that the entity could be required to repay; and
- the associated liability is measured initially at the amount in (ii) above plus the fair value of the guarantee.

The initial fair value of the guarantee is recognised in profit or loss when (or as) the obligation is satisfied in accordance with the principles of IFRS 15 *Revenue from Contracts with Customers Revenue* and the carrying amount of the asset is reduced by any impairment losses. [IAS 39:AG48(a)]

Example 3.4A

Continuing involvement: guarantee over first default losses

Transferor X transfers an asset to Transferee Y. The carrying amount at the date of transfer is CU100, which is also the asset's fair value at that date. Transferee Y pays CU105. Transferor X provides a guarantee to Transferee Y to pay for the first default losses up to a value of CU8. The fair value of the guarantee at the date of transfer is CU5. Expected future losses on the asset are CU12. Transferor X considers that substantially all the risks and rewards of ownership have neither been transferred, nor retained. Transferee Y does not have the practical ability to sell the assets, i.e. Transferor X controls the asset.

Transferor X determines its continuing involvement as the extent to which it continues to be exposed to the changes in the value of the transferred asset, i.e. the lower of:

(i) the carrying amount of the asset (CU100); and

(ii) the maximum amount of the consideration received in the transfer that Transferor X could be required to repay ('the guarantee amount') (CU8).

Transferor X recognises its continuing involvement in the asset at CU8, and derecognises the part of the asset transferred, i.e. CU92. The associated liability is initially measured at CU13, being the guarantee amount (CU8) plus the fair value of the guarantee (CU5). Subsequently, the initial fair value of the guarantee is recognised in profit or loss on a time proportion basis.

The following entries would be recorded at the date of transfer.

		CU	CU
Dr	Cash	105	
Cr	Financial asset		92
Cr	Financial liability		13

To record the transfer of the asset and recognition of the liability associated with the guarantee.

If, at the end of the guarantee period, no amounts have been paid under the guarantee, the following entries will be recorded.

		CU	CU
Dr	Financial liability	8*	
Cr	Financial asset		8

To derecognise the continuing involvement in the asset and the liability associated with the guarantee.

If, at the end of the guarantee period, the full amount of the guarantee is claimed by Transferee Y, the following entries will be recorded.

		CU	CU
Dr	Financial liability	8	
Cr	Cash		8
Dr	Profit or loss	8*	
Cr	Financial asset		8

To record the settlement of the liability associated with the guarantee and derecognition of continuing involvement in the asset.

* the fair value of the guarantee of CU5 will have been fully amortised by the end of the guarantee period

Example 3.4B

Continuing involvement: guarantee over slow payment risk

Entity A transfers short-term receivables to Bank B under a factoring arrangement. Entity A transfers the credit risk of the receivables but retains the slow payment risk up to a maximum of 120 days. If the receivable is outstanding after 120 days, the risk is absorbed by Bank B because the receivable is deemed to be in default. Entity A is charged a market interest rate of 10 per cent for the slow payment risk on the outstanding balance for the period if it is deemed to be a slow paying receivable. At the date of transfer, receivables with a nominal value and amortised cost carrying amount of CU300 million are transferred and the fair value of the late payment guarantee is CU1 million. The total consideration received by Entity A is CU288 million.

Entity A considers that it has neither retained nor transferred substantially of all the risks and rewards of ownership and is deemed to control the receivables because Bank B does not have the practical ability to sell the transferred assets.

Entity A determines its continuing involvement as the extent to which it continues to be exposed to the late payment risk of the transferred asset, i.e. the lower of:

(i) the carrying amount of the asset (CU300 million); and

(ii) the maximum amount of the consideration received in the transfer that Entity A could be required to repay ('the guarantee amount') (CU10 million, being CU300 million x 120/360 x 10%).

Entity A recognises its continuing involvement in the asset at CU10 million, and derecognises the part of the asset transferred (i.e. CU290 million). The associated liability is initially measured at CU11 million, being the guarantee amount (CU10 million) plus the fair value of the guarantee (CU1 million). Subsequently, the initial fair value of the guarantee is recognised in profit or loss on a time proportion basis.

		CU million	**CU million**
Dr	Cash	288	
Dr	Continuing involvement in the transferred asset	10	
Dr	Loss on disposal (profit or loss)	13	
Cr	Receivables		300
Cr	Continuing involvement liability		11

To record the derecognition of the receivables and the recognition of the continuing involvement.

The interest in the continuing involvement asset of CU10 million less the continuing involvement liability of CU11 million is equal to the fair value of the guarantee at the date of transfer (i.e. CU1 million).

3.4.1 Continuing involvement through options

Transfer arrangements often contain written or purchased options, or combinations thereof, so that the transferor neither retains, nor transfers substantially all the risks and rewards of ownership, and controls the transferred asset. This is the case when the option is neither deeply in, nor deeply out of the money at the date of transfer. In such transfer arrangements, with the exception of arrangements that contain a put option written by the transferor when the transferor measures the asset at fair value, the entity's continuing involvement in the asset is the amount of the transferred asset that the entity may repurchase. In the case of an arrangement containing a put option written by the transferor when the transferor measures the asset at fair value, the continuing involvement is the lower of the asset's fair value and the option exercise price. [IAS 39:30(b)] This is because, in such a transfer arrangement, the entity has no right to increases in fair value of the transferred asset above the exercise price of the option.

The table below sets out the measurement bases for the asset and associated liability for transfers that contain written or purchased options, or combinations thereof, when the transferor continues to recognise its continuing involvement in the asset. The manner of settlement of the options, gross or net cash settled, does not affect the accounting analysis below. However, a cash settled option in of itself is less likely to restrict the transferee's practical ability to sell the transferred asset and, therefore, may result in derecognition rather than continuing involvement accounting.

Derivative involved	Measurement basis of transferred asset prior to the transfer	Measurement basis of transferred asset after the transfer	Measurement basis of the associated financial liability
Purchased call option	Amortised cost	Amortised cost	Amortised cost: cost on initial recognition (being consideration received) is adjusted for amortisation of the difference between that cost and amortised cost of the asset on the expiration date of the option.
Written put option	Amortised cost	Amortised cost	Amortised cost: cost on initial recognition (being consideration received) is adjusted for amortisation of the difference between that cost and amortised cost of the asset on the expiration date of the option.
Purchased call option	Fair value	Fair value	When the *option is in or at the money* – the call option exercise price less the time value of the option. When the *option is out of the money* – the fair value of the transferred asset less the time value of the option. This ensures that the net carrying amount of the asset and associated liability is the fair value of the call option right.

Derivative involved	**Measurement basis of transferred asset prior to the transfer**	**Measurement basis of transferred asset after the transfer**	**Measurement basis of the associated financial liability**
Written put option	Fair value	Fair value (limited to the lower of the fair value of the asset and the option exercise price)	Option exercise price plus the time value of the option. This ensures that the net carrying amount of the asset and associated liability is the fair value of the put option obligation.
Collar (combination of purchased call and a written put)	Amortised cost	Amortised cost	Amortised cost: cost on initial recognition (being consideration received) is adjusted for amortisation of the difference between that cost and amortised cost of the asset on the expiration date of the options.
Collar (combination of purchased call and a written put)	Fair value	Fair value	When the *call option is in or at the money* – the sum of the call exercise price and fair value of the put option less the time value of the call option. When the *call option is out of the money* – the sum of the fair value of the asset and the fair value of the put option less the time value of the call option. This ensures that the net carrying amount of the asset and associated liability is the fair value of the options held and written.

The examples below illustrate the application of the requirements set out in the table.

Example 3.4.1

Continuing involvement: options

(a) Out-of-the money purchased call option

Entity A transfers an asset to Bank X and receives US$92. The amortised cost of the asset on the date of transfer is US$98. The amortised cost of the asset on the expiration of the option will be US$100. The fair value of the asset on the date of transfer is US$95. The exercise price of the purchased call option is US$99 (out of the money at the date of transfer) and, therefore, the premium paid to purchase the option consists entirely of the time value, being US$3, at the date of transfer.

The asset is held at amortised cost. On the date of transfer, the asset will continue to be recognised at US$98. The associated liability will be recognised at the fair value of the consideration received, US$92, with the difference between US$92 and US$100 being recognised in profit or loss using the effective interest method.

The asset is held at fair value. On the date of transfer, the asset will continue to be recognised at US$95. The associated liability will be recognised at US$92, being the fair value of the transferred asset, US$95, less the time value of the option, US$3.

(b) In- or at-the-money purchased call option

Entity A transfers an asset to Bank X and receives US$87. The amortised cost of the asset on the date of transfer is US$98. The amortised cost of the asset on the expiration of the option will be US$100. The fair value of the asset on the date of transfer is US$95. The exercise price of the purchased call option is US$90 (in the money at the date of transfer) and, therefore, the premium paid to purchase the option consists of intrinsic value, being US$5, and time value, being US$3, at the date of transfer.

The asset is held at amortised cost. On the date of transfer, the asset will continue to be recognised at US$98. The associated liability will be recognised at the fair value of the consideration received, US$87, with the difference between US$87 and US$100 being recognised in profit or loss using the effective interest method.

The asset is held at fair value. On the date of transfer the asset will continue to be recognised at US$95. The associated liability will be recognised at US$87, being the option exercise price, US$90, less the time value of the option, US$3.

(c) Written put option

Entity A transfers an asset to Bank X and receives US$95. The amortised cost of the asset on the date of transfer is US$98. The amortised cost of the asset on the expiration of the option will be US$100. The fair value of the asset on the date of transfer is US$92. The exercise price of the written put option is US$90 (out of the money at the date of transfer) and, therefore, the premium received for writing the option consists entirely of time value, being US$3.

The asset is held at amortised cost. On the date of transfer, the asset will continue to be recognised at US$98. The associated liability will be recognised at the fair value of the consideration received, US$95, with the difference between US$95 and US$100 being recognised in profit or loss using the effective interest method.

The asset is held at fair value. The asset will be recognised at the lower of its fair value and the option exercise price, i.e. at US$90. The associated liability will be recognised at US$93, being the option exercise price, US$90, plus the time value of the option, US$3.

(d) Collar

Entity A transfers an asset to Bank X and receives US$98. The amortised cost of the asset on the date of transfer is US$98. The amortised cost of the asset on the expiration of the option will be US$100. The fair value of the asset on the date of transfer is US$92. The cost of the collar at the date of transfer is zero. The exercise price of the written put is US$80 (out of the money at the date of transfer) and the exercise price of the purchased call is US$120 (out of the money at the date of transfer).

The asset is held at amortised cost. On the date of transfer, the asset will continue to be recognised at US$98. The associated liability will be recognised at the fair value of the consideration received, US$98, with the difference between US$98 and US$100 being recognised in profit or loss using the effective interest method.

The asset is held at fair value. On the date of transfer, the asset will continue to be recognised at US$92. The associated liability will be recognised at US$92, which is calculated as the sum of the fair value of the asset, US$92, and the fair value of the put option, less the time value of the call. The fair value of the put option will be equal to the time value of the call, because the put option's fair value represents only time value, and the sum of the two premiums on the options (both representing time value only) is zero.

When an option expires unexercised, the transferor derecognises financial assets that were subject to the option and also derecognises the associated liability. The transferee recognises the financial assets and eliminates the receivable due from the transferor.

3.4.2 Continuing involvement in a part of a financial asset

If an entity has a continuing involvement in only a part of a financial asset, the entity allocates the previous carrying amount of the financial asset between the part it continues to recognise under continuing involvement, and the part it no longer recognises, based on the relative fair values of those parts at the date of transfer. [IAS 39:34]

The allocation exercise and the calculation of the gain or loss on the disposal of the part of the asset are done in the same way as is described in **3.2**. In addition to the part retained, the transferor also recognises its continuing involvement in the asset and the associated liability. IAS 39:AG52 contains a numerical illustrative example of continuing involvement in a part of an asset which is reproduced below.

Example 3.4.2

Continuing involvement: part of a financial asset

[Extract from IAS 39:AG52]

Assume an entity has a portfolio of prepayable loans whose coupon and effective interest rate is 10 per cent and whose principal amount and amortised cost is CU10,000. It enters into a transaction in which, in return for a payment of CU9,115, the transferee obtains the right to CU9,000 of any collections of principal plus interest thereon at 9.5 per cent. The entity retains rights to CU1,000 of any collections of principal plus interest thereon at 10 per cent, plus the excess spread of 0.5 per cent on the remaining CU9,000 of principal. Collections from prepayments are allocated between the entity and the transferee proportionately in the ratio of 1:9, but any defaults are deducted from the entity's interest of CU1,000 until that interest is exhausted. The fair value of the loans at the date of the transaction is CU10,100 and the estimated fair value of the excess spread of 0.5 per cent is CU40.

The entity determines that it has transferred some significant risks and rewards of ownership (for example, significant prepayment risk) but has also retained some significant risks and rewards of ownership (because of its subordinated retained interest) and has retained control. It therefore applies the continuing involvement approach.

To apply IAS 39, the entity analyses the transaction as (a) a retention of a fully proportionate retained interest of CU1,000, plus (b) the subordination of that retained interest to provide credit enhancement to the transferee for credit losses.

The entity calculates that CU9,090 (90 per cent CU10,100) of the consideration received of CU9,115 represents the consideration for a fully proportionate 90 per cent share. The remainder of the consideration received (CU25) represents consideration received for subordinating its retained interest to provide credit enhancement to the transferee for credit losses. In addition, the excess spread of 0.5 per cent represents consideration received for the credit enhancement. Accordingly, the total consideration received for the credit enhancement is CU65 (CU25 + CU40).

The entity calculates the gain or loss on the sale of the 90 per cent share of cash flows. Assuming that separate fair values of the 90 per cent part transferred and the 10 per cent part retained are not available at the date of the transfer, the entity allocates the carrying amount of the asset in accordance with IAS 39:28 as follows:

	Estimated fair value	Percentage	Allocated carrying amount
Portion transferred	9,090	90%	9,000
Portion retained	1,010	10%	1,000
Total	10,100		10,000

The entity computes its gain or loss on the sale of the 90 per cent share of the cash flows by deducting the allocated carrying amount of the portion transferred from the consideration received, i.e. CU90 (CU9,090 - CU9,000). The carrying amount of the portion retained by the entity is CU1,000.

In addition, the entity recognises the continuing involvement that results from the subordination of its retained interest for credit losses. Accordingly, it recognises an asset of CU1,000 (the maximum amount of the cash flows it would not receive under the subordination), and an associated liability of CU1,065 (which is the maximum amount of the cash flows it would not receive under the subordination, i.e. CU1,000 plus the fair value of the subordination of CU65).

The entity uses all of the above information to account for the transaction as follows:

	Debit	Credit
Original asset	–	9,000
Asset recognised for subordination of the residual interest	1,000	–
Asset for the consideration received in the form of excess spread	40	–
Profit or loss (gain on transfer)	–	90
Liability	–	1,065
Cash received	9,115	–
Total	10,155	10,155

Immediately following the transaction, the carrying amount of the asset is CU2,040 comprising CU1,000, representing the allocated cost of the portion retained, and CU1,040, representing the entity's additional continuing involvement from the subordination of its retained interest for credit losses (which includes the excess spread of CU40).

In subsequent periods, the entity recognises the consideration received for the credit enhancement (CU65) on a time proportion basis, accrues interest on the recognised asset using the effective interest method and recognises any credit impairment on the recognised assets. As an example of the latter, assume that in the following year there is a credit impairment loss on the underlying loans of CU300. The entity reduces its recognised asset by CU600 (CU300 relating to its retained interest and CU300 relating to the additional continuing involvement that arises from the subordination of its retained interest for credit losses), and reduces its recognised liability by CU300. The net result is a charge to profit or loss for credit impairment of CU300.

A number of observations can be drawn from the example in IAS 39:AG52 reproduced above. A concern that is often cited is that the example advocates 'double-counting', i.e. the continuing involvement in the asset is accounted for twice. This is best illustrated using the numbers in the example above. The transferor continues to recognise a fully proportionate interest in 10 per cent of all cash flows which equals an amortised cost of CU1,000 (being 10% x CU10,000 carrying amount) and also recognises an additional CU1,000 being the 'asset recognised for subordination or the residual interest'. This may appear odd because the interest in the assets is limited to a disproportionate interest in the transferred asset up to CU1,000. However, the reason for presenting the transferor's interest in the transferred asset 'grossed up' is to reflect that the transferor's interest in 10 per cent of the asset is in fact subordinated (and, therefore, is not a fully proportionate interest) because any losses borne by the transferred assets continue to be borne by the transferor until their remaining interest is exhausted. In order to recognise the transferor's continuing involvement liability, the entity needs to 'gross-up' its statement of financial position by recognising a further asset.

Because the transferor's interest in the transferred asset is deemed to be a fully proportionate share of the asset (plus that interest being subordinated), the calculation of the gain/loss on partial disposal of the asset is also based on a fully proportionate basis. On the face of it, this calculation may also appear odd because the entity has not economically sold a fully proportionate share in the asset to the transferee; rather it has retained a disproportionate share of the cash flows of the asset.

The example also recognises another new asset that it refers to as the 'asset for the consideration received in the form of excess spread'. It is worth noting that the amount recognised for the excess spread is equal to the fair value of the excess spread at the date of transfer, being CU40, even though it appears the loans themselves were not originally measured at fair value (i.e. they were originally measured at amortised cost). Because the objective of accounting for continuing involvement is to ensure that the measurement of the net involvement (being the net of the continuing involvement asset and continuing involvement liability) is consistent with the measurement of the transferred assets, it is surprising that the excess spread in the example is initially recognised at fair value rather than amortised cost. It appears possible that this was an oversight when the example was developed.

3.4.3 Accounting by the transferee in the case of continuing involvement

Example 3.4.3

Accounting by the transferee in the case of continuing involvement

Bank S owns a 16 per cent equity stake in a thinly-traded entity. The investment is classified by Bank S as an AFS financial asset. Bank S enters into an agreement with Entity K whereby Entity K pays CU102 to Bank S in return for:

- the 16 per cent equity interest in the thinly-traded entity; and
- a put option that allows Entity K to put the shares back to Bank S for a price of CU96 at a pre-specified date.

On the date of the transfer, the fair value of the shares is CU97 and the time value of the put option is CU5 (CU102 minus CU97), i.e. the option is out of the money at inception.

Transferor accounting

Bank S, the transferor, will apply continuing involvement accounting because it has neither transferred nor retained substantially all the risks and rewards of the shares and Entity K does not have the practical ability to sell the shares because it is a significant holding in an entity that is thinly-traded and, therefore, Bank S is deemed to control the shares.

Because the arrangement involves the transferor writing a put option on an asset that is measured at fair value, the extent of the continuing involvement for Bank S is limited to the lower of the fair value of the shares and the option exercise price. [IAS 39:30(b) & AG48(d)]

At the transaction date, the following entries will be recorded.

		CU	CU
Dr	Cash	102	
Cr	AFS financial asset		1
Cr	Financial liability		101

To record recognition of the liability and adjustment to the asset for continuing involvement.

This entry recognises a liability of CU101, consisting of a strike price of CU96 and time value of the put option of CU5.

The shares continue to be recognised by Bank S and measured as an AFS financial asset, although changes in their value above the strike price of CU96 are not recognised.

If the put option is exercised by Entity K because the share price is below CU96, the following entry will be recorded.

		CU	CU
Dr	Financial liability	96	
Cr	Cash		96

To record the derecognition of the liability on exercise of the put option.

The difference between the opening and the closing carrying amount of the liability of CU5 (CU101 less CU96) will be recognised in profit or loss over the life of the arrangement. Any fair value loss on the AFS investment below CU96 will be recognised in other comprehensive income. Fair value losses recognised in equity will only be reclassified from equity to profit or loss when the asset is impaired or is subsequently derecognised.

If the put option is not exercised by Entity K because the share price is above CU96, the following entry will be recorded.

		CU	CU
Dr	Financial liability	96	
Cr	AFS investment		96

To record derecognition of the liability and the asset on expiry of the put option.

The difference between the opening and closing carrying amount of the liability of CU5 (CU101 less CU96) will be recognised in profit or loss over the life of the arrangement. Any amounts accumulated in the AFS reserve in equity will be reclassified to profit or loss because the AFS investment has been derecognised.

Transferee accounting

Entity K has paid cash of CU102 in return for a right to receive cash of CU96 (through exercise of its purchased put option) and rights to all the upside on the shares above CU96 (i.e. by not exercising its put option and physically retaining the transferred shares). Entity K economically has an investment in shares with no downside risk below CU96.

Entity K should recognise its interest in the arrangement as an AFS financial asset, but not recognise any changes in fair value below the strike price of CU96 because Entity K has no exposure to fair value movements below this amount. This is the inverse of the accounting by the transferor, Bank S. Both parties recognise an AFS investment, with Entity K recognising fair value changes above CU96, and Bank S recognising fair value changes below CU96.

At the date of transfer, the following entry will be recorded.

		CU	CU
Dr	AFS financial asset	102	
Cr	Cash		102

To record initial recognition of the asset.

This entry will recognise the financial asset consisting of the fair value of the shares of CU97 plus the value of the purchased put option of CU5. Increases in the fair value of the AFS investment above CU96 will be recognised in other comprehensive income. The AFS asset and the purchased put will be remeasured in other comprehensive income. Because the purchased put option provides a 'floor' of CU96, changes in fair value of the security below this amount will not be recognised. At maturity of the option, the time value of the option will have been fully eroded resulting in the security either being put at CU96 (and, thereby, being derecognised), or continuing to be measured at fair value in other comprehensive income because the transferee has not exercised the put option. The put option is not measured at FVTPL because, for the transferor, it is not recognised because it is an impediment to derecognition and, for the transferee, it forms part of its involvement in the asset.

If the put option is exercised by Entity K because the share price is below CU96, the following entry will be recorded.

		CU	CU
Dr	Cash	96	
Cr	AFS financial asset		96

To record derecognition of the asset on exercise of the put option.

An amount of CU1 would have already been recognised in other comprehensive income when the fair value of asset had decreased to CU96. Fair value movements below CU96 are not recognised. The CU1 in other comprehensive income is reclassified from equity to profit or loss when the put option is exercised by Entity K and the AFS asset is derecognised.

If the put option is not exercised by Entity K because the share price is above CU96, no further entry will be required to recognise the shares because they are already recognised in Entity K's statement of financial position. After the expiration of the option, all gains or losses on the AFS investment will be recognised in other comprehensive income (except impairment losses recognised in profit or loss) because Entity K will be exposed to movements in the share price in both directions.

3.5 Collateral

A transfer arrangement may require a transferor to provide non-cash collateral (e.g. a debt or an equity instrument) to the transferee. The transferee's entitlement to the collateral is conditional upon the transferor's default and while the transferor continues to perform under the contract, the transferor continues to benefit from substantially all of the collateral's risks and rewards. Normal recognition and derecognition principles apply to the collateral: the transferee is not entitled to recognise the collateral until it becomes contractually entitled to it, which will not be the case until the transferor defaults under the terms of the contract; the transferor retains all of the risks and rewards of ownership of the asset pledged as collateral and, therefore, cannot derecognise it.

If the transferee has the right by contract or custom to sell or repledge the collateral, the asset that has been pledged by the transferor should be reclassified in its statement of financial position separately from its other assets and described as a loaned asset, pledged equity instrument or repurchase receivable. If the transferee uses that right and sells the collateral, it should recognise the proceeds from the sale and a liability measured at fair value for its obligation to return the collateral. [IAS 39:37(b)]

In the event of a default by the transferor, the risks and rewards of the collateral, within the confines of the collateral agreement, are transferred to the transferee. Hence, the transferor derecognises the collateral and the transferee, who after the default becomes contractually entitled to it, recognises the collateral at its fair value, unless the transferee has already sold the collateral, in which case, it derecognises its obligation to return the collateral to the transferor.

3.6 Sale and repurchase agreements and stock lending

A sale and repurchase agreement usually takes the form of an agreement to sell a security (i.e. transfer all the rights attaching to a security) with a simultaneous agreement to repurchase it at a specified price at a fixed future date. The consideration involved is either in the form of cash or security. The repurchase price is normally structured higher than the sale price; alternatively, the two prices can be the same, but with an explicit interest rate charged instead. The transferee will require that it is assured of a lender's return on its investment and the transferor will require that the transferee earns no more than this return. In the event that the transferee is entitled to retain any coupons or dividends that are paid on the asset during the term of the repurchase agreement, the transaction price is adjusted to reflect the fact (see **3.1.6**).

The table below considers some common terms of sale and repurchase transactions and applies IAS 39 derecognition principles to those transactions.

Features	Applying derecognition in IAS 39
The repurchase price is an agreed price higher than the market value at the date of sale.	If the repurchase price results in a lender's return for the transferee, then the transferor has not transferred, but has retained substantially all of the risks and rewards of ownership of the asset. The lender's return earned by the transferee is consistent with the arrangement being a collateralised borrowing for the transferor, and a collateralised lending for the transferee.

Features	Applying derecognition in IAS 39
The repurchase provision is an option for the transferor to repurchase the asset at a fixed price (where the call option is neither deeply in nor out of the money), and the asset is readily obtainable in the market.	The asset is derecognised because the transferor neither transferred nor retained substantially all of the risks and rewards of ownership, and has lost control over the asset since the asset is readily obtainable in the market (i.e., the transferee has the practical ability to sell the asset). The transferor will recognise a stand-alone call option in the statement of financial position at fair value with gains or losses recognised in profit or loss.
The repurchase provision is an option for the transferor to repurchase the asset at a fixed price (where the call option is neither deeply in nor out of the money), and the asset is *not* readily obtainable in the market.	The transferor has neither transferred nor retained substantially all of the risks and rewards of ownership but has retained control of the asset because the asset is not readily obtainable in the market (i.e. the transferee does not have the practical ability to sell the asset). Hence, the transferor continues to recognise the asset to the extent of its continuing involvement: when the asset is measured at fair value and the option is out of the money, the transferor recognises a liability for the fair value of the transferred asset less the time value of the option; when the asset is measured at fair value and the option is at or in the money, the transferor recognises a liability for the option exercise price less the time value of the option; when the asset is measured at amortised cost, the transferor recognises a liability for the consideration received and adjusts it for the amortisation between the consideration received and the amortised cost of the asset on the expiration date of the option.
The repurchase provision is a put option at a fixed price (where the put option is neither deeply in nor out of the money) and the asset is readily obtainable in the market.	The asset is derecognised because the transferor has neither retained nor transferred substantially all of the risks and rewards of ownership, and has lost control over the asset because the asset is readily obtainable in the market (i.e. the transferee has the practical ability to sell the asset). The transferor recognises a stand-alone put option in the statement of financial position at fair value with gains or losses recognised in profit or loss.

Features	Applying derecognition in IAS 39
The repurchase provision is a put option at a fixed price (where the put option is neither deeply in nor out of the money) and the asset is *not* readily obtainable in the market.	The transferor has neither transferred nor retained substantially all of the risks and rewards of the asset and has retained control of the asset; hence, it continues to recognise the asset to the extent of its continuing involvement because the asset is not readily obtainable in the market (i.e. the transferee does not have the practical ability to sell the asset). When the asset is measured at fair value, the transferor recognises a liability equal to the option exercise price plus the time value of the option; when the asset is measured at amortised cost, the transferor recognises a liability for the consideration received and adjusts it for the amortisation between the consideration received and amortised cost of the asset on the expiration date of the option.
The asset sold is subject to the transferor receiving a deferred consideration receipt/payment based on the increases/decreases in the fair value of the asset respectively for a specified period of time.	The deferred consideration passes the changes in the fair value of the asset back to the transferor, thus the transferor has retained substantially all of the risks and rewards of ownership of the asset; hence, the transferor continues to recognise the asset and recognises a liability for the initial cash consideration received.
The asset is subject to a varying repurchase price such that original purchase price is adjusted retrospectively to pass variations in the value of the asset to the transferor.	The variation in the repurchase price so as to pass the changes in the value of the asset back to the transferor means that the transferor retains substantially all the risks and rewards of ownership; hence, the transferor continues to recognise the asset and recognises a liability for the cash consideration received.

Features	Applying derecognition in IAS 39
The transferor provides a residual value guarantee to the transferee or subordinated debt to protect the transferee from falls in the value of the asset.	Provided that the asset has upside potential, the transferor has neither retained nor transferred substantially all the risks and rewards of ownership (transferred the upside, but retained the downside). The transferor continues to control the asset where the guarantee is sufficiently valuable to the transferee and limits its ability to transfer the asset and, therefore, the transferor continues to recognise the asset to the extent of its continuing involvement (i.e. at the date of the transfer the asset is measured at the lower of its carrying amount and the guarantee amount). The transferor recognises an associated liability equal to the guarantee amount plus the fair value of the guarantee. When the guarantee does not restrict the transferee's ability to sell the asset, the transferor derecognises the asset.
The repurchase price, whether put/call or forward, is the market price at the time of repurchase.	The transferor has transferred substantially all of the risks and rewards of ownership of the asset because the transferor can only repurchase it at its fair value. Hence, the asset is derecognised.
Asset repurchased is substantially the same as the asset that is transferred or the transferee can substitute the asset with one that is similar or is of equal fair value.	The transferor retains substantially all the risks and rewards of ownership of the asset and, therefore, derecognition is precluded.

3.7 Debt factoring

Debt factoring is used extensively as a method for obtaining one or more of the following benefits: obtaining financing, bad debt protection or sales ledger administration. A factoring transaction normally takes the form of an entity receiving cash consideration in exchange for the rights to cash collected from its receivables. In many situations, the rights to the cash flows on the receivables are subject to certain restrictions or guarantees. Sometimes the transferee may have recourse to the transferor over the performance of the receivables either up to a certain limit or to the extent to which there is a shortfall of the cash collected on the receivables. In a non-recourse transaction, there is no obligation of the transferor to make good to the transferee for any shortfall on the assets. In order to receive a market return from the receivables (the receivables are collected over time), the transferee charges interest.

The table below sets out some of the common features of debt factoring transactions and application of derecognition principles to a 'vanilla' debt factoring transaction (an entity receives cash consideration in exchange for the rights to cash collected from its receivables) with each of those features. It is assumed that the transferee cannot sell receivables (i.e. the transferor continues to control them).

Features	Applying derecognition in IAS 39
For all receivables not recovered after a certain period (e.g. 120 days), whether due to late payment or default, the transferor provides a guarantee.	The guarantee may represent substantially all the risks of ownership of receivables (e.g. where most receivables are long term due to the credit terms offered). If so, derecognition is precluded. When the transferor has neither transferred nor retained substantially all the risks and rewards of ownership, the transferor continues to recognise receivables to the extent of its continuing involvement, i.e. to the extent that amounts may be repaid under the guarantee.
In the event of a receivable going bad beyond but not prior to a certain period (e.g. the period commencing after 120 days), the transferor provides credit protection on that receivable.	The credit protection may represent substantially all the risks of ownership (e.g. where credit terms are 120 days or more and thus the risk of a receivable going bad stays with the transferor). If it does, derecognition is precluded. Depending on the likelihood of default prior to 120 days and other risks transferred to the transferee, the transferor may determine that substantially all the risks and rewards of ownership are neither transferred nor retained and thus the transferor continues to recognise receivables to the extent of its continuing involvement, i.e. to the extent that amounts may be repaid under the credit protection.

Features	Applying derecognition in IAS 39
The transferor receives an element of non-returnable consideration for the receivables, but either the transferor or the transferee has rights to some further sums from the other party to the transaction. This further sum depends on whether or when cash is collected from the receivables, e.g. through deferred consideration, a retrospective adjustment to the sale price or rebates of certain charges.	When the further sums from the other party are not considered to be substantially all of the risks and rewards of ownership, the transferor has neither transferred nor retained substantially all the risks and rewards of ownership and continues to recognise the receivables to the extent of its continuing involvement. The transferor derecognises receivables to the extent of the non-returnable consideration.
The transferor provides a warranty over the quality/condition of the receivables at the moment of transfer, e.g. at the point of delivery of the goods, the customer had not breached their credit limit.	The warranty provision may result in the transferor retaining some risks and rewards (e.g. if the transferor has to reimburse the transferee should the transferor's representations as to the quality/condition of the asset prove to be wrong). If the warranty results in the transferor neither transferring nor retaining substantially all the risks and rewards of ownership, it continues to recognise the receivables to the extent of its continuing involvement, i.e. to the extent that amounts may be repaid under the warranty. If the warranty as to quality/condition of the assets at the date of transfer results in the entity transferring substantially all the risks and rewards of ownership, then the transferor will derecognise the assets. (The IFRIC (now the IFRS Interpretations Committee) considered conditional transfers in November 2006 – see **section 3.1.4**.)
The transferor continues to service the receivables by administering the sales ledger for a fee that is based upon the total amount of receivables factored at each month end. The charge is at market price. The transferor is not subject to any recourse and the transferor has not retained any residual interest in the receivables.	A servicing arrangement at a market price with no further continuing involvement in the receivables is considered to be a transfer of substantially all of the risks and rewards of ownership of the assets, and, therefore, derecognition by the transferor is appropriate. If the charge for the servicing arrangement is not at market price such that the benefits of servicing the assets are not commensurate with the administration charges, but did not otherwise involve further transfer of exposure to risk back to the transferor, a servicing asset or servicing liability will arise and be recorded separately.

Features	Applying derecognition in IAS 39
The transferor has a call option to purchase outstanding receivables from the transferee at a predetermined price when the amount of outstanding assets falls to a specified level at which the cost of servicing those assets is too high as compared to the benefits of servicing. This is sometimes known as a clean-up call.	Provided that the clean-up call results in the entity neither retaining nor transferring substantially all the risks and rewards of ownership, it precludes derecognition only to the extent of the amount of the assets subject to the call option.

3.8 Securitisations

Securitisation is a means of making use of a portfolio of assets, usually receivables held by an entity (loans, mortgages, credit cards etc.) to obtain cost effective funding. These assets are usually purchased by a transferee who then repackages the receivables as asset-backed securities and sells them on in the market to investors for cash consideration. The normal process is to repackage these securities in a vehicle specifically set up for that purpose, a structured entity (see **3.1.1**). The notes issued to the investors are secured on the underlying assets that have been transferred to the structured entity. It is usual for investors to require a form of credit enhancement which can take many forms:

- subordination: typically the transferor acquires a junior (often the most junior) note issued by the structured entity that absorbs the first losses incurred by the transferred assets;
- over-collateralisation: the face amount of the transferred assets is larger than the funding used to buy the assets;
- excess spread: after all interest has been received and paid and expenses of the structured entity settled, an amount is retained in the arrangement which will absorb first losses should they occur;
- reserve fund: similar to excess spread except a separate fund is created;
- guarantees: the structured entity may obtain guarantees either from the transferor or from third parties, for example from well rated insurance companies;
- letters of credit: the structured entity may obtain letters of credit from well rated banks where the bank will stand ready to reimburse the structured entity for losses incurred up to a specified amount; or
- cash collateral account: similar to a letter of credit except the bank lends cash upfront which is invested in highly rated short-term commercial paper. The structured entity has some credit risk on its investments but this is less than would be the case for a letter of credit where the borrower runs the risk that the lender will fail to meet its lending commitment when demanded by the borrower. Alternatively, the transferor may deposit a percentage of its proceeds from the securitisation in a cash collateral or maintenance account.

Some forms of credit enhancement, like subordination and over-collateralisation and some cash collateral accounts deposited by the transferor, transfer risks and rewards of the transferred asset back to the transferor. Others, like letters of credit and some cash collateral accounts, transfer risks and rewards to third parties. The types of risk transferred determine whether the transferor is able to achieve derecognition for the transferred assets.

As explained in **3.1.1**, it is important to determine whether or not the entity needs to consolidate the structured entity. If the structured entity is consolidated, the extent of derecognition achieved is the same irrespective of whether the transfer is direct to investors or through a consolidated structured entity that obtains the financial assets and, in turn, transfers them to third party investors.

In many securitisations, the structured entity is consolidated and the assets are not transferred to a third party (i.e. the right to receive the cash flows from the assets remains with the group). The group may assume a contractual obligation to pass on those cash flows to ultimate investors in a 'pass-through' arrangement that meets all three conditions detailed in **section 3.1.4**. Nevertheless, the group may still have retained all the risks and rewards of ownership of the assets (e.g. when credit risk is the main risk and credit enhancement provided by the group covers all expected losses) and may still need to continue to recognise the assets. The IASB recognises that many securitisations will not qualify for derecognition either because one of the three conditions in the pass-through test will not be met or because the credit enhancement required by the ultimate investors will mean that the group retains substantially all the risks and rewards of ownership of the assets. [IAS 39:BC63] Where credit enhancement provided by the group is such that the group neither retains nor transfers all the risks and rewards of ownership, the group will continue to recognise the assets only to the extent of its continuing involvement, i.e. the credit enhancement provided.

The table below sets out some of the common features of securitisations where the structured entity that purchases the assets is *not consolidated* by the transferor and application of derecognition principles to securitisations with each of those features. It is assumed that the structured entity cannot sell receivables, i.e. the transferor continues to control them and the transferor has no exposure to the assets other than stated.

Features	Applying derecognition in IAS 39
Credit enhancement is provided for the transferred receivables by an independent third party (e.g. third party credit insurance or guarantee).	The transferor has transferred the rights to receive cash flows on the assets to the structured entity and also transferred substantially all the risks and rewards of ownership of those assets; hence, full derecognition is appropriate.

Features	Applying derecognition in IAS 39
As above, but the transferor acts as the servicing agent on the portfolio of the assets.	The retention of a servicing right at market price does not preclude derecognition, because substantially all of the risks and rewards of the assets have been transferred and, accordingly, derecognition is appropriate. If the charge for the servicing asset is not at market price, such that the benefits of servicing the assets are not commensurate with the administration charges but do not otherwise involve further retention of exposure to risk, a servicing asset or liability arises and is recognised separately.
A call option is held by the transferor that allows it to call back some of the assets from the portfolio. The transferor has the choice of which balances can be recalled but the total amount of balances that can be recalled is restricted.	Assuming the transferor is economically rational, the transferor will repurchase those assets that will yield the highest return, thereby avoiding assets that are expected to default. This interest in the assets indicates that the transferor has neither transferred nor retained substantially all the risks and rewards of ownership, and hence is required to continue to recognise the assets to the extent of its continuing involvement, i.e. the extent to which the transferred assets are subject to the call option.
The transferor has a call option enabling it to insist on the return of some specific assets from the portfolio; the amount of balances that can be recalled is restricted and the transferor cannot choose the balances to be recalled.	Assuming the call option is not deeply in or out of the money, the transferor has neither retained nor transferred all the risks and rewards of ownership and will continue to recognise the assets to the extent of its continuing involvement, i.e. the extent to which the transferred assets are subject to the call option. If the call option is deeply out of the money (e.g. the assets that can be recalled are in default), derecognition is appropriate.
The transferor services the assets and has a clean-up call to purchase outstanding receivables from the structured entity when the amount of outstanding assets falls to a specified level at which the cost of servicing those assets is too high as compared to benefits of servicing.	Provided that the clean-up call results in the transferor neither retaining nor transferring substantially all the risks and rewards of ownership, the clean-up call precludes derecognition only to the extent of the amount of the assets subject to the call option.

The table below sets out some of the common features of securitisations where the structured entity that purchases the assets *is consolidated* by the transferor and application of derecognition principles to securitisations with each of those features. It is assumed that the structured entity has not transferred the assets to a third party, but instead assumed a contractual obligation to pass the cash flows to external investors. Other than indicated, the pass-through tests (see **section 3.1.4**) are met and the group has not retained substantially all the risks and rewards of ownership.

Features	Applying derecognition in IAS 39
The structured entity has provisions for a revolving investment facility (i.e. securitisation of revolving assets such as credit card receivables) in which for a given time period the structured entity reinvests cash receipts in similar assets. This is common when the receivables have a much shorter life than the securitisation programme.	The pass-through conditions are not met because the reinvestment is in assets other than cash and cash equivalents and the cash flows are not passed on without material delay. Derecognition by the group is precluded.
A rebalancing swap is taken on by the structured entity to ensure that the cash flows due on the notes are met at their predetermined payment dates as the timing of cash flows on the underlying assets is often unpredictable.	Short-term advances to the investors from the group do not violate the pass-through tests as long as the investors still bear the risk of recovery of the assets. Hence, provided that the amounts paid to investors are recovered by the group if the group suffers loss on the assets and any advances are only short term, derecognition is appropriate.
The group is granted rights to cash collected from the portfolio of assets and any remaining cash after the payments due on the securities issued to the investor, e.g. deferred sale consideration, dividend payments or other fees.	This right to collect the excess cash flows is often designed to create a similar payoff profile for the group as if the group had retained a subordinated interest in a non-consolidated structured entity. The extent of subordination as compared to expected credit losses on the assets determines whether the group has retained substantially all the risks and rewards of ownership and thus continues to recognise the assets or whether the group has neither retained nor transferred substantially all of the risks and rewards of ownership and thus continues to recognise the assets only to the extent of its continuing involvement, i.e. to the extent of its subordinated interest.

3.9 Loan transfers

A loan transfer is an agreement under which payments of principal and interest collected under the original loan are passed to a transferee or transferees for an immediate cash payment. There are several ways in which a loan transfer can be enacted. The three most common ways are as follows.

(a) Novation – this is normally where the rights and obligations of the loan are cancelled or amended and renegotiated such that the identity of the lender has been changed. In this case, the borrower is released from its obligation to the transferor and instead has an obligation to the transferee.

(b) Assignment – this is a similar process to novation but the original borrower may or may not be made aware of the change in assignment depending on whether or not the assignment is statutory or equitable respectively. Any cash flows paid to the transferor are passed on to the transferee.

(c) Sub-participation – the borrower still has an obligation to the transferor but at the same time the transferor enters into a non-recourse back-to-back agreement with the transferee to pass on the cash flows collected on the original loan.

Under novation, the transferor's rights to the cash flows cease and hence the transferor has transferred the financial asset. Consideration will need to be given to whether the transferor retains some or all of the risk or rewards of ownership of the transferred asset. In an assignment or sub-participation, when the cash flows paid to the transferee reflect in full the collections from the original loan and there is no recourse to the transferor, it is likely that the pass-through tests in **section 3.1.4** are met and the transferor does not retain the risks and rewards of ownership of the assets i.e. derecognition is appropriate.

The table below sets out common features of loan sub-participations and application of derecognition principles to sub-participations with each of those features. Other than indicated, the pass-through tests are met and there is no recourse to the transferor (i.e. risks and rewards are transferred).

Features	Applying derecognition in IAS 39
The terms of the transfer provide that additional funds that are not part of the terms of the original loan will be made available to the borrower in the event of restructuring of the debt; this facility is not provided to the transferee under the terms of the sub-participation.	In the event of restructuring, the entity will not pass all the restructured cash flows to the transferee, i.e. pass-through tests are not met and derecognition is precluded.

Features	Applying derecognition in IAS 39
A proportionate share of all future cash flows on the original loan is transferred, e.g. 40 per cent.	A fully proportionate share of the cash flows from the original loan (40 per cent) constitutes part of the loan. It is assumed that the pass-through tests applied to that part of the loan are met and the transferor has transferred all the risks and rewards of ownership of that part of the loan. Hence, derecognition of the part of the loan is appropriate.
The transferor continues to administer the original loan for a fee.	The servicing right at market price does not preclude derecognition since substantially all of the risks and rewards of the asset have been transferred. If the charge for the servicing asset is not at market price such that the benefits of servicing the asset are not commensurate with the administration charges, but does not otherwise involve further transfer of exposure to risk, a servicing asset or liability arises and is recognised separately.
The assigned loan or sub-participation is floating rate, while the original loan carries a fixed rate coupon.	The pass-through tests are not met because the transferor may be required to pay amounts that are not collected on the original loan to the transferee and equally not all cash flows collected on the original loan are passed to the transferee. Hence, derecognition is precluded.
Both the original loan and the assigned loan or sub-participation are floating rate instruments but they are priced off different floating rate indices, e.g. 6-month LIBOR and 6-month EURIBOR.	The pass-through tests are not met because the transferor may be required to pay amounts that are not collected on the original loan to the transferee and equally not all cash flows collected on the original loan are passed to the transferee. Hence, derecognition is precluded.
The original loan and the assigned loan or sub-participation are in different currencies.	The pass-through tests are not met because the transferor may be required to pay amounts that are not collected on the original loan to the transferee and equally not all cash flows collected on the original loan are passed to the transferee. Hence, derecognition is precluded.

Features	Applying derecognition in IAS 39
The sub-participation is in the same currency, but concurrently the transferor and transferee enter into a cross-currency swap over the same notional as the original loan which converts the payments made to the transferee into a different currency. If the original loan defaults the swap can be terminated at its fair value at the time; the amounts and timing of the payments on the swap are not adjusted to reflect any changes that may occur in the amounts and timing of the cash flows of the original loan.	The sub-participation qualifies for derecognition because all of the risks and rewards of ownership of the original loan are transferred to the transferee. The cross-currency swap is recognised separately as a derivative at FVTPL and may qualify for hedge accounting in the books of the transferee.

3.9.1 Loan syndication

Loan syndication is an agreement between several lenders to fund jointly a large loan. Each lender will advance a loan of a specific amount to the borrower and has the right to repayment from the borrower. Such a syndication agreement does not involve a loan transfer and should be accounted for as recognition of a financial asset by each of the lenders involved.

In some loan syndications, a lead lender may advance cash to the borrower and transfer the loan to a number of other lenders so that repayments by the borrower are made to the lead lender who then distributes the collections to the other lenders in the syndicate. Such loan syndications are just another form of a loan sub-participation and the lead lender would need to consider whether the pass-through tests are met. In other syndications, the pass-through tests are not relevant because the lead lender transfers the contractual rights to a proportion of the loan to third parties.

3.10 Transfers with total return swaps

A total return swap (TRS) is a derivative that transfers the exposure of a referenced asset between two parties. Typically, one entity would pay amounts equal to increases in the fair value of the referenced asset to the counterparty, and at the same time receive amounts equal to decreases in the fair value of the asset plus a floating rate interest return calculated on a fixed notional amount. This floating funding interest compensates the entity for the theoretical cost of borrowing cash in order to buy the referenced asset or, put another way, is equal to a cost that would have been borne by the entity if the entity had instead chosen to expose itself to the referenced asset by acquiring the referenced asset as opposed to entering into the TRS. These types of instruments are common in transfers of financial assets because they allow the transferor some or all of the participation in the underlying asset. As discussed in **3.1.6**, a transfer of an asset for cash consideration and a TRS would not result in the transferor derecognising the transferred asset as the transferor continues to be exposed to substantially all the risks and rewards of ownership as a result of the TRS. However, TRSs can be used in transfer arrangements in other ways. Below are some illustrations which explain the consideration that would need to be given in assessing whether derecognition is appropriate.

Example 3.10

Transfers of financial assets with a total return swap

(i) Transfer of a financial asset with deferred consideration and a total return swap

Transferor A transfers a debt instrument where the transfer agreement requires Transferee B to pay the transferor a fixed sum in six months' time. The transferor and the transferee also enter into a TRS whereby the transferor receives cash equal to increases in fair value of the asset from the transferee and pays cash equal to decreases in the fair value of the asset plus LIBOR plus a fixed spread every quarter based on a notional equal to the fair value of the debt instrument at the date of transfer. The transferee also pays the transferor any interest that it receives on the transferred asset.

Transferor A must first determine whether the contractual rights to cash flows have been transferred to Transferor B in accordance with IAS 39:18(a). Because Transferee B has all rights to cash flows under the asset, the answer is yes. Transferor A must then consider whether it has transferred substantially all the risks and rewards of ownership to Transferor B. The existence of the TRS results in the transferor continuing to be exposed to the risks and rewards of ownership of the transferred asset, being both fair value risk and the interest earned. The risks and rewards are retained by the transferor and, therefore, derecognition is not appropriate even though the transferor has taken on an additional risk that it did not have prior to the transfer, being the credit risk of the transferee who has yet to pay the transferor cash consideration for the transferred asset.

Because the TRS is an impediment to derecognition, it will not be recognised by the transferor in accordance with IAS 39:AG49. Transferor A will continue to recognise the assets until maturity of the TRS. At that date, the TRS will not be an impediment to derecognition because it will have matured and, therefore, the transferor will not have retained substantially all the risks and rewards of ownership, cash consideration for the asset will be received from the transferee and a gain/loss will be recognised by the transferor on disposal.

(ii) Transfer of a financial asset with deferred delivery of the asset at maturity of a total return swap

Entity C enters into a six month TRS with Entity D over Entity C's debt instrument whereby Entity C will pay Entity D cash equal to increases in fair value of the asset and receive from Entity D cash equal to decreases in the fair value of the asset plus LIBOR plus a fixed spread every quarter based on a notional equal to the fair value of the debt instrument at the date of entering into the arrangement. Entity C will also pay Entity D any interest that it receives on the transferred asset immediately after Entity C receives the interest from the issuer of the debt instrument. If Entity C does not receive interest on the debt instrument it has no obligation to pay Entity D. Equally, Entity C does not provide Entity D with any guarantee to pay further amounts. At maturity of the TRS, Entity C will physically deliver the referenced asset to Entity D for a fixed amount of cash determined upon entering into the arrangement.

Entity C must first determine whether the contractual rights to cash flows have been transferred to Entity D in accordance with IAS 39:18(a). Because the transferor retains all the rights to cash flows under the asset, the answer is no. Entity C must then consider whether the pass-through requirements in IAS 39:18(b) & 19 are met. It is clear that *all* the contractual cash flows under the asset are not passed to Entity D because the only cash flows that are passed to Entity D are interest flows on the asset for six months. Because these interest flows are specifically identified cash flows from a financial asset, i.e. they constitute a portion of the asset, under IAS 39:16(a)(i) and the cash flows are immediately paid by Entity C to Entity D when Entity C receives the cash, then Entity C could apply the pass-through requirements to the portion of the asset that represents the interest flows for six months only. Assuming that both the pass-through and risks and rewards tests lead to the conclusion that the portion of the asset representing the interest flows for six months should be derecognised, Entity C would need to recognise a debtor from Entity D as no upfront consideration is received by Entity C. The debtor recognised would be equal to the fair value of the interest flows for the next six months and may differ in amount to the portion of the asset derecognised in the case where the asset is not measured at fair value, i.e. it is measured at amortised cost, with the difference recognised in profit or loss as a gain/loss on disposal.

The remaining portion of the financial asset is not subject to a transfer and, therefore, will continue to be recognised and measured consistently with the period prior to the transaction occurring. The TRS will be recognised at FVTPL. When the referenced asset is physically delivered to Entity D at maturity of the TRS, Entity C transfers the contractual right to cash flows under the asset and derecognises it. This scenario is illustrated below.

- Entity C's fixed rate debt instrument has an amortised cost of €100, and fair value of €110 at 1 January 20X8. The amortised cost of the remaining interest flows, being the present value discounted at the original effective interest rate, is €3, and the fair value, being the present value discounted at current market rates, is €4.
- Entity C enters into a TRS with Entity D for six months over the fixed rate debt instrument. Entity C will pay Entity D increases in fair value of the debt instrument and Entity D will pay Entity C decreases in fair value as well as a funding rate of 6-month LIBOR + 50 basis points set in advance. At the maturity of the TRS Entity C will transfer the debt instrument to Entity D for €110. LIBOR at 1 January 20X8 was 5.5 per cent.
- At 30 June 20X8 the fair value of the debt instrument is €106.

1 January 20X8

		€	€
Dr	Receivable from Entity D	4	
Cr	Debt instrument measured at amortised cost		3
Cr	Profit or loss		1

To recognise the profit on derecognition of the portion of the debt instrument representing the 6-month interest flows that were subject to the pass-through tests.

No further entries are required at 1 January 20X8 because the contractual rights to the cash flows of the remaining portion of the asset have not been transferred and the pass-through requirements for the remaining portion of the asset do not apply.

30 June 20X8

		€	€
Dr	TRS asset	7	
Cr	Profit or loss		7

To recognise the TRS at FVTPL. For illustrative purposes, the fair value of the TRS is equal to the decrease in fair value of the debt instrument (€4) plus 6-month LIBOR accrued for 6 months (6% x 6/12).

		€	€
Dr	Cash	117	
Cr	TRS asset		7
Cr	Debt instrument		97
Cr	Receivable from Entity D		4
Cr	Profit or loss		9

To recognise the consideration received on transfer of the debt instrument with the corresponding derecognition of the TRS, the debt instrument, and the receivable that was recognised on entering into the pass-through arrangement.

The gain on disposal represents the unrealised gain on the debt instrument immediately prior to entering into the arrangement, being €10, less the gain of €1 recognised on 1 January 20X8 upon entering into the pass-through arrangement.

4 Derecognition of a financial liability

A financial liability is derecognised when, and only when, it is extinguished, i.e. when the obligation in the contract is *discharged, cancelled* or *expired*. [IAS 39:39]

An entity discharges its obligation by paying amounts of cash, other financial assets, or by delivering other goods or services to the counterparty. An obligation may expire due to the passage of time (e.g. an unexercised written option). An obligation is cancelled when, through the process of law, or via negotiation with a creditor, an entity is released from its primary obligation to pay the creditor.

Example 4A

Extinguishment of financial liabilities

Situations may arise where a liability is considered unlikely to result in an outflow of economic resources. The following examples illustrate three scenarios in which a liability might never be extinguished absent a statute of limitation in the applicable jurisdiction:

Unredeemed travellers' cheques

Entity A is in the business of issuing travellers' cheques to customers. Historical statistical analysis indicates that five per cent of travellers' cheques will never be redeemed. Travellers' cheques do not have an expiry date.

Because travellers' cheques do not have an expiry date, the entity is obliged to honour the redemption of travellers' cheques on demand. The financial liability will be measured at the amount Entity A can be required to pay on demand. This obligation may carry on indefinitely into the future unless the jurisdiction allows for legal release from that obligation when a specified period of time has passed.

Goods received but not invoiced

Entity B is a media-buying entity that purchases advertising space in newspapers, television and radio on behalf of its customers, thereby incurring a liability to pay for that advertising space. Historical analysis shows that invoices have never been received by Entity B in respect of five per cent of the advertising space purchased. The jurisdiction of Entity B contains a 'statute of limitations' under which the counterparty is no longer able legally to enforce payment if it does not claim payment from Entity B within a period of six years from the date the goods or services are provided.

Until six years have expired since the transaction, Entity B is legally obligated to pay the counterparty if a claim is made. The financial liability will be measured at the amount the Entity B can be required to pay on demand. At the end of six years, Entity B should derecognise the financial liability.

Dormant bank accounts

Bank C cannot locate all its customers that deposit cash with the bank. The depositor may have moved from his or her home without notifying the bank and there have been no transactions on the account for a considerable period of time (the account is dormant). However, the depositor or its legal representatives, including the depositor's executor of the estate, have the right to claim the deposited amounts indefinitely. Historically, five per cent of dormant accounts held with the bank are never reclaimed.

In the absence of a statute of limitation in Bank C's jurisdiction, Bank C will continue to recognise the financial liability to return the cash to the depositor at the amount repayable on demand. In other jurisdictions, the law may allow the bank, or the bank may be forced, to transfer the deposit to a third party (e.g. a government body), after a specified period of time. The legal release on transfer to the government body is a legal release for the bank if the depositor has no recourse to the bank.

When an entity pays another party to assume its obligation under a contract (sometimes referred to as 'in substance defeasance'), the liability is not extinguished until a legal release from the obligation is obtained. [IAS 39:AG59]

Legal release from an obligation extinguishes the liability but if, concurrently, an entity assumes another obligation to a third party or indeed to the original creditor, the new obligation is recognised. For example, an entity may be released from its primary obligation to the creditor, but assumes a guarantee if the party assuming the primary obligation defaults, in which case it derecognises the original liability and recognises the new liability for the guarantee. [IAS 39:AG60]

When a liability is extinguished, the difference between its carrying amount and the consideration paid including any non-cash assets transferred and any new liabilities assumed is recognised in profit or loss. [IAS 39:41] In the above example, the difference between the carrying amount of the liability and consideration paid to the creditor including the fair value of the guarantee provided to the creditor is recognised in profit or loss. When only part of a liability is extinguished (e.g. repurchased by an entity), the allocation of the previous carrying amount between the amount that continues to be recognised and the part that is derecognised is performed by reference to the relative fair values of those parts on the date of repurchase (see **3.2**).

Example 4B

Expiry of embedded written put option

Entity F issues an instrument that contains a written put option embedded in the instrument that allows the holder to redeem the instrument for par in cash three years after the instrument is issued. The instrument also contains an entitlement to a fixed coupon payable at the discretion of the entity to the extent the instrument remains outstanding. If the put option is not exercised by the holder the instrument will remain outstanding in perpetuity. The instrument contains no other financial liability component other than the written put element. In accordance with IAS 32, at initial recognition the difference between the net proceeds and the fair value of the financial liability in respect of the written put option measured at the present value of the strike price of the written put at Year 3, is recognised in equity.

If the put option is exercised by the holder at the end of Year 3, the whole instrument is extinguished and, therefore, is derecognised. Due to the unwinding of the discount on the financial liability recognised in profit or loss, the carrying amount of the financial liability will equal the exercise price of the put option and, therefore, the put option will be settled with no gain or loss.

If the put option is not exercised by the holder at the end of Year 3, the instrument remains outstanding and the written put option is extinguished because it has not been exercised by the holder and is, therefore, derecognised. The financial liability is derecognised at its closing carrying amount and reclassified to equity. In this instance, the terms of the instrument have not changed but the written put option ceases to be a financial liability and starts to be recognised as equity. No gain or loss is recognised on derecognition of the financial liability in this case because the holder has chosen not to exercise its put right to redeem the instrument but rather chose to retain the instrument and have an entitlement to a fixed coupon payable at the discretion of the issuer which is classified as equity.

4.1 Exchange or modification of a financial liability

Often entities will seek to renegotiate debt instruments for a variety of reasons. Sometimes the entity will be seeking more favourable terms from the lender. Sometimes the borrower may be in financial difficulty and need to alter the contractual terms of the liability such as the maturity of the instrument or the coupon on the instrument.

When the existing borrower and lender exchange instruments with terms that are substantially different, the exchange is accounted for as an extinguishment of the original liability and recognition of a new liability. Similarly, modification of the terms of a liability is accounted for as an extinguishment of the original liability and recognition of a new liability where the modification is substantial. [IAS 39:40]

The terms are deemed to be substantially different if the net present value of the cash flows under the new liability, including any fees paid and received, is at least 10 per cent different from the net present value of the remaining cash flows of the existing liability, both discounted at the original effective interest rate of the original liability. Similarly, modification is deemed to be substantial if the net present value of the cash flows under the modified terms, including any fees paid or received, is at least 10 per cent different from the net present value of the remaining cash flows of the liability prior to the modification, both discounted at the original effective interest rate of the liability prior to the modification. [IAS 39:AG62]

IAS 39:AG62 is clear that *fees paid* are included as part of the cash flows of the new or modified liability when performing the 10 per cent test. However, it is not clear whether this relates only to fees paid to the lender or whether this also includes fees paid to third parties (e.g.

third party legal fees). In the absence of further guidance, inclusion or exclusion of third party fees could be justified.

Excluding third-party fees from the calculation is justified based on a view that the 10 per cent test under IAS 39:AG62 is intended to compare the cash flows between the borrower and the lender before and after the modification or exchange. Some of these cash flows may be referred to as 'fees' but, in substance, they are indistinguishable from the other cash flows of the modified debt instrument. Furthermore, inclusion of directly attributable cash flows in the calculation can be justified by analogy to the definition of transaction costs to be included in the initial carrying value of a financial asset or liability which includes, according to IAS 39:AG13, fees and commissions paid to agents (including employees acting as selling agents), advisers, brokers and dealers, levies by regulatory agencies and securities exchanges, and transfer taxes and duties. Accordingly, third party fees should be considered to form part of the cash flows of the modified debt instrument.

On the other hand, fees paid to another party are distinguishable as payments for services other than lending and therefore it can be justified that such fees should not form part of the cash flows used for the purpose of the 10 per cent test.

An entity should adopt an accounting policy, to be applied consistently, to either include or exclude directly attributable fees payable to a third party other than the lender from calculation of the 10 per cent test.

When performing the 10 per cent test described above, the entity must exclude from the original effective interest rate the effects of hedge accounting (whether fair value hedging or cash flow hedging). For example, if the issuer is fair value hedge accounting, the interest rate risk portion of its issued fixed rate debt, the effective interest rate on this debt will reflect current floating rates at the date of exchange. Because the terms of the original debt are fixed, not floating, the original effective interest determined at initial recognition of the debt prior to any hedge accounting, should be the rate that is used in applying the 10 per cent test.

The above treatment for fair value hedge accounting is consistent with applying the original effective interest rate at initial recognition had the issuer designated the debt as at FVTPL. Designating the debt as at FVTPL for subsequent measurement does not negate the issuer determining the original effective interest rate at the date the instrument was initially recognised for the purposes of applying the 10 per cent test.

Example 4.1A

Debt modification: change in interest and term

Entity A borrowed CU1 million on 1 January 20X0, at a fixed rate of 9 per cent per annum for 10 years. Entity A incurred issue costs of CU50,000. Interest on the loan is payable annually in arrears. The original effective interest rate (EIR) is 9.807 per cent. During 20X5, Entity A approached the lender for a modification of the terms of the debt (this modification could have been as a result of a deteriorating financial condition of the borrower or because of a fall in interest rates). The following modified terms were agreed with effect from 1 January 20X6:

- interest rate to be reduced to 7.5 per cent payable yearly in arrears; and
- the original amount, payable on maturity, to remain unchanged but the maturity of the loan to be extended by two years to 31 December 20Y1.

No fees are payable for renegotiating the finance.

	Opening CU	Interest CU	Payments CU	Closing CU
		EIR of 9.807%	(950,000)	
31 Dec 20X0	950,000	93,166	90,000	953,166
31 Dec 20X1	953,166	93,477	90,000	956,643
31 Dec 20X2	956,643	93,818	90,000	960,461
31 Dec 20X3	960,461	94,192	90,000	964,653
31 Dec 20X4	964,653	94,604	90,000	969,257
31 Dec 20X5	969,257	95,055	90,000	**974,312**
31 Dec 20X6	974,312	95,551	90,000	979,863
31 Dec 20X7	979,863	96,095	90,000	985,958
31 Dec 20X8	985,958	96,693	90,000	992,651
31 Dec 20X9	992,651	97,349	1,090,000	0

The present value of the modified debt at the original effective interest rate is calculated as follows.

	Payments CU
31 Dec 20X6	75,000
31 Dec 20X7	75,000
31 Dec 20X8	75,000
31 Dec 20X9	75,000
31 Dec 20Y0	75,000
31 Dec 20Y1	1,075,000
Present value at 1 January 20X6 discounting at original EIR of 9.807%	898,954

The entity must determine whether the modification is considered to be an extinguishment of the original debt. [IAS 39:AG62] Because the difference between the amortised cost of the debt instrument at the date of modification and the present value of the new debt instrument, discounted by the original effective interest rate, is less than 10 per cent, the modification is not considered an extinguishment of the original debt. The difference (CU75,358) will be recognised in profit or loss in future periods through the revised effective interest rate.

For the avoidance of doubt, at the date of modification only, the issuer should not apply IAS 39:AG8, because this will result in an immediate gain/loss in profit or loss on modification which is contrary to the issuer not achieving derecognition. The issuer will apply IAS 39:AG8 following the date of modification if the estimates of future cash flows change. The revised cash flows must be discounted at the revised effective interest rate that was determined at the date of modification.

A modification of debt terms may include changes to any one or a combination of the following:

- stated interest rate for the remaining original life of the debt;
- maturity date or dates;
- face amount of the debt;
- accrued interest;
- recourse or non-recourse features;
- priority of the obligation;
- collateral (requirement for or changes in the type of the collateral);
- covenants and/or waivers;
- currency denomination;
- the guarantor (or elimination of the guarantor); or
- option features.

Example 4.1B

Debt modification: change in notional, interest, term

Entity P borrowed CU100 million on 1 January 20X0 at a fixed interest rate of 10 per cent per annum for 10 years. Entity P incurred no issue costs. Interest on the loan is payable annually in arrears. The original effective interest rate is 10 per cent. At the end 20X4, Entity P is offered a number of alternatives to refinance its issued debt with effect from 1 January 20X0. The current market interest rate including a credit premium for Entity P's credit risk (which has remained unchanged) is 5 per cent for the remaining time to maturity of its existing debt, i.e. half the contractual cash flows on the original debt issued at the start of 20X0.

All proposed new borrowings are with the same counterparty and are used to buy back existing debt with the issue and buy back being in contemplation of one another. Assume for illustrative purposes only, the yield curve is flat at 1 January 20X5.

The fair value of the outstanding debt at 31 December 20X4 is determined as follows.

Period	**Cash flows 10% x CU100m**	**Discount factor at 5%**	**Present value CUm**
20X5	10	0.952	9.52
20X6	10	0.907	9.07
20X7	10	0.864	8.64
20X8	10	0.823	8.23
20X9	110	0.784	86.19
		Fair value	121.65

Scenario 1 – new borrowing at current market interest rate of 5 per cent with notional amount equal to the amount needed to buy back the outstanding debt at market price

Entity P determines the present value of remaining cash flows on its existing debt at the original effective interest rate and compares this with the cash flows on the new debt also discounted at the same original effective interest rate.

The new debt has a notional amount of CU121.65 million and an interest rate of 5 per cent and matures in 20X9.

Period	**Cash flows Existing debt CUm**	**Cash flows New debt 5% x CU121.65m**	**Discount factor at 10%**	**Present value Existing debt CUm**	**Present value New debt CUm**
20X5	10	6.08	0.909	9.09	5.53
20X6	10	6.08	0.826	8.26	5.03
20X7	10	6.08	0.751	7.51	4.57
20X8	10	6.08	0.683	6.83	4.15
20X9	110	127.73	0.621	68.31	79.31
				100.00	98.59

The difference between the present value of the existing and new debt discounted at the original effective interest rate is CU1.41 million (1.41%). Because the difference is within the '10% test' the existing debt will not be derecognised.

Scenario 2 – same as Scenario 1 but term of new debt is extended by one year (assuming yield curve is flat)

The new debt has a notional amount of CU121.65 million and an interest rate of 5 per cent and matures in 20Y0.

Period	Cash flows New debt 5% x CU121.65m	Discount factor at 10%	Present value New debt CUm
20X5	6.08	0.909	5.53
20X6	6.08	0.826	5.03
20X7	6.08	0.751	4.57
20X8	6.08	0.683	4.15
20X9	6.08	0.621	3.78
20Y0	127.73	0.564	72.10
			95.16

The difference between the present value of the existing and new debt discounted at the original effective interest rate is CU4.84 million (4.84%). Because the difference is within the '10% test', the existing debt will not be derecognised.

The difference in the present value calculations of the new debt in scenario 1 and new debt in scenario 2 arises because scenario 2 has an additional interest flow at current market rates and deferral of the principal by a year.

Scenario 3 – same as Scenario 2 but the yield curve is not flat in 20Y0

The yield curve remains flat until 20X9 as in scenario 2 but then falls in 20Y0 and beyond. The 6-year yield curve at 1/1/X5 (i.e. until 20Y0) is 4.85 per cent compared to 5 per cent in scenario 2.

Period	Cash flows New debt 4.85% x CU121.65m	Discount factor at 10%	Present value New debt CUm
20X5	5.90	0.909	5.37
20X6	5.90	0.826	4.88
20X7	5.90	0.751	4.43
20X8	5.90	0.683	4.03
20X9	5.90	0.621	3.67
20Y0	127.55	0.564	71.99
			94.37

The difference between the present value of the existing and new debt discounted at the original effective interest rate is CU5.63 million (5.63%). Because the difference is within the '10% test', the existing debt will not be derecognised.

The difference in the present value calculations of the new debt in scenario 2 and the new debt in scenario 3 has increased because, even though both scenarios 2 and 3 have the same maturity and notional amount, the effective interest rate on the new debt differs. Because the additional contractual interest flows on the new debt extending beyond the term of the existing debt are locking in a lower interest rate environment, this exaggerates the difference in present value calculations between the existing and new debt. If the term was to extend further, and/or interest rates were even lower, then the present value of the new debt may be greater than 10 per cent of the existing debt which would result in derecognition of the existing debt and recognition of the new debt at fair value in accordance with IAS 39:43.

It is possible in a scenario of higher interest rates that when the term of the debt is extended beyond the term of the existing date that the '10% test' is breached and derecognition of the existing debt is required.

Example 4.1C

Debt modification: change in basis of interest

Entity C issued 5 year debt at a fixed rate of interest of 7 per cent on 1/1/X3 at par for €100 million. The debt is measured at amortised cost. On 1/1/X5, the debt is exchanged with the original lender for a new debt instrument that has floating rate, LIBOR, for the remaining three year term that is set annually in advance. The current LIBOR rate is 4 per cent and the yield curve is flat for the next three years. Because interest rates have fallen from 7 per cent to 4 per cent, and credit spreads have remained unchanged, the fair value of the debt has risen above par. In order to put the current debt holders in the same economic position following the debt exchange, the issuer agrees to increase the notional amount of the new debt to €108.70 million.

Entity C applies the 10 per cent per cent test to the debt exchange. Entity C sums the cash flows on the new debt discounted by the original effective interest rate of 7 per cent:

- €4.3 million for three years (4% x €108.70 million, as the LIBOR curve is flat at the date of exchange); and
- the principal of €108.70 million payable at the end of year 3.

The net present value of the new debt discounted using the original effective interest rate is €100 million.

Entity C then sums the remaining cash flows on the old debt of €7 million for three years and a principal of €100 million discounted by the original effective interest rate of 7 per cent, which is also €100 million.

The net present value of the old debt and modified debt discounted by the original effective interest rate are the same, i.e. €100 million. Entity C therefore does not derecognise the old debt.

For the remaining three years, Entity C applies a modified effective interest rate that consists of current LIBOR for the period plus the amortisation from €100 million to €108.70 million based on a constant yield. The internal rate of return for the amortisation is 2.82 per cent per year and represents the current discount to par on the modified debt. This is the same accounting as for a discounted floating rate bond. The amortisation for the remaining three years is as follows.

Period ending 31/12/X5: 2.82% x €100 million = €2.82 million
Period ending 31/12/X6: 2.82% x €102.82 million = €2.90 million
Period ending 31/12/X7: 2.82% x €105.72 million = €2.98 million

At 31/12/X5, Entity C accrues both LIBOR for the period plus the amortisation less the LIBOR interest paid in the period. Because LIBOR is set in advance, the interest payment is €4.3 million, being 4 per cent on the modified notional of the debt of €108.70 million. The period end carrying amount is therefore €102.82 million (being €100 million + €4.3 million + €2.82 million - €4.3 million).

For illustrative purposes, the forecast LIBOR interest rate is assumed to equal to the spot LIBOR rate at the date of modification.

The period end carrying amounts for 31/12/X6 and 31/12/X7 are as follows.

	€ million
1/1/X6	102.82
LIBOR	4.30
Amortisation of discount	2.90
Less cash paid	(4.30)
31/12/X6	105.72
LIBOR	4.30
Amortisation of discount	2.98
Less cash paid	(4.30)
31/12/X7	108.70

At 31/12/X7, Entity C settles the modified debt instrument for €108.70 million, being its par amount.

IAS 39 is not clear whether an entity should forecast future floating interest rates or use the floating spot rate at the date of renegotiation when determining the amount of cash flows to include in the 10% test when either or both of the original or modified financial liability have floating interest rates. In the absence of specific guidance, it is reasonable for an entity to choose one of the two approaches as an accounting policy that should be applied consistently to all financial liability derecognition assessments.

In most instances 'substantially different' will be determined by using the 10 per cent test. However, in limited circumstances, a simple qualitative assessment will be sufficient to establish that the terms of the modified liability are substantially different from those of the original one. One example of modification where a qualitative assessment is relevant is when the denomination of the original liability is changed to a different currency such that the entity is left in a different economic position due to the new currency exposure taken on.

The guidance on renegotiations and exchanges of debt instruments in IFRSs is broadly based on the equivalent guidance in US GAAP. However, US GAAP has a greater amount of guidance in certain areas.

The following guidance included in ASC 470-50 may be relevant in applying the '10 per cent' test under IFRSs:

- the cash flows have to include all cash flows specified by the terms of the new debt instrument (plus any amounts paid by the debtor to the creditor and less any amounts received by the debtor from the creditor as part of the exchange or modification);
- if either the old or the new debt instrument or both have a variable interest rate, an entity has to use the rate effective as at the date of exchange or modification to calculate the cash flows;
- if either the old or the new debt instrument has a call or a put option then separate cash flow analyses for exercise and non-exercise has to be performed and the scenario that generates the smaller change would be used to decide whether the 10 per cent hurdle is breached;
- judgement is to be used when determining the cash flows if the instrument contains contingent payment terms or unusual interest rate terms;
- if the exchanged or modified debt instrument is exchanged or modified again within one year, the terms of the original debt should be used as starting point to perform the '10 per cent' test;
- in the case of an intermediary acting as an agent for the debtor, the assessment of the transaction should "look through" that intermediary; and
- if the intermediary is identified as acting as a principal it is treated like any other creditor.

When an investment bank is used to facilitate a debt exchange, it is important to establish all the terms of the arrangement in order to establish whether the investment bank is acting as agent or principal to the transaction. An investment bank can undertake a number of roles in debt exchanges. For example, if an entity wishes to exchange its issued debt it may request an investment bank to seek out the holders of the debt in order for those holders to be offered the new debt instrument. If the investment bank is remunerated by way of a predetermined fee for this service, it is likely the bank is acting as an agent to enable the issuer to exchange its existing debt instruments.

If the existing debt holders acquire the new debt in exchange for returning the old debt to the issuer, and the investment bank simply facilitates this exchange as an agent of the issuer, then this is considered a debt exchange between the issuer and existing debt holders and, therefore, the 10 per cent test would need to be applied by the issuer. On the other hand, if debt is transferred from one debt holder to another, the issuer's accounting is not affected as long as funds do not pass through the issuer or its agent.

In some instances, the investment bank buys the existing debt from the debt holders by using its own funds and bears market risk of the debt and, therefore, is considered principal to the original debt. If the investment bank subsequently exchanges or modifies the debt with the issuer, the investment bank is considered the original debt holder and the issuer must determine whether the debt exchange between the investment bank and the issuer breaches the 10 per cent test. The investment bank would not be acting as principal (i.e. it would be acting as an agent) if it merely places the new notes in the market and only buys the new debt that it has contractually agreed to sell to others.

If an exchange of debt instruments or modification of terms is accounted for as an extinguishment, any costs or fees incurred are recognised as part of the gain or loss on the extinguishment. When the terms of the new/modified instrument are not substantially different, then any fees or costs paid in the exchange/modification are treated as an adjustment to the carrying amount of the original liability and are amortised over the remaining life of the new/modified liability. [IAS 39:AG62]

There may be very limited circumstances when fees associated with the issue of new debt can be recognised as a reduction in the carrying amount of the new debt at its initial recognition following a substantial modification of a pre-existing debt. When the fees do not relate to the exchange or modification, but rather are an incremental cost of issuing the new debt that is payable to a party other than the lender (e.g. stamp duty or a listing fee for listing the new debt), it can be argued that these costs are a transaction cost of the new debt and, therefore, are appropriately deducted from the carrying amount of the new debt if the new debt is subsequently measured at amortised cost. Examples of this are likely to be limited as many costs incurred relate to the overall exchange or modification and, therefore, cannot be isolated and identified as being specifically related only to the issue of the new debt.

4.2 Exchange of a financial liability for equity

In November 2009, the IFRIC (now the IFRS Interpretations Committee) issued IFRIC 19 *Extinguishing Financial Liabilities with Equity Instruments*. The Interpretation addresses the accounting for entities that issue equity instruments in order to extinguish all or part of a financial liability (often referred to as 'debt for equity swaps'). Debt for equity swaps are more common when the borrower is in financial difficulty and agrees with its lender to forgive amounts due to the lender in return for the lender receiving equity in the borrower.

IFRIC 19 has a limited scope as it only deals with the accounting by the entity that issues equity instruments in order to extinguish, in full or in part, a financial liability. It does not address the accounting by the lender. In addition, the Interpretation is not to be applied in situations where:

[IFRIC 19:3]

(a) the lender is also a direct or indirect shareholder and is acting in its capacity as a direct or indirect shareholder;

(b) the lender and the entity are controlled by the same party or parties before and after the transaction and the substance of the transaction includes an equity distribution from, or contribution to, the entity; or

(c) extinguishing the financial liability by issuing equity shares is in accordance with the original terms of the financial liability.

The IFRIC concluded that the issue of equity instruments to extinguish all or part of a financial liability constitutes 'consideration paid' in accordance with IAS 39:41. The IFRIC observed that the issue of equity instruments to extinguish financial liabilities can be seen as consisting of two transactions: (i) the issue of equity instruments for cash, and (ii) acceptance by the creditor of that amount of cash to extinguish the financial liability. In effect, whether a financial liability is exchanged for equity or equity is issued for cash and the cash is used to extinguish the financial liability, the accounting treatment should be the same.

The IFRIC also concluded that an entity should measure the equity instruments issued as extinguishment of the financial liability at their fair value on the date of extinguishment of the liability, unless that fair value is not reliably measurable. In such circumstances, the equity instruments should be measured to reflect the fair value of the liability extinguished. Therefore, it is not acceptable to simply reclassify the carrying amount of the financial liability to equity (unless the fair value of the equity instruments issued happens to equal the carrying amount of the financial liability at the date of extinguishment).

If only part of a financial liability is extinguished through the issue of equity instruments, the Interpretation states that the entity should assess whether some of the consideration paid represents a modification of the portion of the liability which remains outstanding. If it is determined that part of the consideration paid relates to a modification of the outstanding liability, the entity should apportion the consideration between the portion that has been extinguished and that which remains outstanding. Any difference between the carrying amount of the liability (or the part of the liability) extinguished and the fair value of equity instruments issued is recognised in profit or loss. When consideration is partly allocated to the portion of a liability which remains outstanding, the part allocated to this portion forms part of the assessment as to whether there has been an extinguishment or a modification of that portion of the liability. If the remaining liability has been substantially modified, the entity should account for the modification as the extinguishment of the original liability and the recognition of a new liability as required by IAS 39:40.

Example 4.2A

Liability for equity swap (1)

Entity B issues equity instruments with a fair value of CU90 million to Lender X as extinguishment of the whole of its financial liability to Lender X.

The amortised cost carrying amount of the financial liability on the date of extinguishment is CU100 million.

The following entries would be recorded.

Dr	Financial liability	CU100 million
Cr	Profit or loss	CU10 million
Cr	Equity	CU90 million

To record derecognition of the financial liability, recognition of the equity instruments issued at fair value at the date of issue and recognition of the difference in profit or loss.

Example 4.2B

Liability for equity swap (2)

Entity C issues equity instruments with a fair value of CU35 million to Lender Y as extinguishment of a portion of financial liability to Lender Y. The total financial liability has an amortised cost carrying amount of CU100 million. The portion extinguished has a carrying amount of CU40 million. The issue of equity instruments does not modify in any way the terms of the obligation relating to the portion of the liability which remains outstanding, whose carrying amount is CU60 million (i.e. CU100 million-CU40 million).

The following entries would be recorded.

Dr	Financial liability	CU40 million
Cr	Profit or loss	CU5 million
Cr	Equity	CU35 million

To record derecognition of the portion of the financial liability that is extinguished, recognition of the equity instruments issued at fair value at the date of extinguishment of that portion and recognition of the difference in profit or loss. There is no modification to the remaining portion of the liability of CU60 million; therefore, this portion of the liability is not adjusted or derecognised.

Example 4.2C

Liability for equity swap (3)

Entity C issues equity instruments with a fair value of CU36 million to Lender Z as extinguishment of a portion of its financial liability to Lender Z. The total financial liability has an amortised cost carrying amount of CU100 million. The portion extinguished has a carrying amount of CU40 million. The remaining portion of the financial liability with a carrying amount of CU60 million (i.e. CU100 million - CU40 million) remains outstanding; however, Lender Z agrees to change the contractual cash flows of this portion of the liability.

Entity C determines that, of the issue of equity instruments of fair value CU36 million, CU34 million relates to the extinguishment of the portion of the liability extinguished and the remaining CU2 million is in substance a fee for the change in terms of the portion of the liability which remains outstanding. The entity assesses the new terms of the remaining financial liability, applies the 10% test, and determines that they are not substantially different from the previous terms. Therefore, the entity adjusts the effective interest rate of the portion of the liability which remains outstanding to the rate which discounts the revised future contractual cash flows to the new carrying amount of the financial liability. The fee incurred by the entity (i.e. the portion of equity instruments issued with fair value of CU2 million) adjusts the carrying amount of the liability, and is amortised over the remaining term of the modified liability in accordance with IAS 39:AG62.

The following entries would be recorded.

Dr	Financial liability	CU40 million
Cr	Profit or loss	CU6 million
Cr	Equity	CU34 million

To record derecognition of the portion of the financial liability that is extinguished, recognition of the equity instruments issued at fair value as at the date of extinguishment and recognition of the difference in profit or loss.

Dr	Financial liability	CU2 million
Cr	Equity	CU2 million

To record the adjustment of the carrying amount of the remaining financial liability on modification in accordance with IAS 39:AG62, and recognition of the equity instruments issued at fair value at the date of modification. The effective interest rate of this remaining portion of the liability is recalculated to give the rate that discounts the revised future contractual cash flows to the new carrying amount of this portion of the liability.

When consideration is paid to extinguish a financial liability, and there is a concurrent modification of the remaining contractual cash flows of the financial liability, the consideration paid, in whatever form, is treated as a 'cash flow' that is attributed to the new financial liability when applying the '10% test'. For example, the consideration paid could be in the form of equity instruments issued (see **example 4.2D**). If consideration is instead *payable* in the future these amounts would be included in the 10% test as future cash flows in the relevant period and discounted using the original effective interest rate.

Example 4.2D

Liability for equity swap (4)

Entity D borrowed CU100 million, equal to its par, at an interest rate of 5 per cent from Lender T some years ago. The borrowing matures in 20X5, in 5 years' time. The borrowing is measured at amortised cost. Entity D restructures its borrowing with Lender T by issuing equity instruments as extinguishment for part of the amount due to Lender T and modifying the contractual cash flows on the remaining amounts due.

The equity instruments issued have a fair value of CU50 million at the date of issue. The remaining contractual borrowings are modified so the par is reduced to CU38 million, the interest rate is changed to 8 per cent and the maturity of the borrowing is extended a further year to 20X6. The fair value of the borrowing in its entirety immediately prior to the modification was CU88 million.

Entity D applies the 10% test to determine whether the modified contractual cash flows on the borrowing are substantially different from the contractual cash flows of the original financial liability.

The present value of the remaining contractual cash flows of the original financial liability discounted at the original effective interest rate (EIR) is as follows.

Period	**Cash flows original debt 5.00% x CU100m**	**Discount factor at original EIR of 5%**	**Present value original debt CUm**
20X1	5.00	0.952	4.76
20X2	5.00	0.907	4.54
20X3	5.00	0.864	4.32
20X4	5.00	0.823	4.11
20X5	105.00	0.784	82.27
			100.00

The present value of the new financial liability discounted at the original effective interest rate is as follows.

Period	Cash flows new debt 8.00% x CU38m	Discount factor at original EIR of 5%	Present value new debt CUm
20X0	50.0 (equity instruments issued)	1.000	50.00
20X1	3.04	0.952	2.90
20X2	3.04	0.907	2.76
20X3	3.04	0.864	2.63
20X4	3.04	0.823	2.50
20X5	3.04	0.784	2.38
20X6	41.04	0.746	30.64
			93.81

The difference between the present value of the original and new financial liability discounted at the original effective interest rate is CU6.19 million (CU100 million – CU93.81 million), being 6.19 per cent of the discounted present value of the remaining cash flows of the original liability. Because the difference is within the '10% range', the modified financial liability will not be initially recognised at fair value; instead, the original financial liability will:

(i) be partly derecognised due to the issue of equity instruments; and

(ii) partly continuously recognised with a new effective interest rate used for recognising interest in future periods.

Of the total principal of CU100 million that was originally outstanding at the date of modification, CU62 million has been extinguished. In addition, all future interest payments on that proportion of principal have been extinguished. The fair value of the proportion of the old debt that has been extinguished is CU54.56 million (CU62 million / CU100 million * CU88 million). A gain of CU7.44 million is recognised in profit or loss as the carrying amount of the old debt derecognised (CU62 million) was greater than its fair value (CU54.56 million).

The difference between the fair value of original debt extinguished (CU54.56 million) and the fair value of the total equity instruments issued (CU50 million) represents a fee for modifying the terms of the remaining financial liability which is paid via the revised interest payments and is added to the carrying amount of the liability at the date of modification.

Dr	Financial liability – derecognition of a proportion of the original liability	CU62.00 million
Cr	Financial liability – fee for modification of terms of original liability	CU4.56 million
Cr	Profit or loss	CU7.44 million
Cr	Equity	CU50.00 million

To record the derecognition of the portion of the financial liability that is extinguished, recognition of the fee for modifying the terms of the remainder of the original liability, recognition of the equity instruments issued at fair value as at the date of extinguishment and recognition of the difference in profit or loss.

The effective interest rate on the financial liability that continues to be recognised is revised to reflect the new contractual cash flows as a result of the modification. The modified effective interest rate that discounts all the remaining expected contractual cash flows to the portion of the carrying amount that continues to be recognised (being CU42.56 million at the date of modification) is 5.59 per cent.

	Opening carrying amount	**Effective interest rate at 5.59%**	**Interest and capital paid**	**Closing carrying amount**
	CU million	**CU million**	**CU million**	**CU million**
20X1	42.56	2.38	(3.04)	41.90
20X2	41.90	2.34	(3.04)	41.20
20X3	41.20	2.30	(3.04)	40.46
20X4	40.46	2.26	(3.04)	39.68
20X5	39.68	2.22	(3.04)	38.86
20X6	38.86	2.18	(41.04)	–

If the lender is a direct or an indirect shareholder and is acting in its capacity as a direct or an indirect shareholder, or the lender and the borrower are controlled by the same party or parties before and after the transaction and the substance of the transaction includes an equity distribution from, or contribution to, the borrower, the transaction is not in the scope of IFRIC 19.

If a transaction is outside the scope of IFRIC 19 for the reasons noted above, judgement will be required in determining the appropriate accounting treatment. In such circumstances, it is possible that the fair value of consideration paid (if any) may differ significantly from the fair value of the financial liability that has been extinguished.

Provided that the effects of any significant capital contribution or bonus element are excluded from profit or loss, it will often be acceptable for the borrower to choose one of the following approaches when derecognising the liability.

- **Approach 1:** following the principles underlying IFRIC 19, the borrower may choose to recognise in profit or loss any difference between the carrying amount of the liability derecognised and its fair value at the date of derecognition (as illustrated in **examples 4.2E and 4.2F**). In effect, this is akin to measuring the increase in equity (for shares issued, if any, as adjusted for any capital contribution or bonus element) by reference to the fair value of the financial liability that has been extinguished.

- **Approach 2:** alternatively, the borrower may choose to recognise no gain or loss on derecognition of the liability. In effect, this is akin to measuring the increase in equity (for shares issued, if any, as adjusted for any capital contribution or bonus element) by reference to the carrying amount of the financial liability that has been extinguished, rather than its fair value.

If the fair value of shares issued is significantly less than the fair value of the liability extinguished, the difference between the two should not be recognised as a gain in profit or loss, because it is instead a capital contribution from owners. Similarly, if a liability is extinguished for no consideration, the fair value of the liability extinguished should not be recognised as a gain in profit or loss, because it is instead a capital contribution from owners.

By the same logic, if the fair value of the shares issued is significantly greater than the fair value of the liability extinguished, the difference between the two should not be recognised as a loss; the difference is instead akin to a bonus issue of shares, as illustrated in **example 4.2F**, in that it represents a distribution of additional shares to a parent for no (incremental) consideration.

In some cases, the carrying amount and the fair value of the financial liability may be similar. For example, where a financial liability is repayable on demand by the lender, IAS 39:49 indicates that its fair value is not less than the amount that is repayable on demand. In other cases, the carrying value and the fair value of the financial liability may be different, e.g. where the financial liability is not repayable on demand and the subsidiary is in financial difficulty.

Example 4.2E

Parent waives debt from subsidiary for no consideration

Scenario 1

Subsidiary T is a wholly-owned subsidiary of Parent Y. Parent Y waives a financial liability owed to it by Subsidiary T for no consideration. The carrying amount of the financial liability measured at amortised cost is £100 million. At the date of exchange the fair value of the financial liability is also £100 million.

The difference of £100 million between the fair value of the financial liability (£100 million) and the consideration paid (£nil) should not be reported in profit or loss, because it is instead a capital contribution from owners.

The following entries will be recorded by Subsidiary T.

Dr Financial liability	£100 million	
Cr Equity		£100 million

Being the derecognition of the financial liability and recognition of the capital contribution from the borrower's parent.

Scenario 2

Subsidiary T is a wholly-owned subsidiary of Parent Y. Parent Y waives a financial liability owed to it by Subsidiary T for no consideration. The carrying amount of the financial liability measured at amortised cost is £100 million. At the date of exchange the fair value of the financial liability is £90 million.

An amount should be credited to equity, to reflect the capital contribution that has been made by Parent Y. Subsidiary T should choose an appropriate accounting approach when measuring the amount to be credited to equity.

If Subsidiary T chooses to follow Approach 1, measuring the capital contribution by reference to the fair value of the financial liability that has been extinguished, the following entries will be recorded.

Dr Financial liability	£100 million	
Cr Profit or loss (£100 million - £90 million)		£10 million
Cr Equity		£90 million

Being the derecognition of the financial liability, recognition of the capital contribution from the borrower's parent and recognition of the difference in profit or loss.

If Subsidiary T chooses to follow Approach 2, measuring the capital contribution by reference to the carrying amount of the financial liability that has been extinguished, the following entries will be recorded.

Dr Financial liability	£100 million	
Cr Equity		£100 million

Being the derecognition of the financial liability and recognition of the capital contribution from the borrower's parent.

Example 4.2F

Liability for equity swap (5)

Scenario 1

Subsidiary T is a wholly-owned subsidiary of Parent Y. Subsidiary T issues equity instruments to its lender, Parent Y, as part of extinguishing all of its financial liability owed to Parent Y. The carrying amount of the financial liability measured at amortised cost is £100 million. At the date of exchange the fair value of the financial liability is also £100 million. The equity instruments issued to Parent Y have a fair value of £110 million.

The excess of £10 million of the consideration paid (£110 million) over the fair value and carrying amount of the financial liability (£100 million) should not be reported in profit or loss, because it is instead akin to a bonus issue to owners. Therefore, the overall amount credited to equity should be £100 million.

The following entries will be recorded by Subsidiary T.

Dr	Financial liability	£100 million	
Cr	Equity		£100 million

Being the derecognition of the financial liability and recognition of the equity instruments issued.

Scenario 2

Subsidiary T is a wholly-owned subsidiary of Parent Y. Subsidiary T issues equity instruments to its lender, Parent Y, as part of extinguishing all of its financial liability owed to Parent Y. The carrying amount of the financial liability measured at amortised cost is £100 million. At the date of exchange the fair value of the financial liability is £80 million. The equity instruments issued to Parent Y have a fair value of £90 million.

An amount should be credited to equity, to reflect the equity instruments that have been issued to Parent Y (adjusted for any capital contribution or bonus element). Subsidiary T should choose an appropriate accounting approach when measuring the amount to be credited to equity.

If Subsidiary T chooses to follow Approach 1, measuring the increase in equity by reference to the fair value of the financial liability that has been extinguished, the following entries will be recorded.

Dr	Financial liability	£100 million	
Cr	Profit or loss (£100 million - £80 million)		£20 million
Cr	Equity		£80 million

Being the derecognition of the financial liability, recognition of the equity instruments issued to the borrower's parent and recognition of the difference in profit or loss.

If Subsidiary T chooses to follow Approach 2, measuring the increase in equity by reference to the carrying amount of the financial liability that has been extinguished, the following entries will be recorded.

Dr	Financial liability	£100 million	
Cr	Equity		£100 million

Being the derecognition of the financial liability and recognition of the equity instruments issued.

Scenario 3

Subsidiary T is a wholly-owned subsidiary of Parent Y. Subsidiary T issues equity instruments to its lender, Parent Y, as part of extinguishing all of its financial liability owed to Parent Y. The carrying amount of the financial liability measured at amortised cost is £100 million. At the date of exchange the fair value of the financial liability is £80 million. The equity instruments issued to Parent Y have a fair value of £70 million.

An amount should be credited to equity, to reflect the equity instruments that have been issued to Parent Y (adjusted for any capital contribution or bonus element). Subsidiary T should choose an appropriate accounting approach when measuring the amount to be credited to equity.

If Subsidiary T chooses to follow Approach 1, measuring the increase in equity by reference to the fair value of the financial liability that has been extinguished, the following entries will be recorded.

Dr	Financial liability	£100 million	
Cr	Profit or loss (£100 million - £80 million)		£20 million
Cr	Equity		£80 million

Being the derecognition of the financial liability, recognition of the equity instruments issued to the borrower's parent and recognition of the difference in profit or loss.

If Subsidiary T chooses to follow Approach 2, measuring the increase in equity by reference to the carrying amount of the financial liability that has been extinguished, the following entries will be recorded.

Dr	Financial liability	£100 million	
Cr	Equity		£100 million

Being the derecognition of the financial liability and recognition of the equity instruments issued.

5 Future developments

In response to the global financial crisis and the recommendations made by the Financial Stability Forum, in March 2009, the IASB issued an exposure draft of proposed amendments to IAS 39 and IFRS 7, ED/2009/3 *Derecognition*. The exposure draft proposed derecognition of an asset when:

- the contractual rights to the cash flows expire;
- there is a transfer and the transferor has no continuing involvement in the asset; or

- there is a transfer and there is retention of continuing involvement, but the transferee has the practical ability to transfer the asset for its own benefit.

The exposure draft contained an 'alternative approach' proposed by a significant minority of Board members. Like the model described above, it is based on control. However, the model would require that if a transferor does not have access to *all* the cash flows the transferor recognised prior to the transfer, then the asset is derecognised and a new asset is recognised for any interest in part of the asset transferred.

After considering constituents' comments, the IASB tentatively decided in October 2009 to pursue the alternative approach described in the exposure draft. However, in June 2010, the IASB announced its intention to proceed with a more limited project to issue new disclosure requirements in connection with derecognition which were issued in October 2010 as an amendment to IFRS 7 (see **4.1.5** in **chapter C12**). These amendments are intended to improve the disclosure requirements in relation to transferred financial assets and converge with the requirements in US GAAP.

Following the finalisation of the amended derecognition disclosures the IASB and FASB have agreed not to develop an alternative derecognition model.

C9 Hedge accounting – basics

Contents

1 Introduction

Entities enter into many transactions that aim to reduce risk, and ultimately to reduce the variability in cash flows or earnings that arise from those risks. Entities enter into hedging transactions to hedge risks that are evident in items already recognised in the statement of financial position, as well as to hedge risks for future transactions that have yet to occur.

Hedge accounting is a method of presentation in financial statements that may be voluntarily applied to hedging transactions. The objective of hedge accounting is to ensure that any gain or loss arising on a hedging instrument is recognised in profit or loss in the same period as the item that is being hedged affects profit or loss. In other words, applying hedge accounting results in the 'matched' timing of recognition of gains and losses in profit or loss. When an entity is perfectly hedged, gains and losses arising on a hedging instrument and the hedged item perfectly offset in profit or loss in the same period.

IAS 39 allows an entity to apply hedge accounting if an entity specifically designates the hedging instrument and the hedged item at inception of the hedge accounting relationship. Generally, there are two ways in which hedge accounting achieves the matching of gains and losses arising on a hedging instrument and the hedged item:

- changes in the fair value of the hedging instrument are recognised in profit or loss at the same time that a recognised asset or liability that is being hedged is adjusted for movements in the hedged risk, with that adjustment also recognised in profit or loss in the same period. This is referred to as 'fair value' hedge accounting because it is the exposure to changes in the fair value of the hedged item due to the designated risk that is being hedged; or
- changes in the fair value of the hedging instrument are recognised initially in other comprehensive income and reclassified from equity to profit or loss when the hedged item affects profit or loss. This is known as 'cash flow' hedge accounting because it is the exposure to the variability in future cash flows that is being hedged.

A third and final category of hedge accounting is hedging a net investment in a foreign operation. This is accounted for similarly to cash flow hedges.

There are specific rules in IAS 39 to restrict which financial instruments can be considered hedging instruments and which items can be considered hedged items. In summary, a hedging instrument can be a derivative financial instrument or, for hedges of foreign exchange risk only, a non-derivative financial instrument. The hedged item must be an identified hedged item or a group of items that could affect profit or loss.

When an entity wishes to apply hedge accounting, it must formally document its intention to apply hedge accounting prospectively. Hedge accounting cannot be applied retrospectively. Additionally, hedge accounting must be consistent with the entity's established risk management strategy for that hedge relationship. The hedge documentation must identify the hedging instrument, the hedged item or transaction, the nature of the risk being hedged and specify how the 'effectiveness' of the hedge relationship will be assessed and ineffectiveness measured.

Hedge accounting is only permitted if the hedge relationship is expected to be highly effective and it is actually effective within a quantitative range. To the extent that the hedging instrument and hedged item are not perfectly effective at offsetting each other, this ineffectiveness is immediately recognised in profit or loss.

IAS 39 does not mandate the use of hedge accounting. Hedge accounting is voluntary. If an entity does not wish to use hedge accounting it does not need to designate and document its hedging relationships. An entity may find in some circumstances that the effect on profit or loss of applying hedge accounting is substantially the same as applying the normal recognition, classification and measurement requirements of IAS 39. In such circumstances, the entity may well choose not to apply hedge accounting because there is very little benefit in doing so.

In some circumstances, the fair value option (see **3.1.1** in **chapter C2**) in IAS 39 can be used as an alternative to hedge accounting. If an accounting mismatch exists, which will result in profit or loss volatility, an entity may apply the fair value option to reduce this volatility instead of complying with the onerous conditions of hedge accounting. For example, when a derivative provides an economic hedge of a financial instrument that is not measured at FVTPL, an accounting measurement mismatch exists. In that situation, applying the fair value option to the hedged item would reduce the measurement mismatch. The simplicity of applying the fair value option does, however, come at a cost:

- hedge accounting can be discontinued at any time but FVTPL designation is irrevocable; and
- if the fair value option is used, the entire change in fair value of the designated item must be recognised in profit or loss. This amount will not be an exact offset to the change in fair value of the hedging instrument when the hedging instrument is not hedging all of the risks of the item that is designated under the fair value option. In contrast, because hedge accounting allows the specific hedged risk to be designated, it can achieve a greater reduction in profit or loss volatility.

This chapter discusses the general principles of hedge accounting. The more complex aspects of hedge accounting and detailed examples are included in **chapters C10** and **C11** respectively.

2 Definitions and mechanics of hedge accounting

IAS 39 recognises three types of hedge accounting depending on the nature of the risk exposure:

- a fair value hedge;
- a cash flow hedge; and
- a hedge of a net investment in a foreign operation (net investment hedge).

2.1 Fair value hedge

A fair value hedge is a hedge of the exposure to changes in fair value of a recognised asset or liability or an unrecognised firm commitment, or an identified portion of such an asset, liability or firm commitment, that is attributable to a particular risk and could affect profit or loss. [IAS 39:86(a)]

2.1.1 Examples of fair value exposure

Fair value exposures arise from existing assets and liabilities, including firm commitments. Fixed rate financial assets and liabilities, for example, have a fair value exposure to changes in market rates of interest and changes in credit quality. Non-financial assets have a fair value exposure to changes in their market price (e.g. a commodity price). Some assets and liabilities have fair value exposures arising from more than one type of risk (e.g. interest rate, credit, foreign currency risk).

The following assets and liabilities are commonly fair value hedged:

- fixed rate liabilities such as loans;
- fixed rate assets such as investments in bonds;
- investments in equity securities classified as AFS under IAS 39; and
- firm commitments to buy/sell non-financial items at a fixed price.

Examples of fair value hedges include:

- a hedge of exposure to changes in the fair value of fixed rate debt as a result of changes in market interest rates (such a hedge could be entered into either by the issuer or by the holder);
- a hedge of the foreign currency risk of an unrecognised contractual commitment by an airline to purchase an aircraft for a fixed amount of a foreign currency at a future date; and
- a hedge of the change in fuel price relating to an unrecognised contractual commitment by an electricity utility to purchase fuel at a fixed price at a specified date, with payment in its functional currency.

A detailed illustration of the mechanics of a fair value hedge of interest rate risk of fixed rate debt is included at **2.1** in **chapter C11**.

2.1.2 Fair value hedge accounting

A fair value hedge that meets all of the hedge accounting criteria is accounted for as follows:

[IAS 39:89]

(a) the gain or loss from remeasuring the hedging instrument at fair value (for a derivative hedging instrument) or the foreign currency component of its carrying amount (for a non-derivative hedging instrument) is recognised immediately in profit or loss; and

(b) the carrying amount of the hedged item is adjusted through profit or loss for the gain or loss on the hedged item attributable to the hedged risk. This applies even if the hedged item is an AFS financial asset measured at fair value with changes in fair value recognised in other comprehensive income. This also applies if the hedged item is otherwise measured at cost.

2.1.3 Firm commitment

A firm commitment is a binding agreement for the exchange of a specified quantity of resources at a specified price on a specified future date or dates. [IAS 39:9]

A commitment is binding if it is enforceable either legally or otherwise. If the commitment is with a related party, consideration should be given as to whether in practice the right can be enforced. To be enforceable, the agreement should provide for remedies that are available to the parties to the contract in the event of non-performance, i.e. there is should sufficient disincentive for non-performance. For example, a penalty could be specified at a fixed amount or equal to the change in market price of the item under the contract. Alternatively, the penalty may not be specifically stipulated in the agreement but may otherwise be applicable (e.g. remedies under law). When an entity that is a member of a group is preparing its individual financial statements, the entity needs to consider carefully whether transactions between group entities meet the definition of a firm commitment, because they may not be subject to remedies for non-performance either as part of the contract or under law. In many cases, particularly in the absence of non-controlling interests that may require protection from the controlling interest, an agreement between group entities would not be binding.

Hedges of firm commitments are generally treated as fair value hedges under IAS 39. However, there is one exception; if an entity is hedging the foreign currency risk in a firm commitment, this may be accounted for either as a fair value hedge or a cash flow hedge. [IAS 39:87]

Example 2.1.3A

Hedging foreign currency risk of a firm commitment

Entity B sells machinery at fixed prices in many jurisdictions. Entity B's functional currency is Sterling. Entity B enters into a contract with Entity D, whose functional currency is the Euro, to sell machinery for delivery in six months' time at a fixed price in Euro that is determined today. In other words, Entity B has entered into a firm commitment with Entity D.

Entity B simultaneously enters into a foreign currency forward contract to hedge its future exposure to Euro arising from its firm commitment. This foreign currency forward contract can either be designated as a hedging instrument in a fair value hedge or a cash flow hedge because it is hedging the foreign currency risk of a firm commitment.

Example 2.1.3B

Fair value hedging a firm commitment

Entity E is a discount grocery chain with over 400 stores in the US, which enters into forward contracts to purchase various inventory items for its stores. On 1 June 20X0, Entity E enters into a forward contract to purchase 300,000 bushels of wheat from a wheat producer for a fixed price of US$1.40 per bushel on 1 August 20X0. Entity E will use the wheat in its bakery operations. Entity E intends taking physical delivery of the wheat in accordance with its expected purchase requirements. If Entity E failed to take delivery of the wheat, it would be required to pay for any decrease in the value of the wheat and legal remedies would be available to the wheat producer.

The transaction is a firm commitment because it is a binding agreement for the exchange of a specified quantity of wheat at a specified price on a specified future date. The forward contract is not accounted for as a derivative because Entity E intends to take physical delivery of the wheat and has no past practice of settling similar contracts net. Entity E could enter into a contract to hedge the fair value exposure of the firm commitment due to the change in the price of wheat between 1 June 20X0 and 1 August 20X0 (e.g. a net cash settled forward contract to sell wheat for a fixed price on 1 August). Such a contract would qualify as a hedging instrument in a fair value hedge of a firm commitment.

2.1.4 Fair value hedges of unrecognised firm commitments

When an unrecognised firm commitment is designated as a hedged item, the subsequent cumulative change in the fair value of the firm commitment attributable to the hedged risk is recognised as an asset or a liability with a corresponding gain or loss recognised in profit or loss. [IAS 39:93]

The changes in the fair value of the hedging instrument will also be recognised in profit or loss.

The initial carrying amount of the asset or the liability that results from the entity fulfilling the firm commitment is adjusted to include the cumulative change in the fair value of the firm commitment attributable to the hedged risk that was recognised in the statement of financial position. **Example 2.2** in **chapter C11** demonstrates the entries required when an entity hedges foreign currency risk of a firm commitment.

2.1.5 Discontinuance of fair value hedge accounting

An entity must discontinue prospectively fair value hedge accounting if:

[IAS 39:91]

(a) the hedging instrument expires or it is sold, terminated or exercised. For this purpose, the replacement or rollover of a hedging instrument into another hedging instrument is not an expiration or termination if such replacement or rollover is part of the entity's documented hedging strategy (for a discussion of rollover hedging strategies, see **3.8** in **chapter C10**). Additionally, for this purpose there is not an expiration or termination of the hedging instrument if:

    (i) as a consequence of laws or regulations or the introduction of laws or regulations, the parties to the hedging instrument agree that one or more clearing counterparties replace their original counterparty to become the new counterparty to each of the parties. For this purpose, a clearing counterparty is a central counterparty (sometimes called a 'clearing organisation' or 'clearing agency') or an entity or entities, for example, a clearing member of a clearing organisation or a client of a clearing member of a clearing organisation, that are acting as counterparty in order to effect clearing by a central counterparty. However, when the parties to the hedging instrument replace their original counterparties with different counterparties this paragraph shall apply only if each of those parties effects clearing with the same central counterparty.

    (ii) other changes, if any, to the hedging instrument are limited to those that are necessary to effect such a replacement of the counterparty. Such changes are limited to those that are consistent with the terms that would be expected if the hedging instrument were originally cleared with the clearing counterparty. These changes include changes in the collateral requirements, rights to offset receivables and payables balances, and charges levied.

(b) the hedge no longer meets the hedge accounting criteria (e.g. it is no longer highly effective or its effectiveness is no longer measurable); or

(c) the entity de-designates the hedge relationship.

In June 2013 the IASB issued amendments to IAS 39, *Novation of Derivatives and Continuation of Hedge Accounting*. The amendments shall be applied retrospectively and are effective for annual periods beginning on or after 1 January 2014 with earlier application permitted.

The amendments to IAS 39 introduced IAS 39:91(a)(i) and (ii) in response to widespread legislative changes across many countries requiring over-the-counter (OTC) derivatives to be cleared through central counterparties (CCPs). The IASB concluded that before the amendment novation of a derivative to a CCP would be accounted for as a derecognition of the original derivative and the recognition of a new novated derivative and consequently would lead to the discontinuation of hedge accounting. The IASB noted that this outcome could result in more hedge ineffectiveness, particularly for cash flow hedges, compared to a continuing hedging relationship. This is because the derivative that would be newly designated as the hedging instrument would be on terms that would be different from a new derivative, i.e. it was unlikely to be 'at-market' (for example, a non-option derivative such as a swap or forward might have a significant fair value) at the time of the novation. The IASB also noted that there would be an increased risk that the hedging relationship would fail to fall within the 80–125 per cent hedge effectiveness range required by IAS 39. [IAS 39:BC220E - G]

The IASB believed that accounting for the novated derivative in a continuing hedging relationship would provide more useful information to users of financial statements. As a consequence, it amended IAS 39 to provide relief from discontinuing hedge accounting in the particular circumstances described in IAS 39:91(a)(i) and (ii).

As part of the IASB's deliberations it considered whether voluntary novation to a CCP should be part of the scope of the amendment. The exposure draft that preceded the amendment was limited to circumstances where novation was required by laws and regulations. The IASB concluded that the novation does not have to be required by laws or regulations, however, for hedge accounting to continue voluntary novation to a CCP should be associated with laws or regulations that are relevant to central clearing of derivatives and that the mere possibility of laws or regulations being introduced was not a sufficient basis for the continuation of hedge accounting. [IAS 39:BC220Q]

The IASB acknowledged that permitting relief only where novation is directly to a CCP was too narrow. Consequently, the Board accepted that the relief would also be available if novation is undertaken with the objective of effecting clearing with a CCP. Examples where this may apply are where the novation is to a clearing member in order to transact with a CCP, so called 'indirect clearing'. The Board also observed that an intragroup novation also can occur in order to access a CCP; for example, if only particular group entities can transact directly with a CCP. [IAS 39:BC220R & S]

The IASB notes in IAS 39:BC220W that if an entity had previously discontinued hedge accounting, as a result of a novation, that (pre-novation) hedge accounting relationship could not be reinstated because doing so would be inconsistent with the requirements for hedge accounting (i.e. hedge accounting cannot be applied retrospectively).

Any adjustment to the carrying amount of the hedged item for the designated risk for interest-bearing financial instruments is amortised to profit or loss, with amortisation commencing no later than when the hedged item ceases to be adjusted. [IAS 39:92] The amortisation is based on a recalculated effective interest rate at the date amortisation commences such that the adjustment is fully amortised by maturity.

If amortisation begins as soon as a fair value adjustment exists, the adjustment to the carrying amount affects the effective interest rate calculation for the hedged item. In practice, to ease the administrative burden of amortising the adjustment while the hedged item continues to be adjusted for changes in fair value attributable to the hedged risk, it may be easier to defer amortising the adjustment until the hedged item ceases to be adjusted for the designated hedged risk. This is particularly true when the life of the hedge is the same as that of the hedged item. For example, if a fixed rate loan is issued at par and redeems at par, its fair value will move away from par over its life in response to changes in interest rates but it will be pulled back to par on maturity. Therefore, any fair value adjustments to the carrying amount of the loan under a fair value hedge for interest rate risk will be reversed by the end of the hedge and will not require amortisation.

However, if an interest-bearing instrument is hedged for only a portion of its term to maturity (see **2.2** in **chapter C10** for a discussion of partial term hedging), deferring amortisation until cessation of the hedge relationship will result in a skewed effective interest rate in the remaining years to the maturity of the hedged item.

An entity must apply the same amortisation policy for all of its debt instruments (i.e. it cannot defer amortising fair value adjustments on some items and not on others).

Example 2.1.5

Amortising fair value hedge adjustments

Bank J has a ¥10 million fixed rate loan asset that is classified as an AFS asset in accordance with IAS 39. Bank J hedges the fair value exposure of the asset using a forward contract. As a result of the hedge, the loan asset is adjusted for changes in the fair value of the risk being hedged and that adjustment is recognised in profit or loss. If Bank J does not elect to start amortising the hedging gain or loss while the hedge is outstanding, the adjustment will remain as part of the AFS asset until the loan is sold or until the loan is no longer hedged. If hedge accounting ceases prior to the loan being sold, the fair value adjustment of the loan will be amortised through the revised effective interest over the expected remaining life of the loan.

If an entity discontinues hedge accounting by de-designating the hedging relationship, the entity may elect to designate prospectively a new hedging relationship with the same derivative hedging instrument provided that the new hedging relationship meets the requirements for hedge accounting.

2.2 Cash flow hedge

A cash flow hedge is a hedge of the exposure to variability in cash flows that:

[IAS 39:86(b)]

- is attributable to a particular risk associated with a recognised asset or liability (such as all or some future interest payments on variable rate debt) or a highly probable forecast transaction; and
- could affect profit or loss.

Assets and liabilities and forecast transactions that are commonly cash flow hedged include:

- variable rate liabilities such as loans;
- variable rate assets such as investments in bonds;
- a highly probable future issuance of fixed rate debt;
- forecast reinvestment of interest and principal received on fixed rate assets; and
- highly probable forecast sales and purchases.

An example of a cash flow hedge is a hedge of variable rate debt with a floating to fixed interest rate swap. The variability in cash flow arises due to the reset of interest rates. The cash flow hedge reduces future variability of interest cash flows on the debt. Another example of a cash flow hedge is a hedge of anticipated reinvestment of cash inflows and the anticipated refinancing or rollover of a financial liability. A hedging instrument that swaps one variable rate for another (e.g. LIBOR for EURIBOR) would not qualify in a cash flow hedge relationship because it does not reduce cash flow variability; it merely swaps the debt's existing cash flow variability for cash flow variability determined on a different basis.

2.2.1 Forecast transactions

A forecast transaction is an uncommitted but anticipated future transaction. [IAS 39:9]

It is important to distinguish between forecast transactions and firm commitments because forecast transactions are always cash flow hedged, whereas firm commitments are generally fair value hedged. The following table illustrates some examples of forecast transactions and also illustrates the difference between a forecast transaction and a firm commitment.

Example 2.2.1

Examples of forecast transactions and firm commitments

Forecast transaction	***Firm commitment***
In May 20X1 an entity forecasts the purchase of 100,000 bushels of corn to be used in its manufacturing process in October 20X1.	An entity has signed a legally binding purchase agreement to take delivery of 100,000 bushels of corn on 30 September 20X1 for US$2 per bushel.
Corporate Treasury forecasts the sale of a debt instrument measured at amortised cost at the end of the fourth quarter.	Corporate Treasury signs a legally binding agreement with a third party to sell a specific debt instrument for par on 30 December 20X1.
Corporate Treasury forecasts the purchase of a £25 million bond on 23 March 20X1 from an investment bank.	Corporate Treasury enters into a legally binding purchase agreement with a bank to take delivery of a £25 million bond for par on 23 March 20X1.

Cash flow hedge accounting can be applied to a forecast transaction only if the transaction is highly probable. [IAS 39:88(c)]

The term 'highly probable' is not defined in IAS 39. The probability of occurrence must be significantly in excess of a 50 per cent likelihood, but will not be as high as 100 per cent because it can never be claimed that a transaction to which an entity is not yet committed is guaranteed to occur. IFRS 5:BC81 also refers to 'highly probable' although in a different context. It states that in IFRSs 'probable' is defined as "more likely than not" and that 'highly probable' is regarded as implying a significantly higher probability than 'more likely than not' and as being equivalent to the phrase "likely to occur".

Probability is assessed based on observable facts and the relevant circumstances. In assessing the likelihood that a transaction will occur, consideration should be given to the following:

- the frequency of similar past transactions;

- the financial and operational ability of the entity to carry out the transaction;
- substantial commitments of resources to a particular activity (e.g. a manufacturing facility that can be used in the short-run only to process a particular type of commodity);
- the extent of loss or disruption of operations that could result if the transaction does not occur;
- the likelihood that transactions with substantially different characteristics might be used to achieve the same business purpose (e.g. an entity that intends to raise cash may have several ways of doing so, ranging from a short-term bank loan to a common stock offering); and
- the entity's business plan.

In addition, both the length of time until a forecast transaction is projected to occur and the quantity of the forecast transaction should be considered in determining probability. Other factors being equal, the more distant a forecast transaction is, the less likely it is that the transaction would be considered highly probable and the stronger the evidence that would be needed to support an assertion that it is highly probable. For example, a forecast that a transaction will occur in five years may be less reliable than a forecast of a transaction expected to occur in one year.

Other factors being equal, the greater the physical quantity or future value of a forecast transaction, the less likely it is that the transaction would be considered highly probable and the stronger the evidence that would be required to support an assertion that it is highly probable. For example, it is easier to support forecast sales of 100,000 units in a particular month than to support forecast sales of 300,000 units in that month by an entity, when recent sales have averaged 300,000 units per month for the past three months. [IAS 39:IG.F.3.7]

IAS 39:IG.F.2.4 provides an example of an airline operator that could use sophisticated models based on experience and economic data to project its revenues in various currencies. If it can demonstrate that forecast revenues for a period of time into the future in a particular currency are 'highly probable', it may designate a currency borrowing as a cash flow hedge of the future revenue stream.

To meet the 'highly probable' requirement, an entity is not required to predict and document the exact date a forecast transaction is expected to occur. However, it is required to identify and document the time period during which the forecast transaction is expected to occur within a reasonably specific and generally narrow range of time from a most probable date, as a basis for assessing hedge effectiveness. To determine that the hedge will be highly effective, it is necessary to ensure that changes in the fair value of the expected cash flows are offset by changes in the fair value of the hedging instrument and this test may be met only if the cash flows occur within close proximity to each other. [IAS 39:IG.F.3.11]

A pattern of discovering that hedged forecast transactions are no longer expected to occur would call into question both an entity's ability to predict accurately forecast transactions and the propriety of using hedge accounting in the future for similar transactions. [IAS 39:IG.F.3.7]

A hedged forecast transaction must be identified and documented with sufficient specificity so that when the transaction occurs, it is clear whether the transaction is the designated hedged transaction. Therefore, a forecast transaction may be identified as the sale of the first 15,000 units of a specific product during a specified three-month period, but it could not be identified as the last 15,000 units of that product sold during a three-month period because the last 15,000 units cannot be identified with sufficient specificity: it could be units 20,001 to 35,000 or units 120,001 to 135,000. [IAS 39:IG.F.3.10]

For the same reason, a forecast transaction cannot be specified solely as a percentage of sales or purchases during a period.

While sufficient specificity is required when identifying forecast transactions, a description of the transaction that is *too* specific increases the risk of failure of hedge accounting in its entirety. For example, an entity may have a forecast fixed rate debt issuance of CU100 million in six months' time. The movement in interest rates between the date of designation and the date the debt is to be issued is hedged using a forward starting interest rate swap that will be closed out on the date the debt is issued. Any change in interest rates prior to the date of issuing the debt influences the determination of the fixed rate on that future debt and, therefore, is an eligible hedged risk.

If the entity designated the forecast debt issuance as being a fixed rate debt issuance then, should the forecast debt issuance not occur, the hedge will be entirely ineffective and hedge accounting will not be permitted. This will be the case even if the entity decides at the issuance date to issue floating rate debt instead of fixed rate debt. All gains or losses recognised in other comprehensive income on the forward starting interest rate swap would need to be reclassified from equity to profit or loss because the specific forecast fixed rate debt issuance did not occur, even though, economically, at the date of issuance the entity would be indifferent as to whether it chooses to issue fixed or floating rate debt.

As an alternative, the entity could make its designation a little less specific as to the ultimate basis of interest that will be issued. It could designate the hedged risk more broadly, for example, as changes in interest rates between the date of designation and the date when CU100 million of debt is issued. As long as the debt, when issued, is referenced to the same interest rate as is evident in the forward starting interest rate swap, the hedge will be highly effective (all other things being equal) and, therefore, the entity will continue to recognise the effective gains and losses in the cash flow hedge reserve in equity irrespective of whether the entity chooses to issue fixed or floating rate debt. The amounts recognised in other comprehensive income will be reclassified from equity to profit or loss when the interest affects profit or loss.

2.2.2 Cash flow hedge accounting

A cash flow hedge is accounted for as follows (assuming it meets all other hedge accounting requirements):

[IAS 39:95]

(a) the portion of the gain or loss on the hedging instrument that is determined to be an effective hedge is recognised in other comprehensive income; and

(b) the ineffective portion of the gain or loss on the hedging instrument is recognised immediately in profit or loss.

Specifically:

[IAS 39:96]

(a) the separate component of equity associated with the hedged item is adjusted to the lesser of the following (in absolute amounts):

- the cumulative gain or loss on the hedging instrument from inception of the hedge; and
- the cumulative change in fair value (present value) of the expected future cash flows on the hedged item from inception of the hedge; and

(b) any remaining gain or loss on the hedging instrument (which is not an effective hedge) is included in profit or loss.

An entity may exclude the time value of an option or interest element of a forward contract from the hedge designation, in which case the component of the fair value gain or loss related to that component is recognised in profit or loss. Alternatively, an entity may exclude from the hedge relationship a proportion of a derivative (or a non-derivative instrument for hedges of foreign currency risk) (e.g. 50 per cent of a derivative) or a proportion of a hedged item (e.g. 50 per cent of a debt instrument), in which case the gain or loss on the proportion excluded from the designation is recognised by applying IAS 39's general requirements for the instrument (see **chapter C2** for financial assets and **chapter C3** for financial liabilities).

The effective portion of the gain or loss on the hedging instrument recognised in other comprehensive income is subsequently reclassified from equity to profit or loss in the same period or periods during which the hedged item affects profit or loss, so as to offset the changes in the cash flows of the hedged item for the designated risk (e.g. if sales are hedged, the reclassification from equity to profit or loss will occur when the sales occur).

In April 2009, the IASB issued *Improvements to IFRSs* which amends the description in IAS 39:97 regarding when an amount in equity should be reclassified to profit or loss. IAS 39:97 previously stated that the associated gains or losses that are accumulated in equity should be reclassified into profit or loss in the period during which the asset acquired or liability assumed affects profit or loss (such as in the period in which interest income or interest expense is recognised). The IASB understood that there was some uncertainty about how this paragraph should be applied when the designated cash flow exposure being hedged differs from the financial instrument arising from the hedged forecast cash flows. Accordingly, the IASB clarified the wording by removing the references to an 'asset acquired or liability assumed' and instead referring to the 'hedged forecast cash flows' that affect profit or loss.

Detailed illustrations of cash flow hedges are included in **chapter C11** in the following sections.

- **3.1** Cash flow hedging a forecast sale of a non-financial item
- **3.2** Cash flow hedging a forecast sale for foreign currency risk
- **3.3** Basis adjusting the acquisition of a non-financial item
- **3.4** Cash flow hedging a forecast sale and subsequent receivable
- **3.5** Cash flow hedging variable rate interest with an interest rate swap
- **3.7** Cash flow hedging foreign currency risk of floating rate debt
- **3.8** Cash flow hedging foreign currency risk of fixed rate debt
- **3.9** Cash flow hedging foreign currency risk of zero coupon debt
- **3.10** Cash flow hedging foreign currency risk of the principal only on interest-bearing debt
- **3.14** Cash flow hedging share appreciation rights

In a cash flow hedge of a forecast transaction when the spot foreign exchange rate is being hedged, the effective amount recognised in other comprehensive income is calculated on a discounted basis, i.e. it is based on the present value of the spot element of the derivative. [IAS 39:IG.F.5.6]

When an entity hedges the spot foreign exchange rate in a forecast transaction using a non-derivative hedging instrument (e.g. foreign currency denominated debt), the amount recognised in other comprehensive income should be the undiscounted spot rate because this is the rate used to translate the foreign currency denominated debt in accordance with IAS 21.

A foreign currency monetary item (e.g. a loan) can be cash flow hedged for foreign currency risk for both interest and principal, interest only, principal only, or any proportion thereof.

If an entity hedges both interest and principal with a derivative, in order for the hedging instrument to be highly effective, the derivative will need to have contractual cash flows that match the foreign currency interest and principal flows but swap them into the functional currency equivalent cash flows. An example would be a cross-currency interest rate swap with gross physical exchange of principal at inception and at maturity. **Examples 3.7** and **3.8** in **chapter C11** illustrate this approach for hedging floating rate and fixed rate loans respectively.

If an entity hedges only the interest cash flows with a derivative, in order for the hedging instrument to be highly effective, the derivative will need to have contractual cash flows that match the foreign currency interest flows but swap them into the functional currency equivalent interest flows. An example would be a cross-currency interest rate swap without gross physical exchange of principal at inception and at maturity.

If an entity hedges only the principal cash flows with a derivative, in order for the hedging instrument to be highly effective, the derivative will need to have contractual cash flows that match the foreign currency principal cash flows but swap them into the functional currency equivalent principal cash flows. An example would be a foreign currency forward contract. **Example 3.10** in **chapter C11** illustrates a cash flow hedge of foreign currency risk of the principal only on an interest-bearing debt instrument.

For hedges of forecast transactions, it is permitted, but not required, to adjust the carrying amount of an acquired non-financial asset or a non-financial liability by the effective gain or loss on the hedging instrument as explained below.

2.2.3 Basis adjustments

An entity has a choice of accounting policy regarding the presentation of gains and losses recognised in other comprehensive income if a cash flow hedge of a forecast transaction subsequently results in the recognition of a *non-financial asset* (or a *non-financial liability*), or if a forecast transaction for a non-financial asset or a non-financial liability becomes a firm commitment for which fair value hedge accounting is applied. The accounting policy chosen must be applied consistently to all such hedges. [IAS 39:99]

The entity can either:

[IAS 39:98]

(a) reclassify the associated gains and losses from equity to profit or loss in the same period or periods during which the asset acquired or liability assumed affects profit or loss (such as in the periods that depreciation expense or cost of sales is recognised); or

(b) remove the associated gains and losses that were recognised in other comprehensive income and include them in the initial cost or other carrying amount of the asset or liability (in which case they will automatically affect profit or loss when the item is depreciated or sold).

However, if an entity expects that all or a portion of a loss recognised in other comprehensive income will not be recovered in one or more future periods, it must reclassify the amount that is not expected to be recovered into profit or loss immediately.

IAS 39 only allows a basis adjustment for non-financial items. This exception simplifies the accounting and tracking of gains and losses that would have otherwise been retained in equity. This exception does not apply for financial items because allowing basis adjustments would be contrary to recognising all financial instruments at fair value on initial recognition.

A detailed illustration of a cash flow hedge of a non-financial item where an entity has a policy of basis adjusting is included in **3.3** of **chapter C11**.

2.2.4 Discontinuance of cash flow hedge accounting

An entity must discontinue prospectively hedge accounting if:

[IAS 39:101]

- the hedging instrument expires or is sold, terminated or exercised (the replacement or rollover of a hedging instrument into another hedging instrument is not an expiration or termination if it formed part of the entity's documented hedging strategy from inception);
- the hedge no longer meets the hedge accounting criteria (e.g. it is no longer highly effective or its effectiveness is no longer measurable);
- the forecast transaction is no longer expected to occur; or
- the entity de-designates the hedge relationship.

The cumulative gain or loss on the hedging instrument recognised in other comprehensive income continues to be separately classified in equity until the forecast transaction occurs, at which point it is reclassified from equity to profit or loss.

When a forecast transaction is no longer highly probable but is still expected to occur, it no longer qualifies for cash flow hedge accounting because it does not satisfy the 'highly probable' criterion. Further recognition of fair value gains and losses on the hedging instrument in other comprehensive income is prohibited, i.e. subsequent changes in the fair value of the hedging instrument are recognised in profit or loss.

The cumulative gain or loss on the hedging instrument recognised in other comprehensive income prior to the transaction ceasing to be highly probable remains in equity until the transaction occurs, or until it is determined that the forecast transaction is no longer expected to occur. In the former case, the gain or loss is reclassified from equity to profit or loss when the hedged item affects profit or loss or is used to adjust the initial cost of the carrying amount of a non-financial item. In the latter case, the gain or loss is reclassified from equity to profit or loss as soon as it is determined that the transaction is no longer expected to occur.

Example 2.2.4A

Change in term of forecast debt issuance

Entity D, a Euro functional entity, intends to issue Euro denominated debt in six months' time with a maturity of five years that will pay fixed interest on a six monthly basis. The transaction is highly probable and, therefore, there is a stream of 10 highly probable six monthly interest payments. In order to hedge its future profit or loss exposure as a result of the fixed interest payments on the debt due to changes in the 6-month LIBOR rate between now and the issuance of the debt (in six months' time), Entity D enters into a forward starting receive 6-month LIBOR pay fixed interest rate swap with terms matching the critical terms of the forecast debt issuance such as start date, maturity, notional and payment dates. The entity designates the swap as a cash flow hedge of the profit or loss exposure arising from the series of six monthly interest payments on the forecast issuance of debt. Assuming all conditions necessary for hedge accounting under IAS 39 are satisfied, the effective portion of the gain and loss on the swap will be recognised in other comprehensive income.

On the forecast issue date, Entity D issues 7-year Euro denominated fixed rate debt, rather than debt with a five-year term as previously anticipated. The entity closes out the swap at the date of issuance. Ten forecast highly probable interest payments are still likely to occur, even though they will now be interest payments on debt with a seven-year maturity. The gain or loss recognised in other comprehensive income will be reclassified from equity to profit or loss when the individual interest payments for the first five years of the debt affect profit or loss. An allocation of the amount accumulated in equity when the debt is issued will be required to determine the amount of the swap that relates to the individual interest payments that were forecast and are still expected to occur. Because the fair value of the swap recognised in other comprehensive income consists of the present value of 10 future fixed cash flows, this present value amount is allocated specifically to those 10 future interest periods and, accordingly, is released to profit or loss in those future periods.

When the timing of a transaction moves forward (i.e. the transaction is expected to occur sooner), the forecast transaction continues to be highly probable and, therefore, continues to qualify as a hedged item. [IAS 39:IG.F.5.4]

Example 2.2.4B

Change in timing of forecast sale of a non-financial item

Entity S designates a derivative as a hedging instrument in a cash flow hedge of a forecast sale of silver. The hedging relationship meets all of the conditions for hedge accounting, including the requirement to identify and document the period in which the transaction is expected to occur within a reasonably specific and generally narrow range of time.

In a subsequent period, the forecast transaction is expected to occur in an earlier period than originally anticipated.

The change in timing of the forecast transaction does not affect the validity of the designation. Entity S can conclude that the transaction is the same as the one that was designated as being hedged. However, the change in timing of the hedged transaction may affect the assessment of hedge effectiveness going forward because the hedging instrument must continue to be designated for the whole of its remaining period to maturity. Also, the amount recognised in other comprehensive income up to this point will need to be adjusted to be the lower of the cumulative gain or loss on the derivative from inception of the hedge and the cumulative change in fair value of the future cash flows of the forecast transaction.

If the hedged transaction is no longer expected to occur, then the cumulative amounts in other comprehensive income are reclassified from equity to profit or loss. [IAS 39:101(c)]

Example 2.2.4C

Change in timing of forecast debt issuance

Entity D is hedging the forecast issuance of £100 million of 10-year, fixed rate debt using a rate lock agreement (a derivative). Entity D designates the rate lock agreement as a hedge of the variability in the total cash flows arising on the forecast debt issuance. Entity D expects to issue the debt in the second quarter of 20X0. Entity D's credit rating is BB. In the first quarter of 20X0, the spreads between government and corporate bond rates widen significantly. As a result, Entity D does not expect to issue its bonds in the second quarter. Entity D's advisors believe that the markets may stabilise in the first quarter of 20X1. Entity D will now make a decision on the type of funding in the first quarter of 20X1 and, therefore, closes out its rate lock agreement. At the time of closure, the fair value of the lock agreement is negative.

Entity D should recognise the entire loss in profit or loss because the forecast debt issuance is not expected to occur.

An entity can de-designate a hedge relationship at any point in time. Any gains or losses recognised in other comprehensive income up to the point of de-designation will remain in equity until the forecast transaction occurs. [IAS 39:101(d)] Gains or losses on the hedging instrument after de-designation will be recognised in profit or loss if the hedging instrument continues to be held.

2.2.5 Reclassification from equity to profit or loss after a business combination

Following a business combination, when the acquiree has applied cash flow hedging and recognised gains or losses in other comprehensive income prior to the acquisition, the acquirer will not be able to reclassify those gains and losses to consolidated profit or loss. Because the pre-acquisition reserves of the subsidiary do not exist in the consolidated financial statements of its new parent, any amounts recognised in other comprehensive income by the subsidiary prior to the business combination cannot be reclassified. Thus, the group can only hedge account for the specific relationship prospectively from the date of acquisition and only amounts recognised in other comprehensive income post-acquisition can be reclassified from equity to consolidated profit or loss in accordance with IAS 39:95.

2.2.6 Reclassification of amounts deferred in the cash flow hedge reserve when hedging interest rate risk with an 'off-market' swap

When the hedged risk is cash flow variability from changes in interest rates, the hedged item will often consist of multiple cash flows. For example, if an entity issues floating rate debt with five interest payments, it is common to hedge all five interest payments with a single interest rate swap. If the hedging instrument, when designated, is an 'off-market' interest rate swap (i.e. fair value is not nil) (see **3.7** and **4.1** in **chapter C10**) care needs to be taken to establish the correct amount to reclassify in relation to each cash flow. This is particularly true in the case of an 'under-hedge' (i.e. when the cumulative gain or loss on the hedging instrument accumulated in equity is less than the cumulative gain or loss on the hedged item) because the total amount deferred in the cash flow hedge reserve will not be sufficient to fully offset the variation in the hedged cash flows.

A basic approach to determine the amount to be reclassified from the cash flow hedge reserve for a particular relationship is to first calculate the amount that should remain in the cash flow hedge reserve at the reporting date for that relationship, and then reclassify the difference between that amount and the previous balance in the cash flow hedge reserve.

In a hedge of variability in interest cash flows due to changes in interest rates, the hedged item affects profit or loss through the interest accrual (e.g. interest accrual on debt). Therefore, although it is the full (or 'dirty') fair value gains or losses on the hedged item and hedging instrument that are used to measure the ineffectiveness for the hedge relationship, it is the 'clean' fair value gains or losses that should be used to determine the amounts that remain in the cash flow hedge reserve. The clean fair value is the fair value excluding any accrued interest.

For a swap that has a clean fair value of zero on the date of designation (i.e. an 'on-market' swap), the cumulative clean fair value gain or loss will be equal to the clean fair value. However, if the swap has a non-zero fair value on the date of designation (i.e. an 'off-market' swap), the calculation of the clean fair value gain or loss is more complex. One method of calculating the clean fair value gain or loss is to split the off-market swap into an on-market component swap and an 'embedded financing' component, where the embedded financing component will be a strip of fixed cash flows equal to the difference between the fixed leg on the off-market swap and the fixed leg of the 'on-market' component swap. The on-market component swap has a floating leg that matches the off-market swap and a fair value of zero on the date of designation. The embedded financing component and on-market component swap are determined as of the designation date and are not subsequently adjusted. The cumulative clean fair value gain or loss on the on-market component swap will be equal to the clean fair value of that component. The cumulative clean fair value gain or loss on the embedded financing component will be the cumulative change in clean fair value of the embedded financing component plus the portion of the designation date fair value of the embedded financing cash flows that have been settled and accrued (but not yet settled) since the inception of the hedge.

Therefore, the cumulative clean fair value gain or loss on the hedging instrument as a whole is the cumulative change in the clean fair value of the hedging instrument plus the portion of the designation date fair value of the embedded financing component that has been settled and accrued since the inception of the hedge. There are other acceptable methods of calculating the clean fair value gain or loss that give the same result as the above. For example, calculating the fair value movement for each individual cash flow and deducting the designation date fair value of the settled and accrued cash flows of the on-market component from the fair value gain and loss of those cash flows of the off-market swap that have yet to be settled or accrued.

Examples illustrating the journal entries for a cash flow hedge of floating rate debt using an off-market interest rate swap are included in **3.5B** and **3.5C** of **chapter C11**.

2.3 Net investment hedge

A hedge of a net investment in a foreign operation is a hedge of the foreign currency exposure to changes in the reporting entity's (generally, the group's) share in the net assets of that foreign operation. IAS 21 requires that the group's share of the net assets of a foreign operation be translated into the functional currency of the ultimate parent with the retranslation gain or loss recognised in other comprehensive income. It does not matter which currency the monetary assets and liabilities of the foreign operation are denominated in, because all those monetary items are firstly retranslated into the foreign operation's functional currency. It is the translation of those net assets of the foreign operation into the ultimate parent's functional currency that is the designated hedged risk.

IFRIC 16 *Hedges of a Net Investment in a Foreign Operation* addresses whether the hedged risk in a net investment hedge is the difference between the functional currency of the foreign operation and the presentation currency of the group or rather the difference between the functional currency of the foreign operation and the functional currency of the parent. The IFRIC (now the IFRS Interpretations Committee) consensus was that the hedged risk in a net investment hedge refers to the difference between the functional currency of the foreign operation and the functional currency of the parent. The IFRIC acknowledged that this question is only relevant to the extent that the presentation currency of the group differs from the functional currency of the parent. The IFRIC recognised that there are competing arguments for either view but found that the arguments in favour of looking to the functional currency of the parent were more compelling. The IFRIC concluded that the presentation currency does not create an exposure to which an entity may apply hedge accounting. The functional currency is determined on the basis of the primary economic environment in which the entity operates. Accordingly, functional currencies create an economic exposure to changes in cash flows or fair values; a presentation currency does not. [IFRIC 16:BC14]

A hedge of a net investment in a foreign operation, including a hedge of a monetary item that is accounted for as part of the net investment as defined in IAS 21, assuming it meets all other requirements for hedge accounting, is accounted for similarly to a cash flow hedge:

[IAS 39:102]

(a) the portion of the gain or loss on the hedging instrument that is determined to be an effective hedge is recognised in other comprehensive income; and

(b) the ineffective portion of the gain or loss on the hedging instrument is recognised immediately in profit or loss.

The descriptions of fair value and cash flow hedges in **2.1** and **2.2** respectively make specific reference to the presence of an exposure attributable to a particular risk that could affect profit or loss. The equivalent statement is not made with respect to a hedge of a net investment in a foreign operation. However, this can be seen as simply an omission rather than a substantive difference. The hedged risk in a net investment hedge, being the foreign currency exposure on the retranslation of the reporting entity's share of the net assets of the foreign operation under IAS 21, does affect profit or loss because IAS 21:48 & 48C require the cumulative exchange differences relating to a foreign operation to be reclassified from equity to profit or loss on the disposal (or, in some cases, the partial disposal) of that foreign operation.

Goodwill and any fair value adjustments arising on the acquisition of a foreign operation are treated as assets and liabilities of the foreign operation, expressed in the foreign currency and translated at the closing rate, and thus are considered net assets of the foreign operation. [IAS 21:47] Equally, a monetary item that is receivable from or payable to a foreign operation for which settlement is neither planned nor likely to occur in the foreseeable future is, in substance, part of the entity's net investment in that foreign operation and, therefore, forms part of the net assets of that foreign operation. [IAS 21:15]

Example 2.3

Identifying net assets available to be hedged

Parent A (Sterling functional currency) has a wholly-owned Subsidiary B (US dollar functional currency). Parent A heads Group A. The investment in Subsidiary B was made on 1 January 20X0 when Parent A acquired 100 per cent of Subsidiary B's share capital for US$100 million. At the date of acquisition, the fair value of the identifiable net assets of Subsidiary B was US$70 million. In applying acquisition accounting under IFRS 3 *Business Combinations*, US$30 million of goodwill was recognised in the consolidated financial statements of Group A. At the acquisition date, Parent A extended a loan of £10 million to Subsidiary B when the US$/£spot exchange rate was US$2:£1. Settlement of this loan is neither planned nor likely to occur in the foreseeable future.

At the acquisition date, Group A wishes to designate as a hedged item its net investment in its foreign operation, Subsidiary B, in the consolidated financial statements. The maximum amount of the net investment in the foreign operation that can be designated as a hedged item is US$120 million. This comprises three elements:

- US$70 million of the identifiable net assets of the foreign operation acquired at acquisition;

- US$30 million of goodwill that forms part of the net assets of the foreign operation; and
- US$20 million of additional net assets as a result of the loan extended by Parent A to Subsidiary B, being a monetary item for which settlement is neither planned nor likely to occur in the foreseeable future (i.e. the loan forms part of the net investment in Subsidiary B).

It should be noted that if the loan extended to Subsidiary B was expected to be settled in the foreseeable future, the maximum amount of the net investment in the foreign operation that could be designated would be US$100 million because the loan would not form part of the net investment in Subsidiary B.

The gain or loss on the hedging instrument relating to the effective portion of the hedge that has been recognised in other comprehensive income is reclassified from equity to profit or loss when the net investment affects profit or loss, i.e. on the disposal (or, in some cases, the partial disposal) of the net investment in the foreign operation. [IAS 39:102] This makes it necessary to track the amount of gains and losses on hedging instruments recognised in other comprehensive income in relation to the hedge of each individual foreign operation separately, so as to be able to identify how much of the total amount recognised in other comprehensive income should be reclassified from equity to profit or loss on the disposal or partial disposal of a particular foreign operation. This may be complex in large groups with many foreign operations and with many hedging instruments used over different periods of time.

A more detailed discussion of complex issues that can arise with net investment hedging is included in **section 5** of **chapter C10**.

IAS 21 defines a net investment in a foreign operation as the amount of the reporting entity's interest in the net assets of that operation. [IAS 21:8]

Net investment hedging is only permitted in consolidated financial statements because it is only in consolidated financial statements that the net assets of the foreign operation are recognised. The only exception is a foreign operation that is not a separate legal entity (e.g. branch of the reporting entity that has a functional currency different from the functional currency of the reporting entity). In this case, the investor may apply net investment hedging in its individual financial statements by designating the translation risk of the net assets of the foreign branch. This is acknowledged in IFRIC 16:2.

In August 2014, the IASB issued an amendment to IAS 27 *Separate Financial Statements* to include the equity method as one of the options in IAS 27 to account for an entity's investment in a subsidiary, joint venture or associate in its separate financial statements. As a result, an entity may use the equity method for such investments in its separate financial statements and, to the extent such interests are foreign operations, net investment hedging may be applied. The amendment is effective for annual periods beginning on or after 1 January 2016 (with earlier application permitted).

In the separate financial statements of the investor, an investment in a subsidiary associate or joint venture may alternatively be recognised either at cost or in accordance with IAS 39 (i.e. as an AFS asset or at FVTPL). [IAS 27:10(b)] In such circumstances, the carrying amount will not be equivalent to the net investment in that operation (as defined by IAS 21) and, therefore, net investment hedging cannot be applied.

However, as an alternative, the investor may wish to apply fair value hedge accounting for the foreign exchange risk of its investment in its foreign operation if the investment is not measured at FVTPL under IAS 39. For example, if an investor makes an investment in a foreign operation that meets the definition of a subsidiary, and the investor recognises the investment at cost in its separate financial statements, the investing entity will be exposed to a risk that will affect profit or loss (i.e. the foreign currency risk that arises upon disposal of the foreign subsidiary). If the investing entity has a foreign currency derivative, or a foreign currency denominated liability that was used to fund the investment in the foreign operation, that instrument could be designated as a hedging instrument in respect of a portion of the foreign currency risk of the investment in the subsidiary equivalent to the notional on the hedging instrument. In order to qualify for this treatment, the entity must be able to determine that foreign currency risk with respect to the investment in the subsidiary exists of an amount equal to at least the notional of the hedging instrument. For the entity to make this claim, it must either be able to measure the fair value the investment in local currency terms or, at a minimum, be able to determine that the fair value in local currency terms is not below the notional of the hedging instrument. Applying fair value hedge accounting would result in the gain or loss on the hedging instrument being recognised in profit or loss along with the associated movement in the foreign currency risk on the designated portion of the investment in the subsidiary.

It is worth noting that this approach is very different from applying net investment in a foreign operation hedge accounting at a consolidated level where both the hedging instrument and the foreign exchange translation on the net assets of the foreign operation are recognised in other comprehensive income. Additionally, it should be noted that fair value hedge accounting cannot be applied in the consolidated financial statements to an equity method investment or an investment in a consolidated subsidiary. [IAS 39:AG99] Fair value hedge accounting for such items can only be applied in the separate financial statements of the investor.

2.3.1 Hedging net investments with loans

In the absence of hedge accounting, foreign exchange gains and losses on retranslating the net assets of a foreign operation are recognised in other comprehensive income and taken to a separate component of equity (in accordance with IAS 21), while those on the loan are recognised in profit or loss. This creates a mismatch in foreign currency translation. When net investment hedge accounting is applied, this mismatch is eliminated because the gains and losses on the loan, to the extent effective, are recognised in other comprehensive income.

When the hedging instrument in a net investment hedge is a foreign currency denominated non-derivative financial liability (e.g. a foreign currency denominated loan), it is always the spot retranslation risk that is the hedged risk (as opposed to the forward rate) because it is only the spot rate that is recognised from retranslating the foreign currency non-derivative liability.

2.3.1.1 Loan is less than or equal to the net assets of subsidiary

Example 2.3.1.1

Loan is less than or equal to the net assets of subsidiary

Entity A, a UK entity with a Sterling functional currency, has a US subsidiary with a US dollar functional currency, Entity B. To finance this subsidiary, Entity A has a US$50 million US dollar loan with a third-party bank. Entities A and B have the same 31 December year end and the net assets of Entity B at 31 December 20X1 and 31 December 20X2 are US$70 million.

The loan is designated as a hedging instrument of the first US$50 million of net assets of Entity B. The designation is spot retranslation risk only. The hedge is determined to be highly effective. The US$/£ spot rate on 31/12/X1 is 1.6 and on 31/12/X2 it is 1.7.

On 31/12/X2, the following entries are recorded.

		£ million	**£ million**
Dr	Loan	1.84	
Cr	Other comprehensive income		1.84

To recognise the foreign exchange gain on the loan. This is the difference between US$50 million translated at 1.6 and 1.7.

		£ million	**£ million**
Dr	Other comprehensive income	2.57	
Cr	Net assets		2.57

To retranslate the net assets. This is the difference between US$70 million translated at 1.6 and 1.7.

The entire exchange difference on retranslating the net assets of the foreign operation is taken to other comprehensive income in accordance with IAS 21. The application of hedge accounting results in the remeasurement of the loan being recognised in other comprehensive income rather than profit or loss. No hedge ineffectiveness has been recognised. Hedge ineffectiveness would have arisen if the net assets of the foreign operation fell below US$50 million at the period end.

2.3.1.2 Loan exceeds net assets of subsidiary

Hedge accounting is still possible when the amount of the loan exceeds the net assets of the foreign operation.

Example 2.3.1.2

Loan exceeds net assets of subsidiary

Assume the same facts as in **example 2.3.1.1** except that the loan is US$100 million.

The entity designates US$70 million of the loan as a hedging instrument of the first US$70 million net assets of Entity B. The designation is spot retranslation risk only. The hedge is determined to be highly effective. The US$/£ spot rate on 31/12/X1 is 1.6 and on 31/12/X2 it is 1.7.

On 31/12/X2, the following entries are recorded.

		£ million	£ million
Dr	Loan	3.68	
Cr	Other comprehensive income		2.57
Cr	Profit or loss		1.11

To recognise the foreign exchange gain on the loan.

The entire loan must be remeasured at the closing rate, giving rise to an exchange gain. The exchange gain that relates to the designated and effective hedging instrument (i.e. US$70 million of the loan) is reported in other comprehensive income. The remainder is reported in profit or loss.

		£ million	£ million
Dr	Other comprehensive income	2.57	
Cr	Net assets		2.57

To retranslate the net assets.

2.3.1.3 Net assets of the foreign operation change

The facts in **example 2.3.1.1** and **example 2.3.1.2** were simplified because the net assets of the subsidiary remained the same at the start and at the end of the reporting period. In practice, this will rarely be the case. Because documentation and designation must be in place at inception of the hedge, the hedged item will be based on the opening net asset position. Hedge ineffectiveness arises to the extent to which the net asset position falls below the designated amount of net assets at the date that hedge effectiveness is assessed, which is, at a minimum, at the end of each reporting period.

Example 2.3.1.3

Net assets of foreign operation change

Entity A, a UK entity with a Sterling functional currency, has a US subsidiary with a US dollar functional currency, Entity B. To finance this subsidiary, Entity A has a US$80 million US dollar loan with a third-party bank. The year end of both entities is 31 December. On 31 December 20X1, the net assets of Entity B were US$90 million, and are expected to remain at approximately this level, so the entire loan is designated as hedging the spot retranslation risk associated with the first US$80 million net assets of Entity B.

On 31 December 20X2, the net assets of B are US$75 million. The US$/£ spot rate on 31/12/X1 is 1.6 and on 31/12/X2 is 1.7.

Hedge ineffectiveness arises because US$80 million of net assets are no longer being hedged. Nevertheless, the hedge is assessed as highly effective and hedge accounting is required for the period. Hedge ineffectiveness must be recognised immediately in profit or loss.

		£ million	**£ million**
Dr	Loan	2.94	
Cr	Other comprehensive income		2.76
Cr	Profit or loss		0.18

To recognise the foreign exchange gain on the loan.

The foreign exchange gain that relates to the designated and effective hedging instrument (i.e. the exchange gain on US$75 million) is recognised in other comprehensive income while the ineffective portion is recognised in profit or loss.

On 31 December 20X2, the group may choose to redesignate prospectively the hedging instrument to be only US$75 million of the loan.

In **example 2.3.1.3**, ineffectiveness was caused by the net assets of the foreign operation falling below the level of the loan hedging it. This ineffectiveness can be minimised by monitoring the net assets of the foreign operation and redesignating as appropriate.

2.3.2 Hedging net investments with forward contracts

If no hedge accounting was applied, then the foreign exchange gains and losses on retranslating the net assets of the foreign operation would be taken to other comprehensive income (in accordance with IAS 21:39) and the change in fair value of the forward contract would be recognised in profit or loss.

When hedging net investments with forward contracts, it is important to specify what risk is being hedged: i.e. the forward or the spot foreign currency exchange rate. If the forward rate is hedged, the full change in fair value of the forward contract is recognised in other comprehensive income if it is fully effective whereas, if the spot rate is hedged, the spot element of the forward contract is recognised in other comprehensive income and the remainder (being the forward points) is recognised in profit or loss. Any element recognised in other comprehensive income as an effective gain or loss is reclassified from equity to profit or loss on the disposal (or, in some cases, partial disposal) of the underlying net investment.

For the purpose of both assessing effectiveness and measuring ineffectiveness in net investment hedging, it is possible to identify the spot element of a forward contract as the undiscounted spot. This is because the risk being hedged is the risk of the retranslation of the net assets of the net investment in accordance with IAS 21, which is calculated on an undiscounted basis. This is equally true when an entity designates foreign currency denominated debt as a hedge of a net investment in a foreign operation. In this case, both the hedged item and hedging instrument are retranslated to undiscounted spot in accordance with IAS 21 and, therefore, the hedged risk is the undiscounted spot.

Whether the spot rate or the forward rate is the designated hedged risk, the overall effect on profit or loss is the same, but the timing of the recognition of the fair value of the forward points is different.

It is not permitted in any hedge relationship to amortise any premium or discount on a forward contract. Derivatives must always be measured at fair value in the statement of financial position. Changes in fair value are either recognised in profit or loss or, if the derivative is designated as an effective hedge in a cash flow or net investment hedge, in other comprehensive income. [IAS 39:IG.F.6.4]

A detailed illustration of a net investment hedge using a forward contract is included in the following sections of **chapter C11**.

- **4.1** Net investment hedging the spot foreign currency rate.
- **4.2** Net investment hedging the forward foreign currency rate.

Hedging with cross-currency swaps is very similar to hedging with forward contracts; see **4.3, 4.4** and **4.5** in **chapter C11** for further guidance.

2.4 Exposures and types of hedges: summary

The following table provides examples of assets, liabilities, forecast transactions and firm commitments that may be hedged, and the type of hedge accounting that could apply.

Exposures and types of hedges

Fixed rate assets and liabilities

Examples:

Fixed rate loans

Fixed rate debt securities

Fixed rate issued debt of the entity

Fixed rate deposit liabilities

Exposure	*Hedge accounting*
Overall fair value	FV (Fair value)
Interest rates	FV
Credit of the issuer	FV or CF**
Foreign currency	FV or CF
Termination options	FV

Variable rate assets and liabilities

Examples:

Variable rate loans

Variable rate debt securities

Variable rate debt of the entity

Variable rate deposit liabilities

Exposure	*Hedge accounting*
Overall fair value	FV
Interest rates	FV* or CF (Cash flow)
Credit of the issuer	FV or CF**
Foreign currency	FV or CF
Termination options	FV

Firm commitments to originate loans

Examples:

Issued fixed rate loan commitment

Fixed rate loan commitment held

Exposure	*Hedge accounting*
Overall fair value	FV
Interest rates	FV
Credit	FV

Forecast purchases and sales of financial instruments

Examples:

Forecast purchase of debt

Forecast loan originations

Exposure	*Hedge accounting*
Overall fair value	CF
Interest rates	CF
Credit	CF

Firm commitment to purchase or sell non-financial assets

Examples:

Committed sale of inventory

Committed purchase of inventory

Exposure	*Hedge accounting*
Overall fair value	FV
Foreign currency	FV or CF***

Forecast purchases and sales of non-financial assets

Examples:

Forecast sale of inventory

Forecast purchase of inventory

Exposure	*Hedge accounting*
Overall fair value	CF
Foreign currency	CF

Exposures and types of hedges

Other assets

Examples:

Equity investments classified as AFS in IAS 39

Exposure	*Hedge accounting*
Overall fair value	FV
Foreign currency	FV or CF

* FV hedging is generally permitted for hedging the fair value risk associated with the fixing of interest between floating reset dates.

** CF hedging would only be appropriate if the credit spread on the instrument was variable.

*** IAS 39 recognises that firm commitments create fair value exposure. However, it does allow hedges of the foreign currency risk of a firm commitment to be accounted for as either a fair value hedge or a cash flow hedge. [IAS 39:87]

3 Hedged items

A hedged item is defined as a recognised asset, liability, unrecognised firm commitment, highly probable forecast transaction or net investment in a foreign operation that:

[IAS 39:9]

(a) exposes the entity to risk of changes in fair value or future cash flows; and

(b) is designated as being hedged.

A hedged item can be:

(a) a single asset, liability, firm commitment, highly probable forecast transaction or net investment in a foreign operation;

(b) a group of assets, liabilities, firm commitments, highly probable forecast transactions or net investments in foreign operations with similar risk characteristics; or

(c) in a portfolio hedge of interest rate risk only, a portion of the portfolio of financial assets/liabilities that share the risk being hedged.

The basic application of the rules on qualifying hedged items is covered in the remainder of this section, with more complex issues dealt with in **section 2** of **chapter C10**.

3.1 Unrecognised assets

Unrecognised assets (other than unrecognised firm commitments) cannot be designated as hedged items. For example, it is not possible to hedge account for an unrecognised intangible asset such as a core deposit intangible that is not recognised in the statement of financial position. [IAS 39:IG.F.2.3]

3.2 Intragroup items

As a general rule only assets, liabilities, firm commitments and highly probable forecast transactions that are with a party or parties external to the reporting entity can be designated hedged items. Transactions between entities within the same group can only be designated as hedged items in the entity-only financial statements and not in the consolidated financial statements of the group. This is because intragroup transactions do not generally expose the group to a risk that affects consolidated profit or loss. [IAS 39:80]

There are three exceptions to this general rule. The first is transactions between entities in the same group in the consolidated financial statements of an investment entity, as defined in IFRS 10 *Consolidated Financial Statements*, where transactions between an investment entity and its subsidiaries measured at fair value through profit or loss will not be eliminated in the consolidated financial statements. The second is when the foreign currency exposure of an intragroup monetary item does not fully eliminate on consolidation under IAS 21 (discussed further in **3.2.1**). The third is for the foreign currency risk of forecast intragroup transactions (discussed further in **3.2.2**).

Within a group, an entity exposed to a hedged risk is not required to be party to the hedging instrument if hedge accounting is applied at a group level. An entity may decide not to apply hedge accounting in its individual financial statements, but hedge accounting can be applied in the consolidated financial statements that include that entity. For example, it is common in many groups that trading subsidiaries do not enter into derivative transactions; instead the corporate treasury function does so on their behalf. Unless there are internal derivative transactions between the trading subsidiary and corporate treasury, the subsidiary would not be able to apply hedge accounting in its entity-only financial statements because it has not entered into any hedging instruments. However, hedge accounting may be applied in the consolidated financial statements if the external hedging instrument entered into by the corporate treasury function is an effective instrument at the group level.

3.2.1 Intragroup monetary items and interest

In accordance with IAS 21, foreign currency gains and losses on intragroup monetary assets and liabilities do not fully eliminate on consolidation when the intragroup monetary item is transacted between two group entities that have different functional currencies. Because these gains and losses affect consolidated profit or loss, foreign currency risk on such intragroup monetary assets and liabilities is eligible to be hedged. [IAS 39:80]

Example 3.2.1

Foreign currency risk on intragroup loans

A Sterling functional currency parent makes a 5-year US dollar denominated fixed rate interest-bearing loan to its US dollar functional currency subsidiary. The loan does not form part of the parent's investment in the US subsidiary. In the parent's separate financial statements, this loan will need to be remeasured at the end of each reporting period in accordance with IAS 21, and will give rise to an exchange gain or loss. However, there will be no corresponding foreign currency gain or loss in the subsidiary's financial statements because the loan is denominated in its functional currency.

In the consolidated financial statements, an exchange gain or loss on the intragroup balance will not be eliminated, but will be reported in profit or loss as an exchange gain or loss on a monetary item.

The parent hedges the foreign currency risk of both interest and principal by entering into a cross-currency swap with a counterparty outside of the group under which the parent receives Sterling fixed and pays US dollar fixed on the interest payment dates of the intragroup loan with a gross exchange of US dollar for Sterling at inception and Sterling for US dollar in five years' time equivalent to the US dollar notional amount of the loan.

The loan may be designated as a hedged item in both the parent's separate financial statements and in the consolidated financial statements. In the parent's separate financial statements, the cross-currency swap is expected to be fully effective as a cash flow hedge of the US dollar foreign currency risk arising on the interest and principal of the loan.

However, in the consolidated financial statements, the cross-currency swap will be less effective because the impact on profit or loss in the parent's separate financial statements and the consolidated financial statements differs and, therefore, the hedged risk differs. In the parent's separate financial statements, the impact on profit or loss will be the foreign currency risk associated with both interest and principal cash flows denominated in a foreign currency. In the consolidated financial statements, the hedged risk differs because part of the risk that resides in the parent's separate financial statements does not survive consolidation. The parent's interest income (measured at spot or an average rate) in the parent's separate financial statements and the subsidiary's interest expense (measured at spot or an average rate) in the subsidiary's financial statements should eliminate in the consolidated financial statements. Because the hedged risk differs, the hypothetical derivative will differ, and its fair value will differ from the actual derivative entered into by the parent (for detail on the hypothetical derivative method see **4.4.1** in **chapter C10**). The difference in the actual and hypothetical derivative will need to be determined as part of the prospective hedge effectiveness assessment to establish whether the hedge is expected to be highly effective.

3.2.2 Foreign currency risk of a highly probable forecast intragroup transaction

Foreign currency risk of a highly probable intragroup transaction qualifies as a hedged item in the consolidated financial statements provided that the following two conditions are met:

[IAS 39:80]

- the transaction is denominated in a currency other than the functional currency of the entity entering into that transaction; and
- the foreign currency risk will affect consolidated profit or loss.

The entity can be a parent, subsidiary, associate, joint venture or branch. [IAS 39:AG99A]

In many cases, the forecast intragroup transaction does not affect consolidated profit or loss, as is the case for royalty payments, interest payments or management charges, unless there is a related external transaction. Such transactions for which there are no related external transactions do not qualify as hedged items. By contrast, in the case of forecast sales or purchases of inventories between members of the same group when there is an onward sale of the inventories to a party external to the group, there will be an effect on consolidated profit or loss (see **example 3.2.2B**). Similarly, a forecast intragroup sale of plant and equipment from the group entity that manufactured it to a group entity that will use the plant and equipment in its operation will affect consolidated profit or loss. This is because the amount initially recognised by the purchasing entity for the plant and equipment, and thus depreciated through its profit or loss, will vary with movements in foreign currency prior to the plant and equipment being recognised when the forecast intragroup transaction is denominated in a currency other than the functional currency of the purchasing entity (see **example 3.2.2A**). [IAS 39:AG99A]

If a hedge of a forecast intragroup transaction qualifies for hedge accounting, any gain or loss recognised in other comprehensive income is reclassified from equity to profit or loss in the same period or periods during which the foreign currency risk of the external hedged transaction affects consolidated profit or loss. [IAS 39:AG99B]

Example 3.2.2A

Hedging foreign currency risk of intragroup transactions (1)

Entity A (a Sterling functional currency entity) is expecting, with a high degree of probability, to purchase a machine from Entity B (a Euro functional currency entity) for €10m in 1 year's time. Entity A and Entity B are part of the same group and Entity A will use the machine in its production process to make goods for external sale. The cost of the machine will be capitalised and depreciated over its useful economic life in both the individual financial statements of Entity A and the consolidated financial statements (including both Entity A and Entity B). Entity A enters into a buy Euro sell Sterling forward contract with a third party to hedge the expected foreign currency risk on the forecast purchase.

The forecast intragroup purchase will qualify as a hedged item in the consolidated financial statements in a cash flow hedge of the currency risk because:

- the purchase is highly probable;
- the purchase is denominated in a currency (Euro) other than Entity A's functional currency (Sterling); and
- the depreciation of the machine will result in the foreign currency risk of the forecast transaction affecting consolidated profit or loss. The Euro/Sterling exchange rate at the date of purchase will affect the amount initially recognised in respect of the machinery, and thus will affect the associated depreciation expense.

Example 3.2.2B

Hedging foreign currency risk of intragroup transactions (2)

In all scenarios below, the group has two subsidiaries (Entity C – Euro (€) functional currency and Entity D – US dollar (US$) functional currency).

Scenario 1

Entity C incurs external production costs in € towards goods it manufactures and sells on in € to a fellow subsidiary Entity D. This creates a foreign currency risk in Entity D to the €/US$ exchange rate with regard to its forecast purchase from Entity C (purchase of goods in €). Entity D also intends to sell the goods externally outside of the group in US$. In order to hedge the exposure associated with the forecast purchase from Entity C, Entity D enters into a forward contract with a third party (buy €/ sell US$). The group wishes to designate the forward contract as hedging the foreign currency risk of the forecast intragroup purchase by Entity D from Entity C in a cash flow hedging relationship in the consolidated financial statements.

Scenario 2

The facts are as in Scenario 1 except that the sale of goods from Entity C to Entity D is denominated in US$ and, therefore, there is foreign currency risk for Entity C on the sale of goods to Entity D. Entity C enters into a forward contract with a third party to mitigate its foreign currency risk of the forecast sale to Entity D in US$ (buy €/ sell US$). The group wishes to designate the forward contract as hedging the foreign currency risk of the forecast intragroup sale by Entity C to Entity D in a cash flow hedging relationship in the consolidated financial statements.

Scenario 3

The facts are as in Scenario 1 except that the sale of goods from Entity C to Entity D is denominated in Sterling and, therefore, there is foreign currency risk for Entity C on the sale of goods to Entity D and there is also foreign currency risk for Entity D on the purchase of goods from Entity C. Entity C enters into a buy €/ sell £ forward contract with a third party to mitigate its foreign currency risk of the forecast sale to Entity D, and Entity D enters into a buy £/sell US$ forward contract with a third party to mitigate its foreign currency risk of the forecast purchase from Entity C.

In both Scenarios 1 and 2, the internal transaction being designated is denominated in a currency other than the functional currency of the entity entering into it: in Scenario 1, the forecast intragroup purchase by Entity D (functional currency of US$) is denominated in €; in Scenario 2, the forecast intragroup sale by Entity C (functional currency of €) is denominated in US$. Also, in both cases, the onward sale of the goods by Entity D will affect consolidated profit or loss. Therefore, in both cases, the forecast intragroup transaction could be designated as the hedged item in a cash flow hedge of foreign currency risk in the consolidated financial statements, assuming all other conditions of hedge accounting are met.

In Scenario 3, in the individual financial statements of both entities, cash flow hedge accounting can be applied. With respect to the consolidated financial statements, the possibility of hedging intragroup forecast transactions was included in IAS 39 for situations where one of the parties to the internal transaction passes its foreign currency risk to the other, as in Scenarios 1 and 2 above. This is the currency risk that exists and cannot be avoided because the two parties have different functional currencies. In Scenario 3, the parties to the internal transaction are taking on additional foreign currency risk and, therefore, the hedge accounting cannot be applied. Furthermore, although the sum of the two derivatives result in a net buy €/ sell US$ position, these two derivatives cannot be designated in combination in the consolidated financial statements as a hedge of the external € purchases or a hedge of the external US$ sales, because Entity C does not have a US$ exposure, and Entity D does not have a € exposure.

Example 3.2.2C

Hedging foreign currency risk of intragroup transactions (3)

Entity E (Sterling functional currency entity) has a wholly-owned subsidiary, Entity F (Yen functional currency entity). Entity F generates substantial profits and regularly pays Yen dividends on its ordinary shares to Entity E. In order to hedge the Yen exposure associated with the dividend income, Entity E enters into a series of sell Yen buy Sterling forward contracts. Entity E also expects to pay dividends on its own ordinary shares (classified as equity in accordance with IAS 32 *Financial Instruments: Presentation*) using the proceeds from dividends received from its shareholding in Entity F.

The forecast intragroup transaction (the dividend income in the hands of Entity E) will not qualify as a hedged item in the consolidated financial statements of the group in a cash flow hedge of the currency risk because the foreign currency risk will not affect consolidated profit or loss. Even though Entity E may expect to make an onward declaration and payment of dividends on its own shares, IAS 32 requires that distributions to holders of an equity instrument should be recognised directly in equity and, therefore, this will not give rise to a gain or loss in consolidated profit or loss.

Example 3.2.2D

Hedging foreign currency risk of intragroup transactions (4)

Entity A is a Euro functional currency entity that has a fellow subsidiary Entity B, a US dollar (US$) functional currency entity. Entity A borrows a specified amount of Euro from a party external to the group at fixed interest rates. Entity A lends the proceeds of the borrowing to Entity B on the same terms as the external borrowing. Because Entity B has borrowed in Euro at fixed rates and has a US$ functional currency, it enters into a receive Euro fixed pay US$ fixed cross-currency swap with a party external to the group to hedge the foreign currency risk of the interest and principal payments on its borrowing from Entity A.

In its separate financial statements, Entity B can designate the foreign currency risk arising from the Euro denominated interest payments and principal of its borrowing from Entity A in a hedging relationship with the hedging instrument being the external cross-currency swap.

In the consolidated financial statements, the cross-currency swap cannot be designated as a hedge of the foreign currency risk of the forecast intragroup interest payments by Entity B because the interest payments in Entity B are eliminated against the interest receipts in Entity A. Entity B's interest payments do not affect consolidated profit or loss and, therefore, cannot be designated as a hedged item in the consolidated financial statements.

The foreign currency exposure generated on the intragroup loan will not be fully eliminated on consolidation in accordance with IAS 21 because the loan is measured in Entity B in US$ but measured in Entity A in Euro. It is unlikely that this foreign currency risk could be designated as a hedged item in an effective hedge relationship with the external cross-currency swap as a hedging instrument in the consolidated financial statements because the swap's fair value is derived from both interest and principal payments and receipts whereas the foreign currency risk that survives consolidation is limited to Entity B's translation of the opening and closing carrying amounts of the intragroup loan.

Example 3.2.2E

Hedging foreign currency risk of highly probable forecast intragroup royalty payments

Entity A is the parent of Entity B. Entity A charges Entity B a royalty to compensate for external costs it incurs on behalf of Entity B in respect of technology, brands or other intellectual property. Entity B recovers the royalty cost through the sales price it charges externally whenever it sells the goods/services that utilise the technology, brands or other intellectual property. Entity A and Entity B have different functional currencies. Entity A's functional currency is US dollars (USD);

Entity B's functional currency is Norwegian Krona (NOK). The intragroup royalty payments are denominated in Entity A's functional currency.

Scenario 1: royalty for use of manufacturing process

Entity A has incurred USD1 million in developing a manufacturing process used to make Product X. The manufacturing process is transferred to Entity B, which uses that process to manufacture Product X. Entity A charges Entity B a USD10 royalty for each unit of Product X that Entity B sells externally over a two-year period.

Entity B will sell Product X to customers outside the group at a price in NOK that is substantially in excess of the royalty cost Entity B incurs. Entity B enters into foreign currency forward contracts to hedge the foreign currency risk arising on its forecast intragroup royalty payments relating to highly probable external sales.

Scenario 2: royalty for use of an acquired brand

Entity A acquires an external brand for USD10 million. The group plans to use the newly acquired brand on new products to be sold externally. Some of the newly branded products will be sold by Entity B in NOK and Entity B will be required to pay to Entity A an intragroup royalty payment at a fixed USD amount per unit sold. The royalty payment incurred by Entity B represents no more than 20 per cent of the expected NOK external sales price.

Entity B enters into foreign currency forward contracts to hedge the foreign currency risk arising on its forecast intragroup royalty payments relating to highly probable external sales.

Scenario 3: royalty for use of patented technology

Entity A has developed a patented technology that is used by Entity B as part of its product development for products that Entity B manufactures and sells to customers outside the group in NOK. Entity B pays a USD royalty to Entity A for each unit sold externally which was set at inception of the arrangement at a fixed percentage of the then current external sales price.

Entity B enters into foreign currency forward contracts to hedge the foreign currency risk arising on its forecast intragroup royalty payments relating to its highly probable external sales.

IAS 39:80 states that, in the consolidated financial statements, "the foreign currency risk of a highly probable forecast intragroup transaction may qualify as a hedged item in a [cash flow hedge] provided that (1) the transaction is denominated in a currency other than the functional currency of the entity entering into that transaction and (2) the foreign currency risk will affect consolidated profit or loss". Further, IAS 39:AG99A states that royalty payments, interest payments and management charges between members of the same group will not generally affect consolidated profit or loss (and, consequently, cannot qualify as a hedged item in a cash flow hedge) "unless there is a related external transaction".

In each of the scenarios described, the intragroup royalty cost is an unavoidable part of the highly probable forecasted external sale. Therefore, the foreign currency risk arising from the highly probable forecast intragroup royalty payment may qualify as a hedged item in a cash flow hedge in the consolidated financial statements because (1) the royalty is denominated in a functional currency other than Entity B's and (2) there is a related external transaction that will cause the changes in the royalty payments due to changes in exchange rates to affect consolidated profit or loss.

3.3 Overall business risks

Overall business risk cannot be hedged because it cannot be specifically identified and measured. [IAS 39:AG98] For example, an entity could not apply hedge accounting to a hedge of a risk of a transaction not occurring which will result in less revenue. This is an overall business risk. [IAS 39:IG.F.2.8]

A firm commitment to acquire a business in a business combination cannot be a hedged item, except for foreign exchange risk, because the other risks being hedged cannot be specifically identified and measured. These other risks are general business risks. [IAS 39:AG98]

Example 3.3

Hedging foreign currency risk of a firm commitment to acquire a business

Entity D, a € functional currency entity, is the parent of Group D. Entity D enters into an agreement to acquire Entity E in two months' time for US$50 million. The consolidated financial statements of Group D will include Entity E from the date of acquisition. To hedge the US$ foreign currency risk of the purchase consideration, Entity D enters into a foreign currency forward contract to buy US$50 million and sell € at a specified foreign currency rate that matures in two months.

Because Entity D is hedging the foreign currency risk of a firm commitment, it may designate the foreign currency forward contract as a fair value or as a cash flow hedge.

If Entity D designates the derivative in a fair value hedge, the gains or losses will be recognised in profit or loss, and the movements in the fair value of the firm commitment due to foreign currency risk will also be recognised in profit or loss with the other side of the entry recognised in the statement of financial position. At acquisition, this balance will be derecognised and will adjust the amount of goodwill.

If Entity D designates the derivative in a cash flow hedge, the gain or loss will be recognised in other comprehensive income. As discussed in **2.2.3**, Entity D has a choice as to whether to apply a basis adjustment when cash flow hedging the acquisition of a non-financial item (the acquisition of a business). If Group D applies a basis adjustment, it will remove the gain or loss on the derivative from equity and basis-adjust the goodwill that is recognised on acquisition. The amount of the basis adjustment will affect profit or loss, for example, if any resulting goodwill is impaired. If Group D does not apply a basis adjustment, it will continue to recognise the gain or loss on the derivative in equity until it would have affected profit or loss had goodwill been basis-adjusted.

3.4 Held-to-maturity assets

A held-to-maturity (HTM) investment in the scope of IAS 39 cannot be a hedged item with respect to interest rate risk or prepayment risk. This is irrespective of whether the interest is fixed or variable. To be able to designate an asset as HTM, an entity must be indifferent to future profit opportunities for that asset, i.e. it must have the positive intent to hold the asset to maturity irrespective of changes in its market value (see **3.2** in **chapter C2**). However, an HTM asset can be a hedged item with respect to foreign currency risk and credit risk. [IAS 39:79]

A forecast purchase of a financial asset that an entity intends to classify as HTM can be a hedged item. The prohibition for hedges of interest rate risk and prepayment risk is only for HTM assets already held; until the asset is acquired, it may be a hedged item. [IAS 39:IG.F.2.10]

Example 3.4A

Hedging interest risk for forecast acquisition of a held-to-maturity asset

Entity A forecasts the purchase of a fixed rate financial asset that it intends to classify as HTM. To protect itself against movements in interest rates between now and when the asset is purchased, Entity A enters into a derivative contract that will mature when the forecast transaction occurs with the intent of locking in the current forward rate for the day when the asset is expected to be purchased. The derivative is designated as a hedge of the forecast purchase of the financial asset and qualifies for hedge accounting.

IAS 39 does not prohibit an entity from hedging its forecast interest receipts on debt instruments resulting from the reinvestment of interest receipts from an HTM asset. [IAS 39:IG.F.2.11]

Example 3.4B

Hedging interest risk of forecast reinvestment of cash flows from a held-to-maturity asset

Entity XYZ owns a variable rate asset that it has classified as HTM. The variable interest rate receipts are reinvested in debt instruments. Entity XYZ enters into a derivative to lock in the current interest rate on the reinvestment of the variable cash flows, and designates the derivative as a cash flow hedge of the forecast future interest receipts on debt instruments.

> Entity XYZ qualifies for hedge accounting even though the interest payments that are being reinvested derive from an HTM asset. While an HTM asset itself cannot be hedged with respect to interest rate risk, it is possible to designate the derivative as hedging cash flow risk from debt instruments that were purchased using the interest receipts from the HTM asset. The source of the funds used to purchase the debt instruments in the future is not relevant.
>
> The same would be true if Entity XYZ's HTM assets had been fixed rather than variable rate assets.

3.5 Loans measured at amortised cost

Assets that are classified as loans and receivables under IAS 39 are measured at amortised cost. Even though the financial asset is not measured at fair value, it can still be a hedged item in a fair value hedge or a cash flow hedge. For example, if a loan earns fixed rate interest, it could be hedged for changes in fair value due to movements in interest rates. Further, because there is no presumption of holding the financial asset until its maturity (as is the case for HTM investments as described in **3.4**) it is possible to hedge the cash flows that arise from its future disposal when its disposal is considered to be highly probable.

3.6 Investments in equity instruments

An investment in an equity instrument (e.g. an ordinary share in a third party) may be designated as a hedged item in either a cash flow or fair value hedge if the instrument is not measured at cost or at FVTPL (i.e. if the equity investment is classified as AFS). The instrument is an eligible hedged item because the changes in its fair value will affect profit or loss when the fair value gains or losses initially recognised in other comprehensive income are reclassified from equity to profit or loss on impairment or derecognition.

3.7 Derivatives

Derivatives generally cannot be designated as hedged items. [IAS 39:IG.F.2.1] As an exception, IAS 39 permits a written option to qualify as a hedging instrument if it is designated as an offset to a purchased option, including one that is embedded in another financial instrument (e.g. a written call option used to hedge a callable liability). [IAS 39:AG94]

The inability to designate a derivative as a hedged item will be relevant if an entity attempts to apply hedge accounting to a net risk position that includes a derivative. For example, an entity may enter into a derivative to hedge a debt instrument and then layer on a second derivative to hedge part of the net exposure of the debt and the first derivative. The inclusion of the first derivative as part of the hedged item is prohibited because it would result in the first derivative being a hedged item, rather than it being a hedging instrument.

Example 3.7

Ineligible hedged item

Entity K has a US dollar functional currency. Entity K issues fixed rate Euro denominated 10-year debt. It chooses to issue the debt in the Euro market because it perceives the net interest cost after hedging to be cheaper than issuing directly in the US market. At the date of issue, Entity K immediately swaps all the foreign currency cash flows on the debt into its functional currency by entering into a 10-year receive € fixed pay US dollar floating cross-currency interest rate swap because it does not wish to be exposed to foreign currency risk. Because Entity K has an interest rate policy of fixing interest rates for five years, it also enters into a 5-year receive US dollar floating pay US dollar fixed interest rate swap to fix its interest cost for the five years after issue of the debt.

Entity K is prohibited from designating the interest rate swap as a cash flow hedge of changes in US dollar interest rates of the issued debt and the cross-currency interest rate swap (i.e. the net synthetic US dollar fixed rate debt achieved by swapping all fixed Euro cash flows into US dollar fixed cash flows). The cross-currency interest rate swap is a derivative and, therefore, is not a qualifying hedged item.

However, Entity K could designate the cross-currency swap and the interest rate swap in combination as a partial-term hedge of foreign currency risk of the debt for the first five years and a hedge of foreign currency risk and interest rate risk for the latter five years. IAS 39 permits a combination of derivatives to be designated jointly as a hedging instrument and permits partial-term hedging (see **3.2** and **2.2** in **chapter C10** respectively).

3.8 Designation of financial items

Provided that effectiveness can be measured, it is possible to designate only a portion of either the cash flows or fair value of a financial instrument as the hedged item.

It is possible to designate:

[IAS 39:81]

- one or more contractual cash flows of an instrument;
- one or more portions of one or more contractual cash flows of an instrument; or
- a proportion (i.e. percentage) of the cash flows or fair value of the instrument.

The example below illustrates different permissible hedge designations for a fixed rate bond. For more detailed guidance on hedging portions and partial term hedging see **2.1** and **2.2** in **chapter C10** respectively.

Example 3.8A

Permitted hedge designations of financial items

Entity B has a 5-year fixed rate bond asset. Entity B wishes to hedge part, or all, of the bond. The instrument is not classified as HTM under IAS 39. There are many options available to Entity B in applying hedge accounting. It can choose to:

- hedge the full fair value of the cash flows on the debt (all contractual cash flows);
- hedge the fair value on a proportion of debt, e.g. fair value of 50 per cent of the debt (proportion of all the contractual cash flows);
- hedge the fair value on all cash flows due to the impact of a specific risk only such as the impact of changes in risk-free interest rates (rather than all risks);
- hedge part of the cash flows due to a specific risk, e.g. designate the impact of movements in interest rates on 50 per cent of the cash flows (hedging a specific risk on a proportion of all cash flows);
- hedge an isolated set of cash flows due to all risks, e.g. hedging the fair value movement on the principal only (hedging a portion of cash flows);
- hedge an isolated set of cash flows due to a specific risk, e.g. hedging the fair value movement due to interest rate risk on the principal only (hedging a specific risk only on a portion of cash flows); or
- hedging the full fair value above or below a specified amount, e.g. hedging fair value decreases below a specified amount (hedging a part of the fair value).

IAS 39 does not require risk reduction on an entity-wide basis as a condition for hedge accounting. Exposure is assessed on a transaction basis. [IAS 39:IG.F.2.6]

Example 3.8B

Risk reduction

An entity has a fixed rate asset and a fixed rate liability both measured at amortised cost, each having the same principal amount. The entity receives interest on the asset at 10 per cent, and pays interest of 8 per cent on the liability, with payments and receipts occurring in the same period, so the entity always has a net cash inflow of 2 per cent.

The entity enters into a receive-floating, pay-fixed interest rate swap on a notional amount equal to the principal of the asset and designates the interest rate swap as a fair value hedge of the fixed rate asset. The entity qualifies for hedge accounting even though the effect of the swap on an entity-wide basis is to create an exposure to interest rate changes that did not previously exist. The specific asset being hedged has a fair value exposure to interest rate movements that is offset by the interest rate swap.

3.8.1 Hedge of portions

As illustrated in **example 3.8A**, an entity has many options available to it in dissecting the cash flows of a hedged financial item. An entity may hedge part or all of the cash flows due to all risks inherent in the hedged item, or it may choose to hedge part or all of the cash flows due to specific risks only. This approach is known as 'hedging portions' and is only permitted if the risk can be identified and hedge effectiveness can be assessed and measured reliably.

Hedging portions of cash flows and risks can be helpful in ensuring that the designated terms of the hedged item are similar to the terms of the hedging instrument, which reduces hedge ineffectiveness.

Example 3.8.1A

Hedging interest rate risk portion (1)

Entity A wishes to issue 5-year fixed rate debt. Based on market rates of interest and Entity A's credit rating, it is able to issue debt at 6.5 per cent. This comprises a 5-year interest rate risk of 4.5 per cent, and a credit spread of 2 per cent. Entity A may designate the hedged risk as changes in the fair value of the debt associated with changes in interest rate risk only (i.e. it may exclude from the designation its own credit spread).

Excluding the credit spread from the designation will increase the effectiveness of the hedge relationship because the equivalent credit risk inherent in the debt is not reflected in the terms of the interest rate swap.

An individual leg on an interest rate swap (or other derivative) that is not exactly the same as the cash flows on the hedged item does not necessarily preclude hedge accounting. The fair value of a hedging instrument is determined by the valuation of its net cash flows and, therefore, when determining whether a hedging relationship is effective, an entity would not consider the terms of a single leg of the swap without also considering the impact of the other leg of the swap.

Instead of entering into swaps that receive or pay a LIBOR flat equivalent amount (i.e. LIBOR without a credit spread), entities often enter into swaps where one of the legs exactly matches the cash flows on their debt.

Example 3.8.1B

Hedging interest rate risk portion (2)

Entity Z has a credit rating of B. It issues fixed rate debt at 6 per cent, which includes a credit spread of 100 basis points (i.e. the rate comprises a LIBOR rate of 5 per cent and a credit spread of 1 per cent). To hedge its exposure to changes in interest rate movements, it enters into a receive-fixed, pay-floating interest rate swap.

Instead of entering into a swap where the pay leg exactly matches the equivalent of LIBOR (i.e. receive 5 per cent, pay LIBOR), Entity Z enters into a swap where the fixed leg exactly matches its debt. Because the receive leg is 6 per cent, the pay leg is increased correspondingly to LIBOR + 100 basis points. Because the fair value of the swap is derived from its net settlements, the receive 5 per cent, pay LIBOR swap and the receive 6 per cent, pay LIBOR + 100 basis points will have the same fair value for a given movement in interest rates. Therefore, Entity Z may still designate the LIBOR portion of its debt as the hedged item.

3.9 Designation of non-financial items

If the hedged item is a non-financial asset or liability, it may only be designated as a hedged item:

[IAS 39:82]

(a) for foreign currency risk; or

(b) in its entirety for all risks.

It is often difficult to isolate and measure directly the change in cash flows or fair value associated with a specific risk for a non-financial item, other than foreign currency risk, when compared to measuring separately specific risks of financial items (e.g. interest rate risk). For this reason, IAS 39 only permits hedging of a non-financial item for foreign currency risk or in its entirety for all risks, even though it may be argued that in some cases it is possible to isolate, at least indirectly, the changes in cash flows or fair value attributable to a particular risk. This position was confirmed by the IFRIC (now the IFRS Interpretations Committee) in October 2004 when the IFRIC also noted that to allow separation of a non-financial asset into price risk components with the separate components being designated as the hedged item would require an amendment to IAS 39 rather than an Interpretation.

Example 3.9A

Hedging a forecast acquisition of a non-financial item: foreign currency risk

Entity D, a € functional currency entity, has a highly probable forecast transaction to purchase tyres from an external US dollar functional currency entity. Because the tyres are a non-financial item, Entity D can either hedge the purchase of tyres for all risks or for just the foreign currency risk.

Entity D is able to hedge the foreign currency risk that will arise from buying the tyres because the foreign currency risk between the Euro and the US dollar is identifiable and measurable. However, it is not possible to hedge just the cost of rubber in the purchase of tyres because this is not the entirety of all risks in the forecast transaction.

Example 3.9B

Hedging a forecast acquisition of a non-financial item: all risks

Entity B purchases bronze for use in the manufacture of its products. Entity B enters into a forward contract indexed to copper and wishes to designate it as a hedge of the copper component in forecasted purchases of bronze.

The price of copper is only a portion of the exposure to changes in the price of bronze. Entity B cannot designate as the hedged item changes in the value of the future purchase of bronze due to changes in the price of copper. However, if Entity B is able to demonstrate that the hedging instrument will be highly effective in hedging the price of bronze, it may be able to designate the forward contract as a hedging instrument in hedging the price of bronze. Any hedge ineffectiveness that arises from the hedge relationship must be recognised in profit or loss.

Example 3.9C

Hedging the price of separate base metals in a sale of metal concentrate

Entity A is a mining entity that owns and operates a copper mine. Entity A mines the ore from the mine and processes it into metal concentrate, which contains copper as well as other base metals. Entity A sells the metal concentrate to Entity B. The sales price for the metal concentrate is based on the actual base metal composition of the metal concentrate, which is established through analysis of a sample of the metal concentrate.

Given the guidance in IAS 39:82, is it acceptable for Entity A to designate the price risk of a specific base metal within the metal concentrate (e.g. copper) as the hedged item?

It depends. If the process of extracting the base metals from the metal concentrate is merely a process of disaggregating the different base metals, the metal concentrate in effect represents a collection of different non-financial items for the purposes of IAS 39:82 and, therefore, a specific base metal could be designated as a hedged item. In contrast, if the process of extracting the base metals from the metal concentrate is a process of transformation, the metal concentrate represents a single non-financial item for the purposes of IAS 39:82.

In assessing whether a specific base metal contained within the metal concentrate represents a separate non-financial item, careful judgement and industry knowledge is required. The assessment should include a careful analysis of the following:

- whether the process of extracting the base metals contained within the metal concentrate is a simple process of disaggregation rather than one of transformation;
- whether the quantity of the base metal within the metal concentrate is known with a high degree of certainty;

- whether the pricing of the metal concentrate is based on the actual content of the base metals extracted, rather than on estimated content or a fixed amount price per volume/quantity of the metal concentrate;
- whether the individual base metal components contained within the metal concentrate constitute separate 'units of account' for revenue recognition purposes from the point of view of the seller; and
- whether there are any terms in the sale contract for the metal concentrate that would suggest that the distinct non-financial items cannot be identified easily for the purposes of IAS 39:82; such terms may include any significant element of the pricing of the metal concentrate that cannot be related back to the individual base metals contained within the metal concentrate.

The term 'entirety of all risks' in IAS 39:82 includes variability in cash flows that will be incurred in getting the non-financial item to the condition and location in which it must be delivered when those costs are included by the seller as a single unit price. For example, if an entity has forecast purchases of non-financial items where the buyer is billed for the cost of the non-financial item (which includes some conversion of a commodity into a finished product) plus the delivery of that finished good to the buyer, the entirety of all risks is the entire variability in cash flows, which includes the costs of conversion and delivery.

When transportation is undertaken on behalf of the purchaser by a third-party provider, not the counterparty, the variability in the cost of transportation does not form part of the non-financial item because it is a separate service undertaken by an unrelated party.

The restriction to hedge the item in its entirety for all risks or just foreign currency risk can give rise to practical problems for entities that hedge the purchase or sale of commodities where the grade of the hedging instrument is not equivalent to the grade of the commodity in the purchase. This is often referred to as a 'basis' risk.

Example 3.9D

Hedging a forecast acquisition of a non-financial item: basis risk

Entity E hedges the forecast purchase of cocoa using cocoa futures. The cocoa futures contracts specify cocoa of a quality grade that differs from the quality grade of the forecast purchase of cocoa. The difference in quality grades between the hedged item and the hedging instrument is referred to as basis risk. The basis risk will cause hedge ineffectiveness.

Example 3.9E

Hedging a forecast acquisition of a non-financial item: transportation

Entity C acquires commodities for use in its business. It acquires the commodities at spot prices on the date it requires a commodity for use in its business. The amount it pays to the supplier for the commodity is an amount referenced to the London Metal Exchange (LME), plus an amount for transportation of the commodity from the supplier to the entity.

If an entity designates a non-financial item as a hedged item, it must be designated as a hedged item for (a) foreign currency risk only, or (b) in its entirety.

If Entity C is hedging the cash flow price variability of its future commodity purchases in its entirety, the entity must include the costs, whether fixed or variable, it will pay the supplier in bringing the non-financial item to its current location. If the transportation costs paid to the supplier are variable, this would result in greater cash flow variability that will potentially result in greater hedge ineffectiveness.

If Entity C enters into the hedging instrument to hedge the variability in the LME price only, but the transportation costs also are paid to the supplier and are variable, Entity C may choose to adjust the hedge ratio (i.e. so it is not 1-to-1) to reduce the amount of hedge ineffectiveness that may result from changes in the cash flow variability of transportation costs.

Example 3.9F

Hedging a non-financial item: operating leases

Entity A is a leasing entity that rents out machinery in both operating and finance lease arrangements. Entity A wishes to hedge future lease receipts. The ability to hedge these future receipts depends on whether the lease arrangement is a finance lease or an operating lease. An operating lease is an executory contract committing the lessor to provide the use of an asset in future periods in exchange for cash receipts. Because the lease is a non-financial item, Entity A would need to either hedge account all the risks of the future lease receipts or foreign currency risk only. This is different from a finance lease, because a finance lease is a financial instrument which gives Entity A greater flexibility in designating the hedged item in a qualifying hedge relationship.

Example 3.9G

Hedging a non-financial item: inventory

[Extract from IAS 39.IG.F.3.6]

Can an entity designate inventories, such as copper inventory, as the hedged item in a fair value hedge of the exposure to changes in the price of the inventories, such as the copper price, although inventories are measured at the lower of cost and net realisable value under IAS 2 *Inventories*?

Yes. The inventories may be hedged for changes in fair value due to changes in the copper price because the change in fair value of inventories will affect profit or loss when the inventories are sold or their carrying amount is written down. The adjusted carrying amount becomes the cost basis for the purpose of applying the lower of cost and net realisable value test under IAS 2.

As described in **2.2.3**, IAS 39 permits an accounting policy choice as to whether to basis adjust non-financial items that are subject to a cash flow hedge. As described above, IAS 39:IG.F.3.6 states that a basis adjustment is included in the cost when applying the lower of cost or net realisable value test in IAS 2. If an entity has an accounting policy of not basis adjusting non-financial items subject to a cash flow hedge, IAS 39 does not state that amounts reclassified from the cash flow hedge reserve to profit or loss should be the same as when an entity adopts a policy of basis adjusting.

It is reasonable to assume that this should be the case. Therefore, if an entity does not basis adjust inventory, the reclassification from equity to profit or loss should result in the same net profit or loss amount that would have been achieved had the entity basis adjusted that inventory.

For guidance on other aspects of hedging non-financial items, such as hedging assets held at cost, or hedging for all risks except foreign currency risk, see **2.7** in **chapter C10**.

3.10 Hedging net positions

A hedge of an overall net position does not qualify for hedge accounting because hedge effectiveness is required to be measured by comparing the change in fair value or cash flows of a hedging instrument and a specific hedged item (or group of similar items). However, almost the same effect on profit or loss can be achieved by designating part of the underlying items, assets or liabilities, equal to the net position as the hedged item. [IAS 39:AG101]

Example 3.10A

Hedging a net payable

Entity A, a Sterling functional currency entity, has payables of US$100, and receivables of US$80. Instead of entering into two separate derivatives, it wishes to hedge the net US$20 position for foreign currency risk. IAS 39 does not permit designation of a net position as the hedged item. Instead Entity A can designate US$20 of payables as the hedged item.

Similarly, if an entity has £500 fixed rate assets and £350 fixed rate liabilities and enters into a hedge of the net position, it could designate £150 of assets as being the hedged item in a fair value hedge of interest rate risk.

The net exposure from a forecast purchase and a forecast sale cannot be designated as a hedged item. Once again, almost the same effect on profit or loss can be achieved by designating part of the forecast purchases or forecast sales equal to the net position as the hedged item.

Example 3.10B

Hedging a net sale

Entity A, a UK entity, has highly probable forecast sales of US$100, and highly probable forecast purchases of US$80. Entity A enters into a single foreign currency forward contract to hedge the net exposure of US$20. Although Entity A cannot hedge the net position, it can designate the forward contract as hedging the first US$20 of sales.

An entity cannot hedge net profit because this number results from the netting of many items. If an entity has sufficiently stable net profit margins, it may be able to hedge the net number by designating as the hedged item a portion of sales equal to that amount.

Example 3.10C

Hedging a net profit

Entity A's functional currency is Sterling. One fifth of Entity A's profits are generated in US$ and this exposes Entity A's net profit to foreign currency risk. The US dollar sales are expected to be US$100 million per month and have a relatively stable net profit margin of 15 per cent (i.e. US dollar purchases are expected to be US$85 million per month).

Entity A wishes to hedge the exposure of net profit to changes in US$/Sterling currency rate. Because Entity A cannot hedge a net amount (and, therefore, it cannot hedge the net profit), Entity A chooses instead to designate the hedging instrument as a cash flow hedge of the first US$15 million of US dollar sales per month.

As long as Entity A makes at least US$15 million of US dollar sales per month, the hedge relationship will be effective.

3.11 Hedging own equity

Transactions in an entity's own equity cannot be designated as hedged items. An entity's own equity transactions cannot be hedged because they do not expose the entity to a risk that can affect reported profit or loss. For example, a forecast dividend payment could not be designated as a hedged item, because IAS 32 requires that distributions to owners are recognised directly in equity and, therefore, they do not affect profit or loss. However, a properly declared dividend that has not yet been paid and that is recognised as a financial liability by the payer or as a financial asset by the recipient may qualify as a hedged item for foreign currency risk if it is denominated in a foreign currency because changes in the foreign currency will affect profit or loss. [IAS 39:IG.F.2.7]

An entity may be able to designate share-based payment transactions that are exclusively cash settled in an effective hedge accounting relationship. Even though the amount of cash payable varies by reference to the entity's share price, there is a cash flow variability that will affect profit or loss.

An illustration of the accounting entries recorded for a cash flow hedge of equity price risk arising from an entity's IFRS 2 *Share-based Payment* expense, using an equity call option, is shown at **3.14** in **chapter C11**.

3.12 Hedging issued convertible debt

As explained at **3.1** in **chapter C3**, convertible debt is separated at issue into a financial liability and an equity conversion option which is included in equity. The financial liability is recognised at the present value of the contractual interest flows and principal, discounted at an interest rate for a debt without the equity conversion option. Because the financial liability is measured as if the entity had issued a partly discounted bond, any hedge of the interest rate risk on this financial liability must also take into account this discount. In addition, because the financial liability will be extinguished when the convertible bond is converted, any hedging instrument should mirror this termination feature in order to increase hedge effectiveness.

3.13 Equity-method investments and investments in consolidated subsidiaries

An equity-method investment cannot be a hedged item in a fair value hedge in consolidated financial statements because the equity method recognises the investor's share of the associate's profit or loss, rather than changes in the investment's fair value.

For similar reasons, an investment in a consolidated subsidiary cannot be a hedged item in consolidated financial statements in a fair value hedge because consolidation recognises the subsidiary's profit or loss, rather than changes in the investment's fair value. [IAS 39:AG99]

Although in the consolidated financial statements it is not possible to apply fair value hedge accounting for an equity-method investment or an investment in a consolidated subsidiary, it may be possible to apply fair value hedge accounting to such a hedge in the investor's separate financial statements if the equity method is not applied.

Whether fair value hedge accounting is permitted is dependent on whether the investment in the equity security can actually be fair valued for the hedged risk. It is inconsistent to claim fair value hedge accounting when the fair value of the investment cannot be reliably measured, e.g. when the investment is in an unquoted equity and the variability in the range of reasonable fair value estimates is too high and the entity is attempting to fair value hedge the investment for equity price risk.

A more complex scenario may arise when, in its separate financial statements, the investor attempts to apply fair value hedging with respect to foreign currency risk in relation to an equity investment in a foreign subsidiary. This scenario is discussed in more detail in **2.3**.

A hedge of a net investment in a foreign operation is different because it is a hedge of the foreign currency exposure, not a fair value hedge of the change in the value of the investment. Hedges of net investments in foreign operations are dealt with in **2.3**.

4 Hedging instruments

A hedging instrument is a designated derivative or, for a hedge of the risk of changes in foreign currency exchange rates, a designated non-derivative financial asset or non-derivative financial liability whose fair value or cash flows are expected to offset changes in the fair value or cash flows of a designated hedged item. [IAS 39:9]

Unless a derivative is a written option (see **4.5**), a derivative carried at fair value may always be designated as a hedging instrument, provided that:

(a) it meets the effectiveness requirements (see **section 5**); and

(b) the necessary documentation is in place that supports the hedging relationship (see **section 6**).

Investments in unquoted equity that are carried at cost (because their fair value cannot be reliably measured) and derivatives that are linked to and must be settled by delivery of such an unquoted equity instrument, cannot be designated as hedging instruments. [IAS 39:AG96] This is because a hedging instrument is defined as a designated financial instrument whose fair value or cash flows are expected to offset changes in the fair value or cash flows of a designated hedged item. If an instrument is carried at cost because it is not possible to measure it reliably, there can be no expectation that changes in its fair value or cash flows will offset those of the hedged itcm.

Any derivative, other than one that is linked to and will result in the delivery of an unquoted equity investment, is considered to be measurable with sufficient reliability. Therefore, an entity may designate any derivative as a hedging instrument, assuming all other qualifying criteria are met, even though the derivative's valuation may use a significant amount of unobservable data. However, significant judgement will need to be exercised in these circumstances when assessing hedge effectiveness, determining the gain/loss attributed to the hedged risk for the hedged item in a fair value hedge (pursuant to IAS 39:89(b)), and for cash flow hedges determining the cumulative change in fair value of the expected future cash flows on the hedged item from inception of the hedge.

A derivative may only be designated as an effective hedging instrument if it is a derivative in the scope of IAS 39. The term 'derivative' does not extend to other types of derivatives that are scoped out of IAS 39. For example, a derivative over own equity that meets the definition of equity in accordance with IAS 32 also meets the definition of a derivative in IAS 39 because it has an underlying, it requires a small initial net investment, and it is settled at a future date. However, such a derivative is an equity instrument recognised and measured in accordance with IAS 32 and cannot therefore be designated as a hedging instrument.

The basic application of the rules surrounding qualifying hedging instruments is covered in the remainder of this section, with more complex issues dealt with in **section 3** of **chapter C10**.

4.1 Hedging with non-derivatives

A non-derivative financial instrument may only be designated as a hedging instrument when hedging foreign currency risk. [IAS 39:72] An entity can use foreign currency denominated loans, deposits and other non-derivative financial instruments as hedging instruments. A common example of a non-derivative financial instrument used as a hedging instrument is a foreign currency denominated debt liability used in a hedge of a net investment in a foreign operation (see **2.3.1**).

Example 4.1A

Hedging a financial asset with a non-derivative

Entity J, whose functional currency is Sterling, has issued US$5 million 5-year fixed rate debt. It also acquired a US$5 million 5-year fixed rate bond which it has classified as AFS in accordance with IAS 39.

Entity J cannot designate its US dollar liability as a hedging instrument in a fair value hedge of the entire fair value exposure of its US dollar bond because a non-derivative may only be used as a hedging instrument of foreign currency risk.

Entity J could consider the use of the fair value option (see **3.1.1** in **chapter C2**) at initial recognition of the loan and liability. By designating both items as at FVTPL, this designation would result in substantial offset of gains and losses in profit or loss and, unlike treating the asset as AFS and the liability at amortised cost, it will result in no or little volatility in equity.

If Entity J does not apply the fair value option, it could designate the US$ liability as a hedge of the foreign currency component of the bond (as either a fair value or cash flow hedge), but hedge accounting will not provide any advantage over not applying hedge accounting at all; the foreign currency gains and losses on both the monetary asset and monetary liability are already recognised in profit or loss in the period, in accordance with IAS 21 (i.e. there is already a natural offset of foreign currency risk in profit or loss).

It should be noted that this natural offset would not apply if the hedged item was a non-monetary financial instrument, such as an equity security held as AFS. This is because the foreign exchange gains and losses on an equity security that is recognised at fair value would be recognised in other comprehensive income, and foreign exchange gains and losses from reporting the monetary financial liability would be recognised in profit or loss under IAS 21. An entity could therefore attempt to apply either fair value or cash flow hedge accounting to achieve offset in profit or loss or other comprehensive income respectively, but variations in the US$ fair value of the equity security could result in significant ineffectiveness because the foreign currency component of the shares is derived from the fair value of the shares in local currency, being US dollar.

Example 4.1B

Hedging a firm commitment with a non-derivative

Entity X's functional currency is the Euro. It has issued a US$5 million fixed rate debt instrument that matures in two years, with semi-annual interest payments. Entity X has also entered into a US$5 million fixed price sale commitment of a non-financial item that matures in two years and is not accounted for as a derivative because it meets the exemption as a contract that is entered into and continues to be held for the purpose of the delivery of a non-financial item in accordance with the entity's expected sale requirements.

Entity X cannot designate its US dollar liability in a fair value hedge of the entire fair value exposure of its fixed price sale commitment because a non-derivative liability can only be used in a hedge of a foreign currency risk.

However, Entity X can designate its US dollar liability in a fair value or a cash flow hedge of the foreign currency risk of its fixed price sale commitment.

Note that Entity X cannot designate the fixed price sale commitment as the hedging instrument instead of the hedged item because only a derivative or non-derivative financial instrument can be designated as a hedging instrument in a hedge of a foreign currency risk. The fixed price sale commitment in this case is neither because it is scoped out of IAS 39.

If the foreign currency component of the sale commitment was separated as an embedded derivative that was not considered to be closely related to the sale contract, the embedded derivative could be designated as a hedging instrument of the foreign currency risk of the fixed rate debt instrument. However, applying hedge accounting would not provide the entity with any presentation benefit as both the foreign currency risk on the debt and the embedded derivative hedging instrument would be recognised in profit or loss.

A detailed illustration of a fair value hedge of foreign currency risk on a firm commitment, using a foreign currency denominated deposit is included at **2.2** in **chapter C11**.

A financial asset that is classified as HTM may be designated as a hedging instrument in a hedge of foreign currency risk.

4.2 Splitting a derivative

A hedging relationship must be designated for a hedging instrument in its entirety. This is because there is usually only one fair value for a hedging instrument, and the factors contributing to that fair value are interdependent. Two exceptions to designating a hedging instrument in its entirety are:

[IAS 39:74]

(i) the intrinsic and time value of an option may be separated, with only the intrinsic element designated as the hedging instrument; and

(ii) the interest and spot elements of a forward contract may be separated, with only the spot element designated as the hedging instrument.

In both of these situations, the element of the derivative that is not designated as a hedging instrument (i.e. the time value of an option, or the interest element of a forward contract) will be fair valued through profit or loss.

The above exceptions are permitted because the intrinsic value of an option and the spot element of a forward contract can usually be measured separately. However, the principle of reliable separate measurement cannot be extended. Even if it can be demonstrated that a reliable measure of an element of a derivative can be determined, it cannot be excluded from the hedge designation except if it is one of the two exceptions described above.

As part of a hedge relationship, an entity can choose to designate only a proportion of the derivative as the hedging instrument (e.g. 50 per cent of the notional), and then apply one of the exceptions as described above should it wish to. Designation of proportions of hedging instruments is discussed in **4.3**.

Example 4.2

Fair value hedging with a purchased put option

Entity A has an investment in shares of Entity Y, which it has classified as AFS in accordance with IAS 39. To protect itself against a decrease in the share price, it purchases a put option over those shares. Entity A designates the intrinsic value of the put option as a hedging instrument in a fair value hedge of the Entity Y shares.

The put option has a strike price of CU50 per share – i.e. it allows Entity A to sell the shares at CU50. When Entity A purchased the put option, Entity Y shares were trading at CU55 per share. The put option will be fully effective in offsetting any price decrease below CU50 because Entity A designated only the intrinsic value as a hedging instrument. Any change in price above CU50 is not hedged.

Changes in the fair value of Entity Y shares are recognised in other comprehensive income. To the extent that the shares are hedged, changes in the fair value attributable to the hedged risk are recognised in profit or loss and offset with the gains and losses on the hedging instrument (i.e. the gains or losses on the hedged item below CU50 will be recognised in profit or loss and offset with the gains or losses on hedging instrument). Changes in the fair value of the option that relate to time value will be recognised in profit or loss.

4.3 Designation of portions and proportions of hedging instruments

A proportion of the entire hedging instrument may be designated as the hedging instrument in a hedge relationship. [IAS 39:75]

Example 4.3A

Designating part of a derivative: proportion

Entity A has a pay-fixed, receive-variable interest rate swap that it wishes to designate as hedging its issued variable rate debt. The notional on the swap is CU100 million and the notional on the debt is CU60 million. Entity A may designate CU60 million of the swap (i.e. 60 per cent) as the hedging instrument of the variable rate debt. The remaining CU40 million (i.e. 40 per cent) of the notional of the swap will be measured at FVTPL, unless it is designated as a hedging instrument in another hedge relationship.

A hedging relationship may not be designated for only a portion of the time period that the hedging instrument is outstanding. [IAS 39:75] This restriction is clarified in IAS 39:IG.F.2.17 which indicates that a portion of cash flows of a hedging instrument that is not a fully proportionate part of all cash flows of a financial instrument cannot be designated as a hedging instrument. For example, the cash flows during the first three years of a 10-year borrowing denominated in a foreign currency cannot qualify as a hedging instrument in a cash flow hedge of the first three years of revenue in the same foreign currency. This compares with partial-term hedging where it is permitted to designate all or a fully proportionate part of all cash flows of a hedging instrument in hedging only a portion of the time period to maturity of a hedged item (see **2.2** in **chapter C10**).

Example 4.3B

Designating part of a derivative: portion

Entity A has a pay-fixed, receive-variable interest rate swap that it wishes to designate as hedging its issued variable rate debt. The swap has a 10-year term and the debt has a 7-year term. Entity A cannot designate seven of the ten years of the swap as the hedging instrument.

Note that the converse can be applied because IAS 39 permits partial term hedging. If, in the above example, the terms of the debt and the swap were reversed, it would be possible to hedge the debt for the first seven years of its term. Partial term hedges are discussed further in **2.2** in **chapter C10**.

The inability to designate a hedging instrument for only a portion of the time period that the hedging instrument remains outstanding is an extension of the rule that does not allow derivatives to be split. It is not permitted to designate part of a derivative that is not a proportion of the derivative as a whole, unless the part of the derivative excluded from the hedge relationship is the time value of an option or forward points of a forward contract as discussed in **4.2**.

This should not be confused with designating a hedging instrument for only part of its life if, for that part of its life, it is expected to be a highly effective hedge. For example, it is possible to hedge a 10-year debt instrument using a 10-year interest rate swap, but apply hedge accounting for only one year. Hedge accounting is permitted, assuming the relationship is highly effective, for as long as the designation is applied.

4.4 Hedging more than one risk

A hedging instrument is often designated as hedging one risk only.

However, a hedging instrument can be designated as hedging more than one risk provided that:

[IAS 39:76]

(i) the risks being hedged can be clearly identified;

(ii) the effectiveness of the hedge can be demonstrated; and

(iii) it is possible to ensure that there is specific designation of the hedging instrument and different risk positions.

If a single hedging instrument is hedging more than one risk, and each risk is being hedged using a different form of hedge accounting (e.g. one as a fair value hedge and one as a cash flow hedge), separate disclosures will be needed for each.

Hedging risks in multiple hedged items using a single hedging instrument and hedging with more than one derivative are dealt with in **3.1** and **3.2** in **chapter C10** respectively.

4.4.1 Hedging more than one risk in a single hedged item

IAS 39 allows the use of one instrument to hedge more than one risk. Cross-currency interest rate swaps are commonly used to swap foreign currency floating rate debt into functional currency fixed rate debt, or to swap foreign currency fixed rate debt into functional currency floating rate debt.

If a single derivative hedging instrument is used to hedge multiple risks in a single hedged item or in multiple hedged items and the risks are hedged using different types of hedge accounting (e.g. cash flow hedging, fair value hedging or net investment hedging), the entity will need to isolate the derivative's fair value relating to each type of hedge. In such cases the guidance on hedging multiple hedged items detailed in **3.1.1** in **chapter C10** should be applied.

Example 4.4.1

Hedging both interest rate and foreign currency risk

Entity A, a Sterling functional currency entity, issues floating US dollar debt. To hedge its exposure to foreign currency exchange rates and to interest rate risk, it enters into a cross-currency interest rate swap. The terms of the swap match those of the debt. Under the swap, Entity A receives floating US dollars and pays fixed Sterling. IAS 39 allows the swap to be designated as a cash flow hedge of both US dollar interest rate risk and US$:£ foreign currency risk designated in a single hedge relationship, or a cash flow hedge of US dollar interest rate risk and a fair value hedge of the US$:£ foreign currency risk as two separate hedge relationships. The former designation is preferable to the latter because the entity incorporates two risks in a single cash flow hedge and, therefore, does not need to separate notionally the derivative instrument across multiple hedge relationships.

The latter designation requires notional separation of the derivative across two hedge relationships:

(i) hedge of cash flow variability due to US dollar interest rates in foreign currency terms (being receive US$ floating, pay US$ fixed); and

(ii) a hedge of the foreign currency risk into the entity's functional currency (being receive US$ fixed, pay £ fixed).

The foreign currency hedge may prove more complex because the hedged item does not have fixed US dollar cash flows.

Similarly, Entity A could have issued fixed US dollar debt, and used a cross-currency interest rate swap to convert the position into floating Sterling debt. IAS 39 would permit the entity to designate the swap as a fair value hedge of both the interest rate and foreign currency risk designated as a single hedge relationship, or a fair value hedge of US dollar interest rate risk and a cash flow hedge of the US$:£ foreign currency risk as two separate hedge relationships. The former designation is preferable to the latter because the entity incorporates two risks in a single fair value hedge and, therefore, does not need to separate notionally the derivative instrument across multiple hedge relationships.

The latter designation would require notional separation of the derivative across two hedge relationships:

(i) a fair value hedge of US$ interest rate risk (being receive US$ fixed, pay US$ floating); and

(ii) a cash flow hedge of the foreign currency risk into the entity's functional currency (being receive US$ floating, pay £ floating).

The foreign currency hedge may prove more complex because the hedged item does not have floating US dollar cash flows.

Assuming that all other hedge accounting criteria are met, it is possible to use a single derivative to hedge both foreign currency and interest rate risks if both risks are evident in the hedged item.

4.5 Written options

IAS 39 does not allow a written option to be designated as a hedging instrument unless it is designated as an offset to a purchased option (including one that is embedded in another financial instrument). The written option is not effective in reducing the profit or loss exposure of a hedged item because the potential loss on an option that an entity writes could be significantly greater than the potential gain in value of a related hedged item. [IAS 39:AG94] An instrument containing multiple options (written and purchased) may qualify as a hedging instrument provided it is not a net written option (see **3.3** in **chapter C10** for further detail).

4.6 Purchased options

Unlike written options, a purchased option may be designated as a hedging instrument, provided that all the other criteria for hedge accounting are met. This is because a purchased option has a potential gain equal to or greater than the loss on a hedged item and, therefore, has the potential to reduce profit or loss exposure from changes in fair values or cash flows. [IAS 39:AG94]

Example 4.6

Hedging an available-for-sale asset with a purchased put

Entity Z owns 1,000 shares of Entity C which are publicly traded, and has classified the shares as an AFS asset in accordance with IAS 39. At 1 January 20X0, these shares are trading at CU50 per share and Entity Z has an unrealised gain of CU25,000 accumulated in equity. Entity Z would like to lock in the unrealised gain and purchases a put option on Entity C's shares from Entity A for CU9,000. The purchased put option allows Entity Z to put the 1,000 shares to Entity A at CU50 per share on 31 December 20X2. Subject to the other hedge accounting criteria being met, the purchased put option may be designated as a hedge of the exposure to the decline in the fair value of the investment in Entity C's shares below CU50 per share.

In order to demonstrate that the hedge will be highly effective, Entity Z designates just the intrinsic value of the purchased put option as a hedging instrument so that when the fair value of the shares falls below CU50 the option will be fully effective. When the share price rises above CU50 per share, the put option is out of the money and has no intrinsic value. Accordingly, gains and losses on the 1,000 shares in Entity C above CU50 are not attributable to the hedged risk for the purposes of assessing hedge effectiveness and recognising gains and losses on the hedged item.

Entity Z reports a change in the fair value of the shares in other comprehensive income if it is associated with the price increases above CU50. [IAS 39:55 & 90] Changes in the fair value of the shares associated with price decreases below CU50 form part of the designated fair value hedge and are recognised in profit or loss under IAS 39:89(b). Assuming the hedge is effective, those changes are offset by changes in the intrinsic value of the put option, which are also recognised in profit or loss. [IAS 39:89(a)] Changes in the time value of the put option are excluded from the designated hedge relationship and recognised in profit or loss under IAS 39:55(a). Changes in the intrinsic value of the put option provide protection against the changes in the fair value of the investment in Entity C's shares below CU50 per share. [IAS 39:IG.F.1.10]

A detailed illustration of a cash flow hedge of interest rate risk on variable rate debt, using a purchased interest rate cap, is included in **3.6** of **chapter C11**.

5 Hedge effectiveness

IAS 39 requires a hedge to be 'highly effective', prospectively and retrospectively, for it to qualify for hedge accounting. [IAS 39:88] Highly effective refers to the degree to which the hedge relationship is assessed as having a high level of hedge effectiveness. If hedge accounting is applied in the period, any ineffectiveness is required to be measured and recognised immediately in profit or loss.

Hedge effectiveness assessment is different from hedge effectiveness measurement. An entity is required to *assess prospectively* whether it believes that a hedge relationship will be highly effective. This assessment forms part of the hedge documentation that an entity needs to complete in order to justify the use of hedge accounting. The prospective assessment is forward-looking. An entity is required to *assess retrospectively* whether in any particular period the hedge relationship was highly effective. This retrospective assessment determines whether an entity can apply hedge accounting in the period, i.e. it looks back to establish how well the hedge has performed. If an entity has passed the retrospective assessment it will reflect hedge accounting in its financial statements and recognise any hedge ineffectiveness. Determining the amount of hedge ineffectiveness involves measurement and recognition of hedge ineffectiveness in profit or loss.

5.1 Assessment of hedge effectiveness

The Standard does not prescribe a specific method for assessing hedge effectiveness. [IAS 39:AG107] However, it requires an entity to specify at inception of the hedge relationship the method it will apply to assess hedge effectiveness, and to apply that method consistently for the duration of the hedging relationship. The method specified must be consistent with management's risk management strategy and objective. A method of assessing hedge effectiveness must be applied consistently to all similar hedges unless different methods are explicitly justified. [IAS 39:IG.F.4.4]

Several mathematical techniques can be used to assess hedge effectiveness, including ratio analysis and various statistical methods like regression analysis. The appropriateness of a given method will depend on the nature of the risk being hedged and the type of hedging instrument used.

5.1.1 The 'highly effective' criterion

IAS 39:AG105 specifies that a hedge is regarded as highly effective only if both of the following conditions are met:

(a) at the inception of the hedge, and in subsequent periods, the hedge is expected to be highly effective in achieving offsetting changes in fair value or cash flows attributable to the hedged risk during the period for which the hedge is designated. Such an expectation can be demonstrated in various ways, including a comparison of past changes in the fair value or cash flows of the hedged item that are attributable to the hedged risk with past changes in the fair value or cash flows of the hedging instrument ('ratio analysis' or the 'dollar offset method' – see **5.1.8.1**), or by demonstrating a high statistical correlation between the fair value or cash flows of the hedged item and those of the hedging instrument (for example 'regression analysis' – see **5.1.8.2**). The entity may choose a hedge ratio of other than one to one in order to improve the effectiveness of the hedge (see **4.3.2** in **chapter C10**); and

(b) the actual results of the hedge are within a range of 80-125 per cent.

When actual results are within a range of 80-125 per cent, but not 100 per cent exactly, any deviation from 100 per cent means that the hedge relationship is partly ineffective and ineffectiveness must be recognised in profit or loss.

Hedge ineffectiveness arises in a fair value hedge when the change in the fair value of the hedging instrument differs from that of the hedged risk of the hedged item. Because changes in the fair value of the hedging instrument are recognised in profit or loss so as to offset changes in the fair value due to the hedged risk on the hedged item, all hedge ineffectiveness is automatically recognised in profit or loss in the period. Hedge ineffectiveness is recognised in profit or loss for both under- and over-hedges, i.e. ineffectiveness is recognised when the fair value of the hedging instrument changes, either to a lesser or greater extent respectively when compared to the changes in the fair value of the hedged item.

In a cash flow hedge, the portion of the hedging instrument that is considered to be effective (and, therefore, is recognised in other comprehensive income) is the lesser of:

[IAS 39:96]

(i) the cumulative gain or loss on the hedging instrument from inception of the hedge; and

(ii) the cumulative change in fair value (present value) of the expected future cash flows on the hedged item from inception of the hedge.

In an over-hedge, when the change in fair value of the hedging instrument is greater than the change in fair value of the expected future cash flows on the hedged item, the difference is recognised in profit or loss as hedge ineffectiveness. However, when the change in the fair value of the hedging instrument is less than the change in the fair value of expected future cash flows on the hedged item, the entire change in the fair value of the hedging instrument is recognised in other comprehensive income, i.e. no ineffectiveness arises in an under-hedge unless the hedge is determined no longer to be highly effective.

5.1.1.1 Assessment on cumulative basis

IAS 39 permits the assessment of hedge effectiveness either on a period-by-period basis or cumulatively over the life of the hedging relationship, provided that the approach to be taken is documented formally at inception of the hedge relationship. [IAS 39:IG.F.4.2]

If hedge effectiveness is assessed on a cumulative basis and the hedge is not expected to be highly effective in a particular period, hedge accounting is not precluded if effectiveness is expected to remain sufficiently high over the life of the hedging relationship. The entity is still required to recognise any ineffectiveness in profit or loss as it occurs.

Example 5.1.1.1

Assessment on cumulative basis

Entity S designates a LIBOR-based interest rate swap that resets every 3 months as a hedge of its LIBOR-based borrowing which carries interest at LIBOR plus a credit spread, where LIBOR resets every 6 months. Entity S documents that it will assess hedge effectiveness on a cumulative basis. Over the life of the hedge relationship, the hedge is expected to be almost perfect. However, there will be periods when the variability in cash flows on the borrowing is not perfectly offset by the variability in the interest rate swap.

Entity S is required to recognise any ineffectiveness in profit or loss as it arises. Because it assesses hedge effectiveness on a cumulative basis, Entity S will be able to hedge account for this relationship provided hedge effectiveness is expected to remain sufficiently high over the remainder of the life of the hedge.

5.1.1.2 Effectiveness outside the 80 - 125 per cent range

Effectiveness outside the range of 80 - 125 per cent at any measurement period may preclude hedge accounting not only in the period but also for future periods if it is an indication of further expected ineffectiveness.

A hedge relationship must be discontinued for the period in which the hedge fails to meet the effectiveness criteria. [IAS 39:88] IAS 39:IG.F.6.2 issue (i) states that "if there is a hedge effectiveness failure, the ineffective portion of the gain or loss on the derivative instrument is recognised immediately in profit or loss and hedge accounting based on the previous designation of the hedge relationship cannot be continued. In this case, the derivative instrument may be redesignated prospectively as a hedging instrument in a new hedging relationship provided this hedging relationship satisfies the necessary conditions". Generally, hedge accounting will be discontinued from the previous effectiveness testing date, though when it is possible to identify the event that caused the hedging relationship to fail the effectiveness test and to demonstrate that the hedge was effective before the event occurred, hedge accounting will be discontinued from the date the event occurred. [IAS 39:AG 113]

When hedge effectiveness is outside the 80 - 125 per cent range, hedge accounting in subsequent periods would only be appropriate if a strong historical relationship exists and there is an expectation that the hedge will be highly effective in future periods. The same hedge relationship can be redesignated for hedge accounting prospectively provided that the entity can demonstrate that the new hedge relationship is expected to be highly effective in the future. An entity may wish to change the hedge ratio of the existing hedged item and hedging instrument, designate a new hedging instrument, or utilise the hedging instrument in hedging a different hedged item in order to improve effectiveness.

Where a hedge is redesignated after an effectiveness failure, the previous hedge relationship is considered to be extinguished and a new hedge relationship created. Accordingly, subsequent retrospective effectiveness testing will only assess hedge effectiveness from the date of the new hedge designation and will not be tainted by the poor historical performance. Prospective tests will, nevertheless, be affected where the entity's chosen method of prospective effectiveness testing incorporates historical performance data.

5.1.2 Principal terms of the hedged item and hedging instrument match

If the principal terms of the hedged item and the hedging instrument match, then there is likely to be a high degree of offset between the hedged item and the hedging instrument. The principal terms of a hedged item and a hedging instrument will include: the notional and principal, the maturity, and the underlying. Different hedge relationships will have different principal terms.

For fair value hedges of investments in equity securities, if the underlying of the derivative equals that of the equity security and the derivative has a fair value of zero, there will be an expectation of a high degree of offset in their fair values.

For hedges of interest rate risk there is a greater number of principal terms to consider, in particular depending on whether:

- the notional amount of the derivative matches the principal amount of the interest-bearing asset or liability;
- for cash flow hedges, repricing dates and interest rate indices match;
- the derivative is on-market at inception and, therefore, has a fair value of zero;
- the formula for computing net settlements under the interest rate swap is the same for each net settlement (i.e. the fixed rate is the same throughout the term, and the variable rate is based on the same index and includes either the same constant adjustment or no adjustment, say, for credit spread); and
- if the hedged item has prepayment features, these features are also reflected in the derivative.

For hedges of firm commitments, the principal terms will depend on which risk is being hedged. If the foreign currency risk of a firm commitment is being hedged then the principal terms will include the maturities of the commitment and the derivative, the underlying (i.e. the foreign currency), and the notional of each. When an entity is hedging all the fair value of a firm commitment, the underlying will reflect the exact quality, grade, type, if the underlying is a non-financial item, or exact index, timing of cash flows, if the underlying is a financial item.

Similarly, for cash flow hedges of forecast transactions, the maturity of the hedging instrument is compared to the period when the designated forecast transactions are expected to affect profit or loss. Other principal terms that need to be considered are similar to those described above for hedges of firm commitments. In addition, when a forward contract is designated as a hedging instrument, for the terms to match, either the change in the discount or premium on the forward contract needs to be excluded from the assessment of effectiveness and recognised in profit or loss, or the change in expected cash flows on the highly probable forecast transaction needs to be based on the forward price for the non-financial item.

Even when the principal terms of the hedging instrument and of the entire hedged asset or liability or hedged forecast transaction are the same, an entity cannot assume hedge effectiveness without subsequent effectiveness testing because significant hedge ineffectiveness may arise from other sources, for example, as a result of changes in the liquidity of the hedging instruments or their credit risk. [IAS 39:IG.F.4.7]

Example 5.1.2A

Matched terms: hedge effectiveness not assumed

Entity X enters into a firm commitment to buy 10,000 ounces of gold at the current six-month forward rate of US$310. This contract is not recognised as a financial instrument because it is a purchase for own use requirements contract in accordance with IAS 39:5. On the same day, Entity X enters into a cash settled forward contract to sell 10,000 ounces of gold at the current six-month forward rate of US$310 which is designated as a fair value hedge of all risks with respect to the firm commitment to purchase gold. Hedge effectiveness will be measured based on changes in the six-month forward price of gold.

Because the principal terms of the firm commitment and the forward contract match (quantity of gold, contract maturity, forward rate) Entity X may conclude that the changes in the fair value of the firm commitment are expected to offset the change in the fair value of the derivative. However, ineffectiveness must still be assessed, at a minimum, at the end of each reporting period.

Example 5.1.2B

Matched terms: fair value derived from net settlements

If the form of an interest rate swap is such that the variable leg is adjusted for a fixed spread (e.g. LIBOR + 150 basis points), the adjustment can be considered as an adjustment of the fixed leg of the swap.

For example, for a fair value hedge of a 7 per cent fixed rate issued debt where the credit spread at issue was 1 per cent, the hedged risk, being the LIBOR portion, would be equivalent to 6 per cent. If the terms of the derivative were receive 7.5 per cent, pay LIBOR + 150 basis points, the terms of the swap would not invalidate a conclusion of minimal ineffectiveness as the swap's fair value is derived from its net settlements, and the net receive leg is equivalent to 6 per cent, being the hedged risk.

If the principal terms of the hedging instrument and the hedged item do not match, an entity will be subject to a larger degree of hedge ineffectiveness. For example, if, at inception of a cash flow hedge, the fair value of the swap is not zero (i.e. it is off-market) there will be ineffectiveness due to the interest rate risk on an up-front payment or receipt. For example, when an entity enters into an interest rate swap that has been structured to be significantly in the money at inception, the price paid to purchase the interest rate swap will be reimbursed to the buyer via a higher receive leg, or a lower pay leg. The up-front payment of cash by the buyer of the swap is like financing and, therefore, any costs or income with respect to the financing will result in hedge ineffectiveness.

5.1.3 Minimising ineffectiveness

To improve hedge effectiveness, an entity can elect to designate only certain risks inherent in a hedged item as being hedged. The ability to hedge portions of cash flows or fair value generally applies to hedges of financial items only. The ability to designate only certain risks in non-financial items is limited and is discussed in **3.9**. 'Hedging portions' (i.e. designating an identifiable and separable portion of the risk on the financial asset or liability as the hedged item) can result in a higher degree of effectiveness because the designated risk is a specifically identifiable risk inherent in the hedged item. Designating portions is discussed in greater detail in **3.8** and in **2.1** in **chapter C10**.

Example 5.1.3

Hedging the LIBOR swap rate

Entity A enters into a receive-fixed, pay-variable LIBOR interest rate swap and designates the swap as a fair value hedge of its issued fixed rate debt. Because the interest rate index in the hedging instrument is LIBOR, and the LIBOR rate reflects the credit quality of AA financial institutions, even though Entity A is not an AA-rated entity, it may designate the portion of risk inherent in its issued debt equivalent to this rate, i.e. hedge the LIBOR swap rate only. Entity A designates the risk of fair value movements in respect of the LIBOR swap rate on its issued fixed rate debt. By hedging just this portion of risk, Entity A has excluded from the designation fair value movements of the debt due to movements in its own credit quality.

It should be noted that if Entity A is charged an additional spread on the interest rate swap by the counterparty because Entity A's credit quality relative to the counterparty is poor, this may affect hedge effectiveness. The spread on the derivative will be relatively small when compared to the credit spread charged on the cash instrument, i.e. the debt. The entity will need to monitor the impact of the credit spread of the interest rate swap as part of its assessment of hedge effectiveness.

There are various ways to minimise hedge ineffectiveness. The following sections in **chapter C10** provide further guidance:

- **4.3.1** designating a cash flow hedge in layers;
- **4.3.2** hedging with a ratio other than one to one;
- **4.3.3** hedging on an after tax basis;
- **4.3.4** excluding forward points from forward contracts; and
- **4.3.5** excluding time value from options.

5.1.4 Embedded call, prepayment or termination features

Any derivative feature embedded in the hedged item or features embedded in the hedging instrument will have some impact on the changes in the fair value of these instruments. Differences in terms between the hedged item and hedging instrument will lead to differences in changes in fair value of the respective instruments. A termination, cancellation, call or prepayment feature embedded in the hedged item which is not replicated in the hedging instrument may result in a hedge relationship failing to qualify for hedge accounting.

Example 5.1.4A

Hedging callable issued debt

Entity X issues 10-year fixed rate debt that is callable at the end of the sixth year. It decides to convert the interest payments on the bond from fixed rate to floating rate by entering into a 10-year receive-fixed, pay-floating interest rate swap. The interest rate swap is not cancellable at the end of Year six. Entity X would like to designate the swap as the hedging instrument in a fair value hedge of the interest rate risk only on the fixed rate debt.

The call feature may impede designation of the hedging relationship, particularly if it is probable that during the first six years of the debt it will be in the money. The assessment of whether it will be in the money can be based on a probability-weighted analysis of possible future changes in interest rates. Even if the option is unlikely to be exercised, the fact that there is a possibility of exercise (i.e. time value) will affect the debt's sensitivity to changes in interest rates.

If, during the first six years, interest rates decrease, the gain on the swap will be greater than the loss on the debt because the fair value of the debt will take into consideration the call feature, which will be in the money when interest rates fall below the rate on the debt. Economically, the debt will behave more like 6-year term debt than 10-year term debt. Consequently, the changes in fair value of the debt due to movements in interest rates and the interest rate swap are unlikely to fully offset, potentially resulting in the prospective or retrospective hedge effectiveness tests being failed.

Example 5.1.4B

Hedging puttable issued debt

Entity C has a fixed rate commercial loan maturing in five years. The borrower can prepay the loan without penalty after Year 2.

If Entity C wants to hedge the fair value of the loan due to changes in interest rate risk, it must consider the effect on fair value of the embedded option (a prepayment option forms a sub-component of the overall interest rate risk). A five-year receive-variable, pay-fixed swap might or might not be sufficiently effective to qualify as a hedging instrument. A swap cancellable at Entity C's option after Year 2 with the same terms as the prepayment feature in the loan would be a more effective hedging instrument because it hedges all of the interest rate risk, including the embedded prepayment option.

5.1.5 Credit risk

Changes in credit risk affect the fair value of financial instruments. Because derivative financial instruments are always fair valued, credit risk will directly affect the fair valuation of the instrument and, therefore, will affect hedge effectiveness assessments.

5.1.5.1 Counterparty credit risk

The effect of counterparty credit risk on hedge effectiveness cannot be disregarded. An entity must consider the counterparty's creditworthiness (and changes therein) in assessing hedge effectiveness. [IAS 39:IG.F.4.3] In addition, IAS 39:AG109 states that a hedge of interest rate risk using a derivative would not be fully effective if part of the change in the fair value of the derivative is attributable to the counterparty's credit risk. IAS 39:IG.F.4.7 goes further and states that an entity "cannot assume hedge effectiveness even if the principal terms of the hedging instrument and the hedged item are the same, since hedge ineffectiveness may arise because of other attributes such as the liquidity of the instruments or their credit risk".

Example 5.1.5.1

Cash flow hedge ineffectiveness

[Extract from IAS 39:IG.F.5.2]

Entity A has a floating rate liability of CU1,000 with five years remaining to maturity. It enters into a five-year pay-fixed, receive-floating interest rate swap in the same currency and with the same principal terms as the liability to hedge the exposure to variable cash flow payments on the floating rate liability attributable to interest rate risk. At inception, the fair value of the swap is zero. Subsequently, there is an increase of CU49 in the fair value of the swap. This increase consists of a change of CU50 resulting from an increase in market interest rates and a change of minus CU1 resulting from an increase in the credit risk of the swap counterparty. There is no change in the fair value of the floating rate liability, but the fair value (present value) of the future cash flows needed to offset the exposure to variable interest cash flows on the liability increases by CU50. Assuming that Entity A determines that the hedge is still highly effective, is there ineffectiveness that should be recognised in profit or loss?

No. A hedge of interest rate risk is not fully effective if part of the change in the fair value of the derivative is attributable to the counterparty's credit risk (IAS 39:AG109). However, because Entity A determines that the hedge relationship is still highly effective, it recognises the effective portion of the change in fair value of the swap, i.e. the net change in fair value of CU49, in other comprehensive income. There is no debit to profit or loss for the change in fair value of the swap attributable to the deterioration in the credit quality of the swap counterparty, because the cumulative change in the present value of the future cash flows needed to offset the exposure to variable interest cash flows on the hedged item, i.e. CU50, exceeds the cumulative change in value of the hedging instrument, i.e. CU49.

Dr	Swap	CU49
Cr	Other comprehensive income	CU49

If Entity A concludes that the hedge is no longer highly effective, it discontinues hedge accounting prospectively as from the date the hedge ceased to be highly effective in accordance with IAS 39:101.

Would the answer change if the fair value of the swap instead increases to CU51 of which CU50 results from the increase in market interest rates and CU1 from a decrease in the credit risk of the swap counterparty?

Yes. In this case, there is a credit to profit or loss of CU1 for the change in fair value of the swap attributable to the improvement in the credit quality of the swap counterparty. This is because the cumulative change in the value of the hedging instrument, i.e. CU51, exceeds the cumulative change in the present value of the future cash flows needed to offset the exposure to variable interest cash flows on the hedged item, i.e. CU50. The difference of CU1 represents the excess ineffectiveness attributable to the derivative hedging instrument, the swap, and is recognised in profit or loss.

Dr	Swap	CU51
Cr	Other comprehensive income	CU50
Cr	Profit or loss	CU1

For a cash flow hedge, if it becomes probable that a counterparty will default, an entity will be unable to conclude that the hedge is expected to be highly effective in achieving offsetting cash flows. As a consequence, hedge accounting should be discontinued.

A change in the creditworthiness of the counterparty to the derivative in a fair value hedge would have an immediate impact on the assessment of whether the hedge relationship is effective and qualifies for hedge accounting because the fair value of the hedging derivative will change and will result in immediate recognition of ineffectiveness in profit or loss.

The impact of changes in credit risk on the fair value of a derivative hedging instrument and the resulting impact on hedge effectiveness are easier to understand for fair value hedges than for cash flow hedges. For fair value hedges, the derivative hedging instrument will always be measured at FVTPL and, to the extent the hedge relationship is highly effective, there will be either a full or partial offset in profit or loss with the change in fair value of the hedged risk of the hedged item. The fair value hedge adjustment to the hedged item that is reflected in profit or loss is independent of the change in fair value of the hedging instrument and, therefore, does not reflect the changes in credit risk reflected in the derivative's fair value. The existence of changes in the derivative's fair value due to changes in credit risk, whether counterparty or own credit risk, will directly affect the hedge effectiveness of the hedge relationship.

Cash flow hedges are often hedges of forecast transactions, for example, the foreign currency risk of forecast sales or purchases, or the interest rate risk of variable interest cash flows on floating rate debt. Similar to fair value hedges described above, the hedged item does not incorporate movements in the credit risk of the derivative hedging instrument. The credit risk of the derivative hedging instrument is entirely independent of the change in cash flows of the hedged item. Therefore, when determining hedge ineffectiveness, it is not possible to infer the changes in the credit risk and its impact on the fair value of the hedging instrument onto the hedged item and assume perfect hedge effectiveness. If the fair value of the derivative changes due to changes in counterparty or own credit risk, this change will not be offset by a change in the hedged item and, therefore, hedge ineffectiveness will arise. An entity should monitor the impact of changes in credit risk for both prospective and retrospective hedge effectiveness assessment.

If an entity wished to fair value hedge the counterparty credit risk of a non-derivative asset (e.g. a loan and receivable), hedge ineffectiveness will still arise from changes in the fair value of the derivative hedging instrument. The hedged risk is the credit risk of the counterparty to the loan, but the hedging instrument includes the credit risk of the counterparty and the entity's own credit risk. The counterparty credit risk of the loan differs from the counterparty or own credit risk of the derivative hedging instrument and, therefore, ineffectiveness will arise.

5.1.5.2 Own credit risk

Changes in own credit risk (non-performance risk) will affect hedge effectiveness assessment in the same way as changes in counterparty credit risk described in **5.1.5.1**.

5.1.6 Clean versus dirty prices

'Clean' prices are prices that exclude any interest accruals. 'Dirty' prices include interest accruals.

Although the carrying values recognised in the statement of financial position are dirty prices, clean prices can be used when assessing whether a hedge is expected to be highly effective.

When a retrospective test of hedge effectiveness is performed using dirty prices for a hedge of a debt instrument with an interest rate swap, ineffectiveness will be observed if the test is performed between interest payment dates. The swap's value will include a net interest accrual being the net of the interest receivable on the receive leg and the interest payable on the pay leg. The loan's value will include a gross interest accrual. The accrued interest component of the swap's value will therefore be far smaller than that of the debt causing hedge ineffectiveness.

It is important to note that excluding accrued interest in an effectiveness test does not eliminate the ineffectiveness that can be caused by the first fixing of the swap. When an interest rate swap fixes in advance, the interest rate on the floating leg of the swap is fixed until the next reset date. Therefore, between reset dates, as market interest rates change, this fixed portion of the floating leg builds up value. The build-up of value between reset dates is not mirrored in the fair value movements of the hedged debt. This ineffectiveness is not eliminated by excluding accrued interest from the hedge effectiveness testing.

When measuring the actual results of the hedge (see **5.2**) the dirty value of the instruments must be used.

5.1.7 Frequency of hedge effectiveness assessment

Effectiveness must be assessed, at a minimum, at inception and at the end of each reporting period, including interim reporting periods. [IAS 39:AG106]

5.1.8 Ratio analysis and regression analysis

Hedge effectiveness is the degree to which changes in the fair value or cash flows of the hedged item that are attributable to a hedged risk are offset by changes in the fair value or cash flows of the hedging instrument.

A perfect hedge relationship might be illustrated as follows.

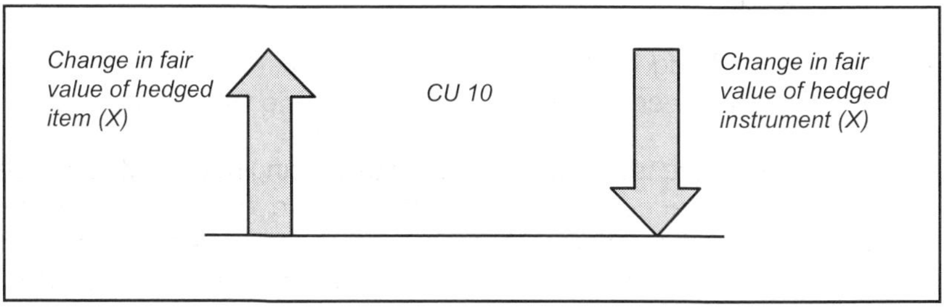

For each CU10 change in value of the hedged item, there is an equal and opposite (CU10) change in value of the hedging instrument (i.e. in this example, the hedging instrument is perfectly negatively correlated with the risk it hedges). The negative sign results from the offsetting effect between the derivative and the hedged item.

Correlation is a term that originates from probability theory and relies on statistical analysis, but it is often estimated from historical data. It is a measure of the extent to which two variables move in relation to one another. The correlation can range from perfectly negative through totally uncorrelated to perfectly positive. Quantitatively, it is expressed as a value ranging from -1 (perfectly negatively correlated) to 1 (perfectly positively correlated).

5.1.8.1 Ratio analysis

Ratio analysis establishes, as a percentage, the extent of effectiveness of the hedging instrument in offsetting the hedged item for the designated risk over a defined period of time, i.e. the degree to which the changes in fair value of the hedging instrument and the hedged item are negatively correlated. It is relatively simple to compute and is well suited for measuring the effectiveness of short term hedges (where there may be insufficient data to perform a statistical test, such as regression) and is also used to measure the level of actual offset.

5.1.8.2 Regression analysis

Regression analysis is a statistical measurement technique for determining the validity and extent of a relationship between an independent and dependent variable. It is more complex than ratio analysis and is explained in more detail in **4.6** in **chapter C10**.

5.2 Measuring hedge ineffectiveness

Section 5.1 considers the various ways in which hedge effectiveness can be assessed. These techniques are used to support the entity's claim that a hedge relationship has been highly effective in the period, and will continue to be so for future periods. Consistent application of these techniques in assessing hedge effectiveness is used to support the continued application of hedge accounting.

Measurement of hedge effectiveness relates to the actual amount of ineffectiveness that needs to be reported in the period's profit or loss.

In many instances, the techniques used for assessing hedge effectiveness (i.e. whether the hedge relationship is effective for this period and future periods) will be different from the technique used in measuring ineffectiveness for the period. The difference arises because recognition of ineffectiveness is based on actual offset. The degree of offset is more consistent with ratio analysis techniques (otherwise known as 'the dollar offset test') as opposed to statistical techniques such as regression. Equally, when clean prices are used for assessing hedge effectiveness, the measurement of the actual results of the hedge must be based on the actual performance of the derivative, i.e. it is not possible to exclude from its measurement a portion of fair value that is due to the interest accrual. This means that measurement of hedge effectiveness is always based on dirty prices.

The extent to which hedge ineffectiveness will be recognised will depend on whether the hedge is a fair value hedge, or a cash flow hedge.

5.2.1 Measurement of fair value hedge effectiveness

Once a fair value hedge has been assessed as being highly effective for the period, and there is an expectation of high effectiveness for future periods, the entity has earned the right to measure the hedged item in a manner consistent with fair value hedging, i.e. adjusting the hedged item for fair value movements in the hedged risk.

Actual measurement of hedge ineffectiveness will be recognised in profit or loss of the period because both the adjustment to the hedged item with respect to fair value movements in the hedged risk and the fair value movements on the hedging instrument are recognised in profit or loss. To the extent that these two amounts do not fully offset, the difference, being hedge ineffectiveness, will be recognised in profit or loss.

If an entity was applying a retrospective assessment of hedge effectiveness using ratio analysis (i.e. dollar offset test) using period-to-period data, then the percentage of hedge ineffectiveness derived from using this technique would be consistent with the measurement of ineffectiveness in the period.

5.2.2 Measurement of cash flow hedge effectiveness

As described in **5.1.1**, measuring the effectiveness for a cash flow hedge is different from measuring the effectiveness in a fair value hedge. With cash flow hedges, no hedge ineffectiveness is recognised in profit or loss if the cumulative gain or loss on the hedging instrument from inception of the hedge is less than the cumulative change in fair value of the expected future cash flows on the hedged item from inception of the hedge. As described in **5.1.1**, this results in hedge ineffectiveness being recognised in profit or loss only when the change in the hedging instrument's fair value exceeds the change in the present value of future cash flows on the hedged item.

If an entity was applying a retrospective assessment of hedge effectiveness using ratio analysis (i.e. dollar offset test) using cumulative data then, in the case of over-hedging, the percentage of hedge ineffectiveness derived from using this technique would be consistent with the measurement of the cumulative ineffectiveness over the life.

6 Documentation

There are several required conditions to achieving hedge accounting under IAS 39. The conditions discussed in the previous sections of this chapter have focused on what is considered to be an eligible hedged item and hedging instrument. Even if the hedge relationship is considered to be eligible for hedge accounting, sufficient documentation of the hedge relationship must be in place at inception of the hedge relationship. Until the necessary documentation is in place, an entity cannot apply hedge accounting. There can be no retrospective designation of a hedge relationship. [IAS 39:IG.F.3.8]

Example 6A

Timing of hedge documentation

Entity A issues fixed rate debt on 1 January. On the same date it enters into a receive-fixed, pay-floating interest rate swap, with all the terms of the debt and swap matching. Entity A does not complete the required documentation until 1 February.

Entity A may adopt hedge accounting from 1 February. From 1 January to 1 February, it will account for the debt and the derivative on the normal measurement basis, i.e. amortised cost for the debt and fair value for the derivative with changes in fair value recognised in profit or loss.

IAS 39 states that at the inception of the hedge there must be formal designation and documentation of:

[IAS 39:88]

- the hedging relationship; and
- the entity's risk management objective and strategy for undertaking the hedge.

That documentation should include identification of:

- the hedging instrument;
- the hedged item or transaction;
- the nature of the risk being hedged; and
- how the entity will assess the hedging instrument's effectiveness in offsetting the exposure to changes in the hedged item's fair value or cash flows attributable to the hedged risk.

Broadly, the documentation requirements fall into two categories:

- specific documentation for every hedge entered into. This will give details of the hedged item, hedged risk, hedging instrument, how effectiveness will be assessed prospectively and retrospectively, and how effectiveness will be measured retrospectively; and
- overall risk management objectives and strategies.

Example 6B

Designating foreign currency deposits as a hedging instrument

Bank B accepts US$-denominated deposits from its depositors; the US$ is not Bank B's functional currency. The deposits are time deposits with a short maturity which can be withdrawn by depositors at the end of their term. Based on historical experience, time deposits are withdrawn and replaced with new time deposits from different depositors or existing depositors roll over their deposits with the bank beyond the contractual maturity. Bank B asserts that the total deposit balance will not be less than US$100 million as a result of deposits being withdrawn and new deposits being made.

Bank B has an investment of US$150 million in a foreign operation that has a US$ functional currency.

Bank B cannot designate the 'first US$100 million' of foreign currency deposits as a hedging instrument in a hedge of Bank B's net investment in its foreign operation because the proposed hedging instrument is not specifically identifiable as is required by IAS 39:88(a). The first US$100 million of foreign currency deposits is not specifically identifiable because it consists of multiple individual financial instruments that are not specified. Further, over time, the individual financial instruments change as deposits are withdrawn and new deposits are received.

An alternative hedge designation that may be permissible is when the individual deposits are specified in the hedge relationship and hedge documentation. However, because of the short-term nature of the deposits, the hedge designation would be limited to a maximum time period equal to the shortest remaining contractual term of any of the specified individual deposit, which might be one day. Consequently, Bank B would need to frequently (possibly daily) designate and document the specified individual deposits that comprise the multiple hedging instruments.

6.1 Risk management objectives and strategies

There are no rules governing this area except that, to achieve hedge accounting, an entity must have documented its objectives and strategies. The hedge relationships that the entity wishes to apply hedge accounting to must be consistent with these stated policies. Therefore, the policies and objectives should as a minimum include a list of the risks that the entity is exposed to and how the entity intends to manage those risks.

6.2 Specific hedge documentation

Below is one example of how the specific documentation requirements for each hedge relationship could be met. It is based on the minimum that could reasonably be provided.

Example 6.2

Entity XYZ

Accounting hedge designation and assessment summary

Policy declaration

This relationship is in accordance with our Risk Management and Accounting Policies for IAS 39 [insert specific reference to policy within the policy manual]. The risk management objective and strategy for undertaking the hedge is as follows [to be inserted].

Risk identification

Nature of risk hedged

e.g. overall fair value, interest, credit, foreign currency, equity risk.

Specific hedged risk

e.g. for overall fair value, commodity price risk, for foreign currency, forward or spot rate; for interest rate risk, specific portion such as the benchmark interest rate

Hedge type

	Yes	**No**
Cash flow hedge		
Fair value hedge		
Net investment hedge		

Date of designation of hedging relationship

Indicate date of designation of the hedging relationship.

Process required for the de-designation of the hedging relationship, including date on which the hedging relationship was de-designated

Indicate process required to formally de-designate the hedging relationship and date of de-designation.

Details of hedging instrument

Nature of hedging instrument

Deal reference number

Contractual parties of the hedging instrument

Start date

Maturity date

Currency

Principal/ notional

Cash flows to be received and paid – amount, basis (e.g. LIBOR) and timing

Amount of Principal/notional designated as a hedging instrument

If non-optional derivative is used, will movements in forward points be excluded?

If optional derivative is used, will the movement in time value be excluded?

Attachments (include any other information to explain the nature and profile of the instrument, e.g. the swap has an amortising notional)

Details of hedged item

Nature of hedged item

Deal reference number (if applicable)

Contractual parties of the hedged item

Start date

Maturity date

Currency, amount (and basis e.g. LIBOR) and timing

Principal/notional

Amount designated as hedged item

Attachments (e.g. if cash flow hedging forecasts sales then sales forecasts will be attached which show the level of designated sales compared with the total forecast sales).

Effectiveness testing

Prospective effectiveness testing

Can hedge effectiveness be reliably measured?

Expectation of hedge effectiveness

Type of test

Period by period or cumulative assessment

Frequency of hedge effectiveness test

Results of prospective effectiveness testing

Date of test

Results of test

Attachments (include any details of the results of the assessment)

Retrospective effectiveness testing

Can hedge effectiveness be reliably measured?

Expectation of hedge effectiveness

Type of test

Period by period or cumulative assessment

Frequency of hedge effectiveness test

Result of retrospective effectiveness testing

Date of test

Results of test

Attachments (include any details of the results of the assessment)

Accounting

Basis adjustment

If the hedge is a cash flow hedge and results in the recognition of a non-financial asset or non-financial liability, whether the gains and losses are reclassified directly out of equity into profit or loss or whether the gains and losses are removed from equity on initial recognition of the non-financial asset or liability and included in the initial carrying amount of the asset or liability.

Reconciliation of gain or loss deferred in other comprehensive income for cash flow and net investment hedges		
	Cash flow hedging	**Net investment hedging**
Balance brought forward in equity as effective gains/losses		
Effective gains and losses recognised in other comprehensive income in period		
Gains and losses reclassified out of equity to profit or loss in the period		
Balance carried forward in equity as effective gains/losses		
Hedge documentation prepared by:	________________	
Hedge documentation reviewed by:	________________	
Date:	________________	

7 Future developments

As part of its project to improve financial instrument accounting with the introduction of IFRS 9, the IASB comprehensively reviewed the hedge accounting requirements in IAS 39 with the objective of more closely aligning the requirements with risk management. In November 2013 this culminated in the introduction of a new set of hedge accounting requirements for general hedge accounting. The Board decided to address improvements to portfolio fair value hedge accounting for interest rate risk (commonly referred to as macro hedge accounting) separately from the general hedge accounting requirements. This led to the issue of a discussion paper, *Financial Instruments: Accounting for Dynamic Risk Management: a Portfolio Revaluation Approach to Macro Hedging*, in March 2014. At the time of writing, the IASB was in the analysis phase of this project and at its May 2015 meeting it tentatively decided:

- that it should first consider how the information needs of constituents concerning dynamic risk management activities could be addressed through disclosures before considering those areas that need to be addressed through recognition and measurement;
- to prioritise the consideration of interest rate risk and consider other risks at a later stage in the project; and
- to establish an Expert Advisory Panel at a later stage in the project.

The IFRS 9 general hedge accounting model introduces significant changes to the requirements in IAS 39, whilst at the same time maintaining some of the basic concepts of IAS 39. For example, IFRS 9 hedge accounting remains elective and requires formal designation of the hedging relationship for it to apply. The three types of hedges, fair value hedges, cash flow hedges and net investment hedges are retained, as is the requirement to measure and recognise any hedge ineffectiveness.

The reforms will make hedge accounting more achievable in practice as some of the restrictions in IAS 39 are removed. For example, a risk component in a non-financial item is eligible as a hedged item provided it is 'separately identifiable and reliably measurable'. Also, synthetic (or 'aggregated') exposures that include cash instruments and derivatives would be eligible hedged items despite the inclusion of a derivative.

The hedge effectiveness assessment requirements are also replaced. IFRS 9 has a principles-based test that requires an entity to demonstrate, on a prospective basis, that an economic relationship exists between the hedged item and hedging instrument. Quantitative testing that demonstrates that a hedge relationship is highly effective would not be required. IFRS 9, compared with IAS 39, will also reduce profit or loss volatility arising from the accounting of certain hedging instruments. For example, when the intrinsic value of an option contract is designated as a hedging instrument, changes in the time value of the option would be recorded in other comprehensive income and recognised in profit or loss on a cost basis. A similar treatment is also permitted for forward points of a forward contract when only the spot element is designated in the hedge and for the foreign currency basis spread in a financial instrument.

Other significant changes include permitting hedge accounting for certain net positions, requiring basis adjustment for cash flow hedges that result in the recognition of a non-financial item, and increased hedge accounting disclosures, including disclosure about an entity's risk management activities. The new requirements also include fair value elections for the hedged exposure as an alternative to hedge accounting to reduce an accounting mismatch when an entity hedges credit risk in a financial item, as well as a fair value election at initial recognition for certain contracts that will be settled with the delivery of non-financial item that meet the own-use criteria.

The mandatory effective date of IFRS 9 is annual periods beginning on or after 1 January 2018 with early application permitted.

As an alternative to applying the new hedge accounting requirements in IFRS 9 when adopting IFRS 9, the Standard permits as an accounting policy to continue to apply the hedge accounting requirements of IAS 39 instead. It is expected that this option will be available until the reforms to macro hedge accounting are complete.

The requirements of IFRS 9 are described at length in *iGAAP 2016 Financial Instruments – IFRS 9 and related Standards – Volume B.*

C10 Hedge accounting – complex

Contents

1 Introduction

Hedge relationships and hedge accounting strategies can range from the basic to the very complex. The purpose of this chapter is to discuss the more complex aspects of hedge accounting. The basic rules of hedge accounting are discussed in detail in **chapter C9** and apply equally to this chapter.

2 Hedged items

The basic requirements governing the qualification of hedged items are discussed in detail in **section 3** of **chapter C9**. This section provides additional application guidance on the basic requirements and also covers less common, more complex scenarios.

2.1 Hedges of portions of a financial instrument

Because it is a requirement for all hedge relationships that effectiveness can be assessed and measured [IAS 39:88(d)], it is essential that the hedged portion is identifiable and separately measurable. For instance, the risk free rate or benchmark interest rate risk component of either a fixed or floating interest-bearing asset or liability is an identifiable and separately measurable portion (as illustrated in **example 3.8.1A** in **chapter C9**). However, in other cases, it may not be possible to establish that a given variable is an identifiable and separately measurable portion if that portion is not identifiable when the instrument was originally issued and priced. This is illustrated in the following example.

Example 2.1A

Ineligible portion of interest rate risk

Entity C has issued Euro denominated debt with a floating interest rate based on the European Central Bank (ECB) rate. It has also entered into a receive EURIBOR pay fixed Euro interest rate swap with a notional equal to the principal of the debt.

The receive EURIBOR pay fixed interest rate swap cannot be designated as a hedge of the portion of the ECB cash flows that is due to changes in EURIBOR. There is no EURIBOR component in the ECB variable cash flows. The interest rate risk that can be designated as the hedged risk is variability in the ECB rate.

Alternatively, Entity C could hedge the variability of the ECB floating interest rate with a EURIBOR swap; however, this is unlikely to be a perfectly effective hedging instrument even if the notional amounts of the two swaps are the same, because of the basis difference between ECB rate and EURIBOR. Changes in the cash flows of the floating interest rate on the debt will not necessarily be offset by variability in EURIBOR on the swap.

It may be possible to adjust continually the number of EURIBOR swaps to be equivalent to the variability in cash flows generated by variability in the ECB rate in order to achieve a highly effective hedge relationship. This is a dynamic hedging strategy. If a sufficiently high correlation can be demonstrated between the EURIBOR and ECB rates then a statistical relationship could be used to adjust the hedge ratio in order to demonstrate prospectively a highly effective hedge in line with the principles described in **4.3.2**.

In July 2008, the IASB issued amendments to IAS 39 titled *Eligible Hedged Items*. The aim of the amendments was to clarify two issues in relation to hedge accounting:

(i) identifying inflation as a hedged risk or portion; and

(ii) hedging with options.

The amendments state that inflation may only be hedged when changes in inflation constitute a contractually-specified portion of cash flows of a recognised financial instrument. This may be the case when an entity acquires or issues inflation-linked debt. In such circumstances, the entity has a cash flow exposure to changes in future inflation that may be cash flow hedged. The amendments, therefore, do not permit an entity to designate an inflation component of issued or acquired fixed rate debt in a fair value hedge – such a component is not deemed separately identifiable and reliably measurable. The amendments also clarify that a risk-free or benchmark interest rate portion of the fair value of a fixed rate financial instrument will normally be separately identifiable and reliably measurable and, therefore, may be hedged.

The clarification on hedging with options is detailed in **3.4**.

When an entity issues debt at a negative spread to LIBOR (i.e. the coupon is set at a rate below the LIBOR rate at inception), it *cannot* designate a 'LIBOR' portion as the hedged risk. This would entail splitting the fixed rate of the debt into a LIBOR portion and a discount to LIBOR (or negative credit spread component). IAS 39 specifies that if a portion of the cash flows of a financial asset or a financial liability is designated as the hedged item that designated portion must be less than the total cash flows of the asset or liability. [IAS 39:AG99C]

Example 2.1B

Fair value hedging sub-LIBOR fixed rate debt

Entity XYZ issues fixed rate debt at 3.75 per cent when LIBOR is 4 per cent. Entity XYZ would like to hedge its debt for interest rate risk arising from changes in the benchmark interest rate, i.e. LIBOR.

Entity XYZ *cannot* designate a LIBOR component (4 per cent) as the hedged risk as this amount is greater than the contractual cash flow on the hedged item. However, Entity XYZ can designate all of the contractual cash flows of the debt instrument as the hedged item and specify that these cash flows are hedged for changes that are attributable to LIBOR. In order for Entity XYZ to have a high expectation of hedge effectiveness, Entity XYZ may need to choose a hedge ratio other than one to one in order to improve the effectiveness of the hedge as described in **4.3.2**.

If an entity enters into a fair value hedge of a fixed rate asset or a liability some time after its initial recognition, IAS 39 permits the entity to designate as the hedged item a portion of the cash flows equal to the benchmark rate (e.g. LIBOR) that is higher than the contractual fixed rate received or paid on the asset or liability, provided that the benchmark rate is less than the recalculated effective interest rate on the asset or liability calculated as if the entity had purchased or issued the instrument on the date it first designates the hedged item. [IAS 39:AG99D]

Assume an entity issues a fixed rate bond at par that will redeem at par. At a later date, it enters into an interest rate swap to hedge its exposure to changes in the fair value of the liability attributable to the benchmark interest rate. If the swap has a fair value of zero at inception and interest rates have fallen since the bond was issued, the coupons on the bond will be higher than the contracted fixed receipts on the interest rate swap. Because the fixed receipts on the swap are lower than the contractual fixed rate coupons on the bond, the entity can designate as the hedged item a portion of each coupon cash flow equal to the fixed receipts of the swap. The fixed receipts of the swap and the cash flows on the designated portion of the bond will match and the hedge is likely to be highly effective.

If interest rates have risen since the bond was issued, the coupons on the bond may be lower than the contractual fixed receipts on the interest rate swap. The entity can designate the bond as hedged for the benchmark interest rate portion of its fair value interest rate risk, provided that the benchmark rate is less than the effective interest rate of the hedged item, calculated based on the assumption that the entity had issued the bond on the date the hedge is designated. [IAS 39:AG99D] This is achieved by designating as the hedged risk both the contractual coupon payments and an amount of discount which is included in the difference between the current fair value of the bond and the amount repayable at maturity. A hedge designated in this way is likely to exhibit ineffectiveness because the fixed cash flows of the swap will have a different profile from the fixed cash flows of the hedged item; the fixed interest cash flows of the swap are composed of equal payments, while the hedged interest cash flows on the bond comprise lower contractual payments and a discount to par. The different cash flow profiles will result in different changes in fair value in response to changes in interest rates.

To minimise ineffectiveness, an entity may need to enter into a swap with a fixed leg rate equal to or lower than the contractual coupons on the bond. Such a swap does not have a zero fair value at inception because it is not entered into at market interest rates. When the upfront payment on the swap is structured to be equivalent to the discount on the bond, the swap will be more effective at hedging the bond.

Example 2.1C

Fair value hedging fixed rate debt when interest rates have moved since issue

Entity F originated a four-year 5 per cent fixed rate loan of CU10,000 on 1 January 20X2, with a maturity date of 31 December 20X5. Of the 5 per cent coupon, 0.4 per cent represents credit spread (i.e. the market rate of interest was 4.6 per cent). Interest is receivable annually. The effective interest rate of Entity F's loan at inception is 5 per cent.

Scenario 1: Interest rates fall between 1/1/20X2 and 31/12/20X2

One year later, interest rates have fallen. At 31 December 20X2, the loan has a fair value of CU10,251. Entity F wishes to protect its loan asset against an increase in interest rates by entering into a fair value hedge of interest rate risk. The current market rate of interest is now 3.5 per cent, rather than 4.6 per cent.

Entity F enters into a receive-variable rate, pay-fixed rate of 3.5 per cent interest rate swap on 31 December 20X2 with a maturity of 31 December 20X5 to hedge its fair value interest rate exposure. The swap is on-market, i.e. it has a fair value of zero at inception.

If Entity F had originated the loan when the hedging swap was entered into, it would not have originated the loan at 5 per cent, but rather at 3.9 per cent, i.e. at the benchmark interest market rate plus the appropriate margin given the counterparty's credit rating (3.5 per cent + 0.4 per cent). In this case, the effective interest rate of the loan would have been 3.9 per cent and not 5 per cent. The benchmark interest rate of 3.5 per cent is lower than the effective interest rate of this 'hypothetical loan' and, therefore, Entity F is permitted to designate as the hedged item a portion equal to the benchmark rate (e.g. LIBOR).

Scenario 2: Interest rates increase between 1/1/20X2 and 31/12/20X2

One year later, interest rates have increased. At 31 December 20X2, the loan has a fair value of CU9,081. Entity F wishes to protect its loan asset against a further increase in interest rates by entering into a fair value hedge of the interest rate risk. The current market rate of interest is now 6 per cent, rather than 4.6 per cent.

Entity F enters into a receive-variable rate, pay-fixed rate of 6 per cent interest rate swap on 31 December 20X2 with a maturity of 31 December 20X5 to hedge its fair value interest rate exposure. The swap is on-market, i.e. it has a fair value of zero at inception.

If Entity F had originated the loan when the hedging swap was entered into, it would not have originated the loan at 5 per cent, but at 6.4 per cent, i.e. at the benchmark interest market rate plus the appropriate margin given the counterparty's credit rating, i.e. the (6 per cent + 0.4 per cent). The benchmark interest rate of 6 per cent is lower than the effective interest rate of this 'hypothetical loan' and, therefore, Entity F is permitted to designate as the hedged item a portion equal to the benchmark rate (e.g. LIBOR) that is higher than the contractual fixed rate received on the asset.

2.2 Partial term hedging

Hedging only a part of a financial instrument's term is an extension of hedging portions of cash flows of the instrument. It is possible to hedge for a shorter period than the term of the whole hedged item, by hedging only selected cash flows in that item. As with all hedge relationships, this is only permitted if hedge effectiveness can be demonstrated and measured (and the other hedge criteria are met). [IAS 39:IG.F.2.17]

Example 2.2A

Partial term hedging fixed rate debt (1)

Entity Q issues 10-year fixed rate debt. To hedge against changes in interest rates, it enters into a 6-year receive-fixed pay-floating interest rate swap. Entity Q may designate the swap as hedging the fair value exposure of the interest payments relating to the first 6 years of the debt and the principal payment due at maturity with respect to movements in interest rates only until the end of year 6.

IAS 39:75 states that a hedging relationship may not be designated for only a portion of the time period during which a hedging instrument remains outstanding. In practice, this prohibition is intended to preclude an entity splitting the fair value of a derivative (other than a fully proportionate share of the entire derivative) and only designating the fair value attributable to a portion of the time period during which it remains outstanding. For example, it would not be permissible to designate the portion of an interest rate swap relating to the next 5 years, when the instrument has a maturity in seven years, as a cash flow hedge of variability in interest rate risk on a debt instrument for the next five years.

The concept of being able to hedge on a partial term basis is driven by the relationship between spot rates and forward rates for any given yield curve. The spot rate today, and the anticipated spot rates in the future periods are used to construct the yield curve today. The yield curve is a reflection of the anticipated rates in the future based on an assessment today.

By dissecting a longer dated current yield curve into 'mini-curves', it is possible to isolate the fair value movements of a longer dated instrument due to movements in the shorter part of the yield curve.

Example 2.2B

Partial term hedging fixed rate debt (2)

Facts as in **example 2.2A**.

At issuance of the bond, Entity Q can obtain the yield curve for the stated maturity of the whole instrument, in this case, a ten year yield curve.

The ten year yield curve can be dissected into mini-yield curves.

- Spot interest rate today (t_0) for interest due in a year (t_1).
- Expected spot interest rate starting in a year's time (t_1) due at the end of that year (t_2) [one-year forward rate starting in a year].
- Expected spot interest rate starting at year 2 (t_2) due at the end of that year (t_3) [one-year forward rate starting in year 2].

If Entity Q wishes to fair value hedge for movements in the interest rate curve that matures in six years' time, it only has to consider movements in the first six years of the ten year yield curve in computing the change in the fair value of the hedged item. Because a six-year interest rate swap is priced off the six-year yield curve, in order to demonstrate hedge effectiveness, the entity discounts the six years of cash flows using the spot rates at the date hedge effectiveness is measured.

In one year's time, Entity Q will compare the change in the fair value of the derivative (with five years remaining) with the change in fair value of the hedged selected cash flows on the bond as well as the principal payment due at maturity to the extent affected by changes in the spot yield curve for the next five years, and so on.

An entity is permitted to partial term cash flow hedge a financial instrument because IAS 39 provides greater flexibility in designating portions when hedging financial instruments compared to hedging non-financial items. For hedges of non-financial items, an entity is limited to hedging all foreign currency risk or all risks in their entirety (see **3.9** in **chapter C9**). An entity that has a derivative with a maturity that is shorter than the timing of the cash flow exposure of the non-financial hedged item must designate all of the derivative (with the exception of the forward points in a forward contract or time value in an option) as hedging all foreign currency risk or all risks in their entirety up to the timing of the cash flow of the hedged item. Because the hedged item is non-financial, the entity cannot designate a derivative for part of the time period until the forecast transaction occurs.

For example, a derivative that matures in nine months' time could be perfectly effective as a hedge of a forecast sale or purchase of a non-financial item that is highly probable of occurring in nine months' time. If the transaction is highly probable of occurring in ten months' time, the same derivative could not be designated as a hedge of the nine month portion of time until the transaction is expected to occur as a non-financial item cannot be partial-term hedged.

2.3 Financial instruments subject to prepayment

An instrument that contains an embedded prepayment option may still be designated as a hedged item. However, the effect of the prepayment option should be considered when designating the hedged item and assessing whether the hedge relationship will be highly effective.

If the entire asset or liability is designated as being hedged, for the hedging instrument to be highly effective it may have to include an equivalent option that coincides with the prepayment option in the hedged item. Inclusion of such an option in the hedging instrument ensures that fair value of the hedging instrument is as sensitive as the hedged item to the designated hedged risk.

Alternatively, the hedging relationship could be designated for just a portion of the term of the instrument prior to the prepayment option being capable of being exercised, provided that the hedging instrument is designated for the entirety of its term. For example, if a debt instrument can be prepaid by the issuer after Year five, the investor may wish to hedge the debt instrument for a period before the prepayment option can be exercised, i.e. for the first five years only.

An investor in a prepayable asset may decide to hedge cash flows in the period in which the prepayment option is exercisable (or in the period after the date on which the option can be exercised). In order to demonstrate that the hedging instrument is expected to be highly effective in the period, the cash flows must be highly probable. For example, cash flows in the period when the prepayment option is exercisable may qualify as highly probable if they result from a group or pool of similar assets (e.g. mortgage loans) for which prepayments can be estimated with a high degree of accuracy or if the prepayment option is significantly out of the money. [IAS 39:IG.F.2.12]

Example 2.3A

Hedging prepayable loans for interest rate risk (1)

Entity A purchases a perpetual debt instrument which pays a fixed rate of interest of 5 per cent on par. The issuer of the debt instrument has an option to prepay the perpetual debt at an amount that is equal to the instrument's par amount after five years. Entity A measures the instrument at amortised cost.

Entity A enters into a non-prepayable swap with Bank B to pay fixed 5 per cent and to receive LIBOR for 20 years. The interest rate swap is designated as a partial term fair value hedge of the LIBOR portion of the perpetual debt instrument for 20 years. Apart from the issuer call prepayment option, all terms and conditions of the swap match those of the hedged item.

Entity A must compare the changes in fair value of the interest rate swap to the changes in the fair value of the perpetual debt instrument, where the latter includes both the change in fair value of the contractual cash flows and the change in fair value of the prepayment option. Hedge ineffectiveness will arise because the hedged item is prepayable while the hedging instrument is not. Hedge ineffectiveness is likely to be so significant in that it will be difficult to demonstrate prospective hedge effectiveness. If five years after the issue, the perpetual debt has not been called by the issuer, Entity A may be able to designate the interest rate swap as a partial term hedge of the LIBOR portion of the perpetual debt for the next 15 years. It is not appropriate to exclude the prepayment risk out of the designation of the hedging relationship because prepayment risk and interest rate risk are closely interrelated.

Example 2.3B

Hedging prepayable loans for interest rate risk (2)

Facts as in **example 2.3A**, except that Entity A enters into a swap with Bank B whereby the swap can be terminated after five years at Entity A's option. The swap will be terminated at the swap's then fair value.

Entity A must compare the changes in fair value of the interest rate swap to the changes in the fair value of the perpetual debt instrument. In both cases, the change in fair value includes both the change in fair value of the contractual cash flows as well as the change in fair value of the prepayment option which for the swap has negligible value because the swap terminates at fair value. Hedge ineffectiveness will still arise because the hedged item is prepayable at par while the hedging instrument can only be terminated at its then fair value, which will include the fair value of the expected future cash flows on the remaining 15 years of the swap. Therefore, changes in the fair value of the hedged item will not be offset by changes in the fair value of the hedging instrument. The lack of offset may be significant enough to prevent hedge accounting.

Example 2.3C

Hedging prepayable loans for interest rate risk (3)

Facts as in **example 2.3A**, except that Entity A enters into a swap with Bank B whereby the swap can be terminated after five years at Entity A's option. The swap will be terminated at zero value.

Entity A must compare the changes in fair value of the interest rate swap to the changes in the fair value of the perpetual debt instrument. In both cases, the change in fair value includes the change in fair value of the contractual cash flows as well as the change in fair value of the prepayment option. The hedging relationship is expected to be highly effective at hedging the interest rate risk of the debt for part of its term because both the hedging instrument and the hedged item are prepayable at par.

2.4 Hedging foreign currency or fair value exposure in equity securities

Available-for-sale (AFS) assets are held at fair value with changes in fair value recognised in other comprehensive income. A non-monetary AFS asset, such as a listed equity security in an unrelated party can be hedged, provided that there is a clear and identifiable exposure to changes in foreign exchange rates. This would normally be the case when:

- the equity instrument is not traded on an exchange (or in another established marketplace) where trades are denominated in the same currency as the functional currency of the entity; and
- dividends received by the investor are not in the same currency as the functional currency of the investor.

If a share is traded in multiple currencies and one of those currencies is the functional currency of the reporting entity, hedge accounting for the foreign currency component of the share price is not permitted. [IAS 39:IG.F.2.19]

Example 2.4A

Hedging foreign currency of an equity security: qualifying

Entity A is a UK-based manufacturing entity. Entity A owns shares in Entity X, which is listed on the New York Stock Exchange. The security is classified as available-for-sale in accordance with IAS 39. Dividends are paid in US dollars and the share price is quoted in US dollars.

Because the shares in Entity X are not traded on a Sterling-denominated exchange and the dividends are not in the functional currency of Entity A, there is a clear and identifiable exposure to changes in foreign exchange rates, and the investment in shares can qualify as a hedged item.

Entity A could hedge its exposure to foreign currency risk by, for example, entering into a forward foreign currency contract to sell US dollars. Additionally, it could choose to designate only a portion of the shares, provided that effectiveness can be measured. For example, if the fair value of the shares was US$1,000, it could designate the foreign currency risk associated with, say, US$800 of the fair value of the shares.

Entity A could designate the forward contract as a fair value hedge of the investment in Entity X, or as a cash flow hedge of the forecast sale of the shares if the timing of the sale is highly probable.

Example 2.4B

Hedging foreign currency of an equity security: non-qualifying

Group A is a group headed by a Japanese resident parent whose shares are publicly traded on the Tokyo Stock Exchange (TSE). Group A has a secondary listing on the New York Stock Exchange (NYSE) where the parent's shares are listed as American Deposit Receipts (ADRs). Trading on the NYSE is comparatively low compared to trading on the TSE because Group A has a small number of US investors. The prices on the NYSE closely approximate the prices of the shares on the TSE multiplied by the current foreign exchange rate between Japanese Yen and US dollars.

An investor is prohibited from hedging the foreign currency risk of an investment in a share denominated in multiple currencies when one of the currencies is the functional currency of the investor. Even when the trading volume is low compared to its primary listing, as in the circumstances described, the parent's shares remain dual listed. Because the investor is a US dollar functional currency investor, and the shares are denominated in US dollars on a stock exchange, the investor cannot hedge its foreign currency risk in respect of the shares acquired from the TSE that are denominated in Japanese Yen. [IAS 39:IG.F.2.19]

2.5 Foreign currency risk of a forecast foreign currency debt issuance

An entity that has a highly probable forecast debt issuance may wish to cash flow hedge the interest rates and/or the foreign currency risk associated with the issuance. Hedging the interest rate risk is permitted and is described in **example 2.2.4A** in **chapter C9** and also in IAS 39:IG.F.5.5.

IAS 39 does not provide guidance on whether a hedge of the variability in functional currency equivalent proceeds attributable to foreign exchange risk that is to be received from a highly probable forecast issue of debt denominated in a currency other than the entity's functional currency can qualify for hedge accounting. It would not appear to be possible to designate the variability in the functional currency equivalent cash flows of a forecast debt issuance in a foreign currency because the foreign currency risk does not affect profit or loss. Foreign currency risk only arises from the date the debt is recognised in the statement of financial position because it is translated thereafter into the entity's functional currency under IAS 21. The quantum of this foreign currency risk that will affect profit or loss following the issue of the debt bears no relation to the quantum of foreign currency risk that arises prior to the date the debt is issued.

Example 2.5

Hedging foreign currency risk of forecast foreign currency debt issuance

On 1 January, Entity C, a US dollar functional currency entity, has a highly probable forecast 10 per cent fixed rate debt issuance of €100 million in one month's time, and wishes to hedge the variability in the US dollar equivalent proceeds that it will receive from the point in time when the hedging instrument is entered into to the point in time when the debt is issued. Entity C will enter into a foreign currency forward contract to sell €100 million and to buy an equivalent amount of US dollars, based on the forward rate for delivery when the debt is expected to be issued. At the date Entity C enters into the foreign currency forward contract, it is expected that the combination of the net cash flows from the forward contract and the Euros to be received from issuing the debt should equal US$100 million, all other things being equal.

Entity C cannot designate the changes in foreign currency risk between the date of entering into the derivative and the date the forecast debt is expected to be issued as a qualifying hedge exposure. This is because the foreign currency risk on the debt will only arise and affect profit or loss from the date it is recognised as a liability and is retranslated from Euro to Entity C's US dollar functional currency during the period it remains outstanding. The gains/losses on the forward contract prior to the debt being issued bear no relationship to the foreign currency gains/losses that will be recognised after the debt is issued. Furthermore, the functional currency amount of interest in future periods is unaffected by movements in foreign currency prior to the debt being issued, as illustrated below.

Assume the foreign currency exchange rate at 1 January is US$1:€1 and at 1 February is US$1.5:€1. Using the 1 January exchange rate, the annual interest in US dollars would be US$10 million. At the rate of exchange prevailing on 1 February, the amount of Euro proceeds necessary to raise US$100 million would be €67 million. The related annual interest, assuming constant interest rates, would be €6.7 million. However, translating € into US dollars, the annual interest is still US$10 million (since €6.7 million x 1.5 = US$10 million). As demonstrated, the annual interest expense in functional currency terms is unaffected by a change in exchange rates between the date the foreign currency forward contract is entered into and the date the debt is issued.

Once the debt is issued, it will be a recognised monetary item and will be retranslated from Euro to US dollars on an ongoing basis in accordance with IAS 21 with any resulting foreign exchange gains or losses recognised in profit or loss. Once recognised, the debt could be designated in either a cash flow or fair value hedge of foreign currency risk.

2.6 Hedging capitalised borrowing costs

Neither IAS 39 nor IAS 23 *Borrowing Costs* provides guidance on whether an entity can cash flow or fair value hedge interest rate risk when the interest is partly or fully capitalised under IAS 23 as part of a qualifying asset. IAS 23 makes reference in its basis of conclusions to the fact that US GAAP does provide specific guidance in this area for fair value hedges. IAS 23:BC21 states that US GAAP "concludes that derivative gains and losses (arising from the effective portion of a derivative instrument that qualifies as a fair value hedge) are part of the capitalised interest cost. IAS 23 does not address such derivative gains and losses".

The capitalisation of borrowing costs in and of itself should not prohibit any entity from applying hedge accounting for interest rate risk for debt that is used to fund a qualifying asset under IAS 23. IAS 39 requires that a hedge must result in the hedged risk affecting profit or loss, which will be the case when interest on debt is capitalised because the qualifying asset will affect profit or loss either through amortisation, impairment or sale.

If an entity applies cash flow hedge accounting it is necessary to consider whether the hedged variable interest cash flows result in the recognition of a non-financial asset as contemplated in IAS 39:98 (see **2.2.3** of **chapter C9**). This is because under IAS 39:98 if a hedged forecast transaction subsequently results in the recognition of a non-financial asset, an entity is required to choose as an accounting policy to either reclassify any deferred gains or losses from the cash flow hedge reserve when the hedged item affects profit or loss; or remove the associated gains or losses from the cash flow hedge reserve and include them directly in the initial cost of the non-financial asset as a 'basis-adjustment'.

It could be argued that because the hedged interest cash flows are capitalised as part of the 'qualifying asset' (i.e. a non-financial asset) the hedged forecast interest payments result in the recognition of a non-financial asset and therefore basis-adjustment can be applied if a policy to basis adjust is chosen.

Alternatively it could be argued that IAS 39:98 was intended for future purchases of non-financial assets and in these circumstances the hedged item is forecast interest payments (i.e. a financial item). Therefore the hedged item is financial in nature and the fact that the interest cash flows are capitalised only changes *when* the hedged forecast interest cash flows affect profit or loss and does not change the financial nature of the forecast transaction. Consequently basis-adjustment under IAS 39:98 is not permitted.

The requirements of IAS 39 are not clear in this regard and an entity should determine as a matter of accounting policy whether the hedged variable interest cash flows required to be capitalised as borrowing costs results in the recognition of a non-financial asset as contemplated in IAS 39:98.

The example below sets out two scenarios where cash flow and fair value hedge accounting of interest rate risk is applied when the interest on the borrowing is capitalised under IAS 23.

Example 2.6

Hedging capitalised borrowing costs

Entity A borrows CU10 million to finance the construction of a 'qualifying asset' in accordance with IAS 23. The related borrowing costs are eligible for capitalisation.

Scenario 1: Entity A borrows at fixed rates

Entity A enters into an interest rate swap (with the same notional and term as the debt) to receive fixed pay 3-month LIBOR and designates this as a hedge of the fair value exposure to changes in interest rates (say 3-month LIBOR) of its debt. Entity A will capitalise under IAS 23 the synthetic floating rate borrowing costs that have been achieved as a result of entering into the effective hedge accounting relationship.

(i) Entity A will determine the effectiveness of the fair value hedge and recognise any ineffectiveness in profit or loss. If the hedge is highly effective, the debt will be fair value adjusted for changes in interest rates with the corresponding entry in profit or loss. The fair value adjustment will be amortised to profit or loss either immediately when the adjustment is made or no later than the debt ceases to fair value hedge adjusted.

(ii) The synthetic floating interest rate that is achieved as a result of the highly effective hedge is capitalised. This amount will include the actual fixed rate on the debt plus the effect of swapping this fixed rate into floating rates.

Scenario 2: Entity A borrows at floating rates

Entity A enters into an interest rate swap to receive 3-month LIBOR pay fixed rates (same notional and term as debt) and designates the swap as hedging the variability in its debt due to changes in 3-month LIBOR. Entity A intends to cash flow hedge the variability in interest rates on its borrowings even though the interest on the borrowings is capitalised under IAS 23.

Entity A can apply cash flow hedge accounting of the interest rate risk on its variable rate borrowings but the gain/loss on the derivative that is recognised in other comprehensive income is reclassified from equity to profit or loss when the interest component of the qualifying asset affects profit or loss.

Entity A will apply the following steps in order.

(i) Capitalise the variable rate interest on the borrowing in accordance with IAS 23.

(ii) Determine the effectiveness of the cash flow hedge and recognise any ineffectiveness in profit or loss. Recognise the effective gain/loss on the derivative in other comprehensive income.

(iii) Depending on the entity's accounting policy (see the guidance immediately before this example), the amount recognised in other comprehensive income will be either: reclassified from equity to profit or loss when the hedged risk affects profit or loss; or capitalised as a basis-adjustment as part of the qualifying asset. If basis-adjustment is applied, the effect would be equivalent to the entity borrowing at fixed rates and capitalising fixed borrowing costs. If basis-adjustment is not applied, the hedged interest that is capitalised as part of the qualifying asset will affect profit or loss when the qualifying asset is amortised, impaired or is sold. Similarly, the net effect in profit or loss from this reclassification will be equivalent to the entity borrowing at fixed rates and capitalising fixed borrowing costs.

If an entity does not apply hedge accounting and, therefore, the derivatives are classified as at fair value through profit or loss, it is not appropriate for the entity to capitalise part of the derivative as part of the borrowing costs under IAS 23. All gains/losses on non-hedging derivatives must be immediately recognised in profit or loss.

2.7 Hedging non-financial items

As described in **3.9** in **chapter C9** a non-financial asset or liability may qualify as a hedged item in limited circumstances. More complex aspects of hedging non-financial items are described below.

2.7.1 Hedging foreign currency risk of non-financial asset held at cost

If an entity is hedging foreign currency risk, this risk must be separately measurable. A non-financial asset that was purchased in a foreign currency cannot be hedged for foreign currency risk because foreign currency risk is not evident in that non-financial item. However, the foreign currency risk associated with a forecasted sale of that non-financial item could qualify as a hedged item.

It is important to distinguish between hedging foreign currency risk of a non-financial item and hedging foreign currency risk in relation to the forecast sale or purchase of that non-financial item.

Example 2.7.1 illustrates that it is not possible to hedge the foreign currency risk of a non-financial item because the foreign currency risk is not evident and not separately measurable. However, if an entity is purchasing or selling a non-financial item in a foreign currency, it is a fixed amount of foreign currency that will be needed to buy or will be received from selling that non-financial item, and a qualifying foreign currency exposure therefore exists.

Example 2.7.1

Hedging a non-financial item: held at cost

Entity A, a Sterling functional currency entity, acquires some plant and machinery in US$ from Entity B, an unrelated third party US dollar functional currency entity. In the financial statements of Entity A, the plant and machinery will be translated at the US$:£ exchange rate at the date of the purchase (i.e. at historical rate).

If Entity A used US dollar borrowing to finance the purchase of the plant and machinery, these US dollar borrowings cannot be used as a hedging instrument in a fair value hedge of the foreign currency risk of the plant and machinery because the hedged item does not contain any separately measurable foreign currency risk.

If Entity A was to demonstrate that the disposal of the plant and machinery in US dollars was highly probable, then the US dollar denominated debt could be used as a hedging instrument against the forecast sale in US dollar provided that the timing of the future cash flows on the debt coincided with the timing of the future cash flow on the disposal.

Non-derivatives can be used as hedging instruments only when hedging foreign currency risk. This is discussed further in **4.1** in **chapter C9**.

2.7.2 Hedging all risks except foreign currency

IAS 39 is clear that hedges of a non-financial instrument are possible for all risks or just foreign currency risk. Therefore, by deduction, it is possible to hedge all risks except foreign currency risk, assuming all other hedge accounting criteria are met. IAS 39:IG.E.3.4 on the interaction between IAS 39 and IAS 21 supports this assertion. For financial instruments, fair value is firstly determined in the currency in which the contract is denominated, and translation of the contract into the functional currency of the entity is secondary. If it can be clearly demonstrated that the exposure to fair value of the non-financial instrument excluding foreign currency risk can be identified and measured, and hedged for all risks except foreign currency risk, such exposure is a permissible hedging designation.

Example 2.7.2

Hedging a non-financial item: all risks except foreign currency

Entity O has an anticipated purchase of 1,000 barrels of oil in six months that is highly probable of occurring. The purchase price will be the market price at the date of purchase and will be priced in US dollars. Entity O's functional currency is the Australian dollar.

Entity O purchases oil futures on 500 barrels of oil to fix the price at US$60 for those 500 barrels. The duration (and other terms) of the forecast transaction and the futures contracts match so that Entity O believes the hedge will be highly effective over its term.

Entity O has two risk exposures: foreign currency risk and fair value risk.

The oil futures hedge price risk only. Entity O does not co-terminously hedge its exposure to the US dollar on the purchase contract.

The oil futures can be designated as a hedge of the forecast purchase of oil (provided that the other hedge accounting criteria are satisfied). A forward purchase of oil (a non-financial asset) does not have inherent foreign exchange risk. The foreign exchange risk arises from the fact that the reporting entity's functional currency is not the US dollar, not from the market price risk inherent in a forward purchase of oil.

2.8 Designation of groups of items

It is possible to group together similar assets or similar liabilities and hedge them as a group, but only if the individual items within the group share the same risk exposure that is designated as being hedged. The change in fair value attributable to the hedged risk of each item in the group must be approximately proportional to the change in fair value attributable to the hedged risk of the entire group. [IAS 39:83]

IAS 39 does not provide specific guidance as to what is approximately proportional. It is reasonable to assume that while it is not expected that the items within a portfolio have exactly the same sensitivity to the hedged risk, the items must show a high degree of similarity for a given movement in the hedged risk.

Investments in debt instruments that have different credit ratings and different maturities can be combined and hedged as a portfolio. In order to comply with the requirement that all items in the portfolio share the same risk exposure for which they are designated and that changes in their fair values are expected to be approximately proportional to the overall change in the fair value attributable to the hedged risk of the group, only portions of risks related to these instruments can be designated as being hedged and only for a portion of their terms that is common to all instruments in the portfolio. For example, the risk-free interest rate component that is shared by these instruments can qualify as being hedged. Alternatively, if an entity wanted to designate the entire risk of each instrument in the portfolio as being hedged, it would have to segregate the loans into portfolios in which each item in the portfolio is similar. This can be done by classifying loans according to their predominant risk characteristics, including:

- date of origination;
- loan type;
- loan size;
- geographical location;
- nature and location of collateral;
- interest rate type (fixed or variable) and the coupon interest rate (if fixed) or the timing of reset dates (if variable);
- scheduled maturity, prepayment history of the loans; and
- expected prepayment performance in varying interest rate scenarios.

Example 2.8

Hedging a group of similar items

On 1 April 20X4, Bank S has a CU100 million portfolio of corporate bonds that have a range of coupons from 7.5 per cent to 9.0 per cent and a maturity range of 10-11 years. Bank S would like to hedge the interest rate exposure on the CU100 million bond portfolio. It performs a sensitivity analysis and determines that the fair value exposure with respect to movement in interest rate risk only of all of the items individually respond within a range of 95 to 105 per cent of the overall change in price of the portfolio as a whole.

Bank S can designate an interest rate swap as a hedge of interest rate risk of the portfolio as a whole because all of the items within the portfolio share the same risk exposure, and the change in value of the items within the portfolio is expected to be approximately proportional to the change in value of the portfolio as a whole.

It is unlikely that a pool of shares could be grouped together and hedged as a portfolio. For example, it would not be possible to hedge a portfolio of shares that equate to the FTSE 100 index with a FTSE 100 total return swap. Although on an aggregated basis the hedge may be highly effective, it is clear that the individual equity securities that make up the portfolio do not share the exposure to risk, in that the fair value of each individual equity share does not move proportionally to the changes in value of the overall FTSE 100 index. [IAS 39:IG.F.2.20]

3 Hedging instruments

The basic requirements governing the qualification of hedging instruments are discussed in detail in **section 4** in **chapter C9**. This section provides additional guidance beyond the basic requirements incorporating less common, more complex scenarios.

3.1 Hedging more than one risk

A hedging instrument is often designated as hedging one risk only.

However, a hedging instrument can be designated as hedging more than one risk provided that:

[IAS 39:76]

(i) the risks being hedged can be clearly identified;

(ii) the effectiveness of the hedge can be demonstrated; and

(iii) it is possible to ensure that there is specific designation of the hedging instrument and different risk positions.

IAS 39 allows the use of one instrument to hedge more than one risk. Cross-currency interest rate swaps are commonly used to swap foreign currency variable rate debt back into functional currency fixed rate debt, or to swap foreign currency fixed into functional currency variable (see **4.4.1** in **chapter C9** for further guidance).

3.1.1 Hedging multiple hedged items

IAS 39 provides limited guidance on how to assess hedge effectiveness when an entity uses a single hedging instrument to hedge multiple hedged items. There are many instances where an entity could use a single derivative financial instrument to hedge one risk (say foreign currency risk) or multiple risks (say foreign currency risk and interest rate risk) where those risks reside in more than one hedged item.

IAS 39:IG.F.1.13 provides an example of an entity hedging two hedged items for the same risk. The example describes a Japanese Yen functional currency entity that has a 5-year floating rate US$ liability and a 10-year fixed rate £-denominated note receivable and chooses to hedge both items with a single foreign currency forward contract where it will receive US$ and pay £ in five years. Because the principal amounts of the asset and liability when converted into Japanese Yen are the same, the entity designates the dual foreign currency forward contract as hedging foreign currency risk for both items. Even though foreign currency risk is defined by reference to the entity's functional currency, and the foreign currency forward contract does not have a cash flow in the functional currency (i.e. Japanese Yen), the foreign currency forward contract may still be designated as hedging *both* foreign currencies as the exposure to both currencies has been eliminated by the forward. Put another way, if the entity entered into a receive US$ pay Japanese Yen forward, and a receive Japanese Yen pay £ forward, each forward could have been designated separately as hedging the foreign currency risk of the liability and asset respectively, the fair value of the two Japanese Yen legs would offset each other perfectly. In a single forward to receive US$ pay £, the receive Japanese Yen leg and the pay Japanese Yen leg do not exist but this does not create hedge ineffectiveness because the fair value of both legs offsets to zero. However, in assessing and measuring hedge effectiveness with a single forward contract, the entity will need to impute the two notional Japanese Yen legs into the hedge designation in order to determine the hedge effectiveness of the two hedges of foreign currency risk. Imputing the two notional cash flows for assessing hedge effectiveness is permitted because doing so does not create any additional cash flows as both notional cash flows offset each other perfectly.

In July 2007, the IFRIC (now the IFRS Interpretations Committee) issued a rejection notice on hedging multiple risks with a single derivative financial instrument. The IFRIC recognised that IAS 39's interpretative guidance does result in an entity needing to impute a notional leg as a means of splitting the fair value of the derivative into multiple components in order to assess hedge effectiveness. The IFRIC considered that this was acceptable in assessing hedge effectiveness because this conclusion did not conflict with IAS 39:IG.C.1 which prohibits an entity from recognising embedded derivatives that result in the *recognition* [emphasis added in the July 2007 *IFRIC Update*] of cash flows that do not contractually exist. The IFRIC's rejection notice highlights that, should any entity need to split notionally a derivative for assessing hedge effectiveness when that derivative is hedging multiple risks, then the process of splitting should not result in any new cash flows or any new risks arising which were not evident in the contractual terms of the derivative.

Example 3.1.1A

Hedging a net investment in a foreign operation and interest rate risk of issued debt

Parent P, a € functional currency entity, has issued a €100 million denominated fixed rate debt. Parent P consolidates Subsidiary S, a US dollar functional currency foreign operation with opening net assets of US$300 million. Parent P's objective is to hedge:

(i) the foreign currency risk of part of its foreign operation (being the € equivalent of US$150 million net assets); and

(ii) the fair value due to changes in interest rates on its issued debt (being interest rate risk on €100 million).

In order to minimise transaction costs, Parent P enters into a single derivative to Receive € fixed on €100 million, Pay US$ 3-month US$ LIBOR on US$150 million with the fair value of the cross-currency interest rate swap equal to zero at the transaction date (i.e. the derivative is on-market).

Parent P designates in the consolidated financial statements the cross-currency interest rate swap as a hedge of the foreign currency risk of Subsidiary S's net assets equal to US$150 million and the fair value interest rate risk on €100 million of its €-denominated debt.

In order to assess hedge effectiveness for net investment hedge and fair value hedge, Parent P notionally splits the derivative into the following:

(i) Receive fixed on €100m, Pay 3-month EURIBOR on €100m (notional derivative 1); and
(ii) Receive 3-month EURIBOR on €100m, Pay 3-month US$ LIBOR on US$150m (notional derivative 2).

Parent P fair values the two notional derivatives at inception and both have a fair value of zero so the sum of the fair values equals the fair value of the actual contractual derivative. Each period, the notional derivatives are fair valued in order to assess and measure hedge effectiveness and to ensure that the sum of these fair values equals the fair value of the actual contractual derivative entered into.

Example 3.1.1B

Hedging cash flow variability of both an asset and liability

Entity B, a Sterling functional currency entity, has issued 3-month LIBOR £200 million denominated debt and has an investment in an inflation-linked bond that receives 3% + UK CPI on a notional of £200 million (the inflation linkage is considered a closely related embedded derivative). The asset and liability have the same five year maturity.

Entity B's objective is to hedge the cash flow variability on both its asset and its liability. In order to minimise transaction costs, the entity enters into 5-year Receive 3-month LIBOR £200 million Pay 3% + UK CPI £200 million and designates this basis swap as a hedge of the cash flow variability of both its assets and its liability.

In order to assess hedge effectiveness, Entity B notionally splits the derivative into the following:

(i) Receive 3-month LIBOR on £200 million, Pay 6% on £200 million (notional derivative 1); and
(ii) Receive 6% on £200 million, Pay 3% + UK CPI on £200 million (notional derivative 2).

Entity B fair values the two notional derivatives at inception and both have a fair value of zero so the sum of the fair values equals the fair value of the actual contractual derivative. Each period, the notional derivatives are fair valued in order to assess and measure hedge effectiveness and to ensure that the sum of these fair values equals the fair value of the actual contractual derivative entered into.

Example 3.1.1C

Hedging cash flow variability of both a foreign currency sale and purchase

Entity C, a Euro functional currency entity, has forecast sales in US dollars and forecast purchases in Japanese Yen. Entity C enters into a series of foreign currency forward contracts under which it receives a fixed amount of Japanese Yen and pays a fixed amount of US dollars every month. The fair value of each forward contract is zero at inception as the terms are on-market at that date. Entity C's objective is to hedge the variability in functional currency cash flows of its US dollar sales and Japanese Yen purchases.

In order to assess hedge effectiveness, Entity C notionally splits the derivative into the following:

(i) receive fixed amount of Japanese Yen, pay fixed amount of Euro (notional derivative 1); and

(ii) receive fixed amount of Euro, pay a fixed amount of US dollars (notional derivative 2).

Entity C fair values the two notional derivatives at inception and both have a fair value of zero so the sum of the fair values equals the fair value of the actual contractual derivative. Each period the notional derivatives are fair valued in order to assess and measure hedge effectiveness and to ensure that the sum of these fair values equals the fair value of the actual contractual derivative entered into.

If the hedge is highly effective, the effective gains/losses on the series of forward contracts will initially be recognised in other comprehensive income and will be reclassified to profit or loss when the sales and purchases affect profit or loss. It should be noted that the timing of the impact to profit or loss of the two hedged items may differ. This is because purchases would normally result in recognition of inventory and the sale of the inventory acquired in Japanese Yen could occur in a period after the sales in US dollars. The entity must allocate the fair value gains/losses accumulated in equity to the two individual hedge relationships so it can determine the appropriate amount to be reclassified to profit or loss when the purchase or sale affects profit or loss.

Judgement is required in determining what is an appropriate split when allocating the fair value of derivatives to multiple hedged items for assessing hedge effectiveness. It would not be appropriate to create multiple notional derivatives which introduce notional legs over risks which did not exist in the contractual derivative or are not specific to the entity entering into the transaction, for example the entity's functional currency. Taking **example 3.1.1A**, the notional legs introduced are in the functional currency of the entity, the Euro, which is a reference point that is specific to the entity; the frequency of reset of EURIBOR on the notional leg is equal to the frequency of reset on the US$-LIBOR leg of the actual derivative. Taking **example 3.1.1B**, the notional legs introduced are the Sterling fixed rate for a 5-year interest rate swap priced off the Sterling 5-year LIBOR curve. In both examples, it would be unacceptable to impute notional legs which, although they could offset each other, would introduce an unrelated risk (say equity prices or an unrelated currency).

If a single hedging instrument is designated as a hedge of more than one risk, the hedge accounting criteria must be satisfied in respect of all the designated hedged risks. If the criteria are not met in respect of one of the risks being hedged, no hedge accounting treatment is allowed for the period. If one designation fails to meet the effectiveness test or no longer exists, continuing hedge accounting would result in split accounting for the hedging instrument, treating one part as a hedge and the other as a trading instrument which is not permitted.

3.2 Hedging with more than one derivative

Two or more offsetting derivatives, or proportions thereof, can be jointly designated as a hedging instrument if none of them are a written or net written option. [IAS 39:77] Further, when hedging foreign currency risk, two or more non-derivatives (or proportions) or a combination of non-derivatives and derivatives can be viewed in combination. Common situations where two or more offsetting derivatives are designated in combination as a hedging instrument are:

- when an entity issues fixed rate debt, swaps the entirety of the debt instrument to floating, and then re-fixes some of the instrument's cash flows;
- when an entity uses a combination of long and short foreign currency forward contracts to hedge its net investments in a foreign operation (e.g. when it manages foreign currency risk on the net assets of the foreign operation where the value of those net assets changes on a frequent basis); and
- when an entity uses a combination of a basis swap and a floating to fixed interest rate swap if there is not enough liquidity directly to enter into a floating to fixed interest rate swap that has a floating leg that matches the specific risk of the hedged item.

Example 3.2A

Hedging with multiple derivatives (1)

Entity A has a forecast purchase of copper. To hedge the price risk associated with the forecast purchase, it enters into a futures contract to buy copper. However, the grade of copper in the futures contract is lower than that required by Entity A. It therefore also enters into a basis swap which swaps between the different grades of copper between the futures contracts and the forecast purchase. Subject to the other hedge accounting criteria being satisfied, Entity A may jointly designate the futures and the basis swap as hedging its forecast purchase of copper.

When a combination of derivatives (or non-derivative instruments with respect to hedges of foreign currency risk only) is used as a hedging instrument, the hedge effectiveness of this relationship is based on the combination as a whole.

Example 3.2B

Hedging with multiple derivatives (2)

Entity X issues fixed rate 10-year debt. At the same time, it enters into a receive-fixed, pay-floating interest rate swap whose terms exactly match those of the debt.

The swap was entered into because Entity X did not want to be exposed to changes in interest rates over the 10-year period of the debt. However, it would like to fix its cash flows for the next 12 months, and so enters into a 1-year receive-floating, pay-fixed interest rate swap. Entity X has now re-fixed its cash flows for the first year of the debt.

Subject to the other hedge accounting criteria being satisfied, Entity X may designate both swaps as a partial term fair value hedge of interest rate risk for years 2 to 10 (even though the second swap partially offsets the effects of the first swap). Partial term hedging is discussed further in **2.2**.

Example 3.2C

Hedging with derivatives and non-derivatives

Entity A, a UK entity, has a US subsidiary, Entity Z. Entity A hedges its net investment in Entity Z in its consolidated financial statements using forward foreign currency contracts and loans. It manages the net asset position quarterly and, as the net asset position changes, it enters into further forward contracts to sell US$ and buy £ that cover the increased exposure (if the US$ net asset position increases), or if the exposure decreases (if the US$ net asset position falls) the entity enters into forward contracts to sell £ and buy US$. In the latter case, any sold US$ forward contracts will partially offset the purchased US$ forward contracts.

The loans and forward contracts may be viewed in combination and jointly designated as a hedge of the spot foreign currency risk of the net investment in Entity Z, even though some of the forward positions may offset each other. This is discussed further in **3.2.1**.

Example 3.2D

Hedging with multiple derivatives (3)

Entity C is a Euro functional currency entity. Entity C issues Mexican Peso floating rate debt. Entity C has a policy of swapping all floating rate debt into fixed and into its functional currency. Because of limited liquidity for Peso/Euro swaps, Entity C does not enter into a Receive Mexican Peso floating, Pay Euro fixed cross-currency interest rate swap. Instead, Entity C enters into a Receive Mexican Peso floating, Pay US dollar floating cross-currency swap, and a Receive US dollar floating, Pay Euro fixed cross-currency interest rate swap, and designates these two swaps in combination as a cash flow hedge of both interest rates and foreign currency of its Mexican Peso floating debt.

In July 2009, the IFRIC (now the IFRS Interpretations Committee) issued a final agenda decision titled *Hedging using more than One Derivative as the Hedging Instrument*. The IFRIC was asked for guidance on how to apply the guidance in IAS 39:IG.F.2.1 *Whether a derivative can be designated as a hedged item*, when an entity issues fixed interest rate foreign currency debt and then swaps it into floating interest rate local currency debt using a cross-currency interest rate swap. The entity also enters into a local currency pay-fixed, receive-variable interest rate swap which has a shorter duration than that of the cross-currency interest rate swap. The request was for guidance as to whether IAS 39:IG.F.2.1 prevents cash flows attributable to a derivative from being designated as the hedged cash flow in a hedge relationship.

The IFRIC noted that IAS 39:77 states that two or more derivatives may be viewed in combination *and jointly designated as the hedging instrument*, including when the risk(s) arising from some derivatives offset(s) those arising from others [emphasis added]. The IFRIC noted that consequently although IAS 39 permits a combination of derivatives to be jointly designated as the hedging instrument in a hedging relationship, it does not allow a 'synthetic hedged item' created by combining one derivative with a non-derivative financial instrument to be designated as the hedged item in a hedging relationship with another derivative.

Given the requirements in IAS 39, the IFRIC concluded that any guidance it could provide would be in the nature of implementation guidance and, therefore, decided not to add this issue to its agenda.

When an entity enters into two derivative transactions at the same time and in contemplation of each other with the same counterparty, so that the terms of the second derivative fully offset the terms of the first one, the two derivatives are viewed as one unit and cannot be used in separate hedge designations. [IAS 39:IG.B.6] This is commonly referred to as 'round-tripping'. However, when there is a substantive business purpose for structuring transactions separately, then the two derivatives are not viewed as one unit. Judgement is applied to determine whether there is a substantive business purpose. Achieving hedge accounting treatment with respect to one of the two derivative transactions is not by itself considered a substantive business purpose. [IAS 39:IG.F.1.14]

Example 3.2E

Roundtripping

[Extract from IAS 39:IG.F.1.14]

Some entities have a policy that requires a centralised dealer or treasury subsidiary to enter into third-party derivative contracts on behalf of other subsidiaries within the organisation to hedge the subsidiaries' interest rate risk exposures. The dealer or treasury subsidiary also enters into internal derivative transactions with those subsidiaries in order to track those hedges operationally within the organisation. Because the dealer or treasury subsidiary also enters into derivative contracts as part of its trading operations, or because it may wish to rebalance the risk of its overall portfolio, it may enter into a derivative contract with the same third party during the same business day that has substantially the same terms as a contract entered into as a hedging instrument on behalf of another subsidiary. In this case, there is a valid business purpose for entering into each contract.

3.2.1 Hedging with a combination of a derivative and a non-derivative

If an entity is hedging foreign currency risk, it may designate a non-derivative as a hedging instrument. An entity can also designate a combination of derivatives or a combination of a derivative and a non-derivative in a hedge of foreign currency risk. If a combination of a derivative and a non-derivative is jointly designated as a hedge of foreign currency risk, the derivative cannot be a written or a net written option. [IAS 39:77]

Example 3.2.1

Hedging with derivatives and non-derivatives

Parent A, a Sterling functional currency entity, has an investment in a Yen functional currency foreign operation. Parent A has US$100 million floating issued debt. Parent A also has a cross-currency swap to receive US dollar floating over a notional of US$100 million, pay Yen floating over a fixed notional of Yen (equivalent to US$100 million on the trade date of the swap). Both the US$ debt and the cross-currency swap have the same maturity. The Yen notional on the swap is less than the net assets of the Yen foreign operation.

Group A can designate the US dollar denominated debt and US$/Yen cross-currency swap jointly as a hedging instrument in hedging the £/Yen foreign currency risk of its net investment in its Yen foreign operation.

Even though the US dollar debt and the US$/Yen swap have a shared risk, being US dollars, that offsets when the two instruments are used in combination, the non-derivative and the derivative may be designated in combination as a hedging instrument of foreign currency risk, being £/Yen foreign currency risk, because the swap is not a written or net written option. It is assumed all other hedge accounting criteria are met.

3.3 Written options and combinations of options

3.3.1 Written options

The Standard does not allow a written option to be designated as a hedging instrument unless it is designated as an offset to a purchased option (including one that is embedded in another financial instrument). The written option is not effective in reducing the profit or loss exposure of a hedged item because the potential loss on an option that an entity writes could be significantly greater than the potential gain in value of a related hedged item. [IAS 39:AG94]

Example 3.3.1A

Hedging an investment with a written call

Entity A owns shares in Entity X, an unrelated entity. It classifies these shares as available-for-sale in accordance with IAS 39. Entity A purchased the shares when the share price was CU10. The share price is currently CU15. Entity A writes an option over its shares in Entity X, allowing the purchaser of the option to acquire the shares for CU17, and for this Entity A receives a premium of CU0.50.

Entity A may not designate the option as a hedge of its shares in Entity X because it is a written option.

All hedging instruments must be assessed to consider whether they contain a written option because this will often disqualify them from being designated as hedging instruments.

Example 3.3.1B

Embedded written options in interest rate swaps

Entity A issues 20-year fixed rate debt. To hedge its fair value exposure to interest rate risk, it enters into a receive fixed, pay floating interest rate swap, such that all the terms of the swap match the debt. Owing to the long-term nature of the swap, the counterparty to the swap, the Bank, inserts a break clause into the swap giving the Bank the option to terminate the swap after ten years so that, on termination, no cash will be exchanged. No cash is exchanged at the start of the transaction.

Entity A has effectively written an option to the bank allowing it to terminate the swap after ten years. While no cash was exchanged up-front, Entity A will have been recompensed for writing this option by receiving a favourable rate on one of the legs of the swap.

The swap cannot be designated as a hedge of the issued debt because it contains a written option. The written option cannot be split out of the swap contract (leaving a vanilla 20-year interest swap) because a derivative must be designated as a hedging instrument in its entirety (with only two exceptions as described in **4.2** in **chapter C9**).

If the terms of the break clause resulted in termination of the swap at fair value at the time of termination, and fair value excluded any additional compensation paid/receivable to either party in excess of the interest rate swap, the swap would still contain a written option, but the value of the option would be zero.

The legs of the swap would be no different from a swap without a break clause. In this case the swap could be used as a hedging instrument.

IAS 39:AG94 states that a written option can only be used as a hedging instrument when it is designated as an offset to a purchased option. The purchased option can be either a stand-alone derivative, or one embedded in another contract. Thus, a written option could be designated as hedging a callable liability where the issuer has the right to call the debt back early.

3.3.2 Net written options

If two options, one written and one purchased, are structured as a single instrument (e.g. as a collar), this instrument must be assessed to see whether overall it is a net written option.

Even when the critical terms and conditions of the written option component and the purchased option component are largely the same (e.g. underlying variable(s), currency denomination and maturity date are the same) a combination of written and purchased options is deemed to be net written (and, therefore, not eligible for designation as a hedging instrument) if:

(i) a net premium is received, either at inception or over the life of the combination of options; or

(ii) the notional on the written option exceeds that on the purchased option. [IAS 39:IG.F.1.3]

Example 3.3.2

Hedging with a collar

Entity A issues CU100 million variable rate debt. To hedge against interest rate increases, it purchases an interest rate collar at the date of issuance of the debt that hedges interest rates above 8 per cent and below 4 per cent. Current fixed interest rates for the same term as the debt are 6 per cent. The collar costs CU0.5 million as forward rates indicate that interest rates are expected to rise over the term of the debt and therefore there is a greater likelihood that the purchased cap will be in the money, when compared to the written floor. The purchased cap at 8 per cent and written floor at 4 per cent included in the collar have the same notional of CU100 million.

Entity A may designate the collar as a cash flow hedge of the variable rate debt because there is no net premium received (there is a net premium payable of CU0.5 million) and the notional on the floor does not exceed that on the cap.

If there was a premium received on the collar, it could not have been designated as a hedging instrument. Equally, if the notional on the floor was greater than CU100 million, the collar could not have been designated as a hedging instrument.

It is not acceptable to split a single instrument that consists of a number of options (e.g. an interest rate collar) and designate just the purchased option component as a hedging instrument. IAS 39:74 specifies that a derivative is designated as a hedging instrument in its entirety except when splitting the time value and intrinsic value of an option and splitting the interest element and spot price on a forward. [IAS 39:IG.F.1.8]

As is the case for all hedging instruments, in order for a combination of interest rate options structured as a single instrument to qualify as a hedging instrument, the combination of options must be expected to be highly effective in achieving offsetting changes in fair value or cash flows attributable to the hedged risk.

3.3.3 Combination of derivatives that includes a written option

Only a combination of separate contractual derivatives that does not include a written or a net written option can be designated as a single qualifying hedging instrument. [IAS 39:77]

When an entity enters into purchased and sold options at the same time, it is necessary to consider, by analogy to the following indicators contained in IAS 39:IG.B.6, whether the two options are separate instruments or the combination of the two options is in substance a single arrangement. Factors that indicate that the instrument is a single arrangement are:

- they are entered into at the same time and in contemplation of one another;
- they have the same counterparty;
- they relate to the same risk; and
- there is no apparent economic need or substantive business purpose for structuring the transactions separately that could not also have been accomplished in a single transaction.

If the combination of options is not considered to be one arrangement, and one of the instruments is a written option or net written option, the combination of options cannot be designated as a hedging instrument.

However, a combination of options structured as a single instrument (that may economically be equivalent to options in a combination of contractually separate instruments) qualifies for designation as a hedging instrument as long as the single instrument is not a net written option as described in **3.3.1**. This is the case for a zero cost collar that combines a purchased option and a written option and passes the test of not being a net written option overall.

3.4 Purchased options

When designating an option in a cash flow hedge accounting relationship, it is common to designate just the intrinsic value of the option as permitted by IAS 39:74(a) and not designate the time value of the option. This approach ensures that when the option is 'in the money', the option is fully effective at hedging the variability in cash flows of the hedged item. Because the time value of the option is not designated as part of the hedge relationship, the gains/losses relating to time value are immediately recognised in profit or loss. These gains/losses are not considered hedge ineffectiveness because time value did not form part of the hedge accounting relationship. Had an entity chosen instead to designate the entirety of the option, the fair value gains/losses that result from changes in time value would cause hedge ineffectiveness, perhaps to such a great degree that the entity could not claim that the hedge is expected to be highly effective.

In July 2008, the IASB issued an amendment to IAS 39 titled *Eligible Hedged Items*. The amendment clarified that a purchased (or net purchased) option can be designated as a hedging instrument in a hedge of a financial or non-financial item. An entity may designate an option as a hedge of changes in the cash flows or fair value of a hedged item above or below a specified price or other variable (a one-sided risk). The amendments make it clear that the intrinsic value, not the time value, of an option reflects a one-sided risk and, therefore, an option designated in its entirety cannot be perfectly effective. The time value of a purchased option is not a component of the forecast transaction that affects profit or loss. Therefore, if an entity designates an option in its entirety as a hedge of a one-sided risk arising from a forecast transaction hedge ineffectiveness will arise. Alternatively, an entity may choose to exclude time value as permitted by the Standard in order to improve hedge effectiveness. As a result of this designation, changes in the time value of the option will be recognised immediately in profit or loss.

If a purchased option or a net purchased option is in the money at the date of designation and the entity excludes time value from the hedge relationship, the question arises as to whether the intrinsic value that exists at the date of designation is itself effective at hedging future cash flows in a cash flow hedge. Changes in this intrinsic value (increases and decreases) could be effective when designated in a hedge, however, the level of hedge effectiveness will depend on how the hedged risk is designated. Alternative designations are illustrated in the example in **3.12** in **chapter C11**.

3.5 Dynamic hedging strategies

IAS 39:74 states that "a dynamic hedging strategy that assesses both the intrinsic value and time value of an option contract can qualify for hedge accounting", i.e. the Standard permits an entity to apply hedge accounting for a 'delta-neutral' or other dynamic hedging strategy under which the quantity of the hedging instrument is constantly adjusted in order to maintain a desired hedge ratio. For example, an entity may wish to achieve a delta-neutral position insensitive to changes in the fair value of the hedged item.

Example 3.5

Delta-neutral hedging

An entity hedges the fair value of an equity security by using a combination of purchased options that aims to achieve a delta-neutral position. As the delta of the options changes, the number of options required will change to ensure the hedge is considered to be highly effective for movements in the fair value of the equity securities. This strategy can qualify for hedge accounting.

To qualify for hedge accounting, all the usual conditions must be met. These will include documenting how effectiveness will be assessed and measured, and demonstrating an ability to track properly all terminations and re-designations of the hedging instrument. Also, the entity must be able to demonstrate an expectation that the hedge will be highly effective for any specified short period of time during which the hedge is not expected to be adjusted. [IAS 39:IG.F.1.9]

3.6 'All-in-one' hedges

A derivative instrument within the scope of IAS 39 that will be settled by physical delivery of an underlying asset at a fixed price can be designated as the hedging instrument in a cash flow hedge of that gross settlement. Without the derivative there would be an exposure to variability in the purchase or sale price. The derivative eliminates this exposure, i.e. it acts as a hedging instrument. [IAS 39:IG.F.2.5] This hedge strategy is suitable when the underlying hedged item, when it is recognised, will not subsequently be measured at fair value.

The rationale for allowing hedge accounting for 'all-in-one' hedges is that an entity should not be disadvantaged by not achieving hedge accounting irrespective of whether a transaction is structured as a single instrument or as a combination of two transactions. Consider the following example.

Entity A normally sells products at variable prices. Entity A could concurrently enter into derivative transactions to fix the price of its forecast sales. Derivative instruments would be recognised at fair value with gains or losses recognised in profit or loss, unless hedge accounting is applied. Assuming the sales are highly probable and cash flow hedge accounting is applied, Entity A would recognise the gains and losses on its hedging instruments in other comprehensive income and reclassify them from equity to profit or loss when the sales occur.

Entity A now decides that it is no longer going to sell its products at variable prices and swap them back into fixed prices via derivatives, but instead is going to fix the sales price today directly with the customer. If the fixed price contract with the customer fell within the scope of IAS 39, it would be recognised at fair value with gains and losses recognised in profit or loss. By applying an all-in-one hedge accounting strategy, Entity A can obtain the same accounting treatment (i.e. recognise gains and losses on the derivative in other comprehensive income until the sale occurs under cash flow hedging), as had been the case in the former scenario where hedge accounting was applied to the derivative and the forecast sale separately.

Example 3.6A

All-in-one hedge of a non-financial item

An entity enters into a fixed price contract to sell a commodity and that contract is accounted for as a derivative under IAS 39. (This may be because the entity has a practice of settling similar contracts net in cash or taking delivery of the underlying and selling it within a short period after delivery for the purpose of generating a profit from short-term fluctuations in price or dealer's margin.) The entity may designate the fixed price contract as a cash flow hedge of the variability of the consideration to be received on the sale of the asset (a future transaction) even though the fixed price contract is the contract under which the asset will be sold.

Example 3.6B

All-in-one hedge of a debt instrument

An entity enters into a forward contract to purchase a debt instrument that will be settled by physical delivery of the debt instrument. The forward contract is a derivative in the scope of IAS 39 because its term exceeds the regular way delivery period in the marketplace. The entity may designate the forward contract as a cash flow hedge of the variability of the consideration to be paid to acquire the debt instrument (a forecast transaction), even though the derivative is the contract under which the debt instrument will be acquired.

Example 3.6C

All-in-one hedge of an equity instrument

Entity P, a US dollar functional currency entity, enters into a forward contract to buy an equity share of Entity X in six months' time at US$10 per share. The current share price of Entity X is US$10. At maturity of the forward contract the share price is US$15 and, therefore, the forward contract has a positive fair value at maturity of US$5 per share.

Entity P cannot designate the forward contract as an all-in-one hedge of the future acquisition of a share in Entity X in six months' time. If the share is measured as at fair value through profit or loss there is no systematic basis in which the hedged risk affects profit or loss and, therefore, Entity P cannot determine how the amount recognised in other comprehensive income can be reclassified from equity to profit or loss.

To illustrate why the forward contract cannot be designated in an all-in-one hedge of a share to be acquired in six months' time that will be measured at FVTPL consider the accounting entries that would result if cash flow hedging was applied:

(i) at initial recognition of the equity security, there would be a gain of US$5 in other comprehensive income that would require reclassification from equity to profit or loss when the hedged risk of the hedged item affects profit or loss; and

(ii) the shares would be recognised at fair value, being US$15 (Dr Shares US$15, Cr Cash US$10, Cr Derivative asset US$5).

If the share price rose or fell and thus affected profit or loss, there would be no basis for determining how much of the gain recognised in other comprehensive income should be reclassified to profit or loss.

3.7 Splitting a derivative to exclude embedded financing

It is not possible to split the embedded financing from a non-optional derivative that has a fair value other than zero at the time of designation and account for it as a separate amortising loan whilst designating the zero fair value derivative as the hedging instrument.

If a non-optional derivative, such as a forward contract or swap, has a fair value other than zero at inception of the hedge, future changes in its fair value are affected by that starting value. The derivative includes an embedded financing element that contributes to its fair value movements and causes them to differ from the changes in fair value of the hedged item when the hedged item does not have an equal and opposite financing element.

IAS 39 does not prohibit non-zero fair value non-optional derivatives being designated as hedging instruments as long as the hedging instrument is expected to be highly effective. In fact, IAS 39 allows hedging instruments to be designated part way through their lives and, therefore, it is quite common for a derivative to have a starting value on designation other than zero. If the derivative can pass the prospective assessment of hedge effectiveness, the non-zero element of the derivative at initial designation will cause ineffectiveness that will be recognised in profit or loss over the term of the hedge. This is particularly the case for cash flow hedges because the 'hypothetical derivative' is deemed to be on-market at the date of designation, which for a non-optional derivative would have a fair value of zero (see **4.1** and **4.4.1**).

The ineffectiveness arises because the embedded financing element is economically similar to a fixed rate amortising loan embedded in the derivative and this 'loan' will change in fair value as interest rates move. By the time the derivative matures, the loan will have been fully eliminated along with the derivative.

3.8 Rollover hedging strategies

A combination of more than one derivative or a derivative and a non-derivative may be used in 'rollover' hedging strategies when applying cash flow hedge accounting. IAS 39 envisages hedging strategies may include the replacement or rollover of one hedging instrument into another as they are referred to in IAS 39:101(a): an entity should discontinue prospectively hedge accounting when "the hedging instrument expires or is sold, terminated or exercised (for this purpose, the replacement or rollover of a hedging instrument into another hedging instrument is not an expiration or termination if such replacement or rollover is part of the entity's documented hedging strategy)" (see **2.2.4** in **chapter C9**).

The benefit of a rollover strategy is that derivatives that have a maturity shorter than the timing of the underlying exposure of the hedged item can be designated as part of a rollover strategy as a hedge of that long-dated exposure. Where the hedged item is a financial instrument this technique offers no advantage because an entity could instead apply partial term hedging, i.e. hedge a risk of the hedged item for part of its life (see **2.2**), but for hedges of non-financial items it is beneficial because, for non-financial items, an entity can only hedge foreign currency risk or all risk in its entirety, i.e. it is not possible to apply partial term hedging.

The following example illustrates how a rollover hedging strategy can be applied in a cash flow hedge relationship.

Example 3.8

Rollover strategies

On 1 January 20X1, Entity A, a Sterling functional currency entity, determines with high probability that it will have US$10 million worth of sales on 30 September 20X1. Entity A enters into short dated forward contracts as part of a rollover strategy in order to hedge the US$:£ risk on its highly probable US dollar sales.

On 1 January 20X1, Entity A enters into a 6-month forward contract (F1) to sell US$10 million and buy £ which is intended to rollover into a new 3-month US$:£ forward contract (F2), also with a notional of US$10 million, to coincide with the timing of the highly probable sales.

Entity A could designate the hedge relationship in one of two ways.

Designation 1

Designate the US$:£ foreign currency *spot* rate risk relating to the first US$10 million of highly probable sales due to occur on 30 September 20X1 with the hedging instrument being the original forward contract (F1) recognised in the statement of financial position at the date of designation and rolled over into a new forward contract (F2) as part of the entity's hedging strategy.

In determining hedge effectiveness (see **section 4** for detail), the hypothetical derivative will be the spot element of an on-market forward contract for US$:£ that is entered into on 1 January 20X1 and matures on 30 September 20X1. The forward points will be excluded from the fair value of the hypothetical derivative as it does not form part of the hedge relationship. The hypothetical derivative has a maturity date of 30 September 20X1 to coincide with the timing of the forecast transaction.

This designation will not be perfectly effective for a hedge of spot rates; there will be some ineffectiveness in the first six months because the fair value of the spot element of F1 will be discounted from 30 June 20X1, whereas the fair value of the hypothetical derivative will be discounted from 30 September 20X1. In the second period, there will be no additional ineffectiveness due to discounting because both F2 and the hypothetical derivative terminate on the same date. Changes in the fair value of the forward points of the derivatives, F1 in the first period and F2 in the second period, will be immediately recognised in profit or loss because forward points do not form part of the hedge relationship.

Designation 2

Designate the US$:£ foreign currency *forward* rate risk relating to the first US$10 million of highly probable sales due to occur on 30 September 20X1 with the hedging instrument being the original forward contract (F1) recognised in the statement of financial position at the date of designation and rolled over into a new forward contract (F2) as part of the entity's hedging strategy.

In determining hedge effectiveness, the hypothetical derivative will be a forward contract for US$:£ that is entered into on 1 January 20X1 and matures on 30 September 20X1 when the forecast transaction is expected to occur.

Because the forward points form part of the hedge relationship, the fair value of this hypothetical derivative will be compared with the fair value of the hedging instrument. Forward points in this case are not excluded from the hedge designation because Entity A is hedging the forward foreign currency exchange rate.

The effectiveness of the hedging relationship will be evaluated by comparing the cumulative change in the present value of the hedged item's cash flows due to the hedged risk (being the *forward* foreign currency exposure), which will equal the hypothetical derivative, with the fair value of the hedging instrument. This hedge will not be perfectly effective. As for Designation 1, the differing maturities of F1 and the hypothetical derivative in the first period will be a source of ineffectiveness. In addition, the forward rate that is locked into F1 will differ from the forward rate implicit in the hypothetical derivative which will be a further source of ineffectiveness.

If F1 is rolled over into a non-derivative financial instrument, a liability to deliver US$10 million on 30 September 20X1, Entity A could apply the following designation.

Rollover of a derivative to a non-derivative

Assume the first derivative, F1, is gross cash settled (gross exchange of US$ and £) and Entity A borrows US dollars at 30 June 20X1 in order to deliver under the gross cash settled derivative, F1, and the borrowing matures on 30 September 20X1. Entity A could intend to designate the anticipated rollover of derivative, F1, into a non-derivative, the US dollar borrowing, as a hedging instrument of the US$:£ foreign currency spot rate relating to the first US$10 million of highly probably sales due to occur on 30 September 20X1. Entity A can only designate the *spot* US$:£ rate, not the *forward* US$:£ rate, because the liability is only subject to spot retranslation under IAS 21. The same level of ineffectiveness would result as per Designation 1.

3.9 Deal contingent derivatives

An entity that expects to enter into transactions whose occurrence depends on a future event sometimes enter into derivatives that mirror the possibility of non-occurrence of the future event, i.e. the derivative has a knock-out option that is exercised if the future event does not occur. These are often referred to as deal contingent derivatives. If the future event occurs the derivative remains outstanding; if the event does not occur, the derivative ceases to exist and no settlements between the parties are made. It is unlikely that these instruments can be considered qualifying hedging instruments as illustrated in the example below.

Example 3.9

Hedging with deal contingent forwards

An entity believes it will enter into a highly likely business combination at a future date where the consideration for the acquiree is specified in a foreign currency. The prospective acquirer is awaiting approval by the acquiree's current shareholders, regulatory agencies, governments, or other parties etc. The prospective acquirer chooses to hedge economically its exposure by entering into a deal contingent foreign currency forward contract, such that if the business combination does not proceed the forward contract knocks-out and is terminated with no cash settlement between the parties. The value of this derivative contract is driven not only by the foreign currency component but also by the probability of the business combination occurring.

The business combination is unlikely to be seen as being highly probable and, therefore, it would be inappropriate to designate the deal contingent forward contract as a hedge of the currency risk of the forecast business combination. The existence of a knock-out option adds strength to the argument that the business combination is not highly probable because the knock-out feature would not be needed if it was. IAS 39 presupposes that if an entity is hedging a transaction that it claims to be highly probable it expects the transaction to occur, while here the entity is economically entering into an additional hedge: the hedge of the non-occurrence of the transaction. The fair value of the deal contingent forward includes the probability that the business combination will not occur which, when compared to the fair value of a hypothetical derivative, a vanilla forward that assumes the transaction will occur, will be different. This difference may be so significant that the entity cannot claim on a prospective assessment of hedge effectiveness that the hedge is expected to be highly effective.

The ineffectiveness cannot be minimised by designating additionally the risk of non-occurrence of the transaction for two reasons:

(i) the risk of non-occurrence is considered to be a general business risk and hence is not eligible to be a hedged item [IAS 39:IG.F.2.8]; and

(ii) with the exceptions set out in IAS 39:74, an entity must designate a derivative instrument in its entirety.

3.10 Internal hedges

In a group that has a central treasury function, a group entity or division that wishes to enter into hedging transactions uses their central treasury function rather than using an external group counterparty. The central treasury function then aggregates all its internal positions and enters into external transactions to offset the internal ones on a net basis thereby taking advantage of any natural offsets and hedging the exposures of the group in a cost efficient way.

At a group level, if the central treasury function enters into external derivatives these can be used as hedging instruments, but only as a hedge of a gross position. As discussed in **3.9** in **chapter C9**, a net position cannot be a hedged item. Therefore, even though the external derivative was entered into to offset a net position, it can be used as a hedging instrument but only if it is designated as hedging (a portion of) a gross position.

Example 3.10A

Hedging an external gross position (1)

Entity A has a central treasury division. The central treasury division aggregates the internal derivative contracts with other group entities, and enters into external derivatives that offset the internal derivatives on a net basis.

Central treasury has three internal receive-fixed, pay-variable interest rate swaps and one internal receive-variable, pay-fixed interest rate swap. It enters into an interest rate swap with an external counterparty that exactly offsets the four internal swaps as follows,

Swap	Counterparty	Description	Notional
1	Internal	Receive-fixed, pay-variable	£100 million
2	Internal	Receive-fixed, pay-variable	£60 million
3	Internal	Receive-fixed, pay-variable	£30 million
4	Internal	Receive-variable, pay-fixed	£150 million
5	External	Receive-variable, pay-fixed	£40 million

Swap 5 cannot hedge an overall net position, i.e. it cannot be used to hedge all of the items that the internal derivatives 1-4 are hedging. IAS 39 states that an overall net position cannot qualify as a hedged item.

However, Swap 5 can qualify as a hedging instrument in a hedge of the underlying hedged items residing in the group companies on a gross basis, i.e. it could hedge £40 million of fixed rate assets or £40 million of variable rate liabilities.

IAS 39:IG.F.1.4 gives further guidance on the use of internal derivatives. The guidance derives from the principles for preparing consolidated financial statements in IFRS 10 *Consolidated Financial Statements*, which require that intragroup balances, transactions, income and expenses shall be eliminated in full.

Only a derivative that is external to the reporting entity, i.e. external to the group or individual entity that is being reported, can be designated as a hedging instrument. In the consolidated financial statements, intragroup derivatives cannot be hedging instruments because these are not external to the reporting entity and they are eliminated on consolidation. However, they may be used in the entity's individual financial statements because, from the individual entity's perspective, such derivatives are with a third party. [IAS 39:73]

Example 3.10B

Hedge accounting in the group versus individual financial statements

Entity A has a 100 per cent subsidiary, Entity B. The group treasury policy requires that only Entity A enters into derivatives with external parties. If Entity B wishes to enter into a foreign currency forward it notifies Entity A. Entity A enters into a forward with a bank (Forward 1), and then enters into an equal and opposite forward contract with Entity B (Forward 2).

From a consolidated perspective, only the forward contract with the bank, Forward 1, can be a designated hedging instrument. In Entity B's individual financial statements, Forward 2 may be designated as a hedging instrument. This would be true even if Entity A had not entered into Forward 1 with the bank.

In Entity A's individual financial statements, there will be two equal and opposite derivatives. These must be presented separately in its statement of financial position. They cannot be offset as they do not meet the offset requirements of IAS 32 (see **section 6** in **chapter C12**).

Entities sometimes enter into netting agreements with a bank such that derivatives held with that bank are settled on a net basis. This does not in itself preclude those instruments from being designated as hedging instruments. [IAS 39:IG.F.2.16]

Example 3.10C

Hedging an external gross position (2)

Entity A has several subsidiaries. Entity A acts as a central treasury function, so that if any subsidiary wants to lay off risk it must do so with Entity A. For each internal derivative, Entity A enters into an equal and opposite external contract with a bank. Thus, if it has a 3-year pay 6 per cent receive LIBOR interest rate swap with a subsidiary, it will enter into a 3-year receive 6 per cent pay LIBOR interest rate swap with a bank, such that all of the terms of the two contracts match. Each internal derivative is hedging a gross exposure.

The external derivatives can be designated as hedging instruments of the underlying gross exposures in the group's consolidated financial statements. This is true even if the external derivatives are settled on a net basis. Provided that the contracts are legally separate and serve a valid business purpose (such as laying off risk exposures on underlying gross positions), they qualify as hedging instruments.

Entities sometimes have external positions that offset each other. This can arise (as in the above example) because there is a policy of hedging every exposure separately (i.e. gross), or because an entity wishes to manage its external portfolio in a certain way.

Example 3.10D

Hedging an external gross position (3)

Continuing with **example 3.10C**, assume Entity A manages the portfolio of offsetting external derivatives separately from other exposures of the entity and enters into an additional, single derivative to offset the risk of the portfolio.

The individual external derivative contracts in the portfolio can still be designated as hedging instruments of the underlying gross exposures even though a single external derivative is used to offset fully the market exposure created by entering into these external contracts.

The purpose of structuring the external derivative contracts in this manner is consistent with the entity's risk management objectives and strategies. As noted in **section 3.2**, external derivative contracts that are structured separately and serve a valid business purpose qualify as hedging instruments. [IAS 39:IG.F.2.16]

Detailed guidance on achieving hedge accounting in the group consolidated financial statements where a central treasury function exists is provided in the Implementation Guidance of IAS 39. Specifically, IAS 39:IG.F.1.5

provides guidance on offsetting internal derivative contracts used to manage interest rate risk, and IAS 39:IG.F.1.6 and IAS 39:IG.F.1.7 provide guidance on offsetting internal derivative contracts used to manage foreign exchange risk.

4 Hedge effectiveness assessment

IAS 39 requires a hedge to be 'highly effective', prospectively and retrospectively, for it to qualify for hedge accounting. [IAS 39:88] The highly effective criterion is used in the assessment of hedge effectiveness. If an entity passes the highly effective criterion and applies hedge accounting in a period, any ineffectiveness is required to be measured and recognised immediately in profit or loss.

The concept of hedge effectiveness and the basic methods for assessing hedge effectiveness are discussed in **section 5** in **chapter C9**. This section discusses techniques to minimise hedge ineffectiveness and explores more advanced methods of assessing hedge effectiveness such as regression analysis.

4.1 Hedge effectiveness – gains/losses versus carrying amount

Assessing hedge effectiveness is based on comparing changes in the fair value of the hedging instrument and changes in the fair value of the hedged item attributable to the hedged risk. In determining the change in fair value of the hedging instrument, an entity considers gains and losses, not the carrying amount of the hedging instrument in the statement of financial position. It is the gains/losses that are recognised in profit or loss, whereas changes in the carrying amount of the hedging instrument may result from receipts or payments of cash which do not affect profit or loss. Similarly for the hedged item, it is the impact of the hedged risk of the hedged item that affects profit or loss and that is, therefore, considered in assessing hedge effectiveness and not the carrying amount of the hedged item itself.

Example 4.1

Cash flow hedge ineffectiveness: off-market swaps

Entity B designates an off-market receive LIBOR, pay 7 per cent interest rate swap in a cash flow hedge of variability on CU100m of its issued variable rate debt attributable to changes in interest rates. The interest rate swap has a notional of CU100m and matures five years after the date of designation. The interest rate swap is off-market at initial designation with a negative fair value of CU8.5m because expectations of interest rates have fallen since the swap was originally priced. The current yield curve for the remaining time to maturity is 5 per cent.

Entity B measures hedge ineffectiveness using the hypothetical derivative method. At the date of designation it determines that a hypothetical derivative that would have a fair value of zero is the same as the actual derivative except that it would receive LIBOR, pay 5 per cent (not receive LIBOR, pay 7 per cent). In assessing hedge effectiveness, Entity B models the actual and hypothetical derivative under various interest rate scenarios and compares the two in reaching its conclusion that the actual derivative, even though off-market, will still meet the hedge effectiveness requirements and therefore can qualify as a hedging instrument in a qualifying hedge relationship. The 2 per cent extra that Entity B will pay on the actual derivative compared to the hypothetical derivative (CU10m in total) will not be equal to the amount of hedge ineffectiveness that will arise in the future periods. The 2 per cent is part of the cash flows of the actual derivative. The total amount of hedge ineffectiveness due to these cash flows over the life of the hedge will be CU1.5m (equal to the difference between the cash paid in respect of the additional 2 per cent and the initial fair value of the derivative). However, this ineffectiveness will only be recognised in profit or loss to the extent there is an over-hedge overall. The amount of hedge ineffectiveness recognised in each period will depend on how future interest rates affect the cumulative fair value gains/losses on the actual derivative from inception of the hedge as compared to the effect they will have on the hypothetical derivative. Another way of viewing the 2 per cent difference between the pay leg of the actual derivative and hypothetical derivative is viewing Entity B as paying loan instalments equal to 2 per cent of the notional of the swap every period (CU2m) to the swap counterparty on an amortising loan. The cash payments on the 'loan' do not affect profit or loss, but changes in fair value of these future cash flows do.

Examples illustrating the journal entries for a cash flow hedge of floating rate debt using an off-market interest rate swap are included in **3.5** of **chapter C11**. Guidance on reclassifying amounts deferred in the cash flow hedge reserve when hedging interest rate risk with an off-market swap can be found at **2.2.6** in **chapter C9**.

4.2 Sources of hedge ineffectiveness

4.2.1 Basis risk

It is not always possible for an entity to find a hedging instrument with exactly the same terms as the item it wishes to hedge. Basis differences result from using a hedging instrument that is based on a specific risk that is similar, but not identical to the risk being hedged in the hedged item. For example, there may not always be an active market for the grade or location of a commodity that an entity is seeking to hedge.

For interest sensitive items, basis differences result from differences in interest indices (e.g. LIBOR versus Treasury rates), in terms (e.g. three-month LIBOR versus 6-month LIBOR), and in credit risk differences.

Example 4.2.1A

Basis risk: commodities

Entity Z has 20,000 therms of natural gas stored at its location in the United Kingdom. Entity Z ultimately intends selling this gas to customers in continental Europe, and is concerned that prices may fall in the future. To hedge the exposure of its sales of natural gas, Entity Z sells the equivalent of 20,000 therms of natural gas under a forward contract (which Entity Z intends on net settling in cash by entering into an offsetting position in the spot market at delivery). The forward contract's price is based on delivery of natural gas at the Zeebrugge gas collection point in Belgium. Because prices in the UK (as based on the price quoted in the UK National Balancing Point, or NBP, market) and at Zeebrugge will differ as a result of regional factors (e.g. location, pipeline transmission costs, and supply and demand), Entity Z cannot assume that the hedge will be highly effective in achieving offsetting changes in fair value. Entity Z appropriately documents the hedging strategy and states that effectiveness will be measured based on the spot prices of natural gas in the UK NBP market and the spot prices at the Zeebrugge hub.

Entity Z is required to demonstrate effectiveness at inception and on an ongoing basis. This is achieved typically through a correlation method such as regression analysis, or ratio analysis. If such analysis does not result in an expectation that correlation would be between 80 - 125%, Entity Z is not permitted to apply hedge accounting. However, even if the effectiveness test is met, Entity Z may have ineffectiveness due to the difference in the basis of the hedged item and the hedging instrument and such ineffectiveness is recognised in profit or loss.

Example 4.2.1B

Basis risk: interest rate resets

Entity D designates an interest rate swap as hedging a debt instrument. The interest rate swap's rate settles every three months but is indexed to the six-month LIBOR rate and the debt settles every three months but is indexed to the three-month LIBOR rate, i.e. the three-month LIBOR index on the debt does not match the six-month LIBOR index on the swap. To the extent that there is high empirical correlation between these rate indices, Entity D may designate the swap as the hedge of the interest rate risk on the debt instrument, but the different rate indexation may result in ineffectiveness that needs to be measured and recognised.

Example 4.2.1C

Basis risk: foreign currency risk

Entity X's functional currency is the Euro. Entity X's forecast purchase of equipment from Brazil is expected to cost R$100,000. Entity X wishes to hedge its foreign currency risk. Because the US$/ Euro currency market is more liquid than the R$/ Euro dollar currency market, Entity X enters into a forward contract to receive US$33,300 and pay €27,000. The US$ will then be converted into Brazilian Real in the liquid spot market for payment to the supplier.

Because the bases of foreign currency for the purchase of the equipment and the foreign exchange forward contract are different (R$ vs. US$), Entity X will have to demonstrate that US$/€ is highly effective in hedging R$/€ both at inception and on an ongoing basis. The entity could use a correlation method to demonstrate the effectiveness of this relationship.

To the extent that there is a basis difference between R$ and US$, hedge ineffectiveness will result and will be recognised in profit or loss.

Further examples

An illustration of the entries for a cash flow hedge of interest rate risk on a forecast debt issuance using an interest rate swap with a different basis to the hedged item is included in **3.13** in **chapter C11**.

4.2.2 Hedge ineffectiveness – forecast transaction occurs earlier than expected

When the forecast transaction that an entity has designated as a hedged item in a cash flow hedge (e.g. a forecast sale of a commodity) is expected to occur in an earlier period than originally anticipated, the entity can conclude that this transaction is the same as the one that was designated as being hedged. The change in timing of the forecast transaction does not affect the validity of the designation. [IAS 39:IG.F.5.4]

However, it may affect the assessment of the effectiveness of the hedging relationship because the hedging instrument would need to be designated as a hedging instrument for the whole remaining period of its existence in order for it to continue to qualify as a hedging instrument. If the forecast transaction was expected to occur prior to the date documented in the hedge documentation, the relationship is likely to be ineffective because the hedging instrument matures after the transaction has occurred. The hedging instrument cannot be split into a part that is fully effective up to the date of the transaction, and a part that is excluded from the designation. However, if the forecast transaction was delayed, and was expected to occur after the date documented in the hedge documentation, the hedge could be redesignated as a hedge for the period up to the date on which the forecast transaction is now expected to occur. The effective part of this hedge will be recognised in other comprehensive income, and reclassified from equity to profit or loss when the transaction affects profit or loss. In the latter case, the hedging instrument is being designated for its full life.

4.3 Minimising hedge ineffectiveness

4.3.1 Designating a cash flow hedge in layers

In order to improve effectiveness, an entity may choose to hedge forecast transactions in layers. For example, instead of hedging a single layer of the first US$1m of forecast sales, an entity could designate the hedge relationship in layers: the first US$0.6m of forecast sales and a second layer of US$0.4m forecast sales. Designation in layers will only result in better hedge effectiveness when, in future periods, the amount of previously designated highly probable forecast transactions falls. In such a situation an entity may be able to recognise a greater amount in other comprehensive income if it designates in layers because hedge effectiveness will be assessed on each individual layer.

Further examples

An illustration of the entries for a cash flow hedge designated in layers for foreign currency risk of forecast revenue using forward exchange contracts is included in **3.11** in **chapter C11**.

4.3.2 A hedge ratio of other than one to one

For the purposes of designating a hedge relationship that satisfies the highly effective criterion, the amount of the hedging instrument designated may be greater or less than that of the hedged item if this improves the effectiveness of the hedging relationship.

For example, if an entity hedges an item with a hedging instrument with a different basis (IAS 39:AG100 uses the example of a transaction based on Brazilian coffee prices hedged with a transaction based on Columbian coffee prices), a regression analysis (see **4.6**) could be performed to establish a statistical relationship between the two items. If a valid statistical relationship between the two variables (i.e. between the unit prices of Brazilian coffee and Columbian coffee) can be demonstrated, the slope of the regression line could be used to establish the hedge ratio that would maximise expected effectiveness.

If the slope of the regression line is, say, 1.02, a hedge ratio based on 0.98 quantities of hedged items to 1.00 quantities of the hedging instrument will maximise expected effectiveness.

Example 4.3.2

Hedge ratio other than one

Entity R periodically issues new bonds to refinance maturing bonds, provide working capital, and for various other purposes. Entity R hedges the risk of changes in the long-term interest rates from the date it decides to issue the bonds to the date the bonds are issued.

Entity R performed historical correlation studies and determined that a treasury bond of the same maturity adequately correlates to the bonds Entity R expects to issue, assuming a hedge ratio of 0.93 futures on treasury bonds to one debt unit. In order to achieve an effective hedge of the future issuance of the bond, Entity R enters into the futures on treasury bonds using this ratio.

Hedge ineffectiveness is measured on the basis of the actual amounts designated. It is not possible to designate an exposure based on a specified notional, but measure ineffectiveness on a different notional.

4.3.3 Hedging on an after-tax basis

IAS 39 permits assessment of hedge effectiveness on an after-tax basis, provided that this approach is documented formally at inception. [IAS 39:IG.F.4.1]

It may be advantageous to assess hedge effectiveness on an after-tax basis when the hedged item and the hedging instrument are taxed differently. However, it must be borne in mind that any subsequent changes in the basis or rate of tax of either the hedged item or hedging instrument will result in hedge ineffectiveness.

Further examples

An illustration of the entries for a net investment hedge of a foreign operation assessed for hedge effectiveness on an after tax basis is included in **4.6** in **chapter C11**.

4.3.4 Forward points

When a forward contract is designated as a hedging instrument in a cash flow hedge of a forecast transaction, the entity can choose to exclude the fair value movements of the forward points from the hedge relationship. In other words, an entity may include in its designation the whole fair value movements of the forward contract, or just the fair value movements of the forward contract that relate solely to movements in spot rates.

Example 4.3.4

Hedging the forward foreign currency rate

Entity X is a Euro functional entity. Entity X makes sales to US customers in US dollars. Entity X wishes to hedge its exposure to US dollars by entering into a forward contract to sell US$ and buy € at a fixed rate at a specified delivery date that coincides with the timing of the sales.

Entity X can choose to designate the hedged risk as movements in either the spot US$/€ rate, or the forward US$/€ rate that terminates when the sales occur and the hedging instrument matures.

If Entity X chooses to hedge the spot rate, then movements in the fair value of the forward contract due to movements in spot rate from period to period are recognised in other comprehensive income (to the extent this is effective). The fair value movements in the forward contract due to the fair value of the forward points will be recognised immediately in profit or loss throughout the hedge relationship.

If the entity chooses to hedge the forward rate, then the full movement in the fair value of the forward contract is recognised in other comprehensive income (to the extent this is effective). Compared to designating the spot rate only, the fair value changes of the forward points are recognised in other comprehensive income (instead of profit or loss) throughout the hedge relationship. If the hedge was perfectly effective over the life, then the fair value of the forward points would never be recognised in profit or loss (at maturity of the hedging relationship and hedging instrument the fair value of the forward points will be zero because there will be no more forward points left). The fair value of the forward contract at maturity will be equivalent to the difference between the spot rate at maturity and the contracted rate.

4.3.5 Time value of options

By splitting the time and intrinsic value of an option that is a qualifying hedging instrument, and designating only the intrinsic value in the hedging relationship, a higher level of effectiveness may be achieved. Depending on the length of time to the maturity of the option, the relative volatility of the option, and other factors that affect the time value, this designation may make the difference as to whether the relationship qualifies for hedge accounting.

Generally, if options are being used to hedge financial instruments that have a linear response to changes in the hedged risk, such as cash instruments, it is beneficial to exclude the time value of the option from the hedge relationship because the time value evident in the option is not evident in the hedged item. Designating the gains and losses on the hedging instrument with respect to intrinsic value only as an offset of the gains and losses on the hedged item creates a greater likelihood that the hedge will be highly effective in achieving offsetting changes in fair value or cash flows attributable to the hedged risk.

The disadvantage of not including time value in the hedge designation is that changes in the value of the component that is not designated in the hedging relationship, i.e. change in time value, must be recognised immediately in profit or loss.

Example 4.3.5

Hedging intrinsic value only

Entity X owns 1,000 shares of Entity A worth CU50 each. Entity X classifies these securities as available-for-sale and recognises changes in the fair value of these securities in other comprehensive income. Entity X would like to hedge its downside equity price risk. Entity X purchases an at-the-money put option (i.e. the put option has a strike price of CU50) on 1,000 Entity A shares expiring in three years' time. The premium paid for the option is CU9,000.

Entity X designates the intrinsic value of the put option as a fair value hedge of its investment in Entity A. The hedge strategy is consistent with Entity X's established risk management strategies. Entity X measures effectiveness by comparing decreases in fair value of the investment below the CU50 strike price with changes in the intrinsic value of the option on a quarterly basis. The time value of the option is not included in the assessment of effectiveness.

Because the hedging instrument and the hedged item have the same basis and are based on the same number of shares, increases in the intrinsic value of the option are expected to be fully effective in offsetting decreases in the fair value of the investment.

In this example, the entire CU9,000 premium is time value because the option purchased was at the money. Changes in the fair value of the time value of the option are recognised directly in profit or loss. Effectiveness of the hedge is assessed based on the intrinsic value rather than the fair value of the option. To the extent that the fair value of the option changes due to other variables such as volatility and the risk free rate, Entity X calculates the fair value of the option and then deducts the intrinsic value to arrive at the 'time' value component. In other words, the time value component reflects the effect of all variables on the option's price other than the intrinsic value. Based on Entity X's designation of effectiveness, the time value component is not part of the hedge relationship and is therefore recognised directly in profit or loss.

When the fair value of the shares falls below the strike price of the option, i.e. CU50, the entity will recognise fair value movements on the hedged item below this amount in profit or loss (instead of other comprehensive income) which will offset the movements in intrinsic value on the hedging instrument that will be recognised in profit or loss in the same period.

The Standard does not provide a definition of time value or intrinsic value for the purposes of identifying these two elements. This raises the question of what should be taken as intrinsic value, especially in the case of European options where the value of the option is driven from the expected price of the underlying in the future, and not its current price. For example, in the case of a cap on an interest rate index that is exercisable at the maturity of the option, the question arises as to whether intrinsic value at any point in time should be measured based on the current level of the given index (i.e. intrinsic value based on the spot rate) or by reference to the forward rate of the index that coincides with the actual exercise date (i.e. intrinsic value based on the forward rate).

The latter view would seem to be more in line with the economic reality for a European option because the intrinsic value of the option is entirely a function of where the rate of interest is predicted to be at the exercise date as opposed to where it currently is, given that the option cannot be presently exercised. This view of intrinsic value is supported by the fact that there is a readily observable prediction of future interest rates, i.e. the forward rates derived from the yield curve. In this respect European options over interest rate indices are different from those over other underlyings such as equity shares. IFRS 2 *Share-based Payment* Appendix A defines the intrinsic value of a share option as the difference between the fair value of the shares and the exercise price of the option, pointing towards a spot based view of intrinsic value, which is consistent with the fact that for equity shares there is no readily observable prediction of future prices as there is for interest rates.

Consider the case of a purchased European interest rate cap in an environment of an inverted interest rate curve (i.e. a yield curve that predicts that future interest rates will be below current levels). An entity may purchase a European interest rate cap at 5 per cent with a maturity of 2 years when the current spot rate is 6 per cent and the current market prediction as illustrated by the yield curve is that the interest rate is expected to be 4.5 per cent at the exercise date of the option. If intrinsic value is based on the spot rate, the intrinsic value will effectively 'build in' an assumption of the interest rate remaining at 6 per cent, i.e. in excess of the cap even though the yield curve predicts that this will not be the case. This will lead to a value being attributed to intrinsic value that is in excess of the total fair value of the option. As a result 'negative' value will be attributed to the time value in order for the sum of the time and intrinsic values to equal the total fair value of the option. It would seem strange that IAS 39 would require an entity to attribute 'negative' time value to a purchased option and, therefore, it is reasonable for an entity to assess intrinsic value based on forward rather than spot interest rates, assuming it documents this as part of its risk management strategy and applies this consistently for similar hedging relationships.

4.4 Methods for assessing effectiveness for cash flow hedges

IAS 39 does not provide specific guidance as to how an entity should measure hedge effectiveness. However, IAS 39:IG.F.5.5 provides an illustrative example of measuring hedge effectiveness in a cash flow hedge of forecast issuance of fixed rate debt. The implementation guidance recognises that there are at least two methods of accomplishing this measurement. The two methods (the 'hypothetical derivative' method and the 'change in fair value' method) are explained in the following section.

4.4.1 The 'hypothetical derivative' method

The hypothetical derivative method measures hedge ineffectiveness by comparing the change in fair value of the actual derivative designated as the hedging instrument and the change in fair value of a 'hypothetical derivative' that would result in perfect hedge effectiveness for the designated hedged item, i.e. the hypothetical derivative would have terms that exactly match the critical terms of the hedged item. For example, for a hedge of a variable rate financial asset or liability, the hypothetical derivative would be a swap with the same notional amount and same repricing dates as the hedged asset or liability. In addition, the index on which the hypothetical swap's variable rate is based would match the index on which the asset or liability's variable rate is based, including, where present, any caps and floors and any other embedded features in the hedged item. Further, it would be an on-market swap, i.e. have a zero fair value at inception.

Under the 'hypothetical derivative method' the change in the fair value of the 'perfect' hypothetical swap is regarded as a proxy for the change in the present value of the expected future cash flows on the hedged transaction.

The determination of the fair value of both the 'perfect' hypothetical swap and the actual swap will use discount rates based on the relevant swap curves.

The amount of ineffectiveness recognised in profit or loss for a cash flow hedge equals the excess of the cumulative change in the fair value of the actual swap over the cumulative change in the fair value of the 'perfect' hypothetical swap.

Example 4.4.1

Identifying the hypothetical derivative

Entity P has a 4-year variable rate loan asset with a notional of €100 and a maturity of 31/12/X5. The benchmark rate on the loan (i.e. the coupon excluding credit spread) is 3-month EURIBOR. Interest is received quarterly. Entity P does not hedge its loan asset on origination, 1/01/X2.

However, at the end of 20X2, Entity P forecasts a fall in interest rates and designates a pay variable overnight indexed swap rate (OIS), receive 5 per cent fixed interest rate swap with a notional of €100 and annual interest payments as a cash flow hedge of the interest rate risk on the loan.

Entity P formally designates the hedging relationship and meets all of the hedge accounting criteria including the prospective effectiveness test.

To measure the effectiveness of the hedging relationship, Entity P compares the change in fair value of the hedging pay variable OIS, receive 5 per cent fixed interest rate swap to the changes in value of the 'hypothetical derivative,' i.e. the derivative that would result in perfect hedge effectiveness for a hedge of the loan. In this instance, the hypothetical derivative is a pay 3-month EURIBOR,

> receive 4.9 per cent interest rate swap with quarterly payment dates. The 4.9 per cent fixed rate for the remaining 3 years is the market EURIBOR swap rate.
>
> Note that the fixed rates on the actual hedging swap and the hypothetical swap differ because they are priced off different yield curves (i.e. OIS versus EURIBOR).

The hypothetical derivative method can be used universally for all cash flow hedge relationships where a derivative is used as a hedging instrument. This method would not be appropriate in the case of hedging foreign currency risk with a non-derivative instrument because clearly the hedging instrument is not a derivative.

The other method discussed below, the 'change in fair value' method, will have greater applicability when determining hedge effectiveness on variable rate financial assets and liabilities and the forecast issuance of fixed rate debt.

The hypothetical derivative method is referred to as Method B in IAS 39:IG.F.5.5.

Hedge ineffectiveness will arise if the timing or amount of a forecast transaction changes because the fair value (present value) of the expected future cash flows on the hedged item from inception of the hedge will not equal the cumulative fair value on the hedging instrument from inception of the hedge.

Determining the degree of hedge ineffectiveness when the timing or amount of forecast transactions change can be a complex exercise. If an entity applies the hypothetical derivative method in assessing hedge effectiveness then this method will also be reapplied when the timing or amount of the hedged item changes. For example, if the timing of the cash flows on the derivative hedging instrument and the hedged item coincide at inception of the hedge and the derivative is deemed to be the hypothetical derivative, then only to the extent that the cash flows continue to coincide will the hedge be fully effective. If the timing of the forecast cash flows changes during the life of the hedge relationship then a new hypothetical derivative needs to be determined which will be equal to the hypothetical derivative that the entity would have determined when they entered into the hedge accounting relationship that reflects the revised timing of the forecast cash flows. Put another way, the revised hypothetical derivative is the one the entity would have determined had it been able to foresee the revised timing of the forecast cash flows. A comparison of the cumulative gain/loss on the actual hedging instrument and the revised hypothetical derivative will determine the degree of hedge effectiveness and the amount of hedge ineffectiveness to be measured under IAS 39:96(a).

Further examples

A detailed illustration of the application of the hypothetical derivative method for a cash flow hedge of interest rate risk on a forecast issuance of debt where the timing of the forecast cash flows changes is included in **3.15** of **chapter C11**.

4.4.2 The 'change in fair value' method

The change in fair value method requires a computation of the change in fair value of the cash flows that would have been achieved had the variable cash flow exposure been a fixed cash exposure. For example, if an entity is hedging variable rate debt, the change in fair value method will compare the cumulative changes in the present value of the fixed cash flows that would have been achieved at inception, discounted at the new interest rate, with the fair value of the derivative that is designated as the hedging instrument.

In the instance that an entity is hedging the variable interest rate risk of a variable rate financial asset or liability, the fair value of the hedged item is generally equal to its par amount, because it is not sensitive to fair value movement when interest rates change. This method overcomes this problem by discounting the cash flows that would have been achieved had the instrument been fixed from inception.

Example 4.4.2

Change in fair value method

Facts as in **example 4.4.1**.

Applying the change in fair value method, Entity P will determine the fixed rate that would have been achieved on 3-year fixed rate loan that is priced off EURIBOR.

The entity will discount the fixed cash flows that would have been achieved on a 3 year fixed rate loan at the new EURIBOR interest rate curve. The cumulative present value of these cash flows will be compared with the fair value of the interest rate swap that is priced off the overnight indexed swap rate. The change in fair value method will recognise ineffectiveness due to the different basis of interest rates between the hedging instrument and the hedged item.

The change in fair value method is referred to as Method A in IAS 39:IG.F.5.5.

4.4.3 The 'change in variable cash flows' method

The change in variable cash flows method compares the floating rate cash flows of the hedged item with the floating rates cash flows on the derivative. For example, if an entity was assessing hedge effectiveness for a variable rate financial asset or liability, the entity would compare the present value of the cumulative changes in the expected future cash flows on the variable leg of an interest rate swap with the present value of the cumulative change in expected future interest cash flows on the hedged item. The fixed rate leg of the interest rate swap is excluded from the analysis because it is assumed that the derivative's fair value that is attributable to the fixed rate leg is not relevant to the variability of the variable cash flows on the hedged item. Such an assumption is only valid when the derivative has a fair value of zero at inception, i.e. it is an on-market instrument, and there is no impact on the fair value of the hedging instrument of non-performance risk of the reporting entity and the derivative counterparty. If the derivative did not have a fair value of zero at inception, the derivative would have a higher or lower fixed rate leg to compensate the entity for the upfront payment or receipt at inception. Because the fixed rate leg is adjusted to reflect this upfront payment or receipt, the fixed rate leg includes a financing element that cannot be ignored. It is for the above reason that IAS 39:IG.F.5.5 purposely prohibits use of the variable cash flows method.

In March 2007, the IFRIC (now the IFRS Interpretations Committee) finalised a rejection notice titled *Assessing Hedge Effectiveness of an Interest Rate Swap in a Cash Flow Hedge*. The IFRIC stated that it was not permissible to consider only the undiscounted changes in cash flows of the hedging instrument and the hedged item in assessing hedge effectiveness in a cash flow hedge of interest rate risk when using an interest rate swap. The IFRIC noted that such a method for assessing hedge effectiveness would not be in accordance with IAS 39:74, which does not allow the designation of a portion of a derivative as the hedging instrument, and would ignore the fact that one of the reasons for ineffectiveness is the mismatch of the timing of interest payments or receipts of the swap and the hedged item.

4.5 Hedge designations in business combinations

Phase 1 of the Business Combinations project that led to the publication of the original version of IFRS 3 *Business Combinations* in 2003 had no specific guidance about whether hedge relationships that exist in the acquiree need to be re-designated by the acquirer should the acquirer wish to continue hedge accounting in the group financial statements. IAS 39 also has no specific requirements with respect to business combinations. Phase 2 of the Business Combinations project that led to the issue of the revised version of IFRS 3 *Business Combinations* in January 2008 has specific guidance on reassessment of contractual arrangements, including financial instruments.

IFRS 3(2008) requires reassessment of classification and designation of all contractual arrangements based on the pertinent conditions as they exist at the acquisition, with the exception of two cases which are classification of leases as finance or operating leases, and the classification of insurance contracts. IFRS 3(2008):16(b) and BC185 specifically refer to designation of a derivative instrument as a hedging instrument in accordance with IAS 39 and require reassessment of classification and designation.

The implication of the requirement to reassess hedge relationships at the date of business combinations is that, without re-designation at the group level, the hedge accounting that may continue to be applied at the level of the acquiree will not be applied by the group. If the group wishes to apply hedge accounting at the group level immediately post-acquisition, a new hedge relationship will need to be designated at the date of the business combination. When designating cash flow hedges, the hypothetical derivative will reflect the conditions that exist at the date of re-designation and, therefore, may be substantially different from the hypothetical derivative that was originally designated in the acquiree's financial statements. Assuming the group attempts to designate the existing derivative of the acquiree in the same hedge relationship as the acquiree, any difference in the hypothetical derivative will result in a different amount of hedge effectiveness recognised at the group level. The hypothetical derivative may be so different from the actual derivative that the group is unable to pass the assessment of prospective hedge effectiveness and therefore is unable to apply hedge accounting post-acquisition. It is worth noting that any re-designation by the group does not affect the acquiree's financial statements assuming the acquiree retains its original hedge designation.

Consideration will need to be given to both hedge documentation and effectiveness where derivative financial instruments are transferred between entities within the same group. This transaction may or may not be part of a transaction that meets the definition of a common control transaction. In the individual financial statements of the entity acquiring the derivative, the instrument will be recognised as a financial instrument for the first time. Should that entity wish to designate that instrument in a hedge accounting relationship a new hedge relationship will need to be determined and documented. In the case of a cash flow hedge, consideration will need to be given to whether the actual derivative is equal to the hypothetical derivative at the date the hedge is designated (for detail on the hypothetical derivative method see **4.4.1**). Hedge ineffectiveness will arise to the extent the actual and hypothetical derivative differs and may be significant enough to prevent the entity passing the prospective hedge effectiveness assessment. This will be the case even if the hedged item (as well as the derivative) is transferred to the acquirer.

When a hedged item and hedging instrument are transferred from one group entity to another group entity and hedge accounting is applied immediately prior to the transfer, the original hedge accounting relationship may continue to apply in the consolidated financial statements if the relationship is highly effective. This will only be the case where there is no period where the hedge accounting relationship ceases and the hedge relationship, including the hedged risk, remains the same. In this limited case, the hypothetical derivative will not need to be reset. Care should be taken in the case where the functional currency of the selling entity and the acquirer differ and foreign currency risk is being hedged as the difference in functional currencies will result in different hedged risks before and after the transfer and therefore a new hedge designation and a new hypothetical derivative will need to be determined in the consolidated financial statements. In some cases, the hedge relationship may no longer qualify for hedge accounting, e.g. if the functional currency of the acquirer is the same as the currency of the hedged item so no foreign currency risk exists, or the hedging instrument does not hedge the foreign currency risk of the hedged item into the acquirer's functional currency.

4.6 Regression analysis

Regression analysis is a statistical measurement technique for determining the validity and extent of a relationship between an independent and dependent variable. It is more complex than ratio analysis and requires appropriate interpretation and understanding of the statistical inferences. Where regression analysis is used, the entity's documented policies for assessing effectiveness must specify how the results of the regression will be assessed. A regression analysis can be used for either a cash flow or a fair value hedge.

Example 4.6

Regression analysis (1)

Where the changes in value of a hedged item in Euros is X(t) and the change in value of the hedging instrument in Euros is Y(t), if Y is a 'good hedge' for X the observed points (X,Y) should be clustered close to a straight line with a slope equal to -1 and intercept equal to the value of the hedged position, C.

$Y(t) - X(t) = C$ or $Y = X + C$

C is the (constant) value of the hedged position.

For the purposes of illustration, assuming a constant of zero, the slope of the regression equation is equivalent to the ratio of effectiveness and, therefore, should lie within the range of -0.8 to -1.25 (corresponding to a ratio of 80 to 125 per cent) for a 1 to 1 hedge relationship. In the absence of further statistical evidence derived from the same data, a correlation coefficient, R^2, between the values of 0.8 to 1 typically is representative of a highly effective offsetting relationship between the hedged item and the hedging instrument. In other words, an R^2 of 0.8 indicate that 80 per cent of the movement in the dependent variable is 'explained' by variation in the independent variable. As the objective of hedge effectiveness is to assess the degree of offset between two variables, a simple linear regression is an acceptable technique for demonstrating the effectiveness of a hedge relationship.

The slope coefficient is the slope of the straight line of best fit of the regression. For a fully effective hedge relationship the slope coefficient will approximate to -1. A slope coefficient of -1 means that for a specified movement in the hedged item the hedging instrument will move by an equal but opposite extent. A slope coefficient of -0.85 means that for every €1 change in the hedged item it will generally result in an opposite change of €0.85 in the hedging instrument.

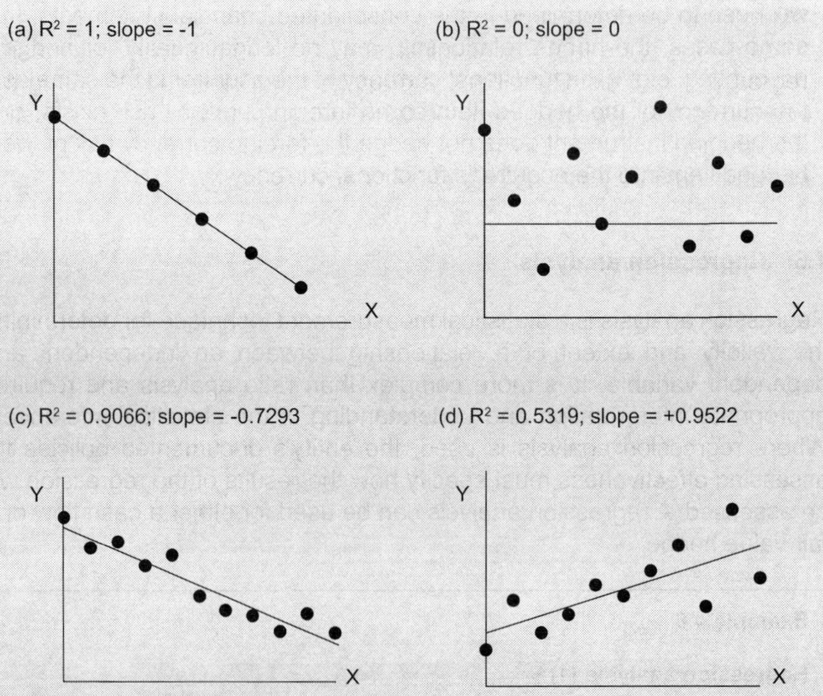

Regression analysis is best suited for measuring the strength of empirical relationships. This relationship can then be used to assess probability of offset, and establish hedge ratios. Such analysis is essential for indirect hedges, i.e. hedges with basis risk where the hedging instrument (e.g. a futures or options contract) has a different underlying to that of the hedged item or transaction. An example is a hedge of petrol prices using oil futures. A simple linear regression may establish a statistical relationship between the two variables, i.e. the price of oil and the price of petrol. The most common method to determine the regression line is called the least squares method. The method finds the best-fitting equation that minimises the sum of the (squared) distances between the data points and the regression line. Where there is a valid statistical relationship, the slope of the regression line can be used to establish the hedge ratio that will maximise expected effectiveness. [IAS 39:AG100]

More complex hedging strategies establish a relationship between one dependent and two or more independent variables by using multiple linear regression. However, as the objective of hedge effectiveness is to compare two variables, namely:

(i) the changes in fair value of the hedged risk of a hedged item with the change in fair value of a hedging instrument in a fair value hedge; or

(ii) the cumulative change in fair value of the expected future cash flows on the hedged item from inception of the hedge with the cumulative gain or loss on the hedging instrument, a simple linear regression will normally be applied.

In order to conclude that the hedging relationship is highly effective using a regression analysis, R^2 should be equal to, or greater than 0.8, and the slope should be between a negative 0.8 and 1.25; and the F and *t* statistics should be evaluated at a 95 per cent confidence level. Only when all of these statistical objectives have been met can an entity claim a highly effective hedge relationship for the period.

The formula for a linear regression is as follows:

$$y = mx + b + x1.$$

where y	—	represents the dependent variable
m	—	represents the slope of the line
x	—	represents the independent variable
b	—	represents the y intercept
x1	—	represents the error term

The table below provides information on how to evaluate the validity of a linear regression.

Factors that prove a regression analysis is valid	**Confidence level or numerical requirement**	**How to evaluate the confidence level or numerical requirement**
R^2	> = 0.8	The R^2 output should be greater than or equal to 0.8. R^2 is the coefficient of determination which is the square of the coefficient of correlation or r. r indicates when two variables are linearly related. The value of r can range from –1 to +1. R^2 measures the proportion of variability in y that derives from x (i.e. how much of the change of y is explained by a change in x). The higher the value the higher the indication that y is related to x. R^2 is always positive as it is a squared number and cannot exceed 1 as x cannot explain more than 100 per cent in the change of y.

Factors that prove a regression analysis is valid	**Confidence level or numerical requirement**	**How to evaluate the confidence level or numerical requirement**
m — slope factor	Between –0.8 & –1.25	In the regression equation, the slope should be in the range provided. The slope of a line is the change in y over the change in x. An increasing or decreasing value indicates the positive or negative change in y for every change in x. For example, a slope of +1 would indicate that y is increasing at a positive rate with each change in x. In a hedging relationship, a hedge is used to achieve offsetting changes in the value of the hedged item, therefore, a regression equation for a hedging relationship should have a negative slope within the range previously specified as an entity will be long the exposure with the hedged item and short the exposure with the hedging instrument or vice versa. Additionally, 'm' represents the optimal hedge ratio for the hedge, indicating you need 'more' or 'less' of the hedging instrument to compensate for changes in the hedged item.
t — Statistic	95 per cent Confidence Level	The t-statistic for the x coefficient evaluates the probability that the slope is zero. A slope of zero indicates that there is no relationship between the x and y variables. A high t-statistic for the x coefficient, positive or negative, generally is a good indicator of correlation and thus a linear relationship. This statistic may be further evaluated by examining the p-value; a statistical output of the t-statistic calculation. A low p-value associated with the t-statistic for the x variable, e.g. less than five per cent, indicates a low probability of the slope being zero and thus a high probability that the independent variable is useful in predicting the dependent variable.
F — Statistic	95 per cent Confidence Level	The F-statistic evaluates the probability that there is no linear relationship between the x and y variables. To achieve a 95 per cent confidence level, the significance of F-statistic should be less than five per cent. If the significance of F-statistic is less than five per cent then there is a less than five per cent probability that no linear relationship is present.

It has to be noted that all the factors have to be considered in determining whether a hedge relationship is highly effective. For example, if R^2 has a value near 1 then an m near the ranges of 80 - 125 per cent can be acceptable and vice versa.

If a hedge ratio other than one-for-one is applied (see **4.3.2**), and historical regression analysis is used to determine this hedge ratio, when an entity actually assesses hedge effectiveness using regression values based on this hedge ratio, the entity would expect the 'perfect hedge' to have a gradient of 1 (not that of the hedge ratio). For example, if an entity has a hedge ratio of 0.7, i.e. 0.7 hedged items to 1 hedging instrument, for the purpose of assessing hedge effectiveness, the entity would still be expecting a gradient of the regression line of 0.8 to 1.25 in order to establish that the hedge was highly effective.

Users of regression must be aware of the concept of autocorrelation (i.e. serial correlation). This concept applies when the data points are correlated to each other over time, i.e. the data points are not random. One of the assumptions of a least squares regression is that the data points are uncorrelated to each other. If the data points are correlated to each other this will affect the output of the regression and will result in the R^2, m slope etc. being misstated. When data points are taken over a period of time autocorrelation can occur if the different data points are sourced from the same period. For example, if one data point is the change in fair value of a derivative from 1 June to 30 August, and the second data point is the change in fair value from 1 August to 31 October, there is autocorrelation with respect to the month of August as it overlaps in both data points. Users of regression should ensure data is taken from discrete periods to avoid the data points being correlated with each other. Statistical techniques like the Durbin-Watson test can be applied to determine whether there is autocorrelation. Other statistical techniques, like the Prais-Winsten test can be used to restate the output from the model by removing the effects of autocorrelation. As IAS 39 provides no guidance on the use of statistical techniques, entities should use established statistical techniques that are known to provide a meaningful output that is consistent with the Standard's objective of assessing hedge effectiveness.

Further examples

An illustration of the accounting entries for a fair value hedge assessed for effectiveness using regression analysis is included in **5.1** in **chapter C11**.

4.6.1 Inputs in a regression analysis

Past data can be used to demonstrate that a hedge relationship is expected to be highly effective in a prospective hedge effectiveness test, and was highly effective in a retrospective hedge effectiveness test.

The data used in a regression is a series of matched-pair observations from a specified period of time. For example, an entity may wish to regress the change in fair value of an interest rate swap with the change in fair value of the interest rate portion of fixed rate debt on the first day of each month for a three year period. This will generate 36 matched-pair observations which will input into the regression model. An entity should apply a consistent number of data points as the regression is updated at a minimum at the end of each reporting period. If an entity is using a regression model for both prospective and retrospective hedge effectiveness tests it should also use the same number of data points in both tests, and should apply this consistently to other similar hedges.

It is typical to regress observations over the same period as the length of the hedge relationship. For example, if an entity is fair value hedging five year fixed rate debt from the date of issue for its full term, an entity would use observations from the last five years to demonstrate prospectively that a five year receive fixed pay floating interest rate swap is highly effective in fair value hedging the interest rate portion of the debt.

The more data points that are included in the data set will generally result in a more robust regression analysis. However, care must be taken not to include so many data points from such a long period that the data set is not representative of the hedge relationship. It is typical to use at least 30 observations, though in theory it is possible to have a highly effective hedge relationship with less than 30 observations when this is supported with an F-statistic and t-statistic that pass the required confidence levels if the underlying distribution can be assumed to be normal or approximately normal. However, as the number of observations must remain fixed throughout the hedge relationship, and therefore must be stated at inception in the hedge documentation, it is beneficial to use at least 30 observations in order to maximise the number of chances of passing the hedge effectiveness test in future reporting periods.

In both prospective and retrospective hedge effectiveness tests an entity will update the regression by adding new observations and excluding the same number of the oldest observations from the data set. This methodology ensures that the regression is consistently updated and interpreted throughout the hedge relationship.

If an entity wishes to designate a hedging relationship at initial recognition of the hedging instrument (in the case of a cash flow hedge) or at initial recognition of the hedging instrument and the hedged item (in the case of a fair value hedge) it will not necessarily have the data history for those particular instrument(s). This would be the case if the contract did not exist prior to the initial recognition date, or historical fair value data is not available for an instrument that did exist but was held by a different party. In this case the entity should consider using data from similar instruments or instead generate data points by calculating the hypothetical fair value of the instrument using historic market data assuming that instrument had existed prior to the initial recognition date.

4.6.2 Differences in the results of regression and ratio analysis

Ratio and regression analysis are clearly very different statistical techniques for assessing hedge effectiveness. Whichever technique is applied, whether for a prospective or/and retrospective assessment of hedge effectiveness, they are unlikely to achieve the same results for each period. The only exception to this perhaps is if the terms of the hedging instrument and hedged item are exactly the same and therefore for all periods the hedge effectiveness assessment would be highly effective. In such instances, entities may have a preference in applying ratio analysis instead of regression because it is simpler.

If an entity chooses to use regression analysis, and therefore must apply this technique consistently throughout the hedge relationship, the entity should be aware of other statistical techniques whose results could call into question the validity of the regression. An example would be a comparison of regression to ratio analysis. If an entity had chosen regression analysis and failed to be highly effective for a period using ratio analysis, it does not mean that the results of the regression are considered not highly effective for that period. Instead, the entity should be aware that if the entity would have failed using ratio analysis on multiple consecutive periods then this does call into question the validity and robustness of the regression analysis. In these instances, the entity should investigate the reasons for the divergence between ratio analysis and regression and if the reasons are not expected to recur in future periods the entity will pass the highly effective test in the current period, and can continue to apply regression analysis in future periods. For example, assume an entity was regressing Brent crude oil prices with aviation fuel prices over a 3 year period as it is hedging its forecast aviation fuel purchases in 3 years' time. After 4 quarters since the start of the hedge relationship, the retrospective hedge effectiveness assessment using regression passed every quarter, but ratio analysis failed every quarter. Upon further investigation of the difference, the entity noted there was a structural event in the market that will result in ratio analysis continuing to fail based on the current hedge designation. It is worth noting that the impact of this structural event will ultimately affect the regression analysis in future periods as new data is added each quarter and the oldest data is removed from the data set. Because the reasons for the divergence in regression and ratio analysis are expected to continue in future periods the entity would not achieve hedge accounting for the period, but the entity could re-designate the hedge relationship using a different hedge ratio and attempt to claim prospective hedge effectiveness based on the new designation.

In November 2006, the IFRIC (now the IFRS Interpretations Committee) issued a rejection notice that addressed testing of hedge effectiveness on a cumulative basis. One of the points made in the rejection notice was if the dollar-to-dollar comparison (i.e. ratio analysis) of the changes in the fair value or cash flows of the hedged items and the changes in the fair value or cash flows of the hedging instrument falls outside a range of 80 - 125 per cent this does not necessarily result in the entity failing to qualify for hedge accounting, provided that the dollar-to-dollar comparison is not the method documented at inception of the hedge for assessing hedge effectiveness.

While this conclusion is certainly logical it is worth noting that the existence of a failing ratio analysis may provide evidence that the data being added to a regression analysis will result in a future failure of regression, which ultimately will affect an entity's ability to pass hedge effectiveness assessment. In short, entities should not be blinded by the output from statistical techniques nor should they look at the output in isolation as this will hinder their ability to assess the quality of the output and the soundness of statistical relationships.

5 Net investment hedge: advanced

Compared to other hedge accounting concepts, net investment hedging is relatively simple. The basic requirements of net investment hedges are described in **2.3** in **chapter C9**. Net investment hedging can become complicated when applied in large groups with multiple entities with different functional currencies. This section discusses some of these complexities and also demonstrates how cross-currency swaps can be used in net investment hedges.

5.1 Hedging net investments with currency swaps

Net investment hedging with loans and forward contracts is discussed in **2.3** in **chapter C9**. Hedging net investments with foreign currency swaps is very similar to hedging with forwards. This is to be expected, as swaps with fixed cash flows are simply a series of forwards. As with forward contracts, it is important to be clear which risk is being hedged (i.e. the spot or forward rate).

While foreign currency swaps that swap from one currency to another can be used as hedging instruments of net investment hedges, it is difficult to get high effectiveness with cross-currency fixed-for-floating interest rate swaps as the interest element of the swap does not reduce foreign exchange risk of the net investment in the foreign operation. This is the case when an entity is swapping currency as well as the basis of interest from floating to fixed rates and vice versa. Furthermore, because a derivative instrument must be designated in its entirety (except for the limited circumstances noted in **4.2** in **chapter C9**), the element that does not reduce foreign exchange risk cannot be excluded from the hedge designation.

When the currency swap is fixed for fixed, or floating to floating, the derivative may qualify as a hedge of a net investment in a foreign operation. Hedging instruments such as floating to floating currency swaps respond closely to movements in spot rates. Thus, provided the notional of such an instrument does not exceed the net investment, it is likely to be an effective hedging instrument for a hedge of the spot risk associated with the net investment.

Fixed for fixed currency swaps may be used as hedging instruments in a hedge of either the forward or spot risk associated with the net investment. In either case there are potentially two ways of designating such an instrument. One would be to hedge an amount of net assets that is equal to the present value of the foreign currency interest and principal. This is in line with viewing the cross-currency swap as comprising a combination of a loan payable in foreign currency and a loan receivable in the other currency. In this case, an amount of net assets equal to the foreign currency principal of the swap should be designated as the hedged item. Alternatively, an amount of net assets equal to the sum of the undiscounted foreign currency principal and undiscounted foreign currency interest payments can be designated as the hedged item. This is in line with viewing the fixed for fixed swap as a combination of forwards with respect to interest payments and final principal exchange at maturity. Note that a greater amount of net assets would have to be available for the second method to be an effective hedge relationship. Whichever approach is applied, it should be applied consistently.

Where the net investment is hedged for the forward foreign currency rate using a fixed for fixed currency swap there are two acceptable approaches with respect to recognition of the interest settlements on the swap in the consolidated financial statements. The first approach is to recognise the net of the interest settlements in profit or loss. Under this approach, the swap is viewed as a combination of a fixed rate foreign currency loan and a fixed rate functional currency deposit (i.e. viewing the two legs of the swap as two gross positions). The interest settlements are recognised in profit or loss because they represent the net financing on the swap. The remainder of fair value gains or losses are recognised in other comprehensive income because they represent the fair value changes in the forward points. The second approach is to recognise the net of the interest settlements in other comprehensive income. Under this approach, the swap is viewed as a string of forward contracts which have been designated in their entirety. Consequently, the net interest settlements on the swap are recognised in other comprehensive income as part of the total fair value gains or losses on the swap. No amount is recognised in profit or loss until the hedged net investment is disposed of.

Irrespective of which approach is applied any hedge ineffectiveness is recognised immediately in profit or loss.

Further examples

An illustration of the entries for a net investment hedge of a foreign operation using a cross-currency interest rate swap that receives and pays:

- floating interest is shown at **4.3** in **chapter C11**.
- fixed interest with interest settlements recognised in profit or loss is shown at **4.4** in **chapter C11**.
- fixed interest with interest settlements recognised in other comprehensive income is shown at **4.5** in **chapter C11**.

5.2 Hedging by multiple parent entities

IFRIC 16 clarified that within consolidated financial statements a parent that hedges a foreign operation can be an immediate parent, intermediate parent, or ultimate parent. The fact that the net investment is held through an intermediate parent does not affect the nature of the economic risk arising from the foreign currency exposure to the ultimate parent entity. [IFRIC 16:12] However, an exposure to foreign currency risk arising from a net investment in a foreign operation may qualify for hedge accounting only once in the consolidated financial statements. Therefore, if the same net assets of a foreign operation are hedged by more than one parent entity within the group (e.g. both a direct and an indirect parent entity) for the same risk, only one hedging relationship will qualify for hedge accounting in the consolidated financial statements of the ultimate parent. [IFRIC 16:13]

If a hedging relationship is designated by one parent entity in its consolidated financial statements, it need not be maintained by another higher level parent entity. However, if it is not maintained by the higher level parent entity, the hedge accounting applied by the lower level parent must be reversed before the higher level parent's hedge accounting is recognised. [IFRIC 16:13] This is not unique to net investment hedging because hedge accounting by a subsidiary or by a sub-consolidated group need not be maintained in the consolidated financial statements that include the subsidiary or a sub-consolidated group. Conversely, hedge accounting could be designated in the consolidated financial statements but is not designated in the subsidiary only financial statements or the financial statements of a sub-consolidated group that forms part of the larger group. This flexibility is possible because hedge accounting is entirely voluntary.

Example 5.2

Hedge designations

The group structure of Group P is as follows.

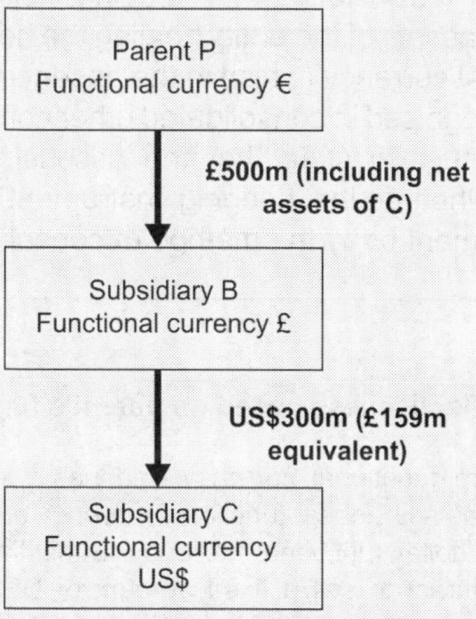

In the consolidated financial statements headed by Group P, the maximum amount of net assets available to be hedged for the respective hedged risk in a qualifying hedge relationship is:

- $300 million net assets for €/US$ risk between P and C; or
- £500 million net assets for €/£ risk between P and B; or
- $300 million net assets for £/US$ risk between B and C; or
- $300 million net assets for £/US$ risk between B and C; and £500 million net assets for €/£ risk between P and B; or
- $300 million net assets for €/US$ risk between P and C; and £341 million net assets for €/£ risk between P and B.

5.3 Location of hedging instrument within the group

IFRIC 16:14 states that the hedging instrument(s) may be held by any entity or entities within the group as long as the designation, documentation and effectiveness requirements of IAS 39:88 for the net investment hedge are satisfied. IFRIC 16 notes that the hedge strategy must be clearly documented because of the possibility of different designations at different levels of the group.

When the hedging instrument resides in an entity that has the same functional currency as the parent that has the investment in the foreign operation the hedge effectiveness calculations are easier to perform as hedge effectiveness is determined as if the parent that has the investment in the foreign operation also had the hedging instrument. Determining hedge effectiveness is more complex when the entity holding the hedging instrument has a different functional currency from that of the parent that has the exposure to the foreign operation. In such circumstances, IFRIC 16 requires hedge effectiveness to not only reflect the gain/loss residing in the entity holding the hedging instrument (which in the absence of hedge accounting would have been recognised in consolidated profit or loss), but also the effect of retranslating that hedging instrument as part of the translation of the net assets of the entity holding the hedging instrument into the parent's functional currency (which in the absence of hedge accounting would have been recognised in consolidated other comprehensive income). The IFRIC goes further to state that the assessment of effectiveness is not affected by whether the hedging instrument is a derivative or a non-derivative instrument or by the method of consolidation. [IFRIC 16:15]

Example 5.3

Assessing hedge effectiveness based on parent's functional currency

Parent P has a Euro functional currency and has two foreign operations, Subsidiary A which has a US dollar functional currency and Subsidiary B which has a New Zealand dollar functional currency. Subsidiary B holds a foreign currency forward contract to sell a fixed amount of US$ for a fixed amount of € at a specific date in the future. Parent P wishes to designate the foreign currency forward as a net investment hedge of its investment in Subsidiary A. The hedged risk is the €/US$ foreign currency exposure with respect to the translation of Subsidiary A's US$ net assets into €.

Parent P wishes to designate the spot foreign currency risk only (not the forward foreign currency risk). The opening net assets of Subsidiary A are US$1,000 and the entire opening net assets are intended to be designated as being hedged by Parent P in its consolidated financial statements. For illustrative purposes the foreign currency forward's fair value is calculated using undiscounted spot rates and the foreign currency spot and forward rate are presumed to be the same (i.e. there is no gain/loss in respect of fair valuing the forward point differential).

	Opening spot rate	Closing spot rate	Average spot rate
€/US$	1.400	1.520	1.460
€/NZ$	2.200	1.850	2.025
US$/NZ$	1.571	1.217	1.394

Parent P's translation of Subsidiary A's designated net assets in the consolidated financial statements:

Opening designated net assets	US$1,000 @ 1.400 = €714
Closing designated net assets	US$1,000 @ 1.520 = €658
Loss on translation of Subsidiary A's net assets	€56

Gain/loss on the foreign currency forward with respect to spot rates in Subsidiary B's financial statements:

Receive €	(Buy €714 @ 1.850) =	NZ$1,321
Pay US$	(Sell US$1,000 @ 1.217) =	NZ$1,217
Gain/loss in the period		NZ$104

Impact of the derivative in consolidated profit or loss in the absence of hedge accounting with respect to the hedged risk:

Gain/loss NZ$104 @ 2.025 (average spot rate) = €51

If the translation of the hedging instrument from Subsidiary B's functional currency, NZ$, to the Parent P's functional currency, €, was ignored, the hedge relationship is partly ineffective. The hedge relationship would be 91% effective (€51/€56). As this remains within the 80 - 125 per cent parameter it would have been deemed highly effective in the period.

IFRIC 16 requires the effectiveness to be determined by reference to the parent's functional currency. The effect of applying this approach is to include the difference between the average spot rate and the closing spot rate that is recognised in consolidated other comprehensive income with respect to the translation of the derivative in Subsidiary B, as part of the assessment of hedge effectiveness.

Gain/loss	NZ$104 @ 2.025 (average rates) =	€51
Gain/loss	NZ$104 @ 1.850 (closing rates) =	€56
Difference	=	€5

When the additional amount described above is included in the assessment of hedge effectiveness the hedge is 100% effective ((€51 + €5) / €56).

Had Parent P held the foreign currency forward, the gain/loss derived from the foreign currency forward would be driven solely by US$ because the € receive leg of the foreign currency forward does not generate foreign currency risk because Parent P has a € functional currency. The gain/loss on the hedging instrument would be an offset to the translation of Subsidiary A's US$ net assets to €. Considered differently, in the group accounts of Parent P the group has a long US$ position being the net assets of Subsidiary A, and a short US$ position being the US$ pay leg of the foreign currency forward contract and, therefore, the derivative would have been fully effective.

In April 2009, the IASB issued *Improvements to IFRSs*, which amended IFRIC 16:14 to allow the hedging instrument to be held by any entity within the group and, thereby, removed the restriction that the foreign operation that is itself being hedged cannot hold the hedging instrument. The basis for conclusions states that the IASB believes that, without hedge accounting, part of the foreign exchange difference arising from the hedging instrument would be included in consolidated profit or loss and, therefore, the restriction that the foreign operation being hedged cannot hold the hedging instrument should be removed.

5.4 Hedging a portfolio of net investments with a single instrument

If a group has multiple foreign operations that have the same functional currency, the group can hedge the foreign operations either as a group, or individually. For example, Parent heads a group that includes two US$ subsidiaries, A and B, each with US$500,000 of net assets, and $1m of third party borrowings. The Parent's interest in subsidiary A and B is held directly, i.e. neither subsidiary is a subsidiary of the other. The group may either designate the borrowings of $1m as a hedge of a group of foreign operations of US$1 million, or designate 50 per cent of the borrowings as hedging US$500,000 of subsidiary A, and 50 per cent of the borrowings as hedging US$500,000 of subsidiary B. When the designation is on a group basis the hedge documentation can be done on a group basis; however, hedge effectiveness must be assessed for each subsidiary individually.

Example 5.4

Hedging a portfolio of net investments with a single instrument

Entity P is a Sterling functional currency entity that has US$400 million foreign currency denominated issued debt which it wishes to designate as a hedging instrument of the net investment in its US dollar foreign operations. The group structure is as follows.

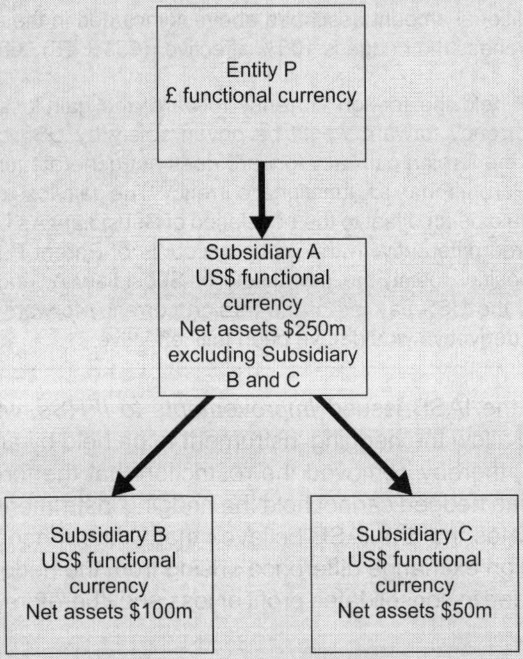

The following designations are permitted by IAS 39:

1. Entity P may designate US$400m debt as a hedging instrument of a net investment in the consolidated net assets of the sub-group headed by Subsidiary A;
2. Entity P may designate relevant proportions of the US$ debt as hedges of net investments in Subsidiary A, Subsidiary B, and Subsidiary C individually, i.e. 62.5 per cent of the US$ debt as a hedge of the net investment in subsidiary A, 25 per cent of the US$ debt as a hedge of the net investment in Subsidiary B, and 12.5 per cent of the US$ debt as the hedge of the net investment in Subsidiary C; or
3. Entity P may designate US$400 million debt as a hedge of a portfolio of net investments in US$ subsidiaries.

IAS 21 *The Effects of Changes in Foreign Exchange Rates* views a net investment in a foreign operation as "the amount of the reporting entity's interest in the net assets of that operation". [IAS 21:8] The 'operation' is not defined and can be considered to be either the consolidated net assets of the sub-group headed by Entity A, or as a collection of net assets held by each of the three subsidiaries.

If Entity P chooses to designate a portfolio (designation 3 in the list above) it must have an expectation that each individual item in the portfolio will change in fair value approximately proportionally to the change in the fair value of the portfolio as a whole. Such an expectation would be appropriate if the net assets of the individual subsidiaries are expected to be stable or increasing, provided the designation is of 'the first US$X million of net assets of a subsidiary'. However, if the net assets of an individual subsidiary are expected to fall below the designated amount, Entity P could not expect that the items in the portfolio will move approximately proportionally to the movement in the portfolio as a whole.

If an entity can demonstrate a high expectation of effectiveness for the portfolio, the group must assess and measure hedge effectiveness based on the individual foreign operations within the portfolio. Therefore, to the extent that the net assets of one of the foreign operations fall below the designated net asset amount, or a subsidiary is sold, ineffectiveness will arise.

It should be noted that the amount of ineffectiveness that will be recognised if Entity P were to use the portfolio designation will be the same as that recognised if designation 2 was adopted where both designations are highly effective. The only comparative advantage of the portfolio method is that the hedging documentation required is done for a portfolio as a whole (though it must include evidence supporting the expectation of approximately proportional movements in the fair value of individual investments in the portfolio to the fair value movements of the portfolio as a whole).

6 Cash flow hedge accounting – portfolio hedge of interest rate risk

An entity may wish to designate a derivative, or portfolio of derivatives, as a hedge of multiple variable interest rate payments or receipts. Instead of allocating each individual derivative to an individual cash inflow or outflow, the derivatives and the hedged cash flows are 'pooled' and hedged as a portfolio. IAS 39:IG.F.6.2 provides a series of questions and answers for an entity wishing to undertake such a hedge accounting strategy. IAS 39:IG.F.6.3 provides an illustrative example of the hedge strategy. The implementation guidance is very detailed and is complex. The objective of this section is to simplify the concepts and highlight some relevant conclusions that can be reached from this implementation guidance.

6.1 Hedged item

As stated in **2.2** of **chapter C9** a recognised floating rate debt instrument can either be hedged as a recognised financial instrument, or instead the floating interest inflows or outflows can be hedged as forecast transactions. If an entity regularly borrows or invests in floating rate debt instruments the entity has an exposure not only from the recognised debt instruments but also the debt instruments that it will invest or borrow in the future. An entity may, for example, borrow through short-term commercial paper, say up to a maturity of 90 days, that has an interest rate that resets monthly, but will rollover the recognised commercial paper into further commercial paper when the recognised commercial paper reaches its maturity. The entity has variability in cash flows with respect to its recognised commercial paper, but also the commercial paper it believes, with high probability, it will borrow in the future.

IAS 39 provides flexibility in hedging forecast cash flows when an entity expects, with high probability, to reinvest cash flows from one instrument into another. When cash flow hedging interest rate risk, say LIBOR, an entity can have cash flow variability with respect to the following:

- the variability in LIBOR inflows or outflows on a recognised acquired or issued debt instrument when the basis of interest is determined by future LIBOR rates; or
- the variability in LIBOR inflows or outflows from a highly probable reinvestment or future borrowing of a new floating rate LIBOR debt instrument. Because future interest inflows or outflows will be derived from future rates of LIBOR, the entity has an exposure to variability in LIBOR; or
- the effective interest rate that will be earned or paid if an entity has a highly probable forecast investment or issuance of fixed rate debt where the debt is priced off the LIBOR curve at the date the debt is issued; or
- the effective interest rate that will be earned or paid if an entity has a highly probable forecast investment or issuance of a fixed rate debt

and the fixed interest rate is determined of the LIBOR curve prior to the debt being issued and, therefore, the amount of proceeds received by the issuer, or paid by the acquirer has not yet been determined, i.e. it is variable. The resulting premium or discount to par at issue will affect profit or loss through the effective interest rate determined when the debt is issued.

The entity can aggregate its floating rate LIBOR exposures from the four examples above and plot them in time buckets so that the entity can determine when the LIBOR cash flows are set (i.e. when they fix), and therefore determine up to what period it has an exposure to LIBOR. For example, if an entity has issued 5-year floating rate 3-month LIBOR debt where the floating rate is set in advance, at the date of issue, the floating rate for the next three months will be determined based on the rate of LIBOR at the date the debt is issued. An entity cannot cash flow hedge the first payment of interest as that first payment is not actually variable as it has been fixed in advance. This payment will be excluded from the hedge designation. (If LIBOR was priced in arrears, or was priced in advance but some of the interest receipts or payments have not yet been set then this is the variability in LIBOR that could be designated.) However, all future interest payments that will be determined in three months' time and beyond, are today all variable, and until those floating rates are set, at the start of each respective quarter, the entity has exposure to LIBOR which it can hedge. As future LIBOR interest payments are set at the start of each quarter, the number of forecast transactions with respect to that debt instrument falls, but is likely to be replaced by more forecast interest exposures in future periods if the entity expects to borrow more floating rate debt.

An entity does not need to state the maturity of the forecast floating or fixed debt it is expecting with high probability to invest in or borrow at. As long as the entity has a high probability of being exposed to LIBOR, because the entity is expected to invest in LIBOR debt instruments or borrow at LIBOR rates, the exact maturity of the instrument is not relevant. If an entity believes it will have an exposure to LIBOR for three years, it does not matter whether the entity expects to invest in a floating rate asset with a maturity of six months that then rolls into another five 6-month term floating rate assets, or whether it expects to invest in a 12-month floating rate asset, and a subsequent investment in a further two 12-month floating rate assets. In both cases, and any other combination, the entity's *future* exposure to LIBOR is the same.

An entity also does not need to state whether it will invest or borrow in floating rate debt instruments, or fixed rate debt instruments, as long as any debt instrument it invests in or borrows is derived from the LIBOR curve. For example, if an entity expects to borrow in six months' time, up to the date it draws down the borrowing, it has an exposure to LIBOR. From today until six months' time, changes in LIBOR will affect the future interest payments on future floating rate debt, or will affect the fixed rate or amount of proceeds that will only be determined at the date the entity draws down the fixed rate borrowing. In both cases, the entity may designate its exposure to LIBOR for the next six months.

The portfolio approach to cash flow hedging interest rate risk is a dynamic approach in that an entity may choose to re-designate, almost on a continuous basis, though more likely every quarter if LIBOR resets quarterly. As the cash flows that are due to fix in the next period fall away from the designation, new forecast cash flows may be added to the designation. As long as the entity can claim these new forecast transactions are highly probable and the entity has qualifying hedging instruments that are expected to be highly effective, the entity can pursue hedge accounting.

6.2 Hedging instrument

When the hedged risk is LIBOR, the hedging instrument could be a LIBOR for fixed rate interest rate swap. Alternatively, it could be a LIBOR-based purchased option. If the entity has an exposure to LIBOR inflows, and it chooses to hedge with a swap, it will have a pay LIBOR receive fixed rate interest rate swap; if the entity has an exposure to LIBOR outflows, and it chooses to hedge with a swap, it will have a receive LIBOR pay fixed rate interest swap. The entity must designate all, or a proportion, of the interest rate swap as a hedging instrument relating to the designated hedged item (forecast LIBOR interest inflows or outflows).

6.3 Hedge designation

In a hedge of forecast interest payments or receipts, an entity will schedule the forecast transactions and will hedge these floating inflows or outflows up to the date they fix, i.e. when LIBOR is set. In more simple hedge designations, the timing of the fixing of the cash flows on the hedged items coincides with the timing of the refixing of the variable rate on the swap. This is considered a full term hedge, compared to a partial term hedge, because the full period up to the date when the forecast transaction is no longer subject to cash flow variability is hedged.

An entity will have exposure to LIBOR as long as the entity has a high probability of investing or borrowing in LIBOR-based debt instruments (whether floating or fixed of the future LIBOR curve). In order to designate all these exposures, an entity can choose to partial term hedge these exposures until the next time LIBOR is set. As described in **6.1**, if a LIBOR interest inflow or outflow is set, it no longer is variable and therefore cannot be hedged. An entity can use partial term hedging to hedge all variable LIBOR exposure for its forecast LIBOR-based transactions from today until the next time LIBOR resets. If LIBOR resets every quarter, the entity can partial term hedge all the future LIBOR exposures for just three months only. After three months, the entity will re-designate, for the next three months, and so on.

Example 6.3

Cash flow hedging the variability in reinvestment: designation

Entity A has a short-term recognised variable rate asset with three months remaining to maturity. At maturity of that asset, Entity A will reinvest the proceeds from the asset into either fixed rate asset(s) or floating rate asset(s) of maturities that are not determined until those instruments are acquired. Entity A forecasts with high probability that it will reinvest for up to four years. Because Entity A is exposed to interest rates from its reinvestment into new assets (irrespective of whether the asset is fixed or floating), it enters into a receive fixed pay floating 3m-LIBOR interest rate swap (IRS) that has a two year maturity (Entity A has a policy of hedging out only two years) to hedge the risk of variability in LIBOR. It is assumed for illustration that the floating rate on the recognised floating rate asset has already been set in advance and therefore there is no cash flow variability that can be hedged.

Entity A does not need to be specific as to the maturity of the future reinvested debt instruments. The instruments could have maturities of three months, six months, nine months etc., and could also be fixed or floating. Up to the date the reinvestment occurs, Entity A has an exposure to LIBOR that it can cash flow hedge.

Entity A plots the notionals for the various time periods over the next two years which will determine the extent to which Entity A is exposed to LIBOR.

	t_0	3m	6m	9m	12m	15m	18m	21m	24m
Specific 3m floating LIBOR asset (notional £m)	100								
Hedged item:									
Non-specific assets that have LIBOR exposure (notional £m)		100	100	100	100	100	100	100	100
Hedging instrument:									
Receive fixed pay 3m-LIBOR (notional £m)	100	100	100	100	100	100	100	100	100

t_0 = 1/1/X0

Because the interest rate swap and the recognised floating rate asset have LIBOR set in advance, in this case on 1/1/X0, there is no cash flow variability on the LIBOR-based asset with three months to maturity. All cash flows of that debt instrument are fixed, not variable, being the principal and one interest payment that have been determined at the date of designation. Therefore, the recognised floating rate LIBOR asset cannot be a hedged item in a cash flow hedge.

Entity A, therefore, can only designate the cash flow variability due to changes in LIBOR with respect to forecast transactions that occur after the first reset date of the swap (the first cash flows under the swap are already fixed at t_0 as LIBOR is set in advance). The forecast transactions that Entity A chooses to hedge are the non-specific forecast exposure to LIBOR from reinvesting in LIBOR-based assets from 1/4/X0 until 31/12/X1 (equal to the maturity of the IRS). At t_0, Entity A designates the exposure of variability in LIBOR that occurs between 1/1/X0 and 31/3/X0 with respect to its forecast transaction (being the LIBOR variability on its forecast transactions occurring from 1/4/X0 to 31/12/X1). The exposure for the subsequent periods is specifically not hedged in this designation. Entity A has entered into a hedge of its exposure to LIBOR with respect to its reinvestment and rollover of LIBOR-based asset that are expected to occur in the 21 month period beginning 1/4/X0, due to changes in LIBOR that occur between 1/1/X0 and 31/3/X0.

Entity A is not specific as to the maturity of its reinvested assets that are acquired after 1/4/X0 as all assets will be subject to exposure to LIBOR until the date they are priced. Because all non-specific forecast transaction are exposed to LIBOR and are deemed as highly probable, Entity A is highly effective on a prospective basis.

6.4 Partial term cash flow hedging

When there is a difference between the timing of the fixing of the LIBOR-based inflows or outflows of the hedged item and the timing of the fixing of LIBOR on the swap hedge ineffectiveness will generally arise as an entity hedges the full term of the forecast transaction, being the time period up to the date the interest receipt or payment is set to LIBOR.

Partial term cash flow hedging is an alternative technique which can be applied to hedged items that are financial instruments. Partial term cash flow hedging does not apply to non-financial items as explained in **2.2**. In this instance, when a forecast variable interest receipt or payment fixes at a date later than the respective fixing on the variable leg of the interest rate swap, an entity can purposely designate a partial term hedge of the period up to the date the variable leg on the interest rate swap refixes. For example, if the variable leg on the interest rate swap fixes for LIBOR on 1 October, yet the hedged item fixes for LIBOR on 1 November, the difference in timing of resetting cash flows is not part of the hedge designation. In this instance, variations in LIBOR between the designation date and 1 October are considered a partial term hedge of the variability in LIBOR that exists on the hedged item that will reset on 1 November. Partial term hedging 'carves' up the period to the next resetting on the hedged item and hedges only part of that period.

IAS 39:IG.F.6.3 endorses this type of designation because it states that "when the interest rate swap is repriced in three months at the then current variable rate, the fixed rate and the variable rate on the interest rate swap become known and no longer provide hedge protection for the next three months. If the next forecast transaction does not occur until three months and ten days, the ten-day period that remains after the repricing of the interest rate swap is not hedged". The term of the hedge designation is only for the next three months. The implementation guidance explains that the "period of the exposure to interest rate changes on the portion of the cash flow exposures being hedged is:

- the period from the designation date to the repricing date of the interest rate swap that occurs within the quarterly period in which, but not before, the forecast transactions occur; and
- its effects for the period after the forecast transactions occur equal to the repricing interval of the interest rate swap".

Because the designation is the variability due to LIBOR prior to the debt instrument being acquired or issued, the fact that following the acquisition or recognition of the borrowing, LIBOR continues to change is irrelevant with respect to this specific partial term hedge designation, because the period following recognition of the asset or liability does not form part of this specific hedge.

6.5 Hedge effectiveness

Hedge ineffectiveness can be greatly reduced by using the above hedge accounting strategy for a number of reasons.

- The entity designates the LIBOR risk only, and excludes credit risk on the hedged items. Changes in the credit risk of the hedged item will not affect the effectiveness of the hedge as credit risk is not a designated hedged risk. The credit risk of the interest rate swap, however, must be monitored as this may be a source of ineffectiveness.
- Duration differences between the interest rate swap and the hedged forecast cash flow are not a source of ineffectiveness as the interest rate risk that is hedged is the risk relating to changes in the portion of the yield curve that corresponds with the period in which the variable rate leg of the interest rate swap is repriced.
- Timing differences between the date the swap resets to LIBOR and the date the hedged item resets to LIBOR are not a source of ineffectiveness when partial term hedging is applied.

Example 6.5

Cash flow hedging the variability in reinvestment: hedge effectiveness

Continuing with **example 6.3**, assuming Entity A is subject to quarterly reporting where the period end coincides with the repricing on the swap, i.e. 31/3/X0, Entity A must perform a retrospective assessment of hedge effectiveness for the period gone, plus a prospective assessment if it wishes to continue to apply hedge accounting.

As part of the retrospective assessment of hedge effectiveness for the period it looks back at the transactions that occurred in the period to determine whether it has been highly effective. As at 1/1/X0, Entity A never claimed it was hedging cash flow variability for the first three months of 20X0 for its recognised asset because LIBOR had already been determined on that floating rate recognised asset and therefore it never formed part of the designation. However, Entity A must assess whether the forecast transactions that it had designated at 1/1/X0, being the full-term hedge of forecast reinvestments after 1/4/X0, is highly effective. Entity A did not need to apply partial term hedging as the date of the LIBOR reset on the interest rate swaps coincides with the date of the LIBOR reset of the forecast reinvestments. When the forecast reinvestments remain highly probable, the hedge will have been fully effective on a retrospective basis, assuming all other criteria are met. Entity A may therefore recognise the full amount of the fair value of the derivative in other comprehensive income at 31/3/X0 in accordance with IAS 39:96.

As part of the prospective assessment of hedge effectiveness at 1/4/X0 Entity A must reassess whether the future exposure to LIBOR is still highly probable. Because the next reset date on the interest rate swap is 1/7/X0, Entity A is hedging those forecast transactions that are subject to LIBOR in the future that reset after 1/7/X0. Any LIBOR-based interest inflows that are fixed at 1/4/X0 are not designated because they are no longer variable, and any interest inflows that fix within the next three months are not part of the designation as they are not subject to variability in LIBOR for the next three months. Entity A can pass the prospective assessment of hedge effectiveness as long as all the forecast transactions are deemed to be highly probable.

7 Fair value hedge accounting – portfolio hedge of interest rate risk

The IASB published an amendment to IAS 39 in March 2004 that details how an entity can apply fair value hedge accounting to a portfolio of financial assets and/or financial liabilities for interest rate risk only. The main reasons for amending IAS 39 and a summary of the amendments are as described below.

7.1 Prepayable financial items

Fixed rate prepayable debt instruments may be prepaid prior to their contracted maturity. When interest rates move the change in the fair value of a prepayable item is caused by changes in the fair value of the contractual cash flows and changes in the fair value of the prepayment option. If the hedging instrument, e.g. an interest rate swap, is not prepayable, changes in the fair value of the hedged item are not expected to be offset by changes in fair value of the hedging instrument. This results in hedge ineffectiveness.

IAS 39 permits prepayable financial assets and liabilities to be hedged for changes in fair value attributable to changes in the hedged interest rate on the basis of expected rather than contractual repricing dates. [IAS 39:81A]

This is achieved by analysing the portfolio of hedged items into time periods based on the expected repricing dates. The expected repricing date of an item is the earlier of the dates when the item is expected to mature or to reprice to market rates. [IAS 39:AG117] As a result, the computation of the effect of a change in interest rates on the fair value of the prepayment option embedded in a prepayable item is not required. Though, if the estimates of the time periods in which items are expected to repay change, ineffectiveness will arise.

7.2 Hedging a portfolio of items

IAS 39 allows similar assets or similar liabilities to be aggregated and hedged as a group only if the individual assets or individual liabilities in the group share the risk exposure that is designated as being hedged. Furthermore, the change in fair value attributable to the hedged risk for each individual item in the group must be expected to be approximately proportional to the overall change in fair value attributable to the hedged risk of the group of items. [IAS 39:83] Because the individual hedged items are expected to behave differently in so far as they may prepay at different times, the change in the fair value of each hedged item cannot be expected to be proportional to the change in the fair value of the portfolio.

The general requirement is modified for a hedge of a portfolio for interest rate risk only. The items in the hedged portfolio must be items whose fair value changes in response to the hedged interest rate and must be items that could have qualified for fair value hedge accounting had they been designated individually. However, an entity is not required to demonstrate that the change in fair value of the individual hedged items is approximately proportional to the overall change in fair value of the portfolio due to interest rate risk. [IAS 39:AG118] For this type of hedge, the designated hedged item is expressed as an 'amount of currency' (e.g. an amount of Sterling, US dollars, Euros etc.) rather than as individual assets or liabilities. [IAS 39:81A]

7.3 Fair value hedge adjustments

IAS 39 requires that in an effective fair value hedge relationship the hedged item is adjusted by the change in its fair value due to the hedged risk. The adjustment to the hedged item may be amortised to profit or loss as soon as the adjustment exists, but should begin no later than when the item ceases to be adjusted for the hedged risk. For a portfolio hedge, this would require an adjustment to many items, as well as tracking the amortisation of the resultant adjustment to profit or loss. In most cases complex systems solutions would be required.

IAS 39 is modified to permit the adjustment to the hedged items for a portfolio hedge of interest rate risk to be recognised in two separate line items within assets or liabilities for those repricing time periods for which the hedged item is an asset or liability respectively. This adjustment should be presented next to financial assets or financial liabilities. [IAS 39:89A] Furthermore, that adjustment may be amortised to profit or loss using a straight line method when amortisation using a recalculated effective interest rate is not practicable. The adjustment should also be amortised to profit or loss by the expiry of the relevant repricing time period. [IAS 39:92]

7.4 Hedging a net position

While IAS 39 prohibits the designation of an overall net position (e.g. the net of fixed rate assets and fixed rate liabilities), entities that hedge the net position in economic terms may designate a proportion of either the assets or liabilities as the hedged item. The net exposure will change each period due to the repricing of items, or through derecognition, impairment and origination of new instruments. It follows that the designated proportion of assets or liabilities will also need to be changed following such changes in the net exposure.

In the case of a portfolio hedge for interest rate risk only, the hedged item may be expressed as a *gross currency amount* of either assets or liabilities rather than as an individual asset (or liability). [IAS 39:81A] The benefit of this approach is that the effect of changes in interest rates on the amount of designated currency is determined in aggregate and not individually for each hedged item. [IAS 39:81A]

7.5 Demand deposits

IAS 39 states that the fair value of a financial liability with a demand feature is not less than the amount payable on demand, discounted from the first date that the amount could be required to be paid. [IAS 39:49] Many entities economically hedge their demand deposits on the basis that a certain core level of the demand deposits is not repaid on demand. For the core deposits, the expected life extends well beyond the demand date and the balance of the portfolio is relatively stable because withdrawals on some accounts are offset by new deposits into others. The hedge relationships are entered into on the basis of the expected repayment dates of the total balance of the portfolio of deposits.

In a fair value hedge, accounting for demand deposits on the basis of their expected repayment dates is inconsistent with the measurement principle for a financial liability with a demand feature. Thus, for fair value hedges, demand deposits cannot be hedged beyond their demand date. Nevertheless, the deposits may be included in determining the entity's net exposure and the designated hedged item with one restriction: if the net exposure is a net liability and that liability is made up entirely or partly of demand deposits, the designated liability can only be up to an amount equal to the amount of non-demand deposit liabilities. The reason for this is that the fair value determined in accordance with IAS 39 of a demand deposit is not affected by changes in interest rates, i.e. there is no fair value exposure to hedge for accounting purposes.

7.6 Hedge ineffectiveness

In a fair value hedge of a portfolio hedge of interest rate risk, in addition to hedge ineffectiveness that arises on other fair value hedging relationships, additional hedge ineffectiveness may arise for the following reasons in a portfolio hedging relationship:

- actual repricing dates differ from those expected, or expected repricing dates are revised; and
- items in the hedged portfolio become impaired or are derecognised.

7.7 Application

IAS 39 sets out a number of steps that should be followed in achieving hedge accounting for a portfolio hedge of interest rate risk. These steps are summarised in the example below.

Example 7.7

Fair value hedging a portfolio of interest rate risk

Step 1: As part of its risk management process, Bank A identifies a portfolio of items whose interest rate risk it wishes to hedge. The portfolio may comprise only financial assets, financial liabilities, or both. Since Bank A hedges its fixed rate originated mortgages, fixed rate liabilities and core deposits on a net basis, it identifies a portfolio containing these items as the portfolio it wishes to hedge. [IAS 39:AG114(a)]

Step 2: Bank A analyses the portfolio into repricing time periods based on expected, rather than contractual, repricing dates. The expected repricing dates are based on historical experience and other available information, including information and expectations regarding prepayment rates, interest rates and their interaction. Whilst the analysis into repricing time periods may be performed by scheduling cash flows into the periods in which they are expected to occur, the Bank schedules the notional principal amounts into all periods until repricing is expected to occur as follows: [IAS 39:AG114(b)]

	T1	**T2**	**T3**
Fixed rate assets	30	40	25
Fixed rate liabilities	(20)	(30)	(15)
Demand deposits	–	–	(35)
Net exposure	10	10	(25)

In addition to complying with all other hedge designation and documentation criteria, Bank A documents:

- which assets and liabilities are included in the portfolio hedge and the basis used for removing them from the portfolio; [IAS 39:AG119(a)]
- how Bank A estimates its repricing dates, including what interest rate assumptions underlie estimates of prepayments rates and the basis for

changing those estimates; the same method is used for both the initial estimates made at the time an asset or liability is included in the hedged portfolio and for any later revisions to those estimates; [IAS 39:AG119(b)] and

- the number and duration of repricing time periods. [IAS 39:AG119(c)]

(for further documentation requirements see steps 3 and 5)

Step 3: Bank A determines the amount it wishes to hedge and designates as the hedged item in each repricing time period a gross currency amount of assets and/or liabilities from the identified portfolio equal to that amount.

	T1	T2	T3
Amount of assets (liabilities) designated as hedged item	10	10	(15)

This amount is converted into a percentage of assets or liabilities from the identified portfolio in each time period, which is used in testing hedge effectiveness. [IAS 39:AG114(c)]

	T1	T2	T3
Net exposure	10	10	(25)
Amount of assets (liabilities) designated as hedged item	10	10	(15)*
Hedge ratio (hedged item as a percentage of amount of qualifying assets (liabilities)	33.33% (10/30)	25% (10/40)	100% (15/15)

* (Note that the amount hedged may only be drawn from the fixed rate liabilities and not from the demand deposits as demand deposits cannot be a hedged item beyond their demand date.)

Bank A is therefore hedging 33.33 per cent of its assets in repricing time period T1, 25 per cent of its assets in repricing time period T2 and 100 per cent of its fixed rate liabilities in repricing time period T3.

In addition to complying with all other hedge accounting criteria, Bank A documents the methodology used to determine the amount of assets or liabilities that are designated as the hedged item, the hedge ratio and the percentage measure used when testing effectiveness. [IAS 39:AG119(e)]

Step 4: Bank A designates the interest rate risk hedged as a particular benchmark rate, e.g. LIBOR. [IAS 39:AG114(d)]

Step 5: Bank A designates one or more hedging instruments for each repricing time period. [IAS 39:AG114(e)] The derivatives designated for a repricing time period may comprise a number of derivatives with offsetting risk positions all of which contain exposure to LIBOR. None of the derivatives however may be a written option, or net written option as the Standard does not permit such options to be designated as hedging instruments except in certain limited circumstances (see **section 3.3** for details). [IAS 39:AG120]

Bank A has three interest rates. Swap 1 pays fixed receives floating and has a notional of 35 that matures in T2; Swap 2 pays fixed receives floating and has a notional of 10 that matures in T3; and Swap 3 pays floating receives fixed and has a notional of 35 that matures in T3.

Bank A designates the following swaps or combination of swaps to hedge each of the time periods:

	T1	**T2**	**T3**
Swap 1	–	–	–
Swap 2	10	10	10
Swap 3	–	–	(25)
Total designated hedging instruments	10	10	(15)

In the above example swap 2 hedges more than one repricing time period and is thus allocated to all the time periods it hedges. [IAS 39:AG120]

Step 6: Using the designations made in steps 3-5 above, Bank A assesses at inception and in subsequent periods, whether the hedge is expected to be highly effective during the period for which the hedge is designated. [IAS 39:AG114(f)] It is not appropriate to assume that changes in the fair value of the hedged item equal changes in the value of the hedging instrument. [IAS 39:AG122] IAS 39 allows the use of either of two techniques to measure the effectiveness of the hedging relationship: Bank A can calculate the effectiveness of the hedging relationship as the difference between the change in the fair value of the hedging instrument and the change in the fair value of the entire hedged item attributable to the hedged risk; [IAS 39:AG126(a)] or it can elect to use an approximation approach. [IAS 39:AG126(b)] Bank A applies this approximation method as is illustrated in steps A to E and step 7 below.

In addition to complying with all other hedge accounting criteria, Bank A documents:

- how often Bank A will test effectiveness (monthly in this case); [IAS 39:AG119(d)]
- which of the two effectiveness testing techniques Bank A is using; [IAS 39:AG119(d)] and
- when effectiveness is tested using the approximation approach, whether effectiveness will be assessed for each repricing time period individually, for all time periods in aggregate, or by using some combination of the two (in this case Bank A elects to assess effectiveness for all time periods in aggregate). [IAS 39:AG119(f)]

After one month, Bank A assesses the effectiveness of the hedging relationship using the approximation approach as follows:

Step A: Fair value changes of the hedged item (before determining the impact of changes in fair value due to revised repayment expectations and ignoring changes in fair value not attributable to interest rate movements) and of the hedging instruments are determined to be as follows:

	T1	T2	T3
Changes in fair value: hedged item	2	3	(1)
% change in fair value (as a percentage of the hedged assets (liabilities))	20% (2/10)	30% (3/10)	6.67% (1/15)
Changes in fair value: hedging instrument	(2)	(3)	1

Step B: A revised estimate of the amount of assets and liabilities in each repricing time period is determined in order to calculate the amount of the hedged item based on the revised estimates. Following a decrease in LIBOR, the assets and liabilities have repaid faster than initially expected. Bank A determines that its portfolio of assets and liabilities is now expected to reprice as follows:

	T1	T2	T3
Fixed rate assets	27	32	20
Fixed rate liabilities	(15)	(20)	(10)
Demand deposits	–	–	(20)
Net exposure*	12	12	(10)

* (Note that the above new net position is irrelevant for the purposes of determining the effectiveness of the hedging relationship for this period. It may however be relevant in the next period in determining the amount of hedged assets and liabilities.)

Step C: The percentage of the assets and liabilities hedged (as determined in step 3 above) is applied to the revised amount of assets and liabilities in each repricing period. [IAS 39:AG126(b)(ii)]

	T1	T2	T3
Hedge ratio (from Step 3)	33.33%	25%	100%
Revised assets	27	32	–
Revised liabilities	–	–	(10)
Revised hedged assets	9 (33.33%*27)	8 (25%*32)	–
Revised hedged liabilities	–	–	(10) (100%*10)

Step D: The change in the fair value of the revised estimate of the hedged item that is attributable to the hedged risk is calculated by multiplying the change in fair value (as determined in Step A) by the new amount of assets (liabilities) in that repricing period (as determined in Step C) [IAS 39:AG126(b)(iii)]:

	T1	T2	T3
% change in fair value (Step A)	20%	30%	6.67%
Revised assets and liabilities (Step C)	9	8	(10)
Changes in fair value of the hedged item	1.8	2.4	(0.667)

Step E: The effectiveness of the hedging relationship is determined by comparing the change in the fair value of the hedging instrument to the change in the fair value of the hedged item:

	T1	**T2**	**T3**
Changes in fair value of the hedged item	1.8	2.4	(0.667)
Change in fair value of the hedging instrument(s)	(2)	(3)	1
Effectiveness (each time period)	90%	80%	66.7%
	(1.8/2)	(2.4/3)	(0.667/1)
Effectiveness (all time periods)		88.33%	
		(1.8+2.4-0.667)/(-2-3+1)	

Because the portfolio hedge is effective for all repricing time periods, in accordance with the documented method of testing hedge effectiveness (see step 6 above), Bank A concludes that the hedge is effective for the designated period.

In this example, for illustrative purposes only, all hedge ineffectiveness is due to changes in the amount of assets and liabilities at the start and the end of the reporting period due to changes in prepayment rates. In practice, ineffectiveness will also result due to impairment of assets, derecognition of assets and liabilities, and other valuation differences between the hedging instrument and hedged item as for any conventional fair value hedge.

Step 7: Bank A measures the change in the fair value of the hedged item attributable to the hedged risk on the basis of the expected repricing dates. Bank A recognises the change in fair value of the hedged item as a gain or loss in profit or loss and in one of two line items in the statement of financial position. Bank A recognises the following entry based on Step D above: [IAS 39:AG114(g)]

Dr	Separate statement of financial position line item (assets) [1.8+2.4]	4.2	
Cr	Separate statement of financial position line item (liabilities)		0.667
Cr	Profit or loss		3.533

Being recognition of the change in fair value of the hedged item attributable to the hedged risk.

Step 8: Bank A measures the change in fair value of the hedging instrument(s) and recognises it as a gain or loss in profit or loss. The fair value of the hedging instrument(s) is recognised as an asset or liability in the statement of financial position. Bank A recognises the following journal entry based on Step A above: [IAS 39:AG114(h)]

Dr	Profit or loss (fair value gains and losses on derivatives)	4	
Dr	Derivative asset	1	
Cr	Derivative liability		5

Being recognition of the change in fair value of the hedging instrument(s).

Step 9: Any ineffectiveness will be recognised in profit or loss as the difference arising from steps 7 and 8. The above hedging relationship resulted in an amount of 0.467 [4-3.533] being recognised in profit or loss as hedge ineffectiveness for the period. [IAS 39:AG114(i)]

Step 10: Bank A then establishes a new estimate of the total assets (liabilities) in each repricing time period, including new assets (liabilities) that have been originated since it last tested effectiveness, and designates a new amount as the hedged item and a new percentage as the hedged percentage. [IAS 39:AG127] The procedures set out above are then repeated at the next date the Bank tests effectiveness.

Step 11: The adjustment determined in Step 7 above should be amortised to profit or loss. Amortisation may begin as soon as an adjustment exists and should begin no later than when the hedged item ceases to be adjusted for changes in its fair value attributable to the risk being hedged. Bank A concludes that amortising the adjustment using a recalculated effective interest rate is not practicable and instead will amortise the adjustment to profit or loss using a straight line approach. The adjustment will be amortised fully to profit or loss by the expiry of the relevant repricing time period. [IAS 39:92] Any amount relating to a particular time period that remains when the repricing time period expires should be recognised in profit or loss at that time. [IAS 39:AG129]

The example above does not account for the instances where, following the calculation of the hedge gain or loss, the hedged items are derecognised (e.g. through earlier than expected prepayment, impairment or sale). Should this occur, then the amount of change in fair value included in the statement of financial position (within a separate line item) that relates to the derecognised item should be removed from the statement of financial position and be included in the gain or loss that arises on derecognition of the item. The knowledge of which repricing time period(s) the derecognised item was included in determines the repricing time periods from which to remove it, and therefore the amount to be removed from the separate line item. If it can be determined in which time period the derecognised item was included, it is removed from that time period. If not, it is removed from the earliest time period if the derecognition resulted from higher than expected prepayments or allocated to all time periods containing the derecognised item on a systematic and rational basis if the item was sold or became impaired. [IAS 39:AG128]

C11 Hedge accounting – examples

Contents

1 Introduction

This chapter includes illustrative examples of hedge accounting.

2 Fair value hedges

The following fair value hedges are illustrated in this section.

Section 2.1 Fair value hedging interest rate risk of fixed rate debt

Section 2.2 Fair value hedging a firm commitment with a non-derivative

2.1 Fair value hedging interest rate risk of fixed rate debt

The following example illustrates the entries for a fair value hedge of interest rate risk of fixed rate debt using an interest rate swap.

Example 2.1

Fair value hedging fixed rate debt

On 1 January 20X0, Entity C issued £100 million of five-year 8 per cent fixed rate debt. Entity C has a BBB credit rating at the issuance date. The fixed interest rate on the debt is 150 basis points higher than the five-year swap rate. Interest on the debt is payable semi-annually. Entity C's interest rate risk policy requires that all debt is at variable rates which is achieved either through issuing variable rate debt or by issuing fixed rate debt and swapping it into variable.

In order to maintain compliance with this policy Entity C entered into an interest rate swap on 1 January 20X0 to 'convert' the debt from fixed rate to variable and designated the swap (identifying and documenting all critical terms) as a fair value hedge of interest rate risk on the fixed rate debt (credit spreads are purposely not hedged). The swap is a five-year pay 6-month LIBOR, receive 6.50 per cent fixed interest rate swap.

Entity C satisfies the hedge accounting criteria.

- The fair value of Entity C's issued fixed rate debt will vary with changes in market interest rates. Such changes could have an impact in profit or loss if the debt is extinguished early. Hence, the debt qualifies for fair value hedge accounting (it is not a non-qualifying exposure).
- Entity C has formally documented the hedging relationship from inception, identifying all critical terms.
- The hedge is consistent with Entity C's risk management policy for that hedging relationship.
- Entity C expects its hedge to be highly effective and has documented this assessment. The primary potential source of ineffectiveness in a fair value hedge of fixed rate debt is credit risk. Entity C is using an interest rate swap to hedge interest rate risk only. Hence, changes in credit spreads between Entity C's BBB rate and swap rates will not generate hedge ineffectiveness.

Note that the principal terms of the hedged item and the hedging instrument match. IAS 39 recognises that if the principal terms of the hedging instrument and the hedged item are the same, then the changes in fair value attributable to the risk being hedged may be likely to offset each other fully, both at inception and afterwards. [IAS 39:AG108] Entity C is required, however to assess effectiveness on an ongoing basis. [IAS 39:IG.F.4.7]

The fair value of the swap and the carrying amount of the debt following the adjustment for changes in fair value attributable to the hedged risk are as follows. Note that the journal entries to recognise interest on the hedged item and the net interest settlements are not presented in this example.

	1/1/20X0	30/6/20X0	31/12/20X0
Issued debt	£(100,000,000)	£(105,000,000)	£(102,000,000)
Swap	£nil	£4,800,000	£1,900,000

The required entries are as follows.

1 January 20X0

		£	£
Dr	Cash	100,000,000	
Cr	Debt		100,000,000

To recognise the issuance of debt.

No entries are required in respect of the swap because it was entered into at the money when the fair value was zero.

30 June 20X0

		£	£
Dr	Profit or loss	5,000,000	
Cr	Debt		5,000,000
Dr	Swap	4,800,000	
Cr	Profit or loss		4,800,000

To recognise changes in the fair value of the debt and of the swap.

The net impact in profit or loss of £200,000 reflects that the changes in fair value of the swap do not fully offset the changes in the fair value of the debt for the designated risk. The difference is due to credit risk of the counterparty bank which is not present in the hedged item.

31 December 20X0

		£	£
Dr	Debt	3,000,000	
Cr	Profit or loss		3,000,000
Dr	Profit or loss	2,900,000	
Cr	Swap		2,900,000

To recognise changes in the fair value of the debt and of the swap.

The net impact in profit or loss of £100,000 reflects that the changes in fair value of the swap do not fully offset the changes in the fair value of the debt for the designated risk.

Note that the carrying amount of the debt in the statement of financial position will not represent its full fair value but will be a hybrid of amortised cost and an element of its fair value which is due to movements in interest rates since the inception of the hedging relationship. Other factors, such as changes in the entity's credit spread, could impact the fair value of the debt, but the hedged item is not adjusted for movements in that risk.

2.2 Fair value hedging a firm commitment with a non-derivative

The following example illustrates the entries for a fair value hedge of foreign currency risk on a firm commitment using a foreign currency denominated deposit as a hedging instrument.

Example 2.2

Hedging a firm commitment with a non-derivative

On 1 January 20X4, Entity B has a firm commitment to purchase equipment (a non-financial asset) from Entity M, a French entity. Entity B's functional currency is Sterling and Entity M's is Euro. The firm commitment requires B to pay €30 million for the equipment for delivery on 1 January 20X5. Entity B has a 31 March year-end.

Entity B currently has €30 million on deposit with a European bank maturing on 1 January 20X5 on which it currently recognises in profit or loss foreign exchange gains and losses at the end of each reporting period. Entity B would like to use its Euro deposit balance as a hedge of its commitment to purchase the equipment.

Entity B can designate the cash deposit as a hedging instrument in either a cash flow or a fair value hedge of the spot foreign currency risk of the firm commitment.

The spot foreign exchange rates are as follows.

Date	Exchange rate	Sterling equivalent of €30m	Movement
1 January 20X4	1.4321	20,948,257	
31 March 20X4	1.4282	21,005,461	57,204
1 January 20X5	1.4511	20,673,971	(331,490)

The entries below do not consider the accounting for the deposit before 1 January 20X4. Up to this date, the monetary asset will have been reported at the spot rate at the end of each reporting period, with exchange gains and losses recognised in profit or loss.

Entity B designates the hedge as a *fair value hedge* of the spot foreign currency risk of the firm commitment.

1 January 20X4

There are no entries. The firm commitment has a fair value of zero.

31 March 20X4

		£	£
Dr	Deposit	57,204	
Cr	Profit or loss		57,204

To recognise the foreign exchange gain on remeasurement of the deposit.

		£	£
Dr	Profit or loss	57,204	
Cr	Firm commitment		57,204

To recognise the change in fair value of the firm commitment relating to the hedged risk (foreign currency spot movements).

1 January 20X5

		£	£
Dr	Profit or loss	331,490	
Cr	Deposit		331,490

To recognise the foreign currency exchange loss on remeasurement of the deposit.

		£	£
Dr	Firm commitment	331,490	
Cr	Profit or loss		331,490

To recognise the change in fair value of the firm commitment relating to the hedged risk (foreign currency spot movements).

		£	£
Dr	Property, plant, equipment	20,948,257	
Cr	Firm commitment		274,286
Cr	Cash		20,673,971

To recognise the acquisition of the asset and derecognition of the firm commitment that has now been extinguished. The carrying amount of the non-financial asset is the Sterling equivalent of €30 million, translated at the spot rate when the hedge was entered into.

		£	£
Dr	Cash	20,673,971	
Cr	Deposit		20,673,971

To recognise the repayment of the deposit upon its maturity on 1 January 20X5.

Entity B designates the hedge as a *cash flow hedge* of the spot foreign currency risk of the firm commitment.

If Entity B has an accounting policy not to apply basis adjustments to non-financial items in cash flow hedges, the amount recognised in other comprehensive income will be retained in equity at the acquisition date of the equipment and will be reclassified from equity to profit or loss in future periods when the depreciation of the equipment will impact profit or loss (see **2.2.3** in **chapter C9**). In this case, the carrying amount of the equipment would be £20,673,971.

3 Cash flow hedges

Because cash flow hedging incorporates the hedging of financial and non-financial items, both recognised in the statement of financial position and forecast transactions that have yet to occur, there are many different examples. This section includes some of the more common examples in detail as well as some complex scenarios.

Section 3.1 Cash flow hedging a forecast sale of a non-financial item

Section 3.2 Cash flow hedging a forecast sale for foreign currency risk

Section 3.3 Basis adjusting the acquisition of a non-financial item

Section 3.4 Cash flow hedging a forecast sale and subsequent receivable

Section 3.5 Cash flow hedging variable rate interest with an interest rate swap

Section 3.6 Cash flow hedging variable rate debt with a purchased interest rate cap

3.1 Cash flow hedging a forecast sale of a non-financial item

The following example illustrates the entries for a cash flow hedge of market price risk on a forecast sale of a non-financial item using a forward contract.

Example 3.1

Forecast sale of a non-financial item

On 4 January 20X0 Entity B has a forecast sale of 500 tonnes of wheat expected to occur on or about 31 December 20X0.

On 4 January 20X0 Entity B designates the cash flows of the forecasted sale as a hedged item and enters into a wheat futures contract to sell 500 tonnes at US$1.1 million on 31 December 20X0.

At inception of the hedge, the derivative is at-the-money (fair value is zero). The terms of the forecast sale and the derivative match. On 31 December 20X0, the wheat futures contract has a fair value of US$25,000 and is closed out. Entity B sells the inventory with a cost of US$1,000,000 for US$1,075,000.

The required entries are as follows.

31 December 20X0

		US$	US$
Dr	Wheat futures contract	25,000	
Cr	Other comprehensive income		25,000

To recognise the wheat futures contract at fair value (note that the changes in fair value of the derivative are recognised in other comprehensive income until the hedged forecast sale occurs).

31 December 20X0

		US$	US$
Dr	Cash	25,000	
Cr	Wheat futures contract		25,000

To recognise the settlement of the wheat futures contract.

		US$	US$
Dr	Cash	1,075,000	
Dr	Cost of goods sold	1,000,000	
Cr	Revenue		1,075,000
Cr	Inventories		1,000,000

To recognise the sale of inventories with a cost of US$1,000,000.

		US$	US$
Dr	Other comprehensive income	25,000	
Cr	Revenue		25,000

To recognise the reclassification of the gain on the hedging instrument from other comprehensive income to revenue.

Revenue of US$1,100,000 is recognised. This represents US$1,075,000 from the sale of wheat at spot prices, plus the gain on the derivative. The sum of the two equals the sale of wheat at the hedged rate.

3.2 Cash flow hedging a forecast sale for foreign currency risk

The following example illustrates the entries for a cash flow hedge of foreign currency risk of a forecast sale using a forward exchange contract.

Example 3.2

Cash flow hedging the foreign currency risk of a forecast sale of a non-financial item

On 4 January 20X2, Entity D has a forecast sale of €4,000,000 of confectionery on or about 31 December 20X2 to a German retail outlet (Entity AG). Entity D has a Sterling functional currency, and Entity AG has a Euro functional currency. On 4 January 20X2, Entity D designates the cash flow of the forecast sale as a hedged item and enters into a currency forward to sell €4 million based on the forecast receipt. The forward contract locks in the value of the Euros to be received at a rate of €1.5:£. At inception of the hedge, the derivative is on-market (i.e. fair value is zero). The terms of the currency forward and the forecast sale match each other. The entity designates the forward foreign exchange risk as the hedged risk.

Potential sources of ineffectiveness include non-occurrence of the forecast transaction and changes in the date of sale. Any ineffectiveness will be recognised in profit or loss.

On 30 June 20X2, the fair value of the currency forward is negative £100,000 because the forward rate has changed, reflecting the fact that the Euro has strengthened against Sterling.

On 31 December 20X2, the transaction occurred as expected. The fair value of the forward is negative £111,111 because the Euro continued to strengthen against Sterling.

The required entries are as follows.

4 January 20X2

No entries are required because the forward was entered into 'on-market', and therefore had a fair value of zero at inception. Normally, there will be margin to be posted, associated with trading on a currency exchange, but this has been ignored for illustration purposes only. There may also be fees if the foreign exchange contract is an over-the-counter (OTC) transaction.

30 June 20X2

		£	£
Dr	Other comprehensive income	100,000	
Cr	Forward		100,000

To recognise the forward contract at fair value, reflecting that the forward contract is fully effective in hedging the forward rate of the forecast transaction.

31 December 20X2

		£	£
Dr	Other comprehensive income	11,111	
Cr	Forward		11,111

To recognise the change in fair value of the forward contract. The forward contract remains fully effective in hedging the forward rate of the forecast transaction.

		£	£
Dr	Forward	111,111	
Cr	Cash		111,111

To recognise the cash paid in settling the forward contract.

		£	£
Dr	Cash	2,777,778	
Cr	Sales		2,777,778

To recognise the receipt of €4m from the sale of confectionery translated at the spot rate of €1.44:£.

		£	£
Dr	Sales	111,111	
Cr	Other comprehensive income		111,111

To recognise the cumulative effective portion of the hedging instrument included in other comprehensive income that is reclassified from equity to profit or loss when the sale occurs.

The net effect of reclassifying the amount from equity to profit or loss when the sale occurred is equivalent to recognising in profit or loss the sale translated at the contracted rate inherent in the forward (i.e. €4,000,000/€1.5:£).

Translation of sale at spot rate at 31 December 20X2	£2,777,778
Reclassified from equity to profit or loss at 31 December 20X2	(£111,111)
	£2,666,667

Note: for the purposes of illustration only, the forward contract has not been discounted.

3.3 Basis adjusting the acquisition of a non-financial item

The following example illustrates the entries for a cash flow hedge of a non-financial item where a policy of basis adjustment is adopted.

Example 3.3

Basis adjusting forecast acquisition of a non-financial item

On 4 January 20X2, Entity D has a forecast purchase of 100,000 kg of cocoa on or about 31 December 20X2 from a Brazilian supplier, Entity B. Entity D has a Sterling functional currency, and Entity B has a US dollar functional currency. On 4 January 20X2, Entity D designates the cash flow of the forecast purchase as a hedged item and enters into a currency forward to buy US$180,000 based on the forecast payment (100,000 kg at US$1.8 per kg). The forward contract locks in the value of the US dollar amount to be paid at a rate of US$1.8:£1. At inception of the hedge, the derivative is on-market (i.e. fair value is zero). The terms of the currency forward and the forecast purchase match each other, and the entity designates the forward foreign exchange risk as the hedged risk.

Potential sources of ineffectiveness include non-occurrence of the forecast transaction and changes in the date of purchase. Any ineffectiveness will be recognised in profit or loss.

On 30 June 20X2, the fair value of the currency forward is positive £10,000 because the forward rate has changed, reflecting the fact that the US dollar has strengthened against Sterling.

On 31 December 20X2, the transaction occurred as expected. The fair value of the forward is positive £12,500 because the US dollar continued to strengthen against Sterling.

The required entries are as follows.

4 January 20X2

No entries are required because the forward was entered into 'on-market', and therefore had a fair value of zero at inception. Normally, there will be margin to be posted associated with trading on a currency exchange, but this has been ignored for illustration purposes only. There may also be fees if the foreign exchange contract is an over-the-counter (OTC) transaction.

30 June 20X2

		£	£
Dr	Forward	10,000	
Cr	Other comprehensive income		10,000

To recognise the forward contract at fair value, reflecting that the forward contract is fully effective in hedging the forward rate of the forecast transaction.

31 December 20X2

		£	£
Dr	Forward	2,500	
Cr	Other comprehensive income		2,500

To recognise the recognition of the change in fair value of the forward contract. The forward contract remains fully effective in hedging the forward rate of the forecast transaction.

		£	£
Dr	Cash	12,500	
Cr	Forward		12,500

To recognise the cash received in settling the forward contract.

		£	£
Dr	Inventories	112,500	
Cr	Cash		112,500

To recognise the payment of US$180,000 to purchase cocoa translated at the spot rate of $1.6:£1.

		£	£
Dr	Other comprehensive income	12,500	
Cr	Inventory		12,500

To recognise the cumulative effective portion of the hedging instrument included in other comprehensive income that is removed from equity and included as a basis adjustment in the initial carrying amount of the inventory.

The net effect of removing the amount from equity and including it in the carrying amount of the inventory is equivalent to recognising the inventory at the contracted rate inherent in the forward (i.e. US$180,000/US$1.8:£1)

Translation of purchase at spot rate at 31 December 20X2	£112,500
Release from equity at 31 December 20X2	(£12,500)
	£100,000

Note: for the purposes of illustration only, the forward contract has not been discounted.

3.4 Cash flow hedging a forecast sale and subsequent receivable

The following example illustrates the entries for a cash flow hedge of foreign currency risk of a forecast sale and the subsequent receivable using a forward exchange contract.

Example 3.4

Cash flow hedging the foreign currency risk of a forecast sale and the subsequent receivable with a forward exchange contract

On 1 January 20X2, Entity A, a Sterling functional currency entity, has a highly probable forecast sale of US$100,000 in June 20X2. The receivable that is due with respect to the sale will be on 6 months credit terms and when recognised will be measured at amortised cost. Entity A wishes to hedge the forecast sale and the receivable for foreign currency risk. Entity A will designate the forward US$:£ exchange rate, as opposed to the spot exchange rate. Entity A enters into a forward contract to sell US$100,000 and buy £50,481. Because the currency, notional amount and maturity of the forward contract coincide with that of the highly probable forecast sale, Entity A expects the hedge relationship to be highly effective.

Date	Spot rate	interest rates	interest rates	Forward rate	Fair value of forward contract	Fair value movement of forward contract
	US$/£	US$	£	US$/£	£	£
1/1/X2	2.000	4%	5%	1.981	0	0
31/3/X2	1.900	5%	6%	1.887	(2,418)	(2,418)
30/6/X2	1.850	4%	6%	1.832	(3,973)	(1,555)
30/9/X2	1.900	7%	8%	1.896	(2,230)	1,743
31/12/X2	2.100	8%	9%	2.100	2,862	5,092

The exchange of US$ at the spot rate at inception, being US$2.0:£, is equal to £50,000. The difference between this amount and the £50,481 contracted in the forward contract is £481 and represents the forward point differential in functional currency terms. This amount can be converted into a daily interest rate for use in allocating the systematic release of forward points to the periods pre and post the sale. The daily forward point differential is 0.0026%, calculated as (1 + (481/50,000))^1/365.

Period	£-equivalent US$	Forward point differential
		£
1/1/X2	50,000	–
1/1/X2 to 30/6/X2	50,238	238
1/7/X2 to 30/9/X2	50,359	121
1/10/X2 to 31/12/X2	50,481	122

Entity A's documentation of the hedge is as follows.

Risk management objective and nature of risk being hedged	Cash flow hedge of the variability in functional currency equivalent cash flows associated with a forecast sale in 6 months and the cash to be paid on resulting receivable due in 12 months with respect to change in forward rates.
Date of designation	1 January 20X2
Hedging instrument	Forward contract entered into on 1 January 20X2 maturing on 31 December 20X2 to buy £50,481 and sell US$100,000.
Hedged item	Forecast US$100,000 denominated sale in June 20X2 with resulting receivable due December 20X2.

Assessment of hedge effectiveness	The critical terms of the derivative match that of the hedged item (in terms of maturity and notional), accordingly there is an expectation of high effectiveness. The entity will assess counterparty credit risk every period.
Measurement of hedge effectiveness	Hypothetical derivative method. The actual hedging instrument is the same as the hypothetical forward with exactly matching terms and therefore, no ineffectiveness is anticipated.

The following table illustrates the accounting entries for the transaction during its life in Sterling. Dr or (Cr) as indicated.

Date		**Profit or loss**	**Receivable**	**Derivative**	**Cash flow hedge reserve**	**Cash**
31/3/X2	Fair value of forward contract			(2,418)	2,418	
30/6/X2	Fair value of forward contract			(1,555)	1,555	
	Sale	(54,054)	54,054			
	Reclassification – spot	4,054			(4,054)	
	Reclassification – forward points	(238)			238	
30/9/X2	Fair value of forward contract			1,743	(1,743)	
	Translation of receivable	1,422	(1,422)			
	Reclassification – spot	(1,422)			1,422	
	Reclassification – forward points	(121)			121	
31/12/X2	Fair value of forward contract			5,092	(5,092)	
	Translation of receivable	5,013	(5,013)			

Date		Profit or loss	Receivable	Derivative	Cash flow hedge reserve	Cash
	Reclassification – spot	(5,013)			5,013	
	Reclassification – forward points	(122)			122	
	Settle receivable		(47,619)			47,619
	Settle forward contract			(2,862)		2,862
		(50,481)	0	0	0	50,481
	Key	**A**			**B**	**C**

Key

A The amounts in profit or loss can be considered as a sale of £50,238 (being a US$100,000 sale at the spot rate) adjusted for the change in spot rates (£4,054 debit) and the portion of the forward points (£238 credit) since the hedge was entered into and the date of the sale); with the remaining net profit or loss impact being the portion of the forward points from the date of the sale to settlement of the receivable. The translation of the receivable in accordance with IAS 21 is perfectly offset by the reclassification of the spot element on the forward contract.

B Nets to zero reflecting that all amounts in the cash flow hedge reserve in equity have been reclassified to profit or loss to offset the sale and the retranslation of the receivable to spot each period.

C Reflects the £-equivalent cash from the receivable plus the receipt under the forward contract.

Entries in the financial statements for 20X2 are as follows.

1 January 20X2

No entry required because the forward contract has a fair value of nil at inception.

31 March 20X2

		£	£
Dr	Other comprehensive income (cash flow hedge reserve)	2,418	
Cr	Derivative		2,418

To recognise the fair value movements of the forward contract and the effective amount recognised in other comprehensive income (and taken to the cash flow hedge reserve in equity).

30 June 20X2

		£	£
Dr	Other comprehensive income (cash flow hedge reserve)	1,555	
Cr	Derivative		1,555

To recognise the fair value movements of the forward contract and the effective amount recognised in other comprehensive income (and taken to the cash flow hedge reserve in equity).

		£	£
Dr	Receivable	54,054	
Cr	Revenue		54,054

To recognise the sale at the spot rate.

		£	£
Dr	Profit or loss	3,816	
Cr	Other comprehensive income (cash flow hedge reserve)		3,816

To recognise the reclassification from equity (the cash flow hedge reserve) to profit or loss.

30 September 20X2

		£	£
Dr	Derivative	1,743	
Cr	Other comprehensive income (cash flow hedge reserve)		1,743

To recognise the fair value movements of the forward contract and the effective amount recognised in other comprehensive income (and taken to the cash flow hedge reserve in equity).

		£	£
Dr	Profit or loss	1,422	
Cr	Receivable		1,422

To recognise the retranslation of the receivable to spot rates in accordance with IAS 21.

		£	£
Dr	Other comprehensive income (cash flow hedge reserve)	1,543	
Cr	Profit or loss		1,543

To recognise the reclassification from equity (the cash flow hedge reserve) to profit or loss.

		£	£
Dr	Derivative	5,092	
Cr	Other comprehensive income (cash flow hedge reserve)		5,092

To recognise the fair value movements of the forward contract and the effective amount recognised in other comprehensive income (and taken to the cash flow hedge reserve in equity).

		£	£
Dr	Profit or loss	5,013	
Cr	Receivable		5,013

To recognise the retranslation of the receivable to spot rates in accordance with IAS 21.

		£	£
Dr	Other comprehensive income (cash flow hedge reserve)	5,135	
Cr	Profit or loss		5,135

To recognise the reclassification from equity (the cash flow hedge reserve) to profit or loss.

		£	£
Dr	Cash	47,619	
Cr	Receivable		47,619

To recognise the settlement of the receivable with the receipt of US$100,000 at the spot rate.

		£	£
Dr	Cash	2,862	
Cr	Derivative		2,862

To recognise the settlement of the derivative with receipt of £2,862 from the derivative counterparty.

3.5 Cash flow hedging variable rate interest with an interest rate swap

The following three examples illustrate the entries for a cash flow hedge of floating rate debt using an interest rate swap. In the first example (**example 3.5A**) the interest rate swap is 'on-market' (i.e. the interest rate swap has a fair value of nil at the date of designation). In the second and third examples the interest rate swaps are 'off-market' (i.e. the interest rate swaps have a fair value other than nil at the date of designation). In the second example (**example 3.5B**) the interest rate swap is an asset at the date of designation. In the final example (**example 3.5C**) the interest rate swap is a liability at the date of designation.

Example 3.5A

Cash flow hedging the variability in cash flows of issued floating rate debt with an interest rate swap that receives floating and pays fixed

On 1 January 20X0, Entity B issues GBP floating rate debt that matures on 30 June 20X2. The principal amount of the debt is £100 million and interest of 6M LIBOR + 123bps is paid semi-annually in arrears.

Period ended	6M LIBOR at start of period %	Interest accrual in period £ '000s
30/06/X0	5.5	(3,365)
31/12/X0	5.0	(3,115)
30/06/X1	1.6	(1,415)
31/12/X1	0.6	(915)
30/06/X2	0.5	(865)

On 1 January 20X0, Entity B also enters into an interest rate swap that matures on 30 June 20X2. Entity B will receive 6M LIBOR and pay 4.77 per cent (per annum) on £100 million. Interest will be settled net semi-annually in arrears. The fair value of the interest rate swap is nil on 1 January 20X0.

	Fair value gain/(loss) during period	Fair value of swap before cash settlement	Cash settlement	Fair value of swap after cash settlement
Period ended	**£ '000s**	**£ '000s**	**£ '000s**	**£ '000s**
30/06/X0	1,549	1,549	(365)	1,184
31/12/X0	(5,841)	(4,657)	(115)	(4,772)
30/06/X1	(829)	(5,601)	1,585	(4,016)
31/12/X1	(199)	(4,215)	2,085	(2,130)
30/06/X2	(5)	(2,135)	2,135	0

On 1 January 20X0, Entity B designates the interest rate swap in a cash flow hedge of the variability of the interest cash flows of the debt due to changes in the 6M LIBOR rate. In this example the hypothetical derivative (which is derived

from the hedged item) is the same as the interest rate swap. The hedge is 100 per cent effective in each period.

The cumulative amount recognised in the cash flow hedge reserve is the lower of the cumulative fair value gain or loss on the hedging instrument and on the hypothetical derivative. The amount remaining in the cash flow hedge reserve, after reclassification, is the lower of the cumulative clean fair value gain or loss on the hedging instrument and on the hypothetical derivative. The cumulative clean fair value gain or loss on the hypothetical derivative is equal to the clean fair value, because the fair value of the hypothetical derivative at the date of designation is nil.

Period ended	Amount remaining in the cash flow hedge reserve £ '000s	Cumulative amount recognised in the cash flow hedge reserve £ '000s	Cumulative reclassification to offset interest accrual £ '000s	Reclassification in the period to offset interest accrual £ '000s
30/06/X0	1,184	1,549	365	365
31/12/X0	(4,772)	(4,292)	480	115
30/06/X1	(4,016)	(5,121)	(1,105)	(1,585)
31/12/X1	(2,130)	(5,320)	(3,190)	(2,085)
30/06/X2	0	(5,325)	(5,325)	(2,135)

The following table illustrates the accounting entries for the transaction during its life in £'000s. Dr or (Cr) as indicated.

Date		Cash	Derivative	Debt	Equity	Profit or loss
01/01/X0	Issue debt	100,000		(100,000)		
30/06/X0	Accrue interest on debt			(3,365)		3,365
	Change in fair value of derivative		1,549		(1,549)	
	Reclassify amounts from equity				365	(365)
	Settlement of interest on the debt and net settlement of derivative	(3,000)	(365)	3,365		
31/12/X0	Accrue interest on debt			(3,115)		3,115

Date		Cash	Derivative	Debt	Equity	Profit or loss
	Change in fair value of derivative		(5,841)		5,841	
	Reclassify amounts from equity				115	(115)
	Settlement of interest on the debt and net settlement of derivative	(3,000)	(115)	3,115		
30/06/X1	Accrue interest on debt			(1,415)		1,415
	Change in fair value of derivative		(829)		(829)	
	Reclassify amounts from equity				(1,585)	1,585
	Settlement of interest on the debt and net settlement of derivative	(3,000)	1,585	1,415		
31/12/X1	Accrue interest on debt			(915)		915
	Change in fair value of derivative		(199)		199	
	Reclassify amounts from equity				(2,085)	2,085
	Settlement of interest on the debt and net settlement of derivative	(3,000)	2,085	915		
30/06/X2	Accrue interest on debt			(865)		865
	Change in fair value of derivative		(5)		5	
	Reclassify amounts from equity				(2,135)	2,135

Date		Cash	Derivative	Debt	Equity	Profit or loss
	Settlement of interest on the debt and net settlement of derivative	(3,000)	2,135	865		
	Settlement of debt	(100,000)		100,000		
		(15,000)	0	0	0	15,000
	Key				**A**	**B**

A Nets to zero reflecting that all amounts in the cash flow hedge reserve in equity have been reclassified to profit or loss to offset recognise interest at the hedged rate.

B Reflects the total interest expense from the debt and derivative. This amount equals the total interest expense that would have been incurred had the entity issued fixed rate debt paying interest at 6 per cent.

Journal entries in the financial statements are provided below for illustrative purposes.

1 January 20X0

No entry required for derivatives because fair value is nil at inception.

		£ '000s	£ '000s
Dr	Cash	100,000	
Cr	Debt		100,000

To recognise the issue of debt.

30 June 20X0

		£ '000s	£ '000s
Dr	Interest expense	3,365	
Cr	Debt		3,365

To recognise the accrual of interest on the debt.

		£ '000s	£ '000s
Dr	Derivative	1,549	
Cr	Equity (cash flow hedge reserve)		1,549

To recognise the change in fair value of the derivative.

		£ '000s	£ '000s
Dr	Equity (cash flow hedge reserve)	365	
Cr	Interest expense		365

To recognise the reclassification from equity to profit or loss.

		£ '000s	£ '000s
Dr	Debt	3,365	
Cr	Derivative		365
Cr	Cash		3,000

To recognise the settlement of interest on the debt and net settlement of interest on the derivative.

Similar entries would be recorded for the remaining term of the hedge relationship.

Example 3.5B

Cash flow hedging the variability in cash flows of issued floating rate debt with an 'off-market' interest rate swap that receives floating and pays fixed, which is an asset at the date of designation.

Assume the same facts as in **example 3.5A** except that on 1 January 20X0, Entity B enters into an 'off-market' interest rate swap that matures on 30 June 20X2. Entity B will receive 6-month LIBOR and pay 3.77 per cent (per annum) on £100 million. Interest will be settled net semi-annually in arrears. Entity B pays £2,323k to enter into the interest rate swap, because the fixed rate on the swap is below the market rate of 4.77 per cent (per annum). Entity B has paid £2,323k in exchange for reducing each net interest settlement on the swap by £500k.

Settlement date	30/06/X0	31/12/X0	30/06/X1	31/12/X1	30/06/X2	Total
	£ '000s	£ '000s	£ '000s	£ '000s	£ '000s	£ '000s
Reduction in net settlement	500	500	500	500	500	2,500
Fair value on 01/01/X0	487	474	464	454	444	2,323

The fair value of the interest rate swap is £2,323k on 1 January 20X0.

	Fair value gain/(loss) during period	Fair value of swap before cash settlement	Cash settlement	Fair value of swap after cash settlement*
Period ended	£ '000s	£ '000s	£ '000s	£ '000s
30/06/X0	1,597	3,920	(865)	3,055
31/12/X0	(5,737)	(2,682)	(615)	(3,297)
30/06/X1	(809)	(4,106)	1,085	(3,021)
31/12/X1	(195)	(3,216)	1,585	(1,631)
30/06/X2	(4)	(1,635)	1,635	0

* The fair value of the swap after cash settlement is equal to the 'clean' fair value, i.e. the fair value excluding any accrued interest.

On 1 January 20X0, Entity B designates the interest rate swap in a cash flow hedge of the variability of the interest cash flows of the debt due to changes in the 6-month LIBOR rate. The hypothetical derivative (which is derived from the hedged item) in this example is the same as the interest rate swap except for the fixed rate, which is 4.77 per cent (per annum). The fair value of the hypothetical derivative is nil on 1 January 20X0.

	Fair value gain/(loss) during period	**Fair value of swap before cash settlement**	**Cash settlement**	**Fair value of swap after cash settlement****
Period ended	**£ '000s**	**£ '000s**	**£ '000s**	**£ '000s**
30/06/X0	1,549	1,549	(365)	1,184
31/12/X0	(5,841)	(4,657)	(115)	(4,772)
30/06/X1	(829)	(5,601)	1,585	(4,016)
31/12/X1	(199)	(4,215)	2,085	(2,130)
30/06/X2	(5)	(2,135)	2,135	0

** The fair value of the hypothetical derivative after cash settlement is equal to the clean fair value, i.e. the fair value excluding any accrued interest.

The cumulative amount recognised in the cash flow hedge reserve is the lower of the cumulative fair value gain or loss on the hedging instrument and on the hypothetical derivative.

	Cumulative fair value gain/(loss) on hedging instrument	**Cumulative fair value gain/(loss) on hypothetical derivative**	**Cumulative ineffectiveness*****	**Ineffectiveness during the period**
Period ended	**£ '000s**	**£ '000s**	**£ '000s**	**£ '000s**
30/06/X0	1,597	1,549	48	48
31/12/X0	(4,140)	(4,292)	0	(48)
30/06/X1	(4,949)	(5,121)	0	0
31/12/X1	(5,144)	(5,320)	0	0
30/06/X2	(5,148)	(5,325)	0	0

*** If the cumulative dirty fair value gain or loss on the hedging instrument is less than that on the hypothetical derivative (i.e. there is an under hedge), the cumulative ineffectiveness will be nil.

The amount remaining in the cash flow hedge reserve, after reclassification, is the lower of the cumulative clean fair value gain or loss on the hedging instrument and on the hypothetical derivative.

Period ended	Cumulative clean fair value gain/ (loss) on hedging instrument****	Cumulative clean fair value gain/ (loss) on hypothetical derivative*****	Amount remaining in the cash flow hedge reserve	Cumulative amount recognised in the cash flow hedge reserve	Cumulative reclassification to offset interest accrual	Reclassification in the period to offset interest accrual
	£ '000s	£ '000s	£ '000s	£ '000s	£ '000s	£ '000s
30/06/X0	1,219	1,184	1,184	1,549	365	365
31/12/X0	(4,659)	(4,772)	(4,659)	(4,140)	519	154
30/06/X1	(3,919)	(4,016)	(3,919)	(4,949)	(1,030)	(1,549)
31/12/X1	(2,075)	(2,130)	(2,075)	(5,144)	(3,069)	(2,039)
30/06/X2	0	0	0	(5,148)	(5,148)	(2,079)

**** The cumulative clean fair value gain or loss on the hedging instrument is the cumulative change in the clean fair value of the hedging instrument plus the portion of the designation date fair value of the off-market component (i.e. the reduction in net interest settlements) that has been settled or accrued since the inception of the hedge, e.g. [£3,055 – £2,323] + £487 = £1,219 in the first period, [-£3,297 – £2,323] + £487 + £474 = £4,659 in the second and so on.

***** The cumulative clean fair value gain or loss on the hypothetical derivative is equal to the clean fair value because the hypothetical derivative has fair value of nil at the date of designation.

The following table illustrates the accounting entries for the transaction during its life in £'000s. Dr or (Cr) as indicated.

Date		Cash	Derivative	Debt	Equity	Profit or loss
01/01/X0	Issue debt	100,000		(100,000)		
	Enter derivative contract	(2,323)	2,323			
30/06/X0	Accrue interest on debt			(3,365)		3,365
	Change in fair value of derivative		1,597		(1,549)	(48)
	Reclassify amounts from equity				365	(365)
	Settlement of interest on the debt and net settlement of derivative	(2,500)	(865)	3,365		

Date		Cash	Derivative	Debt	Equity	Profit or loss
31/12/X0	Accrue interest on debt			(3,115)		3,115
	Change in fair value of derivative		(5,737)		5,689	48
	Reclassify amounts from equity				154	(154)
	Settlement of interest on the debt and net settlement of derivative	(2,500)	(615)	3,115		
30/06/X1	Accrue interest on debt			(1,415)		1,415
	Change in fair value of derivative		(809)		809	
	Reclassify amounts from equity				(1,549)	1,549
	Settlement of interest on the debt and net settlement of derivative	(2,500)	1,085	1,415		
31/12/X1	Accrue interest on debt			(915)		915
	Change in fair value of derivative		(195)		195	
	Reclassify amounts from equity				(2,039)	2,039
	Settlement of interest on the debt and net settlement of derivative	(2,500)	1,585	915		
30/06/X2	Accrue interest on debt			(865)		865
	Change in fair value of derivative		(4)		4	

Date		Cash	Derivative	Debt	Equity	Profit or loss
	Reclassify amounts from equity				(2,079)	2,079
	Settlement of interest on the debt and net settlement of derivative	(2,500)	1,635	865		
	Settlement of debt	(100,000)		100,000		
		(14,823)	0	0	0	14,823
	Key				**A**	**B**

A Nets to zero reflecting that all amounts in the cash flow hedge reserve in equity have been reclassified to profit or loss to offset the interest accrual.

B Reflects the total interest expense from the debt and derivative. This amount equals the total interest expense that would have been incurred had the entity issued fixed rate debt with a par of £100 million paying interest at 5 per cent, at £97,677 (i.e. at a discount).

Journal entries in the financial statements are provided below for illustrative purposes.

1 January 20X0

		£ '000s	£ '000s
Dr	Derivative	2,323	
Cr	Cash		2,323

To recognise the derivative.

		£ '000s	£ '000s
Dr	Cash	100,000	
Cr	Debt		100,000

To recognise the issue of debt.

30 June 20X0

		£ '000s	£ '000s
Dr	Interest expense	3,365	
Cr	Debt		3,365

To recognise the accrual of interest on the debt.

		£ '000s	£ '000s
Dr	Derivative	1,597	
Cr	Equity (cash flow hedge reserve)		1,549
Cr	Interest expense		48

To recognise the change in fair value of the derivative.

		£ '000s	£ '000s
Dr	Equity (cash flow hedge reserve)	365	
Cr	Interest expense		365

To recognise the reclassification from equity to profit or loss.

		£ '000s	£ '000s
Dr	Debt	3,365	
Cr	Derivative		865
Cr	Cash		2,500

To recognise the settlement of interest on the debt and net settlement of interest on the derivative.

Similar entries would be recorded for the remaining term of the hedge relationship.

Example 3.5C

Cash flow hedging the variability in cash flows of issued floating rate debt with an 'off-market' interest rate swap that receives floating and pays fixed, which is a liability at the date of designation.

Assume the same facts as in **example 3.5A** except that on 1 January 20X0, Entity B enters into an 'off-market' interest rate swap that matures on 30 June 20X2. Entity B will receive 6-month LIBOR and pay 5.77 per cent (per annum) on £100 million. Interest will be settled net semi-annually in arrears. Entity B receives £2,323k to enter into the interest rate swap, because the fixed rate on the swap is above the market rate of 4.77 per cent (per annum). Entity B has received £2,323k in exchange for increasing each net interest settlement on the swap by £500k.

	30/06/X0	**31/12/X0**	**30/06/X1**	**31/12/X1**	**30/06/X2**	**Total**
Settlement date	**£ '000s**	**£ '000s**	**£ '000s**	**£ '000s**	**£ '000s**	**£ '000s**
Reduction in net settlement	(500)	(500)	(500)	(500)	(500)	(2,500)
Fair value on 01/01/X0	(487)	(474)	(464)	(454)	(444)	(2,323)

The fair value of the interest rate swap is £(2,323)k on 1 January 20X0.

Period ended	Fair value gain/(loss) during period £ '000s	Fair value of swap before cash settlement £ '000s	Cash settlement £ '000s	Fair value of swap after cash settlement* £ '000s
30/06/X0	1,501	(822)	135	(687)
31/12/X0	(5,945)	(6,632)	385	(6,247)
30/06/X1	(848)	(7,095)	2,085	(5,010)
31/12/X1	(203)	(5,213)	2,585	(2,628)
30/06/X2	(7)	(2,635)	2,635	0

* The fair value of the swap after cash settlement is equal to the clean fair value, i.e. the fair value excluding any accrued interest.

On 1 January 20X0, Entity B designates the interest rate swap in a cash flow hedge of the variability of the interest cash flows of the debt due to changes in the 6-month LIBOR rate.

The hypothetical derivative (which is derived from the hedged item) in this example is the same as the interest rate swap except for the fixed rate, which is 4.77 per cent (per annum) The fair value of the hypothetical derivative is nil on 1 January 20X0.

Period ended	Fair value gain/(loss) during period £ '000s	Fair value of swap before cash settlement £ '000s	Cash settlement £ '000s	Fair value of swap after cash settlement** £ '000s
30/06/X0	1,549	1,549	(365)	1,184
31/12/X0	(5,841)	(4,657)	(115)	(4,772)
30/06/X1	(829)	(5,601)	1,585	(4,016)
31/12/X1	(199)	(4,215)	2,085	(2,130)
30/06/X2	(5)	(2,135)	2,135	0

** The fair value of the hypothetical derivative after cash settlement is equal to the clean fair value, i.e. the fair value excluding any accrued interest.

The cumulative amount recognised in the cash flow hedge reserve is the lower of the cumulative fair value gain or loss on the hedging instrument and on the hypothetical derivative.

Period ended	Cumulative fair value gain/(loss) on hedging instrument	Cumulative fair value gain/(loss) on hypothetical derivative	Cumulative ineffectiveness***	Ineffectiveness during the period
	£ '000s	£ '000s	£ '000s	£ '000s
30/06/X0	1,501	1,549	0	0
31/12/X0	(4,444)	(4,292)	(152)	(152)
30/06/X1	(5,292)	(5,121)	(171)	(19)
31/12/X1	(5,495)	(5,320)	(175)	(4)
30/06/X2	(5,502)	(5,325)	(177)	(2)

*** If the cumulative dirty fair value gain or loss on the hedging instrument is less than that on the hypothetical derivative (i.e. there is an under hedge), the cumulative ineffectiveness will be nil.

The amount remaining in the cash flow hedge reserve, after reclassification, is the lower of the cumulative clean fair value gain or loss on the hedging instrument and on the hypothetical derivative.

Period ended	Cumulative clean fair value gain/ (loss) on hedging instrument****	Cumulative clean fair value gain/ (loss) on hypothetical derivative*****	Amount remaining in the cash flow hedge reserve	Cumulative amount recognised in the cash flow hedge reserve	Cumulative reclas-sification to offset interest accrual	Reclassi-fication in the period to offset interest accrual
	£ '000s	£ '000s	£ '000s	£ '000s	£ '000s	£ '000s
30/06/X0	1,149	1,184	1,149	1,501	352	352
31/12/X0	(4,885)	(4,772)	(4,772)	(4,292)	480	128
30/06/X1	(4,112)	(4,016)	(4,016)	(5,121)	(1,105)	(1,585)
31/12/X1	(2,184)	(2,130)	(2,130)	(5,320)	(3,190)	(2,085)
30/06/X2	0	0	0	(5,325)	(5,325)	(2,135)

**** The cumulative clean fair value gain or loss on the hedging instrument is the cumulative change in the clean fair value of the hedging instrument plus the portion of the designation date fair value of the off-market component (i.e. the reduction in net interest settlements) that has been settled or accrued since the inception of the hedge, e.g. [£(687) – £(2,323)] + £(487) = £1,149 in the first period, [£(6,247) -£(2,323)] + £(487) + £(474) = £(4,885) in the second and so on.

***** The cumulative clean fair value gain or loss on the hypothetical derivative is equal to the clean fair value because the hypothetical derivative has fair value of nil at the date of designation.

The following table illustrates the accounting entries for the transaction during its life in £'000s. Dr or (Cr) as indicated.

Date		**Cash**	**Derivative**	**Debt**	**Equity**	**Profit or loss**
01/01/X0	Issue debt	100,000		(100,000)		
	Enter derivative contract	2,323	(2,323)			
30/06/X0	Accrue interest on debt			(3,365)		3,365
	Change in fair value of derivative		1,501		(1,501)	
	Reclassify amounts from equity				352	(352)
	Settlement of interest on the debt and net settlement of derivative	(3,500)	135	3,365		
31/12/X0	Accrue interest on debt			(3,115)		3,115
	Change in fair value of derivative		(5,945)		5,793	152
	Reclassify amounts from equity				128	(128)
	Settlement of interest on the debt and net settlement of derivative	(3,500)	385	3,115		
30/06/X1	Accrue interest on debt			(1,415)		1,415
	Change in fair value of derivative		(848)		829	19
	Reclassify amounts from equity				(1,585)	1,585
	Settlement of interest on the debt and net settlement of derivative	(3,500)	2,085	1,415		

31/12/X1	Accrue interest on debt			(915)		915
	Change in fair value of derivative		(203)		199	4
	Reclassify amounts from equity				(2,085)	2,085
	Settlement of interest on the debt and net settlement of derivative	(3,500)	2,585	915		
30/06/X2	Accrue interest on debt			(865)		865
	Change in fair value of derivative		(7)		5	2
	Reclassify amounts from equity				(2,135)	2,135
	Settlement of interest on the debt and net settlement of derivative	(3,500)	2,635	865		
	Settlement of debt	(100,000)		100,000		
		(15,177)	0	0	0	15,777
	Key				**A**	**B**

A Nets to zero reflecting that all amounts in the cash flow hedge reserve in equity have been reclassified to profit or loss to offset the interest accrual.

B Reflects the total interest expense from the debt and derivative. This amount equals the total interest expense that would have been incurred had the entity issued fixed rate debt with a par of £100 million paying interest at 7 per cent, at £102,323 (i.e. at a premium).

Journal entries in the financial statements are provided below for illustrative purposes.

1 January 20X0

		£ '000s	£ '000s
Dr	Cash	2,323	
Cr	Derivative		2,323

To recognise the derivative.

		£ '000s	£ '000s
Dr	Cash	100,000	
Cr	Debt		100,000

To recognise the issue of debt.

30 June 20X0

		£ '000s	£ '000s
Dr	Interest expense	3,365	
Cr	Debt		3,365

To recognise the accrual of interest on the debt.

		£ '000s	£ '000s
Dr	Derivative	1,501	
Cr	Equity (cash flow hedge reserve)		1,501

To recognise the change in fair value of the derivative.

		£ '000s	£ '000s
Dr	Equity (cash flow hedge reserve)	352	
Cr	Interest expense		352

To recognise the reclassification from equity to profit or loss.

		£ '000s	£ '000s
Dr	Debt	3,365	
Cr	Derivative		135
Cr	Cash		3,500

To recognise the settlement of interest on the debt and net settlement of interest on the derivative.

Similar entries would be recorded for the remaining term of the hedge relationship.

3.6 Cash flow hedging variable rate debt with a purchased interest rate cap

The following example illustrates the entries for a cash flow hedge of interest rate risk of variable rate debt using a purchased interest rate cap.

Example 3.6

Hedging variable rate debt with a purchased interest rate cap (1)

On 1 January 20X0, Entity X issued a 5-year CU100 million variable rate bond. The bond pays interest based on Sterling LIBOR plus a spread of 200 basis points on an annual basis, reset in arrears on 31 December. Entity X wants to hedge against increases in interest rates by capping the maximum interest rate at 9 per cent (CU LIBOR of 7.00 per cent + 2.00 per cent spread). Entity X purchased an interest rate cap that is indexed to CU LIBOR with a CU100 million notional amount. The interest rate cap has no intrinsic value at inception. The counterparty to the cap pays Entity X the difference between 7 per cent and CU LIBOR if CU LIBOR rises above 7 per cent. The interest rate cap (intrinsic value only) is designated as a cash flow hedge of the variable rate debt. The terms of the cap are as follows.

Notional amount	**CU100 million**
Trade date	01/01/X0
Start date	01/01/X0
Expiration date	31/12/X4
Strike price	7.00 per cent
Index	12 month CU LIBOR, set in arrears
Premium	CU1.44 million
Caplet expirations	31 December 20X0, 20X1, 20X2, 20X3 and 20X4

The payments on each caplet are made at expiration. For example, the caplet that expires on 31 December 20X0 will be paid, if applicable, on that date. The fair value of the cap throughout the term of the cap is summarised below.

Date	**CU LIBOR**	**Cap rate**	**Fair value of cap**	**Intrinsic value of cap**[(1)]	**Time value of cap**	**Cap cash receipts**
			CU	**CU**	**CU**	**CU**
31 December 20X0	5.00	7.00	1,000,000	–	1,000,000	–
31 December 20X1	5.50	7.00	850,000	–	850,000	–
31 December 20X2	7.50	7.00	1,500,000	895,000	605,000	500,000
31 December 20X3	8.00	7.00	1,000,000	600,000	400,000	1,000,000
31 December 20X4	7.00	7.00	–	–	–	–

(1) Intrinsic fair value is computed on a discounted basis.

The following entries are required.

1 January 20X0

		CU	CU
Dr	Cash	100,000,000	
Cr	Financial liability – debt		100,000,000

To recognise the issuance of debt.

		CU	CU
Dr	Financial asset – option	1,440,000	
Cr	Cash		1,440,000

To recognise the purchase of the interest rate cap.

31 December 20X0

		CU	CU
Dr	Interest expense	7,000,000	
Cr	Cash		7,000,000

To recognise the recognition of the interest expense (CU LIBOR at reset plus 200 basis points (5.00 per cent + 2.00 per cent)) on the CU100 million principal amount.

		CU	CU
Dr	Derivative loss	440,000	
Cr	Financial asset – option		440,000

To recognise the cap option asset at fair value with changes in time value recognised in profit or loss (there was no intrinsic value to record).

31 December 20X1

		CU	CU
Dr	Interest expense	7,500,000	
Cr	Cash		7,500,000

To recognise the interest expense (CU LIBOR at reset plus 200 basis points (5.50 per cent + 2.00 per cent)) on the CU100 million principal amount.

		CU	CU
Dr	Derivative loss	150,000	
Cr	Financial asset – option		150,000

To recognise the cap option asset at fair value with changes in time value recognised in profit or loss (there was no intrinsic value to record).

31 December 20X2

		CU	CU
Dr	Interest expense	9,500,000	
Cr	Cash		9,500,000

To recognise the interest expense (CU LIBOR at reset plus 200 basis points (7.50 per cent + 2.00 per cent)) on the CU100 million principal amount.

		CU	CU
Dr	Cash	500,000	
Dr	Financial asset – option	650,000	
Dr	Derivative loss	245,000	
Cr	Other comprehensive income		1,395,000

To recognise the cash receipt and the cap option asset at fair value with changes in time value recognised in profit or loss and changes in intrinsic value recognised in other comprehensive income.

		CU	CU
Dr	Other comprehensive income	500,000	
Cr	Interest expense		500,000

To recognise the reclassification of amounts in equity to profit or loss. The reclassification of amounts from equity ((7.50 per cent CU LIBOR – 7.00 per cent cap rate) × CU100 million) results in an interest expense of 9.00 per cent.

31 December 20X3

		CU	CU
Dr	Interest expense	10,000,000	
Cr	Cash		10,000,000

To recognise the interest expense (CU LIBOR at reset plus 200 basis points (8.00 per cent + 2.00 per cent)) on the CU100 million principal amount.

		CU	CU
Dr	Cash	1,000,000	
Cr	Financial asset – option		500,000
Dr	Derivative loss	205,000	
Cr	Other comprehensive income		705,000

To recognise the cash receipt and the cap option asset at fair value with changes in time value recognised in profit or loss and changes in intrinsic value recognised in other comprehensive income.

		CU	CU
Dr	Other comprehensive income	1,000,000	
Cr	Interest expense		1,000,000

To recognise the reclassification of amounts in equity to profit or loss. The reclassification of amounts from equity ((8.00 per cent CU LIBOR – 7.00 per cent cap rate) × CU100 million) results in an interest expense of 9.00 per cent.

31 December 20X4

		CU	CU
Dr	Interest expense	9,000,000	
Cr	Cash		9,000,000

To recognise the interest expense (CU LIBOR at reset plus 200 basis points (7.00 per cent + 2.00 per cent)) on the CU100 million principal amount.

		CU	CU
Dr	Derivative loss	400,000	
Cr	Financial asset – option		1,000,000
Dr	Other comprehensive income	600,000	

To recognise the cap option asset at fair value with changes in time value recognised in profit or loss and changes in intrinsic value recognised in other comprehensive income.

3.7 Cash flow hedging foreign currency risk of floating rate debt

The following example illustrates the entries for a cash flow hedge of foreign currency risk on variable rate debt using a cross-currency interest rate swap.

Example 3.7

Cash flow hedging the foreign currency risk of issued floating rate foreign currency debt with a cross-currency swap that receives floating foreign currency and pays floating functional currency

On 1 January 20X2, Entity A, a Sterling functional currency entity, issues a US$ LIBOR +100 basis points (bp) floating rate debt instrument denominated in US dollars with a principal amount of US$100,000, that will mature on 31 December 20X6 at par. At 1 January 20X2, the spot rate on the US$/£ is 1.75/1 so the principal of US$100,000 is equivalent to £57,143. On 1 January 20X2, Entity A also enters into a cross-currency swap ('CCS') to exchange interest payments and principal at redemption on the same terms as the above debt and designates the CCS as a hedge of the variability of the Sterling functional currency equivalent cash flows on the debt. The terms are such that on each interest payment date (assume interest is paid annually on 31 December each year for both the debt and the cross-currency swap), Entity A will receive US$ LIBOR + 100 bp on a notional of US$100,000 and pay Sterling LIBOR + 106 bp based on a notional of £57,143. Because the currency, notional, coupons and interest payment dates match on both the CCS and the debt, Entity A expects the hedge relationship to be highly effective.

Date	Spot rate US$/£	Carrying amount of US$ debt in £ after interest settlements	Cross-currency swap fair value £ after interest settlements	Net cash settlement on the swap translated at spot rate £ (£ LIBOR + 106 bp) – (US $ LIBOR + 100 bp)	Net interest payment on the swap translated at average rate £ (£ LIBOR + 106 bp) – (US $ LIBOR + 100 bp)
1/1/X2	1.75	57,143	0	0	0
31/12/X2	1.7	58,824	1,743	1,225	1,259
31/12/X3	1.6	62,500	5,520	1,389	1,476
31/12/X4	1.5	66,667	9,670	1,870	1,952
31/12/X5	1.8	55,556	(1,624)	1,282	1,042
31/12/X6	1.7	58,824	1,681	1,228	1,321

Entity A's documentation of the hedge is as follows.

Risk management objective and nature of risk being hedged	Cash flow hedge of the variability in functional currency equivalent interest and principal cash flows associated with the foreign currency debt due to changes in forward rates.
Date of designation	1 January 20X2
Hedging instrument	Cross-currency swap to exchange US$100,000 for £57,143 at maturity and receive US$ LIBOR + 100bp, pay £ LIBOR + 106bp interest annually over the term of the instrument.
Hedged item	The cross-currency swap is designated as a hedge of the variability in functional currency equivalent interest and principal cash flows associated with the foreign currency debt due to changes in forward rates.

Assessment of hedge effectiveness	The critical terms of the derivative match (exchange of principal at maturity and annual interest payment), accordingly there is an expectation of high effectiveness. The entity will assess counterparty credit risk and probability of cash flows under the swap occurring every period.
Measurement of hedge effectiveness	Hypothetical derivative method. The actual hedging instrument is the same as the hypothetical cross-currency swap with exactly matching terms and therefore, no ineffectiveness is anticipated.

The following table illustrates the accounting entries for the transaction during its life in Sterling. Dr or (Cr) as indicated.

Date		**Cash**	**CCS**	**Debt**	**Cash flow hedge reserve**	**Interest expense**	**Translation loss (gain)**
1/1/X2	Issue debt	57,143		(57,143)			
31/12/X2	Fair value of CCS (before interest settlements)		518		(518)		
	Net settlement of CCS (at spot rate)	(1,225)	1,225				
	Accrue interest on debt (at average rate)			(2,319)		2,319	
	Retranslate debt to spot			(1,715)			1,715
	Reclassify amounts from cash flow hedge reserve				456	1,259	(1,715)
	Settle interest on the debt (at spot rate)	(2,353)		2,353			
31/12/X3	Fair value of CCS (before interest settlements)		2,388		(2,388)		

Date		Cash	CCS	Debt	Cash flow hedge reserve	Interest expense	Translation loss (gain)
	Net settlement of CCS (at spot rate)	(1,389)	1,389				
	Accrue interest on debt (at average rate)			(2,788)		2,788	
	Retranslate debt to spot			(3,763)			3,763
	Reclassify amounts from cash flow hedge reserve				2,287	1,476	(3,763)
	Settle interest on the debt (at spot rate)	(2,875)		2,875			
31/12/X4	Fair value of CCS (before interest settlements)		2,280		(2,280)		
	Net settlement of CCS (at spot rate)	(1,870)	1,870				
	Accrue interest on debt (at average rate)			(2,469)		2,469	
	Retranslate debt to spot			(4,249)			4,249
	Reclassify amounts				2,297	1,952	(4,249)
	Settle interest on the debt (at spot rate)	(2,551)		2,551			
31/12/X5	Fair value of CCS (before interest settlements)		(12,576)		12,576		
	Net settlement of CCS (at spot rate)	(1,282)	1,282				

Date		Cash	CCS	Debt	Cash flow hedge reserve	Interest expense	Translation loss (gain)
	Accrue interest on debt (at average rate)			(2,879)		2,879	
	Retranslate debt to spot			11,351			(11,351)
	Reclassify amounts from cash flow hedge reserve				(12,393)	1,042	11,351
	Settle interest on the debt (at spot rate)	(2,639)		2,639			
31/12/X6	Fair value of CCS (before interest settlements)		2,077		(2,077)		
	Net settlement of CCS (at spot rate)	(1,228)	1,228				
	Accrue interest on debt (at average rate)			(3,171)		3,171	
	Retranslate debt to spot			(3,361)			3,361
	Reclassify amounts from cash flow hedge reserve				2,040	1,321	(3,361)
	Settlement of swap	1,681	(1,681)				
	Settlement of debt	(62,088)		62,088			
		(20,676)	0	0	0	20,676	0
	Key				**A**	**B**	

Key

A Nets to zero reflecting that all amounts in the cash flow hedge reserve in equity have been reclassified to profit or loss to offset retranslation of the debt to spot each period and the recognition of interest.

B Reflects the total interest expense from US$ Debt and CCS. This amount equals the total interest expense that would have been incurred had Entity A actually issued £ debt at inception (£57,143 x (LIBOR + 106bp)) x 5 years = £20,676.

Entries in the consolidated financial statements for 20X2 for illustrative purposes

1 January 20X2

No entry required for CCS because fair value is nil at inception.

		£	£
Dr	Cash	57,143	
Cr	Debt		57,143

To recognise the issue of US$ LIBOR + 100bp debt in £ (retranslated at spot).

31 December 20X2

		£	£
Dr	CCS asset	518	
Cr	Other comprehensive income (cash flow hedging reserve)		518

To recognise the fair value movement in CCS before interest settlement, in other comprehensive income (because 100 per cent effective).

		£	£
Dr	CCS asset	1,225	
Cr	Cash		1,225

To recognise the net settlement of interest on CCS (£ LIBOR + 106bp – US$ LIBOR + 100bp converted at spot rate).

		£	£
Dr	Interest expense	2,319	
Cr	Debt		2,319

To recognise the accrual of interest on US$ debt converted at average rates.

		£	£
Dr	Retranslation loss (profit or loss)	1,715	
Cr	Debt		1,715

To recognise the loss on retranslation of the US$ debt at year end spot rates.

		£	£
Dr	Other comprehensive income (cash flow hedging reserve)	456	
Dr	Interest expense (profit or loss)	1,259	
Cr	Retranslation gain (profit or loss)		1,715

To recognise the reclassification of the effective portion of CCS from equity to profit or loss.

		£	£
Dr	Debt	2,353	
Cr	Cash		2,353

To recognise the payment of interest on US$ debt converted at the spot rate.

Similar entries would be recorded for the remaining term of the hedging relationship (20X3 - 20X6). Interest expense totalling £20,676 is recognised over the term of the hedging instrument and net profit or loss impact is as if Entity A had issued Sterling LIBOR + 106bp debt at inception. The CCS is fair valued at the end of each reporting period (after interest payments have been made because all interest payments are deemed to have taken place on last day of year which is also the reset date for the swap) with amounts recognised in other comprehensive income (and taken to the cash flow hedge reserve in equity). The amount of the CCS is reclassified from equity to profit or loss at the end of each reporting period to offset the amount recognised for retranslation of the US$ debt to Sterling spot rates and finally to offset the translation loss on repayment of principal at maturity of the debt.

3.8 Cash flow hedging foreign currency risk of fixed rate debt

The following example illustrates the entries for a cash flow hedge of foreign currency risk on fixed rate debt using a cross-currency interest rate swap.

Example 3.8

Cash flow hedging the foreign currency risk of issued fixed rate debt with a cross-currency swap that receives fixed foreign currency and pays fixed functional currency

On 1 January 20X2, Entity A, a Sterling functional currency entity, issues a 4 per cent annual fixed coupon debt instrument denominated in US dollars (US$) with a notional amount of US$100,000, that will mature on 31 December 20X6 at par, and therefore the effective interest rate is 4 per cent. At 1 January 20X2, the spot rate on the US$ / £ is 1.75/1 so the notional of US$100,000 is equivalent to £57,143. On 1 January 20X2, Entity A also enters into a cross-currency swap ('CCS') to exchange interest payments and principal at redemption on the same terms as the above debt and designates the CCS as a cash flow hedge of the variability of the Sterling functional currency equivalent cash flows on the debt. The terms are such that on each interest payment date (assume interest is paid annually on 31 December each year for both the debt and the cross-currency swap), Entity A will receive 4 per cent on a notional of US$100,000 and pay 6 per cent based on a notional of £57,143. Because the currency, notional, coupons and interest payment dates match on both the cross-currency swap and the debt, Entity A expects that the hedge relationship will be highly effective.

Date	Spot rate US$/£	Carrying amount of US$ debt in £ after interest settlements	Cross-currency swap fair value £ after interest settlements	Net cash settlement on the swap translated at spot rate £ (£ 6% – US$ 4%)	Net interest on the swap translated at average rate £ (£ 6% – US$ 4%)
1/1/X2	1.75	57,143	0	0	0
31/12/X2	1.7	58,824	2,560	1,076	1,110
31/12/X3	1.6	62,500	7,723	928	1,004
31/12/X4	1.5	66,667	9,513	762	848
31/12/X5	1.8	55,556	(1,452)	1,207	1,004
31/12/X6	1.7	58,824	1,681	1,076	1,143

Entity A's documentation of the hedge is as follows.

Risk management objective and nature of risk being hedged	Cash flow hedge of the variability in functional currency equivalent cash flows associated with the foreign currency debt due to changes in forward rates.
Date of designation	1 January 20X2
Hedging instrument	Cross-currency swap to receive US$ 4 per cent, pay £6 per cent interest annually based on notional of US$100,000 over the term of the instrument and exchange US$100,000 for £57,143 at maturity.
Hedged item	Changes in the £ functional currency equivalent cash flows relating to the changes in foreign currency forward rates related to the debt and to the annual interest payments.

Assessment of hedge effectiveness	The critical terms of the derivative match (exchange of principal at maturity and annual interest payments), accordingly there is an expectation of high effectiveness. The entity will assess counterparty credit risk and probability of cash flows under the swap occurring every period.
Measurement of hedge effectiveness	Hypothetical derivative method. The actual hedging instrument is the same as a hypothetical cross-currency swap with exactly matching terms and therefore, no ineffectiveness is anticipated.

The following table illustrates the accounting entries for the transaction during its life in Sterling. Dr or (Cr) as indicated.

Date		Cash	CCS statement of financial position	Debt	Cash flow hedge reserve	Interest expense	Translation loss (gain)
1/1/X2	Issue debt	57,143		(57,143)			
31/12/X2	Fair value of CCS (before interest settlements)		1,484		(1,484)		
	Net settlement of CCS (at spot rate)	(1,076)	1,076				
	Accrue interest on debt (at average rate)			(2,319)		2,319	
	Retranslate debt to spot			(1,715)			1,715
	Reclassify amounts from cash flow hedge reserve				605	1,110	(1,715)
	Settle interest on the debt (at spot rate)	(2,353)		2,353			
31/12/X3	Fair value of CCS (before interest settlements)		4,235		(4,235)		
	Net settlement of CCS (at spot rate)	(928)	928				
	Accrue interest on debt (at average rate)			(2,424)		2,424	

Date		Cash	CCS statement of financial position	Debt	Cash flow hedge reserve	Interest expense	Translation loss (gain)
	Retranslate debt to spot			(3,752)			3,752
	Reclassify amounts from cash flow hedge reserve				2,748	1,004	(3,752)
	Settle interest on the debt (at spot rate)	(2,500)		2,500			
31/12/X4	Fair value of CCS (before interest settlements)		1,028		(1,028)		
	Net settlement of CCS (at spot rate)	(762)	762				
	Accrue interest on debt (at average rate)			(2,581)		2,581	
	Retranslate debt to spot			(4,253)			4,253
	Reclassify amounts from cash flow hedge reserve				3,405	848	(4,253)
	Settle interest on the debt (at spot rate)	(2,666)		2,666			
31/12/X5	Fair value of CCS (before interest settlements)		(12,172)		12,172		
	Net settlement of CCS (at spot rate)	(1,207)	1,207				
	Accrue interest on debt (at average rate)			(2,424)		2,424	
	Retranslate debt to spot			11,314			(11,314)
	Reclassify amounts from cash flow hedge reserve				(12,318)	1,004	11,314
	Settle interest on the debt (at spot rate)	(2,222)		2,222			
31/12/X6	Fair value of CCS (before interest settlements)		2,057		(2,057)		

Date		Cash	CCS statement of financial position	Debt	Cash flow hedge reserve	Interest expense	Translation loss (gain)
	Net settlement of CCS (at spot rate)	(1,076)	1,076				
	Accrue interest on debt (at average rate)			(2,286)		2,286	
	Retranslate debt to spot			(3,335)			3,335
	Reclassify amounts from cash flow hedge reserve				2,192	1,143	(3,335)
	Settlement of swap	1,681	(1,681)				
	Settlement of debt	(61,177)		61,177			
		(17,143)	0	0	0	17,143	0
	Key				**A**	**B**	

Key

A Nets to zero reflecting that all amounts in cash flow hedge reserve in equity have been reclassified to profit or loss.

B Reflects the total interest expense from US$ debt and CCS. Equals the total interest expense that would have been incurred had Entity A actually issued £ debt at inception (£57,143*6%) * 5 years = £17,143.

Entries in the consolidated financial statements for 20X2 for illustrative purposes

1 January 20X2

No entry required for CCS because fair value is nil at inception.

		£	£
Dr	Cash	57,143	
Cr	Debt		57,143

To recognise the issue of 4 per cent US$ debt in £ (retranslated at spot).

31 December 20X2

		£	£
Dr	CCS asset	1,484	
Cr	Other comprehensive income (cash flow hedging reserve)		1,484

To recognise the fair value movement in CCS before interest settlement, in other comprehensive income (because 100 per cent effective).

		£	£
Dr	CCS asset	1,076	
Cr	Cash		1,076

To recognise the net settlement of interest on CCS (£ 6% – US$ 4% converted at spot rate).

		£	£
Dr	Interest expense	2,319	
Cr	Debt		2,319

To recognise the accrual of interest on US$ debt converted at average rates.

		£	£
Dr	Retranslation loss (profit or loss)	1,715	
Cr	Debt		1,715

To recognise the loss on retranslation of the US$ debt at year end spot rates.

		£	£
Dr	Other comprehensive income (cash flow hedging reserve)	605	
Dr	Interest expense (profit or loss)	1,110	
Cr	Retranslation gain (profit or loss)		1,715

To recognise the reclassification of the effective portion of CCS from equity to profit or loss.

		£	£
Dr	Debt	2,353	
Cr	Cash		2,353

To recognise the payment of interest on US$ debt converted at the spot rate.

Similar entries would be recorded for the remaining term of the hedging relationship (20X3 - 20X6).

Interest expense totalling £17,143 is recognised over the term of the hedging instrument which is equivalent to Entity A having issued Sterling 6 per cent debt at inception.

3.9 Cash flow hedging foreign currency risk of zero coupon debt

The following example illustrates the entries for a cash flow hedge of foreign currency risk of zero coupon debt using a forward exchange contract.

Example 3.9

Cash flow hedging the foreign currency risk of zero coupon debt with a forward exchange contract

On 1 January 20X2, Entity A, a Sterling functional currency entity, issues 5-year US$ denominated zero coupon debt with a notional amount of US$1,812,052 for US$1,419,791. The interest rate implicit in the debt is 5 per cent. The zero coupon debt will mature on 31 December 20X6. On the same date Entity A entered into a forward contract to buy US$1,812,052 for £1,000,000 at the forward rate of US$1.812:£ at 31 December 20X6. The £ interest rate implicit in the forward contract is 6 per cent. The carrying amount of the zero coupon debt at initial recognition in Entity A's functional currency, is £747,258 because spot rates at the date of issue are US$1.90:£.

The entity designates the forward exchange contract as a hedge of the variability of the £ functional currency equivalent cash flows on the zero coupon debt. Because the currency, notional amount and maturity of the forward contract match that of the zero coupon debt, Entity A expects the hedge relationship to be highly effective.

Date	Spot rate US$/£	Forward rate US$/£	US$ amortised cost (effective interest rate of 5%)	Synthetic £ zero coupon debt (effective interest rate of 6%)	Fair value of forward contract £
1/1/X2	1.900	1.812	1,419,791	747,258	0
31/12/X2	1.800	1.733	1,490,780	792,094	36,117
31/12/X3	1.900	1.847	1,565,319	839,619	(15,767)
31/12/X4	1.900	1.900	1,643,585	889,996	(41,196)
31/12/X5	1.900	1.900	1,725,764	943,396	(43,668)
31/12/X6	1.900	1.900	1,812,052	1,000,000	(46,288)

The change in forward rates over the period reflects a combination of factors:

(i) the pull of spot rates to forward rates over the period ending 31/12/X6; and

(ii) an increase in US$ interest rates from 31/12/X4 to 31/12/X6 from 5% to 6%.

Forward rates and spot rates coincide from 20X4 because there is no interest rate differential between US$ and £ because both are 6 per cent.

Entity A's documentation of the hedge is as follows.

Risk management objective and nature of risk being hedged	Cash flow hedge of the variability in functional currency equivalent cash flows associated with the foreign currency zero coupon debt due to changes in US$:£ forward rates.
Date of designation	1 January 20X2
Hedging instrument	Forward contract entered into on 1 January 20X2 maturing on 31 December 20X6 to buy US$1,812,052 and sell £1,000,000.
Hedged item	Zero coupon debt issued on 1 January 20X2 maturing on 31 December 20X6 with a notional amount of US$1,812,052 and issued for proceeds of US$1,419,791.
Assessment of hedge effectiveness	The critical terms of the derivative match those of the hedged item (in terms of currency, maturity and notional), accordingly there is an expectation of high effectiveness. The entity will assess counterparty credit risk every period.
Measurement of hedge effectiveness	Hypothetical derivative method. The actual hedging instrument is the same as the hypothetical forward with exactly matching terms and therefore, no ineffectiveness is anticipated.

The following table illustrates the accounting entries for the transaction during its life in Sterling. Dr or (Cr) as indicated.

Date		Cash	Forward	Debt	Cash flow hedge reserve	Interest expense	Foreign currency loss (gain)
1/1X2	Issue zero coupon debt	747,258		(747,258)			
31/12/X2	Accrue interest on debt			(39,439)		39,439	
	Revalue debt to spot			(41,514)			41,514
	Fair value forward contract		36,117			5,397	(41,514)
31/12/X3	Accrue interest on debt			(39,231)		39,231	

Date		Cash	Forward	Debt	Cash flow hedge reserve	Interest expense	Foreign currency loss (gain)
	Revalue debt to spot			43,590			(43,590)
	Fair value of forward contract		(51,885)			8,295	43,590
31/12/X4	Accrue interest on debt			(41,193)		41,193	
	Fair value of forward contract		(25,428)		16,245	9,183	
31/12/X5	Accrue interest on debt			(43,252)		43,252	
	Fair value of forward contract		(2,472)		(7,676)	10,148	
31/12/X6	Accrue interest on debt			(45,415)		45,415	
	Fair value of forward contract		(2,620)		(8,569)	11,189	
	Settlement of forward	(46,288)	46,288				
	Settlement of debt	(953,712)		953,712			
		(252,742)	0	0	0	252,742	0
	Key				**A**	**B**	

Key

A Nets to zero reflecting that all amounts in the cash flow hedge reserve in equity have been reclassified to profit or loss to offset retranslation of the debt to spot each period and the recognition of total interest in £ at the £ rate implicit in the forward contract of 6 per cent.

B Reflects the total interest expense from the US$ denominated zero coupon debt and the foreign currency forward contract. This is equal to a rate of 6 per cent as applied to the £747,258 (the £ equivalent of the proceeds at the spot rate when the zero coupon debt was issued). The interest amounts comprise two elements:

(i) the underlying 5 per cent interest on the US$ zero coupon debt retranslated into the functional currency; and

(ii) the systematic reclassification of the fair value movements of the forward contract from equity to profit or loss so as to increase the effective interest rate to 6 per cent.

Entries in the financial statements for 20X2 for illustrative purposes:

1 January 20X2

No entry required for forward contract because fair value is nil at inception.

		£	£
Dr	Cash	747,258	
Cr	Debt		747,258

To recognise the issue of the US$ denominated zero coupon debt in the £ functional currency (retranslated at spot).

31 December 20X2

		£	£
Dr	Interest expense (profit or loss)	39,439	
Cr	Debt		39,439

To recognise the accrual of interest on zero coupon debt (5 per cent on US$1,419,791 translated at year end spot rate of US$1.8:£). Translation at year end spot rates is used for illustrative purposes only.

		£	£
Dr	Retranslation loss (profit or loss)	41,514	
Cr	Debt		41,514

To recognise the loss on retranslation of US$ zero coupon debt at year end spot rate.

		£	£
Dr	Forward contract	36,117	
Dr	Interest expense (profit or loss)	5,397	
Cr	Retranslation gain (profit or loss)		41,514

To recognise the fair value movement of the forward contract with the effective gain recognised in other comprehensive income (and taken to the cash flow hedge reserve) together with the appropriate reclassification from equity to profit or loss so as to offset the retranslation of the zero coupon debt to spot and to increase interest expense in profit or loss to total the rate that would have been accrued had the entity issued the zero coupon debt in Sterling.

In this period the effective gain recognised in other comprehensive income is reclassified from equity to profit or loss in the same period and therefore for illustrative purposes only the gross entries of recognising in other comprehensive income and reclassifying to profit or loss are not presented.

Similar entries would be recorded for the remaining term of the hedging relationship (20X3 - 20X6).

Interest expense totalling £252,742 is recognised over the term of the hedging instrument and the net profit or loss is the same as if Entity A had issued £ denominated zero coupon debt for £747,258 on 1 January 20X2 which accrued interest at an effective rate of 6 per cent and matured with a payment of the notional of £1,000,000 at 31 December 20X6.

3.10 Cash flow hedging foreign currency risk of the principal only on interest-bearing debt

If the principal only cash flow of a debt instrument is cash flow hedged for foreign currency risk only part of a derivative's fair value will be reclassified to profit or loss over the period of the hedge relationship because only a part of the carrying amount of the debt instrument that is retranslated into the functional currency represents the principal cash flow (as opposed to future interest flows) that impacts profit or loss. Because the carrying amount of a loan is comprised of the discounted amount of both interest and principal discounted at the instrument's original effective interest rate, the amount that can be reclassified from equity to profit or loss in any given period will not equate to the whole fair value movement of the derivative. The amount to be reclassified will equal the portion of the change in fair value of the derivative equivalent to spot retranslation on the discounted principal at the period end plus the systematic release of forward points to the extent the entity is hedging the forward rate. Over the instrument's life, the proportion of the carrying amount of the loan that equates to the discounted principal only will grow as the principal repayment date nears. It is not permitted to reclassify from equity to profit or loss the entirety of the derivative's fair value movement in the period because this would be overstating the foreign currency risk on the principal portion of the hedged loan. While the retranslation of the entire carrying amount of the loan will impact profit or loss under IAS 21, the principal only forms part of that carrying amount.

The following example illustrates the entries for a cash flow hedge of foreign currency risk of the principal payment only of interest-bearing debt using a forward exchange contract.

Example 3.10

Cash flow hedging foreign currency risk of the principal only on interest-bearing debt

On 1 January 20X2, Entity A, a Euro functional currency entity, issues 3-year US$ denominated debt at par equal to US$100 million for US$100 million. The interest rate implicit in the debt is 5 per cent and is paid annually in arrears. The debt will mature on 31 December 20X4. On the issue date Entity A entered into a forward contract to buy US$100 million for €78.69 million at the forward rate of US$1.27:€ at 31 December 20X4 to hedge the principal payment only. The € interest rate implicit in the forward contract is 5.8 per cent. The carrying amount of the debt at initial recognition in Entity A's functional currency, is €76.92 million because spot rates at the date of issue are US$1.30:€.

The entity designates the forward exchange contract as a hedge of the variability of the € functional currency equivalent cash flows on the principal payment only on the debt at maturity. Because the currency, notional amount and maturity of the forward contract match the currency, notional amount and maturity of the debt, Entity A expects the hedge relationship to be highly effective.

Date	Spot rate US$/€	Forward rate US$/€	US$m amortised cost of the principal only (effective interest rate of 5%)	Synthetic €m amortised cost of the principal only (effective interest rate of 5.8%)	Fair value of forward contract €m
1/1/X2	1.30	1.27	86.38	66.45	–
31/12/X2	1.25	1.21	90.70	70.30	3.22
31/12/X3	1.22	1.21	95.24	74.38	3.87
31/12/X4	1.38	1.38	100.00	78.69	(6.23)

Entity A's documentation of the hedge is as follows.

Risk management objective and nature of risk being hedged	Cash flow hedge of the variability in functional currency equivalent cash flows associated with the principal payment only of interest bearing debt due to changes in US$:€ forward rates.
Date of designation	1 January 20X2
Hedging instrument	Forward contract entered into on 1 January 20X2 maturing on 31 December 20X4 to buy US$100 million and sell €78.69 million.
Hedged item	Principal payment only on interest bearing US$ denominated debt issued at par of US$100 million on 1 January 20X2 maturing on 31 December 20X4.
Assessment of hedge effectiveness	The critical terms of the derivative match those of the hedged item (in terms of currency, maturity and notional), accordingly there is an expectation of high effectiveness. The entity will assess counterparty credit risk every period.
Measurement of hedge effectiveness	Hypothetical derivative method. The actual hedging instrument is the same as the hypothetical forward with exactly matching terms and, therefore, no ineffectiveness is anticipated.

The following table illustrates the accounting entries for the transaction during its life in Euro millions. Dr or (Cr) as indicated.

Date		Cash	Forward	Debt	Cash flow hedge reserve	Profit or loss
1/1/X2	Issue debt	76.92		(76.92)		
31/12/X2	Accrue interest on debt at average rates			(3.92)		3.92
	Revalue debt to spot			(3.16)		3.16
	Pay interest at year end	(4.00)		4.00		
	Fair value forward contract		3.22		(3.22)	
	Reclassify amounts from equity to profit or loss				2.26	(2.26)
31/12/X3	Accrue interest on debt at average rates			(4.05)		4.05
	Revalue debt to spot			(2.02)		2.02
	Pay interest at year end	(4.10)		4.10		
	Fair value of forward contract		0.65		(0.65)	
	Reclassify amounts from equity to profit or loss				1.42	(1.42)
31/12/X4	Accrue interest on debt at average rates			(3.85)		3.85
	Revalue debt to spot			9.74		(9.74)
	Pay interest at year end	(3.62)		3.62		
	Fair value forward contract		(10.10)		10.10	

Date		Cash	Forward	Debt	Cash flow hedge reserve	Profit or loss
	Reclassify amounts from equity to profit or loss				(9.91)	9.91
	Settle forward contract	(6.23)	6.23			
	Settle principal on debt	(72.46)		72.46		
			0	0	0	13.49
	Key		**A**	**B**	**C**	**D**

Key

A Nets to zero reflecting the forward is fully settled at maturity.

B Net to zero reflecting the debt is fully settled at maturity.

C Nets to zero reflecting that all amounts in the cash flow hedge reserve in equity have been reclassified to profit or loss to offset the retranslation of the principal only portion of the debt to spot each period and the systematic release of forward points relating to the principal only portion of the debt.

D The total impact in profit or loss reflects the US$ interest expense on the US$ denominated debt translated at average US$:€ rates, the translation on the US$ denominated debt to closing rates at each period end plus the impact of hedging the principal only from US$ to €.

The amounts reclassified from equity to profit or loss are equivalent to the amounts that would have been reclassified to profit or loss had the entity simply issued a US$100 million denominated zero coupon bond for US$86.38 million and immediately hedged it by exchanging US$100 million at maturity for €78.69 million. Because Entity A only hedged the principal amount of the US dollar denominated debt this is equivalent to hedging a US dollar zero coupon bond with the same maturity.

Entries in the financial statements for 20X2 for illustrative purposes.

1 January 20X2

No entry required for forward contract because fair value is nil at inception.

		€ million	€ million
Dr	Cash	76.92	
Cr	Debt		76.92

To recognise the issue of the US$ denominated debt in the € functional currency (retranslated at spot).

31 December 20X2

		€ million	€ million
Dr	Interest expense (profit or loss)	3.92	
Cr	Debt		3.92

To recognise the accrual of interest on the debt (5 per cent on US$100 million translated at average rates of US$1.28:€).

		€ million	€ million
Dr	Retranslation loss (profit or loss)	3.16	
Cr	Debt		3.16

To recognise the loss on retranslation of US$ debt at year end spot rate. This amount consists of the translation of the opening carrying amount at closing rate compared to opening rate plus the interest accrual at closing rate compared to the average rate.

		€ million	€ million
Dr	Debt	4.00	
Cr	Cash		4.00

To recognise the payment of interest in cash at the year end at the actual rate.

		€ million	€ million
Dr	Forward contract	3.22	
Cr	Other comprehensive income		3.22

To recognise the effective gain on the forward contract in other comprehensive income.

		€ million	€ million
Dr	Cash flow hedge reserve	2.26	
Cr	Profit or loss		2.26

To recognise the appropriate reclassification from equity to profit or loss so as to offset the retranslation of the principal portion of the debt to spot and to release the systematic release of forward points.

Similar entries would be recorded for the remaining term of the hedging relationship (20X3 and 20X4).

The amount of the debt that is hedged and the systematic release of forward points for the period ending 31 December 20X2 is described below.

At 1 January 20X2, the amount attributable to the interest and principal only components of the debt is determined in the foreign currency. This is calculated by discounting the principal cash flow due at maturity at the foreign currency original effective interest rate, US$100 million / ($1.05^{\wedge 3}$) = US$86.38 million, with the balance being attributed to the interest only component (US$13.62 million). At the next period end, 31 December 20X2, the amount attributable to the principal only component is US$90.70 million (US$86.38 million x 1.05), with the balance attributed to the interest only component being US$9.30 million. The foreign currency risk that affects profit or loss, that is being hedged, is the foreign currency translation of the principal only component.

Had Entity A issued the principal component in Euros, the entity's functional currency, as opposed to issuing in US$ (and then hedging the principal component into Euros), the principal component would have a value at issue of €66.45 million (US$86.38 ÷ €:US$1.30 [spot]) and would have an effective interest rate of 5.8%, being the Euro effective interest rate for a 3-year maturity. For the period ending 31 December 20X2, the impact in profit or loss for the principal component denominated in Euros would have been €3.85 million, being €66.45 million x 5.8%.

If the hedge is fully effective the profit or loss for the period will include the impact of the principal only component of the foreign currency debt as if it was issued in Euros. In other words, the effect of hedge accounting should be equivalent to Entity A issuing a Euro-denominated zero coupon bond with a yield of 5.8% for €66.45 million and a 5% US$-denominated interest only strip with a notional of US$100 million for US$13.62 million, as opposed to issuing a 5% US$-denominated debt at par of US$100 million and hedging the principal only component to Euros. Because Entity A is hedging the forward currency rate, not the spot rate, a systematic release of forward points included in the fair value of the forward contract recognised in equity will be reclassified to profit or loss to reflect that the principal only component is economically equivalent to it being denominated in Euros.

A reconciliation of the carrying amount of the debt for 20X2 is illustrated below.

Carrying amount of the debt	**€m**	**Calculation**
Net issue proceeds translated at the spot rate	76.92	US$100m @ US$1.30:€ [opening]
Interest at the effective interest of 5% translated at the average rate	3.92	US$100m x 5% @ US$1.28:€ [average]
Less interest at the effective interest of 5% paid in cash at the period end	(4.00)	US$100m x 5% @ US$1.25:€ [closing]
Foreign currency translation consisting of:		
– period end amortised cost balance in foreign currency translated at the closing rate compared to the opening rate	3.08	US$100m @ US$1.25:€ [closing] less US$100m @ US$1.30:€ [opening]

Carrying amount of the debt	**€m**	**Calculation**
– the difference between the interest at the effective interest rate translated at the average and closing rate	0.08	US$100m x 5% @ US$1.25:€ [closing] less US$100m x 5% @ US$1.28:€ [average]
Carrying amount at 31 December 20X2	80.00	

A reconciliation of the amounts recognised in profit or loss with respect to the principal only component that is cash flow hedged is illustrated below.

Impact on profit or loss	**€m**	**Calculation**
Applying the US$ effective interest on the US$ principal only component	3.37	(US$86.38m x 5%) @ US$1.28: € [average]
Foreign currency translation consisting of:		
– period end amortised cost balance in foreign currency translated at the closing rate compared to the opening rate	2.66	US$86.38m @ US$1.25:€ [closing] less US$86.38m @ US$1.30:€ [opening]
– the difference between the interest at the effective interest rate converted at the average and closing rate	0.08	US$86.38m x 5% @ US$1.25:€ [closing] less US$86.38m x 5% @ US$1.28:€ [average]
Less systematic release of forward points from equity to profit or loss	(2.26)	€66.45m x 5.8% less (3.37+2.66+0.08 above)
Net profit or loss impact had Entity A issued a Euro denominated zero coupon bond at 5.8% for €66.45m instead of issuing the principal only component of the US$ denominated debt at 5% for US$86.38m	3.85	€66.45m x 5.8%

3.11 Designating a cash flow hedge in layers

The following example illustrates the entries for a cash flow hedge designated in layers for foreign currency risk of forecast revenue using forward exchange contracts.

Example 3.11

Designating a cash flow hedge in layers

Entity A, Euro functional currency, has a substantial export business to the United States where Entity A receives US$ receipts from the sales of goods. Entity A is exposed to variability of its future revenue from export sales due to fluctuations in currency rates between US$ and €.

Entity A reports under IFRSs on a semi-annual basis and its period end is 31 December. On 1 January 20X0, Entity A establishes that it will have highly probable US$ sales amounting to US$10 million on 30 June 20X1. In order to hedge its exposure to changes in the US$:€ forward exchange rate it enters into a forward contract to sell US$10 million and buy € on 30 June 20X1. Entity A designates and documents the forward contract as a hedging instrument in a cash flow hedge of the US$:€ forward risk on a designated amount of highly probable US$ revenue.

The changes in the fair value of the derivative are shown in the table below.

Date	Fair value of forward	Fair value change in period
	€ million	€ million
01/01/20X0	0	0
30/06/20X0	0.5	0.5
31/12/20X0	2.5	2.0
30/06/20X1	4.0	1.5

On 31 December 20X0, the entity revises its estimates of the US$ sales that will take place on 30 June 20X1 and determines that now only $7.5 million of sales are highly probable. The entity is unable to identify a single event or change in circumstances responsible for this revision in accordance with IAS 39:AG113. In addition to this, a further $0.5 million of sales is expected to occur (but is not highly probable).

Whether Entity A designates and documents the forecast sales in multiple layers or a single layer does have an impact on the amount of the effective portion of the gain or loss on the derivative that is recognised in other comprehensive income in a cash flow hedge. The impact on profit or loss and other comprehensive income of the two designations is illustrated below.

The entries below are for the 6 months to 30 June 20X0 and 31 December 20X0 only.

Entity A specifies as part of its hedge documentation put in place on 1 January 20X0 that it has two designated hedge relationships, identified by two different layers:

- L1: a 75% proportion of the US$10 million forward is designated as hedging the first $7.5 million of US$ sales that are highly probable of occurring on 30 June 20X1; and
- L2: a 25% proportion of the US$10 million forward is designated as hedging the next US$2.5 million of highly probable US$ sales occurring on 30 June 20X1, i.e. sales US$ US$7.5 million – US$10 million.

6 months to 30 June 20X0

The full $10 million forecast sales remain highly probable and therefore the total fair value movement of €0.5 million will be recognised in other comprehensive income under L1 and L2 (both designations being perfectly effective hedging relationships).

		€ million	€ million
Dr	Derivative asset	0.5	
Cr	Other comprehensive income – cash flow hedge reserve		0.5

To recognise the effective amount of the derivative gain in other comprehensive income.

6 months to 31 December 20X0

(i) Entity A must assess whether any of the amounts recognised in other comprehensive income in equity at 30 June 20X0 should be reclassified from equity to profit or loss in the instance when some of the previously considered highly probable forecast transactions are no longer expected to occur. [IAS 39:101(c)] Because US$8 million of sales are still expected to occur (being US$7.5 million that are highly probable and US$0.5 million that are still expected to occur), compared to US$10 million of sales at 30 June 20X0, 80 per cent of the €0.5 million fair value movement previously recognised in other comprehensive income should remain in other comprehensive income with 20 per cent reclassified from equity to profit or loss. This is in line with the principles outlined at **2.2.4** in **chapter C9**.

		€ million	€ million
Dr	Other comprehensive income – cash flow hedge reserve	0.1	
Cr	Profit or loss		0.1

To recognise the reclassification of a fifth of the cash flow hedge gain from equity to profit or loss as a fifth of previously designated forecast transactions are no longer expected to occur.

(ii) Entity A must assess whether the two hedging relationships (L1 and L2) have been highly effective for the 6 months to 31 December 20X0. Based on the revised estimates at 31 December 20X0 only US$7.5 million of sales are highly probable. The L1 designation is considered to be highly effective because the total fair value movement in the designated proportion of the derivative is €1.5 million (being 75 per cent of the total movement of €2.0 million) and the change in fair value of the hedged cash flows, being US$7.5 million, is €1.5 million. L1 is therefore 100 per cent effective [€1.5 million / €1.5 million = 100 per cent].

All of the fair value movement of designation L2 (€0.5 million, being 25 per cent of total movement of €2.0 million) will be recognised in profit or loss because the hedge relationship is not highly effective due to the fall in the level of highly probable sales. Because the amount of highly probable forecast sales between US$7.5 million and US$10 million is now nil, the hedge relationship is 0 per cent effective.

		€ million	€ million
Dr	Derivative asset	2.0	
Cr	Other comprehensive income – cash flow hedge reserve		1.5
Cr	Profit or loss		0.5

To recognise the effective amount of the derivative gain in other comprehensive income and remainder in profit or loss.

The amount of ineffectiveness recognised in profit or loss in the 6 months to 31 December 20X0 would be different were Entity A to designate the hedge of the forecast sales in a single layer.

Because on 31 December 20X0 only US$7.5 million of sales are considered to be highly probable, the hedging relationship is not highly effective: it is only 75 per cent effective because the total fair value movement in the derivative is €2.0 million and the change in fair value of the hedged cash flows, being $7.5 million, is €1.5 million [€2.0 million / €1.5 million = 75 per cent]. Because hedge effectiveness is outside the range of 80 per cent – 125 per cent the entire fair value movement in the period of €2.0 million will be recognised in profit or loss.

3.12 Cash flow hedging with an 'in the money' option

The following example illustrates the entries for a cash flow hedge of interest rate risk on variable rate debt using a purchased in the money cap. The example illustrates that hedge ineffectiveness can vary depending on the designation of the hedged risk.

Example 3.12

Hedging variable rate debt with a purchased interest rate cap

Entity B has a purchased European-style cap at 6% that matures in 6 months that has a notional of CU100 million that corresponds with issued variable rate debt with the same notional that has a variable interest reset date also in 6 months' time. Entity B wishes to designate the intrinsic value of the option as a hedge of future cash flow variability on its variable rate debt for the next 6 months with respect to changes in interest rates.

At the date of designation, current interest rates are 8% and, therefore, the option is in the money. It is assumed for illustrative purposes that the interest rate curve is flat and, therefore, both current and forward rates are 8%. The intrinsic value would be equal to (8%-6%) x CU100 million discounted for 6 months. The fair value of the purchased cap with respect to intrinsic value will be included in the overall fair value of the derivative asset at the date of designation. At the date of designation, the fair value of the intrinsic value is CU2 million (for illustration purposes only discounting has been ignored throughout this example and fair value movements in time value are excluded because these gains/losses will always immediately be recognised in profit or loss because they are excluded from the hedge designation). Note that in practice the inclusion of discounting would be a source of hedge ineffectiveness.

The date of designation is 1 October 20X9 and the reporting period end is 31 December 20X9. At the reporting period end four scenarios could arise.

The effectiveness of a hedge with an in the money option is dependent on the designation of the hedged risk. This example considers two different hedge designations (A & B) and illustrates the resulting hedge ineffectiveness that would arise. Of the two designations, the first ('Hedge designation A') results in the least hedge ineffectiveness.

Hedge designation A: The purchased interest rate cap is designated as a hedge of

- interest rate increases above 8%; and
- interest rate increases and decreases between 6% and 8%

At the reporting period end four interest rate scenarios are considered.

Scenario 1 – interest rates rise (to 9%)

The option is further in the money.

		CU million	CU million
Dr	Derivative asset	1	
Cr	Other comprehensive income – cash flow hedge reserve		1

To recognise the change in fair value of the derivative.

The option is fully effective at hedging increases in interest rates. In this case increases in interest rates of 1% would result in the at the money option being in the money by CU1 million.

Scenario 2 – interest rates remain the same (at 8%)

The option remains in the money by the same degree as at the date of designation.

No entries are required because intrinsic value has remained the same because there has been no increase or decrease in interest rates. Because there is no change in interest rates the at the money option would continue to be at the money.

Scenario 3 – interest rates fall but remain above the cap (to 7%)

The option remains in the money but by a lesser amount.

		CU million	CU million
Dr	Other comprehensive income – cash flow hedge reserve	1	
Cr	Derivative asset		1

To recognise the change in fair value of the derivative.

The option is fully effective at hedging decreases in interest rates down to 6%. In this case a decrease in interest rates of 1% would result in the loss of CU1m in the intrinsic value of the purchased cap which would match the loss of CU1m on a hypothetical forward rate agreement that would be a perfect hedge of increases and decreases of interest rates between 6% and 8%.

Scenario 4 – interest rates fall below the cap (to 5%)

The option is out of the money.

		CU million	CU million
Dr	Other comprehensive income – cash flow hedge reserve	2	
Cr	Derivative asset		2

To recognise the change in fair value of the derivative.

The purchased cap is fully effective at hedging decreases in interest rates down to 6%. The cap is not designated as a hedge of any decreases below 6% which is permitted in this case because the intrinsic value is nil at 6% and remains nil for any further decrease in interest rates below 6%.

In this case a decrease in interest rates of 3% would result in the loss of CU2m in the intrinsic value of the purchased cap which would match the loss of CU2m on a hypothetical forward rate agreement that would be a perfect hedge of increases and decreases of interest rates between 6% and 8%.

Hedge designation B: The purchased interest rate cap is designated as a hedge of interest rate increases above the current interest rate of 8%. At the reporting period end the same four scenarios from above are reconsidered with this alternative hedge designation.

Scenario 1 – interest rates rise (to 9%)

The option is further in the money.

		CU million	CU million
Dr	Derivative asset	1	
Cr	Other comprehensive income – cash flow hedge reserve		1

To recognise the change in fair value of the derivative.

The option is fully effective at hedging increases in interest rates. In this case increases in interest rates of 1% would result in the at the money option being in the money by CU1 million.

Scenario 2 – interest rates remain the same (at 8%)

The option remains in the money by the same degree as at the date of designation.

No entries are required because intrinsic value has remained the same because there has been no increase or decrease in interest rates. In this case because there is no change in interest rates an at the money option would continue to be at the money.

Scenario 3 – interest rates fall but remain above the cap (to 7%)

The option remains in the money but by a lesser amount.

		CU million	CU million
Dr	Profit or loss	1	
Cr	Derivative asset		1

To recognise the change in fair value of the derivative.

The purchased cap is not effective at hedging changes in interest rates in the instance when interest rates fall below the level that existed when the option was designated. CU1 million cannot be recognised in other comprehensive income because the option is not effective in the period in hedging future variability in interest rates. In this case a fall in interest rates for an at the money option would result in the option being out of the money and therefore no intrinsic value could be recognised in other comprehensive income.

Scenario 4 – interest rates fall below the cap (to 5%)

The option is out of the money.

		CU million	CU million
Dr	Profit or loss	2	
Cr	Derivative asset		2

To recognise the change in fair value of the derivative.

The purchased cap is not effective at hedging changes in interest rates in the instance when interest rates fall below the level that existed when the option was designated. CU2 million cannot be recognised in other comprehensive income because the option is not effective in the period in hedging future variability in interest rates. In this case a fall in interest rates for an at the money option would result in the option being out of the money and therefore no intrinsic value could be recognised in other comprehensive income. In this instance the actual option is out of the money so all intrinsic value that was recognised as an asset in the statement of financial position at the date of designation is recognised in profit or loss in the period.

If Scenario 1 occurred in the first quarter, but in the second quarter interest rates fell below the level of the cap then the amount recognised in the cash flow hedge reserve in the first quarter will be reversed through the cash flow hedge reserve until the cash flow hedge reserve is nil, and any excess is recognised in profit or loss.

If Scenario 4 occurred in the first quarter, but in the second quarter interest rates rose above the level of the cap then the amount recognised in profit or loss in the first quarter will be reversed in the second quarter in profit or loss. Any increase in intrinsic value above CU2 million (being the intrinsic value at the date of designation) will be recognised in other comprehensive income.

3.13 Cash flow hedge ineffectiveness due to basis risk

The following example illustrates the entries for a cash flow hedge of interest rate risk on a forecast debt issuance using an interest rate swap with a different basis to the hedged item.

Example 3.13

Basis risk: interest rate basis

Entity X is expecting to issue €100 million of five-year fixed rate bonds on 30 June 20X0. Entity X has a single A credit rating, it believes that interest rates may increase during the next six months and wants to hedge against such an increase by locking-in existing five-year fixed rates. Entity X enters into a forward starting five-year swap on 1 January 20X0 (the swap starts in six months) with a notional amount equal to the expected principal amount of the anticipated debt issuance. At the date of the hedge, swap rates were 5.50 per cent and five-year single A rates were 5.60 per cent.

Entity X assesses effectiveness based on the cumulative change in fair value of the derivative and the cumulative change in the discounted present value or fair value of expected future interest and principal payments on fixed rate single A bonds. Changes in spreads during the hedge period will result in hedge ineffectiveness. At the inception of the hedge the spread between the swap rates and five-year single A corporate bonds was 10 basis points. Historically there is a high degree of correlation between swaps and single A corporate bonds.

The required entries are as follows.

1 January 20X0

No entry required because the derivative has a fair value of zero.

31 March 20X0

On 31 March 20X0, five-year swap rates are 5.10 per cent and five-year single A rates are 5.15 per cent. The derivative has a negative fair value of €1.744 million as a result of a decrease in five-year swap rates of 40 basis points subsequent to 1 January 20X0. The spread between five-year swap rates and five-year single A corporate bond rates decreased to 5 basis points. Because the hedge underperformed the changes in single A rates, the loss on the hedge is smaller than the present value decrease in expected future interest expense on the anticipated issuance of debt and, therefore, the hedge is fully effective. If the decrease in the expected future interest expense on the anticipated issuance of debt was lower than the loss on the hedge, a portion of the loss on the derivative would be recognised in profit or loss.

		€	€
Dr	Other comprehensive income	1,744,000	
Cr	Derivative liability		1,744,000

To recognise the derivative at fair value with changes in fair value recognised in other comprehensive income.

30 June 20X0

On 30 June 20X0, five-year swap rates are 5.30 per cent and five-year single A rates are 5.40 per cent. The derivative has a negative fair value of €867,000 as a result of an increase in five-year swap rates of 20 basis points from 31 March 20X0; spreads at 30 June 20X0 returned to 10 basis points. The hedge is completely effective on a cumulative basis because the spreads returned to 10 basis points.

		€	€
Dr	Derivative liability	877,000	
Cr	Other comprehensive income		877,000

To recognise the derivative at fair value with changes in fair value recognised in other comprehensive income.

On 30 June 20X0, Entity X issues €100 million of five-year bonds at a rate of 5.40 per cent. Entity X also closes out the derivative.

		€	€
Dr	Cash	100,000,000	
Cr	Debt obligation		100,000,000
Dr	Derivative liability	867,000	
Cr	Cash		867,000

To recognise the debt issuance and close out of the derivative.

The €867,000 debit will be reclassified from equity to profit or loss when the interest on the debt is recognised in profit or loss. It will effectively result in a yield adjustment over the life of the bond (because the bond is issued at a greater discount) and an effective yield on the bond of approximately 5.60 per cent, which is the rate in effect at 1/1/X0, the date the hedge is initiated.

In the example basis risk exists between the risk exposure of the derivative, which is solely interest rates, and the risk exposure of the hedged item, which includes both interest rate risk and credit risk of the debt that has been issued. Even though there is basis risk, in this example, applying cash flow hedge accounting does not result in hedge ineffectiveness in profit or loss (as the hedge underperforms in the first period and is perfectly effective on a cumulative assessment basis for the second period).

3.14 Cash flow hedging share appreciation rights

The following example illustrates the entries for a cash flow hedge of equity price risk arising from an entity's IFRS 2 *Share-based Payment* charge using a purchased equity call option.

Example 3.14

Hedging share appreciation rights

On 1 January 20X1, Entity A awarded its employees exclusively cash-settled share appreciation rights (SARs) that vest and can be exercised at 31 December 20X3 if the employees are still working for the entity on that date. Each of the 100 employees is granted one SAR with a strike price of CU10. Therefore, each right provides for a cash payment equal to the amount by which the share price of Entity A exceeds the strike price on the exercise date. No payment will be made if Entity A's share price is at or below CU10; Entity A's share price on 1 January 20X1 is CU10. Entity A estimates that 85 per cent of employees granted a SAR will be employed at 31 December 20X3 (it is estimated five employees leave the entity each year).

Entity A purchases a net cash-settled call option for CU70 with a strike price of CU10 that can only be settled at maturity on 31 December 20X3. The notional of the call option is over 70 shares, i.e. less than the 85 employees that are expected to be employed at the end of the scheme. Entity A hedges only 70 out of the 85 SARs that are expected to vest in order to reduce the risk over over-hedging should more employees leave than expected. Entity A excludes the time value of the option from the hedge designation to demonstrate prospectively that the relationship is expected to be highly effective. Entity A designates the intrinsic value of the derivative as hedging the cash flow variability of 70 employees' SARs and their profit or loss impact recognised in accordance with IFRS 2. At any given period, the IFRS 2 liability and corresponding cumulative profit or loss charge will be equal to the degree to which the hedging instrument is 'in the money' apportioned for the period from the grant date to the vesting date.

The time value and intrinsic value of the hedging instrument are summarised below:

	1/1/X1	**31/12/X1**	**31/12/X2**	**31/12/X3**
Time value	70	40	20	–
Intrinsic value	–	210	280	140
Fair value	70	250	300	140

All amounts are expressed in CU.

1 January 20X1

		CU	**CU**
Dr	Derivative asset	70	
Cr	Cash		70

To recognise the fair value of the hedging instrument at initial recognition.

31 December 20X1

Entity A's share price is CU13, and three employees have left the entity in the period. Entity A changes its estimate of the number of employees expected to be employed at 31 December 20X3 to 91.

The share-based payment charge and liability is CU91 [((CU13 – CU10) x 91) x 1/3 = CU91].

		CU	**CU**
Dr	Employee expense	91	
Cr	Share based payment liability		91

To recognise the share-based payment expense in the period.

The hedge was highly effective for the period because 70 employees are still expected to be employed at 31 December 20X3, and the hedging instrument provides a perfect offset to the cash flow variability of the liability for the payments to these employees.

		CU	CU
Dr	Derivative asset	180 [250 – 70]	
Dr	Profit or loss	30	
Cr	Other comprehensive income		210

To recognise the fair value movement of the derivative with the time value recognised in profit or loss and the effective portion recognised in other comprehensive income.

The period-end cash flow hedge reserve must be equal to the intrinsic value of 70 employee SARs that are still considered to be highly probable and that have not yet affected profit or loss through the IFRS 2 charge. Because the scheme is one-third through its life, the cash flow hedge reserve at the end of the period is CU140 [((CU13 – CU10) x 70) x 2/3 = CU140].

		CU	CU
Dr	Other comprehensive income	70	
Cr	Profit or loss		70

To recognise the reclassification from the cash flow hedge reserve in equity to profit or loss for the portion of intrinsic value of the derivative as a result of the SAR impacting profit or loss. The amount reclassified is determined as ((13-10) x 70) x 1/3 = 70.

31 December 20X2

Entity A's share price is CU14, and four employees have left the entity in the period. The entity revises its estimates of the number of employees expected to be employed at 31 December 20X3 to 89.

The share-based payment liability is CU237 [((CU14 – CU10) x 89) x 2/3 = CU237].

		CU	CU
Dr	Employee expense	146	
Cr	Share-based payment liability		146 [237 – 91]

To recognise the share-based payment expense in the period.

The hedge was highly effective for the period because 70 employees are still expected to be employed at 31 December 20X3, and the hedging instrument provides a perfect offset to the cash flow variability of the liability for the payments to these employees.

		CU	CU
Dr	Derivative asset	50 [300 – 250]	
Dr	Profit or loss	20	
Cr	Other comprehensive income		70

To recognise the fair value movement of the derivative with the time value recognised in profit or loss and the effective portion recognised in other comprehensive income.

The period-end cash flow hedge reserve must be equal to the intrinsic value of 70 employee SARs that are still considered to be highly probable and that have not yet affected profit or loss through the IFRS 2 charge. Because the scheme is two-thirds through its life, the cash flow hedge reserve at the end of the period is CU93 [((CU14 – CU10) x 70) x 1/3 = CU93].

		CU	CU
Dr	Other comprehensive income	117	
Cr	Profit or loss		117

To recognise the reclassification from the cash flow hedge reserve in equity to profit or loss for the portion of intrinsic value of the derivative as a result of the SAR impacting profit or loss. The amount reclassified is determined as [((14–10) x 70) x 2/3] – 70 recognised in previous period = 117.

31 December 20X3

Entity A's share price is CU12, and five employees have left the entity in the period. In all, 12 employees have left over the three-year period [three in 20X1, four in 20X2, and five in 20X3].

The share-based payment liability is CU176 [((CU12 – CU10) x 88) x 3/3 = CU176].

		CU	CU
Dr	Share-based payment liability	61 [176 – 237]	
Cr	Employee expense		61

To recognise the share-based payment expense in the period.

The hedge was highly effective for the period because 70 employees were employed at 31 December 20X3, and the hedging instrument provided a perfect offset to the cash flow variability of the liability for the payments to these employees.

		CU	CU
Dr	Profit or loss	20	
Dr	Other comprehensive income	140	
Cr	Derivative asset		160 [140 – 300]

To recognise the fair value movement of the derivative with the time value recognised in profit or loss and the effective portion recognised in other comprehensive income.

Since the 70 SARs vested at the period end, no amount should be left in the cash flow hedge reserve. Because the scheme is at the end of its life, the cash flow hedge reserve at the end of the period is CU nil.

		CU	CU
Dr	Profit or loss	47	
Cr	Other comprehensive income		47

To recognise the reclassification from the cash flow hedge reserve in equity to profit or loss for the portion of intrinsic value of the derivative as a result of the SAR impacting profit or loss. The amount reclassified is determined as [((12–10) x 70) x 3/3] – (70 + 117) recognised in period periods = 47.

		CU	CU
Dr	Share-based payment liability	176	
Cr	Cash		176

To recognise the payment to employees on exercise of the SARs [(12–10) x 88].

		CU	CU
Dr	Cash	140	
Cr	Derivative asset		140

To recognise the cash received on settlement of the hedging instrument.

Summary of entries

CU Dr/(Cr)

Description	**Derivative asset**	**Cash-settled share-based payment liability**	**Cash**	**Profit or loss**	**Cash flow hedge reserve**
1/1/X1					
Hedging instrument	70		(70)		
31/12/X1					
Share-based payment		(91)		91	
Hedging instrument	180			(40)	(140)
31/12/X2					
Share-based payment		(146)		146	

Description	Derivative asset	Cash-settled share-based payment liability	Cash	Profit or loss	Cash flow hedge reserve
Hedging instrument	50			(97)	47
31/12/X3					
Share-based payment		61		(61)	
Hedging instrument	(160)			67	93
Share-based payment		176	(176)		
Hedging instrument	(140)		140		
Total	–	–	(106)	106	–

The net cash impact of hedging the cash-settled share-based payments is the total share-based payments of CU176, plus the up-front premium spent to acquire the hedging instrument of CU70, less the cash received on settlement of the hedging instrument of CU140. The profit or loss impact equates to the IFRS 2 charge of CU176 plus the net gain from the hedging instrument of CU70.

The net income in each period is not fully offset for the following reasons.

- Entity A did not hedge all its expected cash-settled share-based payment transactions. The entity hedged the first 70 share-based payment transactions, even though it expected at 1 January 20X1 that 85 of 100 employees would still be employed at 31 December 20X3.
- The time value of the SAR is not designated as part of the hedge relationship, which results in net income volatility in all periods.

In the above example, the entity is negatively exposed to favourable movements in its own share price. The more the share increases in value, the greater the share-based payment liability that must be carried in the statement of financial position in accordance with IFRS 2, and the greater the ultimate cash payout will be at the maturity of the scheme. The cash-settled share-based payment presents an exposure to cash flows that affect profit or loss because the entity's liability under the scheme is remeasured with the movement in the share price. The transaction is deemed highly probable because a number of employees are expected to remain in employment for the period to enable them to exercise their SARs. It is possible to designate the cash flow variability arising from the SARs because the population of forecast transactions is homogenous, i.e. the SARs have the same maturity and the same strike price, and therefore result in the same cash payment at maturity.

To improve hedge effectiveness the time value of the hedging option will generally be excluded from the hedge designation. The effectiveness of the hedge will also be influenced by the number of SARs hedged compared to the number that is expected to, and ultimately does, vest. The effective portion of the gain and loss on the hedging instrument is recognised in other comprehensive income and is subsequently reclassified from equity to profit or loss in the same period during which the hedged item affects profit or loss. The ineffective portion of the gain or loss on the derivative must be recognised in profit or loss immediately.

3.15 Updating the hypothetical derivative

The following example illustrates the application of the hypothetical derivative method for a cash flow hedge of interest rate risk on a forecast issuance of debt where the timing of the forecast cash flows changes.

Example 3.15

Updating the hypothetical derivative

On 1 July 20X1, Entity A considers with high probability that it will issue 5 year fixed rate debt with a notional of CU100 million in six months' time. Interest will be payable semi-annually when the debt is issued. Entity A is concerned that interest rates will change during the next six months and therefore decides to hedge this exposure by entering into a forward starting interest rate swap to receive 6m-LIBOR pay fixed on a notional of CU100 million for five years where the cash flows on the swap will be receivable and payable every six months starting in six months' time. In six months' time, when the fixed rate debt is issued, Entity A will close out the forward starting interest rate swap and settle with the swap counterparty because Entity A will no longer be exposed to changes in interest rates because the fixed rate on the debt will have been determined. The forward starting interest rate swap has a fair value of zero at 1 July 20X1. The hypothetical derivative would have the same terms as the interest rate swap and is deemed to be perfectly effective at hedging changes in the six month forward 5-year LIBOR swap rate which will be an offset to the variability in the then to-be-fixed interest payments on the debt that is forecast to be issued on 1 January 20X2.

The hedging instrument will receive 6m-LIBOR (set in advance) pay 5% every six months starting 1 January 20X2 ending 31 December 20X6. Entity A has a calendar year reporting period and chooses to assess hedge effectiveness every quarter.

1 July 20X1

No entries are required because the fair value of the hedging instrument is zero at inception.

30 September 20X1

The derivative is remeasured to fair value and the effective portion of the gains/losses is recognised in other comprehensive income and taken to the cash flow hedge reserve in equity. Because the timing of the forecast transaction and the credit quality of the counterparty remains unchanged the fair value of the derivative is deemed to be fully effective, i.e. the hypothetical derivative still equals the actual derivative. In the three month period since the derivative was entered into interest rates have fallen and therefore the derivative's fair value is negative, i.e. it is a financial liability. The valuation of the derivative is for illustrative purposes only.

		CU	CU
Dr	Other comprehensive income (cash flow hedge reserve)	450,000	
Cr	Derivative financial liability		450,000

To recognise of the fair value movement of the derivative and the effective amount in other comprehensive income.

Reporting period	Fair value gain (loss) of derivative in the period	Cumulative fair value gain (loss) of derivative	Fair value gain (loss) of forecast transactions in the period	Cumulative fair value gain (loss) of forecast transactions	(Debit) credit in other comprehensive income (taken to cash flow hedge reserve in equity)	(Debit) credit to profit or loss	Hedge effectiveness
1 July to 30 September 20X1	(450,000)	(450,000)	450,000	450,000	(450,000)	–	100%

At 1 October 20X1, Entity A revises its estimates of forecast debt issuance due to changes in its funding needs and considers that the fixed rate debt is no longer expected to be issued at 1 January 20X2 and forecasts a 30 day delay. In addition Entity A no longer believes it will issue CU100 million of debt, rather it will issue CU95 million. All other terms of the debt, e.g. frequency of interest payments, denomination, maturity, remain the same as originally forecast. Two sources of hedge ineffectiveness have arisen:

(i) change in timing of forecast transactions; and

(ii) reduction in amount of the forecast transaction.

Entity A redefines the hypothetical derivative to reflect these changes in expectations. Entity A defines the hypothetical derivative that would have had a fair value of zero at 1 July 20X1 as the forward starting swap that will receive 6m-LIBOR (set in advance) pay fixed every six months starting 1 February 20X2 ending 31 January 20X7 with a notional of CU95 million. The fixed rate that Entity A would have locked into for this revised hypothetical derivative would have been 5.2% (not the 5% fixed that the actual derivative and original hypothetical derivative achieved). The fair value of the revised hypothetical derivative at 1 October 20X1 is CU475,000.

Entity A decides to retain the actual derivative and continue to apply hedge accounting with the actual derivative to the extent that Entity A can be highly effective. The ten forecast interest payments are still expected to occur, though all ten forecast interest payments have shifted back 30 days and will be priced 30 days later because the issue date of the debt is delayed.

31 December 20X1

Interest rates continue to fall during the reporting period ended 31 December 20X1 and the fair value of the actual derivative liability is CU800,000. Entity A fair values the revised hypothetical derivative at 31 December 20X1 and the fair value is equal to (CU780,000). The difference in value between the revised hypothetical derivative and the actual derivative arises because the revised hypothetical derivative has a smaller notional but a higher fixed rate.

Period	**Fair value gain (loss) of derivative in the period**	**Cumulative fair value gain (loss) of derivative**	**Fair value gain (loss) of forecast transactions in the period (revised cash flows)**	**Cumulative fair value gain (loss) of forecast transactions**	**(Debit) credit in other comprehensive income (taken to the cash flow hedge reserve in equity)**	**(Debit) credit to profit or loss**	**Hedge effectiveness**
1 October to 31 December 20X1	(350,000)	(800,000)	305,000	780,000	(330,000)	(20,000)	97.5% (780,000 / 800,000)

		CU	CU
Dr	Other comprehensive income (cash flow hedge reserve)	330,000	
Dr	Profit or loss	20,000	
Cr	Derivative financial liability		350,000

To recognise the fair value movement of the derivative in the period and the effective amount in other comprehensive income and ineffective amount in profit or loss.

The effect of the revision to the change in timing and amount of the forecast transaction is that for the quarter ending 31 December 20X1 not all the gains/losses of the actual derivative are recognised in other comprehensive income (and taken to the cash flow hedge reserve in equity) because the hedge is not fully effective. The hedge is only 97.5% effective and CU20,000 is recognised as ineffectiveness in the period because the cumulative gain/loss on the actual derivative from inception of the hedge is greater than the cumulative gain/loss on the revised hypothetical derivative from inception of the hedge.

At the start of each period for which hedge effectiveness is assessed Entity A would need to demonstrate that prospectively the hedge relationship will be highly effective. Even though the hedge was highly effective for the period ending 31 December 20X1 this of itself is not assurance that the hedge is expected to be highly effective for future periods. On 1 January 20X2 Entity A will perform the prospective hedge effectiveness test that will take into account the revised timing and amount of the forecast transactions.

Had the change in timing and amount of the forecast transaction been so significant that the entity failed hedge accounting in the period then Entity A would need to redesignate the hedge relationship in its entirety. A new hypothetical derivative would be determined for the new hedge relationship which, because an interest rate swap is a non-optional derivative, would have a fair value of zero at the new designation date.

4 Net investment hedges

The following net investment hedges are illustrated in this section.

Section 4.1 Net investment hedging the spot foreign currency rate

Section 4.2 Net investment hedging the forward foreign currency rate

Section 4.3 Net investment hedging with a floating to floating cross-currency swap

Section 4.4 Net investment hedging with a fixed to fixed cross-currency swap with interest settlements in profit or loss

Section 4.5 Net investment hedging with a fixed to fixed cross-currency swap interest settlements in other comprehensive income

Section 4.6 Net investment hedging on an after-tax basis

4.1 Net investment hedging the spot foreign currency rate

Below is an illustration of the accounting entries recorded in a net investment hedge of spot foreign currency risk using a forward contract.

Example 4.1

Net investment hedging the spot foreign currency rate

On 1 November 20X1, Entity XYZ enters into a forward contract to sell US$1,000,000 and buy Sterling at a fixed rate of US$1.57:£1 on 30 January 20X2. Group XYZ has a 31 December year end and is headed by Entity XYZ, which has a Sterling functional currency. The forward contract is entered into to hedge the foreign exchange translation risk associated with movements in the spot rate relating to its investment in its US subsidiary with a US dollar functional currency, Entity ABC, which has net assets of US$1,000,000 in Group XYZ's consolidated financial statements.

The forward and spot US$/£ translation rates are as follows.

	1/11/X1	31/12/X1	30/1/X2
Spot	1.55	1.59	1.61
Forward (to 30/1/X2)	1.57	1.60	n/a

On 30 January 20X2, Entity XYZ closes out the forward contract, and also sells Entity ABC for US$1,200,000 which is equal to £745,342 translated at US$1.61:£1.

Translating US$1,000,000 at the above rates gives the following Sterling amounts.

	1/11/X1	31/12/X1	30/1/X2
Spot	1.55	1.59	1.61
Sterling amount	£645,161	£628,931	£621,118
Forward (to 30/1/X2)	1.57	1.60	n/a
Sterling amount	£636,943	£625,000	

Therefore, the value of the derivative is as follows (for purposes of illustration, ignoring the time value of money).

Date	Derivative value	How calculated
31/12/X1	£11,943	£636,943 – £625,000
30/1/X2	£15,825	£636,943 – £621,118

Movements in the fair value of the premium (or discount) implicitly inherent in the fair value of the forward contract will not give rise to hedge ineffectiveness, because the designated hedged risk is movements in spot rate only and, therefore, those movements are excluded from the designated hedging relationship. However, movements in the fair value of these forward points will give rise to volatility in profit or loss.

The entries are as follows.

31 December 20X1

		£	£
Dr	Other comprehensive income	16,230	
Cr	Net assets		16,230

To recognise the foreign exchange difference on translation of the net assets at the spot rate (i.e. translating the investment at 1.59 rather than 1.55).

		£	£
Dr	Derivative	11,943	
Dr	Profit or loss	4,287*	
Cr	Other comprehensive income		16,230

To recognise the change in the fair value of the derivative, the effective portion in other comprehensive income and the undesignated portion in profit or loss.

* relates to forward points

30 January 20X2

		£	£
Dr	Other comprehensive income	7,813	
Cr	Net assets		7,813

To recognise the foreign exchange difference on translation of the net assets at the spot rate (i.e. translating the investment at 1.61 rather than 1.59).

		£	£
Dr	Derivative	3,882	
Dr	Profit or loss	3,931*	
Cr	Other comprehensive income		7,813

To recognise the change in the fair value of the derivative, the effective portion in other comprehensive income and the undesignated portion in profit or loss.

* relates to forward points

		£	£
Dr	Cash	15,825	
Cr	Derivative		15,825

To recognise the cash settlement of the derivative at its maturity.

		£	£
Dr	Cash	745,342	
Cr	Profit or loss		100,181
Cr	Net assets		621,118
Cr	Other comprehensive income		24,043

To recognise the sale proceeds and profit on disposal.

		£	£
Dr	Other comprehensive income	24,043	
Cr	Profit or loss		24,043

To recognise the reclassification of the hedging gains and losses from equity to profit or loss.

The total, post hedge, profit on disposal is £124,224 (£100,181 + £24,043).

It is assumed for illustrative purposes only that the total net assets of the foreign operation are unaffected by the application of IFRS 5 *Non-current Assets Held for Sale and Discontinued Operations* to the disposal group, i.e. the carrying amount of the net assets is lower than the fair value less costs to sell.

4.2 Net investment hedging the forward foreign currency rate

Below is an illustration of the accounting entries recorded in a net investment hedge of forward foreign currency risk using a forward contract.

Example 4.2

Net investment hedging the forward foreign currency rate

Movements in the fair value of the premium (or discount) implicit in the forward contract, the forward points, will now be recognised in other comprehensive income (rather than in profit or loss) and will therefore give rise to equity volatility. These amounts will be reclassified from equity to profit or loss when the subsidiary is sold.

The required entries are as follows.

31 December 20X1

		£	£
Dr	Other comprehensive income	16,230	
Cr	Net assets		16,230

To recognise the foreign exchange difference on translation of the net assets at the spot rate (i.e. translating the investment at 1.59).

		£	£
Dr	Derivative	11,943	
Cr	Other comprehensive income		11,943

To recognise the change in the fair value of the derivative that is fully effective.

30 January 20X2

		£	£
Dr	Other comprehensive income	7,813	
Cr	Net assets		7,813

To recognise the movements in the investment relating to the spot rate movement (i.e. translating the investment at 1.61).

		£	£
Dr	Derivative	3,882	
Cr	Other comprehensive income		3,882

To recognise the change in the fair value of the derivative that is fully effective.

		£	£
Dr	Cash	15,825	
Cr	Derivative		15,825

To recognise the cash settlement of the derivative at its maturity.

		£	£
Dr	Cash	745,342	
Cr	Profit or loss		100,181
Cr	Net assets		621,118
Cr	Other comprehensive income		24,043

To recognise the sale proceeds and the profit on disposal.

		£	£
Dr	Other comprehensive income	15,825	
Cr	Profit or loss		15,825

To recognise the reclassification of the hedging gains and losses from equity to profit or loss.

The total, post hedge, profit on disposal is £116,006 (£100,181 + £15,825).

Compared to **example 4.1**, the profit on disposal is £8,218 lower because in the previous example the fair value of the forward points was recognised in profit or loss throughout the life of the hedge relationship.

It is assumed for illustrative purposes only that the total net assets of the foreign operation are unaffected by the application IFRS 5 *Non-current Assets Held for Sale and Discontinued Operations* to the disposal group, i.e. the net assets are lower than the fair value less costs to sell.

4.3 Net investment hedging with a floating to floating cross-currency swap

Below is an illustration of the accounting entries recorded for a net investment hedge of a foreign operation, using a cross-currency interest rate swap that receives and pays floating interest.

Example 4.3

Hedging a net investment in a foreign operation with a cross-currency swap that receives floating functional currency pays floating foreign currency

On 1 January 20X2, Entity A, a Sterling functional currency entity, acquires a US subsidiary with a US dollar functional currency which has net assets of US$150,000. Entity A will be subject to foreign currency risk (between the US$ and £) on retranslation of the net investment in the consolidated financial statements and therefore wants to achieve hedge accounting for a specific level (US$100,000) of the net assets in the foreign operation. Entity A wishes to designate the first US$100,000 of net assets as the hedged item in a net investment in a foreign operation. At 1 January 20X2, the spot rate on the US$/£ is 1.75/1 so the notional of US$100,000 is equivalent to £57,143. On the same date, Entity A enters into a cross-currency swap ('CCS') to exchange interest payments and principal at redemption with a notional equal to the designated amount of net assets, and designates the cross-currency swap as a hedge of the variability of the Sterling equivalent cash flows on the US$100,000 of the net assets of the foreign operation. The terms are such that on each interest payment date (assume interest is paid annually on 31 December each year for the cross-currency swap), Entity A will pay US$ LIBOR + 100 basis points on a notional of US$100,000 and receive Sterling LIBOR + 106 basis points based on a notional of £57,143. Because the currency and notional on the swap match the net investment, and the swap is on-market at inception, Entity A expects that the hedging relationship will be highly effective.

Date	Spot rate US$/£	Net assets of foreign operation in US$	Carrying amount of US$100,000 of net assets in £	Cross-currency swap fair value £ after interest settlements	Net cash settlement on the swap translated at spot rate £ (£ LIBOR + 106 bp) – (US $ LIBOR + 100 bp)
31/12/X1	1.75	150,000	57,143	0	0
31/12/X2	1.7	160,000	58,824	(1,743)	1,225
31/12/X3	1.6	141,000	62,500	(5,520)	1,389
31/12/X4	1.5	121,000	66,667	(9,670)	1,870
31/12/X5	1.8	106,000	55,556	1,624	1,282
31/12/X6	1.7	115,000	58,824	(1,681)	1,228

Entity A's documentation of the hedge is as follows.

Risk management objective and nature of risk being hedged	Net investment hedge of the foreign currency exposure (due to US$/£ spot rate) to changes in the reporting entity's interest in the first US$100,000 of net assets in the foreign operation.
Date of designation	1 January 20X2
Hedging instrument	Cross-currency swap to exchange US$100,000 at maturity and pay US$ LIBOR +100bp, receive £ LIBOR +106bp interest annually over the term of the instrument.
Hedged item	The first US$100,000 of net assets in the foreign operation.
Assessment of hedge effectiveness	The critical terms of the derivative (currency, notional) match that of the net investment. Although there are no interest payments from the net investment, the cross-currency float to float swap responds closely to movements in undiscounted spot rates because the interest payments are made at the end of the reporting period. Accordingly there is an expectation of high effectiveness. The entity will assess counterparty credit risk and probability of cash flows under the swap occurring every period.
Measurement of hedge effectiveness	Comparison of the period-to-period retranslation on the first US$100,000 of net assets of the foreign operation using undiscounted spot rates compared to the fair value movement on the CCS.

Period-to-period assessment of hedge effectiveness using the dollar offset test:

Period	**Fair value movement in spot rates in period for first US$100,000 of net assets**	**Fair value movement in CCS in period**	**% effective using period to period fair value movement**	**Hedge accounting permitted in period**
	£	**£**		**(80–125%)**
20X2	1,681	1,743	96%	YES
20X3	3,676	3,777	97%	YES

Period	Fair value movement in spot rates in period for first US$100,000 of net assets	Fair value movement in CCS in period	% effective using period to period fair value movement	Hedge accounting permitted in period
	£	£		(80–125%)
20X4	4,167	4,150	100%	YES
20X5	(11,111)	(11,294)	98%	YES
20X6	3,268	3,305	99%	YES

The hedging relationship is deemed to be highly effective (80%-125%) throughout each period and therefore hedge accounting is permitted. Any ineffectiveness, being the difference between fair value movement of the CCS and the retranslation of the first US$100,000 of net assets using undiscounted spot rates, will be recognised in profit or loss in the period.

The following table illustrates the accounting entries for the transaction during its life in Sterling: Dr or (Cr) as indicated. For illustrative purposes only, the entries have recognised the translation on only US$100,000 of net assets and not actual net assets. IAS 21 would require translation of all net assets of the foreign operation to the cumulative translation reserve. Because the total net assets never fall below US$100,000 at a period end, the illustrative journal for 'Consolidated net assets' is always the retranslation of US$100,000.

31 Dec		Cash	CCS	Consolidated net assets	Profit or loss	Other comprehensive income (cumulative translation reserve)
20X2	Revalue US$100,000 net assets to spot			1,681		(1,681)
	Fair value of CCS		(518)		(1,163)	1,681
	Net interest on CCS	1,225	(1,225)			
20X3	Revalue US$100,000 net assets to spot			3,676		(3,676)
	Fair value of CCS		(2,388)		(1,288)	3,676
	Net interest on CCS	1,389	(1,389)			

31 Dec		Cash	CCS	Consolidated net assets	Profit or loss	Other comprehensive income (cumulative translation reserve)
20X4	Revalue US$100,000 net assets to spot			4,167		(4,167)
	Fair value of CCS		(2,280)		(1,887)	4,167
	Net interest on CCS	1,870	(1,870)			
20X5	Revalue US$100,000 net assets to spot			(11,111)		11,111
	Fair value of CCS		12,576		(1,465)	(11,111)
	Net interest on CCS	1,282	(1,282)			
20X6	Revalue US$100,000 net assets to spot			3,268		(3,268)
	Fair value of CCS		(2,077)		(1,191)	3,268
	Net interest on CCS	1,228	(1,228)			
		6,994	(1,681)	1,681	(6,994)	0
	Key		A	A	B	

Key

A The remaining value on the CCS is the difference between the net assets retranslated at US$1.75/£ (original rate) and the US$1.70/£ (spot rate at termination date of swap). Hence total statement of financial position before final settlement of CCS is (net assets £58,824 – CCS £1,681) = £57,143 at 31/12/X6 which is equivalent to the original US$100,000 net assets at the original spot rate of US$1.75/£.

B Equal to the cash paid out on the CCS.

Entries in the consolidated financial statements for 20X2 for illustrative purposes.

1 January 20X2

No entry required by CCS because fair value is nil at inception.

31 December 20X2

		£	£
Dr	Net assets	1,681	
Cr	Other comprehensive income (cumulative translation reserve)		1,681

To recognise the gain on retranslation of the US$100,000 of net assets at year-end spot rates.

		£	£
Dr	Other comprehensive income (cumulative translation reserve)	1,681	
Cr	Profit or loss		1,163
Cr	Cross-currency swap liability		518

To recognise the fair value movement in CCS before interest settlement with corresponding entries to other comprehensive income (cumulative translation adjustment in equity to offset retranslation of net assets) and remainder recognised in profit or loss.

		£	£
Dr	Cash	1,225	
Cr	Cross-currency swap liability		1,225

To recognise the net settlement of interest on CCS (US$ LIBOR + 100bp – £ LIBOR + 106bp converted at spot rate).

Similar entries would be recorded for the remaining term of the hedging relationship (20X3 - 20X6). The amount in cumulative translation reserve will be reclassified from equity to profit or loss on disposal of the foreign operation.

Income totalling £6,994 is recognised over the term of the hedging instrument in profit or loss because the interest receipts represent the net financing on the swap.

4.4 Net investment hedging with fixed to fixed cross-currency swap with interest settlements in profit or loss

Below is an illustration of the accounting entries recorded for a net investment hedge of a foreign operation, using a cross-currency interest rate swap that receives and pays fixed interest where the interest settlements of the swap are recognised in profit or loss.

Example 4.4

Hedging a net investment in a foreign operation with a cross-currency swap that receives fixed functional currency pays fixed foreign currency

On 1 January 20X2, Entity A, a Sterling functional currency entity, acquires a US subsidiary with a US dollar functional currency which has net assets of US$150,000. Entity A will be subject to foreign currency risk (between the US$ and £) on retranslation of the net investment in the consolidated financial statements and therefore wants to achieve hedge accounting for a specific level (US$100,000) of the net assets in the foreign operation. Entity A wishes to designate the first US$100,000 of net assets as the hedged item in a net investment hedge. At 1 January 20X2, the spot rate on the US$ / £ is 1.75/1 so the notional of US$100,000 is equivalent to £57,143. On the same date, Entity A enters into a cross-currency swap ('CCS') to exchange interest payments and principal at redemption with a notional equal to the designated amount of net assets, and designates the cross-currency swap as a hedge of the variability of the Sterling equivalent cash flows on the US$100,000 of the net assets of the foreign operation. The terms are such that on each interest payment date (assume interest is paid annually on 31 December each year for the cross-currency swap), Entity A will pay 4 per cent on a notional of US$100,000 and receive 6 per cent on a notional of £57,143. Because the currency and notional on the swap match the net investment, and the swap is on-market at inception, Entity A expects that the hedging relationship will be highly effective.

Date	Spot rate US$/£	Net assets of foreign operation in US$	Carrying amount of US$100,000 of net assets in £	Cross-currency swap fair value £ after interest settlements (liability)	Net cash settlement on the swap translated at spot rate £ (£ 6% – US$ 4%)
31/12/X1	1.75	150,000	57,143	0	0
31/12/X2	1.7	160,000	58,824	(2,560)	1,076
31/12/X3	1.6	141,000	62,500	(7,723)	929
31/12/X4	1.5	121,000	66,667	(9,513)	762
31/12/X5	1.8	106,000	55,556	1,452	1,207
31/12/X6	1.7	115,000	58,824	(1,681)	1,076

Entity A's documentation of the hedge is as follows.

Risk management objective and nature of risk being hedged	Net investment hedge of the foreign currency exposure (due to US$/£ forward rates) to changes in the reporting entity's interest in the first US$100,000 of net assets in the foreign operation.
Date of designation	1 January 20X2

Hedging instrument	Cross-currency swap to exchange US$100,000 at maturity and pay US$ 4%, receive £ 6% interest annually over the term of the instrument.
Hedged item	The first US$100,000 of net assets in the foreign operation.
Assessment of hedge effectiveness	The critical terms of the derivative (currency, notional) match those of the net investment. There is an expectation of high effectiveness. The entity will assess counterparty credit risk and probability of cash flows under the swap occurring every period.
Measurement of hedge effectiveness	Comparison of the fair value movement of the CCS and a hypothetical CCS with a notional amount equal to the hedged amount and terms that mirror those of the actual CCS.

The following table illustrates the accounting entries for the transaction during its life in Sterling: Dr or (Cr) as indicated. For illustrative purposes only, the entries have recognised the translation on only US$100,000 of net assets and not actual net assets. IAS 21 would require translation of all net assets of the foreign operation to the cumulative translation reserve. Because the total net assets never fall below US$100,000 at a period end, the illustrative journal for 'Consolidated net assets' is always the retranslation of US$100,000.

For illustrative purposes the hedge relationship is deemed to be fully effective throughout its life.

31 Dec		**Cash**	**CCS**	**Consolidated net assets**	**Profit or loss**	**Other comprehensive income (cumulative translation reserve)**
20X2	Revalue US$100,000 net assets to spot			1,681		(1,681)
	Fair value of CCS		(2,560)			2,560
	Net interest settlements on CCS	1,076			(1,076)	

31 Dec		Cash	CCS	Consolidated net assets	Profit or loss	Other comprehensive income (cumulative translation reserve)
20X3	Revalue US$100,000 net assets to spot			3,676		(3,676)
	Fair value of CCS		(5,163)			5,163
	Net interest settlements on CCS	929			(929)	
20X4	Revalue US$100,000 net assets to spot			4,167		(4,167)
	Fair value of CCS		(1,790)			1,790
	Net interest settlements on CCS	762			(762)	
20X5	Revalue US$100,000 net assets to spot			(11,111)		11,111
	Fair value of CCS		10,965			(10,965)
	Net interest settlements on CCS	1,207			(1,207)	
20X6	Revalue US$100,000 net assets to spot			3,268		(3,268)
	Fair value of CCS		(3,133)			3,133
	Net interest settlements on CCS	1,076			(1,076)	
Total		5,050	(1,681)	1,681	(5,050)	0
	Key		**A**	**A**		**B**

Key

A The remaining value on the CCS is the difference between the net assets retranslated at US$1.75/£ (original rate) and the US$1.70/£ (spot rate at date termination of swap). Hence, the statement of financial position related to the hedge before final settlement of CCS is (net assets £58,824 – CCS £1,681) = £57,143 at 31/12/X6 which is equivalent to the original US$100,000 net assets at the original spot rate of US$1.

B Because at least US$100,000 of net assets existed at each reporting period throughout the relationship, the hedge relationship was fully effective in hedging the first US$100,000 of net assets.

Entries in the consolidated financial statements for 20X2 for illustrative purposes.

1 January 20X2

No entry required because fair value of CCS is nil at inception.

31 December 20X2

		£	£
Dr	Net assets	1,681	
Cr	Other comprehensive income (cumulative translation reserve)		1,681

To recognise the gain on retranslation of the US$100,000 of net assets at year-end spot rates.

		£	£
Dr	Other comprehensive income (cumulative translation reserve)	2,560	
Cr	CCS liability		2,560

To recognise the fair value movement in CCS after interest settlement with corresponding entries to other comprehensive income (cumulative translation adjustment in equity).

		£	£
Dr	Cash	1,076	
Cr	Interest expense		1,076

To recognise the net settlement of interest on CCS (£ 6% – US$ 4% converted at spot rate).

Similar entries would be recorded for the remaining term of the hedging relationship (20X3 - 20X6). The amount in cumulative translation reserve will be reclassified from equity to profit or loss on disposal of the foreign operation.

Income totalling £5,050 is recognised over the term of the hedging instrument in profit or loss because the interest receipts represent the net financing on the swap.

4.5 Net investment hedging with fixed to fixed cross-currency swap with interest settlements in other comprehensive income

Below is an illustration of the accounting entries recorded for a net investment hedge of a foreign operation, using a cross-currency interest rate swap that receives and pays fixed interest where the interest settlements of the swap are recognised in other comprehensive income.

Example 4.5

Hedging a net investment in a foreign operation with a cross-currency swap that receives fixed functional currency pays fixed foreign currency

On 1 January 20X2, Entity A, a Sterling functional currency entity, acquires a US subsidiary with a US dollar functional currency which has net assets of US$150,000. Entity A will be subject to foreign currency risk (between the US$ and £) on retranslation of the net investment in the consolidated financial statements and therefore wants to achieve hedge accounting for a specific level (US$100,000) of the net assets in the foreign operation. Entity A wishes to designate the first US$100,000 of net assets as the hedged item in a net investment hedge. At 1 January 20X2, the spot rate on the US$ / £ is 1.75/1 so the notional of US$100,000 is equivalent to £57,143. On the same date, Entity A enters into a cross-currency swap ('CCS') to exchange interest payments and principal at redemption with a notional equal to the designated amount of net assets, and designates the cross-currency swap as a hedge of the variability of the Sterling equivalent cash flows on the US$100,000 of the net assets of the foreign operation. The terms are such that on each interest payment date (assume interest is paid annually on 31 December each year for the cross-currency swap), Entity A will pay 4 per cent on a notional of US$100,000 and receive 6 per cent on a notional of £57,143. Because the currency and notional on the swap match the net investment, and the swap is on-market at inception, Entity A expects that the hedging relationship will be highly effective.

Date	Spot rate US$/£	Net assets of foreign operation in US$	Carrying amount of US$100,000 of net assets in £	Cross-currency swap fair value £ after interest settlements (liability)	Net cash settlement on the swap translated at spot rate £ (£ 6% – US$ 4%)
31/12/X1	1.75	150,000	57,143	0	0
31/12/X2	1.7	160,000	58,824	(2,560)	1,076
31/12/X3	1.6	141,000	62,500	(7,723)	929
31/12/X4	1.5	121,000	66,667	(9,513)	762
31/12/X5	1.8	106,000	55,556	1,452	1,207
31/12/X6	1.7	115,000	58,824	(1,681)	1,076

Entity A's documentation of the hedge is as follows.

Risk management objective and nature of risk being hedged	Net investment hedge of the foreign currency exposure (due to US$/£ forward rates) to changes in the reporting entity's interest in the first US$100,000 of net assets in the foreign operation.
Date of designation	1 January 20X2
Hedging instrument	Cross-currency swap to exchange US$100,000 at maturity and pay US$ 4%, receive £ 6% interest annually over the term of the instrument.
Hedged item	The first US$100,000 of net assets in the foreign operation.
Assessment of hedge effectiveness	The critical terms of the derivative (currency, notional) match those of the net investment. There is an expectation of high effectiveness. The entity will assess counterparty credit risk and probability of cash flows under the swap occurring every period.
Measurement of hedge effectiveness	Comparison of the fair value movement of the CCS and a hypothetical CCS with a notional amount equal to the hedged amount and terms that mirror those of the actual CCS.

The following table illustrates the accounting entries for the transaction during its life in Sterling: Dr or (Cr) as indicated. For illustrative purposes only, the entries have recognised the translation on only US$100,000 of net assets and not actual net assets. IAS 21 would require translation of all net assets of the foreign operation to the cumulative translation reserve. Because the total net assets never fall below US$100,000 at a period end, the illustrative journal for 'Consolidated net assets' is always the retranslation of US$100,000.

For illustrative purposes the hedge relationship is deemed to be fully effective throughout its life.

31 Dec		**Cash**	**CCS**	**Consolidated net assets**	**Other comprehensive income (cumulative translation reserve)**
20X2	Revalue US$100,000 net assets to spot			1,681	(1,681)
	Fair value of CCS		(1,484)		1,484

31 Dec		Cash	CCS	Consolidated net assets	Other comprehensive income (cumulative translation reserve)
	Net interest settlements on CCS	1,076	(1,076)		
20X3	Revalue US$100,000 net assets to spot			3,676	(3,676)
	Fair value of CCS		(4,234)		4,234
	Net interest settlements on CCS	929	(929)		
20X4	Revalue US$100,000 net assets to spot			4,167	(4,167)
	Fair value of CCS		(1,028)		1,028
	Net interest settlements on CCS	762	(762)		
20X5	Revalue US$100,000 net assets to spot			(11,111)	11,111
	Fair value of CCS		12,172		(12,172)
	Net interest settlements on CCS	1,207	(1,207)		
20X6	Revalue US$100,000 net assets to spot			3,268	(3,268)
	Fair value of CCS		(2,057)		2,057
	Net interest settlements on CCS	1,076	(1,076)		
Total		5,050	(1,681)	1,681	(5,050)
	Key		**A**	**A**	**B**

Key

A The remaining value on the CCS is the difference between the net assets retranslated at US$1.75/£ (original rate) and the US$1.70/£ (spot rate at date termination of swap). Hence, the statement of financial position related to the hedge before final settlement of CCS is (net assets £58,824 – CCS £1,681) = £57,143 at 31/12/X6 which is equivalent to the original US$100,000 net assets at the original spot rate of US$1.75/£.

B Because at least US$100,000 of net assets existed at each reporting period throughout the relationship, the hedge relationship was fully effective in hedging the first US$100,000 of net assets. The net amount in OCI represents the net of the interest settlements of the swap.

Entries in the consolidated financial statements for 20X2 for illustrative purposes.

1 January 20X2

No entry required because fair value of CCS is nil at inception.

31 December 20X2

		£	£
Dr	Net assets	1,681	
Cr	Other comprehensive income (cumulative translation reserve)		1,681

To recognise the gain on retranslation of the US$100,000 of net assets at year-end spot rates.

		£	£
Dr	Other comprehensive income (cumulative translation reserve)	1,484	
Cr	CCS liability		1,484

To recognise the fair value movement in CCS before interest settlement with corresponding entries to other comprehensive income (cumulative translation adjustment in equity).

		£	£
Dr	Cash	1,076	
Cr	CCS liability		1,076

To recognise the net settlement of interest on CCS (US$ 4% – £6% converted at spot rate).

Similar entries would be recorded for the remaining term of the hedging relationship (20X3 - 20X6). The total net interest settlements totalling £5,109 are recognised over the term of the hedging instrument in other comprehensive income along with the effective fair value gains and losses on the hedging instrument. Both these amounts along with the amount in cumulative translation reserve will be reclassified from equity to profit or loss on disposal of the foreign operation.

4.6 Net investment hedging on an after-tax basis

Below is an illustration of the entries for a net investment hedge of a foreign operation assessed for hedge effectiveness on an after tax basis.

Example 4.6

Hedging a net investment in a foreign operation on an after-tax basis

Entity T, a Sterling functional currency, has an investment in a wholly owned subsidiary Entity U, a Euro functional currency. The consolidated financial statements headed by Entity T are presented in Sterling. Entity T's consolidated interest in its foreign operation, Entity U is equal to €840,000 of net assets as of 1/1/X1. Assume that the amount of net assets remains unchanged and that the foreign currency retranslation of the investment in the net assets of Entity U will not attract any taxation. On 1/1/X1, Entity T enters into a forward contract to sell €1,200,000 and buy Sterling at a rate of €1.5: £1 on 31/12/X2. The gain or loss arising on remeasurement of the forward contract at spot rates is subject to current tax at 30 per cent.

The forward and the spot EUR/£ translation rates are as follows.

	1/1/X1	31/12/X1	31/12/X2
Spot	1.4	1.6	1.7
Forward (to 31/12/X2)	1.5	1.66	–

Reporting €1,200,000 at the above rates gives the following Sterling amounts.

	1/1/X1	31/12/X1	31/12/X2
Spot	1.4	1.6	1.7
Sterling amount	£857,143	£750,000	£705,882
Forward (to 31/12/X2)	1.5	1.66	–
Sterling amount	£800,000	£722,892	

Therefore the fair value of the forward is as follows.

Date	Derivative value	Calculated as:
31/12/X1	£77,108	£800,000 – £722,892
31/12/X2	£94,118	£800,000 – £705,882

Note: For illustration purposes only, the fair value of the forward ignores the time value of money.

Reporting €840,000 at the above spot rates gives the following Sterling amounts.

	1/1/X1	31/12/X1	31/12/X2
Spot	1.4	1.6	1.7
Sterling amount	£600,000	£525,000	£494,118

The forward contract is designated as the hedging instrument in an after tax hedge of the spot retranslation risk on the first €840,000 net assets of the investment in the foreign operation in the consolidated financial statements. The notional of the forward contract is purposefully greater than the amount of net assets being designated as a hedged item to compensate for the fact that foreign currency movements on the hedged item (net assets) are not taxable while those on the hedging instrument (forward contract) are. The notional of the derivative of €1,200,000 equals the net assets grossed up for the tax rate (€840,000 / 1 – 0.30 tax rate).

Movements in the fair value due to the forward points will not give rise to hedge ineffectiveness, because the designated hedged risk is movements in spot rate only (on an after-tax basis), i.e. these movements do not form part of the hedging relationship and will be recognised directly in profit or loss.

In accordance with the requirements of IAS 12 *Income Taxes*, the current tax relating to the gain or loss remeasurement of the forward contract at spot rates will be recognised in other comprehensive income because the gain or loss itself is recognised in other comprehensive income.

The required entries are as follows.

31 December 20X1

		£	£
Dr	Other comprehensive income	75,000	
Cr	Net assets		75,000

To recognise the foreign exchange difference on translation of the net assets at the spot rate (i.e. translating the investment at 1.6 rather than 1.4).

		£	£
Dr	Derivative	77,108	
Dr	Profit or loss	30,035*	
Cr	Other comprehensive income		107,143

To recognise the change in the fair value of the derivative, the effective portion in other comprehensive income based on undiscounted spot rates, and the undesignated portion in profit or loss. It is presumed that the hedge relationship is fully effective, so the amount recognised in profit or loss is only the change in the fair value of forward points.

* relates to forward points

		£	£
Dr	Other comprehensive income	32,143	
Cr	Tax liability		32,143

To recognise the tax in respect of the gain on the derivative recognised in other comprehensive income (30% of £107,143).

On a post-tax hedge effectiveness assessment, the hedge relationship has been fully effective. The post-tax foreign exchange loss on the net assets, £75,000, is equal to the post-tax foreign exchange gain on the derivative, £75,000 (£107,143 – £32,143).

31 December 20X2

		£	£
Dr	Other comprehensive income	30,882	
Cr	Net assets		30,882

To recognise the foreign exchange difference on translation of the net assets at the spot rate (i.e. translating the investment at 1.7 rather than 1.6).

		£	£
Dr	Derivative	17,010	
Dr	Profit or loss	27,108*	
Cr	Other comprehensive income		44,118

To recognise the change in the fair value of the derivative, the effective portion in other comprehensive income based on undiscounted spot rates, and the undesignated portion in profit or loss. It is presumed that the hedge relationship is fully effective, so the amount recognised in profit or loss is only the fair value of forward points.

* relates to forward points

		£	£
Dr	Other comprehensive income	13,236	
Cr	Tax liability		13,236

To recognise the tax in respect of the gain on the derivative recognised in other comprehensive income (30% of £44,118).

On a post-tax hedge effectiveness assessment, the hedge relationship has been fully effective. The post-tax foreign exchange loss on the net assets, £30,882, is equal to the post tax foreign exchange gain on the derivative, £30,882 (£44,118 – £13,236).

		£	£
Dr	Cash	94,118	
Cr	Derivative		94,118

To recognise the cash settlement of the derivative at its maturity.

5 Hedge effectiveness assessment techniques

5.1 Regression analysis

Below is a detailed illustration of a fair value hedge where regression analysis is used to assess hedge effectiveness.

Example 5.1

Regression analysis

Bank A owns a €100 million portfolio of 10-year BBB corporate bonds measured at amortised cost. The bonds are eligible to be hedged as a portfolio because each item in the portfolio shares the same hedged risk (interest rate risk) and the change in fair value attributable for each individual item in the portfolio is expected to be approximately proportional to the overall change in the fair value attributable to the hedged risk of the group of items.

On 1 July 20X0, Bank A executes a fair value hedge of the interest rate risk on the bond portfolio using a Euro-bond indexed derivative. To establish a basis for hedge accounting at inception, Bank A computed a historical regression analysis on the monthly results for the previous six months and has assessed offset on a monthly and cumulative basis as summarised below. (For illustrative purposes only six data points have been regressed. As stated in **4.6.1** in **chapter C10** more data points will generally be required.)

Month	Current period gain/(loss) on hedging instrument €	Current period gain/(loss) on hedged item €	(1) Current period R^2	(1) Current period slope	Current period ratio %
January	–700,000	300,000			–233.33
February	1,600,000	–1,500,000	0.970	1.11	–106.67
March	–2,050,000	2,200,000	0.980	0.99	–93.18
April	1,100,000	–1,020,000	0.988	1.00	–107.84
May	3,900,000	–3,980,000	0.995	0.99	–97.99
June	–12,350,000	11,900,000	1.000	1.03	–103.78

(1) Constant set to zero

	Cumulative gain/(loss) on hedging instrument €	Cumulative gain/(loss) on hedged item €	Cumulative ratio %
January	–700,000	300,000	–233.33
February	900,000	–1,200,000	–75.00
March	–1,150,000	1,000,000	–115.00
April	–50,000	–20,000	250.00
May	3,850,000	–4,000,000	–96.25
June	–8,500,000	7,900,000	–107.59

Based on the historical regression analysis, Bank A has a basis for concluding that the hedge is expected to be effective in offsetting changes in fair value. The ratio on a cumulative basis from January to June was within the acceptable 80 to 125 per cent range. Although there were two observations where the cumulative ratio was outside the acceptable 80 to 125 per cent range, based on the per-period ratio results and the strong statistical (regression) results, Bank A could conclude that the hedge was expected to be effective at providing offset. On a per-period basis, the ratio was within the acceptable 80 to 125 per cent range in all periods after the initial period. The regression statistics, with the constant set to zero, were well within the acceptable range of 0.80 to 1.25 for slope, while the range of 0.8 to 1.0 for R^2 indicates that a large element of changes in the fair value of the dependent variable are explained by fair value changes in the independent variable.

The **actual** cumulative and current period changes in fair value of the interest rate risk on the bond portfolio and the Euro-bond indexed derivative, from the date the hedge was initiated on 1 July, are summarised below. The R^2 and slope values were computed using the monthly observations from July to December.

Month	**Current period gain/(loss) on hedging instrument €**	**Current period gain/(loss) on hedged item €**	**(1) current period R^2**	**(1) Current period slope**	**Current period ratio %**	**Current period ineffective portion of hedge**
July	8,575,000	–7,885,000	1.000	1.05	–108.75	€690,000
August	425,000	–765,000	0.998	1.04	–55.56	–340,000
September	750,000	–350,000	0.998	1.05	–214.29	400,000
October	–1,000,000	800,000	0.998	1.05	–125.00	–200,000
November	2,500,000	–2,300,000	0.998	1.05	–108.70	200,000
December [2]	–2,775,000	2,775,000	0.998	1.05	–100.00	0

[1] Constant set to zero

[2] Note that only six observations were used for illustrative purposes to compute the regression statistics. Sufficient data points are required to render the results meaningful. However, there are also instances whereby data sourced over inappropriate lengths of time can obscure a change in the relationship between the hedged risk and the hedging instrument. Therefore, the context of how and why the data points have been sourced should be considered when judging which data should be applied to the assessment of effectiveness.

Month	**Cumulative gain/(loss) on hedging instrument €**	**Cumulative gain/(loss) on hedged item €**	**Cumulative ratio %**
July	75,000	15,000	500.00
August	500,000	–750,000	–66.67
September	1,250,000	–1,100,000	–113.64
October	250,000	–300,000	–83.33
November	2,750,000	–2,600,000	–105.77
December	–25,000	175,000	–14.29

Using a regression test measured on a period basis with the constant set to zero, the hedge was highly effective because the R^2 showed a strong level of explained changes in fair value, i.e. that was due to movements in interest rates, and the slope was within the range of negative 0.8 - 1.25. If the hedge was evaluated using period to period changes, the hedging relationship had periods of ineffectiveness in August and September using a ratio test and was always effective using a regression test. An entity's risk management policy should address when a failure to establish a hedging relationship, using either ratio or regression, would preclude hedge accounting.

Even though on a ratio basis the hedge failed the 80 - 125 per cent test in two months, the entity may conclude that hedge accounting was appropriate based on the strength of historical period to period offset provided that the entity had documented that it would assess hedge effectiveness on a cumulative basis. This assessment would only be appropriate if the entity's risk management policy specifically addresses hedge failures and indicates when such failures preclude hedge accounting.

It should be noted, however, that the measurement and recognition of the ineffective portion, which is computed on a monthly basis in the above example, is based on the degree of offset. Therefore, for example, in July €90,000 is recognised in profit or loss (€75,000 on the hedging instrument plus €15,000 on the hedged item). Although hedge accounting is permitted for the full period, the full extent of ineffectiveness is recognised in profit or loss for each month. For the months in which the effectiveness ratio fell outside the acceptable range, a relatively higher amount of hedge ineffectiveness is recognised in profit or loss.

Further, in this example it has been demonstrated that different methods of assessing hedge effectiveness can be applied, e.g. cumulative or period-to-period. An entity would need to document at the outset of the hedge relationship which method of assessment is going to be applied, and then use this method consistently. This method will also be documented in the entity's risk management strategy. It is not acceptable to switch methods part-way through a hedge relationship in order to 'cherry-pick' the method that produces the more acceptable results.

C12 Disclosure

Contents

1 Introduction

IFRS 7 *Financial Instruments: Disclosures* sets out comprehensive disclosure requirements for financial instruments that apply to all entities complying with IFRSs. The requirements of IFRS 7 apply to an entity's annual financial statements. IAS 34 *Interim Financial Reporting* establishes general principles regarding disclosures in interim financial reports and includes a number of specific requirements regarding financial instruments. These requirements are not included in this chapter.

Since IFRS 7 was originally issued in 2005, the Standard has been subject to a number of amendments, the most significant of which were as follows.

- *Improving Disclosures about Financial Instruments* issued in March 2009 amended the required disclosures for fair value measurement and liquidity risk.
- *Improvements to IFRSs* issued in May 2010 included amendments to IFRS 7 that mostly clarified and refined certain disclosure requirements.
- *Transfers of Financial Assets* issued in October 2010 amended the required disclosures for transfers of financial assets that resulted in continued recognition or derecognition.
- *IFRS 13 Fair Value Measurement* issued in May 2011 removed the fair value disclosures from IFRS 7 and included them, with limited amendment, in IFRS 13.
- *Disclosures – Offsetting Financial Assets and Financial Liabilities* introduced new disclosures for financial assets and financial liabilities that are set-off in accordance with IAS 32 as well as recognised financial instruments subject to an enforceable master netting arrangement or similar agreement, irrespective of whether they are off set in the statement of financial position. These requirements are described in **section 6.7**.

The objective of IFRS 7 is to require entities to provide disclosures in their financial statements that enable users to evaluate:

[IFRS 7:1]

(i) the significance of financial instruments for the entity's financial position and performance; and

(ii) the nature and extent of risks arising from financial instruments to which the entity is exposed during the period and at the end of the reporting period, and how the entity manages those risks.

These disclosures are designed to provide users of financial statements with additional information that may influence their assessment of the financial position, financial performance and of the amount, timing and uncertainty of future cash flows for the reporting entity. Further disclosures are required to enable users to determine what accounting elections and judgements have been made when applying the requirements of IAS 32 and IAS 39, and their impact on the financial statements.

IFRS 7 includes mandatory application guidance (in Appendix B) and is accompanied by non-mandatory Implementation Guidance, with the latter providing illustrative examples and guidance on how the requirements of IFRS 7 may be met.

The extent to which an entity will provide financial instrument disclosures will depend on the entity's use of financial instruments and the associated risks. Because many of the requirements of IFRS 7 are based on information provided internally to key management personnel, the depth of disclosure will reflect partly the information provided for use within the business. Entities with few financial instruments and associated risks will provide less disclosure than those entities that have significant financial instruments and related exposures to financial risk.

2 Scope

IFRS 7 is applicable to *all* entities and to *all* risks arising from *all* financial instruments, whether recognised or unrecognised, except where specifically mentioned below. Recognised financial instruments include financial assets and financial liabilities that are within the scope of IAS 39. Unrecognised financial instruments include some financial instruments that, although outside the scope of IAS 39, are within the scope of IFRS 7, such as certain loan commitments that are not designated or required to be carried at FVTPL. [IFRS 7:4]

While a loan commitment may eventually give rise to a recognised financial asset for the lender, to the extent that funds have not been drawn down by the counterparty, the commitment to lend meets the definition of a financial liability because the lender is *contractually obligated to deliver cash or another financial asset to another entity.* [IAS 32:11] When this commitment is not recognised and measured in accordance with IAS 39, it is considered to be an unrecognised financial liability to which IFRS 7's disclosure requirements apply. Similarly, the party with the right to draw down funds (the borrower) under a loan commitment has an unrecognised financial asset (to the extent that the funds have not yet been drawn down) to which IFRS 7's disclosure requirements apply.

IFRS 7 applies to the financial statements of subsidiaries. There is no exemption even if full disclosures are provided in the consolidated financial statements in which the subsidiary is included. The IASB considers when an entity prepares any financial statements in accordance with IFRSs, users of those financial statements should receive information of the same quality as users of general purpose financial statements prepared in accordance with IFRSs. [IFRS 7:BC11]

The table included in **section 2** of **chapter C1** summarises whether certain arrangements are in the scope of IFRS 7 or not.

Regular way sales and purchases of financial assets accounted for using a settlement date accounting policy may also give rise to unrecognised financial assets or liabilities that are within the scope of IFRS 7 (see **2.2** in **chapter C8** for settlement date accounting).

IFRS 7 includes within its scope any lease which meets the definition of a financial instrument. Finance leases are financial instruments, whereas operating leases are not (except as regards individual payments currently due and payable). For further discussion, see **3.4** in **chapter C1**.

IFRS 7 applies to the financial statements of subsidiaries. There is no exemption even if full disclosures are provided in the consolidated financial statements in which the subsidiary is included. The IASB has stated that, when an entity prepares any financial statements in accordance with IFRSs, users of those financial statements should receive information of the same quality as users of general purpose financial statements prepared in accordance with IFRSs. [IFRS 7:BC11]

IFRS 7 applies to all contracts linked to interests in subsidiaries, associates or joint ventures that meet the definition of a derivative unless they meet the definition of an equity instrument in IAS 32. [IFRS 7:3(a)]

IFRS 7 scopes out derivatives over own equity that meet the definition of equity. This will include derivatives over shares in a subsidiary that meet the definition of equity in the consolidated financial statements. IFRS 7 does not appear to have a scope exception for non-derivative instruments classified as equity from the perspective of the issuer, such as ordinary shares and certain preference shares. This appears to be an oversight in the drafting of the Standard because IFRS 7:BC8 states that the scope of IFRS 7 is intended to be the same as IAS 32 (which included disclosure requirements for financial instruments prior to IFRS 7 being issued) with one exception, namely "derivatives based on interests in subsidiaries, associates or joint ventures if the derivatives meet the definition of an equity instrument in IAS 32". The Basis for Conclusions justifies the exclusion of such derivatives by stating that these instruments are not remeasured and hence "do not expose the issuer to balance sheet and income statement risk", and that the disclosures about the significance of financial instruments for financial position and performance are not relevant to equity instruments. In addition, IFRS 7.BC8 states that these instruments are excluded from the scope of IFRS 7, but they are within the scope of IAS 32 for the purpose of determining whether they meet the definition of equity instruments. It seems reasonable that the scope exclusions for derivatives over own equity that meet the definition of equity would also apply to non-derivatives that meet the definition of equity because the justification in the Basis for Conclusions would be equally relevant.

Consolidated financial statements include all financial instruments of subsidiaries except those intragroup financial instruments that are fully eliminated on consolidation. Only if the financial instrument is fully eliminated on consolidation is it excluded from the scope of IFRS 7 in the consolidated financial statements.

IFRS 7 does not apply to an investment in an associate or joint venture accounted for under the equity method because the carrying amount represents the investor's initial cost adjusted for the post-acquisition changes in the investor's share of net assets of the investee.

It is less clear whether IFRS 7 applies to the share of any financial instruments of a joint operator held in a joint operation under IFRS 11. The application of IFRS 11 on joint operations means that the statement of financial position of the joint operator includes its share of the assets that it jointly holds and its share of the liabilities for which it is jointly responsible. [IFRS 11:20] Because the assets and liabilities will include the joint operator's share of financial instruments that are recognised and measured in accordance with IAS 39, it would seem reasonable that these financial instruments are subject to the disclosure requirements of IFRS 7.

IFRS 5 *Non-current Assets Held for Sale and Discontinued Operations* specifically states in paragraph 2 that the classification and presentation requirements of IFRS 5 apply to all non-current assets (or disposal groups) classified as held for sale and discontinued operations. A question arises as to whether IFRS 7 disclosures are also required for financial assets and financial liabilities classified as held for sale or that form part of disposal groups because there is no scope exemption in IFRS 7 in this respect. The IASB issued *Improvements to IFRSs* in April 2009, which clarified that IFRS 5 specifies the disclosures required in respect of non-current assets (or disposal groups) classified as held for sale or discontinued operations. IFRS 5:5B states that disclosures in other IFRSs do not apply to such assets (or disposal groups) unless those IFRSs require:

[IFRS 5:5B]

(a) specific disclosures in respect of non-current assets (or disposal groups) classified as held for sale or discontinued operations; or

(b) disclosures about measurement of assets and liabilities within a disposal group that are not within the scope of the measurement requirement of IFRS 5 and such disclosures are not already provided in the other notes to the financial statements.

Additional disclosures about non-current assets (or disposal groups) classified as held for sale or discontinued operations may be necessary to comply with the general requirements of IAS 1 *Presentation of Financial Statements*, in particular IAS 1:15 & 125. [IFRS 5:5B]

Therefore, in the context of IFRS 7, IFRS 5.5B means that the disclosure requirements of IFRS 7 apply to stand-alone non-current financial assets held for sale and to financial assets/liabilities that form part of a disposal group *to the extent that those disclosure requirements relate to measurement*.

The specific disclosure requirements of IFRS 7 that apply should be determined as a matter of judgement. In some circumstances, the applicable disclosures about measurement may be limited to:

- the accounting policies and measurement bases for financial assets and liabilities; [IFRS 7.21] and
- the carrying amount of each category of financial asset and liability; [IFRS 7.8]

In some cases it could be argued that, for example, the liquidity risk, credit risk and market risk disclosures, amongst others, are not relevant to financial assets held for sale and financial assets/liabilities within a disposal group in the scope of IFRS 5's presentation and disclosure requirements.

It is important to remember that contracts to buy or sell non-financial items that may not be typically considered financial instruments are within the scope of IFRS 7 if they are in the scope of IAS 39. Guidance on the recognition and measurement of contracts over non-financial items is set out at **2.5** in **chapter C1**.

The extent to which an entity will provide financial instrument disclosures will depend on the entity's use of financial instruments and the associated risks. Because many of the requirements of IFRS 7 are based on information provided internally to key management personnel, the depth of disclosure will reflect partly the information provided for use within the business. Entities with few financial instruments and associated risks will provide less disclosure than those entities that have significant financial instruments and related exposures to financial risk.

3 Classes of financial instruments

IFRS 7 specifies a number of disclosure requirements to be provided by 'class of financial instrument'. These include:

- derecognition of financial assets (see **4.1.5**);
- allowance account for credit losses if an entity chooses under IAS 39 to have a separate allowance account (see **4.1.7**);

- impairment losses in the period (see **4.2.5**);
- 'day 1 profit or loss' (see **4.3.3.8**); and
- credit risk (see **5.2.1**).

IFRS 13 also requires fair value disclosures by class of assets and liabilities (see **4.3.3**).

IFRS 7 requires entities to group financial instruments into classes that are appropriate to the nature of the information disclosed and that take into account the characteristics of those financial instruments. The classes are to be reconciled to the line items presented in the statement of financial position. [IFRS 7:6] The classes are determined by the entity and are distinct from the categories of financial instruments specified by IAS 39. [IFRS 7:B1] At a minimum, the classes are required to distinguish between those financial instruments that are measured at amortised cost and those that are measured at fair value. The entity should treat as a separate class or classes those financial instruments that are outside the scope of IFRS 7 (when the entity wishes to provide disclosures regarding such financial instruments in addition to the requirements of IFRS 7). [IFRS 7:B2] In many instances, classes of financial instruments will be more granular than the categories of financial instruments specified by IAS 39. For example, 'loans and receivables' is a financial instrument category in IAS 39 that could comprise various classes such as home loans, credit card loans, unsecured medium term loans etc.

IFRS 13 provides some additional guidance on determining classes for the basis of fair value disclosures. In addition to considering the nature, characteristics and risks of the asset and liability (as with IFRS 7) it states that consideration should be given to the level of the fair value hierarchy within which the fair value measurement is categorised. The number of classes may need to be greater for fair value measurements categorised within Level 3 of the fair value hierarchy because those measurements have a greater degree of uncertainty and subjectivity. IFRS 13 notes that where classes of assets and liabilities differ to line items in the statement of financial position an entity shall provide information sufficient to permit reconciliation to the line items presented in the statement of financial position. [IFRS 13:94]

The preparer of the financial statements must strike a balance between providing excessive detail and obscuring information as a result of too much aggregation. [IFRS 7:B3]

IFRS 7 is not clear whether the same classes of financial instruments are applied universally to all the disclosures that IFRS 7 requires by class. An advantage of using the same classification for financial instruments across all the required disclosures is that it enhances comparability and understanding between disclosures. However, such an approach may be in conflict with IFRS 7 in the following instances.

(i) Disclosure by class is required for certain quantitative disclosures, and IFRS 7:34 requires this information to be consistent with that provided internally to key management personnel. If the information provided to key management for the quantitative disclosures required by the Standard is aggregated differently, depending on the applicable risk disclosure, this information must be disclosed. It would be inappropriate to aggregate classes differently to the aggregation provided to key management personnel.

(ii) IFRS 7:IG21 indicates that, in determining classes for credit risk disclosures, entities should group financial instruments that share economic characteristics with respect to the risk being disclosed (e.g. residential mortgages, unsecured consumer loans and commercial loans). This implies that classes vary depending on the type of information being disclosed. The classes applied to credit risk disclosure, therefore, may not be appropriate for the classes of financial instruments applied to fair value disclosure (e.g. the specific disclosures required for 'day 1 profit or loss' – see **4.3.3.8**). If only a small number of items are included in the day 1 profit or loss disclosure, but the characteristics of the instruments or valuation techniques differ, an entity may consider it more appropriate to choose classes for the specific disclosure that differ to other required disclosures.

Care should be taken to ensure that the determination of classes is relevant to the disclosure requirement and provides the most meaningful information. If different classifications of financial instruments are used for different disclosures, the entity should place greater emphasis on making clear how the classes are reconciled to the statement of financial position and between notes.

Because IFRSs do not prescribe line items for the statement of financial position, other than specified minimum requirements set out in IAS 1 and a number of other Standards, an entity could choose to use its IFRS 7 classes of financial instruments as the basis for the line items in its statement of financial position. Such an approach would be likely to result in the presentation of many more line items in the statement of financial position that would be the case if the entity uses IAS 39's categories for financial assets as the basis for line items in its statement of financial position.

4 Significance of financial instruments

One of the two key objectives of IFRS 7 is to require entities to provide disclosures in their financial statements that enable users to evaluate the significance of financial instruments for the entity's financial position and performance. To achieve this objective, disclosures are required relating to the statement of financial position, statement of comprehensive income and equity.

4.1 Disclosures relating to the statement of financial position

IFRS 7 requires specific disclosures in respect of items included in the statement of financial position. Some are very broad (e.g. disclosing financial assets and financial liabilities by classification category) and others are very specific (e.g. disclosures regarding collateral and derecognition).

4.1.1 Categories of financial assets and financial liabilities

An entity is required to disclose the carrying amount for each financial instrument category as defined by IAS 39 either in the statement of financial position or in the notes to the financial statements. The carrying amounts of each of the following categories are specifically required to be disclosed:

[IFRS 7:8]

(a) financial assets at fair value through profit or loss, showing separately (i) those designated as such upon initial recognition and (ii) those classified as held for trading in accordance with IAS 39;

(b) held-to-maturity investments;

(c) loans and receivables;

(d) available-for-sale financial assets;

(e) financial liabilities at fair value through profit or loss, showing separately (i) those designated as such upon initial recognition and (ii) those classified as held for trading in accordance with IAS 39; and

(f) financial liabilities measured at amortised cost.

These disclosures are intended to assist users in understanding the extent to which accounting policies affect the amounts at which financial assets and financial liabilities are recognised. [IFRS 7:BC14] Together with the disclosure of gains and losses by category of financial instrument, the disclosure of the carrying amounts for each category of financial instrument allows users to appraise management on its decisions to buy, sell or hold financial assets and to incur, maintain or discharge financial liabilities.

Recognised derivative financial instruments other than those that are designated and effective hedging instruments are included within the FVTPL category. Derivatives that are designated as effective hedging instruments, however, are excluded from that category and IAS 39 does not include them in any other category or create a specific category for them. It is reasonable, however, to include derivatives that are effective hedging instruments as a separate category in order to facilitate reconciliation between disclosures by category and the statement of financial position. Some entities choose to show derivatives in effective hedging relationships in a separate caption both in the statement of financial position and in the notes.

4.1.2 Financial assets at FVTPL

An entity that designates a loan or receivable (or a group of loans or receivables) as at FVTPL (see **3.1.1** in **chapter C2**) is required to provide extensive disclosures. These disclosures are required because the application of the fair value option to these instruments may have a significant impact on the financial statements as a result of fair value movements and, in particular, those movements caused by changes in credit risk.

IFRS 7 requires disclosure of:

[IFRS 7:9]

(a) the maximum exposure to *credit risk* of the loan or receivable (or group of loans or receivables), at the end of the reporting period;

(b) the amount by which any related credit derivatives or similar instruments mitigate that maximum exposure to credit risk;

(c) the amount of change, during the period and cumulatively, in the fair value of the loan or receivable (or group of loans or receivables) that is attributable to changes in the credit risk of the financial asset determined either:

   (i) as the amount of change in its fair value that is not attributable to changes in market conditions that give rise to *market risk*; or

   (ii) using an alternative method the entity believes more faithfully represents the amount of change in its fair value that is attributable to changes in the credit risk of the asset.

   Changes in market conditions that give rise to market risk include changes in an observed (benchmark) interest rate, commodity price, foreign exchange rate or index of prices or rates; and

(d) the amount of the change in the fair value of any related credit derivatives or similar instruments that has occurred during the period and cumulatively since the loan or receivable was designated.

In addition, an entity should disclose:

[IFRS 7:11]

(a) the methods used to comply with the requirements in (c) above; and

(b) if the entity believes that the disclosure it has given to comply with the requirements in (c) above does not faithfully represent the change in the fair value of the financial asset attributable to changes in its credit risk, the reasons for reaching this conclusion and the factors it believes are relevant.

The maximum exposure to credit risk for a derivative is its carrying amount. [IFRS 7:BC50] The Standard is not clear whether the maximum exposure to credit risk for loans and receivables can also equal the carrying amount, which is fair value, when an entity designates those assets as at FVTPL.

The information to be disclosed regarding the maximum exposure to credit risk depends on whether exposure to credit loss is viewed as a 'cash loss' or a loss that will be recognised in the statement of comprehensive income. Credit risk is defined as "the risk that one party to a financial instrument will cause a financial loss for the other party by failing to discharge an obligation". [IFRS 7:Appendix A] If the maximum exposure to credit risk is viewed as a cash loss, then the amount to be disclosed would be the amount owed (e.g. if the fair value of the debt is CU70 and the amount owed is CU100, then the maximum 'cash loss' is CU100). If, however, the maximum exposure to credit risk is viewed as a loss that will be recognised in the statement of comprehensive income, then the carrying amount (i.e. the fair value of the assets in this instance) will be the amount that is required to be disclosed.

While either approach is supportable, an entity must apply a consistent policy in disclosing the maximum exposure to credit risk for loans and receivables designated as at FVTPL.

Example 4.1.2

Portfolio of assets designated at FVTPL

Entity A acquired at the beginning of the prior period a portfolio of 9 per cent non-amortising unsecured long-term loans with five years remaining to maturity. The loans meet the definition of loans and receivables. Entity A chooses to designate the loans as at FVTPL. The loans were acquired for CU905 million when the effective interest rate was 10 per cent, consisting of 8 per cent benchmark interest rate and 2 per cent credit spread. The par amount of the loans is CU1 billion. At the date of acquisition, Entity A entered into a credit default swap with a financial institution to provide credit protection on the loans with a notional of CU500 million. The credit default swap had an initial fair value of zero and remains outstanding at the end of the reporting period.

At the end of the reporting period:

- the fair value of the loans is CU896 million (prior year: CU852 million);
- benchmark interest rates for the remaining maturity are 8 per cent and credit spreads are 2.5 per cent (prior year: 9 per cent and 3 per cent respectively); and
- the fair value of the credit default swap is CU35 million (prior year: CU46 million).

The items to be disclosed in accordance with IFRS 7:9 are as follows.

(a) Maximum exposure to credit risk at the end of the reporting period

If maximum exposure to credit risk is viewed as being the loss that will be recognised in the statement of comprehensive income, then the amount to be disclosed would be CU896 million (prior year: CU852 million), being the fair value of the loans at the end of the reporting period.

If the maximum exposure to credit risk is viewed as being equal to a cash loss, then the amount to be disclosed would be CU1 billion (prior year: CU1 billion), being the amount owed by the borrower at the end of the reporting period.

Note: the entity cannot offset the loans and the credit default swaps because there is no right of set-off and the financial instruments are with a different counterparty.

(b) Amount by which any related credit derivatives or similar instruments mitigate that maximum exposure to credit risk

The credit default swap provides credit protection for half of the loans. On a fair value basis, the maximum protection is equivalent to 56 per cent (prior year: 59 per cent) and on a cash loss basis is equivalent to 50 per cent (prior year: 50 per cent).

(c) Amount of change, during the period and cumulatively, in the fair value of loans that is attributable to changes in credit risk

The cumulative change in fair value due to credit risk of the loans is a CU16 million loss (prior year: CU27 million loss). The change in fair value due to credit risk for the period is a CU11 million gain.

(d) Change in the fair value of any related credit derivatives

The cumulative change in fair value of the credit default swap is a CU35 million gain (prior year: CU46 million gain). The change in fair value of the credit default swap for the period is a CU11 million loss.

4.1.3 Financial liabilities at FVTPL

When an entity has designated financial liabilities as at FVTPL, IFRS 7:10 requires extensive disclosures and, in particular, disclosures about creditworthiness. These disclosures have been included to help alleviate concerns that users may misinterpret the profit or loss effects of changes in the issuer's credit risk. The perceived 'anomaly' of recognising gains in profit or loss when the entity's credit rating deteriorates is partially mitigated by disclosure of the changes in fair value attributable to credit risk.

IFRS 7 requires disclosure of:

[IFRS 7:10]

(a) the amount of change, during the period and cumulatively, in the fair value of the financial liability that is attributable to changes in the credit risk of that liability determined either:
   (i) as the amount of change in its fair value that is not attributable to changes in market conditions that give rise to market risk; or
   (ii) using an alternative method the entity believes more faithfully represents the amount of change in its fair value that is attributable to changes in the credit risk of the liability.

   Changes in market conditions that give rise to market risk include changes in a benchmark interest rate, the price of another entity's financial instrument, a commodity price, a foreign exchange rate or an index of prices or rates. For contracts that include a unit-linking feature, changes in market conditions include changes in the performance of the related internal or external investment fund; and

(b) the difference between the financial liability's carrying amount and the amount the entity would be contractually required to pay at maturity to the holder of the obligation.

IFRS 7:BC22 states that the fair value may differ significantly from the settlement amount (i.e. the amount contractually required to be paid at maturity), in particular for financial liabilities with a long duration when an entity has experienced a significant deterioration in creditworthiness since the issue of those financial liabilities. In order to comply with the requirements of IFRS 7:10(b) (see above), the amount contractually required to be paid at maturity should be an undiscounted amount, not affected by the entity's own credit risk. To the extent that the amount payable at maturity is subject to variability (e.g. because the principal is index-linked), an estimation of this amount should also be included, whether or not the index-linked feature is a separately accounted for embedded derivative. This is consistent with the principle applied for liquidity risk disclosures (as discussed in **5.2.2**) where the effects of any embedded derivatives are included on an undiscounted basis based on conditions existing at the end of the reporting period (incorporating forward rates as applicable).

The Standard also requires disclosure of:

[IFRS 7:11]

(a) the methods used to comply with the requirements in IFRS 7:10(a) above; and

(b) if the entity believes that the disclosure it has given to comply with the requirements in IFRS 7:10(a) above does not faithfully represent the change in the fair value of the financial liability attributable to changes in its credit risk, the reasons for reaching this conclusion and the factors it believes are relevant.

Example 4.1.3

Financial liabilities designated as at FVTPL

On the first day of its current financial period, Entity B issued a 5-year bond in order to finance the expansion of its operations. The bond trades on a recognised bond exchange. Entity B's year end is 31 December 20X1.

Details of the bond are as follows.

Maturity date:	31 December 20X5
Nominal value:	CU500 million
Coupon:	9%, payable annually on 31 December in arrears
Issue price (1 January 20X1):	CU450 million
Fair value (31 December 20X1):	CU400 million
5-year LIBOR (1 January 20X1):	10.5%
4-year LIBOR (31 December 20X1):	12.75%

As permitted by IFRS 7:B4, Entity B determines the amount of change in the fair value of the financial liability that is attributable to changes in the liability's credit risk as the change in the liability's fair value that is not attributable to changes in market conditions that give rise to market risk. This is appropriate as the only relevant changes in market conditions for the liability are changes in the observed (benchmark) interest rate. Entity B calculates the amount of change in the fair value of the financial liability that is attributable to changes in the liability's credit risk as follows.

(a) Determine the liability's internal rate of return (IRR) at the start of the period using the observed market price of the liability and the liability's contractual cash flows at the start of the period.

Year 0	Year 1	Year 2	Year 3	Year 4	Year 5
450,000,000)[1]	45,000,000[2]	45,000,000[2]	45,000,000[2]	45,000,000[2]	545,000,000[3]

1 The bonds are recognised initially at fair value (CU450 million).

2 Yearly cash flows are determined as being 9% x CU500 million.

3 The terminal cash flow is determined as the nominal value of the bonds plus the interest coupon.

The IRR, equal to the effective interest rate, at the issue date is 11.76%.

(b) Deduct the observed (benchmark) interest rate at the start of the period from the IRR to arrive at an instrument-specific component of the IRR (i.e. the portion of the effective interest that relates to credit risk).

11.76% - 10.5% = 1.26% instrument specific component of the IRR

(c) Compute the present value of the cash flows of the liability using the liability's contractual cash flows at the end of the period and a discount rate equal to the sum of the observed benchmark interest rate at the end of the period and the instrument-specific component of the internal rate of return determined in (b).

Remaining cash flows to be discounted using an IRR of 14.01% (12.75% + 1.26%)

Year 2	Year 3	Year 4	Year 5
45,000,000	45,000,000	45,000,000	545,000,000

Present value is equal to CU427,059,828 as at the end of the reporting period.

(d) Compute the change in the fair value of the liability that is not attributable to changes in the observed (benchmark) interest rate as the difference between the observed market price of the liability and the amount determined above.

Change in fair value due to changes in credit risk is determined as CU27,059,828 (CU427,059,828 - CU400,000,000).

The required disclosures may be provided as follows.

Financial liabilities

During the year, the group issued a commercial bond with a nominal value of CU500 million with a maturity of five years that was designated as at fair value through profit or loss at initial recognition. The fair value and the change in that fair value that can be ascribed to changes in underlying credit risk are set out below.

	31 December 20X1	31 December 20X0
Fair value of commercial bond	CU400,000,000	–
Change in fair value of commercial bond not attributable to changes in market conditions	CU(27,059,828)	–
Difference between carrying amount and amount contractually required to be paid at maturity	CU100,000,000	–

The group estimates changes in fair value due to credit risk by estimating the amount of change in the fair value that is not due to changes in market conditions that give rise to market risk.

Example 4.1.3 assumes that changes in the fair value arising from factors other than changes in the bond's credit risk or changes in interest rates are not significant. Had the bond contained an embedded prepayment option, then the change in the fair value of the embedded derivative would need to be excluded in determining the amount to be disclosed. [IFRS 7:B4] Whether or not IAS 39 requires separation of the embedded derivative the effects of the embedded derivative need to be excluded.

The methodology illustrated in **example 4.1.3** is a reasonable approach to determining the extent to which fair value movements are attributable to changes in credit risk for vanilla debt instruments. When other factors affect the change in the instrument's fair value (e.g. embedded derivatives), then alternative methods may be used. Such methods are required to be disclosed, as well as why those methods provide a more faithful representation than the method described in IFRS 7. [IFRS 7:BC21(a)] Liabilities, such as unit-linked insurance contracts (for which the amount of the liability reflects the performance of a defined pool of assets) present particular challenges.

4.1.4 Reclassification

IFRS 7 requires extensive disclosures when financial assets are reclassified from one measurement category to another.

When an entity reclassifies financial assets in accordance with the requirements of IAS 39:51 – 54 (from cost or amortised cost to fair value, or vice versa), the entity is required to disclose the amount that has been reclassified into and out of each category, together with the reason for that reclassification. [IFRS 7:12] This disclosure will be relevant when financial assets are reclassified from the HTM to the AFS category, and vice versa, and when an investment in, or derivative that results in the physical delivery of, an unlisted equity instrument becomes or ceases to become reliably measurable.

Some classification decisions are made on the basis of management's intent (e.g. classification as HTM investments). Reclassifications from cost/amortised cost to fair value, and vice versa, may occur in limited circumstances and it is important for users to understand the reasons for such reclassifications in order to assist the users in judging how management follows through with its stated intentions. Such information is also useful to users in understanding the performance of the entity because reclassifications of such instruments can have a significant effect on their measurement. [IFRS 7:BC23]

IFRS 7:12 requires disclosure regarding financial assets reclassified from cost or amortised cost to fair value, and vice versa. While reclassification of financial liabilities is also permitted, the disclosure requirements in IFRS 7:12 do not refer to financial liabilities.

Although IFRS 7:12 appears not to require the same disclosures regarding financial liabilities that are reclassified, it is preferable to provide similar disclosures. For example, if an entity has written a call option over a non-listed third-party equity security, where a fixed amount of the equity security would be delivered to the option holder upon exercise, the derivative instrument (call option) is a financial liability. If the entity had previously measured the call option at cost because it could not measure the fair value of the instrument reliably, and a reliable measure subsequently becomes, the entity would be required to remeasure the derivative liability at fair value with changes in fair value recognised in profit or loss. [IAS 39:53] Information regarding the amount reclassified and the reason for the reclassification would be equally relevant in such circumstances as it would be for a reclassification of an asset.

IAS 39 permits non-derivative financial assets to be reclassified out of the held for trading category and reclassification of AFS debt instruments to loans and receivables subject to meeting specified criteria (see **section 4** of **chapter C2**). IFRS 7 requires the following disclosures for such reclassifications:

[IFRS 7:12A]

(a) the amount reclassified into and out of each category;

(b) for each reporting period until derecognition, the carrying amounts and fair values of all financial assets that have been reclassified in the current and previous reporting periods;

(c) if a financial asset was reclassified in accordance with paragraph 50B, the rare situation, and the facts and circumstances indicating that the situation was rare;

(d) for the reporting period when the financial asset was reclassified, the fair value gain or loss on the financial asset recognised in profit or loss or other comprehensive income in that reporting period and in the previous reporting period;

(e) for each reporting period following the reclassification (including the reporting period in which the financial asset was reclassified) until derecognition of the financial asset, the fair value gain or loss that would have been recognised in profit or loss or other comprehensive income if the financial asset had not been reclassified, and the gain, loss, income and expense recognised in profit or loss; and

(f) the effective interest rate and estimated amounts of cash flows the entity expects to recover, as at the date of reclassification of the financial asset.

The IASB requires extensive disclosures for reclassifications out of FVTPL and out of AFS to loans and receivables because of the significant effect these reclassifications can have on the financial statements. [IFRS 7:BC23A]

4.1.5 Transfers of financial assets

When an entity transfers financial assets they may continue to be recognised, derecognised in full, or partly derecognised to the extent of the transferor's continuing involvement. The derecognition requirements of IAS 39 are extensive and are discussed at length in **chapter C8**.

IFRS 7 requires specific disclosures relating to transfers of financial assets because it is considered to be important for users of financial statements to be able to evaluate the significance of such transactions and the risks retained, the nature of the risks and rewards to which the entity continues to be exposed, and the extent of its continuing involvement with the transferred asset.

Irrespective of whether an entity applies the October 2010 amendments, IAS 1.122 requires an entity to disclose the judgements that management has made in the process of applying its accounting policies. IAS 1:123(b) makes specific reference to disclosure of the judgements made in determining when substantially all the significant risks and rewards of ownership of financial assets and lease assets are transferred to other entities.

The disclosures for transfers of financial assets required by IFRS 7 are by class of financial asset and can be provided either by type of financial assets (i.e. differentiating by characteristics of the assets) or by type of risks or rewards of ownership to which the entity remains exposed.

In October 2010, the IASB issued amendments to IFRS 7, *Disclosures – Transfers of Financial Assets*, which substantially changed the disclosure requirements regarding transfers of financial assets. These extensive disclosures are required to be presented in a single note in the financial statements for all transferred financial assets that are not derecognised and for any continuing involvement in a transferred asset, existing at the reporting date, irrespective of when the related transfer transaction occurred. [IFRS 7:42A] This has the effect of requiring extensive disclosures regarding transfers that arose in periods prior to the comparative period.

The objective of the disclosures is to help users of financial statements:

[IFRS 7:42B]

(a) to understand the relationship between transferred financial assets that are not derecognised in their entirety and the associated liabilities; and

(b) to evaluate the nature of and risks associated with the entity's continuing involvement in derecognised financial assets.

In addition to the specific disclosures required under IFRS 7:42D - 42G, an entity is required to disclose any information that it considers necessary to meet the disclosure objective described in IFRS 7:42B. [IFRS 7:42H] The scope of the disclosure requirements extend to all transfers of all or part of a financial asset ('the transferred asset') if, and only if, either the transferor:

[IFRS 7:42A]

(a) transfers the contractual rights to receive the cash flows of that financial asset; or

(b) retains the contractual rights to receive the cash flows of that financial asset, but assumes a contractual obligation to pay the cash flows to one or more recipients in an arrangement.

The scope of IFRS 7's disclosure requirements regarding transferred financial assets (as set out in IFRS 7:42A immediately above) differs from the definition of a transfer in IAS 39:18 for the purposes of determining whether the transferred asset is derecognised; IFRS 7:42A(a) is the same as IAS 39:18(a), but IFRS 7:42A(b) is not the same as IAS 39:18(b). An arrangement whereby the transferor retains the contractual rights to receive the cash flows of the financial asset but assumes an obligation to pay the cash flows to one or more recipients is only regarded as a transfer under IAS 39 if it passes all three of the pass-through tests in IAS 39:19. Meeting the pass-through tests is not a requirement for the arrangement to fall within the scope of IFRS 7:42A because the IFRS 7 disclosure requirements are intended to be broader and to capture transactions where the all three of the pass- through tests are not necessarily met.

In September 2014, the IASB issued *Annual Improvements to IFRSs 2012-2014 Cycle*. The amendment clarifies how an entity should apply the guidance in IFRS 7:42C to a servicing contract in order to decide whether a servicing contract is 'continuing involvement' for the purposes of applying the disclosure requirements in IFRS 7:42E-H. Servicing agreements can arise when an entity transfers a financial asset but retains the right to service that asset for a fee. The amendment provides an example where a servicer will have continuing involvement in the transferred asset if the servicing fee is dependent on the amount or timing of the cash flows collected from the transferred asset. Another example provided notes that a servicer has continuing involvement if a fixed fee would not be paid in full because of non-performance of the transferred financial asset. In these two examples, the servicer has an interest in the future performance of the transferred asset.

The amendments apply retrospectively for annual periods beginning on or after 1 January 2016, except for any period presented that begins before the annual period for which the entity first applies the amendments. Earlier application is permitted in which case an entity shall disclose that it has applied those amendments for an earlier period.

The disclosure requirements in IFRS 7 prior to the October 2010 amendments (contained in IFRS 7:13 – see **4.1.5.1**), relating to assets that continue to be recognised in part or in full, are retained in the revised IFRS 7 because the Board considers that these requirements still provide relevant information to users of financial statements. The amendments to IFRS 7 introduce additional disclosure requirements regarding the nature of the relationship between transferred assets and associated liabilities, including restrictions on the transferor's use of the transferred asset, and additional disclosures when the transferee has recourse only to the transferred assets. Following the October 2010 amendments, all of these requirements are set out in IFRS 7:42D.

When a transferred asset is not derecognised in its entirety, the transferor is required to disclose:

[IFRS 7:42D]

(a) the nature of the transferred assets;

(b) the nature of the risks and rewards of ownership to which the entity is exposed;

(c) a description of the nature of the relationship between the transferred assets and the associated liabilities, including restrictions arising from the transfer on the reporting entity's use of the transferred assets;

(d) when the counterparty (counterparties) to the associated liabilities has (have) recourse only to the transferred assets, a schedule that sets out the fair value of the transferred assets, the fair value of the associated liabilities and the net position (the difference between the fair value of the transferred assets and the associated liabilities);

(e) when the entity continues to recognise all of the transferred assets, the carrying amounts of the transferred assets and the associated liabilities; and

(f) when the entity continues to recognise the assets to the extent of its continuing involvement (see IAS 39:20(c)(ii) & 30), the total carrying amount of the original assets before the transfer, the carrying amount of the assets that the entity continues to recognise, and the carrying amount of the associated liabilities.

The Board considered that additional disclosures regarding the nature of the relationship between the transferred assets and associated liabilities was necessary in order for users to understand the economic benefit generated by assets of an entity that cannot be used in an unrestricted manner. Without this disclosure, users could incorrectly conclude that, because transferred assets continue to be recognised, the transferor has unlimited rights to the economic benefits from those assets, even though as a result of the transfer the transferee has a part or a full beneficial interest in the economic benefits of the transferred assets. Further, requiring additional disclosures when associated liabilities will be settled entirely from the proceeds received from the transferred assets ensures that users understand whether a transferee only has claims against the transferred assets as opposed to having claims against the assets of the transferor in general. [IFRS 7:BC65H]

Prior to the October 2010 amendments to IFRS 7, the disclosure requirements in IFRS 7 only related to transfers of assets where the transferred asset continued to be recognised either in full or partly to the extent of the transferor's continuing involvement. The amendments to IFRS 7 retain this focus but also add extensive disclosure requirements for transfers of financial assets that are derecognised. The introduction of disclosures regarding derecognised assets where the transferor retains some continuing exposure to the transferred asset provides a more comprehensive picture of the entity's exposure to risk as a result of transferring financial assets.

Example 4.1.5A

Transferred financial assets that are not derecognised in their entirety

[IFRS 7:IG40C]

Illustrating the application of IFRS 7:42D(d) and (e)

	Financial assets at fair value through profit or loss		**Loans and receivables**		**Available-for-sale financial assets**
	CU million		**CU million**		**CU million**
	Trading securities	**Derivatives**	**Mortgages**	**Consumer loans**	**Equity investments**
Carrying amount of assets	X	X	X	X	X
Carrying amount of associated liabilities	(X)	(X)	(X)	(X)	(X)
For those liabilities that recourse only to the transferred assets:					
Fair value of assets	X	X	X	X	X
Fair value of associated liabilities	(X)	(X)	(X)	(X)	(X)
Net position	X	X	X	X	X

The disclosure requirements of IFRS 7:42D apply only in respect of transferred assets that have not been derecognised in full. A transferred asset will not be derecognised in full if either (a) the transferor retains substantially all the risks and rewards of ownership of the transferred asset, or (b) the transferor neither transfers nor retains substantially all the risks of rewards of ownership of the transferred asset but continues to control the transferred asset. Examples of arrangements that would meet these requirements and, therefore, be subject to the disclosures requirements of IFRS 7:42D are:

- a transfer of a financial asset with an obligation to repurchase the transferred asset in the future at a fixed price;
- a transfer of a financial asset where the transferor has an option to buy the transferred asset back at a fixed price and, at the date of transfer, the option strike price is deeply in the money;
- a transfer of a financial asset where the transferee has the right to require the transferor to repurchase the transferred asset back at a fixed price and, at the date of transfer, the option strike price is deeply in the money.
- a transfer of a financial asset where the transferor has an option to buy the transferred asset back at a fixed price and, at the date of transfer, the option strike price is neither deeply in nor deeply out of the money and the asset is not readily obtainable in the market;
- a transfer of a financial asset where the transferee has the right to require the transferor to repurchase the transferred asset back at a fixed price and, at the date of transfer, the option strike price is neither deeply in nor deeply out of the money and the asset is not readily obtainable in the market;
- a transfer of a financial asset where the transferor has written a financial guarantee (or provided other credit enhancement) to the transferee agreeing to reimburse the transferee for credit losses suffered on the transferred asset and, at the date of transfer, the financial guarantee contract results in the transferor retaining substantially all the risks and rewards of ownership; and
- a transfer of a financial asset where the transferor has written a financial guarantee (or providing other credit enhancement) to the transferee agreeing to reimburse the transferee for credit losses suffered on the transferred asset and, at the date of transfer, the financial guarantee contract results in the transferor neither retaining nor transferring substantially all the risks and rewards of ownership of the transferred asset, and the transferor controls the transferred assets.

If a transferred asset is derecognised and the transferor retains a 'continuing involvement' in the transferred financial asset IFRS 7 requires the transferor to provide extensive disclosures. A transferor has a continuing involvement in the transferred asset if, as part of the transfer, the transferor retains any of the contractual rights or obligations inherent in the transferred financial asset or obtains any new contractual rights or obligations relating to the transferred financial asset. The following do not constitute continuing involvement:

[IFRS 7:42C]

(a) normal representations and warranties relating to fraudulent transfer and concepts of reasonableness, good faith and fair dealings that could invalidate a transfer as a result of legal action;

(b) forward, option and other contracts to reacquire the transferred financial asset for which the contract price (or exercise price) is the fair value of the transferred financial asset; or

(c) an arrangement whereby an entity retains the contractual rights to receive the cash flows of a financial asset but assumes a contractual obligation to pay the cash flows to one or more entities and the conditions in IAS 39:19(a)-(c) are met.

The use of the term 'continuing involvement' for IFRS 7 disclosures should not be confused with the continuing involvement derecognition requirements in IAS 39:20(c)(ii) & 30. An asset that is derecognised to the extent of the transferor's continuing involvement in accordance with IAS 39 would be subject to the disclosure requirements in IFRS 7:42D described above because the transferred asset is not derecognised in its entirety. This compares with the specific disclosures required in IFRS 7:42E-H when an asset is derecognised but the transferor retains some continuing involvement. It is unfortunate that both terms are used to apply to transfers of financial assets, one for applying the derecognition requirements and one for applying the disclosure requirements, but their application applies to different subsets of transferred assets.

When the transferor derecognises the transferred asset in its entirety but has some continuing involvement in the asset, the transferor is required to disclose, as a minimum, for each type of continuing involvement at each reporting date:

[IFRS 7:42E]

(a) the carrying amount of the assets and liabilities that are recognised in the entity's statement of financial position and represent the entity's continuing involvement in the derecognised financial assets, and the line items in which the carrying amount of those assets and liabilities are recognised;

(b) the fair value of the assets and liabilities that represent the entity's continuing involvement in the derecognised financial assets;

(c) the amount that best represents the entity's maximum exposure to loss from its continuing involvement in the derecognised financial assets, and information showing how the maximum exposure to loss is determined;

(d) the undiscounted cash outflows that would or may be required to repurchase derecognised financial assets (e.g. the strike price in an option agreement) or other amounts payable to the transferee in respect of the transferred assets. If the cash outflow is variable, then the amount disclosed should be based on the conditions that exist at each reporting date;

Example 4.1.5B

Transferred financial assets that are derecognised in their entirety

[IFRS 7:IG40C]

Illustrating the application of IFRS 7:42E(a)-(d)

	Cash outflows to repurchase transferred (derecognised) assets	**Carrying amount of continuing involvement in statement of financial position**			**Fair value of continuing involvement**		**Maximum exposure to loss**
	CU million	**CU million**			**CU million**		**CU million**
Type of continuing involvement		**Held for trading**	**Available-for -sale financial assets**	**Financial liabilities at fair value through profit or loss**	**Assets**	**Liabilities**	
Written put options	(X)			(X)		(X)	X
Purchased call options	(X)	X			X		X
Securities lending	(X)		X	(X)	X	(X)	X
Total		X	X	(X)	X	(X)	X

(e) a maturity analysis of the undiscounted cash outflows that would or may be required to repurchase the derecognised financial assets or other amounts payable to the transferee in respect of the transferred assets, showing the remaining contractual maturities of the entity's continuing involvement;

Example 4.1.5C

Transferred financial assets that are derecognised in their entirety

[IFRS 7:IG40B]

Illustrating the application of IFRS 7:42E(e)

Undiscounted cash flows to repurchase transferred assets

	Maturity of continuing involvement CU million							
Type of continuing involvement	**Total**	**less than 1 month**	**1-3 months**	**3-6 months**	**6 months - 1 year**	**1-3 years**	**3-5 years**	**more than 5 years**
Written put options	X		X	X	X	X		
Purchased call options	X			X	X	X		X
Securities lending	X	X	X					

(f) qualitative information that explains and supports the quantitative disclosures required in (a) – (e).

The disclosures required by IFRS 7:42E may be aggregated in respect of a particular asset if the transferor has more than one type of continuing involvement in that derecognised financial asset, and reported under one type of continuing involvement. [IFRS 7:42F]

In many cases, the existence of a continuing exposure to a transferred asset will result in the asset not being derecognised, in which case the disclosure requirements of IFRS 7:42E-H do not apply. The disclosure requirements of IFRS 7:42E-H should be applied in circumstances where, even though the transferor retains a continuing exposure to the transferred asset, the transferred asset is still derecognised. This is the case when the transferor either (a) does not retain substantially all the risks and rewards of ownership of the transferred asset following the transfer or, (b) if it did not transfer or retain substantially all the risks of rewards of ownership of the transferred asset, it also does not control the transferred asset. Examples of arrangements that would result in derecognition of the transferred asset despite some continuing involvement and which, therefore, would be subject to the disclosure requirements of IFRS 7:42E-H are:

- a transfer of a financial asset where the transferor has an option to buy the transferred asset back at a fixed price but, at the date of transfer, the option strike price is deeply out of the money;
- a transfer of a financial asset where the transferee has the right to require the transferor to repurchase the transferred asset back at a fixed price but, at the date of transfer, the option strike price is deeply out of the money;
- a transfer of a financial asset where the transferor has an option to buy the transferred asset back at a fixed price but, at the date of transfer, the option strike price is neither deeply in nor deeply out of the money and the asset is readily obtainable in the market;

- a transfer of a financial asset where the transferee has the right to require the transferor to repurchase the transferred asset back at a fixed price but, at the date of transfer, the option strike price is neither deeply in nor deeply out of the money and the asset is readily obtainable in the market;
- a transfer of a financial asset where the transferor has written a financial guarantee (or other credit enhancement) to the transferee agreeing to reimburse the transferee for credit losses suffered on the transferred asset, but, at the date of transfer, the financial guarantee contract does not prevent the transferor from transferring substantially all the risks and rewards of ownership; and
- a transfer of a financial asset where the transferor has written a financial guarantee (or other credit enhancement) to the transferee agreeing to reimburse the transferee for credit losses suffered on the transferred asset, but, at the date of transfer, the financial guarantee contract results in the transferor neither retaining nor transferring substantially all the risks and rewards of ownership of the transferred asset and the transferor does not control the transferred assets.

For each type of continuing involvement, the transferor is also required to disclose:

[IFRS 7:42G]

(a) the gain or loss recognised at the date of transfer of the assets;

(b) income and expenses recognised, both in the reporting period and cumulatively, from the entity's continuing involvement in the derecognised financial assets (e.g. fair value changes in derivative instruments); and

(c) if the total amount of proceeds from transfer activity (that qualifies for derecognition) in a reporting period is not evenly distributed throughout the reporting period (e.g. if a substantial proportion of the total amount of transfer activity takes place in the closing days of a reporting period):

    (i) when the greatest transfer activity took place within that reporting period (e.g. the last five days before the end of the reporting period);

    (ii) the amount (e.g. related gains or losses) recognised from transfer activity in that part of the reporting period; and

    (iii) the total amount of proceeds from transfer activity in that part of the reporting period.

Entities are required to provide this information for each period for which a statement of comprehensive income is presented.

The Board considered that disclosure of the gain or loss on derecognition and the timing of recognition of that gain or loss as required by IFRS 7:42G(a) is useful information because it illustrates the proportion of an entity's profit or loss that arises from transferred financial assets in which the entity also has a continuing involvement. This information is useful in assessing the extent to which an entity generates profits from transferring financial assets while retaining some form of continuing involvement and thus exposure to risk. [IFRS 7:BC65M]

The requirement for extensive disclosure if the transfer activity during the period is not evenly distributed was introduced to highlight instances of potential 'window dressing' where the transfer transaction might have been undertaken for the purpose of altering the appearance of the statement of financial position at the reporting date rather than for an ongoing commercial or financing purpose. [IFRS 7:BC65N]

4.1.6 Collateral

An entity is required to disclose the carrying amount of financial assets it has pledged as collateral (non-cash financial assets) for liabilities or contingent liabilities, including amounts the transferor has reclassified in accordance with IAS 39:37(a) when the transferee has the right to sell or pledge the collateral. The entity is also required to disclose the terms and conditions relating to its pledge. [IFRS 7:14] The terms and conditions may include:

- how much collateral needs to be maintained as security for the loans; and
- the type of collateral that needs to be provided as security for the loans.

When an entity holds collateral (both financial and non-financial assets) as security for financial assets loaned to another entity and it is permitted to sell or repledge in the absence of default by the owner of the collateral, the entity is required to disclose:

[IFRS 7:15]

- the fair value of the collateral held;
- the fair value of any such collateral that has been sold or repledged, and whether the entity has an obligation to return it; and
- the terms and conditions associated with its use of the collateral.

The disclosure of the existence of such collateral is important because it provides information to users of the financial statements regarding the amount of collateral used and available for use that may not be recognised in the statement of financial position of the entity.

Disclosure of collateral that the entity does not have the right to sell or pledge in the absence of default by the borrower is required in the credit risk disclosures note – see **5.2.1.2**.

4.1.7 Allowance account for credit losses

When financial assets are impaired by credit losses, and the entity recognises the impairment in a separate allowance account rather than by directly reducing the carrying amount of the assets, the entity is required to present a reconciliation of changes in that allowance account during the period. [IFRS 7:16] This disclosure is required by class of financial asset. The reconciliation is useful in assessing the adequacy of the allowance for impairment losses and enables comparison between entities.

IFRS 7 does not, however, specify which components of the reconciliation are required to be separately presented in order to allow preparers flexibility in determining the most appropriate format for their needs. [IFRS 7:BC26]

For example, the reconciliation of the allowance account for credit losses could be presented with the following line items.

Opening balance	XX
Plus: impairment losses recognised	XX
Less: reversals of impairment losses	XX
Less: amounts written off during the year	XX
Plus/less: exchange gains and losses on foreign currency denominated items	XX
Plus: unwind of discount	XX
Closing balance	XX

Entities may wish to expand on each of the above items. For instance:

- impairment losses recognised could be analysed between losses due to breach of contract, bankruptcy of the underlying debtor, adverse changes in payment status of borrowers and national or local economic conditions that correlate with defaults on the assets in the group, and increases due to increases in effective interest rates (floating rate debt);
- reversals of impairment losses could similarly be analysed according to the underlying cause of the reversal; and
- amounts written off during the year could be analysed, for example, by type of exposure, type of client, geographical or industry segment.

The allowance account may be expanded to include any other items that the preparer of the financial statements considers to be material to users' understanding of the financial statements.

4.1.8 Compound financial instruments with multiple embedded derivatives

IAS 32 prescribes how a compound financial instrument should be separated into its liability and equity components. For a compound financial instrument, the value of the debt or equity component may be affected by the other component. For instance, for convertible debt, the value of the debt component may depend in part on the relative attractiveness of early conversion. Therefore, the aggregate fair value of the convertible bond could differ from the sum of the estimated fair values of the debt and equity components if these were valued independently. IAS 32 assigns the full value of these interdependencies to the liability component and treats equity as the residual. This allocation is arbitrary and could be argued to misstate the amount of the liability and, thereby, misstate the 'true' interest cost.

The interdependencies become even more significant when a compound instrument contains multiple embedded features whose values are also interdependent. For example, the values of an embedded purchased call option and a written equity conversion option in a callable convertible debt instrument depend in part on each other; because the equity conversion option is extinguished if the issuer exercises its purchased call option to redeem early, and vice versa, the value of the issuer purchased call option depends on the likelihood that the holder will exercise its right to convert early into shares. Because of the importance of these features, IFRS 7:17 requires an issuer of a compound instrument that has multiple embedded derivatives whose values are interdependent to disclose the existence of those features.

4.1.9 Defaults and breaches

For loans payable recognised at the end of the reporting period, disclosure is required of any defaults during the period of principal, interest, sinking fund, or redemption terms. In addition, the entity is required to disclose the carrying amount of any such loans that are in default at the end of the reporting period and whether the default was remedied, or the terms of the loans payable were renegotiated, before the financial statements were authorised for issue. [IFRS 7:18] Loans payable are defined as "financial liabilities, other than short-term trade payables on normal credit terms". [IFRS 7:Appendix A] It is important to note that disclosure regarding defaults is required even when those defaults were rectified by the end of the reporting period.

If, during the period, there were breaches of loan agreement terms other than those described in the IFRS 7:18 (see previous paragraph), the entity is required to disclose the same information as required by IFRS 7:18 if those breaches permitted the lender to demand accelerated repayment (unless the breaches were remedied, or the terms of the loan were renegotiated, on or before the end of the reporting period). [IFRS 7:19] Examples of such defaults include breaches of collateral requirements or loan covenant features, or a failure to administer the loan in terms of the loan agreement.

Such disclosures are designed to provide the users with relevant information about the entity's creditworthiness and its prospects for obtaining future loans. [IFRS 7:BC32]

The presentation of such loans as either current or non-current in accordance with the requirements of IAS 1 may also be affected by such defaults.

4.2 Disclosures relating to the statement of comprehensive income

IFRS 7 requires disclosure of specified income, expense, gains or loss items either in the statement of comprehensive income or in the notes to the financial statements.

4.2.1 Net gains or net losses

An entity is required to disclose in the statement of comprehensive income or in the notes the net gains or net losses for:

[IFRS 7:20(a)]

(i) financial assets or financial liabilities at fair value through profit or loss, showing separately those relating to financial assets or financial liabilities designated as such upon initial recognition, and those relating to financial assets or financial liabilities that are classified as held for trading in accordance with IAS 39;
(ii) available-for-sale financial assets, showing separately the amount of gain or loss recognised in other comprehensive income during the period and the amount reclassified from equity to profit or loss for the period;
(iii) held-to-maturity investments;
(iv) loans and receivables; and
(v) financial liabilities measured at amortised cost;

The disclosures required by IFRS 7:20(a) are intended to assist users in understanding the extent to which accounting policies affect the performance of the entity and in understanding the nature of such gains and losses. [IFRS 7:BC33] The disclosures also provide useful financial information, together with the disclosure of the carrying amounts by category of financial instruments, which is designed to allow users to appraise management on the manner in which it has classified financial instruments and, ultimately, its decisions to buy, sell or hold financial assets and to incur, maintain or discharge financial liabilities.

IFRS 7:BC33 states that the disclosure of gains and losses analysed by IAS 39's measurement categories complements the disclosures regarding the statement of financial position described in **section 4.1**. Despite this claim, it would appear that there is a difference between the disclosure requirements regarding the statement of financial position and the statement of comprehensive income. As explained in **section 4.1**, IFRS 7:8 requires disclosure of the carrying amounts of: financial assets *and* financial liabilities designated at FVTPL upon initial recognition, as well as financial assets *and* financial liabilities classified as held for trading in accordance with IAS 39. The equivalent requirements regarding the statement of comprehensive income refer to financial assets *or* financial liabilities. It is reasonable to presume this difference in wording was an oversight in the drafting and, therefore, an entity should disclose information on net gain or net losses in relation to *both* financial assets *and* financial liabilities.

Derivative financial instruments (or non-derivative financial instruments when hedging foreign currency risk) that have been designated as effective hedging instruments are not included in any of the financial instrument categories. Instead, any fair value movements relating to those instruments will be reported under the hedge accounting disclosure requirements.

4.2.2 Interest income and interest expense

IFRS 7 requires disclosure of total interest income and total interest expense, determined using the effective interest method, for financial assets or financial liabilities that are not classified as at fair value through profit or loss. [IFRS 7:20(b)]

Total interest expense is a component of the finance costs that are required to be disclosed as a line item in the statement of comprehensive income in accordance with IAS 1:82(b). Finance costs that are required to be disclosed in accordance with IAS 1 may also include amounts that arise on non-financial liabilities such as pension liabilities and income taxes. Separate disclosure of total interest expense allows users of the financial statements to understand the extent to which financial instruments contribute to finance costs.

4.2.3 Fee income and expense

IFRS 7 requires disclosure of fee income and expense, other than those amounts that are included in determining the effective interest rate, that arise from financial assets or financial liabilities that are not at fair value through profit or loss. [IFRS 7:20(c)(i)] Such items include:

[IAS 39:AG8C]

(a) fees charged for servicing a loan;

(b) commitment fees to originate a loan when the loan commitment is outside the scope of IAS 39 and it is unlikely that a specific lending arrangement will be entered into; and

(c) loan syndication fees received by an entity that arranges a loan and retains no part of the loan package for itself (or retains a part at the same effective interest rate for comparable risk as other participants).

In addition, disclosure is required of trust and other fiduciary activities that result in the holding or investing of assets on behalf of individuals, trusts, retirement benefit plans, and other institutions. [IFRS 7:20(c)(ii)] This information indicates the level of such activities and helps users to estimate possible future income of the entity. [IFRS 7:BC35]

The extent of disclosure required under IFRS 7:20(c)(i) will depend on the type of business. Lenders are likely to be subject to a significant level of disclosure. Examples of fees will include annual membership fee income for credit cards (payable irrespective of whether the card holder uses the card); interchange fees received each time a credit card is used; merchant service commission fees for processing debit and credit transactions; fees for withdrawing cash on a credit card; overdraft fee income received irrespective of whether the borrower utilises the overdraft facility etc. Many fees with respect to specific borrowing and lending will meet the definition of a transaction cost and, therefore, will form part of the effective interest rate (and, thereby, will not be subject to separate disclosure).

4.2.4 Interest on impaired financial assets

IFRS 7 requires interest income on impaired financial assets to be disclosed. The interest income is determined using the rate of interest used to discount the future cash flows for the purposes of measuring the impairment loss. [IFRS 7:20(d)]

The requirements of IFRS 7:20(d) merit careful consideration in the context of financial assets impaired on a portfolio basis (see **5.2.4** in **chapter C6**).

If a loan within a portfolio is not individually assessed as being impaired, but is impaired on a collective basis prior to the loan being individually identified, and all cash flows with respect to the impaired loan are not recoverable, then no interest income will be disclosed in accordance with IFRS 7:20(d). In such circumstances, following the impairment loss, there is no interest income on the loan as the loan is fully impaired (because no cash flows are expected).

In contrast, the entity may determine that an impairment loss is required in circumstances where some, but not all, cash flows on unidentified loans are not recoverable. For disclosure of interest income on impaired financial assets, the entity should use the effective interest rate that was used to discount the cash flows in determining the impairment loss. Even though the loans that are impaired are not yet identified, the entity is still required to disclose the amount of interest on the portfolio of loans that is impaired.

If an impairment loss is recognised in the period but is reversed prior to the end of the period, an entity should still disclose the interest that arose during the part of the reporting period that the loan was impaired. Because interest will be recognised throughout the instrument's life, the entity will need to isolate the period immediately following the impairment event and prior to the impairment loss being reversed and determine the interest that was recognised during that period.

4.2.5 Impairment losses

IFRSs require disclosure of the amount of any impairment loss for each class of financial asset. [IFRS 7:20(e)]

4.3 Other disclosures

4.3.1 Accounting policies

IAS 1.117 requires disclosure of the measurement bases used in preparing the financial statements and the other accounting policies used that are relevant to an understanding of the financial statements. For financial instruments, these would normally include:

[IFRS 7:B5]

(a) for financial assets or financial liabilities designated as at fair value through profit or loss:
   - (i) the nature of the financial assets or financial liabilities that have been designated as at fair value through profit or loss;
   - (ii) the criteria for so designating financial assets or financial liabilities on initial recognition; and
   - (iii) how the entity has satisfied the criteria in IAS 39 for such designation. That disclosure includes a narrative description of the circumstances underlying the measurement or recognition inconsistency that would otherwise arise and a narrative description of how designation at fair value through profit or loss is consistent with the entity's documented risk management or investment strategy where applicable.

(b) the criteria for designating financial assets as available for sale.

(c) whether regular way purchases and sales of financial assets are accounted for at trade date or at settlement date;

(d) when an allowance account is used to reduce the carrying amount of financial assets impaired by credit losses:

  (i) the criteria for determining when the carrying amount of impaired financial assets is reduced directly (or, in the case of a reversal of a write-down, increased directly) and when the allowance account is used; and

  (ii) the criteria for writing off amounts charged to the allowance account against the carrying amount of impaired financial assets;

(e) how net gains or net losses on each category of financial instrument are determined (e.g. whether the net gains or net losses on items at fair value through profit or loss include interest or dividend income);

It appears that the objective of the Standard in requiring an entity to disclose whether interest or dividends are shown separately from other fair value gains/losses is to make clear how interest and dividends are presented in income for non-derivative instruments that are carried at FVTPL. It is reasonable that if a derivative is not in a qualifying hedge relationship and, therefore, is classified as a held for trading instrument, movements in its fair value is a single number recognised in income and should not be split further across other profit or loss captions. This view is consistent with the SEC's view of US GAAP that if a derivative does not qualify for hedge accounting, income, expenses and fair value changes related to that derivative (whether realised or unrealised) must be presented in one line item in the financial statements and this line item must not change.

For non-derivative financial instruments carried at FVTPL, some entities include interest income and expense and dividend income in gains and losses on financial assets and financial liabilities respectively and others include them in separate line items for interest and dividends. The disclosure regarding whether net gains and losses on financial assets or financial liabilities that are carried as at FVTPL include interest income and expense or dividend income is designed to aid comparability between entities.

It seems reasonable to have a separate policy for interest-bearing instruments (e.g. debt) and non-interest-bearing instruments that earn a dividend (e.g. equity securities), but it is not acceptable to have a separate policy for interest-bearing assets and a separate policy for interest-bearing liabilities because this could result in overstating or understating interest income and expense.

(f) the criteria the entity uses to determine that there is objective evidence that an impairment loss has occurred;
(g) when the terms of financial assets that would otherwise be past due or impaired have been renegotiated, the accounting policy for financial assets that are the subject of renegotiated terms.

The disclosure required under IFRS 7:B5(g) is the entity's policy as to how it accounts for renegotiated debt assets; specifically, the entity should disclose how it determines whether the renegotiated debt is considered new debt (and, therefore, old debt is derecognised), or whether it is considered the original debt with the original effective interest rate and the carrying amount adjusted according to IAS 39:AG8 at the date of renegotiation. This disclosure would be relevant because the only guidance in IFRSs regarding the accounting for debt modifications relates to financial liabilities (in IAS 39:40 & AG62), and no guidance is provided for financial assets other than in the case of impairment. [IAS 39:IG.E.4.3]

Information that includes a description of the manner in which debt is renegotiated and the terms and conditions of the renegotiated debt may also provide valuable information.

4.3.2 Hedge accounting

Disclosures are required for entities that apply hedge accounting in accordance with IAS 39. [IFRS 7:22 - 24]

Hedging activities are integral to an entity's financial risk management and are often significant. Hedge accounting for such activities is a matter of choice under IAS 39 and this accounting choice can have a significant impact on the financial statements. In the absence of hedge accounting, changes in the fair value of all derivatives would be reflected in profit or loss as they arise, often creating a mismatch with the timing of recognition of the gains and losses on the exposure that is being hedged. Hedge accounting corrects this measurement or recognition mismatch.

Hedge accounting disclosures are provided to allow users of the financial statements to understand the nature of the entity's hedge relationships and the effect of those hedge relationships on the performance of the entity both during the current period and anticipated in future periods.

For each type of hedge accounting applied (fair value hedge, cash flow hedge, or a hedge of net investment in a foreign operation), the entity must disclose the following:

[IFRS 7:22]

(a) a description of each type of hedge;

(b) a description of the financial instruments designated as hedging instruments and their fair values at the end of the reporting period; and

(c) the nature of the risks being hedged.

Additional disclosures are required for cash flow hedges because the entity has to make significant judgements about the expectation of future cash flows that are being hedged. Also, because cash flow hedging requires recognition of gains/losses in other comprehensive income and frequent reclassification from equity to profit or loss, the Standard requires these amounts to be transparent. For cash flow hedges, an entity is required to disclose:

[IFRS 7:23]

(a) the periods when the cash flows are expected to occur and when they are expected to affect profit or loss;

(b) a description of any forecast transaction for which hedge accounting had previously been used, but which is no longer expected to occur;

(c) the amount that was recognised in other comprehensive income during the period;

(d) the amount that was reclassified from equity to profit or loss for the period, showing the amount included in each line item in the statement of comprehensive income; and

(e) the amount that was removed from equity during the period and included in the initial cost or other carrying amount of a non-financial asset or a non-financial liability whose acquisition or incurrence was a hedged highly probable forecast transaction.

IFRS 7 requires an entity to disclose the extent to which hedge accounting has been effective in the period. For cash flow hedges and hedges of a net investment in a foreign operation, the amount of ineffectiveness must be disclosed. [IFRS 7:24(b) & (c)]. This can be disclosed either in the statement of comprehensive income (because all hedge ineffectiveness is recognised in profit or loss) or alternatively in a note to the financial statements.

The disclosure requirements for fair value hedges are somewhat different, although the objective of disclosing hedge ineffectiveness is the same. In a fair value hedge, the gain or loss on the hedging instrument and the gain or loss on the hedged item are immediately recognised in profit or loss in all periods. The net of these amounts is equivalent to the hedge ineffectiveness that is recognised in profit or loss in the period. IFRS 7, therefore, requires an entity to disclose separately the gains or losses on the hedging instrument and on the hedged item that are attributable to the hedged risk. [IFRS 7:24(a)] These may be disclosed either in the statement of comprehensive income or alternatively in a note to the financial statements.

If a fair value hedge is not highly effective (i.e. hedge effectiveness is outside the 80-125 per cent range), then hedge accounting cannot be applied for the period. The entity has not achieved hedge accounting and, consequently, is not required to disclose hedge ineffectiveness for that period with respect to that designated hedge.

For cash flow hedges and hedges of a net investment in a foreign operation, if the hedge is not highly effective in the period (i.e. it is outside the 80 - 125 per cent range), hedge accounting is not applied in the period. The gains or losses on the hedging instrument will be recognised directly in profit or loss. The entity is not required to disclose hedge ineffectiveness. If previously designated forecast transactions are no longer expected to occur, this will generally result in reclassification from equity to profit or loss for some or all of the cumulative gains/losses brought forward from the prior period recognised in other comprehensive income (and accumulated in the cash flow hedging reserve in equity). This amount must be disclosed along with the other disclosures listed above.

4.3.3 Fair value

IFRS 7 requires fair value information to be provided for all financial assets and liabilities (with limited exceptions, see **4.3.3.1**). An entity is required to disclose the fair value of that class of assets and liabilities in a way that permits it to be compared with its carrying amount. In disclosing fair values, an entity shall group financial assets and financial liabilities into classes, but shall offset them only to the extent that their carrying amounts are offset in the statement of financial position. [IFRS 7:25 & 26]

IFRS 13 requires disclose of information that helps users of its financial statements assess both of the following:

[IFRS 13:91]

(a) for assets and liabilities that are measured at fair value on a recurring or non-recurring basis in the statement of financial position after initial recognition, the valuation techniques and inputs used to develop those measurements.

(b) for recurring fair value measurements using significant unobservable inputs (Level 3) (see **7.3** in **chapter C7**), the effect of the measurements on profit or loss or other comprehensive income for the period.

To meet the objectives above, an entity shall consider all the following:

[IFRS 13:92]

(a) the level of detail necessary to satisfy the disclosure requirements;

(b) how much emphasis to place on each of the various requirements;

(c) how much aggregation or disaggregation to undertake; and

(d) whether users of financial statements need additional information to evaluate the quantitative information disclosed.

To meet the objectives in IFRS 13:91 the standard requires minimum disclosures that are aggregated by class of assets and liabilities. If the disclosures provided in accordance with IFRS 13 and other IFRSs are insufficient to meet the objectives described above in IFRS 13:91, an entity shall disclose additional information necessary to meet those objectives.

The amount of the disclosure required by IFRS 13 depends on whether IAS 39 requires the financial asset or financial liability to be measured at fair value in the statement of financial position. The greatest amount of disclosure is required for those assets or liabilities subsequently measured at fair value in the statement of financial position on a recurring basis. Most, but not all, of these disclosures are required for those assets and liabilities that are measured at fair value on a non-recurring basis. A recurring fair value measurement is where IFRSs require or permit in the statement of financial position the asset or liability to be subsequently measured at fair value at the end of each reporting period. A non-recurring fair value is where IFRSs require or permit in the statement of financial position the asset or liability to be subsequently measured at fair value in particular circumstances, i.e. not necessarily at the end of each reporting period. [IFRS 13:93(a)]

Financial instruments subsequently measured in the statement of financial position at fair value are generally recurring fair value measurements. Examples include financial assets and financial liabilities that are measured at fair value through profit or loss and investments in equity instruments designated as at fair value through other comprehensive income. IAS 39 permits non-recurring fair value measurement in limited circumstances. An example is the practical expedient offered in IAS 39:AG84 where an entity may determine impairment of a financial asset carried at amortised cost on the basis of an instrument's fair value using an observable market price.

Recurring and non-recurring fair value measurements include only those assets or liabilities measured at fair value in the statement of financial position. Financial instruments measured at amortised cost that are fair value hedge adjusted are not recurring or non-recurring fair value measurements because they are not measured at fair value.

4.3.3.1 Exceptions from fair value disclosures for financial instruments

IFRS 7 provides limited exceptions from fair value disclosures for financial instruments. IFRS 7:29 does not require disclosure of fair value:

- when the carrying amount is a reasonable approximation of fair value, for example, for financial instruments such as short-term trade receivables and payables;
- for a contract containing a discretionary participation feature (as described in IFRS 4) if the fair value of that feature cannot be measured reliably.

However, when fair value cannot be measured reliably, additional disclosures are required to assist users of the financial statements in making their own judgements about the extent of possible differences between the carrying amount of those financial assets or financial liabilities and their fair value. These disclosures include:

[IFRS 7:30]

- a statement that fair value information has not been disclosed for these instruments because their fair value cannot be measured reliably;
- a description of the financial instruments, their carrying amount, and an explanation of why fair value cannot be measured reliably;
- information about the market for the instruments;
- information about whether and how the entity intends to dispose of the financial instruments; and
- if such instruments are subsequently derecognised, the carrying amount at the date of disposal, the fact that fair value could not be reliably measured, and the gain or loss that results.

4.3.3.2 Summary of fair value disclosures

The minimum disclosures required by IFRS 13 that relate to financial instruments are summarised below. Many of the disclosures are based on the fair value hierarchy as described in IFRS 13 which is described in detail in **section 10** in **chapter C7**.

	Assets and liabilities measured at fair value in the statement of financial position after the date of initial recognition		
Required disclosure:	**Recurring**	**Non-recurring**	**Fair value disclosed in the notes to the financial statements**
Fair value at the reporting date. [IFRS 13:93(a) & 97, IFRS 7.25]	✓	✓	✓
Reason for the fair value measurement. [IFRS 13:93(a)]		✓	
The level of the fair value measurement in the fair value hierarchy. [IFRS 13:93(b)]	✓	✓	✓

	Assets and liabilities measured at fair value in the statement of financial position after the date of initial recognition		
Required disclosure:	**Recurring**	**Non-recurring**	**Fair value disclosed in the notes to the financial statements**
For assets and liabilities held at the end of the reporting period, amounts of any transfers between Levels 1 and 2 (separately for transfers into and out of each level), the reasons for those transfers, and the entity's policy for determining that a transfer has occurred. [IFRS 13:93(c)]	✓		
For Levels 2 and 3 measurements, a description of the valuation techniques and inputs used. [IFRS 13:93(d)]	✓	✓	✓
For Level 2 and 3 measurements for which there has been a change in valuation technique, the nature of that change and the reason for it. [IFRS 13:93(d)]	✓	✓	✓
Information sufficient to permit reconciliation between the amounts disclosed for classes of assets and liabilities by level of the fair value hierarchy and the line items presented in the statement of financial position. [IFRS 13:94]	✓	✓	Not required by IFRS 13 but for financial instruments required by IFRS 7:6
If an entity chooses as its accounting policy to use the portfolio valuation exception permitted by IFRS 13:48, that fact. [IFRS 13:96]	✓		

	Assets and liabilities measured at fair value in the statement of financial position after the date of initial recognition		
Required disclosure:	**Recurring**	**Non-recurring**	**Fair value disclosed in the notes to the financial statements**
For a liability measured at fair value, the existence of any credit enhancement and whether it is reflected in the fair value measurement of the liability. [IFRS 13:98]	✓	✓	
The following disclosures only apply to Level 3 fair value measurements:			
Quantitative information about the significant unobservable inputs used in the fair value measurement. [IFRS 13:93(d)]	✓	✓	
Reconciliation of movements in fair value from opening to closing balances, showing separately: • total gains and losses recognised in profit or loss (including the line items in profit or loss); • total gains and losses recognised in other comprehensive income (including the line items in other comprehensive income); • purchases, sales, issues, settlements (each disclosed separately); and • the amounts of transfers into and out of Level 3 separately (including the reasons for those transfers and the entity's policy for determining that a transfer has occurred). [IFRS 13:93(e)]	✓		

	Assets and liabilities measured at fair value in the statement of financial position after the date of initial recognition		
Required disclosure:	**Recurring**	**Non-recurring**	**Fair value disclosed in the notes to the financial statements**
Amount of total gains or losses for the period recognised in profit or loss that is attributable to the change in unrealised gains or losses for those assets and liabilities held at the end of the reporting period, and the line items in profit or loss in which the gains or losses are recognised. IFRS 13:93(f)]	✓		
Description of the valuation processes used, including a description of how an entity the entity decides on valuation policies and procedures and how it analyses changes in fair value from period to period. [IFRS 13:93(g)]	✓	✓	
Narrative description of the sensitivity of the fair value measurement to changes in unobservable inputs if a change in those inputs might result in a significantly different fair value measurement and a description of the interrelationships between those inputs, if any, including how those interrelationships might magnify or mitigate the impact on fair value arising from changes in such inputs. The narrative description of the sensitivity should include, at a minimum, all significant unobservable inputs used in the fair value measurement. [IFRS 13:93(h)(i)]	✓		

	Assets and liabilities measured at fair value in the statement of financial position after the date of initial recognition		
Required disclosure:	**Recurring**	**Non-recurring**	**Fair value disclosed in the notes to the financial statements**
For financial assets and liabilities, when a change in one or more of the unobservable inputs to reflect reasonably possible alternative assumptions would change fair value significantly, that fact, the effect of those changes, and how the effect of such a change is calculated. [IFRS 13:93(h)(ii)]	✓		

The quantitative disclosures required by IFRS 13 shall be presented in a tabular format unless another format is more appropriate. [IFRS 13:99]

In addition, IFRS 7 requires specific disclosures in respect of 'day 1 profit or loss' which are detailed in **4.3.3.8**.

4.3.3.3 Financial instruments measured at fair value

For recurring and non-recurring fair value measurements an entity is required to disclose the fair value at the end of the reporting period and level within the fair value hierarchy within which the fair value measurement is categorised in their entirety (i.e. Level 1, 2 or 3). For non-recurring fair value measurements the reason for the measurement shall be disclosed. [IFRS 13:93(a) & (b)]

IFRS 13:IE60 provides an illustrative example of the disclosures required by IFRS 13:93(a) & (b)in the case of assets measured at fair value. The example has been reproduced below, however, excludes non-financial items that are not within the scope of this volume.

Example 4.3.3.3

Financial assets measured at fair value

[IFRS 13:IE60]

(CU in millions)		**Fair value measurements at the end of the reporting period using**		
		Quoted prices in active markets for identical assets	**Significant other observable inputs**	**Significant unobservable inputs**
Description	**31/12/X9**	**(Level 1)**	**(Level 2)**	**(Level 3)**
Recurring fair value measurements				
Trading equity securities[(a)]:				
Real estate industry	93	70	23	
Oil and gas industry	45	45		
Other	15	15		
Total trading equity securities	153	130	23	
Other equity securities[(a)]:				
Financial services industry	150	150		
Healthcare industry	163	110		53
Energy industry	32			32
Private equity fund investments[(b)]:	25			25
Other	15	15		
Total other equity securities	385	275		110
Debt securities:				
Residential mortgage-backed securities	149		24	125
Commercial mortgage-backed securities	50			50
Collateralised debt obligations	35			35
Risk-free government securities	85	85		
Corporate bonds	93	9	84	
Total debt securities	412	94	108	210
Hedge fund investments:				
Equity long/short	55		55	
Global opportunities	35		35	
High-yield debt securities	90			90

(CU in millions)		Fair value measurements at the end of the reporting period using		
		Quoted prices in active markets for identical assets	Significant other observable inputs	Significant unobservable inputs
Description	**31/12/X9**	**(Level 1)**	**(Level 2)**	**(Level 3)**
Recurring fair value measurements				
Total hedge fund investments	180		90	90
Derivatives:				
Interest rate contracts	57		57	
Foreign exchange contracts	43		43	
Credit contracts	38			38
Commodity futures contracts	78	78		
Commodity forward contracts	20		20	
Total derivatives	236	78	120	38

(a) On the basis of its analysis of the nature, characteristics and risks of the securities, the entity has determined that presenting them by industry is appropriate.

(b) On the basis of its analysis of the nature, characteristics and risks of the investments, the entity has determined that presenting them as a single class is appropriate.

(Note: A similar would be presented for liabilities unless another format is deemed more appropriate by the entity.)

IFRS 13 also requires that the amounts of transfers between Levels 1 and 2, the reasons for those transfers, and the entity's policy for determining when transfers between levels are deemed to have occurred shall be disclosed. [IFRS 13:93(c)]

The Standard provides guidance on what policy may be applied in determining when within the reporting period a transfer between levels of the fair value hierarchy occurs. An entity is required to disclose and consistently follow its policy for determining when those transfers have deemed to occur. This applies to both transfers in and out the levels. Examples of policies for determining the timing of transfers include the following:

[IFRS 13:95]

(a) the date of the event or change in circumstances that caused the transfer;

(b) the beginning of the reporting period; and

(c) the end of the reporting period.

The policy chosen should be applied consistently to transfer in and out of the levels in the hierarchy with transfers in and transfers out disclosed and discussed separately.

In the case of a compound financial instrument (i.e. an instrument including a financial liability and equity component as described in **section 3** of **chapter C3**), the disclosures regarding fair value will relate only to the financial liability component of the compound instrument because the equity component is scoped out of IFRS 7 (see **section 2**). The fair value of the financial liability component will incorporate interest rate risk and the entity's own credit risk but will exclude any consideration of equity price risk.

4.3.3.4 Valuation techniques and inputs

IFRS 13 requires certain disclosures about valuation techniques which are used in fair valuing both recurring and non-recurring fair value measurements for assets and liabilities. The Standard requires a description of the valuation technique(s) and inputs used as well as disclosure if there has been a change in valuation technique, disclosing the change and the reason(s) for making the change. [IFRS 13:93(d)]

4.3.3.5 Level 3 fair value measurements

In addition to the disclosures on valuation techniques described in **4.3.3.4**, IFRS 13 requires further disclosure for Level 3 fair value measurements. IFRS 13 requires greater disclosure for Level 3 fair value measurements compared with Levels 1 and 2 fair value measurements because determining their measurement is more subjective.

For recurring and non-recurring fair value measurements that are categorised within Level 3 of the fair value hierarchy an entity shall provide quantitative information about the significant unobservable inputs used in the fair value measurement. An entity is not required to create quantitative information to comply with this disclosure requirement if quantitative unobservable inputs are not developed by the entity when measuring fair value (e.g. when an entity uses prices from prior transactions or third-party pricing information without adjustment). However, when providing this disclosure an entity cannot ignore quantitative unobservable inputs that are significant to the fair value measurement and are reasonably available to the entity. [IFRS 13:93(d)]

In addition to the quantitative information required by IFRS 13 it states an entity shall consider whether additional information shall be disclosed in order for users of financial statements to evaluate the quantitative information disclosed. [IFRS 13:92(d)] The illustrative examples contained in IFRS 13 describe some or all of the following information an entity must disclose in order to meet the requirement.

[IFRS 13:IE64]

(a) the nature of the item being measured at fair value, including the characteristics of the item being measured that are taken into account in the determination of relevant inputs. For example, for residential mortgage-backed securities, an entity might disclose the following:
   (i) the types of underlying loans (e.g. prime loans or sub-prime loans);
   (ii) collateral;
   (iii) guarantees or other credit enhancements;
   (iv) seniority level of the tranches of securities;
   (v) the year of issue;
   (vi) the weighted-average coupon rate of the underlying loans and the securities;
   (vii) the weighted-average maturity of the underlying loans and the securities;
   (viii) the geographical concentration of the underlying loans;
   (ix) information about the credit ratings of the securities.

(b) how third-party information such as broker quotes, pricing services, net asset values and relevant market data was taken into account when measuring fair value.

For recurring Level 3 fair value IFRS 13 requires a reconciliation of the opening and closing balances. The Standard requires the following to be included in that reconciliation:

[IFRS 13:93(e)]

(i) total gains or losses for the period recognised in profit or loss, and the line item(s) in profit or loss in which those gains or losses are recognised.

(ii) total gains or losses for the period recognised in other comprehensive income, and the line item(s) in other comprehensive income in which those gains or losses are recognised.

(iii) purchases, sales, issues and settlements (each of those types of changes disclosed separately).

(iv) the amounts of any transfers into or out of Level 3 of the fair value hierarchy, the reasons for those transfers and the entity's policy for determining when transfers between levels are deemed to have occurred (see **4.3.3.3**). Transfers into Level 3 shall be disclosed and discussed separately from transfers out of Level 3.

Physically settled commodity derivative instruments within the scope of IAS 39 that do not meet the 'own-use' exception (see IAS 39:5 and 6(c)) are treated the same as financial commodity derivatives.

For financial commodity derivatives, economic performance is demonstrated by the changes in fair value and results in net settlement or settlements that occur over the life of the instrument. Gains or losses for net-settled financial derivatives are determined based on the cash settlement activity. In contrast, physically settled commodity derivatives feature a gross exchange of a physical commodity and cash or another financial asset based on a pre-determined price. However, the objective of the Level 3 roll forward reconciliation remains the same – that is, to provide information about the economic performance and position of the derivative in value terms, irrespective of the settlement provisions. Consequently, for physical settled commodity derivative contracts "settlements" includes the cash or another financial asset paid or received under the contract as well as the physical commodity delivered in exchange.

Example 4.3.3.5

Level 3 reconciliation

Entity A has the following two financial derivatives.

	Financial derivative 1 (CU)	**Financial derivative 2 (CU)**
Beginning balance	100	Not applicable as entered into during the period
Change in fair value	10	250
Cash received	110	Not applicable
Closing fair value	–	250

The contracts are part of the same class for the purposes of IFRS 13:94 and, consequently, are reported in a single column of the reconciliation table.

	Financial contracts CU
Beginning balance	100
Total gains or losses (realised and unrealised) recognised in profit or loss (i) (ii)	260
Total gains or losses recognised in other comprehensive income (i)	–
Purchases	–
Sales	–
Issuances	–
Settlements (iii)	(110)
Transfers into Level 3	–
Transfers out of Level 3	–
Closing balance	250

(i) The entity should also disclose the line item in profit or loss/other comprehensive income in which these gains or losses are recognised.

(ii) Represents the change in fair value of Derivative 1 (CU10) and change in fair value of Derivative 2 (CU250).

(iii) Represents cash received on settlement.

Entity A also has two physically settled commodity derivatives. Physical derivative 1 is a sale of 100 mmbtu of Natural Gas at CU8 per mmbtu. Physical derivative 2 is a sale of 100 mmbtu of Natural Gas at CU12 per mmbtu.

	Physical derivative 1 (CU)	**Physical derivative 2 (CU)**
Beginning balance	100	Not applicable as entered into during the period
Change in fair value	10	250
Cash received	800	Not applicable
Market value of commodity delivered	690	Not applicable
Closing fair value	–	250

The contracts are part of the same class for the purposes of IFRS 13:94 and, consequently, are reported in a single column of the reconciliation table.

	Physical contracts CU
Beginning balance	100
Total gains or losses (realised and unrealised) recognised in profit or loss (i) (ii)	260
Total gains or losses recognised in other comprehensive income (i)	–
Purchases	–
Sales	–
Issuances	–
Settlements (iii)	(110)
Transfers into Level 3	–
Transfers out of Level 3	–
Closing balance	250

(i) The entity should also disclose the line item in profit or loss/other comprehensive income in which these gains or losses are recognised.

(ii) Represents the change in fair value of Derivative 1 (CU10) and change in fair value of Derivative 2 (CU250).

(iii) Represents settlement of the fixed price forward component of the physical derivative. The fixed price is the cash received on gross settlement (CU800) that is offset against the market spot price for gas (underlying the physical derivative) at settlement. In this example, the spot price is assumed to be CU6.9 per mmbtu or CU690.

In addition, an entity is required to disclose the amount of the total gains or losses recognised in profit or loss in the period that is included in the Level 3 reconciliation that is attributable to the change in unrealised gains or losses relating to those assets and liabilities held at the end of the reporting period, and the line item(s) in profit or loss in which those unrealised gains or losses are recognised. [IFRS 13:93(f)]

4.3.3.6 Valuation processes for Level 3 fair value measurements

For recurring and non-recurring fair value measurements categorised within Level 3 of the fair value hierarchy an entity is required to disclose a description of the valuation processes used by the entity (including, for example, how an entity decides its valuation policies and procedures and analyses changes in fair value measurements from period to period). [IFRS 13:93(g)] The illustrative examples contained in IFRS 13 contain an example of the disclosures an entity might include in order to meet the requirement:

[IFRS 13:IE65]

(a) for the group within the entity that decides the entity's valuation policies and procedures:
   (i) its description;
   (ii) to whom that group reports; and
   (iii) the internal reporting procedures in place (e.g. whether and, if so, how pricing, risk management or audit committees discuss and assess the fair value measurements);

(b) the frequency and methods for calibration, back testing and other testing procedures of pricing models;

(c) the process for analysing changes in fair value measurements from period to period;

(d) how the entity determined that third-party information, such as broker quotes or pricing services, used in the fair value measurement was developed in accordance with the IFRS; and

(e) the methods used to develop and substantiate the unobservable inputs used in a fair value measurement.

4.3.3.7 Information about sensitivity to changes in significant unobservable inputs for Level 3 fair value measurements

For recurring fair value measurements categorised within Level 3 of the fair value hierarchy an entity must disclose a narrative description of the sensitivity of the fair value measurement to changes in unobservable inputs if a change in those inputs to a different amount might result in a significantly higher or lower fair value measurement. If there are interrelationships between those inputs and other unobservable inputs used in the fair value measurement, an entity shall also provide a description of those interrelationships and of how they might magnify or mitigate the effect of changes in the unobservable inputs on the fair value measurement. To comply with that disclosure requirement, the narrative description of the sensitivity to changes in unobservable inputs shall include, at a minimum, the unobservable inputs disclosed when complying with IFRS 13:93(d) (see **4.3.3.5**). [IFRS 13:93(h)(i)]

Example 4.3.3.7

Information about sensitivity to changes in significant observable inputs

[IFRS 13:IE66]

The significant unobservable inputs used in the fair value measurement of the entity's residential mortgage-backed securities are prepayment rates, probability of default and loss severity in the event of default. Significant increases (decreases) in any of those inputs in isolation would result in a significantly lower (higher) fair value measurement. Generally, a change in the assumption used for the probability of default is accompanied by a directionally similar change in the assumption used for the loss severity and a directionally opposite change in the assumption used for prepayment rates.

For financial assets and financial liabilities, if changing one or more of the unobservable inputs to reflect reasonably possible alternative assumptions would change fair value significantly, an entity shall state that fact and disclose the effect of those changes. The entity shall disclose how the effect of a change to reflect a reasonably possible alternative assumption was calculated. For that purpose, significance shall be judged with respect to profit or loss, and total assets or total liabilities, or, when changes in fair value are recognised in other comprehensive income, total equity. [IFRS 13:93(h)(ii)]

4.3.3.8 Day 1 profit or loss

IAS 39 requires that no gain or loss should be recognised on initial recognition of a financial instrument if the fair value at initial recognition is neither evidenced by a quoted price in an active market for an identical asset or liability (i.e. a Level 1 input) nor based on a valuation technique that uses data from observable markets. A gain or loss should be recognised subsequently only to the extent that it arises from a change in factor (including time) that market participants would take into account when pricing the asset or liability. As noted at **7.1** in **chapter C7** there is little clarity as to when day 1 profit or loss should be recognised because the Standard does not specify how entities should account for those initial differences in subsequent periods. Disclosure is required, by class of financial instrument, of the accounting policy for recognising in profit or loss the difference between the fair value at initial recognition and the transaction price to reflect a change in factors (including time) that market participants would take into account when pricing the financial instrument. [IFRS 7:28(a)] The aggregate difference yet to be recognised in profit or loss at the beginning and end of the period should be disclosed together with a reconciliation of the changes in the balance during the period. [IFRS 7:28(b)] In addition, disclosure is required as to why the entity concluded that the transaction price was not the best evidence of fair value, including a description of the evidence that supports the fair value. [IFRS 7:28(c)]

5 Nature and extent of risks arising from financial instruments

IFRS 7 has two key objectives: firstly to show the significance of financial instruments as discussed in **section 4**; and, secondly, to require entities to disclose information that enables users of its financial statements to evaluate the nature and extent of risks arising from financial instruments to which the entity is exposed at the end of the reporting period as discussed below.

Both qualitative and quantitative disclosures are required regarding the risks that arise from financial instruments and how those risks have been managed. The risks typically include, but are not limited to, credit risk, liquidity risk and market risk. [IFRS 7:32] The disclosures provided should depend on the extent of an entity's use of financial instruments and the extent to which it assumes associated risks, although certain minimum disclosures are required for all entities. The guidance on how the disclosures should be provided has been developed so as to be consistent with the Basel Committee disclosure requirements for banks (generally referred to as 'Pillar 3' of Basel II) to allow banks to prepare a single set of co-ordinated disclosures about financial risk. [IFRS 7:BC41] It is of note that Pillar 3 disclosures are broader than those required under IFRS 7 because they include operational risks.

The disclosures should either be provided in the financial statements or incorporated by clear cross-reference from the financial statements to some other statement (e.g. a management commentary or risk report). Such a report must be available to users on the same terms as the financial statements and be available at the same time. Without such information, the financial statements are incomplete. [IFRS 7:B6]

> If the disclosures are provided in a separate statement, the information should be clearly referenced as being part of the IFRS financial statements.

5.1 Qualitative disclosures

For each type of risk to which an entity is exposed, disclosure is required regarding:

[IFRS 7:33]

- the exposures to the risk and how those exposures arose;
- the entity's objectives, policies and processes for managing the risk and the methods used to measure it; and
- any changes in the information disclosed under the previous two bullets from the previous period.

Providing qualitative disclosures in the context of quantitative disclosures enables users to link related disclosures and, as a result, to form an overall picture of the nature and extent of risks arising from financial instruments. The interaction between qualitative and quantitative disclosures contributes to disclosure of information in a way that better enables users to evaluate an entity's exposure to risks. [IFRS 7:32A]

Disclosures may be provided on both a gross basis and net of any risk transfer and other risk-mitigating transactions. [IFRS 7:IG15(a)] Such information is useful because it highlights the relationships between financial instruments and provides users of the financial statements with information to understand the effect of those relationships on the nature, timing and uncertainty of future cash flows.

Disclosure of the entity's policies and processes for accepting, measuring, monitoring and controlling risk may include disclosure of the following:

[IFRS 7:IG15(b) & (c)]

- the structure and organisation of the entity's risk management function;
- the scope and nature of risk reporting or measurement systems;
- policies for hedging or mitigating risk, including policies and procedures for taking collateral;
- the entity's processes for monitoring the continuing effectiveness of such hedges or mitigating devices; and
- the policies and procedures undertaken to avoid excessive concentrations of risk.

An entity is required to disclose any changes in the qualitative information from the previous period. Such changes may result from changes in the entity's exposure to risk or from changes in the way in which the exposures are managed. [IFRS 7:IG17] This information is important because users of the financial statements need to understand the effect that such changes have on the nature, timing and uncertainty of future cash flows.

One of the objectives of the disclosure requirements is to enable users to evaluate an entity's ability to generate returns, and to appreciate the risks and uncertainties of those expected returns. This evaluation can only be meaningful if it is carried out in the context of the entity's risk management policies.

5.2 Quantitative disclosures

For each type of risk arising from financial instruments, IFRS 7 requires an entity to provide quantitative information about exposure to that risk at the end of the reporting period, based on information reported internally to key management personnel. [IFRS 7:34(a)] If more than one method is used to manage and report information about risk exposures, then the method that provides the most relevant and reliable information should be disclosed. [IFRS 7:B7] The advantages of basing disclosures on management information are that such disclosures:

[IFRS 7:BC47]

- provide a useful insight into how risk is viewed and managed by the entity;
- are based on information that has a more predictive value than information based on assumptions and methods that management does not use; and
- adapt to changes in the manner in which risk is measured and managed and allows users to use the same data that management uses to measure and manage risk.

Key management personnel are defined as "those persons having authority and responsibility for planning, directing and controlling the activities of the entity, directly or indirectly, including any director (whether executive or otherwise) of that entity". [IAS 24:9]

Following the definition, any director, whether executive or non-executive, will be considered to be key management personnel. The definition of key management personnel is, however, wider than just directors of an entity. Key management personnel might, in some instances, include directors of subsidiaries who are not directors of the parent entity and senior managers who are not directors. Other managers may be included as key management personnel in some circumstances, and not in others. Consideration needs to be given to the relative autonomy of management and whether their decisions are subject to the approval of the board of directors. For example, a Treasury Manager in an organisation may unilaterally review exposures and act independently following only guidelines and objectives established by the board of directors. In such circumstances, the Treasury Manager may be considered to be part of the key management personnel of that entity. In contrast, if the Treasury Manager operates purely in accordance with detailed treasury risk policies set out and approved by the board of directors, then that person is more likely to be excluded from the definition of key management personnel. In order to arrive at an appropriate determination, it is always necessary to obtain a thorough understanding of the manager's role within the organisation and the extent of his or her authority.

In addition to the disclosures under IFRS 7:34(a) (see above), which are based on information provided to key management personnel, IFRS 7:34(b) requires disclosures regarding credit, liquidity and market risk to the extent that these are not covered by the disclosures under IFRS 7:34(a) (see **5.2.1** to **5.2.3**).

Disclosures regarding concentrations of risk are also required to be provided if not apparent from the disclosures provided in accordance with IFRS 7:34(a) & (b). [IFRS 7:34(c)] Concentrations of risk arise from financial instruments that have similar characteristics and are affected similarly by changes in economic or other conditions. The identification of concentrations of risk requires judgement and must take into account the specific circumstances of the entity. Disclosures may include:

[IFRS 7:B8]

- a description of how management determines concentrations;
- a description of the shared characteristic that identifies each concentration (e.g. counterparty credit rating, geographical distribution, industry sector and other risks such as liquidity and market risks); and
- the amount of the risk exposure associated with all financial instruments that share that risk characteristic.

In all circumstances, the quantitative information should be provided for the risk exposures that exist at the end of the reporting period. When such information is unrepresentative of the exposure to financial risk during the period, an entity should provide additional information, which may include, but not be limited to, disclosure of the highest, lowest and average amount of risk the entity was exposed to during the period. [IFRS 7:IG20]

5.2.1 Credit risk

Credit risk is defined as "the risk that one party to a financial instrument will cause a financial loss for the other party by failing to discharge an obligation". [IFRS 7:Appendix A] IFRS 7 disclosure requirements regarding credit risk are substantial and are discussed in detail below. These disclosures are intended to provide users of the financial statements with a sufficient understanding of the net risk position of financial assets at all stages and the extent of financial assets that are more likely to become impaired in the future.

5.2.1.1 Disclosure of the maximum exposure to credit risk

For each class of financial asset, disclosure is required of the amount that best represents the entity's maximum credit risk exposure at the end of the reporting period, *excluding* the effect of any collateral and other amounts that do not qualify for offset in accordance with IAS 32. This disclosure is not required for financial instruments whose carrying amount best represents the maximum exposure to credit risk. [IFRS 7:36(a)]

These disclosures are designed to provide users of the financial statements with a consistent measure of the amounts exposed to credit risk and to allow for the possibility that the maximum exposure to loss may differ from the carrying amount of financial assets recognised at the end of the reporting period. [IFRS 7:BC49] The disclosure requirement focuses on the entity's exposure to credit risk that is not already reflected in the statement of financial position. [IFRS 7:BC49A]

For financial assets exposed to credit risk, an entity's maximum exposure to credit risk is typically the gross carrying amount of those financial assets, net of any amounts offset in accordance with IAS 32 and any impairment losses recognised in accordance with IAS 39. [IFRS 7:B9] In the case of a derivative that is measured at fair value, an entity's maximum exposure to credit risk at the end of the reporting period will equal its carrying amount. [IFRS 7:B10(b)]

A derivative that will result in the delivery or receipt of an unquoted equity security where the fair value of the underlying security cannot be determined with sufficient reliability will be measured at cost in accordance with IAS 39:46(c) & 47(a). IFRS 7 does not state how to determine an entity's maximum exposure to credit risk when a derivative is measured at cost. For example, a gross physically settled purchased call option over an unquoted equity security has a maximum exposure to credit risk equal to the value of the equity security that will be physically delivered to the entity less the exercise price to be paid. However, because the fair value of the instrument cannot be determined with sufficient reliability, and cost will generally be unrepresentative of the maximum exposure to credit risk, narrative disclosure of the terms of the instrument and the underlying would seem appropriate.

The maximum exposure to credit risk for financial guarantees that have been granted is equal to the maximum amount the entity would have to pay if the guarantee is called upon, irrespective of the likelihood of the guarantee being exercised. This amount will generally be significantly greater than the amount recognised as a liability. [IFRS 7:B10(c)]

Irrespective of whether a financial guarantee is accounted for under IFRS 4 or IAS 39, similar disclosures are required. IFRS 4 requires disclosure of information about the credit risk associated with such contracts in the same manner as IFRS 7 requires credit risk disclosures for instruments that are measured in accordance with IAS 39. [IFRS 4:39(d)]

The maximum exposure to credit risk for a loan commitment that is irrevocable over the life of the facility, or is revocable only in response to a material adverse change, and that cannot be settled net in cash or another financial asset, is the full amount of the commitment. This is because it is uncertain whether the amount of any undrawn portion may be drawn upon in the future. Therefore, the amount of the maximum exposure to credit risk for a loan commitment may be significantly greater than the amount recognised as a liability. [IFRS 7:B10(d)] Loan commitments that will be settled net in cash or other financial instruments are treated as derivative financial instruments and, consequently, an entity's maximum exposure to credit risk in respect of such loan commitments will be equal to their carrying amount.

While loan commitments that will not be settled net in cash or other financial instruments are outside the scope of IAS 39, they are within the scope of IFRS 7 because they are unrecognised financial assets or financial liabilities. [IFRS 7:4] If a loan commitment cannot be settled net, but is designated as at FVTPL and, therefore, is within the scope of IAS 39, IFRS 7 is not clear whether it is possible to consider the entity's maximum exposure to credit risk in respect of that loan commitment as being its fair value (as is the case for other derivative financial assets). Because a loan commitment that cannot be settled net will always result in the origination of a loan if the commitment is exercised by the borrower, the most appropriate amount representing the entity's maximum exposure to credit risk would seem to be the maximum that can be borrowed under the commitment. Disclosing this amount is consistent with the majority of gross settled loan commitments that are outside the scope of IAS 39.

The exposure under the loan to be originated under a loan commitment is the same as the exposure under a financial guarantee that can be claimed if the loan is in default. From the lender's perspective, both have credit risk.

IFRS 7:B10(c) states that the maximum exposure to credit risk for a written guarantee is the amount the entity could have to pay if the guarantee is called upon. It is reasonable to conclude that this amount should be based on the amount that could be required to be paid if the guarantee was called upon in its entirety, as opposed to the amount that could be claimed under the guarantee at the end of the reporting period based on the then level of lending that the lender has made to the borrower. This approach applies equally to loan commitments.

Example 5.2.1.1A

Maximum exposure to credit risk: loan commitment

Bank A issues a loan commitment to Entity B for US$100 million. The maximum exposure to credit risk that will be disclosed in Bank A's financial statements with respect to the loan commitment will be equal to the full amount of the loan that has been offered (i.e. US$100 million). Assume that Entity C issues a financial guarantee to Bank A relating to Bank A's loan commitment to Entity B over US $100 million. The guarantee will provide protection against Entity B defaulting on its loan to Bank A should Entity B draw down on the loan commitment. The maximum exposure to credit risk for Bank A is US$100 million, being the maximum potential loss under the loan ignoring the guarantee it has acquired to reduce this potential loss. This amount will be disclosed at the end of the reporting period even if no draw-down on the loan commitment is made by Entity B.

Entity C has credit risk on the financial guarantee written to Bank A. The maximum exposure to credit risk is also US$100 million because this is the maximum amount Entity C could have to pay to Entity A if the guarantee is called upon.

Example 5.2.1.1B

Maximum exposure to credit risk: receivables

Group F is a listed retail group with a large customer base. Customers purchase goods under the group's standard credit terms. Group F also purchases goods from some of its major customers.

	30 June 20X2 US$	30 June 20X1 US$
Gross trade receivables	365,500	323,700
Impairment loss	(14,620)	(12,948)
Net carrying amount	350,880	310,752
Amounts owed to customers	(75,500)	(62,250)

Group F has an agreement with its customers to set off amounts owed by customers and amounts owed to customers, but only if the customer defaults. Group F does not meet the requirements to offset the asset and liability and there is not the intention and legal ability to set off the recognised amounts.

Group F's maximum exposure to credit risk at the end of each reporting period is the gross amount due from its customers less the allowances recognised for impairment losses. The payables are excluded from the analysis because they are not offset in the statement of financial position.

Example 5.2.1.1C

Maximum exposure to credit risk: financial guarantee contracts

Entity B is a wholly-owned operating subsidiary of Entity A, the ultimate parent of Group A. To finance its working capital requirements, Entity B has short-term banking facilities of €300 million with various banks. Entity A has issued a variety of guarantees on behalf of its subsidiary and in favour of the banks which meet the definition of financial guarantee contracts. The schedule below details the drawn-down banking facilities of Entity B and the amounts guaranteed by Entity A at 30 June 20X2 and 30 June 20X1.

	30 June 20X2 € million	30 June 20X1 € million
Short term banking facilities drawn down at year end	100	100
Guarantees issued by Entity A to lenders	250	250

The following amounts will be disclosed as the maximum exposure to credit risk in Entity B's financial statements, Entity A's separate financial statements, and Group A's consolidated financial statements.

- Entity B: € nil (20X1: € nil) because Entity B is the borrower, it does not have an exposure to credit risk.
- Entity A (separate financial statements): €250 million (20X1: €250 million) being the full amount of the guarantee that would be required to be paid if the guarantee is called upon. [IFRS 7:B10(c)]
- Group A: € nil (20X1: nil) because, from a group perspective, the group is the borrower and it does not have exposure to credit risk. The amount repayable is the same irrespective of whether Entity B repays the debt or Entity A repays the debt on Entity B's behalf.

5.2.1.2 Disclosure of collateral held as security and other credit enhancements

IFRS 7 requires disclosures regarding collateral held as security and other credit enhancements. [IFRS 7:36(b)] These requirements may be met by disclosing:

[IFRS 7:IG22]

- the policies and processes for valuing and managing collateral and other credit enhancements obtained;
- a description of the main types of collateral and other credit enhancements (examples of the latter being guarantees, credit derivatives, and netting agreements that do not qualify for offset in accordance with IAS 32);
- the main types of counterparties to collateral and other credit enhancements and their creditworthiness; and
- information about risk concentrations within the collateral or other credit enhancements.

IFRS 7 requires an entity to provide a description of collateral held as security and of other credit enhancements, and their financial effect (e.g. a quantification of the extent to which collateral and other credit enhancements mitigate credit risk) in respect of the amount that best represents the maximum exposure to credit risk (whether disclosed in accordance with IFRS 7:36(a) or represented by the carrying amount of a financial instrument). [IFRS 7:36(b)]

5.2.1.3 Disclosures regarding the credit quality of financial assets that are neither past due nor impaired

Information should be provided regarding the credit quality of financial assets that are neither past due nor impaired. [IFRS 7:36(c)] A financial asset is not past due when the debtor has not missed a contractual payment (interest or capital) when contractually due [IFRS 7:Appendix A], and a financial asset is not impaired when there is no objective evidence of impairment. [IAS 39:59] In order to meet these disclosure requirements, the following information may be provided:

[IFRS 7:IG23]

(a) an analysis of credit exposures using an external or internal credit grading system;

(b) the nature of the counterparty;

(c) historical information about counterparty default rates; and

(d) any other information used to assess credit quality.

Such disclosures provide useful information and greater insight into the credit risk of assets and allow users to assess whether assets are more or less likely to become impaired in the future. Because all entities are different, each entity may determine its own way of providing the required information. [IFRS 7:BC54]

When an entity considers external ratings for managing and monitoring credit quality, the entity might disclose information about:

[IFRS 7:IG24]

(a) the amounts of credit exposures for each external credit grade;

(b) the rating agencies used;

(c) the amount of an entity's rated and unrated credit exposures; and

(d) the relationship between internal and external ratings.

When an entity considers internal credit ratings for managing and monitoring credit quality, the entity might disclose information about:

[IFRS 7:IG25]

(a) the internal credit ratings process;

(b) the amounts of credit exposures for each internal credit grade; and

(c) the relationship between internal and external ratings.

Disclosing information regarding exposures by credit grade reflects the strength of the debtors, especially when that debt is rated externally. Disclosures regarding an entity's internal credit rating process together with disclosing exposures by credit rating provide a useful insight into how the credit risk of financial assets is monitored internally and reflects how management measures and manages credit risk. Because comparative financial information will also be provided, users of the financial statements will be able to understand how the credit risk of those financial assets that are neither past due nor impaired has changed over the financial period.

5.2.1.4 Disclosures regarding financial assets that are either past due or impaired

Financial information regarding financial assets that are either past due or impaired should be provided by class of financial asset. [IFRS 7:37]

A financial asset is past due when the counterparty has failed to make a payment when contractually due. [IFRS 7:Appendix A] Past due status can trigger various actions such as renegotiation, enforcement of covenants, or even legal proceedings. [IFRS 7:IG26] The new terms and conditions of debt that has been renegotiated apply in determining whether the financial asset is past due for the purposes of this disclosure item. [IFRS 7:IG27]

There is a subtle distinction between 'past due' and 'impaired'. A financial asset is considered to be 'past due' when a payment that was contractually due is not made. This may not necessarily be equivalent to an impairment because the late payment may be added to the outstanding balance, with interest applied to the outstanding payment missed that is still deemed recoverable so that, from the lender's perspective, the recoverable amount of the asset is the same (i.e. there is no impairment).

Disclosures regarding financial assets that are either past due or impaired should include an analysis of the age of financial assets that are past due but not impaired at the end of the reporting period. [IFRS 7:37(a)] An entity should use its judgement to determine an appropriate number of time bands. [IFRS 7:IG28]

Because the quantitative disclosures made under IFRS 7 should be based on the information that is provided internally to key management personnel of the entity, the disclosures for the ageing analysis should be based on internally reported time bands where available.

Providing an analysis of the age of financial assets that are past due but not impaired, as at the end of the reporting period, allows the users of the financial statements to understand the extent of financial assets that are more likely to become impaired because they are past due. This, in turn, assists users in estimating the level of future impairment losses. [IFRS 7:BC55(a)]

The disclosure of past due items may be particularly onerous for entities with accounts receivable. For example, if an entity has debtor repayment terms of 30 days from invoice date, but it is customary for payment to be received after 60 days, then those receivables that remain outstanding at the end of the reporting period that are older than 30 days should be disclosed as past due. This disclosure requirement is more onerous than that for breaches of loans payable, where short-term trade payables on normal credit terms are specifically excluded.

The disclosures regarding financial assets that are either past due or impaired should include an analysis of financial assets that are individually determined to be impaired at the end of the reporting period and the factors that were considered in determining that those assets were impaired. [IFRS 7:37(b)] Such an analysis may include the carrying amount, before deducting any impairment losses, the amount of any related impairment losses, and the nature and fair value of collateral available and other credit enhancements obtained. [IFRS 7:IG29]

An analysis of impaired financial assets other than by age is useful because it helps users to understand why the impairment occurred. [IFRS 7:BC55(b)]

5.2.1.5 Disclosures regarding collateral and other credit enhancements obtained

When an entity obtains financial or non-financial assets by taking possession of collateral or calling on other credit enhancements (e.g. financial guarantee contracts) at foreclosure, and such assets are required to be recognised at the reporting date in accordance with IAS 39 or another Standard, disclosure should be provided regarding the nature and carrying amount of those assets. When the assets are not readily convertible into cash, then the entity's policies for disposing of the assets or using them in its operations should also be disclosed. [IFRS 7:38] Disclosures regarding collateral are useful in such circumstances because they provide information about the frequency of such events and the entity's ability to obtain and realise the value of the collateral.

IFRSs do not define what is meant by 'readily convertible to cash'. Consideration should be given to the type of assets that are obtained as collateral and the ability to sell those assets. The mere fact that the collateral consists of listed securities does not indicate that it is readily convertible to cash because the liquidity of those assets and the size of the holding should be considered.

Example 5.2.1.5

Collateral and other credit enhancements obtained

Scenario 1

Bank A lends CU100,000 to a homeowner with property specified as collateral for the loan. During the period, the homeowner defaults under the loan and the property meets the criteria for recognition in the statement of financial position of Bank A before being disposed of. Bank A must comply with the disclosure requirements of IFRS 7:38 as noted above.

Scenario 2

Bank B lends CU1,000 to a retail customer. Concurrently, it enters into a financial guarantee contract with Entity C under which, if the retail customer fails to make payments under the loan agreement when due, Entity C will reimburse Bank B the CU1,000 in cash. During the period, the retail customer defaults under the loan and Bank B claims under the financial guarantee contract. The amount of CU1,000 is required to be disclosed under the requirements of IFRS 7:38.

5.2.2 *Liquidity risk*

Liquidity risk is defined as "the risk that an entity will encounter difficulty in meeting obligations associated with financial liabilities that are settled by delivering cash or another financial asset". [IFRS 7:Appendix A]

If a financial liability is exclusively settled in the issuer's own equity instruments (e.g. a variable number of equity shares equal to a fixed monetary amount), then the financial liability will not be included in the liquidity risk disclosures. Equally, if the issuer has the right to deliver its own equity instruments instead of cash or another financial asset, the financial liability is deemed not to have liquidity risk because the issuer can avoid the delivery of cash or another financial asset by electing to deliver its own equity instruments. If the counterparty to the financial liability can demand cash or another financial asset, even if there is an equity-settlement alternative, the financial liability must be included in the liquidity risk disclosures because the issuer cannot avoid settlement in cash or another financial asset if the counterparty chooses this settlement alternative.

If an entity has a contractual arrangement recognised as a financial liability where the entity is required to deliver a non-financial item only (e.g. gold), or the entity has a choice of delivering a non-financial item instead of cash or another financial asset, then the financial liability is excluded from the liquidity risk disclosures, because the non-financial item is not cash or another financial asset (even if the non-financial item is regarded as readily convertible into cash). This will typically be the case for contracts for the delivery of non-financial assets that are included within the scope of IAS 39 because they are deemed net settled in accordance with IAS 39:5 - 7 (see **2.5** in **chapter C1**). Such instruments are generally classified as derivatives as at FVTPL and may be financial liabilities at the reporting period end.

Liquidity risk also arises because of the possibility (which may often be remote) that the entity could be required to pay its financial liabilities earlier than expected.

5.2.2.1 Quantitative liquidity risk disclosures

IFRS 7 requires an entity to disclose summary quantitative information provided internally to key management personnel regarding its exposure to liquidity risk and how this data is determined. If the outflows of cash or another financial asset included in the data could occur significantly earlier or be for significantly different amounts than indicated in the data, this fact should be disclosed and additional quantitative information should be provided to enable users of the financial statements to evaluate the risk. [IFRS 7:B10A] The example provided in IFRS 7 is where data on derivatives assumes net settlement but where the counterparty has the option to require gross settlement. However, additional quantitative information is not required if it is already included in the maturity analysis disclosure.

5.2.2.2 Maturity analysis

IFRS 7:39 requires disclosure of:

(a) a maturity analysis for non-derivative financial liabilities (including issued financial guarantee contracts) that shows the remaining contractual maturities;

(b) a maturity analysis for derivative financial liabilities. The maturity analysis should include the remaining contractual maturities for those derivative financial liabilities for which contractual maturities are essential for an understanding of the timing of the cash flows (see IFRS 7:B11B); and

(c) a description of how the entity manages the liquidity risk inherent in (a) and (b).

IFRS 7:B11B provides two examples where a quantitative maturity analysis for derivative financial liabilities showing remaining contractual maturities is deemed essential for an understanding of the timing of the cash flows. The first example is an interest rate swap with a remaining maturity of five years in a cash flow hedge of a variable rate financial asset or liability. The second example is all loan commitments.

A contractual maturity analysis is not required in respect of derivative liabilities if the information is not essential for an understanding of the timing of cash flows. This may be the case when an entity frequently buys and sells derivatives (e.g. derivative liabilities included in a trading book in a financial institution). Showing the contractual maturities may not be essential for understanding the timing of cash flows because the derivative liabilities will be settled through sale rather than through the payment/receipt of the contractual cash flows under the instrument until its contractual maturity. In such circumstances, the entity is still required to show a maturity analysis for derivative financial liabilities, but the analysis could be presented on an alternative basis; for example, it could be based on expected maturities, or even on fair values at the end of the reporting period when the entity's expectation is that the carrying amount of the derivative liability (i.e. its fair value) will be payable as a result of a disposal shortly after the reporting date.

An entity should exercise its judgement in determining the appropriate number of the time bands in the maturity analysis prescribed in IFRS 7:39 (a) and (b) (see above).

Because quantitative information is required to be reported based on information reported to key management personnel, the time bands should, where applicable, be equivalent to those reported internally. Some entities may have many more time bands than others; for examples, some banks disclose liquidity for 1 day, 1-3 days, 3-7 days, 7-30 days etc. In any event, the entity should evaluate whether the liquidity analysis provides sufficient disclosure regarding its liquidity requirements by considering the relative timing of its liquidity needs. For example, an entity may have significant obligations due in a month's time, in which case aggregating all obligations for the first year into one band will not be appropriate.

5.2.2.3 Contractual maturity analysis: determining which time band

When a counterparty has a choice regarding when an amount is required to be paid, the liability is included on the basis of the earliest date on which the entity can be required to pay (e.g. demand deposits should be included in the earliest time band because the deposit holder can require repayment on demand). [IFRS 7:B11C(a)] Therefore, American-style written options that can be exercised by the holder at any time should be disclosed in the earliest time band in which the holder can exercise, while a European-style option, which is only exercisable by the holder at maturity, should be included in the time period equivalent to its maturity date.

When the counterparty has the choice regarding when an amount is to be paid, the liquidity analysis should be based on the 'worst case' scenario, i.e. the earliest date on which the entity could be required to pay. [IFRS 7:BC57] This also has implications for the treatment of financial liabilities that are callable by the issuer. IFRS 7:BC57 would seem to imply that an issuer call option is not taken into account for the purposes of the liquidity analysis. Therefore, for liquidity risk purposes, perpetual fixed rate debt that can be called by the issuer will be presented as if the call feature were absent and, therefore, the issuer has an obligation to pay cash flows into perpetuity. Similarly, if a financial liability has a maturity of 10 years but is callable by the issuer after 5 years, the cash flows included in the liquidity analysis would assume the instrument will remain outstanding until its contractual maturity. This approach applies even if it is highly likely that the issuer's call option will be exercised and also if the effect of the call option has been included in the determining the effective interest rate of the liability for the purpose of its measurement at amortised cost (see **4.1** of **chapter C6** for details).

When an entity is committed to make amounts available in instalments, each instalment is allocated to the earliest period in which the entity can be required to pay it (e.g. an undrawn loan commitment should be included in the time band containing the earliest date that it can be drawn down). [IFRS 7:B11C(b)] If loan commitments can be drawn by the holder at any time, they should be included in the earliest time period.

While the loan commitment is undrawn, it is generally an unrecognised financial liability. However, IFRS 7:4 is clear that unrecognised financial liabilities are included within its scope. The requirement for the writer of the loan commitment (i.e. the potential lender) to include in the contractual maturity analysis of liquidity risk its potential obligation to pay cash under undrawn loan commitments in the time band that reflects the earliest period the holder can draw down under the loan commitment is reasonable because it demonstrates the timing and amount of cash that the entity may be committed to pay to a borrower.

The approach applied to written loan commitments is equally applied to written financial guarantee contracts. The maximum amount that the writer could be required to pay to the holder of the guarantee should be included in the time band that reflects the earliest period in which the guarantee could be called. [IFRS 7:B11C(c)]

If an entity has issued perpetual debt, the entity must consider how the cash flows that are due to perpetuity will be included in the maturity analysis. Because the cash flows are perpetual, it would be reasonable to determine the number of time bands based on all other financial liabilities that are not perpetual (i.e. that are term liabilities) and include undiscounted interest cash flows in relation to perpetual liabilities as appropriate in these time bands. In addition, it will be necessary to make clear through additional disclosure (in narrative form or a combination of an additional column with narrative disclosure) that the entity is subject to a stream of interest cash flows in relation to the perpetual instrument into infinity with disclosure of the key terms of the perpetual instrument (such as the rate of interest and the notional amount).

5.2.2.4 Contractual maturity analysis: amount to include in the time band

The amounts to be presented in the contractual maturity analysis are contractual, undiscounted cash flows. These amounts will differ from the amounts disclosed in the statement of financial position for financial liabilities, which are typically discounted amounts. [IFRS 7:B11D]

Although not specifically mentioned in IFRS 7, the financial liabilities to be disclosed as part of the liquidity risk analysis should be after any amounts offset in accordance with IAS 32.

Examples of amounts included on an undiscounted basis include:

[IFRS 7:B11D]

- gross finance lease obligations, before deduction of finance charges;
- prices specified in forward agreements to purchase financial assets for cash;
- net amounts for pay (receive) floating/receive (pay) fixed interest rate swaps for which net cash flows are exchanged;
- contractual amounts to be exchanged in a derivative financial instrument, such as a cross-currency swap, for which gross cash flows are exchanged; and
- gross cash flows in respect of loan commitments.

For foreign currency denominated fixed- or floating-rate debt instruments, the disclosure of principal and interest in the appropriate time bands is determined based on the interest rates curves in the foreign currency interest rate environment. These amounts may be disclosed in the foreign currency. Alternatively, they may be disclosed in the functional currency when preparing entity-only financial statements, or alternatively disclosed in the group presentation currency when preparing consolidated financial statements.

When the amount payable is not fixed, as is the case for issued debt that has a variable interest rate, the amount to be disclosed should be determined by reference to the conditions existing at the end of the reporting period. If the amount payable varies with changes in an index, the amount disclosed may be based on the level of the index at the end of the reporting period. [IFRS 7:B11D]

What is not clear from IFRS 7:B11D is whether "conditions existing at the end of the reporting period" is referring solely to the absolute level of the index at the end of the reporting period (e.g. the LIBOR rate at the end of the reporting period), or whether it is referring to conditions relating to future LIBOR that exist at the end of the reporting period.

The former would result in, say, a five-year LIBOR-based issued debt having five interest payments of the same amount, whereas the latter would have five interest payments based on the prevailing forward curve at the end of the reporting period (i.e. based on expectations of future LIBOR). The most appropriate disclosure would seem to be the latter because it recognises the conditions at the period end relating to the entity's expected payments of cash or another financial asset.

A derivative may be an asset in one period and a liability in another period depending on its fair value at each reporting date. In order to provide some comparability, an entity may choose to project the undiscounted cash flows on the derivative (whether it is settled net or gross) and disclose these undiscounted cash flows in the appropriate time bands, irrespective of whether in a particular time band the entity is expecting a net cash inflow or a net cash outflow.

In the case of gross-settled derivatives that are liabilities at the end of the reporting period, the Standard only requires disclosure of the gross outflow leg. However, an entity may wish to disclose these derivatives separately from net-settled derivatives so that users of the financial statements can distinguish the derivatives that will be accompanied by a gross inflow. An entity may also choose to provide the information in relation to the accompanying gross inflow to make clear the total cash flows on derivative instruments.

Disclosure of the gross outflow leg of gross-settled derivative liabilities is required even if the outflow leg is not a cash leg, but the outflow is still the delivery of a financial instrument. For example, an entity may have entered into a forward contract to sell a particular corporate bond in exchange for CU100 million cash in 9 months' time with the contract being exclusively gross-settled through delivery of the bond and receipt of the cash.

Consideration needs to be given as to how to present optional derivative financial liabilities that are not written loan commitments or financial guarantee contracts (whether stand-alone or embedded) in the maturity analysis. For example, if a written credit default option that does not meet the definition of a financial guarantee contract because the payout under the contract is driven not only by non-payment of a debtor but also by the credit rating of the borrower, it will be measured at FVTPL. The fair value of the written option will, at each reporting date, comprise intrinsic value and time value. In determining the amount to be included in the liquidity analysis, it would seem reasonable to draw on the principle in IFRS 7:B11D and disclose an undiscounted amount that represents the expected payout under the option based on conditions at the end of the reporting period. Under this, an amount of nil would be disclosed for options that are out of the money (based on forward rates, if applicable) at the end of the reporting period. For options that are in the money (based on forward rates, if applicable) the amount of the expected payout would be included in the liquidity risk analysis. It should be noted that this amount will not take account of any of the option's time value because the time value is not payable by the writer to the counterparty, and will also differ from the intrinsic value of the option because this will include the effect of discounting.

If an entity is preparing a contractual maturity analysis and has a hybrid (combined) financial instrument, it should not separate an embedded derivative for the purposes of including cash flows in the maturity analysis. [IFRS 7:B11A] The entity will instead include the cash flows in the maturity analysis based on the terms of the whole arrangement (i.e. based on it being a non- derivative financial liability, whether or not embedded derivatives in the instrument are separately accounted for). If the hybrid (combined) financial instrument is a recognised financial asset, an entity should disclose cash flows in the maturity analysis based on the terms of the whole arrangement if that information is necessary to enable users of its financial statements to evaluate the nature and extent of liquidity risk (see **5.2.2.5**). [IFRS 7:B11E]

The guidance in IFRS 7:B11A applies to hybrid (combined) financial instruments. An example would be an issued equity-linked bond or an issued debt instrument where the interest payments breach the 'double-double' test (see **7.3** in **chapter C5**).

IFRS 7 does not refer to the inclusion or exclusion of an embedded derivative that is a financial liability at the reporting date that is embedded in a non-financial arrangement that is outside the scope of IFRS 7 (e.g. a separately recognised embedded derivative in an unrecognised executory contract to receive a non-financial item). Because the embedded derivative financial liability is fully within the scope of IFRS 7, it would appear that it should be included within the maturity analysis if the embedded derivative results in the entity delivering cash or another financial asset. However, including the embedded derivative in the maturity analysis would appear to be in conflict with the principle in IFRS 7:B11A that requires an entity to consider the outflows of the whole contractual arrangement. Because the whole contractual arrangement is not in the scope of IFRS 7 (only the embedded derivative liability is) and the embedded derivative liability recognised may include imputed (not contractual) cash flows as a result of separating out part of the arrangement from the host contract, it is reasonable to exclude the embedded derivative from the maturity analysis.

Example 5.2.2.4

Liquidity risk disclosure: maturity analysis of financial liabilities

Bank M is a financial institution with a 31 December 20X1 reporting date. Bank M accepts deposits from a wide range of investors with a variety of rates and maturities. The bank manages its exposure to liquidity risk through a separate and independent liquidity risk management board which reports monthly to the board of directors with a maturity analysis based on the term structure of its deposit book. Bank M uses interest rate swaps to economically hedge its net interest margin. The interest rate swaps are not part of a trading book where there is frequent buying or selling. Bank M considers that the inclusion of cash flows on its interest rate swaps in its liquidity risk maturity analysis is essential in order for users of the financial statements to understand the timing of cash flows.

The schedule below sets out the financial liabilities at 31 December 20X1 (ignores comparative amounts and assumes that all figures quoted in the table are the notional amounts only, where applicable).

Instrument type	**CU'000**
5.35% 15-day notice deposits[1]	4,550
4.5% demand deposits[2]	6,750
Fixed rate deposits[3]	6,200
10% preference shares[4]	5,000
LIBOR-based financial liabilities[5]	10,000
Interest rate swaps[6]	1,200
Total	**33,700**

1 The notice deposits have a clause that allows for a depositor to elect to liquidate his/her deposit within 15 days. At the end of the reporting period, 40 per cent of the outstanding balance is in respect of depositors who have made this election.

2 The demand deposits are repayable within 30 days of notice being given. No persons had given notice at the end of the reporting period.

3 The fixed rate deposits are for periods ranging between 60 days, 90 days and 120 days at varying rates. The balance at the reporting date is made up as follows.

4 The preference shares are redeemable after five years. The interest on the preference shares is paid yearly on 31 December.

5 The LIBOR-based financial liabilities pay interest monthly with the interest rate resetting to LIBOR in advance, with a bullet repayment of principal in one year's time. The forward curve at the reporting date was as follows.

6 The interest rate swaps are settled net on a quarterly basis. The undiscounted future cash flows for all interest rate swap liabilities based on the forward curve at the reporting date were as follows (negatives represent cash inflows).

Maturity	Rate	Notional amount (CU'000)
60 days	4.90%	1,240
90 days	6.50%	1,860
120 days	7.36%	3,100

Interest is payable on maturity.

Month	Interest rate
January 20X2	5.53%
February 20X2	5.61%
March 20X2	6.12%
April 20X2	6.57%
May 20X2	6.59%
June 20X2	6.69%
July 20X2	6.71%
August 20X2	6.95%
September 20X2	7.06%
October 20X2	7.06%
November 20X2	7.30%
December 20X2	7.18%

Month	Net cash flow CU'000
March 20X2	600
June 20X2	500
September 20X2	400
December 20X2	350
March 20X3	300
June 20X3	200
September 20X3	100
December 20X3	50
March 20X4	(100)
June 20X4	(150)
September 20X4	(250)
December 20X4	(300)

Liquidity risk – maturity analysis CU'000

	≤1 month	1–≤3 months	3–≤12 months	1–≤3 years	3–≤5 years
Notice deposits	4,560[1]				
Demand deposits	6,775[2]				
Fixed deposits		3,140[3]	3,175[3]		
Preference shares			500[4]	1,000[4]	6,000[4]
LIBOR-based financial liabilities		142[5]	10,520[5]		
Interest rate swaps		600[6]	1,250[6]	(150)[6]	
Total	11,335	3,882	15,445	850	6,000

1 (4,550 x 5.35% x 40% x 15/365) + (4,550 x 5.35% x 60% x 16/365) + 4,550 = CU4,560

While 40% of the depositors have indicated they will liquidate their deposits, on a worst case scenario basis, the remaining 60% will also all liquidate their deposits by giving notice the next day for their funds to be repaid within the following 15 days. Therefore, the total liability would be settled within a month, and the disclosure will need to include the principal plus interest due.

2 (6,750 x 4.5% x 30/365) + 6,750 = CU6,775

On a worst case basis, all of the demand deposits will be called within the following month. The amount to be disclosed will be the principal plus the interest for 30 days.

3 60 days: (1,240 x 4.90% x 60/365) + 1,240 = CU1,250

90 days: (1,860 x 6.50% x 90/365) + 1,860 = CU1,890

The fixed deposit is payable in tranches. The first two tranches fall due within the first 3 months. Total for 1-3 month time period = CU3,140.

120 days: (3,100 x 7.36% x 120/365) + 3,100 = CU3,175

The fixed deposit is payable in tranches. The last tranche falls due in 120 days' time, i.e.: 3-12 month period.

4 1 year: (5,000 x 10%) = CU500

2, 3 years: (5,000 x 10% x 2) = CU1,000

4, 5 years: (5,000 x 10% x 2) +5,000 = CU6,000

The interest payment for the preference share falls due at the end of each year, with the capital being repaid at the end of 5 years.

5 Interest due is determined using the yield curve at the end of the reporting period, and is calculated as the product of the notional of the loan, the interest rate and the number of days.

Total for 1-3 months.

6 The undiscounted forecasted cash flow for:

March 20X2 = CU600

June, September and December 20X2 = CU1,250

March 20X3 to December 20X4 = (CU150)

Amounts determined as follows.

Month	**Days**	**Time band**	**Rate**	**Cash flow CU'000**
January 20X2	31	1–3 months	5.53%	47.00
February 20X2	28	1–3 months	5.61%	43.00
March 20X2	31	1–3 months	6.12%	52.00
Total				142.00

Total for 3-12 months

Month	**Days**	**Time band**	**Rate**	**Cash flow CU'000**
April 20X2	30	3–12 months	6.57%	54
May 20X2	31	3–12 months	6.59%	56
June 20X2	30	3–12 months	6.69%	55
July 20X2	31	3–12 months	6.71%	57
August 20X2	31	3–12 months	6.95%	59
September 20X2	30	3–12 months	7.06%	58
October 20X2	31	3–12 months	7.06%	60
November 20X2	30	3–12 months	7.30%	60
December 20X2	31	3–12 months	7.18%	61
December 20X2	–	3–12 months	–	10,000
Total				**10,520**

5.2.2.5 Liquidity risk management

An entity is required to describe how it manages the liquidity risk inherent in the financial liabilities included in the maturity analysis (see **5.2.2.2**). An entity should disclose a maturity analysis of financial assets it holds for managing liquidity risk (e.g. financial assets that are readily saleable or expected to generate cash inflows to meet cash outflows on financial liabilities), if that information is necessary to enable users of its financial statements to evaluate the nature and extent of liquidity risk. [IFRS 7:B11E]

There is an apparent conflict between IFRS 7 which requires the disclosure of a liquidity analysis for all *financial liabilities* and IAS 1:65 which states that "IFRS 7 requires disclosure of the maturity dates of *financial assets and financial liabilities*" [emphasis added]. An entity is not required to disclose a maturity analysis for financial assets in all cases. The minimum required disclosure is for a maturity analysis for financial liabilities only. However, a maturity analysis should be disclosed for financial assets if the entity holds financial assets for managing liquidity risk and that information is necessary to enable users of its financial statements to evaluate the nature and extent of liquidity risk. [IFRS 7:B11E]

Other factors that an entity may wish to disclose in describing how it manages its liquidity risk include, but are not limited to, whether the entity:

[IFRS 7:B11F]

(a) has committed borrowing facilities (e.g. commercial paper facilities) or other lines of credit (e.g. stand-by credit facilities) that it can access to meet liquidity needs;

(b) holds deposits at central banks to meet liquidity needs;

(c) has very diverse funding sources;

(d) has significant concentrations of liquidity risk in either its assets or its funding sources;

(e) has internal control processes and contingency plans for managing liquidity risk;

(f) has instruments that include accelerated repayment terms (e.g. on the downgrade of the entity's credit rating);

(g) has instruments that could require the posting of collateral (e.g. margin calls for derivatives);

(h) has instruments that allow the entity to choose whether it settles its financial liabilities by delivering cash (or another financial asset) or by delivering its own shares; or

(i) has instruments that are subject to master netting agreements.

5.2.3 Market risk

Market risk is defined as "the risk that the fair value or future cash flows of a financial instrument will fluctuate because of changes in market prices. Market risk comprises three types of risk: currency risk, interest rate risk and other price risk". [IFRS 7:Appendix A] Each of these risks is defined as follows.

[IFRS 7:Appendix A]

(a) **Currency risk:** the risk that the fair value or future cash flows of a financial instrument will fluctuate because of changes in foreign exchange rates. Currency risk arises on financial instruments that are denominated in a different currency to the entity's functional currency.

(b) **Interest rate risk:** the risk that the fair value or future cash flows of a financial instrument will fluctuate because of changes in market interest rates. Interest rate risk arises on interest-bearing financial instruments that are recognised in the statement of financial position (e.g. debt instruments acquired or issued), and on some financial instruments that are not recognised in the statement of financial position (e.g. some loan commitments).

(c) **Other price risk:** the risk that the fair value or future cash flows of a financial instrument will fluctuate because of changes in market prices (other than those arising from interest rate risk or currency risk), whether those changes are caused by factors specific to the individual financial instrument or its issuer, or factors affecting all similar financial instruments traded in the market.

Examples of other price risks include equity price risk, commodity price risk, prepayment risk and residual value risk.

For a financial asset or a liability that is classified as at FVTPL, whether a non-derivative or a derivative, credit risk will be a factor affecting its fair value and will affect profit or loss. For a debt security classified as AFS in accordance with IAS 39, credit risk associated with the security will affect equity. However, it is questionable whether credit risk is a 'market price risk' in the same way as an equity price, foreign exchange rate or interest rate. Also, because credit risk is specifically covered by a different set of detailed disclosures in IFRS 7 (see **5.2.1**), it is reasonable to assume that credit risk was not intended to be included in market risk. While changes in the likelihood of the obligor defaulting under a financial instrument would not be treated as a type of *other price risk*, changes in the fair value of an instrument due to, or cash flow payments contractually linked to, a variable such as a credit index which is not based on the ability of the obligor to meet its obligations under the financial instrument, will be viewed as a type of *other price risk*.

Market risk sensitivity analysis is required for each type of market risk to which the entity is exposed at the end of the reporting period showing how profit or loss and equity would have been affected by changes in the relevant risk variable that were reasonably possible at the end of the reporting period. In addition, disclosure should be provided of the methods and assumptions used in preparing the sensitivity analysis, any changes from the previous period in the methods and assumptions used, and the reasons for those changes. [IFRS 7:40]

An entity will need to decide how it should aggregate information to present a comprehensive analysis without combining information with different characteristics about exposures to risks from significantly different economic environments. For example:

(a) an entity that trades financial instruments might disclose this information separately for financial instruments held for trading and those not held for trading; and

(b) an entity that is exposed to market risks from areas of hyperinflation and areas of very low inflation would disclose the information sensitivity for the two areas.

If an entity is exposed to only one type of market risk in only one economic environment, it would not show disaggregated information. [IFRS 7:B17]

The sensitivity analysis provides useful information because it is relatively easy to calculate and understand, is suitable for all entities, and highlights the nature and extent of risks that arise from financial instruments. [IFRS 7:BC59]

It is not necessary to prepare an analysis that reflects inter-dependencies between risk variables (e.g. in preparing an interest rate sensitivity analysis, an entity does not need to determine the impact of changes in interest rates would have on the relative strengthening and weakening of the currency with other currencies). Rather, a simple sensitivity analysis that shows the change in only one variable is sufficient. [IFRS 7:BC60]

The preparation of a market risk sensitivity analysis requires the following steps.

(i) Identify risk exposures

(ii) Identify the exposures at the end of the reporting period and how those exposures affect the sensitivity analysis

(iii) Determine what is a reasonably possible change in the relevant risk variable

(iv) Determine the appropriate level of aggregation that should be provided in the disclosures

(v) Calculate and present the sensitivity analyses

Each of these steps in considered in detail below.

(i) Identify risk exposures

All market risks to which the entity is exposed need to be identified.

(ii) Identify the exposures at the end of the reporting period and how those exposures affect the sensitivity analysis

All financial instruments at the end of the reporting period whose fair value and/or cash flows are affected by changes in risk factors need to be identified.

Examples of financial instruments and their impact on profit or loss are set out below.

- Floating rate debt instruments, whether assets or liabilities, are sensitive to interest rates. The entity will flex interest rates for floating rate instruments outstanding at the period end showing how profit or loss would have varied in the period assuming the instruments at the reporting date were outstanding for the entire period.

- Foreign currency denominated debt instruments are sensitive to foreign currency rates because monetary items are retranslated into the functional currency of the entity at the reporting date. The sensitivity to foreign currency rates applies irrespective of whether the instrument is an asset or a liability, and whether it is measured at fair value or amortised cost. This includes intragroup foreign currency denominated loans that are expected to be repaid in the foreseeable future when the foreign currency risk does not eliminate on consolidation.
- For financial instruments held at the reporting date that are designated as at FVTPL or are held for trading, sensitivities will depend on the underlying risks of the instrument. A debt instrument may be sensitive to changes in interest rate and foreign currency risk, whereas an equity instrument may be sensitive to changes in equity prices and foreign currency risk.
- All derivatives in designated and qualifying fair value hedge accounting relationships are sensitive to the underlying risks of the instrument.
- Fixed rate debt instruments that are hedged items in qualifying fair value hedges of interest rate risk are sensitive to changes in interest rates.

Examples of financial instruments and their impact in other comprehensive income are set out below.

- Foreign currency denominated debt instruments that are designated as a qualifying hedging instrument in a foreign currency cash flow or net investment hedge are sensitive to foreign currency rates.
- Intragroup foreign currency denominated debt instruments to or from a foreign operation that are not expected to be repaid in the foreseeable future in accordance with IAS 21:15 are sensitive to foreign currency rates when the foreign currency risk does not eliminate on consolidation. Even though the debt instrument may form part of the foreign operation, in accordance with IAS 39:102 it remains within the scope of IAS 39 and IFRS 7 and, therefore, should be included in the sensitivity analysis.
- Derivatives and embedded derivatives designated as effective hedging instruments in a cash flow hedge or a hedge of a net investment in a foreign operation are sensitive to the underlying risks of the instrument.
- Foreign currency denominated equity securities classified as AFS are sensitive to foreign currency rates and equity prices.
- Debt securities classified as AFS in accordance with IAS 39 are sensitive to interest rate risk and credit risk, and may also be sensitive to foreign currency risk.

Any recognised financial instrument at the end of the reporting period whose cash flows are contractually linked to a variable or whose fair value is dependent on a variable should be included in a sensitivity analysis to the extent that changes in the variable will affect profit or loss or equity. For example, if an entity has issued debt that is contractually linked to inflation, where the inflation linkage is considered a closely related embedded derivative, the carrying amount of the debt and its impact on profit or loss will depend on the level of inflation throughout the reporting period and at the period end. Alternatively, if the inflation linkage is not closely related, the instrument will affect profit or loss through its remeasurement as a derivative at FVTPL.

An example of a financial instrument that has no impact on profit or loss or equity is a fixed rate debt instrument, whether an asset or a liability, measured at amortised cost, that is denominated in the entity's functional currency, which does not require any embedded derivatives to be separated. Changes in interest rates or currency rates in respect of this instrument do not impact profit or loss or equity.

IFRS 7:Appendix A defines currency risk as "the risk that the fair value or future cash flows of a financial instrument will fluctuate because of changes in foreign exchange rates. IFRS 7:B23 states that currency risk (or foreign exchange risk) arises on financial instruments that are denominated in a foreign currency, i.e. in a currency other than the functional currency in which they are measured". The Standard is clear that any foreign currency monetary item held at the reporting date should be included in the foreign currency risk sensitivity analysis. What is less clear is whether IFRS 7 requires an entity to also include in the foreign currency risk sensitivity analysis the extent to which the effective interest rate that is recognised in profit or loss in the period in respect of the monetary item held at the reporting date would have differed had foreign currency rates differed. The foreign currency interest recognised in profit or loss is usually translated using the average monthly foreign currency rate and, therefore, profit or loss is sensitive to changes in foreign currency rates irrespective of whether the loan has fixed or floating foreign currency interest. Because the monetary item affects profit or loss through the recognition of interest, as well as the translation of the carrying amount at the reporting date, it would be meaningful to include both interest and principal of a monetary item within the foreign currency sensitivity analysis. This approach is consistent with the view that foreign currency interest is variable in the functional currency of the entity.

Financial instruments that are classified as equity in accordance with IAS 32 are not remeasured and, therefore, do not affect profit or loss or equity when sensitivity analysis is performed. [IFRS 7:B28]

It should be noted that if the entity is party to derivatives over own equity that are not classified as equity (e.g. if the entity has issued warrants with an exercise price in a currency other than the functional currency of the entity), then its own equity price risk will be a relevant example of an 'other price risk'. Because the instruments will be accounted for as derivatives at FVTPL with the underlying being the entity's own equity price, they will need to be considered for the purposes of the sensitivity analysis.

(iii) Determine what is a reasonably possible change in the relevant risk variable

An entity needs to determine what it considers to be a reasonably possible change in the relevant risk variable, and should consider both the economic environment in which it operates and the time frame over which it is making the assessment. A reasonably possible change in a relevant risk variable in one environment may not be the same in another environment (e.g. a reasonably possible change in interest rates may be 100bp for Sterling denominated debt, but the same could not be said for Yen denominated debt, for which a reasonably possible change may be substantially smaller). Entities are required to judge what those reasonably possible changes are and should not include remote or 'worse case scenarios' or 'stress tests'. A reasonably possible change in the relevant risk variable should be assessed over the time frame until the entity will next present these disclosures, which is usually until the end of the entity's next annual reporting period. [IFRS 7:B19]

While the range of reasonably possible changes may be wide, disclosure is not required for each change within that range. It is sufficient to disclose the effects of the changes at the limits of the reasonably possible range. [IFRS 7:B18(b)]

IFRS 7 requires comparative information to be presented. If the volatility of a given risk variable changes and, therefore, an entity alters its view of what is a reasonably possible change, this would not prompt restatement of the comparative risk disclosures. The entity should, however, carefully disclose the fact that there has been a change in what is considered to be a reasonably possible change in the risk variable.

(iv) Determine the appropriate level of aggregation that should be provided in the disclosures

An entity should aggregate the output from sensitivity analysis in order to provide a broad view of the entity's overall sensitivity to market risk but without combining information with different characteristics about exposures to risks from significantly different economic environments. Disclosures may, for example, be provided separately for financial instruments that are held for trading from those that are not. Alternatively, disclosures may be disclosed for each risk. As a minimum, sensitivity analyses for each currency to which an entity has a significant exposure should be provided. [IFRS 7:B24]

An entity should provide sensitivity analyses for the whole of its business but may provide different types of sensitivity analysis for different classes of financial instruments. [IFRS 7:B21]

An entity could provide different types of sensitivity analysis for different parts of its business if this is consistent with how it manages risk internally. For example, a financial institution may comprise a retail banking division and an investment banking division. The entity could choose to provide a conventional sensitivity analysis, as described in the steps above, in relation to the retail banking division and a value-at-risk (VaR) analysis in relation to the investment banking division, if the latter analysis is used for internal risk management purposes within the investment banking division. However, the entity in this case would need to consider carefully how to treat any transactions and exposures between the two divisions so that the disclosure is not misleading (see (vi) below for discussion of VaR as an alternative disclosure of market risk).

(v) Calculate and present the sensitivity analyses

Entities should disclose the effect on profit or loss and equity for exposures at the end of the reporting period assuming that a reasonably possible change in the relevant risk variable had been applied to those exposures at the end of the reporting period. [IFRS 7:B18]

The sensitivity may be reported separately for different lines in profit or loss or for consolidated profit or loss and equity. An entity might disclose a sensitivity analysis for interest rate risk for each currency in which the entity has material exposures to interest rate risk. [IFRS 7:IG34]

The sensitivity of profit or loss and the sensitivity of other comprehensive income should be disclosed separately. [IFRS 7:B27]

The sensitivity analysis is prepared based on financial instruments that are recognised at the end of the reporting period. This is the case even when those exposures did not exist for the entire period or when the exposure changed materially during the period.

For example, an entity is building a road. To finance the construction of the road, it negotiates a floating rate debt facility. The entity starts to draw down on the facility half-way through the year and, by year end, it has fully drawn down the facility. A sensitivity analysis will be prepared for the loan showing profit or loss sensitivity assuming that the loan was in place for the entire period. A similar situation would arise in the case of an amortising loan where the exposure has reduced over the period due to part repayment of the principal. In that instance, the sensitivity analysis would be prepared on the basis of the exposure at the end of the reporting period, notwithstanding the significantly higher exposures during the period.

IFRS 7:35 does state that if the quantitative data disclosed as at the end of the reporting period is unrepresentative of an entity's exposure to risk during the period, the entity should provide further information that is representative. For sensitivity analysis, an entity may provide supplementary disclosures illustrating the impact on profit or loss and equity based on the timing of recognition and derecognition of financial instruments in the period, in addition to the analysis based on financial instruments recognised at the period end.

While IFRS 7 provides some guidance on the determination of reasonably possible changes in the relevant risk variable, no guidance is available on whether the degree of change at the end of the reporting period in the relevant risk variable should be extrapolated to the risk variables during the period, or whether the change should be determined as a fixed amount of change.

For example, an entity has a floating rate liability at the reporting date. The current LIBOR rate is 5 per cent, and the entity estimates that a reasonably possible change in LIBOR is 100bp. During the year, LIBOR was 2 per cent in the first half of the year, 3 per cent at half-year and 4 per cent during the second 6 months. The volatility in cash flows during the year may either be expressed as:

(a) an *absolute change* of 100bp's to all rates. Thus, the sensitivity would be of 100bp increase and decrease to the loan's cash flows during the year; or

(b) a *percentage change*, where the change at the end of the reporting period is 20 per cent (1/5) and, hence, all rates should change by 20 per cent during the period. Thus, the volatility in cash flows will be determined as the change of the above interest rate of 1.6 and 2.4 per cent, 2.4 and 3.6 per cent and 3.2 and 4.8 per cent (all increased and decreased by 20 per cent).

While either approach would be acceptable under IFRS 7, approach (a) provides information that seems more relevant and reliable than approach (b), because the sensitivity analysis will be more comparable with past periods. Whichever approach is used, the methods and assumptions used should be disclosed.

IFRS 7 requires disclosure of a sensitivity analysis showing how profit or loss and equity would have been affected by changes in the relevant risk variable. The Standard is not clear whether sensitivity analysis should be provided on a pre- or post-tax basis. Because equity is defined in IAS 32 as the residual interest in the assets of the entity after deducting all of its liabilities, and tax on gains or losses recognised in other comprehensive income (and accumulated in equity) will also be recognised in other comprehensive income (and accumulated in equity), it is reasonable to assume that for the purposes of the sensitivity analysis the analysis should be net of tax. Additionally, IFRS 7:IG36 provides an example of a sensitivity analysis that is determined on an after-tax basis.

Example 5.2.3A

Market risk disclosures: sensitivity analysis

Company D (ZAR functional currency) is a diversified oil and gas group. The earnings of the group are exposed to movements due to changes in market interest rates, equity prices, exchange rates and commodity prices. The entity expects the following to be reasonably possible changes in the relevant risk variable at the end of the reporting period.

ZAR market interest rates =	**100 basis points**
ZAR equity prices =	8%
ZAR/USD exchange rate =	15%
USD Brent crude price =	25%

Assume a tax rate of 30%. Profit after tax for the year ended 31 December 20X0 was ZAR 2,750 million and equity was ZAR 1,000 million. Company D has the following financial instruments that have an exposure to the relevant risk variable at the end of the reporting period.

(1) USD denominated short term accounts receivable with a carrying amount of ZAR 235 million are held at amortised cost.

(2) ZAR denominated listed equity investments that are classified as held for trading with a carrying amount of ZAR 500 million.

(3) ZAR denominated listed equity investments that are classified as AFS with a carrying amount of ZAR 200 million.

(4) ZAR denominated fixed rate cash deposits with a carrying amount ZAR 1,245 million. The cash deposits are classified as loans and receivables and return a rate of 10 per cent per annum. The deposits were initially recognised at the beginning of the year.

(5) ZAR denominated treasury bonds that have a fixed rate of interest of 12 per cent per annum with a carrying amount of ZAR 765 million. The bonds are designated as at FVTPL. A 100 basis point change in market interest rates is equivalent to a 4 per cent change in the fair value of the bond.

(6) Purchased Brent crude futures denominated in USD that are classified as held for trading and have a carrying amount of ZAR 490 million. A 100 basis point change in the ZAR market interest rate is equivalent to a 1 per cent change in the fair value of the futures and a 25 per cent change in the Brent crude oil price is equivalent to a 20 per cent change in the fair value of the futures.

(7) USD denominated fixed rate borrowings initially recognised at the beginning of the year. The interest rate is 10 per cent. The borrowings have been classified as a liability to be carried at amortised cost. The weighted average exchange rate during the reporting period was ZAR7:$1.These borrowings were designated as a hedge of a net investment of its foreign operation and had a carrying amount at year end of ZAR 730 million (USD100 million at a closing exchange rate of ZAR7.3:$1).

(8) ZAR denominated floating rate borrowings of ZAR 350 million that are classified as a financial liability held at amortised cost and were entered into at the beginning of the year for an amount of ZAR 350 million. The floating interest resets on a quarterly basis in advance, with the quarterly rates during the past reporting period being as follows,

Month	Rate
1 January 20X0	14%
1 April 20X0	13%
1 July 20X0	12%
1 October 20X0	13%
1 January 20X1	14%

Company D wishes to present its sensitivity analysis by risk variable. Comparative financial information has been ignored for the purposes of this example.

The following represents the calculation of the market risk sensitivity analysis as required by IFRS 7:40.

Market interest rates

Items (1), (2), (3) and (4) do not affect profit or loss or equity, if market interest rates change. In the case of item (4), the ZAR denominated fixed rate cash deposits that are classified as loans and receivables do not affect profit or loss or equity given a reasonably possible change in market interest rates since they are neither measured at fair value nor do they contain variable cash flows.

Item (5), the ZAR denominated fixed rate bonds that are designated at fair value through profit or loss will result in sensitivity in profit or loss of ZAR 765 million x 4% = +/-**ZAR 30.60 million**.

Item (6), the Brent crude futures will result in sensitivity in profit or loss of +/- ZAR 490 million x 1% = +/-**ZAR 4.90 million**.

Item (7), the USD denominated fixed rate liability is designated as a hedging instrument for foreign currency risk only, with the carrying amount in foreign currency measured at amortised cost. This liability does not affect profit or loss or equity if market interest rates change since it is neither measured at fair value nor does it contain variable cash flows.

Item (8), the ZAR denominated floating rate borrowings are subject to floating interest rates. If market rates changed by 100 basis points during the period the sensitivity in interest cash flows would be 1.0% x ZAR 350million = +/-**ZAR 3.50 million**.

The treasury bond assets and the issued floating rate borrowings have the same directional sensitivity to interest rates with respect to their impact on profit or loss. As interest rates rise, the treasury bond assets fall in value, resulting in a loss in profit or loss, and the floating rate borrowing results in a higher interest expense in profit or loss. The reverse is equally true when interest rates fall. Total profit or loss sensitivity as a result of changes in ZAR market interest rates is +/-**ZAR 27.30 million** after tax (30.60+4.90+3.50) x (1-30%).

ZAR Equity prices

Items (1), (4) – (8) do not affect profit or loss or equity if ZAR equity prices change.

Item (2), the ZAR listed investments that have been classified as held for trading will result in profit or loss sensitivity of ZAR 500 million x 8% = +/-ZAR 40.00 million.

Item (3), the ZAR listed investments that have been classified as available for sale will result in equity sensitivity of ZAR 200 million x 8% = +/-ZAR 16.00 million.

Total profit or loss sensitivity as a result of changes in ZAR equity prices is +/-**ZAR 28.00 million** after tax 40.00 x (1-30%).

Total equity sensitivity as a result of changes in ZAR equity prices is +/-**ZAR 11.20 million** after tax 16.00 x (1-30%).

ZAR/USD exchange rate

Items (2), (3), (4), (5) and (8) do not affect profit or loss or equity if ZAR/USD exchange rates change.

Item (1), the USD denominated accounts receivable will result in profit or loss sensitivity of ZAR 235 million x 15% = +/-ZAR 35.25 million.

Item (6), the USD denominated Brent crude derivatives will result in profit or loss sensitivity of ZAR 490 million x 15% = +/-ZAR 73.50 million.

Item (7), the USD denominated borrowings will result in equity sensitivity of ZAR 730 million x 15% = +/-ZAR 109.50 million, being the retranslation of the borrowings at the end of the reporting period. Sensitivity of profit or loss due to recording interest cash flows during the year at a different exchange rate is determined as USD 100million x 10% interest rate x weighted average exchange rate during the year of ZAR7:$1 x sensitivity of 15% = ZAR 10.50 million.

Total profit or loss sensitivity as a result of changes in the ZAR/USD exchange rate is +/-**ZAR 68.78 million** after tax (35.25+73.5-10.5) x (1-30%).

Total equity sensitivity as a result of changes in the ZAR/USD exchange rate is +/-**ZAR 76.65 million** after tax (109.5) x (1-30%).

USD Brent crude price

Items (1) – (5), (7) and (8) do not affect profit or loss or equity if USD Brent crude prices change.

Item (6), the USD denominated Brent crude futures will result in profit or loss sensitivity of ZAR 490million x 20% = +/-ZAR 98.00 million.

Total profit or loss sensitivity as a result of changes in the Brent crude price is +/-ZAR 68.60 million after tax 98.00 x (1-30%).

Disclosure

For financial instruments held, the entity has used a sensitivity analysis technique that measures the change in the fair value and cash flows of the entity's financial instruments for hypothetical changes in all relevant market risk variables.

The amounts generated from the sensitivity analysis are forward-looking estimates of market risk assuming certain market conditions. Actual results in the future may differ materially from those projected results due to the inherent uncertainty of global financial markets. The methods and assumptions used are the same as those applied in the previous reporting period.

The sensitivity of profit or loss and equity due to changes in the relevant risk variables as at 31 December 20X0 are set out in the table below. The methods and assumptions used in calculating are set out in note X1 to the financial statements.

The estimated change in fair values and cash flows for changes in market interest rates are based on an instantaneous increase or decrease of 100 basis points at the end of the reporting period, with all other variables remaining constant.

The estimated change in fair values for changes in ZAR equity prices are based on an instantaneous increase or decrease of 8 per cent for instruments at the end of the reporting period, with all other variables remaining constant.

The estimated change in fair values for changes in the ZAR/USD exchange rate are based on an instantaneous increase or decrease of 15 per cent for instruments at the end of the reporting period, with all other variables remaining constant.

The estimated change in fair values for changes in Brent crude prices are based on an instantaneous increase or decrease of 25 per cent for instruments at the end of the reporting period, with all other variables remaining constant.

The above-mentioned changes in the risk variables may result in non-proportional changes in fair values or cash flows due to the specific terms and nature of the relevant risk exposures.

The sensitivity analysis is for illustrative purposes only - in practice market rates rarely change in isolation and are likely to be interdependent.

The sensitivity of the relevant risk variables, on an after tax basis is as follows.

Market risk exposure	Profit or loss sensitivity ZAR million	Equity sensitivity ZAR million
Market interest rates	+/–27.30	–
ZAR equity prices	+/–28.00	+/–11.20
ZAR/USD exchange rates	+/–68.78	+/–76.65
USD Brent crude	+/–68.60	–

Example 5.2.3A includes only non-optional derivatives (in this case, Brent crude oil futures). Other non-optional derivatives include swaps and forward contracts. If non-optional derivatives do not contain options embedded within their contractual terms (such as knock-out or knock-in options, early termination clauses that terminate at an amount other than at fair value), the sensitivity to the underlying is likely to be the same irrespective of whether the price of the underlying moves up or down. This would not be the case for optional derivatives like options, or derivatives that are constructed using combinations of options (e.g. collars). Because an option addresses one-directional exposure (e.g. protection against rising interest rates), the fair value sensitivity of the option to increasing interest rates will be different from the sensitivity to falling interest rates. The fair value sensitivity of optional derivatives will vary depending on the directional movement in the underlying market risk. The fair value sensitivity of an option to the underlying market risk will also depend on the price of the underlying at the end of the reporting period compared to the strike price of the option. If an option is nearly at the money, it will have a greater sensitivity to changes in market risk when compared to an option that is deeply out of the money.

Impairment of financial assets can also be affected by changes in an underlying market risk. However, it seems appropriate that for debt instruments only changes in existing impairment losses should be considered in the determination of the market risk sensitivity analysis. An entity should not project additional impairment losses that might occur given a movement in an underlying market risk. For example, if a loan is not impaired at the period end it will not be treated as impaired for the purposes of the sensitivity analysis.

If an AFS debt instrument in the scope of IAS 39 is impaired at the end of the reporting period and all the accumulated loss has been recognised in profit or loss in accordance with IAS 39:67 - 68, the sensitivity of the fair value of the debt instrument to changes in interest rates will affect the extent of impairment recognised in profit or loss. Had interest rates been higher or lower, the amount of impairment recognised in profit or loss in the period would have been different because a different market interest rate would have resulted in a different fair value.

If an AFS debt instrument in the scope of IAS 39 is not impaired at the end of the reporting period, changes in the relevant risk variable should not result in the recognition of an impairment loss. For example, the increased likelihood of a borrower defaulting in a higher interest rate environment should not result in the lender recognising an impairment loss in its interest rate sensitivity analysis. This view is consistent with the view that credit risk is not a market risk, as discussed at the start of this section.

If a floating rate financial asset is impaired at the end of the reporting period, the amount of interest income in the period will be sensitive to changes in the floating rates for the period. If the floating rate cash flows are themselves impaired, as opposed to the principal cash flow, then changes in the floating rate will affect the amount of impairment at the period end. This is not the case for a fixed rate asset because all cash flows are fixed and the effective interest rate is not sensitive to changes in interest rates.

In the case of sensitivity analysis to equity price risk of non-monetary AFS financial assets in the scope of IAS 39, it is necessary to consider carefully whether a reasonably possible change in the relevant equity price would affect equity or profit or loss. Consider the case of an investment in an equity security that has already suffered an impairment loss by the end of the reporting period. Because reversals of impairment on equity securities classified as AFS may not be recognised through profit or loss, in such a case a reasonably possible downward fall in the equity price would be shown as affecting profit or loss, but an equivalent upward shift would be shown as affecting equity. The fair value of an AFS equity security that has not previously been impaired could become impaired depending on what is considered a reasonably possible downward shift in equity prices (based on a significant or prolonged decline in fair value of an investment in an equity security below cost in accordance with IAS 39:61). In such a case, consideration must be given to whether a reasonably possible downward movement in the equity price would affect equity or profit or loss, taking into account an entity's impairment policy.

(vi) Provide additional disclosures

When the sensitivity analysis is unrepresentative of a risk inherent in a financial instrument, that fact is required to be disclosed together with the reason why the entity believes the sensitivity analysis is unrepresentative. [IFRS 7:42] Examples of circumstances where this may occur include the following.

[IFRS 7:IG37 - IG39]

(a) Financial instruments contain terms and conditions whose effects are not apparent from the sensitivity analysis (e.g. options that are deeply out of (or in) the money for the chosen change in risk variable). In this situation, additional disclosures might include the terms and conditions of the financial instruments, the effect on profit or loss if the option were exercised.

(b) Financial assets are illiquid so that the calculated changes in profit or loss are difficult to realise when there are low volumes of transactions or lack of counterparties to trade at those prices or rates. In this situation, additional disclosures might include the reasons for the reasons for the lack of liquidity and how the entity hedges the risk.

(c) An entity has a large holding of a financial asset that would be sold at a discount or premium to the quoted market price. In this situation, additional disclosures might include the nature of the security (e.g. the entity name), the extent of holding, the effect on profit or loss and how the entity hedges the risk.

IFRS 7:IG38(b) states that when financial instruments contain terms and conditions whose effects are not apparent from the sensitivity analysis, an entity may wish to state the effect on profit or loss if the term or condition were met. An entity may also wish to state the impact on equity because this is consistent with the objective of sensitivity analysis of providing users of financial statements with the impact on profit or loss and equity. For example, an entity may have designated a purchased interest cap as a cash flow hedge of highly probable forecast floating interest payments where the option is so deeply out of the money at the period end that no intrinsic value is recognised in other comprehensive income. Because the option is so deeply out of the money, a moderate change in interest rates has little fair value sensitivity. If interest rates were to increase significantly, movements in the option's fair value would be reflected in profit or loss, and potentially would result in part of the fair value being recognised in other comprehensive income (and accumulated in equity) if interest rates are higher than the strike price of the cap. Because the derivative is an effective hedging instrument in a cash flow hedge, illustrating the impact on equity is equally appropriate to illustrating the impact in profit or loss.

The sensitivity analysis may not give a true presentation of exposure to risk in cases where the hedging instrument is in the scope of IFRS 7 but the hedged item is not. An example is a hedge of a net investment in a foreign operation. Changes in the sensitivity of the fair value of derivatives or foreign currency risk for non-derivative financial instruments will be reported in other comprehensive income if it is a qualifying hedging instrument in a net investment hedge. The changes in the hedged item, being the retranslation of the net assets in accordance with IAS 21 *The Effects of Changes in Foreign Exchange Rates*, is not required to be reported in the sensitivity analysis because it is not a financial instrument within the scope of IFRS 7. An entity may choose to provide additional disclosure to explain that the retranslation of the net assets of the foreign operation would reduce the sensitivity of the hedging instrument in equity. For example, if the entity designates spot foreign currency risk as being hedged and the hedge is fully effective, the gains and losses on the hedging instrument recognised in other comprehensive income (and accumulated in equity) will be offset by the losses and gains on foreign currency translation on the net assets of the foreign operation, which are also recognised in other comprehensive income (and accumulated in equity).

Similarly, additional disclosure may be appropriate for cash flow hedges or fair value hedges of non-financial items (including unrecognised 'off balance sheet' items). An entity may designate a foreign exchange forward contract in a highly effective hedge of a firm commitment to acquire plant and equipment, with the hedged risk being spot foreign currency risk. The forward contract will be included in the sensitivity analysis, while the fair value adjustment to the firm commitment to acquire a non-financial item will be outside the scope of IFRS 7. Additional disclosures may be useful to explain that the retranslation of the firm commitment at spot rates reduces the sensitivity of the hedging instrument in profit or loss.

Example 5.2.3B

Interest rate risk

[IFRS 7:IG36]

At 31 December 20X2, if interest rates at that date had been 10 basis points lower with all other variables held constant, post-tax profit for the year would have been CU1.7 million (20X1 – CU2.4 million) higher, arising mainly as a result of lower interest expense on variable borrowings, and other comprehensive income would have been CU2.8 million (20X1 – CU3.2 million) higher, arising mainly as a result of an increase in the fair value of fixed rate financial assets classified as available for sale. If interest rates had been 10 basis points higher, with all other variables held constant, post-tax profit would have been CU1.5 million (20X1 – CU2.1 million) lower, arising mainly as a result of higher interest expense on variable borrowings, and other comprehensive income would have been CU3.0 million (20X1 – CU3.4 million) lower, arising mainly as a result of a decrease in the fair value of fixed rate financial assets classified as available for sale. Profit is more sensitive to interest rate decreases than increases because of borrowings with capped interest rates. The sensitivity is lower in 20X2 than in 20X1 because of a reduction in outstanding borrowings that has occurred as the entity's debt has matured (see note X).

Foreign currency exchange rate risk

At 31 December 20X2, if the CU had weakened 10 per cent against the US dollar with all other variables held constant, post-tax profit for the year would have been CU2.8 million (20X1 – CU6.4 million) lower, and other comprehensive income would have been CU1.2 million (20X1 – CU1.1 million) higher. Conversely, if the CU had strengthened 10 per cent against the US dollar with all other variables held constant, post-tax profit would have been CU2.8 million

(20X1 – CU6.4 million) higher, and other comprehensive income would have been CU1.2 million (20X1 – CU1.1 million) lower. The lower foreign currency exchange rate sensitivity in profit in 20X2 compared with 20X1 is attributable to a reduction in foreign currency denominated debt. Equity is more sensitive in 20X2 than in 20X1 because of the increased use of hedges of foreign currency purchases, offset by the reduction in foreign currency debt.

As an alternative to sensitivity analysis, disclosure may be provided of a value-at-risk (VaR) analysis that reflects interdependencies between risk variables. An entity may only disclose value-at-risk analysis when the entity uses such a model to manage risk internally. Disclosures should include an explanation of the method used in preparing such an analysis, how the model works (such as whether the model is based on a delta- normal variance-covariance approach, historical simulation or Monte Carlo simulation), the main parameters and assumptions underlying the data provided such as the holding period, confidence interval, historical observation period and weightings assigned to the observations, how options are dealt with and which volatilities and correlations are used. The objective of the method used and the limitations that may result in the information not fully reflecting the fair value of the assets and liabilities involved should also be disclosed. [IFRS 7:41 & B20]

The value-at-risk analysis used internally may measure the potential for loss or gain including the effects of items that are outside the scope of IFRS 7 (e.g. contracts to buy or sell non-financial items outside the scope of IAS 39, hedged items that are outside the scope of IFRS 7 or risks such as credit risk that are not market risks). In contrast to conventional sensitivity analysis as described above, a value- at-risk analysis including such items would, if used as a model to manage risk internally, satisfy the requirements of the Standard. If such items are included, this fact should be clearly disclosed as part of the method used in preparing the analysis.

Example 5.2.3C

Market risk disclosures: value at risk

The Group manages the market risk in its trading and treasury portfolios through the use of value-at-risk (VaR) limits as well as stress testing, position and sensitivity limits. VaR is a technique that produces estimates of the potential negative change in the market value of a portfolio over a specified time horizon at a given confidence level. The table below sets out the trading and treasury VaR for the Group, which assumes a 95 per cent confidence level and a one-day time horizon. The VAR model uses largely historical data from the preceding three years to simulate scenarios of the future.

Year	Period end CUm	Minimum CUm	Maximum CUm	Average CUm
Trading VaR				
20X1	17.2	13.4	24.3	19.1
20X0	16.2	14.0	22.3	18.1
Treasury VaR				
20X1	8.1	6.6	12.1	9.5
20X0	8.0	6.9	13.1	8.5

The Group's VaR should be interpreted in light of the limitations of the methodologies used. These limitations include the following.

- Historical data may not provide the best estimate of the joint distribution of risk factor changes in the future and may fail to capture the risk of possible extreme adverse market movements which have not occurred in the historical window used in the calculations.
- VaR using a one-day time horizon does not fully capture the market risk of positions that cannot be liquidated or hedged within one day.
- The Group largely computes the VaR of the trading portfolios at the close of business and positions may change substantially during the course of the trading day. Controls are in place to limit the Group's intra-day exposure such as the calculation of VaR for selected portfolios.
- VaR using a 95 per cent confidence level does not reflect the extent of potential losses beyond that percentile.

These limitations and the nature of the VaR measure mean that the Group can neither guarantee that losses will not exceed the VaR amounts indicated nor that losses in excess of the VaR amounts will not occur more frequently than once in 20 business days.

6 Offsetting financial assets and financial liabilities

6.1 General principle

IAS 32 requires that a financial asset and a financial liability should be offset as a net amount in the statement of financial position when, and only when, both of the following conditions are satisfied:

- the entity currently has a legally enforceable right to set off the recognised amounts of the asset and liability; and
- the entity intends to settle on a net basis, or to realise the asset and settle the liability simultaneously.

In the case of a transfer of a financial asset that does not qualify for derecognition under IAS 39, the entity should not offset the transferred asset and the associated liability (for further details on derecognition refer to **3.3** in **chapter C8**). [IAS 32:42]

When offset is applied, the entity has the right to pay or receive a single net amount in relation to the two instruments, and intends to do so; therefore, in effect, the entity only has a single financial asset or financial liability. If the conditions for offset are not met, the two financial instruments are presented separately. Whether or not a financial asset and a financial liability are offset, they should be measured in accordance with the normal measurement principles with respect to financial assets and financial liabilities.

It should be noted that offsetting a financial asset and a financial liability (and the consequent net presentation in the statement of financial position) is different from derecognition of those financial instruments. In contrast to offsetting, derecognition of a financial asset or a financial liability not only removes the financial instrument from the statement of financial position, but also may give rise to a gain or loss on derecognition. [IAS 32:44] Offset does not result in the asset or liability being removed from the statement of financial position, but in net presentation of the asset and liability as either a net asset or a net liability. A gain or loss does not arise because of the offsetting requirements, although it may arise because of the measurement requirements applicable to the asset or liability, respectively.

In December 2011 the IASB issued amendments to IAS 32 *Offsetting Financial Assets and Financial Liabilities*. Concurrently the IASB introduced new offsetting disclosures by amending IFRS 7 which is described in **section 6.7**. The amendments to IAS 32 introduce further application guidance which was intended to address inconsistencies in applying some of the offsetting criteria. This included clarifying the meaning of 'currently has a legally enforceable right of set-off' and that some gross settlement systems may be considered equivalent to net settlement. [IAS 32:BC78] These amendments are reflected in the sections below. The amendments are effective for annual periods beginning on or after 1 January 2013.

In September 2014 the IASB issued *Annual Improvements to IFRSs 2012-2014 Cycle*, which amended IFRS 7:44R to clarify that the additional disclosure required by the amendments to IFRS 7 *Disclosure – Offsetting Financial Assets and Financial Liabilities* is not specifically required in condensed interim financial statements that are prepared in accordance with IAS 34 *Interim Financial Reporting*. However, the additional disclosure is given when its inclusion would be required in accordance with the general principles in IAS 34. The amendment applies retrospectively for annual periods beginning on or after 1 January 2016. Earlier application is permitted in which case an entity shall disclose that it has applied those amendments for an earlier period.

6.2 Legal right of offset

The first part of the offset criteria is that the reporting entity 'currently has a legally enforceable right to set off the recognised amounts' [IAS 32:42]

IAS 32 defines the right of offset as a debtor's legal right, by contract or otherwise, to settle or otherwise eliminate all or a portion of an amount due to a creditor by applying against that amount an amount due from the creditor. Because the right is specifically a legal right, the circumstances that give rise to such a right will vary from one legal jurisdiction to another. Thus, for each relationship between the two parties (the debtor and the creditor), it will be necessary to consider the particular laws applicable to it. [IAS 32:45]

The amendments to IAS 32 acknowledge that a right of set-off may be currently available or it may be contingent on a future event (for example, the right may be triggered or exercisable only on the occurrence of some future event, such as the default, insolvency or bankruptcy of one of the counterparties). Even if the right of set-off is not contingent on a future event, it may only be legally enforceable in the normal course of business, or in the event of default, or in the event of insolvency or bankruptcy, of one or all of the counterparties. [IAS 32:AG38A]

The Standard makes clear the characteristics that a currently legally enforceable right to set-off the recognised amounts should have. The right of set-off:

[IAS 32:AG38B]

(a) must not be contingent on a future event; and

(b) must be legally enforceable in all of the following circumstances:

   (i) the normal course of business;

   (ii) the event of default; and

   (iii) the event of insolvency or bankruptcy of the entity and all of the counterparties.

The nature and extent of the right of set-off, including any conditions attached to its exercise and whether it would remain in the event of default or insolvency or bankruptcy, may vary from one legal jurisdiction to another. Consequently, it cannot be assumed that the right of set-off is automatically available outside of the normal course of business. For example, the bankruptcy or insolvency laws of a jurisdiction may prohibit, or restrict, the right of set-off in the event of bankruptcy or insolvency in some circumstances. [IAS 32:AG38C] The reference to default, insolvency or bankruptcy are broad and are intended to describe scenarios where an entity will not or cannot perform under the contract. [IAS 32:BC81]

The laws applicable to the relationships between the parties (for example, contractual provisions, the laws governing the contract, or the default, insolvency or bankruptcy laws applicable to the parties) need to be considered to ascertain whether the right of set-off is enforceable in the normal course of business, in an event of default, and in the event of insolvency or bankruptcy, of the entity and all of the counterparties (as specified in IAS 32:AG38B(b)). [IAS 32:AG38D]

The amendments to IAS 32 in this area arose following feedback on the exposure draft that revealed inconsistencies in the application of this criterion. In amending IAS 32 the IASB made clear that where set-off only arises if a contingent event occurs it is not acceptable to offset financial assets and financial liabilities. Even where the right to set-off is not dependent on a contingent event the right to set-off must apply in all circumstances, i.e. not just in the normal course of business but also in bankruptcy, default or insolvency. This means that the right must apply in cases where the reporting entity (or counterparty) ceases to operate as a going concern.

Uncertainties about the amount to be paid (and/or received) under the set-off arrangement do not preclude an entity from currently having a legally enforceable right to set-off. Similarly, the passage of time is not considered a contingent right that would prevent offsetting. [IAS 32:BC83]

For example, if a receivable and payable are contractually due on the same date and there is an enforceable right to set-off on that date, the fact there is no right to enforce net settlement (and potentially simultaneous settlement) prior to that date does not prevent offset as prior to that the receivable and payable are not due. However, in order for the offset criteria to be met the reporting entity must be able to demonstrate that there is a currently enforceable right to set-off the recognised amounts on the settlement date which would apply in all circumstances, i.e. in the normal course of business or in the case of default, insolvency or bankruptcy of either party.

If the right of set-off is not exercisable during a period when amounts are due and payable, then the entity does not meet the offsetting criterion as it has no right to set off those payments. [IAS 32:BC84] For example, a right to set-off the recognised amount that only applies say at the reporting period end, but not throughout the reporting period(s) would not meet the offset criterion.

Similarly, a right of set-off that could disappear or that would no longer be enforceable after a future event that could take place in the normal course of business or in the event of default, or in the event of insolvency or bankruptcy, such as a ratings downgrade, would not meet the currently legally enforceable criterion in IAS 32:42(a). [IAS 32:BC84]

In some circumstances, the debtor may have a legal right to apply an amount due from a third party against the amount due to a creditor provided that there is an agreement between the three parties that clearly establishes the debtor's right to offset. [IAS 32:45]

Legal rights do not need to be established in a single document between the three parties. For example, a debtor might obtain set-off rights separately from the third party and from the creditor. In establishing the validity of the legal right to set-off, it is necessary to understand the terms of the particular contracts, as well as the context within which set-off is to be applied. The legal right to set-off could, inter alia, be evidenced with reference to a legal opinion, or be established by statutory or regulatory provisions which have been clearly demonstrated as applicable to and governing the particular transaction.

Assessing whether the entity has a legal right to set off the recognised amounts is independent from assessing how the reporting entity intends to settle the arrangement. The requirement to have a currently legally enforceable right to set off the recognised amounts in effect means that the reporting entity can enforce settlement of the net amount and can do so in all situations (i.e. the exercise of this right is not contingent on a future event). The Board clarified in the Basis for Conclusions that the ability to exercise this right 'is assured' [IAS 32:BC86]. This right must exist and be assured irrespective if the entity does not intend to settle the net amount, but instead (as permitted by IAS 32) intends to settle the asset and liability simultaneously (see **6.3**).

For a discussion of considerations surrounding master netting agreements refer to **6.6**.

6.3 Intention to settle on a net basis, or to realise the asset and settle the liability simultaneously

The second part of the offset criteria is that the reporting entity 'intends to settle on a net basis, or to realise the asset and settle the liability simultaneously'. [IAS 32:42]

The existence of the legal right of offset (while it affects the entity's rights and obligations and may affect its credit exposure) is not sufficient in itself for offsetting. When there is a legal right, and an entity intends to exercise the right of offset (i.e. to settle net), or to settle simultaneously, the entity is, in effect, exposed to a net amount, which reflects the timing of the expected cash flows and the risks to which those cash flows are exposed and, therefore, presentation of the financial instruments on a net basis is appropriate. [IAS 32:46]

The intention by one or both parties to settle on a net basis without the legal right to do so is not sufficient to justify offsetting a financial asset and a financial liability. This is due to the fact that the legal rights and obligations pertaining to the individual financial assets and financial liabilities are not altered. [IAS 32:45]

Intention may be demonstrated through management representations that are not contradicted by past experience or other relevant circumstances (e.g. normal business practices, requirements of financial markets, circumstances that limit the ability to settle net) and also may take into account reference to the entity's risk management policies, if appropriate. There is no requirement for an assessment of the counterparty's intent, however, if the counterparty was able to restrict the reporting entity's right to enforce the set-off of the recognised amounts this prevents the reporting entity from meeting the offset criteria.

Example 6.3

Offset: unmatched payments and receipts

Assume that the legal right of offset exists in the following scenario.

Company X owes Company Y four payments of CU10 million each at the end of each calendar quarter (31 March, 30 June, 30 September, 31 December), totalling CU40 million. As part of another contract, Company Y owes Company X two payments of CU15 million at 30 June and 31 December, totalling CU30 million.

The intention to settle simultaneously can only be demonstrated in respect of the 30 June and 31 December cash flows. At the beginning of the year, Company X will, therefore, reflect a financial liability of CU20 million (being the 31 March and 30 September payments) and a separate financial asset of CU10 million (representing the difference between the CU10 million payable and CU15 million receivable from Company Y on 30 June and 31 December). Although Company X's net position over the whole year is a financial liability of CU10 million, because it cannot demonstrate the intention to settle net or simultaneously for all payments, the criteria for offset are not satisfied in respect of those unmatched payments and separate presentation is required. Company Y correspondingly has an asset of CU20 million and a liability of CU10 million.

It is common for entities to have amounts on deposit with a financial institution and simultaneously have a drawn-down borrowing facility, sometimes referred to as an 'overdraft', with the same financial institution. The entity has a separate financial asset and a financial liability with the same counterparty. It is usually not possible to achieve offset for the asset and the liability because, in most cases, the entity cannot assert that the asset will be used to settle the liability. The asset will rise and fall as the entity places further cash on deposit or withdraws cash to settle other obligations. Although the asset at the reporting date could be used to settle the overdraft, the entity cannot claim offset because the entity does not have the intention at the reporting date to settle the overdraft liability with the deposit asset. Rather, the entity's intention is to use the deposit asset at the reporting date, and potentially draw down more borrowings if needed to meet its working capital needs.

The amendments to IAS 32 clarified when simultaneous settlement of gross amounts can meet the second part of the offset criterion in IAS 32:42. This will be the case where the gross settlement mechanism has features that eliminate or result in insignificant credit and liquidity risk, and that will process receivables and payables in a single settlement process or cycle. For example, a gross settlement system that has all of the following characteristics would meet the net settlement criterion in IAS 32:42(b):

(a) financial assets and financial liabilities eligible for set-off are submitted at the same point in time for processing;

(b) once the financial assets and financial liabilities are submitted for processing, the parties are committed to fulfil the settlement obligation;

(c) there is no potential for the cash flows arising from the assets and liabilities to change once they have been submitted for processing (unless the processing fails-see (d) below);

(d) assets and liabilities that are collateralised with securities will be settled on a securities transfer or similar system (for example, delivery versus payment), so that if the transfer of securities fails, the processing of the related receivable or payable for which the securities are collateral will also fail (and vice versa);

(e) any transactions that fail, as outlined in (d), will be re-entered for processing until they are settled;

(f) settlement is carried out through the same settlement institution (for example, a settlement bank, a central bank or a central securities depository); and

(g) an intraday credit facility is in place that will provide sufficient overdraft amounts to enable the processing of payments at the settlement date for each of the parties, and it is virtually certain that the intraday credit facility will be honoured if called upon.

[IAS 32:AG38F]

The Basis for Conclusions recognises that simultaneous settlement is included as a practical exception to net settlement as there may be cases when an entity currently has a legally enforceable right and desire to settle net, but may not have the operational capabilities to effect net settlement. The gross positions would be settled at the same moment such that the outcome would not be distinguishable from net settlement. [IAS 32:BC95] The requirements introduced in IAS 32:AG38F were included to clarify that certain gross settlement mechanism with features that both (i) eliminate credit and liquidity risk; and (ii) process receivables and payables in a single settlement process may meet the simultaneous settlement criteria in IAS 32:42(b). [IAS 32:BC99].

The Board was conscious not to mandate that arrangements with all clearing houses or other similar organisations would meet the simultaneous settlement criteria as arrangements will vary with different organisations. Therefore care should be taken in analysing the contractual arrangements with clearing houses and other similar organisations against the strict criteria in IAS 32:AG38F.

6.4 Unit of account to which offsetting applies

IAS 32 does not provide specific guidance whether the offset requirements are to be applied to the unit of account as included in the statement of financial position (i.e. the entire financial instrument) or whether it is applied to individual identifiable contractual cash flows that make up the financial instrument.

The IASB considered this issue when developing the amendments to IAS 32 but decided to provide no further guidance. The IASB acknowledges that some industries, e.g. energy producers and traders, apply the offsetting criteria to individual identifiable cash flows whereas others do not. The Board noted that some entities such as financial institutions would find it impractical and burdensome to apply offsetting to individual identifiable cash flows. [IAS 32:BC106]

The Board acknowledged that the focus of the offsetting model is the entity's net exposure and expected future cash flows from settling the related financial instruments. [IAS 32:BC107] The Board did consider clarifying the application guidance in IAS 32 to indicate that offsetting should apply to individual identifiable cash flows of financial instruments, however, it decided against such an approach because of the need to add an exemption from this requirement for some entities on the grounds of operational complexity. The Board concluded that applying either approach, being the entire financial instrument or individual identifiable cash flows of the financial instrument, does not result in inappropriate application of the offsetting criteria and therefore chose to not provide any further guidance. [IAS 32:BC110 & BC111]

In light of the IASB's view that it is appropriate to apply offsetting to either an entire financial instrument or individual identifiable cash flows, entities should apply one of these approaches as a consistently applied accounting policy.

There may be circumstances where the offset requirements are met only in relation to some of the cash flows of a contractually single financial asset and a contractually single financial liability. In such circumstances, the offset requirements are applied to the extent that the conditions are met. This is illustrated in the following example.

Example 6.4

Offset: partial offset of cash flows

Company A and Company B are independent entities. On 1 January 20X1, Company A borrows CU100 from Company B (Instrument 1). The terms of Instrument 1 require repayment after six years (at 31 December 20X6) of CU100 and annual interest of 6 per cent on the notional of CU100. One year later, on 1 January 20X2, Company A lends CU50 to Company B (Instrument 2) on terms that require repayment of CU50 after five years (at 31 December 20X6) and annual interest of 6 per cent on the notional of CU50.

The terms of the instruments give both parties the legally enforceable right to settle the principal amounts repayable on a net basis on maturity of the instruments (i.e. through Company A paying a net amount of CU50 to Company B on 31 December 20X6). Both parties intend to settle the principal amounts on this basis. In respect of the 6 per cent interest payments/receipts over the life of the two instruments there is no ability to settle on a net basis.

Company A measures both the financial liability (Instrument 1) and the financial asset (Instrument 2) at amortised cost, using the effective interest method.

Company A should offset the financial asset and financial liability to the extent that the financial asset and financial liability meet the conditions for offset. The offset conditions are met in respect of a proportion of the principal payments on the two instruments at 1 January 20X2 onwards. Therefore, offsetting is appropriate in respect of these amounts. However, offsetting is not appropriate in respect of the interest amounts.

Assume the amortised cost carrying amount of Instrument 1 (before considering offset) at 1 January 20X2 is CU100, which comprises an amount of CU75 being the present value of the principal payment and an amount of CU25 being the present value of the interest payments. Similarly, the amortised cost carrying amount of Instrument 2 (before considering offset) comprises an amount of CU37.50, representing the present value of the principal payment and an amount of CU12.50 representing the present value of the interest payments.

Applying offset to the proportion of principal payments but not to the interest components of the financial asset and financial liability will result in a liability of CU62.50 and asset of CU12.50 being shown in the statement of financial position of Company A. This balance is summarised below.

	CU	CU
Asset		
Present value of interest flows on Instrument 2		12.50
Liability		
Present value of interest flows on Instrument 1		25
Present value of principal flow on Instrument 1	75	
Less offset of principal flow on Instrument 2	(37.50)	
Net principal flow		37.50
		62.50

The offset that is achieved by Company A can equally apply to Company B; Company B will present a liability of CU12.50 to Company A, and a loan and receivable of CU62.50 from Company A.

6.5 Circumstances in which offsetting is usually not appropriate

Because the conditions outlined in **6.1** are not met, offsetting is specifically identified in IAS 32 as not being appropriate when:

[IAS 32:49]

(a) several different financial instruments are used to emulate the features of a single financial instrument (known as a 'synthetic instrument');

Example 6.5

Offset: synthetic instrument accounting

Assume an entity issues long-term floating rate debt in the market and concurrently enters into an interest rate swap with the bank that involves receiving floating rate payments and making fixed rate payments with a maturity equal to that of the debt. The combination of the issued debt and the interest rate swap could be seen as synthetically amounting to fixed rate long-term debt.

Each of the two instruments (floating rate liability and receive floating rate pay fixed rate interest rate swap) represent contractually separate arrangements with their own terms and conditions and each may be transferred or settled separately. Moreover, each of the two instruments will be exposed to risks that differ from those to which the other instrument is exposed. The offset conditions are not met because there is no legal right of set-off and, while the cash flows under the two instruments may occur within a short space of time, they are not simultaneous. Therefore, the debt and the swap are not presented on a net basis in the entity's statement of financial position.

(b) financial assets and financial liabilities arise from financial instruments with the same primary risk exposure (e.g. assets and liabilities within a portfolio of forward contracts or other derivative instruments) but with different counterparties;

(c) financial or other assets are pledged as collateral for non-recourse financial liabilities;

(d) financial assets are set aside in trust by a debtor for the purpose of discharging an obligation without those assets having been accepted by the creditor in settlement of the obligation (e.g. a sinking fund arrangement); or

(e) obligations incurred as a result of events giving rise to losses are expected to be recovered from a third party by virtue of a claim made under an insurance policy.

6.6 Master netting agreements

An entity that undertakes a number of financial instrument transactions with a single counterparty may enter into a 'master netting agreement' covering all of its transactions with that counterparty. Such an agreement creates a legally enforceable right of offset that comes into effect and affects the realisation of individual financial assets and settlement of individual financial liabilities only on the occurrence of a specified event of default, or other events not expected to happen in the normal course of business. Such agreements are typically used by financial institutions to provide a degree of protection in the event of bankruptcy or other circumstances that render a counterparty unable to meet its obligations. Once the triggering event takes place, the contract will typically provide for a single net settlement of all financial instruments covered by the agreement.

The existence of a master netting agreement does not in itself provide a basis for offsetting assets and liabilities covered by the agreement: firstly, the master netting agreement creates only a conditional right to set off recognised amounts, which falls short of the IAS 32 requirement that the entity must have a *currently enforceable* legal right to set off recognised amounts; and, secondly, the entity may not have the intention or ability to either settle on a net basis or realise the asset and settle the liability simultaneously. [IAS 32:50]

Example 6.6A

Offset: master netting agreement

Bank X, an investment bank, enters into several swap transactions with different reset dates to manage the interest rate risk arising from its corporate loans portfolio. Although these transactions are with a range of other banks as counterparties, Bank X's systems aggregate all exposures on a daily basis to enable them to recognise the net profit or loss due to the change in fair value of all open (i.e. unexpired) contracts. Certain contracts have a positive fair value while others are in a loss position. ISDA (International Swaps and Derivatives Association) Master Netting Agreements are in place with some, but not all, of these counterparties. Bank X does not net the settlements across swap positions with counterparties on reset dates.

Bank X does not meet the criteria for offsetting financial assets and liabilities related to its swap positions. It does not settle on a net basis and, due to the mismatch in reset dates across its swaps book, cannot demonstrate the simultaneous settlement of swap cash flows. Additionally, the ISDA Master Netting Agreements are not, in themselves, sufficient to provide Bank X with the legal right to set off its settlement cash flows across contracts except in the conditional event of default or termination by one of the parties.

Example 6.6B

Offset: options

Company X, a gold producer in South Africa, manages its exposure to changes in the gold price and locks in the cost of funding future capital expenditure by entering into option strategies with several investment banks. These strategies require Company X to both purchase call options and to write put options at various strike prices and with various maturity dates. The transactions are expected to be settled in cash and, therefore, are measured at FVTPL in IAS 39.

The investment banks require Company X to enter into ISDA Master Netting agreements which give either party the legal right of offset on termination of the contract, or on default of the other party. These agreements do not provide for the offset of settlements in the ordinary course of business.

Company X may not offset the financial assets and financial liabilities arising from the premiums paid and received and subsequent measurement of these options to fair value. The master netting agreement establishes a legally enforceable right of offset only in the event of a contingent event (i.e. default or on termination by one of the parties) and not in respect of ongoing settlements. Additionally, by virtue of the different maturity dates, Company X does not demonstrate the intention to settle on a net basis or to realise the asset and settle the liability simultaneously. Therefore, the requirements in IAS 32 are not satisfied. Even in the case where the premiums are settled on the same date, the continuing exposure to credit risk on the party writing the option precludes set-off.

6.7 Offset disclosures

The amendments to the offsetting requirements in IAS 32 that were issued in December 2011 were accompanied with amendments to IFRS 7 that introduced specific offsetting disclosure requirements. Prior to these amendments IFRS 7 did not have any specific disclosure requirements for offsetting financial assets and financial liabilities. The aim of the disclosures is to enable users of an entity's financial statements to evaluate the effect or potential effect of netting arrangements, including rights of set-off associated with the entity's recognised financial assets and financial liabilities, on the entity's financial position. [IFRS 7:IN9]

An entity shall retrospectively apply the amendments to IFRS 7 for annual periods beginning on or after 1 January 2013 and interim periods within those annual periods. [IFRS 7:44R]

The transition guidance as stated in IFRS 7:44R does not address whether it permits early application. However, the transition guidance as stated in IAS 32:97L does require an entity to apply the IFRS 7 amendments if it early applies the amendments to IAS 32. Therefore, an entity that early applies the IAS 32 amendments must also early apply the IFRS 7 amendments at the same time. The standards do not address whether they permit an entity to apply the IFRS 7 amendments on their own, i.e., without also applying the IAS 32 amendments at the same time. However, in light of the IFRS 7 amendments not being in conflict with the pre-amended disclosure requirements in IFRS 7 it would be reasonable for an entity to provide such information as additional information without stating that it has early applied those amendments.

6.7.1 Scope

The scope of the offsetting disclosure requirements are designed to be broad. The disclosure requirements have been designed to capture not only financial assets and financial liabilities that are offset in the statement of financial position but also recognised financial instruments that are subject to an enforceable master netting arrangement or similar agreement where the financial assets and financial liabilities are not offset. [IFRS 7:13A] As the amendments to IFRS 7 arose out of a convergence project with the U.S. Financial Accounting Standards Board one of the aims of broadening the scope of the disclosures was to ensure that users of IFRS and US GAAP financial statements would benefit from converged disclosures even though the requirements to achieve offsetting in the statement of financial position were not the same.

However, following stakeholder feedback, the FASB issued ASU No. 2013-01, *Clarifying the scope of disclosures about offsetting assets and liabilities*, which limits the scope of the offsetting disclosure requirements to derivatives (including bifurcated embedded derivatives), (reverse) sale and repurchase agreements, and securities borrowing and lending transactions. IFRS 7 was not subject to an equivalent amendment and therefore following the amendment by the FASB, IFRS 7 has a broader scope.

Typical enforceable master netting arrangements arise with derivative financial instruments where multiple derivatives with the same counterparty are subject to an agreement that dictates the netting of these multiple contracts in the case either party defaults on its obligations. The 'similar arrangements' referred to in IFRS 7:13A includes derivatives clearing arrangements, global master repurchase agreements, global master securities lending arrangements, and any related rights to financial collateral. [IFRS 7:B41]

The types of financial instruments and transactions that would typically be subject to the disclosures if subject to an enforceable master netting arrangement or similar arrangement would be derivatives, sale and repurchase agreements, reverse sale and repurchase agreements, securities borrowing, and securities lending agreements. Financial instruments that are not within the scope are loans and customer deposits at the same institution (unless they are set off in the statement of financial position), and financial instruments that are subject only to a collateral agreement. [IFRS 7:B41]

6.7.2 Offsetting disclosure requirements

An entity shall disclose information to enable users of its financial statements to evaluate the effect or potential effect of netting arrangements on the entity's financial position. This includes the effect or potential effect of rights of set-off associated with the entity's recognised financial assets and recognised financial liabilities that are within the scope as described above. [IFRS 7:13B] To meet this objective, an entity shall disclose, at the end of the reporting period, the following quantitative information separately for recognised financial assets and recognised financial liabilities:

[IFRS 7:13C]

(a) the gross amounts of those recognised financial assets and recognised financial liabilities;

(b) the amounts that are set off in accordance with the criteria in IAS 32:42 when determining the net amounts presented in the statement of financial position;

(c) the net amounts presented in the statement of financial position;

(d) the amounts subject to an enforceable master netting arrangement or similar agreement that are not otherwise included in paragraph (b) above, including:

   (i) amounts related to recognised financial instruments that do not meet some or all of the offsetting criteria in IAS 32:42; and

   (ii) amounts related to financial collateral (including cash collateral); and

(e) the net amount after deducting the amounts in (d) from the amounts in (c) above.

The information above shall be presented in a tabular format, separately for financial assets and financial liabilities, unless another format is more appropriate.

The total amount for an instrument that is disclosed in accordance with (d) above is limited to the amount in (c) above for that instrument. [IFRS 7:13D] For example, if the amount in (c) is a net financial asset, then deducting the amount in (d) will not result in the balance being disclosed as a net financial liability. Conversely, if the amount in (c) is a net financial liability, then deducting the amount in (d) will not result in the balance being disclosed as a net financial asset. By limiting the amount in (d) to be less or equal to the amount in (c) for financial instruments subject to an enforceable master netting arrangement or similar arrangement the amounts in (e) represent the net credit exposure after reflecting the impact of the netting arrangement as the amounts in (d) act as a credit risk mitigant for the amount in (c).

A description and the nature of the rights of set-off associated with the entity's recognised financial assets and recognised financial liabilities subject to enforceable master netting arrangements and similar agreements that are disclosed in accordance IFRS 7:13C(d) shall be disclosed [IFRS 7:13E]

If the information required by IFRS 7:13B - 13E is disclosed in more than one note to the financial statements, an entity shall cross-refer between those notes. [IFRS 7:13F]

IFRS 7 includes some illustrative examples within its implementation guidance:

Example 6.7.2

Disclosures (paragraphs 13A - 13F and B40 - B53)

[IFRS 7:IG40D]

Background

An entity has entered into transactions subject to an enforceable master netting arrangement or similar agreement with the following counterparties. The entity has the following recognised financial assets and financial liabilities resulting from those transactions that meet the scope of the disclosure requirements in paragraph 13A.

Counterparty A:

The entity has a derivative asset (fair value of CU100 million) and a derivative liability (fair value of CU80 million) with Counterparty A that meet the offsetting criteria in paragraph 42 of IAS 32.

Consequently, the gross derivative liability is set off against the gross derivative asset, resulting in the presentation of a net derivative asset of CU20 million in the entity's statement of financial position.

Cash collateral has also been received from Counterparty A for a portion of the net derivative asset (CU10 million). The cash collateral of CU10 million does not meet the offsetting criteria in paragraph 42 of IAS 32, but it can be set off against the net amount of the derivative asset and derivative liability in the case of default and insolvency or bankruptcy, in accordance with an associated collateral arrangement.

Counterparty B:

The entity has a derivative asset (fair value of CU100 million) and a derivative liability (fair value of CU80 million) with Counterparty B that do not meet the offsetting criteria in paragraph 42 of IAS 32, but which the entity has the right to set off in the case of default and insolvency or bankruptcy. Consequently, the gross amount of the derivative asset (CU80 million) and the gross amount of the derivative liability (CU80 million) are presented separately in the entity's statement of financial position. Cash collateral has also been received from Counterparty B for the net amount of the derivative asset and derivative liability (CU20 million). The cash collateral of CU20 million does not meet the offsetting criteria in paragraph 42 of IAS 32, but it can be set off against the net amount of the derivative asset and derivative liability in the case of default and insolvency or bankruptcy, in accordance with an associated collateral arrangement.

Counterparty C:

The entity has entered into a sale and repurchase agreement with Counterparty C that is accounted for as a collateralised borrowing. The carrying amount of the financial assets (bonds) used as collateral and posted by the entity for the transaction is CU79 million and their fair value is CU85 million. The carrying amount of the collateralised borrowing (repo payable) is CU80 million.

The entity has also entered into a reverse sale and repurchase agreement with Counterparty C that is accounted for as a collateralised lending. The fair value of the financial assets (bonds) received as collateral (and not recognised in the entity's statement of financial position) is CU105 million. The carrying amount of the collateralised lending (reverse repo receivable) is CU90 million.

The transactions are subject to a global master repurchase agreement with a right of set-off only in default and insolvency or bankruptcy and therefore do not meet the offsetting criteria in paragraph 42 of IAS 32. Consequently, the related repo payable and repo receivable are presented separately in the entity's statement of financial position.

Illustrating the application of IFRS 7:13C(a) - (e) by type of financial instrument

Financial assets subject to offsetting, enforceable master netting arrangements and similar arrangements

CU million						
As at 31 December 20XX	**(a)**	**(b)**	**(c)=(a)–(b)**	**(d)**		**(e)=(c)–(d)**
				Related amounts not set off in the statement of financial position		
	Gross amounts of recognised financial assets	**Gross amounts of recognised financial liabilities set off in the statement of financial position**	**Net amounts of financial assets presented in the statement of financial position**	**(d)(i), (d)(ii) Financial instruments**	**(d)(ii) Cash collateral received**	**Net amount**
Description						
Derivatives	200	(80)	120	(80)	(30)	10
Reverse repurchase, securities borrowing and similar agreements	–	–	90	(90)	–	–
Other financial instruments	–	–	–	–	–	–
Total	290	(80)	210	(170)	(30)	10

Financial liabilities subject to offsetting, enforceable master netting arrangements and similar arrangements

CU million

As at 31 December 20XX	(a)	(b)	(c)=(a)–(b)	(d)		(e)=(c)–(d)
				Related amounts not set off in the statement of financial position		
	Gross amounts of recognised financial liabilities	Gross amounts of recognised financial assets set off in the statement of financial position	Net amounts of financial liabilities presented in the statement of financial position	(d)(i), (d)(ii) Financial instruments	(d)(ii) Cash collateral pledged	Net amount
Description						
Derivatives	160	(80)	80	(80)	–	–
Repurchase, securities lending and similar agreements	80	–	80	(80)	–	–
Other financial instruments	–	–	–	–	–	–
Total	240	(80)	160	(160)	–	–

Illustrating the application of IFRS 7:13C(a) - (c) by type of financial instrument and IFRS 7:13C(c) - (e) by counterparty

Financial assets subject to offsetting, enforceable master netting arrangements and similar arrangements

CU million

As at 31 December 20XX	(a)	(b)	(c)=(a)–(b)
	Gross amounts of recognised financial assets	Gross amounts of recognised financial liabilities set off in the statement of financial position	Net amounts of financial assets presented in the statement of financial position
Description			
Derivatives	200	(80)	120
Reverse repurchase, securities borrowing and similar agreements	90	–	90
Other financial instruments	–	–	–
Total	290	(80)	210

Net financial assets subject to offsetting, enforceable master netting arrangements and similar arrangements

CU million

As at 31 December 20XX	**(a)**	**(d)**		**(e)=(c)–(d)**
		Related amounts not set off in the statement of financial position		
	Net amounts of financial assets presented in the statement of financial position	**(d)(i), (d)(ii) Financial instruments**	**(d)(ii) Cash collateral received**	**Net amount**
Counterparty A	20	–	(10)	10
Counterparty B	100	(80)	(20)	–
Counterparty C	90	(90)	–	–
Other	–	–	–	–
Total	210	(170)	(30)	10

Financial liabilities subject to offsetting, enforceable master netting arrangements and similar arrangements

CU million

As at 31 December 20XX	**(a)**	**(b)**	**(c)=(a)–(b)**
	Gross amounts of recognised financial liabilities	**Gross amounts of recognised financial assets set off in the statement of financial position**	**Net amounts of financial liabilities presented in the statement of financial position**
Description			
Derivatives	160	(80)	80
Repurchase, securities lending and similar agreements	80	–	80
Other financial instruments	–	–	–
Total	240	(80)	160

Net financial liabilities subject to enforceable master netting arrangements and similar agreements, by counterparty

CU million				
As at 31 December 20XX	**(c)**	**(d)**		**(e)=(c)–(d)**
		Related amounts not set off in the statement of financial position		
	Net amounts of financial liabilities presented in the statement of financial position	**(d)(i), (d)(ii) Financial instruments**	**(d)(ii) Cash collateral pledged**	**Net amount**
Counterparty A	–	–	–	–
Counterparty B	80	(80)	–	–
Counterparty C	80	(80)	–	–
Other	–	–	–	–
Total	160	(160)	–	–

C13 First-time adoption of IFRSs

Contents

1 Introduction

A first-time adopter of IFRSs is an entity that prepares its first IFRS annual financial statements containing an explicit and unreserved statement of compliance with IFRSs. [IFRS 1:3] The date of transition to IFRSs for a first-time adopter is the beginning of the earliest period for which an entity presents full comparative information under IFRSs in its first IFRS financial statements. [IFRS 1:Appendix A]

In general, IFRS 1 *First-time Adoption of International Financial Reporting Standards* requires a first-time adopter to comply retrospectively with each IFRS effective at the end of the reporting period for its first IFRS financial statements. [IFRS 1:7] IFRS 1 grants limited exemptions from these requirements in specified areas, including financial instruments (see **section 2.7**) and prohibits retrospective application in others, also including financial instruments (see **section 3**).

The general requirements of IFRS 1 are dealt with in detail in **chapter A3** of **Volume A**, Deloitte's companion volume for this manual. These include the requirements regarding the information to be disclosed in order to explain how the transition from previous GAAP to IFRSs has affected the entity's reported financial position, financial performance and cash flows. The scope of this chapter is limited to an exploration of the impact of some of the requirements of IFRS 1 on an entity's accounting for financial instruments that are within the scope of IAS 32 and IAS 39, namely:

- the requirement to identify, classify and measure as appropriate all financial instruments in the scope of IAS 32 and IAS 39 (see **sections 2** to **2.6**, **2.8** and **2.9**);
- IFRS 1's elective exemption from retrospective application of IAS 32 to compound instruments when the liability component is no longer outstanding (see **2.7**); and
- IFRS 1's mandatory prohibitions from retrospective application of IAS 39 in respect of derecognition, hedge accounting, and estimates (see **sections 3.1**, **3.3** and **2.5**).

2 Transition to IFRSs with respect to financial instruments

At the date of transition to IFRSs, a first-time adopter is required to identify, recognise, classify and measure as appropriate all financial assets and financial liabilities that qualify for recognition in accordance with IAS 32 and IAS 39, and to treat any adjustment to the carrying amount of a financial asset or financial liability resulting from the adoption of these Standards as a transition adjustment to be recognised in the opening balance of retained earnings at the date of transition to IFRSs. [IFRS 1:IG58A]

IAS 8 *Accounting Policies, Changes in Accounting Estimates and Errors* applies to adjustments resulting from changes in estimates. If a first-time adopter is unable to determine whether a particular portion of the adjustment is a transition adjustment or a change in estimate, it should be treated as a change in accounting estimate under IAS 8, with appropriate disclosures. [IFRS 1:IG58B]

At the date of transition to IFRSs, a first-time adopter is required to derecognise assets and liabilities that do not qualify for recognition in accordance with IAS 32 and IAS 39 (e.g. gains and losses deferred as assets and/or liabilities in the statement of financial position in respect of hedge relationships under previous GAAP that do not qualify for recognition as assets and liabilities under IFRSs – see **section 3.3**).

2.1 The key steps to conversion to IFRSs for financial instruments

The key steps to ensure that an entity complies with IAS 32 and IAS 39 on first-time adoption can be summarised as follows:

(a) identify all financial instruments and other contracts that fall within the scope of IAS 32 and IAS 39 which may or may not be accounted for as financial instruments under previous GAAP, including embedded derivatives and other contracts scoped into those Standards (see **chapter C1** and **section 2.2**);

(b) recognise and classify all financial instruments in accordance with the financial asset and liability classifications in IAS 39 and the rules on equity and liability classification in IAS 32 (see **chapters C2** and **C3**);

(c) derecognise items if IAS 32 and IAS 39 do not permit their recognition (e.g. gains and losses deferred as assets and/or liabilities in the statement of financial position in respect of hedge relationships under previous GAAP that do not qualify for recognition as assets and liabilities under IFRSs – see **3.1**);

(d) designate and document qualifying hedge relationships on or before the date of transition to IAS 39 to ensure these comply with IAS 39's hedge accounting criteria should an entity wish to apply hedge accounting prospectively from the date of transition to IAS 39 (see **section 3.3** and **chapters C9** and **C10**);

(e) apply IAS 32 and IAS 39 in measuring all financial assets and financial liabilities in accordance with their classification (**2.4** and **chapters C2**, **C3**, **C6** and **C7**); and

(f) design and implement controls and procedures for continued compliance with (a) to (e) above.

2.2 Identification of all financial assets and financial liabilities on first-time adoption

Typically a number of items would *not* have been recognised under previous GAAP compared to IFRSs. These include:

(a) all derivatives, including:

  (i) contracts to buy or sell a non-financial item, scoped into IAS 39 if they can be settled net in cash or another financial instrument, or by exchanging financial instruments, and are not entered into or held in accordance with the entity's expected purchase, sale or usage requirements (see **2.5** in **chapter C1**);

  (ii) issued guarantees falling within the scope of IAS 39 that do not meet the definition of a financial guarantee contract (see **2.3.3** in **chapter C1**);

  (iii) derivatives on an interest in a subsidiary, associate or joint venture unless they meet the definition of an equity instrument of the entity in accordance with IAS 32 or because they will result in a business combination at a future date (see **2.1** and **3.2** in **chapter C1**);

  (iv) derivatives based on climatic, geological or other physical variables unless they meet the definition of an insurance contract and are within the scope of IFRS 4 (see **2.3** in **chapter C1**); and

  (v) loan commitments that can be settled net in cash or another financial instrument, loan commitments that the issuer designates as financial assets or liabilities at FVTPL or loan commitments to provide a loan at a below-market interest rate (see **3.5** in **chapter C1**);

(b) all embedded derivatives that are required to be separately accounted for as required by IAS 39 (e.g. an embedded derivative in a financial liability that is not measured at FVTPL when the embedded derivative is not closely related to the non-derivative financial liability host contract – see **chapter C5**);

(c) other interests, such as servicing rights or servicing liabilities, retained after a derecognition transaction and still existing at the date of transition to IFRSs (see **chapter C8**); and

(d) financial instruments that are held in subsidiaries that were not consolidated under the previous GAAP, but are consolidated under IFRSs because the entity controls the entity at the date of transition to IFRSs (see **3.1.1** in **chapter C8**).

2.2.1 Embedded derivatives

First-time adopters need to assess all contractual arrangements for embedded derivatives. IAS 39 requires separate accounting for embedded derivatives not closely related to the host contract, where the entire contract is not one measured at FVTPL.

Full retrospective application of IAS 39 is required in this area. IFRIC 9 *Reassessment of Embedded Derivatives* clarifies that a first-time adopter should make its assessment as to whether an embedded derivative is to be separated on the basis of conditions that existed at the later of the date it first became party to the contract and the date (if any) when the contract is substantially modified (for a discussion of the 'substantially modified' criterion, see **section 3** of **chapter C5**).

If there has been no substantial modification of the arrangement, the assessment as to whether the embedded derivative is closely related is made on the basis of conditions that existed at the date when the entity first became party to the contract and not on the date of transition to IFRSs. The initial carrying amounts of the embedded derivative and the host contract reflect circumstances at the date the whole instrument satisfied the recognition criteria of IAS 39. [IFRS 1:IG55] Once the carrying amount at initial recognition of an embedded derivative that is not closely related to the host contract is separately determined (see **section 12** of **chapter C5**), it is then possible to determine the appropriate carrying amounts at the date of transition. These adjustments are recognised in the opening balance of retained earnings at the date of transition to IFRSs.

If the entity cannot determine the initial carrying amounts of the embedded derivative and host contract reliably, it treats the entire combined contract as a financial instrument as at FVTPL (see **section 12** of **chapter C5**). [IFRS 1:IG55]

2.3 Recognition of all financial instruments on first-time adoption

Subject to the exception discussed in **3.1** relating to the retrospective application of IAS 39's derecognition rules, at the date of transition to IFRSs an entity is required to recognise all financial assets and financial liabilities that qualify for recognition under IAS 39 (e.g. certain derivative instruments) that have not yet qualified for derecognition under IAS 39, except non-derivative financial assets and non-derivative financial liabilities derecognised in accordance with previous GAAP before the date of transition to IFRSs. For example, an entity that does not apply IFRS 1:B3 (see **3.1**) does not recognise assets transferred in a securitisation, transfer or other derecognition transaction that occurred before the date of transition to IFRSs if those transactions qualified for derecognition in accordance with previous GAAP. However, if the entity uses the same securitisation arrangement or other derecognition arrangement for further transfers after the date of transition to IFRSs, those further transfers qualify for derecognition only if they meet the derecognition criteria of IAS 39. [IFRS 1:IG52 - 54]

An entity does not recognise financial assets and financial liabilities that do not qualify for recognition in accordance with IAS 39, or have already qualified for derecognition in accordance with IAS 39. [IFRS 1:IG54]

2.4 Classification and measurement of financial assets and financial liabilities on transition

A first-time adopter applies the classification and measurement criteria of IAS 39 to its financial assets and its financial liabilities at the date of transition to IFRSs.

For those financial assets and financial liabilities classified at the date of transition in an amortised cost category, an entity determines their amortised cost on the basis of circumstances existing when the assets and liabilities first satisfied the recognition criteria in IAS 39. However, if the entity acquired those financial assets and financial liabilities in a past business combination, their carrying amount under previous GAAP immediately following the business combination is their deemed cost under IFRSs at that date. [IFRS 1:IG57]

Example 2.4A

Determining classification and measurement at date of transition to IFRSs

Entity ABC has a 31 December year end and is a first-time adopter in 20X2. Its date of transition to IFRSs is 1 January 20X1. How should Entity ABC apply the requirements of IAS 39 in respect of the classification and measurement of its financial assets and financial liabilities?

At 1 January 20X1, Entity ABC applies IAS 39's classification and measurement criteria to its financial assets and financial liabilities as if it had initially recognised those financial assets and financial liabilities in accordance with the Standard as illustrated.

- Entity ABC can classify financial assets meeting the criteria for classification as HTM investments (see **3.2** in **chapter C2**) in that category; the classification should reflect Entity ABC's intent and ability to hold such assets to their maturity at the date of transition. [IFRS 1:IG56(a)] Entity ABC recognises any adjustment to financial assets classified in the HTM category to measure them at the appropriate amortised cost balance, as if that measurement basis had been applied from the date they first qualified for recognition in accordance with IAS 39, directly in retained earnings. It follows that sales or transfers of HTM investments before the date of transition to IFRSs do not trigger the 'tainting' rules (see **3.3** in **chapter C2**).
- It can classify financial assets as 'loans and receivables' provided they meet the definition of loans and receivables (see **3.4** in **chapter C2**) when they first satisfied the recognition criteria. [IFRS 1:IG56(b)] Entity ABC recognises any adjustment to financial assets classified in the loans and receivables category to measure them at the appropriate amortised cost amount, as if that measurement basis had been applied from the date they first qualified for recognition as loans and receivables in accordance with IAS 39, directly in retained earnings.
- Entity ABC can designate any non-derivative financial asset that is not held for trading and required to be measured at fair value through profit or loss,

as AFS (see **3.5** in **chapter C2**). [IFRS 1:29 & D19] Like the designation of AFS assets at initial recognition, the designation in this category on transition to IFRSs is irrevocable. The fair value gain or loss on transition for assets designated as AFS financial assets on the date of transition is taken to a separate component of equity as if those assets had been accounted for since initial recognition as AFS financial assets, except for impairment losses, foreign exchange gains or losses on monetary assets and interest income calculated using the effective interest method on those assets. [IFRS 1:IG59]

- Entity ABC recognises any derivative financial assets and derivative financial liabilities that are in the scope of IAS 39 at fair value (see **3.1.2** in **chapter C2** and **7.1.1** in **chapter C3**) with fair value gains or losses on transition accounted for as an adjustment to retained earnings, except for derivatives that were part of a net investment hedge or cash flow hedge under previous GAAP of a type that qualifies under IAS 39. [IFRS 1:B5 and IG60B]
- Entity ABC classifies non-derivative financial assets and non-derivative financial liabilities in its opening IFRS statement of financial position as held for trading (and, therefore, measured at FVTPL) if the assets or liabilities were: (i) acquired or incurred principally for the purpose of selling or repurchasing in the near term; or (ii) at the date of transition to IFRSs, part of a portfolio of identified financial instruments that were managed together and for which there was evidence of a recent actual pattern of short-term profit-taking. [IFRS 1:IG56(d)] The fair value gain or loss on transition is accounted for as an adjustment to retained earnings.
- At the date of transition to IAS 39, Entity ABC is also permitted to designate any financial asset or financial liability as one to be measured at FVTPL if specified criteria are met, i.e. the 'fair value option' (see **3.1.1** in **chapter C2** and **7.1.2** in **chapter C3**) is available as a one-off choice on transition. [IFRS 1:D19(b)] The fair value gain or loss on transition for financial assets or financial liabilities designated as at FVTPL at the date of transition is accounted for as an adjustment through retained earnings, i.e. the assets or liabilities are accounted for as if they were designated as at FVTPL at the date of initial recognition. Entity ABC must disclose the fair value of any financial assets or financial liabilities designated into the 'financial assets at fair value through profit or loss' and 'financial liabilities at fair value through profit or loss' categories and their classification and carrying amount in its previous financial statements. [IFRS 1:29]
- Entity ABC classifies financial liabilities that are not measured at FVTPL, either because the 'fair value option' has not been applied or because the items are not held for trading, as other financial liabilities measured at amortised cost (see **section 7** in **chapter C3**). It recognises any adjustment to measure them at the appropriate amortised cost amount as if that measurement basis had been applied since the date they first qualified for recognition in accordance with IAS 39, in retained earnings.

Example 2.4B

Derivative not measured at fair value under previous GAAP

Entity P is a first-time adopter of IFRSs and is preparing its first annual IFRS financial statements for the year ended 31 December 20X2.

Entity P has some derivative financial instruments. Under previous GAAP, these instruments were not recognised at fair value in the statement of financial position because they were considered to be hedging instruments. The derivatives were instead held on an accruals basis and were included in the carrying amount of the item being hedged. At the date of transition the instruments have a fair value of CU(2) million and do not qualify as hedging instruments in accordance with IAS 39 as they are net written options.

On Entity P's date of transition to IFRSs (1 January 20X1), it recognises the derivative liability in its statement of financial position with the corresponding entry recognised in retained earnings. The entity cannot include the loss in a cash flow hedge accounting reserve because the derivative is not a qualifying hedging instrument under IAS 39.

Under previous GAAP, the derivatives had been netted against the item being hedged. Not only is the measurement basis not compliant with IFRSs, but also the financial instruments could not be offset unless the criteria for offset in IAS 32 were met (see **section 6** of **chapter C12**). An adjustment will be required to the hedged items to recognise them at the appropriate carrying amounts.

Example 2.4C

Determining amortised cost

Entity MNO is a first-time adopter of IFRSs and is preparing its first annual IFRS financial statements for the year ended 31 December 20X8. Therefore, its date of transition to IFRSs is 1 January 20X7. Entity MNO has the following two zero coupon bond assets, which are not quoted in an active market.

- Bond 1 was purchased at original issuance on 1 January 20X5 for €1,000. It is redeemable in 5 years' time at €1,250. The effective interest rate on this instrument is 4.56 per cent.
- Bond 2 has the same terms as Bond 1, but the bond was acquired in a business combination on 1 January 20X6. The fair value of the bond on the date of the business combination was €1,100. The bond has risen in value since it was issued because of the unwinding of discount and because interest rates have fallen since the bond was issued. The effective interest rate calculated at the time of the business combination is 3.25 per cent.

The bonds are not quoted in an active market and the entity chooses not to designate the bonds as AFS financial assets. Therefore, at its date of transition to IFRSs (1 January 20X7), Entity MNO classifies both bonds as loans and receivables (see **3.4** in **chapter C2**) measured at amortised cost. Entity MNO determines the carrying amount of Bond 1 as if it had been accounted for at amortised cost since acquisition using the bond's effective interest rate of

4.56 per cent. The amortised cost on 1 January 20X7 is €1,093, reflecting two years of amortisation at 4.56 per cent.

Entity MNO determines the carrying amount of Bond 2 as if it had been accounted for at amortised cost since it was acquired in the business combination using the bond's effective interest rate of 3.25 per cent. The amortised cost on 1 January 20X7 is €1,136, reflecting 1 year of amortisation at 3.25 per cent.

Alternatively, the fair value option could be applied to the bonds on transition to IFRSs if the specified criteria in IAS 39:9 and 11A are met.

2.5 Impairment and other estimates

IFRS 1 prohibits retrospective application of IFRSs in respect of estimates (after adjustments to reflect any difference in accounting policies), unless there is objective evidence that previous estimates were in error. [IFRS 1:14]

The principal area where estimates are involved in the measurement of financial instruments is in the assessment of impairment. IFRS 1:IG58 confirms that an entity's estimates of loan impairments at the date of transition to IFRSs are consistent with estimates made for the same date under previous GAAP (after adjustments to reflect any difference in accounting policies), unless there is objective evidence that those assumptions were in error. It is important to distinguish between a change in estimate and a change in accounting policy for the purpose of recognition of impairment on transition. For example, a change in accounting policy would be moving from an undiscounted basis for measuring impairment under previous GAAP to a discounted basis under IFRSs. The effect of such a change in accounting policy would be reflected in the adjustment to the opening balance of retained earnings on transition.

Generally, reconsidering the extent of cash flows that are then subject to discounting under IFRSs is a reassessment of an estimate. Such a change in estimate would not be reflected in the adjustment to the opening balance of retained earnings on transition. An exception may arise in the case where there are purchased guarantees. An adjustment to the carrying amount of loans and, potentially, retained earnings on transition arise because IFRSs may include the potential recovery under the guarantee as part of the impairment analysis whereas previous GAAP may not. Impairment is described in greater detail in **section 5** of **chapter C6**.

2.5.1 Change in impairment policy

Example 2.5.1

Change in impairment policy

Under previous GAAP, Entity A measured impairment of financial assets carried at cost on an undiscounted basis. Entity A is a first-time adopter of IFRSs.

IAS 39 requires impairment losses to be measured using discounted cash flows. [IAS 39:63] Therefore, at the date of transition to IFRSs, Entity A makes an adjustment to the carrying amount of those financial assets that are measured at amortised cost under IAS 39 to reflect the effect of discounting expected future cash flows.

This adjustment is recognised as an adjustment to the opening balance of retained earnings at the date of transition in accordance with IFRS 1 in accordance with IFRS 1:11, 14 & IG58 as the adjustment arises as a result of a change in accounting policy in respect of impairment of financial assets.

2.6 Classification as a financial liability or equity

In its opening IFRS statement of financial position, an entity applies the criteria in IAS 32 to classify financial instruments issued (or components of compound instruments issued) as either financial liabilities or equity instruments in accordance with the substance of the contractual arrangement when the instrument first satisfied the recognition criteria in IAS 32:15, without considering events after that date other than changes to the terms of the instruments. [IFRS 1:IG35]

Example 2.6

Assessing terms at date of transition to IFRSs

Entity P issued a capital instrument on 1 January 20X1 which is required to be settled in cash in specified circumstances. Entity P's date of transition to IFRSs is 1 January 20X3. If IAS 32 had been applied at the date of issue of the instrument, the instrument would have been classified as a liability because the instrument's contingent settlement provision (requiring redemption in cash) would have been judged to be genuine (i.e. the event that would trigger redemption would not have been considered to be extremely rare). At 1 January 20X3, circumstances have changed such that it is now considered that the event that would trigger redemption is extremely rare (there has been no change in the terms of the instrument).

In accordance with IFRS 1:IG35 (see above), the classification of the instrument as either a financial liability or as equity should be determined based on conditions at the date of issue (1 January 20X1). Entity P should classify the instrument as a financial liability on transition notwithstanding the fact that if it issued an instrument with the same terms at 1 January 20X3 it would recognise an equity instrument.

2.7 Compound instruments

IFRS 1 provides some relief for first-time adopters when applying IAS 32 for the first time. To the extent that the liability component of a compound instrument is no longer outstanding at the date of transition to IFRSs, retrospective application of IAS 32's requirement to split the instrument is not required. [IFRS 1:D18]

This exemption is justified on the basis of expediency. The only effect of retrospective application of IAS 32 in the circumstances described would be the separation of two components of equity: one portion representing the cumulative interest accrued on the liability component during its life using the effective interest method (which would normally reside in retained earnings) and the second portion representing the original equity component that would have been separated on initial recognition of the instrument.

Example 2.7A

Convertible debt outstanding at date of transition to IFRSs

Entity H is a first-time adopter in 20X4. Entity H issued 2,000 convertible bonds on 1 January 20X1. The bonds have a four-year term, and were issued at par with a face value of CU1,000 per bond, giving total proceeds of CU2 million. Interest is payable annually in arrears at an annual interest rate of 6 per cent. Each bond is convertible, at the holder's discretion, at any time up to maturity into 250 ordinary shares. When the bonds were issued, the market interest rate for similar debt without the conversion option was 9 per cent.

How should Entity H account for its convertible debt on first-time adoption of IFRSs?

An entity that has an issued compound instrument outstanding at the date of transition to IFRSs determines the initial carrying amounts of the liability and equity components based on circumstances existing when the instrument was issued. [IFRS 1:IG36]

IAS 32 requires that the liability component be valued first. The liability component is calculated as the present value of the contractual cash flows using the discount rate of 9 per cent, which was the market interest rate for similar bonds with the same credit standing having no conversion rights when the bonds were issued. The difference between the proceeds of the bond issue and the fair value of the liability at the time of original issuance is assigned to the equity component. The equity component is not remeasured. An adjustment in the opening balance of retained earnings is required to measure the liability component at its appropriate amortised cost at the date of transition.

Example 2.7B

Convertible debt not outstanding at date of transition to IFRSs

Entity Q is adopting IFRSs for the first time in its annual financial statements for the year ending 31 December 20X7, with a date of transition to IFRSs of 1 January 20X6. Entity Q issued a convertible bond on 1 January 20X1. The bond had a three-year term, was convertible at any time up to maturity into 250 ordinary shares of the entity, and was redeemed at maturity.

How should Entity Q account for its convertible bond on first-time adoption of IFRSs?

The liability component of Entity Q's convertible bond is no longer outstanding at Entity Q's date of transition to IFRSs. Therefore, Entity Q is not required to separate the two components of equity that would have resulted if full retrospective application had been applied. [IFRS 1:D18]

Example 2.7C

Convertible debt redeemed after date of transition to IFRSs

Using the facts as in **example 2.7B**, if Entity Q's convertible bond had a maturity of 1 January 20X7 (i.e. it had a six-year term and was expected to be redeemed on its maturity on 1 January 20X7), would Entity Q be exempted from full retrospective application of IAS 32 for its convertible bond?

No. Entity Q's date of transition to IFRSs is 1 January 20X6. In this example, the liability component of Entity Q's convertible bond is still outstanding at the date of transition. Therefore, Entity Q would be required to apply IAS 32 retrospectively to its convertible bond and to separate out the equity component that would have been separated on initial recognition of the instrument in accordance with IAS 32.

2.8 Designation of previously recognised financial instruments

An entity is permitted to designate any financial asset, other than an asset that meets the definition of held for trading, as an AFS financial asset at the date of transition to IFRSs. An entity is also permitted to designate a previously recognised financial asset or financial liability as at FVTPL if it meets the criteria for designation as at FVTPL in IAS 39:9 & 11A. [IFRS 1:29]

A first-time adopter of IFRSs must de-designate financial assets and financial liabilities that under previous GAAP were designated as at FVTPL but do not qualify for such designation under IAS 39, and apply the measurement requirements of IFRSs retrospectively.

Example 2.8

Date of designation for instruments acquired after the date of transition

Entity B prepares its first set of IFRS financial statements for the year ended 31 December 20X2; its date of transition to IFRSs is 1 January 20X1. In February 20X1, Entity B issued fixed rate debentures that were measured at amortised cost on initial recognition. At the same time, Entity B used the proceeds of the debt to acquire a portfolio of fixed rate assets which it designated as AFS with changes in fair value recognised in other comprehensive income. The fair value changes on the assets tend to offset the fair value movements on the debenture liabilities. During 20X1, Entity B realises that there is a measurement and recognition inconsistency in measuring the fixed rate debt

> liability at amortised cost while measuring the fixed rate assets at fair value with gains and losses recognised in other comprehensive income.
>
> Entity B cannot re-designate the fixed rate debt instruments after initial recognition. At initial recognition, in February 20X1, Entity B chose to designate the fixed rate debentures at amortised cost and not at FVTPL. A designation as at FVTPL must be made at the later of initial recognition and date of transition to IFRSs.
>
> If the fixed rate debentures were acquired prior to the date of transition to IFRSs (i.e. prior to 1 January 20X1), Entity B could have designated those fixed rate debentures as at FVTPL at the date of transition to IFRSs if the specified criteria were met.

Entities are required to disclose the fair value of the financial assets or financial liabilities designated into each category (AFS or at FVTPL) at the date of designation and their classification and carrying amount in the previous financial statements. [IFRS 1:29]

2.9 Fair value measurement of financial assets or financial liabilities

Because all financial assets and financial liabilities, except for trade receivables that do not have a significant financing component (determined in accordance with IFRS 15 *Revenue from Contracts with Customers*), are required to be initially recognised at fair value, an entity must consider the specific guidance in IFRS 13 on fair value when determining the carrying amount of financial assets and financial liabilities at the date of transition to IFRSs.

IAS 39 limits upfront gain/loss recognition unless the fair value of the instrument is evidenced by comparison with other observable current market transactions in the same instrument (i.e. without modification or repackaging) or based on a valuation technique whose variables include only data from observable markets. This is often referred to as 'day 1 P&L' and is discussed in more depth at **7.1** in **chapter C7**. IFRS 1:D20 has specific transition requirements when applying the day 1 P&L guidance. IFRS 1 permits an entity to apply the day 1 P&L guidance (with specific reference from IFRS 1 to the last sentence of IAS 39:AG76 and to IAS 39:AG76A) prospectively to transactions entered into on or after the date of transition to IFRSs. Alternatively the requirements are applied retrospectively.

2.10 Extinguishing financial liabilities with equity instruments

IFRIC 19 *Extinguishing Financial Liabilities with Equity Instruments* addresses the accounting for entities that issue equity instruments in order to extinguish all or part of a financial liability (often referred to as 'debt for equity swaps'). The requirements of IFRIC 19 are discussed in **4.2** of **chapter C8**.

The transition provisions of IFRIC 19 require that an entity should apply any change in accounting policy arising from the application of the Interpretation from the beginning of the earliest comparative period presented.

IFRS 1 permits first-time adopters to apply the transition provisions in IFRIC 19. [IFRS 1:D25]

First-time adopters therefore have a choice between full retrospective application of IFRIC 19 and application of the transition provisions of IFRIC 19. The option selected will have no impact on amounts reported for the first IFRS reporting period and for the comparative period, but full retrospective application could result in some additional reclassifications within equity.

In finalising IFRIC 19, the IFRIC (now the IFRS Interpretations Committee) concluded that it was preferable to require entities that could apply the Interpretation retrospectively to do so, rather than requiring all entities to apply it prospectively to future transactions; the Committee made specific reference to IAS 8's guidance on circumstances in which retrospective application might be impracticable. To simplify transition, the IFRIC also concluded that it should require retrospective application only from the beginning of the earliest comparative period presented because application to earlier periods would result only in a reclassification of amounts within equity. [IFRIC 19:BC33]

3 Prohibition on retrospective application of IAS 32 and IAS 39

In the course of developing IFRS 1, the IASB identified a number of circumstances where it believed retrospective application of IFRSs is not necessary or should not be permitted. The exceptions from retrospective application relate to:

- derecognition of financial assets and financial liabilities (see **3.2**);
- hedge accounting (see **3.3**); and
- government grants (see **3.4**).

3.1 Transitional requirements on derecognition for first-time adopters

A first-time adopter is required by IFRS 1:B2 to apply the derecognition rules in IAS 39 prospectively from the date of transition to IFRSs unless it chooses to apply the derecognition rules of IAS 39 retrospectively from a date of its choosing in accordance with IFRS 1:B3 (see **3.2**). Therefore, if a first-time adopter derecognised financial assets under its previous GAAP in a securitisation, transfer or other derecognition transaction that occurred before the date of transition to IFRSs, it does not recognise those assets and liabilities at the date of transition (even if they would not have qualified for derecognition under IAS 39), unless they qualify for recognition as a result of a later transaction or event.

However, a first-time adopter must recognise any financial interest retained as a result of a derecognition transaction prior to the date of transition to IFRSs that still exists at the date of transition to IFRSs (e.g. any derivatives and other interests, such as servicing rights or servicing liabilities).

Furthermore, the exemptions from retrospective application of the derecognition requirements do not extend to consolidation. A first-time adopter must consolidate all subsidiaries (as defined in IFRS 10 *Consolidated Financial Statements*), unless IFRS 10 requires otherwise. [IFRS 1:IG26] Therefore, although a group may have derecognised financial assets under its previous GAAP as a result of a transfer of assets to an entity occurring before the date of transition to IFRSs, those assets may be consolidated back into the group's statement of financial position if the entity to which the financial assets were transferred is deemed to be controlled by the group in accordance with IFRS 10 and the entity did not derecognise the assets under its previous GAAP. If this is the case, the IAS 39 derecognition decision tree will be applied to the new group as defined by IFRSs.

Example 3.1

Transfers to a structured entity

Entity X is part of Group Y. The date of transition to IFRSs for Entity X and for Group Y is 1 January 20X5. The entity and the group do not apply the election available under IFRS 1:B3 (see **3.2**) to apply the derecognition rules to transactions derecognised prior to the date of transition to IFRSs.

Entity X derecognised financial assets under its previous GAAP on 30 September 20X3. These assets were transferred to Entity Z. Entity Z was not considered a member of Group Y under previous GAAP. Entity Z is a structured entity that issues beneficial interests in the underlying financial assets transferred to it by Entity X to unrelated third-party investors, and provides servicing of those financial assets.

On the date of transition to IFRSs, in accordance with IFRS 10, Entity Z is now considered to be part of Group Y and must be consolidated by Group Y.

Individual financial statements of Entity X under IFRSs

Because Entity X derecognised the financial assets under its previous GAAP in a transaction occurring prior to the date of transition to IFRSs, the transferred assets continue to be derecognised under IFRSs.

Group Y's financial statements under IFRSs

Because Group Y now includes Entity Z, the derecognition requirements must be applied to the enlarged group. If Entity Z could not derecognise the financial assets under its previous GAAP, and the assets continue to be recognised under IFRSs, then Group Y continues to recognise those assets. If Entity Z did derecognise the financial assets under its previous GAAP, the assets will remain derecognised under IFRSs because they were derecognised under previous GAAP in a transaction occurring prior to the date of transition to IFRSs.

When the entity and group have made the election available under IFRS 1:B3 to apply the derecognition requirements of IAS 39 to derecognition transactions occurring before the date of transition to IFRSs (see **3.2**), the derecognition requirements of IAS 39 would apply to the transaction on 30 September 20X3.

3.2 Option to apply derecognition rules retrospectively from a chosen date

Notwithstanding the requirement to apply IAS 39's rules on derecognition prospectively from the date of transition to IFRSs, an entity may choose to apply them retrospectively from a date of the entity's choosing, provided that the information needed to apply IAS 39 to financial assets and financial liabilities derecognised as a result of past transactions was obtained at the time of initially accounting for those transactions (see **example 3.1B**). [IFRS 1:B3]

3.3 Hedge accounting

IFRS 1 prohibits retrospective application of IAS 39 in respect of hedge accounting. [IFRS 1:B4 - B6] This is consistent with the general hedging requirements of IAS 39 under which hedge accounting is only ever available prospectively if the hedge relationship is appropriately designated, documented, is expected to be highly effective and satisfies all other hedge accounting criteria (see **chapters C9** and **C10**).

At the date of transition to IFRSs, an entity must measure all derivatives at fair value and eliminate all deferred gains and losses arising on derivatives that were reported under previous GAAP as assets or liabilities in the statement of financial position in respect of hedge relationships under previous GAAP because these do not qualify for recognition as assets and liabilities under IFRSs. [IFRS 1:B4]

If, before the date of transition to IFRSs, a transaction had been designated as a hedge of a type that qualifies for hedge accounting under IAS 39 but the hedge does not meet all the specific conditions for hedge accounting in IAS 39, the requirements of IAS 39:91 and IAS 39:101 should be applied to discontinue hedge accounting. [IFRS 1:B6]

The designation and documentation of a hedge relationship must be completed on or before the date of transition to IFRSs if the hedge relationship is to qualify for hedge accounting from that date. Hedge accounting can be applied prospectively only from the date that the hedge relationship is fully designated and documented. [IFRS 1:IG60]

3.3.1 Re-designation or discontinuation of hedge relationships that do not comply with IAS 39

When a first-time adopter has a hedge relationship of a type that does not qualify for hedge accounting under IAS 39 (e.g. when the hedging instrument is a cash instrument or written option or when the hedged item is a net position, or the designated risk is interest rate risk in a HTM investment (see **sections 3** and **4** of **chapter C9** on qualifying hedged items and qualifying hedging instruments respectively)), the entity should not reflect that hedge relationship in its opening IFRS statement of financial position. However, if an entity designated a net position as a hedged item under previous GAAP, it may designate an individual item within that net position as a hedged item under IFRSs, provided that it does so no later than the date of transition to IFRSs and provided that all other hedge accounting criteria are met. [IFRS 1:B5]

3.3.1.1 Fair value hedge under previous GAAP of a type that does not qualify as a fair value hedge under IFRSs

Example 3.3.1.1A

Non-qualifying hedge (1)

Entity H applies IAS 39 in classifying and measuring its financial assets. Entity H is fair value hedging a fixed rate debt instrument for interest rate risk under previous GAAP. Entity H intends to classify the instrument as HTM under IFRSs. HTM investments cannot be hedged items with respect to interest rate risk under IFRSs because designation of an investment as HTM requires an intention to hold the investment till maturity without regard to the changes in fair value attributable to changes in interest rates. Therefore, the hedge relationship does not qualify for hedge accounting under IAS 39, and the entity is not permitted to reflect the hedge relationship in its opening IFRS statement of financial position. [IFRS 1:B5] Under IFRSs, the HTM debt security will be accounted for at amortised cost.

How should the previous fair value adjustments to the carrying amount of the hedged item be accounted for on the first-time adoption of IFRSs and, thereby, the initial application of IAS 39?

Because the HTM investments are not qualifying hedged items under IFRSs in respect of interest rate risk, the carrying amount on the date of transition to IFRSs should reflect the balance that would have existed had the entity always applied IFRSs (i.e. the balance that would have existed had the entity never applied hedge accounting). Since the HTM investment will be measured at amortised cost and thus any previous adjustments recognised under previous GAAP should be reversed to the extent that they have resulted in a carrying amount that differs from the amortised cost that would have been reported had the entity applied IFRSs and measured the item at amortised cost throughout its life.

The derivative will be recognised in the statement of financial position at its fair value with an adjustment to retained earnings on the date of transition.

Example 3.3.1.1B

Non-qualifying hedge (2)

Entity J is fair value hedging a fixed rate, non-prepayable debt instrument for interest rate risk under previous GAAP with an interest rate swap whereby Entity J receives a fixed rate of interest and pays LIBOR. The interest rate swap contains an option for the Bank to cancel the swap at any time at a settlement amount of zero (the bank will cancel the swap when it is out of the money to them). Under IFRSs, the debt instrument will be carried at amortised cost.

How should this relationship be accounted for on first-time adoption of IFRSs?

Entity J has written an option embedded in the swap. A written option or net written option does not qualify as a hedging instrument unless it is designated as an offset to a purchased option, including one that is embedded in another financial instrument. [IAS 39:77 and IAS 39:AG94] Because the debt is non-prepayable and, therefore, does not have an equal and opposite embedded purchased option, the hedging instrument is not a qualifying instrument. [IAS 39:AG94] The difference between the fair value of the interest rate swap and its previously reported carrying amount, together with the difference between the debt's amortised cost and its previously reported carrying amount, should be recognised directly in opening retained earnings. No fair value hedging adjustment to the hedged debt is allowed.

3.3.1.2 Cash flow hedge under previous GAAP that does not qualify as a cash flow hedge under IFRSs

Example 3.3.1.2

Non-qualifying hedge (3)

If a forecasted transaction is not expected to occur at the date of transition to IFRSs, how should any net cumulative gains or losses arising on measurement at fair value of the hedging instrument be accounted for at the date of transition?

If, at the date of transition to IFRSs, the forecasted transaction is not expected to occur the hedge does not qualify as a cash flow hedge. A first-time adopter reclassifies any net cumulative gain or loss reported in other comprehensive income under previous GAAP to retained earnings at the date of transition in accordance with IFRS 1:11.

If the derivative instrument was carried at cost, and no changes in value of the derivative were recognised in other comprehensive income, the full amount of the adjustment to the derivative asset or liability necessary to recognise the derivative at fair value should be recognised in retained earnings if hedge accounting is not permitted. If the derivative instrument was carried at an amount other than fair value with a deferred debit or credit in the statement of financial position recognised as an offset, that deferred debit or credit should be reversed through retained earnings if it does not meet the appropriate recognition criteria under IFRSs, and the value of the derivative brought up to its fair value at the date of transition.

3.3.2 Hedge relationships of a type that continue to qualify under IAS 39

For a hedge relationship to continue to qualify as a hedge relationship at the date of transition to IFRSs, it must meet all of the hedge accounting criteria (see **chapters C9** and **C10**). In particular, the designation and documentation of a hedge relationship must be completed on or before the date of transition to IFRSs if the hedge relationship is to qualify for hedge accounting from that date. Hedge accounting can be applied prospectively only from the date that the hedge relationship is fully designated and documented.

For a first-time adopter of IFRSs, this may be a significant change from previous GAAP which may not have required such rigorous hedge designation and documentation. Hedge accounting under IAS 39, and hence on first-time adoption of IFRSs, can only be applied prospectively from the date that the hedge relationship is fully designated and documented, subject to all other hedge accounting requirements of IAS 39 being met.

If an entity designates and documents a hedge relationship in accordance with IAS 39 on or before the date of transition to IFRSs the effective start date of the hedge relationship for the purpose of deriving the hypothetical derivative (used to measure the hedged item, see **4.4.1** in **chapter C10**) could be a date before the date of transition to IFRSs. This is because the combination of the hedge accounting transition adjustments posted for qualifying cash flow hedges (see **3.3.2.2**) and application of hedge accounting from the date of transition to IFRSs has a similar effect to applying hedge accounting from the point the hedge relationship first came into existence. However, if the hedge relationship is documented and designated on a date after the date of transition to IFRSs the date of documentation and designation would be used as the start date of the hedge for the purpose of deriving the hypothetical derivative. This is illustrated in the following example.

Example 3.3.2

Determining the hypothetical derivative

Entity A is a first time adopter of IFRSs. Its date of transition to IFRSs is 1 January 20X8. At the date of transition, Entity A has an issued 1-month LIBOR floating rate bond outstanding which will be measured at amortised cost under IAS 39 and an interest rate swap with matching critical terms that pays fixed interest and receives 1-month LIBOR which in the absence of hedge accounting would be measured at FVTPL. The bond was issued, and the swap was entered into, on 1 September 20X5 and under its previous GAAP the entity accounted for the swap by only accruing the net cash flows of the swap (i.e. it did not recognise the swap at FVTPL).

Entity A wishes to apply cash flow hedge accounting from the date of transition to IFRSs and documents and designates the cash flow hedge on 1 January 20X8. Consequently, from the date of transition to IFRSs the IAS 39 cash flow hedge accounting requirements apply (see section **2.2** in **chapter C9**). For the period up to the date of transition to IFRSs, the cash flow hedge accounting transition requirements apply (see **3.3.2.2**).

To measure the change in present value of the hedged item for changes in the hedged risk from the date of transition, Entity A uses the hypothetical derivative method. A critical feature of the hypothetical derivative is that it has nil fair value on the date of designation. In this scenario, because of the transition adjustments for the cash flow hedge and the fact that the hedge was designated under IAS 39 on the date of transition to IFRSs it could be argued that the hedge relationship is effectively a continuing hedge from 1 September 20X5. Consequently it would be appropriate to use 1 September 20X5 as the designation date for the purpose of deriving the hypothetical derivative.

This treatment would not be appropriate if Entity A had not documented and designated the hedge on or before the date of transition to IFRSs. For example, if Entity A designated the hedge on 1 February 20X8, then it could not be argued that the hedge is effectively a continuing hedge since 1 September 20X5 because of the break in the hedge relationship between 1 January 20X8 and 1 February 20X8. Instead, the hypothetical derivative would be derived using the designation date of 1 February 20X8.

3.3.2.1 Qualifying fair value hedges

Under its previous GAAP, an entity may have deferred or not recognised gains and losses on a fair value hedge of a hedged item that is not measured at fair value. In these circumstances, IFRS 1 requires an adjustment (in the opening balance of retained earnings) to the carrying amount of the hedged item at the date of transition provided that the hedge is of a type that would be a qualifying hedge relationship under IAS 39. This adjustment is the lower of:

[IFRS 1:IG60A]

(a) that portion of the cumulative change in the fair value of the hedged item that reflects the designated hedged risk and was not recognised under previous GAAP; and

(b) that portion of the cumulative change in the fair value of the hedging instrument that reflects the designated hedged risk and, under previous GAAP, was either (i) not recognised or (ii) deferred in the statement of financial position as an asset or liability.

These requirements result in the hedged item being adjusted by the cumulative change in the fair value of the hedged item due to the designated risk when the fair value of the hedging instrument is more than the exposure on the hedged item. This entry is equivalent to the entry that would have been recognised had the entity always applied IFRSs.

If the fair value of the derivative is less than the exposure of the hedged item, the hedged item is adjusted to the value of the derivative which would have been different had the entity always applied IFRSs.

Example 3.3.2.1

Qualifying fair value hedges

Assume for both of the following scenarios that the hedge relationship is one that is a qualifying hedge relationship under IAS 39 and, therefore, qualifies for hedge accounting at the date of transition to IFRSs.

Scenario A

Entity D has an issued fixed rate bond (CU100 million) and a receive fixed rate CU pay floating 3-month CU LIBOR interest rate swap that it has designated in a fair value hedge of the fixed rate bond (with the designated risk being fair value interest rate exposure due to changes in 3-month CU LIBOR). Under Entity D's previous GAAP, changes in the fair value of the swap were not recognised in the financial statements and the carrying amount of the debt was not adjusted for changes in fair value attributable to the designated risk (3-month CU LIBOR).

At the date of transition to IFRSs, the fair value of the bond is CU70 million. Of the CU30 million cumulative changes in the value of the bond since its issue (when its fair value was CU100 million), CU20 million is determined to be due to changes in the 3-month CU LIBOR interest rate while CU10 million relates to changes in Entity D's credit risk. At the date of transition to IFRSs, the cumulative changes in the fair value of the swap (not reflected in the financial statements under previous GAAP) amount to CU21 million of which CU19.5 million is attributable to the hedged risk (changes in the 3-month CU LIBOR rate).

In accordance with IFRS 1:IG60A, on transition to IFRSs, the hedged item (the fixed rate bond) is adjusted by CU19.5 million such that its carrying amount in the opening statement of financial position is CU80.5 million (CU100 million less the adjustment of CU19.5 million). The CU19.5 million adjustment is the lower of the portion of the cumulative change in the fair value of the hedged item due to the designated hedged risk and the portion of the cumulative change in the fair value of the hedging instrument due to the designated hedged risk (CU20 million and CU19.5 million respectively).

At the date of transition Entity D makes the following entries.

		CU million	CU million
Dr	Fixed rate bond	19.5	
Cr	Retained earnings		19.5

To adjust the hedged item for the designated risk.

		CU million	CU million
Dr	Retained earnings	21.0	
Cr	Derivative liability		21.0

To recognise the swap at fair value.

Scenario B

Entity F has a fixed rate investment that is not classified as HTM that it originally acquired for CU100 million some years ago. On acquisition of the investment, Entity F also entered into a receive floating 1-month CU LIBOR pay fixed CU interest rate swap that it designated under previous GAAP as a hedging instrument in a fair value hedge of the fixed rate investment (with the hedged risk being fair value interest rate risk due to changes in the 1-month CU LIBOR rate).

At the date of transition to IFRSs, the fair value of the fixed rate investment is CU115 million. Changes in the fair value of the investment have not been recognised under previous GAAP. Of the CU15 million cumulative change in the value of the fixed rate investment since it was acquired (when its fair value was CU100 million), CU13 million is determined to be due to fair value changes due to changes in the 1-month CU LIBOR rate while CU2 million relates to changes in the issuer's credit risk. At the date of transition, the cumulative change in the fair value of the swap (not reflected in the financial statements under previous GAAP) amounts to CU12 million, all of which is determined to relate to the hedged risk (changes in the 1-month CU LIBOR rate).

At the date of transition, the fixed rate investment is adjusted by CU12 million such that its carrying amount in the opening statement of financial position is CU112 million (CU100 million plus the adjustment of CU12 million). This adjustment is the lower of the portion of the cumulative change in the fair value of the hedged item due to the designated hedged risk and the portion of the cumulative change in the fair value of the hedging instrument due to the designated hedged risk (CU13 million and CU12 million respectively).

On transition Entity F makes the following entries.

		CU million	CU million
Dr	Fixed rate investment	12	
Cr	Retained earnings		12

To adjust the hedged item.

		CU million	CU million
Dr	Retained earnings	12	
Cr	Derivative liability		12

To recognise the swap at fair value.

3.3.2.2 Qualifying cash flow hedges

An entity may have deferred gains and losses on a cash flow hedge of a forecast transaction. If, at the date of transition to IFRSs, the hedge relationship is of a type that would be a qualifying hedge relationship under IAS 39 and it is still expected to occur, the entire deferred gain or loss on the hedging instrument is recognised in equity. [IFRS 1:IG60B] Note that this initial entry in or reclassification into equity (depending on whether the gains and losses were either previously not recognised or deferred in the statement of financial position outside of equity) comprises the entire cumulative gain or loss on the hedging instrument as at the date of transition regardless of its effectiveness up to that date.

Any net cumulative gain or loss that is reclassified to equity on initial application of IAS 39 remains in equity until:

(a) the forecast transaction subsequently results in the recognition of a non-financial asset or non-financial liability and the amount deferred in equity, depending on the accounting policy choice of the entity, is either included in the initial carrying amount of the non-financial asset or non-financial liability (i.e. it is accounted for as a basis adjustment to the item), or remains in equity and is reclassified from equity to profit or loss when the hedged forecast cash flows affect profit or loss (see **2.2.3** in **chapter C9**);

(b) the forecast transaction affects profit or loss and the amount deferred in equity is reclassified from equity to profit or loss (e.g. when a hedged highly probable forecast sale actually occurs); or

(c) the forecast transaction is no longer expected to occur, in which case any related net cumulative gain or loss is reclassified from equity to profit or loss.

Example 3.3.2.2

Qualifying cash flow hedges

Prior to the date of transition, a Sterling functional currency entity expects, with a high degree of probability, to sell goods to one of its customers for €1 million on a date after the date of transition to IFRSs. The entity enters into a forward contract to sell €1 million and buy £ at a forward rate of £0.7:€1 on the expected date of sale of the goods. Under previous GAAP, the entity did not recognise the fair value of the forward contract in its statement of financial position.

Assume that on date of transition:

- the fair value of the forward contract is £(200,000), i.e. it is a liability; and
- the sale of goods for €1 million at the date originally forecast is still a highly probable forecast transaction.

At the date of transition, the entire cumulative loss on the forward contract to date is recognised in equity as follows.

	£	£
Dr Equity	200,000	
Cr Forward contract		200,000

To recognise the fair value of the forward contract.

After the date of transition to IFRSs, the accounting treatment depends on the likelihood of the forecast transaction occurring.

(a) If the forecast transaction is no longer expected to occur, the entire cumulative gain/loss on the forward contract deferred in equity until that date (including that portion deferred on transition) is immediately reclassified from equity to profit or loss.

(b) If after the date of transition the forecast transaction becomes no longer highly probable but it is still expected to occur, the hedged transaction no longer qualifies for hedge accounting (because it is no longer highly probable). Therefore, subsequent gains and losses on the forward contract are recognised in profit or loss. However, the cumulative gain/loss on the forward contract deferred in equity (including that portion deferred on transition) up until the forecast transaction is no longer highly probable, remains in equity until either the transaction takes place (see (c) below) or it is no longer expected to occur (see (a) above).

(c) The highly probable forecast transaction takes place as expected. The cumulative gains/losses on the hedging instrument (including that portion deferred on transition) will be released to profit or loss at the same time as the highly probable forecast transaction (in the form of Euro denominated revenues) affects profit or loss (i.e. when the Euro denominated sale occurs).

3.3.2.3 Qualifying net investment hedges

Neither IAS 39 nor IFRS 1 contains any explicit guidance as to the transitional requirements in respect of hedges of a net investment in a foreign operation.

In accordance with IAS 39:102, hedges of a net investment in a foreign operation are accounted for similarly to cash flow hedges. It may, therefore, be argued that similar transitional provisions to those for cash flow hedging should be applied in the case of hedges of a net investment in a foreign operation. This would imply that, provided that the hedge relationship qualifies for hedge accounting under IAS 39, the cumulative gain/loss on the hedging instrument at the date of transition (that under previous GAAP may or may not have been recorded in the statement of financial position) is recognised in equity. Therefore, for a derivative hedging instrument (e.g. cross-currency swap or foreign currency forward contract) not previously reflected in the statement of financial position under previous GAAP, the following journal entry is required.

Dr/Cr	Fair value of derivative (statement of financial position)	X
Cr/Dr	Equity	X

This amount classified in equity is reclassified to profit or loss upon disposal of the foreign operation in accordance with the requirements of IAS 39:102 (see **2.3** in **chapter C9** for more details on hedging a net investment in a foreign operation). The reclassification of the deferred fair value gains/losses on the hedging instrument from equity to profit or loss will offset either fully or partially the foreign exchange gains/losses recognised in other comprehensive income arising on the retranslation of the net assets of the foreign operation in accordance with IAS 21 *The Effects of Changes in Foreign Exchange Rates*.

Pre-transition gains and losses recognised in equity will not be reclassified from equity to profit or loss in accordance with IAS 39:102 when an entity has elected to reset the cumulative translation reserve in equity to zero in accordance with IFRS 1:D13. Applying the exemption in IFRS 1:D13, the cumulative translation differences for all foreign operations are deemed to be zero at the date of transition and, therefore, only subsequent translation differences that arise after the date of the transition will be reclassified from equity to profit or loss on disposal of the foreign operation. If an entity has applied net investment hedge accounting in the consolidated financial statements under previous GAAP, and the related hedging reserve is set to zero at the date of transition to IFRSs, the gains and losses on the hedging instrument prior to the date of transition should be recognised in the opening balance of retained earnings.

3.4 Government grants

A first-time adopter shall classify all government loans received as a financial liability or an equity instrument in accordance with IAS 32 *Financial Instruments: Presentation*. Except as permitted by IFRS:B11, a first-time adopter shall apply the requirements in IAS 39 *Financial Instruments: Recognition and Measurement* and IAS 20 *Accounting for Government Grants and Disclosure of Government Assistance* prospectively to government loans existing at the date of transition to IFRSs and shall not recognise the corresponding benefit of a government loan at a below-market rate of interest as a government grant. Consequently, if a first-time adopter did not, under its previous GAAP, recognise and measure a government loan at a below-market rate of interest on a basis consistent with IFRS requirements, it shall use its previous GAAP carrying amount of the loan at the date of transition to IFRSs as the carrying amount of the loan in the opening IFRS statement of financial position. An entity shall apply IAS 39 to the measurement of such loans after the date of transition to IFRSs. [IFRS 1:B10]

Despite IFRS 1:B10, an entity may apply the requirements in IAS 39 and IAS 20 retrospectively to any government loan originated before the date of transition to IFRSs, provided that the information needed to do so had been obtained at the time of initially accounting for that loan. [IFRS 1:B11]

The requirements and guidance in IFRS 1:B10 and B11 do not preclude an entity from being able to use the exemptions described in IFRS 1:D19 - D19D (see **2.8**) relating to the designation of previously recognised financial instruments at fair value through profit or loss. [IFRS 1:B12]

Index